Digital Platforms - From Technical Foundations to Legal and Economic Implications

Roberto Bocchini
Editor

Digital Platforms - From Technical Foundations to Legal and Economic Implications

Volume 1

Springer

Editor
Roberto Bocchini
University of Naples "Parthenope"
Naples, Italy

ISBN 978-3-032-07977-0   ISBN 978-3-032-07978-7 (eBook)
https://doi.org/10.1007/978-3-032-07978-7

This Springer imprint is published by the registered company Springer Nature Switzerland AG
The registered company address is: Gewerbestrasse 11, 6330 Cham, Switzerland

Preface: The Research Project

The research, which is offered in these pages to the scientific community, originated in December 2020 at the height of the COVID pandemic when, barricaded in our homes in defence of the virus that was wielding men and women, together with a number of scholars Antonio Albanese, Riccardo Omodei Salè, Valeria Falce, Alessandra Bellelli, Lourdes Fernández del Moral Domínguez and Roberto Carleo, we started, precisely through information technology, the first reflections on a subject that was beginning to enter the horizons of scholars and in particular of jurists.

The platforms appeared as a *world apart*, the e-Agoras as a virtual world.

The study of digital platforms was uncertain in its boundaries and articulations and the multidisciplinary topic was receiving its regulatory basis from Europe with a series of proposed Regulations and Directives. Over the course of five years of research, the proposals became law with the exception of the Artificial Intelligence (AI) Liability legislation that was withdrawn by the European Union probably as a result of the election of Donald Trump as President of the United States of America. These legislative bases, which are identical throughout the European Union, have provided a foundation of positive law for our research and have allowed us to lay a much more solid foundation for future research.

In short, the research began when not even Artificial Intelligence legislation had found life and now ends with a proliferation of publications on the subject.

The decision to conduct the investigation with a multidisciplinary slant meant that the investigation was not limited to a collaboration of jurists with economists, in order to identify a composite indicator to meet the challenge of measuring articulated and multidimensional phenomena, as already emphasised in the scientific literature and therefore with an approach typical of *Law and Economics*. It seemed opportune to broaden the horizons of the research to other sciences under the ethical, computer science, philosophical and corporatist profile with the contribution of the Communications Guarantee Authority, also as the coordinator of digital services under the Digital Services Act (DSA), which, with its study, monitoring, regulatory and supervisory activities, also aims to accelerate digitalisation processes in order to attract investments in accordance with the objectives of digital access for all Italian households and businesses.[1]

The multidisciplinary nature of the treaty made it particularly difficult to take a scientific approach to give homogeneity to the treatment of the topic.

Digital platforms or e-Agoras, in the imaginative metaphor of our treatise, have in the twenty-first century redefined the way we live, work and interact. From simple technological tools, they have become essential infrastructures that permeate our daily lives, influencing the economy, politics and society. Their regulation is a central challenge for contemporary law: how to guarantee fairness, security and transparency in a context where a few global players manage billions of users and huge volumes of data, how to ensure that economy and capital are fairly distributed with rules that identify common values at least in Europe.

Technology is in danger of becoming the planetary power of the future, recalling Asimov's films. And so it is necessary to investigate the technological instrument on the level of law so that through legal analysis we can better investigate its functions and, therefore, rebalance the totalising capitalist power in the hands of a few, thus setting a virtuous course. We want to avoid that, in the name of economic efficiency (albeit useful and necessary), the personal essence (as a human connotation) is expropriated.

The scientific itinerary has, therefore, made it possible to recompose the *e-Agoras* through the prism of the various sciences in order to cross the frontiers of knowledge, allowing the scholar not to be a Pirandellian character in search of an author, living poised between reality and fiction, unable to grasp the meaning of time.

The awareness of the epochal turning point must overcome the limits of a sectorial study by placing the centrality of Man in the development of markets. The *market* does not protect Man, but protects itself for its broader and deeper development, which, however, must be *Sustainable* in order to allow the greatest growth in the interest of *Man* himself.

In the Treaty, research also takes on an epistemological function, an exploration that is not limited to the ascertainment of phenomena, but breaks down boundaries and allows us to redefine the meaning of the time we live in, creating value beyond mere profit or technological efficiency.

In concrete terms, *online* platforms are defined by the DSA as an 'information storage service which, at the request of a recipient of the service, stores and disseminates information to the public, except where that activity is a minor and purely ancillary function of another service or a minor functionality of the main service and, for objective and technical reasons, cannot be used without that other service and provided that the integration of that function or functionality into the other service is not a means of circumventing the applicability of this Regulation' (Art. 3(i)).

The complexity of the mere definition and the linguistic style of the legislator, far removed from our own, highlight the difficulty of the approach not only of the jurist, but of the scholar in general by highlighting the multiple profiles that even the

[1] On this point see, AGCOM, *Annual Activity Report*, 2024, 3 ff.

legislative definition highlights: the *subjects*, *goods* and *services* that the platform embraces with its activity.

Today, the majority of the Union's citizens use information society services and this not only economic profile emerges prominently, intersecting communication and technological innovation. The impact on society of global giants such as Google, Amazon, Facebook, Microsoft and Apple, which manage billions of pieces of information, is in profound and continuous evolution as they are not mere technological tools, but *autonomous ecosystems*, capable of shaping user behaviour and dictating the rules of the market, highlighting the dilemma of whether they are autonomous entities or mere information dissemination services.

In any case, platforms are *not neutral*, as *technology* '*is not neutral*'[2] and, therefore, they are not just 'means', but actively modify the reality in which they operate by becoming algorithms that influence economic and political decisions: they are *business* models that redefine the structure of labour and production, they are *consumption logics* that change the very concept of property and value. They are not neutral because they are created by Man and, therefore, are *tools*,[3] but, through the algorithms that manage them, they are directed!

The *economic and informational power* of these companies that manage the platforms emerges in a preponderant and certainly not invisible way, as the control of the information, which crystallises in the data, becoming persistent, determines the knowledge by the few companies that administer it, do not compete with each other, but establish access rules and dominate entire sectors. Over time, there is a tendency to state that the mere storage and dissemination of information *is a minor and purely ancillary function of another service*, which may seem static, but when combined with the service and its functionality opens the horizon to new technical and practical approaches.

In order, the treatise inevitably starts from the purely technological approach to first understand how the infrastructure we call the platform is created. The latter comprises both *hardware* and *software* because it is structure and function together. It is designed to provide a variety of services and technological tools, thus enabling the distribution, management and creation of both free and paid-for digital content and services.

The same structure is built to connect different systems accessible to users through exemplified interfaces in order to improve information control management. Digital platforms are technologically created to be true e-Agoras of the third millennium as virtual learning environments, training *learning* systems, collaborative work environments and more are created within them. In the e-Agoras, the community interacts by sharing a reference conceptual architecture that consists of four fundamental layers: (1) contact points for user involvement; (2) API (*Application Programming Interface*) services, i.e. a set of definitions and protocols for the

[2] Pope Francis.

[3] Pope Francis in his speech to the G7 dedicated to artificial intelligence held in Borgo Egnazia on 17 June 2024 and available at https://www.vatican.va/content/francesco/it/speeches/2024/june/documents/20240614-g7-artificial-intelligence.html.

creation and integration of information; (3) data management; and (4) information storage.

For e-Agoras to be populated, the digital platform must offer user-friendly services to engage users in an effective and unobtrusive manner. With this simple approach, the digital population is involved in the *marketplace* and the platform begins to manage information flows related to the participants and their transactions. Thus, communication protocols are used that are capable of performing sophisticated analyses, but with simple and appealing interfaces. The registration system then makes use of information storage media that act as authoritative sources of data or information storage and are responsible for the integrity and validity of the data and their transactions, which are then legally binding for the parties.

In a nutshell, the technological infrastructure is created to involve as many subjects as possible in e-Agoras by offering a variety of services in a simplified manner through mobile *apps* and *websites*: it thus facilitates the integration of subjects, but then manages the information verified in the data in a professional manner and creates a technologically sophisticated digital ecosystem for the management of all information.

First, an immediate and intuitive access for users and then, an extremely sophisticated data management system, often invisible, but capable of determining economic, social and political dynamics.

The part of the treatise devoted to information technology therefore delves into the creation of digital platforms, the enabling technologies that created the European data space, and advanced data processing with the most technologically innovative systems in a simple way.

Having thus identified the structure and technology through which it is possible to transform information into data with *bits* and *hash* strings, the need to investigate how mankind can enter the *web* has emerged. An apparently limited technical apparatus can, therefore, generate a transformation that is not only material, but spiritual and value-based, so that data leaves a trace creating 'the archive of recorded humanity' (Ferraris). The recording of human life, transformed into data, creates a new capital by creating the *ichnosphere*, i.e. the sphere of the trace, which then becomes the infosphere, i.e. the set of information found on the *web* and, then, the docusphere, which is found within the infosphere and which is represented by the domain of the recording and capitalisation of acts that, transformed into data, represent the heritage of humanity. This philosophical approach has been fundamental in understanding the historical passage that human beings make, as mentioned, through the equalisation of information into data and its registration that determines the new value and capital of the third millennium.

From IT to philosophy and from this to economics. Under the direction of Antonio Garofalo and Massimiliano Agovino, the survey then delved into composite indicators, such as the Corporate Economic and Financial Health Index, in order to interpret the mechanisms of a constantly evolving economy with an indication of the economic-financial *performance* of the main digital platforms, allowing for the identification of intervention strategies that can also improve the regulatory environment and incentivise their sustainable development. This part of the treatise has thus made it possible, in the global context, to highlight how digital and technological competences represent a key factor for the success of digital companies and for their affirmation on the market through Artificial Intelligence systems that allow, with data analysis, broad technological innovation that strengthens productivity and operational efficiency.

And, therefore, this part of the research also broadened the scientific path to understand that economic value is not only generated by goods and services, but also by the interactions between users that generate the information that determines the efficiency of the digital ecosystem.

The treatise then delved into the profiles *of* platform *management*, by Franco Calza, Adele Parmentola and Annalisa Sorrentino, who elaborated on how digital transformation, with reference to all tools and technologies, is able to improve and renew business processes, replacing classic production methods with more innovative ones, to increase business efficiency. A new management and cultural model has been analysed, through the digitisation of processes, to free up time, introduce new skills, track data. The managerial level involves a change in *leadership*, a different way of thinking, new *business* models and greater use of technology to improve the experience of employees, customers, suppliers, partners and all *stakeholders*.

This is a revolution that does not only affect operational processes, but also people, so it is crucial for companies to invest in new professionals and to rethink skills in a digital key. In conclusion, on a theoretical level, the treatise shows that the digital transformation is therefore based on three fundamental pillars: people, company and technology.

Last but not least, the treatise has had the privilege of delving into the subject with the attentive eye of scholars such as Benedetta Liberatore and Mario Staderini, with a large group of legal practitioners who, on the basis of their professional work experience accumulated over the years, including as managers of the Communications Guarantee Authority, have deepened their research on a pivotal theme that unites all the contributions, namely the regulation of digital platforms between user protection and the promotion of new rights from the always attentive viewpoint of a dynamic analysis within the guidelines outlined by the European Union legislator, moving between regulation and self-regulation with the aim of achieving an effective balance between different, sometimes opposing interests.

At this point, the investigation delved into the more properly legal part with the examination of the various profiles useful for understanding how the rules can rebalance the disvalues that the market creates with its own march. And so the theme of the contract was explored first with the Naples Parthenope unit, then the theme of civil liability with the Catholic University of Milan, then the theme of *soft law* and co-regulation with which Europe intends to balance democratic rights and competitiveness in the digital market, then the profile relating to public and private actors for a more adaptable and innovative risk management with respect to traditional regulations with the University of Perugia, then the intellectual property profiles with the European University of Rome and, finally, the data protection profiles with the University of Verona.

But without prejudice to these more strictly private law aspects, it seemed appropriate to extend the research to tax law, labour law, public law, European Union law and administrative law profiles.

The breadth and complexity of the Treaty makes a synthesis that does not err on the side of simplicity impossible.

Yet some profiles emerge clearly and indicate the *common thread* that the various sciences bring to the reader's attention: (a) the *evolution of information* as knowledge that becomes a *legal* asset with its own legally relevant patrimonial value that crystallises in *data*; (b) *the control of* data: the ability to collect, analyse and monetise information on users; (c) *digital intermediation*: more and more sectors depend on these platforms to operate (advertising, *e-commerce*, financial services); (d) the challenge between *regulation* and *decentralisation*.

The results of the research are, therefore, the future challenges of scholars in the third millennium and the pages of the treatise are the sap of future studies because the *e-Agorà* are not *a world apart*, but the commercial marketplaces or digital ecosystems that precisely because they are already regulated by those who created them and invisibly govern them, as they are legally accountable to the regulators, cannot be left to self-regulation.

The forces of *Nature*, unlike *Digital* forces, are governed by heteronomous laws that are independent of the human will since the natural world is governed by self-organised and often unpredictable dynamics, whereas the digital world is constructed and modelled by man, following artificial and algorithmic logics. Hence, data control and digital intermediation must find rules that can rebalance the asymmetries. Their regulation is essential to ensure a balance between technological innovation and the protection of democratic rights.

Lastly, it is worth mentioning that the treatise was born out of the concerted activity, as mentioned at the end of this brief introduction, of five study groups, characterised first and foremost by private law scholars, who have intensely cooperated scientifically over the course of these years at the Universities of Naples Parthenope, the Catholic University of the Sacred Heart in Milan, the European University of Rome, the Universities of Verona and Perugia, made up of numerous scholars and legal practitioners from different schools and cultural and scientific backgrounds, who were joined by other jurists from administrative, tax, labour, public and European Union law, and many scholars from different disciplines: computer scientists, philosophers, economists, corporatists enabling the cultural and scientific breadth of the treatise.

The activity of these groups, coordinated by the undersigned, was fruitful because it had the privilege of the valuable scientific input of the most accredited scholars in the field, Antonio Albanese, Giovanni D'Angelo, Riccardo Omodei Salè, Valeria Falce and Alessandra Bellelli, who were the scientific heads of the research in the individual academic venues.

The complex coordination work was carefully and diligently supervised by Dr Franco Trubiani to whom we extend our heartfelt thanks for this articulate and tireless day and night work that confirms his organisational capacity and dedication to study and research.

The work of editing and adapting the English language version to the editorial criteria was skilfully coordinated and directed by Dr Clara Tuccillo, to whom we owe the careful verification of the coherence and accuracy of the translation, as well as the coordination of the work carefully and punctually carried out by Drs Antonella Caia, Annamaria Carrato and Lorenzo Trapani in adapting the editorial criteria.

Since I cannot remember individually all the people who, as doctoral students, colleagues, professionals and administrative staff, have made an essential contribution to the success of these years of research and collaboration, I would like to address my sincerest and deepest appreciation to each one. Their commitment, dedication and enthusiasm have been a lifeblood for the progress of our mission.

To each and every one of them, goes my heartfelt wish: that this experience may not only be a meaningful memory, but also a starting point to continue on the difficult and compelling road of scientific research and university with renewed passion. Their contribution has been, and is, a fundamental pillar in facing the challenges of an ever-evolving knowledge.

The progress of the research has had numerous confrontation *steps* through the fruitful conference activities, which have taken place over the years at the various university venues, and which have made it possible to verify the progress of the research, which will conclude with the final conference to be held in June this year at the Parthenope University in Naples.

Naples, Italy
July 2025

Roberto Bocchini

The original version of the book has been revised: Copyright year has been updated. A correction to this book can be found at https://doi.org/10.1007/978-3-032-07978-7_38

Foreword: Platforms Between Science and Conscience

1. Introductory Notes

The search for something that can tell us about the human being and explain to us who he really is and what role he plays in this world is one of the questions that has always gripped mankind. The search for a meaning that we can offer to the things that happen to us in life, but also the search for our identity, is particularly difficult in the historical period of digital platforms or *e-Agoras*.

We inhabit a world mediated by these new entities that risk making us the protagonists of a radical anthropological mutation. Emerging and converging technologies, in fact, can transform humans at our will. Hence, the importance of safeguarding the common human so that it is not manipulated by technology. We speak too easily of the post-human, the transhuman and so on. The risk is not far off that the new technologies may change our way of being and thus also of thinking and acting. It is essential, therefore, to question the quality of the relationship we must have with these new means of communication that connect us with the whole world. The entities that surround us, such as new technologies, become part of us as enabling tools of our way of thinking. Platforms not only extend our experience but also redefine our relationships and our very identity.

It must be made clear from the outset that progress in science and technology must be regarded as a positive human achievement. They should, therefore, not be demonised a priori. I say this starting from the first book of the Bible, *Genesis*, where we read that 'the Lord God took the man and put him in the garden of Eden, that he might cultivate it and keep it' (Gen 2:15). This was well before original sin. Work, understood in a broad sense, is by no means a punishment. On the contrary, it is part of the dignity of the human person whom God created 'in his image and likeness' (Gen 1:27), hence with a capacity that is also 'creative' and 'generative', although not in an absolute sense. We always remain 'creatures'. Woe betide the temptation to be 'like God'—it was the sin that Adam and Eve committed, they wanted to be like God; we are, however, created in His image, hence 'creatures capable of creation'. This is the meaning of the task that God has entrusted to man and woman: to be responsible for 'creation' and to work the 'garden' to make it beautiful and habitable for all. It is, therefore, not only a matter of preserving but also of developing the life of both creation (the 'garden') and the human family. Man and woman have received from God himself the appropriate energy for this lofty mission. It is obvious that their task is not to hurt or, worse, to destroy life. On the contrary, they have the responsibility to promote sustainable development so that the 'common house' is made habitable for all. Freedom is the responsibility to put ourselves at the service of creation and the care of human relationships.

Pope Francis himself, in his message for Peace Day on 1 January 2024, teaches in this regard: 'In the pastoral constitution *Gaudium et Spes*, the Second Vatican Council reaffirmed this truth, declaring that 'by his work and ingenuity man has always sought to develop his own life'. When human beings, 'with the help of technology', strive to make the earth a dwelling worthy of the whole human family, they are acting in accordance with God's plan and cooperating with His will to bring creation to completion and to spread peace among people. Even the progress of science and technology, insofar as it contributes to a better order of human society, to increasing freedom and fraternal communion, thus leads to the betterment of man and the transformation of the world'.[1]

A new human condition is emerging through an unprecedented and simultaneous increase in technological power and planetary interdependence. For the first time in human history, machines have been created that can reach conclusions previously reserved for humans and the human mind. The frontier of artificial intelligence is a great achievement, but one whose dangers we also know. But we must not allow ourselves to be frightened by this discovery, which is, in any case, the work of man.

2. Humanising Technology

Keeping well in mind the ontological limits of Science and Technology, through digital platforms and with the enabling tool of artificial intelligence and 'cobots' (the new collaborative robots), we have, however, reached the threshold of a new era, in which digital devices, transcending the circumscribed spaces of industrial production (or military organisation), enter the social sphere and domestic life, proposing possible increasingly flexible functions. In this framework, the risk of human beings being technologised and not just assisted, as they should be, in carrying out their activities appears real. It is important to reiterate that 'intelligent machines' are tools created by man to perform specific tasks efficiently, but they do not have emotions, consciousness or a genuine understanding of the world as the human mind has. They are limited to processing data through predetermined rules, and everything that seems 'intelligent' is the result of complex mathematical calculations.

[1] Pope Francis (2024) *Artificial Intelligence and Peace. Message for the LVII World Day of Peace.*

Accepting this distinction is essential to avoid unnecessary disappointment and to be aware of the real potential and challenges of 'intelligent' machines. On the other hand, recognising their limitations allows us to develop ever more useful and effective technologies, focusing on what they can do best without setting unrealistic expectations. Ultimately, we must bear in mind that artificial devices capable of simulating human capabilities actually lack a 'human quality'.

The speed of computing and the technologies associated with artificial intelligence open up new and unprecedented scenarios, for which an ethical approach is certainly urgently needed. It is also indispensable to organise a regulatory framework at a global level to establish the boundaries of what can be done, what should not be done and in what ways to think together—scientists, governments and public opinion—to reach shared forms of decision-making.

To understand whether artificial intelligence truly respects the fundamental principles of human dignity and freedom of persons, we can take the perspective of those who choose not to use it. In fact, if using these tools becomes compulsory—otherwise, one is a sort of technological pariah and therefore cut off from access to care, health and the benefits of essential services for citizens—perhaps we are building a society that excludes the less technologically capable or, the less affluent when they find themselves unable to equip themselves with equipment that is not always affordable.

It is, therefore, a question of guaranteeing an adequate exercise of freedom and recognition of the dignity of all human beings. How will those who decide not to use certain assistive devices, which they consider inconsistent with their conception of the person and human relations, be protected?

Will it be possible to choose a human nurse, even if it means giving up a higher level of efficiency in exchange for humanity, or will the health service be compelled to provide robotic agents, take it or leave it? For those introduced into healthcare protocols, even diagnostic ones, impartiality criteria must be guaranteed or the *bias* that so often characterises algorithms will have discriminatory effects.

Similarly, we could argue about *big data*: will it be possible for everyone and different communities to have some intuitive and practicable mode of access, more or less analogous to the one that today allows even the elderly to access the Internet to compose their own picture of information, research, contacts? Or, with the development of artificial intelligence, will access and processing be selectively reserved for economic *holdings*, public security systems and political *governance* actors? In other words, will it be possible to search for information in a fair manner, or will the sophistication of services be automatically taken away from those who routinely live in society and the communities to which they belong, further widening the already manifold forms of divide?

3. The Human Brain: Emotions, Creativity, Consciousness

Concerning the technological innovations we are talking about, the irreducibility between man and machine, between the brain and artificial intelligence, must be emphasised. First of all, on a biological level. The human brain—it is very useful to read Giulio Maira's book, *Il cervello è più grande del Cielo*[2]—possesses dimensions, qualities and characterising traits that are the result of an evolution lasting millions of years and that perhaps machines will never be able to emulate. The first trait is the ability to *experience emotions, such as excitement, anger, fear or* love. Emotions are so important that, without them, the rational part of the brain would never have had the drive that has enabled man to achieve all the works we know. Emotions also play essential roles in every decision-making process: our whole life is an escape from what frightens us and an attraction to what we love. Finally, emotions have the great function of allowing us to be selective in our learning, to continually set fixed points in the endless series of events that characterise our lives. Another peculiar characteristic of the human brain is *creativity*, the companion of curiosity and imagination. If we imagine it as an expression of the free contamination of ideas, can a computer driven by rigid algorithms ever express it? Curiosity, which generates questions, is the authentic machine learning of the human mind, far more effective than that of a computer. And then there is *consciousness*, without which all the above (emotions, creativity) could not exist. Consciousness encompasses a multitude of aspects, including self-awareness, awareness of the reality around us, a moral perspective on the world, the ability to think critically and reflect on one's thoughts, and many more, making it challenging for an algorithm to replicate it. Will a machine ever feel the need to watch a sunset, feel an inner pleasure listening to a Chopin nocturne or simply savour a grape? And can we call machines incapable of constructing a representation of the world or bringing creative processes to life 'intelligent'?

Finally, no matter how much progress technology may make, there will always remain an irreducible difference between the human being and the artificial intelligence (A.I.). As the ancient philosophers already understood, the specificity of the human being, like that of every living creature, consists in the fact that the brain is an integral part of a body that is a permanent source of emotions, interacting unpredictably with other bodies and with the vast environment that surrounds us. Interaction and empathy constitute the very essence of our intelligence and humanity. It is through these interactions that decisive structures are formed that will make the brain of each of us a unique structure unlike any other.

---

[2] Maira (2019) *Il cervello è più grande del cielo, passim*. The author writes about the brain: 'A network [...] a crucial point in all this takes place at the junction between two cells, where the transmission of information takes place. This junction between two cells, where the endings of the two neurons face each other, is called a synapse'. In an adult human brain, there are more than 150 trillion synapses, and the axons, the long fibres connecting cells, the brain's superhighways, and the white substance cover a length of about 160,000 kilometres: 'Put together, they are equal to one-third of the distance between the Earth and the Moon'.

And it is thanks to the action of emotional intelligence and the function of mirror neurons, these extraordinary biological mechanisms that make us empathise with another person and suffer with them for their pain, that when confronted with the famous, terrible photograph of the little girl hit by napalm in Vietnam, human intelligence immediately grasps the meanings and makes us cry, while A.I., basing its answers on numbers and probabilities, would not even be able to understand the drama that the photograph conceals.

As I said at the beginning of these reflections, however, we must not give in to a pessimistic view of this scientific and technological progress. Suppose we only concern ourselves with the difference between man and machine, without careful reflection. In that case, we risk missing another important question: what can we say about ourselves in this twenty-first century of technology and globalisation? The question is broad and challenging. There are two reductions that the current discourse on A.I. seems to impose on reflection on the human.

The first is that if we are concerned about these systems, it is because they emulate specific processes that we associate with human intelligence. And so we work to mark the difference as if our humanity resides in these faculties. This is not true: we are not our intelligence alone, and any discourse that goes in this direction is reductive. Secondly, we are not our data alone either. Dataism (a pseudo-religious form that springs from the incredible predictive power of *machine learning* systems) wants to reduce us to the (innumerable) traces we leave behind. But it does not.

Machines, designed by man, can change and adapt their behaviour in even unpredictable ways according to the conditions and circumstances in which they operate. The fact that, technologically, within the framework of human-machine interaction, the possibility of unpredictable adaptation or change can occur does not mean that the machine is autonomous.

Autonomy in its original ethical sense can only be attributed to human beings. Autonomy means the capacity to act according to moral values, but it also represents the point where duty and the freedom to act meet.

The term ‘autonomy’ cannot be applied to artefacts, even very advanced, complex or even ‘intelligent’ systems, as it is not really autonomy but rather independence or unpredictability. The terminology of ‘autonomous’ systems is, however, widely used in the scientific literature and in public debate (e.g. autonomous driving machines) to refer to the highest degree of automation in terms of operations and decisions.

Machines ‘support’ and ‘assist’ human decisions, technologically and cognitively, but do not ‘replace’ them. It is worth repeating: A.I. is a mechanical system produced by man that ‘simulates’ and ‘replicates’ human intelligence, performs actions, reasoning and behaviour, and ‘performs functions’, such as comprehension, language, translation, organisation and decision-making. Machines can also reduce cognitive errors and achieve superior performance results in terms of cognition, especially at the quantitative level (gathering and correlation of information; calculation), compared to humans. However, certain characteristics remain specifically human and irreplaceable. Artificial intelligence/machine is placed in the world of *doing*, man in the world of *being*.

It is, however, essential to maintain human control of the machine; the so-called technological delegation issue must be avoided. An expert system that suggests 'decisions' to man poses the risk of diminishing human attention with the possible consequence of reducing human skills (de-professionalisation), reducing responsibility (deresponsabilisation), moving towards the artificialisation of choices that may impoverish and even eliminate the inter-subjective relationship (dehumanisation).

The machine can be an intelligent 'support' that allows humans to maintain focus, supervision and responsibility. I repeat, artificial intelligence can be more efficient, precise and quicker; it may be desirable to introduce A.I. for specific tasks and activities that are considered repetitive, tedious, dangerous or tiring. If used correctly, A.I. could reduce the time professionals have to spend on merely routine or bureaucratic tasks, or activities that expose them to avoidable dangers or humiliate them, allowing them less (physical-psychic) risk and more time.

The problem is not in the progress of science and technology, which aim at the enhancement of humans. The problem lies in the subjection to the soulless thing, concealed by the excitement of its enjoyment.[3]

The deployment of pseudo-religious and pseudo-humanistic rhetoric, which feeds the myth of a science capable of simulating the human outside itself, calls for the careful vigilance of a more shrewd and honest reason. The irruption of natural science into the sphere of organic and combinatorial processes, which can be associated with the so-called higher functions of the human, occurred against the backdrop of a genuine lack of familiarity with the complexity of philosophical ontology and the developments in phenomenological anthropology.

Religious experiences can help us grasp the meaning of human existence and its ultimate destination. It is in its cords to help humanity orient the world of affections that qualify the human: the addition of reality that historical life receives from it is not simply empirical, logical or virtual. The meaning of existence and its destination is qualified by the evangelical provocation of the primacy of the love of neighbour, far from the cold neuronal and digital pseudo-religion of post-modernism. Obviously, theology must go far beyond a tired and simple repetition of the articles of the Creed. What is needed is a witness that also imposes itself through a force of attraction, reducing the rhetoric of single-mindedness that is interested in holding on to enchantment.

A.I. systems, taken up in their deepest anthropological challenge, require us to revisit discussions about men and their bodies. The topic we should develop with greater attention is the reality of the body, of the 'flesh', one might say. A field, this one, that Christians must hold in high regard. Christianity, in fact, has the mystery of the 'incarnation' as one of its cornerstones. The 'carnal' dimension of the Christian story is anchored in the Gospel, in the mystery of a God who becomes 'flesh', man, a non-virtual corporeal reality, we might say. It is on a resurrected body that the faith of the apostle Thomas is played out. And it is no coincidence that the

[3] Baricco (2018), *passim*.

ancient Christian thinker, Tertullian, on the basis of the mystery of the resurrection of the flesh—following that of Christ—affirmed: *Caro cardo salutis* ('the flesh is the hinge of salvation').

The custody of the flesh is among the urgent tasks of Christians in this digital age. An announcement, that of the irrepressibility of bodies, which must be passionate, almost carnal. Owning a body means recognising our finitude, accepting our creatureliness and declaring our fragility. From a theological perspective, this means admitting that we are creatures and not creators of ourselves and that whenever we attempt to remove this essential difference between us and God, we endanger human destiny. Acceptance of creaturality does not in any way mean demonising science and technology. I said this at the beginning of these pages.

Man is called upon to develop his full potential. Of course, a positive view of science and technology—and thus also of the A.I. phenomenon—does not exempt us from the need to regulate and conduct such a powerful and transversal phenomenon. This is a concern that is growing, fortunately, globally, albeit at different times and in various ways.

Recently, even the United Nations itself set up a group of experts on the subject. The contribution of all towards a new awareness and, thus, a new responsibility is the path that must be pursued with determination and creativity.

4. A New Humanism for Digital Platforms

We are in the midst of a change of epoch, as Pope Francis often says. In any case, technological development, due to its global significance, must be geared towards the common good, according to a perspective that brings the various disciplines together in an interdisciplinary manner. An ethical framework for A.I. technologies is indispensable and urgent, so that it can be governed and governable towards a vision of the common good. It is no coincidence that the draft law implementing the Artificial Intelligence (A.I.) The Regulation, known as the Artificial Intelligence Act (A.I. Act), in Article 1 aims to promote the correct, transparent and responsible use, in an anthropocentric dimension, of artificial intelligence, with the goal of seizing its opportunities while ensuring vigilance over the economic and social risks and the impact on fundamental rights of artificial intelligence.

First of all, let us not forget that intelligence belongs to the human, to the flesh, to the body. Not to a machine. In spite of the great novels and stories of the science fiction genre, the intelligent robot—possessing a positronic brain, according to the neologism coined by Isaac Asimov—that interacts, learns, acts and decides according to rules imprinted in its circuits is an artefact far from being a reality. And perhaps it will always remain a product of literature. The work of the future will focus on the development of networks of interconnected computers with great capacities for calculation and data analysis, perhaps capable of suggesting solutions, according to the perspective coined by Arthur C. Clarke and Stephen Baxter in the three novels of the Time Odyssey cycle, in which the 'legal machine' is called 'Aristotle', with a protected *status at* the legal level, capable of helping mankind in decision-making processes. In essence, it is a sophisticated network of computers that any person can access. And already in these cycles, one glimpses the limits and possibilities of development according to the coordinates of automatic systems conceived with the idea of helping mankind. On the one hand, perhaps we will never have intelligent machines capable of moving in the world (robots). On the other hand, maybe we will have systems to help us make decisions.

However, we are still far from a shared ethical approach. We must consider the systems we have, to which I refer in these pages. The most important roles are programming and engineering, which require an ethical direction from the perspective of what is called *ethics by design*. That is, ethics must be integrated into the design and development of a product from the outset. This is the only way to ensure that new solutions, technologies and innovations align with society's norms and values. A step in this direction must be taken.

The UN Agenda 2030 reaffirms the need to balance the three dimensions of sustainable development, the economic, social and environmental dimensions, as indivisible factors for the full realisation of human rights for all.

A reflexive, anticipatory and multidisciplinary approach is necessary to identify medium- and long-term risks and capitalise on the opportunities of innovation itself. It is possible to start from the stages of choosing and extracting the materials that will be used to build the artefacts that we call artificial intelligence systems. It is well known that these are precious, relatively rare minerals, the processing of which can contribute to further polluting our planet. Therefore, an ethical approach begins with sustainability, continues by ensuring the working conditions and wages of workers employed in such activities and then focuses on the characteristics that programmers and engineers impart to the product during the design phase and the purpose of the artificial intelligence system.

It is essential to recognise that the extraordinary resources of science and technology enable the creation of genetically modified and technologically equipped life forms, including the human organism, in ways that are unprecedented in comparison to those of the human subject hitherto known. For this reason, the ethical sensibility relating to the care of life, traditionally linked to respect for the natural limits of the human being, now finds itself engaged with an unprecedented type of challenge which precisely questions these limits. And not only for what concerns birth and death but also the good and the bad, the just and the unjust, the injunction and the freedom that concern life as such.

The horizons of moral reflection must be broadened: this is the meaning of global bioethics. It is no longer possible to circumscribe a local event within the narrow confines of a region: both the pandemic and the conflicts unfolding worldwide exhibit phenomena that affect the biosphere or alter international relations, impacting the planet's population as a whole and necessitating systemic responses.

The anthropocentric turn with technology brings us back to the fundamental question: what is human? The panorama widens and calls into question the very concept of 'nature' and thus also of 'human nature'.[4]

Faced with the enormous challenges we face and which the application of artificial intelligence amplifies, we cannot continue to repeat the same old thinking wearily. There is an urgent need to creatively address the new scenarios that technological development and anthropological changes have presented to us. And it is a task that must be carried out in an open dialogue between all the different components of society, including the religious ones. Pope Francis never ceases to remind us of this and to urge us to promote a deeper dialogue between the intelligence of faith and the thinking of the human. We need a new spirit of fervour for the different communities—political, cultural, intellectual, administrative and beyond—to get involved in shaping a new planetary humanism.

I hope that world politics will soon become aware of the enormous responsibility that rests on its shoulders.

The United Nations is undertaking a careful reflection in this field. And we must hope that the agreement will hasten and expand. The European Union has offered an excellent example of both research and political determination.

The hope is that all world institutions, including religions, will commit themselves to this horizon. Without such a perspective, I ask myself: what is the point of conflicts between states and struggles over national borders while the world is networking with ever closer and tighter connections? And what will happen to the cultures present in our world if a new awareness of the planet's common future does not mature? And again, how can we prevent technological and cultural Westernisation from engulfing minorities, dialects, cultural oases and different possibilities of living and relating to our world? Numerous other questions could be listed.

Could the work done so far, with the help of the Rome Call for A.I. Ethics, also put pressure on the United Nations, for example, to encourage the world's governments to adopt new technologies that follow the path of sustainable development for the entire human family? Pope Francis is among the world leaders to offer a vision that everyone can grasp from his universal perspective. His presence at the G7 is the most explicit testimony of a path that must be travelled by all the heads of government of the countries of the planet.

The Bari experience encourages us to continue on this path by involving other governments. We can draw inspiration from the assembly that took place in Paris in 2015, which saw the participation of the governments of all the countries sitting in the United Nations. The reason for that extraordinary gathering was the conviction that a global agreement on the climate emergency could no longer be delayed. Out of that assembly came an essential international treaty, known as the Paris Agreement, which was ratified the following year in New York by almost all the countries on Earth. It marked the beginning of a major global effort in response to a shared emergency.

---

[4] V. Paglia (2022), *passim*; Casalone et al. (2024), *passim*.

Shouldn't something similar be created to regulate new technologies? Why not also imagine it in Rome, where the *Rome Call* was signed? The presence of the pope, together with the leaders of all religions, could accompany this truly global assembly for a future that is favourable to all.

5. The *A.I. Rome Call on Ethics*

Artificial intelligence (A.I.) induces and will induce profound changes in human life. It offers great potential for enhancing social coexistence and personal well-being, amplifying human capabilities and facilitating numerous tasks that can be performed more efficiently and effectively. But these results are not guaranteed.

The transformations taking place are, in fact, not only quantitative but also, above all, qualitative, as they affect the way we perform these tasks and perceive reality, and even human nature itself, to the point of influencing mental and relational habits. It is necessary to direct research and the production of new technologies according to criteria that effectively place them at the service of the entire 'human family'[5] in respect of the inherent dignity of each of its members and of all natural environments, bearing in mind the needs of the most fragile. The objective is not only to exclude no one, but also to expand those spaces of freedom that could be threatened by algorithmic conditioning.

A new step forward, also on a cultural and religious level, towards the creation of a so-called Algoretic, i.e. an ethical debate and reflection on the use of algorithms. A path, the one launched in 2020 with the signing of the *Rome Call for A.I. Ethics*, the document created within the Pontifical Academy for Life with FAO, IBM, Microsoft and the Italian Ministry of Innovation, which has set itself the mission of developing and promoting an ethical approach to the development and use of I.A. A commitment, the one launched with the *Rome Call for A.I. Ethics*, which has seen FAO and the Vatican working to put A.I. also at the service of sustainability and food security, and which is open to subscription not only by digital platforms but also by universities and other research bodies.

To achieve these goals, we must start by developing each algorithm with an 'algorithm-ethical' vision, i.e. ethics *by design*. Designing and developing A.I. systems that can be trusted requires that policymakers, researchers, academics and representatives of non-governmental organisations converge on ethical principles that can be infused into these technologies. For this reason, the promoters of the *Call* express their willingness to work together, in this context as well as on national and international platforms, to promote 'algor-ethics', i.e. an ethical use of A.I., which can be identified in the following principles.

[5] *The preamble* to the *Universal Declaration of Human Rights*.

1. *Transparency*: A.I. systems must be (in principle) explainable.
2. *Inclusion*: Looking at the totality of the needs of all human beings so that everyone can benefit and so that all individuals can be given the best conditions to express themselves and develop.
3. *Responsibility*: The people who design and deploy the A.I. must be responsible for its operation.
4. *Impartiality*: Not creating or acting according to *biases*, safeguarding human dignity.
5. *Reliability*: A.I. systems must be able to function reliably.
6. *Security and privacy*: A.I. systems must operate securely and with respect for users' *privacy*.

Given the novelty and complexity of the demands involved in digital transformation, the collaboration of all stakeholders and the representation of the different needs affected by A.I. are required.

This *Call* is a step in the direction of growing in participatory understanding and seeking a shared language and standard solutions. On this basis, it will be possible to recognise and assume responsibilities that consider the entire path of technological innovation, from its design to its deployment and use, fostering a practical commitment to the concreteness of different situations. In the long run, it will be the values and principles that we succeed in instilling in A.I. that will help establish a framework of regulation and reference for a digital ethic that guides action, favouring the use of technologies for the benefit of humanity and the environment.

Today, more than ever, it is necessary to ensure a vision of A.I. development whose focus is not technology but the good of humanity and the environment: of the typical home and its inseparably connected human inhabitants. A vision, in other words, in which human beings and nature are at the centre of the development of digital innovation, supported and not progressively replaced by technologies that behave as rational actors but are in no way human subjects. It is now a matter of preparing a future of Technological Humanism in which humans and machines will increasingly work together, but where it is clear that technological progress confirms the genius of the human and remains subordinate to his ethical integrity.

The development of A.I. in the service of humanity and the planet must be translated into norms and principles that protect people, especially the weak and the last, and the natural environment. The ethical commitment of all those involved is an indispensable threshold. An essential complement for the realisation of this horizon are legal norms and principles that support, structure and accompany this process.

It is no coincidence that with the entry into force of the first articles of the European regulation, the obligation to become literate in the field of artificial intelligence has been initiated, which is not a mere bureaucratic fulfilment but rather an invitation to promote a critical and conscious understanding of artificial intelligence, not only from a technical point of view but also about its implications, be they ethical, social or legal.

Providers and users of A.I. systems should ensure a sufficient level of A.I. literacy among their personnel as well as any other persons involved in the operation and use of A.I. systems on their behalf. Thus, concrete steps should be taken to ensure that anyone working with A.I. systems has the necessary skills to understand their operation, limitations and potential risks.

Literacy goes through concrete training that is not limited to technical aspects, but includes awareness of the ethical and social implications of using A.I. In order to develop and implement A.I. systems that benefit humanity and the planet, as well as tools for building and maintaining international fraternity and peace, it is necessary that A.I. development goes hand in hand with robust digital security measures.

For A.I. to be a tool for the good of humanity and the planet, it is necessary to put the issue of protecting human rights in the digital age at the centre of the public debate. One must question whether new forms of automation and algorithmic action do not require the development of new forms of human rights. In particular, it will be indispensable to think about forms of 'right to explanation': one must think about being able to make comprehensible not only the decision criterion but also the purpose and objectives of the algorithmic agent based on I.A. systems. Such devices must be able to guarantee the person's information on the logic of the algorithms used to make decisions so as to improve transparency, traceability and accountability and make machine-assisted decision-making more valid.

This opens up the reflection of Man through scientific research of a transdisciplinary nature, and the treatise introduced here represents a truly important moment of common reflection.

Pontifical Academy for Life Mons. Vincenzo Paglia

References

Baricco A (2018) The game. Torino

Casalone C et al. (2024) La gioia della vita. Un percorso di etica teologica: Scrittura, tradizione, sfide pratiche, Città del Vaticano

De Beistegui M (2024) Truth and Genesis. Philosophy as Differential Ontology. Bloomington

Desmond W (1995) Being and the Between. Albany

Guglielminetti E (2011) La commozione del bene. Una teoria dell'aggiungere. Milano

Maira G (2019) Il cervello è più grande del cielo. Milano

Paglia V (2022), Etica teologica della vita. Città del Vaticano

Pope Francis (2024) Artificial Intelligence and Peace. Message for the LVII World Day of Peace. www.vatican.va/content/francesco/it/messages/peace/documents/20231208-messaggio-57giornatamondiale-pace2024.html

Tourpe E (2020) Donation et réciprocité. L'Amour, point aveugle de la philosophie. Parigi

Contents

Personal Data Protection

Contributors

Antonio Albanese Catholic University of the Sacred Heart of Milan, Milan, Italy

Giulio Andreotti University of Naples "Parthenope", Naples, Italy

Emanuela Arezzo University of Teramo, Teramo, Italy

Maria Barela University of Tuscia, Tuscia, Italy

Pierfrancesco Bartolomucci University of Naples "Parthenope", Naples, Italy

Maria Letizia Bixio European University of Rome, Rome, Italy

Roberto Bocchini University of Naples "Parthenope", Naples, Italy

Silvia Bonetti University of Verona, Verona, Italy

Luigi Cameriero University of Rome "G. Marconi", Rome, Italy

Roberto Carleo University of Naples "Parthenope", Naples, Italy

Angelo Ciaramella University of Naples "Parthenope", Naples, Italy

Valentina Citarella University of Naples "Parthenope", Naples, Italy

Luigi Coppolino University of Naples "Parthenope", Naples, Italy

Salvatore D'Antonio University of Naples "Parthenope", Naples, Italy

Lourdes Fernández del Moral Domínguez University of Naples "Parthenope", Naples, Italy

Antonio di Biase University of Foggia, Foggia, Italy

Giovanni Di Lorenzo University of Rome "La Sapienza", Rome, Italy

Mirko Faccioli University of Verona, Verona, Italy

Valeria Falce European University of Rome, Rome, Italy

Nicola M. F. Faraone European University of Rome, Rome, Italy

Stefano Gatti University of Verona, Verona, Italy

Rosaria Giampetraglia University of Naples “Parthenope”, Naples, Italy

Raffaele Montella University of Naples “Parthenope”, Naples, Italy

Salvatore Monticelli University of Naples “Parthenope”, Naples, Italy

Francesca Morri Catholic University of the Sacred Heart of Milan, Milan, Italy

Matteo Nuzzo University of Naples “Parthenope”, Naples, Italy

Agostino Nuzzolo General Counsel TIM, Milan, Italy

Matteo Ortino University of Verona, Verona, Italy

Abigail Owusu Lawyer, Verona, Italy

Valerio Pescatore University of Rome “La Sapienza”, Rome, Italy

Laura Guffanti Pesenti Catholic University of the Sacred Heart of Milan, Milan, Italy

Maria Pia Pignalosa University of Rome “Foro Italico”, Rome, Italy

Luigi Romano University of Naples “Parthenope”, Naples, Italy

Marina Romano University of Naples “Parthenope”, Naples, Italy

Riccardo Omodei Salè University of Verona, Verona, Italy

Sara Scola University of Verona, Verona, Italy

Mauro Tescaro University of Verona, Verona, Italy

Stefano Troiano University of Verona, Verona, Italy

Franco Trubiani University of Naples “Parthenope”, Naples, Italy

Clara Tuccillo University of Naples “Parthenope”, Naples, Italy

Francesca Zagaria University of Rome “La Sapienza”, Rome, Italy

Information Technology

Digital Platforms

Luigi Romano and Salvatore D'Antonio

Contents

Abstract This chapter analyzes digital platforms, detailing their architecture and diverse models (marketplaces, services, payments, investment, and art). It underscores their role in fostering business innovation alongside significant legal challenges. A key contribution is the exploration of digital sovereignty, showing how traditional state control adapts to the digital era, particularly with sovereign cloud solutions ensuring national data and operational autonomy.

L. Romano (✉) · S. D'Antonio
University of Naples "Parthenope", Naples, Italy
e-mail: luigi.romano@uniparthenope.it; salvatore.dantonio@uniparthenope.it

R. Bocchini (ed.), *Digital Platforms - From Technical Foundations to Legal and Economic Implications*, https://doi.org/10.1007/978-3-032-07978-7_1

1 The Concept of a Digital Platform

A digital platform is a technological infrastructure, which can be *hardware and/*or *software*, designed to provide a variety of technological services and tools. These platforms enable the distribution, management, and creation of digital content and services, both free and paid.[1]

Digital platforms connect different systems and make them accessible to users through simplified interfaces, such as mobile *apps* or *websites*. This facilitates the integration and analysis of data from different sources, improving information management and control. In practice, digital platforms can be used to create virtual learning environments, *e-learning* training systems, collaborative work environments, and more.

They can also offer informational, interactive, file sharing, *streaming*, and multimedia communication services. The essential part of any digital platform is the community that interacts with it. Advanced technologies such as artificial intelligence, *machine learning*, *cloud*, and *Internet of Things* can also be used.

2 Architecture of a Digital Platform

Regardless of the specific function performed and despite differences in the selection and implementation of the technologies employed, most digital platforms share a reference conceptual architecture, which consists of four basic layers: (1) customer engagement touch points; (2) Application Programming Interface (API) services; (3) data management; and (4) information storage.

The touch point layer for customer engagement is of paramount importance. Indeed, a digital platform must offer easy-to-use services, such as mobile applications, *websites*, and so on, to engage the customer effectively and unobtrusively. This layer represents the interface of the system to the users, and its proper design and implementation is crucial to the market success of the products and/or services offered.

Of equal importance are API services. The acronym API stands for Application Programming Interface. An API is a set of definitions and protocols for creating and integrating *software* applications.

Also essential (and always present) is a data management layer. This layer is responsible for the efficient management of information flows related to master records and transactions.

Event-based communication protocols are used to obtain real-time operational *reports* on updated data in order also to perform sophisticated analysis.

[1] Harvard Business School Online (2024).

Finally, the recording system makes use of information storage media, which serve as authoritative sources for specific data elements or information. This layer is responsible for the integrity and validity of data and transactions. Many platforms use the *facilities* offered by *cloud* technology to achieve this goal.

Digital platforms can take different forms depending on the specific purposes they are intended to serve. Several models or categories can be distinguished. In the following sections, we briefly present some of the most popular digital platforms, grouped into the categories: marketplace, services, payments, and art.

3 Digital Platform Models

3.1 Digital Marketplace Platforms

Digital marketplace platforms (Table 1) represent one of the most prevalent models in the contemporary digital ecosystem, facilitating the matching of supply and demand for goods and services through structured virtual environments. The prevailing economic model is based on fees charged on completed transactions, with variations reflecting different positioning strategies.

Amazon represents a case of transformative evolution in the industry. Starting as a specialized online bookstore, it gradually expanded its offerings to become a generalist marketplace, and then further extended its ecosystem with cloud services (Amazon Web Services; AWS), streaming content, and proprietary devices. This evolutionary path illustrates how a platform can transcend its original concept, creating a vertically integrated system that generates multiple sources of value and competitive advantages.

In sharp contrast to this expansive model, Etsy has instead demonstrated the effectiveness of a specific strategic focus. By focusing exclusively on handcrafted, vintage, and handmade products, it has built a distinctive *community* around shared values, demonstrating how specialization can be a viable alternative to generalist models, especially in niches characterized by strong cultural identity.

eBay introduced a fundamental innovation in transaction mechanisms, basing its model on online auctions before also integrating fixed-price purchase options. This system brought about a paradigm shift, introducing elements of dynamic pricing and *gamification* into *e-commerce*, anticipating trends that would become relevant in later years.

On the promotional models front, Groupon represented a break with its predecessors by introducing the concept of collective buying. This approach subverted the traditional logic of *e-commerce* by creating interdependencies between consumers and incentivizing viral behavior, with significant implications for demand formation dynamics.

AliExpress has revolutionized the geography of digital trade, creating a direct bridge between Chinese producers and global consumers. This model has

Table 1 Summary of digital platforms by marketplace

Name	Business innovation	Controversial aspects of a legal nature
Amazon	From digital library to multidimensional integrated ecosystem with vertical and horizontal integration strategies	Transnational antitrust regulations and abuse of dominant position;[a] third-party product liability; personal data processing; labor law protection in logistics centers
eBay	Pioneering paradigm of electronic auctions and *peer-to-peer* transactions	Combating counterfeiting and trade in illicit goods; liability of the intermediary; differentiated tax regime between private and professional sellers; buyer protection
Etsy	Focusing on the arts and crafts segment and creating community ecosystem	Intellectual property protection for handmade creations; tax qualification of casual sellers; certification of authenticity; categorization of *handmade* products
AliExpress	*Supply chain* disintermediation by direct connection Chinese manufacturers-global consumers	Jurisdiction and applicable law in cross-border disputes; compliance with EU/US standards; customs evasion; supply chain traceability
Groupon	Innovative collective purchasing model with gamification elements	Transparency of commercial communications; validity of standardized clauses; specific withdrawal rights; liability for services provided by third parties
ManoMano	Vertical specialization in DIY with integration of sectoral expert consulting	Regulation of non-professional technical advice; liability for potentially hazardous products; certification of recommended installers
Zalando	Regionalized adaptation of *fashion e-commerce* model with European logistics strategy	Optimized returns management; environmental impact of *e-commerce fashion*; biometric data protection; personalized *marketing* and *privacy* regulations
Vinted	C2C marketplace for *secondhand* clothing with circular economy concept	Delimitation of liability in transactions between private individuals; warranties for used products; tax implications for casual sellers; compliance with personal data regulations
Shein	*Ultra-fast fashion* model with accelerated production cycles, competitive pricing and advanced digital *marketing*	Environmental sustainability and jurisprudential conditions; compliance with safety *standards*; compliance with international customs and tax regulations

[a]European Commission (2020)

dramatically reduced traditional intermediary barriers, redefining global value chains and introducing new competitive dynamics to Western markets.

Technological Insight: Architectural Evolution
The evolution of marketplace platforms reflects the gradual shift from monolithic architectures to microservice-based distributed systems, with increasingly specialized solutions to cope with increasing volumes of data and scalability requirements.

Amazon has led technology innovation by developing a distributed microservices-based architecture that has redefined industry standards. The infrastructure relies on globally distributed proprietary data centers with advanced load balancing and data replication systems. This approach has not only supported the exponential growth of the platform, but also generated an independent technology offering (AWS) that has transformed the global cloud landscape.

The technological evolution of eBay represents an exemplary case of incremental transformation. Starting with a monolithic architecture in the early 1990s, the platform has gone through multiple stages of modernization, maintaining *legacy* components while progressively integrating modern microservices. This coexistence of technologies from different generations illustrates the technology evolution challenges that many mature platforms face.

Regarding optimization for specific markets, the case of AliExpress is exemplary, which with the adoption of *Progressive Web App*[2] (PWA) and lightweight protocols developed technical solutions specifically designed for emerging markets with limited connectivity. This technological approach has supported the global expansion of the platform into areas previously marginal for *e-commerce*.

Newer platforms such as ManoMano highlight the potential of serverless architectures, using services such as AWS Lambda[3] for specific components and achieving significant benefits in terms of operational costs and elastic scalability. This evolution represents an important trend toward infrastructure abstraction and the *pay-as-you-go* model.

3.2 *Digital Platforms for Services*

Digital platforms for services constitute an evolution within the digital economy, marking a significant shift in the analytical axis from the mere transaction of tangible goods to the provision of intangible services and activities.

Unlike traditional *marketplaces*, in which intermediation concerns precipitously tangible products, service platforms play a facilitating function in the matching of supply and demand for skills, time availability and operational capabilities,

[2] Fortunato and Bernardino (2018), pp. 1–6.

[3] AWS (2024).

generating innovative *business* models based on the principle of temporary access and use rather than proprietary acquisition. These platforms are based on processes of digitizing and parceling out activities traditionally performed in physical settings, making them accessible *on-demand* and on a global scale.

The underlying economic model is frequently articulated through commission systems for each service provided, periodic subscription structures, or hybrid schemes that integrate multiple revenue sources. In order to delineate with greater analytical precision the variety and scope of such digital infrastructures, a taxonomy is proposed divided into core categories, each distinguished by specific innovations and distinctive operating models.

Platforms for Mobility and Transportation

Platforms pertaining to this domain have brought about a radical transformation in the dynamics of contemporary urban mobility.

The fundamental innovation lies in the conceptual reconfiguration of the use of private vehicle and other means of transportation, converting them into services characterized by high flexibility and accessibility through digital interfaces. Uber has introduced a particularly sophisticated model, implementing dynamic *match-making* algorithms between demand and supply of transportation services. This innovation, together with the complete dematerialization of the user experience, has redefined the industry's operations.

In dialectical contrast, FreeNow (formerly called *mytaxi*) is characterized by synergistic integration with traditional non-scheduled public transportation operators. While Uber generated a marketplace in which any entity could assume the function of a carrier, FreeNow opted for an integration with the pre-existing cab system, offering users the ability to book services with professional drivers equipped with the necessary administrative authorizations. In addition to these examples, multiple other mobility platforms—including BlaBlaCar, Lime and Citymapper—have introduced elements of profound innovation in the sector, implementing models that integrate heterogeneous modes of transportation and promoting solutions characterized by greater environmental sustainability and responsiveness to the needs of contemporary urban contexts.

Hospitality and Accommodation Platforms

Platforms operating in this area have led to a redefinition of the tourism and hospitality market. The main innovation consists of the functional conversion of real estate units originally intended for residential use into accommodation facilities of a temporary nature, considerably expanding the offer available to users.

Airbnb established a global *marketplace* for short-term rentals, setting itself up as the most emblematic example of this operating model. In parallel, Booking.com has gradually expanded its offerings, initially focused on conventional hotel accommodations, to include private homes and self-contained residential units, converging on a related model and expanding its platform to form an all-inclusive system for reservations inherent to the travel experience.

The distinctive innovation of these platforms lies in the design of user interfaces characterized by high intuitiveness for the search and booking of housing solutions, the implementation of two-way review and rating systems (*reputation systems*) aimed at the consolidation of mutual trust, and the fully digitized management of economic transactions and communication flows.

Food *Delivery and* Delivery *Platforms*

Platforms belonging to this category have introduced elements of profound innovation in the food service and home delivery sector. The central innovation is the expansion of the availability of food and other consumer goods to an extended user base through the development of *just-in-time* delivery models characterized by high logistical efficiency.

Deliveroo, Just Eat, and Glovo have distinctive specificities in their operating model and the extent of territorial coverage, setting themselves up as examples in this field. Technological innovation is embodied in the optimization of distribution logistics through advanced *routing* algorithms, the use of *rider* geolocation systems, and the development of digital applications for real-time order and delivery management, ensuring high parameters of efficiency and timeliness in service delivery.

Platforms for Freelance *and* On-demand *Work*

Platforms operating in this segment have generated new markets for self-employment (freelancing) and professional services delivered *on-demand*. The key innovation is the creation of a digital infrastructure that facilitates the matching of economic actors (businesses and individuals) and independent professionals with a wide range of skills.

Upwork and Fiverr stand as established marketplaces in the industry, while TaskRabbit has adopted a focus on primarily operational and task-specific activities, further expanding the type of services that can be brokered.

The peculiar innovation lies in the design of global platforms aimed at identifying and engaging independent professionals, the adoption of advanced *project* management and compensation management systems, and the implementation of sophisticated mechanisms for reputational assessment and certification of professional skills, facilitating the matching of supply and demand for labor services in a context characterized by high digitization and global dimension (Table 2).

Table 2 Summary of digital platforms by services

Platform category	Business innovations	Controversial implications of a legal nature
Mobility and transportation platforms (Uber, FreeNow, BlaBlaCar, Lime, Citymapper)	Conceptual reconfiguration of private vehicle use into accessible service through digital interfaces; implementation of dynamic matchmaking algorithms between supply and demand; complete dematerialization of user experience; integration of heterogeneous transportation modes	Ambiguities in the employment law qualification of vehicular operators; competitive asymmetries with the regulated non-scheduled public transport sector; licensing and administrative issues
Hospitality and accommodation platforms (Airbnb, Booking.com)	Functional conversion of residential real estate units into temporary accommodations; creation of global *marketplaces* for short-term rentals; implementation of two-way *reputation* systems; fully digitized management of economic transactions and communication flows	Structural impact on local real estate markets resulting in higher residential rental rates; phenomena of urban gentrification and *overtourism*; asymmetric competition with the traditional hotel sector subject to more stringent regulations; fiscal issues related to taxation of short leases
Delivery and *food delivery* platforms (Deliveroo, Just Eat, Glovo)	Expansion of food availability through *just-in-time* delivery models; optimization of distribution logistics through advanced *routing* algorithms; implementation of operator geolocation systems; development of real-time management applications	Precariousness of *riders'* labor-law conditions; disputes over contractual framing of riders (subordination vs. autonomy); inadequacy of traditional social protection schemes; issues related to responsibility for quality and safety of delivered products
Platforms *for freelance* and *on-demand* work (Upwork, Fiverr, TaskRabbit)	Creation of digital infrastructure for matching economic actors with independent professionals; conception of global marketplaces for identifying and engaging specialized skills; development of reputational assessment mechanisms and certification of skills; facilitation of access to a global talent pool	Acceleration of *gig economy* phenomena resulting in the precarization of intellectual and operational labor; issues related to the protection of social security and welfare rights of independent workers; issues of social *dumping* and *regulatory arbitrage*

3.3 Digital Platforms for Payments

Digital payment platforms constitute a major structural component in the architecture of the contemporary digital economic ecosystem. These infrastructures perform a technological intermediation function aimed at facilitating electronic financial transactions among multiple economic actors, overcoming the inherent limitations of traditional payment systems based on the use of cash or physical payment instruments.

The hallmark of these platforms lies in their ability to efficiently interconnect buyers and sellers, financial institutions, and third-party service providers within an integrated ecosystem, leading to significant optimization and acceleration of digitized monetary flows.

The nature of such platforms is manifested through the standardization of APIs, the delivery of services characterized by high modularity and composability, and the creation of an environment conducive to innovation and incremental integration of advanced functionality.

Digital payment platforms have distinctive features such as high speed of transaction execution, sophisticated security protocols for the protection of financial data, complete traceability of monetary flows, and significant advantages in terms of operational efficiency for users and economic operators. In order to delineate with greater analytical precision the variety and functional specificities of such infrastructures, a taxonomy is proposed that is divided into the following basic categories.

Payment Gateways

These platforms take the form of technological interfaces that establish a functional connection between the digital infrastructure of electronic commerce (websites and applications) and payment networks, enabling the authorization and processing of transactions made using credit cards, debit cards, and additional electronic payment methods.

Stripe and Square represent examples of payment *gateways* that have resulted in significant simplification of online payment system integration for enterprises of diverse sizes, offering programming interfaces characterized by high flexibility, comprehensive technical documentation, and advanced tools for transaction management and implementation of anti-fraud protocols.

PayPal, although originally conceived as a digital wallet system, has gradually implemented payment *gateway* capabilities for integration with e-commerce platforms.

The distinctive innovation of these platforms lies in democratizing access to digital payment systems for economic entities, significantly reducing the technical and operational complexity involved in implementing these systems, and offering advanced instrumentation for transaction security and financial data analysis.

Digital Wallets

These platforms carry out a digitization of the functions traditionally performed by the physical wallet, enabling users to securely store payment information (card credentials, bank details, digital certificates) and carry out monetary transactions in online and physical contexts via mobile devices or Web interfaces.

Apple Pay, Google Pay, and Amazon Pay are representative examples of digital wallets that have integrated payment systems natively within the architectures of mobile operating systems and e-commerce ecosystems, implementing technologies such as *Near Field Communication* (NFC), QR codes, and biometric authentication systems in order to streamline and speed up the payment process.

The distinctive innovation of these platforms is manifested in the convergence of *online* and *offline* payment modes, the significant improvement of the user experience by increasing the speed and usability of the systems, and the enhancement of security protocols by implementing advanced tokenization and authentication mechanisms.

Buy Now Pay Later (BNPL) Platforms

These platforms offer consumer credit solutions that are organically integrated into the online purchasing process, allowing consumers to defer payment for purchases in periodic installments, frequently featuring no interest or the application of flexible repayment plans.

Klarna represents an example in the BNPL sector, having introduced elements of significant innovation in the consumer credit model through integration with e-commerce platforms, implementation of real-time risk assessment systems, and simplification of credit approval processes. Other platforms operating in this segment, such as Afterpay and Affirm, adopt similar operating models with distinctive specificities.

The distinctive innovation of these platforms lies in the expansion of consumer credit accessibility for specific market segments, increased conversion rates for merchants, and the customization of financing proposals according to users' risk profiles and preferences (Table 3).

Table 3 Summary of digital platforms for payments

Platform category	Business innovations	Controversial implications of a legal nature
Payment gateways (Stripe, PayPal, Square)	Democratization of access to payment systems; reduction of technical complexity; advanced tools for security and data analysis; comprehensive technical documentation; anti-fraud protocols	Concentration of market power; *privacy* issues and management of sensitive data; liability for fraud; tax tracking; freezing of funds and suspension of services
Digital wallets (Apple Pay, Google Pay, Alipay)	Online/*offline*; improved user experience; advanced tokenization and authentication; integration into *e-commerce* operating systems and ecosystems	Dependence on proprietary ecosystems; interoperability issues; transactional data *privacy*; competitive constraints; geopolitical risks in international expansion
Buy Now Pay Later (Klarna, Affirm, Afterpay)	Expanded accessibility to consumer credit; integration of financing into the purchasing process; real-time risk assessment; increased conversion rates; merchant fees	Over-indebtedness risks; applicability of traditional credit regulations; need for robust risk assessment methods; insolvency management; data protection

Technology Insight: Security Mechanisms

Digital payment platforms implement sophisticated security mechanisms to protect transactions and users' financial data. Some of the main ones include:

- *End-to-end encryption*:[4] This system ensures the protection of sensitive data during the entire transmission path, from the user's device to the infrastructure of the platform and financial institutions, through the use of advanced cryptographic protocols. This protection extends to all stages of the transaction, ensuring the confidentiality of information.
- *Tokenization*:[5] This technique involves replacing sensitive payment card data with unique, non-reusable "tokens." In the event of a systems breach or data interception, the *tokens* are unusable for committing fraud, as they do not contain sensitive financial information, significantly reducing the risk of data theft and misuse.
- *Multi-Factor Authentication (MFA)*:[6] To prevent unauthorized access and fraudulent transactions, platforms implement multi-factor authentication (MFA) systems. These systems require verification of the user's identity through at least two authentication factors belonging to different categories, such as a combination of a password (knowledge), an OTP code sent via SMS (possession), or biometric data (inherency), greatly increasing the security of access and transactions.
- *Fraud Detection and Prevention Systems*:[7] Digital payment platforms integrate sophisticated machine learning and behavioral analysis systems that operate in real time to identify suspicious transactions and block fraudulent activity. These systems analyze a vast number of parameters and behavioral variables to detect anomalies and patterns indicative of fraud, providing proactive and dynamic protection.
- *Security Standards Compliance (PCI DSS)*: To ensure a high and uniform level of payment card data protection, platforms adhere to stringent security standards defined by the payment industry, such as the *Payment Card Industry Data Security Standard*[8] (PCI DSS). Compliance with these standards is often certified by external audits and is a prerequisite for operating in the industry.

(continued)

[4] IBM (2024).

[5] Tripathi (2024), pp. 1848–1850.

[6] Ometov et al. (2018), p. 1.

[7] Chang et al. (2022).

[8] Chippagiri and Ramesh (2025), pp. 1258–1266.

(continued)

- *Know Your Customer (KYC) and Anti-Money Laundering (AML) Procedures*: In compliance with international regulations on the prevention of money laundering and terrorist financing, the platforms implement procedures for identifying and verifying the identity of users (*Know Your Customer*, KYC) and for constantly monitoring transactions (*Anti-Money Laundering*, AML). These procedures are critical in trying to ensure transparency of financial flows and regulatory compliance.[9]

3.4 Digital Platforms for Investment

Digital investment platforms constitute a segment characterized by rapid expansion in the contemporary financial landscape. These infrastructures employ advanced technological solutions in order to democratize access to financial markets and simplify investment processes for a wide range of users, from small savers to highly experienced and knowledgeable investors.

In their conceptual essence, these platforms establish a direct connection between investors and capital allocation opportunities, leading to significant disintermediation from traditional financial players (such as banking institutions and conventional *brokers*) and offering solutions characterized by high levels of innovation and greater efficiency in terms of operational costs and timing of execution.

The nature of the platforms manifests itself through the modularity of the services offered, the intensive implementation of digital interfaces accessible via *web* and mobile devices, the automation of processes characterized by high complexity, and the customization of investment proposals according to the investor's risk profile and financial objectives.

Digital investment platforms have distinctive features such as greater information transparency, potentially lower operating costs than traditional channels, continuous (24/7) accessibility, and advanced analytical tools to support decision-making processes inherent in capital allocation.

In order to delineate with greater analytical precision the variety of operational models and strategic approaches, a taxonomy is proposed that is divided into the following basic categories:

[9] Anti-Money Laundering AML Policy (2019).

Online Trading *Platforms*

These digital infrastructures have led to a transformation in access to *trading* financial instruments, offering significantly reduced or entirely eliminated commission structures and interfaces characterized by high intuitiveness for investors with different levels of experience and expertise.

E-Toro is distinguished by its implementation of the innovative *copy trading* feature, which allows users to replicate investment strategies adopted by other traders in an automated way, democratizing access to potentially highly sophisticated strategies and introducing a dimension of social interaction within the *trading* ecosystem. The platform offers a broad spectrum of financial instruments, from traditional equities to digital *assets*.

Degiro has adopted a strategic focus on offering particularly competitive commissions for *trading* in equities and exchange-traded funds (ETFs), making equity investment more accessible and cost-effective, with particular reference to investors characterized by high operational activity or oriented toward extended time horizons.

Robinhood, a pioneer in the implementation of the explicit commission-free *trading* model, has attracted a large audience of *retail* investors, with particular reference to younger demographic cohorts, due to the implementation of an interface characterized by significant simplicity and the elimination of traditional economic barriers. However, this operating *model* has raised questions about the sustainability of the *business model* and potential conflicts of interest related to the *payment for order flow* mechanism.

Interactive Brokers, although geared more toward highly experienced investors, is characterized by access to a wide range of global markets and the availability of advanced tools, shaping itself as a comprehensive and sophisticated platform for international *trading* and the implementation of strategies characterized by high complexity.

The technological innovation peculiar to these platforms lies in the implementation of simplified user interfaces accessible via *web* and mobile channels, the development of high-performance trading infrastructure, the availability of real-time market data, the provision of advanced charting tools, and, in specific cases, the integration of social features and *copy trading* mechanisms.

Cryptocurrency Investment Platforms

These platforms present a specialization in offering services for the purchase, sale, exchange, and custody of cryptocurrencies and other digital *assets*, tapping into the growing market interest in this innovative asset class.

Coinbase is considered a particularly suitable platform for users initially approaching the cryptocurrency ecosystem, due to the implementation of an interface characterized by high intuitiveness, significant ease of use, and the integrated offering of training materials, which provide structured support in the initial stages of approaching digital *asset trading*.

Binance, configuring itself as one of the most relevant cryptocurrency trading platforms globally, offers a broad spectrum of digital assets and instruments characterized by high sophistication, attracting experienced traders and institutional players due to the considerable depth of the market and the comprehensiveness of the services offered (derivatives, *futures*, *staking*, and additional features).

Kraken is strategically positioned as a platform geared toward more experienced *traders*, offering advanced *trading* features and options for *staking*, a mechanism that enables the generation of returns through participation in transaction validation processes on the *blockchain* infrastructure.

The distinctive technological innovation of these platforms focuses on the implementation of security protocols for the safekeeping of digital *assets* (*wallets*), the development of high-frequency, low-latency *trading* infrastructure, the availability of APIs for algorithmic *trading*, and the implementation of interfaces for conversion transactions between fiat currencies and cryptocurrencies or between different types of digital *assets*.

Robo-Advisor Platforms

These services have resulted in a significant democratization of financial advice and asset management, making these activities accessible even to investors with limited capital availability through automated solutions with low cost structures.

Moneyfarm offers an automated financial advisory service and the construction of portfolios characterized by high diversification, based on the analysis of the user's risk profile and goals. The platform implements a hybrid approach, combining automated processes with advisory support provided by professionals.

Betterment is distinguished by the implementation of automated investment management characterized by a highly personalized approach, adapting allocation strategies according to the user's specific goals (retirement planning, real estate purchase, and other purposes) and optimizing the management of tax implications.

Wealthfront, with similarities to Betterment, places an accentuated focus on integrated financial planning and offering investments characterized by low costs, automating not only portfolio management but also additional aspects of personal financial planning.

The technological innovation peculiar to robo-advisors lies in the implementation of sophisticated algorithms for *asset allocation* and dynamic portfolio rebalancing, the application of artificial intelligence for strategy customization, the development of user interfaces characterized by high intuitiveness, and the implementation of advanced systems for *reporting* and *performance* monitoring.

Crowdfunding Platforms and Alternative Investments

These platforms have ushered in new ways of financing *startups*, small businesses, and innovative projects, and expanded investment opportunities in alternative *assets* such as *peer-to-peer lending* and fractional real estate investment.

Crowdcube and Seedrs represent flagship platforms in the *equity crowdfunding* (*equity*) segment, enabling *retail* investors to allocate capital directly into unlisted startups and small businesses, acquiring corporate stakes and potentially benefiting from the growth of these economic entities.

Bondora presents a specialization in *peer-to-peer lending*, allowing users to invest in personal loans provided to individuals, earning potentially higher returns than traditional bond investments, against the assumption of higher credit risk.

Housers has introduced elements of innovation in real estate investment, making this asset class accessible even with low capital allocations, through the mechanism of real estate *crowdfunding*, which enables participation in projects in the real estate sector by splitting the investment among a plurality of users.

The distinctive technological innovation of these platforms is based on the implementation of *web* infrastructure for project submission and evaluation, the development of due *diligence* and risk assessment systems, digitized transaction management, and the implementation of platforms for direct communication between issuers and investors.

ESG (Environmental, Social, Governance) Investment Platforms

These platforms respond to the growing demand for sustainable and responsible investments by integrating environmental, social, and *governance* (ESG) criteria into capital allocation strategies.

Ethic offers customized investment solutions based on ESG criteria, enabling users to align their capital allocations with their ethical and environmental values by selecting companies and funds that meet specific sustainability standards.

Impakter has adopted a specific focus on sustainable and green transition-oriented investments, promoting companies and projects that contribute to the development of an economy characterized by greater environmental sustainability.

The distinctive innovation of these platforms lies in the integration of ESG data and *ratings* into traditional financial analysis, the construction of customized portfolios based on sustainability criteria, information transparency regarding the environmental and social impact of investments, and the promotion of an approach to finance characterized by greater social and environmental responsibility (Table 4).

3.5 Digital Platforms for Art

Digital platforms for art represent an evolutionary segment characterized by transformations in the processes of creation, distribution, and marketing of artistic works. These infrastructures have introduced innovative ways of interconnecting actors in the art ecosystem, reconfiguring traditional value chains through disintermediation of established processes, broadening market accessibility and democratizing creative opportunities.

Table 4 Summary of digital platforms by investment

Category of platforms	Business innovations	Controversial implications of a legal nature
Online trading (eToro, Degiro, Robinhood, Interactive Brokers)	Simplified multichannel interfaces; commission reduction/elimination; high-performance infrastructure; real-time data; *social* and *copy trading* capabilities; democratization of complex strategies	Behavioral risks from simplified interfaces; herd effect in *copy trading*; transparency of *payment for order flow*; uninformed *trading* increase; *gamification* of investment experience
Investments in cryptocurrencies (Coinbase, Binance, Kraken)	Security protocols for digital *wallets*; low-latency *trading* infrastructure; API for algorithmic trading; DeFi and *staking* capabilities; passive performance from validation	Inherent *asset* volatility; *cybersecurity* risks; regulatory uncertainty; AML issues; disputes with regulators; complexity for inexperienced investors; *margin trading* risks
Robo-advisor (Moneyfarm, Betterment, Wealthfront)	Algorithms for allocation and rebalancing; AI for strategy personalization; intuitive interfaces; automation and human support integration; personalization based on risk profile	Limitations of algorithmic advice; transparency of decision-making algorithms; need for independent validation; cost/value ratio; handling exceptional market events
Crowdfunding and alternative investments (Crowdcube, Seedrs, Bondora, Housers)	Infrastructure for project evaluation; digital due diligence systems; direct issuer-investor communication; democratizing *equity* and *venture capital*; access to fractional real estate investments	Illiquidity of unlisted investments; risks of *startup* failure; complexity of due *diligence* for *retail*; non-professional investor protection; *pre-money* valuation issues; insolvency risks in P2P *lending*
ESG investment (Ethic, Impakter)	Integration of ESG *ratings* into analyses; portfolios based on sustainability criteria; transparency on environmental/social impact; alignment of capital with ethical values	Objective definition of ESG criteria; *greenwashing* risks; *performance/impact trade-off*; need for independent verification; sectoral focus

The nature of such platforms is manifested through highly interactive interfaces, integration of emerging technologies such as *blockchain* and artificial intelligence, highly connective virtual communities, and innovative ways of tokenizing works. Distinctive features include the removal of geographic barriers, transactional transparency, and the redefinition of the concepts of originality and authenticity.

Platforms for Buying and Selling Physical Artwork

These platforms have transformed the marketing of traditional art, partially disintermediating physical galleries and expanding market accessibility.

The key innovation lies in digitizing the exhibition experience and reducing information asymmetries. Artsy connects international collectors and galleries through recommendation algorithms and *online* auctions. Saatchi Art enables independent artists to directly market their works with transparent commission structures. Singulart focuses on international contemporary artists while Artspace specializes in modern and contemporary art with a focus on limited editions. Technological innovation includes HD virtual galleries, augmented reality viewing tools, sophisticated transactional systems, and digitized processes for authenticating works.

Digital Art Platforms and NFT

These platforms have ushered in an innovative concept by introducing verifiable scarcity and ownership in the digital environment through *blockchain* and non-fungible tokenization (NFT), structurally reconfiguring the concepts of originality and collectibility. OpenSea features an open architecture with interoperability between different *blockchains* and support for a wide range of digital *assets*. Foundation adopts a selective approach with invitation system and auction mechanisms with decreasing price increment. SuperRare focuses on unique works of high quality with rigorous artistic selection. Rarible implements a democratic approach by allowing artists to create and customize their own *tokens* with high autonomy.

Technological innovation includes *smart contracts* for automated *royalties*, decentralized *marketplaces*, and integrated *wallets for token* and cryptocurrency management.

Platforms for Art Learning and Discovery

These platforms have democratized access to artistic knowledge and cultural heritage, disintermediating the traditional museum experience and breaking down geographic and economic barriers.

Google Arts & Culture has digitized collections from more than 2000 cultural institutions, implementing virtual museum tours and interactive tools for thematic exploration of art history. Artland has developed a model focused on connecting collectors and galleries with three-dimensional virtual tours of exhibitions and fairs. MoMA online courses offer structured training on modern and contemporary art through an interactive *e-learning* infrastructure. Technological innovation includes ultra-high resolution digitization, immersive virtual and augmented reality experiences, and algorithmic semantic navigation of collections.

Platforms for Creating and Sharing Art

These platforms have generated digital ecosystems for sharing and promoting artistic productions, creating virtual communities, and democratizing access to skilled *feedback* and professional opportunities. DeviantArt has established itself as one of the most extensive digital art communities, implementing an infrastructure for multidisciplinary sharing and monitoring of unauthorized use of works.

Behance, acquired by Adobe, focuses on professional art portfolios with algorithmic curation and advanced *engagement* metrics. ArtStation specifically targets digital artists, illustrators, and designers with a dedicated ecosystem for job opportunities in digital entertainment.

Technological innovation includes portfolio management tools, content discovery algorithms, statistical *engagement* analysis, and intellectual property protection technologies.

Platforms for **Crowdfunding** *Art Projects*

These platforms have introduced innovative systems in financing artistic production through distributed micro-mecenatism, disintermediating traditional channels, and democratizing access to capital for experimental projects. Kickstarter pioneered an "all or nothing" model with predefined goals and graduated rewards. Patreon has developed a recurring subscription system for ongoing support with access to exclusive content. Indiegogo offers more flexibility by allowing pledgers to receive funds raised regardless of goal achievement.

Technological innovation includes scalable infrastructure for decentralized fundraising, reward management systems, analytical tools for campaign optimization and project feasibility verification (Table 5).

3.6 Digital Platforms, Data Sovereignty, and Digital Sovereignty

The advent of digitization has brought about the need for a profound conceptual reformulation of the notion of sovereignty in the context of the contemporary digital age.

The issue of digital sovereignty, understood as the preservation and application of the fundamental principles of territoriality and state hierarchy in the domain of digital activities, has become increasingly relevant as digital platforms have become more widespread and pervasively integrated into economic and social fabrics.

The inherently global dimension of the digital ecosystem, which transcends traditional physical and jurisdictional boundaries, poses novel and complex challenges to established models of governance and state-derived regulatory architectures.

The dialectical tension between the transnational nature of data flows and digital transactions, on the one hand, and the need to preserve sovereign prerogatives in the regulation and supervision of these activities, on the other, have led to the emergence of an articulate debate on how to reconcile these two seemingly antithetical aspects. In this context, digital sovereignty is configured not merely as a transposition of traditional concepts of state sovereignty into the digital domain, but as an

Table 5 Summary of digital platforms for art

Category of platforms	Business innovations	Controversial implications of a legal nature
Purchase and sale of physical artwork (Artsy, Saatchi Art, Singulart, Artspace)	HD virtual galleries; reducing information asymmetries; partial disintermediation; accessibility for emerging artists; recommendation algorithms; transparent commissions; digitized logistics management; augmented reality visualization	Authenticity verification without physical inspection; platform liability in disputes; cross-border tax implications; digital reproduction rights; due *diligence* and AML obligations
Digital Art and NFT (OpenSea, Foundation, SuperRare, Rarible)	*Blockchain* for verifiable ownership; non-fungible tokenization; *smart contracts* for automatic *royalties*; decentralized *marketplaces*; integrated *wallets*; auction mechanisms with dynamic *pricing*	Regulatory uncertainty; qualification of NFTs; intellectual property rights; separation of *token* ownership/playback *rights*; tax implications; *blockchain* environmental impact; long-term persistence
Art learning and discovery (Google Arts & Culture, Artland, MoMA Online Courses)	HD digitization of museum collections; immersive virtual tours; global educational content; virtual/augmented reality experiences; algorithmic semantic navigation	Intellectual property rights in massive digitization; equitable cultural heritage representation; differential access premium content; ethical implications for sensitive cultural heritages
Creating and sharing art (DeviantArt, Behance, ArtStation)	Ecosystems for sharing and promotion; specialized social networks; *feedback* democratization; digital wallets; content discovery algorithms; statistical *engagement* analysis	Ownership rights uploaded works; implicit licenses sharing; artistic moderation and censorship; protection of minors; cultural appropriation; representation marginalized communities
Crowdfunding art projects (Kickstarter, Patreon, Indiegogo)	Distributed micro-patronage; direct creator-supporter connection; disintermediation traditional channels; accessibility capital experimental projects; graduated rewards system	Legal qualification of contributions; contractual obligations to supporters; disputes over delays/failure to complete projects

evolved concept that requires a reconceptualization of the fundamental notions of jurisdiction, control, and decision-making autonomy.

From a strictly technological point of view, the first concrete responses to the need to implement effective digital sovereignty mechanisms have mainly taken the form of developing and offering *cloud* services characterized by national sovereignty.

These services, offered by leading global *cloud* infrastructure providers, are based on the provider's assumption of specific contractual commitments designed to ensure that storage processes and, in certain cases, even data processing operations take place exclusively within infrastructures physically located in the territory of a specific state entity, or in a predefined set of national jurisdictions.

Amazon Web Services (AWS), configuring itself as one of the leading players in the *cloud* infrastructure sector, offers its users the ability to select with high granularity the geographic region in which to execute their computational *workloads* (*workloads*), also announcing the imminent implementation, expected by the end of the year 2025, of AWS *European Sovereign Cloud.*[10] This initiative is a significant testament to the increasing attention being paid to the digital sovereignty needs expressed in particular by European Union institutions and member states.

The offering elaborated by Google, called *Google Sovereign Cloud*,[11] presents an even more articulated structuring, proposing a broad spectrum of features that implement the three conceptual pillars on which the company bases its digital sovereignty strategy: data sovereignty (*Data Sovereignty*), conceived as control over the physical location and access mechanisms to data; operational sovereignty (*Operational Sovereignty*), understood as autonomy in the management and control of technical operations; and application sovereignty (*Software Sovereignty*), defined as the ability to maintain control over the applications and digital services used.

However, it is crucial to note that the solutions currently available in the market, while representing a significant advancement toward addressing digital sovereignty needs, offer—in their optimal configuration—effective responses predominantly in relation to the essential digital sovereignty requirements expressed by national governmental entities and public institutions in specific geopolitical contexts, with particular reference to countries belonging to the European Union. This effectiveness, however, appears to be mainly focused on the dimension of data sovereignty, leaving the further conceptual dimensions of digital sovereignty partially unexplored.

The complexity and heterogeneity of the application scenarios of digital platforms mandate for a more comprehensive approach to issues of digital sovereignty, i.e., in a conceptual context characterized by greater breadth and articulation. In this broader perspective, sovereignty over data (*Data Sovereignty*), while maintaining a position of primary importance in the conceptual architecture of digital sovereignty, needs to be integrated and balanced with the more general issue of sovereignty over digital tools and infrastructures in their systemic complexity.

Therefore, the full achievement of digital sovereignty requires the adoption of a holistic view that includes not only the aspects of physical location and legal protection of data, but also the dimensions of technological control, operational autonomy, and the ability to generate and implement innovation in the digital domain. In this context, the need emerges to develop multidimensional approaches, which consider the different facets of digital sovereignty, contemplating not only technical and infrastructural aspects, but also regulatory, economic, and socio-cultural ones.

---

[10] Amazon Web Services (2024).

[11] Google (2024).

References

Amazon Web Services (2024) AWS Digital Sovereignty. https://aws.amazon.com/compliance/digital-sovereignty/. Accessed 2 June 2025

Anti-Money Laundering AML Policy (2019) Know Your Customer (KYC) and anti-money laundering (AML) policy. Policy. https://vastu-hfc-website.s3.ap-south-1.amazonaws.com/uploads/public/assets/pdf/policies/kyc-and-aml-policy.pdf. Accessed 2 June 2025.

AWS (2024) lambda/. https://aws.amazon.com/it/lambda/. Accessed 2 June 2025

Chippagiri S, Ramesh A (2025) PCI DSS: a critical analysis of implementation, effectiveness, and legislative impact in payment card security. Int J Sci Res Comput Sci Eng Inf Technol 11(1):1258–1266. https://doi.org/10.32628/CSEIT251112115

European Commission (2020) STATEMENT/20/2082. https://ec.europa.eu/commission/presscorner/detail/en/STATEMENT_20_2082. Accessed 2 June 2025

Fortunato D, Bernardino J (2018) Progressive web apps: an alternative to the native mobile Apps. In: 2018 13th Iberian Conference on Information Systems and Technologies (CISTI), pp 1–6. https://doi.org/10.23919/CISTI.2018.8399228

Google (2024) GoogleSovereign Cloud. https://cloud.google.com/sovereign-cloud. Accessed 2 June 2025

Harvard Business School Online (2024) What is a Digital Platform? https://online.hbs.edu/blog/post/what-is-a-digital-platform. Accessed 2 June 2025

IBM (2024) end-to-end-encryption. https://www.ibm.com/it-it/topics/end-to-end-encryption. Accessed 2 June 2025

Ometov et al (2018). Multi-factor authentication: a survey. Cryptography 2(1):1. https://doi.org/10.3390/cryptography2010001

Tripathi P (2024) Tokenization strategy implementation with PCI compliance for digital payment in the banking. Int J Sci Res Eng Trends 10(5):1848–1850. https://doi.org/10.61137/ijsret.vol.10.issue5.235

Chang et al. (2022). Digital payment fraud detection methods in digital ages and Industry 4.0. Comput Electr Eng, 100, 107734. https://doi.org/10.1016/j.compeleceng.2022.107734

Enabling Technologies

Luigi Coppolino and Luigi Romano

Contents

Abstract This chapter examines the EU's strategic initiatives, like European Data Spaces and the Data Governance Act, to foster secure, ethical, and sovereign data ecosystems. It details how federated environments, supported by connectors and intermediary services, facilitate transparent data sharing while retaining ownership. The chapter also highlights the crucial role of security modules, identity management systems, audit services, cryptography, and blockchain in ensuring data protection and traceability within these innovative paradigms.

L. Coppolino (✉) · L. Romano
University of Naples "Parthenope", Naples, Italy
e-mail: luigi.coppolino@uniparthenope.it; luigi.romano@uniparthenope.it

R. Bocchini (ed.), *Digital Platforms - From Technical Foundations to Legal and Economic Implications*, https://doi.org/10.1007/978-3-032-07978-7_2

1 The European Data Space

In the global economic context, the intrinsic value of data is reaching unprecedented levels. In any modern economy, the management and utilisation of ever-growing volumes of data pose significant challenges, both from a technological and regulatory perspective. The evolution of increasingly data-driven systems and the development of artificial intelligence models, such as large language models (LLMs), further encourage the pursuit and accumulation of information, which is regarded as a strategic resource for creating value-added services. The European Union has acknowledged this trend and initiated a regulatory and strategic process to ensure the creation of secure and reliable ecosystems for the management, exchange, and use of data. Within this framework, the Data Governance Act[1] represents a significant effort to establish a regulatory framework enabling innovative data-sharing methods compared to traditional paradigms, which have typically been characterised by bilateral and centralised exchanges.

In parallel, the European Union's vision encompasses the establishment of the *European Data Spaces*,[2] an initiative aimed at creating a common data market based on the principles of ethics, trust, and digital sovereignty, in full compliance with European regulations. This approach seeks to foster a collaborative ecosystem in which data circulation is governed by transparency and security criteria, thereby promoting sustainable and innovative economic growth.

1.1 The Concept of Data Space

Data sharing is a central issue in the current digital economy, marked by an increasing need to ensure data security, ownership, and sovereignty, especially in transnational multi-stakeholder contexts. It is important to distinguish between data sharing and data exchange: while exchange involves the permanent transfer of ownership and control of data from one entity to another, sharing allows the original owner to retain ownership and control over the data, regulating access and use by third parties.

This approach means that even when data is shared, the owner can continue to exercise their rights over it. Moreover, when discussing data sharing, the concept of data sovereignty is indispensable. This refers to the ability of the owner to autonomously determine how their data is used, accessed, and protected, in compliance with applicable regulations.

In a transnational context, data sovereignty is critical to ensuring that data is managed according to principles of ethics, transparency, and security, avoiding

[1] Pathak (2024).

[2] European Commission (2024).

misuse or unauthorised access. Data sovereignty is not merely a matter of technical control; it is also a fundamental safeguard for protecting the digital rights of individuals and organisations.

In this context, the concept of a *Data Space* emerges as an innovative paradigm aimed at overcoming the limitations of traditional approaches to data management. A Data Space can be defined as a federated environment where different organisations collaborate to share data in a secure and regulated manner, while retaining control over its ownership and sovereignty.

This infrastructure not only facilitates data sharing in compliance with applicable regulations but also lays the groundwork for the development of a secure and transparent data market. The objective, as illustrated in Fig. 1, is to ensure that data is regarded as a strategic asset, capable of generating economic and social value without compromising the principles of trust and ethics.

Fundamental components of a Data Space are the connectors. Their primary function is to facilitate connections between participants, ensuring security and interoperability during data sharing. Functionally, connectors enable data access among entities that may use heterogeneous systems and formats. They ensure that data can flow freely within the Data Space while maintaining its integrity and confidentiality, even in highly complex environments.

Another key feature of Data Spaces are the intermediary services. These services act as facilitators for discovering and accessing available data. Their main role is not to store data directly but to manage metadata that describes the datasets and services offered within the Data Space. Through these services, participants can identify the resources they are interested in and access them according to predefined usage rules and rights, contributing to a transparent and regulated ecosystem.

The metadata managed by intermediary services can, for instance, support the creation of a federated service catalogue. This catalogue provides participants with

Fig. 1 Data Spaces as part of the European Data Strategy [https://digital-strategy.ec.europa.eu/en/policies/strategy-data]

a comprehensive and organised overview of the available datasets and functionalities, making it easier to identify opportunities for collaboration or strategic data use. Moreover, the metadata goes beyond merely describing the content of the data, encompassing information about accessibility, licences, security requirements, and usage restrictions. This comprehensive metadata framework supports negotiation and access processes within the Data Space.

Technical Insights: Aspects of Connectors

To enable scalable and flexible management, connectors are released in the form of *Helm Charts*, a well-established standard for *deployment* on *Kubernetes* clusters.[3] This release method simplifies the deployment and configuration of connectors, making them easily integrable into existing infrastructures.

Connectors are designed with a *microservices architecture*, allowing for high modularity and scalability. Each microservice is responsible for a specific function, such as access control, data encryption, or communication protocol management. This separation of responsibilities enhances the overall resilience of the system and ensures more efficient operation.

From a functional perspective, while connectors and their microservices form the core of data sharing, the *governance framework* constitutes the regulatory backbone of the Data Space. This framework is essential to ensure that all parties involved adhere to shared rules regarding the use and management of data. Functionally, governance establishes a set of policies, guidelines, and contracts that clearly define the rights and responsibilities of participants. These regulated elements include access terms, data usage restrictions, and applicable sanctions for violations. This approach balances flexibility and control, fostering a collaborative environment where data can be used ethically and responsibly.

To ensure the security of Data Spaces, various security modules are employed to manage authentication and authorisation, safeguarding data access and ensuring compliance with governance rules. These modules are often integrated with Multi-Factor Authentication (MFA) systems to enhance security and mitigate risks associated with unauthorised access.

Additionally, *Identity Management Systems* (IMS)[4] play a critical role in ensuring that every action within the Data Space is securely recorded and traceable. These systems provide centralised management of participants' identities and credentials, facilitating the verification of access rights and enforcement of security

[3] Zerouali et al. (2023), pp. 523–533.

[4] Identity management systems (IDMS) are frameworks that handle the creation, maintenance, and removal of digital identities and their associated access rights within an organisation or system. They ensure that only authorised entities gain access to specific resources and systems, protecting sensitive information and enhancing security. IDMS also manages aspects like user onboarding, role assignments, and access control policies.

Fig. 2 Key elements for Data Space security: access management, data protection, and traceability

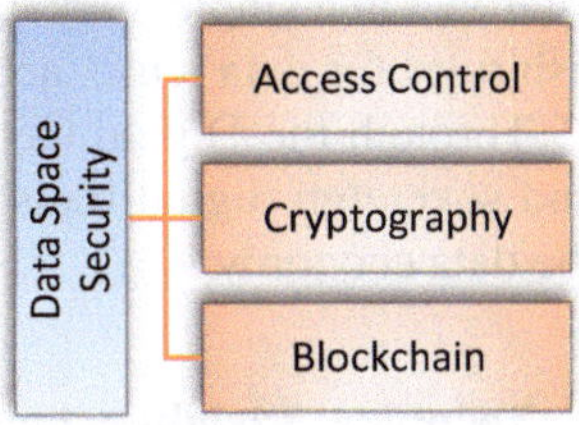

policies. This integrated approach enables strict access control, preserves data security, and strengthens trust among participants.

> **Technical Insights: Access Control Aspects**
> From a functional perspective, security modules ensure that only authorised participants can access data and that every operation is verifiable and compliant with *security policies*. To achieve these objectives, established technologies such as OAuth 2.0 for access delegation and X.509 digital certificates for secure authentication are employed.

To conclude, audit and monitoring services complete the security architecture by providing transparency and ensuring that all operations within the Data Space comply with established regulations and policies. Functionally, these services track every operation performed on the data, maintaining a verifiable and immutable record of all activities. This is essential not only for identifying potential anomalies or security incidents but also for demonstrating compliance with applicable regulations.

Figure 2 illustrates the key elements of Data Space security.

> **Technical Insights: Audit and Monitoring Services**
> From a technological perspective, *audit* and *monitoring* services leverage advanced tools for logging and log analysis. *Blockchain*-based technologies are often employed to ensure the immutability and transparency of records, providing a robust foundation for traceability.[5]

1.2 European Initiatives

In recent years, the European Union has prioritised the development of a data economy, recognising its key role in driving innovation and competitiveness. Among the main initiatives, the European Strategy for Data aims to create a secure and

[5] Coppolino et al. (2021).

interoperable single market, while the Data Governance Act and the Data Act establish rules for data reuse, access, and sharing, ensuring both protection and trust.

Through the Digital Compass 2030, the EU outlines its goals for a sustainable and sovereign digital transformation, reinforcing its position as a global leader in the data economy.

Technical Insights: The Data Governance Act and the Role of the Intermediary
The Data Governance Act establishes a regulatory framework for data management, focusing on secure data sharing and data altruism. Central to this framework is the role of the intermediary, a neutral entity that facilitates data exchange between parties while ensuring transparency and security. Intermediaries operate within a regulated context, avoiding conflicts of interest and ensuring compliance with data protection regulations. This mechanism aims to foster trust and innovation within the European single data market.

Aligned with the European Union's goal of creating a single data market that promotes trust and transparency, various organisations are developing technological infrastructures and operational models to enable innovative services. Among these, the International Data Spaces Association (IDSA) plays a key role in setting standards for Data Spaces, offering a model that ensures data sovereignty and direct control by data owners. Through shared architectures and governance tools, IDSA facilitates the creation of ecosystems where data can be securely shared across sectors and regions.GAIA-X, another significant initiative, stands out for its approach to federating cloud infrastructures, fostering a European ecosystem that ensures compliance with digital sovereignty and existing regulations. By promoting interoperability and transparency, GAIA-X enables secure data sharing and its strategic use to enhance the competitiveness of European businesses. These initiatives are essential components in developing a European data economy that combines innovation and security, strengthening the EU's leadership in a context increasingly reliant on the value of data.

1.3 Example of a Data Space

Catena-X[6] is one of the first practical examples of a Data Space implemented in an industrial context, specifically for the German automotive sector. The primary goal of Catena-X is to enhance collaboration along the value chain by enabling secure data sharing among manufacturers, suppliers, and logistics partners. This platform

[6] Catena-X (2024).

increases efficiency in production processes, reduces operational costs, and improves sustainability through optimised resource utilisation.

The management of the supply chain through a Data Space like Catena-X relies on a federated model that allows stakeholders to share data securely and in a controlled manner, while maintaining full sovereignty over their information. This system is particularly beneficial in complex, multi-stakeholder environments where manufacturers, suppliers, logistics companies, and other partners collaborate across the entire value chain.

In the traditional model, information sharing often occurs in a fragmented manner, typically via manual exchanges of documents, emails, or dedicated portals. These approaches create information silos and limit the effectiveness of collaboration. In contrast, a Data Space such as Catena-X provides a shared technological infrastructure that ensures interoperability between different systems and centralised management of access mechanisms. Each participant can decide what data to share and with whom, leveraging integrated governance rules that ensure regulatory compliance and protect sensitive data.

Compared to traditional methods, Catena-X removes technological barriers between stakeholders, allowing real-time access to the information necessary for operations. The decentralised control of data is another distinctive feature, as each participant retains full ownership of their information, mitigating the risks of misuse or unauthorised access. Furthermore, this system enhances transparency and facilitates the identification of inefficiencies or anomalies, promoting more agile and resilient supply chain management.

Technical Insight: Practical Example of Catena-X Usage

A practical example showcasing the benefits of a Data Space like Catena-X in a multi-stakeholder context involves the production and distribution of vehicles in an industry characterised by a complex and interconnected supply chain. Consider a scenario involving an automotive manufacturer, multiple component suppliers, logistics companies, and a recycling partner, all connected through Catena-X.

In the traditional model, each actor manages their data in isolation, often using proprietary and non-interoperable systems. Communication relies on emails or manual data exchanges, leading to delays, duplications, and potential errors. In contrast, Catena-X enables each stakeholder to share the necessary data selectively and securely, using a common and standardised language.

For instance, component suppliers upload data to the Data Space regarding part availability, production timelines, and product quality. This information is immediately accessible to automotive manufacturers, who can monitor order status in real-time, plan production schedules, and respond quickly to

[7] STMicroelectronics (2021).

issues such as delivery delays or manufacturing defects. Simultaneously, logistics companies continuously update the system with data on cargo location and transport conditions, enabling more precise planning for downstream operations, such as final assembly.

Another significant advantage arises when the recycling partner becomes involved. At the end of a vehicle's lifecycle, the partner can access technical data on the materials used, facilitating the recovery and reuse of resources such as steel or batteries.

This level of cross-functional collaboration would not be possible without an ecosystem like Catena-X, which ensures interoperability among diverse stakeholders while preserving each participant's data sovereignty.

2 Cryptography: Key Elements

Cryptography[7] is a discipline that provides mechanisms to protect information, ensuring its confidentiality, integrity, and authenticity. In this context, cryptography is the means through which it is ensured that only authorised parties can access certain data (confidentiality), that information is not altered during transmission or storage (integrity), and that the origin of the data can always be verified (authenticity). To achieve these results, cryptography uses a data transformation mechanism based on pairs of secret codes. The first secret, called key, can be imagined as a sort of code used to transform data into an unreadable format, known as encryption. A second secret code can be used to return the data to its original state, referred to as decryption. There are two main approaches to cryptography: symmetric and asymmetric (Fig. 3).

Symmetric cryptography requires that the two secrets, the one for encryption and the one for decryption, are the same and are referred to as a "symmetric key." A single key is therefore shared between the sender and the receiver, the one who encrypts and the one who decrypts. This method is fast and efficient, particularly

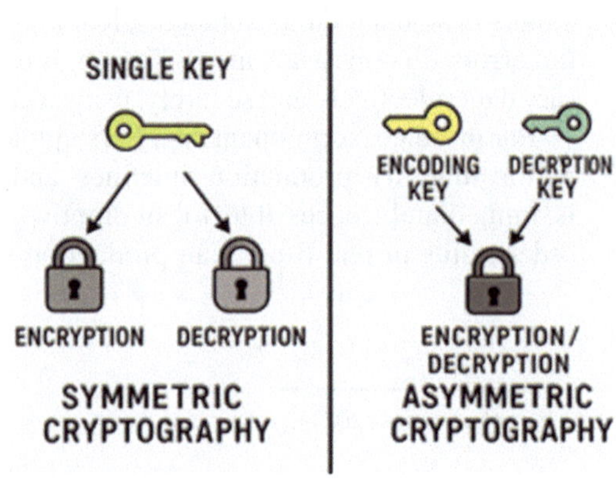

Fig. 3 Symmetric and asymmetric cryptography

suitable for protecting large amounts of information, but presents challenges in the secure management of keys. In distributed systems, in fact, it becomes complex to ensure that the shared key remains secret and protected.

In the case of asymmetric cryptography, however, the two codes are different: one key, generally called "public," because it can be freely shared, is used to encrypt the data. A second key, uniquely linked to the first and generally called "private," because it should remain secret, is used to decrypt it. This approach overcomes many limitations of symmetric cryptography related to key distribution but requires greater computational resources, making it less suitable for managing large volumes of data. It should be noted, in fact, that anyone who wants to send a message whose confidentiality is to be preserved can retrieve the public key, encrypt the message, and transfer it to the holder of the corresponding private key, who will be the only person able to decrypt and read the message.

The key pair, public/private, can be used inversely: it is, that is, possible to encrypt the message with the private key and decrypt it with the public key. In this case, while anyone can decrypt the message, given the availability of the public key, only the holder of the private key could have encrypted it. This scheme makes it possible, therefore, to verify the identity of the entity that generated the encrypted message and is the basis of the well-known mechanism of the "digital signature."

Another mechanism made available by cryptography is that of "hash functions." This mechanism allows any digital content to produce a single fixed-length sequence of characters called a "hash" or "digital fingerprint." Calculating the hash of a document multiple times will always result in the same digital fingerprint; however, even the smallest change to the original document would result in a completely different digital fingerprint. Storing digital content alongside its hash thus allows verification that the document has not been altered.

Technical Insight: Post-Quantum Cryptography

Modern cryptography relies on complex mathematical problems, such as the factorisation of large numbers or discrete logarithms, which require vast amounts of time to solve using traditional computers. These problems underpin the security of cryptographic techniques currently in use, such as asymmetric cryptography, which protects sensitive communications and online transactions. However, the advent of quantum computers poses a significant threat to this security. Quantum computers, with their ability to solve complex problems much faster, could potentially break current cryptographic systems.

Post-quantum cryptography has been developed to address this challenge, creating new algorithms that remain secure even against the capabilities of quantum computers. These algorithms are based on mathematical problems that, according to current knowledge, cannot be easily solved even by quantum computers, such as lattice problems or hash functions. The primary challenge is to ensure that these solutions are not only secure but also efficient and compatible with existing systems, enabling a gradual and reliable transition to a future where quantum computers are a reality.

2.1 Blockchain and Non-Fungible Tokens

To fully grasp the potential and risks of a technology like non-fungible tokens (NFTs), which is both widespread and often misunderstood, it is crucial to analyse the fundamental problem this technology seeks to address. This is an age-old issue common to many fields: ensuring the authenticity and veracity of information within a community. NFTs aim to provide a solution to this need.

Some examples of information for which one might wish to prove authenticity include: the ownership of an asset (demonstrating that it belongs to a specific individual), the authorship of a work (recognising that it was created by a specific author), and the repudiation of authorship (asserting that a work is not attributable to a specific individual).

Traditionally, to provide proof of authenticity for such information, a centralised model has been employed. In this system, a central entity, often a public authority, acts as the guarantor of the community's trust. This entity, referred to as a trusted third party (TTP), uses its authority to certify the veracity of the information. Examples of this approach include the issuance of an identity card by a public authority to attest to a person's identity or the certification of an economic transaction by a bank (Fig. 4).

As an alternative to the centralised approach, information can be certified through a distributed consensus mechanism. In this model, the validity of information is guaranteed by the community itself, acting as a collective guarantor. If a sufficient number of network participants recognise the authenticity of the information, it is accepted as valid. The robustness of this system relies on the difficulty of influencing or compromising a significant portion of participants without detection. This "difficulty" underpins the operation of blockchain technology. A blockchain is a digital ledger that records a sequence of transactions by linking them together. Each new transaction is stored by combining its information with the hash calculated from previous transactions, creating a chain where each element depends on the preceding one. Any alteration to an already recorded transaction renders the hashes

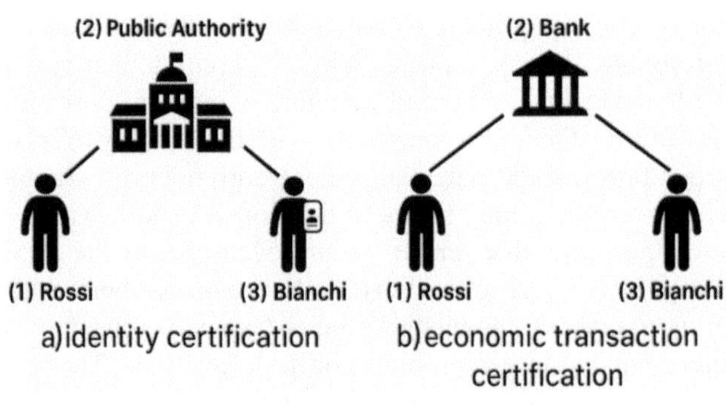

Fig. 4 (**a**) Identity certification in a centralised model; (**b**) Certification of an economic transaction in a centralised model

of all subsequent transactions inconsistent, making any tampering immediately evident. This ledger is distributed across multiple network nodes, which synchronise to ensure the integrity and consistency of the information. Different implementations of blockchain exist, such as Bitcoin, Ethereum, and Solana, which differ in how they manage transaction creation and inclusion in the chain. Some blockchains, like Ethereum, also allow the use of smart contracts, which are programs that automatically verify the validity and presence of transactions.

A key feature of blockchain technology is its ability to prevent the alteration of recorded transactions and certify new information solely through network consensus. However, over time, the community supporting a blockchain may split, creating a fork. This event generates two distinct branches of the chain, each with its own unsynchronised transactions. After the fork, the integrity of each branch can only be verified by the part of the community that supports it, reducing the uniqueness of the shared ledger.

Technical Insight: Risks Associated with Loss of Consensus

The strength of a blockchain lies in the number of nodes participating in the network: the greater the number of nodes, the more difficult it becomes for an alternative group to coordinate and achieve a level of reliability comparable to the original network. Blockchain nodes are generally managed by voluntary users who provide computational resources, often in exchange for economic incentives or, in some cases, without any direct return. However, the sustainability of this participation depends on the popularity of the network itself.

The technology is not immune to sudden shifts in interest. History is filled with examples of systems that were initially widespread but experienced rapid decline, as seen with some platforms or technologies that fell out of public favour. If a blockchain were to lose popularity, the number of nodes supporting it would decrease, jeopardising the entire network. A smaller community would be more vulnerable to the formation of an alternative group large enough to develop a competing chain.

This scenario, known as the risk of loss of consensus, can lead to the fork of the blockchain, resulting in two distinct chains supporting conflicting information. In the absence of clear consensus, it becomes impossible to determine which chain represents the "truth."

An interesting example of blockchain application is its use in the creation and management of unique digital certificates, known as non-fungible tokens (NFTs). These tools are designed to represent the ownership of digital or physical objects, addressing the issue of certifying and tracing the uniqueness and authenticity of an asset.

To clarify the concept, consider the case of a work of art, which could be either digital content or a physical object. In the case of a digital work, it is possible to generate a hash that represents its unique and unrepeatable fingerprint. This hash, along with information about ownership transfers, is recorded on the blockchain, thereby creating an NFT. This token becomes an unalterable certificate that certifies the ownership and authenticity of the work. The *blockchain* ensures that this certificate is verifiable and cannot be altered or duplicated without network consensus. If the work is physical, the process requires a preliminary digitisation phase. Digitisation can be achieved, for example, through high-definition scanning or the creation of a three-dimensional model, producing a unique digital representation of the work. From this representation, a *hash* is generated, and the process follows the same steps as the digital case, resulting in the creation of an NFT. This system allows physical works to be certified by associating them with a certified digital representation. However, it raises questions about the relationship between the original work and the digital copy. In some cases, the digital copy may acquire independent artistic value, particularly if the original is destroyed or becomes inaccessible.

Insight: The Banksy Case[8]
The artist Banksy brought the debate around NFTs into the spotlight with a provocative act involving his famous work "Girl with Balloon." After creating an NFT linked to the piece, the physical original was destroyed. This event highlighted how, in the digital age, the value of a work can be entirely transferred to a certified digital representation. The destruction raised questions about authenticity and the art market, demonstrating how a non-existent physical piece can continue to be traded through its NFT.

2.2 *Cloud Computing*

Cloud computing[9] allows the use of computing resources such as servers, storage, and applications over an Internet connection without the need to purchase or directly manage them. This model is based on three main paradigms that define the services offered. The first is Software as a Service (SaaS), which enables access to applications directly via the web, removing the need for installation and management by the user. Solutions like email platforms or productivity tools fall under this category.

The second paradigm is Platform as a Service (PaaS), which provides a complete platform for developing and managing applications, simplifying developers' work with preconfigured infrastructure. Lastly, Infrastructure as a Service (IaaS) offers access to virtualised hardware resources, such as servers and networks, that users

[8] BBC (2021).
[9] Sunyaev (2024).

can configure and manage according to their specific needs. These paradigms make cloud computing a versatile solution for various technological requirements. The flexibility of SaaS is particularly useful for organisations needing ready-to-use tools without managing the underlying infrastructure, while PaaS is ideal for companies developing customised applications, allowing them to focus on innovation without worrying about platform maintenance. IaaS, on the other hand, is a suitable choice for those needing full control over their infrastructure, providing the ability to configure tailored virtual environments.

Beyond these paradigms, cloud computing has evolved to support new approaches such as continuum computing, which integrates resources between central cloud and peripheral devices (known as edge). This approach processes data closer to its origin, reducing latency and improving system efficiency, a crucial aspect for real-time applications such as the Internet of Things (IoT) or Industry 4.0. As data and application complexity increases, the integration of public cloud, private cloud, and edge computing has led to hybrid models that balance scalability, efficiency, and control over sensitive data.

References

BBC (2021) Banksy art burned, destroyed and sold as token in 'money-making stunt'. BBC News. https://www.bbc.com/news/technology-56335948

Catena-X (2024) Catena-X. https://catena-x.net/en/1/. Accessed 2 June 2025

Coppolino et al. (2021) Facing the blockchain endpoint vulnerability, an SGX-based solution for secure eHealth auditing. In: 5th Italian Conference on Cybersecurity - CEUR Workshop Proceedings, 2940, pp 298–308

European Commission (2024) European data spaces. https://digital-strategy.ec.europa.eu/en/policies/data-spaces. Accessed 2 June 2025

Pathak M (2024) Data governance redefined: the evolution of EU data regulations from the GDPR to the DMA, DSA, DGA, data act and AI act. Eur Data Protect Law Rev (EDPL) 10(1). https://doi.org/10.21552/edpl/2024/1/8

STMicroelectronics (2021) MOOC, Security Part2: Basics of cryptography [YouTube playlist]. https://www.youtube.com/playlist?list=PLnMKNibPkDnFSFh57UFTZLpy-7lZiwTHh. Accessed 2 June 2025

Sunyaev A (2024) Cloud computing. In: Internet computing. Springer, Cham. https://doi.org/10.1007/978-3-031-61014-1_6

Zerouali et al. (2023) Helm charts for kubernetes applications: evolution, outdatedness and security risks. In: 2023 IEEE/ACM 20th International Conference on Mining Software Repositories (MSR), 523–533. https://doi.org/10.1109/MSR59073.2023.00078

Advanced Data Elaboration

Angelo Ciaramella and Raffaele Montella

Contents

Abstract The aim of this chapter is to explore the intersection of big data, artificial intelligence (AI), machine learning (ML), and high-performance computing (HPC), highlighting their synergies and challenges. The first section examines big data and data analytics, addressing the five key challenges in big data analytics, the process

A. Ciaramella (✉) · R. Montella
University of Naples "Parthenope", Naples, Italy
e-mail: angelo.ciaramella@uniparthenope.it; raffaele.montella@uniparthenope.it

R. Bocchini (ed.), *Digital Platforms - From Technical Foundations to Legal and Economic Implications*, https://doi.org/10.1007/978-3-032-07978-7_3

of data transformation, and the different types of data. The discussion then shifts to artificial intelligence, providing an overview of its historical evolution. The third section delves into machine learning and deep learning, covering various learning paradigms, advancements in Generative AI, and the technologies and platforms enabling deep learning. Finally, the chapter discusses the critical role of high-performance computing in supporting these data-intensive and AI-driven processes. By integrating these domains, the study underscores their collective impact on modern computational and analytical capabilities, offering insights into future technological advancements.

1 Big Data and Data Analytics

The locution big data ("large [masses of] data") generally refers to a set of large digital data, characterized by volume, velocity, and variety, which require specific technologies and analytical methodologies to extract information or knowledge. The term is often associated with the ability to analyze and correlate massive amounts of heterogeneous data, both structured and unstructured.

Big data analytics refers to the systemic collection, processing, and analysis of large volumes of data, known as big data. This process allows for the identification of trends, patterns, and correlations within complex and diverse data sets, providing analysts and business decision-makers with evidence-based information. Through the application of advanced analytical techniques, such as *machine learning* (ML), *artificial intelligence* (AI), and predictive analytics, raw data can be transformed into strategic knowledge.

The practice of big data analytics is particularly relevant in an environment where the amount of data generated from heterogeneous sources, such as IoT (*Internet of Things*) sensors, social media, financial transactions, and smart devices, is growing exponentially. This ability to extract value from data consents organizations to optimize processes, improve operational efficiency, anticipate market trends, and make informed decisions, thereby contributing to a competitive advantage in an increasingly data-driven landscape.

Advances in software and hardware capabilities have made it possible for organizations to collect and manage large amounts of unstructured data since the early 2000s. With this explosion of useful data, communities have developed frameworks to store and process this data. Together with appropriate tools and libraries, big data frameworks can be utilized for:

- *Predictive modeling*, which incorporates artificial intelligence (AI) and statistical algorhythms
- *Statistical analysis* for in depth exploration of data and to uncover hidden models

- *What-if* analysis for simulating different scenarios and explore potential outcomes;
- *Processing of different data sets*, including structured, semi-structured, and unstructured data from various sources.

The main difference between big data analytics and traditional data analytics lies in the type of data handled and the tools used to process it. Traditional data analytics focuses primarily on structured data, typically stored in relational databases. In contrast, big data analytics deals with significantly larger volumes of data in heterogeneous formats, including structured, semi-structured, and unstructured data, requiring more advanced and sophisticated analytical techniques. Big data analytics makes use of methodologies such as *machine learning* (ML) and data mining to extract information from large, complex data sets. It also often makes use of distributed processing systems, such as Hadoop, to efficiently manage the huge volume of data involved.

The four methods of data analysis in big data:

- *Descriptive analysis*. The focus is on summarizing and describing data to understand its basic characteristics.
- *Diagnostic analysis*. Diagnostic analysis identifies the underlying patterns and trends observed in descriptive analysis.
- *Predictive analysis*. This uses historical data, statistical modeling, and machine learning to predict trends.
- *Prescriptive analysis*. Prescriptive analysis goes beyond prediction to make recommendations for optimizing future actions based on intuitions derived from all precedents.

1.1 The Five Challenges in Big Data Analytics

The five main challenges of big data analytics are Volume, Velocity, Variety, Veracity, and Value. *Volume* refers to the enormous amount of data generated, which often exceeds the capabilities of traditional storage and processing solutions. Cloud-based storage platforms are an effective answer, enabling organizations to manage and store large volumes of data in a more scalable and efficient manner.

Speed relates to the rapid pace at which data are produced and must be processed, requiring infrastructure capable of acquiring, processing, and providing accurate analysis in near-real time. *Variety* reflects the diversity of data formats and sources, ranging from structured and numeric data to unstructured content such as text, video, and images from heterogeneous sources such as social media and video surveillance systems. To manage this heterogeneity, flexible systems, such as Not Structured Query Language (NoSQL) databases, data lakes, and schema-on-read technologies, are needed to integrate and analyze different types of data effectively.

Veracity emphasizes the importance of data reliability and accuracy, as decisions based on incomplete or inaccurate information can lead to negative results. This dimension includes aspects such as data quality, noise, and anomaly detection, making tools and techniques for data cleaning, validation, and verification essential. Ensuring data integrity is essential to support informed, evidence-based decisions.

Finally, *Value* represents the final goal of big data analytics: transforming large volumes of data into meaningful, actionable information. This process makes it possible to support strategic decisions, identify new opportunities, and foster innovation, generating tangible impact for organizations.

1.2 Data Transformation Process

A *Data Warehouse* is a system that aggregates data from different sources into one central and coherent data storage to support data analysis, *data mining*, *artificial intelligence*, and *machine learning*.

The process of transforming raw data into useful information consists of several key stages: data collection, processing, cleansing, and analysis. The initial phase involves the collection of data, which can come from heterogeneous sources, such as cloud, mobile applications, and IoT sensors, and come in both structured and unstructured formats. Next, the collected data are processed, i.e., organized, extracted, transformed, and uploaded to a storage system, a crucial step in ensuring the accuracy of analytical results.

Regardless of their size, data require cleaning to ensure their quality and relevance. This process includes such operations as proper formatting, elimination of duplicates, and removal of irrelevant information. *Data cleaning* is essential to prevent errors in the output and maintain the reliability and accuracy of the information.

Finally, the processed and cleaned data are subjected to advanced analysis, which may include techniques such as data mining, predictive analytics, machine learning, and deep learning. These approaches enable deep data exploration, extracting meaningful insights and supporting informed decisions.

1.3 Types of Data

Data can be classified primarily into three categories: *structured*, *unstructured*, and *semi-structured*.

Structured data refer to information that is highly organized, easily searchable, and typically stored in relational databases or spreadsheets. This data follows a rigid schema, in which each element is clearly defined and accessible within a specific field of a record or file. The main advantage of structured data lies in its simplicity of entry, search, and analysis, often done through SQL queries. However, despite their usefulness, structured data represent only a small fraction of the total data generated today, due to the rapid growth of the big data universe.

Unstructured data, on the other hand, do not follow a predefined pattern and are therefore more complex to collect, process, and analyze. They represent most of data currently generated and include formats such as textual content (emails, documents), multimedia content (images, video, audio), and data from IoT devices. The main challenge associated with unstructured data is its lack of uniformity, which requires advanced methods for indexing, searching, and analysis.

Semi-structured data lies somewhere in between structured and unstructured data. Although they are not stored in relational databases, they contain markers or tags that define hierarchies and relationships between elements, as in JSON (JavaScript Object Notation) or XML (eXtensible Markup Language) files, or in NoSQL databases. This feature makes semi-structured data more flexible than structured data, but easier to analyze than unstructured data, representing a particularly effective solution for web applications and data integration processes.

2 Artificial Intelligence

Artificial intelligence (AI) is the ability of a machine to exhibit human capabilities such as reasoning, learning, planning, and creativity.[1]

AI enables systems to understand their surroundings, interact with what they perceive, solve problems, and act in a targeted way to achieve specific goals. The computer receives data, which may be pre-processed or collected through sensors, processes it, and provides a response. AI systems can adapt their behavior by analyzing the outcomes of previous actions, operating autonomously, and improving their performance over time.[2]

Based on the level of sophistication, two types of AI can be defined, weak and strong. *Weak AI*, also known as "narrow AI," defines AI systems designed to perform a specific task or set of tasks (e.g., "smart" voice assistant, such as Amazon's Alexa or Apple's Siri, social media chatbots, or Tesla's promised autonomous vehicles). *Strong AI*, also known as "general artificial intelligence" or "general AI.," possesses the ability to understand, learn, and apply knowledge across a wide range of tasks at a level equal to or greater than human intelligence.

[1] Negnevitsky (2005).

[2] Russell and Norvig (2020).

2.1 History of AI

To understand the evolution of AI, it is essential to examine some of the major historical milestones that have marked its development. AI emerged as an academic discipline in the 1950s, going through phases of increasing interest and periods of stalemate related to its ability to solve concrete problems.

In 1943, Warren S. McCulloch and Walter H. Pitts published a paper entitled "A logical calculus of the ideas immanent in nervous activity," introducing the concept of the artificial neuron as a model for simulating brain function. This model, based on fixed synaptic weights, did not yet include a learning mechanism.

In 1949, Canadian psychologist Donald O. Hebb, in his book *The organization of behavior*, theorized the first learning rule, known as "Hebb's rule," supported by physiological evidence.

In 1950, Alan Turing published "Computing Machinery and Intelligence," asking a fundamental question, "Can machines think?" Turing proposed a test, known today as the "Turing Test," in which a human interrogator tries to distinguish between a computer-generated response and one from a human. Despite criticism, this test remains a mainstay in the history of AI and the philosophy of mind.

It was John McCarthy, in 1956, who coined the term *artificial intelligence* during a lecture at Dartmouth College. In the same year, Allen Newell, J.C. Shaw and Herbert Simon developed Logic Theorist, the first working AI program.

In 1958, Frank Rosenblatt formalized the *perceptron* model, an artificial neural network, and built the Perceptron Mark 1, the first computer based on a neural network capable of trial-and-error learning. In 1960, Bernard Widrow and Marcian Hoff created ADALINE, a neural network model that used the descending gradient rule for learning. At the same time, in 1965, Lotfi Zadeh introduced fuzzy logic, which allowed control systems to be built in a more intuitive and general way.

The golden age of AI ended in 1969, when Marvin Minsky and Seymour Papert demonstrated the limitations of the perceptron in solving complex problems, such as the XOR problem. This marked the beginning of a period of stalemate, known as the *AI Winter*, that lasted until 1986, when David Rumelhart, Geoffrey Hinton, and Ronald Williams introduced the multilayer perceptron (MLP) and the backpropagation algorithm, revolutionizing the training of neural networks.

In 1995, Vladimir Vapnik and Corinna Cortes developed support vector machine (SVM), a new machine learning model. In the same year, Stuart Russell and Peter Norvig published *Artificial Intelligence: A Modern Approach*, which has become a landmark text for the study of AI.

In 1997, IBM's Deep Blue system defeated world chess champion Garry Kasparov, marking a milestone in AI. In 2004, John McCarthy proposed a definition of AI that is still widely cited today. With the advent of big data and cloud computing, organizations began to handle increasing volumes of data, critical for training AI models.

In 2006, Geoffrey Hinton and Ruslan Salakhutdinov introduced the concept of *deep neural network* and *pre-training*, giving the field a significant boost. In 2011,

IBM Watson defeated the champions of *Jeopardy!*, and in 2015, Baidu's *Minwa* supercomputer used a convolutional neural network to classify images with greater than human accuracy.

In 2016, DeepMind's *AlphaGo*, powered by a deep neural network, beat Go world champion Lee Sedol in a historic game. This success was particularly significant given the complexity of the game, with more than 14.5 trillion possible moves after only four rounds. Google acquired DeepMind for $400 million, further accelerating the development of AI.

After 2017, the introduction of the *Transformer* architecture and increased investment in AI led to rapid and continuous progress, known as the *AI boom*. In 2022, *large language models* (LLMs), such as OpenAI's *ChatGPT*, revolutionized AI performance, opening new possibilities in the field of generative AI. These models, pre-trained on massive amounts of data, have demonstrated unprecedented potential in business value creation.

Today, AI underpins high-profile applications, such as advanced search engines (e.g., Google Search), recommendation systems (e.g., YouTube, Amazon, Netflix), virtual assistants (e.g., Google Assistant, Siri, Alexa), autonomous vehicles (e.g., Waymo), generative tools (e.g., ChatGPT), and superhuman analysis in strategy games (e.g., chess and Go). Recent trends include multimodal models, which can process different types of data (text, images, audio), and smaller but efficient models, which are reducing reliance on models with too many parameters. AI continues to evolve, promising new revolutions in the near future.

3 Machine Learning and Deep Learning

Machine learning (ML) represents one of the fundamental methodologies of AI. It involves creating models by training algorithms, with the goal of making predictions or making decisions based on data. There are several ML techniques and algorithms, including linear regression, logistic regression, decision trees, random forests, support vector machine (SVM), k-nearest neighbor (KNN), and clustering. Each of these approaches is suitable for solving specific types of problems and handling different data structures, offering targeted solutions based on analytical needs.[3]

One of the most popular methodologies in ML is *neural network* (NN). NNs are *computational intelligence* models inspired by the structure and functioning of the human brain. They are composed of interconnected layers of nodes, called artificial neurons, that collaborate to process and analyze complex data. These networks are particularly effective in tasks that require the identification of intricate patterns and relationships within large volumes of data.

Deep learning is a subset of ML that uses multilayer NNs, known as *deep neural networks*. These networks more accurately simulate the human brain's

[3] Goodfellow et al. (2016).

decision-making process by having an input layer, numerous hidden layers (which can range from a few to hundreds), and an output layer. Unlike traditional NNs, which usually include only one or two hidden layers, deep networks are able to automatically extract features (characteristics) from the data, facilitating more accurate and detailed pre-views.

Deep learning is distinguished by its ability to operate without the need for direct human intervention, making it ideal for large-scale machine learning. It is widely used in areas such as *natural language processing*, *computer vision*, and other applications that require rapid and accurate identification of complex patterns within large data sets.

3.1 Types of Learning

Deep learning also makes it possible to be able to use different types of learning:

- *Supervised learning*. The simplest form of learning, which involves using labeled data to train methodologies to classify, do regression or prediction. The goal is to allow the model to learn the mapping between input and output in the training data so that it can predict the labels of new, unseen data.
- *Semi-supervised learning*. Combines supervised and unsupervised learning using labeled and unlabeled data to train models for classification and regression tasks.
- *Self-supervised learning*. Generates implicit labels from unstructured data rather than relying on labeled data sets.
- *Reinforcement learning*. Learns by trial and error and with reward features rather than by extracting information from hidden patterns.
- *Transfer learning*. Knowledge gained through one task or data set is used to improve model performance on another related task or on a different data set.
- *Generative AI*. Deep learning models capable of creating complex original content, such as long text, high-quality images, realistic video or audio, and more, in response to a user request or query. At a high level, generative models encode a simplified representation of their training data and then draw from that representation to create new work that is similar, but not identical, to the original data.

3.2 Generative AI and Advanced Deep Learning Models

Generative models have been used for years in statistics to analyze numerical data, but in the past decade they have evolved to analyze and generate more complex types of data through *deep learning*. This evolution has coincided with the emergence of three sophisticated types of deep learning models:

- *Variational autoencoders* (VAEs), introduced in 2013, have enabled models that can generate multiple content variations in response to a prompt or instruction.
- *Diffusion models*, first seen in 2014, which add "noise" to images until they are unrecognizable and then remove the noise to generate original images in response to prompts.
- *Transformers*, which are trained on sequential data to generate extended sequences of content (such as words in sentences, shapes in an image, photograms of a video, or commands in software code). Transformers are the basis of most of today's most popular generative AI tools, including ChatGPT and GPT-4, Copilot, BERT, Bard, and Midjourney.

3.3 Deep Learning Technologies and Platforms

Major technology companies, including Google, Microsoft, Amazon, and Apple, are investing significant resources in deep learning methodologies and technologies, with the goal of developing hardware and software innovations that improve the performance and efficiency of next-generation products.

One of the most successful technologies in this area is *TensorFlow*. Initially released by Google in late 2015, TensorFlow reached version 1.0.0 in early 2017. This framework offers Application Programming Interface (APIs) for languages such as Java, C++, Go, and Python and is designed for computation on dataflow graphs, where nodes represent operations and arcs are multidimensional arrays (tensors). TensorFlow supports computation on multiple CPUs (central processing units) and GPUs (graphics processing units), with optional extensions such as Compute Unified Device Architecture (CUDA) and SYCL. In addition, TensorFlow Lite was developed specifically for machine learning on mobile and embedded devices, providing an API for neural networks on Android. TensorFlow is particularly performant in multi-threaded server environments (more than eight threads).

Another significant framework is deep learning for Java (DL4J), an open source distributed deep learning solution for the Java Virtual Machine (JVM) contributed to the Eclipse Foundation. DL4J is designed to be usable in commercial contexts, supports Java and Scala APIs, operates in distributed environments, and integrates with Apache Hadoop and Spark. In addition, it can import models from other frameworks such as TensorFlow, Caffe, and Theano. DL4J includes implementations of advanced algorithms, such as restricted Boltzmann machines, autoencoders, and recursive neural networks, which in other platforms would require custom development.

Theano, a Python library developed primarily for academic purposes, was one of the first successful platforms in the field of deep learning. However, support ceased after the release of version 1.0.0 in November 2017. Born in 2007, Theano was designed to perform mathematical operations on multidimensional arrays and optimize code compilation, outperforming libraries such as NumPy in terms of speed and stability. It supported tensor operations, GPU computation, and parallelism via

Basic Linear Algebra Subprograms (BLAS) and Single Instruction Multiple Data (SIMD).

Torch is another scientific computing framework focused primarily on GPU-accelerated computing. Implemented in C, it uses a Lua-based scripting language called LuaJIT. Torch is supported primarily on Mac OS X and Ubuntu 12+, while implementations for Windows are unofficial. Despite being optimized for GPUs, benchmarking studies have shown that Torch does not significantly outperform other frameworks such as CNTK (Microsoft Cognitive Toolkit), MXNet, and Caffe in terms of performance on single or multi-GPU, while remaining ideal for some types of neural networks.

The *Microsoft Cognitive Toolkit* (CNTK), developed in mid-2015, is a versatile framework that can be integrated into Python, C#, and C++ programs or used independently with the BrainScript scripting language. It supports the open-source ONNX format, which allows the transfer of models between frameworks such as Caffe2, PyTorch, and MXNet. CNTK is designed to be scalable and production-ready, with performance competitive with other more established platforms.

Caffe, developed by Berkeley AI Research (BAIR) and the Berkeley Vision and Learning Center (BVLC), is designed for image classification and offers an expressive architecture with GPU support. Based on C++ and CUDA, Caffe can be used through command-line interfaces, Python and MATLAB. It has been extended for use in environments such as Apache Hadoop with Spark. Caffe2, developed by Facebook, extended the functionality of Caffe by adding a Python API and support for multiple platforms, including Mac OS X, Windows, Linux, iOS, and Android. Apache MXNet, launched in mid-2015, supports APIs for Python, R, Scala, Julia, C++, and Perl, as well as the new Gluon API. MXNet is designed to be scalable and reduce I/O complexity, demonstrating high efficiency in single- and multi-GPU implementations, although performance on CPU is less optimized. Finally, *Keras* is not a stand-alone deep learning framework, but it provides a high-level API that integrates with TensorFlow, Theano, and CNTK. The strength of Keras is the ease of prototyping, thanks to a modular and intuitive interface. It supports both CPU and GPU, convolutional (CNN) and recursive neural networks (RNN), and can be integrated with libraries such as scikit-learn for Python. Keras is particularly valued for its speed of development and flexibility.

4 High-Performance Computing

High-performance computing (HPC) uses supercomputers and computer cluster to solve complex problems, as distinguished from high-throughput computing (prolonged use of resources) and many-task computing (intensive but brief use). HPC is a multidisciplinary field that combines advanced hardware, parallel programming, and systems administration. Although the term "HPC" is later than "supercomputing," the two are often considered synonymous. However, *supercomputer* can refer to machines specifically designed for high performance. HPC is critical for scientific research, computational engineering, and business applications, particularly in artificial intelligence and big data analysis. HPC technologies are essential in many areas, including quantum mechanics, weather forecasting, mineral exploration, molecular modeling, pharmaceutical research, cryptanalysis, and advanced physics simulations. Governments and research centers employ it to study climate, fusion energy, galaxy formation, and to improve the accuracy of weather forecasting.

4.1 Basic Concepts

Supercomputing involves running multiple computers as a single unit, dividing the work among them for parallel processing.

Scalability

Theoretically, doubling the computing power halves the execution time of a problem, but in practice the gain is limited by the communication between nodes and the size of the problem, which must be scaled appropriately. A parallel algorithm is scalable if the execution time remains constant by proportionally increasing the number of processors and the size of the problem.

Speedup

Speedup measures the performance improvement of an algorithm running on a system with more computing resources. According to Amdahl's law, speedup grows with the number of processors, but not illimited. In rare cases, superlinear speedup occurs, where performance improves more than expected, for example, due to cache memory hierarchy or efficient Random Access Memory (RAM) management in applications such as computational genomics and parallel backtracking.

Domain Decomposition

Partitioning the data of a problem among multiple processors is essential for parallel computing. Although HPC and distributed computing share many technologies, they differ in the interconnection technologies between nodes, which affect communication management. For an efficient HPC application, specific enablement of parallel algorithms and a co-creation engineering approach, in which software and hardware are designed in together to maximize performance, is required.

Performance Measurement

Performance in HPC systems is measured in FLOPS (floating-vehicle operations per second), a unit better suited for scientific computations than generic operations per second (OPS). FLOPS is often expressed in its multiples as MFLOPS (millions), GFLOPS (billions), TFLOPS (trillions), etc.

4.2 *Brief History of Supercomputing*

The term *Supercomputing* first appeared in 1929 in the New York World, referring to IBM tabulators at Columbia University. In the 1950s–1960s, universities and companies developed the first high-performance computers, such as the Manchester Atlas (1962) and the IBM Stretch (1962). Seymour Cray becomes a key figure, designing the CDC 6600 (1964), considered the first true supercomputer, and the CDC 7600 (1968). The Cray-1 (1976) becomes the most successful supercomputer, introducing innovations such as vector register chaining.

The Cray X-MP (1982) and Cray-2 (1985) improve vector computation and memory management. The 1980s saw the emergence of the first massively parallel systems based on Multiple Instruction stream Multiple Data stream (MIMD) and SIMD architectures. In 1993, the TOP500 classification, which evaluates the performance of global supercomputers, is launched. ASCI Red (1996) is the first supercomputer to exceed 1 TFLOPS.

IBM's Blue Gene and Earth Simulator (2004) mark an evolution in distributed computing and energy efficiency. China takes the lead with the Tianhe-I (2010) and the Sunway TaihuLight (2016). In 2020, Japan's Fugaku becomes the world's fastest with 442 PFLOPS. Frontier (2022), the first exascale supercomputer, surpasses 1 EFLOPS. El Capitan (2024) becomes the most powerful supercomputer with 2746 EFLOPS, followed by Frontier and Aurora. Microsoft Eagle (2024) marks a breakthrough as the first virtual supercomputer in the cloud.

The evolution of supercomputers has been driven by increased parallelization, miniaturization, and energy efficiency, with an increasing focus on artificial intelligence and scientific simulation.

4.3 *GPU Acceleration*

General Purpose GPU (GPGPU) is the use of GPUs (graphics processing units), typically intended for graphics, to perform general purpose computations that were traditionally performed by the CPU. Due to their massively parallel architecture, GPUs offer high computing power, greatly accelerating scientific and artificial intelligence applications.

The concept of using graphics processors for general-purpose computations dates back to 1987 with Conway's Game of Life on the Commodore Amiga and Atari ST. In the early 2000s, the increasing programmability of GPUs and support for floating-point computation made GPGPU more accessible. In 2003, it was shown that GPUs could solve linear algebra problems faster than CPUs. The year 2007 marks a turning point with the release of NVID-IA's CUDA, which simplifies programming GPUs without having to treat them as graphics hardware. OpenCL (Apple/Khronos Group) and DirectCompute (Microsoft) offer alternatives to CUDA, with OpenCL supporting CPUs, GPUs, FPGAs (field-programmable gate array), and other accelerators. OpenACC is a programming model that allows parallelization of CPU and GPU code by mitigating the vendor lock-in problem imposed by NVIDIA.

GPUs are fundamental to artificial intelligence, accelerating model training and inference. GPGPU is used in numerous areas, from scientific data analysis to image processing and physical simulations. Today, the use of GPUs for high-performance computing is strategic and indispensable for many computational disciplines.

4.4 Acceleration via FPGA

An FPGA (field-programmable gate array) is an integrated circuit that can be configured and reprogrammed after manufacture, used for custom applications in telecommunications, automotive, aerospace, industrial, and high-performance computing (HPC).

An FPGA contains programmable logic blocks connected by a reconfigurable grid. It can function as an accelerator, similar to GPUs, through code offloading and data offloading. It can be programmed through hardware description languages (HDL) such as VHDL, to create custom circuits. It is used in hardware/software co-design for prototyping and simulation of embedded systems. FPGAs support the design of ASICs, accelerating the simulation process.

The first FPGAs were made available in 1984 through Altera introduces the first reprogrammable logic device. In 1985 Xilinx launched the first commercial FPGA (XC2064).

In the 1990s the growth of use in telecommunications and networking, with expansion into consumer and industrial areas defines FPGAs of strategic interest. In the second decade of the new millennium, Xilinx, Altera, and Actel dominate the FPGA market.

FPGAs are widely used within computational architectures dedicated to HPC and artificial intelligence. Microsoft has been using FPGAs since 2014 to accelerate Bing and has been integrating them into the Azure cloud since 2018. Amazon Web Services (AWS) offers virtual machine instances with FPGAs.

FPGAs are widely used in AI, especially to accelerate inference operations. FPGAs offer flexibility, energy efficiency, and high performance, making them essential tools for advanced computing and emerging applications in artificial intelligence and HPC.

4.5 Acceleration by Tensor Processing Unit

The Tensor Processing Unit (TPU) is an application-specific integrated circuit (ASIC) developed by Google to accelerate machine learning based on neural networks, optimized for the TensorFlow framework. Google began using them in 2015 and in 2018 made TPUs available to third parties via Google Cloud Platform and dedicated hardware. TPUs feature a systolic array architecture for tight interconnection between compute nodes. They are optimized for operations on arrays and tensors, improving speed over CPUs and GPUs. Usually, development and testing are done through proprietary technologies, with access through Google Cloud TPU and standalone hardware solutions. AlphaGo and AlphaZero are two software used for the game of Go, Chess, and Shogi. TPUs have been used in the Google Street View environment: text recognition on millions of images in a few days. The Google Photos application accelerated through TPUs has been used to evaluate the performance of a single TPU that can process over 100 million images per day. Google uses TPUs to optimize search engine results. TPUs are integrated into Google's cloud services Kaggle and Colaboratory. There are standalone hardware versions with M.2 and PCI-express connections.

4.6 TOP500 and GREEN500

The TOP500 project ranks the 500 most powerful supercomputers in the world, based on performance as measured by the high-performance LINPACK (HPL) benchmark. Started in 1993 by Jack Dongarra, Hans Meuer, Horst D. Simon, and Erich Strohmaier, the ranking is updated twice a year: in November at the Supercomputing Conference in the United States and in June at the International Supercomputing Conference in Europe.

Not all supercomputers are included because some cannot run HPL or because owners choose not to participate (e.g., for security or strategic research reasons). LINPACK is criticized because it provides a partial measure of a supercomputer's performance. To overcome these limitations, the HPC Challenge benchmark was developed, which incorporates more comprehensive tests, but the TOP500 remains the main benchmark because of its ease of interpretation.

As of November 2024, the most powerful supercomputer is El Capitan (USA) with 2746 EFLOPS. The United States dominates the ranking with 173 supercomputers, followed by China (63) and Germany (40). Italy ranks ninth with CINECA's Leonardo supercomputer, which was the fourth in the world in November 2022.

The Green500: measures the energy efficiency of supercomputers. The High Performance Conjugate Gradients (HPCG): assesses I/O bandwidth.

The TOP500 remains the global benchmark for HPC, despite its limitations, and is essential for monitoring trends and progress in supercomputing.

4.7 High-Performance Cloud Computing

Traditionally, HPC has involved infrastructure, investing in supercomputers or clusters of computers connected to each other through high-performance networks. Over the past decade, cloud computing has grown in popularity because of the provision of computational resources that can be accessed democratically through the pay-as-you-go paradigm, through which the initial investment cost is zeroed out and all fixed maintenance costs are converted into variable costs tied to the actual use of computing and storage systems. Some features, such as scalability and containerization, have also attracted interest in academia in contextualizing high-performance cloud computing.

Major players in the cloud market provide tools for creating on-demand HPC virtual infrastructure through optimization of dedicated structures, minimizing the impact of virtualization on overall performance. Currently, the use of high-performance cloud computing is beneficial, from a performance perspective, for a small number of nodes (currently 256 is considered the convenient number of nodes beyond which the weight of communications affects performance).

The fact that an HPC system can be instantiated on demand and be up and running after a few minutes of waiting, coupled with the simple payment for the resources used in compute time without investment costs and, most importantly, without the time it takes to acquire a physical machine, leads to the choice of HPC systems on the cloud for all non-routine tasks.

Added to this is the advantage that ad hoc network configurations such as three-dimensional toroids or meshes are configurable via software through an application-specific or generic scripting language such as Python. Another advantage is the ability to use accelerators (GPU, FPGE, TPU) that are difficult to obtain on the market due to cost or availability. Finally, the cloud-based HPC approach frees the user from the burdens related to the costs of power, cooling, and, most importantly, machine maintenance and preventive replacement of obsolescing parts.

However, some criticisms cloud the use of HPC systems on cloud. Foremost among them is the fact that costs can become significant in the case of computing tasks performed on a routine basis or need for storage of large amounts of data for a long time. In addition to natural performance-related criticisms due to connectivity, in the case of distributed-memory high-performance parallel computing, some concerns arise from the virtual and shared nature of virtual machine instances on cloud.

Although the players in the cloud market ensure the utmost determination to apply everything necessary for the minimization of risks due to malicious actions, often the specific requirements of some applications do not allow the use of this particular approach. It should be noted, however, that in the specific case of training large AI models using deep neural networks, transformers, and other tools for generative artificial intelligence, often the HPC option on the cloud is the only really feasible one.

4.8 Cluster Beowulf

Although supercomputers and HPC clusters have hardware and software differences, they share the principle of parallel processing. Supercomputers cost between $2 million and $10 million, while HPC clusters range between $50,000 and $2 million, with opportunities for low-cost mini HPC clusters for experimentation and education. Beowulf Clusters were born in 1994 at NASA, built with consumer hardware and open source software. They use Linux and the MPI (Message Passing Interface) library for parallelization. Many TOP500 supercomputers are derived from this architecture, but with engineered solutions to maximize performance and efficiency. The Raspberry Pi is a low-cost single board computer (SBC) used for HPC experimentation. In 2017, the UK Government Communications HeadQuarters (GCHQ) created OctaPi, a cluster of eight Raspberry Pi 3Bs for teaching STEM subjects. There are advanced clusters using Raspberry Pi such as the Turing Pi that allow multiple Compute Modules to be connected to simulate mini HPC. In 2019, Oracle built a cluster of 1060 Raspberry Pi 3B+, with over 4200 cores. HPC clusters and solutions with Raspberry Pi offer cost-effective alternatives to supercomputers, fostering experimentation and education in parallel computing and HPC.

References

Goodfellow I et al (2016) Deep learning. The MIT Press, Cambridge

Negnevitsky M (2005) Artificial intelligence: a guide to intelligent systems, 2nd edn. Addison Wesley, London

Russell S, Norvig P (2020) Artificial intelligence: a modern approach, 4th edn. London

The Contract

Models of Contract in the Platform Economy

Lourdes Fernández del Moral Domínguez and Clara Tuccillo

Contents

Abstract The chapter aims to present the various contractual models through which the main commercial transactions are carried out via platforms and the mandatory relationships that arise between all parties involved. This overview leads to further reflection on the peculiarities associated with the platform's involvement in the finalisation of such contracts.

Sections 3, 4, 4.1 and 5 are attributed to Lourdes Fernández del Moral Domínguez; Sects. 1, 2 and 4.2 and 4.3 are attributed to Clara Tuccillo.

L. F. del Moral Domínguez (✉) · C. Tuccillo
University of Naples "Parthenope", Naples, Italy
e-mail: lourdes.delmoral@uniparthenope.it; clara.tuccillo@studenti.uniparthenope.it

R. Bocchini (ed.), *Digital Platforms - From Technical Foundations to Legal and Economic Implications*, https://doi.org/10.1007/978-3-032-07978-7_4

1 Introduction

From a legal perspective, digital platforms are online structures that facilitate interaction between different actors, creating an environment in which goods, services, or information can be exchanged. Their legal nature varies according to the type of service provided, the way in which users interact and the contracts governing the relationship between the parties involved.

Digital platforms are primarily characterised by the use of membership contracts, which are generally non-negotiable, that users accept to access the services offered. These contracts regulate the rights and obligations between the platform and users, as well as between the platform and service providers or sellers of goods. Platforms also frequently act as 'intermediaries', as they facilitate the connection and interaction between two or more parties (e.g. between consumers and sellers, or between service providers and recipients). Their intermediary function entails legal responsibilities that may relate to consumer protection, personal data protection and the regulation of financial transactions. Digital platforms are subject to rules that vary according to the type of service provided. For instance, e-commerce platforms are subject to e-commerce regulations, while sharing economy platforms are regulated by specific laws governing the renting or sharing of goods. Additionally, social media platforms must comply with data protection and content liability regulations.

This chapter sets out to analyse in detail the different types of digital platforms that populate today's market, focusing in particular on the modes of interaction they allow between users. To this end, the main models of existing platforms on the market will be explored, distinguished according to the functions they offer, the types of relationships they establish and the services they allow users to enjoy.

Subsequently, attention will shift to examining the contracts that characterise transactions within these platforms, which fall into three distinct types: the contract that binds the user to the platform, the contract between the platform itself and the vendors or service providers and, finally, the contract between the vendor or provider and the end user. The objective is to understand how each of these contractual dynamics affects the regulation of interactions and mutual responsibilities between the various actors involved.

2 The Different Types of Existing Digital Platforms and Their Characteristics

Given the impossibility of dealing with every type of digital platform on the market, a targeted selection has been made, recognising that the analysis will necessarily be incomplete. Although the distinguishing criteria of the platforms are different (these, in fact, can be distinguished according to the structure of the users involved, the type of value generated, the mode of access and remuneration, the network dynamics, the use of data, etc.), the analysis that follows will be organised according to the type of service or function that each platform offers.

The first type of platform under consideration—which differs from the others in the type of interaction it offers users—is the membership (or registration) platform. This allows users who register to actively participate in the virtual space (e.g. commenting on content, purchasing products, or sharing thoughts) or simply access exclusive content. Only after providing their e-mail address and creating a username—thus outlining their individual 'profile' within the platform—can the user enjoy a personalised experience, including suggestions based on their preferences or past activities: this is the case on platforms such as Netflix, a streaming platform where, as is well known, a subscription is required to access video content and receive personalised suggestions based on viewing preferences; or Spotify, where although it is possible to listen to music on a limited basis without registration, to access advanced features such as personalised playlists, offline listening and to remove advertising, users must register and choose a subscription plan.

Profiles keep track of users' interactions, preferences and activities. Membership platforms allow users to interact with each other through messages, comments, reviews, posts or shares, thus creating a social network, or community of people, with similar interests. The most suitable example is Facebook, where users are invited to 'follow' or 'become friends' with other people and share content. Membership platforms also include Instagram since, although it offers content that can be viewed without registration, it allows registered users to actively interact with photos, videos and stories, follow other profiles, create posts and receive personalised notifications.

Some platforms offer different levels of membership, each of which allows access to specific functionalities. Thus, basic free access may limit certain options, while a premium or paid plan may unlock advanced features or exclusive content. An example is LinkedIn, a professional platform that famously allows members to connect with other professionals, post career updates, and search for or offer job opportunities. A free account will enable them to communicate with others, while a premium membership offers advanced features, such as a more in-depth job search and networking tools.

Membership of these platforms also entails the collection of users' personal data, as the use of this information enables the customisation of content and offers, as well as marketing analysis. Any processing must be carried out following the privacy regulations.[1]

[1] As is well known, platforms are obliged to comply with the General Data Protection Regulation (GDPR), which states that personal data must be processed lawfully, fairly and transparently. They must ensure that data is collected for specific and legitimate purposes, and not subsequently processed in a manner incompatible with those purposes. Furthermore, platforms must obtain the user's explicit consent for the processing of his or her personal data, which must be specific, informed and revocable at any time. In some circumstances, data processing may take place without consent, for example when it is based on other legal justifications, such as the performance of a contract or the fulfilment of a legal obligation. Users have the right to access their personal data, rectify them, erase them (right to be forgotten), object to their processing, request their portability

Although membership platforms offer numerous advantages—such as the ability to collect information about users to improve the experience through more relevant content, recommendations and notifications, and allow for personalised interaction, participation in a community, building relationships and sharing ideas and content—user privacy raises concerns due to the continuous collection and profiling[2] of personal data that these platforms perform.[3]

The examination continues by delving into sharing platforms, which allow users to exchange content or resources, such as files, photos, videos and other information, adopting a model based on the collaborative economy. First of all, sharing platforms differ from membership platforms in that the latter aim to create an ongoing relationship between the platform and the user, who can take advantage of content, services or functions customised according to his or her preferences; in sharing platforms, on the other hand, although registration may be required, the primary focus is not on creating an ongoing relationship, but on facilitating the exchange or sharing of resources between users.

Sharing platforms have transformed the way we interact, collaborate and access online resources, allowing us to exchange information, content and even monetise digital assets. Sharing can take place in public or private mode: users can choose whether to share files or documents with others via links, e-mail or through dedicated access groups (platforms supporting this mode include Google Drive,[4]

---

and restrict their processing in certain situations. Platforms are required to provide clear and comprehensible information about data processing, the purposes of collection and users' rights. To ensure data security, platforms must take appropriate measures to protect data from unauthorised access, accidental loss or damage, including encryption and anonymisation techniques. They must also comply with the *ePrivacy* Directive (2002/58/EC), which regulates *privacy* in electronic communications and integrates with the GDPR, particularly with regard to the protection of data related to *cookies* and traffic information. Platforms must obtain users' consent before storing or accessing *cookies* or similar technologies on their devices, unless strictly necessary for the operation of the service. Platforms are also required to ensure that users' information is not used for unauthorised *marketing* purposes without their consent. In addition, each EU Member State may adopt specific regulations that complement the GDPR. In Italy, the Personal Data Protection Code (Legislative Decree No. 196/2003) has been updated to align with the GDPR and the Italian Data Protection Authority is the body responsible for enforcing *privacy* regulations and supervising compliance with the GDPR.

[2] Profiling is defined in Article 4 of the EU Regulation of the European Parliament and of the Council of 27 April 2016, No. 679, on the protection of natural persons with regard to the processing of personal data and on the free movement of such data and repealing Directive 95/46/EC, published in *Official Gazette*, 4 May 2016, No. 119 (so-called GDPR) as 'any form of automated processing of personal data consisting of the use of such personal data to evaluate certain personal aspects relating to a natural person, in particular to analyse or predict aspects of that natural person's professional performance, economic situation, health, personal preferences, interests, reliability, behaviour, location or movements'. On the concept of data 'profiling' see Cassano (2024), p. 1575.

[3] See Schönberger and Cukier (2013), *passim*.

[4] Google Drive is a *cloud* storage service that allows users to save, share and access files and documents from any device connected to the Internet. It also offers collaborative features, allowing users to work on documents in real time with other users.

Dropbox[5] and OneDrive[6]); or upload and distribute multimedia content, such as photos, videos, audio and music, through specialised platforms such as YouTube[7] (for videos), SoundCloud[8] (for music) and Vimeo[9] (for professional-quality videos).

Sharing platforms can also foster the exchange of knowledge and resources, allowing users to share information, ideas and resources in a structured manner through articles, tutorials, discussion forums or databases. These platforms are often used for knowledge crowdsourcing, with multiple users contributing in specific areas. An emblematic example is Wikipedia, a shared encyclopaedia platform.

In addition, sharing platforms can enable users to share experiences, opinions, reviews and ratings of products or services, helping others to make informed decisions. These platforms are prevalent in e-commerce, travel and catering. Examples include TripAdvisor[10] (for travel and restaurant reviews) and Amazon[11] (for product reviews).

Sharing platforms are not limited to digital content, but also extend to physical goods and services. These platforms, known as sharing economy platforms, allow people to share or rent resources such as cars, homes, tools and more, promoting an economic model that favours sharing rather than ownership. In this way, a peer-to-peer market is created that reduces the need for individual asset ownership and encourages access to assets rather than ownership. Examples of such platforms include Airbnb[12] (for renting accommodation), Uber[13] (for ride-sharing) and

[5] Dropbox is a *cloud* storage platform that allows you to save, synchronise and share files between different devices. It also offers collaboration features, allowing you to work together on documents and projects in real time.

[6] OneDrive is a Microsoft *cloud* storage service that allows users to save, synchronise and share files across multiple devices. It also integrates Office applications, facilitating real-time collaboration on documents and projects.

[7] YouTube is one of the main video-sharing channels, allowing users to upload, watch and interact with video content of various kinds. This platform is discussed in more detail in Part III, Title III, Section IV.

[8] SoundCloud is a music *streaming* platform that allows users to upload, discover and share audio tracks. It is used by independent and professional artists to disseminate their music and reach a global audience.

[9] Vimeo is a video sharing platform that allows users to upload, view and share high-quality content. It is particularly appreciated by creative professionals for its focus on video quality and customisation tools.

[10] TripAdvisor is an *online* platform that provides reviews and information on hotels, restaurants, tourist attractions and activities around the world. Users can share their experiences and consult the opinions of other travellers to plan their stays.

[11] Amazon is the world's largest *e-commerce* platform. However, it is also a sharing platform through user reviews. Customers, in fact, can write and share their opinions on the products they purchase, thus helping other consumers to make informed decisions. This platform is analysed in Title III, Section IV.

[12] Airbnb is an *online* platform that allows individuals to rent houses, flats and rooms to travellers worldwide. It is better described in Title III, Section IV.

[13] The Uber platform was conceived as a tool to connect drivers and passengers in order to facilitate private car transportation. Uber today offers a variety of services, including Uber Rides, which

TaskRabbit[14] (for sharing work services). However, these platforms also have limitations, as sharing content without proper copyright recognition can generate legal issues for content creators.[15]

Along with membership and sharing platforms, there is also the category of e-commerce platforms. The latter have transformed how businesses and consumers interact, extending commerce beyond the confines of traditional physical shops and thus offering the service of facilitating the buying and selling of goods and services between sellers and buyers via the Internet.

Indeed, e-commerce platforms provide a virtual environment where users can purchase a wide range of products or services via online transactions, organised in categories to simplify navigation (such as clothing, electronics, food, etc.). During the purchasing process, each user has the option of adding items to a virtual 'shopping cart', which allows them to review their purchases before finalising their order. E-commerce platforms offer a wide range of payment methods, including credit/debit cards, PayPal, bank transfers, payments on delivery, and, more recently, payments via cryptocurrencies or digital wallets (such as Apple Pay or Google Pay). They handle the logistics and shipping of purchased products, sometimes offering various shipping options (standard, express, international) and managing returns.

---

allows booking private transport via the app; Uber Eats, which deals with home food delivery; and Uber Freight, which focuses on freight transport.

[14] TaskRabbit is an *online* platform that allows users to find professionals to perform various jobs, such as assembling furniture, cleaning or home repairs. Taskers offer their services according to the specific needs of customers, making it easier to manage daily tasks.

[15] To date, there are no known provisions in national laws or international copyright agreements that are dedicated to the metaverse as such. However, for a long time there has been a system of basic rules applicable globally, which has been progressively adapted to the development of digital technology: well before the aforementioned TRIPs Agreement, the minimum level of copyright protection was regulated by the Berne Convention (Paris Act) for the protection of literary and artistic works—signed on 9 September 1886, Paris Act of 24 July 1971, ratified by Italy with law no. 399 of 20 June 1978—and by the Rome Convention for the protection of performers and artists—signed on 9 September 1886, Paris Act of 24 July 1971, ratified by Italy with law no. 399 of 20 June 1978. 399-and by the Rome Convention for the Protection of Performers, Producers of Phonograms and Broadcasting Organisations—signed in Rome on 26 October 1961, ratified by Italy by Law no. 866 of 22 November 1973. 866-which were joined by the two World Intellectual Property Organisation (WIPO) treaties of 1996 WCT and WPPT (WIPO *Copyright Treaty* and *WIPO Performances and Phonograms Treaty*), as well as the Beijing Treaty on Audiovisual Performances of 2012, Council Decision of 10 June 2013 on the signing, on behalf of the European Union, of the Beijing Treaty on Audiovisual Performances (2013/275/EU). At the EU level, the two WIPO Treaties of 1996 were transposed through Directive 29/2001/EEC (Infosoc Directive) with the aim of ensuring a harmonised revision of the national laws of the member countries. More recently, Directive (EU) 719/2019 on Copyright and Related Rights in the Digital Single Market (CDSM Directive) added further 'harmonised' chapters to the EU IP *acquis*. The international framework on the subject is dealt with in Ginsburg and Treppoz (2005), *passim*; in a more in-depth and general way the subject is dealt with in Ricketson and Ginsburg (2022), *passim*; Rosati (2014), p. 585 ff.; Musso (2020), p. 411 ff., in particular p. 412 ff.; Goglia (2022), p. 83; Cavani and Ercolani (2023), p. 154.

A distinctive feature of e-commerce platforms is the possibility to consult user reviews, which often influence purchasing decisions, as consumers tend to rely on the experiences of others. Furthermore, the shopping experience is customised thanks to recommendation algorithms, which suggest products to customers based on their past shopping habits or searches. For example, platforms such as Amazon show personalised suggestions in the 'Recommended Products' section or 'Customers who have purchased this product have also purchased…'.

E-commerce platforms can be classified according to the type of business interaction they facilitate. The main categories include B2C (Business to Consumer) platforms, the most popular e-commerce model, where companies sell directly to consumers, who can browse thousands of products, select the ones they want and receive them directly at home (examples of these platforms are Amazon, eBay and Zalando); B2B (Business-to-Business) platforms, which encourage sales between companies, mainly to wholesalers, manufacturers or suppliers who sell to other companies rather than to end consumers (examples of B2B platforms include Alibaba, Made-in-China and ThomasNet); C2C (Consumer to Consumer) platforms, where consumers sell directly to other consumers. In these cases, platforms provide the infrastructure for selling and handling transactions, thus acting as intermediaries (C2C platforms include eBay and Etsy). The different types of contracts concluded on such platforms will be discussed in more detail on the following pages.

Also facilitating direct contact between people or companies and the goods, services or resources they need, acting as intermediaries between two or more parties, are the so-called intermediation platforms (or marketplaces). The latter facilitate transactions, agreements, exchanges, and collaborations, often in real-time, and are used in numerous sectors, such as commerce, finance, professional services, logistics, and others. However, they differ from e-commerce in that intermediary platforms are not directly involved in managing goods or services, but rather facilitate contact and exchange between supply and demand. Buyers purchase from third-party sellers and the platform only offers the necessary tools for the process (e.g. payment management, reviews, advertising, etc.). The e-commerce platform, on the other hand, is often the owner of the catalogue of products or services that are offered, and is also responsible for managing the sale, payments, logistics and delivery.

A feature that characterises both brokerage and e-commerce platforms is the possibility of leaving reviews and ratings. These so-called feedback systems are crucial for establishing trust between users and service or product providers.

Reviews and reputation help select suppliers and ensure that users have a positive experience, creating a community of trust. Furthermore, both of these virtual spaces use algorithms to optimise the matching process between supply and demand. For instance, based on user preferences, geolocation or past transactions, the platform can automatically suggest the best solution for each case.

Brokerage platforms can be of different kinds depending on the goods, services or resources they broker; in particular there are: intermediation platforms that connect freelance workers or independent professionals with clients in need of specific services; intermediation platforms for transport (ride-sharing), which connect drivers and passengers by allowing users to book a trip with drivers who offer their own vehicles for transport; intermediation platforms for hospitality (short-term rentals), which allow owners of houses, flats or rooms to get in touch with those looking for short-term accommodation, such as travellers marketplaces, which facilitate the interaction between sellers and buyers, enabling producers of products to offer them for sale to a wide audience of consumers; financial intermediation platforms (crowdfunding, peer-to-peer lending), which connect investors and borrowers;[16] on-demand services intermediation platforms, which connect professionals (such as plumbers, electricians, tutors, etc. with customers who need services) with clients who require specific services; real estate brokerage platforms, which connect those seeking to buy, sell, or rent real estate with agents, owners, or buyers, handling listing, property search, negotiation and sometimes legal documentation.

Yet another category is that of payment platforms, i.e. digital systems that facilitate and manage the transfer of money between buyers and sellers in a secure and efficient manner.

These platforms facilitate economic transactions, allowing users to make payments for goods or services online, transfer money between bank accounts or manage payment transactions, both domestic and international, in real time. They also simplify the purchasing process and ensure secure handling of sensitive information, such as credit card data.

There are different types of payment platforms in the current landscape: among the most common are those for e-commerce, which are integrated into online shops to facilitate transactions during the purchasing process (e.g. PayPal); those that are digital wallets (e-wallet[17]), which allow users to store payment information digitally and make purchases or transfers without having to enter credit card data each time; and peer-to-peer (P2P) money transfer platforms, which allow users to send money directly to other people via their smartphone or computer, often used for micro-transactions, such as paying small debts between friends or transferring money to family members. Payment platforms provide security, convenience and ease of use in online financial transactions for both private and corporate users.

Another interesting category is that of cloud computing platforms, digital infrastructures that allow data to be stored, managed and processed through remote servers accessible via the Internet.

Cloud computing platforms are essential for the functioning of modern businesses and organisations, as they offer access to advanced computing resources, without the need to manage expensive and complex physical infrastructures, from

[16] On *equity crowdfunding* for small and medium-sized enterprises, see: Mozzarelli (2019), p. 650 ff.; Macchi (2017), p. 555 ff.; Fregonara (2016), p. 2287 ff.; Vella (2019), p. 251 ff.; Lamberti (2015), p. 23 ff.; Laudonio (2014); Stefanelli (2019), p. 177 ff.; Vitali (2014), p. 371 ff.; Laudonio, (2019), p. 1237 ff.; Guccione (2024), p. 1348.

[17] An e-wallet is a digital application that allows you to store money and make *online* transactions, such as purchases and transfers, securely. It supports different payment methods, such as credit, debit and cryptocurrency cards.

wherever there is a network connection. Security is one of the most critical aspects in cloud computing platforms. Cloud service providers adopt advanced security measures to safeguard user data, including data encryption (both in transit and at rest), multi-factor authentication, firewalls[18] and continuous activity monitoring.

Cloud computing platforms[19] offer several service models, each designed to meet specific business and technology needs. The main ones are: Infrastructure as a Service (IaaS), which provides core computing resources such as servers, storage and networking on demand so that users can rent these resources and manage them at the operating system and application level, without worrying about the underlying hardware; Platform as a Service (PaaS), which provides a complete development environment where developers can build, deploy and manage applications without worrying about managing the underlying infrastructure; Software as a Service (SaaS), which offers software applications via the cloud that users can use through a web interface without having to worry about managing the infrastructure or IT resources; Function as a Service (FaaS), also known as serverless computing, which allows developers to run individual functions or blocks of code without worrying about managing the infrastructure. The cloud can also be public, when resources are provided by an external cloud provider and are shared among multiple users; private, when resources are dedicated to a single organisation, which can choose to manage them internally or through an external provider; or hybrid, in which case public and private cloud resources are combined, allowing companies to manage some applications in a private environment and others in the public cloud. Finally, when multiple cloud providers are used simultaneously, we refer to a multi-cloud environment. Cloud computing platforms offer a wide range of advantages in terms of efficiency, flexibility and cost reduction; however, they entail certain risks and challenges, especially in terms of privacy and security.

Finally, a further type of digital platform, included in this classification on the basis of the function or service offered, deserves to be mentioned: those dedicated to gaming. Gaming platforms represent a digital environment where users can play, download, buy, sell and interact with games and gaming-related content. Such platforms offer a wide range of services and features, including multiplayer online games, social features and live game streaming.

In conclusion, technological evolution has led to the creation of new business models and, consequently, various types of platforms, each with its own specific purpose and a range of services tailored to the needs of users.

These may be offered free of charge or subject to a payment of a specified amount, which can be made on a weekly, monthly, quarterly or yearly basis. In this case, a periodic payment is required to access a wide range of exclusive content, services or goods that are not available for free or through one-time purchases.

[18] *Firewalls* are computer security devices that monitor and control incoming and outgoing network traffic, preventing unauthorised access. They can be hardware or software and protect systems from external attacks and internal threats.

[19] Cf. Trubiani (2022), p. 395 ff.

These may include access to music, films and TV series, software, news, training courses, consultancy and much more.

Subscription platforms typically offer unlimited or extended access to specific content or functionalities for the duration of the subscription, with the option to cancel or modify it at any time (if applicable). Moreover, users can enjoy the services on any Internet-connected device, such as smartphones, tablets or computers.

Platforms offering subscription-based services include: video and music streaming platforms, which provide access to multimedia content, such as films, TV series, music and podcasts, for a subscription fee (e.g. Netflix and Amazon Prime Video, for video content, or Spotify and Apple Music, for music); so-called Software as a Service (SaaS) platforms, which provide software and applications online via subscription (well-known examples include Google Workspace, Adobe Creative Cloud and Dropbox, tools frequently used by companies, professionals, teams for productivity, management and business management); and Software as a Service (SaaS) platforms, which provide software and applications online via subscription (known examples include Google Workspace, Adobe Creative Cloud and Dropbox). Software as a Service (SaaS), which provide online software and applications by subscription (well-known examples include Google Workspace, Adobe Creative Cloud and Dropbox, tools frequently used by companies, professionals and teams for productivity, project management, data analysis, marketing and other areas); those that have editorial content and news and, therefore, offer access to articles, reports, newsletters, and in-depth analysis for a periodic payment. In addition, there are online training and course platforms, which offer learning courses on a wide range of topics and which users can subscribe to in order to obtain certificates and study materials (examples include Master Class or LinkedIn Learning); and online game subscription platforms, which offer access to games or extra content (such as expansions or in-game benefits) for a periodic payment (one of these is PlayStation Plus).

The dynamics described so far of the different types of platforms highlight how contracts in the platform economy regulate complex, tripartite relationships, which simultaneously involve: the platform, which, while sometimes acting as a neutral intermediary, exercises strong control over market dynamics; end users, who access services or purchase products; and third parties, such as service providers (e.g. riders or drivers) or sellers of goods.

Let us now examine the contracts governing these relationships.

3 Digital Platforms and Contracts Concluded in Digital Marketplaces

In recent years, digital platforms have profoundly transformed the way contracts are concluded and regulated in digital markets. Online purchases, subscriptions to digital services, collaborative economy contracts: everything happens at the click of a button, often without the user having a clear understanding of the contractual terms he or she is accepting.

This development raises important legal questions: how are contracts concluded online qualified? What is the liability of platforms? What protections are afforded to consumers? And again, how to ensure that the system is fair and transparent for all actors involved? The answer to these questions is not simple, as the law often struggles to keep pace with technological innovation.

Regarding the contractual aspect, numerous transactions occur within digital marketplaces via platforms, which may lead to the conclusion of various types of contracts. These can basically be classified into two main categories.

Firstly, there are contracts through which platforms directly offer a service or good to end users. The basic scheme of such contracts, therefore, involves two parties in a contractual relationship, the platform (or digital service provider, such as Netflix, Spotify, Dazn, etc.) and the end user. The discipline to be applied will differ according to the qualification of the party concluding the contract with the platform: whether it is a business user or a consumer user. The nature of the good or service covered by the contract will also contribute to determining the applicable discipline. Contracts that have as their object the provision of one or more information of society services are subject to a specific set of rules, which, as we shall see, differ from those governing other types of services provided on the web.[20]

In addition to this category of contracts, contracts concluded between users of the platform and by means of the platform (so-called marketplaces, e.g. Amazon, eBay, etc.) are extremely widespread today.

---

[20] The complexity that often characterizes the role exercised and the function performed by the platform sometimes makes the boundary separating the figure of the entity that performs the information society service from the entity that through the platform provides goods or services to end users unclear. The Commission has set out certain criteria to be applied in individual cases in order to determine whether the platform acts only as an intermediary or must also be regarded as the provider of the underlying service, even though formally the service offering comes from another entity. These criteria relate in particular to the decisive influence exercised by the platform in determining the price to be paid by the end user, the provision of binding instructions to the service provider that are included in the content of the contract that the latter formally enters into with the end user, and the ownership of the goods necessary for the provision of the service. This does not exclude the possibility of using other criteria if in individual cases they may be revealing of the particular relationship established between the parties involved in the economic transaction.

The question became apparent in relation to the service offered by *Uber*, which was resolved by the Court of Justice in its judgment of 20 December 2017 in Case C-434/15, in which it can be read: 'An intermediary service having as its object the bringing together, by means of a *smartphone* application, for remuneration, of non-professional drivers, using their own vehicle, with persons wishing to make a journey in the urban area, must be regarded as inextricably linked to a transport service and therefore falling within the classification of "services in the field of transport" within the meaning of Article 58(1) TFEU. Such a service must, accordingly, be excluded from the scope of application of Article 56 TFEU, EC Dir. No. 123/2006 and EC Dir. No. 31/2000' (see *Nuova giur. civ. comm.*, 2018, 1085 ff., with note by Turci (2018), p. 330 ff.; Camardi (2021), p. 893 ff.; Zeno-Zencovich (2018), p. 141 ff. There are also some subsequent measures on the topic, CJEU, C-320/16, *Uber France* (2018); CJEU, C-390/18, *Airbnb Ireland* (2019); CJEU, C-62/19, *Star Taxi App* SRL v. *Unitatea Amministrativ teritoriale municipiul bucureşti prin Primar General and Consiliul General al Municipiulni Bucarest* (2020).

In relation to such contracts, the platform plays the role of intermediary, creating the online space where supply and demand meet and the contract is concluded. The services provided by the platform, in a nutshell, allow its users (traders, consumers and, in some cases, both belonging to the same category) to enter into contact, to make use of the digital infrastructure for the eventual conclusion of contracts and, often, allow for the performance of some if not all of the services deriving from the contract itself such as, for example, payment management, logistics, etc.

This type of transaction is characterised, basically, by being at least a trilateral relationship. On the one hand, the platform which, in carrying out the activity of intermediation, establishes a contractual relationship with both the users, suppliers of the services or goods and the end users of the same. On the other hand, the user supplier of the services or goods who concludes a contract (which we may call an underlying contract) through the platform with another user, the final recipient of the transaction. This latter party may be, from time to time, a business user or a consumer user, and this qualification will affect the discipline to be applied.

The individual contracts concluded via the platform, for instance, will also be subject to very different rules depending on the service or good they cover. These may be information society services or, as is often the case, services to be performed offline.[21]

This distinction is crucial because it affects the role played and the legal liability of the platform. A pure marketplace, for instance, might not be liable for defects in products sold by third parties, whereas a platform that handles the sale directly (such as Amazon with its products) must be liable like a normal seller.

4 Contractual Relations Arising on Digital Platforms

A contract concluded online follows the same basic rules as a traditional contract: there must be an agreement between the parties, with a clear and conscious manifestation of will. However, in digital markets, the formation of consent takes place in a different manner than in traditional contracts.

Platforms generally prepare a set of general terms and conditions, made public on their own site under a very varied denomination, among which the terminology 'Terms of Use' or 'Terms of Use' is often used, which must be accepted by anyone who wants to make use of the platform to disseminate advertising, commercial communications and/or offers of their own products or services through it, and by those who, on the other hand, want to search for and, possibly, purchase the same. These are, therefore, uniform general terms and conditions of contract, unilaterally drawn up by the platform and without having been the subject of individual

[21] On models of contracts concluded through a digital platform, see Quarta and Smorto, (2024), p. 201 ff.; Alvarez Moreno (2021), p. 53 ff.; Camardi (2021), p. 881 ff. On the nature of agreements between users and digital platforms in the context of *social networks*, see especially, Perlingeri (2014), p. 36 ff.

negotiation, generally, neither with the commercial user who is the supplier of the good or service nor, even less so, with the end user (whether commercial or consumer). Often, therefore, it is not possible to identify separate telematic documents with two different contracts: one between the platform and the user supplying the goods or services and another between the platform and the end user. In some cases, moreover, it is not even possible to detect a specific document in which the full text of the contract between the business user and the end user recipient can be found. Everything is contained in a single telematic space and, sometimes, in several spaces as the contractual conditions are allocated in different 'places' of the site, corresponding to the different sections concerning the different aspects of the service to which they refer.[22]

However, it is possible to extrapolate and identify the different obligatory relationships that arise in connection with this type of negotiation.

4.1 Contractual Relations Between the Platform and the Service Provider User

The intermediation contract between the platform and the business user consists of an exchange between an information society service and a monetary consideration.

The platform undertakes to make available a telematic space in which it puts its users in contact with each other, thus enabling the business user to offer its products or services in exchange for a fee to a wide audience of consumer users who, if interested, can conclude purchase contracts through the same platform.

The main service, therefore, which is the subject of the platform's obligation concerns an online intermediation service, which Article 2.2 of Reg. (EU) 2019/1550, 20 June, defines according to the following requirements: (a) an information society service within the meaning of Article 1(1)(b) of Directive (EU) 2015/1535 of the European Parliament and of the Council; (b) a service by which business users are enabled to offer goods or services to consumers, with the aim of facilitating the initiation of direct transactions. (b) of Directive (EU) 2015/1535 of the European Parliament and of the Council; (b) a service by which 'business users are enabled to offer goods or services to consumers, with the aim of facilitating the initiation of direct transactions between those business users and consumers, regardless of where those transactions are concluded'; (c) a service provided 'to business users on the basis of contractual relationships between the provider of those services and the business users offering goods and services to consumers'.

Regarding the legal qualification of the negotiation relationship, doctrine has pointed out that certain characteristics of the contract bring it closer to mediation. In

[22] Battelli (2022b), p. 563 ff.; Foltran (2019), p. 163 ff.; Quarta (2017), p. 558 ff.; Smorto (2020), p. 59 ff.

fact, the content of the platform's obligations, which aim to facilitate and promote the meeting of supply and demand for a product or service with a view to concluding a contract, would seem to suggest placing this negotiating figure within the scope of mediation.[23]

However, there are many aspects that characterise the role and legal position of the platform that make this contractual relationship peculiar.

Among the aspects that characterise this type of intermediation contract and differentiate it from mediation is the circumstance that there is no provision, at least in a large proportion of cases, for an obligation on the part of the business user to pay a fee to the platform only upon the actual conclusion of the contract, which makes clear the difficulty of definitively framing it within the margins of the mediation contract.

The remuneration, in most cases, is linked to the promotion and advertising activity carried out by the platform and the presentation of the commercial user's offer within it. However, the market presents an enormous variety of ways of determining this remuneration. In addition to the activity carried out by the platform in each case or the possible commission for the contracts actually concluded, the number of potential end users who have viewed or visited a specific web page, link or the provider's advertising often also affects the determination of remuneration.

Moreover, the platform's obligation often extends to a much broader scope than simply connecting its users and providing them with the opportunity to conclude a contract using its telematic infrastructure. The platform places the commercial user's advertising, commercial communications and offers within its own online structure, promotes its offers in a digital marketplace among a huge number of potential customers, and undertakes to ensure the integrity and dissemination of messages, but also stable and continuous access to potential customers and the ability to interact in the telematic space made available. It is also common for the platform to undertake to use search engines within its application (by means of algorithms set up by the platform itself) to link offers to customer enquiries, on the basis of criteria and filters activated by the target users, or to set up the telematic infrastructure necessary for the business user to be able to fulfil all the information obligations binding on him and to prearrange all the activities necessary for the conclusion of the contract and, frequently, also those for the performance of the contract itself. In cases where the good or service to be delivered or performed is telematic, execution often takes place through the same platform, as on the other hand is the case with the payment of the monetary consideration. Even in some cases where the performance is not digital, however, the execution is expected to be handled by the platform (think, for instance, of the case of Uber).

Other possible obligations consist in organising and ranking the offers of goods or services, drawing up rankings of products or business users, collecting and processing the opinion and comments of end users and making them public, or even,

[23] On the legal qualification of the activity of platforms, see Alvarez Moreno (2021), p. 53 ff.; De Artiñano Marra (2023), p. 88 ff.; Di Sabato (2020), p. 9 ff.; Fernández García de la Yedra (2024), p. 121 ff.; Perlingieri (2015), p. 201 ff.

for instance, in managing the reservation system for the good or service contracted between users.

It is rarely possible to classify the platform as a merely extraneous entity that remains on the sidelines of the contract concluded between the provider and the end user. It is very frequent that the platform, in unilaterally drawing up the general contractual terms and conditions to be accepted by the commercial user and the end user, lays down conditions affecting the content of the contract to be established between them. In addition to the very frequent eventuality in which the platform competes with the offeror, proposing goods or services that are complementary to those offered by the business user.

Undoubtedly this mediation contract presents peculiar features that not only enrich the basic scheme of mediation but also connote it in a very special way, making it 'atypical', a particular figure of mixed contract. With mediation, it shares the essential characteristic of the absence of a contractual bond with one of the parties to which it undertakes to protect their interests. This does not detract, however, from the fact that the mediation activity carried out by platforms may be conditioned by the marketing strategies of this or that particular business, which do not exclude the granting of particular advantages to a certain category of users in order to increase their interaction with the platform.

Platforms, for their part, may reserve the right to offer goods that are accessory or complementary to those offered by commercial users.

The contractual relationship between the platform and the commercial user is normally governed by an adhesion contract, unilaterally prepared by the platform and formulated through a set of general conditions. In any case, the contract is also subject to the general rules of the Civil Code concerning general terms and conditions and, therefore, to the rules of Article 1341 of the Civil Code and the other rules intended to protect the contracting party that has not prepared the contractual terms and conditions.[24]

Also in relation to the contractual relationship that is established between the platform and the business user, of particular relevance is Regulation No. 2019/1150 of the European Parliament and of the Council of 20 June 2019 promoting fairness and transparency for business users of online intermediary services, the scope of which is specifically focused on contracts concluded between platforms and business users (Art. 1(2)).

This legislation introduces for the first time the application of a regulation on general terms and conditions about contracts between traders with the specific aim of helping to ensure transparency and fairness in the contract.[25]

Particularly relevant is the rule that states that the general terms of the contract do not lose this connotation and, therefore, do not cease to be subject to the relevant discipline whatever their name or form, provided that they have been determined

---

[24] Battelli (2022b), p. 563 ff.

[25] Alvarez Moreno (2021), p. 51 ff.; Cavaceppi (2021), p. 157 ff.; Fernández García de la Yedra (2024), p. 157 ff.; Martinelli (2023), p. 147 ff.; Quarta and Smorto (2024), p. 207 ff.; Ruggeri (2021), p. 397 ff.; Tripodi (2022), p. 17 ff.

unilaterally by the platform. To enable this to be ascertained, it will be decisive to make an overall assessment, 'for which the relative size of the parties concerned or the fact that a negotiation took place or that certain provisions thereof may have been subject to such a negotiation jointly by the supplier and the business user concerned' (Article 2(10)) is not in itself decisive.

The current relevance of the digital market, driven by network effects based on the use and processing of data, is attracting more and more business users to this sector, who want to avail themselves of the services offered by platforms, which, in turn, are seeing their market presence increase at the same time. This, however, also increases the risk for commercial users, suppliers of goods and services, to be subjected to the superior bargaining power of platforms and, therefore, to have to accept unfair agreements. The need to provide protection for the weaker party, which, in this case, is the business user who wants to make use of the platform's intermediation service, has therefore become evident.

Consistent with the purpose of the rules outlined in the Regulation and set forth therein, these rules aim to protect the transparency and fairness of the content of contracts between these parties, ensuring accessibility, transparency and knowledge of the contractual clauses.

In this perspective, Article 3, which deals with the terms and conditions of use unilaterally prepared by the platforms, states that they must be drafted in simple and comprehensible language and be easily available online, even before the conclusion of the contract with the platform (sub-paragraphs a and b), is particularly important.

In relation to another issue of great relevance to the business user concerning the platform's ability to suspend, cease or limit the provision of online brokerage services, which results in the deactivation or suspension of the account of the person concerned, Article 3 provides that the terms of the contract must accurately state the conditions that may justify these measures. Moreover, in the event of their adoption, the platform must communicate them to the business user in advance, using a durable medium, then indicating the reasons underlying the measures. In the event of a definitive termination of the brokering service, the notice shall be at least 30 days from its effective implementation. The business user may lodge a complaint against the deactivation, following the new procedure described in Article 11 of the Regulation.

In justifying the decision to initiate such measures, it is not sufficient to put forward generic grounds. The Regulation, in fact, requires that in communicating the reasons the platform must make concrete reference to specific facts and circumstances in such a way as to put business users in a position to assess whether there is room to contest the decision. Recital 22 of the Regulation itself about the manner in which the platform must state the concrete reasons for the decision requires a 'reference in a proportionate manner to the relevant circumstances, including third party notifications, that led to that decision'. It may be inferred from reading the aforesaid recital and the text of Article 4(5) that the assessment of the degree of specificity with which the facts or circumstances that led the platform to take the decision to suspend, limit or interrupt the brokering service provided up to that point must be made explicit requires a case-by-case assessment taking into account all the circumstances that concur in that particular context.

The general terms and conditions must also contain information concerning any additional distribution channels and potential affiliate programmes through which platforms may market the products and services offered by commercial users. To comply with the purpose of the rule, all information concerning the conditions of access to these channels, the particular characteristics of these means, and their functionality, as well as any additional costs, must be deemed to be subject to the platform's obligation.

All 'general information on the effects of the terms and conditions on the ownership and control of commercial users' intellectual property rights' should be the subject of the general terms and conditions.

Any amendments to the contract must, under penalty of nullity, be communicated to the business user by means of a durable medium and with at least 15 days' notice, and may not enter into force and be applied before the expiry of the term, so that the business user may possibly withdraw from the contract before the expiry of the term. The termination shall take effect within 15 days of receipt of the notification of the change that the platform intends to make, unless a shorter period is stipulated in the contract.

The business user, once he has received the notice, may renounce it. He shall be deemed to have renounced it if, during the period of the notice period, he offers new goods or services on the platform, unless the notice period is longer than 15 days, as changes in the conditions may require the business user to make technical updates to his services or information provided.

Terms and conditions that do not comply with the requirements of the Rules are null and void. It is in any case a nullity that can be considered to protect the weaker party, in this case the business user, and consequently subject to the regime of possible partial nullity and limitation of active legitimacy to the exercise of the relative action.

The Regulation also addresses the issue of the positioning of goods and services by the platform, aware of the significant impact this can have on consumer choice and, therefore, on the outcome of the activities carried out by the business user. Positioning refers to how the different offers of commercial users are presented, organised or communicated by platforms or online search engine providers, or the relevance that is attributed to them, deriving from the use of algorithmic systems of sequential sorting, from the communication of the results of ratings or reviews, from the management of visual evidence or other detection tools rather than from a combination of all these elements.

Platforms organise the positioning of all the offers they manage in a way that is not arbitrary but based on certain parameters. In this important aspect, the Regulation imposes an obligation on platforms to communicate to the providers of the goods or services the main parameters determining their positioning and the reasons behind these choices (Art. 5(1)) and to include them in the platform's terms of use. By main parameter it is reasonable that it should mean any general criterion, process, specific signal taken into account by the algorithms or any other adjustment or retrocession mechanism used to determine the positioning.

The description of these parameters provided by the platforms should be clear, comprehensible and up-to-date, based on actual data. Even if the interpretation of this obligation does not necessitate the disclosure of the detailed functioning of the positioning mechanisms, including the algorithms, it should be clear and comprehensible. In fact, Article 5(6) itself confirms the application in this area of Directive (EU) 2016/943 of the European Parliament and of the Council of 8 June 2016 on the protection of confidential know-how and confidential business information (trade secrets) against the unlawful acquisition, use and disclosure of that type of information.

Article 8 of the Regulation lists the specific contractual clauses that the terms of use of intermediary platforms must contain in order to ensure that the relationship with the commercial user is characterised by the principles of good faith and fairness. These include the clause by which the platform undertakes not to impose retroactive changes to the terms of use; the clause indicating the conditions under which business users may withdraw from the relationship with the platform; and, finally, the conditions relating to technical and contractual access to the information provided or generated by the business user and which are retained by the platform even after the contract expires.

Another very relevant issue that must be addressed in the terms of use concerns the conditions relating to technical and contractual access, or the impossibility of access, by commercial users to personal and non-personal data provided by commercial users or consumers for the use of the brokering services carried out by the platform. In this same line of transparency, the Regulation requires in the terms of use the inclusion of information concerning the provision or non-provision to third parties of the aforementioned data, when such sharing is not indispensable for the proper functioning of the online brokering services, the purpose of such sharing and the possibilities for the business user to opt out.

Article 11 focuses on the internal complaint handling system that the brokerage platform must offer to the business user. It must be easily accessible, free of charge and must ensure that the complaint is acknowledged within a reasonable time. The Rules set out a list of issues that, should they occur during the relationship, could be the subject of a complaint by the business user through the internal complaints handling system: these are possible failures by the platform to fulfil its obligations under the Rules; technological problems affecting the provision of the brokerage service; and, finally, measures and conduct adopted by the platform during the execution of the contract that have had negative consequences for the business user.

In the Regulation, however, there is no useful indication of the internal complaints management system, which is therefore left to the autonomy of the platform: Article 11(2) mentions very general indications that do not constitute real guarantees for the business user. The only obligation that the Regulation places on the platform concerns the publication of information on access and the operation of the internal complaints management system, as outlined in the terms of use.

On the other hand, Regulation (EU) 2019/1150 does not apply to the contractual relationship between the platform and a provider of goods or services who is not a trader but a party offering a peer-to-peer exchange. In these cases, in addition to the common law and the data processing regulations, Reg. (EU) 2022/2065, Digital Services Act, applies.

The latter regulation applies to all contractual relations between platforms and users of the intermediation service, including commercial users, non-commercial users, and consumer users. As Article 1 itself points out, the DSA (Digital Services Act) deals especially with the issue of content management, regulating the powers of platforms to act on illegal content and content provided by the recipient that it deems incompatible with its policy, and the imposition of specific duties of care to promote a transparent and safe online environment.

In this sense, platforms must include in their general terms and conditions 'information on the restrictions they impose about the use of their services with regard to information provided by service recipients. Such information shall cover, inter alia, the policies, procedures, measures and tools used for the purpose of content moderation, including algorithmic decision-making and human verification, as well as the procedural rules of their internal complaint handling system'. In imposing such restrictions, platforms must act in a 'diligent, objective and proportionate manner', taking into account the rights and legitimate interests of all stakeholders (Art. 14(3)).

The Regulation insists on the obligation for platforms to draft the general terms and conditions in a clear and comprehensible manner, 'easily usable and unambiguous', in a format that is easily accessible to the public and machine-readable (Art. 14(1)), and on the obligation to inform the recipients of the service of any significant unilateral changes to the general terms and conditions.

Among the obligations imposed on platforms to ensure greater transparency, there are the obligations to inform about their content moderation activities (Article 14), the obligation to set up a mechanism through which any person can notify the presence of illegal content in their information service, process the reports received and take the relevant decisions (Article 15). If the decision entails a restriction on the information provided by the service recipient, the platform must provide a clear and specific justification to all concerned service recipients (Article 17).

Other obligations imposed on platforms relate to the adoption of an easily accessible and effective internal complaints handling system, as indicated in Article 20, which can significantly affect the position of individual users through a number of decisions.

Further transparency obligations concern advertising (Art. 26), recommendation systems (Art. 27) and the protection of minors (Art. 28). Of particular importance is the obligation to trace traders. Before allowing a trader to use the platform to advertise or offer products or services to consumers, the platform must have received certain information from him by which it is possible to identify him, to know his contact details and his main business data, as well as his signed commitment to offer only products or services that comply with EU law.

On this point, the DSA lays down particularly strict rules with regard to VLOP platforms (Very Large Online Platforms) and VLOSE search engines (Very Large

Online Search Engines), i.e. online platforms or search engines that have more than 45 million users per month in the EU, precisely because of their size and impact on the market and society.

The DSA requires platforms to make 'the greatest possible effort to assess' whether the information received from the trader 'is reliable and complete, using any freely accessible official online database or interface made available by a Member State or the Union'.

The role of the platform in informing the end user of a transaction of the qualification, as a trader or not, of the supplier of goods or services is therefore essential.

4.2 Contractual Relations Between the Platform and the User

The contract between the digital platform and the user constitutes one of the legal agreements that govern the rights and obligations of the parties in the context of using online services. This type of contract may vary depending on the nature of the platform and the services offered; however, most contracts between digital platforms and users are adhesion contracts, in which one party (the platform) draws up the general terms and conditions of the contract, while the other party (the user) can simply accept or reject these conditions, without the possibility of modifying them.

This agreement raises questions regarding the potential vexatiousness of the clauses, as the user is often confronted with conditions that may be unfair, such as the platform's limitation of liability clauses, which exclude the platform's liability for direct or indirect damages resulting from the use of the service.[26]

The consumer is protected by the Consumer Code (Legislative Decree No. 206/2005), which is the primary Italian legislation governing consumer protection in contracts with professionals, including digital platforms. In particular, Article 33 of the Consumer Code, also applicable to online contracts, states that clauses that impose excessive obligations on the consumer without adequate counterbalance or that unfairly limit his rights are considered null and void if the user has not explicitly accepted them in a clear and comprehensible manner.[27]

[26] The regulatory source legitimising such clauses is European Directive 2000/31/EC, better known as the e-Commerce Directive, according to which *hosting* platforms (such as those hosting user-generated content) are not held liable for the content they host, unless they have actual knowledge of the illegal content.

[27] Furthermore, it pursues the objective of ensuring that platforms do not abuse their dominant position, an aspect that also includes the control of unfair terms, the recently adopted (2019/1150) Digital Market Regulation (EU) (known as the Digital Markets Act), which aims to promote fair competition in the digital sector by limiting unfair practices of *online* platforms. Finally, consumer protection is entrusted to the Antitrust Authority for Competition and the Market (AGCM), which is in charge of monitoring unfair commercial practices, including those related to digital platforms, and has the power to intervene with sanctions in the case of the detection of unfair terms or misleading practices.

In the context of digital platforms, such clauses could concern, for instance, not only the seller's liability limitations, but also conditions for returning products or dispute resolution. Platforms should ensure that such clauses are clearly separated from the rest of the contract and presented in a way that allows users to easily read them and decide whether to accept them. If there is no clear and explicit acceptance by the user, the clauses could be considered null and void.

Contracts between the digital platform and the user may be explicit or implicit, depending on the way they are concluded. If the user clicks 'I accept' after having read the contract and formally acknowledges the conditions, the contract is explicitly concluded. Conversely, when acceptance of the conditions occurs tacitly, such as when use of the platform automatically entails acceptance of its conditions, the contract is considered implicit.

Mutual rights and obligations arise from the concluded contract. The platform's main duty is to provide a specific service (e.g. access to games, products, information, social features), to which are added commitments relating to security, protection of personal data and the reliability of the service itself. The user, for its part, undertakes to use the service in compliance with the law, not to infringe intellectual property rights, not to engage in fraudulent activities or activities that are harmful to the platform and other users, and to respect the platform's policies, such as those relating to content and conduct.

Intellectual property rights shall be deemed to be infringed if the user uploads or distributes copyrighted content without due authorisation, uses trademarks or patents of others without the necessary licence, or copies and distributes software, music, videos or other copyrighted material without the express consent of the owners.

As far as fraudulent activities are concerned, this refers to acts such as the creation of false accounts or the use of misleading information to gain access to services, the carrying out of fraud in the commercial sphere, such as payment scams, as well as the carrying out of phishing operations[28] or the attempt to unlawfully obtain sensitive data belonging to other users (e.g. by means of forged e-mails or websites).

Behaviour detrimental to the platform and users is defined as sending spam messages, promoting unauthorised commercial activities or unsolicited advertising, spreading viruses, malware, spyware or other dangerous software that may compromise the security of the platform or users, as well as acts of attack or interference with the normal operation of the platform, such as hacking or tampering with the platform software.

Inappropriate behaviour would also include conduct that harasses or intimidates other users, creates intentional conflicts, participates in bullying or discrimination, and abuses the platform's functionalities to damage the reputation of other users or the platform itself.

[28] *Phishing* techniques are deceptive practices employed by malicious individuals with the intent to defraud victims in order to obtain personal, confidential or sensitive information, such as login credentials (*username, password*), bank details, credit card numbers and other private information.

Finally, there would be a violation of the content policy if users posted offensive, discriminatory, threatening or hateful material, uploaded content promoting violence, sexual abuse, illegal activities or criminal behaviour, and shared data that violated the privacy of others, such as images or personal information without the consent of the persons concerned.

The protection of personal data is a crucial aspect in digital contracts. Platforms are required to comply with the General Data Protection Regulation (GDPR), which establishes clear rights for users regarding the processing of their data, including the rights of access, rectification, deletion and portability. Users must provide informed and explicit consent for the processing of their data, with the option to revoke it at any time. Platforms are obliged to inform users about the types of data collected, the purposes of the processing and the third parties with whom the data may be shared. Furthermore, they must take appropriate measures to protect data from unauthorised access or accidental loss. Suppose platforms utilise third-party services, such as payment providers, cloud servers or management technologies. In that case, it is essential that these arrangements are clearly defined in the contract to avoid liability issues related to the services provided. For instance, if an e-commerce platform utilises an external payment system (such as PayPal or Stripe), the contract must clearly specify the payment arrangements and responsibilities of each party involved.[29]

4.3 Contractual Relations Between the Seller or Service Provider and the User

In a contract concluded between a seller and a user via a digital platform, the platform acts primarily as an intermediary, ensuring that the entire contractual process is carried out in compliance with applicable regulations.

In general, the contract between the seller or service provider and the user also takes the form of a contract of adhesion, an agreement in which the user has little opportunity to negotiate the terms, since the conditions are usually set unilaterally by the seller. However, this does not imply that the contract should not respect the principles of fairness and transparency, which are fundamental to consumer protection.

The principle of transparency, laid down in the main Italian and European regulations,[30] requires that even in this type of contract the clauses be drafted in a way that is clear, comprehensible and easily accessible to the average user. Digital

[29] The analysis of the terms and conditions of *online* contracts is developed in Tuccillo (2025), in this book.

[30] They aim to ensure that information is easily understandable and accessible to users, promoting consumer protection and fairness in transactions, the Consumer Code (Legislative Decree no. 206/2005), Directive 93/13/EEC of the European Parliament and of the Council (Directive on unfair terms in consumer contracts), Regulation (EU) 2016/679 or GDPR (*General Data Protection*

platforms must therefore ensure that their terms and conditions are expressed in plain language, avoiding technicalities and ambiguities that could prevent users from making an informed decision. In particular, clauses covering crucial issues such as privacy, personal data management, payment methods, withdrawal rights, guarantees and liability limitations should be clearly highlighted so that the user can easily understand his or her rights and obligations. Ambiguous or unclear language may in fact render some clauses null and void, as it is considered to hinder an informed decision.

The conclusion of a contract through a digital platform generally takes place through an opt-in system, in which the user, after having read all the contractual terms and conditions, confirms his or her acceptance by clicking on a box or otherwise providing consent (e.g. by pressing an 'I accept' or 'Confirm' button). This act of acceptance implies that the user has understood and accepted the terms and conditions of sale or use of the service, marking the formation of the contract.

In contracts concluded between a seller or service provider and online users, a series of mutual obligations arise, governing the rights and obligations of the parties involved, in order to ensure a fair exchange of goods and services, as well as consumer protection and full compliance with applicable legal regulations.

First and foremost, the seller has an obligation to provide clear, complete and truthful information about the product or service offered, including the terms of payment, additional costs and rights of withdrawal. Furthermore, it is obliged to deliver the good or service by the contract, respecting the agreed specifications in terms of quality, quantity and other characteristics. The product or service must correspond exactly to what is stated in the contract or in the pre-contractual information, thus meeting the legitimate expectations of the user. It is always the seller's responsibility to fulfil his obligation to deliver the good or complete the service within the agreed time and to provide the legal guarantee against conformity defects, which covers this for a period defined by law. Finally, it is the seller's responsibility to provide adequate and transparent mechanisms for the resolution of any disputes, in full compliance with consumer protection regulations.[31]

The user, for their part, is obliged to examine the terms and conditions of use with due attention and accept them before proceeding with the purchase or accessing the service, to avoid potential problems arising from unfair terms. Furthermore, he/she is obliged to pay the agreed amount for the purchased good or service,

---

Regulation), Directive 2000/31/EC or E-Commerce Directive and Directive 2011/83/EU on consumer rights.

[31] The seller must offer, where provided for by European and national regulations, *Alternative Dispute Resolution* (ADR) mechanisms, such as mediation or arbitration, which allow for a quick and inexpensive resolution of disputes without the need for formal court proceedings. In addition, in accordance with the European Directive 2013/11/EU (as updated by Directive (EU) 2019/2161), the seller must ensure access to *Online* Dispute *Resolution* or ODR platforms, which allow consumers to submit complaints quickly and easily via the web, without the need for complex legal intervention. The European Union has made available an ODR platform accessible *online*, which facilitates interaction between consumers and sellers for the resolution of disputes related to *online* purchases.

respecting the terms and timeframe established in the contract. The user also has a duty to receive the product or service in accordance with the contractual provisions. He is obliged to scrupulously comply with the conditions stipulated in the contract, including those relating to the use of the product or service, the prohibition of resale or improper use, as well as compliance with the rules of conduct. In the event that the product is defective or does not meet the stipulated specifications, the user is obligated to notify the seller of the issue, following the procedures for exercising the right of guarantee or withdrawal.

Both parties are obliged to scrupulously observe the applicable regulatory provisions, including those relating to the protection of personal data (such as the GDPR), the safeguarding of consumer rights, the security of financial transactions and the prevention of misleading advertising. It is essential that both parties are fully aware of the dispute resolution methods outlined in the contract, which may include arbitration or other alternative forms of mediation.[32]

Likewise, both parties have to comply with the regulations concerning the handling and protection of personal data. In particular, the seller or service provider is obliged to ensure the protection of the user's information, while the latter is obliged to provide true and timely updated data. These mutual obligations are of fundamental importance for the proper conduct of online contracts and to ensure a fair and transparent business relationship between seller/service provider and user. Failure to comply with these obligations may result in serious legal consequences, including termination of the contract, compensation for damages and the application of sanctions.

5 The Peculiarities of Contracts Concluded Through Digital Platforms

Electronic commerce has long since undergone considerable development and diffusion. Proof of this is the proliferation of regulations, both at European and national level, issued to protect the weaker party in this field of trade. Therefore, it is legitimate to ask oneself about the specificities of trade through digital platforms, what are the particularities that characterise the commercial activities that take place through platforms and that have given rise to so many new interventions by legislators and doctrine.

Contracts concluded with or through platforms pose issues that go beyond the perimeters of the individual telematic contract and even the more recent smart contract.

The use of digital platforms has simplified contract conclusion and made the market more accessible, but it has also introduced new legal challenges. Traditional

[32] For the arbitration clause see Chapter "Terms and Conditions of Services as Expressions of the Normative Power of Online Platforms" by C. Tuccillo in this handbook, volume II.

rules of contract law have to adapt to an environment where transactions are fast, automated and often transnational.[33]

The European legislator has attempted to address this issue with regulations such as the Digital Services Act and the Digital Markets Act, which aim to ensure greater transparency and user protection. However, the real challenge will be to strike a balance between innovation and the protection of fundamental rights in an ever-changing digital ecosystem.

The commercial activities of platforms directly affect the very structure of markets and contractual practices, generating an enormous impact, particularly in relation to the matching of supply and demand.

Platforms, in fact, by facilitating such a meeting, enable the end user to reduce search and negotiation times, exponentially multiplying the possibilities for the latter to evaluate and purchase among a multiplicity of goods or services conveniently, without economic and time costs, allowing him/her to compare prices and characteristics of a plurality of offers easily.

Trading through digital platforms enables companies to reach new markets, thus facilitating their exponential growth. It also encourages greater interaction between businesses, facilitating the collaborative implementation of aggregations of services offered to users, increasingly intensifying the ability of platforms to exploit network effects. These effects are magnified disproportionately when the value of a platform increases as more users join, creating a positive feedback loop.

The impact on the market and competition with traders who conduct their business in presence are obvious and have already been discussed at length.

Their influence, however, has recently become even more decisive as platforms not only facilitate the encounter between supply and demand but also direct and channel these encounters through the management of search engines through which the end user's search is oriented and filtered. They therefore intervene in an increasingly incisive manner in the decision-making process of the end user of goods and services, guiding the process of identifying the good or service sought.

Through their system of interaction with users, moreover, the digital platforms improve the possibility of involving them in the articulation of the services offered, making it possible to increase the customisation of the offer, thereby increasing customer satisfaction and, therefore, their attractiveness, promoting greater loyalty and also favouring monitoring that facilitates the selection of the offer intended for individual users.

Platforms end up, therefore, by conditioning market trends insofar as they also intervene in questions concerning the security conditions of contracting, the reliability of suppliers of goods and services and the transactions themselves. Suffice it to consider, from this point of view, the decisive role they play in the collection of customer opinions, in their publication and in the drawing up of rankings between

[33] Alvarez Moreno (2021), p. 7 ff.; Carleo (2022), p. 74 ff.; Conti (2020), p. 32 ff., p. 63 ff.; De Artíñano Marra (2023), p. 72 ff.; Di Sabato (2020), p. 9 ff.; Martinelli (2023), p. 7 ff.

operators or between products or services. They manage, therefore, the reputational mechanisms that have a very strong influence on market orientations.

All this makes clear the enormous impact that the spread of platforms has had on competition between companies and how this can generate new possible forms of distortion of free competition in the market, which have been the subject of attention by the European legislator.

Another fundamental aspect of the phenomenon of digital platforms and contracting through them is the vast amount of data they collect from all interactions with various users, both commercial and end users.

This phenomenon, now increasingly consolidated, ultimately develops into an immensely profitable data market for platforms, which, in terms of size and complexity, contributes to further increasing their potential and gives them market power hardly comparable to that of other commercial operators in the past.[34]

On the other hand, as experience has already shown, this power, driven further by the enormous and in part as yet untapped potential of artificial intelligence, goes beyond the perimeter of the market understood in the traditional sense and is capable of conditioning much wider spheres of society such as freedom of the press, information, politics, international conflicts and even democracy itself.

Today, platforms are one of the privileged players in the acquisition, management and circulation of a mass of data of, sometimes, planetary dimensions.

Some manifestations of this potential of platforms can also be found at the contractual level. Today, contrary to what end users used to believe in the past, it has become evident that the supply of goods and services that are offered to users without a specific claim to pecuniary consideration, but with the sole claim of providing their data and, sometimes, answering a simple questionnaire, are not 'free' contracts but contracts for consideration whose consideration is nothing more than the set of data that the user provides, often unaware that he is transmitting a value in this way: a value of which the user, most of the time, is unable to appreciate the extent because it is not easy for him to hypothesise the elaboration process in which the individual data will be inserted and processed for subsequent implementation. All this highlights the end-user-contractor's lack of effective control over the balance of the exchange between the service they aspire to obtain and the provision of their data. It is clear, how, in this context, the general terms and conditions on privacy take on particular relevance and, therefore, the importance of these being accessible to a careful reading by those concerned.[35]

In addition to the incidence of platforms, from the perspective of the market for goods and services and the market for data, which will be the subject of attention

---

[34] Stanzione (2022), *passim*; Addante (2020), p. 890 ff; Camardi (2021), p. 876 ff; Irti (2021), p. 45 ff; De Franceschi (2017a), p. 17 ff; Miridi (2021), p. 111 ff.; Resta and Zeno Zencovich (2018), p. 436 ff.; Ricciuto (2019), p. 23 ff.; Id. (2020), p. 642 ff.; Stazi and Corrado (2019), p. 443 ff.; Versaci (2020), p. 27 ff.

[35] Battelli (2022a), p. 55 ff.; De Franceschi (2017b), p. 1405 ff.; Di Cerbo (2021), p. 185 ff.; Giannone Codiglione (2017), p. 418 ff.; Perlingieri (2015), p. 55 ff., and p. 66 ff.; Resta and Zeno-Zencovich (2018), p. 412 ff.; Ricciuto (2023), p. 21 ff.; Tosi (2023), p. 189 ff.

later, it is not possible to overlook the impact that the intervention of these commercial operators also has on the individual contracts concluded through the spaces they make available to users.

Firstly, the platform often unilaterally arranges the content or part of the content of the contract, not only that between the platform and the end user, but also that between the supplier of the goods and services and the end user.

Platforms prepare and make accessible the information received from the supplier of goods and services, as well as instructions for concluding the contract and often for its performance, especially if the contracted good or service is also digital. Very frequently, they also provide the payment procedure and service, or other services required for the performance of the main service by the business user, such as the booking service or the procedures for carrying out any communications between the end user and the supplier of the goods or services. In many cases, the platform also operates a special system for resolving any conflicts that arise after the contract is concluded.

Therefore, based on these elements, it is no longer possible to consider the platform as an extraneous party to the relationship between commercial users and end users, since its intervention becomes decisive both for the definition of the applicable rules and for the very course of the contractual programme and, indeed, sometimes even for settling issues that may subsequently arise.

It is therefore a digital contract, but no longer a bilateral one, like the basic scheme that essentially preoccupied the first legislator of electronic commerce, but a subsequent evolution of such a contract that poses new legal questions to which an answer must be sought. Not the least of these is the peculiar multilateral setup of interests, about which there is a clear risk of particular imbalances between the parties, more complex than those present in the first phase of e-commerce development. In particular, the position of the business user as a weaker contracting party, which previously existed sporadically and only in specific circumstances, is being consolidated in this area.

It is clear that the discipline of the European matrix is concerned with protecting users, whether commercial or consumer, in the face of situations of imbalance, but it cannot be its task to resolve questions concerning the identification of the particular rights and obligations incumbent on each of the contractual parties in these multilateral transactions. These questions are to be settled based on the general rules of the contract, which remain within the scope of the laws of the member states. It is the task of the interpreters in each jurisdiction to unravel this interweaving of legal situations, in order to clarify for each participant the party against whom they may claim a right or have a duty to perform an obligation.

Among the issues that arise, therefore, the need to ensure clarity and transparency in relation to the actors involved, their role, the function each of them is called upon to perform and the rights and obligations of each.

A need that becomes even more pressing, as the reality of the market demonstrates, when it is not only the three entities we have referred to so far that are involved in the commercial transaction, but others, as is often the case.

Indeed, the contract between the supplier of the main good or service and the end user, concluded via a platform, is not infrequently supplemented by other contractual relationships with different subjects offering goods or services that are accessory or complementary to the main object of the first contract. In this context, there are many examples: the insurance that is taken out with the rental of a car, the excursion that is booked along with the reservation of a hotel room, or an airline ticket, which may also be associated with an airport transport service or entry to a show, the maintenance of the purchased good or the supplement of the guarantee of the regular operation of the purchased household appliance, the cleaning service of the rented clothes, etc.

It is also possible that the platform itself entrusts certain services to third parties such as, for instance, payment service providers or cloud server providers, and, in such cases, the end user does not even have the possibility of deciding to exclude these further contractual relationships as they are strictly linked to the conclusion of contracts with the platform and the selected business user.

Therefore, clear and easily accessible information on the identification of different contractual relationships and the respective contracting parties, along with their obligations and responsibilities, becomes increasingly important.

Platforms, which by their very nature perform the function of a marketplace, not only provide a virtual space, but also promote a negotiating link between contracts concluded by different parties. The risk for the end user of not fully grasping the structure of the different contractual relationships they are quickly concluding with a series of clicks is particularly high; therefore, information concerning this aspect should be equally clear. And the platform cannot be considered an outsider in this respect since it is the one that presents all offers, arranges their display and communication to the end user.

In this perspective, Article 3(5) of Regulation (EU) 2019/1150 places an obligation on platforms to ensure that the identity of the business user providing the goods or services is 'clearly visible'. Compliance with this rule requires making it particularly comprehensible, even visually, to an average end user that the new service constitutes the subject of a new contract with another party, as well as the identity of the latter with an indication of all necessary information about him or her.

Similarly, it is of the utmost importance to properly inform the user who is the recipient of the service and, in particular, to whom he or she may address any complaint in the event of non-performance or inexact performance of the service.

References

Addante A (2020) La circolazione negoziale dei dati personali nei contratti di fornitura di contenuti e servizi digitali. Giust. civ. 4:890 ff

Alvarez Moreno MT (2021) La contratación electrónica mediante plataformas en línea: modelo negocial (B2C), régimen jurídico y protección de los contratantes (proveedores y consumidores). Madrid

Battelli E (2022a) I modelli negoziali di business degli operatori digitali a “prezzo zero” non sono “gratuiti”. Contratti 3:55 ff
Battelli E (2022b) Questioni aperte in materia di contrattazione nelle piattaforme on line. Contratti 5:563 ff
Camardi C (2021) Contratti digitali e mercati delle piattaforme. Un promemoria per il civilista. Jus civile 4:893 ff
Cassano G (2024) Protection of the person v. company. when the ‘transfer’ of personal data might suffice. the case of personalised advertising, in Il Diritto di Famiglia e delle Persone, 4, 1575.
Carleo R (2022) Piattaforme digitali e contratto. EJPLT, p 74 ff
Cavaceppi C (2021) La tutela dei consumatori delle piattaforme digitali. In: Contaldo A (ed) Le piattaforme digitali. Profili giuridici e tecnologici nel nuovo ecosistema. Pisa, p 157 ff
Cavani G, Ercolani S (2023) Mondi virtuali e sfide reali proprietà intellettuale (pi) e metaverso. Riv. dir. ind., p 154
Conti G (2020) Lineamenti di Diritto delle piattaforme digitali. Santarcangelo di Romagna (RN), P 32 ff and p 63 ff
De Artiñano Marra P (2023) Régimen jurídico de las plataformas de mediación electrónica: Nuevas perspectivas para un fenómeno en constante desarrollo. Pamplona, p 88 ff
De Franceschi A (2017a) La circolazione dei dati personali tra privacy e contratto. Napoli, p 17 ff
De Franceschi A (2017b) Il «pagamento» mediante dati personali. In: Cuffaro C et al. (eds) I dati personali nel diritto europeo. Torino, p 1405 ff
Di Cerbo A (2021) Il corrispettivo dei servizi digitali: i dati personali. EJPLT 2:185 ff
Di Sabato D (2020) Il ruolo delle piattaforme digitali nello svolgimento delle attività economiche in rete. Annali della Facoltà Giuridica dell’Università di Camerino-Studi 9:9 ff
Fernández García de la Yedra A (2024) Régimen jurídico de las plataformas en línea de alojamiento. Madrid, p 121 ff
Foltran F (2019) Professionisti, consumatori e piattaforme on line: la tutela delle parti deboli nei nuovi equilibri negoziali. MediaLaws 3:163 ff
Fregonara E (2016) L’“equity based crowdfunding”: un nuovo modello di finanziamento per le “start up” innovative. Giur. it., p 2287 ff
Giannone Codiglione G (2017) I dati personali come corrispettivo della fruizione di un servizio di comunicazione elettronica e la “consumerizzazione” della privacy. Dir. inf., p 418 ff
Ginsburg J, Treppoz E (2005) International Copyright Law: U.S. and E.U. Perspectives – Text and Cases. Cheltenham
Goglia L (2022) Le eccezioni e le limitazioni nei contesti digitali e transfrontalieri. In: Lavagnini S (ed) Il diritto d’autore nel mercato unico digitale. Direttiva (UE) 2019/790 e d.lgs. n. 177/2021 di recepimento. Torino, p 83
Guccione AV (2024) L’equity crowdfunding delle piccole-medie imprese. Giur. comm., 6:1348
Irti C (2021) Consenso “negoziato” e circolazione dei dati personali. Torino, p 45 ff
Lamberti A (2015) Il finanziamento di nuove imprese: le peculiarità della “start-up innovative” e l’”equity-based crowdfunding” in Italia. Il Nuovo dir. soc
Laudonio A (2014) La folla e l’impresa: prime riflessioni sul “crowdfunding”. In: Orizzonti dir. comm
Laudonio A (2019) “Equity-based crowdfunding”: la protezione degli investitori nel prisma delle legislazioni europee e latino-americane. In: Riv. soc., p 1237 ff
Macchi F (2017) Corporate law and economics of equity crowdfunding. Giur. comm., p 555 ff
Martinelli S (2023) I contratti delle platform Economy. Ruoli e responsabilità delle piattaforme. Torino, p 147 ff
Miridi M (2021) Le piattaforme e il potere dei dati (Facebook non passa il Reno). Dir. inf. 2:111 ff
Mozzarelli MCM (2019) L’equity crowdfunding in Italia. Dati empirici, rischi e strategie. Banca, borsa, tit. cred., p 650 ff
Musso A (2020) Eccezioni e limitazioni ai diritti d’autore nella direttiva UE n. 790/2019. Dir. inf., p 411 ff
Perlingeri C (2014) Profili civilistici dei social network. Napoli

Perlingieri C (2015) Gli accordi tra i siti di social networks e gli utenti. In: Perlingieri C, Ruggieri L (eds) Internet e diritto civile, Napoli, p 201 ff
Quarta A (2017) Il ruolo delle piattaforme digitali nell'economia collaborativa. Contr. e impr. Eur., p 558 ff
Quarta A, Smorto G (2024) Diritto privato dei mercati digitali. Milano
Resta G, Zeno Zencovich V (2018) Volontà e consenso nella fruizione dei servizi in rete. In: Riv. trim. dir. e proc. civ., p 436 ff
Resta G, Zeno-Zencovich V (2018) Volontà e consenso nella fruizione dei servizi in rete. In: Riv. trim. dir. proc. civ., p 412 ff
Ricciuto V (2019) La patrimonializzazione dei dati personali: Contratto e mercato nella ricostruzione del fenomeno. In: Cuffaro C et al. (eds) I dati personali nel diritto europeo. Torino, p 23 ff
Ricciuto V (2020) Il contratto ed i nuovi fenomeni patrimoniali: il caso della circolazione dei dati personali. In: Riv. dir. civ., p 642 ff
Ricciuto V (2023) Lo scambio dei dati con i contenuti e i servizi digitali: una nuova modalità di contrarre?. EJPLT, 1, p 21 ff
Ricketson S, Ginsburg J (2022) International Copyright and Neighbouring Rights. Oxford
Rosati E (2014) Copyright in the EU: in search of (in)flexibilities. J Intual Prop Law Pract, p 585 ff
Ruggeri F (2021) Regole di trasparenza e rapporti tra imprese nei mercati digitali: Il Regolamento (UE) 2019/1150 sull'intermediazione on line e i motori di ricerca. Dir. infor., 2:397 ff
Schönberger M, Cukier K (2013) Big Data. Una rivoluzione che trasformerà il nostro modo di vivere. E già minaccia la nostra libertà. Milano
Smorto G (2020) La tutela del contraente debole nella platform economy dopo il Regolamento UE 2019/1150 e la Direttiva UE 2019/2161 (c.d. Omnibus). In: Falce V (ed) Fairness e innovazione nel mercato digitale. Torino, p 59 ff
Stanzione P (2022) I "poteri privati" delle piattaforme e le nuove frontiere della privacy. Torino
Stazi A, Corrado F (2019) Datificazione dei rapporti socio-economici e questioni giuridiche: profili evolutivi in prospettiva comparatistica. Dir. inf., p 443 ff
Stefanelli MA (2019) 'Regtech' e 'equity crowdfunding'. sperimentazioni nella regolazione giuridica del mercato finanziario digitale. Percorsi cost., p 177 ff
Tosi E (2023) Circolazione contrattuale dei dati personali tra GDPR e nuovo codice del consumo. Dir. inf., p 189 ff
Tripodi M (2022) Verso un nuovo quadro di riferimento per il commercio digitale. In: Fimmanò et al (eds) E-commerce. Regole, applicazioni, insidie, opportunità. Milano, p 17 ff
Trubiani F (2022) I contratti di cloud computing: natura, contenuti e qualificazione giuridica. Dir. inf., 2:395 ff
Tuccillo C (2025) Terms and Conditions of Services as Expressions of the Normative Power of Online Platforms". In: this handbook, volume II
Turci (2018) Nuova giur. civ. comm., 1085 ff
Vella F (2019) Crescere su mercati e piattaforme: le piccole medie imprese tra regole e politica industriale (Relazione al Convegno "Società a responsabilità limitata, piccola e media impresa mercati finanziari: un mondo nuovo?", Courmayeur, 14-15 settembre 2018). In: Merc. conc. reg., p 251 ff
Versaci G (2020) La contrattualizzazione dei dati personali dei consumatori, Napoli, p 27 ff
Vitali ML (2014) "Equity crowdfunding": la nuova frontiera della raccolta del capitale di rischio. In: Riv. soc., p 371 ff
Zeno-Zencovich V (2018) Uber: modello economico e implicazioni giuridiche. MediaLaws 1:141 ff

Sources: General Framework and Specific Rules

Roberto Carleo and Valerio Pescatore

Contents

Abstract The chapter aims to examine the complex system of sources of the digital ecosystem by referring to the methodological problems of building a system of effective rules that are adequate to the current technological context. The reflection then moves on to the possible positive effects of soft law in this field.

Sections 1, 4, 5 and 6 are attributed to Roberto Carleo and Sects. 2 and 3 to Valerio Pescatore.

R. Carleo · V. Pescatore (✉)
University of Naples "Parthenope", Naples, Italy
e-mail: roberto.carleo@uniparthenope.it; valerio.pescatore@uniroma1.it

R. Bocchini (ed.), *Digital Platforms - From Technical Foundations to Legal and Economic Implications*, https://doi.org/10.1007/978-3-032-07978-7_5

1 Introductory Notes. The Digital Ecosystem and the Sources of Law

The construction of a digital ecosystem first of all comes up against the problem of the relationship between law and technology:[1] with the latter seemingly overriding the former, within which, however, there is a strong need to introduce new sources, capable of regulating increasingly complex matters and situations.

The problem, moreover, is dealt with differently in the different territories of the world: in the Chinese model, total control of the digital data circulating in the network is centralised in the state;[2] in the (North) American model, the investment (mainly) of private subjects and the economic initiative of digital platforms within a free market are favoured.[3] Finally, in the European system, an attempt has been under way for some years now—not without some clamorous setbacks[4]—to dictate rules aimed at guaranteeing the development of digitalisation and the new artificial intelligence systems from an *anthropocentric* perspective: that is, attentive to the protection of the fundamental rights of the individual.[5]

The path of regulation is full of questions and uncertainties which, as will be seen, derive in particular from the inevitably limited territorial sphere of application of the law,[6] as well as from the progressive, often disorderly, affirmation of new sources (above all of *soft law*, co-regulation or 'participatory regulation'[7]), which, however, become necessary especially in view of the almost unlimited global power of the large digital platforms.[8] These platforms, erupting on the world stage as a sort of autonomous order (even more penetrating than the state), reveal themselves to be endowed with their own intrinsic regulatory power; all the more intense because they are exercised in a de-institutionalised economic and legal system, 'crowded with new modes of law, which go beyond or circumvent state boundaries,

[1] In general, around the debate on the relationship between law and technique, on the unstoppable primacy of technique, which influences law but can and must also be guided by it, it is always fundamental to start from the dialogue between Natalino Irti and Emanuele Severino (joined by Luigi Mengoni), on which cf. Irti and Severino (2001).

See also Galimberti (1999) p. 5 according to whom what technology 'knows is only the appropriateness of the means to the respective objectives, while what it does not know and around which it is incompetent is whether the objectives should be pursued or not. Here are the roots of the disagreement between technique and ethics, between what can be done and what must be done'.

[2] On this point Cerrina Feroni (2023), p. 3.

[3] Pollicino (2023), pp. 436–438.

[4] This refers to the withdrawal (announced on 11 February 2025) of the proposal on the *AI Liability Directive*.

[5] See e.g. recital 6 of the *AI Act* (Regulation (EU) 1689/2024).

[6] As long noted by Irti (2001).

[7] Bassan (2023), pp. 1103–1132.

[8] Attention should be paid to the so-called over the top platforms (namely the largest ones, the so-called VLOPs, *Very Large Online Platforms*). On the types of platforms, see Sect. 3.

reinventing their own space and functions, as well as their relationship with politics and technology'.[9]

2 The European Digital Strategy

Faced with the sudden evolution of the digital ecosystem, within which platforms are the main *players*, bearers of technological innovation, in recent years the European legislator has intervened with multiple regulations (more or less defined),[10] of a general or sectoral nature. At present, the main normative acts of reference are:

1. Regulation (EU) 2022/2065 (so-called Digital Services Act, DSA). It undoubtedly constitutes the main discipline on the subject, aimed as it is—through the reform of the previous directive on electronic commerce—at broadening both the transparency and the liability of platforms, with the purpose of ensuring effective protection of consumers and of the fundamental rights they hold in the digital ecosystem, also in order to obtain their less exposure, on the net, to illegal content. It can therefore be said that the specific objective of this discipline is to identify a new balance between innovation and user protection, which is based on a system of asymmetric obligations: in the sense that they burden *providers* in direct proportion to their role and size.

2. Regulation (EU) 2022/1925 (the so-called Digital Markets Act, DMA). This is the other regulatory intervention with which the European legislator intended to create the Digital Single Market. In particular, it aims to create a competitive (hence contestable) and fair digital sector, allowing innovative companies to grow, while at the same time requiring that *online* users be guaranteed security and breadth of choice, also through the prohibition of unfair practices.

3. Regulation (EU) 2023/1114 (so-called MiCA Regulation). This covers cryptocurrency markets and establishes uniform rules for issuers of crypto assets not regulated by other acts and for service providers for crypto assets. It regulates the issuance, public offering and admission to trading of crypto-assets, as well as the

[9] Thus Ferrarese (2006); see also, with reference to speculative investment funds that have become stronger than individual states by exploiting and accelerating '*the process of dismantling welfare states and privatising society*', Volpi, (2024). On the problem of the sources of law on the Internet and the decline of the law and the state monopoly in the production of legal rules in the current new systems of globalised economy, see Finocchiaro (2001), pp. 571–610; Clarizia (2024), pp. 5–8; Ciacci (2023), pp. 11–13, who recalls the multiple names attributed to the autonomous order of extra-state sources that regulate the Internet according to *soft law* instruments, following the path of the experience of the *lex mercatoria*: *lex electronica, lex informatica, lex networkia*. On the role of private law in the new forms of sovereignty, see Caruso (2006).

[10] That the EU aims, instead of following or adapting disciplines dictated in non-European countries or contexts, to strengthen its digital sovereignty and set its own rules, focused on the regulation of data, technology and infrastructure, is clear from the strategy for 2019–2024. *A Europe ready for the digital age*, available at https://ec.europa.eu/info/strategy/priorities-2019-2024/europe-fit-digital-age_en.

provision of services related to crypto-assets, the types of which it defines by distinguishing between 'e-money *tokens*' (which stabilise their value in relation to a single official currency), asset-linked *tokens* (which stabilise their value in relation to other assets or a basket of assets) and crypto-assets other than asset-linked tokens or e-money *tokens*.

4. Regulation (EU) 2022/868 (the so-called Data Governance Act). It lays down the conditions for the reuse, within the Union, of certain categories of data held by public bodies, with the aim of creating a secure environment in which data can nevertheless be exploited for the purposes of innovation and research: consistent, therefore, with the basic idea of a digital market inspired by the principles of competition, user security and the promotion of technological innovation.

5. Regulation (EU) 2023/2854 (the so-called Data Act). It contains harmonised rules on fair access to data, with the aim of growing the *data economy* in the Union, making more data available to businesses, citizens and public administrations, and establishing rules on their use and access, in all economic sectors, supporting the digital transformation. It also regulates, in particular, the sharing of data generated by the use of connected products (*Internet of Things*, IoT) or related services; users' access to the data they generate; as well as, for businesses, fair compensation for making data available and the prevention of abuses arising from contractual imbalances.

6. Regulation (EU) 2024/1689 (the so-called Artificial Intelligence Act, AI Act). Its main objective is to create a regulatory framework that promotes the development and safe and reliable use of artificial intelligence systems, while protecting the health, safety and fundamental rights of citizens. In a nutshell, it provides for a precise classification of artificial intelligence systems, lays down specific and diverse obligations for operators and establishes measures to increase transparency and innovation.

7. Regulation (EU) 2024/1083 (the so-called European Media Freedom Act). It establishes a common framework for media services within the internal market, aiming to foster transparency, editorial freedom and independence of media service providers, to ensure that they can operate more easily across borders and to benefit from the digital transformation of the media space, also with a view to pluralism. It also aims to create forms of protection for media service providers and journalists from external interference.

At least a nod then and there:

8. The proposal for a directive COM/2022/495 on so-called Product Liability. Not yet approved, with the declared aim of adapting the liability rules to the products of the digital age, in order to ensure the most efficient functioning of the market, effective competition between operators and a high level of health and consumer protection.

9. The proposal for a directive on artificial intelligence liability. Also dating back to 2022, it promised to introduce specific provisions on damage caused, precisely, by artificial intelligence systems, on the assumption that the existing national liability rules did not guarantee citizens adequate protection in the event of damage caused by these particular products and services. The objective of more intense

protection was pursued mainly through two technical solutions: the so-called presumption of causality, as a result of which the injured party would have been facilitated with respect to the burden of proving the elements constituting the tort; the further facilitation, in certain cases, of access to information and circumstances, in certain categories of companies or suppliers, that could constitute evidence. As mentioned, however, this proposal was abruptly withdrawn by the EU Commission on 11 February 2025.[11]

Even beyond the incompleteness of this concise list, rather than analytically examining the detailed content of each of these sources of information—inevitably destined, in a subject dominated by unstoppable technological progress, to rapid obsolescence—it seems more useful to dwell on the general and common characteristics of the new sources of production and the objectives that the European legislator intends to pursue with them.

Thus, the choice, made in most cases, to use the instrument of the Regulation should be emphasised. This evidently responds to the need, perceived as necessary and urgent, to create a uniform discipline for all member states. Another effect of the extraordinary diffusion and pervasiveness of technologies, therefore, is the tendency to abandon the directive instrument, which by definition leaves more or less ample margins of autonomy to internal legislators, which cannot be easily governed, with consequent, inevitable differences in application.

The use of the Regulation instrument also shows the implicit (political) intention of the European legislator to set itself up as a 'model' of the rules on the subject, as opposed to the other world systems, mentioned above, inspired by technological and economic power. The aforementioned recent *Artificial Intelligence Act* can undoubtedly be traced back to this choice: based (like Regulation No. 2016/679 on the protection of personal data, the so-called General Data Protection Regulation; GDPR) on the so-called risk-based approach, it imposes obligations that differ according to the level of risk (low, medium or high) that artificial intelligence systems are likely to create for the maintenance of the fundamental rights of the individual.

Characteristic of European legislation, moreover, is the choice to draw a framework of principles, so as to orient and delimit the intervention of national legislators, and also to establish, in the aforementioned *anthropocentric* perspective, a set of fundamental user rights.

If a first core of these digital rights has been commonly derived from the general systems of guarantees established by the GDPR, a further, newer catalogue is taking shape, at present on the level of *soft law*, as a result of the *European Declaration on Digital Rights and Principles for the Digital Decade* (2023/C 23/01).

In light of this, the new rights for the digital decade should include:

- The right to connectivity; the right to a neutral and open Internet, where applications, services and content are not blocked, suspended or unjustifiably degraded in quality.

[11] See footnote 5.

- The right to education, training and lifelong learning for basic and advanced digital skills.
- The right to disconnect, so as to ensure a work-life balance in the digital environment.
- The right to digital public services *online.*
- The right not to be subjected to burdens of inquiry (in the sense that no one should be asked, while accessing digital public services, to provide unnecessary data).
- The right to an accessible, secure and trustworthy digital identity.
- The right to large-scale access and reuse of public administration information.
- Freedom of choice in interactions with artificial intelligence algorithms and systems (in the sense that everyone should be able to enjoy the benefits of artificial intelligence, making informed choices in the digital environment and being protected from risks to fundamental rights).
- The right to transparency regarding the use of algorithms and artificial intelligence (in the sense that anyone interacting with them is autonomous, informed and responsible).
- The guarantee that algorithmic systems are based on adequate data sets, suitable to avoid unlawful discrimination and allow for human supervision of the results; this also means the guarantee of digital and artificial intelligence systems that are secure and managed in full respect of fundamental rights.
- The right to protection of personal data *online*.

3 The Types of Platforms

Digital platforms are defined by Article 2 of Regulation (EU) 2019/1150 as providers of *online* intermediary services. This provision thus qualifies the relevant activity as the subject of *information society services*, within the meaning of Article 1(1) (b) of Directive 2015/1535, itself taken from Article 2(a) of Directive 2000/31 on electronic commerce: a service '*normally provided for remuneration, at a distance, by electronic means and at the individual request of a recipient of services*'.

Depending on the case, intermediation is understood as an activity interposed between the provider and the user of the service or (even) as an activity directly assimilated to the provision of the service. In such cases, the distributor is thus identified with the producer.[12]

A classification of the various types of platforms, based on the purpose of use, is becoming more widespread. Thus, one can identify: *online* intermediaries (i.e. *marketplaces* such as Amazon and eBay); digital services (pertaining to the *sharing economy*, such as Uber, or other public utility services, such as platforms belonging to public administrations); payment services (i.e. digital infrastructures designed for

[12] See Alpa (2024) p. 973.

peer-to-peer money transfers, such as PayPal); investment *marketplaces* (operating mainly in *equity crowdfunding*, i.e. the collective investment system supporting innovative *start-ups*).

It has to be said, however, that such a distinction is not particularly relevant, since the European legislator adopts a different, certainly more significant differential criterion: that of size.

Hence the identification of the so-called over the top platforms (the largest, i.e. the so-called VLOPs, *Very Large Online Platforms*),[13] capable of playing the role of *gatekeeper* of the entire digital ecosystem. With respect to which, however, there is the different, delicate, but related problem of clarifying what role they actually play, in the digital markets, with respect to users.[14]

The reference legislation for *online* platforms is the DSA, whose objective is to ensure security and protection of fundamental rights in the digital single market by regulating the activities of *online intermediaries*: Article 3 defines intermediary services as a general category, to which *online* platforms and *online* search engines are also attributable.[15]

These two subcategories of intermediary services, platforms and search engines are also subject to special rules and made the addressees of additional obligations if they fall within the definition in Article 33 concerning *Very Large Online Platforms and Very Large Online Search Engines*.

These are the platforms that reach more than 45 million active users per month in Europe, and are therefore exposed to the greatest risks related to the dissemination of illegal content and related widespread harm.[16]

Also linked to size parameters is the procedure for designating Very Large Platforms (so-called VLOPs) and Search Engines (so-called VLOSEs), to which additional obligations apply. Conversely, micro and small enterprises are exempted from the general obligations of transparency, communication and annual reporting that apply to all providers of intermediation services, albeit with some caveats under Article 29. While entities qualified as VLOPs and VLOSEs fall under the direct and exclusive competence of the Commission.

Lastly, Directive (EU) 2024/1760 of 13 June 2024, in regulating liability for production chains, has also adopted a size parameter to identify companies established in the Union that are bound by sustainability-related duties of care.[17]

---

[13] Liberatore (2023) p. 179.

[14] On this point, see Trubiani, in this *Book*, p. 157 ff.

[15] More specifically, see Schepisi (2025), in this *Book*, p. 1155 ff.

[16] On 25 April 2023, the EU Commission designated 17 *Very Large Online Platforms* (VLOPs) and 2 *Very Large Online Search Engines* (VLOSEs).

[17] See recital 28: '*Companies established in the Union with, on average, more than 1 000 employees and a worldwide net turnover of more than EUR 450 000 000 in the last financial year for which annual accounts were adopted or should have been adopted should be required to comply with the due diligence requirements of this Directive. Companies which have concluded franchise or licensing agreements in the Union in exchange for licensing rights with independent third party companies should also be required to comply with the due diligence obligations set out in this*

4 The Problem of Regulating a New and a-Territorial Technical Phenomenon

It has been mentioned that the territoriality limits of state laws, unable to regulate the global space of the network, have led to experimentation with the use of more modern and effective regulatory techniques: 'self-regulation',[18] 'co-regulation',[19] 'participatory regulation'[20] and regulatory *sandboxes*,[21] all based on the principle of subsidiarity under Article 118 of the Constitution.[22]

The enormous power—economic, factual, contractual—acquired by digital platforms imposes the problem of their subjection to the legislation of states, whose territorial sovereignty cannot easily impose heterodetermined rules, thus favouring

---

Directive, where such agreements ensure a common identity, a common business concept and the application of uniform business methods and where such licensing rights amount to more than EUR 22 500 000 in the last financial year in which the annual accounts were adopted or should have been adopted, and provided that the company had a worldwide net turnover of more than EUR 80 000 000 in the last financial year in which the annual accounts were adopted or should have been adopted'.

[18] See Bellelli, in this *Book*.

[19] See Rabitti (2022) p. 119.

[20] Bassan (2023), pp. 1103–1132, which explains what co-regulation is and what the author calls 'participatory regulation'. 'Participatory regulation' is a new form of co-regulation, in which the roles of regulators and the market are less defined and can be reversed, with cooperation between market participants, regulators and legislators beginning immediately. In other words, while in the classic co-regulation mechanisms the process begins with the authorities drawing up texts and proposals for rules, which the market then comments on, taking part in consultation procedures; on the other hand, in 'participatory regulation', legislators, regulators and operators work together right from the initial phase of product and service creation, to draw up together the minimum requirements deemed suitable to guarantee compliance with continental European *welfare*, which the market must then comply with, according to the so-called regulatory circle of rules that originate from the market and return to the market (i.e. first the market tends to align itself with *best practices* that are transformed into *standards* by national authorities, which then share them in European fora, transforming them into European *standards*, in some cases even into *technical rules*, which then in turn return to the market.

[21] In Italy, the first rule providing for the *regulatory sandbox* was included in Article 36, paragraph *2-b* is of Decree-Law No. 34/2019 (so-called Growth Decree) delegating to the Ministry of Economy and Finance ('MEF') the issuance of one or more decrees to regulate fintech experimentation '*aimed at the pursuit, through new technologies such as artificial intelligence and distributed ledgers, of service and product innovation in the financial, credit, insurance and regulated markets sectors*'. Subsequently, on 17 July 2021, the implementing decree of the MEF came into force, establishing at it a *Fintech* Committee whose main function is to define the objectives and mediate between sector operators and supervisory authorities. In concrete terms, the Italian *sandbox*, along the lines of the English model, consists of an environment in which *fintech* operators are confronted with the competent supervisory authorities by experimenting for a limited period of time with innovative products and services in the banking, insurance and financial sectors, against a simplified regulatory regime.

See also Article 57 of the *Artificial Intelligence Act*, which stipulates that each member state has to establish at least one space for regulatory experimentation for AI at national level and that this space has to be operational by 2 August 2026 (on this point, see Sect. 6).

[22] See Nuzzo (2014).

the use of co-regulation and *soft law* instruments, aimed at the creation of shared rules, which make it possible to overcome the limits of the sovereignty of states.[23]

This overwhelming de facto power has to some extent legitimised the thesis according to which the most important digital platforms could be characterised in terms of 'private orders', which calls for experimenting with new sources of regulation, such as co-regulation or 'participatory regulation'.[24]

New sources of regulation are thus emerging (mostly *soft law*) based precisely on co-regulation, 'participatory regulation' and experimentation, according to the modern model of the regulatory *sandbox.*

The rule must also function in an a-territorial space, such as the Internet, which tends to escape the sovereignty of state law, in force only in the territory of reference,[25] and therefore requires new protection criteria, which allow for the 'disconnection between law and territoriality'.[26]

Indeed, a new, effective instrument has been experimented by the European legislator with reference to the protection of personal data, in an attempt to adopt rules that can also be applied outside the European territory, by adopting a so-called protection *by design*, i.e. specifically constructed to tailor the most appropriate processing on a case-by-case basis. In this way, a system of data protection is adopted that is not actually regulated in detail by the legislator, who merely indicates the objectives to be achieved, leaving the choice of the appropriate processing to the responsibility of the *data controller*, according to the principle of *accountability*: which represents one of the most important innovations of the GDPR.[27]

The legislative affirmation of this principle marks a new regulatory technique capable of extending the effectiveness of personal data protection regulation anywhere in the network space, even beyond the limits of European territory.[28]

The legislator, in other words, abandons the rule of detail and entrusts an 'empowered regulator'—the *data controller*—with the choice of the most suitable solutions for achieving the objective, the suitability of which the *data controller* will then be called to account if problems arise. And so it is that—thanks to this expedient, which allows the aforementioned 'disconnection between law and

---

[23] Carleo (2022), pp. 73–81.

[24] See Bassan (2023).

[25] Hugenholtz (2010), p. 310.

[26] Thus Floridi (2020), p. 28 praises on this point the method introduced by the European legislator with the GDPR (*General Data Protection Regulation*) 'which, in an ingenious way, overcomes the post-Westphalian disconnect, exploiting instead the welding … between personal identity and data, to justify the fact that, wherever a European citizen's data are processed, European law applies in any case'. The Author continues: 'The GDPR binds the data to the source and not the law to the territory, a bit like the logic of the passport, which does not give the right to expatriate (e.g. sometimes a visa is needed) but to repatriate, tying the bearer to his nationality, like a rubber band'. On this point see also Amato Mangiameli (2017), p. 147.

[27] See for all Poletti (2019), pp. 43–45.

[28] With reference to the regulation of artificial intelligence see Finocchiaro (2024), pp. 69–74; Bertolini (2025), pp. 10–20.

territoriality'[29]—the protection of personal data should be ensured regardless of the territory of states, i.e. even in an a-territorial space, such as that of the Internet.

5 Instruments of Regulation Compared: Prohibition and Persuasion

The regulatory technique used by the European legislator is, moreover, varied. It takes the form not only of prohibition rules, i.e. prohibition rules (so-called pure prohibition rules), and preceptive rules, which (also) indicate positive conduct, but also of *persuasion* rules, i.e. non-binding regulations based on persuasion, rather than on prohibition assisted by administrative sanctions, such as codes of conduct and other so-called soft law interventions. The objective of inducing digital platforms to behave in a precise manner is pursued through the elaboration with *stakeholders* of co-regulatory rules, as well as practices and best practices: thus introducing rules that are also tested through regulatory *sandboxes*, i.e. in controlled environments, in which the effectiveness of the provisions can be tested.[30]

Reference is first and foremost made to the 'nudge' (or 'gentle nudge'), which could represent an interesting norm-setting profile stemming from bargaining autonomy, as it introduces into the system behavioural rules of practical training,[31] which have recently been gaining ground in certain areas of the legal system.[32]

In this regard, however, it has been pointed out that 'there is no coincidence between persuasive regulation and *nudge*: the former encompasses but is not resolved in the latter'.[33]

[29] See footnote 29.

[30] Bocchini (2024), p. 599 who notes that 'the differences between prohibitive and persuasive regulation, however, concern not only the space of choice given to the recipient, but also the moment of their application … Systems that allow the regulated (or representative organisations of the regulated) to question the regulator *ex ante* (before any violation) on what constitutes compliant conduct reduce uncertainty without necessarily restricting the regulated space of freedom … Systems that limit regulatory intervention to the phase following the violation allow the regulated a wider margin of choice without, however, reducing uncertainty as to the boundaries between prohibited and permitted. From a legal point of view, persuasive regulation is considered less invasive than prohibitive regulation. It is characterized not by the compression of faculties and rights, but by guiding the addressee in his choices, which remain, however, within his sphere of control. Moreover, it seems better to express the technical content of regulation rather than the political value of regulation.

[31] Thaler and Sunstein (2008), p. 11 where the observation was that: 'in many cases individuals make bad decisions: decisions they would not have made if they had paid full attention and possessed full information, unlimited cognitive capacity and total self-control'.

[32] See, for example, in administrative law, Zito (2021), p. 85 where he outlines a different notion of administrative power that includes the power *of influencing* associated with governmental power.

[33] Cafaggi (2022), p. 493.

And the same doctrine has identified different regulatory techniques in relation to prohibition and persuasion,[34] suggesting that these opposing instruments of regulation (which differ not only in terms of their respective areas of coercion or freedom of choice, but also because a political content emerges in prohibition, while in persuasion a technical content of regulation emerges)[35] are *jointly* employed to promote behavioural changes (despite the authoritative and traditional thesis that advice and command are two mutually exclusive notions, the latter alone constituting a legal rule).[36]

The hypothesis put forward is that prohibitions mainly employ incentives, including rewards and sanctions, while persuasion relies on the motivational systems of individuals and organisations. In this way, the complementarity between prohibitive and persuasive regulation would avoid the phenomenon of *crowding* out the latter, which would occur when the latter is directed at promoting the desired behaviour while the former is directed at preventing the adoption of the prohibited behaviour.

6 The Spaces for Regulatory Experimentation and the Contribution of Soft Law

So-called co-regulation, according to the expression currently in vogue, already emerges in Regulation (EU) 2019/1150, which promotes fairness and transparency for business users of *online* brokerage services.

It should be noted that the Regulation applies to all digital intermediary services offered within the European Union, regardless of whether the providers are established in an EU member state or outside the EU.

[34] Cafaggi (2022), p. 495 where he specifies that 'At least four regulatory techniques can be identified in relation to prohibition and persuasion: the authorisation of permitted conduct that prohibits any other conduct; the prohibition of prohibited conduct that permits any other conduct; the definition of prohibited conduct accompanied by the recommendation of desired conduct; the definition of desired conduct without any reference to prohibitions or impositions. These are ideal-typical models, each of which may be subject to further articulations that define not only the space but also the quality of the choice allowed to the recipient of regulation. This choice must be informed by the type of cognitive distortions and social norms and the belief systems they reflect'.

[35] Cafaggi (2022), p. 497 where he points out that: 'The origin of regulatory indications from technical bodies suggests that they can be configured as recommendations with a persuasive character except when they are incorporated into binding normative acts in order to change their legal status. A typical example of persuasive technical regulation is that of technical standards. Such standards become binding only when a legal norm makes them so, transforming technical regulation from persuasive into prescriptive. Of course, they can also become binding by contract when the parties undertake to comply with them'.

[36] See also Sacco (1960), p. 12 where the relations between juridicality, compulsion and coercion are reconstructed in philosophical literature starting with Kant.

According to Article 17(1), '*the Commission shall encourage providers of* online *brokering services and their representative organisations and associations to develop codes of conduct, together with business users, including Small and Medium-sized Enterprises and their organisations, aimed at contributing to the correct application of this regulation, taking into account the specificities of the different sectors and the specific characteristics of SMEs*'.

The mission entrusted to codes of conduct consists, as already noted, in performing an integrative, complementary function to the regulation. The regulation does not come exclusively from the platforms, but is produced through the participation of those involved, i.e. together with business users and their organisations, in order to better compose and balance the different interests at stake, and is targeted to the specific particularities of the individual sector. Moreover, it should be noted that it is necessary, in order for co-regulation to function properly, 'expressing its function as a curb to the mere "privatisation" of regulatory enforcement', that it postulates a clear distinction between the different interests at stake and the specifics of each sector,[37] that it postulates a clear distinction of roles and functions, but above all the predetermination and comprehensibility of the deliberative process.[38]

With regard to existing codes of conduct, Article 17(3) of Regulation (EU) 2019/1150 textually states that the Commission shall encourage *online* intermediary service providers to adopt and apply sector-specific codes of conduct, where such sector-specific codes of conduct exist and are widely used. One can infer from this provision an implicit recognition of the legal value of codes of conduct in terms of effectiveness. In fact, the adoption of existing codes is only promoted and encouraged if they are widely used and concretely applied.[39]

Ample space is reserved for codes of conduct by the *Digital Services Act*[40] (Arts. 45-47). A general regulation, aimed at promoting and regulating codes of conduct in the world of digital services (Art. 45), is followed by specific regulations concerning codes of conduct for *online* advertising (Art. 46) and codes of conduct aimed at improving accessibility to services for people with disabilities (Art. 47).

A plurality of stakeholders is involved in the formation of these codes: in addition to *online* platform providers and other service providers (such as, for *online* advertising, intermediary service providers and other actors involved in the value chain of programme advertising), organisations representing the recipients of the service, civil society organisations and competent authorities. It should be noted that, as already mentioned, all actors in the *online* advertising value chain, who are called upon to participate in the drafting of codes of conduct, are also encouraged by the Commission to subscribe to them and to observe their rules (Art. 46(4)).

---

[37] Simoncini (2022), p. 1048.

[38] Di Porto and Zuppetta (2021), p. 272.

[39] On this point, see more fully Bellelli, Soft law *and* co-regulation, cit. in this *Book*.

[40] Regulation (EU) 2022/2065 of the European Parliament and of the Council of 19 October 2022 on a single market for digital services and amending Directive 2000/31/EC on electronic commerce.

From the systematic set of provisions just mentioned it is clear that for these codes of conduct the Commission's action is more incisive; despite the recurring use of the verb 'encourage', as for the other codes, it seems, however, that here the Commission, rather than encouraging, essentially imposes the drawing up of the rules of self-discipline, also defining their modalities and content.

The main features of the codes of conduct provided for in the recent European legislation on digital services provided by *online* platforms are, therefore, the following:

- *Speciality*, as these are sector codes
- The drafting of rules on the basis of *consultation* between the different stakeholders
- *The co-regulatory function*, i.e. the integration of regulatory acts
- *The not exclusively private nature*, given the European Commission's powers of impulse, direction and control.

Particularly interesting is the creation of the so-called sandboxes,[41] the regulatory *experimentation spaces* already mentioned (Art. 57 ff. AI Act, *Regulatory Experimentation Spaces for I.A.*), where authorities and *stakeholders* of a specific sector can experiment the application of new rules and practices without risking sanctions. It will be up to the states to create them and they will be managed by the authorities designated by the member states, AgID (*Agenzia per l'Italia Digitale*) and ACN (*Agenzia per la cybersecurity nazionale*) in the Italian case, with the technical assistance of the Commission.

Article 57(5) states: '*Regulatory testing spaces for IA established in accordance with paragraph 1 shall provide a controlled environment that promotes innovation and facilitates the development, training, testing and validation of innovative IA systems for a limited period of time prior to their placing on the market or putting into service in accordance with a specific testing space plan agreed between potential suppliers and the competent authority. Such regulatory test spaces may include tests under real-world conditions subject to control within the test space*'.

It is intended to develop, experiment and test novel technologies for a limited period of time, with the aim of promoting innovation by the companies involved and, more generally, the development of artificial intelligence and its adoption.

Given that, as has just been mentioned, experimentation takes place before the product or service is placed on the market, under the guidance of the competent authority, it follows that *sandboxes* use a *bottom-up* approach, characterised by interaction between developers and regulators, with a regulatory option, so to speak, in anticipation.

The mechanism is, in some respects, opposite to that of the *accountability* principle, adopted, for instance, in the GDPR, which gives the data controller the freedom to choose the measures that are appropriate to achieve the objectives imposed

[41] This is not entirely new, as the tool of regulatory *sandboxes* has previously been employed in the fintech sector (see footnote 23).

by the legislator in order to guarantee the rights and freedoms of data subjects.[42] Therefore, while in the case of *accountability* the assessments made by the data controller can then be scrutinised by the Data Protection Authority (which could sanction the controller if the measures are not deemed sufficient to prevent the risks associated with the use of those personal data), on the contrary, in the case of the AI Act *sandboxes*, the supervisory authority assesses ex ante the risk exposure of the technology tested. And in fact, the AI Act provides that, during the *testing* phase, although the persons admitted to the *sandbox* are liable for damages caused to third parties, according to the ordinary rules of tort, they cannot be subject to administrative sanctions by the supervisory authority.[43]

The process of regulatory creation through *sandboxes is* also a clear expression of the principle of subsidiarity,[44] even more so in view of the *certifications* that can be issued to providers by the authority *under* Section 57(7) of the AI Act. These certifications attest to the favourable outcomes of controlled experiments, which, in prospect, could be used as documentary evidence of compliance with the obligations under the Regulation, thus constituting technical norms (i.e. regulatory *standards* to measure the diligence of conduct, such as the guidelines on medical liability), on which the decision of any disputes (e.g. on liability) could depend.

References

Alpa G (2024) Amazon in Tribunale. In Contr. e impr., p 973

Amato Mangiameli AC (2017) Techno-regulation and law. Brief notes on limits and differences In Dir. inf., pp 147–150

Bassan F (2023) Digital platforms and Blockchains: the age of participatory regulation. Eur Bus Law Rev 34(7):1103–1132

Bertolini A (2025) Artificial Intelligence and Civil Liability. Problem, system, functions, Il mulino, Bologna, pp 10–15

Bocchini R (2024) Le categorie giuridiche nell'economia digitale: il terzo paradiso In Jus civile, pp 596–624

Cafaggi F (2022) Prohibiting, permitting, persuading. Appunti di viaggio nella regolazione contemporanea. In Mercato Concorrenza Regole, pp 491–499

Carleo R (2022) Digital Platforms and Contract. EJPLT, pp 73–81

Caruso D (2006) Private law and state-making in the age of globalization. In: Boston University School of Law, Public Law. Research Paper

Cerrina Feroni G (2023) Intelligenza artificiale e sistemi di scoring sociale. Tra distopia e realtà. In Dir. inf., pp 3 ff

Ciacci G (2023) Le fonti del diritto dell'informatica. In: Bocchini R (ed) Manuale di diritto privato dell'informatica, Esi, Naples, pp 11–21

Clarizia O (2024) Lex mercatoria, lex informatica e self-regulation della tecnologia virtuale. Teoria e Storia del Diritto Privato XVII:1–9

[42] *See back*, para. 4, end, and footnotes 29 and 30.

[43] Riccio (2024); Ranchordas (2021).

[44] See para. 4, footnote 24.

Di Porto F, Zuppetta M (2021) Co-regulation and algorithmic disclosure for digital platforms. Policy Soc 40:272
Finocchiaro G (2001) Lex mercatoria e commercio elettronico. Il diritto applicabile ai contratti conclusi su Internet. In Contr. e impr., pp 571–610
Finocchiaro G (2024) Artificial Intelligence. Quali regole?, Il mulino, Bologna, pp 69–74
Floridi L (2020) Il verde e il blu. Idee ingenue per migliorare la politica, Raffaello Cortina Editore, Milan
Galimberti U (1999) Psyche and Techne. L'uomo nell'età della tecnica (Man in the age of technology), Feltrinelli, Milan
Hugenholtz PB (2010) Codes of conduct and copyright enforcement in cyberspace. In: Stamatoudi IA (ed) Copyright Enforcement and the Internet, pp 303–305
Irti N (2001) Norma e luoghi, problemi di geo-diritto, Roma-Bari, 2001
Irti N, Severino E (2001) Dialogo su diritto e tecnica, Laterza, Roma-Bari
Liberatore BA (2023) Le piattaforme digitali. In: Bocchini R (ed) Manuale di diritto privato dell'informatica. Esi, Naples, pp 179–182
Nuzzo M (ed) (2014) Il principio di sussidiarietà nel diritto privato, vol I and II. Giappichelli, Turin
Poletti D (2019) True challenges and false myths of the GDPR. In Nuovo dir. civ., 2019, pp 32–33
Pollicino O (2023) Potere digitale. In Enc. dir., I Tematici, Potere e Costituzione, directed by M. Cartabia and M. Ruotolo, V, Lefevbre Giuffrè, Milan, pp 436–437
Rabitti M (2022) Le regole di supervisione nel mercato digitale: considerazioni intorno alla comunicazione Banca d'Italia in materia di tecnologie decentralizzate nella finanza e cripto-activitià. In Riv. trim. dir. econ., pp 119–122
Ranchordas S (2021), Experimental lawmaking in the EU: Regulatory Sandboxes. In University of Groningen Faculty of Law Research Paper 12:1–3
Riccio GM (2024) A.I. Act and sandbox: a good choice, still leaving many doubts. In Altalex, pp 1–8
Sacco R (1960) Coercion and Coercibility. In Enc. dir., Lefevbre Giuffrè, Milan, 1960, p 12
Schepisi S (2025) The Private Enforcement of the Digital Markets Act. In this Book Vol. II
Simoncini A (2022) The co-regulation of digital platforms. In Riv. trim. dir. pubbl., p 1048
Thaler RH, Sunstein (2008) Nudge. The Gentle Push. The new strategy to improve our decisions about money, health, happiness. Yale University Press, New Haven
Volpi A (2024) I padroni del mondo. How financial funds are destroying the market and democracy, Laterza, Roma-Bari
Zito A (2021) La nudge regulation nella teoria giuridica dell'agire amministrativo. Presupposti e limiti del suo utilizzo da parte delle pubbliche amministrazioni, Editoriale scientifica, Naples, pp 85–88

Legal Subjects of the Digital Economy

Franco Trubiani

Contents

Abstract The contribution aims to investigate the legal profiles related to the subjects of the digital economy that also include new figures such as influencers and content creators. The author also focuses on the possible contribution of behavioral economics to clarify the legal boundaries of the notion of consumer.

F. Trubiani (✉)
University of Naples "Parthenope", Naples, Italy
e-mail: franco.trubiani@uniparthenope.it

R. Bocchini (ed.), *Digital Platforms - From Technical Foundations to Legal and Economic Implications*, https://doi.org/10.1007/978-3-032-07978-7_6

1 Introductory Notes. The Digital Ecosystem and Its Players

Technological evolution, concomitant with the perpetual expansion of digital platforms, has given rise to a digital ecosystem, as is well documented. This ecosystem comprises a diverse array of participants, each contributing to the realization of the digital market in its own unique manner.

Indeed, the necessity to discern and examine the emergent demands for legal safeguards concerning particular subjects, which were once deemed a novel form of agreement within the offline market, had already manifested itself.

As Giuseppe Benedetti, a renowned expert in civil law, articulated two decades prior, the multifaceted nature of roles—whether hegemonic or subordinate—that coexist within an individual renders it impracticable for that individual to adopt a definitive stance. Those who produce in one area are consumers in another'.[1]

This assumption remains particularly salient in today's digital economy, where, as will be discussed in greater detail below, the boundaries between consumer and professional figures, as dictated by consumer discipline, appear increasingly blurred and undefined.

Indeed, until recently, the examination of the subjective qualification of contracting parties was regarded as a "novelty" for the interpreter under the Italian civil code.[2] However, with the advent of consumer law and the broader issue of safeguarding the interests of the "weaker" contracting party (e.g., consumers and micro-businesses), it has been determined that the subjective qualification of the contracting parties becomes pertinent not only at the time of contract conclusion, but also during its execution.

The conclusion of a contract by digital means, in fact, does not allow for the identification of the contracting party, thereby hindering the determination of whether the contracting party is, for instance, a consumer, a minor, an elderly individual, or an AI-managed system.

The study of contracting parties in the contemporary context no longer poses a significant novelty for civilists in the strict sense. The introduction of consumer law, and more broadly, the broader topic of safeguarding the "weak" contracting party (such as micro-businesses, associations, third sector entities, energy communities, etc.) has led to a resurgence of interest in the legal ramifications of the subjective status of contracting parties, with particular emphasis.

In this regard, our civil code, in fact, as is well known, is characterized by a certain "subjective indifferentiation," i.e., the subjective characteristics of the parties to a contract were and are for the most part irrelevant for the purposes of the rules

[1] Benedetti (1998), pp. 21 ff.

[2] Note correctly Zoppini (2022), p. 313, how "the traditional conception of the contract is founded on the ideological axioms made proper by the bourgeois codes assumed, insofar as consistent with the nature of things, as unassailable data and not in need of any further specification: the formal equality of the subject of law."

applicable to it: consequently, as already noted in doctrine, a study on the figures of the contracting parties in the civil code would have little systematic impact.

As of several years ago, however, the Italian legislator, following the introduction of consumer legislation, included among the qualifying elements of the case and its regulation precisely the subjective qualities of the contracting parties.

It In light of the progressive spread of the Internet, which gave rise to the telematic market and subsequent evolution, the concept becomes increasingly evident. This evolution is further influenced by the distinctive characteristics of digital contracting. It is evident that the prevailing legislative definitions of "consumer" and "professional," among others, are inadequate to adequately delineate the legal framework governing certain subjects within the digital economy.

Indeed, whereas the digital marketplace was previously characterized by sales conducted through websites, contemporary digital platforms now offer a diverse array of tools, including *shops* and *marketplaces,* that enable any individual to engage in the exchange of goods and services.

However, further analysis reveals additional factors to consider.

Alongside digital platforms, new figures are emerging that are, for the most part, unfamiliar to the law. These include influencers and content creators, who are playing an increasingly significant role in the expansion of the economy, particularly in the digital economy.

In essence, the ongoing discourse surrounding the predominant figures of the European digital market remains a pivotal exercise, not only to comprehend the evolution of business practices but also to acknowledge the inherent challenges of the law in grasping the evolving social and technological landscape. This analysis is further complicated by the inherent challenges in formulating effective regulatory frameworks to address the multifaceted nature of digital business operations.

2 The Figure of the Average Consumer Under Article 20 of the Italian Consumer Code and the Broadening of the Notion of Vulnerable Consumer

The initial figure to be examined is undoubtedly that of the consumer-user of digital platforms.

The consumer has become fragmented due to the implementation of various sectoral regulations. This phenomenon has become a well-established reality and is also increasingly reflected in case law.

The experience of banking, finance, insurance, and, most recently, the energy market and tourism has broadened the scope of definitions. This expansion has particularly facilitated a link between sectoral disciplines and the "general" principles expressed in the Consumer Code.

A particularly salient starting point, one that is more clearly delineated than in other sectors, can be found in the realm of consumer protection, particularly in the energy sector and the tourism sector. These sectors serve as valuable case studies for examining the interplay between horizontal and vertical disciplines. This interplay necessitates a consideration of novel developments, which, however, do not invariably completely overshadow existing and enduring practices.

Indeed, significant challenges emerge when one endeavors to implement the criterion of speciality to resolve antinomies between the Consumer Code and disciplines that, according to alternative systematizing logics, appear to be autonomous segments. However, these disciplines must be interconnected within a more extensive and intricate legal framework.

Nevertheless, each new definition appears to evoke, to employ the elegant imagery provided by a meticulous author, "a stone propelled with escalating vigor into the water of a pond." Indeed, the expansion of the circles' perimeter is determined, and these circles are added to one another. However, since they are concentric, they do not completely negate the centrality of the consumer in the expansion of a figure that expands, though not overwhelming, the primitive configuration.

It is therefore imperative to identify suitable criteria to accurately discern the relationships between the various disciplines.

In addressing the matter of consumer freedom of choice, understood in its various dimensions, it is crucial to acknowledge the emergence of a further multiplication, stemming from the polymorphism of information obligations.

Information obligations are one of the pillars, but certainly not the only one, on which awareness is based. These obligations manifest in diverse forms, assuming varied connotations and degrees of relevance across specific consumer activities. Nevertheless, it is indisputable that they are directed towards a shared objective.

The notion of fragmentation and reaggregation, which are characteristic of consumer and consumer awareness, also resurface in this context. Therefore, when examining the average consumer, it is essential to consider the fundamental principle that guides all reasoning on this subject. Indeed, we observe the necessity of consumer awareness to inform choices, a concept that must be incorporated into the definition of the average consumer. These figures should collectively encompass this concept.

The case of which it is based for a recent order issued by the Italian Council of State (10 October 2022, no. 8650)[3] involves customers of a financial company who allege that the company engaged in the practice of product tying, which is defined as the practice of offering one product or service in conjunction with another, often for the purpose of increasing sales. The case is notable for its application of two distinct legislative disciplines: insurance law and the provisions of a particular Article 120 *quinquies* cod. ass. ("Tying"), as introduced by Legislative Decree No. 68 of 21 May 2018 of "Implementation of Directive (EU) 2016/97 of the European Parliament and of the Council of 20 January 2016 on insurance distribution" and that relating to unfair commercial practices introduced by Dir. 2005/29/EU and transposed by the Consumer Code in Articles 18 ff. cons. code.

[3] Italian Council of State, 10 October 2022, no. 8650.

Indeed, it is this so-called transversal discipline to which the insurance discipline appears to be linked.

Furthermore, by underscoring consumer awareness, it appears to have transcended the "paternalistic" paradigm, even at the regulatory level. This shift has frequently accompanied the regulation of consumer contracts, thereby enhancing the "sovereign" role of the consumer. This phenomenon, in essence, transcends the literal interpretation of the act itself. The objective is to expand the scope to encompass a more extensive dimension. In comparison with traditional legal concepts, this approach encompasses a more extensive scope.

In this regard, it appears decisive to point out how this discipline has opened up a new consideration of the decision-making processes of consumers,[4] already taking into account the openings that must mark the figure of the average consumer. In fact, with Article 20 of the Consumer Code, the legislator states that: "*1. A commercial practice shall be unfair if it is contrary to professional diligence, and is false or is likely to distort to an appreciable extent the economic behaviour of the average consumer whom it reaches or to whom it is addressed, or of the average member of a group where the practice is directed to a particular group of consumers. 2. Commercial practices which, while reaching broader groups of consumers, are likely to appreciably distort the economic behaviour only of a clearly identifiable group of consumers who are particularly vulnerable to the practice or the product to which it relates because of their mental or physical infirmity, age or credulity in a way that the trader could reasonably be expected to foresee, shall be assessed from the perspective of the average member of that* group."

In particular, where there is a group of consumers particularly vulnerable to the practice or the good or service to which it relates which is clearly identifiable (in its identity and in the factors which determine its weakness), and provided that the trader can reasonably foresee that the commercial practice resorted to by reason of its characteristics or the nature of the good or service which is the subject of it is likely to influence to an appreciable extent the decisions of the persons likely to be included in that group the ability of the practice to distort the economic behaviour of consumers for the purposes of its possible classification as unfairness must be ascertained from the point of view of the average member of the group of consumers who is particularly vulnerable, notwithstanding the fact that the practice is addressed to the generality of consumers and not only to persons belonging to that group.

Therefore, it is evident that, although not solitary, unfairness undoubtedly functions as a counterbalance to the rules that aim to regulate the market by prescribing appropriate behavior. These rules are predicated on a fundamental aspect of prevention.[5]

---

[4] Caterina (2011), p. 123.

[5] On this point see Camilleri (2024), p. 200, according to which "just in the endiadi that links such terms (good faith *and* fairness), preceded, in the municipal provision, by the reference to the general principles of the sector of activity of the professional - in place of the reference to honest practices referred to in the text of the directive - the propulsive factor of objective rules of conduct,

From this perspective, it is essential to examine the pivotal role of awareness in shaping consumer choices. In this context, the profile of the manipulation of information provided to the consumer that can influence their consumption choices becomes evident. It is crucial to consider not only the consumer's weakness, but also their potential vulnerability.

The significance of the manipulation of information presented to the consumer that may influence their consumption decisions is evident, considering that both the consumer's weakness and their potential vulnerability must be taken into account in this context.

This is particularly salient when a group of consumers is susceptible to the practice or the good or service to which it relates and is clearly identifiable in terms of its identity and the factors that determine its vulnerability.[6] Furthermore, the trader's capacity to foresee that the commercial practice, given its characteristics or the nature of the good or service in question, will likely influence the decisions of the consumers within the group must be taken into account. The determination of whether a practice distorts the economic behavior of consumers for the purposes of its possible classification as unfair must be made from the perspective of the average member of the group of consumers who are particularly vulnerable. Notwithstanding the fact that the practice is addressed to the general public and not exclusively to members of that group.

In practice, the vulnerability of the consumer is considered in relation to the good or service that is the object of the practice, the market in which the conduct is carried out, and the general context in which it occurs. It is evident that the digital market is a particularly risky terrain for the "vulnerable" consumer: just think, e.g., of the adoption by companies of increasingly sophisticated techniques that seek to manipulate users and induce them to make unwanted choices (the so-called dark patterns).

A dark pattern is defined as an interface design choice of a website that is deliberately and consciously deceptive, with the purpose of inducing the user of that site to perform an action that he or she would otherwise not have performed, or conversely, not to perform actions that he or she would like to perform, but that are unfavorable to the owner of that site.

To illustrate, a dark pattern may take the form of an interface designed to encourage subscription to a newsletter or a specific service, accompanied by the assertion that unsubscribing is possible at any time, yet in reality, it is rendered highly difficult to do so.

The numerous European-style regulatory prescriptions provide for strong formal and informational obligations. These regulations are designed to ensure the full expression of individual freedom of choice. The concept of the "average consumer"

---

duties of information and protection that the professional is required to observe in any market context is in fact revealed, without prejudice to the additive relevance of the *best practices* of the given professional context, as well as of the more specific behavioural rules eventually prescribed for the single sector."

[6] Trubiani (2023), p. 117.

serves as the foundational principle for this endeavor, providing a rational basis for the pursuit of autonomy. This archetype of the rational subject is understood as the foundation for the validation of both general legislation on unfair commercial practices and specialized legislation on the sale of "bundled" insurance products.

It can be posited that the general legislation on unfair commercial practices and the specialized legislation on the sale of "bundled" insurance products may find common ground.

The sale of a "bundled" product can be regarded as a particular instance of a more extensive category of unfair commercial practices. This category encompasses all behaviors implemented by a contracting party that is presumed to possess specialized knowledge or information. This encompasses actions that compromise the contractual integrity and legal binding of the agreement. The objective of this scheme is to obtain an advantage through unjust means, thereby placing the "weaker" counterparty at a disadvantage. It should be noted that the latter is often represented in subjects who are presumed to be in a state of particular psychological vulnerability due to their economic circumstances.[7]

This dynamic poses a significant risk, as it has the potential to influence consumers' economic decisions by altering their ability to make informed choices, or by imposing limitations through the use of pressure or psychological manipulation. This is facilitated by the persuasive advantage derived from the consumer's anticipation of the outcomes associated with financing practices.

The technical intricacy of financial and insurance contracts, which has become increasingly pronounced over time, has resulted in a marked disparity between the negotiating positions of professionals and consumers. This has resulted in consumers often facing a significant disadvantage compared to professionals, who possess the capacity to prepare the contractual text and to unilaterally conform "the very utilities that, hypothetically, that relationship is capable of procuring for the client."

The proliferation of sectoral regulations has led to a significant increase in the complexity of regulatory frameworks. These regulations are designed to enhance the information provided to consumers. However, it appears that this endeavor has not adequately addressed consumers' protection needs. The quantitative increase in information, especially that which is over-standardized, may pose a risk to consumers. This phenomenon, characterized by the proliferation of information, carries with it the potential to induce perplexity among consumers and clients. This is particularly salient in the financial-insurance sector.[8]

---

[7] This aspect is plastically outlined in numerous AGCM measures: among others, see Provv. no. 28159 (Unicredit—Sale coupled with mortgages), in Boll. no. 11 of 18 February 2020; Provv. no. 20883 (Crefin Money—Advertising loans), in Boll. No. 10 of 10 March 2010; Prov. No. 20005 (Ambrosiana Finanziamenti), in Boll. No. 26 of 25 June 2009; Prov. No. 18723 (Cerruti Multiservice Group—Financing Costs), in Boll. No. 31 of 7 August 2008, all available at www.agcm.it.

[8] See Court of Justice. EU, 23 April 2015, C-96/14, which states that transparency must also be understood as an understanding of the clause not only in terms of its lexical meaning, but also of its possible impact on one's economic sphere; ECJ, 20 September 2017, C-186/16.

Information that lacks clarity may result in a decrease in the amount of usable knowledge.[9] In addition to the manner, the how is relevant: an excess of information may lead to an inability to select important news and produce a result similar to that of an absence of information.

The paradigm of protection shifts from the preventive level to the subsequent one, since it is necessary to have recourse to remedies and to prove in concrete terms that the inadequate information caused real prejudice to the consumer and/or that it affected his consent. In the absence of such proof, the consumer himself will be considered negligent or at least lazy.[10] The shift in protection from the preventive level to the subsequent level necessitates the recourse to remedies and the demonstration of concrete harm to the consumer, resulting from inadequate information. Absent such evidence, the consumer is deemed negligent or, at the very least, indolent, thereby forfeiting the specific protection and remedies afforded by law.

Consequently, in the event of negligence on his part (perhaps even due to carelessness or superficiality), the existence of any detrimental consequences that can be compensated by way of damages must be excluded.

In this regard, the necessity arises not only to identify appropriate methods of promoting awareness but also to ascertain the underlying principles that guide this awareness. In this regard, it is essential to examine the prevailing understanding of the average consumer.

Indeed, the central issue concerns the interpretation of the notion of average consumer under Article 20 of the Consumer Code for the purposes of applying the rules on unfair commercial practices.[11]

In the aforementioned decision, The Council of State posits a query to the Court of Justice of the European Union, inquiring whether the concept in question ought not to be articulated in accordance with the best science and experience, and thereby not exclusively adhere to the traditional conception of homo oeconomicus but also encompass the most recent theoretical frameworks of bounded rationality, which have demonstrated how people often act by reducing the necessary information with decisions that are "unreasonable" when compared to those that would be taken by a hypothetically attentive and circumspect subject.

Acquisitions that impose a greater need for consumer protection in the case. This is an increasingly recurrent phenomenon in modern market dynamics, and it is associated with the danger of cognitive conditioning. The perils of cognitive

---

[9] See ECJ, 7 April 2022, C-249/21.

[10] Rossi Carleo (2010), p. 688.

[11] It should be noted that the expression "average consumer," without its own definition, is commonly used in European regulatory texts: see, most recently, EU Reg. no. 2065 of 19 October 2022 (so-called Digital Services Act), whose Article 6, para. 3 ("*Storage of information*") states that "*Paragraph 1 shall not apply in relation to liability under consumer protection legislation for online platforms that enable consumers to conclude distance contracts with traders, where those online platforms present specific information or otherwise make possible the specific transaction in question in such a way as to lead an average consumer to believe that the information, or the product or service that is the subject of the transaction, is provided by the platform itself or by a recipient of the service acting under its authority or control.*"

conditioning have become a recurring theme in contemporary market dynamics. A thorough examination of this subject reveals the mounting imperative to consider the evolution of behavioral economics research. It is noteworthy that the legislator has incorporated behavioral economics into numerous recent measures, thereby integrating it into the system. This integration necessitates a comprehensive and nuanced examination of the subject, taking into account its multifaceted nature.

One of the merits of the ordinance is that it acknowledges the elevated discourse surrounding the notion of the average consumer in a sector regarded as "Law in a Changing Society." This discourse has been ongoing for some time, not only in Europe, but also in other regions.[12]

A comprehensive discussion of this multifaceted topic is beyond the scope of this analysis. However, it is worthwhile to offer some key considerations that serve to contextualize the issue, while also acknowledging the historical underpinnings that are pertinent to this discourse on the so-called irrational consumer.

The archetypal consumer, as depicted in previous literature, has been characterized by a model of an informed, reasonably observant, and circumspect (though not specialized) subject. This archetype is typically characterized by a comprehensive understanding of the relevant circumstances, enabling them to anticipate the actions of professionals in specific situations.

The average consumer is thus characterized as a per relationem figure, meaning that their actions are contingent upon the specific conditions of the consumer in a given transaction and situational context.

This objective matrix parameter may evoke the concept of the "good father" archetype within the codified tradition.[13] This is particularly evident in the degree of caution exhibited when engaging with the market of reference during consumer decision-making.[14] This is necessary to maintain a balance between making a conscious choice and assuming personal responsibility.

---

[12] Rabitti (2019), p. 351, points out, dwelling precisely on the possibility of overcoming a conception of the average consumer based exclusively on *homo oeconomicus*.

[13] A figure that, according to the teaching of a master of civil law, "*constitutes the yardstick of the activity directed to the protection or realisation of others' interests, so that the idea of a special solicitude that must guide the obligor in his activity is inherent in it*," thus posits Giorgianni (1968), p. 597; with broader reference to the subjectivistic theory of liability for breach of contract see Giorgianni (1975), pp. 188 ff.

[14] On the notion of professional diligence and the relationships between diligence, fairness, and good faith see Piraino (2010), pp. 1117 ss.

3 The Contribution of Behavioral Economics

The notion of the "homo oeconomicus" as a paradigm consumer has been adopted as a reference model. This notion is understood as a model of a rational actor, and it has become a "source of production of implicit legal rules."[15] This phenomenon is particularly evident in the context of unfair commercial practices, including those that take place within the digital market.

The conceptualization of the "average consumer" model, which serves as the foundation for evaluating the appropriateness of marketing techniques, has been influenced by the jurisprudence of the EU Court of Justice. The court has demonstrated a consistent association with the concept of the "homo oeconomicus" irrespective of the contributions of behavioral sciences.

This is in spite of the fact that, for several years, a segment of the economic literature has contended that consumer behavior is aimed at maximizing individual well-being and is to some extent based on impulsive and emotional elements.[16] Nevertheless, a considerable body of research in the field of economics has contended that consumer behavior is intended to optimize individual well-being and is, to a certain extent, influenced by impulsive and emotional factors. Furthermore, consumer choice is presumed to be constrained by cognitive and decision-making processes, resulting in outcomes that are deemed to be irrational.

Conversely, as established doctrine has previously noted, the market itself "constitutes not merely an offer of goods, but also an offer of suggestive, emotional, and cognitive data." The necessity to critically evaluate the conventional agent model of neoclassical economics, predicated on "a system of interdependent markets, independent of external regulation," has been acknowledged within legal doctrine.

Consequently, the focus of reflection has shifted to the legal aspects of the psychology of decision-making.[17] A divergent model of "homo heuristicus" emerged. This model is regarded as the foundation of the concept of the average consumer. This concept is reminiscent of a paradigm of choice that is also characterized by mental shortcuts that simplify individual choices, while at the same time proving to be harbingers of misperceptions that can compromise their outcomes.

The term "limited rationality"[18] is employed to denote the notion that the cognitive abilities of individuals are constrained by their own limitations in terms of the number of stimuli to which they are exposed, their capacity to sustain attention over

---

[15] The exception is the "Tekanne" ruling (ECJ, 4 June 2015, C-195/14), albeit with reference to the different field of food labeling. The case on which the ruling was based concerned an infusion that, while bearing the graphic reference to raspberry and vanilla on the label, only listed the presence of fruit flavorings in the list of ingredients. The Court held that it was correct that the *packaging* could have been misleading because it could have led an "average consumer" to believe that the fruit was present as such rather than just the flavorings. On this point, for a more detailed commentary, see Gonzalez Vaquè (2015), pp. 43 ff.

[16] Zoppini (2020), p. 208.

[17] Thaler (2015).

[18] Simon (1985).

extended periods, and their ability to retain the memory of all information received. The term “limited rationality” signifies that the decision-making capacity of human beings is influenced by the constraints of their cognitive abilities. These limitations pertain to the number of stimuli received, the capacity to sustain attention over time, and the ability to retain the memory of all received information.

This phenomenon, termed “limited rationality” has been demonstrated to induce “distortions” in decision-making processes.[19]

A substantial body of research has demonstrated that individuals’ choices can be considerably influenced by the manner in which a given problem is presented to them or by the manner in which a set of alternatives is presented to them (so-called framing effect). In essence, people tend to underestimate the negative consequences of actions that produce a positive effect in the immediate future (so-called present bias); moreover, in gathering and selecting information, individuals tend to prefer information that confirms their initial hypotheses, rather than information that might undermine them (so-called confirmation bias).[20]

This phenomenon underscores the limitations of a rigid legislative notion, such as that of consumer protection, and highlights the need for a more nuanced and informed approach to addressing consumer issues. This notion has become obsolete in the face of the evolution of commercial techniques. Rather than a mere restatement, a comprehensive reevaluation is imperative. A fundamental rethinking is necessary, as evidenced by the growing focus on vulnerable consumers.

In its ruling of 14 November 2024, in Case C-646/22, the Court of Justice of the European Union (CJEU)[21] reaffirmed that the concept of the “average consumer” as defined in Directive 2005/29 on unfair commercial practices refers to an individual who possesses a level of information that can be reasonably expected to be known to all consumers. This determination is made with consideration for pertinent social, cultural, and linguistic factors, and does not encompass information that is specific to the particular transaction in question.

The Court holds, however, that “*such a definition does not exclude ... that an individual’s decision-making capacity may be distorted by limitations such as cognitive distortions.*”

Finally, the Court states that the commercial practice consisting in the simultaneous offer to the consumer of a loan and an insurance product not linked to that loan cannot be classified as an unfair commercial practice in any event, the black list of Dir. 2005/29 constituting an exhaustive list.

The point of law expressed by the Court on the average consumer therefore appears to be the expression of a clear principle of “European private law”:[22] the reference model of the average consumer remains the so-called homo oeconomicus

[19] Tversky and Kahnemann (1974), pp. 1124 ff.

[20] Thaler and Sunstein (2009), pp. 5 ff.

[21] Court of Justice of the European Union, 14 November 2024, C-646/22, available in https://eur-lex.europa.eu/legal-content/EN/TXT/?uri=celex:62022CJ0646.

[22] Zaccaria (1997), p. 377.

even the notion under consideration continues to express a certain vivacity by also accepting, case by case, the instances linked to so-called cognitive distortions.

While certain observers may interpret the ruling as a missed opportunity, it is arguably the most equitable resolution of the competing interests that lie at the heart of the issue.[23] This outcome serves to affirm the EU Court of Justice's role as the primary arbiter of legal principles within the European Union. This principle is regarded as a cornerstone of legal certainty and predictability.[24]

Nevertheless, the necessity for the predictability and calculability of the law appears to be progressively recognized, even within this particular sector. This necessity is particularly pronounced in the context of rapid technological advancement. See, e.g., artificial intelligence emotion recognition systems, i.e., software systems aimed at identifying or inferring emotions or intentions of natural persons on the basis of their biometric data.

This progression has led to the emergence of a rapid and pervasive system of commerce, intertwined with substantial digital platforms. Within this context, the legislative framework pertaining to legal entities and, consequently, the legitimate boundaries of actions permitted to economic operators are delineated with clarity and precision. Undoubtedly, this constitutes the primary form of consumer protection.

As previously articulated in the context of the order of referral, this approach serves as a foundational element in ensuring the integrity and security of commercial activities within the digital landscape. The risk associated with an unconditional openness to the contribution of the behavioral sciences was that of a possible return, in attenuated form, of a consumer paternalism updated to today's times. This scenario would entail the potential diminution of personal autonomy, a fundamental principle underpinning the effective operation of the European market. It is imperative to identify an equilibrium between the competitive nature of the market and the provisions for consumer protection.

One potential approach to achieving this balance could involve a re-examination of consumer education, as outlined in Articles 2(d) and 4 of the consumer code, as a fundamental right of the consumer.[25] It is also imperative to consider the dictates of Article 169 TFEU, which establishes information as a pivotal element capable of determining that balance, thereby enabling the effective exercise of autonomy by the parties involved. This article further emphasizes the significance of education and information in this regard.

Furthermore, a reevaluation of the "homo oeconomicus" paradigm should encompass the recognition that, within the European policy framework of solidarity-based and sustainable growth, consumers are endowed with a "power of choice" that transcends mere economic convenience, encompassing additional and varied

---

[23] ECJ, 4 June 2015, C-497/13. More recently, see ECJ, 17 May 2022, C-693/19 and C-831/19.

[24] Irti (2016).

[25] On this point see Rossi Carleo (2005), pp. 14 ff.

criteria.[26] In this regard, an emphasis on behavioral economics has the potential to unveil novel perspectives. The prevailing paradigm is characterized by the pervasive influence of network entities on the decision-making process of the average consumer.

These entities, through their sophisticated behaviors, exert a significant impact on choices that ought to be immune to such influences. Consequently, it becomes imperative to undertake a comprehensive examination of the factors that influence decision-making capacity and the limitations that can be imposed to safeguard the interests of the average consumer. This examination should be conducted during the preventive phase rather than in the subsequent and compensatory phase, which, as has been repeatedly demonstrated, has minimal effectiveness in the digital realm.

4 Social Platforms, Influencers, and Content Creators

In the digital economy, novel actors such as influencers and content creators have witnessed a marked increase in presence in recent years.

This phenomenon, often termed "influencers" has garnered significant attention in contemporary discourse. These individuals have achieved a notable degree of visibility within the digital landscape, thereby assuming a pivotal role in the communication sphere.[27] They have come to wield significant influence over the decisions of social media users, encompassing both passive consumers and active participants in the digital ecosystem. *Content creators*, on the other hand, are creative experts who are in charge of devising, structuring, and realizing an *online* communication project: they produce digital content of all kinds—texts for *blogs* and *websites*, *posts* for *social networks*, videos for *social* platforms such as YouTube, Instagram, TikTok (with its *scrolling* activity), or Twitch containing *live streaming* video content.

Although in reality, in most operational contexts, the profile in question deals with the creation of any type of digital content, on a theoretical level there are several categories of *content creators*, i.e., profiles specialized in certain areas, such as *copywriters*, *video makers*, and *graphic designers*.

In particular, *influencers* assume actual relevance in many cases due to the experience and knowledge they have gained in a given product sector (such as, for instance, everything related to travel, fashion, and cooking, but sometimes also financial products and crypto-assets) and, in others, also due to their participation in those groups created around a company, i.e., the so-called brand communities. According to "*Guidelines aimed at ensuring compliance with the provisions of the*

[26] Once again, without going into a subject that would require a great deal of reflection, it would seem sufficient, by way of simplification, to refer to the so-called ethical choices, which, as is widely believed, could leverage ethics as a *marketing* tool. For a basic reflection on the subject, we refer to the now classic book of Bauman (2007).

[27] Trubiani (2024), p. 385 ss.

Consolidated Act by influencers and establishment of a special technical table" introduced by Resolution no. 7/24 Italian Authority for Communications (AGCOM) and which only apply to *influencers* with at least 1 million *followers*, the main purpose of the service offered is "*the provision of content, created or selected by the influencer, which informs, entertains or educates and which is likely to generate income directly in execution of commercial agreements with producers of goods and services or indirectly in application of the monetisation agreements applied by the platform or social media used.*"

The most recent studies in the field of legal business have elucidated how influencers have become increasingly adept at influencing their followers' consumption decisions. This influence is facilitated by the direct and unfiltered interaction between influencers and their followers, which is facilitated by the publication of posts, reposts, stories, and direct streaming, often aimed at promoting a specific brand. This phenomenon encompasses a wide spectrum of activities, including the strategic alternation of moments in which the influencer's daily life is showcased.

A distinguishing feature of influencer marketing is the vast and potentially infinite audience for advertising messages, as evidenced by the scrolling activity on TikTok. It has been posited that influencers may exert a form of psychological pressure on consumers/users through the use of emotional stimuli. This emotional manipulation is often disproportionate to the actual needs of the consumers and can significantly impact their decision-making capacity. In some cases, the use of emotional advertising can be regarded as a form of aggressive commercial practice.

In instances where commercial information or context is distorted, consumer decision-making may be compromised. Consequently, the consumer's decision-making process may be compromised.

As is well understood, the Unfair Commercial Practices Directive 2005/29/EU also aims to prevent the exploitation of consumers whose characteristics, such as age, physical or mental infirmity, or credulity, make them particularly susceptible to unfair commercial practices or the underlying products (e.g., minors or the elderly). In instances where a commercial practice is designed to target a vulnerable group of consumers, it is imperative to assess its impact from the perspective of the average consumer within that group. This evaluation, however, has been the subject of critical discourse within the prevailing doctrine for an extended period.

In the context of the digital market, however, there appears to be a shift in focus towards the significant risk of user vulnerability to commercial practices implemented through influencers. This emergent phenomenon manifests particularly among consumers and users of social media, whose vulnerability appears to transcend the confines of intrinsic weakness or fragility. Instead, it is evident that this vulnerability is intricately intertwined with broader contexts of situational or relational vulnerability, necessitating a reevaluation of established frameworks. This phenomenon necessitates a reevaluation of established categories by interpreters. It is imperative to maintain a constant vigilance against the potential for a paternalistic shift in perspective that may emerge in the process of broadening the concept of vulnerability. This phenomenon, however, concomitantly restricts the "positive freedom" of the consumer. This resolution occurs within the consumer's awareness.

The European Commission's guidelines stipulate, in the first instance, that influencers possess the capacity to impart guidance on the requisite conduct. The European Commission's guidelines stipulate that influencers are capable of imparting guidance on appropriate conduct. Additionally, it is asserted that the magnitude of an influencer's audience is of negligible concern, provided that the influencer engages in such practices with regularity and receives compensation for promoting a product.

When assessing the professional nature of an influencer's marketing activities, it is essential to consider all the circumstances of the individual case, including regularity, frequency, information asymmetry, profit-seeking, and turnover.

A preliminary evaluation indicates that the digital influencer market exhibits a dynamic environment, necessitating the consideration of multiple variables. Some influencers engage in consistent collaborations with specific companies, while others engage in commercial agreements only sporadically.

Furthermore, the manner in which influencers are compensated for their promotional services is multifaceted. They may receive a fixed sum of money, a reward based on the number of sales they generate in the context of affiliate marketing, free products, or a discount code for the purchase of a specific company's products. Consequently, in some cases, it will be evident that the influencer has the status of a professional, while other influencer marketing scenarios will not be so defined and clear.

However, drawing parallels with the context of the collaborative economy reveals the impracticality of establishing quantitative thresholds at the European level. Such thresholds would encompass the level or percentage of income derived from influencer activities, with the aim of distinguishing between professional and non-professional influencers. This challenge arises due to the variability in income levels across EU Member States and the unique characteristics of influencer marketing.

The second assessment, i.e., determining whether the influencer acts in the name of or on behalf of a professional, concerns two profiles. First, as previously mentioned, when a professional or non-professional influencer acts as an intermediary, the professional who initiated the activity will be held responsible for compliance with the Unfair Commercial Practices Directive. Secondly, the question of whether the influencer is acting in the name of or on behalf of a professional is pivotal in determining the applicability of the Unfair Commercial Practices Directive to a specific commercial practice carried out by the influencer in the interest of that professional 20 ff. of the Consumer Code, and thus whether the influencer will be subject to the obligations imposed by the directive in relation to that specific commercial practice.

A number of variables may potentially play an important role in this matter. First of all, the nature of the agreements between the influencer and the company can take different forms. Some influencers have to adhere to extensive and detailed instructions on the content required by the company. Conversely, in other instances, such as the case of Balocco and Ferragni, the balance of power is tipped in favor of the influencer. Furthermore, the duration of the collaboration can be a determining factor: in some cases, influencers only enter into an occasional contractual agreement with a company, whereas in others they are involved in long-term partnerships as so-called brand ambassadors. Finally, the nature of the incentive received by the influencer to promote the products of a particular company must be considered. This could also be taken into account.

The analysis of the recent "Balocco/Ferragni" case is particularly salient in elucidating the multifaceted nature of influencer marketing contracts, which often exhibit a lack of singularity and are instead comprised of a series of interconnected contractual relationships. Instead, it is more common to find a series of interdependent bundles of contractual relationships. These arrangements may encompass the licensing of the influencer's brand, the particulars of sponsorship negotiations, and other related activities. The licensing of the influencer's brand, the negotiation of sponsorship, and the endorsement (in which the combination of the public image of the well-known person and the brand creates "a symbolic interference between the personal identity of the well-known person and the personal identity of the person who is not a well-known person") are all relevant factors.

The juxtaposition of the public image of the well-known person and the trademark creates a symbolic interference between the personal identity of the dispatcher and the activity exercised by the authorized company.

A particularly salient provision within this legislative framework is that of Loi no. 451 of 9 June 2023, which establishes regulatory frameworks for influencer marketing within the French jurisdiction. Article 3 of this decree includes legal persons within the definition of influencer. This solution effectively addresses the ambiguities previously identified in the interpretation of the influencer concept. Consequently, French law offers a novel approach to addressing the legal ramifications of the intricate contractual relationships underlying agreements between brands, agencies, and influencers.

In this regard, the subsequent Article [7] stipulates: 7, which delineates the agencies activity as those consisting in representing, for consideration, natural or legal persons exercising the activity of an influencer, is also consistent. Article 8 stipulates that the agent is obligated to ensure that the activities are in accordance with the established legal norms and is jointly and severally liable with the influencer and the commissioning party for compensation for damages caused to third parties in the performance of the contract. This is undoubtedly consistent.

The marketing activities of influencers or content creators on social media are undoubtedly encompassed within the purview of the business practices of a professional.

Article 18(1)(d) of the Consumer Code defines commercial practices as "any act, omission, course of conduct or representation, commercial communication including advertising and marketing of the product, by a trader, in relation to the promotion, sale or supply of a product to consumers."

The discipline in question, as is well understood, aims to safeguard the consumer's freedom of choice. However, this freedom is not protected by Directive 2005/29 in the context of the individual relationship. Rather, it is protected by the traditional remedial technique that has always characterized European consumer law. The consumer's freedom of choice is, in fact, protected at the general level of the market. This protection is an essential component of the proper functioning of competition.

It is widely acknowledged that legislation pertaining to unfair commercial practices is interpreted as regulating not the act itself but rather the activity. It is evident that commercial communications, encompassing advertising and marketing activities, occurring prior to or subsequent to the execution of a contract, may be deemed as commercial practices within the purview of the directive.

However, this would only be the case if the commercial communication is "directly related to the promotion, sale, or supply of a product to consumers."

To ascertain the applicability of the Unfair Commercial Practices Directive to the marketing activities of influencers, a distinction must be made between two scenarios: (a) the influencer promoting their own products, and (b) the influencer promoting the products of a third company. The latter category must be further subdivided into two subcategories: (b1) influencers acting in the name of or on behalf of the third company, and (b2) influencers not acting in the name of or on behalf of the third company.

The dissemination of commercial messages pertaining to the influencer's products is subject to the provisions of the Unfair Commercial Practices Act (UCP) if the influencer fulfills the criteria of a "trader." This status is determined by the presence of specific criteria, as outlined above. Furthermore, the commercial messages must be integral to the influencer's business strategy and must be directly associated with the promotion, sale, or supply of the influencer's products to consumers.

The aforementioned principles may be invoked in instances such as when the influencer provides their followers with a discount code to purchase their products or organizes a giveaway (i.e., an online competition to win their products). In other scenarios, such as when the influencer wears his or her products in a photo or video, it is less clear whether a direct connection with the promotion, sale, or supply of the influencer's products within the meaning of the Directive can be established. However, if the influencer shares marketing content related to the products of a third company and is acting in the name of or on behalf of that third company, the content must be directly linked to the promotion of the products of the company in question for the Unfair Commercial Practices Directive to apply.

A direct connection is present if the content provides information about a discount offer or a complimentary gift, for example. This is analogous to an influencer promoting its own products.

This principle finds its foundation in the EU Court of Justice's ruling in the Peek & Cloppenburg case.[28] The discipline on unfair commercial practices is applicable to the publication of a post or story in which an influencer invites their followers to a private sales evening organized by a third-party company. It can be posited that the publication of sponsored editorial content by the influencer, operating as a media operator, is not inherently associated with the promotion of the medium through

[28] ECJ, 2 September 2021, C-371/20, in *DCPE online*, 2021.

which the content is disseminated (e.g., the influencer's blog, Instagram profile, or YouTube/TikTok channel).

A direct link to the influencer's product might be present, for instance, when the influencer organizes a giveaway concerning the third company's products, requiring people who want to participate to follow or subscribe to the influencer's profile on social media. The EU Court of Justice's jurisprudence in the Kamenova case provides specific criteria for determining the professional status of an influencer-seller.[29]

The aforementioned criteria include regularity, frequency, asymmetry of information, profit motive, and turnover. Once these criteria are met, the influencer-seller is designated as a professional. The application of the unfair commercial practices (UCP) discipline to the influencer is contingent upon the existence of a direct link between the promotion of the influencer's products and the influencer's actions. This link is established when the influencer promotes their products themselves or when they act through another person on their behalf.

However, the UCP discipline also applies to the influencer if they act through another person. According to the general clause in Article 6 of Directive 2005/29, as is well known, a commercial practice shall be regarded as misleading if it contains false information and is therefore untruthful or in any way, including overall presentation, deceives or is likely to deceive the average consumer, even if the information is factually correct, in relation to a number of essential elements, such as the existence or nature of the product, the main characteristics of the product or the nature, attributes and rights of the trader or his agent. A commercial practice is considered deceptive if it involves the marketing of a product that creates confusion with the products, trademarks, trade names, or other distinguishing marks of a competitor or if the trader fails to comply with commitments contained in codes of conduct to which the trader has committed.

Furthermore, it must be shown that the commercial practice induces or is likely to induce the consumer to take a transactional decision that he would not otherwise have taken.

The shift in perspective from the act to the activity must not, however, lead one to underestimate the concrete incidence that the professional's activity exerts on the individual acts of consumption that the consumer does or does not perform. In fact, Article 18(m) of the Consumer Code, as amended by the decree transposing Directive 2005/29, in outlining the definition of the "decision of a commercial nature" taken by the consumer under the influence of the unfair practice, refers to the choice of whether or not to purchase the product, to the terms and conditions of the purchase itself, and to the *amount* and terms of payment of the price.

It is clear from the wording of Article 18(m) of the Consumer Code that the concept of "decision of a commercial nature" is broadly defined. In the *Trento Sviluppo* case, the EU Court of Justice held that the concept includes not only the decision to purchase or not to purchase a product, but also any decision directly related to that

[29] ECJ, 4 October 2018, C-105/17, in *Giur. it.*, 2019, p. 1813 ss.

decision. In this sense, the concept of a decision of a commercial nature also includes decisions prior to purchase, such as the decision to enter a physical shop or a *website/web* platform.

In the context of influencer marketing, Article 7 of the Unfair Commercial Practices Directive presents an additional mechanism for addressing deceptive advertising and other unjust influencer marketing practices. However, the content of the influencer is only considered a misleading omission under Article 7 if it causes or is likely to cause the consumer to make a transactional decision that they would not have otherwise made. This is not always the case with the commercial practices listed above. Moreover, national authorities must evaluate each case individually to ascertain whether the relevant information has been omitted, given that the influencer's commercial communication generally does not constitute an invitation to purchase.[30] The assessment will also determine whether the influencer has complied with the transparency requirements of Article 7 of the Misleading Omissions Directive.

For instance, a social media post in which an influencer promotes a skin care product could potentially contravene the prohibition of misleading actions under Article 6 Dir. 2005/29 when the influencer employs a beauty filter to exaggerate the effect of the product, particularly when the influencer states the contrary (e.g., by using the hashtag #nofilter). However, the assessment of whether the content is misleading and may have an impact on the consumer's commercial decision must be conducted on a case-by-case basis.[31]

The "classic" regulatory sources do not exhaust the complex system of rules governing the phenomenon of influencer marketing. The rules of the Code of Self-Discipline of the Institute of Advertising Self-Discipline (IAP) also have an important place in this sector. Article 7 of the Code stipulates that Commercial communication must always be recognizable as such. In media and forms of commercial communication that disseminate other content and information, commercial communication must be distinctly separated by employing suitable devices. With regard to certain forms of commercial communication disseminated via the Internet, the main appropriate devices are set out in the Digital Chart Regulation.

The Digital Chart, in this case, provided specific operational suggestions to enable two groups of users to recognize promotional content as opposed to other types of content. The first group was comprised of users of the digital tool. The second group was comprised of operators. These operators were able to create transparent and correct messages in order not to incur sanctions.

The Digital Chart stipulates that when an endorser engages in a form of commercial communication, it is subject to all the provisions of the C.A.P. that pertain to offline advertising, particularly the provisions outlined in Article 7 concerning the principle of transparency and recognizability. As indicated by the Digital Chart,

---

[30] Riefa and Clausen (2019), p. 66 ff.

[31] European Commission, Guidance on the interpretation and application of Directive 2005/29/EC [2021] OJ C 526/1, p. 40.

advertising content disseminated by the endorser on social networks is required to contain the phrase "Advertising" or "Promoted by" in the initial part of the post… brand/Promoted by…brand or "Sponsored by… brand/Sponsored by…brand" or "in collaboration with …brand" or "in partnership with …brand" xml-ph-0001@ deepl.internal. Alternatively, or in addition, one of the following words must be included in the first three hashtags (#): "#Advertising" or "#Sponsored by … brand" or "#ad" together with "brand."

On 1 June 2023, an updated and amended version of the Digital Chart was published, in which the principle of recognizability of advertising content was strengthened. This stipulation indicates that the indication of the advertising nature of content shared or reposted on other platforms or online interfaces must be maintained.

Additionally, the Digital Chart acknowledges the potential for influencers to encompass both human and virtual entities, thereby subjecting them to the same transparency obligations as the former. In this latest iteration, it is imperative that all online content, whether disseminated through posts or communications, be clearly marked as either "Advertising/Advertising" or "Sponsored by…brand/Sponsored by…brand."

The IAP has stipulated that in the context of "call to action," the influencer and/or the company must encourage users to acknowledge the promotional character of the content. Furthermore, in instances pertaining to the utilization of discount codes or the practice of "affiliate marketing," the influencer is obligated to incorporate a warning that is conspicuously visible, thereby underscoring the promotional character of the content in question. Recently, AGCOM, through Del. 7/24/Cons., approved the Guidelines to regulate influencers' product advertising promotion activities and to identify the provisions of the Consolidated Text on Audiovisual Media Services ("TUSMA"). The aforementioned guidelines will be compulsory for influencers to adhere to. The Resolution also established a Technical Table, with the mission of drafting a specific Code of Conduct that will define the concrete measures and methods to ensure compliance with the relevant provisions of the TUSMA by influencers.

Social platforms wield considerable influence in the promotion of content published on their platforms. In this regard, Section 26 of the Digital Services Act (DSA) stipulates that platforms must ensure that users can discern the true nature of each advertisement, and that specific sanctions are to be imposed in the event of a violation of this obligation.

The aim behind this provision is to try to make platforms more accountable in the case of situations where there is a concrete risk of misleading the advertising message conveyed through the platform towards consumers/users.

Digital platforms assume the role of a "guardian of the web" in the context of the new regulation. Consequently, in the event that advertising content disseminated through influencers is found to be deceptive in practice, these digital platforms are obligated to intervene, while taking into account the distinction between content that is "only" potentially misleading, such as advertising messages conveyed through influencers, and content that is illegal in the strict sense, such as content concerning cyberbullying practices.

A uniform stance on this matter is articulated by Article 7 of the DSA, which establishes the "Good Samaritan rule."[32] This provision stipulates that voluntary investigations conducted by intermediary service providers in good faith and with due diligence, with the objective of identifying, removing, or disabling access to illegal content, do not constitute a basis for exemption from liability with respect to activities involving mere transport, temporary storage, or long-term storage (Articles 4, 5, and 6). Furthermore, this rule does not apply to the adoption of measures necessary to comply with Union law or national rights. The fourth, fifth, and sixth points in question pertain to the failure to adopt the requisite measures to comply with the stipulations of both Union law and national legislation.[33] In any event, through this provision, the European legislator establishes a principle of proactivity on the part of digital platforms. This principle could also be applied concretely in the domain of influencer marketing.

In addition, the provisions of Articles 19–22 of the DSA on trusted flaggers can be exploited. The term "trusted flagger" refers to those third parties who make use of the tools made available by online service providers to report content that, in their view, should be subject to moderation or removal.

The qualification of trustworthy reporter is recognized by the coordinator of digital services of each Member State (in our system, the AGCOM), as designated by Article 15 of Legislative Decree no. 123 of 15 September 2023, which was converted into Law no. 159 of 13 November 2023, at the request of entities that have demonstrated, inter alia, that they have special skills and expertise in the fight against illegal content and that they carry out their activities in a diligent, accurate, and objective manner.[34]

In the context of digital platforms, a separate category of rules of a private nature is also added to the standards. Indeed, most platforms provide specific community guidelines that influencers should also adhere to. These rules of a private nature, the nature of which is the subject of reflection in doctrine, are of particular concern.

These guidelines, often termed "community standards" or "terms of use," represent an additional layer of content moderation governance. This layer of governance is intended to complement the existing regulatory framework. The purpose of this study is to promote the adoption of best practices in influencer marketing, ensuring that promotional content does not exceed the bounds of fair and reasonable advertising.

An initial analysis of the content moderation policies adopted by various technology giants reveals an interesting finding: not all platforms directly address the issue of surreptitious and/or misleading marketing in their guidelines. Moreover, the

[32] Nozick and Routley (1962), p. 377 ff.

[33] Buiten (2020).

[34] Recital no. 61 DSA.

remedies proposed by these platforms do not appear to be effective in combating the phenomenon in question.

For instance, Facebook and Instagram have established guidelines aimed at ensuring the transparency of marketing activities within the influencer marketing ecosystem.[35] In the most recent iteration of its terms of use, Instagram formally acknowledges the definition of "commercial user" as outlined in Article 2(21) EU Reg. 2022/1925 (DMA), with the objective of notifying the user that they have the option to utilize the alternative dispute resolution mechanism outlined in Article 6(12) DMA.

Failure to adhere to these platform guidelines can result in specific sanctions, including content removal, account suspension, and even banishment.

Therefore, it is imperative for brands to comprehend and adhere to these platform guidelines, particularly in regard to banned or restricted products, such as alcohol and tobacco. It is imperative to note that both Facebook and Instagram explicitly prohibit any activity that contravenes legal statutes. The terms of service for both platforms unequivocally stipulate that influencers may be held accountable for engaging in unlawful actions, which can result in permanent expulsion from the platform.

It is noteworthy that the guidelines and terms of use of Meta platforms do not provide for any form of monitoring and control of advertising content expressed through influencers, with the exception, as previously noted, of a few specific products.

TikTok[36] has also established its own guidelines to regulate influencer marketing. Influencers and brands are obligated to clearly disclose any promotional collaborations using features such as the "Branded content toggle" tag or through direct disclosure in video captions ("#Ad"). TikTok has also established a set of guidelines for specific regulated products, including alcohol, tobacco products, firearms, sexual services, counterfeit goods, and gambling. Violations of these guidelines can result in the removal of content deemed illicit and, in certain cases, a permanent ban for the influencer. It is important to note that, in the absence of the aforementioned listed cases, there is an absence of any form of monitoring or control.

It is evident that the rapid evolution of marketing and advertising techniques on social media platforms gives rise to novel and continually evolving challenges in consumer protection. In light of these developments, the conventional instrument of so-called hard law (i.e., laws, regulations, and directives) is insufficient to adequately regulate this phenomenon, necessitating the effective implementation of

---

[35] Meta Platforms Inc, "*Facebook Community Standards: The Facebook Community Standards outline what is and isn't allowed on Facebook*" (Meta Platforms Inc, 2024) available in https://transparency.fb.com/en-gb/policies/community-standards/; Meta Platforms Inc, Instagram: Community Guidelines' (Meta Platforms Inc, 2023) in https://help.instagram.com/477434105621119?Mcms_id=477434105621119.

[36] TikTok Inc, "Regulated Goods and Commercial Activities" (TikTok Inc, 2024) in https://www.tiktok.com/community-guidelines/en/regulatedcommercial-activities/.

co-regulation initiatives.[37] These initiatives, as previously mentioned, likely constitute the predominant form of public regulatory intervention within the market. These measures are arguably the most consistent with the prevailing evolution of the digital market.[38]

5 Micro-Enterprises in the Digital Market

In the digital economy, in addition to "physical" actors, legal entities are also becoming mobile, particularly micro-enterprises.

These entities have identified in the digital market a natural conduit for their business operations, either through direct sales on their own platforms or indirect engagement via marketplace platforms.

It is precisely with regard to this latter hypothesis that we observe the proliferation of contracts between large platforms and micro-enterprises.

Consequently, the focus shifts to the realm of micro-enterprise contracts and the ensuing challenges in their execution, which characteristically entail long-term contractual commitments.

As in the offline market, unfair conduct to the detriment of micro-businesses can also occur in the digital market. Examples of such practices can be identified in the operations of digital platforms, which, due to their dominant market position, have the capacity to impose disadvantageous contractual provisions on suppliers. A notable example of this is the requirement to offer certain products at below cost prices for a specified duration, with the threat of exclusion from sale if the products are not offered at these prices.

A notable instance of this was observed in the case of AGCM Provv. 9 December 2021, A-528. In the "Amazon Logistics" case, the well-known platform Amazon had linked the use of its logistics service to access to a set of advantages essential for gaining visibility and better sales prospects on Amazon.it. Among these exclusive advantages is the Prime label, which facilitates sales to the most loyal and high-end consumers who are members of Amazon's loyalty program of the same name. The Prime label facilitates seller participation in popular Amazon special events, including Black Friday, Cyber Monday, and Prime Day. It also increases the likelihood that an offer will be selected as a "Featured Offer" and displayed in the "Buy Box."

---

[37] Bassan (2021).

[38] Busch (2019), according to which "a future regulatory framework for the platform economy should not only address platform operators as market intermediaries, but should also consider their role as actors participating in the regulatory chain…In this sense a future EU policy for platform regulation should be focused on a co-operative regulatory approach combining elements of regulated self-regulation and regulatory intermediation"; see also Fink (2018), p. 47 ff.; Harvey (2017).

Consequently, Amazon has restricted third-party sellers from utilizing the Prime label in conjunction with offers not managed through the FBA (Fulfilled by Amazon) label.

The AGCM investigation determined that these were features of the Amazon.co.uk platform that were instrumental in the success of sellers and in increasing their sales. A notable finding was that third-party sellers utilizing the FBA service were not subject to the same stringent performance measurement system applied to non-FBA sellers. This system, if not met, can result in the suspension of an account.

Accordingly Amazon has had a deleterious effect on competing e-commerce logistics operators by preventing them from offering themselves to online sellers as service providers of comparable quality to Amazon's logistics. Consequently, this behavior has exacerbated the disparity in market power between Amazon and its competitors in the e-commerce order delivery sector.

Consequently, competing marketplaces have also been adversely affected, as sellers are deterred from offering their products on other online platforms due to the cost of duplicating warehouses and the logistical challenges associated with offering a broad range of products.

The authority considered this abusive strategy particularly serious and, also in view of its duration, the effects already produced, and the size of the group, sanctioned Amazon under Article 102 TFEU for abuse of a dominant position and decided to impose the record fine of more than EUR 1 billion.

Regarding the qualification of possible abuses along the supply chain of the digital market, there is also the provision of the "abuse of economic dependence in digital markets" (as amended by Article 33 l., 5 August 2022, no. 118).

The legislative reform of 2022, in fact, introduces a presumption of economic dependence in which the company would find itself when it "uses the intermediation services provided by a digital platform," rather than the prescription of the prohibition of abuse of economic dependence on the platform operator.

6 The Role of Digital Platforms and the Contribution of the EU Court of Justice

In the recently implemented framework, the consumer discovered that they were utilizing a technical infrastructure with which they had limited familiarity and which was not subject to any regulatory oversight.

It is evident that the digital platform in question is a legal entity capable of leveraging its dominant position to its benefit by establishing a substantial information imbalance. This imbalance primarily manifests in the quality of the service, particularly with regard to the comprehensibility of the reference parameters used to evaluate the quality of the service, the clarity and transparency of the terms and conditions of the service, the method of contract conclusion, the duration of the contract, the tracking and security methods of the economic transaction of the payment, and the method of processing personal data.

Secondly, and particularly in regard to the nature of the service provided, information asymmetry is also associated with the placement of the offer on the electronic search channel. It is imperative for consumers to have access to the technical parameters that determine a provider's placement on the platform. Moreover, it is essential to ascertain whether this advantageous position is a consequence of any form of compensation or consideration. This information disparity consequently engenders a substantial imbalance of contractual power with respect to the following aspects: (a) the terms and the exercise of the right of withdrawal; (b) the possibility of reimbursement; (c) the possibility of a complaint; (d) the presence of an additional assistance service in the provision of the service; (e) the possibility of suspension/termination of the provision of the service; (f) the provision and legitimacy of clauses exempting from liability for damages; and (g) the remedies relating to termination for non-performance and lack of quality of the service provided.

Digital platforms facilitate exchanges by allowing a high level of interaction between users, thus describing forms of social commerce. This phenomenon has appeared alongside more "traditional" operators such as eBay and Amazon on the digital market in the form of social networks (e.g., Facebook, initially with Marketplace and now with Shops), then e-commerce platforms (e.g., Shopify, PrestaShop, or OpenCart) and, more recently, with the development of the so-called sharing economy, the so-called collaborative economy platforms (e.g., Airbnb, BlaBlaCar, Etsy, Couchsurfing, Gnammo, or Jobba), which present such characteristics as to make their classification among the intermediaries of a relationship between private individuals aimed at sharing goods or services insufficient.

Digital platforms play a crucial role in the digital economy, as digital content, digital services, and goods with digital elements are conveyed through these platforms. This system appears to challenge the market functioning models established in the "non-digital" economy and the rules that regulate them. Indeed, the basis of many peer-to-peer sharing practices is the absence of intermediaries and selective distribution networks.

Technological innovation has prompted the restructuring of production and sales processes, rendering traditional intermediaries redundant in numerous sectors and giving rise to previously non-existent markets (e.g., the services offered by BlaBlaCar, Gnammo, or Jobba).

A thorough examination reveals that certain collaborative platforms do more than simply facilitate the alignment of user supply and demand; they also establish the modalities of service delivery. This raises the question of whether the service provider's autonomy in performing the service is truly intact.

Digital platforms are the foundational infrastructure of the collaborative economy, establishing an open market for the temporary use of goods or services, often provided by private individuals.[39] These platforms connect two groups of actors: service providers and users.

Each occupying a different side of a "two-sided market."[40] This configuration is designed to facilitate communication and collaboration between participants from different sides of the market, thereby ensuring that individuals on one side have access to the group on the other side, and vice versa. This approach entails the execution of two distinct activities by the platform.

On the one hand, it facilitates the convergence of two or more parties for the purpose of concluding a transaction by establishing a "virtual space" where supply and demand can interact. On the other hand, it provides the foundational support for the formation of the contractual relationship.

These include, but are not limited to, the following: (a) the electronic payment system through which the user can remunerate the service provider for the service purchased; (b) the creation of a space in which users can evaluate the service they have used, giving rise to a reputational mechanism that can guide their consumption choices; and (c) the setting up of specific tools to channel communication between the parties.

The legal position of digital platforms depends on their definition: they are qualified as *online* intermediary service providers by Article 2 of EU Reg. 2019/1150.

This rule qualifies the activity as the subject of "information society services," within meaning of Article 1(1)(*b*) of Directive 2015/1535, itself taken over from Article 2(*a*) of Dir. 2000/31 on electronic commerce: a service "normally provided for remuneration, by electronic means and at the individual request of a recipient of services."

The problem that arises in connection with this market is that there is essentially a kind of "legal vacuum" that causes uncertainty as to who is the addressee of the rules in this "triangular' contractual relationship.

The question arises in the following terms: the operation of consumer protection normally presupposes the presence of a "professional." In the event that it is a "private individual" (i.e., a person who does not operate within an organized activity) who provides the service (e.g., Airbnb) or sells the good (e.g., Etsy), the classic professional-consumer relationship is superseded by a *peer-to-peer* relationship and the purchaser could be, at least in a strictly theoretical way, deprived of the protections provided by the consumer protection system.

The problem is not insignificant: especially when the platform encompasses both "private individuals" (or, so to speak, "trader users") and "professionals," the (supposed) consumer may not easily understand whether the other party is to be considered, in relation to the individual and concrete negotiation exchange, as a professional or a consumer: even more so if the purchaser is comforted by the trust generated by the platform itself and does not realize that he is deprived of specific negotiation protections.

[39] Busch (2016), p. 225.

[40] Rochet and Tirole (2003), p. 990.

It is therefore important to clarify the role of these platforms in the negotiation transactions in question and in particular to identify the elements whose occurrence may affect their qualification as counterparty to the consumer.[41] Whether or not the platform is a party to the contract with the consumer will have to be ascertained on the basis of what is stated in the general terms and conditions of the contract, which to tell the truth are often very incomplete (given also, in several cases, the linguistic difficulties that require a rather approximate translation), but also on the basis of the relational context in which the conduct was implemented.

On this point, see Communication from the Commission *A New Deal for Consumers*, COM(2018) 183 *final* of 11 April 2018, expressly provides for the platform's obligation to specify: (i) whether the third party offering goods, services, or digital content is a professional or not, on the basis of the third party's declaration on the *online* marketplace; (ii) whether or not consumer rights stemming from Union consumer protection legislation apply to the contract concluded; and (iii) in case the contract is concluded with a professional, which professional is responsible for ensuring, in relation to the contract, the application of consumer rights stemming from Union consumer protection legislation.

Similarly, Recital No. 27 of dir. 2019/2161/EU (transposed into our law by Legislative Decree No. 26 of 18 March 2023) stipulates that providers of *online* marketplaces must inform consumers whether the third party offering goods, services, or digital content is a professional or not, on the basis of the declaration made to them by the third party.

In the event that the third party offering goods, services, or digital content claims to be a non-professional, *online* marketplace providers should provide a short statement to the effect that consumer rights under Union law on consumer protection do not apply to the contract concluded. In addition, consumers should be informed about how the contractual obligations are shared between the third party offering goods, services, or digital content and the *online* marketplace provider. This information should be provided in a clear and comprehensible manner and not only by means of *standard* terms and conditions or similar contractual documents.

The EU Commission recently intervened with dir. 771/2019/EU, transposed into our law by legislative decree no. 170 of 4 November 2021, which amended Article 128 of the Consumer Code, in paragraph 2, lett. c, which included within the notion of seller also "*the platform provider if it acts for purposes within the framework of its activity and as a contractual counterparty of the consumer for the supply of digital content or digital services.*"

More specifically, with reference to contracts for the supply of digital content and digital services, the notion of professional also includes "*the platform provider if he acts for purposes within the scope of his business and as the contractual counterparty of the consumer for the supply of digital content or digital services.*"

Recently, the Court of Justice of the EU intervened in the case of the offering on platforms of products not put into circulation by the manufacturer, and delivered to

[41] Busch (2018), p. 2 ff.

Amazon by other manufacturers with the ruling "Louboutin"[42], a manufacturer of women's footwear with registered trademarks, invoking an infringement of the exclusive rights deriving to it from the trademark in question, had brought an action for infringement of its trademark against Amazon before the *Tribunal d'arrondissement de Luxembourg*. Louboutin requested that Amazon be declared liable for the infringement of the trade mark and that it cease, on pain of a fine, to make use in the course of trade of signs identical with the trade mark throughout the territory of the European Union, and that it be ordered to pay compensation for the damage allegedly caused by such use.

The Court upheld the appeal and resolved the question in Louboutin's favor. The Court ruled as follows: "*the provider of an online sales website, which includes, in addition to its own sales offers, an online marketplace, can be considered to use a sign identical with another person's European Union trade mark for goods identical with those for which that mark is registered, where third-party sellers offer for sale on that marketplace, without the consent of the proprietor of that mark, such goods bearing that sign, if a reasonably well-informed and reasonably observant user of that website establishes a link between the services of that operator and that sign; which is the case in particular where, taking account of all the elements characterising the situation in question, such a user might have the impression that it is that operator which markets, in its own name and on its own behalf, the goods bearing that sign. What is relevant in that regard is the fact that that operator uses a uniform method of presentation of the offers published on its website, displaying at the same time the advertisements relating to the goods which it sells in its own name and on its own account and those relating to goods offered by third-party sellers on that market, that it displays its logo as a well-known distributor on all those advertisements and that it offers to third-party sellers, in the context of the marketing of the goods bearing that sign, additional services consisting, in particular, in the storage and dispatch of those goods.*

7 Conclusions

In conclusion, it is possible to draw the threads of the discourse with some final considerations that, however, do not claim to exhaust complex issues raised in the practical application of a conspicuous new regulatory apparatus that evidently also needs the interpretative contribution of the European judge. Primarily, it is evident that a rigid legislative notion, such as that of consumer, is inadequate. This notion has become obsolete in the face of the evolution of commercial techniques and the emergence of new needs. A thorough and proper reconsideration is imperative.

In any event, it is evident that the European legislator has recognized the necessity to implement specific safeguards for the legal entities within the digital

[42] Corte Giust. UE, 22 dicembre 2022, C-148/21 e C-184/2021.

ecosystem, encompassing both user-consumers and micro-businesses. However, these protections are subject to a distinct regulatory framework, given the heterogeneity of the vulnerabilities inherent in the contractual relationships between digital platforms and users, as well as between platforms and micro-businesses.

It is evident that the risk of manipulating the information provided to the consumer may influence their consumption choices, particularly within the context of the digital market. In this environment, seemingly neutral information can elicit specific expectations in the consumer-user regarding the implicit meaning of its subtext. This phenomenon, often termed "dark patterns" has garnered significant attention in the field of user experience design, particularly in the context of digital platforms.[43] These patterns frequently manifest within the user interface of the platform itself. However, it is important to note that Article 25 of the Digital Services Act (DSA) expressly prohibits such practices.

This development prompts a critical examination of the legal mechanisms designed to safeguard consumers and users, which were primarily developed for the offline context (e.g., the regulatory framework for unfair terms as outlined in Directive 93/13/EU, which recently commemorated its 30th anniversary since its integration into European legislation[44]) and the discipline on unfair commercial practices as per directive 2005/29/EU) that do not seem to be better adapted to the online market, which brings with it some decidedly peculiar characteristics and probably require, with the law unchanged, a new effort to reconceptualize the current legal categories ex dir. 2005/29/EU) that do not seem to fit best as far as the online market is concerned, which brings with it some decidedly peculiar features and which probably impose, with the law unchanged, a new effort to reconceptualize the current consumer legal categories and the relative forms of protection.

Technological evolution, particularly the emergence of new AI systems in the digital market, underscores the need for both legislators and interpreters to maintain a high level of vigilance. This is particularly salient when considering the pronounced information asymmetry that underlies bargaining between users and platforms that possess technological power.

References

Bassan F (2021) Digital platforms and global law. Elgar

Bauman Z (2007) Homo consumens. Lo sciame inquieto dei consumatori e la miseria degli esclusi. Trento

Benedetti G (1998) Tutela del consumatore e autonomia contrattuale. Riv Trim Dir Proc Civ pp 21 ff

Buiten M (2020) The Digital Services Act: From Intermediary Liability to Platform Regulation. Available at SSRN https://papers.ssrn.com/sol3/papers.cfm?abstract_id=3876328

[43] Orlando (2024), p. 64 ss.

[44] Pagliantini (2024).

Busch C (2016) Crowdsourcing consumer confidence. How to regulate online rating and review systems in the collaborative economy. In: De Franceschi A (ed) European contract law and the digital single market. The implications of the digital revolution. Intersentia, Cambridge, p 225
Busch C (2018) European model rules for online intermediary platforms. Nomos, p 2 ff
Camilleri E (2024) Unfair commercial practices, safety net and new vulnerabilities: perspectives and limits. Nuove leggi civ comm, p 200
Caterina R (2011) Pratiche commerciali scorrette e psicologia del consumatore. In Studi in onore di Aldo Frignani. Nuovi orizzonti del diritto comparato europeo e transnazionale, Naples, p 123 ff
Fink M (2018) Digital co-regulation: designing a supranational legal framework for the platform economy. Eur Law Rev, p 47 ss
Giorgianni M (1968) Buon padre di famiglia. Noviss Dig It II:597
Giorgianni M (1975) L'inadempimento. Corso di diritto civile, Milan
Gonzalez Vaquè L (2015) El TJUE confirma y precisa su jurisprudencia sobre la eficacia informativa de la lista de ingredientes: la sentencia "Teekanne" de 4 de junio de 2015. Riv Dir Alim, pp 43 ff
Harvey D (2017) Collisions in the digital paradigm: law and the rule making in the Internet age. Hart, Oxford
Irti N (2016) Un diritto incalcolabile, Turin
Nozick R, Routley R (1962) Escaping the Good Samaritan paradox. Mind, p 377 ff
Orlando S (2024) A proposito dei deceptive designs (già dark) patterns. Mercato digitale e tutela dei consumatori. Prove di futuro, a cura di G. Grisi e S. Tommasi, Turin, p 64 ff
Pagliantini S (2024) Le clausole abusive nei contratti dei consumatori. Trent'anni di direttiva 93/13. Piacenza
Piraino F (2010) Diligence, good faith and reasonableness in unfair commercial practices. Eur Dir Priv pp 1117 ff
Rabitti M (2019) Il diritto dei consumatori. In: Lemme G (ed) Diritto ed economia del mercato, Padua, pp 349–351
Riefa C, Clausen C (2019) Towards fairness in digital influencers' marketing practices. J Eur Consum Mark Law, p 66 ff
Rochet JC, Tirole J (2003) Platform competition in two-side markets. J Eur Econ Assoc p 990 ff
Rossi Carleo L (2005) Sub art. 4 - Educazione del consumatore. In Alpa G, Rossi Carleo L (eds) Codice del consumo. Commentario, Naples, pp 14 ff
Rossi Carleo L (2010) Consumatore, consumatore medio, investitore cliente: frazionamento e sintesi nella disciplina delle pratiche commerciali scorrette. Eur Dir Priv 2010, p 688
Simon H (1985) Models of bounded rationality. MIT Press, Boston
Thaler RH (2015) Misbehaving. The birth of behavioural economics, Norton, New York
Thaler RH, Sunstein CR (2009) Nudge: the gentle way to improve decisions. Yale University Press
Trubiani F (2023) Le incerte sorti del 'consumatore medio' tra condizionamenti cognitivi e nuove aperture della giurisprudenza. Accademia, p 117 ff
Trubiani F (2024) Influencer marketing: libertà della scelta di consumo nel mondo digitale. Dir Inf p 385 ff
Tversky A, Kahnemann D (1974) Judgment under uncertainty: heuristics and biases. Science, p 1124 ff
Zaccaria A (1997) Il diritto privato europeo nell'epoca del postmoderno. Riv Dir Civ p 377
Zoppini A (2020) Il diritto privato e i suoi confini. Bologna, p 208
Zoppini A (2022) Contratto ed economia comportamentale. Enc Dir I Tematici, Milan, p 313 ff

Contract Formation

Rosaria Giampetraglia, Maria Pia Pignalosa, and Francesca Zagaria

Contents

Sections 1, 2, 3 and 4 are attributed to Rosaria Giampetraglia, Sections 5, 6, 7 and 8 to Maria Pia Pignalosa, and Sections 9, 10, 11 and 12 to Francesca Zagaria.

R. Giampetraglia (✉) F. Zagaria
University of Naples "Parthenope", Naples, Italy
e-mail: rosaria.giampetraglia@uniparthenope.it;
francesca.zagaria@collaboratore.uniparthenope.it

M. P. Pignalosa
University of Rome "Foro Italico", Rome, Italy
e-mail: mariapia.pignalosa@uniroma4.it

R. Bocchini (ed.), *Digital Platforms - From Technical Foundations to Legal and Economic Implications*, https://doi.org/10.1007/978-3-032-07978-7_7

Abstract The contribution analyses the issue of contract formation in the digital world, focusing on the dynamics relating to the process of agreement formation. The authors also dwell on the purchases of minors on the web, highlighting the profiles concerning the provision of digital consent by the minor.

1 From Contracts in General to the New Cases Born of the Digital Revolution: A Transition in Progress

The rapid pace of digital transition,[1] especially in recent years, has significantly complicated the task of legally regulating phenomena, including economic activities, associated with technological innovations. In this context, the digital revolution[2] has inevitably impacted the fundamental concept of private patrimonial autonomy. As a result, it has become necessary to reconsider whether the traditional configuration of the contractual instrument[3] remains adequate for providing coherent solutions in a landscape marked by such profound transformations.[4] The commercialisation of the Internet[5] characterised by its universal and non-territorial nature,[6] the proliferation of electronic transactions[7] and the sudden shift from a

[1] On this concept, which can be defined as 'the path towards the widespread diffusion of information technologies in everyday life, mostly regarded as engines of collective progress', see Troiano (2022), p. 51 ff. For an interesting insight into computer, telematic and digital progress see Tosi (2010).

[2] See, for further discussion on the topic, *ex pluribus*, De Franceschi and Schulze (2019); Tulli (2020). For a discussion of the new risks and dangers brought about by this development, see Rodotà (2012), p. 312 ff.; Pirozzoli (2018), p. 213.

[3] See Zeno-Zencovich (2018), p. 99 ff.; Poncibò (2020), p. 4; Maggiore and Assenza (2024), p. 3 ff. on this point.

[4] It is undeniable that the increasingly widespread and pervasive use of the Internet has profoundly transformed the traditional paradigms of commercial relations. It has significantly expanded both the category of consumers (the so-called mass demand) and that providers of goods and services (so-called mass supply) while also introducing new mechanisms and faster rhythms of wealth circulation. These changes clearly influence the dynamics of bargaining. Cf. Solinas (2018), D'Elia (2021), p. 2.

[5] This definition refers to the role assumed by the Internet and virtual space in facilitating the exchange of goods and services, the foundation of e-commerce and their gradual evolution into a strategic component of the economic systems of technologically advanced countries. On this point, see, Tosi (2014), p. 1264 ff.

[6] See Battelli (2022a), p. 86.

[7] See, on this point, Piraino (2020).

property-based society to one focused on access to content,[8] with new mechanisms for the use of goods and services[9] have undoubtedly contributed, if we follow a possible chronological progression, to the emergence of the so-called telematic contract. In this case digital innovation has primarily impacted the mechanisms surrounding the conclusion of contracts particularly with regard to the formation of the agreement and the fulfilment of formal requirements.

Subsequently, with the emergence of the 'contract involving digital object (or content)', it is the digital element itself that becomes the subject of the contract, governing the purchase, use, ownership or exchange of goods, services or rights that exist and function in digital form.[10] Finally, with the recent development of the so-called algorithmic contract or artificial intelligence contract,[11] the digital component takes the form of an algorithm or computational protocol capable of replacing the will or actions of the parties in the formation or execution phases of the contractual scheme.[12]

The widespread adoption of these new contractual forms has naturally raised the timely question of whether they require specific regulation or whether, and to what extent, traditional conceptual categories, such as those governing the formation of agreement, remain adequate.[13]

As a matter of principle, it should be noted from the outset that the advancement of technology and multimedia, even within the contractual sphere, has not been deemed[14] to necessitate radical changes to the existing legal framework to date, as there is no break with the recognised cardinal principles of the regulatory framework.[15]

The digital element, in fact, primarily affects the mode of communication, rather than the substance of the contract itself,[16] regardless of whether it is concluded in the physical world or in a virtual environment.[17] This confirms the adaptability of

---

[8] For a more detailed discussion of this topic, see Auletta (2009).

[9] On this point, the progressive dematerialisation of the object of the contract has driven the development and spread of new markets based on novel rights of use, conditional upon compliance with strict regulatory constraints stemming from the need to ensure adequate protection of digital content. See Tosi (2010), p. 1268. For a discussion on the regulation of access contracts, see Palmieri (2022).

[10] Cf. Finocchiaro (2017), p. 189.

[11] By this definition, we refer to contracts based exclusively on the use of AI programmes. For further discussion, see, Alpa (2020); Taddei Elmi and Contaldo (2020); Ruffolo (2020).

[12] On this point, see Benedetti (2021), p. 413. For a more in-depth exploration of the distinction between the cases under consideration see Perlingieri and Lazzarelli (2016), p. 269 ff.; Salito (2019), p. 394 ff.; Tosi (2021), p. 210 ff.

[13] Cf. Gemma (2007), p. 237 ff.

[14] On this topic, see, among others, Gambino (1997); Delfini (2020); Tosi (2005).

[15] Cf. Camardi (2021), p. 875.

[16] See, Perlingieri (2011a), p. 272 ff.

[17] Gibson's (1984) description, p. 63, is noteworthy and particularly evocative: 'He tapped himself on the keyboard as he penetrated it and found an infinite blue space where colour-coded spheres were aligned, hanging from a tightly meshed grid of pale blue fluorescent light. In the non-space

traditional legal categories,[18] which continue to demonstrate a flexible capacity to respond to the significant pressure generated by emerging exogenous factors in an increasingly digital and interconnected society.

Nonetheless it is clear that, in light of ongoing technological advancement and the widespread adoption of technology-driven contractual models, the legal system must continue to explore its boundaries[19] in order to ensure the provision of adequate and timely responses. This will likely require targeted updates to contractual regulatory policies,[20] particularly considering the high level of technical complexity inherent in digital developments and the unique challenges posed by the growing use of artificial intelligence—whose disruptive potential to reshape the world as we know it remains difficult to fully grasp.[21]

Within this framework, and given the extraordinary pace of these evolutionary processes, any targeted regulatory interventions entrusted to the legislator should be guided by the principle of technological neutrality. That is, such interventions should avoid tailoring legal rules too closely to specific applications or forms of information technology, in order to prevent the vicious cycle of rapid obsolescence affecting both the regulated technologies and the corresponding regulatory instruments.[22]

2 The Dynamics of Contract Formation: Preliminary Phase and Information Obligations

The conclusion of *online* contracts, and the various stages leading up to it, represents, to date, one of the most distinctive aspects in the analysis of e-commerce.[23]

It is therefore appropriate to reflect on the digital meeting of wills upon which contractual agreements between parties are based. The issue remains central to the current legal debate,[24] especially in light of the need to safeguard fundamental rights and protect a wide range of values of particular importance, such as consumer protection and the safeguarding of personal data. These rights may be jeopardised by the speed at which digital technologies facilitate and accelerate the

---

of the matrix, the interior of the construct of certain data possessed unlimited subjective dimensions'.

[18] For an in-depth study of the evolutionary *process* of the aforementioned civil law categories, see, *ex pluribus*, Lipari (2013).

[19] On this issue, the analysis by Roppo (2020), p. 153, is particularly interesting.

[20] Even within the European Union, given the scale of the phenomena in *question.*

[21] Astone (2021), p. 3 ff.

[22] See, on this point, Troiano (2022), p. 59.

[23] See, Adamo (2022), p. 158.

[24] For an overview, see, *ex pluribus*, Benedetti (2005), p. 323 ff.; Cavalaglio (2006); Favale (2013), p. 2555 ff.; Delfini (2020); Pascuzzi (2020); Perlingieri et al. (2020); Perlingieri and Lazzarelli (2016), pp. 281–286; Perlingieri (2011b), p. 274; Tosi (2010).

formation of contractual consent.[25] Within the e-commerce sphere, different contractual models can be identified, each involving a varying degree of legal protection: (a) *business to business* (B2B);[26] (b) *business to consumer* (B2C);[27] (c) *consumer to consumer* (C2C);[28] (d) *business to administration* (B2A);[29] (d) *peer to peer* (P2P).[30]

The procedure for forming telematic contracts, irrespective of the ongoing debate regarding the exact legal classification of negotiations, is governed by the provision of Articles 12 and 13 of Legislative Decree 70/2003. This regulatory framework has been significantly reinforced, particularly in the context of B2C contracts, by Legislative Decree 21/2014, implementing Directive 2011/83/EU on consumer rights, as well as by EU Regulation 2018/302.[31]

Given their nature, these types of contracts are also subject to both the provisions of the Consumer Code and those of Legislative Decree 185/1999 concerning consumer protection in distance contracts.

More specifically, Article 3 of the aforementioned decree, in line with principles also established at the European Union level, mandates that the professional must comply with a comprehensive set of information obligations aimed at protecting the consumer[32] with whom the contract is intended to be concluded.[33]

Accordingly, the other party must be informed by the professional[34] prior to the conclusion of the contract, and must subsequently receive confirmation of such information in writing or 'on another durable medium available and accessible to

---

[25] See Addante (2016), p. 41.

[26] Also known as a 'third contract', this term refers to an agreement concluded between professionals, a commercial relationship between two companies with one of which is interested in purchasing the products of the other. See, Gitti and Villa (2008).

[27] The reference here is to contracts concluded between a professional and a consumer.

[28] This category includes contracts concluded between consumers who are both acting outside their professional activities (e.g. *online* auctions).

[29] This therefore refers to all relationship between business and government, where the contract in this case is between a professional and a public entity.

[30] *Social lending* (or P2P *lending*) is one of the most common types of contracts and involves lending between private individuals via the Internet.

[31] The following aspects fall within the scope of these information obligations: the identity of the professional, the identification of the services, the regulation of the established relationship and the right of withdrawal, the clarification of the methods for resolving possible disputes, and the specification of the functional characteristics of the digital products. Additional information obligations are also set out in Legislative Decrees No. 59/2010 and No. 70/2003, alongside further requirements established by the legislator (in accordance with Article 6(8) of Directive 2011/83/EU). See Trezza (2021), p. 295.

[32] For a discussion of pre-contractual information obligations, see, among others, Di Donna (2008).

[33] See Adamo (2022), p. 159.

[34] As stated in the second paragraph of the same article: 'in a clear and comprehensible manner, by any means appropriate to the technique of distance communication used, observing in particular the principles of good faith and fairness in commercial transactions, assessed in the light of the need to protect particularly vulnerable categories of consumers'.

them' either before or at the time of performance of the contract, regarding[35] '(a) the identity of the supplier and, in the case of contracts requiring prepayment, the supplier's address; (b) the essential characteristics of the good or service; (c) the price of the good or service, including all taxes and levies; (d) the delivery costs; (e) the arrangements for payment, delivery of the good or provision of the service and any other manner of performance of the contract; (f) the existence of the right of withdrawal or its exclusion pursuant to Article 5(3); (g) the procedures and times form the return or withdrawal of the good in case of exercise of the right of withdrawal; (h) the cost of using the distance communication technique, when calculated on a basis other than the basic rate; (i) the duration of the validity of the offer and of the price; (j) the minimum duration of the contract in cases of contracts for the supply of goods or provision of services with continuous or periodic performance'. Similarly, Article 4, imposes additional information obligations on the trader prior to the execution of the contract, concerning: '(a) information on the conditions and procedures for exercising the right of withdrawal under Article 5, including the cases referred to in Article 5(2); (b) the geographical address of the supplier's place of business to which the consumer may submit complaints; (c) information regarding existing after-sales services and commercial guarantees; (d) the conditions for withdrawing from the contract in the case of an indefinite duration or exceeding one year'. Even more specific, then, is the legislation governing e-commerce which, as noted, also applies to online contracts. Reference is made to legislative decree 70/2003 enacted in implementation of the relevant European Directive and applicable, unless otherwise agreed between the parties, also to subjects other than consumers. Article 12 of this decree sets forth further detailed information obligations, requiring the professional to inform the consumer in a 'clear, comprehensible and unequivocal manner' of the following: '(a) the various technical steps to be followed to conclude the contract; (b) the manner in which the concluded contract will be stored and how it can be accessed; (c) the technical means made available to the consumer to detect and correct input errors prior to submission of the order to the supplier; (d) any codes of conduct to which the professional adheres and the means to access them electronically; (e) the languages available to conclude the contract in addition to Italian; (f) an indication of the means for dispute resolution'.

It is also worth noting that, as provided under Article 13 of these provisions, the aforementioned rules apply where the recipient of an 'information society' good or service transmits his or her order electronically; however, they do not govern 'contracts concluded exclusively by exchange of email messages or equivalent individual communications'.[36]

As will be detailed below, the new European Regulation on Digital Services impacts this regulatory framework. With the objective of ensuring consumer protection, it establishes a range of information obligations for digital market operators, aimed at informing users of the terms of service and associated requirements. Moreover, it prohibits platforms from engaging in misleading practices capable

[35] This is in accordance with the provisions of Article 4 of Legislative Decree 185/1999.

[36] See Adamo (2022), p. 160.

of influencing consumer choices. As will be further detailed below, the new European Regulation on digital services[37] impacts this regulatory framework. With the objective of ensuring consumer protection, it establishes a range of information obligations for digital market operators, aimed at informing users of the terms of service and associated requirements. Moreover it prohibits platforms from engaging in misleading practices capable of influencing customer choices. This regulation further emphasises the need to guarantee transparency in online contracting and to prevent unfair commercial practices. For instance, it provides that commercial users will be granted access to data generated within platforms holding a dominant market position (so-called gatekeepers), in order to advertise their offers and conclude contracts outside of the *gatekeeper*'s own platform's ecosystem.[38]

3 Contract Formation Dynamics: The Conclusion of the Contract

Given that under our legal system, pursuant to Article 1326 of the Civil Code,[39] the moment of formation of the contractual agreement is identified in the exchange of offer and acceptance,[40] it becomes essential to assess whether the traditional civil law frameworks may be seamlessly applied to online contract[41] as well.

[37] The so-called Digital Service Act in the intentions of the EU legislator aims, among other things, to ensure a safe and trustworthy *online* environment, protecting the fundamental rights of users of digital services, and combating disinformation and the dissemination of illegal content. Coming into force in November 2022, the framework will apply to all intermediary service providers from 17 February 2024. However, already as of 25 August 2023, the Regulation has applied to large platforms and search engines as identified by the European Commission Very Large Online Platform (VLOP) and Very Large Online Search Engine (VLOSE) . For a more detailed discussion, see, among others, Tripodi (2022), p. 33 ff.; Del Gatto (2023), p. 724 ff.; Tommasi (2023), p. 279 ff.

[38] In the event of non-compliance, potential infringements are subject to stringent sanctions, as the European Commission is empowered to impose fines up to 10% of the *gatekeeper*'s total worldwide turnover in the preceding financial year. In cases of repeated infringements, such penalties may be increased to a maximum of 20% of the total worldwide turnover in the preceding financial year.

[39] Moreover, it is expressly provided that the agreement shall be deemed perfected at the moment the offeror receives notice of offeree's acceptance.

[40] The prevailing scholarly opinion held that, owing to the inherent peculiarities of the Internet—marked by the absence of dialogue, spoken words and gestures—the formation of a legally binding agreement could not be recognised. As it was argued, 'l'uso telematico delle parole non è uso del linguaggio, ma di meri simboli, fungibili con altri, e destinati a offrire soluzioni alternative, tra le quali si compirà la scelta'. Irti (1999a), p. 364; Irti (1999b), p. 273; Irti (2000), p. 601; *contra* Oppo (1984), p. 525; Bianca (2002), p. 43.

[41] On this matter, two prevailing doctrinal approaches can be identified. According to the first view, the traditional offer-and-acceptance framework would not be applicable to contracts concluded

In such contracts, the parties agree to exchange goods or services for consideration, which today is no longer necessarily and exclusively monetary. Rather, consideration may also consist of the user's provision of personal data in favour of the operator of the online service.[42] It is the operator who subsequently monetises such data, through targeted advertising tailored to consumer preferences, as inferred from the data generated by the users in the course of using the service[43] which today is no longer necessarily or exclusively monetary. Rather, consideration may also consist of the user's provision of personal data in favour of the operator of the online service. At the outset, it is appropriate to observe that the legislature, in the wording of Article 67(2) of the Consumer Code, by specifying that the civil law provisions concerning the validity, formation and effectiveness of contracts may be applied in matters not expressly governed by the Code itself, bears witness to the enduring suitability of the 1942 Code in addressing the evolving needs of modern society. Similarly, Article 13(1) of Legislative Decree No. 70/2003 clarified that 'the rules on the conclusion of contracts also apply in cases where the recipient of a good or an information society service places his order by telematic means'. Accordingly, as confirmed by authoritative legal scholarship, the technical specificities of computer-based systems of distance communication do not, in themselves, require the adoption of new or innovative procedures for the conclusion of the contract.[44] The mechanisms governing contract formation remain, those provided for under the Civil Code, albeit potentially subject to reinterpretation in light of the specific characteristics of the telematic medium.[45]

In this context, a simple click on a product image displayed on a device screen, depending on the circumstances, is equated with a request for information

online. This is due to the extreme rapidity inherent in electronic communications, whereby the transmission and receipt of acceptance occur virtually simultaneously. Cf. Pasquino (2002), p. 69 ff. In contrast, a second line of scholarship contends that the provisions of Article 1326 of the Italian Civil Code remain applicable even in the context of electronically concluded contracts. This position is grounded in the observation that electronic mail (email) services may deliver messages with a temporal delay, such that the acceptance does not necessarily coincide with the moment of its transmission. The email provider, in fact, may process and route the message after a lapse of time, thereby maintaining a distinction between dispatch and actual receipt of acceptance. See Adamo (2022), p. 161; Tosi (2003), p. 101 ff.

[42] At the moment of contract formation, personal data and information are disclosed which, on the one hand, are acquired by the contractual counterparty for the purpose of performing the agreement, and, on the other hand, are retained by the platform operator who, although a third party to the contract, provides the technological infrastructure enabling the execution of the relevant transactions. See, on this point, Camardi (2021), p. 877. More generally, on the creation and control of personal data with respect to contracts, Quarta (2020); Versaci (2020).

[43] On this point, Major and Absence (2024), p. 9.

[44] Mazzamuto (2017), p. 218. The author clarifies that the use of information technology in contractual negotiation requires specific regulation solely in relation to obligations of information and the right of withdrawal, with the aim of preventing potential abuses of contractual power by the professional party.

[45] Ricciuto (2004), p. 13.

(pre-contractual phase), a purchase request (invitation to offer) or a request for the dispatch of goods (acceptance of the offer).

That said, there are essentially two prevailing methods through which the finalisation of *online* contracts may occur.

In so-called direct communication contracts, the exchange of the parties' declarations of intent, aimed at reaching a contractual agreement, and subject to the applicable regulatory framework, takes place through mechanisms and tools, such as, but not limited to, email, messaging services, online forums or other instruments capable of enabling an effective (*one-to-one*) communication between the parties.[46] In such cases, the contract is considered concluded according to the traditional scheme outlined in Article 1326 of the Civil Code: a proposal made by one party is followed by the corresponding acceptance of the other. For instance, where the parties communicate via email, the contract is deemed concluded at the moment the acceptance reaches the proposer's email address.[47] Contracts involving indirect communication, such as so-called click-wrap[48] or point and click[49] agreements, are, by contrast, far more prevalent than those based on direct exchanges. In particular, in such cases, an offer published on an e-commerce site, which is complete and contains all the essential elements of the agreement, constitutes an offer to the public.[50] Accordingly, the general

---

[46] Foderini (2021), p. 21.

[47] Accordingly,, the contract is formed in accordance with the codified model governing agreements entered into between absentees through the application of the rule set forth in Article 1335 of the Civil Code. On this point, see Battelli and Brizzolari (2024), p. 111.

[48] In such cases, acceptance is effected through the positive act of clicking the virtual button signifying adherence to the contractual terms.

[49] Battelli (2014), p. 1054.

[50] This includes instances in which online sales platforms offer electronic catalogues listing goods or services available for purchase, which the consumer may acquire by completing and submitting an electronic form to the offeror. This includes cases in which *online* sales platforms offer electronic catalogues listing goods or services available for purchase, which the consumer may acquire by completing and submitting an electronic form to the offeror. A part of legal scholarship observes that where an offer is made telematically to an indeterminate number of recipients, such conduct constitutes a contractual proposal *ad incertam personam.* Conversely, where the contractual framework is unilaterally determined by the offeror, leaving no room for negotiation on the part of the other party, the resulting legal relationship qualifies as a contract of adhesion perfected at the moment of the recipient's acceptance. Furthermore, contractual liability may also arise on the part of the information society service provider when the user places an order via the online platform. On this point, it is worth noting that, in the context of distance communications implemented through telematic means: 'è possibile riscontrare strumenti interattivi di comunicazione molto avanzati in grado di permettere al consumatore di dialogare e negoziare il contenuto dell'accordo con l'imprenditore offerente, andando ben oltre una semplice scelta, peraltro normalmente imposta, tra aderire o rifiutare la proposta pubblicizzata mediante *website*'. In such scenarios, the manifestation of the consumer's intent does not occur through the so-called point and click mechanism applied to a contract rigidly predetermined in all its element. Rather, the user may be afforded the opportunity to select among various, potentially modifiable, options and, where available, to insert freely formulated content through textual input fields. See Battelli (2014), p. 1065 ff.

rule under Article 1326 of the Civil Code applies, requiring the offeror to receive the acceptance in order for the contract to be validly formed.[51]

Consent, therefore, is expressed by the simple act of clicking and the contract, together with its general terms and conditions, if any, is finalised through the selection of a virtual checkbox (the so-called box ticking) and/or the activation of a virtual 'I accept' button.

This final act is, on the one hand, commonly preceded by the users' completion of an online registration form, typically involving the creation of a personal account with a 'user ID' and 'password' and consequent acceptance of the contractual terms unilaterally prepared by the platform and, on the other hand, in certain cases, this act is subsequently followed or reinforced by conclusive conduct, within the meaning of Article 1327, of the Italian Civil Code, such as the transmission of debit or credit card details necessary to complete the transaction. Conversely, where the online offer is incomplete—as may be the case in auctions concluded in favour of the highest bidder—one is confronted with an *invitatio ad offerendum*[52] by the platform. In such scenarios, the party intending to purchase online assumes the role of offeror. The contract will, in that instance, be deemed concluded upon the buyer's receipt of the seller's acceptance of the proposal.[53]

Also falling within the category of contracts concluded through indirect communication are so-called browse-wrap agreements.[54] In this case, the formation of the contractual bond is deemed to occur by the mere performance of the *online* transaction, such as submitting an order or simply continuing to browse the website—despite the absence of any prior and express acceptance of the contractual terms and conditions.[55]

---

[51] In this sense, see, Delfini (2020), p. 90; Battelli (2014), p. 1063.

[52] This is the approach adopted by Amazon, which classifies its listings as mere invitations to treat rather than offers to the public, as can be inferred from the first clause of the General Conditions of Sale contained in the 'Legal Policies' section of its marketplace. In particular, it is expressly stated that the order shall be deemed accepted—and the contract consequently concluded—only upon the dispatch of the shipping confirmation email, pursuant to Amazon's terms and conditions. It has been observed, however, that each product listing on Amazon's platform includes an indication of the essential contractual elements, including price and availability, which may allow the purchaser's order to be construed as an act of acceptance. In this view, Amazon's dual confirmation process (comprising both the order receipt and the shipping confirmation emails) may be interpreted as a contract that is perfected immediately upon acceptance, but whose effectiveness remains subject to a suspensive condition—namely, verification of actual stock availability and subsequent dispatch.

[53] Although they share certain common features, the institutions under consideration differ in that, in the former case, all the constituent elements of a formal offer addressed to a plurality of recipients are present, whereas in the latter, by contrast, the proponent merely invites multiple potential purchasers to submit an offer.

[54] In this case, however, acceptance by browsing is relevant.

[55] With regard to the valid manifestation of consent to the general terms and conditions of an online contract, it is both necessary and sufficient that such terms be made knowable to the contracting party.

4 The Balance in *Online* Contracting: General Terms and Conditions and Unfair Terms

In the wake of the evolution of consumer protection mechanisms,[56] Legislative Decree No. 21/2014 introduced a set of pre-contractual and contractual information obligations applicable to contracts concluded by electronic means. These provisions must, in any case, be interpreted in light of the overarching principles of good faith enshrined in in Articles 1337 and 1375 of the Civil Code. The legislative intervention in question specifies the type of information that must be provided to the consumer, which is further supplemented by the obligations set forth in Legislative Decree No. 70/2003. These include not only the disclosures expressly required by law, but also any information likely to influence the formation of consent by the contracting parties.

By imposing such disclosure and documentation duties[57] on the professional trader, the consumer is, on the one hand placed in a position to make informed choices, and on the other, enabled to retain access to such information in order to assert their rights, even at a later stage, should the need arise.[58]

In this context, two aspects are undoubtedly of particular relevance and worthy of closer examination: first the knowledge and/or knowability of the general terms and conditions[59] governing telematic contracts, and second, the specific acceptance, within such contracts, of unfair terms—namely, clauses which, pursuant to Article 33 of the Consumer Code, despite the requirement of good faith, cause a significant imbalance in the parties' rights and obligations to the detriment of the consumer.[60] With regard to the first issue, prevailing case law, in the context of *point-and-click* contracting, it is not necessary for the general conditions of contract to be displayed within each screen forming the contractual pathway up to acceptance. It is generally deemed sufficient that the terms be accessible via a hyperlink to a dedicated or, alternatively, that they appear in a scrollable window prior to the finalisation of consent. Conversely, where the contract is concluded through an exchange of individual communications, the general conditions must be contained in a specific individual message.[61]

---

[56] Necessary in the context of a relationship marked by structural imbalance, wherein the economically dominant party, the professional, is in a position of advantage to the detriment of the consumer, who, as a weaker party, suffers from significant technical and informational asymmetries and is therefore endowed with reduced contractual power. See, on this point, *ex pluribus*, Roppo (2018), p. 695 et seq.; Roppo (2001), p. 23 et seq.; Zorzi and Galgano (2012), p. 76 et seq., Battelli (2022c), p. 939 et seq.

[57] See, Ricci (2005), p. 392.

[58] See Gambino (2020), p. 179; Moscarini (2001).

[59] The same principle, in the context of online contracting, may be articulated in various forms, as is evident from para. 3 of Article 10 of Directive 2000/31/EC, according to which, quite simply, 'le clausole e le condizioni generali del contratto proposte al destinatario devono essere messe a sua disposizione in un modo che gli permetta di memorizzarle e riprodurle'. See, Gemma (2007), p. 276.

[60] On this point, D'Elia (2021), p. 24.

[61] See, Gemma (2007), p. 276.

More problematic, however is the matter of the specific written approval of unfair terms by the adhering party. According to a minority view, in the context of online transactions, the consumer's 'double-click'—or the act of selecting a check-box followed by the activation of a confirmation button—may be considered functionally equivalent to a written signature,[62] thereby satisfying the requirements of Article 1341, paragraph 2, of the Civil Code.[63]

Part of the doctrine has, however rejected this interpretation, asserting that the unfair terms contained in telematic contracts may only be validly accepted through the use of an electronic signature, and more precisely, a digital one.[64]

However, considering the requirement of form *ad substantiam* and the validity of abusive clauses contained in a telematic contract as being subject to the user's signature by means of one of these electronic signatures raises issues of compatibility with the provisions laid down in Articles 33 and 34 of the Consumer Code. At this point, recourse may be had to the concept of protective nullity, a legal category designed to safeguard the consumer in cases involving the inclusion of unfair terms. In general, Article 36 of the Consumer Code provides that 'clauses considered unfair pursuant to Articles 33 and 34[65] are null and void, while remainder of the contract remains valid', while, the paragraph 3 of the same provision further specifies that 'nullity operates solely for the benefit of the consumer and may be declared ex officio by the judge', which must therefore assess the unfairness of the clause in light of the imbalance between the rights and obligations arising from the agreement.

The discipline in question, establishes a partial and relative nullity, which is actionable solely by the consumer and may be raised *ex officio* by the judge, capable of rendering ineffective exclusively the specific contractual provision that is *contra legem*;[66] in any event, this framework modifies the traditional characteristics of nullity as governed by Article 1419 of the Civil Code, particularly with respect to the notions of absoluteness, total ineffectiveness of the contract and standing to initiate

[62] The Civil Court of Cassation, Labour Section, has affirmed that the reproduction of a file or digital document prepared by a professional and intended for use in an indefinite number of legal relationships also constitutes the use of a standard form. See Court of Cassation 22 March 2006 no. 6314 in *Foro.it,* 7–8, 2006, 2035.

[63] See Addante (2016), p. 81.

[64] See Battelli (2014), p. 1079.

[65] More specifically, Article 33(2) of the Consumer Code sets out a list of clauses included in the so-called grey list, whose unfairness is presumed, albeit rebuttably. In such cases, it is for the professional to demonstrate that the clause is not unfair, either because it reproduces the content of legislative provisions or of one of the sources referred to in Article 34, paragraph 3 of the Consumer Code, or because it was the result of an individual negotiation allowing the consumer to influence its formulation. Conversely, Article 36 of the Consumer Code identifies further clauses, falling under the so-called black list, in respect of a conclusive (*iuris et de iure*) presumption of unfairness operates thereby excluding any possibility of rebuttal. More generally it should be noted that unfair terms constitute an open category: the consumer, therefore, may demonstrate that a clause, although not expressly listed by statute, nonetheless creates a significant imbalance between the parties in the rights and obligations under the contract in breach of the principle of objective good faith. Thus, Caringella and Buffoni (2025), p. 1103.

[66] To this effect, Mazzamuto (2017), p. 257.

proceedings.[67]Consequently, with regard to the issue of *online* contracts, under consideration, it may happen that the contract is perfected through the *point and click* system and the unfair clauses, pursuant to Art. 1341, second paragraph, of the Civil Code, will be effective only if made specifically approvable by electronic signature. However, in contracts with consumers, even the use of a qualified or digital signature may be deemed inadequate to demonstrate the negotiation necessary for the approval of such unfair clauses.

5 The Procedural Private Autonomy and the Receipt of the Order pursuant to Article 13, Legislative Decree 9 April 2003, no. 70

The purpose of these pages is to ascertain whether, and within what limits, the parties may affect the procedure described in Article 13, legislative decree no. 70/2003 by modifying it: (i) i.e. by transforming, under a configurative contractual clause, the acknowledgement of receipt from a post-contractual obligation to a final act of the contractual procedure; (ii) and whether they may transform, what is conceived by the legislature as a consensual contract, into a real contract by the will of the parties (or of the professional alone).

For the first eventuality mentioned, the formula of the agreement would become more complex than the general scheme under Art. 13, Legislative Decree No. 70/2003, as it would contain an additional element: agreement = offer (to the public) + acceptance + confirmation of the order.[68]

Under the scheme outlined, therefore, the contract would be concluded, not when the acceptance of the public offer reaches the offeror's address, but only if and when the consumer receives confirmation of his order-acceptance from the other contracting party.

Those who have delved into the study of configuration clauses have recognised how the procedure described should be considered admissible insofar as it would not affect superior or unavailable interests.[69]

It is also noted that the scheme described, although it aggravates the process of contract formation, better serves the interests of the parties.

Suffice it to say that the consumer does not run the risk of seeing his order unsatisfied because of the scarcity of the goods concerning the acceptances (because according to this procedure the contract will be concluded only when the receipt of the order reaches the consumer's address) and the trader, for his part, is not exposed to compensation for damages, to which he would be obliged if, having concluded the contract under Art. 1326 of the Civil Code, because of the scarcity of the goods,

[67] See Tosi (2014), p. 278 ff.

[68] Benedetti (2005), p. 408; in the same sense also Tosi (2010), p. 199.

[69] Tosi (2010).

he is unable to fulfil his obligation to all those who have subscribed to the offer to the public.

This procedural variation would not be precluded by the letter of the provision either. The exceptions prohibited by Article 13 Legislative Decree 70/2003 are only those that diminish the level of protection it provides.[70] Paragraph 2 of the provision in question, in prescribing that in the relationship between consumer and professional, the latter must without undue delay acknowledge receipt of the recipient's order, does indeed lay down a post-contractual obligation that cannot be derogated from (when one party is a consumer), but it does not state that the parties cannot transform this obligation into an element of the formation procedure.

The interpreters who have suggested this solution on the basis of a careful and in-depth study have recognised a power of procedural autonomy for the parties.[71] Taking their cue also from the contractual practice that has developed in the field of *e-commerce* and on the basis of some significant positive indices, this doctrine has questioned the traditional notion [72,73] of private autonomy, hypothesising that it may also be expressed in the field of the ways in which a contract is formed.[74]

Retracing some passages of a much more complex and articulated reasoning, carried out in a monographic work a few years ago, the author—in setting himself the objective of verifying in what situations and within what limits private autonomy can affect the manner of construction of the contractual agreement—moves from the analysis of the provisions dedicated to the formation of the contract and among these he elects the classic sequence of proposal and acceptance as a model.[75]

---

[70] Benedetti (2002), p. 409; Tosi (2010), p. 199.

[71] Benedetti (2002).

[72] On the notion of private autonomy see, among many others, the contributions of Sacco (1987); Pugliatti (1959), p. 366; Scognamiglio (1984), p. 88 ff. See, finally, Di Raimo (2003) (2023), p. 83.

[73] On this subject, see Benedetti (1969), p. 35, where we read that 'Private autonomy is essentially the power to fashion different types. Not procedures'. But read also the more recent Id., *La formazione del contratto e l'inizio di esecuzione. Dal codice civile ai principi di diritto europeo dei contratti, in Eur. e dir. priv.,* 2005, 2, 337; Betti (1966), p. 5; Ferri (1970), p. 141 ff.

[74] Romano (1961), p. 80, was among the first to recognise a 'freedom to configure' contractual procedures for private individuals. Perlingieri (2007), p. 65. More recently, Conte (2017), p. 596, where he investigates, precisely with regard to e-commerce and contracts regulated by Article 51(2) of the Civil Code, what are the spaces in which private procedural autonomy can express itself. Until Benedetti's monographic study (2002), *passim*, the relationship between private autonomy and the formation of the contract had not yet been investigated through a systematic investigation and on a general level, but in relation to specific profiles. In this more specific perspective see the contributions of Nuzzo (1972), p. 549 ff; Zimatore (1985), p. 129 ff; Di Gravio (1989), p. 68 ff; Cenni (1998); D'Amico (1996), p. 17; more recently see Cicero (2019), p. 16 ff.

[75] Benedetti, p. 28, states that the scheme outlined in Art. 1326 of the Civil Code, far from representing the rule, as opposed to the exceptions that would be constituted by the subsequent particular schemes, is rather one of the ways of concluding the contract. The author points out how widespread among interpreters is the tendency to assign to Art. 1326 of the Civil Code a role of pre-eminence with respect to the rules governing the conclusion of the contract: Roppo (2001),

Article 1326 Civil Code represents the paradigm against which to measure the variations introduced not only by the other formative schemes, but also by the contracting parties themselves through pacts, clauses and conventions. Compared to the model indicated, one distinguishes between simpler procedures, which dispense with acceptance, contenting themselves with execution or silence (Art. 1327 Civil Code and Art. 1333 Civil Code, respectively) and heavier schemes for which the agreement must be accompanied by delivery or must be consecrated in a given form.[76] In relation to the other procedures, Art. 1326 Civil Code would have both a general and a residual value: whenever another (simplified or aggravated) scheme is applicable, the general rule yields to the particular scheme.

The discretional criterion to be referred to in order to elaborate a *summa divisio* within the category of contracts would be that centred on simplified agreement contracts and aggravated agreement contracts.

Each procedure is designed according to a criterion of expediency that serves to protect the different interests of the parties that justify different choices as to the way in which the completion of the contract can be achieved.[77]

Having attributed to the agreement the connotation of a normative fact,[78] the author clarifies that this circumstance does not bring with it the typicality of the acts capable of achieving it. There would be no historical or systematic reasons justify-

pp. 96–97, orders the different regulatory schemes according to a hierarchical relationship. From the rules one would derive a 'general scheme, intended to apply in principle to the generality of contracts: the scheme defined by Art. 1326, with the important addition of Art. 1335. And particular schemes are derived, which apply to particular classes of contracts in derogation from the general scheme'; Bianca (2002), p. 227, uses the expression 'ordinary scheme' to describe the conclusion procedure described by Art. 1326 of the Civil Code; for Gorla (1956), p. 926 ff., the scheme of Art. 1326 of the Civil Code is that of 'exchange'.

[76] Benedetti (2002), p. 20, borrowing Irti's terminology on form, states that, even with regard to agreement, strong cases could be recognised, described through the equation agreement = will of the parties + form or delivery; the strength of which would be measured in relation to the weak reference scheme for which the law considers the mere meeting of wills sufficient.

[77] Benedetti (2002), p. 23 ff., recalling the plurality of the formation procedures as well as the flexibility of the agreement, functional to guaranteeing the different interests of the parties involved, observes how 'sometimes the interest in knowing the will of the offeree is privileged (this is the scheme of art. 1326 Civil Code: agreement = exchange of declarations); sometimes it is preferred to guarantee a rapid conclusion of the transaction (art. 1327: agreement = proposal + execution). Sometimes again the type and content of the proposal justify the adhesive value of non-refusal (art. 1333 Civil Code: agreement = proposal + omission)'; see also the reflections of Benedetti (1969), p. 20.

[78] Benedetti (2002), p. 22, specifies that agreement as a normative fact means that its realisation is to be ascertained on the basis of exclusively legal criteria and parameters, eschewing ideological conceptions that cannot be used as criteria for solving problems. For the criticism of the concept of the 'mystical meeting of the wills', the words of Gorla (1956), p. 924 ff. are well known; Gorla (1966), p. 225 ff.; Benedetti (1969), p. 23 ff., is among the first to carry out an in-depth examination of the techniques, objectively considered, through which, according to positive law, consent is formed; Nuzzo (1972), p. 558, places himself in the same perspective. See also Maggiolo (2012), p. 80 ff.

ing the existence of a principle of typicality of the procedures for the formation of the contract.The manner of its formation, on the other hand, would respond to concrete needs in relation to which it is stated, 'it does not seem scandalous to envisage some explicative possibility for the autonomy of private individuals'.[79]

The rules on the formation of the contract would be characterised by a certain degree of ductility that would allow the parties, through the exercise of typical and atypical faculties, to adapt its content to the interests of which they are bearers, and this both through a greater simplification of the procedure and, conversely, through an aggravation of the time and forms of agreement (where the greater or lesser complexity is assessed based on the scheme taken as a model: Article 1326 of the Civil Code).

In examining the 'legally permissible voluntary aggravation of the procedure'[80] the interpreters note how now the offeror and now the parties have typical faculties through which they are empowered to direct the contract formation procedure. In particular, the offeror would enjoy a particularly privileged position because he is recognised as having the power to condition the *an of* the conclusion of the contract; he may fix the time limit within which the proposal remains effective, and he may provide that acceptance must be dressed up in a given form.

In this regard, it should be noted that these determinations often take the form of clauses that do not concern the content of the agreement but rather regulate the manner, time and form through which the agreement will be formed and that exhaust their effects within the contract formation procedure. The proposal could have a composite content: along with the essential elements of the contract to be concluded, there could also be rules of procedural content affecting the 'manner' by which the contract formation process will end.

Beyond the hypotheses in which it is the law itself that gives the proponent or the parties the power to determine the timing[81] and the forms[82] of acceptance, we recall by way of example certain clauses connected with the contract of sale by which the parties aggravate the procedure,[83] such as 'subject to confirmation', 'subject to sale', 'subject to approval of the house'.

---

[79] Benedetti (2002), p. 32, footnote 79.

Paying attention to the procedural interests underlying Art. 1327 of the Civil Code, Benedetti (1969), p. 333.

[80] Benedetti (2002), p. 279.

[81] Benedetti, p. 355 ff., focusing his attention on the contract of sale, which is so rich in procedural clauses, recalls the *reservation of approval under* Art. 1520 of the Civil Code with which, he observes, 'the legislator has regulated "faculties" by exercising which one of the parties can vary - aggravating it - the general scheme under Art. 1326 of the Civil Code'.

[82] Benedetti, p. 311 ff., cites the covenant on form regulated by Art. 1352 of the Civil Code as one of the hypotheses of 'voluntary aggravation legally permissible by constraints of form'.

[83] Benedetti, p. 365, note 5, clarifies that aggravating the procedure 'means taking away the value as a contractual fact from a set of declarations or conduct that, according to the law, should be sufficient to give rise to the contractual bond'.

These are clauses that, albeit to varying degrees, affect the 'determination of a moment or element that makes the contractual agreement final and complete'.[84]

An examination of the aforementioned legislative provisions shows us how the law, directly or through typified faculties, provides for numerous cases of aggravated agreement.

Consumer legislation, in particular, would be a very pertinent example of a trend inclined to aggravate the contract formation process through a considerable use of formal burdens and information requirements.

5.1 Continued. The Aggravated Agreement by Will of the Parties

With regard to the 'aggravated agreement by the will of the parties'[85] the doctrine under review proposes to ascertain 'whether and to what extent the agreement - as a sufficient element for the creation of the bond - places some limit on atypical aggravation'.[86] The survey data show how 'legal simplification never derogates from the principle of the agreement as a necessary element of the contract'; on the other hand, it would be the law itself that would derogate from the rule of the 'sufficiency of the agreement, where an interest - general or particular - justifies or imposes its abandonment'.

Even the Courts of legitimacy do not doubt the validity of a procedural aggravation that is brought about by a contractual clause. On several occasions, the judges of the Supreme Court have recognised the power of private autonomy to regulate the conclusive moment of the contract in a way that differs from what is prescribed by Art. 1326 and 1335 of the Civil Code.[87]

Applying the results of the survey to the procedure described in Article 13 of Legislative Decree No. 70/2003 and, having ascertained that the receipt of the order is not conceived by the legislature as a mechanism to aggravate the procedure of the formation of the contract for the protection of the consumer, the doctrine examined recognises the power of the parties themselves to regulate the procedure by making it more complex, i.e. by transforming a post-contractual

---

[84] Benedetti, p. 280.

[85] Benedetti, p. 364, highlights how 'the agreement, as a sufficient factor for the creation of the contractual bond, seems to give way in the face of derogations from private sources, due to interests that suggest an aggravation of the formative procedure'.

[86] Where, it bears repeating, the expression *aggravating the proceeding* means, as Benedetti, *Autonomia privata*, cited above, p. 365, footnote 5, 'to take away the value of a contractual fact from a set of declarations or conduct that, according to the law, should be sufficient to give rise to the contractual bond'.

[87] In this connection, among the most relevant are: Cass., 4 February 2000, no. 1239, *Assicuraz. Generali v. Quirci*, in *Giust. civ.*, (2001), p. 1361; Court of Cassation, 14 February 1992, no. 1823, *Cacciamani v. Mirenghi*, in *Nuova giur. civ.* comm. (1993), p. 13.

obligation to provide information into a phase of the process of the conclusion of the contract. The solution adopted does not affect the right to post-contractual information which is in any event guaranteed by Art. 51(7) of the Consumer Code itself, under which the professional is obliged to give confirmation of the contract concluded to the consumer.

In transforming the receipt of the order from a post-contractual obligation to a final act in the contractual formation procedure, the parties do not contradict the basic idea animating the 2011 directive on *Consumer Rights*: to protect the consumer also by burdening the contractual formation procedure; on the contrary, the configuration clause under consideration would confirm this logic.

In conclusion—if one moves from the conviction that the formation of a contract 'is not a matter of alleged logical or dogmatic principles, but delineates an area in which the concrete interests of those who, wishing to conclude a contract, are about to perform the acts necessary for its formation' dominate—it may be recognised that the parties have the power to conclude a new contract, albeit within the described limits, the power to fashion a new procedure for the formation of the contract, using a clause that does not concern the terms of the agreement, but rather, as in the case at hand, concerns the time when the contractual agreement will be formed.

The parties themselves may decide that the consumer's acceptance will be ineffective until the consumer receives the trader's notice confirming, for instance, the availability of the goods and thus the conclusion of the contract (as is the case with the 'subject to availability of goods' clause).

This is a mechanism reminiscent of the conditional mechanism and, in particular, that of the condition precedent, with the not inconsiderable difference, however, that in this case the occurrence of the event affects not the effectiveness but the conclusion of the contract.[88]

The procedure of reservation of approval also comes to mind, for which, on the other hand, it is the law itself to establish, *pursuant to* Art. 1520(1) of the Civil Code, that the 'contract is not perfected until the approval is communicated to the seller'.

The practice of online commerce confirms these conclusions when it is observed that the finalisation of the contract is largely left to procedural private autonomy.

Suffice it to observe how it is sometimes the same general terms and conditions contained in the application form that indicate that confirmation of the order form is the act that closes the contract formation process. This circumstance should not be surprising since e-commerce is governed by the power of the provider to design the site and guide the user towards the conclusion, a circumstance that seems to have been taken into consideration by the legislature itself when, in laying down, pursuant to Article 12 of Legislative Decree No. 70/2003, the information that the provider must provide to the consumer before placing the order, it indicates precisely

[88] See in the same vein, but with respect to late acceptance that is ineffective *under* Art. 1326 of the Civil Code, pending the offeror's finding that it is effective, cancels the defect of tardiness and thus determines the conclusion of the contract, with retroactive effect, Benedetti (2002), p. 301.

'the various technical stages to be followed for the conclusion of the contract' (Article 12, Legislative Decree No. 70/2003, letter a).

6 Procedural Private Autonomy, Real Contracts by the Will of the Parties (or of the Professional Alone): Crisis of Cooperation and Real Contracts with 'Inverted Parties'

Anyone who has purchased a good or service online by accessing the trader's site is well aware that there is a disconnect between the rule and the fact.[89] Indeed, what happens in the reality of trade is quite different from what the legislator envisaged in Article 51(2) of the Consumer Code.

The professional who, it must be reiterated, 'designs' the site and guides the consumer in the purchase, 'window' after 'window', protects himself not using the principle of execution under Article 1327 of the Civil Code, but by requesting the entire execution of the pecuniary performance by the party whose performance would be more uncertain if the contract were concluded under Article 1326 of the Civil Code, as well as by Art. 1327 of the Civil Code, and this is because, for this hypothesis, it is not trivial to recall that the commencement of performance, the continuation of which constitutes the subject matter of a contractual obligation, is already sufficient to integrate the scheme under Art. 1327 of the Civil Code.

And precisely to avert this risk, in the name of efficiency, the practitioner avails himself of the realities of the contract, transforming an obligation of performance into a co-element (together with consent) necessary for the completion of the contract.

The professional seems to be aware of the *crisis of cooperation*[90] already announced by Betti at the beginning of the 1950s, and taken up again in recent studies on the obligatory relationship and general principles;[91] *cooperation*[92] is understood not only as the obligation of the debtor to behave in a certain way to satisfy the interest of others, but also as the fulfilment of a duty that allows the interest of society to be satisfied at the same time. Betti's intuition, once purified of a neo-idealist vein, captures the feature that characterises modern consumer society, the so-called global market, i.e. speed, the hallmark of the times that connotes thought, action and results.

---

[89] As pointed out, Pietro Perlingieri already in 1969 pointed out the risks that the progressive separation of theory and practice brings with it; in this regard see: Perlingieri (1969), p. 455 ff., now in Perlingieri (1989), p. 8 ff. More recently, among others, see Orlandi (2016), p. 5.

[90] Already Betti (1953), pp. 28–29, denounced *the crisis of cooperation*, seeing the reasons, among others, in the idea that technique no longer has an instrumental function, but is elevated to an ultimate goal; recently Zaccheo (2019), p. 5 ff.

[91] Benatti (2018), p. 5 ff.

[92] Giorgianni (1968), p. 194 ff.; Natoli (1984), p. 1 ff.

And it is no coincidence that there is a certain melancholic mistrust in doctrine, perhaps dictated by the pessimism of intelligence that leads one to state that it is 'no longer time for reflection, because the result must be here and now'.

The time would therefore seem to be ripe for a '*restart from* slowness'.

And the European legislator, as mentioned above, has made itself interpreter of this need by designing, not by chance and precisely with the intention of protecting the weaker party, a series of contract formation procedures designed to make it heavier, to aggravate it in order to 'slow down' the speed of the means of communication employed (think of the choices made in the field of *teleselling*,[93] even before the contracts under consideration).

Picking up on Giuseppe Benedetti's teaching,[94] it should then be noted that the examination of the procedures[95] for concluding a contract cannot stop and exhaust itself in the exquisitely technical or aesthetic explanation of them, since it must also involve the interests that underlie the specificity of each procedure.

It is well known that the model described by Art. 1327 of the Civil Code, in which the principle of performance and the conclusion of the contract coincide (so much so that perfection takes place precisely at the place and time where performance has begun) was conceived by the legislature to guarantee urgency and effectiveness, derogating not from a substantive balance, but from the procedural balance concerning the party that performs without already having behind it a contract that is perfected, precisely, only with performance.

Over the protection of consent (under the combined provisions of Articles 1326 and 1335 of the Civil Code) in Article 1327 of the Civil Code prevails that of the efficiency of the mechanisms for organising companies and therefore the market.[96]

Something significantly different happens in the reality of e-commerce. And on this diversity we need to stop our attention.

As mentioned above, the professional does not make use of Art. 1327 of the Civil Code, and only rarely makes use of Art. 1326 of the Civil Code for the purpose of perfecting the contract. Rather, precisely in order to combine the protection of *consent and the efficiency of the organisation*,[97] the telematic contract under consideration is configured as a real contract by the will of the professional.

In the practice of *online* commerce, in fact, the purchaser is not 'only' asked to order, i.e. to manifest his consent, or 'only' to execute—if one agrees with the idea of attributing a solutory value to the typing of credit card details;[98] but most of the

---

[93] For the problems raised by the evanescence of communication by telephone and for a discussion of the process of concluding the telephone agreement, see my (2024), p. 937 ff.

[94] Benedetti, p. 333; in the same vein, among others, Di Raimo (2003), pp. 90–91.

[95] He uses the category *procedure* as opposed to the category of *case* for the formation of the contract: Benedetti, pp. 314–315, aware that 'the two categories constitute the two points of view for investigating the problems that are stirred up in the dynamic dimension of the formation of the agreement'.

[96] Di Raimo (2003), *op. loc. ult. cit.*

[97] Among the first to point out how organisational activity aims to make bargaining more efficient and economic: Maggiolo (2012), p. 64.

[98] Di Gravio (1989), p. 56.

time one is asked to do both: both to order (by filling in forms expressing the will to purchase a certain good) and to execute by paying.

In conclusion, both co-elements characterising real contracts coexist in the model described: consent and delivery. But with the not inconsiderable peculiarity that, unlike what happens in the real contract par excellence—the loan (but similar observations can also be extended, and at least, to the commodity)—in our case it is not the economically strong subject who anticipates the performance at the time of the conclusion of the contract, but it is the economically weak subject, also economically—and who should be better protected—who concludes the contract through delivery (which in our case is represented by the payment of the price).

Thus, a *real contract* is configured *in reverse to* the mortgage and commodity, to recall the 'classic' figures of real contracts.

This would not be an eccentric or original hypothesis. Suffice it to think of what happens, this time at the behest of the legislature itself (a circumstance that is perhaps trivial to recall) in the contract of deposit in which, as has been pointed out by careful doctrine,[99] a notable similarity can be recognised precisely about the inversion of the roles of the parties, the position of the *accipiens* being also in this case the one considered most worthy of protection, as is proved by the use of the verb *receive* instead of *deliver* in the relevant defining rule.

Thus, in electronic commerce using access to the site, the actual contract combines consent and efficiency to the sole benefit of the trader and thus inevitably would seem to disturb, even on first reflection, not only *the procedural balance to* which Giuseppe Benedetti alludes, but also, and more seriously, the substantive one. This is because the certainty and *speed* inherent in relations between entrepreneurs cannot always be transposed to relations with consumers without an unjustified sacrifice of their contractual position.[100] But we will return to this profile at greater length below.

7 Procedural Private Autonomy and Typical Faculties in the Sale

Once what happens in reality has been described, and after attempting to put the facts into concepts, a critical analysis cannot be neglected: asking what are the legal, even before the economic, consequences of what has been said.

If it is accepted that the online contract using access to the site is, for the reasons described above, a real contract, it follows that precisely because of the circumstance that payment is not an obligation, but a necessary co-element for the

[99] In a similar vein, but with regard to Article 1327 of the Civil Code, Di Raimo (2003).

[100] The literature on the subject is vast; we will merely point out (in chronological order) the contributions of particular relevance to our investigation. Among the works that devote attention to the general characters of the sale, see: Ferri (1984); Gardani Contursi Lisi (1988); Perlingieri et al. (1991).

conclusion of the contract, the relevant contract for the purchase of a good or service does not, once finalised, generate any obligation on the part of the consumer purchaser, who has already 'handed over' the money precisely using the delivery/payment of the price.

If we were to stop at a superficial analysis, at a suggestion, we would be tempted to register a paradox: the telematic sale 'would no longer be a sale' when, precisely because of the procedure for concluding the contract chosen by the professional—or by agreement between the parties, or if you wish according to custom—payment of the price is no longer qualifying as an obligation, but becomes a necessary co-element for the completion of the contract.

However, on a less hasty observation, this impression seems to be eclipsed, overshadowed by the positive fact from which we need to start by asking: what qualifies the sales type?[101]

By virtue of the defining provision in Art. 1470: '(Notion) A sale is a contract for the transfer of ownership of a thing or the transfer of another right in return for a price'.

The transfer is a constitutive element of the fact, of the normative type 'constituted' by the legislature with the description in Article 1470 of the Civil Code 'which draws to its consideration the fact of sale insofar as it is directed to the realisation of the "transfer of ownership of a thing or the transfer of another right'.

The consideration for the right transferred is the payment of the price, which is not only the principal obligation of the buyer but also an essential element of the contract of sale, which cannot exist without it. If instead of the price, there were an obligation of a different content or a different object, we would be faced with another type of contract for consideration.

It should also be recalled that, unlike the multiplicity of the seller's obligations and the variety of their content and object—especially with regard to the nature of the right transferred and of the thing—the price obligation is uniform because of the constancy of its object: money. The buyer's other possible obligations are, concerning it, incidental and secondary.

Concentrating our attention on the aspects that most directly concern us for the present article, it is useful to stop the analysis at the time of payment, starting first of all from the positive datum, and in particular not from para. (according to which, as is well known, if the contract provides for a term for the payment of the price, it is this term that must be observed), but from para. (2) of the cited provision, from which it follows that in the silence of the contract there may be usages (general or local, and possibly special to certain categories of persons or things) which establish a given term for the payment of the price, or even that it must be paid immediately although, according to the same usage or by contract, a deferment for the delivery of the thing is granted. Then, and always subject to the contract, the law requires compliance with these usages (Art. 1498(2) of the Civil Code).

---

[101] Ruperto (2019), pp. 124–125.

Where there is also a lack of usage in this respect, the law provides that the price must be paid at the time of delivery of the thing; Art. 1498 of the Civil Code thus links payment to the time when delivery must take place, by the principle of simultaneity which safeguards the interest of both parties.

It is also well known that purchase and sale is the chosen terrain of that power that is usually identified with the autonomy of configuration of the contract formation process, and it is no coincidence that the author[102] who was the first to recognise the configurative freedom of private individuals arrived at these results by taking advantage of the study he had just completed on the purchase and sale contract, being well aware of the numerous clauses and variables that, widely diffused in practice, intend to enrich the most elementary version of the typological scheme of this contract.[103]

Focusing on clauses dealing with the time of payment, it is now accepted that most of them derogate from the rule of Art. 1498(2) of the Civil Code. One example, as far as we are concerned, is the clause providing for an advance payment, which includes any case in which payment is to be made before delivery.

As a rule, payment is then due at the very moment of the conclusion of the contract (order payment), and in this sense the clause should be interpreted if it is not better specified in this respect; but a time limit may also be fixed, but it expires before the time fixed for delivery of the thing.

In the sale, in particular, it must be reiterated, the law-will separation is not so clear-cut, since it is precisely the legal schemes that—as the doctrine most sensitive to these profiles observes—'open up' to modifications and variations that the parties themselves can avail themselves of first and foremost through typical faculties.[104]

It is thus precisely the law that recognises and offers typical faculties to private individuals, which, as has been duly noted, it is not even correct to think of as derogations from legal norms, since they are, rather, legal faculties (i.e. legislatively regulated), some of which are left to the unilateral initiative of the proponent, while others, on the other hand, are attributable to initiatives agreed upon by the parties.

One example is the clause 'subject to the availability of the goods' with which, as already noted, the occurrence of the event affects not the effectiveness but the conclusion of the contract, as is the case with the sale subject to approval, for which, on the other hand, it is the law itself to establish, under Art. 1520(1) of the Civil Code, that the 'contract is not concluded until the approval is communicated to the seller'.

On the other hand, the so-called conventional reality is different, an expression used to describe the case in which it is the parties themselves—in derogation of the principle of consensualism that characterises the formation of that particular

---

[102] The reference is of course to Romano (1960), *passim*.

[103] This was recently recalled by Conte (2017), p. 582.

[104] Benedetti (2002), p. 434.

contract—to attribute to the delivery of the goods the role of element perfecting the *vinculum iuris* between them.[105]

8 The Elasticity of the Sales Type

The analysis of the typical clauses and faculties conducted above suggests that we should think of the sale as a flexible scheme, sufficiently elastic to encompass various species. Elasticity, as observed by the best doctrine,[106] is usually invoked to broaden the scope of application of the type discipline. And it is precisely in this perspective that the interpreter is willing to tolerate 'deviations' from the regulatory model, provided that they are compatible with the type and therefore do not distort it. It is then necessary to verify the scope of this elasticity, ascertaining to what extent the presence of new elements does not compromise the ascribability of the contract to the type. In other words: to what extent does the typical scheme tolerate intrusions without losing its physiognomy.

In the case of the online sale that ends in the reality of the exchanges with the delivery/payment of the price, there does not seem to us to be an escape from the type, from the codified model.

Indeed, as has been observed, constituent elements of the regulatory type described in Art. 1470 of civil code are, it should be recalled, the transfer of ownership of a thing or the transfer of another right in return for the payment of a price. There can be no doubt that the contract at issue transfers the right of ownership; it is then on the consideration that one must reason. But on closer inspection, as is shown by the reading of Art. 1498 of the Civil Code, although the price is an essential element of the sale contract, the time, i.e. when, of the payment of the price is not a rigid element, binding on the parties: only in the absence of usage or a different contractual choice will the rule of contextuality apply. And the clauses on the time of payment, frequently included in sales contracts, are further proof of this. Suffice it to recall the aforementioned clause providing for a so-called advance payment, which includes any case in which payment is to be made before delivery.

The professional seller chooses reality thus confessing that he no longer believes in cooperation and in this perspective adopts a contractual procedure that, as mentioned, manages to combine consensus and efficiency to the sole benefit of the professional.

---

[105] The subject has been variously addressed by interpreters. In particular, they recognise the power of private autonomy to aggravate the formative scheme of a contract governed by the principle of consensualism, introducing elements of 'realism', among others, Palermo (1991), p. 46 ff.; Mancini (1999), p. 445 ff.; Cenni (1998), p. 103 ff.; Benedetti (2002), p. 382 ff., who considers that the rule of the sufficiency of the agreement can only be abandoned by means of an agreement between the parties, and not by virtue of a unilateral initiative. Conte (2017), p. 600 ff.

[106] De Nova (1974), p. 15 ff., where it is stated: 'the more the interpreter is willing to tolerate deviations from the legislative scheme (…) the more he widens the scope of application of the type'. With reference to the 'elasticity' of the type of loan, in a monographic study on the purpose loan, see for all Zimatore (1985), p. 228 ff.

At first impression, the dynamic described would seem to disturb not only the procedural balance, to which Giuseppe Benedetti alludes, but also the substantive one.

Undoubtedly, if we were to stop our attention at the time and how the contract is concluded according to the model described, we would be tempted to denounce the arbitrariness, if not the overpowering of one party, the professional to the detriment of the consumer.

But this conclusion would prove to be short-sighted, if not naive, because it would confess an error of method: isolating the formation of the telematic contract, thus a distance contract, from the more complex regulatory context that the legislator has designed precisely to protect the consumer.

Let us not forget that although the procedure chosen, or sometimes even imposed by the professional, benefits him in the sense of enabling him to obtain an immediate and secure (since without risk; which would be the case if the professional relied on the consumer's cooperation) transfer of wealth to his benefit, at the same time it is the legislature itself that recognises on the other hand the consumer, and only the consumer, the right to regret his choice and withdraw from the contract that has already been concluded not only by consent but also by the execution of the payment of the price. Therefore, if one recognises the power of private autonomy to attribute to the delivery of the goods (which in our case is specified in the payment of the price), which constitutes the object of a contractual obligation, the different role of an essential element of the contract, it may be affirmed that in the case at hand, it is precisely the simultaneous presence of the right of withdrawal that balances the positions of the parties, excluding the possibility of arbitration by the professional to the detriment of the consumer.

9 Online Purchases by Minors

The ease and immediacy with which adolescents and even children access the Internet, often beyond any effective control and without the appropriate age verification mechanisms, give rise to specific technical and legal challenges. This situation underscores the imperative to safeguard this vulnerable segment of consumers who represent an attractive market, particularly for companies marketing products specifically dedicated to them.

The child is inundated with constant advertisements and product offers and, given the widespread availability of various technological tools, often has the tangible possibility of directly concluding online purchases.[107] After all, the formation of a contract in a digital environment may occur through actions marked by a level

[107] Already in 2004, Alpa (2004), p. 517, observed that 'I contatti e i contratti si moltiplicano non solo per effetto delle nuove tecnologie che hanno rivoluzionato le modalità di distribuzione di beni e servizi, ma anche per effetto delle nuove modalità con cui si effettuano le pratiche commerciali contratti conclusi fuori dei locali commerciali, contratti a distanza, contratti conclusi mediante la

of awareness that is undeniably lower than that which typically characterises contract formation in the physical world.

The need therefore arises to identify appropriate rules to govern contract concluded online by minors, who often access e-commerce platforms without adult supervision,[108] in order to address the issue of their legal validity and the remedies that may be invoked. In other words, legal scholars are called upon to investigate the true content of the individual legal institutions and their consequent suitability, or otherwise, to regulate in a fruitful manner the spurts of progress. '*il vero contenuto dei singoli istituti giuridici e la loro conseguente idoneità, o meno, a regolamentare in maniera proficua gli slanci del progresso*'.[109]

The complexity of the issue is heightened by the necessity to balance the conflicting interests involved: on the one hand, the personal and patrimonial interests of the minor, who may be incapable of providing truly informed consent due to a lack of sufficient experience and discernment to adequately assess the various aspects of the transaction; on the other hand, the need to safeguard commercial interests, consumer confidence and the stability of transactions.

10 The Regulation of Minors' Purchases, Evolutionary Trends

It is an indisputable fact that minors under the age of 18 routinely enter into *online* contracts, acquiring a broad spectrum of goods and services,[110] frequently through actions carried out without full awareness or understanding. A salient example is the acceptance of standard terms and conditions required to 'download' an application onto personal devices or purchases made on *online marketplaces*.

The problem thus arises of determining whether minors are capable of exercising the rights in question and, consequently, of assessing the validity and binding nature of the acts performed.

---

rete informatica costituiscono un veicolo straordinario di penetrazione nel mercato destinato specificamente ai minori e nel mercato degli adulti ai cui i minori hanno un più facile accesso'.

[108] The topic is extensively examined by Spangaro (2014), p. 219 ff.

[109] As expressed by one of the pioneering scholars who analysed the relationship between law and new technologies: Borruso (1988), p. 265.

[110] The record shows that the highest expenditure was incurred in the purchase of the games, Bird (2023); Hannah and Andrews (2020).

Our civil code (Article 2)[111] still establishes that full legal capacity is acquired at the age of 18.[112]

Prior to attaining the age of majority, an individual is deemed legally incapacitated, regardless of the degree of personal maturity or the ability to safeguard their own interests. Pursuant to the provisions of the Civil Code, a minor is presumed incapable of making decisions appropriate to the protection of their interests and the administration of their assets; hence the incapacity to negotiate, that is, the inability to perform acts of negotiation affecting their legal sphere, which must therefore be carried out by the legal representative.

The legislature, with the aim of protecting minors, provides (article 1425, para. 1, Civil Code) that a contract entered into by a person lacking contractual capacity is voidable, regardless of any harm suffered by the incapacitated party and irrespective of the other contracting party's knowledge or constructive knowledge of the incapacity.[113]

The act is therefore voidable but remains effective until a constitutive judgement of annulment is issued by the court.[114]

Since annulment is intended to protect the minor, the relevant action may be brought on behalf of the minor by their legal representative or by the minor themselves upon reaching the age of majority, but not by the other contracting party.

In other words, the contract provisionally produces legal effects that can be nullified or become definitive on the basis of a choice dictated by an assessment of the convenience of the transaction formulated by the legal representative or by the party concerned once they have reached the age of majority.[115] On this basis, the effects

[111] Tutto il primo comma dell'art. 2 c.c. ha i tratti di una regola ormai inadeguata, a partire dall'unica sua parte che suona diversa dal testo originario e che individua il dato anagrafico della 'maggiore età' nel 'compimento del diciottesimo anno' Si tratta di una rigida cesura che spezza la vita umana in due periodi drasticamente contrapposti, in ossequio ad un'antica logica di certezza, fatalmente destinata ad esigere il sacrificio delle sfumature che accompagnano il percorso dell'uomo verso la maturità, Giardina (2012), p. 361. For a comprehensive reconstruction of the meaning and function of legal capacity to act, see Giardina (2019), p. 171 ff.

[112] Legal incapacity to act is clearly designed to protect the weaker party, Falzea (1960), p. 8.

[113] Some scholars have argued that in the present case, the will of one of the two parties is entirely lacking, and consequently the requirement of consent set forth by Article 1325 of the Civil Code is not met. Therefore the contract should be declared null and void pursuant to Article 1418(2) of the Civil Code. However, denying legal validity to contracts concluded by minors would irreparably undermine commercial certainty and would not be advantageous either for the minor or for the community, which would see contracts concluded by persons who, practice, actively participate in commerce, rendered ineffective. On this point, Kötz and Patti (2017), p. 183 ff.

[114] On this point, Tommasini (1988), p. 1 ff., with regard to protected interests and legal standing, see Bianca (2019a), pp. 625–626 and Id. (2002), pp. 235–236.

[115] Precisely because it is dictated by the rationale *of* protecting the incapacitated minor, the annulment of the contract cannot give rise to contractual liability on the part of the minor. In this sense Stolfi (1968), p. 271; Franzoni (2005), p. 188. Case law, Court of Cassation, 21 July 1954, no. 2616, in *Foro pad.*, 1955, I, c. 438, and in *Foro it*, 1955, c. 339; on this point it stated that 'L'art. 1338 cod. civ., sulla responsabilità di chi non ha dato notizia, all'altra parte, della causa d'invalidità del contratto, è inapplicabile al minore di età'.

on the contract of the lack of capacity have been effectively framed by the expression 'patologia discreta del contratto annullabile'.[116]

However, acts performed by a minor who has concealed his or her age by deception and induced the other party to believe that they were contracting with an adult are not voidable.[117]

In such circumstances, there is no need to protect the minor who, having the capacity to mislead an adult and capable counterpart, demonstrates a level of maturity *that renders them* undeserving of the protection afforded by the legal system to persons *lacking capacity to act* (*malitia supplet aetatem*).[118]

On the other hand, from the perspective of balancing the opposing interests at stake, particular importance attaches to the need to protect the good faith of the competent contracting party misled by the fraudulent machinations of the minor, through which the latter has demonstrated intellectual *maturity beyond* that typical of their age, thereby overcoming the legal presumption of incapacity to manage their own interests.[119] The legislator in Article 1426 clarifies that the mere declaration of being of age is not sufficient to prevent an action for annulment; consequently, for the requirement of 'deception' to be met, active conduct aimed at misleading the other party is necessary.[120]

From a certain interpretative standpoint, the legal regime governing the incapacity of minors to act appears as an impairment of the individual's autonomy.[121]

---

[116] Maiello (2003), p. 329 ff.

[117] On the basis of the exceptional rule governing regulating the fraudulent conduct of the minor, see Roppo (2001), p. 770.

[118] Falzea (1960), p. 38 ff.; 'In linea di principio, la furbizia del minore configura uno stato di capacità naturale che può diventare presupposto eccezionale di validità di un atto giuridico altrimenti annullabile' See Andreola (2018), p. 965. On this point, see Cass. 4 July 2012 no. 11191 in *Giust. civ. mass.* 2012, 7-8, 881; *Dir. fam. pers*, 2014, 39, in *Giur. it.*, 2013, 1544; in *Contr.*, 2012, 771 that expressly states 'L'art. 1426 cod. civ., il quale stabilisce la non annullabilità del contratto concluso dal minore, che con raggiri abbia occultato la sua minore età, costituisce una norma di carattere eccezionale. Ne consegue che detta deroga al regime dell'annullabilità per incapacità legale non può essere estesa all'ipotesi del malizioso occultamento del proprio stato da parte dell'interdetto o dell'inabilitato, sia perché la condizione di questi ultimi non è equiparabile a quella del minore, il quale può essere naturalmente capace di intendere e di volere e dimostrare per la sua precocità una particolare astuzia, sia perché tale malizioso occultamento appare difficilmente conciliabile con la situazione di incapacità in cui l'interdetto e l'inabilitato versano, trattandosi di condotta che postula la lucida rappresentazione del proprio stato e la consapevole volontà diretta a mascherarlo'.

[119] Some scholars recognise the rule in question as having a sanctioning function towards the child perpetrator. In this sense Franzoni (2005), p. 207 ff.

[120] For example, by altering the date of birth on the identification document. In this sense, Bianca (2002), p. 236. In this regard, Messineo (1958), p. 476., considers that the deception must consist in an 'efficiente macchinazione' similar to that provided for in Article 1439, Section 1, Civil Code. According to this interpretation latter, the provision serves as a warning to exercise caution and prudence when contracting with individuals whose physical appearance clearly suggests young age. In such a cases, it is the explicit responsibility of the other party to request reliable proof of majority.

[121] Bianca (2002).

Deprived of the capacity to independently initiate or determine transactions that affect their legal sphere, the minor is effectively excluded from any meaningful form of active participation in social life.

This consideration has led part of the legal doctrine to partially temper the rigidity[122] of the incapacity regime, acknowledging as validly undertaken by the minor those acts in which the fundamental freedoms of the person are exercised.[123]

In our legal system, the once monolithic notion of legal incapacity to act has progressively been eroded, especially in the domain of personal rights and, in certain well-defined instances, also with regard to rights of a patrimonial nature.[124]

Apart from the cases expressly provided for by statute, legal scholarship recognises that minors possess the capacity to perform legal acts of minor patrimonial content, i.e. the so-called necessary acts of daily life.[125] These are acts of limited economic value which, by virtue of their routine and non-prejudicial nature do not determine the need for protection of the incapacitated person.[126]

---

[122] On this point Stanzione (2014), p. 123.

[123] Busnelli (1982), p. 54 ff.

[124] In the first place, a minor who has reached the age of 16 is allowed to enter into an employment contract and, pursuant to the second paragraph of Article 2 of the Civil Code, is qualified to exercise the rights and actions arising from such contract; furthermore, on the basis of the provisions of the second paragraph of Art. 84 of the Civil Code, the Court at the request of the interested party, having ascertained his or her psycho-physical maturity and the validity of the reasons put forward, and having heard the Public Prosecutor, the parents or the guardian, the Court may, by decree issued in chambers, authorise the marriage of anyone who has reached the age of 16. Even before the child reaches the age of 16, with the authorisation of the judge, he may directly recognise his or her child (Art. 250, § 5 of the Civil Code, Law n° 633 of 22 April 1941). Pursuant to Art. 108 of law no. 633 of 22 April 1941, the author of an original work, who has reached the age of 16 years, has the capacity to perform all the legal acts relating to the works he has created and to exercise the actions deriving therefrom. Moreover, law no. 194 of 22 May 1978 allows, in health care facilities and counselling centres, the administration to minors, on medical prescription, of the means necessary to carry out 'the purposes freely chosen with regard to responsible procreation' (Art. 2 para. 3 law no. 194 of 22 May 1978). On the basis of Article 120 of Presidential Decree No 309 of 9 October 1990, a minor who uses psychotropic substances may personally request to undergo diagnostic tests and a socio-rehabilitation programme.

[125] On this point, Stanzione (2014), p. 1238, adopts a jusrealist perspective as opposed to a jusformalist one, emphasising how, in everyday life, 'i minori, ogni giorno, concludono con tratti di scambio che non sono invalidati. Nei fatti della vita reale essi scelgono, contrattano, concludono molti rapporti negoziali che, non essendo annullati o non potendo esserlo per ragioni di prescrizione, producono effetti'. In line with this view, G. Alpa, *I contratti del minore. Appunti di diritto comparato*, cit., 519, points out that the case law on the subject 'sia esigua, per certi aspetti inesistente, al punto da lasciar intendere che la scarsa rilevanza economica del singolo atto, l'agevole sistemazione dei conflitti in via conciliativa, l'eccessivo costo del ricorso alla macchina della giustizia o, più semplicemente, il difetto di interesse a invalidare il contratto tendano da un lato a scoraggiare la litigiosità, dall'altro a riflettere un uni verso sommerso di rapporti che prosperano senza creare problemi di qualche consistenza'. See also Caterina (2016); Carbone (2019), p. 1086 ff.; Giardina (1990), p. 2; Id. (2012), p. 361.

[126] In this sense, Anzani (2009), p. 509 ff.; Carbone (2019), p. 1086, states that la categoria extralegislativa dei c.d. atti minuti della vita quotidiana è tradizionalmente associata alla disciplina legislativa dell'incapacità di agire, rispetto alla quale ha sempre operato come limite interno, con funzione moderatrice'.

However, the lack of specific legal provisions and case law on this matter[127] renders it somewhat problematic to clearly delineate the characteristics of the type of the acts in question.

The characteristics of the minute acts of daily life that may be performed by the minor have been identified by legal doctrine in the reduced economic and patrimonial relevance and in the low impact on interests deserving protection;[128] falling within this category, for example, are acts such as the purchase of newspapers, books and various gadgets distributed at newsstands, various stationery, sports goods, video games, clothing, foodstuffs, the purchase of tickets for means of transport, sporting events or cinema and theatre, hotel stays and tourist trips.

Some scholars have legally framed the rule of the validity of acts of daily life performed by the child within the scope of representation under Article 1389 of the Civil Code. In the absence of an express provision of law, the minor, with specific reference to the performance of the aforementioned acts, has been regarded as acting on behalf of his or her parents, in view of the fact that, in our legal system, for the validity of the contract concluded by the representative it is sufficient that he or she has the capacity to understand and to form intent, having regard to the nature and content of the contract itself, but it is necessary that the represented person be legally capable of acting.[129]

Such an interpretation, however, may provide a formal legal basis for the purchase of goods in the interest (also) of the parents or in general for the family, but cannot serve as a valid justification for purchases made exclusively in the minor's own interest such as a newspaper or a toy. The recourse to the legal concept of representation, which inherently presupposes the conferral of power to act in the interest of another, appears wholly inadequate to justify acts performed by the minor for their own benefit and under their own initiative.[130]

Such a reconstruction would lead to the assumption that the assets acquired are the property of the parents and the obligations assumed will be borne by them. From this perspective, the child would thus be deprived of any capacity to act in the patrimonial field.[131] Indeed, the recognition of the capacity to perform acts of everyday

---

[127] Alpa (2004), p. 519. See also Caterina (1990), p. 2.

[128] 'Quando trattisi di piccole spese, affari bagatellari, servizi di modesto importo economico, per così dire di «atti giuridici della vita quotidiana» la griglia dei rimedi e lo schermo delle finzioni appaiono da un lato effetto di una vera e propria superfetazione dei principi sistematici e dall'altro un corredo eccessivo e d'impaccio alla normale soddisfazione dei bisogni della vita'. Thus Alpa (2004). In relation to this, Carbone (2019), p. 1099, observes that the acts of 'everyday contractuality' which a minor can validly perform must be identified according to an objective criterion **defined** in the minimal dimension recognisable by all, so that protection and socialisation are harmoniously combined. However, the objectivity of the criterion does not entail rigidity in its application: indeed the minor's everyday negotiation displays a recognisable elasticity depending on the type of agent, in line with the evolutionary progression associated with age related maturation. **This negotiation capacity thus** has fundamentally evolutionary nature, almost developing year by year **as the minor grows older**.

[129] Art. 1389 (1) of the Civil Code.

[130] See, on this point, Ruscello (2000), p. 72.

[131] Stanzione (2014), p. 1247.

contractuality would find a valid justification in the observation that, for the child, it would constitute an essential and indispensable tool for establishing social relations that constitute an inviolable right protected under Article 2 of the Constitution. Thus, from a constitutionally oriented interpretation of Article 2, paragraph 1 of the Civil Code, which appears to implicitly recognise that minors under-18 may be deemed capable for specific categories of acts,[132] it follows that legal incapacity no longer explains its effects on all acts for which a different age is not established, but on those acts for which the legal institution serves a clear and enduring protective function.[133] This requirement does not apply to all contracts, and in particular it appears not to extend to minute acts of everyday life.

This reconstruction is confirmed in the amended Article 409 of the Civil Code, which, in regard to 'amministrazione di sostegno', allows the beneficiary to perform, in any case, the acts necessary to meet the needs of his or her daily life. A category once considered vague and elusive thus finds a normative foundation: that of minute acts which, even if contractual, no longer appear capable of justifying protective measures. The aforementioned *provision appears* to underpin the same principles that justify recognising the child's capacity to validly perform acts of daily life, thereby ensuring an incompressible space of autonomous action, indispensable for exercising constitutionally guaranteed inviolable rights. In this context, it is considered appropriate to define everyday contractual acts objectively, both to avoid excessively broadening the scope of unprotected actions, and to allow their clear identification by the general public, thereby safeguarding the legitimate reliance interests of counterparties.[134]

It therefore appears possible to recognise a broader scope for the exercise of patrimonial rights by minors than that which the legal system traditionally attributes to them.

Having outlined the general framework governing acts performed by minors under the current legal system, it is now necessary to examine how, and within what limits, the principles and rules, formulated with reference to traditional modes of contracting that allow a straightforward and immediate ascertainment of the parties' capacity to act, apply to the conclusion of contracts not made at the newsagent's or neighbourhood grocery store, but rather concluded, through different techniques, in an agile and immediate manner on online platforms.[135]

---

[132] Carbone (2019), p. 1098.

[133] Giardina (1990), p. 394.

[134] Carbone (2019).

[135] In fact, the depersonalised and anonymous character of telematic declarations led part of the doctrine to consider contracts concluded by means of telematic instrument as 'scambi senza accordo', Irti (1998), p. 362 ff. According to this view, in online negotiation the exchange does not arise from agreements understood as declarations addressed by one party to the other but rather from acts directed at the object and inscribed in a market system, such acts serving exclusively to display and select a thing. However, over time this approach has been superseded by the thesis that considers the general rules governing the formation of consent, defects of the will and incapacity also applicable to the exchange of telematic declarations, albeit with due regard to the peculiarities of the communication medium. Indeed, in the system of concluding contracts by means of point

11 The Contract Concluded *Online* by the Minor: Requirements for Protection and Available Remedies

The main challenges posed by the regulation of the purchase of goods or services on *online* platforms stem from the fact that these are contracts concluded between absentees,[136] which complicates the identification of the party who has manifested the will to contract and to whom the legal statement must be attributed, even though the technological tools used to transmit the communication may be traceable.

On the other hand, the method of concluding the contract, lacking any direct physical interaction between the minor and the good or service, which can only be perceived through the images specifically designed to induce purchase, further strengthens the need for enhanced protection of minors.

At the outset, one must consider how the provisions of our legal system are to be applied in such cases.

As previously noted, the particular features of online contracting and, in particular, its inherently depersonalised nature render it especially difficult to ascertain both the identity and the age of the contracting parties. This facilitates the ability of minors to conceal their true age or to adopt a false identity in order to circumvent the legal restrictions associated with their incapacity.

The acuity and specific abilities that often characterise younger individuals, *as well as* the maturity reached by those *approaching the age of majority, call for a careful assessment of the applicability of existing legal rules to online contracting.* The above considerations have led part of the legal doctrine to question whether the codified rules *on legal capacity, particularly those concerning the validity of juridical acts, should be revised, placing emphasis on the actual maturity attained by the acting* subject.[137] *While one may, in abstract terms and de iure condendo, agree on the desirability of such an evaluative approach, in practice, the current positive law provides clear, rigid and binding rules on legal incapacity, which cannot be disregarded in the cases under consideration.* It is, however, possible to identify certain areas in which juridical acts performed by minors may be deemed valid.

and click, even in the absence of an express declaration of will identifiable in the exchange of emails, an act of manifestation of will cannot be excluded since, for the conclusion of a non-formal contract, the will may also be inferred from concluding facts. See, to this effect, Oppo (1998), p. 525 ff. On the relevance of consent in the telematic contract see Sacco and De Nova (2016), in particular pp. 125 ff. and 333 ff.; Clarizia (2018), p. 95 ff.

136 Bianca (1998), p. 1038.

137 On this issue see Longo (2006), p. 396 et seq. The author, starting from an analysis of the legislation and case law that recognise the capacity of minors with sufficient discernment to make decisions concerning highly personal and non-transferable rights, including the right to health, questions the reasons why a minor who has been acknowledged as possessing adequate discernment should be deemed incapable of performing acts of a patrimonial nature. Berti De Marinis (2016), p. 48, considers this position excessively rigid and even in conflict with the principles underlying the constitutional system.

Firstly, in the case of goods of modest value or those necessary for everyday life, traditional doctrine, already with reference to in-person transactions, as noted in the preceding pages, holds that acts performed by a minor who is capable of understanding are valid. There do not appear to be sufficient reasons to reach a different conclusion with respect to online transactions.

A minor possessing natural capacity may therefore *validly* conclude *online* the so-called minute acts of daily life, precisely because such acts are not likely to cause pecuniary harm to the minor. *As a result, the protective rationale* underlying the rules on annulability does not apply.

At this stage, the discussion—focused on contracts involving goods that cannot be classified among acts typical of everyday contractual dealings (such as the purchase of technological devices, clothing or particularly costly accessories)—requires a clear distinction between two fundamentally different scenarios. The first scenario involves a minor making a purchase in their own name, by providing their personal information. The second scenario concerns a minor acting in the guise of another person (e.g. a parent), by using someone else's account, device, email address, credit card details, or by completing the platform registration form with false information. In the latter case, the issue arises of a contract concluded under a false name.

In this case, it is not possible to speak of representation as there is no indication of substitution in the legal sphere of another person, given the absence of any evidence that the minor is acting on behalf of someone else. On the contrary, the agent presents themselves as the person whose identity they are unlawfully using. Since the minor is not contracting in their own name, the legal act cannot be attributed to them. In particular, if the conduct of the person whose identity has been used can be objectively construed as authorising the transaction,[138] the contract may be deemed valid and attributable to that person.

Conversely, if the so-called dominus is to be regarded as entirely uninvolved in the legal activity carried out in their name, the contract must be considered null and void due to the absence of consent, pursuant to Articles 1325(1) and 1418 of the Civil Code.

---

[138] That is to say, when, in addition to the use of the name, there are identifiable elements unequivocally identificative of the consent of the holder of the spent name—attributable to his or her omissive or commissive conduct (such as the use of a credit card or identification mechanisms)—liability will arise on the part of that holder, and the need to protect the reasonable expectations of the other contracting party will come into play. In such cases, the contract will be valid and attributable to the person who appears to have made the declaration. In other words, if there is conduct objectively expressing the party's adherence to the agreement, the holder of the spent name will be deemed bound by the contract. Conversely, in the absence of any elements capable of indicating the subject's involvement in the agreement, the contract will be null and void for lack of consensus. See also p. 118, considers it appropriate to examine this case in light of the principle of so-called culpable appearance according to which the effects of the contract are imputable to the apparent contracting party only when the latter, by failing to use the instruments provided by law to protect their legal sphere, tolerates the misuse of their identification instruments or digital identity by third parties, thereby generating, in the contracting party, a reasonable expectation regarding the attainment of the legal effects.

The case where the minor enters into a contract in their own name is of a different nature and requires the distinction between different various hypotheses.

In the first instance, where the platform does not require the disclosure of the user's age at any point prior to the conclusion of the contract and the incapacitated party remains silent on the matter, the contract shall be considered voidable since the omission of the minor's age cannot be construed as deception under Article 1426 of the Civil Code.

If the minor at the time of registration on the platform, or upon explicit request, provides their personal data and correctly discloses their age, the contract is clearly voidable pursuant to Article 1425 of the Civil Code. Furthermore, even in cases where the minor misrepresents their age—by, for instance, selecting a false date of birth or affirming majority status through a dropdown menu—the contract remains voidable, since pursuant to Article 1426 of the Civil Code, the mere declaration of being of age is not an obstacle to challenging the contract.

Regarding the entry of credit card details in the name of a parent, it should be noted that it constitutes a payment in performance of the contract.[139] Accordingly, the electronic transmission of the order to the seller shall be deemed performance within the meaning of Article 1327 of the Civil Code and qualifies as 'prompt notice' within the meaning of the second paragraph of the same article.[140]

An *online* contract entered into by a minor is subject to the provisions of the Civil Code as well as those of the Consumer Code. Moreover, a contracting party under 18 years of age, by virtue of the structural vulnerability inherent in the consumer's position, combined with the particular weakness attributable to their youth, is deemed worthy of a heightened level of protection, as established for vulnerable consumers.

In particular, the Consumer Code is concerned, by regulating unfair commercial practices, to protect individual subjects deemed 'particularly vulnerable' on account of 'their age or naivety' (Art. 20 of the Consumer Code), 'children or adolescents' (Article 21 of the Consumer Code, fourth paragraph).

Moreover, the Consumer Code allows a minor who has concluded an *online* contract, qualifiable as a distance contract, or their legal representative, to validly exercise the right of withdrawal pursuant to Articles 52 et seq.,[141] 'without having to provide any reason and without incurring any costs other than those related to the return of the goods'.

The deadline for *exercising* the right of withdrawal is 14 days, unless the trader has failed to provide the consumer with the required information about the right of withdrawal. In that case, the period is extended to 12 months from the end of the

---

[139] In this sense, Gambino (1997), p. 240 holds that the payment of the price is part of the contractual performance and its execution by sending the order to the company issuing the credit card integrates the hypothesis referred to in Article 1327 of the Civil Code.

[140] Andreola (2018), p. 980 et seq., considers that the use of the parent's credit card by the minor child may constitute a presumption of prior waiver, on the part of the individual exercising parental responsibility, to challenge the contract.

[141] As amended by Legislative Decree No 21 of 21 February 2014 implementing Directive No 2011/83/EU.

initial withdrawal period.[142] If the trader provides the consumer with the required information within this 12-month period, *the withdrawal deadline expires 14 days after the day on which the consumer receives that information.*

This institution allows the consumer, after a more careful evaluation of the convenience or the actual advisability of the purchase, to eventually free themselves from the contractual obligation. Similarly it enables parents who may not have been aware of the contract's conclusion at the time to also release themselves from the obligation. This is particularly justified given that the legally prescribed time frame for exercising this right is generally considered reasonable. Moreover, modern security measures facilitate real-time awareness of payments, such as instant notifications sent directly to the *smartphone* of the payment instrument holder, or through the mandatory order confirmation pursuant to Article 51 paragraph 7 of the Consumer Code.

In addition, by prescribing a relatively brief period for the exercise of the right of withdrawal, the legislation serves not only to uphold the principles of legal certainty and the stability of commercial relations, but also to safeguard the legitimate reliance interests of the counterparty.

In this regard, it should be further noted that the supply of sealed audio or video recordings or sealed computer software which have been unsealed after delivery (Article 59 of the Consumer Code, subparagraph i) as well as the supply of digital content delivered through non-material means where performance has begun with the consumer's express consent accompanied by acknowledgement of the consequent loss of the right of withdrawal (subparagraph o)—constitute explicit exceptions to the right of withdrawal under Article 59 of the Consumer Code. These exceptions are particularly significant, as they concern types of purchases most frequently concluded by minors. As such, the withdrawal regime reveals a substantial gap in the protective framework afforded to this vulnerable category of consumers.

It should be noted, however, that the remedy of avoidance is, in practice, hindered by the evidentiary burden borne by the party required to prove the minority of the purchaser.

Pursuant to the general principle governing the allocation of the burden of proof as set forth in Article 2697 of the Civil Code, the burden lies with the party seeking to assert the invalidity of the contract. That party must provide full proof that the act was referred to a person who had not yet attained the age of majority.

The evidentiary burden is significantly heightened where the agent either withholds identifying information or provides false data. In such circumstances, it becomes feasible only to trace the technological instrument from which the purchase order originated. Consequently, the claimant bears the onerous task of demonstrating—an undertaking fraught with difficulty—that access to the platform was effected by the minor, or that the digital device in question was operated by the minor at the material time.[143]

---

[142] Pursuant to Art. 53 of the Cons. Code.

[143] In this sense, Grossi (2003), p. 13, in particular emphasises the role of anonymisation techniques that enable incognito surfing, as well as the application of confidentiality rules throughout the *e-contract* process and Seminara (1996), p. 208.

It cannot, however, be deemed appropriate to consider the parent's timely withdrawal as the most suitable remedy, solely on the grounds of the practical difficulties associated with bringing an action for annulment.[144] First, annulment and withdrawal are not interchangeable remedies.[145] Second, such an interpretation would imply the validity of the contract concluded online by an individual lacking legal capacity, which would contradict general principles of contract law.[146]

In fact, in the specific sphere of purchases made by minors and, more broadly, with regard to their protection when accessing digital platforms and the digital universe, the identification of valid *age verification* tools becomes of fundamental importance.

12 The Minor's Digital Consent to the Processing of Personal Data

One notable example of the erosion of the traditional concept of the legal incapacity of individuals under 18 is found in Article 8 of the GDPR.[147] This provision allows minors to give valid consent to the processing of their personal data in the context of the direct offer of information society services, provided they are at least 16 years old. This reflects a shift towards recognising a more nuanced and context-dependent legal capacity in minors, particularly in the digital environment.[148]

However, the regulation allows Member States to set a lower age for this purpose by law, provided that is not below 13 years.

In this context, the national legislator has established the minimum age for validly giving 'digital consent' at the age of 14.[149] Below this age threshold, the

[144] Follieri (2005), p.188.

[145] Cinque (2007), p. 25.

[146] Andreola (2018), p. 980.

[147] Acronym for the *General* Data *Protection* Regulation *GDPR* Regulation 2016/679/EU of 27 April 2016 of the European Parliament and of the Council on the protection of natural person with regard to the processing of personal data and on the free movement of such data and repealing Directive 1995/46/EC.

[148] Recital 38 of the GDPR specifically examines the special situation of children expressly recognises that 'Children merit specific protection with regard to their personal data, as they may be less aware of the risks, consequences and safeguards concerned and their rights in relation to the processing of personal data. Such specific protection should, in particular, apply to the use of personal data of children for the purposes of marketing or creating personality or user profiles and the collection of personal data with regard to children when using services offered directly to a child. The consent of the holder of parental responsibility should not be necessary in the context of preventive or counselling services offered directly to a child'.

[149] In fact, Legislative Decree No. 101 of 10 August 2018 on provisions for the adaptation of national legislation to the provisions of Regulation (EU) 2016/679 supplemented the Personal Data Protection Code issued by Legislative Decree No. 196 of 30 June 2003.

processing of personal data is lawful only if consent is provided by those exercising parental responsibility.[150]

Although *social* platforms explicitly state the minimum age for consent in their 'terms of use',[151] they do not, in practice, verify the accuracy or truthfulness of users' declarations.[152] As a result, so-called young minors are granted access, despite lacking the cognitive maturity required to be able to comprehend certain content, language and topics.

Both European and national legislators, aiming to provide specific protection for younger users, require the data controller, when obtaining consent, to use 'simple and clear language that a child can easily understand'[153] as well as a 'concise, transparent, intelligible, and easily accessible form, with simple and clear language, particularly in the case of information specifically intended for children'.[154]

On the other hand, serious doubts have been raised regarding the suitability of consent, even when complying with the aforementioned obligations, to ensure an adequate level of protection.[155]

Paragraph 3 of Article 8 of the GDPR, which sets the age limit for the expression of valid consent to data processing, clarifies that 'the general provisions of the

---

[150] Art. 8(2) provides that the data controller shall take all reasonable steps to verify in such cases that consent is given or authorised by the holder of parental responsibility over the child, having regard to the available technology', but it does not specifically state how the verification of parental age is to be carried out.

[151] *Instagram*'s terms of use provided in Article 4.1. Who can use Instagram? 'We want our Service to be as open and inclusive as possible, but we also want it to be safe, secure and in accordance with the law'. Therefore, the user is required to comply with certain legal restrictions. 'To be part of the *Instagram* community the user must be at least 13 years old'. A similar provision can be found in *Facebook*'s terms of use: 'Our goal is to make *Facebook* available to everyone, but its use is prohibited in the following cases: for users who are under 13 years old'. The general terms and conditions of *TikTok* in Art. 4.3. minimum age states that 'To use the Platform, users must be at least 13 years old. We carry out checks to ensure compliance with age limits and, in the event of reasonable suspicion, we order the closure of the profile of users who are under 13 years of age or who allow users under 13 years of age to use their profile. Our decision to order profile closure for an age violation can be challenged if it is deemed that there has been a mistake'. In short: users must be at least 13 years old to use the platform. In addition, the use of *live streaming* functions is subject to the age of 16 or older with the full permission of parents or legal guardians. Only users who are 18 years of age or older (or of legal age according to their own legislation) may purchase virtual 'Coins' or 'gifts'.

[152] Meta platforms, i.e. *Facebook* and *Instagram*, only ask for age during registration, while allowing the creation of **profiles for minors** under the management and supervision of parents or possibly guardians. ***TikTok***, on the other hand, implements more stringent age verification measures conducting periodic checks on the consistency between the declared age and the nature of the content **searched and** published, as well as on user interactions and reports. In cases of well-founded suspicion that the account holder is under the legally required age, the platform may request the presentation of an identity document, use of a credit card, or submission of a selfie with a parent or legal guardian. Should such suspicion be confirmed, TikTok promptly blocks and disables the account.

[153] Recital 58 GDPR.

[154] Art. 12 paragraph 1 GDPR and Art. *2d* Privacy Code.

[155] Gambino (2020), p. 298.

contract law of the Member States, such as the rules on the validity, formation or effect of a contract in relation to a child' remain unaffected.

From a reading of this provision, it appears that the legislator's intention is to establish a distinct set of rules for the provision of valid consent to the processing of personal data—which constitutes an exercise of fundamental rights—different from those applicable to acts of a patrimonial nature.

Scholars have expressed differing views on the act of registering on social platforms particularly with regard to the nature of the consent given for data processing.

The classification of such consent as an act of authorisation is based on the need to prevent a personality right from acquiring the characteristics of an economic interest. However, the increasingly sophisticated techniques of profiling have led a significant portion of legal scholarship[156] to consider personal data as legal assets capable of being the object of disposal.

According to this line of reasoning, it would be impossible not to recognise the contractual nature of the act whereby the user in exchange for access to the platform grants the platform operator the right to economically exploit his data.[157] This interpretation has in fact been endorsed by the Italian AGCM (Autorità Garante della Concorrenza e del Mercato)[158] and supported by jurisprudence[159] which challenge the view that personal data are protected solely as a fundamental right of the indi-

[156] Thobani (2019), p. 131 ff.; Battelli (2022b), p. 356, on this point argues that la prospettiva della valorizzazione economica dei dati personali non vada posta in contrapposizione con quella della protezione dei dati nell'ottica della tutela della persona. Al contrario, le rispettive discipline devono essere considerate l'una complementare all'altra, arricchendo l'esigenza di salvaguardia del dato come attributo della persona e, al tempo stesso, quale risorsa economica oggetto di valorizzazione tramite lo strumento di circolazione della ricchezza per eccellenza: il contratto'.

[157] Ricciuto (2022), p. 55; Id. (2018), p. 689 ff.; Perlingieri (2014), p. 88.

[158] The AGCM, in its meeting of 11 May 2017, recalling the well-established guidance of the European Commission (European Commission, 'Guidelines for the implementation/application of Directive 2005/29/EC on unfair commercial practices', Brussels, 25.5.2016 28, and, with respect to Case No. COMP/M.7217 - FACEBOOK/WHATSAPP, §13) aiming to recognise that personal data, consumer preferences and other user-generated content have a *de facto* economic value and are sold to third parties, formally recognises the pecuniary significance of social media user data considered as 'non-pecuniary consideration' for the services offered.

[159] See Tar Lazio, 18 December 2020, no. 260, in *Foro amm.*, 2020, 99 ff. Moreover, the administrative judges have clarified that the phenomenon of the 'monetisation' of personal data, which is a hallmark of the new digital market economies, requires operators to comply, in the context of related commercial transactions, with the obligations of clarity, completeness and non-deceptiveness of information as established by consumer protection legislation. The consumer must be made fully aware of the reciprocal exchange underlying the conclusion of a contract for the use of a service, such as that offered by a social network. **Moreover, the** Supreme Court of Cassation, Cass, 2 July 2018, No. 17278, in *Law Guide* 2018, f. 42, 75, and in *GiustiziaCivile.com*, 21 March 2019, with a footnote by Ruggeri, has held that consent to data processing is validly given only if it is freely and specifically expressed in relation to a clearly identified processing activity. This allows the operator of a website offering a fungible service—one that the user may forego without significant burden (in the case at hand, a 'newsletter' service concerning finance, taxation, law and employment topics)—to make the provision of such service conditional upon the processing of personal data for advertising purposes, provided that consent is unequivocally and individually given with regard to this specific purpose. This, in turn, entails the necessity, at a minimum, of indicating the commercial sectors or services to which the advertising messages will relate.

vidual. Instead, they argue that such an approach reflects a limited understanding of the potential inherent in the exploitation of personal data, which may also constitute a negotiable asset, subject to economic exploitation, and therefore capable of functioning as 'consideration' in the technical sense of contract law.

Granting a child the ability to give valid consent for the processing of their personal data amounts to recognising a form of special contractual capacity which, however, does not affect the general provisions governing the validity of contracts.

As a consequence, a minor under the age of 18 may be allowed to register on a platform but would not be legally capable of entering into valid contracts for the purchase of goods or services. In such cases, references must be made to the general rules outlined in the preceding paragraph regarding the validity of these contractual acts.

This approach also appears consistent with the contractual terms of the major social platforms which distinguish between the age required to consent to data processing for registration purposes and the age required to enter into commercial transactions on marketplace services.[160]

Attributing a form of 'digital capacity' to minors in the upper age brackets is fully consistent with the legal framework outlined in the preceding pages which recognises that individuals who have reached the age of 14 are entitled to autonomously exercise certain rights. This development aligns with the progressive affirmation of minors' right to self-determination provided they possess sufficient capacity for discernment, particularly in light of the fact that 'the new means of digital communication have become the primary tools for social interaction and personal development, through which users from a young age construct their identity and exercise a range of fundamental rights'.[161]

This approach is also consistent with the findings of the most attentive legal scholarship, which has observed that young and very young individuals frequently make purchases that go unquestioned, insofar as such acts are considered necessary to meet the ordinary needs of their daily lives.

It cannot be denied that, in practical terms, the question of whether contracts enabling the use of information society services should be included in the aforementioned categories is a complex matter, as it also involves the educational choices made by parents with regard to their children.[162]

In this respect, it should be noted that the European legislator explicitly recognises the protection of minors as a key policy objective of the Union.[163] To this end, it requires providers of intermediary services that are primarily intended for and predominantly used by minors to explain in a manner that is understandable to them, the conditions and restrictions applicable to the use of

[160] The platform states in Article 3.1. of the terms of use that 'We try to ***make Facebook*** broadly ***available*** to ***everyone***, ***but*** you cannot ***use Facebook*** if: you are under 13 years old (or the minimum age required in your country). (…) For users who are under 13 years of age, in the information concerning the use of the *marketplace*, it clarifies 'You must be of legal age, according to the laws of your country, to use *Facebook Marketplace*'.

[161] Garaci (2021), p. 811. See also Bianca (2019b), p. 150.

[162] See Quarta and Smorto (2024), p. 205.

[163] Considering No. 71 DSA.

such services.[164] Furthermore these providers are required to adopt appropriate and proportionate measures to ensure a high level of privacy, security and protection for minors.[165]

Moreover, very large *online* platforms and search engines[166] are required to conduct an annual assessment of the potential risks faced by minors using their services[167] and to adopt effective measures to mitigate those risks. Such measures may include the implementation of age verification systems, parental control tools or mechanisms that enable minors to report abuse or seek support.[168]

Finally, with regard to the protection of minors in the digital environment, the so-called Caivano Decree[169] has imposed an obligation on website operators and platform providers that disseminate video content not suitable for minors to verify users' age. In this context, the Communications Regulatory Authority (AGCOM), tasked with identifying the technical methods and procedures to be adopted for such verification—after consulting the Data Protection Authority[170]—clarified in its draft regulation[171] (approved during the session of 24 September 2024) that it intends to follow a neutral approach.

This approach would apply not only to video content but also to all services requiring age verification, such as the online sale of alcoholic beverages and online gambling.

References

Adamo G (2022) La contrattualistica per il commercio elettronico. In: Tripodi-F EM, Fimmanò-B. Tassone (eds) E-commerce. Regole, applicazioni, insidie, opportunità, Milano

---

[164] Art. 14(3) DSA.

[165] Art. 28 paragraph 1 DSA states that where the provider is aware, with reasonable certainty, that the recipient of the service is a minor, he may not present on his *online* interface advertising based on user profiling, and these measures must be taken from the design of the interface and do not imply the need to collect additional personal data of the user to assess whether the recipient of the service is a minor, nor do they necessarily require verification of the age of the user of the platform, unless the service offered *online* is prohibited to minors. In the latter case, it would instead be appropriate to intervene on the structure of the platform so as to allow verification of the user's age. In this regard, the Commission in 2022 within the framework of the new European strategy for children and minors BIK+(Better Internet Kids) published *best practices* concerning age verification and *parental control* settings, to which the DSA itself refers.

[166] That is, platforms whose number of recipients exceeds 45 million or a number equivalent to 10% of the population of the European Union (see Recital No. 76 of the DSA).

[167] Art. 34 DSA.

[168] Art. 35 lett j DSA.

[169] Decree Law No. 123 of 15.09.2023 converted into law with amendments by Law No. 159/2023, Art. 13 *bis*.

[170] Art. 13 *bis* d.l. No. 123/2023.

[171] In the pursuit of the aforementioned objectives, AGCOM will be required to ensure a level of security appropriate to the risk and in compliance with the minimisation of personal data collected for this purpose.

Addante A (2016) Tutela del consumatore nei contratti telematici e nuove frontiere del diritto europeo della vendita, Padova
Alpa G (2004) I contratti del minore. Appunti di diritto comparato In Contr
Alpa G (ed) (2020) Diritto e intelligenza artificiale, Pisa
Andreola E (2018) Gli acquisti online del minore tra invalidità dell'atto e responsabilità dei genitori In Contr. impr
Anzani G (2009) Capacità di agire e interessi della personalità. Nuova Giur Civ Comm
Astone F (2021) Intelligenza artificiale e diritto civile. In: V. Cuocci-F.P. Lops-C. Motti (eds) La circolazione della ricchezza nell'era digitale, Pisa
Auletta K (2009) Googled: the end of the world as we know it. New York
Battelli E, Brizzolari V (2024) Il contratto online. In: Battelli E (ed) Diritto privato digitale in, in collaborazione con G. d'Ippolito-T. Pellegrini, Torino
Battelli E (2014) Riflessioni sui procedimenti di formazione dei contratti telematici e sulla sottoscrizione on line delle clausole vessatorie. Rass Dir Civ 4
Battelli E (2022a) Vulnerabilità della persona e debolezza del contraente. Riv Dir Civ 5
Battelli E (2022b) I modelli negoziali di business degli operatori digitali a "prezzo zero" non sono "gratuiti". Contr
Battelli E (2022c) La contrattazione online. In: Battelli E (ed) Diritto Privato digitale, Torino
Benatti F (2018) L'"obbligazione" (un cammino). Nuovo Dir Civ, 3
Benedetti AM (2021) Contratto, algoritmi e diritto civile transnazionale: cinque questioni e due scenari. Riv Dir Civ
Benedetti M (2005) La formazione del contratto e l'inizio di esecuzione. Dal codice civile ai principi di diritto europeo dei contratti. Eur Dir Priv
Berti De Marinis G (2016) Autodeterminazione e capacità di discernimento del minore: profili di diritto civile. In Actualidad Jurídica Iberoamericana
Betti E (1966) La tipicità dei negozi giuridici romani e la cosiddetta atipicità del diritto odierno. Ann Macerata I:5
Bianca CM (1998) I contratti digitali, in Studium iuris
Bianca CM (2002) Diritto civile. 1. La norma giuridica. I soggetti, Milano
Bianca CM (2019a) Diritto civile. 3. Il contratto, Milano
Bianca M (2019b) Il minore e i nuovi media. In: Senigaglia R (ed) Autodeterminazione e minore di età, Pisa
Bird N (2023) Roblox: Ten-year-old spent £2,500 of mum's money without her knowing, bbc.com
Borruso R (1988) Computer e diritto, Milano
Busnelli FD (1982) Capacità ed incapacità di agire del minore, in Dir. fam. e pers
Camardi C (2021) Contratti digitali e mercati delle piattaforme, in Jus Civile, 4
Carbone E (2019) Contrattualità quotidiana e dignità della persona, in Riv. dir. civ
Caringella F, Buffoni L (2025) Manuale di diritto civile. Roma
Caterina R (2016) Le persone fisiche. Torino
Cavalaglio L (2006) La formazione del contratto. Normative di protezione ed efficienza economica, Milano
Cenni D (1998) La formazione del contratto tra realtà e consensualità. Padova
Cicero C (2019) Il problema dell'inosservanza del patto sulla forma. In: D'Angelo A, Roppo V (eds) Annuario del contratto. Torino
Cinque M (2007) Il minore e la contrattazione telematica tra esigenze del mercato e necessità di apposite tutele. in Nuova giust. civ. comm.
Clarizia R (2018) Informatica e contratto: la identificazione dei contraenti. In: Dialoghi con Guido Alpa, Roma
Conte G (2017) Sulla libertà dei privati di configurare il procedimento di formazione del contratto, in Giust. Civ
D'Amico G (1996) Regole di validità e principio di correttezza nella formazione del contratto. Napoli
D'Elia P (2021) Il procedimento atipico di formazione del consenso nella contrattazione online: profili evolutivi nella disciplina comunitaria e interna. in Dir., Mercato e Tecnologia
De Franceschi A, Schulze R (2019) Digital revolution – new challenges for law. München
De Nova G (1974) Il tipo contrattuale. Padova

Del Gatto S (2023) Il Digital Services Act: un'introduzione. in Giorn. dir. amm., 6
Delfini F (2020) Forma digitale, contratto e commercio elettronico. Milano
Di Donna L (2008) Obblighi informativi precontrattuali, vol 1. La tutela del consumatore, Milano
Di Gravio V (1989) Teoria del contratto reale e promessa di mutuo. Milano
Di Raimo V (2003) Autonomia privata e dinamiche del consenso. Napoli
Falzea A (1960) voce Capacità (Teoria generale). Enc. dir., VI, Milano
Favale R (2013) La conclusione del contratto telematico, in Giur. merito
Ferri GB (1970) Ordine pubblico, buon costume e teoria del contratto. Milano
Ferri GB (1984) La vendita in generale. In: Rescigno P (ed) Trattato di dir. priv., 11, Torino
Finocchiaro G (2017) Il quadro d'insieme sul Regolamento europeo. In: G. Finocchiaro (diretto da), Il nuovo regolamento europeo sulla privacy e sulla protezione dei dati personali, Bologna
Foderini A (2021) E-commerce e contratti telematici: la rimodulazione della contrattazione codicistica. Cammino diritto, 3
Follieri L (2005) Il contratto concluso in Internet, Napoli
Gambino AM (1997) Il contratto telematico, Milano
Gambino AM (2020) Big data e fairness. Il ruolo delle authorities. Nuovo dir. civ
Garaci I (2021) Il superiore interesse del minore nel quadro dello sviluppo sostenibile dell'ambiente digitale, in Nuove leggi civili comm
Gardani Contursi Lisi L (1988) La compravendita. In: Giur. sist. civ. e comm., fondata da Bigiavi W. Torino
Gemma A (2007) L'accordo telematico. In: Clarizia R (ed) I contratti informatici, Milano
Giardina F (1990) voce Minore (dir. civ.), in Enc. giur., XX, Roma, 2
Giardina F (2012) Commento all'art. 2 c.c. Maggiore età. Capacità di agire. In: Barba A, Pagliantini S (eds) Commentario del Codice Civile
Giardina F (2019) Il minore e il contratto. In: Senigaglia R (ed) Autodeterminazione e minore di età, Pisa
Giorgianni M (1968) L'obbligazione. Milano
Gitti G, Villa G (eds) (2008) Il terzo contratto. L'abuso di potere contrattuale nei rapporti tra imprese, Bologna
Gorla G (1956) Il dogma del «consenso» o «accordo» e la formazione del contratto di mandato gratuito nel diritto continentale. In: Riv. dir. civ., I
Grossi E (2003) La tutela del minore nel commercio elettronico e nella rete internet. LIUC Papers
Hannah F, Andrews J (2020) Loot boxes: I blew my university savings gaming on Fifa. BBC. https://www.bbc.com
Irti N (1999a) È vero, ma... (Replica a Giorgio Oppo). Rivista di diritto civile
Irti N (1999b) Scambi senza accordo. Rivista trimestrale di diritto e procedura civile
Irti N (2000) Lo scambio dei foulards (Replica semiseria al prof. Bianca). Rivista trimestrale di diritto e procedura civile
Kötz H, Patti A (2017) Diritto europeo dei contratti. Giuffrè, Milano
Lipari N (2013) Le categorie del diritto civile. Milano
Longo I (2006) Capacità e incapacità delle persone di età minore: alcuni spunti sul contratto telematico. Cyberspazio e diritto
Maggiore M, Assenza A (2024) I contratti online. In: Maggiore M (ed) Il commercio elettronico (pp. xx–xx). Torino
Maiello U (2003) La patologia discreta del contratto annullabile. Rivista di diritto civile
Mancini C (1999) La realità come scelta atipica. Rivista di diritto commerciale
Mazzamuto S (2017) Il contratto di diritto europeo. Torino
Messineo F (1958) Annullabilità e annullamento. In: Enciclopedia del diritto (Vol. II). Milano
Moscarini LV (2001) Diritti ed obblighi di informazione e forma del contratto. In: Diritto privato e interessi pubblici. Milano, pp xx–xx
Natoli U (1984) L'attuazione del rapporto obbligatorio. Tratt. dir. civ. comm. Cicu-Messineo. Milano
Nuzzo M (1972) Predisposizione di clausole e procedimento di formazione del contratto. In: Studi in onore di F. Santoro Passarelli. Napoli
Oppo G (1984) Disumanizzazione del contratto, in Riv. dir. civ
Palmieri A (2022) I contratti di accesso. Milano

Pascuzzi G (2020) Il diritto dell'era digitale Bologna
Pasquino T (2002) La conclusione del contratto nella direttiva sull'e-commerce In Ricciuto V Zorzi N (a cura di) Il contratto telematico. In: Galgano F (a cura di) Trattato di diritto commerciale e di diritto pubblico dell'economia Vol XXVII. Padova
Perlingieri C (2014) Profili civilistici dei social networks. Napoli
Perlingieri G (2011a) Il contratto telematico. In: Valentino D (ed) Manuale di diritto dell'informatica. Napoli
Perlingieri G (2011b) La convalida delle nullità di protezione e la sanatoria dei negozi giuridici. Napoli
Perlingieri G Lazzarelli F (2016) Internet e il contratto In Valentino D (a cura di) Manuale di diritto dell'informatica. Napoli
Perlingieri P Giova S Prisco I (2020) Il trattamento algoritmico dei dati tra etica diritto ed economia. Napoli
Piraino F (2020) Il commercio elettronico. In: Pasquino T, Rizzo A, Tescaro M (eds) Questioni attuali in tema di commercio elettronico. Napoli
Pirozzoli A (2018) Il libero accesso alla rete un diritto in espansione. In Diritto dell'informazione e dell'informatica
Poncibò C (2020) Il diritto comparato e la Blockchain. Napoli
Quarta A (2020) Mercati senza scambi La metamorfosi del contratto nel capitalismo della sorveglianza. Napoli
Quarta A Smorto G (2024) Diritto privato dei mercati digitali II ed Firenze p 205
Ricci F (2005) Sub Art 52 Informazioni per il consumatore. In Codice del consumo Commentario Napoli
Ricciuto V (2004) Il contratto telematico e i pagamenti elettronici l'esperienza italiana e spagnola a confronto. Milano
Ricciuto V (2018) La patrimonializzazione dei dati personali. In Diritto dell'informazione e dell'informatica
Ricciuto V (2022) La patrimonializzazione dei dati personali Contratto e mercato nella ricostruzione del fenomeno. In: Cuffaro V, D'Orazio R, Ricciuto V, (eds) I dati personali nel diritto europeo Torino
Rodotà S (2012) Il diritto di avere diritti. Bari
Roppo V (2001) Il contratto. In: Iudica G, Zatti P (eds) Trattato di diritto privato. Milano
Roppo V (2018) Parte generale del contratto contratti del consumatore e contratti asimmetrici. In Rivista di diritto privato
Roppo V (2020) Il contratto del duemila. Torino
Ruffolo U (a cura di) (2020) Intelligenza artificiale Il diritto i diritti l'etica. Milano
Ruperto S (2019) La dinamica giuridica. Un itinerario di diritto privato. Torino
Ruscello F (2000) Potestà genitoria e capacità dei figli minori dalla soggezione all'autonomia. In Vita notarile
Sacco R (1987) Autonomia nel diritto privato In Digesto delle discipline privatistiche I. Torino
Sacco R De Nova G (2016) Il contratto. Torino
Salito G (2019) Smart contract. In: Digesto delle discipline privatistiche Sezione civile Aggiornamento XII. Torino
Scognamiglio A (1984) La capacità di agire del minore. Studi in onore di De Nova
Seminara S (1996) La pirateria su Internet e il diritto penale. AIDA
Solinas C (2018) Il contratto amministrato La conformazione dell'operazione economica privata agli interessi generali. Napoli
Spangaro A (2014) Tutela dei minori e delle fasce deboli. In: Finocchiaro G, Delfini F (a cura di) Diritto dell'informatica. Milano
Stanzione F (2014) I contratti del minore. Europa e diritto privato
Stolfi G (1968) Sulla responsabilità precontrattuale del minore. Rivista di diritto commerciale
Taddei Elmi A, Contaldo A (eds) (2020) Intelligenza artificiale Algoritmi giuridici Ius condendum o fantadiritto. Pisa
Thobani S (2019) Il mercato dei dati personali tra tutela dell'interessato e tutela dell'utente. MediaLaws

Tommasi S (2023) Digital Services Act e Artificial Intelligence Act tentativi di futuro da armonizzare. Persona e mercato 2

Tommasini R (1988) voce Annullabilità e annullamento II Diritto privato. Enciclopedia giuridica II Roma

Tosi E (2003) Contrattazione telematica e conclusione del contratto virtuale. In: Rossello C, Finocchiaro G, Tosi E (eds) Commercio elettronico documento informatico e firma digitale (la nuova disciplina). Torino

Tosi E (2005) Il contratto virtuale. Milano

Tosi E (2010) Contratti informatici telematici e virtuali Nuove forme e procedimenti formativi. Milano

Tosi E (2014) La dematerializzazione della contrattazione. Il contratto virtuale con i consumatori alla luce della recente novella al Codice del Consumo di cui al D Lgs 21 febbraio 2014 n 21. Contratto e impresa

Tosi E (2021) Diritto privato delle nuove tecnologie. Milano

Trezza R (2021) Il contratto nell'era del digitale e dell'intelligenza artificiale. www.ildirittodelleconomia.it

Tripodi EM (2022) Verso un nuovo quadro di riferimento per il commercio digitale. In: Tripodi EM, Fimmanò F, Tassone B (eds) E-commerce Regole applicazioni insidie opportunità

Troiano S (2022) Il contratto tra analogico e digitale. Pactum Rivista di diritto dei contratti 1

Tulli E (2020) Filosofia e rivoluzione digitale Echi dal futuro. Bari

Versaci G (2020) La contrattualizzazione dei dati personali dei consumatori. Napoli

Zaccheo M (2019) Principi generali e obbligazioni. Nuovo diritto civile

Zeno-Zencovich V (2018) La "datasfera". In: Scaffardi L (ed) I "profili" del diritto Regole giuridiche per il mondo digitale rischi e opportunità nell'era digitale. Torino

Zimatore A (1985) Il mutuo di scopo Problemi generali. Padova

Zorzi N Galgano F (2012) I contratti di consumo e la libertà del consumatore. Padova

The Requirements of the Contract

Marina Romano

Contents

Abstract The chapter proposes to analyse the tightness of the discipline on contract requirements in the digital reality, distinguishing between hypotheses that are still attributable to the will of the parties and those where, on the contrary, the entire transaction is governed by AI and where Regulation (EU) 2024/1689 offers a relevant interpretative cue.

M. Romano (✉)
University of Naples "Parthenope", Naples, Italy
e-mail: marina.romano@uniparthenope.it

R. Bocchini (ed.), *Digital Platforms - From Technical Foundations to Legal and Economic Implications*, https://doi.org/10.1007/978-3-032-07978-7_8

1 The Impact of New Contractual Models on Contract Requirements

Recent decades have witnessed an epochal transformation in human existence due to the advent of the Internet, which has completely abolished space-time distances and opened up possibilities that were unimaginable just a few years before.

Technological innovations have followed one another with great rapidity, and if the advent of the Internet was considered a great change until recently, it now seems almost normal compared to what is happening with the transition to the so-called digital era and AI with increasingly complex algorithmic systems, endowed with an autonomous and progressive capacity for self-learning.

These systems are programmed by humans, but are no longer limited to being merely tools to assist human activity, as they are structured in such a way that they learn themselves and then make decisions in total autonomy: we have thus moved on to so-called generative Artificial Intelligence.

That said, in terms of exchanges, it is an absolutely incontrovertible fact that almost all of them now take place via the new digital tools.

The landscape is very diverse, ranging from contracts concluded *online*[1] with or through digital platforms, to those in which the parties may delegate the definition of part of the negotiation content to Artificial Intelligence, as may be the case, for example, for setting the price of air transport or insurance services,[2] to fully automated contracts such as *smart contracts.*

In all these models, although very different from each other, there is nevertheless a minimum common denominator, constituted by the fact that they are all, in a more or less direct way, traceable to human action, according to an anthropocentric perspective[3] in which technology, although very complex and sophisticated, is always dominated by man, who is the initial engine of every digital process.

On the other hand, an entirely different scenario appears to be emerging in reality as a result of the ever-increasing spread of generative Artificial Intelligence systems, in which even the initial decision to act is taken by the algorithm, which is now

---

[1] Think of contracts concluded between a user and a supplier directly by accessing the latter's site. For example, in the tourism sector, the tourist enters his data and the service chosen in a *form* provided by the hotelier. With the latter's confirmation, the hotel contract is concluded; the *form* also always requires the indication of credit card details, together with a warning that cancellation after a certain deadline would entail a penalty charge; thus, for all, Santagata (2025), pp. 184 ff.

[2] In the insurance sector, the amount of the premium can be defined as a result of monitoring through *apps* on the way the insured drives the vehicle, speed, risk, etc., or in the financial markets, the AI can manage the orders and quantities of securities to be traded.

[3] The anthropocentric view was confirmed by the European legislator in Regulation (EU) 2024/1689-AIA, in which, verbatim in Recital 1, it is made clear that 'the Union shall promote the deployment of anthropocentric and reliable artificial intelligence', as well as in Recital 6, where it is reiterated that 'AI should be an anthropocentric technology. It should serve as a tool for people, with the ultimate goal of improving the well-being of human beings'.

capable of pursuing its own objectives, completely unpredictable and unrelated to the programmer himself.

With regard to the first group of contracts, as mentioned above, on closer inspection, the entire process can always be traced back to man to some extent, even when it entails effects that are unforeseeable for him: it is, in fact, always man who made the initial choice concerning the technological modalities by which the entire relationship must be conducted.[4]

This consideration is possible because, although in the digital age, exchanges take place in a virtual space, the need that drives them is still attributable to man, who, through this system, pursues his own interests.[5] In other words, the network still serves the realisation of the interests of individuals.

In this field, a leading role is entrusted to the interpreter who, having to deal with the various and numerous implications of this new reality, such as the profile of the identification of the parties and the manner of concluding the contract, copyright, personal data protection, etc., must first of all orient himself among the traditional legal categories, whose suitability to provide adequate answers to the phenomenon must be verified, in the light of the numerous rules of European derivation that have followed one another over the years.

From a first observation, it emerges that we are in the presence of several contractual models,[6] each deserving of separate and in-depth analysis, which, however, is beyond the scope of these brief notes; here, instead, under the specific profile of the requirements of the contract, the content of Art. 1325 of the Civil Code must necessarily be connected with the peculiarities of the phenomenon,[7] especially as regards the requirement of consent, given that it is the one most directly dependent on the manner in which the contract is concluded.

Precisely by taking as a reference the numerous models observed in reality, the principles on the subject of contractual requirements must be interpreted differently depending on whether we are in the presence of contractual models in which their formation is still directly ascribable to man,[8] or those in which the algorithm governs the entire relationship; in the latter case, the interpreter is confronted with novel problems, for the framing of which, as will be pointed out, Regulation (EU) 2024/1689-AIA represents a solid point of reference.

---

[4] Thus, Spatuzzi (2023), p. 407.

[5] In this sense, Scognamiglio (2002), pp. 159 ff.

[6] The use of digital technologies would seem, in fact, to have produced a wide range of ways in which consent can be deemed to be expressed; therefore, an elastic reading of the contractual paradigm is suggested. Thus, Spatuzzi and Tosi (2021), pp. 201 ff.

[7] In this regard, the doctrine speaks of contracts without space and time: Finocchiaro (2018b), p. 191; Battelli (2022), p. 564.

[8] Consider, moreover, that authoritative doctrine has proposed a distinction between telematic contracts, cybernetic contracts and algorithmic contracts on the basis of the relevance of the requirement of will; thus, Gentili (2022), pp. 705 ff.

2 The Problem of Will Imputation in *Online* Contracts

In contractual models in which it is still possible to trace back to human action, the discipline may have unitary features insofar as they are all distance contracts and the platform (algorithm) is the means by which the conclusion of the contract takes place, or the contract is concluded directly with the platform.

In this area, the interpretative effort is facilitated by the circumstance that the contract is essentially still attributable to the will of the parties, albeit mediated by technology; in essence, in them, there is a negotiating will regarding the good or service[9] which is governed first and foremost by the rules on the imputation of the electronic document to the parties, as set out in Articles 20 ff. c. amm. dig.[10]

The provision of digital services, on the other hand, is regulated by Directive (EU) 770/2019, transposed by Legislative Decree No. 173 of 4 November 2021, which supplemented the Consumer Code[11] on the subject of contracts between professionals and consumers concerning this type of provision.

Online contracts are a species of the *genus of* distance contracts; in them, a fundamental role is played by digital platforms that essentially allow the sharing of content and the exchange of goods and services.[12] The manner in which the exchange takes place does not seem to alter its substance since in all of them the contractual will of the parties can be seen,[13] albeit manifested in peculiar ways.

Rather, it is a matter of considering the different segments of relations between the network users and the platform.[14] In fact, if the contract is concluded with the platform, which thus assumes the role of negotiating counterparty, one can have either the relationship segment (P2C),[15] or the relationship segment (P2B)[16] depending on whether the user is a consumer or a professional.

---

[9] Thus, Gentili (2022), pp. 705 ff.

[10] On this subject, see Bianca (2000), pp. 301 ff.; see also Finocchiaro (2018a), pp. 452 ff.

[11] With the insertion of Chapter *I-bis* after Chapter I of Title III of Part IV of the Consumer Code. For an initial discussion, Versaci (2023), pp. 2244 ff.

[12] It has, moreover, been pointed out that digital platforms, in addition to the service of connection and virtual showcase of goods and services, are essentially also capable of directly affecting the market through the offer of additional assistance and information services. Thus, Battelli (2022), p. 563.

[13] Thus, Caggiano (2018), pp. 1152 ff.; Finocchiaro (2018b), p. 192.

[14] On this subject, Battelli (2022), pp. 568 ff.

[15] In this hypothesis, the platform is positioned as a sort of virtual showcase where the characteristics of the goods and services are illustrated and where all the technical information relating to them is provided, as well as offering a series of assistance services functional to the execution of the main transaction, such as the guarantee of payment or the return/replacement phase of the good. On this subject, Smorto (2020), pp. 49 ff.

[16] This area of trade is governed by Regulation (EU) 2019/1150, also known as The P2B Regulation. It introduced into European law a new set of rules intended to ensure conditions of transparency and, above all, predictability for business users of *online* intermediary services and for users owning business websites that are in connection with *online* search engines.

If, on the other hand, the platform plays the role of a mere intermediary, then the relationship segment (P2P) will be.[17]

With regard to *online* contracts entered into between a professional and a consumer, these fall, as is well known, within the scope of application of the directive on electronic commerce, transposed by Legislative Decree No. 70 of 9 April 2003,[18] by which the services of the information society in the internal market were regulated in compliance with the general principle of the free movement of services. Here, the rules on the conclusion of the contract were expressly referred to in Art. 13(1),[19] and the contractual agreement between the parties, in this case the service provider and the recipient of the service,[20] is deemed to have been reached with the exchange of the order and the receipt thereof in accordance with the provisions of Art. 13(2); the order and receipt are deemed to be known to the addressee when the parties 'have the possibility of accessing them' pursuant to Art. 13(3), where the connection between the concept of 'knowledge of the proposal and acceptance' and that of 'access to the order or receipt' is made unequivocally, which occurs when telematic means are used.[21]

A clarification is necessary, however, since order and receipt rather mark the process of the conclusion of the contract, which, in this case, takes place when the offeror notifies the buyer/receiver that he has received his acceptance, and sends the receipt of the order in accordance with Art. 13(2).[22] At the level of individual contractual intentions, on the other hand, the provider makes his consent clear by presenting the offer in the virtual shop window, while the recipient accepts at the moment when he begins to follow a series of steps consisting of: opting for the chosen good or service, filling in all the fields that gradually 'open up', and carrying out the executive behaviour consisting of payment (typing in the credit card details). The subsequent moment of sending the order receipt would, therefore, in this procedure, have the function of assuring the addressee that the contract has been

[17] On this point, Battelli (2022), p. 568.

[18] Recently amended by Legislative Decree No. 50 of 25 March 2024, 'Integrative and corrective provisions of Legislative Decree No. 208 of 8 November 2021, containing the Consolidated Text on Audiovisual Media Services in view of changing market realities, implementing Directive (EU) 2018/1808 amending Directive 2010/13/EU'. On e-commerce, among many others, Signoretta (2023), pp. 116 ff.; Piraino (2023), pp. 146 ff.

[19] On Art. 13, however, consider what Benedetti (2006), p. 79. points out, who emphasises that the reference made by the legislature in it to the codified rules on the conclusion of contracts is the result of a compromise, intended to reassure the interpreter.

[20] Article 2 of Legislative Decree No. 70/2003 on the subject of definitions, qualifies the provider as the natural or legal person providing an information society service, and the recipient of the service as the person who, for professional or non-professional purposes, uses an information society service, in particular to search for or make accessible information.

[21] On this point, reference must again be made to the considerations expressed by Benedetti (2006), p. 79, who points out that the rapidity with which exchanges take place makes it, in fact, impossible to prove that one did not have knowledge without fault of what was expressed by the other party, according to the parameter of Art. 1335 of the Civil Code.

[22] For all, Benedetti (2006), p. 81.

concluded and that the entire operation has been successful (including that of payment). This strengthens the recipient's position, since virtual contracts are contracts dominated by the provider who has unilaterally arranged the entire procedure leading to the exchange, and which the purchaser cannot govern, but is obliged to follow.[23]

As distance contracts, they also fall within the scope of Directive 2011/83/EU implemented by Legislative Decree No. 21 of 21 February 2014, as well as within the scope of Directive 2019/2161/EU implemented by Legislative Decree No. 26 of 7 March 2023.

With regard to Directive 2011/83/EU,[24] it is part of the interventions of the European legislator aimed at strengthening consumer protection by broadening the concept of distance contract which, in the new rules, has been qualified as *any* contract, including a contract for an indefinite period of time, concluded between a trader and a consumer under an organised distance sales or service-provision scheme without the simultaneous physical presence of the parties, through the exclusive use of one or more means of distance communication.

Directive 2019/2161/EU, the so-called *omnibus* directive,[25] was also intended to introduce new provisions to strengthen consumer protection in the case of unfair terms, unfair commercial practices,[26] unfair competition or untruthful commercial communications, as well as to implement and adapt to the evolution of *business* models and *online* transactions the entire sanctioning system,[27] to ensure maximum harmonisation at the European level in the protection apparatus.

---

[23] Thus, Benedetti (2006), p. 79, who observes that the formative procedure of the contract has received a 'forward shift' in the interest of the offeree, the weaker party to the whole operation. This occurs in the sense that the contract is concluded when the offeree-recipient has knowledge that his order has been received, and this is attested by the sending of the order receipt by the lender.

[24] The decree transposing Directive 2011/83/EU made changes to the Consumer Code, replacing Chapter I of Title III, limited to Arts. 45 to 67. For an initial commentary on this decree, Gambino and Nava (2014). On the directive, Finocchiaro (2018b), p. 200.

[25] Legislative Decree No. 70 of 7 March 2023 transposing the directive made changes to the Consumer Code with the replacement in Part II, Title II, Chapter III of the heading of Section I entitled: 'Price Indication'. For an initial commentary on Directive 2019/2161/EU, Camilleri (2024), pp. 197 ff.

[26] Specifically, the system of unfair commercial practices has been enriched with the provision of a new typology qualifying as a misleading practice in the case of the promotion of a good, in one Member State, as identical to a good marketed in other Member States, although significantly different in composition or characteristics (so-called *dual quality*).

[27] Specifically, Art. 1 of Legislative Decree No. 26/2023 amended Arts. 27 and *37-bis* of the Civil Code.

3 The Proceduralisation of the Agreement Based on Information Obligations

The core of the aforementioned set of rules concerns the provision of a series of information obligations on which would be based a system aimed at rebalancing the position of the user-recipient who is exposed to the pitfalls of the network, against which he or she has no adequate means of protection.

The system of information obligations in force in digital exchanges is the one that most directly affects the requirements of the contract, since if on the one hand through this system of information it is possible to 'determine or make determinable' the requirement of the subject matter of the contract,[28] on the other hand the contractual will of the addressee seems to be reduced to a procedure consisting of correctly and carefully following the instructions unilaterally prepared by the proposer.

The offer prepared by the professional is, in fact, displayed on the virtual showcase, and when it is opted for by a potential buyer, a scheme is set up, as already noted, characterised by various chain steps that the recipient/buyer is obliged to follow if he intends to proceed with the purchase. It is in these terms that his willingness to accept is *proceduralised* according to a unilateral choice that is the sole responsibility of the professional.[29]

That being said, the information obligation system thus fulfils the function of eliminating the *gap in which* the network user finds himself, represented by the purely virtual nature that necessarily accompanies the preliminary phase, in which any form of negotiation between the parties would be completely absent.[30]

The pre-contractual information obligations that must be provided in advance to the user are, in fact, functional for the exact determination of the subject matter of the contract; it is a matter of defining the services to be provided by the parties with regard to delivery terms, shipping costs, payment of the price and the terms of payment, the possibility of access to discounts or promotions, as well as, of course, the

[28] Indeed, the subject of the object of the contract has been put in different terms based on the consideration that virtual reality is immaterial; in it, the traditional canons of space and time have lost their intrinsic meaning. In essence, a new reality has arisen where relations are characterised by the physical absence of the parties. In this context, the object of the contract is itself immaterial, in the sense that it becomes the computer code, susceptible to being used by an unlimited number of users. According to this approach, therefore, this dematerialisation of the object of the contract, together with the dematerialisation of space and time, characterises what is defined as virtual contracting. In this sense, E. Tosi, *Il contratto virtuale con i consumatori*, in *Studium iuris*, 2, 2014, 150 ff.

[29] Thus, Benedetti (2006), p. 79; Finocchiaro (2018b), p. 193.

[30] Thus, Battelli (2022), p. 564.; Gentili (2022), p. 705. On this subject, see also the considerations set out by Finocchiaro (2018b), p. 192.

technical characteristics of the good or service and the existence of the right of withdrawal.[31]

This phase is also, in turn, functional to the externalisation of an informed contractual consent, to the extent that, if the information is omitted or provided inexactly or incompletely, the will may be vitiated.[32] Nevertheless, it has been observed that these information obligations cannot include the obligation to send the addressee/buyer the offeror's receipt of the order, since this would constitute a mere procedural burden[33] since, as noted above, the contract has already been concluded with the payment of the price by the addressee.

The function of information obligations is also to obviate the problem of the certain identification of users on the net, given that the virtual context is the ideal environment for concealing or falsifying one's true identity.[34] Information obligations, therefore, include those relating to the identity of contracting parties, as well as a number of others of various kinds.

A preponderant role is played by pre-contractual information, as anticipated; in this regard, it is provided that the trader must provide or make available the information in an 'appropriate' manner in view of the medium used, pursuant to Art. 12(1)(a) of Legislative Decree No. 70/2003.

The consumer must also be informed of the possibility reserved for him to correct any errors before the order is sent to the other party, as provided for in Art. 12(1).

With regard to the aspect of the user's accessibility of this information, it is possible to proceed by 'referring' it to a *web* page, or 'sending' it, for example, by *e-mail* to his *e-mail* address; this option may facilitate the trader's commitments, but it must be implemented in such a way that the information must in any case be fully compliant with the requirements of transparency and 'accessibility' by the consumer, given that it becomes an integral part of the type of contract to be concluded subsequently.

If a durable medium is used, this information must be readable, subject to the limitations of the medium.

The burden of proof relating to the fulfilment of the information obligations falls on the professional, this being behaviour that conforms to the principle of accountability in terms of making the subjects responsible for compliance with the regulations on the subject.[35] In fact, the system of sanctions provided for by Art. 21 of Legislative Decree No. 70/2003 transposing Directive 2000/31/EU, and subsequently by Legislative Decree No. 26/2023 transposing Directive 2019/2161/EU, in addition to compensation for damages for breach of the principle of good faith, is in this direction.

---

[31] On the information concerning the exercise of the right of withdrawal under Directive 2011/83/EU, see Finocchiaro (2018b), pp. 200 ff.

[32] On this point, see Gentili and Battelli (2012), pp. 371 ff.; Finocchiaro (2018b), p. 194.

[33] In this sense, Benedetti (2006), p. 80.

[34] Thus, Finocchiaro (2018b), p. 192.

[35] On this point, see Carleo (2021), pp. 349 ff.

4 The Different Assessments in the Case of Algorithms *That Are 'Mere Tools' or Have the 'Ability to Learn and Decide'*

At first analysis, the phenomenon appears to have different peculiarities in the case of contracts characterised by varying degrees of automation, where an algorithm is also capable of autonomously making negotiation choices; these are hypotheses in which a programme is capable of managing the formation as well as the execution of the contract.[36]

In this context, given the absence of any negotiation between the parties,[37] the central point is the imputation of the will expressed by the algorithm.

In the case of algorithms that are '*mere* tools', i.e. that constitute an instrument for the transmission of a negotiating will attributable to man, the question is whether the algorithm can constitute a declaration, tacit, of negotiating will, or whether it constitutes a beginning of the execution of the contract.[38] In either case, however, there seems to be no doubt that we are in the presence of a case that can still be ascribed to man from the point of view of the imputation of the negotiating will.[39]

On the other hand, the formation of a contract always implies a procedure, i.e. a sequence of human behaviours that must comply with regulatory provisions. Not only can different procedural schemes coexist in the legal system, but these can also change over time due to new provisions that intervene to regulate the matter;[40] and this is exactly what has happened with the transition to the digital era, where new European-derived rules have regulated the formation of contracts concluded by telematic means.

If anything, the analysis should be directed towards identifying the consequences in the event of algorithm malfunctioning, where it has been noted that the question could be posed in terms of liability[41] in its management by the programmer; this approach would also be in line with Regulation (EU) 2024/1689-AIA, whereby the European legislator set the regulation of Artificial Intelligence on a system based on the risk connected to the use of such systems, imposing constraints proportionate to the dangers that the use of this technology may cause to society.[42]

---

[36] The impact of technology is such that the programme 'is the contract', thus, verbatim, Benedetti (2021), p. 413. The author proposes a further classification between algorithmic negotiation, which would be functional to the formation of the contract or the determination of the object, and *smart contracts*, which would instead be functional to the execution phase of the contract.

[37] Thus, Gentili (2022), p. 705.

[38] Thus, Caggiano (2018), p. 1156.

[39] On this subject, see also the considerations of Gentili (2022), p. 710.

[40] Thus, for all, Roppo (2024), p. 375.

[41] On the subject, Caggiano (2018), p. 1156.

[42] Broadly speaking, it is envisaged that systems containing only a limited risk will be subject to very light transparency requirements, whereas high-risk systems—used for instance in critical infrastructure, education, human resources or law enforcement—will be subject to more stringent requirements. This risk-structured system has been variously articulated; specifically, the new regulation proposes a risk-based subdivision of AI systems. First, there are the AI systems charac-

In the most up-to-date version, some algorithms are now able to define the content of the contract themselves and thus essentially the obligations incumbent on the parties, as in the case of *smart contracts*[43] where there is a high degree of automation.

Smart contracts have aroused a great deal of interest in doctrine; as far as the perspective of these brief notes is concerned, it should be premised, very briefly, that these are computerised procedures, which make use of a particular technology[44] through which it is possible to implement the precise will of the parties regarding the production of predetermined effects.

The peculiarity of *smart contracts* is the automaticity of their effects and the unmodifiability of their content, which translates into an undoubted advantage in terms of the certainty and precision of the relations between the parties and vis-à-vis third parties, since it would be known to all parties involved that the mechanism is based on the 'if-this-then-that'.[45]

They also entail considerable cost savings, due to the exclusion of any intermediary or approval figure; in them, the margin of error[46] is minimised, as is that of non-performance[47] or invalidity of the contract.[48]

---

terised by unacceptable risk, which are therefore prohibited because they are considered contrary to the fundamental values of the EU. Then there are the high-risk systems, where the Regulation intervenes in a more punctual and exhaustive manner, going on to define a series of quality requirements that these systems must meet, as well as a whole series of compliance obligations incumbent on all the operators that, for various reasons, enter into the supply and delivery chain of that AI system: the supplier, the distributor, the user, the importer of AI systems from countries outside the EU, and the authorised representatives. Basically, high-risk systems are those on which the greatest attention is focused, as they can potentially have negative repercussions on people's security or their fundamental rights; for these, it is necessary, according to the objective of the legislation, to reduce the risks to acceptable levels.

For an initial insight into the novelties of the Regulation, among many contributions, Smorto (2024), pp. 208 ff.; Petruso and Smorto (2024), pp. 989 ff.

[43] There are now many contributions on *smart contracts,* including Maugeri (2021); Battelli (2020), pp. 681 ff.; Finocchiaro (2020), pp. 4 ff.; Fauceglia (2020), pp. 591 ff.; Pardolesi and Davola (2019), p. 195; Di Sabato (2017), pp. 317 ff.; Caggiano (2018), p. 1154.

[44] One of the most widespread technologies underlying the functioning of *smart contracts* is the *blockchain*, which guarantees the realisation of divided effects upon the occurrence of pre-set conditions; on this topic, among many contributions, Contaldo and Campara (2019), pp. 30 ff.; Caggiano (2018), p. 1154.

This particular technology has been the subject of in-depth analysis in terms of its relationship with the system of rules that govern social reality. In this direction, the question has indeed been raised as to whether such a technology could have the potential to regulate the conduct of individuals itself, in the sense that the procedure contained in the code would become an unmodifiable rule that is automatically executed; Thus, Caforio (2023), p. 151. For an in-depth discussion on the functioning of the *blockchain* and the key system connected to it, Spatuzzi (2023), p. 408.

[45] Thus, Benedetti (2006), p. 414.

[46] Thus, Caforio (2023), p. 152.

[47] Extensively on this point, Di Sabato (2017), pp. 318 ff.

[48] On this point, Caggiano (2018), p. 115, points out that this efficiency of the *smart contract* functioning system leads to a more limited application of the remedies on the subject of contract pathology.

In terms of the requirements of the contract *pursuant to* Art. 1325 of the Civil Code, and specifically of the contractual will, it is certainly possible to detect the total absence of it in the phase of operation of the computer code. On the other hand, as in normal contracts, even in this hypothesis, the will of the parties exists, and it is the will of the effects that the contract will produce at the end of the procedure; in other words, it is possible to detect that we are in the presence of a will translated into computer code.

The legislature defined *smart contracts* in Art. *8-ter* of Decree-Law No. 135 of 14 December 2018 by framing them within the framework of 'distributed ledger-based technologies', as a 'computer programme' to the results/effects of which it recognises binding validity between the parties.

In this regard, the very letter of this provision[49] has given rise to different conclusions by the doctrine regarding the legal qualification of *smart contracts*.

Given the peculiar nature of *smart contracts*, one part of the doctrine, basing itself on the definition given by the legislator who qualified them as computer programmes, concluded that they would constitute mere instruments for the realisation of previous agreements reached between the parties.[50]

Another part of the doctrine, on the other hand, considered that these computer codes would have the function of translating the will of the parties into technical language, thus conferring greater importance on the reference made by the legislator to the bond arising between the parties. *Smart contracts* would thus be contracts[51] endowed with their own peculiarities as regards the arising of the contractual will.[52]

With regard more specifically to the subject matter requirement, one may conclude that it would, in any event, be determinable to the extent that the parameters for its determination have been provided for in the *smart contract*;[53] this also on the basis of Art. 1349 of the Civil Code, according to which the determination of the subject matter of the contract may be entrusted to a third party, provided that the parties have determined both the essential core of the relationship and the criteria for its determination.[54]

---

[49] Admittedly, it has been pointed out that the tenor of the provision would make the binding nature of the *smart contract* dependent on the execution of the IT procedure, thus meaning that the agreement on the effects would be an antecedent event. Thus, Cerrato (2020), p. 382.

[50] Thus, Contaldo and Campara (2019), p. 42; Cuccuru (2017), p. 111; Caggiano (2018), p. 115. On this topic, see also Cerrato (2020), p. 374.

[51] In this sense, Di Sabato (2017), p. 392; Gambino (2019), p. 1169.
Benedetti (2021), p. 415.

[52] However, it should be considered that a more precise legal qualification of *smart contracts* must presuppose a careful assessment of how the computer code works in the specific case, as it has been highlighted that there can be *smart contracts* in which the implementation of a previous agreement between the parties is more evident, from hypotheses in which, instead, certain aspects are expected to be the result of an automatic application of the programme; in this sense, A. Stazi, *Automazione contrattuale e 'contratti intelligenti'*, Torino, 2019, 107.

[53] On the subject, Finocchiaro (2018a), p. 456.

[54] Thus, Bianca (2000), pp. 327 ff.

On the other hand, it should be noted that in general it would never be possible in a contract for the parties to plan every aspect of the contractual affair; indeed, it has been pointed out that the role of the will is indeed central, but not entirely exhaustive,[55] which does not mean, however, that the result obtained is not in any case in keeping with the interests of the parties.

This observation would thus also be valid for highly automated contracts, when the algorithm system is particularly complex and can lead to results that were *unforeseeable a priori* for the parties; what must be noted, however, is that from the outset there must have been a concerted will to use *that* computerised procedure, which implies that from the outset the contractual parties voluntarily accepted its consequences.[56]

Based on these findings, *smart contracts*, although endowed with a certain degree of automation, would still be attributable to man; in this case, the decision-making complexity of the algorithms would therefore *still* not exclude the will of man.

They would ultimately represent an agreement between the parties on the technique (algorithm) chosen to manage the relationship;[57] a contract on the contract, to which it would be possible to attribute the value of a framework contract.[58]

5 The Legal Qualification of the Bargaining Will Resulting From 'Computer Instructions'

However, as initially pointed out, we are now in the era of algorithms with the '*ability to learn and decide*', i.e. the so-called generative Artificial Intelligence, capable of trading characterised by a maximum degree of automatism, an example of which can be represented by the automated algorithmic trading of financial instruments[59] in which even the choice of whether or not to initiate the order, as well as the timing and price, is attributable to the algorithm.[60]

In essence, these are not systems that transmit orders to trading venues, or confirm orders that have already been placed, or even manage the post-trade phase, as they have an autonomous ability to determine trading parameters.

Another example may be the interconnected algorithmic systems capable of ordering goods in depletion,[61] still autonomously settling the monetary transaction

---

[55] Thus, Di Giovanni (2019), p. 1684.

[56] On this subject, see, moreover, the considerations of Spatuzzi (2023), p. 412, on the remedies provided by the legal system in the event that the parties' action gives rise to results that differ substantially from those expected.

[57] Thus, Benedetti (2021), p. 416.

[58] Thus, Di Ciommo (2019), p. 261.

[59] As referred to in Art. 1, paragraph *6-quinquies*, TUF.

[60] See Caggiano (2018), p. 1155.

[61] It is Amazon's Dash Replenishment (DRS) service.

on behalf of the user. In these hypotheses, one could still reason in terms of imputability to the user of the entire operation, essentially holding him responsible for having concluded a contract with an undetermined object, and considering him exposed to the consequences arising from the operation[62] in terms of fulfilment of obligations; in particularly complex systems, however, it is not always easy to have a 'human' user as a reference.

There is also high-frequency algorithmic trading (HFT) based on algorithmic systems capable of implementing precise *marketing* strategies based on price.[63] They are enabled to autonomously set the price of a good or service on the basis of external variables that they can instantaneously process, such as: the number of views of the supplier's site by the user before the purchase, the time of day, his profiling, and his habits. This list is, however, only indicative, as this technology is spreading rapidly in all sectors of the economy.

In this context, it is less easy to define the terms of the question in terms of verifying the impact of new technologies on the regulation of contracts, as the whole process lacks any human *input* of which technology can still be considered to be the conduit.

In this context, we are in the presence of a machine/programme that has its own decision-making and operational autonomy.[64] As it is endowed with the capacity for self-learning, it is progressively capable of reproducing the decision-making process and human intelligence.

Even in the case of algorithms endowed with the '*ability to learn and decide*', as previously noted for *smart contracts*, it must be concluded that the will is absent and the entire process consists of a series of *imputations* of an exclusively computerised type, endowed with the ability to function autonomously of its user. The difference consists, on the other hand, in the circumstance that for *smart contracts,* it was possible to find that the will, so to speak 'human', was present insofar as it had been translated into a computer code, as a will expressed in a non-conventional language.

In the case of generative Artificial Intelligence, in which the degree of automation is therefore the maximum that technology allows at the moment, the interpreter is presented with a scenario that is completely unprecedented in many respects, in which the AI system's ability to autonomously adopt decisions relevant to the conclusion of contracts is only one of many aspects to be examined.

At present, the doctrine's effort to frame the phenomenon within the traditional legal categories has consisted, first and foremost, in attempting to recognise to the AI system a sort of legal subjectivity with the attribution to it of an electronic personality, which, however, upon careful examination has turned out not to be

---

[62] Thus, Finocchiaro (2018a), pp. 441 and 456.

[63] It has been pointed out, in this regard, that *marketing* strategies based on *dynamic pricing* make markets extremely volatile and complex, with respect to which normal operators are no longer aware; thus, Caggiano (2018), p. 1155. This consideration seems rather indicative of the circumstance that in certain sectors of the economy, the supremacy of the algorithm is already a reality.

[64] Authoritative doctrine has qualified this technology as *computable contracts*, thus, Benedetti (2021), p. 413.

feasible;[65] not even the recognition of a robotic representation has been considered conceivable,[66] given that any form of representation is based on the priority attribution of the capacity to understand and want to the representative to then be able to transfer the effects of the act concluded in the legal sphere of the represented.

Moreover, the profile of imputation of liability connected with the risk of the actions of the I.A. in the performance of the contractual activity was also considered a non-exhaustive interpretative option in light of the unforeseeable consequences that could occur.[67]

It is necessary, therefore, in this attempt at reconstruction to start from a fixed point that can be represented by Regulation (EU) 2024/1689,[68] which reaffirmed the centrality of the anthropocentric perspective that must, therefore, be duly taken into account by the interpreter when re-examining the institutions of contract law in the light of a new reality in which technology dominates.

In this perspective, the IA's negotiating activity can be regarded as a kind of integrative will[69] with respect to the main/contractual will of the parties, which is necessary for a certain transaction to be realised through the use of an AI system.

Ultimately, the use of complex algorithmic systems in contractual activity entails significant repercussions on the requirements of the contract and calls the interpreter to a considerable interpretative effort; in those models where it is possible, even mediately, to impute the contract to the will of the parties, the interpretative activity was easier as it was essentially a matter of re-examining the contractual rules in light of the peculiarities of the technology used.

In the hypothesis, on the other hand, of generative Artificial Intelligence systems in which the entire operation is substantially dominated by the machine/programme, recourse has been made to the anthropocentric perspective according to the indications recently provided by the European legislator in Regulation (EU) 2024/1689. This perspective has made it possible to point out that an AI system, with maximum automation, can be endowed, with respect to the negotiation event, with operational autonomy, in the function of integration[70] of the will of man, which is therefore positioned only in the background with respect to that of the machine, but does not

---

[65] For a careful analysis of the obstacles to such a solution, for all, Bravo (2024), pp. 1073 ff.

[66] For all, Sartor (2003), p. 485; Benedetti (2021), pp. 424 ff., who a few years ago called for a new 'Vienna Convention' to be entrusted with the task of hypothesising a world code of the algorithmic contract to safeguard the higher values of equality and solidarity.

For the extensive arguments against accepting a kind of robotic representation, Bravo (2024), pp. 1077 ff.

[67] For all, Finocchiaro (2018a), pp. 455 ff. Again, for arguments against the acceptance of this solution, Bravo (2024), pp. 1081 ff.

[68] It has been observed that the Regulation does not contain any provisions relevant to contract law. Only a *disclosure* obligation on suppliers would be provided for in Art. 50 when an AI system is intended to deal with natural persons, thus, Bravo (2024), p. 1093.

[69] For all, Bravo (2024), pp. 1089 ff., the author hypothesises the use of AI systems in the conclusion of contracts as a recourse to a voluntary, objective source of contractual integration.

[70] Thus, Bravo (2024), p. 1076.

vanish; in these terms, the case in point can still be brought back within the scope of Art. 1325 of the Civil Code.

References

Battelli E (2020) Le nuove frontiere dell'automatizzazione contrattuale tra codici algoritmici e "big data": gli "smart contracts" in ambito assicurativo, bancario e finanziario. In: Giust. civ., p 681 ff

Battelli E (2022) Questioni aperte in materia di contrattazione nelle piattaforme online. In Contratti, p 564, che rinviano a Irti N (1998) Scambi senza accordo. In Riv Trim Dir Proc Civ 2:347 ff

Benedetti AM (2006) Autonomia privata procedimentale e formazione del contratto virtuale: annotazioni sull'art. 13 del d.lgs. 70/2003. In: Diritto dell' internet, p 79–81

Benedetti AM (2021) Contratto, algoritmi e diritto civile transnazionale: cinque questioni e due scenari. Riv Dir Civ p 413 ff

Bianca CM (ed. 2°) (2000) Diritto civile, 3, Il contratto, p 301 ff

Bravo F (2024) Intelligenza Artificiale, autonomia contrattuale e meccanismi di controllo. Contr. e impr., p 1073 ff

Caforio G (2023) *La* blockchain *determina difficoltà nel determinare l*e regole da applicare e la giurisdizione competente. Dir Ind pp 151–152

Caggiano IA (2018) Il contratto nel mondo digitale. In Nuova giur. civ. comm. 2:1152 ff

Camilleri E (2024) Pratiche commerciali scorrette, safety net e nuove vulnerabilità: prospettive e limiti. In Nuove leggi civ. comm. p 197 ff

Carleo R (2021) Il principio di accountability nel GDPR: dalla regola all'auto- regolazione. In Nuovo Dir Civ, p 349 ff

Cerrato SA (2020) Appunti su smart contract e diritto dei contratti. In Banca, borsa, tit. cred., 3:374 ff

Contaldo A, Campara F (2019) Blockchain, criptovalute, smart contract, industria 4.0. Registri digitali, accordi giuridici e nuove tecnologie, Pisa, p 30 ff

Cuccuru P (2017) Blockchain ed automazione contrattuale. Riflessioni sugli smart contract. In Nuova Giur Civ Comm., p 111

Di Ciommo (2019) Smart contract e (non-) diritto, Il caso dei mercati finanziari. Nuovo Dir, p 261

Di Giovanni F (2019) Attività contrattuale e Intelligenza Artificiale. In Giur. it., p 1684

Di Sabato D (2017) Gli smart contracts: robot che gestiscono il rischio contrattuale. In Contr. e impr., p 317 ff

Fauceglia G (2020) Il problema dell'integrazione dello smart contract. Contratti, p 591 ff

Finocchiaro G (2018a) Il contratto nell'era digitale. In Riv. trim. dir. proc. civ., 2:452 ff

Finocchiaro G (2018b) Il perfezionamento del contratto on line: opportunità e criticità. In Dir. com. scambi internaz., p 191 ff

Finocchiaro G (2020) *Riflessioni sugli* "smart contracts" e sull'intelligenza artificiale. www.giustiziacivile.com, p 4 ff

Gambino AM (2019) Vizi e virtù del diritto computazionale. Dir Inf, p 1169

Gambino AM. e Nava G (2014) (a cura di) I nuovi diritti dei consumatori. Commentario al d.lgs. 21/2014, Torino

Gentili A (2022) La volontà nel contesto digitale: interessi del mercato e diritti delle persone. In Riv. trim. dir. proc. civ., p 705 ff

Gentili A, Battelli E (2012) Le patologie del contratto telematico. In: Tosi E (ed) La tutela dei consumatori in internet e nel commercio elettronico, Milano, p 371 ff

Maugeri M (2021) Smart contracts e disciplina dei contratti. Bologna

Pardolesi R, Davola A (2019) "Smart contract"*:* lusinghe ed equivoci dell'innovazione purchesia. In Foro it., p 195

Petruso R, Smorto G. (2024) Il Regolamento europeo sull'intelligenza artificiale: una prima lettura. Nuova giur. civ. comm., 4:989 ff

Piraino F (2023) La responsabilità dei prestatori di servizi di condivisione di contenuti online. Nuove leggi civ. comm., p 146 ff

Roppo V (ed. 9°) (2024) Diritto privato, Torino, p 375

Santagata R (2025) Manuale di diritto del turismo. p 184 ff

Sartor G (2003) Gli agenti software e la disciplina degli strumenti cognitivi. Dir Inf p 485

Scognamiglio R (2002) L'adempimento dell'operazione economica telematica tra "realtà virtuale" ed "interessi dei contraenti". In: Ricciuto V, Zorzi N (eds) Il contratto telematico, in Tratt. dir. comm., directed by Galgano, Padova, 2002, p 159 ff

Signoretta C (2023) La responsabilità civile degli intermediari internet. Danno Resp, p 116 ff

Smorto G (2020) La tutela del contraente debole nella platform economy, dopo il Regolamento UE 2019/1150 e la Direttiva UE 2019/2161 (c.d. Omnibus). In: Falce V (ed) Fairness e innovazione nel mercato digital*e*. Torino, p 49 ff

Smorto G (2024) Distribuzione del rischio e tutela dei diritti nel Regolamento europeo sull'intelligenza artificiale. Una riflessione critica. Foro It V:208 ff

Spatuzzi A (2023) Algoritmi e automazione: la notte del contratto? Notar 4:407–412

Tosi E (2021) Diritto privato delle nuove tecnologie. Milano, p 201 ff

Versaci G (2023) Contratti di fornitura di contenuti e servizi digitali: scioglimento, restituzioni e obbligazioni post-contrattuali. Giur It 10:2244 ff

Contract Form

Valentina Citarella

Contents

Abstract This work examines the forms of computer documents, starting from the classification of digital signatures and, therefore, the simple electronic signature, the advanced electronic signature, the qualified electronic signature, the digital signature and, finally, the authenticated electronic signature as defined pursuant to Legislative Decree No. 82 of 7 March 2005, the Digital Administration Code and, for brevity, CAD, which is the new legislative text of reference on computer documents and digital signatures. The examination of the forms of digital contracts then continues with the public digital deed drawn up by the Notary Public and addresses the issues relating to the public official's obligation to ascertain the validity of the digital signature certificates and the filing and preservation obligations of the public digital document on the part of the aforementioned professional.

V. Citarella (✉)
University of Naples "Parthenope", Naples, Italy
e-mail: vcitarella@notariato.it

R. Bocchini (ed.), *Digital Platforms - From Technical Foundations to Legal and Economic Implications*, https://doi.org/10.1007/978-3-032-07978-7_9

1 The Formal Requirement in the Digital Contract

The examination of the formal requirement of the digital contract presupposes a defining premise concerning the qualification of the digital document.

It has historically been pointed out that three elements characterise the document: the subject matter, the medium and the content. As for the first of these three elements, it is substantiated by any material that is capable of bearing witness to the fact that, in historical experience, it has always been paper, whereby the document *tout court* was identified with the paper document.[1]

The paper document has been joined, over time, by the electronic document that appeared for the first time in our legal system with the issuance of the Regulation containing criteria and methods for the formation, filing and transmission of documents by computer and telematic means, Presidential Decree No. 513 of 10 November 1997, later transfused into the Consolidated Text of legislative and regulatory provisions on administrative documentation, Presidential Decree No. 445 of 28 December 2000.[2]

This body of legislation was then further repealed in its central part, relating to the regulation of computerised documents, with effect from 1 January 2006 by the CAD, Legislative Decree No. 82 of 7 March 2005, in fact the new reference legislative text on computerised documents and digital signatures.[3]

The Digital Administration Code, CAD for brevity, defines the computerised document in Art. 1, para. 1, letter p), as: '*the document that contains the computer representation of acts, facts or legally relevant data*' in dualistic opposition to the analogue document which, in the subsequent letter p)-*bis*, is defined as '*the non-computerised representation of acts, facts or legally relevant data*'.

The subsequent Art. 20 of the CAD, in a certain sense, completes the aforementioned definition by specifying that: '*The computer document by whoever formed,*

---

[1] Carnelutti (1975), p. 86.

[2] La normativa in materia di documento informatico e firma digitale era essenzialmente contenuta nel d.P.R. 28 dicembre 2000, n. 445, *Testo Unico delle disposizioni legislative e regolamentari in materia di documentazione amministrativa*, che ha incorporato le disposizioni del d.P.R. 10 novembre 1997, n. 513, *Regulation containing criteria and methods for the formation, filing and transmission of documents by computer and telematic means*, and in Presidential Decree No. 10 of 23 January 2002, which implemented in our country Directive 1999/93/EC on the *Community framework for electronic signatures*, all as amended by Presidential Decree No. 137 of 7 April 2003, containing *Coordination Provisions on electronic signatures*.

[3] Legislative Decree No. 82 of 5 March 2005, published in the *Official Gazette*, 16 May 2005, No. 112 – enacted pursuant to Delegated Law No. 229 of 29 July 2003 – supplemented and corrected by Legislative Decree No. 159 of 4 April 2006, published in the *Official Gazette*, 29 April 2006, No. 99, which, from the date of its entry into force, scheduled for 1 January 2006, repealed Legislative Decree No. 10 of 23 January 2002, as well as Articles 1(1)(t), (u), (v), (vi), (vii) and (vii) of the same Decree. (t), (u), (v), (z), (aa), (bb), (cc), (dd), (ee), (ff), (gg), (hh), (ii), (ll), (mm), (nn), (oo); 2, para. 1, last sentence, 6; 8; 9; 10; 11; 12; 13; 14; 17; 20; 22; 23; 24; 25; 26; 27; *27-bis*; 28; *28-bis*; 29; *29-bis*; *29-ter*; *29-quater*; *29-quinquies*; *29-sexies*; *29-septies*; *29-octies*; 36, paras. 1, 2, 3, 4, 5 and 6; 51 of d. Presidential Decree No. 445 of 28 December 2000.

the recording on computer support and the transmission by telematic means are valid and relevant for all legal purposes, if they comply with the provisions of this code'.

Computer representation, therefore, as opposed to analogue representation, is understood as the mode of imprinting a computer impulse, defined as a bit, stored on an electronic support that is converted into language graphemes (mainly letters of the alphabet) having as its object acts, understood as behaviour attributable to a legal subject, facts, occurrences of material reality, or data, and therefore, codified descriptions of phenomena that have legal relevance.

The term *computerised representation of* the CAD was then supplemented by the concept of *electronic representation* ascribable to the Regulation of the Parliament and of the Council of 23 July 2014, No. 910, the so-called *eIDAS* Regulation (*electronic IDentification Authentication and Signature*), which defines an electronic document as '*any content stored in electronic form, in particular text or sound, visual or audiovisual recordings*'.

It follows from the defining premise that the digital form, or electronic form, is therefore a mode of expression that, through the computer technology described, allows statements to be made in written form that are stored on a durable electronic medium.

The digital formal requirement, like the analogue one, is not, however, a unitary concept; therefore, it is more correct to speak, with reference to the formal requirement, of *computerised documents* and not of *computerised documents.*

The classification made for the types of computer documents follows directly from the way in which they are signed and, therefore, from the type of electronic signature used for their formation, and, to this effect, one must speak not of *electronic form* but of *electronic forms.*

1.1 Electronic Signatures and the Resulting Forms of Electronic Private Contracts

In the legal tradition of our legal system, for a document to be attributable to a subject, it must be signed. What, precisely, makes a document attributable to a specific subject is the signature; it consists of the placing of one's name and surname at the bottom of the document and typically fulfils three functions: indicative—in that it makes it possible to identify the author of the document, declarative—in that it implies the assumption of authorship of the document—and, finally, probative of the authenticity of the document itself.[4]

The essential characteristic of the signature of a paper document is, therefore, autographity, i.e. the fact that it is written in the author's own hand: only in this way does it fulfil the functions traditionally associated with it, the indicative one, in that

---

[4] Bechini (2003), pp. 24 ff.

it serves to identify the person who affixed it, and the declarative one of assuming the authorship of the document.

In the digital context, on the other hand, the authorship of an electronic document is resolved through the use of a technical device that is at the disposal of a specific person and that is affixed to the digital document, thus determining the traceability of the document to the owner of the device used.

The electronic signature, therefore, is nothing more than a complex operation of encryption and encoding of the document or, rather, of its imprints by means of asymmetric encryption keys, which then allows, through an inversion of the cryptographic signature process, to verify a posteriori the integrity and provenance of the document itself.

Having defined electronic signatures, it is possible to distinguish the following categories of electronic signatures, to which as many categories of computer documents can be ascribed.[5]

The CAD dedicates the entire Chapter II to the regulation of computer documents and electronic signatures, whereas the *eIDAS* Regulation dedicates Chapter IV to the electronic document and Section IV of Chapter III to electronic signatures (Art. 25–34), but both sources have in common the classification criterion, i.e. *as many electronic signatures as computer documents.*

Analysing the aforementioned sources according to a unitary classification, it is possible to deduce that the signing of computerised documents can take place with five distinct electronic signature models.

First, the *simple electronic signature as* referred to in Art. 3, No. 10, aIDAS Regulation and Art. 20, para. *1-bis*, CAD. Second, *the advanced electronic signature* pursuant to Art. 3 No. 11, aIDAS Regulation and Art. 20, para. *1-bis* and Art. 21, para. *2-bis*, CAD. Third, the *qualified electronic signature* regulated under Art. 3 No. 12 and 25(2), aIDAS Regulation and Art. 20(*1-bis*) and 21(*2-bis*) CAD. The fourth category is that of *digitally signed documents* under Art. 1(s), Art. 20(*1-bis*), Art. 21(*2-bis*) and Art. 24, CAD. Finally, the final classification is that of documents with *recognised signatures* under Art. 25, CAD.

The *simple electronic signature*, defined in the *eIDAS* Regulation (Art. 3, para. 1, no. 10) as those '*data in electronic form, attached to or connected by logical association with other electronic data and used by the signatory to sign*' is linked to Art. 20, para. *2-bis*, CAD, which, in the second sentence, defines '*the suitability of the electronic document to satisfy the requirement of written form and its probative value are freely assessable in court in relation to the characteristics of security, integrity and unchangeability*'. The simple electronic signature, therefore, identifies the electronic data of a specific subject that—by means of a technical device—is affixed to the computer document, thus determining the traceability of a document to the holder of that data. The technical device in question may be a *password* or a

[5] For an examination of the categories of digital signature, let us refer to Andreotti (2023), pp. 321 ff; Finocchiaro (2014), pp. 309 ff; Tosi (2021), pp. 344 ff.

For an examination of the categories of digital forms, let us refer to Andreotti (2023), pp. 337 ff; Delfini (2014), pp. 251 ff.; Martoni (2020), pp. 224 ff.

magnetic card, otherwise known as a *smart card*, in the possession of a specific person. The simple electronic signature can thus be defined as certainly useful for the formation of free-form contracts for which, that is, the legal system does not provide for the formal requirement *ad substantiam* and *ad probationem*.

The difference, however, between the private contract and the digital document signed with a simple signature lies in the different probative efficacy. If, in fact, Art. 2702 of the Civil Code attributes to private deeds signed on paper by the parties the effectiveness of full proof on the origin of the declarations contained therein, in the case of computer documents with simple signatures, it will only be *the judicial authority that will assess*, in court, the suitability of that computer document to *satisfy the requirement of the written form, taking into account its characteristics of security, integrity and immodifiability.*[6]

Turning to the *advanced electronic signature* (FEA), this is defined in the *eIDAS* Regulation, Art. 3(1)(11), as '*an electronic signature that meets the requirements of Art. 26, i.e.: a) it is uniquely linked to the signatory; b) it is capable of identifying the signatory; c) it is created by means of electronic signature creation data that the signatory can, with a high level of security, use under his sole control; d) it is linked to the subscribed data in such a way that any subsequent change to that data can be identified*'.

From the regulatory definition, it can be deduced that the advanced electronic signature, like the simple electronic signature, also consists of the affixing of a computer datum—by means of an electronic device—on a computer document, but reinforces the attributability of the signature computer datum to the person who is the holder. The requirement of being able to uniquely identify the signatory is inherent in the greater technological complexity of the electronic signature device, such that there is a greater guarantee that the signature with an advanced electronic signature is made by the holder of the signature. In relation to the evidentiary effectiveness regime, the document with an advanced electronic signature is equated with the provisions of Art. 2702 of the Civil Code, such that the computerised writing with an advanced signature is fully in keeping with the origin of the declarations contained therein. Article 20, para. *1-bis*, first sentence, CAD, in fact, expressly provides: '*the computer document satisfies the requirement of written form and has the effectiveness provided for in Article 2702 of the Civil Code when a digital signature, another type of qualified electronic signature or an advanced electronic signature is affixed to it...*'. This is therefore an *ex lege* presumption and not a matter for discretionary verification by the courts.

Turning to the examination of the nature of the written form for the digital document with an advanced signature, it is clear that the same integrates the formal requirement for free form contracts, with *ex lege* presumption of authorship to the relative author, but contracts for which the legislator requires the written form *ad substantiam* can also be signed with an advanced digital signature. The reference is

[6] It has been observed that a type of advanced electronic signature is the signature affixed by means of the Public Digital Identity System or SPID. In this sense Andreotti (2023), p. 328; Finocchiaro (2014), p. 316.

to Art. 21, para. *2-bis*, second sentence, CAD, by virtue of which *contracts for which the legislature requires the ad substantiam form, identified in Art. 1350 no. 13 of the Civil Code, may be signed with advanced electronic signatures*, since the contracts referred to in Art. 1350 no. 1 to 12 may only be signed with qualified electronic signatures or authenticated signatures.

Moving on to the discussion of the *qualified electronic signature* (FEQ), Art. 3(1)(12) of the *eIDAS* Regulation, according to which it is '*an advanced electronic signature created by a qualified electronic signature creation device and based on a qualified certificate for electronic signatures*'. It is therefore an advanced electronic signature to which is added a qualification requirement represented by the existence of a 'qualified certificate' and a 'qualified signature creation device'.

The aforementioned device is regulated by Art. 29 of the *eIDAS* Regulation and Art. 35 CAD and represents an electronic device that ensures secrecy of the signature and attributability to its author. Qualified certificates are defined as an '*electronic attestation linking the electronic signature validation data to a natural person and confirming at least the name or pseudonym*' (Art. 3, no. 14, *eIDAS* Regulation). In relation to the evidentiary effect, Art. 25(2) of the *eIDAS* Regulation comes into play, according to which a qualified electronic signature has the equivalent legal effects of a handwritten signature. From the foregoing definition and as already noted for advanced electronic signatures, digital documents signed with a qualified electronic signature have the evidentiary effect referred to in Art. 2702 of the Civil Code with *legal* presumption.

The fourth type of electronic signature is the *digital signature* and is defined in Art. 1, para. 1, letter s) of the CAD as '*A particular type of qualified signature based on a system of cryptographic keys, one public and one private, correlated with each other, which allows the holder of the electronic signature by means of the private key and a third party by means of the public key, respectively, to make manifest and verify the provenance and integrity of an IT document or a set of IT documents*'. The digital signature is thus a qualified electronic signature with a system of operation with two distinct cryptographic keys. A private key, which pursuant to Art. 24(1) CAD *must refer uniquely to a single subject and to the document or set of documents to which it is affixed or associated*, representing the first segment of a secret identification code and a second public segment that allows the authenticity of the writing to be verified, which will be verified when the public key matches the private one through a signature verification system.

The evidentiary effectiveness regime of the digital document signed with a digital signature is that of Art. 2702 of the Civil Code—already pointed out—for which the author of the declaration, whose authenticity is verified, is presumed to be the holder of the private key unless disavowed and, therefore, the presumption of authenticity will be overcome by contrary proof in the event of an action of disavowal, all as provided for by Art. 20, para. *1-ter*, CAD, according to which '*The use of the signature device is presumed to be attributable to the holder, unless he provides proof to the contrary*'.

The requirement of the nature of the written form that is the subject of this contribution will be analysed—in view of the unity of the legislative provision—at the same time for both qualified electronic and digital signatures. The reference standard is Art. 21, para. *2-bis*, CAD, according to which '*The computer document signed with a qualified electronic signature or with a digital signature, formed in compliance with the technical rules established pursuant to Art. 71, which guarantee the identifiability of the author, the integrity and immodifiability of the document, is presumed to be attributable to the owner of the signature device pursuant to Article 21, paragraph 2, and in any case satisfies the requirement of written form, also in the cases provided for, under penalty of nullity, by Article 1350, first paragraph, numbers 1 to 12 of the Civil Code*'. According to the aforementioned definition, therefore, both the qualified electronic signature and the digital signature are suitable for integrating the hypotheses of written form *ad substantiam* as listed pursuant to Art. 1350, nos. 1 to 12 of the Civil Code, i.e. the hypotheses of contracts having as their object rights in rem in immovable property, as well as the residual category of Art. 1350, no. 13, for which, as already mentioned, an advanced digital signature is also sufficient.

The last hypothesis of electronic signature that will be considered in this analysis relates to the *authenticated electronic signature*. Article 25(1) CAD, according to which an advanced electronic signature can be authenticated by a notary public or other authorised public official, is applicable to this signature. This authentication takes place '*in the attestation, by the public official, that the signature has been affixed in his presence by the holder after ascertaining his personal identity, the validity of the electronic certificate used, if any, and the fact that the document signed is not contrary to the legal system*'. It is clear from the definition that the digital document authenticated in the terms indicated is legally recognised *pursuant to* Art. 2703 of the Civil Code and, therefore, will be full proof until a claim of forgery of the origin of the declarations made.

2 The Public Digital Deed Drawn Up by a Notary Public

The notarial deed drawn up in digital format was introduced in 2010, with Legislative Decree No. 110 of 2 July 2010,[7] which inserted into the Notarial Law No. 89/1913, Art. *47-bis*, according to which '*The provisions of this law and those issued in implementation thereof shall apply to the public deed referred to in art. 2700 of the Civil Code, drawn up by means of computerised procedures*'.

The introduction of the computerised public deed has brought about an important regulatory coordination between what is provided for by the CAD on the

[7] Legislative Decree No. 110 of 2 July 2010 on *Provisions on the subject of the public electronic deed drawn up by the Notary Public*, implementing the delegated law contained in Art. 65 of Law No. 69 of 18 June 2009, in accordance with the general provisions contained in the CAD.

subject of the authenticated electronic signature and what is provided for by the notary law on the subject of the formal requirements of the (analogue) public deed.[8]

From a formal point of view, the changes introduced in the notarial law concerned, first, the notary's obligation to equip himself, *for the exercise of his functions, with the digital signature referred to in Article 1(1)(s) of Legislative Decree No. 82 of 7 March 2005, issued by the National Council of Notaries*[9] (Art. *23-bis* of the Notarial Law).

The provision of the digital signature must also be extended, in cases where its use is provided for by law, to the parties, trustworthy interpreters and witnesses. Textually Art. *52-bis*, Notary Law, as introduced by the aforementioned Legislative Decree No. 110/2010, in fact, states that: '*The parties, the guarantors, the interpreter and the witnesses shall personally sign the computerised public deed in the presence of the notary with a digital signature or with an electronic signature, consisting also of the digital acquisition of the handwritten signature*' and that the '*Notary shall personally affix his digital signature after the parties, the interpreter and the witnesses and in their presence*'. In relation to the digital signature with which the notary must equip himself, it is provided that the notary must use a qualified certificate that, at the time of signing, is not expired, revoked or suspended, and it is established that through the qualified certificate the validity of the certificate itself, as well as the identification elements of the holder and the certifier and any limits on its use, in accordance with the technical rules established pursuant to Art. 71 CAD, must be detected.

The notary law then provides that the qualified certificate issued to the notary must contain *an indication of the specific qualification of the holder, particularly the title of notary and the relevant registration.* The certificate must also indicate the relevant suspension and revocation, in the event of suspension or termination of the notary's functions for any reason, including transfer to another district. There is, on the other hand, no need for such revocation in the event of a transfer within the same district.

Still in relation to the obligation to verify the validity of digital signature certificates, the public official is also required to certify the validity of the signature certificates used by the notaries. In this regard, in fact, the provision has been introduced in Art. *47-ter*, para. 3 of the Notary Law, according to which '*The notary public in the public deed and in the authentication of signatures must also certify the validity of any signature certificates used by the* parties'.[10] It is also considered that the

[8] For an examination of the introduction of the computerised public deed, see Petrelli (2010); Stucchi et al. (2017); Chibbaro (2006), pp. 1765 ff.

[9] With regard to the regulation of digital signatures, reference may be made to section 5.1.2 above.

[10] It has been observed that the parties are permitted—unlike the notary—to sign not only with a digital signature, with the notary checking the certificate of validity, but also with a non-qualified electronic signature. Pursuant to Art. *52-bis*(1) of the Notary Law, the electronic signature of the parties may *also* consist of '*digital acquisition of the handwritten signature*'. In this sense, therefore, the parties (and any witnesses, guarantors and interpreters) may affix their own handwritten signature to a paper support (containing the text of the public deed), which will subsequently be

aforementioned attestation of the validity of the signature certificate by the notary must be specifically mentioned in the authentication of the signature.[11]

With regard to the time of the aforementioned verification of the validity of the parties' digital signature certificate, the rules require that the verification in question be carried out by the notary at a time subsequent to the time at which the parties affix their digital signature, and obviously before the notary himself affixes his own. This is the only way to ensure certainty with regard to the validity of the signature certificate.

The necessary coordination resulting from the introduction of the computerised public deed and the discipline envisaged until then for the analogue deed, also passes through the affirmation of the centrality of the role and personality of the notary's services also in the digital deed.[12]

Of extreme relevance, in this regard, is the provision of the third paragraph of Art. *23-ter*, Notary Law, pursuant to which the notary must '*personally*' keep and use the signature device (so-called *smart card*), in accordance with Art. 32 CAD.

On this point, it has been specified that the reading of the deed is carried out by the notary *through the use and personal control of computer tools and, therefore*, such reading will take place directly '*from the computer screen*' or, in any case, it will also be possible to read the text on paper, in view of the necessary correspondence of the text read by the notary with the text to be signed by the parties, and, therefore, it will be necessary for the notary to have personally printed in the presence of the parties.

Having completed the analysis of the formal prerequisites, it should be noted that all those 'substantive' provisions of the notary law apply to the authentication of digital and electronic signatures in computerised public deeds, the rationale of which is general, and regardless of the type of medium used—paper or computerised.

In conclusion, therefore, at the outcome of the necessary coordination between Art. 25 of the CAD, which as analysed contains the definition of digital signature,

---

'scanned', and then, once thus transformed into a computer document, signed by the notary with their own digital signature, Petrelli (2010).

[11] In this sense, it has been pointed out that the law does not attach any consequences to the failure to mention the verification of the validity of the parties' signature certificates, in accordance with Art. 28 CAD, either in terms of the validity of the public deed, or in terms of disciplinary consequences for the notary public, Petrelli (2010).

[12] It is believed that the rule of the receipt of the deed in the presence of the parties and, possibly, two witnesses also applies to the computerised public deed, as does that of subsection 2 of Art. 47, according to which '*The notary shall investigate the will of the parties and under his own direction and responsibility take care of the complete completion of the deed*'. Although not specifically referred to, Art. 28 of the Notary Law concerning the legality check of the content of the electronic deed and Art. 54 of the Notary Regulation concerning the verification of authorisations, legitimation and powers of representation obviously also apply to the electronic public deed. More generally, *all those 'substantive' provisions of the notarial law*, the rationale of which is of *a general nature and regardless of the type of medium used (paper or computer), apply to the computerised public deed.*

Art. 2703 of the Civil Code, relating to the legal nature of the (analogue) public deed, and the provisions of the notarial law, as supplemented following the entry into force of the regulations on the subject of the electronic public deed drawn up by the Notary (Legislative Decree No. 110 of 2 July 2010), it is possible to state the following.

In the digital deed, the notary's prior verification will concern, first, the personal identity of the parties; second, the validity of the electronic certificate used by the parties, in the terms indicated above, and, third, the necessary control of legality entrusted to the notary, which is an indefectible prerequisite regardless of the use of the analogue or computerised instrument used. Lastly, it is considered necessary to mention the aforementioned verification of the validity of the signature certificate in addition to the mandatory verification of the identity of the appearing parties in an analogue document.

Continuing on, the authentication of the digital or electronic signature of the parties must consist of an '*attestation*' by the notary that may be contained in the same computer document, or in an additional computer document linked to the one bearing the digital or electronic signatures of the parties.[13]

As to the content of this attestation, it must first show the notary's declaration that the party's digital or electronic signature was affixed in his presence. This is to ensure that the signature device (*smart card*) is actually used by its holder, and not by a third party who unlawfully holds it for any reason whatsoever, and, in addition, the indication of the date and place of the attestation (Art. 72(1) of the Notary Law).

To complete the discussion, the preservation of the computerised public deed drawn up by the notary will be dealt with.

The preservation of the documents drawn up by the notary is one of the notary's main tasks, as can be seen from Art. 1, Notary Law, according to which: '*Notaries are public officials instituted to receive deeds between living persons and of last will, to bestow public faith, and to preserve their deposit*', and can be deduced from the entire notarial system, and in particular from Art. 61, Notary Law, which lays down rules for preservation and limited cases of exemption from this obligation, from Art. 72 of the Notarial Regulation.

The legislative focus on the preservation of the notarial document is explained by its importance in the system of civil evidence. Documentary evidence is undoubtedly the reigning evidence in civil proceedings, and within this particular value and importance is given to the public deed, Art. 2699 Civil Code, to the notarised private deed, Art. 2703 Civil Code, and to copies issued by public depositories and public officials, Art. 2714 ff Civil Code.

The notarial deed is then, in addition to being an instrument of proof, a title for legal real estate and commercial publicity on which the certainty of legal transactions in our country is based.

On the basis of these brief premises, it has been observed, therefore, that in the transition from paper to computerised documents, the same security requirements to

[13] Argument inferable *from* Articles 1(1)(q), 23(3) and (5), 24(1) CAD.

protect the proper conduct of legal transactions remain unaffected. The computerised notarial deed must, therefore, combine the characteristics of legal security of the notarial document with those of legal and technological security necessary for the computerised document and its preservation.

The preservation of computerised notarial acts is provided for, particularly by Art. *62-bis* and *62-ter*, Notary Law, as amended in 2010.

Article *62-bis* provides that '*The notary shall make use, for the preservation of computerised deeds, of a structure set up by the National Council of Notaries and that the specific technical rules necessary for the implementation of this provision shall in any case comply with the requirements of the digital administration code*'. Thus, the need to coordinate the general regulations on the preservation of computerised documents with the regulations of the Notarial is also fulfilled in the area of computerised document preservation.

The decision to centralise the structure, but not the archives, which remain at the exclusive disposal of the notary until the termination of practice in the district, is dictated by the need to ensure maximum security in the preservation of data, entrusting a public body with the preparation and management of the necessary infrastructure.

The preservation structure will be technically managed by the National Council of Notaries, which will operate in accordance with the principles established by the CAD for public administrations, particularly Art. 50, which lays down general rules to ensure interoperability between public administrations and their respective databases.

The preservation of computerised public acts, therefore, remains entrusted to the notary, as public depositary, for as long as it is in operation and will then be centralised by the National Council of Notaries.

References

Andreotti G (2023) Le firme elettroniche. In: Bocchini R (ed) Manuale di diritto privato dell'informatica, p 321 ff

Bechini U (2003) Efficacia, rilevanza formale e rilevanza probatoria. In: Firme elettroniche – Questioni ed esperienze di diritto privato, p 24 ff

Carnelutti F (1975) Documento (teoria moderna). Novissimo Digesto Italiano VI:86

Chibbaro S (2006) Codice dell'Amministrazione digitale, firme elettroniche ed attività notarile. Studi del Consiglio Nazionale del Notariato, n 2006-G, in Studi e Materiali CNN 2, p 1765 ff

Delfini F (2014) Documento informatico, forma analogica e forma digitale: dalla scrittura privata autenticata all'atto pubblico informatico. In: Finocchiaro G, Delfini F (eds) Diritto dell'informatica, p 251 ff

Finocchiaro G (2014) Firme elettroniche e firma digitale. In: Finocchiaro G, Delfini F (eds) Diritto dell'informatica, p 309 ff

Martoni M (2020) Il documento informatico e le firme elettroniche nel codice dell'Amministrazione Digitale. In: Di Cocco C, Sartor G (eds) Temi di diritto dell'informatica, p 224 ff

Petrelli G (2010) L'atto notarile informatico. In: Rassegna Novità Normative, II semestre

Stucchi E, Manente M, Chibbaro S (2017) Il Documento Digitale nel tempo. In: Studi del Consiglio Nazionale del Notariato, novembre
Tosi E (2021) Forme elettroniche. In: Diritto privato delle nuove tecnologie digitali. p 344 ff

New Digital Services and Goods

Roberto Bocchini

Contents

Abstract The contribution analyses the subject of digital assets, highlighting, first, the problem of their classification within the traditional legal categories. The author qualifies digital movables as movable assets under Art. 812 (3) of the Civil Code, further subdividing them into persistent movables and dynamic movables.

The reconstructive hypothesis is then tested by analysing the main assets in the digital ecosystem.

R. Bocchini (✉)
University of Naples "Parthenope", Naples, Italy
e-mail: roberto.bocchini@uniparthenope.it

R. Bocchini (ed.), *Digital Platforms - From Technical Foundations to Legal and Economic Implications*, https://doi.org/10.1007/978-3-032-07978-7_10

1 The Configuration of Legal Assets in the Elaborations of Doctrine—Digital Entities: Problems of Legal Framing

The development of the tertiarisation of the economy and the affirmation of the digital society have determined the incessant conceptual evolution of the category of legal goods that the jurist must redesign, even concerning the boundaries evoked by the word itself, starting from the consideration, nowadays widespread, that the goods of most significant value have become first and foremost *data*. To recall the words of an illustrious philosopher, Maurizio Ferraris,[1] although data cannot be considered, as Clive Humby stated, the oil of the third millennium, they represent the so-called docusphere and the new form of capital that is expressed in *software*, digital currencies, *cloud* services, digital financial services, etc.: in short, to use an almost obsolete language, in the *new properties.*[2]

It is no coincidence that abstract entities, mainly represented by the service sector, according to the US S&P Global Composite Index (PMI), which measures the activity of the manufacturing and service industries, have increased over the past year to 56.6%, in contrast to manufacturing activity, which has been declining. This exponential growth contributes to the creation of the so-called information society,[3] in which services are linked to information, which is considered a strategic resource and an instrument of value creation.[4]

The immateriality and intangibility *of assets*, which distinguish the digital economy from the traditional one, determine that transactions take place *online* and concern packages of *files*, rather than physical assets. However, it is precisely the immateriality of content and its real-time global dissemination that raises numerous legal issues, representing one of the main challenges of the digital economy and necessitating a reflection on the assets subject to transfer.

The affirmation of *new properties*, for which 'there is no unitary general theory'[5] is an inescapable fact insofar as technological progress has determined digital *platform capitalism*[6] or *platform society*[7] or rather immaterial capitalism[8] in which digital companies exercise the real power of control over all intangible digital entities in

[1] Ferraris (2021).

[2] On this topic, one can refer, for all, to the studies by De Nova (1991), pp. 13 ff.; Gambaro (2004), pp. 675 ff.; Bellelli and Cianci (2008), pp. 145 ff.; Vari (2023), p. 25; Tosi (2024), p. 411; as well as, in perspective to the goods of the knowledge and communication economy, including information and certain administrative 'positions' Zoppini (2000), pp. 185 ff.; Candian (2003), pp. 291 ff.; more recently, Colangelo (2012).

[3] A term coined by Bell (1976) that indicates a society, having reached the peak of industrialisation to continue to develop must concentrate its efforts towards the production no longer of tangible goods but of intangible services.

[4] De Laurentiis (2021).

[5] De Nova (1991), p. 16.

[6] On this topic, see Srnicek (2017).

[7] Van dijck et al. (2018).

[8] The term is borrowed from Quintarelli (2019).

a veritable 'market of the immaterial'[9] dedicated to traditional non-material economic values. It follows that the capitalism of the third millennium is no longer represented by goods that have physical consistency, but by immaterial consistencies and, therefore, it is necessary to identify on which objects, *or rather* goods, this economic wealth is based to identify the most efficient legal rules through which to regulate the transfer of digital entities: particularly, one must verify the possibility that the new digital entities can be placed in the legal category of goods and how the concept of 'what' should be interpreted in the new reality.

It must therefore be sounded out whether it is possible to place the new assets within our legal categories to be able to adequately regulate social and legal relations in the digital society in the face of the speed of technological progress and the realisation that the most excellent value is less and less represented by real estate, but rather by assets understood as intangible assets and digital assets.[10]

If, therefore, the subjects represent the terms of reference of the relationships that the legal system deals with, with the attribution of subjective legal situations, then it must be verified whether the objective profile, represented by the goods, as entities capable of satisfying interests considered worthy of consideration for the protection of the legal system (legal assets), can be traced back to the definition of Art. 810 of the Civil Code, which, by limiting the definition of legal assets 'to things that can form the subject matter of rights', understood as entities capable of satisfying relevant interests, seems to limit the category to *things* only, in their naturalistic and material meaning, proper to a conception of the economy and law that is distant in time.

In reality, to give definitive affirmation to the new goods within the codified categories,[11] it is necessary to provide an account of the framework of doctrine, discounting the vice of any simplification, concerning the different theories that have followed on the conception of legal goods[12] which can be grouped into two major strands: (a) realist theories; (b) formalist theories.

(a) The theory defined as *realist*[13] considers that the transition of an entity from a de facto interest, not legally qualified, to a protected/qualified interest and, therefore, from a 'thing' in the economic sense to a 'thing' in the legal sense, takes place by the economic and/or social transformation of the thing, which becomes a legal good when, again on the financial plane, it acquires the characteristics of separability,

---

[9] Ferrarese (2002), p. 12; Galgano (2001), p. 229.

[10] Battelli (2023), p. 46. For a discussion in comparative perspective on intangible property, see also, among others, Rahmatian (2020), p. 186.

[11] Camardi (2018), p. 962, indeed, highlights how reflection on the acquisition of relevance in terms of a *legal good* is fundamental for the legal system, not only to test the latter's resilience, but also as a protection technique, in the author's opinion, 'perhaps the most effective', from new demands for protection.

[12] On this subject, we refer to Bocchini (2018), pp. 23 ff.

[13] Patti (1979), p. 147, according to whom the passage from the meta-legal to the juridical is governed by the same dynamics of reality, subsumed by the legal system according to parameters and indices more or less expressly inferred from a purported economic-social concept of the good.

utility and scarcity. According to this theory, therefore, an entity becomes a juridical good when it provides economic utility and, at the same time, is not present in sufficient quantity to satisfy the needs of all community members.

Utility and scarcity of the good in the marketplace are, therefore, the two presuppositions that determine the interest of the right in the good and condition the qualification of the good as legal. This doctrine, in support of this reconstruction, which permits the widening of the range of legal assets, emphasises that the literal wording of Art. 810 of the Civil Code makes a generic reference to things and is therefore susceptible to extension. It has also been pointed out[14] that the assumptions of this theory are constituted by the extension of the semantic value of the term 'thing' beyond its usual minimum conditions of use and by the denial of any normative value to the expression 'which may form the subject matter of rights'.[15]

The consequence of this reconstruction is that the interpreter or, rather, the judge is authorised to define an entity as a legal good and to grant it protection, simply by asserting its usefulness and its economic rarity. This elaboration has not been without criticism. It has been said[16] that it would not be possible to configure the notion of a thing in the legal sense, based on the material or economic relevance given to the thing by the subject who claims to have appropriated it and wants to use it to satisfy his needs, without the legal system recognising, selecting and typifying, with a blank fundamental legal norm, such a thing.

(b) The second theory, elaborated by the doctrine about the definition of the content of Art. 810 of the Civil Code, could be defined as *formal-objectivist* and considers that the passage from de facto utility to legally protected interest is represented by a sort of reservation of law, whereby for the qualification of an interest in terms of utility, thing or value the mere intervention of any normative protection constitutes a necessary and sufficient requisite, regardless therefore of the so-called subjectivisation of such protection in the hands of an individual. It would thus be the legal system that determines and identifies legal goods when it renders them worthy of legal protection.

The rationale of the provisions of Art. 810 of the Civil Code,[17] would reside in the fact that, only after verifying which requirements, interests and needs the legal system considers worthy of protection, would it be possible, to recognise to certain portions of material reality or economic utilities the quality of legal goods, not vice versa. It is necessary to identify a universal and generic scope of the legal system, as there are norms that have objective relevance to anyone in a legally relevant situation involving a specific good as their object.

[14] Barcellona (1987), p. 608, according to the explanation offered by the realist theory of the rule in Art. 810 of the Civil Code is taken up and supported by that part of the doctrine in favour of the inclusion of new entries in the catalogue of legal assets without much discussion.

[15] On the risk, in general, of confusion between the notion of a thing in the legal sense and a good in the legal sense, see, among others, Piraino (2012), pp. 469 ff., who notes, in the words of Nicolò, (1936), p. 78, how the two concepts are 'overlapping' and the risk arising from this phenomenon.

[16] Costantino (1982), p. 1.

[17] Costantino (1982), p. 10.

Opposed to this theory was[18] the criticism of the excessive dilatation of the concept of legal good.

(c) Then there is the theory that has been defined as *weak formal-subjectivism*, according to which the attribution of legal significance to an asset in the economic sense as a legal asset would depend exclusively on the intervention of a subjectivised protection by the legal system. This protection would be conferred using formal structures (so-called subjective situations) that are differentiated and flexible, such as to transpose in some way the dynamics of reality: the transition from good in the economic sense to good in the legal sense would thus be governed by typical subjectivisation legal structures[19] by which the legal system attributes the good to a subject.

The theory of those who propose to distinguish between a *broad* notion of legal good 'as the object of legal protection per se taken' (i.e. considered in an objective sense) and a *narrow* notion of legal good 'as the object of legal protection intended for a given subject' (i.e. considered in a subjective sense, and explicitly attributed to that subject as his subjective situation) can also be traced back to this position.

The theory, therefore, goes so far as to consider the concept of legal good as a 'synthesis between the particular interest protected and the subjective situation predisposed by the legal system as an instrument of protection intended for a particular subject'.

However, this more restricted notion of legal asset would include not only 'things', which can be the object of absolute real rights, but also what can be the object of rights on so-called intangible goods and, above all, what can be the object of relative subjective rights. And, following this perspective, it would be precisely these 'personal' subjective structures, which go beyond the requirement of materiality proper to the term 'thing', that would open up the notion of a legal good to the new utilities formed with economic development.[20]

It has thus been pointed out that the reference to personal subjective situations, to determine the definition of a good, and the subsequent development of the legal concept of services,[21] extends to the field of legal goods the 'open' techniques of qualification, peculiar to obligation and contract.[22]

(d) The theory defined as *strong formal-subjectivism* holds, on the other hand, that the attribution of legal significance to a good of an economic nature depends exclusively on the intervention of a subjectivised protection, rigorously and rigidly reserved to the legislature, i.e. on an 'original and autonomous' attribution for which

---

[18] Barcellona (1987), p. 608.

[19] Pugliatti (1957), p. 187.

[20] Pugliatti (1957), p. 176, most recently on this line of thought Camardi (2018), p. 1018, who in identifying certain entities as 'of administrative creation' states that such goods are not formally but only descriptively qualifiable as intangible goods as the usefulness of the model represented by Art. 810 of the Civil Code persists for which an entity becomes a legally relevant good insofar as it is qualified as such by a norm, and in relation to a qualified situation of belonging.

[21] For an examination of the concept of service, let us refer to Bocchini (1999), pp. 24 ff.

[22] Barcellona (1987), p. 611.

the legislature itself would have exclusive and, above all, direct and singular competence. According to this theory, therefore, the passage of economic entities or, in general, of social values, financial or otherwise, into the group of legal goods would take place exclusively through express normative decisions that, from time to time, recognise and guarantee certain absolute subjective situations to a subject.

From this conception emerges a narrow definition of legal good as 'any entity currently qualified by the legal system that considers it the object of an absolute subjective situation'.[23] From this definition, it follows that: 'if an entity is useful and solicits human interests, but is not qualified by the legal system, it remains legally irrelevant'.

The good in the legal sense exists only through an absolute subjective situation, since the concept of a legal good relates to the immediate and direct management of appropriation. Indeed, the form through which the legal system protects and guarantees to subjects the appropriation of the use value of a good is identified with absolute rights, due to their suitability as an instrument through which the legal system performs to a subject the fundamental and original attribution of an entity, which becomes legally relevant for this.

Vice versa, according to this theory, relative rights could not assume relevance for the theory of legal assets, since they pertain to the circulation of wealth and always presuppose, but never realise, an original attribution of the asset in the same way as limited real rights, which logically and chronologically presuppose the existence of a property right, once again solving the problem of qualifying an entity as a good. In conclusion, the determination of a legal asset is the exclusive competence of the legislature, so that no intervention in this sense can be made by the interpreter or the judge, and presupposes a fundamental and original attribution.

(e) The picture of the theories set out so far would not be complete without considering two other theories, one so-called legislative and the other so-called theoretical.

In short, there are two theories, one of which holds that the notion of legal good is a 'legislative' and non-theoretical notion, and the other, on the contrary, that the idea of legal good is exclusively a theoretical and, therefore, technical notion in legal terms. For the first theory, a concept has a legislative nature when it is established by the legislature to perform specific normative functions; various interpretations have been proposed for this meaning.

According to a first reading key, the definition of Art. 810 of the Civil Code has a sectorial interpretative content, i.e. it only serves to determine the scope of application of Articles 812–831 of the Civil Code, and, therefore, the discipline of movable and immovable property, i.e. the scope of application of the general discipline of the right of ownership to which Book III of the Code is devoted. In short, the definition in Art. 810 of the Civil Code implies that the subject of the right of ownership can only be movable or immovable things.

---

[23] Scozzafava (1982), pp. 128 ff.

A second interpretation of the so-called normative theory of the legal asset attributes to Art. 810 of the Civil Code a broader interpretative task, i.e. relating not only to the regulation of property, but also to all rights generally understood as exclusive forms of appropriation of resources. Based on this understanding, intangible goods would also fall under Art. 810 of the Civil Code. Thus, the distinction between the terms 'thing' and 'good' has been elaborated. According to this doctrine,[24] in fact, the normative function of the term 'good' can only be that of intermediate qualification. All the rules referring to 'goods' apply to what is defined as a good by Art. 810 of the Civil Code and, therefore, to all entities that can form the object of exclusive appropriation. Instead, the normative function of the term 'thing' is different and consists in designating all the entities that may form the object of exclusive appropriation, even if not proprietary. They are goods, then, certainly all the entities that can form the object of exclusive appropriation. But it should be added that only entities that are 'things' can be the object of exclusive appropriation.[25]

According to a third key of interpretation of the normative theory under consideration,[26] Art. 810 of the Civil Code would have the function of a closing rule of the system and the legislative definition of legal asset would thus have a general interpretative task in the sense that Art. 810 of the Civil Code serves to delimit the scope of the law, i.e. of the conflicts that assume legal relevance concerning legal assets, understood as the entities that can form the subject matter of a right. Interpreting and defining the concept of legal good in the light of Art. 810 of the Civil Code, therefore, means determining the object of the right, i.e. that which may assume legal significance for the legislature.

According to a final interpretation of the normative concept of legal good, this latter notion is, quite simply, the object of a classificatory oversight on the part of the legislature.[27] It has therefore been observed that not only would Art. 810 of the Civil Code be useless, but the concept of 'legal asset', as a legislative concept, would also be useless, because it would designate neither an element, even partial, of a series of cases already defined by the legislature with other norms, nor a general criterion of legal relevance.[28]

(f) Lastly, another theory holds that the concept of legal good could have only theoretical and not normative relevance. In this sense, therefore, disregarding the literal datum of Art. 810 of the Civil Code, the elaboration of its content would be

---

[24] Barcellona (1987), p. 620.

[25] To the contrary is Piraino (2012), p. 493, who understands the concept of 'thing' as 'a negative limit of nomogenetic discretion for a sort of "factual constraint" in this case coinciding with the social perception of those entities, material and otherwise, to be considered things. Thus, the relation of genus to species traditionally established between goods and things is inverted: the latter acquire the rank of *genus* of which the former are a partition'.

[26] In this sense, Barcellona (1987), p. 622.

[27] Pugliatti (1957), p. 80.

[28] In this sense, Barcellona (1987), p. 623.

reserved to legal science[29] since the legislature '*iubet non docet*' and the defining norms are devoid of practical cogency. A theoretical concept designates either a set of norms unified by the homogeneity of facts, about the type of problem that the social environment proposes to the legal system that they are deputed to resolve, or a set of facts unified by the unitary character of a norm, or instead by the circumstance that a norm, or more often a set of standards, gives rise to a conjunctive plurality of effects.

In the first case, the legal concept is essentially valid for operating a functional unification, which is primarily based on the identity of the type of problem posed to the system. It can, therefore, with some reason, be said to be systemic. In contrast, in the second case, the legal concept is mainly valid for operating a formal unification, founded primarily on the identity, even relative to a minimum nucleus, of the normative treatment. It can, therefore, with some reason, be said to be *classificatory*.

This doctrine extends to the point of structuring a dual meaning of legal good in a theoretical sense.

A first meaning attributes to the legal asset a partial systemic character with the task of representing the problem of the so-called legal distribution of resources and the range of solutions that the legal system provides to this problem. In this meaning, the theoretical ambit of the concept of the legal asset coincides with the area of the attributive function of the legal system, i.e. with the area of that particular function of the legal system that is expressed in determining which resources appropriation is guaranteed and in what manner, and to whom, it is guaranteed. Entities, interests, and values that are not linked to the economic dimension of so-called corporeal and incorporeal things and to the legislator's decision to consider them, precisely because of the form of use and exchange value they may take, would remain extraneous to this concept of legal good.[30]

The second meaning attributes a general systemic value to the theoretical concept of the legal good, with the task of representing the distinction between relevant and irrelevant legal, not only concerning the problem of the legal distribution of resources, but also in general. On this condition, in fact, the concept of the legal asset would incorporate that functional identity that alone is capable of making it scientifically significant as a systemic concept: it would express the unitary foundation of the private law system, the unification of all its fundamental disciplines around the ordering of wealth and would therefore be able to provide significant information both on the type of fundamental problem entrusted to the legal system and on the identity of the formal principles of relevance assumed by each of the

[29] Belfiore (1983), pp. 859 ff. Commenting on this reconstruction, it has been observed: 'Such a concept would not, then, have any normative value, i.e. it would not designate anything that is not already designated by certain norms or by the entire legal system (and that cannot be autonomously derived from one or the other by means of scientific analysis), but would be worth conceptualising, representing in theoretical form the system from the point of view of the utilities, interests, wealth, and values to which it gives legal form', Barcellona (1987), p. 623.

[30] Messinetti (1985), p. 363.

functions performed by the various forms of protection that contribute to the solution of this problem.

2 Evaluation and Perspectives: Digital Assets as Legal Goods

It is necessary to pull the strings of the discourse that has been conducted so far. From the proposed reconstructions, a dichotomy has emerged between representing legal goods as an open category or a closed category. The first presupposes an atypicality of legally relevant resources so that all valuable and scarce economic entities are legal goods. The second, rigidly closed categorisation limits, on the other hand, the range of legally relevant interests and, therefore, defines legal goods more narrowly: legal goods are entities subject to legal regulation or subjective rights, even relative ones, or only absolute subjective rights.

The two theoretical approaches have limitations. And, indeed, the open categorisation lends itself to the observation that the atypical nature of the legally relevant resources means that it is not possible to distinguish between qualified interests and so-called de facto interests, according to specific formal indices. The legal system would thus turn out to be an apparatus of procedures whose conditions of application would be largely left to the free determination of the judge, and, therefore, a system of solutions to problems would be created, which would not be selected by the legal system, not even indirectly.[31]

Theories, on the other hand, that consider legal goods to be a rigidly closed category on the assumption that the legal classification of a good is determined solely and exclusively by the legal system, expose themselves to the observation that, according to this analysis, the notion of legal goods remains indeterminate because there is no agreement on the type of legal regulation that is capable of attributing to economic entities the qualification of legal goods.

It therefore seems reasonable to hold that this line of thought, which does not qualify as goods all useful and scarce economic entities, but only those economic entities that the legal system recognises and qualifies, can be valid on condition that a dual notion of goods is posited: legal good in the broad sense, which occurs when any objective discipline regulates economic entities; legal good in the strict sense, which occurs when a discipline recognises the ownership of that entity, attributing to a given subject a relative or absolute subjective right. The literal datum of Art. 810 of the Civil Code seems not to be in line with this conclusion since for this rule all things that 'may form the subject matter of rights' and not only real rights are

[31] On this point, see Luhmann (1983). See also Zaccaria (1985), pp. 206 ff. In Italy, the best doctrine has long felt the importance of systemic theory for understanding law as a system and for legal science in general; on this point, see Irti (1987), p. 174.

goods. In this case, the *voluntas legislatoris* has not been translated into *voluntas legis.*[32]

If, therefore, the evolution of doctrine also follows a direction whereby both tangible and intangible things are to be considered assets,[33] in consideration of the economic utility for the persons who use them,[34] then in the most essential of categorisations: immovable assets are the things that can be the subject of rights, movable assets are all other assets (Art. 812, para 3, Civil Code) and intangible assets are intellectual works and industrial inventions. This represents a milestone in doctrine and jurisprudence, marking the overcoming of the correspondence between tangible things and the objects of rights. In fact, for some time now, doctrine has recognised[35] that intangible assets are legal assets insofar as the asset is identified with the sign or with the patent idea, and therefore, intangible assets represent the maximum abstraction in terms of property concerning the thing, as understood in Roman law. It appears, thus, evident that the legislator, with the recognition of intangible assets, intended to protect not the mere *res*, but *the utility* that the asset produces to its owner so that, it was noted that, in the most technologically advanced sectors, the intangible aspect of the product becomes prevalent and the emergence of an economic and legal system centred on intangible property and contractual circulation is, therefore, at the heart of the problem.[36]

It is, therefore, a shared arrest that immateriality is not a limit for the ownership of the good and the category of goods in that the signs and ideas that are identified and represented identify the good to be protected, regardless of the physicality of the thing on which (trademark) or through which (patent) they are defined. The abstraction of the thing to the good does not appear to be a limitation for the qualification of digital entities and resources that, as new goods, represent the real wealth of the third millennium.

It is evident that the legislator of 1942 could not have imagined that technological evolution, through information technology, electronics, telecommunications and the Internet, would create such a large number of new goods that apparently do not seem to find a place in the Civil Code, but which, on the contrary, with proper

---

[32] On the other hand, in this sense, Demolombe (1855), pp. 4–6 stated that 'Let us say, goods to be the things that can be useful to man for the satisfaction of his needs or his enjoyment. It has been pointed out that in this respect the word "good" expresses only an abstraction, which denotes less the thing in itself than a simple quality of it, that is to say, the utility which the person procures and the result of the rights to which he is subject. We conclude, therefore, that in evaluating and qualifying a good, in law, it is less necessary to dwell on the material elements of the thing than on its external conformation and the resulting purpose'.

[33] On tangible and intangible entities: Stella Richter Jr. (2013), p. 1244.

[34] Tommasini (2012), p. 153.

[35] Albeit with a progressive path: cf. Santoro Passarelli (1995), p. 55; Barbero (1962), p. 297; Scozzafava (1999), pp. 12 ff.; Gambaro (2004) p. 675. In a different sense, albeit limited to administrative creation rights that 'are not formally, but only descriptively, qualifiable as intangible goods', see Camardi (2018), pp. 1009 ff.

[36] Tosi (2024), p. 411.

reconstruction, could find appropriate lodging in the various existing categories such as, for example, among movable property.

Indeed, in the *online* world, data, as will be explained below,[37] represent the information of the *offline* world and are an asset susceptible to appropriation, with their own patrimonial value at the moment when, through the *bits* that become *hashes*, they take on their own physicality even in the *offline* world with their persistence. Thus, the data of the *online* world are subject to circulation and reproduction, so that digital data can be categorised as movable goods that acquire their own economic value within the digital environment.

Data, therefore, as we shall see, as a digital resource,[38] although it is debated whether an exclusive right is established in their favour,[39] are undoubtedly movable goods falling within the scope of the third paragraph of Art. 812 of the Civil Code since, also and not only, from a Romanistic point of view, they are the object of appropriation. Indeed, data has its own connotation that allows it, even in the *offline* world, to be persistently and physically appropriated as *res*. This normative reference enables us to understand how, within the elasticity of civil law categories, it is possible to fill, through a process of adaptation, an apparent void that seems to exist in the qualification of these goods and digital entities. Through Art. 812 (3) of the Civil Code, they can be systematised as movable assets, thus attributing their ownership to the subject who owns the asset, which undoubtedly derives utility from them, also having the characteristics of separability and scarcity, and being able to rise, even as a physical entity, to the status of a legal asset.

It follows that these new assets do not seem to be identifiable as intangible assets, while it seems more appropriate to categorise them as movable assets rather than intangible assets, which represent the highest abstraction of property and have, moreover, obtained legitimate recognition. The essential referent for recognising the interests that access them is the deservingness of those interests according to the legal system.

[37] See para 4.

[38] According to Busacca (2023), p. 38: ‘information, as well as data and knowledge, belongs to a sub-category of digital goods called precisely *information goods*’.

[39] Without claiming to be exhaustive, on the one hand, Ottolia (2017), p. 158, argues that the establishment of an exclusive right in favour of data would facilitate the circulation of data. *Contra* Szilágyi (2021), pp. 180 ff., argues that such an exclusive right could violate the *numerus clausus*.

3 From New Properties as Legal Goods Under Art. 810 of the Civil Code to Services in the Theory of Legal Goods – Difference Between Static Goods and Dynamic Goods

The examination and identification of digital goods, understood as static entities in the digital world, which do not also require the cooperation of a subject for their functioning, must not lead one to overlook the fact that in the digital world there are numerous goods in respect of which the cooperation of other subjects is, on the other hand, necessary to be able to enjoy the utility offered. It is no coincidence that with the DSA,[40] Europe has equipped itself with a uniform regulatory framework for *online* intermediaries (i.e. all digital services that connect consumers with goods, services or content, including *online* marketplaces and *social networks*; content sharing platforms and *online* travel and accommodation platforms; *app stores*, *cloud* and *web hosting* services; collaborative economy platforms), ensuring transparency and traceability of *online* content, protection of consumers' rights (by ensuring their safety), combating the dissemination of illegal content, information manipulation and *online* disinformation.[41]

The use of digital content, through contracts for the sale and supply of content on digital services and goods, represents, from an economic point of view, an important frontier that differentiates the digital good, in itself, from digital content for the use of which the cooperation of the party that has to provide the service is required. For instance, contracts for digital services *(such as cloud, hosting, and streaming) have an active functional profile, involving constant digital interaction with an intermediary who provides updates* and maintenance of the service itself.

In this sense, the European legislator, through two Directives (No. 770 and 771/2019), provided certain definitions that were then incorporated into the Consumer Code in Art. *135 sections of the Consumer Code relating to (a) digital content, (b) digital services* and (c) goods with digital elements, which appear to be particularly useful for this in-depth study.

Digital content is defined by Art. 2 of Directive 770/2019/EU as all data produced and supplied in digital format.

Digital service has been defined as (a) a service enabling the consumer to create, transform, store or access data in digital format or (b) a service enabling the sharing of data in digital format uploaded or created by the consumer or other users of that service or any other interaction with such data.

Goods with digital elements have been defined as any tangible movable property that incorporates or is interconnected with digital content or a digital service in such a way that the absence of said digital content or digital service would prevent the performance of the functions of the good.

---

[40] Regulation (EU) 2022/2065.

[41] Falce (2023), p. 70.

Therefore, the connection or demarcation line between the two Directives, as has been correctly stated,[42] is constituted by the prevalence of the digital or material element in relation to which the autonomy of the goods and the instrumentality, more or less necessary, of the digital content with respect to it is of primary importance since, whereas Directive No. 770 concerns the supply of digital content and services, Directive No. 771 concerns the sale of movable goods, among which, goods with digital elements are expressly taken into consideration.

This dividing line is highlighted in recital 16 of Directive No. 771, which states that if the absence of the digital content or the digital service, whether incorporated or interconnected, does not prevent the goods from performing their proper functions, or if the consumer concludes a contract for the supply of digital content or digital services which is not part of a contract of sale concerning goods with digital elements, that contract should be distinct from the contract for the sale of goods, even if the seller acts as an intermediary in relation to that second contract with the third economic operator, and may therefore fall within the scope of Directive No. 770. For example, if a consumer downloads a game application from an app store onto a smartphone, the contract for the supply of the game application is distinct from the contract for the sale of the *smartphone*.

Directive No. 771 should therefore only apply to sales contracts concerning the *smartphone*. In contrast, the provision of the game's application should fall under Directive No. 770 if the conditions of that directive are fulfilled.

Another example may be the case where it is expressly agreed that the consumer buys a *smartphone* without a specific operating system and subsequently concludes a contract for the supply of an operating system by a third party. In such a case, the supply of a separately purchased operating system would not be part of the sales contract and, therefore, would not fall within the scope of Directive No. 771; instead, it might fall within the scope of Directive No. 770.

For the economy of the present work, it therefore appears useful to identify when a good is digital with respect to a service, since the static utility that the good is acknowledged to have is different from the dynamic utility that the user of the service acquires when, in addition to acquiring a good with digital content, within the meaning of Directive No. 771, he also acquires a digital service interconnected with it.

The digital good, understood as digital content, and which finds its origin in the data, produced and supplied in digital format, is a movable good *under* Art. 812 (3) of the Civil Code—as identified above—and is therefore present in the *offline* world in the sense that such an asset can be used independently of access to the *online* world.

The digital service, on the other hand, is understood to be a good in the sense that it is an element of the data being transferred in a contract, whereby the service enables data to be created, transformed, stored, accessed, or shared.

[42] Addis (2021), p. 11.

As has been observed,[43] the European legislator does not refer to the general category of digital goods, but relates to the data that, as digital content, is connected to and embedded in the mobile good, making its functioning possible. A differentiation must then be made: on the one hand, data, as products supplied in digital format, i.e. digital content understood as goods; on the other hand, digital services and goods with digital elements.[44]

The same Directive No. 771 does not provide, unlike Directive No. 770, for the enucleation of a new category of goods, as it emphasises the functional aspect of incorporating and connecting the digital element for the purposes of the contract of supply and/or sale for consumption. It becomes, therefore, fundamental the automated service that, connected to the digital content, determines the creation of a new good that is not static, but dynamic insofar as the data, united to the automated digital service, determines the creation of a good that is reified with the machine and is different from the digital movable good *ex* Art. 812, para 3, Civil Code.

In this sense, in further investigation, it is necessary to differentiate personal services from automated services in that, while services in their personal dimension,[45] unlike data, cannot circulate since they do not pre-exist their provision, since at the moment they are provided, they are exhausted. On the other hand, automated services[46] are rendered to the market automatically and mechanically by 'automated things' (*ex re* services), in the information society, and, therefore, the service becomes the object of the contract and, as a good, becomes reified. In this sense, Directive No. 770, in recital 12, states that it does not define the legal nature of contracts for the provision of digital content or digital services, and it should be for national law to determine whether such contracts constitute, for example, a contract of sale, service, rental or a *sui generis* contract. This is without prejudice to national rules that do not specifically deal with consumer contracts and that provide for specific remedies for certain types of defects that were not apparent at the time of the conclusion of the contract, i.e. national provisions that may lay down specific rules on the liability of the trader in case of hidden defects.[47]

It follows that the same Directive No. 770 does not seem to deal with contracts, but identifies the digital content, the digital service and the good with digital elements, making it emerge that the service, reified in the company, is provided

---

[43] Busacca (2023), p. 85.

[44] Quarta (2019), p. 1013.

[45] Personal services are those rendered personally by the service provider (*ex homine* services) or are rendered by the service provider through its own activity or, in any event, the personal activity of its employees, possibly with the aid of machines, but with an auxiliary function with respect to the performance of the service debtor. The human activity of the obligor is therefore necessary during the rendering of the service, so that the mere provision of a machine to perform the contractual performance is not sufficient.

[46] We refer to Bocchini (1999), p. 79.

[47] It goes on to say: 'This Directive should also be without prejudice to national laws providing for non-contractual remedies available to the consumer in the event of lack of conformity of digital content or the digital service with respect to persons at earlier stages in the chain of commerce, or to other persons performing the obligations of such persons'.

independently of the company itself in the sense that the provision of a service by reason of the automation of its production transforms an infungible service into a fungible service, therefore the element of *intuitus personae* of the *doing* of the service provider is attenuated to the point of disappearing. In contracts for automated services, the service is rendered by the functioning machine providing the service and not by the person who is made available to the other party.[48]

Mechanisation, by allowing the standardisation of the service, actually renders the latter fungible in the sense that it renders completely irrelevant the personal performance of the service by the debtor, which is no longer necessary and indispensable for the satisfaction of the creditor's interest. Through this process of *reification*, all services of the digital age become goods in the legal sense, in that the performance of the service, which was previously infungible, becomes fungible.

The conclusion that may be reached is that, in contracts for automated services, the very process of *reifying the service* permits, in another respect, specific performance and hence the application of Art. 2931 of the Civil Code. This is because, in recognition of the interest of the debtor and the creditor, objectified in the reality of the individual obligatory relationship, it appears reasonable that the equivalence of the service rendered by the machine supplied by the debtor with that rendered by 'another machine' that is identical or equivalent.

Naturally, what has been said so far concerning the applicability or non-applicability of Art. 2931 of the Civil Code to long-term contracts for automated services is also reflected on the applicability of Art. 700 of the Code of Civil Procedure to the case under consideration.[49]

In such cases, precautionary protection complements and anticipates the function of specific performance, providing the aggrieved party (the active party) with a broader guarantee to obtain the object of the obligation in full. On the other hand, in the case of non-performance, in contracts of duration having as their object personal services, there is non-performance of infungible obligations to perform, so that the object of the obligation, which is intended to satisfy the creditor's interest, can only be produced by the personal activity of the debtor.[50] In such a case, it has been said,

---

[48] Bocchini (1999), p. 89.

[49] It has indeed been observed in doctrine (see, for all, Montesano (1965), p. 116) that the non-performance of fungible obligations to perform, and such are the obligations having as their object mechanised automated performances, does not entail the absolute impossibility of satisfying the interest of the active party, the application of the rules on specific performance under Art. 2931 of the Civil Code being possible.

[50] Trib. Napoli (ord.), 31 March 1993, in *Giust. civ.,* 1993, I, 2245. The order of the Neapolitan court is very interesting: it concerned a case in which the parties had entered into a long-term contract for services under which a company was to carry out an activity of control over the quality of the raw materials used by the producing company in the manufacture of the products then sold to the public. As a dispute arose regarding the termination of the contract, the company that carried out the control of raw materials appealed to the judicial authority *pursuant to* Art. 700 of the Code of Civil Procedure, claiming that the contract between the parties had not been terminated in due time, and therefore requested that the designated judge authorise it to carry out its activity at the defendant company's premises. The court rejected, however, with a detailed order, the appeal argu-

no more could be obtained provisionally by means of the injunction than can be obtained definitively by the use of ordinary protection. But the jurisprudence[51] and the doctrine[52] now seem to be oriented towards admitting emergency protection regardless of the infungible or non-infungible content of the relevant service. Automated services receive enhanced legal protection, i.e. similar to the protection that real services receive from the legal system (i.e. not only injunctive protection, but also possessory and precautionary protection) by virtue of the holder's right over the business.

If, then, the digital service represents a further development with respect to the digital movable good, in that it enables the consumer to create, transform, store data

ing that it is not possible to order *under* Art. 700 of the Code of Civil Procedure an infungible performance of do or do not do, since, since it cannot be compulsorily enforced, the measure adopted would be *useless* from a precautionary point of view. As a matter of fact, according to the interpretation of the Neapolitan judicial authority, a different solution to the problem would entail the operativeness, in our legal system, of the *astreintes,* coercive measures aimed at ensuring the performance also of infungible performances, operativeness that, instead, *de iure condito*, must be excluded. In the same sense, see Trib. Palermo, (ord.) 28 July 1995, in *Foro it.*, 1996, c. 2252.

[51] Trib. Roma, ord. 17 February 2000 in *Foro it.*, 972 and *Giur. it.*, 2001, 300; Trib. Roma, ord. 23 July 2003 in *Giur. it.*, 2004, 1195; Trib. Trieste, ord. 20 September 2006 in *Giur. it.*, 2007, 1737; Trib. Bari, ord. 30 June 2009; Trib. Catania, ord. 9 July 2009 in *Foro it*, I, 2009, 2813; Trib. Cagliari, ord. 19 October 2009; Trib. Verona, ord. 9 March 2010, according to which the precautionary protection is admissible *under* Art. 700 c.p.c. is admissible 'in consideration of the absence of limits of admissibility in the wording of the aforementioned provision, of the possibility (in some cases) of obtaining the enforcement of the precautionary measure by means of instruments of indirect coercion and of the suitability to justify the utility of the precautionary measure of the mere prospect of a spontaneous fulfilment, induced by the power of conviction by the judicial ruling'. More recently, Trib. S. Maria Capua V., ord. 27 January 2021; Trib. Brindisi, ord. 7 June 2016; Trib. Siena, ord. 21 November 2015; Trib. Roma, ord. 25 June 2015. Moreover, it should be noted that the legislator introduced the remedy of the so-called *astreintes* by Law No. 69 of 18 June 2009, in Art. *614-bis* c.p.c. .: on this point see, Trib. Palermo, ord. 29 March 2014; Tribunal of Naples, ord. 30 July 2021, according to which 'the remedy under Article *614-bis* of the Code of Civil Procedure was provided for precisely with reference to non-fungible services [...] and in the case law there is no doubt that it is an instrument that can also be applied in interlocutory proceedings'. On the applicability of the remedy *ex* Art. *614-bis* c.p.c. in the context of the emergency measures provided for *by* Art. 700 c.p.c. see. Trib. Milan, ord. 22 February 2021, available on *giurisprudenzadelleimprese.it*, which defines the instrument of Art. *614-bis* c.p.c. as the 'discipline providing for general means of indirect coercion ancillary to judicial measures having as their object the condemnation of obligations to do and, therefore, also applicable in the case of orders to do adopted *pursuant to* art. 700 c.p.c. and, as such, susceptible of anticipatory effects of the condemnation without requiring the consolidation thereof by means of the introduction of a judgement on the merits'.

[52] For a survey of the most recent literature, G. Arieta (2005), p. 644 ff. On this point, indeed, it is considered admissible to adopt condemnation measures *pursuant to* Art. 700 of the Code of Civil Procedure with an injunction content, also based on traditional doctrine, regardless of the impossibility or difficulty of giving them coercive implementation, since they have as their object an infungible performance of a *task*, since the judicial pronouncement alone would exert a psychological coercion on the condemned party, such as to induce him to perform. Moreover, the admissibility of the precautionary measure, if granted and disregarded, may be useful to the holder of the right to invoke further legal consequences, including a claim for damages.

or to share them in digital format within the meaning of Art. 2(2)(a) and (b) of Directive No. 770, then it is clear that the digital good connected with the service represents a different good in that it is dynamic and not merely static, but still identifiable as a movable good *within the meaning of* Art. 812 of the Civil Code.

And, therefore, it is necessary to identify the new digital goods according to this categorisation:

(a) static goods that can be enjoyed, used and circulated *offline*, such as data, and which can be understood as static persistent digital goods;
(b) dynamic assets for which the cooperation of the intermediary debtor is necessary to use the asset, including, in an automated manner, such as virtual currency, *e-wallets, Non-Fungible Tokens, hosting, streaming, cloud computing*, determining this partition as a different criterion for the protection of such assets.

4 The New Static Digital Goods: Data

The use of as much data as possible, through digitisation, makes the *training of* generative Artificial Intelligence systems possible, as the input of millions of data represents the greatest resource, so strategic that one can even theorise about the evolution of the essential market structures.[53]

Data, as illustrated above, becomes such in a digital format, separating itself from the context in which it was born and transferring from the mind and inner psyche of man into a form of knowledge that transforms the economy, society, and culture. When stored digitally, facts take on a different morphology.

The category from which to start, to then place the data in the context of the code, is the fact understood as knowledge of law and the relevance of information as a legal asset. The studies of a Master[54] have highlighted the distinction between empirical knowledge and scientific knowledge, considering that the nature of knowledge is presented as a form of psychic fact, characterised by the concurrence of consciousness and will. However, the fact of knowledge in the sphere of law necessitates an in-depth examination of its role in relation to the normative values of conduct, which in law are regulated, thereby giving them a different connotation. Human knowledge in law becomes knowing consciousness with respect to which in ‘law it is what is known and not the form of knowing that is relevant’.[55]

Knowledge thus assumes relevance both as a functional element in the process of realising legal values and as a factual situation influencing the very constitution, modification and distinction of those values.

[53] Alaimo and Kallinicos (2024).

[54] Pugliatti (1961), p. 45.

[55] Falzea (1978), p. 537.

Human knowledge is therefore considered in two ways: sub specie facti, highlighting human interests that require protection, and sub specie effecti, being able to constitute a condition for the realisation of the interests highlighted by the fact.[56]

This determines that the object of legal knowledge is the juridically relevant reality; the appropriate expertise is parameterised on the capacities of conscious human cognition.

It follows that this legally relevant reality can be viewed both in relation to legal relations considered in an individual dimension, and in relation to scientific knowledge in relation to the progress of the community and the pursuit of interests and values of a super-individual character. In reality, scientific knowledge, the fruit of research and human activity, can be directed towards a profile of commercial exploitation that must find a balance, as a value within the community.

Knowledge, therefore, becomes information mediated through the human being: the evolution of information as a legal asset confers a legally relevant patrimonial value on facts and expertise. *Knowledge*, in fact, as a set of *information* that an individual accumulates within his own being, in economic evolution, becomes a *datum*, bringing with it a value in commercial and economic terms.

If, therefore, at the basis of the datum is the fact of knowledge, which assumes relevance both with respect to the human interests requiring protection and with respect to the realisability of the interests underlying the fact,[57] the object of legally relevant knowledge becomes, through scientific knowledge, a balancing point of the interests of individuals and the community.[58]

In this sense, information, as a fact of knowledge, has its own identification with the characteristics of immateriality, dynamism and modifiability, posing a problem of ownership and exclusive enjoyment of the asset 'information' as knowledge of a fact and, therefore, an intangible asset, also about its transmissibility to third parties.

From another perspective, it is worth noting that the market is a decentralised and spontaneous information system that can fail due to a series of externalities, among which the information asymmetries of the agents at the time of decision-making stand out. The economic role of the state is also to reduce, if not limit, the information asymmetries of the individual agent at the time of the decision, and more generally, the uncertainty of the market that causes its failure.[59] If, therefore, the state must reduce information asymmetries through the efficient and fair allocation of resources to protect the weak subject with an information deficit, it follows that information symmetry is a factor in the allocation of resources that the jurist must protect by safeguarding the weak interest of the information *deficit*. This presupposes,

---

[56] Busacca (2023), p. 185.

[57] Busacca (2023), p. 185.

[58] Busacca (2023), p. 1181, considers that the datum in its raw representation emerges in a prejudicial dimension, indeed in some ways in the sphere of juridical irrelevance, representing a sensorial and intellectual perception that through an activity of cognitive consciousness can take on the value of information or knowledge and thus a good/object juridically relevant to the subject through a process of goods/objects functional to human interests.

[59] Bocchini (2011), p. 15.

therefore, that information represents a patrimonial value that, with the characteristics of immateriality and modifiability, accesses the market and, thus, as an asset with patrimonial value, must be brought within a mechanism of appropriation and ownership.

Information, as a good crystallised in data, becomes even more susceptible to appropriation in the context of the patrimonial circulation of goods. In this sense, utility becomes evident when information, through data, becomes not only multiple and contextual, but also exclusive enjoyment, at the very moment it is stored.

Digital data is identified as information expressed in sequential numbers produced by a computer or, in any case, as a reinterpretable representation of information in a format conventionally suitable for communication, interpretation or processing. Data is the representation of information in a digital format, which is crystallised and becomes a legal asset. The digital datum makes it even more possible to identify the asset, which, moreover, can then be manipulated, giving evidence of the patrimonial value of the information that becomes data in the digital age and, therefore, a mobile asset.

This is true insofar as the *fact*, also understood as information, exists in a historical context in which it is exhausted and lives in an abstract dimension not being editable and performative, because it finds its external manifestation in the human mind, internal to man. When data is digitised, through platforms and with the use of the algorithms that process them, different relationships are created with the data itself, as it is not the human mind that generates the correlations and knowledge between the data. Still, it is digitisation that first crystallises the data and then, by connecting them, generates a different relationship between them.

In this way, information becomes a value that is crystallised in data and confirms its suitability to be considered a legal good according to the fact-information-goods-data scheme,[60] all identified as belonging to the same sub-category of digital goods known as *information goods*, according to *marketing* and innovation economics studies.

Indeed, data, like information, is an asset susceptible to appropriation, with its own patrimonial value subject to the forms of circulation and reproduction. Even more so, manipulated digital data is a legal asset that, in the digital environment, has its own economic value.

The computational valorisation of digital data aims to liberate personal data from a merely personalistic approach, recognising its contractual dimension in the context of an increasingly digital economy, and, as noted, as the primary object of telematic business activity.

Data are not neutral, meaning that the choices that produce and enhance them are relative to the value systems of the cultural and institutional histories of those who have designed the methods for collecting and using them. Data analysis is not

---

[60] Some, to describe the transformation of data into information, resort to the figure of the so-called *DIKW* pyramid (*Data, Information, Knowledge, Wisdom*), see Van Meter (2020), p. 77.

merely a matter of statistics and technology, and the risk of cultural homogenisation cannot be a roadblock for the evolution of the system.

First, it is necessary to realise that there are different needs underlying the circulation of the various categories of data, which can be identified as personal data and non-personal data, from which a different qualification as legal goods derives.

International doctrine, moreover, has also classified data in a third category, that of so-called synthetic data, which can be qualified as a-personal data, i.e. created by AI tools with no referents in the material reality that, in addition to their commercial aspect, present such characteristics as to make them suitable for taking a position in the protection and defence of super-individual and community interests, enhancing them as *commons*.

The tripartition of the data category becomes functional for the objectification of data, for its valuation as a legal asset, and for its economic evaluation in terms of market transactions between operators and between operators and stakeholders.

5 The New Dynamic Digital Goods: Virtual Currencies and E-Wallets

The process of identifying digital goods involves examining those goods for which the cooperation of another party is required to enjoy their utility and digital content.

One of the dynamic digital assets par excellence is cryptocurrencies or virtual currencies (of which *Bitcoin* is the best known), which, like *Non Fungible Tokens* (NFTs), require the cooperation of an intermediary for their use.

The impact of these assets on the market is economically significant, as monthly activity on the blockchain of compliant *tokens* increased from approximately USD 200 million per month in June 2024 to over USD 5 billion in November 2024. The *business* of *cryptoassets* is fostered in a competitive and innovative digital ecosystem through the recognition of *blockchain* technology and distributed ledger (DLT). The realisation of a single market, which is still unrealised as far as capital and services are concerned, involves simplifying the processes of raising capital and speeding up the ways of financing and payment for SMEs on our continent through cross-border transactions, which, at present, still require intermediaries.

The so-called *token economy*,[61] understood as the complex of economic phenomena based precisely on the use of these *cryptoassets*, still presents a specific regulatory fragmentation, and an initial, almost shared definition of *cryptoassets* is offered by Regulation (EU) 2023/1114 (MiCA)[62] which, in an attempt to rationalise the

[61] Voshmgir (2021), pp. 30 ff.; Sunyaev et al. (2021), pp. 457 ff.; Cong and Wang (2019), pp. 1 ff.; Lee (2019), pp. 773 ff.; Nieves Pacheco Jiménez (2019), pp. 61 ff.; De Caria (2021), pp. 90 ff. From an engineering perspective, see Wang (2022), pp. 710 ff.

[62] Regulation No. 1114 of 31 May 2023 on cryptocurrency markets and amending Regulations (EU) 1093/2010 and (EU) 1095/2010 and Directives 2013/36/EU and (EU) 2019/1937 operative in Italy by Legislative Decree No. 129 of 5 September 2024.

regulatory system, describes them as: 'a digital representation of a value or right that can be transferred and stored electronically, using distributed ledger or similar technology'.

In particular, the virtual currency has been disseminated since 2009 through the so-called *Bitcoin*[63] *software* has now established itself as the virtual currency of the metaverse.[64] It is a cryptocurrency generated by a *software* programme belonging to a private issuer and not to a public body recognised as a legal tender issuer, which is why it cannot have a legal fulfilment function unless private individuals conventionally accept it through a *peer-to-peer* transaction.[65]

Bitcoin is based on the *blockchain*, the decentralised and distributed digital ledger that stores transactions on many computers in a *peer-to-peer* network. Each group of transactions is grouped into a 'block', and these blocks are linked together in a chain (hence the term '*blockchain*') that is decentralised, meaning there is no single point of control. The data is distributed over numerous nodes[66] (computers) in the network, and this makes the *blockchain* resistant to attacks and tampering, but at the same time ensures transparency of transactions, as they are permanently recorded and visible to all participants in the chain. These features of the system reduce the risk of fraud by guaranteeing, for the entire *blockchain* community, security through the use of advanced cryptographic techniques to protect data. Transactions must be verified and agreed upon by most of the nodes in the network, and once a block is added to the chain, its information cannot be changed. This ensures that recorded transactions are permanent and cannot be altered.

This simple yet technologically advanced mechanism enables the system's efficiency through automation, leading to the apparent removal of intermediaries. This, in turn, would further reduce transaction times and costs, which are still long and burdensome due to the presence of intermediaries.[67]

Bitcoin can, therefore, be identified as a communication protocol based on cryptography, which represents a multifunctional exchange system with multiple

[63] Its characteristic of being a 'decentralised' currency does not make it subject to the MiCA Regulation in certain respects, cf. Annunziata (2024), available at *ssrn.com*, observes that *Bitcoin*: '*falls outside the scope of rules contained in MiCAR on the issuance and offering of tokens. Nonetheless, decentralised crypto-assets remain subject to the MiCAR framework in relation to service providers, where the provisions governing crypto-asset services extend to those involving fully decentralised assets*' in commenting on the content of recital 22 of MiCA Reg.

[64] Bocchini (2017), pp. 28 ff.

[65] Pasquino (2023), p. 225; Rubechini (2023), p. 263.

[66] There are different categories of nodes. One tripartition distinguishes between nodes that 'validate' operations and keep the entire register (so-called *full nodes*), nodes that verify and send operations without keeping the entire register, but only some information (so-called *light nodes*), and nodes that keep the entire register (so-called *archive nodes*): Mayer et al. (2020), p. 1284 ff. Other classifications distinguish between *miners* (i.e. *full nodes* that, in addition to preserving the register, compete to confirm the transaction and be remunerated), *full nodes*, and *light nodes*: Ismail and Huned (2019), p. 4; Gong et al. (2020), p. 782.

[67] Bocchini (2017), p. 37.

application possibilities, also with a variable legal nature depending on the uses and economic activities performed with its use.

It follows that *Bitcoin* is undoubtedly a digital asset, consisting of a *hash* string, composed of *bits*, used through one of the electronic processors, belonging in turn to a *network*,[68] autonomous concerning the processor, which circulates from one user to another. Still, it can be considered neither a movable asset under Art. 812 (3) of the Civil Code as it is not persistent, nor an intangible asset as it is exchangeable exclusively by telematic means through subjects operating on the *web* and in custody in special digital wallets (*e-wallets*).[69]

In light of the reconstruction of case law,[70] cryptocurrencies should not even be considered a currency, but at most financial products, i.e. forms of investment with an intrinsic financial value.[71] However, despite the debate on the qualification, the giving of cryptocurrency would not have a solutary function of a pecuniary obligation, since it would not be a payment *under* Art. 1277 of the Civil Code, but—if the creditor allows it—would only be worth *datio in solutum* (Art. 1197 of the Civil Code).

Concerning our study profile, we need to investigate whether these undoubtedly digital assets can be considered as *static* digital assets or *dynamic digital* assets, and this also with respect to the profile of custody activity in electronic wallets, so-called *e-wallets*, which act as personal accounts and through *wallet providers* allow crypto-assets to be easily operated through intuitive interfaces, on a telephone or

---

[68] Fauceglia (2020), p. 1254.

[69] A distinction is made, depending on the type of medium, between off-network custody (so-called *cold storage*), in the absence of an Internet connection, by means of media ranging from *paper wallet* to USB key (so-called *hardware wallet*), and on-network custody (so-called *hot storage*) by means of *software* and applications (so-called *software wallet*), with variants linked to security levels for access (e.g. *userid*, *password*, PIN, two-factor authentication, etc.). On these aspects: Morone (2018), pp. 1 ff.; Deloitte, *A Market Overview of Custody for Digital Assets*, June 2020, 7. All custody modes present risks and benefits; that is why hybrid modes are spreading, which, through the use of multiple *online* and *offline* keys held by clients and intermediaries, try to avoid the most common criticalities.

[70] Cass. pen., sec. II, 22 November 2022, no. 44378, in *Pactum*, 2023. To the contrary, Trib. Brescia, Sec. I, decr., 24 October 2018, no. 207, in *Società*, 1, 2019, pp. 26 ff. held that – in relation to its payment function – cryptocurrency should be considered, to all intents and purposes, as currency.

[71] Rulli (2019), p. 121, who reconstructs the regulation of *tokens* by highlighting similarities and differences with the category of securities. Fava (2024), p. 129, who, in commenting on the so-called *Fintech* Decree, points out that the issuance of financial instruments through registrations on a distributed registry for their digital circulation represents an innovative way of incorporating and transferring the relative rights. This process, made possible by technological advances, marks a significant change, paving the way for the 'tokenization' of financial instruments on DLT, a possibility hitherto excluded from our legal system. Caloni (2023), p. 135, argues that cryptocurrencies, by virtue of incorporation, would be ascribable to a category with the same distinguishing feature, that of securities. In this regard, the author emphasises how, in the case of both cryptoassets and debt securities: 'from a strictly civil law perspective [...] the security can circulate on the market as a movable thing, legitimising the person who becomes its possessor (according to the circulation rules laid down by law) to exercise the right'.

computer, through which orders can be placed. Transactions realised, values and balances noted.

With regard to the first profile, relative to the verification of whether they are static or dynamic digital assets, it appears evident that the *hash* string composed of *bits*, which identify the digital asset, allows the latter to be classified among the dynamic movable assets *pursuant to* Art. 812 (3) of the Civil Code, insofar as it is only possible to use *Bitcoin* with the aid of the platform, not being persistent goods and, therefore, of an intermediary, who, by his activity, makes possible both the identification of the *Bitcoin* to be transferred from one person to another and the transfer between different *e-wallets*. Therefore, virtual currency must be traced back to that category of digital entities that, to be operational, need the *online* digital world and the cooperation of subjects that enable the fruition of the *Bitcoin* asset.

Regarding the second profile, however, one of the network's main services needs to be explored: *Bitcoin* storage.

According to a recent doctrine,[72] the *e-wallet*, which contains the computer data of all cryptocurrencies, can be qualified as a contract *under* Art. 1782 of the Civil Code, as an irregular deposit.[73] This type of contract would commit the platform operator to the safekeeping of identifiable cryptocurrencies, such as those with their own serial numbers, thanks to the unique algorithmic strings that comprise them.

Therefore, these are certainly fungible movable assets insofar as the intermediary will have to guard and return to the depositor *the tantundem eiusdem generis et qualitatis* of the *Bitcoin* present in the *e-wallet* that the debtor-depositary will have to pay to the creditor. Thus, an additional irregular deposit contract between the depositor and the debtor would be created alongside the original agreement between the creditor and the debtor, and only with the cooperation of the third party (the digital wallet platform) will it be possible to transfer the *Bitcoins* that the depositor has placed in the *e-wallet* in favour of the third party.

Despite the scarcity of rulings on the subject, one agrees, therefore, with the idea that the *e-wallet* can be traced back to the figure of the irregular deposit, and indeed not of the loan,[74] but the point remains that the cooperation of a third party is necessary in the identification of the *Bitcoin* asset, the depositary platform, which turns

---

[72] Fauceglia (2020), p. 1276.

[73] Trib. Firenze, sez. fall., 21 January 2019, no. 18, states that: 'Cryptocurrency is a monetary unit similar to a currency, which, however, is not qualified as legal tender; it is a consumable asset by reason of its use (when it is spent); it is a fungible asset because the individual units composing it are of the same nature and quality, as they belong to the same computer protocol, and are subject to the same rationale as other assets enabling payments. By reason of their fungibility, cryptocurrencies if kept in a general fund, not bearing distinctive elements as to their belonging to individual users, give rise to an irregular deposit, from which follows the specific obligation for the depositary to keep the full quantity at the disposal of the depositors at all times, with a cash coefficient of 100%'. TAR Lazio, 27 January 2020, in *Le società*, 2020, 566, qualified virtual currencies as intangible 'goods', as they do not perform the typical functions of currency, albeit conventional, of unit of account and store of value, due to their extreme volatility, as well as their lack of releasing power in payments.

[74] Fauceglia (2020), p. 1284.

out to have a decisive role in the performance of the performance by the debtor, since the latter does not have the possibility of discharging its obligation without the intermediary, so that even in this case the *e-wallet* asset can be traced back to a dynamic movable asset *pursuant to* Art. 812 (3) of the Civil Code.

5.1 Continued: The *Non-Fungible Tokens*

The economic value of such digital assets has emerged in a disruptive manner in recent years: a single NFT was auctioned at Christie's for the sum of 69 million dollars as was the case with the purchase of the work by Beeple, (born Mike Winkelmann) entitled '*Every Day: The First Five Thousand Days*' and on this wave, the NFT of Jack Dorsey's first Tweet was sold for an impressive 2.9 million dollars. The virtual world, therefore, has now reached a materiality, in terms of economic values, that is truly impressive. On a strictly artistic level, the circumstance that the object of the collection is not the work of art itself, but rather the certificate of authenticity that concerns it, while the work itself ends up being usable by the entire community, raises the question as to whether, in this different dimension, the emotional relationship that has hitherto characterised the relationship with an original work of art should be considered definitively surpassed, with the consequent placing of the artistic dimension on a different level.

To legally frame NFTs, it is first necessary to understand their technological profiles to attribute their ownership and authorship correctly. NFTs must be divided into two categories: those that exist exclusively on distributed records and those that, on the other hand, constitute a representation of physical works existing in nature. So-called *native smart properties* are assets created and intended to exist exclusively on a digital platform, as they are created on that platform and are intended to circulate solely on it.

Then there are the NFTs reproducing works/goods existing in nature, which are to be counted among the so-called *non-native smart properties*.

In light of this initial classification, it is first necessary to understand how such assets are generated within the digital world. They arise from the need to convey information to a community of reference through a medium that can assure that the information is authentic and truthful. Whereas until some time ago this information was based on the centralised model and a public authority existed, with the advance of digitised systems, on the other hand, it is possible to certify information utilizing a distributed consensus mechanism through which in a community, if a sufficient number of subjects recognise the identity of a certain subject, this will be valid as proof of that subject's actual identification.

This principle originates from a widespread consensus mechanism using technology that is not centralised, but is shared by the cybernaut community and is called *blockchain*. It derives from the cryptographic hash, which is understood to be a unique, fixed-length summary of a digital document, as illustrated in the context of cryptocurrencies. The *hash* enables the creation of a transaction that, when linked to the next transaction, forms the well-known *blockchain*. While the use of a chain prevents the alteration of the single replica of the chain and the single transaction, it also prevents new information from being certified without participation in the chain. The digital work or the digitised physical work becomes a *hash* that, together with the information regarding the transfer of the digital work from one party to another, acts as a certificate of ownership of the work in the hands of the party to whom it is transferred.

Having briefly illustrated the technical mechanism through which the NFT comes into being in the digital world, we can now delve into its legal nature to frame what the digital good, represented by *the hash of* the NFT, consists of in the legal world.

There is no real legal definition of NFT and to reconstruct its meaning, it is possible to start from the MiCA Regulation,[75] according to which[76] infungible crypto-assets are those assets whose value can be attributed to the unique characteristics of each crypto *asset* and the utility it offers to the *token* holder. The same Regulation[77] specifies that fractions of a unique and non-fungible crypto-asset should not be considered unique and non-fungible.

The issuance of crypto-assets as non-fungible *tokens* in a large series or collection should be considered an indicator of their fungibility. The mere attribution of a unique identifier to a crypto-asset is not in itself sufficient to classify it as unique and non-fungible because for it to be considered unique and non-fungible, the assets or rights represented should also be unique and non-fungible.

The exclusion of unique and non-fungible crypto-assets from the scope of application of the MiCA Regulation is without prejudice to the qualification of such crypto-assets as financial instruments, as it should also apply to crypto-assets that appear to be unique and non-fungible, but whose *de facto* characteristics or features that are linked to their *de facto* uses would make them fungible or non-single. In this regard, when assessing and classifying crypto-assets, competent authorities should adopt a substance-over-form approach, whereby the characteristics of the crypto-asset determine its classification, rather than its designation by the issuer.

Hence, the underlying digital good may also be concretely infungible, and hence the infungibility of the *token*. The NFT differs from the object, or rather, the underlying digital good, and thus it may well be the case that the person who owns the copyright on the digital effect is not the owner of the NFT.[78] The person who has realised the NFT of a digital object protected by someone else's trademark may be prevented from using the NFT by the actual owner of the trademark.[79]

---

[75] Regulation (EU) 2023/1114 of the European Parliament and of the Council of 31 May 2023 on cryptocurrency markets and amending Regulations (EU) 1093/2010 and (EU) 1095/2010 and Directives 2013/36/EU and (EU) 2019/1937.

[76] Recital 10 of Regulation (EU) 2023/1114.

[77] Recital 11 of Regulation (EU) 2023/1114.

[78] Sirgiovanni (2024), p. 242.

[79] Trib. Rome, ord. 20 July 2022.

The rationale of copyright law is therefore completely different from the principles of NFT because. In contrast, copyright protects the creator of the work irrespective of its registration, as the expression of the work is protected; NFT protects the person who has digitally recorded that work, irrespective of authorship. It is therefore necessary, in the context of the analysis at hand, to differentiate native NFTs from non-native NFTs. In both cases of native and non-native works, the NFT of the work, together with the information regarding its transfer, represents a transaction that can be linked to the blockchain, thereby becoming irrefutable evidence, known as an NFT. From this moment on, the NFT acts as a *certificate of ownership of the work* by the person who owns the NFT, and this applies both in the case of a digital native work and in the case of a physical work that has been digitised by means of a high-definition scan of the work, even possibly three-dimensional. Therefore, both the NFT of an originally digital work and the NFT of a subsequently digitised physical work only allow the ownership of that *hash to be* attributed to the person who owns it. If from the same non-digital, but physical work, i.e. from two distinct digital versions of the work, two distinct *hashes*, completely different, and therefore two NFTs, two different ownerships of the work would be realised on two different *blockchains*.

The author of the work, therefore, as in the case of multiples of art photographs, where, for example, twelve copies of a subject are made and sold, should indicate how many copies of that digitised or physical work were made.

The NFT does not represent the work, but only the title of possession of the same and, therefore, the guarantee for the purchaser with respect to the value of the work that is purchased can only be given by a contract through which the parties grant to each other the authority to be the author of the work and the transfer of the same to the purchaser. If, therefore, the NFT does not integrate the certificate of authenticity of the work, then the digital asset, i.e. the *hash*, which is identified through the NFT, constitutes only the means of identification of the digital native work through which the person acquires the exclusive right of availability of the asset.

The exclusive attribution of the object to the owner of the NFT is different from the copyright on the digital object that belongs to the author of the work. The owner of the copyright and, therefore, of the digital work has the same rights as the author of the painting or sculpture on the work itself, so that the person who acquires the NFT is only the owner of the reproduced work.

It can therefore be said that the copyright law applies with respect to the NFT of a digital native work, with the only difference being that the representation of the work takes place in digital format through a service rendered by a third party to allow the owner and also the users of the work to enjoy the work of art digitally represented in the NFT. In fact, the *hash of* the NFT can only be used with the cooperation of another party, through the use of the described chain that prevents the alteration of the single replica of the chain and the single transaction, and prevents new information from being certified without participation in the chain. Therefore, the cooperation of the third party is necessary and indispensable.

In this sense, therefore, in our categorisation, *it is a dynamic mobile asset* because for its fruition, as with *Bitcoins,* the activity of an intermediary is required, as the *bits* and the *hash* chain cannot be enjoyed on an external autonomous persistent medium.

A further issue concerns the identification of the asset related to an NFT of a physical work that is replicated in a digital manner, insofar as the copy of the physical work, becoming a virtual asset, takes on its own autonomy as a work and, therefore, as a legal asset. In this case, the realisation of the work through the NFT determines that, even though that static movable asset exists through the *tokenization*[80] of the physical work to be able to use the work itself, the cooperation of a third party is necessary since the *hash* realised cannot be used by the owner of the property right without the cooperation of the third party who must allow the 'viewing' of the NFT and therefore one cannot speak of a movable asset *pursuant to* Art. 812, para 3, of the Italian Civil Code.

5.2 Next: Cloud, Streaming and Hosting Services

Among dynamic mobile goods are certainly *cloud computing, streaming* and *hosting* services, which represent, in the above categorisation, the dynamic goods of the third millennium. If, in fact, one examines the services that are offered with these types of contracts, it becomes clear that storage services (*cloud*), continuous live broadcasting or over the Internet, such as *webcasting* (*streaming*), or *hardware* leasing *(hosting)* represent some of the many dynamic goods that are used daily in *cyberspace*.

Indeed, the automated digital service, which becomes a good because it is reified through the company and as the utility of an automated service rendered by the machine, thus allowing such services to be considered dynamic goods, emerges easily precisely from the examination in these contracts of *cloud*, *streaming* and *hosting*. As will be seen, with a closer examination of the case in point, through such services, the user can create, transform, store data or access them in digital format or share them in digital format uploaded or created by the user himself or have any other interaction with such data, through the cooperation of an intermediary who allows the user of the service to receive a dynamic good since the data, combined with the digital service, determines the creation of a different good with respect to the digital movable good *pursuant to* Art. 812, para 3, of the Civil Code, since these are automated services rendered to the market automatically and mechanically by 'things automated' (services *ex re*), in the information society. The service, therefore, becomes the object of the contract and as a good is reified. Let us test this line

[80] On this point, see Rainone (2022), p. 489, who defines the NFT as the 'digital *alter ego*' of any tangible or intangible good and with regard to this 'process' qualifies it as both 'legal and cryptographic by which a tangible or legal good is transformed' and 'once tokenized, a good can be the object of disposition through the means of *tokens*, which are, for example, linked and transferred by means of *smart contracts* and recorded in distributed form'.

of thought with regard to the technological phenomenon of so-called *cloud computing*.

As has been convincingly stated, cloud computing services, or more simply 'cloud', represent the latest frontier of computerised information systems through the use of distributed computing devices. This term refers to on-demand reallocated access to a shared computing system (e.g. networks, *servers, data centres*, storage, applications and services) through which data and functions can be quickly shared. This mode enables all users to access large computing power without incurring considerable economic effort. Therefore, it requires providers to adapt to the language of computing, such as the standards established by the owners of *cloud* distribution platforms. These services may be offered jointly by the same provider or, as usual, by several providers; indeed, the contractual network of relationships involved is referred to by North American doctrine as 'contractual chains of *cloud providers*'.

One of the reasons behind the proliferation and widespread use of cloud computing is the wide range of unparalleled opportunities it provides. These opportunities include the optimisation and scalability of *storage*, as well as *software* and application support.

Cloud service providers often not only offer end-users *software* applications or, more generally, content, such as music, videos or books produced or sold by the providers themselves, but also make their platform available to other providers to sell their services on it, a fact that is now fully recognised and that increasingly leads the interpreter to think about the possible solution of unprecedented problems arising from the use of a technical infrastructure, the operation of which the user in general (consumer or not) was mostly unaware of until a few years ago, and whose activities were not subject to any kind of regulation.

Cloud computing does not really consist of a new technology, but rather of 'a combination of already known technologies that generate a new way of offering services',[81] making storage space, *software* or development environments available without the related resources residing in the user's computer systems (*cloud consumer*), since only the connection to remote *servers* managed by the provider (*cloud service provider*) is necessary. More specifically, this is a set of services, accessible *on demand* and in *self-service* mode via the *web*, based on shared resources, characterised by considerable flexibility of the infrastructure, 'capable of responding quickly and automatically to even significant variations, either increasing or decreasing, in the demand for resources by users'.[82] In *cloud computing*, the *provider* offers

[81] So correctly Martini (2020), p. 970.

[82] The definition was drawn up by the *National Institute for Standards and Technology*. P. Mell-T. Grance, *The NIST Definition of Cloud Computing. Recommendation of the National Institute of Standards and Technology*, (NIST), U.S. Department of Commerce, January 2011. *NIST* highlights five characteristics of the *cloud*: (i) On-demand *self-service*: a customer can unilaterally request, within the constraints set by the contract, IT resources without direct intervention by the service providers themselves; (ii) Broadband access: resources are accessible via the Network, whose bandwidth must be adequate for the specific use requested, and are accessed

services that can be classified into distinct models based on the mode of delivery. According to the NIST document's description, these models can be distinguished into three main categories.[83]

A peculiar element that characterises *cloud* models, therefore, is the provision of a service: the *cloud*, in fact, is a model centred not on the proprietary dimension,[84] but precisely on the provision of IT services by third-party providers, according to a paradigm already widely investigated in economic literature, which in this regard has spoken of a 'culture of access'.[85]

Similarly, with regard to *streaming* contracts, although there is no normative definition of *streaming*, doctrine and jurisprudence have identified it as an indirect continuous transmission, such as *live streaming*, or a television transmission over the Internet, such as *webcasting*.

In fact, Directive (EU) 2019/790, later transposed into Legislative Decree No. 177 of 8 November 2021, states in recital 62 that the definition of *online* content sharing service provider should only include *online* services that play an important role in the *online* content market, in competition with other *online* content services such as *online* audio and video *streaming* services for the same recipients. With this directive, it was intended to frame the phenomenon of *streaming* as that activity of an information society service provider whose main purpose is to store and give public access to large amounts of copyright-protected works or other protected material uploaded by its users, which the service organises and promotes for that purpose (recital 62 and Art. 2(1)(6)).

These are, therefore, audiovisual *media* services through an undertaking that merely offers the viewing of live *streaming* television programmes over the Internet, not by providing an electronic communication network, but instead by offering only access to the content of audiovisual services provided over the electronic communication network.

Therefore, the fundamental characteristic of *streaming* is its progressive usability, the quasi-real-time of the flow of audio and video data that only determines a temporary storage within the destination device, for the sole purpose of their

---

through mechanisms that allow them to be used with diversified and heterogeneous platforms; (iii) Shared resources: the provider's computing resources are organised to serve multiple customers, using the *multi-tenant* model, in which physical and virtual resources are dynamically allocated according to customer demand. The resources offered are independent of their physical location, i.e. the customer generally has neither control nor knowledge of where they are located; (iv) Elasticity: resources can be rapidly and elastically provisioned, and in some cases even automatically, to quickly increase computational capacity; (v) Monitored services: *cloud* systems automatically monitor and optimise resource utilisation, exploiting the ability to measure resource utilisation at the level required for the type of service. The monitoring of service utilisation is very important to enable the provider to react to any peaks in demand in order to guarantee the promised quality of service to the customer.

[83] On this point, see Trubiani (2022), pp. 403 ff.

[84] This consideration is accepted in doctrine cf. Noto La Diega (2014), 577. On this point, see also Trubiani (2022), p. 94.

[85] The reference, of course, goes to Rifkin (2011).

immediate reproduction. These data, therefore, travel in a compressed manner and are then decompressed and reproduced by the PC without storing a copy on the device through which the transmission service is used. In jurisprudence with respect to this technical fact, however, the problem has arisen as to the legitimacy of the use of such content through the *mere conduit* or *hosting* service whereby the intermediary receives the data flow and transmits it, in turn, to the service user's computer. The profile relative to the typical liability of Art. 5 of the DSA and the relative infringements, through this system of copyright, of those who generate the transmission with respect to the final user of the service was then examined in depth.

Without prejudice, therefore, to the profiles of the legitimacy or otherwise of the *streaming* activity,[86] as far as the present work is concerned, it is clear that this is an enduring automated service, through which the service user obtains the goods and the audiovisual service from a third party. This is the classic example of an automated broadcasting service: the service user needs an automated intermediary who, through the company that generates the service itself, makes the service user enjoy the final good.

The EU Court of Justice itself[87] has held that an undertaking that merely offers *streaming* and live television programme viewing over the Internet does not provide an electronic communications network, but instead offers access to the content of audiovisual services provided over electronic communications networks. It is thus clear from that the service is provided by an undertaking in an automated manner, to such an extent that the Court, in this judgment, notes that the undertaking may also carry out the service of retransmitting television channels using, for consideration, a communications infrastructure owned by other economic operators and states that that does not, however, preclude those activities from being regarded as a service of providing content, to which the universal service obligations laid down by that directive do not apply.

As far as our reasoning is concerned, it clearly emerges that this pronouncement establishes that such supply services are automated and can be carried out by companies not only on their own telecommunications networks, but also on the networks of others.

Finally, we come to the *hosting* service, which is perhaps the most widely used service in the digital world, as it is necessary for storing information. It is now extensively regulated by Art. 6 of the DSA. It consists in the provision to users, by network intermediaries, of a space on the *server*, i.e. on the *hard disk* under their

---

[86] Among studies conducted by the content industry, the IFPI (International Federation of the Phonografic Industry) states that digital music revenues of record companies internationally grew by 25% to USD 3.7 billion in 2008. Digital platforms now account for 20% of the market, up from 15% in 2007. The continued growth of digital sales has helped limit the damage of the decline in the recorded music market. Single file downloads grew by 24% in 2008 to 1.4 billion units, continuing to lead the *online* market, while digital albums also grew by 37%. Despite these results, the Federation states that *online* music piracy accounts for 95% of the total global music market (IFPI Digital Music Report 2009).

[87] Court of Justice. EU, 11 December 2019, Case C-87/19, cited above.

own management, or for the input of data that can be used by all network users. In this way, a *web* space is provided by the intermediary, in an automated manner (free of charge or in return for a fee) and the information is stored, in an enduring manner.

From the point of view of liability, the service provider shall be held liable for the information stored when: (a) it has actual knowledge of illegal activities or content and, with regard to claims for damages, is unaware of facts or circumstances that make the illegality of the activity or content apparent; or (b) as soon as it becomes aware of such illegal activities or content or becomes aware of such facts or circumstances, it fails to act immediately to remove the illegal content or to disable access to it.

Well, also in this case, it is clear, in the light of what has been argued with regard to the *e-wallet*, that the user of the service, to be able to enjoy the good, needs the cooperation of the intermediary who, in an automatic manner, makes the *server* available for the service user to enjoy the dynamic mobile good.

References

Addis F (2021) Spunti esegetici sugli aspetti dei contratti di vendita. Nuovo Dir Civ p 13 ff

Alaimo C, Kallinicos J (2024) Data rules, reinventing the market economy. Cambridge

Annunziata F (2024) Taxonomy of Crypto-assets and financial instruments: where do we stand? In: Bocconi Legal Studies Research Paper. Milan

Arieta G (2005) I provvedimenti d'urgenza ex art. 700 c.pc. In Montesano L-Arieta G, Tratt. dir. proc. civ., III, 1. Milano, p 644 ff

Barbero D (1962) I beni immateriali come oggetto di diritto. Riv Dir Ind, p 297

Barcellona M (1987) Attribuzione normativa e mercato nella teoria dei beni giuridici. In: Quadrimestre, p 608

Battelli E (2023) La patrimonializzazione dell'immateriale (anche nella prospettiva del moderno diritto d'impresa). In: Maniaci A (ed) Nuovi beni e new properties, Pisa, p 46

Belfiore A (1983) I beni e le forme giuridiche di appartenenza. A proposito di una recente indagine. Riv Crit Dir Priv, p 856

Bell D (1976) The coming of post-industrial society. New York

Bellelli A, Cianci AG (2008) Beni e situazioni giuridiche di appartenenza. Tra diritti reali e new properties. Torino, p 145 ff

Bocchini E (2011) Diritto commerciale nella società dell'informazione. Napoli, p 15

Bocchini R (1999) La somministrazione di servizi. Padova, p 24 ff

Bocchini R (2017) Lo sviluppo della moneta virtuale: primi tentativi di inquadramento e disciplina tra prospettive economiche e giuridiche. Dir Inf, p 28 ff

Bocchini R (2018) La tutela assoluta dei servizi. Napoli, p 23 ff

Busacca A (2023) I beni digitali nella tassonomia dei beni giuridici. Bari

Caloni A (2023) Criptoattività e contratti delle piattaforme: inquadramento civilistico e profili di diritto finanziario. In: Imbrosciano C, Lorenzini M, Zulberti M (eds) Criptovalute. Profili storico-economici e giuridici, Torino, p 135

Camardi C (2018) Cose, beni e nuovi beni, tra diritto europeo e diritto interno. Europa e Dir Priv, p 962

Candian A (2003) Rapport Italien-Les nouveaux biens, in La Propriété. Journées Vietnamiennes-Travaux de l'Association Henri Capitant, Parigi, p 291 ff

Colangelo M (2012) Creating property rights: law and regulation of secondary trading in the European Union. Leiden-Boston.

Cong LW, Wang L (2019) Tokenomics: dynamic adoption and valuation, in Columbia business school research paper, p 1 ff
Costantino M (1982) I beni in generale. In Tratt. dir. civ., directed by P Rescigno, vol. VII, Torino, p 1
De Caria R (2021) L'impatto della tokenizzazione sui diritti di proprietà. In: Media laws, p 90 ff
De Laurentiis R (2021) Economia digitale. Torino
De Nova G (1991) I nuovi beni come categoria giuridica. In: De Nova G, Inzitari B, Tremonti G, Visintini N (eds) Dalle res alle new properties. Milano, p 13 ff
Demolombe G (1855) Corso di Codice civile. trad. De Filippo e Tucci, V, Napoli, pp 4–6
Falce V (2023) Piattaforme ed ecosistemi digitali. La regolazione europea. In: Bocchini R (edited by), Manuale di diritto privato dell'informatica. Napoli, p 70 ff
Falzea A (1978) Fatto di conoscenza. In Studi in onore di Salvatore Pugliatti, vol. I. Milano, p 537
Fauceglia D (2020) La moneta privata, le situazioni giuridiche di appartenenza e i fenomeni contrattuali. In Contr. e impr., p 1254
Fava R (2024) La nuova forma di "incorporazione" digitale degli strumenti finanziari. In Banca e borsa, p 129
Ferrarese MR (2002) Il diritto al presente. Bologna, p 12
Ferraris M (2021) Documanità. Filosofia del mondo nuovo. Bari-Roma
Galgano F (2001) Lex Mercatoria. Bologna, p 229
Gambaro A (2004) Dalla new property alle new properties (Itinerario con avvertenze, tra i discorsi giuridici occidentali. In: Scalisi V (ed) Scienza e insegnamento del diritto civile in Italia, Milano, p 675
Gong X, Liu E, Wang R (2020) Blockchain-Based IoT Application Using Smart Contracts: Case Study of M2M Autonomous Trading, 2020 5th International Conference on Computer and Communication Systems (ICCCS), p 782
Irti N (1987) L'età della decodificazione, Milano
Ismail L, Huned H (2019) A review of Blockchain architecture and consensus protocols: use cases, challenges, and solutions. In Symmetry, p 4 ff
Lee JY (2019) A decentralized token economy: How blockchain and cryptocurrency can revolutionize busineff. Business horizons, p 773 ff
Luhmann N (1983) Illuminismo sociologico. Milano
Martini A (2020) Dalla "nuvola" al negozio: il contratto di cloud computing. Nuova giur. civ. comm., p 970
Mayer H, da Costa C, Da Rosa Righi R (2020) Electronic health records in a Blockchain: a systematic review. Health Inf J, p 1284 ff
Messinetti D (1985) Voce Personalità (diritti della). In: Enc. dir., vol. XXXIII, Milano, p 363
Montesano L (1965) Condanna civile e tutela esecutiva. Napoli, p 116
Morone M (2018) Bitcoin e successione ereditaria: profili civili e fiscali. In: giustiziacivile. com, p 1 ff
Nicolò R (1936) L'adempimento dell'obbligo altrui. Camerino
Nieves Pacheco Jiménez M (2019) De la tecnología blockchain a la economía del token. In: Derecho PUCP, p 61 ff
Noto La Diega G (2014) Il Cloud computing. Alla ricerca del diritto perduto nel web 3.0. In Eur. dir. priv., p 577
Ottolia A (2017) Big Data e innovazione computazionale. Torino, p 158
Pasquino T (2023) Le monete virtuali. In: Bocchini R (ed) Manuale di diritto privato dell'informatica, Napoli, p 225
Patti S (1979) La tutela civile dell'ambiente, Padova, p 147
Piraino F (2012) Sulla nozione di bene giuridico. Riv Crit Dir Priv, p 469
Pugliatti S (1957) voce Beni (teoria generale). In Enc. dir., V, Milano, 1957, p 187
Pugliatti S (1961) voce Conoscenza. In: Enc. dir., IX, Milano, p 45
Quarta A (2019) La dicotomia bene-servizio alla prova del supporto digitale. In: Contr. e impr., p 3

Quintarelli S (2019) Capitalismo immateriale. Le nuove tecnologie digitali e il nuovo conflitto sociale, Torino

Rahmatian A (2020) Debts, money, intellectual property, data and the concept of dematerialised property. JIPITEC, p 186

Rainone A (2022) Uso illecito del marchio altrui sulla blockchain: il principio di neutralità tecnologica e la rivoluzione mancata dei registri distribuiti. Dir Ind p 489

Rifkin J (2011) L'era dell'accesso. Milano

Rubechini P (2023) Criptoattività e blockchain. In Giorn Dir Amm p 263

Rulli E (2019) Incorporazione senza res e dematerializzazione senza accentratore: appunti sui token. In Orizz Comm p 121

Santoro Passarelli F (1995) Dottrine generali del diritto civile. Napoli

Scozzafava OT (1982) I beni e le forme giuridiche di appartenenza. Milano, p 128 ff

Scozzafava OT (1999) Dei beni. In Comm Schlesinger, Milano, p 12 ff

Sirgiovanni B (2024) Il non fungible token nella cripto-arte: la 'recinzione' dell'oggetto digitale. NLCC, p 242

Srnicek N (2017) Capitalismo digitale. Google, Facebook, Amazon e la nuova economia del web. Roma

Stella Richter M. Jr (2013) Tullio Ascarelli e i beni immateriali. In: Fusar Poli E, Sciumé A (eds) Afferrare... l'inafferrabile: i giuristi e il diritto della nuova economia industriale fra Otto e Novecento, Milano, p 1244

Sunyaev N, Kannengießer N-R, Beck H, Treiblmaier M, Lacity J, Kranz G, Fridgen-Luckow A, Spankowski U (2021) Token economy. Bus Inf Syst Eng, p 457 ff

Szilágyi F (2021) The necessity of data allocation: A plea for a private law (property law) perspective. EPLJ, p 180

Tommasini R (2012) I servizi come beni. Raff Dir Civ p 153

Tosi GM (2024) L'emersione dei beni immateriali digitali: rilettura dell'art. 810 c.c. alla luce del diritto privato europeo. Dir Inf p 411

Trubiani F (2022) I servizi di cloud computing fra innovazione tecnologica e sostenibilità digitale. Tecn Dir, p 94

Van dijck J-T, Poell M, De Waal (2018) The platform society. In: Public Values in a Connective World, Oxford

Van Meter HJ (2020) Revising the DIKW pyramid and the real relationship between data, information, knowledge, and wisdom. In: Law, technology and humans, vol. 2. Brisbane, p 77

Vari B (2023) New Properties e Noveaus Biens nelle prassi discorsive dei giuristi. In: Maniaci A (ed) Nuovi beni e new properties, Pisa, p 25

Voshmgir S (2021) Token economy. Lussemburgo, p 30 ff

Wang YC (2022) Efficient token circulation strategies against misers in device-to-device relay using token-based incentive mechanisms. IET Communications, p 710 ff

Zaccaria G (1985) Ermeneutica e giurisprudenza. Saggio sulla metodologia di Jossef Esser, Milano, p 206 ff

Zoppini A (2000) Le «nuove proprietà» nella trasmissione ereditaria della ricchezza (note a margine della teoria dei beni). Riv Dir Civ p 185 ff

Developments in the Contractual Relationship

Maria Barela and Giulio Andreotti

Contents

Abstract The purpose of this contribution is to analyse the events affecting platform contracts. The focus is on the constitutive, modifying and extinguishing moments of the contractual relationships, dwelling, in the light of the national and

Sections 1–5 of this chapter are attributable to Maria Barela; Sections 6–7 are attributable to Giulio Andreotti.

M. Barela
University of Tuscia, Tuscia, Italy
e-mail: mariabarela@libero.it

G. Andreotti (✉)
University of Naples "Parthenope", Naples, Italy
e-mail: giulio.andreotti@uniparthenope.it

R. Bocchini (ed.), *Digital Platforms - From Technical Foundations to Legal and Economic Implications*, https://doi.org/10.1007/978-3-032-07978-7_11

supranational regulations, on the various events, including those peculiar to digital realities, that affect, at one and the other moment, the relationships themselves and their effectiveness.

1 Foreword

We begin our investigation into the effects of the contract entered into through the *online* intermediary. We start from the simple observation that access to the platform and the activity carried out therein by the user generate a series of legal relationships, each with its own vicissitudes, differing from one another in object and subject matter.[1]

Furthermore, as is well known, the individual contract concluded *online* is no longer merely the instrument for achieving a result of a financial nature, but becomes the occasion for the release of the user's personal information and data both for the performance of the relationship and for other purposes that are now well known, such as profiling, *marketing*, *pricing* or other uses of a commercial nature; this entails, therefore, the production of effects in addition to the legal effects intrinsic to the contract itself, these data processing activities generate further legal consequences.

This data collection and storage operation is normally carried out by the *online* intermediary, the *platform*—the core around which our study revolves—i.e. the subject that enables exchanges to take place by setting up a virtual *ad hoc* apparatus such as a digital *marketplace*. It is here that infrastructures are set up and organised to enable the various categories of users to meet, distinguished by commodity sector and/or exchange characteristics.

Before delving into the thicket of the events produced by the contract, it is then necessary to understand the concept of the 'market', which, in the present case, corresponds to a virtual place where sellers and buyers converge, each to obtain the most advantageous terms of exchange and compare prices and characteristics of similar products.

This virtual place might nostalgically evoke the territorial market, where merchants and patrons gather, all hoping to do good business, but of course, for little reflection, these are completely different worlds, where the undisputed protagonist of the marketplace, located in a physical place, is completely missing in the digital marketplace, namely the *trading* activity.

[1] It remains to be established whether, in some cases, the contract may be considered *ab origine* as trilateral or even plurilateral, depending on the number of parties that take part in it, thus giving rise to as many relationships, but on the subject of contract formation, see chapter 'Contract Formation' by Giampetraglia et al. (this volume).

In the digital *marketplace*,[2] not only is any possibility of negotiation, which traditionally characterises the territorially localised market, completely absent, but the comparison of products travels at an infinitely higher speed, through images, technical information of the service or product and accurate descriptions. Moreover, as mentioned above, in digital markets, exchanges produce effects 'beyond' the mere constitution of the legal relationship, so that in platforms, the legal-economic space filled by the rules that constitute the statute of exchanges and are applied there,[3] is much enlarged compared to other types of markets.

In fact, if the contract is concluded in the virtual place set up by the intermediary—technically a third party with respect to the parties, but 'master' of the technological interface in which those exchanges take place—each contract stands as a fragment of a more complex system, in which the intermediation activity between supply and demand is professionally carried out by the digital platform.[4]

From the point of view of the contractual regulation established between the parties, the real novelty of the *marketplace* lies in the position of strength assumed by the *online* intermediary vis-à-vis both traders and consumers, since the platform dictates the contractual conditions, which the operator could also unilaterally modify during the course of the relationship, following new requirements.

As a result, the order of contractual positions, which has undergone alternating phases over the last two centuries, has once again been overturned: from the position of equality between the contracting parties, a hard-won achievement of the nineteenth century codes, which became part of the current civil code following the unification of civil and commercial law, we have moved on to the subsequent phase of reconsideration of the contractual synallagma, through the ascertainment of the unbalanced position of the parties in consumer contracts, with the consequent slow path leading to the separation of the latter from civil contracts.

Well, today we are witnessing a new phase, in which the real protagonist of the bargaining process is precisely the *online* intermediary, with respect to whom the contracting parties are both in a position of 'weakness'.

In view of the peculiarities of this form of contract, jurists and legal practitioners had to take into account the difficulty of applying purely and simply in the virtual world the rules regulating contractual events in the physical world and thus proceed to elaborate a new system, which would obviously consider, primarily, the a-territoriality of that new space, separated from any physical-territorial ties and dominated by technology that becomes the protagonist, leaving human will in the background. Nonetheless, account had to be taken of the risks associated with the dissemination of personal data on the Internet and thus of the need to identify new forms of protection, without neglecting the different ways of executing the contractual relationship, both in terms of price payment and product delivery.

---

[2] On the subject, Quarta and Smorto (2024), *therein* an extensive bibliography; Quarta (2020); for an overview of the problems opened up by digital platforms, Battelli (2022b), p. 563.

[3] Inescapable reference on the subject, Irti (1998a).

[4] A detailed analysis of the issues relating to contracts concluded electronically is offered by Camardi (2021), pp. 915 ff.

Within this perspective, we intend to offer some food for thought on the events of this contract, in due consideration of those profiles that have led to irreversible forms of objectification and 'proceduralisation' of the relationship,[5] not only under the profile of its formation,[6] consequent to uniform and repetitive conclusive conduct, but also and above all under the profile of the multiplication of the effects relating to the release of personal data, as well as to the pre-determination of the contractual terms and conditions (especially by the intermediary),[7] so that the constitution of the legal relationship no longer constitutes the result of the 'free determination' of the parties, with good reason for the Art. 1322 of the Italian Civil Code, but the mere adherence of the latter to the content prepared by the platforms.

2 Variety of Legal Relationships and Contractual Integration in the Digital Marketplace

It must be clarified that in the digital *marketplace*, every single 'transaction'[8] entails the establishment of several relationships, which, for the sake of classification, have been collected by doctrine into various categories, moving from the subjective profile.

If we consider, for example, a transaction occurring between a trader and a consumer, we have to take note of the constitution of at least three distinct relationships, for each of which requires the identification of the applicable legal framework and its effects: (1) the relationship between platform and trader (P2B-Platform *to business*); (2) that between platform and consumer (P2C-Platform *to consumer*); (3) that between trader and consumer (B2C-Business *to Consumer*).[9]

In additions to this category of economic operations, which imply the aforementioned threefold relationship, there is the series of P2P (*Peer to Peer*) contracts, always managed by the *online* intermediary, who, also in this case, plays a central role, establishing the rules of access, contract conclusion, regulation of the relationship and production of the effects, which often results in a trilateral relationship. This is the expanding sector of the *sharing economy*,[10] centred on the concept of

---

[5] Note the precursor pages by Oppo (1998), pp. 525 ff., and the reply by Irti (1999), pp. 273 ff.

[6] Irti (1998b), pp. 347 ff., who almost 30 years ago observed the '*dissolution of the agreement*' in some contracts.

[7] On the role of the intermediary, see Pisani (2023).

[8] From a terminological point of view, it should be noted that in the digital and financial world, the use of the term '*transaction*' to indicate a *contract*, an *exchange*, has become widespread, it being understood that in our legal system, 'transaction' has the well-known and precise meaning of a typical contract to end a dispute.

[9] For a comprehensive analysis of these contractual categories, see, for all, Smorto (2020), pp. 49 ff.

[10] We are referring here to that form of 'collaborative economy', practised through the platform and essentially inspired by the cooperative principle, with all its advantages. Some have believed they see in this type of economy a form of social solidarity, but in reality, even here, the profit motive

shared use, which disregards the ownership of property rights over things. This is where the figure of the *prosumer* is born, i.e. the consumer who becomes producer/trader precisely through the communication channels established by the *online* infrastructure, which has now become an irreplaceable commercial tool, even for the most distrustful of new technologies.

To complete the picture of the constituent events of platform-based relationships, two further contractual categories must be considered: (1) automated contracting, to which both *smart contracts*[11] and *computable contracts*[12] belong, where the former are governed entirely by Artificial Intelligence, which can perform the entire contractual cycle by itself,[13] including the execution of contractual performances, whereas in the latter the chain of the execution process could be interrupted by human intervention; (2) *social network* services or those of search engines, which likewise constitute commercial operations and entail the establishment of platform/user and user relations between them.[14]

Faced with such a variety of relationships established through the platform, there are numerous regulatory sources, both European and national, that must be taken into consideration when examining the contractual regulation, which is not only the result of the platform operator's determinations and the conditions dictated by the commercial operator, but also and above all arises from the multiplicity of rules concerning both the contractual regulation of the relationship and the management of the information and personal data released during the service access phase. With the consequent production of favourable and unfavourable effects, for various reasons, on all the subjects involved, thus configuring a 'contract imposed, arranged, but integrated with the rights and remedies that heteronymous sources impose on private authorities'.[15]

Thus, for the sake of argument, those simple and rapid actions that each one of us now performs on a daily basis (and even mechanically) to take advantage of the services offered by platforms operating in the most varied sectors—from commercial products to tourist services, banking services, but also health or sports, and so on up to *social networks*—entail a myriad of effects, deriving from the numerous

---

dominates, since through this instrument, users can achieve substantial savings compared to the exclusive use of the same service, which would entail much higher costs. Also in this sector, we have B2B, B2C and C2C models. See Quarta and Smorto (2024), pp. 55 ff.

[11] The scholarly production on the subject to date is endless. Among the most recent investigations into the constitution of the relationship, Di Sabato (2024), p. 360, which summarises the history of *smart contracts*, pointing out that the contractual clauses agreed upon are included in a cryptographic code and can be read directly by *hardware*: the programme applies the clauses, performs the services due, models their execution according to the different needs and adequately manages the different events that occur during the course of the contract; Maugeri (2021); see, also, Maugeri and Grasso (2022).

[12] The definition is attributable to Surden (2012), pp. 629 ff.

[13] The process is made crystal clear by Carleo (2019). On this point, Di Giovanni (2019), pp. 1677 ff., draws attention to the distinction between automation and autonomy.

[14] Battelli (2022b), p. 568.

[15] Thus Camardi (2021), pp. 915 ff.; see also Quarta (2020).

applicable disciplines, in compliance with a rule that comes to assume, at this point, a position of central importance, namely that on the integration of the contract, referable to the revitalised Art. 1374 of the Italian Civil Code.

It appears singular how this provision, conceived by the 1942 legislator with a function of closing the regulation of the contractual relationship, within the framework of the Italian Civil Code (where the contractual effects were *primarily* those agreed upon by the parties), now becomes the keystone of the contractual regulation, which is largely made up of the provisions applicable to the telematic contract, while the scope of the individual transaction remains in the background, from which reciprocal rights and obligations arise between the parties to the exchange, and between each of them and the platform, in compliance with the pre-packaged contractual regulation including the disciplines that apply thereto.

3 Production of Effects Resulting from EU Regulations

The problem then arises to ascertain which are the main regulatory disciplines involved in the production of contractual effects, breaking down the analysis for the different groups of relationships established through the[16] platform.

In principle, the two most recent European regulations that aim precisely to regulate relations arising on the *web*, particularly those arising via platforms, namely the DMA (*Digital Market* Act-Regulation (EU) 2022/1925, entered into force on 2 May 2023) and the DSA (*Digital Service* Act-Regulation (EU) 2022/2065, entered into force on 25 August 2023)[17] are worth considering.

1. From the point of view of P2B contracts, which are capable of constituting long-term relationships between platforms and traders, a prominent place is certainly occupied by the entire body of legislation protecting correct information and transparency, starting with Regulation (EU) 2019/1150, issued to '*promote fairness and transparency for business users of online intermediation services in the various areas of* digital *markets*'[18] and applicable only in the presence of services involving a contractual relationship with consumers.

   The regulation imposes transparency and information obligations, for the entire duration of the relationship, in favour of the commercial operator and at the expense of the intermediary, who, on the one hand, is obliged to make the information regarding the distribution channels of the products and the intellectual property rights of the commercial users easily accessible and, on the other

[16] Battelli's (2022a) analysis by contractual categories is precise, pp. 85 ff.

[17] It should be recalled that the aforementioned regulations, which today constitute the indispensable regulatory reference in this matter, find their ancestor in Directive 2000/31/EC on electronic commerce, transposed into Italian law by Legislative Decree No. 70 of 9 April 2003.

[18] On the relationship between the platform and the practitioner, see Ruggeri (2021), pp. 397 ff.; Camardi (2019), p. 499; Sartoris (2021).

hand, is obliged to justify and motivate, by means of prior notice, any possible modification of the contractual conditions that may become necessary during the course of the relationship itself. Correspondingly, the commercial operator is given the right to terminate the contract, to be exercised following the notice sent by the intermediary, and within the relevant deadline.

2. Where, on the other hand, the figure of the consumer as contractual party comes into play (in P2C, B2C contracts[19]), the above-mentioned Digital Service Act, which aims to regulate content and liability, as well as Directive 2019/2161/EU, the so-called Omnibus Directive and Directives (EU) 770 and 771/2019, on consumer protection and correct information, will certainly apply. *Omnibus*,[20] as well as Directives (EU) 770 and 771/2019, on the subject of consumer protection and correct information, not forgetting, of course, the regulations transfused in the Consumer Code, all of which supplement and complete the contractual regulation, determine additional effects with respect to those posed by the parties.

   It must be emphasised that, from the point of view of correct information, the *Omnibus* Directive 2019/2161/EU (Art. 4) has placed on the *online* intermediary an obligation of particular importance, namely that of communicating to the public of users the nature of the subject offering goods and services through the platform (based on the declarations provided by the offeror himself), particularly by declaring whether he is a private individual or a professional: this is a communication of no small importance, since from it will derive the application or non-application of all consumer protection legislation, especially the discipline relating to the exercise of the right of withdrawal,[21] which certainly constitutes one of the most important events in the legal relationship, especially in the area of consumer contracts.

3. But certainly the most interesting category to examine in the context of the vicissitudes of the relationship, starting from its constitution, is that of P2P contracts, entered into between private parties through the *online* intermediary.

The position of parity between the contracting parties, which now seemed to have been relegated to the restricted sphere of civil contracts, a prerogative of the regulations of the 1942 Code, re-emerges here in an important manner. So-called collaborative economy or *sharing economy*,[22] which was previously unknown to the market, a sector where contracting parties meet virtually and conclude contracts unfailingly through digital infrastructure, thereby establishing a three-way relationship.

---

[19] Pagliantini (2022), pp. 1499 ff.

[20] On this subject, see Gentili and Battelli (2011), pp. 379 ff.

[21] For a discussion of the right of withdrawal as an incident of the platform contract, see Nuzzo (2025).

[22] See Di Sabato and Lepore (2018), p. 509.

Here emerges the figure of the prosumer,[23] placed at the centre of the new markets *characterised precisely* by the peer-to-peer model, in whose contractual regulation the rules valid for P2C and B2C contracts cannot evidently converge, since the figure of the 'consumer' proper is absent here, as the economic counterpart of the company, with the consequent greater freedom of the intermediary to decide terms and conditions, taking into account however the *limitations imposed* by the Digi*tal* Market Act against the web giants—the so-called *gatekeepers*[24]—precisely to contain possible abuses of the dominant position assumed by the large *online* intermediaries.

This type of contract, rightfully placed in the category of platform-based exchanges, constitutes perhaps its most innovative model, certainly sharing the manner in which the relationship is constituted and the substantial lack of party autonomy in determining the contractual regulation and effects,[25] since the rules of the exchange are dictated, for the most part, by the *online* intermediary.

The latter, here more than elsewhere, plays a fundamental role in preparing the contractual conditions to which users wishing to use the services offered by the digital infrastructure[26] will adhere. Think, for example, of the *Vinted* or *Airb&b* platforms,[27] where the *online* intermediary establishes the criteria for offering products and even the price *ranges*.

The particularity of this contract lies, on the one hand, in the triplicity of the relationship that derives from it and, on the other hand, in the duplicity of the type of effects produced, concerning both the service provided electronically (service provided in the information society) and the material services that will be implemented in the real world.

On the other hand, the relationship constituted for the purpose of obtaining digital services[28] through the platform, including *social networks*,[29] finds full development on the *web,* in the knowledge that the latter still belong to the category of

---

[23] The term is chorally attributed to the American sociologist Alvin Toffler and has been used since the 1980s (Toffler 1987). As is well known, the term *prosumer* refers to a natural person who is both consumer and producer of a good or service; Sartoris (2022), p. 962.

[24] The *DMA* (*Digital Market Act*) aims to prevent the abuse of a dominant position by large platforms—*gatekeepers*—on whom certain limits are imposed in the performance of their activities to avoid unfair commercial practices, so that this legislation has several points of contact with the competition protection regulation: on this subject, see Bania (2022).

[25] On this subject, Benedetti (2002).

[26] Pinelli (2024), pp. 451 ff.

[27] On the *AirB&B* model in relation to platform law, see Hatzopoulos and Roma (2017), who note the need to standardise national disciplines; see also Colangelo (2020), p. 291, footnote to CJEU, Judgment 19 December 2017, *AirB&B Ireland*, C-390/18.

[28] A digital service is defined in Art. 128 of the Consumer Protection Code as '*1) a service enabling the consumer to create, transform, store or access data in digital format; 2) or a service enabling the sharing of data in digital format uploaded or created by the consumer or other users of that service or any other interaction with such data*'.

[29] On the legal nature of *social networks*, see Perlingieri (2015); Caterina (2011). More recently, Manganelli (2023), p. 883.

peer-to-peer relationships: here, there is no exchange of goods, but only an exchange of information according to the rules established by the digital infrastructure. In this regard, the scenario of events concerning so-called *hate speech* would open up with the application of the relevant rules, the matrix of which is unanimously found in Art. 14 of the ECHR. Ideally, the Budapest Convention on Cybercrime (2003), the Charter of Fundamental Rights of the European Union (2000) as well as the *Digital Service Act* mentioned above, in the part in which it pays particular attention to content exchanged on the net, can be traced back to it; in addition, there is the 2016 *Code of Conduct to combat illegal forms of online hate speech*, dictated by the major IT companies to share the European Commission's position on the matter.

Now, rules from different sources, heteronomous and autonomous, produce legal relations that somehow 'accompany' relations on the *web* or become an integral part of them, creating a network of intersecting events, thus making the applicable contractual regulation extremely complex.

4 The Reputational Mechanisms of *Peer Reviewing* or *Peer Monitoring* and Their Effects on the Competitive Relationship

From the legal relations that 'complement' the main relationship to some extent, let us move on to examine an affair that has implications that are anything but trivial in terms of the balance between the positions of the parties to the contractual relationship (platform and users of it in various capacities), namely that concerning the mechanisms of *peer reviewing* or *peer monitoring*.

By virtue of the aforementioned mechanisms, in fact, the user of the services, particularly the consumer, having shed the guise of the 'weaker party' in the contract,[30] can instead take on a leading role by himself, providing information on the products and services he has used, intended for other *web* users with a 'word-of-mouth' speed that only the platform can allow.[31]

This is an unprecedented instrument in the hands of the consumer, who sees his or her position as economic counterpart of the professional strengthened in a concrete manner, acquiring in relation to the supplier of goods and services, and to the platform itself, an extraordinary power that by other means would certainly be exercisable in a more laborious and slower manner: here, however, the immediacy and wide diffusion of the feedback constitute, if you like, one of the most powerful means of publicity currently conceivable. To give an example, let us think of the provision of services offered by accommodation facilities: the *rating* given by the guest to the facility at the end of their stay determines the rise or fall in position in the ranking prepared by the platform, so that all possible users are placed in a

---

[30] On the balance between contractual parties, Foltran (2019), pp. 165 ff.

[31] See Smorto (2020), p. 69; Smorto (2017), pp. 119 ff.; Battelli (2022b), p. 571.

position to immediately access the information offered by the consumer and rely on it to make their choice.

From the perspective of the smooth functioning of the principle of competition and the affirmation of the most deserving in the market, certainly, this instrument set up by the platform is the most suitable and efficient.

Well, the possibility for the consumer (or *prosumer*) to express his satisfaction in the digital *marketplace* is at the centre of a legal event that has an extraordinarily important effect on the competitive relationship between the companies operating in the 'relevant market' and also constitutes the official recognition of the consumer/user of the role that has always been his, that of 'arbiter of the market': said function—which Tullio Ascarelli had already recognised to the consumer since the middle of the last century[32]—now finds an easy way of implementation through the digital infrastructure, which advertises and disseminates on the *web* the consumer's preference, thus determining the growth or vice versa the decline in the market of the products and services offered on (or by) the platform itself.

That simple *click on* the computer keyboard, which we are asked to do in front of a screen crowded with indignant or smiling 'smiley faces', can produce—together with the *clicks* of other users of the same platform—excellent or devastating consequences for each commercial operator, also taking into account the possible 'domino effect', which is not at all uncommon on the *web*,[33] where the *like* becomes the unavoidable unit of measurement of any object placed on the network.

It should be noted, however, how the *peer reviewing* or *peer monitoring* affair, linked to the establishment of the *online* relationship, is still managed by the platform, which establishes the modalities of its performance: in this aspect, the strong position of the *online* intermediary is therefore further confirmed, already expressed in dictating upstream the rules of access, navigation and possible exchange through the general terms and conditions of contract, most often accepted by the user without even being read.[34]

Now, it is precisely this disparity of position that has led the European legislator to enact a regulation designed to reduce the enormous power of platforms, namely the aforementioned *Digital Market Act*, which aims to prevent the abuse of the

[32] We recall, in this regard, the famous essay forerunner of the times, *Teoria della concorrenza e interesse del consumatore (prolusione al corso di Diritto industriale nella Facoltà di giurisprudenza dell'Università di Roma, delivered on 27 November 1953)*, in *Riv. trim. dir. proc. civ.*, 1954, 873, in which consumers were called '*men and not children to be guided from above*'.

[33] Think of the phenomenon of the *influencer*, who dictates trends and fashions, whose activity is fuelled by '*likes*', i.e. preference, satisfaction/ dissatisfaction with products, services, news, comments, behaviour and personal attitudes.

[34] It is to be noted that among the main effects characterising the relationship established on the platform, to which the user consents by accepting the c.g.c, we find cases of *ius variandi* in the hands of the platform: for example, the right to unilaterally modify the contract, to dissolve the contractual bond, to suspend a user's account or, again, to remove a product from the *online* offer or, even, to determine the service to be used to make the payment (so-called *bundling* clause) as well as the obligation to use certain ADRs for dispute resolution: on this subject, Camardi (2021), p. 870.

dominant position of the *web* 'giants', at the same time having its effects on both the competitive relationship between operators and on the protection of platform users and the protection of personal data 'processed' by the *online* intermediary.

To this end, the aforementioned EU Regulation affects the contractual content decided by platform operators, placing certain obligations on them: by way of example, (1) to treat their own services and products favourably compared to similar services or products offered by third parties on their platform; (2) to prevent consumers from contacting companies outside the platform; (3) to keep track of users' personal data for advertising purposes without the prior consent of the persons concerned.

Of course, this evaluation tool may also apply to the platform itself, even if it is managed directly by the latter,[35] with the setting of terms and conditions for the granting of *feedback*, which must therefore fall within the pre-established *standards*.

It should be noted, however, that while the *peer review* mechanism may have extraordinary beneficial effects on the functioning of competition, it could, on the other hand, produce disastrous consequences if it is misused: in such a case, it could only be classified as unfair competition[36] and the most effective remedy would undoubtedly be an injunction.[37]

5 Events Relating to the Release of Personal Data

Last, but certainly not least, we must mention the matter mentioned at the outset and certainly the most important among those that relate to the establishment of the contractual relationship via the digital platform, i.e. the collection and processing of the user's personal data.

It has already been mentioned that the contract thus concluded constitutes the occasion for the release of the data collected and managed by the *online* intermediary.[38] Indeed, the release of the data often constitutes the 'consideration' for a digital product that prima facie would appear to be offered free of charge.

Well, the communication of data (and of the so-called metadata[39]) can take place in the most varied ways: when 'registering' on the platform, in the selection of

[35] Smorto (2016), p. 199; Carota (2017), p. 624; Vizzoni (2018), p. 706.

[36] See, Cons. di Stato, sec. VI, 15 July 2019, no. 4976, which emphasises the trust placed in the user. In the case law on the merits, Trib. Milano, sez. impr., 22 March 2024, in *De Iure Giuffrè* database; Trib. Roma 21 September 2020, ibid.

[37] Most recently, Barba (2025), p. 821. On the brokerage of reviews, D'Auria (2024), p. 1408.

[38] For a more extensive discussion of data protection versus platform law, see Omodei Salè (2025).

[39] We understand metadata as 'information about information', i.e. those attributes that can specify and contextualise the meaning of individual data, reading them in a cross-referenced manner. Most recently, Irti (2025), pp. 149 ff. On the subject, Camardi (2023), pp. 59 ff.

filters in searches carried out or through the filling in of questionnaires, in the choice of additional services and so on up to traceability in simple Internet surfing.[40]

The transmission of information on the occasion of the conclusion of the contract thus entails the establishment of a legal relationship between the user and the *online* intermediary, which arises *alongside the* contractual relationship and by reason thereof.

To understand what effects are produced on the data controller and, correlatively, on the data subject, it is necessary to recall the successive disciplines on the protection of personal data, among which the reference constituted by the *GDPR*[41] is inescapable, as an inescapable normative source of the modalities of data processing by anyone who comes into possession of such data and must use them for some legitimate reason.

Certainly, the platform is a full-fledged data controller within the meaning of Art. 4 of the GDPR, so that at the time of access, with the release of the data, the further legal relationship arising from the relevant legislation is established; and there is no doubt that the event originating from the communication of the user's data is one of the main and most complex among those arising from the conclusion of the telematic contract and, in particular, that concluded on the platform.

It is, again, a matter that accompanies the contract and follows a path, we would say, almost parallel to that which strictly concerns the essential elements of the Internet 'transaction'.

In this regard, let us start from the consideration that the guiding principle of the regulations issued by the European legislator through the GDPR is that of the *functionality of* the processing with respect to the intended purpose, subject to the acceptance of the data subject, so that in principle, the use of the data that goes beyond the purpose for which they are provided or the lack of adequate protection with respect to the same purpose could be affected by the illicit qualification, taking into account the size of the platform and the power it enjoys. The principle in question brings in the so-called *accountability*,[42] i.e. *making* the data controller *responsible for* the use and precautions taken to protect the data, with a view to stemming the phenomenon of *deregulation* that has characterised the use of personal data for too long.

Consequently, the data controller will not be subject to obligations with well-defined contours and contents, but will be under a general obligation to adopt the most appropriate measures for the best protection of data in each context:[43] the provision of this obligation will have its most significant effect in terms of proof, i.e. the need to demonstrate *a posteriori*, before the Supervisory Authority, that he complied with the most suitable measures for the concrete protection of data, in accordance with the type of processing and the context in which it takes place.

[40] D'Ippolito (2021).

[41] *General Data Protection*, or Regulation (EU) 2016/679, enacted by the European Parliament and Council on 27 April 2016.

[42] This principle is provided for in Art. 24 GDPR. For all, Galli (2023), pp. 137 ff.

[43] This is referred to as *Data Protection by default and by design*, in accordance with Art. 25 of the GDPR.

Not to be overlooked, moreover, on the subject of communication and transparency, is the aforementioned Regulation (EU) 2019/1150, which aims to regulate mainly the *platform-to-business* relationship, placing some specific obligations in this regard on the *online* intermediary, a key player in the information society and thus in the management of an indefinite amount of personal data.

Finally, it should be emphasised that the step from data protection regulation to *antitrust* regulation is a short one, so that it seems appropriate to point out, lastly, the obligations imposed on *web* giants and aimed at avoiding abuse of a dominant position precisely because of the use of the information collected.[44]

6 Events of Modification of the Legal Relationship

Leaving to the discipline of the governing law (i.e. to the discipline applicable from case to case according to the type of relationship) the modifying events that may affect the contracts entered into, through the intermediation of platforms, between sellers/suppliers and buyers, the modifying events that refer to the contracts entered into by the platforms with the users raise questions. What comes to the fore are: objectively, changes in the relationship associated with the *ius variandi*; subjectively, changes in the relationship arising from the assignment of the contract *inter vivos* and from succession *mortis causa*.

6.1 *Modifications of an Objective Nature: The* Ius Variandi *of the Platforms*

As a rule, the contracts entered into by platforms with users are based on general conditions of contract (i.e. 'terms of service') prepared unilaterally by the platforms, corresponding to the provision of clauses (in the same general terms and conditions) authorising the platforms to exercise the power of *ius variandi.* Thus, in the case of relationships whose duration is projected over time, the platforms insert clauses whereby they are granted the power to unilaterally change the contractual clauses in the course of the relationship.[45]

These provisions, which often address users indiscriminately (without, thus, distinguishing between sellers/suppliers and buyers), are formulated with a more or

---

[44] In this respect, reference is made to the decision of the *Bundeskartellamt* (German Data Protection Authority) in *Facebook Inc. and C. v. Berlin*, 2019, which required the Zuckerberg giant to renounce the collection and aggregation of data relating to its customers through services provided by third-party sites, in the absence of explicit consent from the data subjects. The decision was upheld by the European Court of Justice (3 October 2019 in Case C-18/18). See Osti and Pardolesi (2019), pp. 194 ff.

[45] See Codiglione (2022), p. 299.

less articulated content: one goes from cases, where platforms reserve the power of *ius variandi* to themselves without limits,[46] to others, where platforms instead make the exercise of *ius variandi* conditional upon the occurrence of certain circumstances.[47] Moreover, while in some cases it is stipulated that platforms must always directly notify users, with a certain amount of notice, of changes.[48] In other cases, it is stipulated, conversely, that direct notification to users, with an accompanying notice, must take place only for substantial changes, a general *online* publication being sufficient for non-substantial changes.[49] At the same time, there is no lack of common features: on the one hand, there is frequently the provision whereby, in the face of changes, there is '*a presumption of acceptance on the part of the users deriving from their continuous use of the platform*';[50] on the other hand, users are, in any case, recognised as having the right to withdraw from the relationship (i.e. to deactivate their account), in the sense that they are granted the right to dissolve the negotiation bond if they do not agree with the changes.[51]

The critical issue then is to ask whether, and to what extent, clauses of this kind, insofar as they endow platforms with the power of *ius variandi*, conform with the law. Can platforms be holders of such power?

Certainly, the power of *ius variandi*, although it represents a derogation from the principle of agreement, does not appear to be itself prohibited by the law: there are, in fact, various hypotheses in which the legislator legitimises the exercise of this power (e.g. Art. 118 Testo Unico Bancario, among many others). More. It is precisely with respect to platforms that the exercise of the power of *ius variandi* may reveal a physiological connotation: taking into account, in fact, that the relationships between platforms and users tend to unfold over long durations (thus, the relationships are often of indefinite duration), the need for platforms to make changes to the clauses of the relationship, whether for objective reasons (e.g. the need to adapt to ius superveniens) or strategic reasons (e.g. adaptation to market requirements or business models or technological processes), seems conceivable.[52]

Notwithstanding this, the possibility of platforms becoming holders of the power of *ius variandi* is defined in the legal system by a series of limits, since it is not conceivable, due to the obvious risks of abuse, that platforms could *a priori* unilaterally change the terms of the relationship. In this regard, the legislative framework comes out, since a distinction must be made according to whether the users, in comparison with the platforms, qualify as 'business users', consumers or others.

With respect to 'business users', the notion of which, mirroring that of professionals, identifies '*any private individual acting in a commercial or professional*

---

[46] See, e.g. Art. 6, X Terms of Service.

[47] See, e.g. Art. 4, Meta Terms of Service.

[48] See, e.g. Art. 16, Uber User Terms and Conditions.

[49] See, e.g. Art. 15, Airbnb Terms of Service for European Users.

[50] Smorto (2020), p. 60. For an example, see Art. 5, Amazon Conditions of Use.

[51] See, e.g. Art. 16, eBay User Agreement.

[52] See Restelli (2022), pp. 111–112.

capacity who, or any legal person which, through online intermediation services offers goods or services to consumers for purposes relating to its trade, business, craft or profession' (Art. 2(1)(1)), Regulation (EU) 2019/1150 comes into focus. Article 3(2) and (3), specifically regulating *the ius variandi* power of platforms (framed as 'providers of online intermediations services'), provides by the way: that platforms must notify 'business users' of proposed changes to '*their terms and conditions*' with a notice period, normally of at least 15 days; that 'business users' have '*the right to terminate the contract*' during the notice period; that 'business users' may waive the notice period, also in the sense that '*During the notice period, submitting new goods or services to the online intermediation services shall be considered affirmative action to waive the notice period*'; that, where these regulatory requirements are not met, changes to the relationship '*shall be null and void*'.

As far as 'business users' are concerned, therefore, the legislator, in legitimising the power of *ius variandi* for platforms, subordinates its regulation to a combination of notice and withdrawal.[53] The Regulation, in particular, without demanding that the exercise of the power by the platforms needs to be linked to the recurrence of particular conditions (this choice seems to follow the logic—in reality, doubtful—that 'business users' are subjects endowed with greater power than mere consumers), requires, under penalty of nullity, that platforms, where they intend to make unilateral changes to the relationship, give notice to 'business users', who then, in turn, if they disagree, may terminate the contract. Interesting, at the same time, is the equation, made directly by the legislator, between conduct of platform use and acceptance of the changes, there being here a direct legislative recognition that the use of the platform, by means of the offer of new goods or services, by the users, is a conduct valid to determine the waiver of the notice period or, therefore, the acceptance of the proposed changes.[54]

Turning, on the other hand, to consumers (in this group, for the present purposes, we also allow the so-called *prosumers* to be included[55]), it is the consumer discipline of 'unfair terms' that comes into play. The list of unfair terms, in fact, pursuant to Art. 33 of the Italian Consumer Code, also includes clauses which, in the context of the *ius variandi*, allow the professional either '*to unilaterally amend the terms of the contract ... without a justified reason indicated in the contract itself*' (subpara m) or to '*increase the price of the good or service without the consumer being able to withdraw if the final price is excessively high compared to the price originally*

[53] See Camardi (2021), p. 903.

[54] Cf. Falce (2022), p. 189.

[55] The category of '*prosumers*' (see also Battelli 2022b, pp. 569–570), in identifying natural persons, who, operating outside their working activity (professional, commercial, etc.), turn to platforms to offer goods or services (not, therefore, to purchase them: e.g. an offer to rent a flat or sell a suit), flows, for the purposes of this case, into that of consumers. Prosumers, in fact, when looking at the contractual relationship with the platforms, can be qualified as consumers, as they are subjects who, 'from outside' the work context, enter into a contract aimed at acquiring from the platforms, as professionals, the provision of certain intermediation services (see Martinelli 2023, p. 42, footnote 96).

agreed upon' (subpara o). It follows that, where consumers are concerned, platforms, to be legitimately endowed with the power of *ius variandi*, must respect the limits allowed, under penalty of nullity, by the unfair terms: therefore (unless the presumption of unfairness of the clauses is overcome), the exercise of the power is permitted, where it concerns changes to the clauses of the contract, in the presence of the recurrence of a justified reason, while, where it concerns excessive price changes, upon recognition of the consumer's right of withdrawal.[56]

Moreover, this discipline is now complemented by Art. 14(2) of the *Digital Services Act*, according to which platforms (in the terms of 'providers of intermediary service') have a duty to inform '*the recipients of the service of any significant change to the terms and conditions*'.[57] Without prejudice to the above-mentioned limits to the exercise of the power of *ius variandi*, platforms are so also called upon, on the basis of the rule, to provide information, thus having to ensure that consumers are specifically informed if significant changes are made to the general terms and conditions (this hypothesis occurs, for example, according to recital 45 of the DSA, when platforms '*modify the rules on information that is permitted on their service*' or introduce 'other *changes which could directly impact the ability of the recipients to make use of the service*').[58]

Finally, the attention goes to the category of users who are identifiable neither as 'business users' nor as consumers. This group, in essence, always includes professionals, but it is here that professionals, with respect to platforms, do not operate, according to the qualification of 'business users', as subjects who offer goods or services, but rather, according to that of subjects who purchase goods or services.[59]

In this hypothesis, the legislator has not prescribed a particular discipline, thus lacking a rule that singularly regulates the *ius variandi* power of the platforms. The doubt might then arise that the legislator did not intend to allow room for *ius variandi* there, but the perplexity is immediately removed: if the legislature, in fact, allows the *ius variandi* of platforms both towards 'business users' and towards consumers, why should it not also be the same towards professionals who act as purchasers of goods or services?

The key to the answer, therefore, in line with the general profiles of the configurability *of ius variandi* clauses,[60] seems to pass right through the disciplines ruled for the other categories of users. That is to say, the legislator, between 'business users' and consumers, renders legitimate the *ius variandi* power of the platforms where this power, being circumscribed, is either accompanied by the occurrence of a justified reason (Art. 33(1) of the Consumer Code) or is assisted by the recognition

---

[56] See Alpa (2022), p. 737.

[57] For 'business users', Art. 3 of Regulation (EU) 2019/1150 continues to apply as a rule that specifically prescribes the discipline regime for 'business users' themselves.

[58] Still in the consumer ambit, with reference to 'contracts for the supply of digital content and digital services', a particular discipline is ruled by Art. *135-vicessemel* of the Italian Consumer Code for the case of 'modifications of the digital content or the digital service'.

[59] In this sense, see Smorto (2020), p. 59.

[60] See, on this subject, Roppo (2011), pp. 523 ff.

of the right of withdrawal (Art. 3, Regulation (EU) 2019/1550 or Art. 33(o) of the Consumer Code). It follows that, given the absence of a specific regulation, both solutions appear to be envisaged also with respect to the professionals under examination: in their regard, in other words, provisions conferring the power of *ius variandi* to the platforms may be said to be admissible, provided that the same power is therefore delimited, through the provision, alternatively, of the need for a justified reason or the possibility of withdrawal. Moreover, the applicability of Art. 14(2) of the *Digital Services Act* is valid here too: the rule, given its general content (the disposition concerns, indiscriminately, '*the recipients of the service*'[61]), is indeed capable of including in its ambit also the professionals in question, thus determining, even in this case, the duty for the platforms to specifically notify changes to the general conditions that are significant.

To conclude the discourse, the clauses through which the platforms, in their general conditions of contract, assume the power of *ius variandi* towards the users require, in the face of the varied formulation that they may concretely assume, a comparison with the regulatory framework of reference. This power, thus, to answer the question raised, is legitimate under the law, but requires, to be validly constituted and exercised, that the various limits associated with the subjective qualification of users must be respected.

6.2 *Modifications of a Subjective Nature: The* Inter Vivos *Assignment of the Contract*

Turning to the modifications of a subjective character, the analysis goes, first, to the hypothesis (less frequent in practice) of the assignment of the contract *inter vivos*. In this respect, what comes into play, from the point of view of discipline, is the general legal regime of Art. 1406 et seq. of the Italian Civil Code, according to which a contract may be assigned to a third party to the extent that the other party agrees or has previously authorised the assignment.[62]

Within this framework, platforms, within the general terms and conditions, are used to move in two directions.

Thus, on the one hand, platforms, in relation to users, tend to place prohibitions on the transfer of the contract (*alias*, of the *account*). To prevent users from circulating the contract, or to preserve control over the subjective identity of the users themselves, the general conditions usually contain clauses precluding users (regardless of subjective qualification) from assigning the contract to third parties, unless

[61] The notion of 'recipient of the service' includes, according to Art. 3(a), '*any natural or legal person who uses an intermediary service, in particular for the purposes of seeking information or making it accessible*'.

[62] According to the majority view, the assignment of a contract, in its legal regime, is admissible for any type of contract (whether onerous or gratuitous), unless, as a limitation, the effects of the transaction have been completely exhausted: see Clarizia (2005), pp. 22 ff.

specific consent is given by the platform:[63] the assignment of the contract is not in itself excluded, but requires going through the platform and its agreement.

On the other hand, platforms, with respect to themselves, generally leave open the assignment of the contract. Recurring, in other words, are clauses by means of which the general terms and conditions provide that the platforms are free, by allowing themselves to be replaced, to assign the contract to third parties: what operates here, therefore, is the mechanism of prior authorization given that the users, by means of acceptance of the general terms and conditions, express their authorization with respect to future assignments of the contract by the platforms.[64] The implication, then, is twofold: on the one side, it seems necessary to have a specific acceptance of these clauses of the general terms and conditions by the users, given that they are required, in line with Art. 1407 of the Italian Civil Code, to give prior consent to a (possible) assignment of the contract;[65] on the other side, if the users are consumers, Art. 33 of the Italian Consumer Code comes into play, including, under letter s), among the unfair terms, also those that allow '*the professional to substitute a third party for himself in the relations deriving from the contract, even in the case of prior consent of the consumer, if the protection of the latter's rights is diminished*'.

6.3 Follow-Up: Succession *Mortis Causa*

The subject of *mortis causa* succession in contracts with platforms is one of those that gives rise to the greatest doubts. In other words, the possibility that, in the event of the death of the user, the contractual relationship, instead of being interrupted, passes into the hands of a successor to the *de cuius*, continuing its course, is debated.

The difficulties stem from the circumstance that platforms often set the general conditions in such a way that, if the user dies, the relationship is destined to end, with the consequent power of the platforms to deactivate the *account* and destroy its data. Thus, the general conditions include clauses explicitly endowed with this content[66] or even clauses where, in a twist, on the one hand it is stated that users cannot transfer the contract (see, *supra*, para 4.2) and, on the other hand, it is added that, in the event of termination of the relationship, the platform will proceed to delete the

---

[63] See, e.g. Art. 4.5, Meta Terms of Service, and Art. 7, Meta Commercial Terms of Service.

[64] See, e.g. Art. 24.4, Airbnb Terms of Service for European Users, and Art. 16.3, Uber Terms and Conditions for Users.

[65] The requirement under Art. 1407 of the Italian Civil Code, that the contracting party give its prior consent to the assignment of the contract (see Bianca 2019, pp. 680–682), does not seem to be satisfiable, given its specific character, either by the mere knowledge/acceptance of the general terms and conditions under Art. 1341(1) of the Civil Code or by their general acceptance (*contra,* Court of Cassation, 10 June 1986, no. 3845, in *Giur. it.*, 1987, I, 1, 1012).

[66] See, e.g. Art. 3, Yahoo Terms of Service.

account and its contents:[67] thus, in one way or another, death is considered under the general conditions as an event valid to determine the termination of the relationship, with the consequent deactivation of the *account* and data by the platforms.

The doubts, which arise in this respect, precisely concern the legitimacy of such clauses. It appears controversial, in fact, that platforms, in the event of the death of users, may dissolve contracts, thus preventing successors (or interested third parties) from continuing the relationship and/or having access to the data stored in the *accounts*.[68]

The difficulty of the issue is intensified to date by the lack of a uniform legal framework. Given the (if we may say so) 'recent' nature of the phenomenon, there is currently no common supranational discipline and, in most cases, no specific national disciplines have been dictated either. The 'field' is, therefore, covered by the solutions adopted by the platforms in the general conditions and the analyses provided by the scrutiny of doctrine and jurisprudence.

The indications, which are drawn at the level of comparison, are divergent.[69]

In the United States, therefore, what emerges is a greater propensity, inspired by the strict protection of the principle of private autonomy, to deem valid the disciplines, for the dissolution of contractual relations, laid down by the platforms. In various decisions, which have made the headlines (among many others, mention should be made of the well-known case, decided by the Oakland County Probate Court in judgment no. 2005/296, 651-DE, concerning the request, formulated by the parents of a dead Marine, to have access to their son's e-mail account), the courts have thus rejected the requests of third parties to have access to the *accounts* of the deceased, since the choice, to deactivate the *accounts* upon the death of the user, was the one regulated in the general conditions and accepted by the *deceased*, thus responding to his negotiating will.[70]

In Europe, on the other hand, the orientation is somewhat different, the need being more felt, despite the disciplines outlined by the platforms, to preserve the individual freedom of the *de cuius* to be able to decide on the fate of his (or her) contractual relations and data for the period after death. For example, it comes the experience of France, which, through the enactment of a legislative reform (Art. 63(2), *Loi* 7-10-2016, no. 2016-1321, *pour une République Numérique*), laid down a rule to the effect that the data subject has the right to '*establish general or special directives, always revocable, concerning the processing of his or her personal data post mortem*', so that '*any clause contained in general terms and conditions of contract that limits or excludes the prerogatives granted to the data subject with regard to the posthumous governance of his or her digital identity is deemed to be*

[67] See, e.g. Articles 13.5 and 24.4, Airbnb Terms of Service for European Users. and Articles 3 and 11.3, eBay User Agreement.

[68] See Cinque (2020), pp. 76 ff.

[69] See Resta (2019), pp. 89 ff.

[70] See Carleo (2023), pp. 560–566.

unwritten'.[71] Similarly, jurisprudence has moved in Germany: in a well-known decision, rendered in 2018, the German Supreme Court (BGH)[72] granted the request made by the parents to access their dead daughter's *account*, given the consideration that, regardless of any contrary clauses provided for in the general terms and conditions (i.e. regardless of any clauses aimed at ordering the termination of the relationship), the parents, in their capacity as heirs, were entitled to succeed *mortis causa* to the *deceased* in the contract with the platform, thus taking over the ownership of the *account*.[73]

What, then, for the Italian legal system? On closer inspection, the discourse must be conducted on two levels. When, indeed, we speak of clauses that, in the event of the death of users, provide for the deactivation of *accounts* and the destruction of data, there are, from a legal point of view, two different profiles to be considered.

The one profile, which concerns the *account*, relates to the contract itself, i.e. the fate of the contractual relationship between users and platforms. The other profile, which concerns data, relates to content, i.e. the fate of user data contained in *accounts*.[74]

So, starting with the first profile, which is the one that defines properly the destiny of the contractual relationship between users and platforms, the legal regime of reference brings into play the inheritance discipline. Thus, the general rule is such that, upon death, the contractual relations of the *de cuius* continue in the hands of the successors, unless they are strictly personal relations.[75]

It follows that it is the personal or non-personal nature of the relationship that is discriminating. Where, indeed, the contracts between platforms and users are based on strictly personal relationships (for instance, email *accounts*, devoted to the exchange of correspondence, or *social accounts*, devoted to the management of personal thoughts or photos), then it is physiological that the contractual relationships do not continue beyond the death of the users: the personality of the relationships implies, in fact, that the death of the users automatically entails the relationships to termination, without a *mortis causa* succession in the ownership of the *accounts* by third parties being configurable. Where, on the other hand, the contracts between platforms and users do not take basis on strictly personal relationships (for example, a *marketplace account*, through which purchases/sales of goods or services are managed), the discourse is reversed: given that we are not dealing here with relationships denoted by personality, then the contracts open to succession, so that to succeed in the relationship with the platforms, that is to say in the ownership of the *accounts,* are the successors of the *de cuius*.[76]

---

[71] Nardi (2020), p. 597.

[72] BGH (2019), pp. 691 ff.

[73] Cf. Confortini (2021), pp. 1189 ff.

[74] Cf. Camardi (2018), pp. 73 ff.

[75] See Padovini (2009), pp. 525 ff.

[76] See Marino (2022), pp. 167 ff.

In this way, the clauses designed to provide for the closure of *accounts* in the event of the death of users can be evaluated. In some cases, such clauses linearly reflect the personal nature of the relationship. In other cases, differently, the clauses themselves affect, in a covenant mode, the duration of the relationship, precluding, as vice versa would be the case, the relationship from continuing beyond the death of the users: to be more precise, where the non-personal nature of the contract would theoretically make possible a continuation of the relationship *post mortem*, nothing then seems to prohibit, *ex adverso*, the contract between platforms and users being regulated by clauses linking the duration of the contract to the life of the users; thus, in the presence of clauses of this type, the relationship, upon the death of the users, comes to an end, not opening itself, consequently, to an inheritance phenomenon.

Turning, then, to the second profile, the gaze moves to the data side. Without prejudice to the fate of the contract, there is a different matter as regards data, since what comes into play here is not the relationship between users and platforms, but the more or less extensive group of data, owned by users, contained in the *accounts*.[77]

The basic consideration that the data belong to users implies that the clauses of the general terms and conditions, authorising platforms, after the death of users, (not only to deactivate *accounts*, but also) to delete their data, incur possible grounds for invalidity, both with respect to the succession regime and to the rights of third parties.[78]

In this regard, first, the mind goes to the data, forming part of the content of the *accounts*, which can be traced back to *digital assets*: this is the case of digital goods, endowed with an economic value, such as intellectual works (a literary work), digital currencies or the materials produced by an *influencer*.[79] These assets, we note, are part of the users' patrimony and can therefore be included among the assets, existing in the patrimony, which the users have the right to dispose of, by way of succession *mortis causa*, in favour of their successors (heirs or legatees).

Hence, clauses authorizing platforms *sic et simpliciter* to destroy data upon the death of users do not appear, with respect to digital assets, to be valid (nor, therefore, such as to enable platforms to oppose requests for access to digital assets by persons who are their successors *mortis causa*): on the one hand, there is a defect of form, given that, to dispose of the inheritance rights over digital assets, users, without being able to rely on contractual provisions, must proceed by means of a testamentary deed; on the other hand, there is a defect of substance, given that negotiated agreements, which lead users to authorize the destruction of their digital assets upon death, appear to incur the prohibition of 'covenant of succession' under Art. 458 of the Italian Civil Code, as provisions by which '*a person disposes of its own succession*'.[80]

---

[77] Cf. Tampieri (2021), pp. 554 ff.

[78] Cf. Carleo (2023), pp. 554 ff.

[79] Cf. Nardi (2020), pp. 598–600. On the topic, see chapter 'New Digital Services and Goods' by Bocchini (this volume) (also, Bocchini 2023, pp. 167 ff.).

[80] Delle Monache (2020), pp. 464–465.

Thus, the mind goes, generally, to the totality of 'personal data' located in *accounts*. Under this aspect, the clauses, which authorize the destruction of the data by the platforms, require to be confronted with the particular discipline on personal data of deceased persons prescribed by law and such for which, according to the combined provisions of Art. 9, para 3, of the Italian Privacy Code and Art. *2-terdecies*, Legislative Decree 10 August 2018, No. 2: on the one side, the legislator recognizes the right of third parties to access the personal data of deceased persons where it is necessary to act to protect their own interest or an interest of the data subject (on the basis of a mandate) or for family reasons deserving protection; on the other side, the legislator requires the data subject, should he wish to exclude this right of third parties, to provide contrary provisions by means of an unequivocal, specific, free, informed and express manifestation of will, to be communicated in writing to the data controller.[81]

The corollary is that, here too, the clauses designed to allow the deletion of *account* data *post mortem* may be invalid. Unless, in fact, the users, in compliance with the legal requirements, have specifically communicated to the data controller their will to the contrary, the clauses, under penalty of violation of the law, cannot preclude access to the personal data by legitimate third parties, thus including either the relatives of the *de cuius* who, *iure proprio,* intend to access the data for family reasons or the subjects who, *iure proprio* or *iure successionis*, intend to access the data to protect their own interest or that of the data subject.[82]

A series of merit judgments have reached this conclusion in recent years. Jurisprudence, in fact, has been called upon to rule in cases where the relatives of deceased users, relying on the aforementioned provisions of the Italian Privacy Code and Legislative Decree No. 2/2018, have brought disputes against platforms, given the prohibition imposed by them, by virtue of the clauses authorizing the destruction of users' data, to access the users' data contained in the *accounts*. Those judgments, upholding the claims of the relatives, so found that the clauses in question were invalid, because the legislative provisions allow '*that third parties with interests "for family reasons deserving of protection" may retrieve the personal data of deceased persons*'[83] and also because the clauses themselves, if included in the general terms and conditions, cannot be considered as a manifestation of will contrary to access by users: in other words, '*The acceptance of the general terms and conditions by the deceased at the time of purchase of the device (in this case, a mobile telephone) is not capable of precluding access to the personal data contained therein, since mere adherence to the general terms and conditions does not satisfy the substantive and formal requirements expressed by Art. 2 of Legislative*

[81] See Quarta and Smorto (2024), p. 276.

[82] See, also with critical remarks, Resta (2021), pp. 678 ff.

[83] Trib. Milan 9 February 2021, *in Ilfamiliarista.it*, 28 June 2021. Equally: Trib. Bologna 25 November 2021, in *Dir. informazione e informatica*, 2022, 1, 19; Trib. Milano 20 June 2022, in *Nuovo dir. civ.*, 2022, 3, 1117 ss.; Trib. Como 27 July 2023, in *Pactum online*, 2023.

Decree No. 101/2018'[84] for the *de cuius* (i.e. the user) to specifically express the will to prohibit third parties from accessing his or her data.

It is worth adding that some platforms, to prevent the occurrence of such difficulties, have, over time, introduced particular solutions aimed, according to mechanisms based on users' choices, at regulating and managing the fate of *accounts* after the death of users. The best known example is Meta's 'memorial' *account*, whereby: upon the news of the user's death, the platform transforms the *account* into memorial mode, provided that the user, during his or her lifetime, has not otherwise communicated to the platform the decision to delete the *account* upon his or her death; the memorial *account* remains visible online, allowing its consultation by those who had access to it (including the possibility for 'friends' to share memories); at the same time, the platform allows the user to identify, during his or her lifetime, a 'legacy contact', who, if appointed, will be a person authorized to exercise a series of—but not all—features related to the memorial *account* (e.g. it is permissible to change the cover image or make a post in the profile, but not to read messages or remove 'friends').[85,86]

7 Events of Termination of the Legal Relationship: Physiological and Pathological Hypotheses

If, with respect to contracts concluded, through platforms, between sellers/suppliers and buyers, reference is always made (as it has been observed with respect to events of modification) to the governing law and so to the rules proper to the agreements according to their nature, the subject of termination events evokes the circumstances from which the termination of the contracts concluded between platforms and users may result, with the consequent dissolution of the legal relationship.

A distinction can be made between physiological and pathological hypotheses.

Moving from the first aspect, the point comes back to the fact that platform contracts, being destined to project over time, assume the conformation of relationships of duration. So, the contracts, according to the physiological course of the relationship, are destined to expire: if a term has been attached to the contracts, upon the expiry of the term, thus allowing also for the case that the contracts have been anchored, as a period of duration, to the life of the users or to their death; if the contracts have not been attached to a term (indefinite duration), upon the exercise of the right of withdrawal by one of the parties (being, in this case, necessary to

[84] Trib. Rome 10 February 2022, in *Quot. Giur.*, 2022.

[85] Cf. Barba (2017), pp. 341 ff.

[86] Another issue, which is under discussion, concerns the nature of the provisions whereby the testator gives instructions to a person to manage the passwords to his or her *accounts*: there is debate as to whether to qualify these provisions as inheritance in nature (legacy of passwords, executor) or as a *post mortem* mandate *ad exequendum* (see, on this subject, Damiani 2020, pp. 87 ff.; Vesto 2020, pp. 171 ff.).

recognize a right of withdrawal to the parties given the radical impossibility of profiling a perennial contractual bond).

This right of termination, moreover, characterises platform contracts as a rule. The general terms and conditions, in fact, whether the contracts are of indefinite duration or not, usually grant the contracting parties the right to terminate the relationship by withdrawing from it.[87,88]

As far as users are concerned, therefore, the general conditions normally provide for a free withdrawal right.[89] The 'attractiveness' of platforms, that is, implies that platforms leave users free to choose whether to keep active *accounts*. Hence, users—without prejudice to the applicability to them, where they qualify as consumers, of the *ius poenitendi* of consumer derivation (Articles 52 ff. Italian Consumer Code)[90]—are recognised, where they wish, the power to exercise free withdrawal from contracts.[91]

As for platforms, then, the discourse is similar. To be more precise, sometimes the general terms and conditions also grant platforms, like users, the right to withdraw freely from contracts.[92] At other times, the general terms and conditions provide that the right of withdrawal, to which platforms are entitled, is subject to the occurrence of particular circumstances, as regulated in the *account* suspension/deactivation clauses, which we will return to below (see, *below*, next section).[93]

Turning to the second side, the causes of extinction of the legal relationship are the various pathological events that can functionally affect the execution phase of contracts.[94]

The reference goes, first, to the non-performance of the parties, which may lead to the termination of the contracts for non-performance pursuant to Articles 1453 et seq. of Italian the Civil Code (or, if the requirements of the consumer discipline on the 'contracts for the supply of digital content and digital services' are met, pursuant to Articles *135-septesdecies* et seq. of the Italian Consumer Code). To be added, therefore, although these are cases that are quite remote to envisage, are the further legal hypotheses: the other cases of termination, referable to the supervening impossibility of performance and excessive onerousness, and the rescission thus comes into play.[95]

---

[87] See Codiglione (2022), p. 300.

[88] For specific references on the right of withdrawal, see Sect. 10 of this chapter.

[89] See, e.g. Art. 15, Amazon Conditions of Use.

[90] See Quarta and Smorto (2024), p. 193.

[91] To ensure that no undue hindrances are placed in the way of users, Art. 6(13) of the DMA provides: '*The gatekeeper shall not have general conditions for terminating the provision of a core platform service that are disproportionate. The gatekeeper shall ensure that the conditions of termination can be exercised without undue difficulty*'.

[92] See, e.g. Art. 13.2, Airbnb Terms of Service for European Users.

[93] See, e.g. Art. 4, X Terms of Service.

[94] For specific references on the subject of remedies, see Sect. 11 of this chapter.

[95] See Astone (2023), p. 436 (where the author, with critical remarks, also considers that to be evocable also are '*the principles of associative contracts and, in particular, the rules of internal*

Nonetheless, here too the field is again often covered by withdrawal clauses. Indeed, for users who wish to withdraw from contracts in the face of a breach of contract by the platforms, the right of withdrawal, where provided for, is the quickest way to terminate the contracts, without prejudice to the possibility of exercising against the platforms any other remedies (e.g. compensation for damages). For the platforms, at the same time, the aforementioned *account* suspension/deactivation clauses return: in these clauses, in fact, which require particular scrutiny, it is also usually provided that platforms have the power to unilaterally terminate contracts in the case of non-performance by users.[96]

7.1 Account Suspension and Deactivation Clauses

Account suspension/deactivation clauses constitute one of the clauses through which platforms can impose their contractual force. The platforms, in fact, given the technical availability of the infrastructure, reserve for themselves, through these clauses, the possibility of presiding over the course of the relationship, to the point of having, therefore, the power to unilaterally determine the termination of contracts, through the disconnection of users' *accounts*.[97]

The wording of the clauses is, as a rule, wide-ranging. On the one hand, the assumptions on which the clauses base the power granted to the platforms are varied: these range from situations of a mere factual nature, such as the inactivity of users for a certain period of time or the non-confirmation of *accounts* after registration,[98] to situations of an economic nature, based on the failure to achieve *performance* standards,[99] up to situations of breach nature, linked to the violation by users of the obligations prescribed for them by the general conditions, including the *policies* of the platforms.[100] On the other hand, the platforms' ways of intervening are also varied: according to a gradual approach, platforms reserve the right, when one of these conditions is met, either to adopt more mitigated decisions, such as that of determining a temporary or partial suspension of *accounts* (or even the removal

---

justice regarding cases of exclusion of the associate').

[96] Against the risk for users that, in case of termination of the relationship, the platforms will delete the data contained in their *accounts* (this is, as we have seen in the previous paragraph, the solution generally provided for by the general conditions), there is the right to data portability. This right, which allows users to request that their data are made available in a format suitable for transferring them elsewhere, is increasingly protected by the EU legislator, being recognised both by Art. 20 of the GDPR, with respect to personal data, and by Art. 6(9) of the DMA, with respect to the data of 'end users' towards the *gatekeepers*.

[97] See Battelli (2022b), p. 572.

[98] See, e.g. Art. 13.2, Airbnb Terms of Service for European.

[99] See, e.g. Art. 4.2.6, eBay User Agreement.

[100] See, e.g. Art. 4.2, Meta Terms of Service.

of individual contents), or to adopt stricter decisions, such as that of terminating contracts, permanently deactivating *accounts*.[101]

The clauses under examination raise multiple questions.

To begin, it is an issue of qualification that arises, since it is necessary to assess what legal nature the clauses have. The answer seems bivalent. In other words, if the clauses in the general terms and conditions are formulated as a unit, they, in reality, appear to respond to a dual nature, which varies according to their application requirements.[102]

Where, that is, the clauses anchor the power of the platforms to situations of non-performance, the clauses seem to take on the profile of express termination clauses, as clauses that, in the presence of non-performance, legitimise the platforms to terminate the contracts. Where, *ex adverso*, the clauses base the power of the platforms on situations of mere fact or on situations of an economic nature, the clauses seem, on the contrary, to designate withdrawal clauses, such as clauses that, upon the occurrence of specific terms (which do not go so far as to identify a breach), allow the platforms to terminate the relationship.[103]

In another aspect, then, comes the issue of transparency and defence. Faced, indeed, with the circumstance that platforms, through clauses, can, on their own initiative, deactivate *accounts* and, therefore, exclude users, the need arises to guarantee protection to those users.

This aspect is now ruled by EU regulations. First, the mind goes to Regulation (EU) 2019/1150, which, with respect to the relationship between platforms and 'business users' (see, *supra*, para 4.1), establishes a discipline aimed at providing, in accordance with a joint protection of transparency and defence: (1) that the general conditions must '*set out the grounds for decision to suspend or terminate or impose any other kind of restriction upon, in whole or in part, the provision of their online intermediation services*' (Art. 3, para 1, lett. c); (2) that the platforms, where they intend to exercise the power to suspend or deactivate *accounts*, must communicate the decision to the users, giving them reasons and at least 30 days' notice (Art. 4, paras 1 and 2); (3) that the users, in their protection, have the right to challenge the platforms' decision, explaining their defences (Art. 3, para 3); (4) that, to this end, the platforms must set up appropriate internal complaint-handling systems (Art. 11).[104] The DSA, then, intervenes in a similar way.[105] The DSA, in fact, referring more generally to the relations between platforms and 'recipients of the service',[106] establishes a discipline of similar content, requiring, again for the cross-protection of transparency and defence: (1) that the general conditions must provide information on '*any policies, procedures, measures and tools used for the purposes*

[101] See, e.g. Art. 4.1.6, eBay User Agreement.

[102] See Camardi (2021), p. 900 (footnote 59).

[103] See Quarta and Smorto (2024), p. 194.

[104] See Martinelli (2023), pp. 182–183.

[105] See Finocchiaro (2023), pp. 734–735.

[106] For the notion of 'recipient of the service', see footnote 61.

of content moderation ... as well as the rules of procedure of ... internal complaint handling system' (Art. 14(1)); (2) that decisions to suspend or deactivate *accounts* must be reasoned (Art. 17); (3) that users must be granted the right to defence by lodging complaints against platform decisions through internal complaint-handling systems (Art. 20).[107,108]

Finally, the issue of the validity limits of the clauses arises. To be understood is how far the clauses can go in substance, legitimately giving platforms the power, by deactivating *accounts*, to terminate contracts.

In this regard, a number of specific constraints come into play, first, in the particular cases where the clauses are to be identified (as seen above) as withdrawal clauses.[109] It is to say: if the users have the nature of consumers, it operates, according to the Italian Consumer Code (Art. 33), the presumption of unfairness of the clauses allowing '*only the professional and not the consumer to withdraw*' (sub-para g, first part) or allowing the professional, who has exercised withdrawal, to withhold consideration for services not rendered (sub-para g, second part) or allowing '*the professional to withdraw from contracts of indefinite duration without reasonable notice, except in the case of just cause*' (sub-para h); then, pursuant to Art. 1341(2) of the Italian Civil Code, clauses provided for in general terms and conditions which grant the right of withdrawal to the principal require specific approval in writing.[110]

The thorny point, however, is another. Given the heterogeneity of the assumptions identified as the basis of the clauses, it is controversial whether, in some hypotheses, platforms are allowed to arrogate to themselves the power to deactivate *accounts*. In other words, if in many cases the legitimacy of the clauses does not seem questionable, since it is certainly possible that platforms, in the case of factual situations or, even more so, in the case of breach, may be entitled to terminate relations, the same cannot be said for other cases, which particularly involve users' fundamental rights.

One example, which is of more interest to business users, concerns hypotheses where clauses link the power to deactivate *accounts* to situations of an economic

---

[107] Another legislative provision, within the area of consumer discipline, is regulated by Art. *135-noviesdecies*, para 6, of the Italian Consumer Code for 'contracts for the supply of digital content and digital services'.

[108] To adapt to these regulatory disciplines, the platform's general terms and conditions consequently provide that the platforms' decisions on *account* suspension and deactivation must pass through mechanisms of prior communication to users and adversarial discussions with them: see, e.g. Articles 13 and 14, Airbnb Terms of Service for European Users.

[109] With respect to the norms, regulating withdrawal clauses, which we shall immediately cite below in the text, it is excluded that the withdrawal clauses themselves may include, in their ambit, also express termination clauses, since they are clauses of a different kind: see, in case law, among many others, Cass. 5 July 2018, no. 17603, in *Giust. civ. Mass.*, 2018 and Cass. 11 November 2016, no. 23065, in *Just. civ. Mass.*, 2017.

[110] See, in case law, precisely with reference to clauses prescribed in the general conditions of platforms, Trib. Catanzaro 30 April 2012, in *Dir. informazione e informatica*, 2012, 6, 1174 and Trib. Messina 7 July 2010, in *Dir. inf.*, 2011, 1, 118.

nature, based on non-compliance with *performance* standards (which depend, thus, on sales parameters, disputes, delivery delays, etc.).

Now, the idea that platforms, on their side, can demand certain levels of quality of performance from business users, to guarantee their reliability on the *marketplace*, must be calibrated with the consideration that platforms, on the other hand, themselves become channels of access to the market: economic operators, to access the market, *aka* to exercise their freedom of economic initiative pursuant to Art. 41 of the Italian Constitution, may find themselves forced to go through platforms, not otherwise having the effective capacity to compete.[111]

The limit, then, to the validity of the clauses emerges from the point that the power, conferred on platforms, to deactivate *accounts* in the event of failure to meet *performance* standards, cannot transcend, to the detriment of the freedom of economic initiative of business users, into an abuse.[112]

The clauses, therefore, according to their content, must neither entail an abuse of a dominant position nor determine, according to the most recent regulatory interventions: on the one hand, an abuse of economic dependence, which, following the reform of Art. 9 of Law No. 192/1998 (provided for by Law No. 118/2022), now also includes, by hitting them, the '*abusive practices carried out by digital platforms*';[113] on the other hand, a violation of the obligations imposed on platforms (or, better, on large platforms qualifying as '*gatekeepers*') by the Digital Markets Act, such as obligations aimed at ensuring that the markets are fair and contestable (Art. 1), including, above all, the obligation to guarantee business users '*fair, reasonable and non-discriminatory*' conditions of access to services (Art. 6, para 12).

Another example, then, which arouses—in a multidisciplinary ambit[114]—some of the most heated debates, is the one concerning the hypotheses in which the clauses base the power to deactivate *accounts* on the 'moderation' of content by the platforms: otherwise to say, if users publish content of an illegal nature or otherwise contrary to the platforms' *policies*, then the platforms, identifying a breach, are authorized to detach *accounts*.

Again, at the interface, there are conflicting needs.[115] Platforms, on the one hand, have an interest in avoiding (the regulation on the liability of *providers* governed by the DSA comes into play as a counterpoint) that users convey content contrary to the law through them. Users, on the other hand, have an interest in being able to exercise their freedom of manifestation of thought *pursuant to* Art. 21 of the Italian Constitution, which today finds in platforms a fundamental mode of expression.[116]

[111] Cf. Martinelli (2022), p. 85.

[112] See Quarta and Smorto (2024), p. 195.

[113] On this subject, please refer specifically to the following section of this chapter (as well as to Zinno 2024, pp. 631 ff.).

[114] See Gabrielli and Ruffolo (2024), p. 441.

[115] See Resta (2022), pp. 371 ff.

[116] Cf. Manganelli (2023), pp. 899 ff.

So, difficulties emerge in the 'grey areas'.[117] Indeed, no one doubts that platforms certainly have the legitimacy to react when faced with illicit content, such as offensive content (hate speech) or content inciting crime, hatred, racism, etc. The crux of the matter, however, is in the borderline territories, such as those that are linked to the expression of political ideas, especially if of an extreme nature or dissimilar to the prevailing public opinion or not in accordance with the *policies of* the platforms: suffice it to think, to cite among the most notorious cases, of President Trump's affair over the events on Capitol Hill or the events of the Italian political movements CasaPound and Forza Nuova.[118]

Here, reasoning according to a view that is more widespread in America, the autonomy of the platforms should be favoured: as private subjects, they would be free to establish the 'rules of the game', thus defining, at their discretion, the terms within which users can publish content on the platforms themselves.[119] Nevertheless, counter to this view, comes the consideration that platforms do not seem to be able to be reputed as mere private entities. Platforms, indeed, insofar as they manage infrastructures that enable the continuous exchange of billions and billions of contents, reveal a supra-individual dimension, settling, precisely, as 'channels' that allow individuals to interact with third parties, expressing their freedom of manifestation of thought.

Therefore, even in this respect, what seems to emerge is a limit to the validity of the clauses. The clauses, that is, which allow platforms to deactivate users' *accounts* in the face of content moderation, are subject to the constraint that the clauses

---

[117] Cf. Ruffolo (2023), p. 102.

[118] These Italian cases demonstrate the difficulty of the subject. The CasaPound affair is particularly indicative, given that, dealing with the deactivation measure of the political movement's *account* ordered by Facebook and thus challenged, the Court of Rome: in the precautionary phase, censured the platform's decision, considering that '*The Facebook-user contract is a contract with a social character that obliges the defaulting provider to reintegrate the 'media square' according to the principles of pluralism and equal access to political debate. The deactivation (default) of a political party's page produces damage to the entire system of membership (media plaza) by depriving user-visitors-thirds of the right to pluralist information and depriving the user-contractor of equal access to political debate*' (Trib. Roma 12 December 2019, in *Dir. & giust.*, 16 December 2019; conf., Trib. Roma 29 April 2020, in *Foro it*, 2020, 9, I, 2889); in the merit phase, found, on the contrary, the validity of the platform's decision, considering that '*In the event of publication within a social media platform of content characterised by hate speech based on race or ethnicity and of symbols representing or praising an organisation that incites hatred or that incites violence, according to the contractual conditions governing the service, the platform provider may suspend or permanently disable the user's access to his personal account. Such content not only violates the contractual conditions, but is unlawful under the entire national and European regulatory system and the platform provider, once it becomes aware of it, has a legal duty to remove it*' (Trib. Roma 3 December 2022, in *Dir. informazione e informatica*, 2023, 2, 213). As regards, instead, the Forza Nuova affair, what comes to the fore is the decision made by the Court of Rome with the order of 23 February 2020 (in *Dir. informazione e informatica*, 2020, 3, 552), which, in this case, considered the *account* deactivation measure taken by Facebook to be legitimate, relying on the circumstance that the activities of the political movement were to be associated with a '*hate organisation*'.

[119] See Codiglione (2022), pp. 317 ff.

themselves may not determine an unjustified restriction of the freedom of manifestation of thought pursuant to Art. 21 of the Italian Constitution (in support, there is also Art. 14, para 4, of the DSA, which includes freedom of expression, together with the fundamental values of the Charter of Nice, in the list of principles that platforms must respect with reference to content moderation activities).[120] Hence, platforms may claim that a user's content is illicit, assuming the commission of a non-performance or a violation of the *policies*, insofar as the content itself does not represent a legitimate manifestation of the user's freedom of expression or thought.[121,122]

References

Alpa G (2022) Sul potere contrattuale delle piattaforme digitali. Contr e impr, p 737

Astone F (2023) Social network e rapporti contrattuali. In: Bocchini R (ed) Manuale di diritto dell'informatica, p 436

Bania K (2022) Fitting the Digital Markets Act in the existing legal framework: the myth of the "without prejudice" clause. Eur Competition J

Barba V (2017) Interessi post mortem tra testamento e altri atti di ultima volontà. Riv dir civ, pp 341 ff

Barba A (2025) Tutela inibitoria del consumatore e trasparenza dei modelli omogenei di contrattazione. Accademia, p 821

Battelli E (2022a) Diritto privato digitale. Torino, pp 85 ff

Battelli E (2022b) Questioni aperte in materia di contrattazione nelle piattaforme on line. I contratti, p 563

Benedetti AM (2002) Autonomia privata procedimentale. La formazione del contratto fra legge e volontà delle parti, Torino

BGH (2019) 12 luglio 2018, III ZR 183/17. Nuova giur civ comm, pp 691 ff

Bianca CM (2019) Diritto civile. 3. Il Contratto. Milano, pp 680–682

Bocchini R (2023) Nuovi beni digitali e mondi dematerializzati. In Bocchini R (ed) Manuale di diritto dell'informatica. Napoli, pp 167 ff

Bocchini R (this volume) New digital services and goods. In Bocchini R (ed) Digital platforms - from technical foundations to legal and economic implications, vol I. Springer, Cham

Camardi C (2018) L'eredità digitale tra reale e virtuale. Dir informazione e informatica, pp 73 ff

Camardi C (2019) Prime osservazioni sulla Direttiva (UE) 2019/770 sui contratti per la fornitura di contenuti e servizi digitali. Operazioni di consumo e circolazione di dati personali. Giust civ, p 499

Camardi C (2021) Contratti digitali e mercati delle piattaforme. Un pro memoria per il civilista. Jus civile, pp 915 ff

Camardi B (2023) "Gigantismo" e disuguaglianze nell'economia dei dati. Appunti sulla governance europea delle relazioni digitali. Ianus dir e fin, pp 59 ff

Carleo A (2019) (ed) Decisione robotica, Bologna

[120] Pinelli (2024), p. 34.

[121] Codiglione (2022), pp. 332 ff.

[122] If users suffer unlawful *account* deactivation by platforms, they are entitled to damages: see, in confirmation, App. L'Aquila 9 November 2021, no. 1659, in *Dir. & giust.*, 2022, 15 February and Trib. Bologna 10 March 2021, in *Foro it.*, 2021, 4, I, 1421.

Carleo R (2023) La successione digitale. In: Bocchini R (ed) Manuale di diritto dell'informatica, pp 554 ff
Carota L (2017) Diffusione delle informazioni in rete e affidamento sulla reputazione digitale dell'impresa. Giur comm, p 624
Caterina R (2011) Cyberspazio, social network e teoria generale del contratto. AIDA
Cinque M (2020) L'«eredità digitale» alla prova delle riforme. Riv dir civ, pp 76 ff
Clarizia R (2005) La cessione del contratto. Artt. 1406-1410. Comm cod civ Schlesinger, Varese, pp 22 ff
Codiglione GG (2022) Il contratto dell'utente con il social network: i limiti dello schema negoziale nell'esercizio dei diritti fondamentali. In: Stanzione P (ed) I "poteri privati" delle piattaforme e le nuove frontiere della privacy. Torino, p 299
Colangelo M (2020) Piattaforme digitali e servizi alla società dell'informazione: il caso AirB&B Ireland. Dir inf, p 291, nota a CGUE, sent. 19 dicembre 2017, AirB&B Ireland, C-390/18
Confortini V (2021) L'eredità digitale (appunti per uno studio). Riv dir civ, pp 1189 ff
D'Auria M (2024) Il fenomeno delle recensioni nel prisma della concorrenza sleale. NGCC, p 1408, nota a trib. Milano 21.03.2024
D'Ippolito G (2021) Profilazione e pubblicità targettizzata on line. Real-Time Bidding e behavioural advertising, Napoli
Damiani E (2020) I legati. In Comm. Scialoja-Branca, Bologna-Roma, 87 ss
Delle Monache VS (2020) Successione mortis causa e patrimonio digitale. Nuova giur civ comm II:464–465
Di Giovanni F (2019) Attività contrattuale e intelligenza artificiale. Giur it, pp 1677 ff
Di Sabato D (2024) Tecnologia algoritmica e attività negoziale smart. Contr e impr 2:360
Di Sabato D, Lepore F (2018) Sharing economy. Profili giuridici, Napoli
Falce V (2022) Piattaforme ed ecosistemi digitali. Scelte pro-concorrenziali. Riv dir ind, p 189
Finocchiaro G (2023) Responsabilità delle piattaforme e tutela dei consumatori. Giorn dir amm, pp 734–735
Foltran F (2019) Professionisti, consumatori e piattaforme online: la tutela delle parti deboli nei nuovi equilibri negoziali. In MediaLaws, 3, pp 165 ff
Gabrielli E, Ruffolo U (2024) Introduzione. In: Gabrielli E, Ruffolo U (eds) Piattaforme e content moderation. Giur it, p 441
Galli F (2023) Il principio di accountability. In: AA.VV. (ed) La protezione dei dati personali: natura, garanzie e bilanciamento di un diritto fondamentale. Torino, pp 137 ff
Gentili A, Battelli E (2011) I contratti di distribuzione del commercio elettronico. In: Bocchini R (eds) I contratti di somministrazione e di distribuzione. In Trattato dei contratti Rescigno-Gabrielli, Torino, pp 379 ff
Giampetraglia R et al (this volume) Contract formation. In Bocchini R (ed) Digital platforms - from technical foundations to legal and economic implications, vol I. Springer, Cham
Hatzopoulos, Roma S (2017) Caring for sharing? The collaborative economy. Common Mark Law Rev 54:81, 86
Irti N (1998a) L'ordine giuridico del mercato, 1ª edn. Bari
Irti N (1998b) Scambi senza accordo. Riv trim dir proc civ, pp 347 ff
Irti N (1999) È vero ma… (Replica a Giorgio Oppo), ivi, I, pp 273 ff
Irti C (2025) La protezione dei dati personali degli utenti nelle piattaforme digitali. In: AA.VV (ed) Il diritto privato nell'economia digitale. Torino, pp 149 ff
Manganelli A (2023) Piattaforme digitali e social network tra pluralità degli ordinamenti, pluralismo informativo e potere di mercato. Giur cost, p 883
Marino VG (2022) Mercato digitale e delle successioni mortis causa, pp 167 ff
Martinelli S (2022) Piattaforme: problematiche e responsabilità. In: Magri G, Martinelli S, Thobani S (eds) Manuale di diritto privato delle nuove tecnologie, Torino, p 85
Martinelli S (2023) I contratti della platform economy. Torino, p 42, nota 96
Maugeri M (2021) Smart contract e disciplina dei contratti, Bologna

Maugeri M, Grasso G (eds) (2022) Contratto, contratti e mercati. In Collana della Scuola superiore della magistratura
Nardi S (2020) Successione digitale e successione nel patrimonio digitale. In: Del Prato E (ed) Le successioni. Torino, p 597
Nuzzo M (2025) Il recesso., in questo Trattato
Omodei Salè R (2025) (ed) La tutela dei dati personali, sez. V. In questo Trattato
Oppo G (1998) Disumanizzazione del contratto? Riv dir civ, I, pp 525 ff
Osti B, Pardolesi R (2019) L'Antitrust ai tempi di Facebook. Merc conc reg, pp 194 ff
Padovini VF (2009) Le posizioni contrattuali. In: Bonilini G (ed) Trattato delle successioni e delle donazioni, I. Milano, pp 525 ff
Pagliantini S (2022) La nuova disciplina dei contratti B-to-C per la fornitura di contenuti e servizi digitali. Nuove leggi civ comm, pp 1499 ff
Perlingieri C (2015) Profili civilistici dei social networks, Napoli
Pinelli C (2024) Poteri e diritti nelle piattaforme. Problemi di una prospettiva costituzionale. Giur it, pp 451 ff
Pisani G (2023) Piattaforme digitali e autodeterminazione. Relazioni sociali, lavoro e diritti al tempo della governamentalità algoritmica, Modena
Quarta A (2020) Mercati senza scambi. La metamorfosi del contratto nel capitalismo della sorveglianza, Napoli
Quarta A, Smorto G (2024) Diritto privato dei mercati digitali, 2ª ed. Le Monnier
Resta G (2019) La successione nei rapporti digitali e la tutela post-mortale dei dati personali. Contr e impr, pp 89 ff
Resta G (2021) L'accesso post mortem ai dati personali: il caso Apple. Nuova giur civ comm, II, pp 678 ff
Resta F (2022) Le piattaforme e la visibilità del potere. In: Stanzione P (ed) I "poteri privati" delle piattaforme e le nuove frontiere della privacy, pp 371 ff
Restelli ER (2022) Le piattaforme digitali. Milano, pp 111–112
Roppo V (2011) Il contratto. In Tratt. dir. priv. Iudica-Zatti, Milano, pp 523 ff
Ruffolo U (2023) Il contrasto alla disinformazione e alle fake news. In: Pinelli C, Ruffolo U (eds) I diritti nelle piattaforme, Torino, p 102
Ruggeri F (2021) Regole di trasparenza e rapporti tra imprese nei mercati digitali: il regolamento (UE) 2019/1150 sull'intermediazione online e i motori di ricerca. Dir inf, pp 397 ff
Sartoris C (2021) Trasparenza e piattaforme online alla luce del Regolamento (UE) 2019/1150. In: Orlando S, Capaldo G (eds) Osservatorio Giuridico sulla Innovazione Digitale
Sartoris C (2022) Piattaforme digitali e tutele: dal "consumer" al "prosumer". Actualidad Jurídica Iberoamericana, n 16:962
Smorto G (2016) Reputazione, fiducia, mercati. Eur dir priv, p 199
Smorto G (2017) Economia della condivisione e antropologia dello scambio. Dir pubbl comp eur, pp 119 ff
Smorto G (2020) La tutela del contraente debole nella platform economy, dopo il Regolamento UE 2019/1150 e la Direttiva UE 2019/2161 (c.d. Omnibus). In: Falce V (ed) Fairness e innovazione nel mercato digitale. Torino, pp 49 ff
Surden H (2012) Computable Contracts. UC Davis Law Rev, pp 629 ff
Tampieri M (2021) Il patrimonio digitale oltre la vita: quale destino? Contr e impr, pp 554 ff
Toffler A (1987) La terza ondata, Milano
Vesto A (2020) Successione digitale e circolazione dei beni online. Napoli, pp 171 ff
Vizzoni L (2018) Recensioni non genuine su Tripadvisor: quali responsabilità? Resp civ prev, p 706
Zinno M (2024) L'abuso di dipendenza economica "digitale". Dir di int, pp 631 ff

Issues of Economic Dependence

Giovanni Di Lorenzo

Contents

Abstract The chapter investigates the prohibition of abuse of the economic dependence of a company that makes use of the intermediation services of a digital platform, and offers an exegesis of Art. 9 Law No. 192/1998, also in the light of the recent sentence rendered by the Council of State in the case Siae v. Meta. The investigation on economic dependence also unveils the delicate problem of the coordination of Art. 9 of the aforementioned law with the DMA.

G. Di Lorenzo (✉)
University of Rome "La Sapienza", Rome, Italy
e-mail: giovanni.dilorenzo@uniroma1.it

R. Bocchini (ed.), *Digital Platforms - From Technical Foundations to Legal and Economic Implications*, https://doi.org/10.1007/978-3-032-07978-7_12

1 The Prohibition of Abuse of Economic Dependence and Intermediary Services Rendered by Digital Platforms

The extension of the prohibition of abuse of economic dependence to companies providing intermediation services via digital platforms, introduced in 2022 within Art. 9 of the Industrial Subcontracting Act,[1] is part of the relatively recent initiatives taken by the European institutions to '[...] *safeguard a fair and innovation-friendly business environment*' in the digital single market;[2] and is in addition to the provisions of Regulation (EU) 2019/1150 ('promoting fairness and transparency for business users of *online* intermediary services') and Regulation (EU) 2022/1925 (on the regime 'relating to fair and contestable markets in the digital sector', hereinafter also referred to as DMA for brevity) to protect businesses that are users of services rendered by platforms.[3]

As soon as one approaches the reading of Art. 9 mentioned above, one becomes aware of the numerous doubts that arise. Not only because of the questionable language chosen to describe the hypotheses regulated, but also and above all because of the difficulty of coordinating the rule prohibiting the abuse of economic dependence with the DMA.

Hence, the following pages will offer a brief inventory of the main interpretative issues that the exegesis unveils, not only of Art. 9 l. s., but also of Art. 1 DMA, which coordinates the European rules enclosed therein with the competing national sources. Investigation, this one, allows for identifying the space that the prohibition of abuse of economic dependence can be assigned in the broader framework of the legal rules that aim to counter the abuse of the economic power of the operators of digital platforms.

2 The Status of Economic Dependence

The most innovative contribution of the 2022 reform mentioned above would seem to reside in the introduction of the presumption of economic dependence in which the company would find itself when it 'uses the intermediation services provided by a digital platform', rather than in the prescription imposed on the platform operator.

---

[1] Hereinafter, for the sake of brevity, also l. s.

With reference to the reform of Art. 9 l. s. introduced by Art. 33 Law 118 of 5 August 2022, see Libertini (2023), p. 10; Colangelo and Minervini (2023), *passim*; Bachelet (2023), pp. 39 ff.; Licastro (2022), *passim*; Falce (2021), p. 189; Monterossi (2021), pp. 919 ff.

[2] In this regard, see Communication from the Commission to the European Parliament, the Council, the European Economic and Social Committee and the Committee of the Regions, 25 May 2016, in *Online platforms and the digital single market opportunities and challenges for Europe*, 13.

For a more extensive treatment of the issues mentioned below in the text, see Libertini (2022), pp. 1069 ff.

[3] Hereinafter also referred to as DMA for brevity.

In fact, in line with the most widespread interpretation in the civil law literature,[4] Art. 9 l. s. regulates not only the subcontracting contract industrial, but all relations between companies characterised by asymmetrical contractual strength.

Now, some doubts arise when examining the prerequisites of economic dependence. Indeed, some focus the investigation on the '[...] situation in which an undertaking is able to bring about an excessive imbalance of rights and obligations in its commercial relations with another undertaking'.[5] Others 'also' on the '[...] real possibility for the abusing party to find satisfactory alternatives on the market'.[6]

The latter thesis seems more convincing, not only because it corroborates the use of the conjunction 'also' and is more faithful to the enunciation under consideration, but also because it proposes to reconcile the protection of the weaker contracting party with self-responsibility for the consequences of choices made freely and consciously.[7] If economic dependence resulted implicitly from the mere imbalance of rights and obligations, the law would also provide protection to those who, faced with the alternatives available in the market, consciously accept an unsuitable contract. Yet, authoritative doctrine warns, as soon as the contract is concluded, '[...] the individual is no longer free to escape the consequences, good or bad for him [...]. The effect of the act is also directed against its author, who remains bound and as if imprisoned by it'.[8] Hence, the idea that the excessive imbalance of rights and obligations constitutes only one of the indicators of economic dependence and

---

[4] On this point, see Bianca (2019), p. 405; Roppo (2011), p. 870; Orlandi (2008), p. 144; Fabbio (2006), p. 102; Macario (2005), p. 683; Gentili (2004a), p. 40; Barba (1998), p. 298; Maugeri (2003), p. 10; Prosperi (2002), p. 269; Albanese (1999), p. 1179; Camardi (2005), p. 549; Battelli (2007), p. 180; Spolidoro (1999), p. 204.

May I also refer to Di Lorenzo (2009), p. 37; Di Lorenzo (2014), p. 567.

Also widespread in case law is the idea that the prohibition of the abuse of economic dependence, although dictated by the law on subcontracting in manufacturing activities, can be applied to all contracts that achieve the so-called vertical integration of the supply chain and, therefore, to factual hypotheses that are much broader than those described by Art. 1 l. s. In this sense, Cass. 22 July 2024, no. 20270; Cass. 13 September 2024, no. 24680; Cass, sez. un., 25 November 2011, no. 24906, in *Giur. it.*, 2012, col. 2054; Trib. Forlì 27 October 2010, in *Foro it.*, 2011, I, 1578; Trib. Roma 30 November 2009, in *Foro it.*, 2011, I, 256.

To the contrary, see Trib. Rome 17 March 2010, in *Danno e resp.*, 2010, 1175, with note by Colangelo; Trib. Taranto 22 December 2003, in *Foro it.*, 2004, I, 262; Trib. Bari 2 July 2002, in *Foro it.*, 2002, I, 3208, with note by Palmieri. In this sense, also, Scarso (2006), p. 219; Musso (2003), p. 484.

[5] Maffeis (1998), p. 79; Scarso (2006), p. 219; Agrifoglio (2008), p. 1361.

[6] Libertini (2023), p. 30; Fabbio (2006), p. 126. May I also refer to my *Abuso di dipendenza economica e contratto nullo*, cit., pp. 21 ff.

[7] As has been aptly observed, '[...] those who do not withdraw from the bargain despite the out-of-market price, are either under duress, and it is up to legislation to assess the decisive weight and social ethical relevance; or they find convenience, at least *aliunde*, so that their transfer of wealth is not as unmotivated as claimed. If (and when) the latter is true, a review of the reason for exchange is not justified [...]'. In this sense, see Gentili (2004a), p. 51.

[8] Betti (1994), p. 162.

The relevance of freedom and consciousness of choice in market regulation is also emphasised by Irti (1996), p. 97; Gentili (2004b), p. 557; Messinetti (2009), pp. 615 ff.

assumes legal importance when it is caused by the impossibility '[...] of finding satisfactory alternatives on the market'.

2.1 *The Presumption of Economic Dependence of the User Undertaking: The Case of Meta v. Siae*

It is far from straightforward to indicate the assumptions of the presumption of economic dependence of the user enterprise.

In fact, Art. 9(1) l. s. omits to specify, on the one hand, the meaning of the syntagma 'digital platform'; and neglects, on the other hand, to clarify whether 'intermediation services' include only *online* e-commerce marketplaces, in line with the hypotheses regulated by Art. 1 of Regulation (EU) 2019/1150, or also the additional services listed in Art. 2 of the DMA.

In another respect, the provision of the 'known' fact to which the presumption under examination is anchored does not appear to be unequivocal either, particularly the provision of the 'decisive role in reaching end users or suppliers'.[9] Rather than the description of a fact, this phrase postulates a judgment entrusted to the interpreter in the absence of a precise parameter of assessment.

Moreover, if the known fact coincided with the ascertainment of the 'indeclinable' nature of the platform, and, therefore, with the demonstration that recourse to it constituted a *condicio sine qua non* for 'reaching end users or suppliers', the rule in question would end up placing on the user company the burden of proving the absence of the 'real possibility [...] of finding satisfactory alternatives on the market' and, therefore, the traceability of the concrete fact to the case of economic dependence. Therefore, this leads to the contradictory outcome of logically making the known fact coincide with the unknown fact, disregarding the intention of introducing a presumption to protect the user company.[10]

Hence, the idea, proposed by attentive doctrine, of referring '[...] the "determining position" [...] to an entire market' and of placing the burden of proof on the user undertaking that '[...] access to the services of the digital platform in question constitutes an economically necessary choice (even if this does not exclude the possibility of recourse to some other alternative platform, with a lesser market presence, or to online sales on its own site, or to other commercial methods)'.[11]

The need to reconcile the protection of the contracting party with private autonomy is also emphasised by Navarretta (2014), p. 566: '[...] one cannot fall into the temptation of automatically considering the discriminated party to be a weak party: it will only be so if reasons of actual contractual weakness occur, linked either to the lack of alternatives on the market or to contingent factors that invalidate its full autonomy, according to the *unfair exploitation* model'.

[9] On this point, see, more recently, Cons. Stato 2 July 2024, no. 5827, in *Foro it.*, 2024, 9, 417.

[10] The remark is also proposed by Libertini (2023), p. 28.

[11] Libertini (2023), p. 29.

Now, such an idea could lead to the application of the presumption whenever the basic platform service is rendered by one of the *gatekeepers* designated by the EU Commission pursuant to Art. 3(1) of the DMA; and, thus, whenever it is established that the operator, in addition to providing a 'basic platform service constituting an important *gateway for business users to reach end users*, is a *gateway operator*', the operator is not only a '*gateway operator*', but also a '*gateway operator*'. 1, DMA;[12] therefore, whenever it is established that the operator, in addition to providing a 'basic platform service which constitutes an important *gateway* for business users to reach end users', has 'a significant impact on the internal market' and holds '[...] an established and durable position in its own business, or is likely to acquire such a position in the near future'.

But such an outcome presupposes, however, that the DMA leaves room for the national rule under scrutiny also with regard to *gatekeepers*; and that the application of the prohibition does not preclude the fragmentation of the internal market that the European regulation seeks to prevent (see *below*, para 4).

Indeed, useful indications regarding economic dependency vis-à-vis a *gatekeeper* are provided by the relatively recent ruling by the Council of State at the outcome of the case between Meta and Siae.[13]

This judgement reformed the ruling by which the Lazio Regional Administrative Court (TAR),[14] ascertaining the legitimacy of a precautionary measure issued by the Competition and Market Authority,[15] had found Meta's decision to interrupt negotiations for the renewal of licences for the use of musical works managed by SIAE to create an audio *library* to enrich the videos created and shared within the *social network to* be arbitrary under Art. 9 of the law.

The Council of State, particularly after having noted that the purpose of the negotiation was not '[...] the granting of the licence to disseminate and distribute music content through the platform to end users', but the '[...] collection of music content protected by SIAE in the *audio library* [...] to enrich videos or *reels*', denied that Meta provided an intermediation service to reach end users of musical works;[16] and that, therefore, SIAE's economic dependence on the *social network* operator can be presumed.

[12] An explicit reference to the position of economic dependence of the user undertaking vis-à-vis *the gatekeeper* is contained in recital 75 DMA.

[13] Cons. Stato 2 July 2024, no. 5827, cit., 418.

[14] Tar Lazio sez. I 30 October 2023, no. 16069.

[15] AGCM 20 April 2023, no. 30606, in *Foro it.*, 2023, III, 416, with a note by Lopopolo (2024), pp. 151 and 769, with comments by Meo (2024) and Fabris (2024).

[16] The Council of State points out that the '[...] Meta platforms do not offer a streaming service or a music listening service (it is a well-known fact that there are major web giants that compete for large market shares in the sector), but limit themselves to making available to their users an archive, represented by the audio library implemented by the contents acquired by virtue of the licence, without precluding in any way those (including authors) who intend to use social networks for the dissemination of videos already equipped with background music or who intend to access the same contents on the web'.

In this respect, the ruling moves from the idea that economic dependence cannot be presumed every time the user undertaking avails itself of a service rendered by a *gatekeeper*; but it postulates a careful verification of the concrete circumstances with regard to the specific service offered by the *gatekeeper*, to ascertain whether the network effects of the platform contribute to making the role assumed by the gatekeeper 'decisive' to reach end users or suppliers.

Now, without prejudice to the need for such a concrete ascertainment, the wording of Art. 9 l. s. would seem to allow, in other respects, to find a 'determining position' also in respect of an operator not designated by the European Commission as a *gatekeeper*. In fact, in describing this position, the aforementioned article alludes to the 'network effects' or 'data availability' permitted by the services rendered by the digital platform.[17] Therefore, it would seem to attribute relevance, on the one hand, to the quantitative data offered by the number of 'customers and suppliers' who can be found through the operator and who contribute to increasing the value of the platform; and, on the other hand, to the degree of transparency offered by the operator with regard to all the information gathered through access to the digital platform (see *infra,* para 3).

But even this perspective raises the doubt as to what the threshold of relevance of the quantitative datum is, or that offered by the degree of transparency, given that Art. 9 l. s. does not offer the interpreter any precise criteria to which to anchor the ascertainment of the alleged economic power of the operator of the digital platform.

3 The Abuse of Economic Dependence

Equally ambiguous are the indications that Art. 9, para 2, l. s. offers to identify the abuse of the operator when it provides '[...] insufficient information or data on the scope or quality of the service provided'. In fact, the provision in question, while intercepting the importance that the processing of data assumes in the formation of the economic power of the operators of digital platforms, does not clarify what the threshold of relevance of reticence is and, in particular, what information must be provided to the user who avails himself of the intermediation services.

In this respect, the provision under consideration moves from the awareness that the availability of the aggregate data collected through the use of the platform services offers the operator a position of certain advantage within the market, if one

---

[17] The economic literature makes it clear that the services provided through digital platforms are characterised by a very significant *network effect*, i.e. the number of users using a service favours, in itself, the increase of the same. This *network effect* is due to the fact that, normally, digital platforms operate in a market characterised by two or more sides (*multi-sided market*), i.e. by at least two different categories of users who are, at the same time, *the* users of a service offered in one side and, so to speak, the 'product' sold to the users of the other side.

A characteristic feature of digital platforms is the crucial role of data, which are the core *assets* of such enterprises. The greater the number and variety of data, the faster and more precisely algorithms process and produce services for users.

considers the possibility that the latter offers not only the *online* brokerage service, but also goods or services in competition with the user companies.[18] Therefore, it would appear to contain a general clause capable, not only of encompassing the more punctual prescriptions that Articles 5, 6 and 7 DMA impose on *gatekeepers*, but also of permitting a review of the adequacy of the information offered by the platform operator and of the entire private structure of interests divided by the contract that allows the user undertaking access to the digital platform.

This review, which Art. 9 of the Act also allows when it prohibits the manager from '[...] demanding undue unilateral benefits not justified by the nature or content of the activity performed'.

Indeed, this provision, which takes its cue from the practice of platform operators in preparing their general terms and conditions, specifies, on the one hand, the more general hypothesis of the 'imposition of unjustifiably onerous contractual terms and conditions'; and, on the other hand, describes in broader terms the so-called tying practices more specifically listed in Art. 5(7) and (8) DMA.[19]

Likewise, 'unjustifiably burdensome' are '[...] practices that inhibit or hinder the use of different providers for the same service', particularly *lock-in* practices that confine the user to the intent of the digital ecosystem, precluding in whole or in part the possibility of migrating to competing platforms.

In that respect, Art. 9 l. s. would appear to contain a general clause, capable of intercepting cases additional to those more precisely described by Art. 7 DMA, which alludes to the interoperability of number-independent interpersonal communication services. From another point of view, it would seem to refer to practices that inhibit or hinder only the use of services offered by a 'different provider', but not also those that interfere with the possibility for the user to undertake to use its own sales channels.

---

[18] On this point, see Libertini (2022), pp. 1069 ff.; Manzini (2021), p. 48; Monterossi (2021), p. 951.

[19] So-called tying practices include business strategies whereby an undertaking makes the sale of one product or service (the main product or service) conditional on the purchase of another product or service (the tied product or service) that is to be used in conjunction with the first (e.g. a computer and a screen, or a car and servicing) and is offered by the same or a related undertaking.

The EU Commission—in *Guidelines on the Commission's enforcement priorities in applying Article 82 of the EC Treaty to abusive exclusionary conduct by dominant undertakings, OJEU* C 45, 24 February 2009, 7–20, pp. 47 ff.—distinguishes *tying* practices from tying and bundling. 'Tying' includes cases where customers purchase the tying product together with the tying product of the dominant undertaking. 'Bundling', on the other hand, refers to the manner in which products are offered by the dominant undertaking and the manner in which that undertaking sets the price. It is referred to as 'pure' where the products are only sold together and in fixed proportions; or 'mixed' where the products are also available separately, but where the sum of the individual selling prices is greater than the aggregate price.

4 The Coordination with the DMA

Even more controversial would seem to be the coordination of the rule prohibiting abuse of economic dependence with the DMA.[20]

It is well known, in fact, that the aforementioned European source, in an attempt to avoid the 'fragmentation of the internal market', assigns to the EU Commission the role of 'the only authority with the power to apply the Regulation' (recital 91); and '[…] is also without prejudice to the application […] of national competition rules prohibiting other forms of unilateral conduct insofar as they are applied to undertakings other than *gatekeepers* or amount to the imposition of further obligations on *gatekeepers* […]'.

In the face of such a provision, it could be considered that the application of the prohibition in question is confined to undertakings other than *gatekeepers*, provided that the rule dictated by Art. 9 l. s. is counted among the 'national competition rules'.[21] In the above-mentioned perspective, therefore, the application of the prohibition at issue would not even envisage the need for coordination between the national antitrust authority and the EU Commission, as outlined in Art. 38 DMA.

Supporting this solution, which is inclined to include the rule dictated by Art. 9 under review among the 'national competition rules', is the sentence of para *3-bis* of the aforementioned article, which admits the possible 'relevance for the protection of competition and the market' of the abuse of economic dependence; and which assigns the Competition and Market Authority the competence to ascertain the abuse as well as to impose the correlative sanctions provided for by antitrust law.[22]

This incidence supports the idea that the prohibition of abuse of economic dependence also supports the need for the proper functioning of the market, and not only the fairness of the private arrangement of interests contained in a contract between undertakings.

From another point of view, a different reading of the coordination between the opposing sources under consideration could lead to the idea that the rule prohibiting

---

[20] On the subject, Colangelo (2023), p. 3. In a broader perspective, Gentili (2024), pp. 342 ff.

Indeed, a problem of coordination also arises with reference to the aforementioned Regulation (EU) 2019/1150, 'promoting fairness and transparency for business users of online intermediation services'. As to the relationship with national laws, Art. 1(4) of the aforementioned Regulation '[…] is without prejudice to national legislation which, according to Union law, prohibits or sanctions unilateral conduct or unfair commercial practices in so far as the relevant aspects are not covered by this Regulation. This Regulation is without prejudice to national civil law'. Similarly to the DMA, therefore, Regulation No. 2019/1150 provides that, in case of overlapping, European rules apply exclusively, while national rules remain effective for the regulation of 'aspects not covered' by the Regulation.

The fundamental difference to the DMA lies, however, in the fact that Regulation 2019/1150 provides for decentralised application by the Member States.

[21] Such is the solution proposed by Libertini (2023), p. 20. On the points of contact between DMA and antitrust law, see Scalzini (2023), p. 15.

[22] On the subject, Guzzardi (2023), p. 309; Pisani Tedesco (2023), p. 194.

the abuse of economic dependence aims at protecting the 'weak' undertaking and allows for the review of the contractual balance regardless of the general requirements of competition regulation.

In this perspective, Art. 1(5) DMA could come into play, which, as is well known, allows '[…] Member States to impose obligations on undertakings, including undertakings providing basic platform services, in *matters outside the scope of this Regulation*'. At least in *private enforcement* cases entrusted to the jurisdiction, a competition between national and European law would be conceivable against a *gatekeeper* appointed by the EU Commission.

References

Agrifoglio G (2008) Abuso di dipendenza economica e asimmetria nei contratti tra imprese. Contr Impr Eur, p 1333

Albanese A (1999) Abuso di dipendenza economica: nullità del contratto e riequilibrio del rapporto. Eur dir priv, p 1179

Barba A (1998) Libertà e giustizia contrattuale. In: Studi in onore di Pietro Rescigno. Milano, III, p 298

Battelli E (2007) Servizi di telefonia e violazione della libertà di contrarre. Corr merito, p 180

Bachelet V (2023) Il rafforzamento del contrasto agli abusi di posizione "non dominante" delle piattaforme digitali. Nuove leggi civ comm, pp 39 ff

Betti E (1994) Teoria generale del negozio giuridico. Rist, 1998

Bianca CM (2019) Diritto civile. 3, Il contratto, III edn. Milano, p 405

Camardi C (2005) Contratti di consumo e contratti tra imprese. Riflessioni sull'asimmetria contrattuale nei rapporti di scambio e nei rapporti «reticolari». Riv crit dir priv, p 549

Colangelo G (2023) Regolazione dei mercati digitali e neutralità dei gatekeepers: il tramonto dell'antitrust? Il caso della dottrina dell'essential facility e della dipendenza economica, AIDA, p 3

Colangelo G, Minervini V (eds) (2023) La nuova stagione dell'abuso di dipendenza economica, Bologna

Di Lorenzo G (2009) Abuso di dipendenza economica e contratto nullo. Padova, p 37

Di Lorenzo G (2014) Contratto e divieto di discriminazione. Nuova giur civ comm I:567

Fabris D (2024) La nuova disciplina dell'abuso di dipendenza economica nei mercati digitali alla luce della direttiva Digital Copyright. Osservazioni a margine del caso Meta vs Siae. Annali it dir autore, p 769

Fabbio F (2006) L'abuso di dipendenza economica. Milano, pp 102, 126

Falce V (2021) Rapporti asimmetrici tra imprese e soluzioni pro-concorrenziali. Riv dir ind, p 189

Gentili A (2004a) De jure belli: l'equilibrio del contratto nelle impugnazioni. Riv dir civ I:40

Gentili A (2004b) Informazione contrattuale e regole dello scambio. Riv dir priv, p 557

Gentili A (2024) Le fonti del diritto d'impresa: un tentativo di sistema. Contr e impr, pp 342 ff

Guzzardi G (2023) L'abuso di posizione dominante nel mercato dei servizi digitali. Nuova giur civ comm, p 309

Irti N (1996) Intervento. In: Vettori G (ed) Persona e mercato. Padova, p 97

Licastro A (2022) La riscoperta dell'abuso di dipendenza economica nell'era dei mercati digitali. Federalismi.it

Libertini M (2022) Il Regolamento europeo sui mercati digitali e le norme generali in materia di concorrenza. Riv trim dir pubbl, pp 1069 ff

Libertini M (2023) La presunzione di dipendenza economica nei mercati digitali. Un commento all'art. 33 della l. 5 agosto 2022, n. 118. In: Orizzonti del Diritto commerciale, 1, pp 10, 20, 28, 29, 30
Lopopolo S (2024) L'abuso di dipendenza economica alla prova dei mercati digitali tra presunzione e misure cautelari. Annali it dir autore, p 151
Macario F (2005) Abuso di autonomia negoziale e disciplina dei contratti tra imprese: verso una nuova clausola generale? Riv dir civ I:683
Maffeis D (1998) Sub art. 9. In: De Nova G (ed) La subfornitura: legge 18 giugno 1998, n. 192. Milano, p 79
Manzini P (2021) Equità e contendibilità nei mercati digitali: la proposta di Digital Market Act. In: Annali della Associazione Studiosi di Diritto dell'Unione Europea, p 48
Maugeri M (2003) Abuso di dipendenza economica e autonomia privata. Milano, p 10
Meo C (2024) Dipendenza economica tra società di gestione collettiva e social networks: spunti alla luce del caso Meta c. Siae. Annali it dir autore, p 769
Messinetti R (2009) Il "falso" problema normativo della giustizia contrattuale. Riv crit dir priv, pp 615 ff
Monterossi M W (2021) La tutela dell'utente commerciale nei mercati digitali. Contr e impr, pp 919 ff e p. 951
Musso A (2003) La subfornitura, nel Commentario Scialoja-Branca, Suppl. legge 18 giugno 1998, n. 192. Bologna, p 484
Navarretta E (2014) Principio di uguaglianza, principio di non discriminazione e contratto. Riv dir civ I:566
Orlandi M (2008) Dominanza relativa e illecito commerciale. In: Gitti G, Villa G (eds) Il terzo contratto. Bologna, p 144
Pisani Tedesco A (2023) L'abuso di dipendenza economica, tra avanzamenti del Legislatore e incertezze giurisprudenziali. Nuova giur civ comm, p 194
Prosperi F (2002) Il contratto di subfornitura e l'abuso di dipendenza economica: profili ricostruttivi e sistematici. Napoli, p 269
Roppo V (2011) Il contratto, nel Trattato Iudica-Zatti, II edn. Milano, p 870
Scarso A (2006) Il contraente «debole». Torino, p 219
Scalzini S (2023) Digital Markets Act e tutela della concorrenza. Annali it dir autore, p 15
Spolidoro M S (1999) Riflessioni critiche sul rapporto fra abuso di posizione dominante e abuso dell'altrui dipendenza economica. Riv dir ind, p 204

Control Over the Act and the Regime of Invalidity

Salvatore Monticelli and Antonio di Biase

Contents

Section 1 was edited by Antonio di Biase; Section 2 by Salvatore Monticelli.

S. Monticelli (✉)
University of Naples "Parthenope", Naples, Italy
e-mail: salvatore.monticelli@uniparthenope.it

A. di Biase
University of Foggia, Foggia, Italy
e-mail: antonio.dibiase@unifg.it

R. Bocchini (ed.), *Digital Platforms - From Technical Foundations to Legal and Economic Implications*, https://doi.org/10.1007/978-3-032-07978-7_13

Abstract In a modern global economy, the widespread use of digital platforms, accelerated by the recent dramatic 'pandemic' events, has had a significant impact on the structure of the contract and requires a general reconsideration of the civil law profiles of the discipline, also with reference to the aspects, the subject of the present reflections, relating to the control over the content of the deed and the consequences of the presence of any flaws in the formation phase of the transaction.

1 Contract Formation and Invalidity Rules: The Role of Digital Platforms

1.1 Digital Platforms and Identification of the Rules of Formation of the Act: Introductory Premises

The phenomenon of digital platforms has assumed an unprecedented centrality in the global economy. Platforms are (but not limited to) digital *marketplaces*, i.e. virtual meeting spaces, which essentially play a role in facilitating and promoting the meeting of supply and demand, i.e. they represent a place where different categories of economic operators converge and cross paths, who are, so to speak, 'attracted' by this *online* space, within which a series of collateral services, so to speak, are provided by the same platforms, all aimed at achieving the final objective, in the short term, of the conclusion of the individual transaction and, in the medium to long term, of promoting and facilitating future transactions: One thinks, for example, of the possibility offered to potential buyers of goods or services to compare the various offers available, comparing their conditions; to select the product identification filter; to read the reviews left by other customers; to watch video *tutorials* on how to use and employ the chosen good; to send comments, questions and whatever else the platform allows them to do; up to the release of a *feedback* of the service received, which is the premise for future subsequent transactions.[1]

Platforms are all this and much more: one can thus have *e-commerce* platforms, which allow companies to sell their products *online* (possibly in competition not only with products of other professionals, but also with those offered by the same

[1] For more in-depth studies, the following contributions can be mentioned: Foltran (2019), p. 165; Palmieri (2019), pp. 49 ff.; Speziale (2020), pp. 441 ff.; Contaldo (2021); Camardi (2021); Battelli (2022), pp. 563 ff.; Martinelli (2023); Pisani (2023); Irti (2024), pp. 5 ff.; Ruffolo (2024), pp. 442 ff.

platform); *streaming* platforms, aimed at the provision of audiovisual services; intermediation in the encounter between labour demand and supply, so-called freelance platforms; collaborative or shared economy, where parties rent and 'share' movable or immovable goods; social media, allow users from all over the world to rent and 'share' movable or immovable goods; social media, which would enable users from all over the world to use the platform for the provision of audiovisual services; and social media, which allow users from all over the world to use the platform for the provision of services; so-called *freelance* platforms; collaborative or *shared* economy platforms, where parties rent and 'share' movable or immovable goods; *social media platforms*, allow users from all over the world to connect and interact with each other, sharing information and content of various kinds, and so on.

These platforms may also envisage the intervention of third parties, who may carry out a series of additional and related activities, such as, for instance, providing faster and safer payment instruments (so-called payment platforms), additional forms of guarantee for any faults or defects in the goods, technical and after-sales services, and even forms of financing for the acquisition of the good or service. Or, like *crowdfunding* platforms, they can be aimed at promoting collective actions, such as fundraising for certain purposes, whether entrepreneurial or charitable. Other times, the platform operator itself directly offers goods and services in competition with those offered by professional users, acquiring the position of a real contractual partner. Also fundamental is the role of data analysis played by platforms, i.e. the collection and analysis of the data of users accessing them. *Big data*.

Without going into detail on the subject, the concept of *online* platform is therefore difficult to define, encompassing a potentially unlimited series of services, even considerably different from each other, the purpose of which is to facilitate the meeting and interaction between users, or to facilitate the access and dissemination of data, or even the exchange of goods, services or content of various kinds: The 'globality', complexity and dimension of the phenomenon makes platforms, and the relationships established through them, difficult to catalogue and identify the applicable legal framework: according to some, even, digital platforms would be '*over the top*', i.e. above the laws and sovereignty of individual states.[2]

That being said, the increasing diffusion of services offered by *online* platforms has radically transformed the way goods and services are acquired, leading to the emergence of new contractual models and, above all, new ways of forming the agreement and, more generally, deviations from the 'traditional' schemes of contract law. Generally, contracts entered into with or through digital (or *online*) platforms are contracts entered into and concluded in peculiar ways, i.e. through computer and telematic means and, above all, in an 'aterritorial' and 'supranational' place, with no time or space,[3] which is the *web*, removed from the possibility of

[2] In this regard, there has been talk of a crisis of public governance of the economy and the emergence of a self-regulating commercial contract law that can no longer be circumscribed within predefined territorial boundaries. Thus, variously: Draetta (2001), pp. 57 ff.; Rosciano (2002), pp. 559 ff.

[3] Thus, Irti (1998), pp. 347 ff.; Irti (2001).

exact identification and geopolitical connotation. Many contractual models are used, both to regulate relations between the subjects that 'meet' on the platform, i.e. the suppliers of goods and services and the buyers/users of the same (horizontal relations); and to regulate relations between the platform itself and its users (vertical relations)—a topic, that of the identification of negotiation models, is outside the scope of this contribution.

What is important for the present work is to highlight that the now 'massive' use of digital platforms, accelerated by the recent and dramatic 'pandemic' events, has had a significant impact on the structure of the contract and requires a general reconsideration of the civil law profiles of the discipline, also with reference to the phase, the subject of the present reflections, of the control over the content of the deed and the consequences of the presence of any flaws in the formation phase of the transaction. In the context of platforms, the legal analysis of the invalidity of digital contracts and the related controls is developed through the lens of several issues: the difficulty at times of applying the traditional rules on invalidity in a context characterised by constantly evolving technologies; the balance between contractual freedom and the need to protect the most vulnerable parties; the growing concern for the protection of consumer rights, and so on.

The answer to the question of the problem of control over the act and the invalidity regime passes through the analysis of at least three orders of problems, logically and chronologically succeeding one another: (*a*) first, there is the need to identify the sources that can dictate *rules on the content of* the contract or the deed in general; (*b*) second, to identify the *consequences* that derive from the violation of these rules and in particular to verify whether, in addition to compensatory consequences (more easily hypothesised), demolishing effects on the deed are also conceivable; (*c*) finally, to investigate the *subjects* and *authorities* required to verify compliance with the rules.

The following comments are devoted to the second and third of the above questions.

1.2 New Contract Formation Rules Between Technological Innovation and User Protection

Before addressing *funditus* the issue of control over the deed and the invalidity regime, it is necessary to make a very brief premise regarding the identification of the most significant sources that dictate rules on the formation of the deed, the violation of which must then be investigated to determine what consequences it leads to. The preliminary issue, therefore, is that of identifying the sources, which, evidently—given the already highlighted 'trans-territoriality' and 'globality' of digital platforms—cannot be (only) national ones, but must be sought, in the absence of regulation at a global level, primarily at a European level. In any case, even if the platforms can be considered as private subjects operating within a transnational space with planetary extension, it obviously appears impossible to deny, at least for the 'portion' or contractual phase that exerts its effects on EU territory, the application of the discipline dictated by the European Union, as well as the rules of the domestic law of the individual states concerned.

With regard to the Community discipline, it should be mentioned that after years of *deregulation*, the European legislator has recently issued a series of regulations that, with a view to containing the phenomenon of 'gigantism'[4] of the *corporations* that dominate the digital market, aim to set limits, obligations and responsibilities for operators (in some cases in proportion to their size) in order to allow the efficient application of technological innovations, while protecting the interests of users and, more generally, of the users of digital platforms.

Since it is impossible here to make an exhaustive survey and to limit ourselves to the most significant regulations, our thoughts turn, first of all, to the European Regulation 2019/1150/EU (so-called *platform-to-business* regulation) aimed at promoting 'fairness and transparency for business users of online intermediation services',[5] which lays down rules on the act—i.e. at the stage of contract formation between *online* intermediation service providers and businesses that use platforms to offer goods and services to the public—providing that the contract must have a certain mandatory 'minimum' content.[6]

Again with regard to the control over the contract formation phase, particularly the removal of information asymmetries between the parties, mention must be made of the so-called *Digital Service Act*, i.e. European Regulation 2022/2065/EU of 19 October 2022 on the single market for digital services, which became fully enforceable on 17 February 2024, which, with a view to promoting a single market for digital services and the protection of users, introduces new obligations for platforms that impact on the content of individual contracts.[7] This legislation, together with the so-called *Digital Market Act*, i.e. Regulation 2022/1925/EU on fair and contestable markets in the digital sector, is part of the so-called *Digital Service* Package, i.e. a 'package' of regulations that has the general twofold objective, on the one hand, to create a safer and more secure digital space, and, on the other, to promote

[4] An expression that probably goes back to Camardi (2023), pp. 59 ff. A 'gigantism'—warns Irti (2024), p. 8—that 'not only occupies market spaces, but ends up occupying spaces of freedom'.

[5] For an initial commentary, see Ruggieri (2021), pp. 397 ff.

[6] Article 8 provides that 'In order to ensure that contractual relations between online brokering service providers and business users are conducted in good faith and with fairness, online brokering service providers: *(a)* not impose retrospective changes to their terms and conditions, except where they are required to comply with a legal or regulatory obligation or where retrospective changes are beneficial to business users; *(b)* ensure that their terms and conditions include information on the conditions under which business users may terminate their contractual relationship with the *online* intermediary service provider and (c) include in their terms and conditions a description of the technical and contractual access, or lack of such access, to the information provided or generated by the business user, which they retain after the expiry of the contract between the online brokering service provider and the business user'.

[7] For more details, see Stucchi (n.d.). See also Casolari (2024), pp. 462 ff.

a level playing field for the development of innovation, growth and competitiveness in both the European and global single market.

Particularly, as regards what is of interest here, it is important to recall that, with a view to the broader protection of a principle of transparency and 'good information', Art. 14 of Regulation 2022/2065/EU imposes an obligation on intermediary service providers to include, in their general terms and conditions of contract, a series of information 'on the restrictions they impose in relation to the use of their services with regard to the information provided by the recipients of the service'. This information—which may concern, for example, 'the policies, procedures, measures and tools used for content moderation purposes, including algorithmic decision-making and human verification, as well as the procedural rules of their internal complaint handling system'—must be drafted using 'clear, simple, understandable, easily usable and unambiguous language' and must also be made available to the public 'in an easily accessible and machine-readable format'.

1.3 Standardisation of Contracts and the **'Point and Click'** *Rule: General Terms and Conditions and Nullity* **Under** *Article 1341 of the Civil Code*

Once the rules on the act have been established, the problem arises in identifying the *consequences* of violating these rules, particularly the possibility of identifying demolition remedies, as well as compensation for damages.

Circumscribing the investigation to the consequences of invalidity due to original defects of the deed, the traditional civil law categories of invalidity must be reconsidered and reinterpreted in the light of a type of contract that is very different and varied, but which has the common trait of negotiation and/or stipulation at a distance and using telematic instruments. What we wish to make clear right away is that, although the civil law categories remain the same, a considerable hermeneutic effort must be made to adapt them to the peculiarities of the *online* contract: just to give an easily understandable example, think of the question relating to the form of the contract, which in the context of digitalisation has undergone a profound rethinking and has been affected by regulations aimed at ensuring full equivalence of the 'dematerialised' form to the written form.[8]

It is also necessary to distinguish between bargaining relationships in relation to which platforms are third parties, merely acting as a 'virtual shop window', i.e. 'hosting' and enabling, so to speak, the conclusion of contracts between other parties; and bargaining in which platforms take on the role of bargaining counterparty, offering goods and services in competition with other professional users, and which in turn are divided into *platform-to-business (P2B)* models, characterised by bargaining in which the counterparty of the platform operator is also a businessman or

[8] For more details, see, *ex plurimis*, Berti de Martinis (2013), pp. 67 ff.; Battelli (2022), p. 565.

trader; and *platform-to-consumer (P2C)* models, in which the counterparty is a *cyber* user consumer.

Within the sphere of contracts concluded by third parties by means of platforms—also distinguishable, from a subjective point of view, in contracts between professionals (*B2B*) or between professionals and consumers (*B2C*), to which are added contracts in which both parties are consumers (*C2C*)—the so-called peer-to-peer platform models, the 'collaborative' or 'sharing economy', in which subjects, all formally consumers, participate to satisfy needs outside the performance of their professional activity, are particularly important. Models of *peer-to-peer platform*, of 'collaborative' or '*shared*' economy, in which the subjects, all formally consumers, participate to satisfy needs unrelated to the performance of a professional activity: one thinks, for example, of the *AirB&B* sharing platform, a short-term accommodation service that allows one to place an advertisement for the rental of a house or a room, thus coming into contact with people who wish to rent it.

These distinctions are important because, as will be seen in a moment, alongside a common discipline, of general application to all contracts, the profile of invalidity is also influenced by the application of sectoral regulations, with particular reference to consumer protection.

As to the rules of universal application that may affect the validity of the deed, one may assume a broad use of the rules set forth in Articles 1341 and 1342 of the Civil Code, given the generalised unilateral drafting of contractual clauses by the supplier of the goods or services, without any possibility for the user to intervene on its content.[9]

And if the requirement of knowability *under* Art. 1341(1) of *the Ci*vil Code—which is pendant, on the subject of e-commerce contracts, Art. 12(3) of Legislative Decree No. 70/2003, pursuant to which the clauses and the general terms and conditions of the contract proposed to the addressee 'must be made available to him in such a way that he is allowed to memorise and reproduce them'—is substantially complied with the publication on the platform of the general terms and conditions of the contract, provided that they are expressly referred to by means of links or other direct connections (it is difficult to consider the *requirement* of knowability pursuant to Art. 1341 of the Civil Code as comp*lied with in th*e case where, for example, the general terms and conditions are only traceable through a tortuous and non-intuitive virtual path). In the event that, for example, the general terms and conditions are only traceable through a tortuous and non-intuitive virtual path[10], a serious problem of nullity/ineffectiveness may arise,[11] pursuant to the second paragraph of the rule, of unbalancing clauses, such as those limiting the liability of the

[9] General Terms and Conditions which, pursuant to Art. 3 of Regulation 1150/2019/EU, must be drafted in simple, comprehensible language and easily available, also in pre-contractual terms.

[10] In this case, according to the general rules, general terms and conditions that are not cognisable would not form part of the content of the contract, would be considered *tamquam non esset* and would have to be disapplied, even ex officio, by the court.

[11] This is certainly not the place to deal with the question of the identification of the exact consequences resulting from the non-signing of the clause *under* Art. 1341(2) of the Civil Code, with

platform,[12] or which give the latter the power to suspend or terminate users' *accounts* on the basis of generic and standardised reasons, or which provide for the tacit renewal of the service in the absence of express termination, to be communicated within predetermined time limits. These clauses, pursuant to general civil law, should probably be considered null and void if not previously and specifically signed, by means of a digital signature or other equivalent means, by the user, for which purpose the mere '*click*' of approval of the contractual text[13] does not seem sufficient.

In fact, it is held that although the '*point and click*' technique, i.e. the ticking of the virtual negotiation button, represents the concluding behaviour expressive of the intention to conclude the contract and is the moment in which the will of the contractual parties meets, thus perfecting the contract itself.[14] This mode of operation is sufficient, for the purposes of validity, only in the case of a free-form transaction, i.e. a contract for which the law does not require a different form. When, on the other hand, as in the case of unfair *terms under* Art. 1341 of the Civil Code, when, on the other hand, as in the case of unfair terms under Art. 1341 of the Civil Code, written form is required for the validity of the agreement, it should not be sufficient merely to press or 'tick' the 'I accept' (or similar) button, but a specific further activity will be required, such as the affixing of a digital signature or other equivalent instrument, which must in some way precede the '*click*' on the '*I accept*' button: This is because the affixing of a digital signature constitutes an activity subsequent to the *online* acceptance of the contract proposal, an activity that must necessarily be performed *offline* and at a time prior to the actual acceptance.

This solution, although to some extent 'proceduralising' the conclusion of the contract, providing for a further activity that may constitute an obstacle to the speed of digital commercial transactions, nevertheless seems to the writer to be preferred—because it better guarantees the position of the adhering party—to an

reference to the following fundamental doctrinal contributions: Genovese (1954), pp. 232 et seq.; Dossetto (1959), III, 1112; Ferri (1977), pp. 11 et seq.

[12] On the question of the validity of the liability limitation clauses of the major *online* platforms, such as *Google*, *Amazon* and *Facebook*, see Alpa (2022), pp. 733 ff.

[13] In this sense, Trib. Catanzaro 30 April 2012, in *Resp. civ. prev.*, 2013, 2015 ss., with a note by De Leo (2013), pp. 2015 ff, which ruled on the vexatiousness (inter alia) for lack of specific signature *pursuant to* Art. 1341 of the Civil Code of a clause, contained in the general terms and conditions of the contract between the *eBay* platform and a professional user, which gave the *provider* the power to unilaterally withdraw from the contract in the event of a serious breach by the counterparty of the rules on 'Seller's breach' present on the portal *www.ebay.it.* The issue had arisen because *eBay* had suspended the seller's *account* by invoking the aforementioned clause contained in the 'User Agreement' generically accepted by the counterparty, in telematic mode, at the time of registration on the platform. The Court, in declaring the nullity of the clause, expressly stated that 'in free-form telematic contracts, the contract is perfected by means of the virtual negotiation key, but the vexatious clauses will be effective and binding only if specifically approved with a digital signature'. Giudice di Pace di Partanna, 1 February 2002, no. 15, in www.altalex.it. On this point see, among others: Minussi (2006), pp. 445 ff.; Ventrella (2013), pp. 9 ff.

[14] For more details on this *online* contract conclusion technique, see Sforza (1997), p. 89; Cassano (2005), p. 186.

opposite solution, which considers it sufficient, for the purposes of the validity *under* Art. 1341 of the Civil Code of the vexatious clause, the affixing of a double *click* on the special virtual button by the adherent: a first *click* for the purpose of acceptance of the contract *in its entirety*, a second *click* for the purpose of approval of the specific vexatious clause (or a specific *click* for each vexatious clause).[15]

Finally, a peculiar hypothesis of nullity was then introduced by Art. 3 del Regolamento 1150/2019/UE, nel caso in cui le condizioni generali di contratto predisposte dai fornitori di servizi di intermediazione *online* non rispettino anche uno dei seguenti requisiti, ossia: non siano redatte in un linguaggio semplice e comprensibile; non siano facilmente reperibili dagli utenti commerciali in tutte le fasi del loro rapporto commerciale con il fornitore di servizi di intermediazione *online*, anche in fase precontrattuale (con ciò ricalcando quanto previsto, nel nostro Paese, dal già citato comma 1 dell'art. 1341 c.c.); do not indicate the reasons justifying decisions to suspend, cease or otherwise limit, in whole or in part, the provision of *online* brokering services to business users; do not include information on any additional distribution channels and potential affiliate programmes through which *online* brokering service providers may market the products and services offered by business users; finally, do not contain general information on the effects of the terms and conditions on the ownership and control of business users' intellectual property rights. Furthermore, pursuant to the aforementioned provision, all clauses amending the general terms and conditions that are effective before the expiry of a reasonable period, not less than 15 days, during which the user is entitled to terminate the contract, shall be null and void.

In all these cases, specific partial nullity cases apply in contracts where one of the parties is a provider of *online* brokering services,[16] and the other party is a business user, i.e. a professional, natural or legal person.

[15]Thesis upheld, for example, by the Justice of the Peace of Partanna, 1 February 2002, no. 15, in *Contr.*, 2002, 869 ff., with note by Cassano and Cimmino (2002), p. 869. For further discussion see, among others: Minussi (2006), pp. 445 ff.; Ventrella (2013), pp. 13 ff.

[16]That is, according to Art. 2 of the Regulation, 'a natural or legal person who provides, or offers to provide, online brokering services to business users'. *Online* intermediation services' means, according to the same provision, 'services that meet all of the following requirements: (a) they are information society services within the meaning of Article 1(1)(b) of Directive (EU) 2015/1535 of the European Parliament and of the Council; (b) they enable business users to offer goods or services to consumers, with the aim of facilitating the initiation of direct transactions between those business users and consumers, regardless of where those transactions are concluded; (c) they are provided to business users on the basis of contractual relationships between the provider of those services and the business users offering goods and services to consumers'.

1.4 Platforms and Consumer Protection: Nullity Protection and the Role of the 'Prosumer'

In the event that the contract entered into *with the* platform or *through* the platform sees as counterparty a person qualifying as a consumer—i.e. as is well known, a natural person acting for purposes unrelated to any entrepreneurial, commercial, handicraft or professional activity carried on—the rules, including those on the invalidity of the act, change significantly. There can be no doubt, in fact, that the contract concluded between professionals—which category also includes platforms, whenever they take on the role of contractual counterparties—and consumers, including through *online* brokerage services, is drawn within the scope of application of the European legislation on consumer contracts, transposed in Italy mainly with Legislative Decree No. 206/2005, the so-called Code of Conduct for the sale of consumer goods.

This discipline, in fact, is applicable to all contracts between professionals and consumers regardless of the medium—in person or *online*—used, and thus both to contracts concluded between any consumer and a professional 'meeting' in the telematic platform and to the relationship between the consumer and the platform operator for access or use thereof. Added to this is the circumstance that contracts concluded with or through platforms certainly fall within the macro-category of distance contracts, i.e. those concluded without the simultaneous physical presence of the professional and the consumer,[17] for which the specific regulations set forth in Art. 45 et seq. of Legislative Decree No. 206/2005 may also be invoked.

Thus, and remaining on the subject of invalidity, one can hypothesise the application of the discipline *pursuant to* Art. 33 et seq. of Legislative Decree No. 206/2005 to obtain the declaration of *nullity* (*of protection*) of a series of vexatious clauses, such as, to hypothesise the most frequent, those concerning the platform's liability exemption or limitations, or concerning the right of withdrawal of the strong party alone, the competent court, the possibility of unilateral amendment of the contract by the platform alone, and so forth. In this perspective, doubts of validity may also concern the so-called *bundling* clauses, through which the contracting parties undertake to avail themselves exclusively of certain services connected to the platform's activity and offered by the latter, such as electronic payment systems, communication channels or logistics.

Moreover: the so-called 'warranty clauses', often included in the general contractual terms and conditions, by means of which specific limitations and/or exclusions of the guarantee of quality, proper functioning or suitability, with respect to a given purpose, of a certain good or service are introduced, must be carefully scrutinised on the basis of the principles and rules just mentioned. In the same perspective of the protection of the adherent, all those clauses can be considered as 'smelling' of unfairness that in some way predetermine the damage that can be indemnified in the event of non-performance or in relation to certain breaches, quantifying and

[17] As defined in Art. 45(1)(g) of Legislative Decree 206/2005.

limiting it to amounts lower than what normally occurs in reality, or even excluding the indemnifiability of damages that are technically defined as 'indirect'.

This form of protection, it should be pointed out, is guaranteed to the weaker party in the relationship even if the platform or other professional in question, at the time of the stipulation, 'chooses', as the applicable law, a law other than that of the state in which the consumer/user resides: this option, although legitimate, cannot in fact deprive the consumer of the greater protection that may be provided by the legislation of the state of residence, since Art. 6 of Regulation No. 593/2008 of the European Parliament and Council of 17 June 2008 on the law applicable to contractual obligations (the so-called 'Rome Regulation') provides that the parties may derogate from the rule that the law applicable to the contract of the consumer/user is the law of the state in which the contract is concluded. Regulation No. 593/2008 of the European Parliament and of the Council of 17 June 2008 on the law applicable to contractual obligations (the 'Rome Regulation') provides that the parties may derogate from the rule that the law applicable to the consumer's contract is the law of the country in which the consumer has his habitual residence, provided that this derogation does not deprive the consumer of the protection granted to him by the mandatory rules of his national law.

Similarly, on the subject of jurisdiction, Articles 17 ff. of Regulation (EU) 1215/2012 reaffirm the right of the consumer to bring proceedings against a professional before the authorities of the state of domicile.

Lastly, mention must be made of the question, which to date has not yet found an unequivocal solution, concerning the qualification, as consumers or not, for the application of the relevant protectionist legislation, of the so-called 'producer-consumers', or, using a term that is so fashionable today, 'prosumers', i.e. those web operators who play an active role in the offer of goods or services, even though they act outside the scope of the protectionist legislation. *Producer-consumers*, or, using a term nowadays so much in vogue, '*prosumers*', i.e. those *web* operators who play an active role in the offer of goods or services, although acting outside of a business activity in the strict sense of the word and therefore cannot be technically qualified as 'professionals'. These are, in other words, subjects of the so-called 'digital and collaborative economy', or 'shared economy' (sharing economy in English), who, although not organised in the form of a company, through *online* platforms likewise exercise an activity directed at offering goods or services to the community.[18] Just to

[18] For more on the notion of *prosumers*, please refer to the extensive Anglo-Saxon literature on the subject, including the following contributions: Ritzer and Jurghenson (2010), pp. 13 ff. In Italy, we refer, *ex plurimis*, to Quarta (2017), pp. 667 ff.; Foltran (2019), pp. 164 and 170, who stresses that the qualification of *prosumers* as professionals 'would produce disincentive effects, for instance, for platforms dedicated to the *sharing economy*, burdening *prosumers* with obligations in some respects contrary to the very philosophy underlying the sharing economy; on the other hand, especially in the case of mixed-sharing platforms, the exclusion of the application of the consumer code would deprive the consumer of some important guarantees. This could lead to a loss of confidence in such services if the nature of the negotiating counterparty and its consequences are not adequately disclosed - prior to the conclusion of the transaction'. Lastly, see Bocchini (2021), pp. 246 ff.

give an easily perceptible example, think of the figure of the '*private host*' in the digital platform *Airbnb*, who, while not professionally carrying out the activity of renting flats, nevertheless often acts in the platform in an increasingly structured, organised and 'consciously informed' manner, offering the service of renting houses or rooms in competition with professionals: In such a situation, one wonders whether it is really reasonable to treat this subject as a consumer, as he formally is—and therefore to apply to his contractual relationship with users exclusively the codified discipline of common law—or whether, on the contrary, to the contract stipulated between this subject and any user of the network, who is perhaps looking for accommodation for his own seaside holiday, it would not be fairer to apply the consumer protection legislation.

This has obvious consequences with regard to the invalidity of the contract and the applicability or otherwise of the system of protective nullity.

1.5 The Nullity of Contracts Concluded Through Digital Platforms Between 'Ordinary' and 'Special' Invalidity Hypotheses

The question of the applicability or otherwise of consumer legislation—with the grey areas relating, as we have seen, to the 'hybrid' figure of *producer-consumers*—is intertwined with another question, namely that the causes of invalidity of the contract concluded with or through digital platforms can be traced back to two different categories: the *ordinary* one, so to speak, which refers to the traditional civil law hypotheses of nullity and/or annulment; the *special* one, that is, deriving from the peculiarities of this particular category of contract. The field of investigation of the interpreter is therefore twofold, as the interpreter must ascertain, on the one hand, whether the general rules on invalidity are logically also applicable to contracting through telematic platforms; on the other hand, whether and what are the possible deviations from the common law rules.

With regard to the first question, it is hard to see why the possibility should be excluded that the contract under consideration presents grounds for nullity under Art. 1418 of the Civil Code, such as the unlawfulness of the cause and/or object, as in the case of *online* sales of pornographic material concerning minors, or material inciting racial hatred or discrimination in general, the commission of crimes, terrorism and so on. Think again of the possibility of the application of the codictic discipline on the subject of nullity of the transaction in fraud against the law in the case of telematic contracts concluded in violation of mandatory rules.[19]

[19] The opposite is expressed by part of the doctrine, which arrives at the peremptory affirmation that, unlike traditional contracts, the *smart contract* cannot be affected by grounds for nullity. Tommasini (2022), p. 4.

It may be more difficult, however, to imagine *in rerum natura* a nullity of the *online* contract due to the impossibility or vagueness of the object, but nothing detracts from the theoretical applicability of this nullity hypothesis as well.

In contracting with or by means of a digital platform, specific hypotheses of nullity will then be conceivable, which cannot be configured in the common discipline of the contract. For example, the hypothesis of the nullity of a signature with a digital signature in cases in which the person who has disavowed the signature proves that it was affixed in an abusive manner (e.g. in the case in which a person steals the *smart card* or other device from its owner, or uses the owner's '*user id*' and '*password*' without authorisation[20]) by a person other than the owner of the certificate;[21] or to cases where an agreement signed with the affixing of a digital signature *tamquam non esset*, because it is based on a revoked, expired or suspended electronic certificate.[22]

In fact, the digital signature, unlike the handwritten signature, is not materially inseparable from the person and the text to which it is affixed, so that it lends itself, more than the latter, to being affixed by third parties and thus to questions of 'authorship' of the document.[23]

In such cases, on closer inspection, there is a delicate question of balancing the interests of, on the one hand, the person who suffers an abusive use of the signature and, on the other hand, the recipient of the declaration, who legitimately relies on the origin of the declaration by the person who appears to be its author. A balanced solution could be to start from a sort of *iuris tantum* presumption of the provenance of the digital signature by its owner, who could 'reject' the effects of the act and have it declared null and void only where he proves not only the abusive use of the device, but also that he has correctly fulfilled the obligations of diligent preservation of the signature and protection of the *software* that the law, particularly Art. 32 of

[20] On the other hand, the different hypothesis in which the third party has been legitimised by the proprietor to use the electronic device but has done so in contravention of the instructions given to him by the proprietor does not seem to be able to be traced back to the abusive use of the signature, because, in this case, 'there remains a connection between the key holder and the manifestation of will, even if the latter is expressed in a different manner'. Thus, Gentili and Battelli (2012), pp. 419–431.

[21] Trib. Roma 23 January 2017, no. 1127, in *www.dejure,it,* decided in this sense, according to which Art. 21, para 2, of the digital admissions code places the burden of proving that the digital signature was not affixed on the person who disavows the signature. Once the required proof is provided, the contract signed by a person other than the holder of the digital signature certificate must be declared null and void. In doctrine, for more details see Ciacci (2002) pp. 67 ff.; Gentili and Battelli (2012), pp. 419 ff. Denying the possibility of a disavowal of the digital signature, among others, Graziosi (1998), pp. 515 ff.

[22] Hypothesis expressly contemplated by the repealed Art. 21(3) of Legislative Decree No. 82/2005 (CAD).

[23] For further discussion, see Di Benedetto (2009), pp. 331 ff.

the CAD,[24] imposes on him.[25] Nullity in these cases would have to be declared pursuant to the second paragraph of Art. 1418 of the Civil Code, for lack of agreement, since there is no will on the part of one of the parties;[26]or, according to a possible alternative reconstruction, pursuant to the first paragraph of the same rule, for violation of the mandatory rule, of a penal nature, in this case Art. 494 of the Criminal Code, which would prohibit such conduct.[27]

A solution that is even more respectful of the third party's innocent trust and the principle of the free circulation of goods and rights could be that of considering, in the case of abusive use by third parties of the digital signature, the contract invalid only where the absence of a legitimate trust in the validity of the act on the part of the other party is also demonstrated, who, if he had acted diligently and carefully, could have realised the real situation and 'unmasked' the abuse. Since, however, it is fair to imagine that such proof is very difficult to provide, in the writer's opinion this thesis would de facto always render the abusive use of the digital signature unenforceable against the other party and would end up by binding to the contract, always and in any event, a person who, it must not be forgotten, did not participate in any way in the deed.

1.6 The Annulment of the Contract

As to the hypotheses of the annulment of the contract, it is difficult to conceive the existence of the prerequisites for the applicability of the remedy of annulment on the ground of incapacity *pursuant to* Art. 428 of the Civil Code, if only because it appears difficult to imagine the counterparty's bad faith, in view of the peculiar modalities of conclusion of this type of contract, which takes place at a distance and with 'depersonalised' modalities, which make it extremely difficult to find detailed

---

[24] Pursuant to the first paragraph of Art. 32 of Legislative Decree No. 82/2005, in fact, 'the holder of the signature certificate is required to ensure the safekeeping of the signature device or of the computer authentication tools for the use of the signature device remotely, and to adopt all organisational and technical measures suitable for avoiding harm to others; he is also required to use the signature device personally'.

[25] Gentili and Battelli (2012), p. 423, among others, consider the filing of a false claim to be necessary.

[26] According to Rizzo (2004), p. 404, on the other hand, in such cases the contract would be voidable under Art. 1429(2) on the ground of an essential mistake as to the identity of the other contracting party.

[27] Pursuant to Art. 494 of the criminal code, which punishes the offence of substitution of person, the offence is punished as follows: 'Whoever, in order to procure for himself or for others an advantage or to cause damage to others, misleads someone by unlawfully substituting his own person for the person of another, or by attributing to himself or to others a false name, or a false status, or a quality to which the law attributes legal effects'. See Nappi (1989).

information on the user (beyond, of course, those relating to generalities and those voluntarily entered by the latter) and, therefore, to perceive his possible natural incapacity. In other words, it is plausible to imagine that one of two things is possible: either the subject, despite his incapacity, succeeds in correctly completing the telematic path envisaged, 'clicking' correctly on the required settings and filling in exactly the *format* present on the site, and then there can probably be no room for recognition and consequent exploitation of the incapacity; or the subject, perhaps because of his incapacity, fails to enter the required data and complete the telematic path, and then the contract is not even concluded. Without taking into account that it is often possible to imagine the absence of the other requirement of Art. 428 of the Civil Code, i.e. the presence of the serious prejudice deriving from the bargain for the incapacitated person, at least with reference to the 'micro bargains' that take place daily via the *web*.

Having clarified this, for other cases of voidability, it will be a matter of applying common law principles, but adapting them to the peculiarities of this particular instrument, that is, the contract concluded with or by means of telematic platforms.[28]

One thinks, for instance, of the rules on the annulment of the contract following the peculiar vice of consent represented by the *error*: in the case of contracts concluded through digital platforms, both the traditional hypotheses of 'vice error' and 'obstruction error' are conceivable. Consider, in the first case, a person who, due to an error in the process of forming the will, purchases a good other than the one actually wanted (e.g. an imitation instead of an original work of art); in the second case, a person who, when placing an order *online*, mistakenly enters a datum that does not correspond to the real one.

Here, too, the general codictic discipline must come to the interpreter's aid, and thus such errors may lead to the annulment of the contract only if there is proof of

[28] On the subject of contract annulment, it was generally noted that the discipline outlined by the civil code appears difficult to apply to *smart contracts*, at least to those inserted in *blockchain*: 'the content of the blocks of the chain, once they have been validated by the *miners*, cannot be modified. The immutability of the computer code, made valid by the other nodes of the chain, appears hardly compatible with the possibility of subsequent external intervention; hence, the doubts about the governability of *smart contracts* through ordinary civil law remedies'. Thus, Proto (n.d.), who considers that a possible solution 'could be found through recourse to the so-called *kill code*, a function capable of definitively removing the blockade from the chain, which can be activated by the parties jointly or by the party that has victoriously asserted its reasons in court. Through the removal of the block, the *kill code* would make it possible to restore the situation prior to the conclusion of the *smart contract*; leaving open, however, the problem relative to the rights acquired by third parties in good faith'.

the recognisability[29] and essentiality[30] of the same. With the clarification that—if the information has been correctly and exhaustively disclosed—it will not be easy to prove the existence of these prerequisites, with particular reference to that of recognisability, it being legitimate to presume, on the contrary, that the seller's reliance on the validity of the contract derives from the buyer having correctly completed the purchase procedure. In other words, if the information was provided correctly and the user made the purchase by carrying out the operations required by the platform, then it would appear difficult to assume and prove that his counterpart, notwithstanding this, realised the essential error which the user had incurred.

Coming to specific hypotheses that are peculiar to the sector, different solutions could be reached in cases where an error occurs in the transmission of the order or data resulting from an alteration made by the *provider* or, more generally, from defects in the operation of the programme or platform: imagine, for instance, the situation in which a malfunction of the *software* used causes an *e-mail* or other declaration to be sent to a person other than the one to whom the declarant's will was addressed. In these cases, a fair balancing of the opposing interests could be found in the application of the well-known principle, elaborated by jurisprudence and doctrine, of the 'culpable appearance'.[31] In the light of which, without prejudice to any liability for damages on the part of the third party, the contract would generally be invalid (because it was not intended or not intended under those conditions), being capable of being upheld only where the declarant's culpable conduct is proved to have given rise to a legitimate expectation on the part of the other party as to the validity of the contract.[32]

---

[29] The doctrine has pointed out that the requirement of the recognisability of the mistake is different in the case of professional users or consumers: in the former case, in fact, 'the requirement of recognisability may be considered to be easily fulfilled and therefore the annulment of the contract may be requested; in the latter case this eventuality must be considered to be more difficult to realise empirically'. Thus, Bevivino (2024), pp. 407–408. This is so because—Tommasini (2022), p. 4—if the party receiving the message is a professional to analyse the requirement of recognisability, a greater effort is required of him than that required of an 'ordinary' person, and this in consideration of the circumstance that a professional in the sector can more easily understand 'the logical procedures that the programme carries out and study its algorithms'. If, on the other hand, the user is a person 'who does not know the computer language or the logical processes that cause the computer to generate the declaration and is not capable of carrying out any *reverse engineering* operations, it will be almost impossible for him to notice any errors in the processing or transmission of the *smart contract*. The non-professional user, therefore, will be unable to do anything if the error is not recognisable from the transmitted text or other forms of *output*'.

[30] As for the requirement of the essential nature of the error, it has been held that this poses fewer problems than the requirement of recognisability, and this inasmuch as 'it will be necessary to verify, in a wholly syllogistic manner, whether the concrete hypothesis taken into consideration and verified in practice, with reference to the pathological process of the formation of the will, corresponds to the abstract hypotheses taken into consideration by the legislature'. Thus, Bevivino (2024), p. 408.

[31] Without being able to give any account here of the very extensive bibliography on this point, we refer to the following encyclopaedic entries: Besson and Di Paolo (1988), pp. 1 ff.; D'Amelio (1957), pp. 714 ff.; Falzea (1958), pp. 682 ff.; Moschella (1973).

[32] For further interesting insights, see Gentili and Battelli (2012), pp. 403 ff.

Conversely, the application of the rules on the cancellation of a contract could not reasonably be invoked in the hypotheses in which an *e-mail* proposing or accepting a telematic contract is sent, by mistake of the sender himself, since on the contrary a principle of self-responsibility of the social meaning of one's declarations and, consequently, of acceptance of the 'computer risk' applies, whereby the user who decides to carry out any telematic transaction accepts the rules of the chosen negotiating instrument and will be bound according to the rules of the negotiating instrument used.

Again, in the different case of an error in the execution of the order resulting from an erroneous calculation operation performed by the seller's programme or by the platform, one might think of having recourse to the discipline on the subject of the rectification of the contract pursuant to Art. 1430 of the Civil Code and thus consider that such a counting error may give rise, as a rule, to a mere rectification of the contract.[33] Obviously, the simpler the contract that the machine has to process, the fewer combinations of instructions that have to be provided and, consequently, the less chance of errors.[34]

Scrolling through the other hypotheses of defects of will, as to ***malice***, part of the doctrine has pointed out that, since the so-called 'smart contracts' of e-commerce are *self-executing*, there would be no room for such a defect of consent, as well as for violence, since they would be difficult to reconcile with the automatisms that characterise this type of contract.[35]

Against this reconstruction, however, it may be objected that, even if technological translation takes place by activating a mechanical and automatic process, these vices, particularly wilful misconduct, may nevertheless intervene in the phase of the formation of the will, leading to the expression of a consent that is neither free nor conscious: therefore *to* exclude a priori the application *tout* court of the rules on violence and wilful misconduct seems, in the opinion of the writer, an apriorism that is difficult to justify.

Thus, there is nothing to prevent the possibility of the occurrence of artifices and deceptions, whether decisive or incidental, perpetrated through the use of new

---

[33] For more details, see Perlingieri (2011), pp. 320 ff.; Bevivino (2024), pp. 409–410.

[34] See Tommasini (2022).

[35] Thus, Tommasini (2022), who specifies that, if anything, violence or malice could be exercised on the programmer, who is responsible for installing the *software*. More precisely: 'If violence is used on the programmer, since there is no possibility on the part of the contracting party to make a conscious choice on the opportunity to avoid the threatened evil since the threat is not addressed to his person' (Art. 1435 of the Civil Code), the regulation on the annulment of the contract does not appear to be applicable to the above hypothesis. If, on the other hand, deception is exercised on the planner, a distinction must be made according to the identity of the person who has perpetrated it. If it is the other party who deceived the planner in the service of the other party, the latter, if the deception was decisive for the conclusion of the contract, may request its avoidance pursuant to Art. 1439(1) of the Civil Code. If, on the other hand, the author of the fraud is a third party, the second paragraph of Art. 1439 of the Civil Code, which provides for the annulment of the contract, may be applied only if the deception perpetrated by the third party is known to the contracting party who has taken advantage of it.

technologies, such as, for example, the preparation of 'convoluted' and not very 'crystalline' paths that suddenly lead the user, with the umpteenth '*click*' required to go on, to express his definitive consent to the conclusion of the contract without having been made aware, by means of clear wording (such as, for example, the '*order confirmation*' window), of the irreversibility of the choice. Imagine the case in which, among the various icons placed on a *website*, there is one designed in such a way as to lead the user to suppose that it gives rise to information on a particular product, whereas his '*click*' instead directly leads to the sending of a request for immediate supply of the goods.

More generally—but this is a broader issue—the problem arises on the *web of* the adoption, by certain actors, of '*dark patterns*' techniques, i.e. the use of manipulative and deceptive *design* strategies implemented in 'user interfaces' to induce users to perform actions (or perhaps not to perform actions!). A typical example is the difficulty of 'unsubscribing' from a *mailing list*, the *link to* which cannot be found or is perhaps written in tiny letters in the *footer* of a *newsletter*, contrary to their interests or their real will.

Generally, and returning to wilful misconduct, it can be said that the conceivable conduct and the modalities of manifestation of the artifice or deception in 'real' life can be replicated in the abstract in virtual platforms, even if some specificity can be found in the practical case history and in the consequences arising therefrom.

To exemplify, a specific hypothesis of deception or artifice made possible by the telematic tool is the one highlighted by a recent judgment of the Criminal Court of Cassation, which even considered as constituting the offence of fraud the conduct of a person who—taking advantage of the peculiar characteristics of the *online* sales operation, based on the buyer's failure to see the goods, who relies on the correctness of the advertised offer—has put up for sale 'a object at an extremely convenient price in the absence of the same, or, without the subsequent non-delivery being due to specific factors intervening and adequately exposed by the seller, where the same also omits the due return of the price'.[36]

[36] Cf. Criminal Cass., 6 November 2019, No. 45115, at www.dejure.it. This is the key passage: '*online* sales are based on the buyer's reliance on the seller's offer, which is advertised exclusively through an internet portal. It follows that the seller cannot see the goods he is buying and relies entirely for the indication of the characteristics, the qualities of the product and the sale price on the indications that are advertised by the seller. It is precisely this particular feature of online sales that determines the nature of artifice and deception of the offering for sale of an object at an extremely convenient price in the absence of the same, that is, without the subsequent non-delivery being due to specific factors intervening and adequately set out by the seller, where the same also omits the due return of the price. Such conduct, in fact, stigmatises the presence of the initial intent to defraud since it clearly manifests the absence of any real intention to proceed with the sale on the part of the person who, having forfeited the price, omits the shipment, refuses to return the sum and also fails to indicate any circumstance justifying such wilful conduct. And from an objective point of view, the artifice and deception are to be found in the registration on an *online* sales portal, in the publication of the advertisement together with the description of the goods, in the indication of a convenient sale price, all of which are factors intended to capture the purchaser's good faith and to mislead him'.

Following this line of argument, it can indeed be concluded that, generally, the 'virtual' world of platforms lends itself more to alterations or manipulations of reality potentially capable of misleading the public, as occurs, to further exemplify, in cases where the offer of a good is accompanied by videos or photographic surveys that are faked through the use of 'filters' or other tools designed to enhance, beyond all reasonable measure, its qualities, or to conceal its flaws beyond the limit of the so-called dolus bonus, which, as is well known, marks the dividing line between legally permissible and conduct that significantly vitiates consent dd. *dolus bonus*, which, as is well known, marks the dividing line between what is legally permissible and conduct that significantly vitiates consent. This is obviously conduct that is easier to carry out and has a higher 'deceptive' potential in the telematic and remote realities than in the physical reality in person.

Lastly, as regards the third and last vice of consent, namely *moral violence*, this form of coercion of consent is perhaps rarer to occur—but certainly not to be excluded *a priori*—in the context of telematic contracting, if only because of the distance existing between the parties and the consequent greater difficulty in identifying an activity of threatening an unjust and considerable evil in the case of failure to conclude the contract or its conclusion on conditions other than those imposed.[37]

1.7 Breach of Information Obligations and Possible Invalidating Consequences for the Transaction

A peculiar problem that comes to the interpreter's attention relates to the consequence of the breach of the information obligations that, for various reasons, must precede the phase of the conclusion of the contract stipulated through or with a digital platform. Without wishing to address the issue of the identification of individual information obligations and their sources, an issue that would go well beyond the scope of the present work, one need only mention here the circumstance that over the years—in an attempt to reduce the gap between face-to-face and remote contracting, especially in an IT context, and to offer adequate protection to the 'digital' consumer with respect to his professional counterpart—many laws have introduced a series of information obligations for the latter.[38] This is with the declared aim of

[37] To this must be added, Gentili and Battelli (2012), p. 410, warn the circumstance that the recourse to anonymity and the use of fictitious *names (so-called nike names)*, which characterise the relationships between subjects on the *web*, makes it highly unlikely that the threat of an unjust and considerable evil can be considered such as to 'make an impression on a sensible person', as instead Art. 1435 of the Civil Code requires for the purposes of contract annulment.

[38] Just to simplify, consider Directive 2011/83/EU, which was followed, with specific reference to the digital market, by Directive 2019/2161/EU (the so-called *omnibus* directive), Directive 2019/770/EU (implemented in Italy by Legislative Decree No. 173/2021) and Directive 2019/771/EU (implemented in Italy by Legislative Decree No. 170/2021). Even earlier, it is worth mentioning Articles 7 et seq. of Legislative Decree No. 70/2003, implementing in Italy Community Directive 2000/31/EC.

ensuring that, through the provision of detailed, clear information offered on a durable medium, the user is put in a position to accurately assess the quality of the product or service he intends to purchase or use and is thus bridged, or at least reduced, that structural and inevitable information *gap* between the parties that characterises distance and *online* contracting, either because the purchaser is not in a material position to physically see and touch the goods he/she acquires, or because the services in question may have a content that is, so to speak, 'opaque', 'intangible' and difficult to understand in its fullness.

Well then, the unquestionable proceduralisation of the agreement, due to the need to provide the user with precise and detailed information, cannot but raise the question of what happens in the event of violation of the rules of formation of the contract and, as far as we are concerned here, whether it is possible to hypothesise, in addition to compensation for damages (which appears difficult to deny), some form of total or partial invalidity of the contract stipulated downstream. Furthermore, one must ask oneself whether the contractual agreement may also be vitiated in the event that, although the information obligations are formally observed, the provisions on the manner in which such information must be provided are not complied with.

Having set forth the problem in these terms, it should be briefly recalled that the issue of the consequences of the breach of disclosure obligations has been *funditus* addressed by two well-known 'twin' judgments of the Court of Cassation in United Sections,[39] which, albeit pronounced on the specific matter of securities brokerage,[40] set forth a precept of general application, affirming the principle[41] of the non-interference between *rules of validity*—the breach of which gives rise to invalidity of the contract—and *rules of conduct*—the breach of which instead gives rise to liability[42]—and brought the rules on disclosure obligations under the second of the two categories, with the consequent inapplicability of the remedy of nullity in the event of breach thereof. For this reason, the lack of due information, although

[39] These are: Cass., sec. un., 19 December 2007, nos. 26724 and 26725. The first of the two pronouncements can be found in *Foro it.*, 2008, I, 784 ff., with a note by Scoditti (2008), pp. 784 ff., with note by Rozzi and Bruno (2008), pp. 1175 ff., with note by Nappi (2008), pp. 525 ff., with note by Roppo (2008), pp. 353 ff., with note by Cottino (2008), pp. 691 ff., with note by Mazzini (2008), pp. 1189 ff., with note by Calisai (2008). The second ruling is published in *Resp. civ. prev.*, 2008, 547 ff., with note by Greco (2009), pp. 133 ff., with note by Bove (2009), pp. 133 ff. See also the commentary by Febbrajo (2008), pp. 2775 ff.

[40] The United Sections of the Court were called upon to rule on the specific question as to the consequences of the financial intermediary's failure to comply with the rules of conduct and the disclosure obligations imposed on him by the reference legislation and particularly whether the contract relating to the financial investment may be deemed void in such cases. See the order of referral to the United Sections: Cass. 16 February 2007, no. 3683, in *Foro it.*, 2007, I, 2093 ss., with a note by Scoditti (2007).

[41] Already supported in the past by authoritative doctrine. See, among the most significant contributions: Barcellona (1962), pp. 221 ff.; Pietrobon (1990), pp. 104 ff.; D'Amico (1996), pp. 44 ff.; D'Amico (2002), pp. 37 ff.; Scognamiglio (2008), pp. 599 ff. With specific reference to the area of securities brokerage, see, on all, Di Majo (1993), pp. 291–310.

[42] Unless, of course, otherwise provided by law.

constituting the violation of a mandatory rule, should, according to the court of legitimacy, be assessed not on the level of the validity of the transaction, which could not be considered invalid for that reason alone, but on that of the liability for damages.

This, in a nutshell, was the Court's *dictum*, followed unhesitatingly by the subsequent jurisprudence of legitimacy.[43]

Now, if the conclusion just seen may be valid as a general principle and therefore also apply to contracts concluded through or by means of digital platforms, whenever, from a subjective point of view, the parties to the transaction are a professional and a consumer, one may take a different view and refer to the regulations of the Consumer Code on distance and off-premises contracts, to which macro-category the contracts at issue in the present study certainly belong, since they too are concluded 'under an organised distance sales or service provision scheme without the simultaneous physical presence of the trader and the consumer, through the exclusive use of one or more means of distance communication', as provided for in the definition of 'distance contract' in Art. 45(1)(g) of Legislative Decree No. 206/2005.

Well then, once the legislation on distance contracts is deemed applicable, Art. 49(5), according to which pre-contractual information '*forms an integral part of the contract*', i.e. 'enters' *ex lege* into the structure and content of the contract, thus becoming rules of validity of the same; consequently, the violation of pre-contractual information obligations would be converted into a defect in the structure of the contract, i.e. a violation of a rule of validity of the same, thus opening the door to the application of the remedy of the nullity of the shop.[44]

Concluding on this point: if in contracts in which all the parties are professionals or consumers, the principle developed by jurisprudence that sees the violation of information obligations sanctioned only at the level of compensation for damages may be maintained, in *business/platform-to-consumer* contracts a different solution may be hypothesised and consider that the lack of or false provision of information may determine the nullity of the contract. A nullity that, consistently with the underlying consumer protection *rationale*, should be qualified as 'protective', with the application consequences of Art. 36 of the Consumer Code.

A final consideration: if the conclusions just seen apply in the case of non-compliance with a duty to inform 'pure and simple', in cases where such a breach is accompanied by further circumstances nothing detracts from the possibility of invoking the other form of civil law invalidity, i.e. the annulment of the contract, whenever the consumer or customer (even if professional) succeeds in proving the existence of a defect of consent, such as (excluding for obvious reasons violence) error, provided that he proves that this is essential and recognisable, or fraud, when it can be proved that the other party adopted artifices or deception aimed at

[43] Thus, most recently: Cass. 3 November 2021, no. 31494, at www.dejure.it; Cass. 31 May 2021, no. 15099, *therein*; Cass. 19 February 2021, no. 4484, *therein*; Cass. 22 May 2020, no. 9468, in *Guida dir.*, 2020, no. 38, 54 ff.; Cass. 24 April 2018, no. 10111, at www.dejure.it; Cass. 8 February 2016, no. 2414, *therein*, 2016, no. 15, 46 ff.

[44] For more details see Trezza (2021), pp. 297–298.

obtaining the other party's consent, *pursuant to* Articles 1439 and 1440 of the Civil Code. The voidability of the contract for fraudulent intent, in particular, seems to be admissible both in the hypothesis of active conduct on the part of the professional or service provider, i.e. where the latter has provided false information that has induced the other party to enter into a contract that otherwise would not have been entered into; and, according to some, in the hypothesis where this information has been fraudulently concealed, constituting, the violation of a specific and mandatory obligation to provide information, a reticence that leads to fraudulent omission.[45]

1.8 Control Over the Content of the Contract and the Role of Platforms

Once the rules on the formation of the contract have been established and the profile of the possible consequences (in the sole perspective of invalidity, not also of compensation) of the violation of these rules has been investigated, it is important to ask *who should* and *how should* guarantee the application of these rules. Another topic of investigation is the problem of the subject to whom the power/duty of *control* over the content of the contract should be delegated, given the already highlighted trans-nationality of contracts concluded through digital platforms.

Turning to the specifics, it is necessary to seek an answer to the question of whether a check on the content of the contract can also be entrusted to the same company operating the digital platform, which acts as a mere intermediary and not as a counterparty to the contract (in the latter case, no problems arise, since the platform is part of the contract).

The question seems to have to be answered, in principle, in the negative, since at Community level the principle applies—already 'codified' by Community Directive 2000/31/EC, the so-called '*e commerce* directive', and confirmed by the more recent Art. 6 of Regulation (EU) 2022/2065—of the so-called *safe harbour*, according to which intermediaries are generally not liable for the contents hosted on their services, unless they are aware of the manifestly illegal contents (the rule in fact speaks of 'manifest' illegality) of the same, or they do not immediately remove or block access to such contents once they become aware of them. Thus, intermediary service providers cannot be considered to have a general duty to monitor the content of the contract, let alone to actively ascertain facts or circumstances indicating the presence of illegal activities.

The situation may change, however, in the event that the platform has not played the role of mere 'host' of the transaction between the parties, but has assumed a position such as to lead an 'average' consumer or user to believe that the

[45] Cf. Gentili (2000), p. 762, according to whom, since there is an obligation to inform, the supplier's reticence, which is silent about a circumstance that the other party ought to have known, constitutes wilful misconduct.

information, or the product or service that is the subject of the transaction, is provided by the platform itself or by a recipient of the service acting under its authority or control: in this case, in fact, a sort of legitimate reliance operates on the part of the consumer or user on the role and responsibility assumed by the platform, a reliance that may generate, on the part of the latter, a real obligation of control, the breach of which may be a source of compensatory liability.

Apart from the latter situation, if *online* platforms do not generally assume a role of guarantor of the content and control over the act, it is nevertheless true that they are obliged to set up '*notice and take down*' mechanisms, essentially aimed at facilitating the submission of reports of possible illegal content of the contract: Art. 16 of Regulation (EU) 2022/2065 in fact imposes on 'providers of information storage services', i.e. precisely on *online* platforms (Art. 3, lett. i),[46] the obligation to set up mechanisms, easy to access and use, 'to allow any person or entity to notify them of the presence in their service of specific information that that person or entity considers to constitute illegal content'.

Once the presence of illegal content of interest to the individual contract has been reported and/or verified, the platforms have a duty to take action on the matter, adopting a series of measures, provided for by Art. 17, which may range from (*a*) the adoption of restrictions on the visibility of specific information, including the removal of content, the disabling of access to the content or the downgrading of the same, (*b*) the suspension, termination or other limitation of monetary payments; (*c*) the total or partial suspension or termination of the provision of the service, up to and including (*d*) the suspension or termination of the *account* of the recipient of the service. Furthermore, if the platform has an 'inkling' that an offence is being committed or is about to be committed through the contract (e.g. contracts for the exchange of child pornography or subscription to child pornography services), it is obliged under Art. 18 below to immediately notify the authority of the Member States concerned, and to provide all possible cooperation.

In the case of a '*marketplace*' platform, i.e. a provider of an *online* platform that enables consumers or users to conclude distance contracts with traders, there are additional obligations, which may even go as far as having to inform buyers that the contract concluded through the platform contains an illegal product or service, i.e. has an unlawful object (Art. 32 Regulation (EU) 2022/2065).

Even more stringent obligations are imposed on the so-called *very large online* platforms and *very large online search engines*, i.e. *online* platforms and *online* search engines with an average monthly number of active recipients of the service in the Union equal to or greater than 45 million, identified and designated by a specific

[46] Pursuant to Art. 3(i) of Regulation (EU) 2065/2022, an '*online* platform' is defined as 'an information storage service which, at the request of a recipient of the service, stores and disseminates information to the public, unless that activity is a minor and merely ancillary function of another service or a minor functionality of the main service and, for objective and technical reasons, cannot be used without that other service and provided that the integration of that function or functionality into the other service is not a means of circumventing the applicability of this Regulation'.

decision of the European Commission:[47] these subjects, in fact, pursuant to Articles 33 et seq. of the Regulation in question, are required to carry out periodic evaluations and analyses of the '*systemic risk*' arising from the design or operation of their service and its related systems, taking into consideration a series of factors, including that of the possibility of the dissemination of illegal content, and are also obliged to adopt risk mitigation measures, under penalty of the applicability of specific sanctions and of the rules on damages. In fact, if it is true that the large platforms must assess the risk of illegal content being disseminated through their services and must adopt consequent countermeasures, then it is legitimate to assume, at the expense of these subjects, some obligation to control the content of contracts that 'transit' through or by means of their services: In short, to put it bluntly and by way of example, if the large platform is required to assess the risk that contracts with an illegal object are entered into, such as the supply of child pornography or the dissemination of sensitive data, then it is difficult to deny the existence of an obligation of diligent and continuous monitoring, and therefore control, of the contracts entered into through its network, albeit limited, as mentioned above, to the verification and detection of illegal profiles.

Lastly, it should be noted that a control on the content of the contract with illegal content can also be configured in the hands of other entities, to which the same Regulation (EU) 2022/2065 attributes powers and duties to control compliance with the obligations provided for: this is a *governance* system based on close cooperation between the European Commission and the individual national states, which are required to appoint a digital services coordinator, i.e. a 'digital services coordinator' (a role attributed, in Italy, to the Authority for Guarantees in Communications[48]), in charge of supervising digital platforms and compliance with regulatory standards, with the function of coordinating the other competent national authorities.

2 The Regulation of the Market and the Contract Conforming Powers of the Independent Authorities

2.1 The Sale, Concluded Through Platforms, of Goods and Services Relating to 'Sensitive' Sectors

The discussion so far cannot fail to consider the further aspect that the marketing of certain products through IT platforms intercepts the competences of independent authorities. One alludes, for instance, to the wide and varied energy sector, the telecommunications sector, and the water supply sector.

[47] This includes platforms and search engines such as, for instance, *Facebook, Google, Instagram, Amazon, Ali baba, Booking* and so on.

[48] The appointment of the Authority for Guarantees in Communications took place with Art. 15, Law Decree No. 123/2023 (known to the media as the '*Caivano Decree*'), conv. by Law No. 159/2023.

Widely used are platforms that compare the various domestic utility suppliers, indicating the most favourable prices at the moment and allowing users to click directly on the icon for the chosen supplier, thus setting in motion the mechanism aimed at concluding a supply contract.[49]

The same applies to platforms that refer to the comparison of offers and prices with regard to the insurance sector, especially with regard to motor liability, health policies, life policies, etc., as well as, with regard to the banking sector, especially with regard to basic products such as current accounts and forms of remunerated deposits, partly similar to current accounts, the so-called deposit account.

The market for these types of supplies and products is, to a certain extent, regulated not only by the respective national sector disciplines but also by the independent Authorities.[50] These authorities, being so-called sensitive sectors whose control they are variously entrusted with, break into the area of private autonomy by means of a congeries of 'acts' represented by the so-called directives, circulars, guidelines, recommendations, regulations and expressions of the so-called polycentrism of regulation that characterises the system of sources of production of law.[51]

This is a varied instrumentarium, difficult, not to say, at times, almost impossible for precise connotation and/or legal categorisation, which the interpreter finds difficult to categorise with certainty in the hierarchy of sources. Often hybrid figures, such as, for example, the guidelines, which even administrative law scholars find uncertain between law, regulation and administrative measure, which obviously has repercussions on the possibility of appeal by the interested parties, but above all, and this is what is most interesting here, with regard to the repercussions on contracts of non-compliance by market operators.

The subject, as is all too evident, involves complex and relevant issues for civil law scholars, first and foremost that of the regulatory and conformative power of the independent administrative authorities, given that private autonomy is guaranteed by a reservation of the law under Art. 41(3) of the Constitution.[52] The provision states that 'social and general utility in the economic field must be pursued within the framework of the institutional principles of the rule of law'.[53] Therefore, as has been effectively pointed out,[54] the contractual validity of the measures of the independent authorities necessarily passes through the *subtle crux* of the identification of the scope of the reservation of law, and, therefore, of the resolution of the preliminary question 'whether the regulation of contracts (especially where it entails

---

[49] By way of example and just to mention the best-known platforms, see *Comparasemplice.co.uk*, *Segugio*.co.uk, *Comparatore*.co.*uk*.

[50] On the market regulation function and the conformative powers exercised by the Independent Authorities in the various sectors the book, Angelone and Zarro (2022), pp. 13 ff., and more recently AA.VV., *Conformazione del contratto e Autorità Indipendenti nel diritto Italo-Europeo*, Atti del XVI Convegno Nazionale SISDIC, Napoli, 2023.

[51] See, in this regard, Cons. Stato 14 February 2006, no. 11603.

[52] On this point, for further study, please refer to Monticelli (2023), pp. 161 ff.

[53] Merusi (2006), pp. 44–62.

[54] Roppo (2001), p. 86.

restrictions on contractual freedom) is reserved to primary sources; and whether the reservation is absolute or relative'. A debate that, moreover, has particularly developed with reference to two very peculiar hypotheses, respectively, in the banking and financial sphere. Article 117(8) of the Consolidated Banking Law (TUB), according to which 'the Bank of Italy may prescribe that certain contracts or securities, identified by means of a particular name or based on specific qualifying criteria, have a typically determined content. Differing contracts and securities are null and void', and Art. 23 TUF which, in para 1, after stating that 'Contracts relating to the provision of investment services, and, if provided, contracts relating to the provision of ancillary services, shall be in writing, in accordance with the provisions of the delegated acts of Directive 2014/65/EU, and a copy shall be given to the clients' allows/delegates to Consob the possibility to provide by regulation, after consulting the Bank of Italy, 'that, for justified reasons or in relation to the professional nature of the contracting parties, particular types of contract may or must be concluded in another form, ensuring in respect of retail clients an appropriate level of guarantee. In cases of non-compliance with the prescribed form, the contract is null and void'.

These are rules that find a common denominator in their underlying purpose of protecting weaker contracting parties through a delegation that invests the delegated Authorities with the power to prescribe models (Art. 117(8) TUB) and differentiated formal charges (Art. 23 TUF) that integrate the so-called form/content of the contract.[55]

This is a case where, while it is true that there is a very generic delineation of the regulatory precept through the technique of reference to the determinations that will be made by a secondary source[56] (in fact, the cited provisions lack any indication as to the choice of the type of contract on which the delegated Authority can operate the so-called typifying intervention[57]). Thus, configuring the unprecedented category of 'blank nullity', it is equally true that at least an explicit reference is made, without prejudice to the admissibility or otherwise of a contractual nullity deriving from the violation of mandatory rules of a secondary source.[58] But it is equally true that at least there is an explicit reference, without prejudice to investigating the admissibility or otherwise of the configurability of a contractual nullity deriving from the violation of mandatory rules of a secondary source.

---

[55] In this regard, it is hardly worth mentioning that Art. 117(8), cited above, is located in Title 6 of the Consolidated Banking Act concerning the 'transparency of contractual terms and conditions and customer relations'.

[56] Significantly, Amadio (2006a), pp. 220–224, highlights the peculiarity of the hermeneutic itinerary envisaged by the above rules: in them, unlike what happens in the case of virtual nullity contemplated by Art. 1418(1) of the Civil Code, where it is left to the interpreter to identify the possible civil law sanction of nullity from a well-defined prohibitive or preceptive provision, the legislator, on the other hand, 'moves … from an express provision of the sanction to go in search of the precept, generically outlined by the rule through the technique of reference to another determination'. An inverted perspective, therefore, which leads to the conclusion that we are faced with hypotheses of textual nullity with a 'virtual case'.

[57] Cf. Cass. 28 November 2013, No. 26672, in *Jur. comm.*, 2, II, 156, regarding Art. 117(8), Tub.

[58] Amadio (2006b), but also Viti (2013), p. 107.

On the other hand, the value of the independent authorities' *dicta*, in relation to compliance with the principle of legality, is a subject also addressed by administrative justice, in view of the function they perform of regulating the sector they are responsible for. In this regard, the Council of State[59] has expressly admitted, in relation to the regulatory acts of the Independent Authorities, that they can be substantiated in the exercise of implicit powers inasmuch as it is not possible for the legislative source, in sensitive sectors such as those entrusted to the Authorities, to predetermine all aspects of the future of administrative action, leaving the latter to pursue the objectives with the exercise of powers implicitly inferred from the regulatory source establishing the individual Authorities.[60] At the same time, it has also highlighted, in a recent arrest, the advisability 'that the legislature should intervene to regulate, with more pregnant measures, modulated in light of the subject matter regulated, also the sectors falling within the competence of the independent Authorities to reduce the scope of implicit powers and ensure a more certain constitutional compatibility'.[61] And, with reference to the guidelines, particularly those of Anac, it ruled out the possibility that they could be classified as regulations in the proper sense but should be considered as general administrative regulatory acts, as such, 'justiciable' before the administrative court.

In this magmatic and above all very slippery context for legal practitioners, certainly for civilists, it is a fact that the independent authorities, in key market sectors, produce determinations addressed to the operators of the sectors concerned to whom they 'recommend' the general and widespread adoption of specific contractual and procedural models.

Form and content requirements, therefore, which, by often also providing for documentary enclosures as a necessary accompaniment to the contract or, in any case, the adoption, in the text of the contract, in writing, of a series of warnings, prescriptions, clauses expressly pre-packaged by the independent Authorities themselves, result in the phenomenon now known as 'neo-formalism' in negotiations.

However, it is easy to see that, on the one hand, such so-called recommendations/directives/provisions/regulations are for the most part devoid of an explicit enunciation of the civil law consequences for non-compliance, and on the other hand, only in an absolutely episodic manner, such as those potentially evoked in Art. 117(8) TUB and Art. 23(1) TUF, are they governed by an express legislative delegation conferred on the independent Authorities to which the power to conform or typify is explicitly attributed. 23(1) of the Consolidated Law on Finance, are governed by an express legislative delegation conferred on the Independent Authorities, which are

[59] Cons. Stato, 2 May 2012, no. 2521, in *Foro amm. CDS*, 2012, 5, 1284.

[60] See, also, Cons. Stato, comm. spec., opinion no. 1920 of 14 September 2016, where it is pointed out that the independent Authorities are vested with regulatory power as a 'corollary of the powers granted to them by the law, closely linked to the element of independence that characterises them' and translates into 'the recognition of the power to directly exercise the regulatory and control tasks in the sectors they are responsible for safeguarding'. On the powers of independent Authorities in general see, among others, Amato (1997); Clarich (2003), pp. 49–69.

[61] Cons. Stato 15 December 2020, no. 7972, in *Giur. comm.*, 2022, 1, II, 152.

explicitly vested with a conforming or typifying power,[62] and finally, in no case, to the best of our knowledge, except for the cases referred to above, is the consequence of the nullity of the contract or of individual clauses that conflict with the preceptive indications provided by the Independent Authorities made explicit.

Having said this, it would appear useful to continue the examination by attempting to distinguish the hypotheses that may be envisaged and the possible repercussions with regard to the possible invalidity of contracts concluded through information technology platforms, with respect to the so-called sensitive sectors falling within the competence of the independent Authorities. It should, in fact, be considered that the conclusion of a contract through platforms has a standardised, particularly rapid and depersonalised procedure, where it is not always easy for the user to understand the real advantage of the contract as well as the obligations he or she enters into. In such a context, which is not always entirely transparent, the observance by the supplier of the goods or services of the formal and documentary attachment obligations indicated by the sectoral authority acquires particular importance.

2.2 *The Formal and Documentary Prescriptions of the Independent Authorities Between Express Delegation and Reservation of the Law* Pursuant to *Article 41(3) of the Constitution*

The first hypothesis to be considered is that of a formal and/or documentary prescription contained in a regulation, directive of the independent authority that, for non-compliance, commits the nullity of the contract by virtue of express delegation found in a primary source.

To the best of my knowledge, the only regulatory hypothesis that expressly delegates to an independent authority, in this case Consob, the indication of particular formal prescriptions under penalty of nullity is, as already noted, that contained in Art. 23(1) of the Consolidated Law on Finance.

As mentioned above, the provision, after stating that ‘Contracts relating to the provision of investment services, and, if provided for, contracts relating to the provision of ancillary services, shall be in writing’, provides for the possibility that the ‘Consob, having consulted the Bank of Italy’, may provide ‘by regulation that, for justified reasons or in relation to the professional nature of the contracting parties, particular types of contract may or must be stipulated in another form, ensuring in respect of retail clients an appropriate level of guarantee. In cases of non-compliance with the prescribed form, the contract is null and void’.

[62] See Cass. 28 November 2013, no. 26672, cited above; similarly Cass. 6 December 2013, no. 27380, in *Foro it.*, 2014, 2, I, 499; Cass. 4 November 2015, no. 22446, in *Mass. Just. civ.*, 2015; Cass. 24 June 2016, no. 13164, in *De jure*.

Beyond any consideration of the concrete scope of the delegated authority, it should be noted that the provision, like the aforementioned provision of Art. 117(8) of the Consolidated Banking Act, contains the provision of a blank nullity as a consequence of the failure to comply with the formal prescriptions laid down by the delegated authority in the aforementioned contracts.

It has already been pointed out that the aforementioned rules represent unique hypotheses, and in particular, Art. 117, para 8, TUB, has not substantially found concrete application.[63] However, one must agree with what has generally been observed[64] with respect to them, i.e. that the admissibility of so-called 'blank' primary nullity rules and of the consequent specification measures (of secondary rank) issued by the Authorities may be recognised only in the presence of the conditions and limits of the existence of an express delegation containing the attribution to the secondary rank of the Authority of the power to issue the specific measures, and of the consequent (secondary) specification measures issued by the Authorities can be recognised only in the presence of the conditions and limits of the existence of an express delegation of authority that contains the attribution to the secondary source of the power to imperatively order nullity for non-compliance.[65] Furthermore, the correspondence between the function of the authoritative act and the interests underlying the delegation of power can be ascertained in concrete terms.[66]

In the absence of such requisites to be found in the delegating provision, the secondary-ranking specification measures issued by the delegated authorities

[63] On the other hand, with regard to the aforementioned Art. 23 of the TUF, Consob issued Intermediaries Regulation No. 20307/2018, Art. 37(1) of which states: 'Intermediaries shall provide their investment services, including investment advice *which provides for the performance of a periodic assessment of the suitability of the financial instruments or services recommended*, on the basis of a specific written contract; a copy of this contract shall be delivered to the client'. The way the regulatory provision is written, it would seem that the burden of form would not apply to investment advisory contracts for which the 'suitability' rules do not apply (according to some, they are only applicable when they are addressed to a retail client, and not also when they are addressed to an eligible counterparty or a professional client). Consequently, in a singular countertrend with respect to operational practice, the Independent Authority, with the second-degree rule, while resolving the long-standing issue of the applicability of the form requirement also to consultancy contracts, excludes the necessity of compliance with the written form for those contracts, whether investment or consultancy, for which the adequacy test is not compulsory, i.e. for contracts with so-called professional subjects. On this point, see, usefully, Fauceglia (2021), pp. 238–240.

[64] Screws (2013), p. 114.

[65] It is interesting, precisely in this regard, that the case law debate has developed with reference to Art. 38, para 2, of the Consolidated Banking Act ('The Bank of Italy, in accordance with the resolutions of the CICR, determines the maximum amount of financing, identifying it in relation to the value of the mortgaged assets or the cost of the works to be performed on the same, as well as the hypotheses in which the presence of previous mortgage registrations does not prevent the granting of financing') in comparison with Art. 117(8) TUB, the subject of the very recent decision of the Sezioni Unite, 16 November 2022, no. 33719, in *Mass. Giust. civ.*, 2022.

[66] The question remains as to whether, for the purposes of the configurability of an express delegation, there is a need for the protected interest to be specified in the individual rule containing the delegation or, conversely, whether the more general assignment of functions provided for in the laws establishing the authorities is sufficient in this regard.

cannot be recognised as having the legitimacy to impose the nullity of the contract[67] nor even to supplement it;[68] this is precluded by the aforementioned reservation of the law contained in Art. 41, para 3, of the Italian Constitution, which requires that the measure of the authority find its attributive foundation in a formal legislative provision[69] that represents the title and legitimation of the provision of lower rank[70] just as it happens, on the other hand, for substitute interventions *pursuant to* Art. 1339 of the Civil Code by a secondary source.[71]

---

[67] See, among others, Farace (2012), pp. 656–670.

[68] Monticelli (2023), p. 165.

[69] That it must be a formal law is effectively reaffirmed by Cass. 30 July 2009, no. 17746, in www.inps.it, but previously Cass. 29 September 2004, no. 19531, in *Mass. Giust. civ.*, 2004, 9. In this regard, the reflections of Perlingieri (1999), p. 284, deserves full agreement, who points out that 'reserved regulatory power must reckon with the law's reservations and with the fundamental values of the Constitution: such authorities are suspected of constitutional illegitimacy, especially when they come to limit the individual positions of individual subjects'.

[70] Amadio (2006a), pp. 220–224.

[71] In this sense, the jurisprudence of the Council of State (see, among others, Cons. Stato, section VI, 13 October 2021, no. 6892, in the *De jure* database), which reiterates that the secondary administrative source must necessarily operate upon express delegation by the legislature. The necessary intermediation of the law is inferred not only from the relative nature of the reservation set forth in Articles 41 and 42 of the Constitution (the freedom to make contracts instrumental to the exercise of economic initiative is in fact constitutionally protected to the same extent that economic initiative receives protection, i.e. to the same extent that the ownership of the negotiated goods is protected), but also from the relevant provisions of the Civil Code. Article 1372 of the Civil Code, in attributing 'force of law' to the manifestation of will supported by common intention, excludes the possibility of modifying 'administratively' the structure of interests established by the parties, unless such power is provided for by law (Art. 1374 of the Civil Code) or prefigured in the agreement itself. In short, since the power of self-regulation of private parties is conferred by law, the 'administrative conformation' of the contract requires a normative foundation having equal rank in the system of sources. Article 1339 of the Civil Code, according to a well-established interpretative orientation, refers not only to the case in which the law itself directly identifies the clause to be inserted in the contract, but also to the hypothesis in which the law provides that the identification of the clause is made by a regulatory source authorised by it. That being said, the delegation of legislation cannot be summarised in the mere attribution of administrative competence, but must be accompanied by a 'minimum' set of substantive guidelines referring (at the very least) to the purposes, subject-matter and prerequisites, consistent with the principle of substantive legality underlying the rule of law, by virtue of which 'it is not sufficient that the power be aimed by law at the protection of a good or a value, but it is indispensable that its exercise be determined in its content and modalities, so as to constantly maintain a, albeit elastic, legislative coverage of administrative action' (Constitutional Court, Const., judgment no. 115/2011). 'For the same reasons, the possibility of inferring implicit powers of ab externo incision on the contract from provisions that merely identify the purposes of administrative action must be excluded'.

2.3 *The Debate on the Value of Formal and Documentary Requirements in the Absence of Delegation*

As noted elsewhere,[72] the above flat conclusions must, however, come to terms with the objection, also authoritatively sustained, according to which independent authorities, by virtue of the rules establishing them and the market sector they are responsible for, could consider themselves authorised, even without an express delegation, and in relation to the results to be achieved, to issue measures recommending or even imposing the widespread adoption of formal or documentary burdens.

This opens up the further and consequential question whether non-compliance with the measure, directive, recommendation, etc. issued by the Authority may result, by express provision contained therein, in the nullity of the contract, or, in the absence of an express provision, in the sanction of nullity for non-compliance, in the contract being void. Issuances by the Authority may result, by an express provision contained therein, in the nullity of the contract, or, in the absence of an express provision, the sanction of nullity for non-compliance, may in any event be inferred from an axiological interpretation of the powers attributed to the Authorities for the purposes of the objectives of protecting the market or the users of the reference market entrusted to them, and, as a consequence of the foregoing, the court is required to proceed to adjust the contract in the light of the prescriptions contained in the Authority's measures.

In this regard, as mentioned above, it has been argued[73] that, in sensitive areas such as those entrusted to the authorities, it is not possible for the legislative source to predetermine all aspects of the future of administrative action, leaving it to the latter to pursue objectives through the exercise of powers implicitly inferred from the regulatory source.

At the same time, at the strictly civil law level, the same jurisprudence, also with the support of the unified sections of the Supreme Court of Cassation, appears increasingly oriented towards favouring, with respect to the prescription of certain formal obligations, an interpretative key aimed at identifying the functional value attributable to the form, in relation to the contract or contractual model for which it is provided. An axiological reading, therefore, that prescinds from abstract positions on the exceptional or non-exceptional character of the rules prescribing a given form, or of its derogable or mandatory character, but rather aims at deducing these features from an 'interpretative procedure that depends on the place that the rule receives in the system, on the ratio that it expresses, on the value that it represents for the legal system'[74] in relation to the effectiveness of the protection of the interests underlying the prescription of the formal or documentary burden. Form and

---

[72] Monticelli (2023), p. 165.

[73] See Cons. Stato 2 May 2012, no. 2521, in *Foro Amm. CDS*, 2012, 5, 1284; Cons. Stato Comm. Spec., Opinion 14 September 2016, no. 1920.

[74] Cass., sec. un., 17 September 2015, no. 18214, in *Mass. Just. civ.*, 2015.

proceduralisation that, therefore, from mere dressing of the contract, can expand to include the very content of the contract and the interconnections with the cause.[75]

This interpretative option is undoubtedly to be shared but with a complication that specifically concerns the issue at hand, represented by the relevant circumstance that, in the case at hand, the prescription of the formal or documentary burden and, where provided for, the sanction of nullity for non-compliance, does not derive from a primary law but from a secondary source, which, however, in the primary law would find its foundation and its finalistic or axiological inspiration, as one may wish.

Analysing the two hypotheses envisaged, it must be agreed with those who hold[76] that, generally, if the rule establishing the Authorities can certainly legitimise them to introduce content and, as far as we are concerned, form prescriptions in contracts relating to the sectors of operation, it cannot, however, implicitly legitimise them, in the absence of an express delegation, to impose for non-compliance the sanction of nullity of the contract or of individual clauses because they lack the prescribed formal or documentary obligation, since in such a case the direct effect would derive directly from a regulatory administrative act, i.e. from a secondary source, which would be in clear conflict with the reservation of the law expressed by Art. 41(3) of the Constitution.

However, this conclusion, which in its general lines appears shareable and respectful of the hierarchy of sources, may, with reference to specific concrete hypotheses, not be so obvious: Think of the case in which the prescription of formal or documentary charges, such as, for example, the attachment of prospectuses to the contract, is intended, as is usually the case, to inform the consumer/user or, in any case, the contracting party not predisposing of the choices he makes by signing the contract, of the services he can actually make use of, of the rights he has vis-à-vis the service provider in the sector in which the Authority operates, and of the obligations he assumes. In these cases, the prescription found in the administrative measure or regulation issued by the Authority responds to the obvious purpose of filling an information gap that places the user at a disadvantage. It is therefore reasonable to assume that the *dicta* contained in the secondary source in fact implies a protective function aimed at rebalancing the positions of the parties,[77] as well as the conscious exercise of private autonomy by the non-precipient.

It is in this perspective that the regulatory activity of the independent Authorities should be viewed: and so, it seems equally reasonable to assume that the secondary source may express, in the case in point, that form-function placed at the protection/preservation of the real exercise of private autonomy. This would make it possible to affirm that the administrative regulation issued by the Authority, especially in the

[75] Cf. Canton (n.d.).

[76] Cf. Amadio (2006a), p. 224, who picks up on the thought of Villa (1993), pp. 114 ff., and emphasises that what is precluded from the administration's power is to affect private autonomy with an act of 'independent' regulation; not when 'rules of administrative origin… are delegated by ordinary law to regulate' that same autonomy.

[77] On this point, see Napolitano and Zoppini (n.d.), pp. 137 ff.

mostly recurring hypothesis in which it follows a prior discussion with the entrepreneurs and the associations representing the consumers/users of a given market, may contain a prescription aimed at identifying a procedure designed to ensure, also through the adoption of formal indications or documentary allegations (so-called forms of protection), a parameter of contract transparency aimed at revealing to the user non-competitive conditions or contractual disparity. A requirement, therefore, which, regardless of its suitability or, better yet, its inability to have a direct and binding effect on private autonomy, is placed to protect the market and the weaker party in the relationship and, therefore, a series of primary rules, expressed in Articles 1375 and 1175 of the Civil Code, as well as the principle of solidarity expressed in Art. 2 of the Constitution, which, taken together, constitute the foundation of the effective exercise of private autonomy which, in turn, is expressly recognised in Art. 41 of the Constitution.

Now, if the foregoing appears plausible, the justified denial to the independent authorities of the implied power to impose contractual nullity does not, therefore, *necessarily* exclude that such nullity may in any event result not from any provision expressed in the secondary provision, but from an assessment by the court carried out in the light of Art. 1322 of the Civil Code. To be considered not only as to para (1) but also as to para (2) of that article. And indeed, it is true that the rule, in para (1), expressly refers to 'the limits imposed by law', which has for the most part led interpreters to consider the 'limit' to exist where the breach concerns a mandatory rule. However, it has been pointed out elsewhere[78] that this reading is extremely reductive, since, for example, the concept of a limit may well include an unjustified derogation of a dispositive rule, especially where there is a contractual relationship between parties in an asymmetrical position and where the so-called 'strong contractor' has arranged for the breach to be committed by the party in question—so-called strong contracting party arranging general terms and conditions in derogation of the dispositive right, for the sole purpose of gaining an unjustified advantage. On the other hand, even from a strictly textual point of view, the concept of 'limit imposed by law' does not necessarily seem to exclude that it may be found, with the clarifications to be made below, in a secondary source, when, for example, to remain on the subject of form, it is prescribed to supplement the content of the contract for the purpose of rebalancing the position of the parties, also by reason of the frequent inclusion in the contractual text of so-called atypical clauses.

In these hypotheses, therefore, the secondary source, while confirming itself as per se unsuitable for directly founding the nullity of the contract or of clauses thereof and for compulsorily supplementing its content or form/content,[79] would represent a relevant index of the emergence of an abuse and/or a distorted use in the

---

[78] Monticelli (2021), pp. 5 ff. and 33 ff.

[79] On this point, Addis (2006), pp. 111 ff., notes that 'the authoritative source of the contract cannot be understood exclusively with reference to normative or administrative acts capable of generating rules that dictate an authoritative discipline of the contractual relationship… On the contrary, the connotation of authoritativeness could be exhausted in the source without being transferred also to the regulation of the relationship, *thus giving rise to a set of dispositive rules*'.

exercise of contractual autonomy by the operators of the sector, and could therefore represent a parameter for assessing, in concreto, the failure by them to comply with the aforementioned primary rules protecting private autonomy, authorising on that basis the intervention of the court.

Thus, an osmotic relationship is accredited between primary sources (of general or sectoral rank) and secondary sources, with the latter drawing inspiration from the former, and, therefore, the need for an overall unitary reading of this network of sources to correct possible market distortions and mitigate the effects of the so-called 'information asymmetry' between the parties.

On the other hand, it is precisely to an osmotic relationship between the sources, while respecting the hierarchical relationship between them, that the current text contained in Art. *37-bis* of the Consumer Code seems to allude, on the subject of administrative protection against the insertion of unfair terms in contracts, and attributing to the Competition and Market Authority the preventive and subsequent power to ascertain unfairness. An instrument of *public enforcement*, in addition to the private models already present in the Consumer Code, with which the legislator 'intended to help encourage the spread of contractual models capable of ensuring that all market players have rules of greater fairness and transparency and, therefore, of greater efficiency both for the consumer and as regards the proper competitive game'.[80] Well then, it is not disputed that the Authority cannot impose civil sanctions or inhibit the use of clauses judged unfair, which, notwithstanding their ascertained vexatiousness, will continue to be considered valid and effective until they are declared null and void by the judge *pursuant to the* Civil Code, nevertheless the negative assessment made by the Authority cannot but be taken into account by the judge hearing the *quaestio nullitatis* in relation to the concrete case and also for the purposes of a subsequent conformation of the contract in a protective key.[81]

2.4 The Residuality of the Remedy of Contract Avoidance and the Remedy of Damages

The considerations made so far, however, require further clarification: It seems appropriate to point out that just as the requirement of form or documentary annexation do not permit, in the absence of the express provision of nullity for non-compliance, to disregard the investigation of the proper function of the rule—whether primary or secondary—to accredit or exclude the directing effect, so likewise they do not permit any automatism that would certainly evoke the demolishing effect of

[80] Trubiani (2022), pp. 20–21; but see also Camardi (2013), pp. 305 ff., who also appropriately highlights the critical issues for the consumer that may arise from the AGCM's control of unfair terms.

[81] On the role of independent authorities for the purpose of contract conformation in a protective key, see Perlingieri (2017), pp. 214 ff., Angelone (2012), pp. 199 ff.

the contract or part thereof[82] and, consequently, also the conforming effect in line with the provisions in question. In fact, such an approach is neither automatic nor taken for granted and, on the contrary, it must in principle be deemed to be normally residual with respect to the remedies available for non-compliance with formal or documentary obligations not expressly provided for in primary provisions under penalty of nullity, given the clear wording of Art. 1325(4) of the Civil Code and, as regards formal obligations deriving from secondary sources, the oft-cited reservation of the law contained in Art. 41(3) of the Constitution.

In this regard, one cannot fail to subscribe to the criticisms finally made by the SS.UU[83] with regard to the excessively casual use by jurisprudence of the category of nullity, as an instrument of reaction by the legal system with respect to forms of negotiated programming allegedly damaging fundamental legal values, forgetting that the use of such remedy must be founded on clear and solid dogmatic foundations, just as, likewise, on such solid foundations must be based the contractual compliance activity by the court, eschewing creative constructions that do not take due account of the precise hierarchy, binding on the interpreter, dictated by Art. 1374 of the Civil Code in determining the integration of the contract.[84]

The interpretative investigation obviously cannot be carried out in the abstract but with reference to the concrete case to verify the function concretely pursued by the prescription of form or documentary allegation, in the light of the distinction between rules of conduct and rules of validity. It must, in fact, be considered that the breach of the former, generally deriving precisely from failure to comply with information obligations, mostly affecting the pre-contractual phase, permits, according to a shareable teaching[85] followed also by the well-known decisions of the United Sections,[86] normally, though not necessarily, access only to the indemnification remedy,[87] it being necessary, beyond any consideration as to the legitimacy under

[82] Cass., sez. un., 16 January 2018, no. 898, in *Foro it.*, 2014, 4, I, 1283, where it is stated: '*in the context of what has been defined as neo-formalism or negotiation formalism, it must be understood according to what is the proper function of the rule and not automatically recalling the general discipline on nullity*'.

[83] Cass., sez. un., 15 March 2022, no. 8472, in *Foro it.*, 2022, 5, I, 1650, but see, also, sez. un., 16 November 2022, no. 33719, in *Mass. Giust. civ.*, 2022.

[84] On this point, let us refer to Monticelli (2021), pp. 33 ff.

[85] Mengoni (1997), p. 9 of a different opinion, however, Sacco (1975), pp. 669 ff.

[86] Cass., sec. un., 19 December 2007, nos. 26724 and 26725, commented by: Albanese (2008), pp. 107 ff.; Gentili (2008), p. 393; Mariconda (2008), pp. 230 ff.; Sangiovanni (2008), pp. 231 ff.; Salanitro (2008), pp. 445 ff.; Scoditti (2008), pp. 784 ff.; Galgano (2008), pp. 1 ff.

[87] On this point, with extreme clarity, Trib. Salerno, sez. I, 13 February 2010, *Drafting Giuffrè 2011*, where we read: In financial transactions, the rules governing information obligations, both prior and after the conclusion of the contract, fall within the rules of conduct, the non-observance of which may give rise to a liability of a compensatory nature where it results in a form of incorrect performance of the general duty of protection. In fact, there is a distinction between rules of conduct and rules of contract validity, since only the latter can be attributed a mandatory character, hence their inclusion by right in the contract and their sanctionability with the nullity of contracts pursuant to Art. 1418 of the Civil Code, while for the former, their violation could only lead to a

the dogmatic profile of the principle of non-interference,[88] to deem devoid of reasonableness[89] and, above all, lacking in proportionality,[90] if not sometimes even conflicting with the user's interest itself, the destructive or partially destructive remedy of nullity of contract.

2.5 *Analysis of Certain Cases*

In view of the foregoing, the recent issuance by the Private Insurance Supervisory Authority (IVASS) of the renewed Regulation No. 40 of 2 August 2018, effective as of 31 March 2021, in compliance with the European IDD Directive, and the Insurance Code, is brought to our attention. According to the aforementioned Regulation, insurance distributors are obliged to deliver to the customer/insured person a whole series of documents to supplement/correspond to the insurance contract.[91] The protective function of such a documental requirement on the part of the

---

possible termination of the contract for breach in the existence of all the conditions set forth in Art. 1453 et seq.

[88] On the subject, with different perspectives, see, among others, Scognamiglio (n.d.). Scognamiglio (2008), pp. 599 ff.; Vettori (2008), pp. 104 ff.; Gentili (2008) p. 393; Maffeis (2008), pp. 403 ff.; Perlingieri (2013), who points out that to establish 'whether or not a mandatory rule affects the validity of the contract it is necessary not only to investigate the relationship existing between the area of the fact and the area of value and to understand whether or not the misconduct has penetrated the regulation of interests determining a structural or functional disvalue of the act, but also to analyse the interests implicit in the rule and those involved in the concrete case so as to enucleate the remedy most suited to satisfy those interests' (p. 112). To this end, the author points out, it is necessary to consider the consequences to which the application of each of the remedies abstractly available leads, giving preference to the one that guarantees, in the light of the parameters of reasonableness, adequacy and effectiveness, a considered balancing between the conflicting needs and the prevalence of the interest that, in the light of the system, appears worthy of implementation (p. 115). In a much more radical perspective, see, instead, D'Amico (2006), pp. 1004 ff., according to whom 'the invalidity of the act may derive exclusively from the occurrence of a case outlined by the legislature, but never from a case constructed by the judge in the application/concretion of the general clause of good faith'.

[89] Cf., on this point, Polidori (2014), p. 654, who, taking up the author's thought, agrees that, with reference to a series of cases considered by the author, 'nullity does not constitute an adequate remedy for the violation of rules of conduct, which are no longer considered in the light of a non-existent principle of non-interference, but rather of the unreasonable consequences to which its application would lead'.

[90] It is precisely the principle of proportionality, whose canon must guide the judge when investigating the meaning of the law, that inspires the above-mentioned decision of the SS.UU. No. 898 of 16 January 2018, where it points out that to derive the sanction of the nullity of the contract from the intermediary's failure to sign the framework contract would mean moving '*in an exasperatingly sanctioning* direction', reaching '*a result that is manifestly disproportionate to the function for which the form is preordained here*'.

[91] Specifically: a document called 'INFORMATION ON THE DISTRIBUTOR- ANNEX 3, IVASS REG. 40/2018', containing the list of the main information obligations aimed at ensuring maximum transparency in the relationship; this document must be provided to the customer or potential

customer is evident, since, as in other hypotheses, it is aimed, for the most part, at bridging an information *gap* and permitting a conscious exercise of private autonomy. Now, the aforesaid Regulation does not impose civil law sanctions for non-compliance with the aforesaid prescriptions, and it must reasonably be considered that such non-compliance cannot, in any respect, affect the validity of the contract, not even from the point of view of the aforesaid abuse in the exercise of private autonomy; however, such non-compliance, in addition to the administrative sanctions contemplated, is capable of determining the insured party's right to compensation for damages, provided that he proves the existence thereof.

It is also worth recalling that Art. 166 CAP already required, as a general rule, the drafting of the insurance contract and the related documents 'in a clear and exhaustive manner' (para 1), highlighting with 'particularly prominent features' the clauses indicating forfeitures, nullity, limitation of guarantees or burdens to be borne by the policyholder or the insured (para 2). Evidently, this is a formal requirement integrating an objective rule aimed at responding to the need for insurance contracts to be fully comprehensible by the addressees, often characterised by a gap in professionalism or, more generally, in information.[92] The Court of Cassation recently expressed an opinion on the effects of this provision,[93] which highlighted how the requirement for clauses to be readable has been standardised in a general way, establishing that the relative violation, as a violation of a rule of conduct, gives rise to compensation for damages for breach of good faith.[94]

---

customer at the first meeting. A document called 'LIST OF THE DISTRIBUTOR'S RULES OF BEHAVIOUR ANNEX 4-TER, IVASS REG. 40/2018', containing the list of the obligations expected of intermediaries, to be displayed on the premises or published on the website and to be given to the customer only in the case of off-premises/distance sales; this document must be given to the contracting party before the conclusion of the contract or, if applicable, the signing of the proposal. A document entitled 'LIST OF INSURANCE UNDERTAKINGS WITH WHICH THE INTERMEDIARY HAS OR MAY HAVE BUSINESS RELATIONSHIP'. A suitability questionnaire (for policyholders only): containing a grid of questions aimed at identifying, through an effective dialogue between the Intermediary and the policyholder, the insurance product that is consistent with the policyholder's requests and needs Copy of the pre-contractual documentation and the Information Set.

[92] On this point, very clearly, the intervention of the Secretary General of Ivass, De Polis (2021) in https://www.ivass.it/media/interviste/intervista/sdp-sapienza-22-02-21/.

[93] Cass. 11 June 2019, No. 15598, in *Guida dir.*, 2019, 39, 60.

[94] The judgment states: 'the formal requirement laid down in Art. 166 D. Lgs. 209 of 2005 (…) does not extend the list of vexatious clauses, but standardises in a general way the need for the requirement of legibility of the clauses (which is now typified and formalised)' and established, with regard to the consequences of the violation of the rule in question, that 'the failure to comply with the formal requirement, as a violation of a rule of conduct, can only give rise to compensation for damages for breach of good faith, It may integrate a pre-contractual liability, with compensatory consequences where such violations occur in the phase preceding or coinciding with the conclusion of the contract, or a contractual liability that may possibly lead to the termination of the contract, where the violations concern the further implementation of the contractual provisions'.

Similarly, on the subject of intermediary liability in financial intermediation contracts, the jurisprudence[95] is, in agreement, oriented towards configuring the breach of the duties of informing the customer and of the proper execution of contractual procedural transactions that the law places on persons authorised to provide financial investment services in accordance with the provisions of primary legislation and the Consob regulation, in terms of pre-contractual liability, with compensatory consequences, where such violations occur in the phase preceding or coinciding with the conclusion of the financial intermediation contract intended to regulate the subsequent relationship between the parties (so-called framework contract), and in terms of contractual liability, with possible termination of the contract, where it concerns breaches relating to investment or disinvestment transactions carried out in performance of the financial intermediation contract.[96] In any event, jurisprudence excludes the possibility that the breach of the aforementioned duties of conduct may give rise, pursuant to Art. 1418(1) of the Civil Code, to the nullity of the brokerage contract or of the individual acts of negotiation entered into pursuant thereto.

2.6 Concluding Remarks

Obviously, this cannot be the place for an analysis of the many contractual cases involving the prescriptions of form and proceduralisation of the contract dictated by the independent authorities, in the various market sectors in which they intervene. However, the aforementioned hypotheses, like many others that can be envisaged, identify prescriptions—originating from secondary sources—aimed at regulating the so-called pre-contractual phase and the formation of the contract. However, the aforementioned hypotheses, like many others that may be envisaged, identify prescriptions—originating from secondary sources—aimed at regulating the so-called pre-contractual and agreement formation phase, and sometimes the executive phase of the contract, imposing on the operators behaviours and procedural burdens, in a protective key, that do not directly affect the content and structure of the contract; and, therefore, in such cases, in the event of violation by the operators of the supervised sector, they are the cause of the mere liability of the latter,[97] without prejudice, of course, to the possibility for the user to invoke the annulment of the contract for error, provided the prerequisites exist. The latter remedy, which, as mentioned in Sect. 1 of this chapter, may find, precisely because of the peculiarities that charac-

[95] For jurisprudence of legitimacy, see, among others, Cass. 16 May 2016, no. 9981, in *Guida dir.*, 2016, 36, 74; Cass. 26 October 2015, no. 21711, in *Guida dir.*, 2016, 4, 59; Cass. 10 April 2014, no. 8462, in *Giust. civ. Mass.*, 2014; for jurisprudence on the merits, among the most recent, Trib. Ascoli Piceno, 3 August 2022, no. 520, *Maximum drafting Giuffrè* 2022; App. Bari 12 January 2022, no. 47, *Giuffrè drafting maxim*, 2022; Trib. Ancona 30 July 2021, no. 1002, *Giuffrè drafting maxim*, 2021.

[96] On this topic, see, most recently, Di Biase (2023), pp. 145 ff.

[97] See Cass. 22 May 2020, no. 9468, in *Guida dir.*, 2020, 38, 54.

terise the formative *process* of contracts concluded through platforms, ample room for application for both the traditional hypotheses of 'defect error' and 'obstructive error'.

In the hypothesis, on the other hand, where the secondary source clearly tends to affect the structure of the contract by laying down prescriptions pertaining to the so-called form-content, the decisive effect cannot be said to be excluded *a priori* on the sole ground that the secondary source is incapable of overcoming the reservation of the law contained in Art. 41(3) of the Constitution. In fact, in the light of what has been said above, this approach may be legitimately called into question by the court's assessment of the concrete case in the light of Art. 1322 of the Civil Code and of a non-preconceived reading of the regulatory sources, first of all identifying the nature of the interests underlying the form requirement coming from the secondary source[98] and attributing to it, if not the direct suitability to affect the validity of the contract, the value of a relevant index of an abnormal and/or abusive use of private autonomy and, therefore, for the purposes of the examination of the legality and merits of the contract. Scrutiny to be carried out in the light of a series of primary rules, expressed in Articles 1375 and 1175 of the Civil Code, as well as the principle of solidarity expressed in Art. 2 of the Constitution, to guarantee the effective exercise of private autonomy.

How demanding this heuristic task is is intuitive to perceive; how much it must be exercised by the judge with extreme caution and without illegitimate forward races is equally obvious. Indeed, it is incumbent on the interpreter to use with extreme caution the remedy of nullity, which, albeit in the polyformism that now connotes it, still represents an extreme *ratio*, the use of which, too often nonchalant and not always founded on solid normative foundations capable of overcoming the silence of the legislator,[99] is apt to undermine the security of trade and even, at times, to become what has been effectively defined as[100] 'a surreptitious way for the parties (or rather the party that has an interest in it) to escape from the contractual bond'.

References

Addis F (2006) La produzione di clausole d'uso e la loro efficacia nei settori di mercato sottoposti al controllo di autorità indipendenti. In: AA VV (ed) L'autonomia privata e le autorità indipendenti, pp 111 ff

Albanese A (2008) Regole di condotta e regole di validità nell'attività di intermediazione finanziaria. Corr giur, pp 107 ff

Alpa G (2022) Sul potere contrattuale delle piattaforme digitali. Contr impr 2022:733 ff

[98] For a comprehensive and interesting analysis with reference to multiple cases, see Fauceglia (2021), pp. 255 ff.

[99] The point is well highlighted in the recent arrest of the SS.U., 16 November 2022, no. 33719, cited above, with reference to so-called virtual nullities.

[100] Delfini (n.d.), pp. 1 ff., 176.

Amadio G (2006a) Autorità indipendenti e invalidità del contratto. In: Gitti G (ed) L'autonomia privata e le autorità indipendenti. Bologna, pp 220–224
Amadio G (2006b) Forma, causa ed oggetto del contratto: tratti comuni e profili differenziali. https://www.iurisprudentia.it
Amato G (1997) Le autorità indipendenti nella Costituzione economica. In: AA VV (ed) Regolazione e garanzia del pluralismo. Le Autorità indipendenti. Milano
Angelone M (2012) Autorità indipendenti e eteroregolamentazione del contratto. Napoli, pp 199 ff
Angelone M, Zarro M (eds) (2022) Diritto civile della regolazione. Conformazione degli atti di autonomia e disciplina dei mercati. Jovene, Napoli
Barcellona P (1962) Profili della teoria dell'errore nel negozio giuridico, Milano
Battelli E (2022) Questioni aperte in tema di contrattazione nelle piattaforme on line. Contr, pp 563 ff
Berti de Martinis G (2013) La forma del contratto nel sistema di tutela del contraente debole. Napoli, pp 67 ff
Besson M, Di Paolo M (1988) Apparenza. Enc giur. Roma, pp 1 ff
Bevivino G (2024) Smart contracts e 'assestamenti' della disciplina generale del contratto. Contr impr 2024:407–408
Bocchini R (2021) La polivalenza delle posizioni contrattuali nella sharing economy. Nuovo dir civ 1:246 ss
Bove A (2009) Le violazioni delle regole di condotta degli intermediari finanziari al vaglio delle Sezioni Unite. Banca borsa 2:133 ff
Calisai F (2008) La violazione degli obblighi di comportamento degli intermediari finanziari: il contratto di intermediazione davanti ai giudici, fino alla tanto attesa (o forse no) pronuncia delle Sezioni Unite della Corte di Cassazione. Resp civ prev, pp 547 ff
Camardi C (2013) La protezione dei consumatori tra diritto civile e regolazione del mercato. A proposito dei recenti interventi sul codice del consumo. Jus Civile 6:305 ff
Camardi C (2021) Contratti digitali e mercati delle piattaforme. Un promemoria per il civilista. www.juscivile.it
Camardi C (2023) "Gigantismo" e disuguaglianze dell'economia dei dati. Appunti sulla governance europea nelle relazioni digitali. Ianus Diritto e Finanza 27:59 ff
Casolari F (2024) Il Digital Services Act e la costituzionalizzazione dello spazio digitale europeo. Giur it 2024:462 ff
Cassano G (2005) Diritto dell'internet. Il sistema di tutele della persona. Milano, p. 186
Cassano G, Cimmino IP (2002) Contratto via internet e tutela della parte debole. Contr 2002:869
Ciacci G (2002) La firma digitale. Milano, pp 67 ff
Clarich M (2003) Per uno studio sui poteri normativi della Banca d'Italia. Banca Impresa Soc 3:49–69
Contaldo A (2021) Le piattaforme digitali
Cottino G (2008) La responsabilità degli intermediari finanziari e il verdetto delle Sezioni Unite: chiose, considerazioni e un elogio dei giudici. Dir banca merc finanz 1:691 ff
D'Amelio M (1957) Apparenza del diritto. Noviss Dig it I:714 ff
D'Amico G (1996) Regole di validità e principio di correttezza nella formazione del contratto. Napoli, pp 44 ff
D'Amico G (2002) Regole di validità e regole di comportamento nella formazione del contratto. Riv Dir Civ I:37–60
D'Amico G (2006) La responsabilità precontrattuale. In: Roppo V (ed) Trattato del contratto, V, Rimedi, 2, Milano, pp 1004 ff
De Leo F (2013) Sospensione dell'account da parte di eBay. Nota a Trib. Catanzaro 30 aprile 2012. Resp civ prev 2013:2015 ff
De Polis S (2021) La semplificazione dei contratti assicurativi. Consenso, Forma e Trasparenza dall'età dell'emergenza all'età digitale. Disponibile su. https://www.ivaffit/media/interviste/intervista/sdp-sapienza-22-02-21/

Delfini F (n.d.) Il controllo ex art. 4, legge n. 287/1990, dell'autorità antitrust sul contenuto del contratto. In: AA VV (ed) L'autonomia privata e le autorità indipendenti, pp 1 ff
Di Benedetto G (2009) Scrittura privata e documento informatico. Riconoscimento, disconoscimento, verificazione. Milano, pp 331 ff
Di Biase A (2023) Gli obblighi informativi dell'intermediario finanziario nella prestazione dei servizi d'investimento. Torino, pp 145 ff
Di Majo A (1993) La correttezza dell'attività di intermediazione mobiliare. Banca Borsa I:291–310
Dossetto M (1959) Condizioni generali di contratto. Noviss Dig it III:1112
Draetta U (2001) Internet e commercio elettronico nel diritto internazionale dei privati, pp 57 ff
Falzea A (1958) Apparenza. Enc dir II:682 ff
Farace D (2012) Art. 1339 cod. civ., provvedimenti delle Autorità indipendenti ed eterointegrazione del contratto. Nuova Giur Civ Comm II:656–670
Fauceglia D (2021) I mercati regolati e l'integrazione dei contratti di impresa. Napoli, pp 238–240
Febbrajo T (2008) Violazione delle regole di comportamento nell'intermediazione finanziaria e nullità del contratto: la decisione delle Sezioni Unite. Giust civ, pp 2775 ff
Ferri GB (1977) Nullità parziale e clausole vessatorie. Riv dir comm I:11–ss
Foltran F (2019) Professionisti, consumatori e piattaforme on line: la tutela delle parti deboli nei nuovi equilibri negoziali. www.MediaLaws.eu, p 165
Galgano F (2008) Il contratto di intermediazione finanziaria davanti alle Sezioni Unite della Cassazione. Contr impr, pp 1 ff
Genovese A (1954) Le condizioni generali di contratto. Padova, pp 232 ff
Gentili A (2000) L'inefficacia del contratto telematico. Riv Dir Civ, pp 762–778
Gentili A (2008) Disinformazione e invalidità: i contratti di intermediazione dopo le Sezioni Unite. Contratti, pp 393 ff
Gentili A, Battelli E (2012) Le patologie del contratto telematico. In: AA VV (ed) Le tutele dei consumatori in internet e nel commercio elettronico. Milano I, pp. 419–431
Graziosi A (1998) Premesse ad una teoria probatoria del documento informatico. Riv trim dir proc civ 1998:515 ff
Greco F (2009) Intermediazione finanziaria: violazione di regole comportamentali e tutela secondo le Sezioni Unite. Banca borsa 2:133 ff
Irti N (1998) Scambi senza accordo. Riv trim dir proc civ, pp 347 ff
Irti N (2001) Norma e luoghi. Problemi di geo-diritto, Roma
Irti C (2024) Piattaforme digitali, contratti e protezione dei dati personali. Contr, pp 5 ff
Maffeis D (2008) Discipline preventive nei servizi di investimento: le Sezioni Unite e la notte (degli investitori) in cui tutte le vacche sono nere. Contratti, pp 403 ff
Mariconda V (2008) L'insegnamento delle Sezioni Unite sulla rilevanza della distinzione tra norme di comportamento e norme di validità. Corr giur, pp 230 ff
Martinelli S (2023) I contratti della. Platform Economy
Mazzini F (2008) L'ambito applicativo della nullità virtuale e gli obblighi di astensione dell'intermediario nella sentenza delle Sezioni Unite. Riv dir comm obbligaz 2:1189 ff
Mengoni L (1997) Autonomia privata e costituzione. Banca borsa titoli di credito, p 9
Merusi F (2006) Il potere normativo delle autorità indipendenti. In: Gitti G (ed) L'autonomia privata e le autorità indipendenti. Bologna, pp 44–62
Minussi D (2006) Riproduzione di un documento informatico e clausole vessatorie. Dir internet 2006, pp 445 ff
Monticelli S (2021) Il ruolo "ambivalente" della norma dispositiva nel contratto. Nuovo diritto civile, 2:5 ff e 33 ff
Monticelli S (2023) Procedimentalizzazione contrattuale e «neoformalismo». In: AA VV (ed) Conformazione del contratto e Autorità Indipendenti nel diritto Italo-Europeo. Atti del XVI Convegno Nazionale SISDIC. Napoli, pp 161–169
Moschella R (1973) Contributo alla teoria dell'apparenza giuridica, Milano
Napolitano G, Zoppini A (n.d.) Regolazione indipendente dei servizi pubblici e garanzia dei privati. In: AA VV (ed) L'autonomia privata e le autorità indipendenti, pp 137 ff

Nappi A (1989) Falsità personale. Enc giur XIV:1
Palmieri A (2019) Profili giuridici delle piattaforme digitali
Perlingieri P (1999) Relazione conclusiva. In Authorities e tutela della persona. Napoli, pp. 284–290
Perlingieri P (2011) Il contratto telematico. In: Valentino D (ed) Manuale di diritto dell'informatica. Napoli, pp 320 ff
Perlingieri G (2013) L'inesistenza della distinzione tra regole di comportamento e di validità nel diritto italo-europeo, Napoli
Perlingieri P (2017) "Controllo" e "conformazione" degli atti di autonomia negoziale. Rassegna di diritto civile, pp 214 ff
Pietrobon V (1990) Errore, volontà e affidamento nel negozio giuridico, Padova
Pisani G (2023) Piattaforme digitali e autodeterminazione
Polidori S (2014) Recensione a G. Perlingieri, L'inesistenza della distinzione tra regole di comportamento e di validità nel diritto italo-europeo, Napoli, 2013. Rassegna di diritto civile, 2, p 654
Proto M (n.d.) Questioni in tema di intelligenza artificiale e disciplina del contratto. Revista Actualidad Jurídica Iberoamericana
Quarta A (2017) Il diritto dei consumatori ai tempi della peer economy. Prestatori di servizi e prosumers: primi spunti. Eur dir priv 2017:667 ff
Ritzer G, Jurghenson N (2010) Production, consumption, prosumption. The nature of capitalism in the age of the digital "Prosumer". J Consum Cult 10:13 ff
Roppo E (2001) Il contratto. Milano, p 86
Rosciano M (2002) La conclusione del contratto telematico: tutela attuale e prospettive future. Verso una nuova dimensione della contrattazione. In: AA VV (ed) Diritto delle nuove tecnologie informatiche e dell'Internet, edited by G. Cassano, Milano, pp 559 ff
Ruffolo U (2024) Piattaforme e content moderation negoziale. Giur it, pp 442 ff
Ruggieri F (2021) Regole di trasparenza e rapporti tra imprese nei mercati digitali: il regolamento (UE) 2019/1150 sull'intermediazione online e i motori di ricerca. Dir inf, pp 397 ff
Salanitro U (2008) Violazione della disciplina dell'intermediazione finanziaria e conseguenze civilistiche: ratio decidendi e obiter dicta delle Sezioni Unite. Nuova giurisprudenza civile commentata, pp 445 ff
Sangiovanni V (2008) Commento a Caff S.U. 19 dicembre 2007, n. 26724 e 26725. Contratti, pp 231 ff
Scoditti E (2008) La violazione delle regole di comportamento dell'intermediario finanziario e le Sezioni Unite. Foro italiano I:784 ss
Scognamiglio C (2008) Regole di validità e di comportamento: i principi e i rimedi. Europa e diritto privato, pp 599 ff
Scognamiglio C (n.d.) Regole di validità e regole di correttezza nel nuovo diritto dei contratti. Quaderni della Fondazione Italiana del Notariato
Sforza F (1997) Conclusione del contratto e strumenti informatici. Contr, p 89
Speziale I (2020) La Dir. 2019/2161/UE tra protezione dei consumatori e promozione della competitività sul mercato unico. Corr giur, pp 441 ff
Stucchi M (n.d.) DSA: le nuove regole per le piattaforme online
Tommasini MF (2022) Lo smart contract e il diritto dei contratti. www.juscivile.it, p 4
Trezza R (2021) Il contratto nell'era del digitale e dell'intelligenza artificiale. Dir Economia 2021:297–298
Trubiani F (2022) Poteri regolatori dell'AGCM ed efficacia conformativa del contratto. In: Angelone M, Zarro MC (eds) Diritto civile della regolazione. Conformazione degli atti di autonomia e disciplina dei mercati. Napoli, pp 20–21
Ventrella T (2013) La validità del contratto online: "ipertrofia" delle tutele o mero formalismo? www.archivioceradi.luiffit, pp 9 ss e 13 ff
Vettori G (2008) Regole di validità e di responsabilità di fronte alle Sezioni Unite. La buona fede come rimedio risarcitorio. Obbligazioni e contratti, pp 104 ff
Villa G (1993) Contratto e violazione di norme imperative. Milano, pp 114 ff
Viti V (2013) Il contratto e le autorità indipendenti. Napoli, p 107

Right of Withdrawal

Matteo Nuzzo

Contents

Abstract The chapter analyses the rules governing withdrawal in the context of digital platforms, distinguishing between withdrawal from participation in the platform and withdrawal from individual contracts signed through it. The discussion begins with the European regulatory framework, particularly EU Regulation 2019/1150, known as the Platform to Business Regulation, and EU Regulation 2022/2065, known as the Digital Services Act, highlighting how European legislators tend to favour alternative instruments to withdrawal, such as suspension or limitation of service, leaving definitive termination as a residual option.

The author investigates the three main sources of withdrawal: general legal, specific legal and contractual, highlighting how the exercise of withdrawal differs

M. Nuzzo (✉)
University of Naples "Parthenope", Naples, Italy
e-mail: matteo.nuzzo@uniparthenope.it

R. Bocchini (ed.), *Digital Platforms - From Technical Foundations to Legal and Economic Implications*, https://doi.org/10.1007/978-3-032-07978-7_14

according to the nature of the platform (small or large), the status of the subject (supplier, commercial operator or consumer), and the structure of the legal relationship (continuous, occasional or contractually defined).

A coherent set of rules on withdrawal is then reconstructed, also by analogy, in the light of the principles of fairness, transparency and proportionality. The chapter highlights the tension between economic freedom and the protection of user trust, emphasising the importance of notice procedures, justification and data retention even after withdrawal, particularly for platforms of systemic importance. Finally, an evolutionary interpretation of withdrawal as an ordinary instrument of contractual self-determination is proposed, even in digital relationships, in response to the growing standardisation and automation of online legal relationships.

1 Withdrawal from the Digital Platform and Withdrawal from the Contract Concluded Through the Digital Platform

The regulation of the relationship between the provider and recipient of services of *online* platforms,[1] in promoting participation in these according to principles of fairness and transparency, does not contain a systematic regulation of the withdrawal[2] of the recipients of the services, whether they are traders[3] or consumers.

The Regulation of the European Parliament and of the Council 2019/1150, known as the Regulation Platform to Business or P2B,[4] merely states that, in the event that the provider of *online* intermediation services decides to exercise a right of withdrawal—based on compelling reasons under national law in accordance with Union law—the 30-day notice period provided for in the case of termination of the supply to the business user does not apply. On the other hand, the business user is given the power to terminate the contract with the *online* intermediary service provider, pending the notice period provided for in the event of a change in the terms and conditions of the service applicable to him.

[1] Alpa (2022), pp. 721 ff.; Carleo (2022), pp. 73 ff.; Bocchini (2002), pp. 471 ff.; Tosi (2021), pp. 283 ff.; Giannone Codiglione (2022), pp. 283 ff.

[2] The absence of a specific regulation of withdrawal in the new system of digital services is also highlighted by Morotti (2020), pp. 1369 ff. who, in this perspective, investigates in particular cases of abuse of the instrument of protection.

[3] Bocchini (2021), pp. 246 ff.

[4] Among the earliest comments on the P2B Regulation, see Ruggeri (2021), p. 319, who highlights among the most innovative features of this legislative intervention the perspective of protection of the weaker party addressed to companies, [*rectius* the commercial operators] as new weak subjects in the economy of platforms and, only '*by reflex, also to protection of the final recipients of consumer offers*'.

The Regulation 2022/2065, known as the Digital Service Act (DSA), on digital platforms essentially takes up the pattern of the previous P2B Regulation by giving the service provider the power to make decisions affecting the recipient of the service, including the termination of the service or the closure of the *account*.

The even more recent Directive No. 2831/2024 on the improvement of working conditions in work through digital platforms,[5] despite its recognition of the need to protect workers and improve working conditions in algorithmic management, to promote transparency, fairness, human supervision, safety and accountability of work performed through digital platforms, merely establishes the cases in which digital work platforms restrict[6] the account of the employee without terminating the relationship.

Regarding online brokerage services, in fact, the European legislator seems to prefer alternative solutions to termination by introducing figures that affect operators' participation in the digital platform, such as limitation and suspension of the service or account, leaving the definitive termination of the relationship a residual role.[7]

---

[5] Donini (2019) and Smorto and Donini (2024). Digital work platforms differ from other *online* platforms in that they use automated monitoring systems or automated decision-making systems to organise the work performed by individuals at the request, *one-off* or repeated, of the recipient of a service provided by the digital platform. These characteristics make digital work platforms a distinct form of organising the provision of services by professionals as opposed to more traditional forms of organising the provision of services, such as the classic forms of DRT or dispatching transport services. This way of organising work through digital platforms often entails a wide range of different and complex multilateral relationships that expose service providers to the absence of the legal protections provided for the activity performed. In order to counteract this potential prejudice, this directive introduces a legal presumption of an employment relationship in favour of persons performing work through digital platforms by allowing the application of the relevant discipline as defined by law, collective agreements or practice in force in the Member States, taking into account the case law of the Court of Justice, where facts indicating direction and control are found.

[6] *Account* limitation is any restriction imposed on a person to perform work via digital platforms through the *account*, including limiting access to the *account* or work assignments. In such cases, according to the directive, digital work platforms shall provide, without undue delay and no later than the day on which the decision takes effect, a written justification for any decision taken or supported by an automated decision-making system to limit, suspend or close the person's account, any decision not to remunerate the work performed, any decision regarding the contractual situation, any decision with similar effects or any other decision affecting the essential aspects of the employment or other contractual relationship.

[7] It is a complex and delicate question to establish whether the platform constitutes only the place where the *peer-to-peer* matching of supply and demand of the service takes place or whether an employment relationship can be configured between the platform and those who perform, on its behalf, the service requested in favour of the users. Communication COM 356/2016 from the Commission to the European Parliament, the European Economic and Social Committee and the Council of the Regions of 2 June 2016, A European agenda for the collaborative economy, at *https://ec.europa.eu/transparency/regdoc/rep/1/2016/EN/1-2016-356-EN-F1-1.PDF*, 13, points out that '*the boundaries between self-employed and employed workers are becoming increasingly blurred*' and suggests that the existence or otherwise of an employment relationship should be

An analysis on withdrawal must therefore, first, investigate whether, within these cases, the institution, while retaining a residual nature in favour of the preservation of the concluded legal transaction, constitutes an exceptional hypothesis only in the cases expressly provided for by the legislature or must assume a different role on account of the needs of the operators and the purposes of the overall discipline on the subject of *online* intermediation services on a digital platform.

At the operational level, this translates into the assertion that the 'bare' definition of termination included in the aforementioned legal texts is exhaustive of the hypotheses applicable in practice to the power of unilateral termination of the relationship, or whether it should be supplemented with the set of specific and general legal provisions on termination provided for in the European and national legal order, attributing to termination a role and function other than exceptional.

Inducing in the latter direction are the specific legal data—which places the termination exercised for compelling reasons under national provisions among the cases in which the termination of the relationship by the service provider does not require prior notice, which may be understood as a general reference[8] to the regulation of termination already operating in the individual national systems—and the general data on the purpose of the regulation of digital platforms and coordination with national systems.

The European legislator, in fact, indicates among the purposes of *online* intermediation services to be determining elements for entrepreneurship and new *business* models, trade and innovation, as they can contribute to improving consumer welfare.[9] These tools offer access to new markets and business opportunities, allowing businesses to explore the advantages of the internal market and consumers a greater choice of goods and services, as well as more competitive prices, so much so that most EU citizens now use these services daily, with the consequent new risks and challenges for businesses and society.

The sector-specific rules must therefore recognise and safeguard the considerable innovation potential of the whole economy of *online* platforms and allow for healthy competition that provides consumers with more choice without undermining national civil contract law, notably on the validity, formation, effects or

established on a case-by-case basis on the basis of three essential criteria: - the existence of a relationship; - the nature of the work; - the presence of remuneration.

[8] The textual datum expressly refers only to termination based on compelling reasons, but the specification of the reference to reasons of a higher order is justified by the derogation to the rules on notice considered by the European legislator to be essential in order to guarantee fairness and transparency in relations. Nothing therefore seems to preclude an interpretation of the text that identifies a general reference to the cases of termination provided for by national law as a valid cause for the termination of the relationship between supplier and user in compliance with the procedure and the 30-day notice period, and a specific reference to the overriding cases of termination under that law as justification for the derogation from the aforementioned notice period.

[9] On the operation of trading platforms and the clarity of information Gentili and Battelli (2011), pp. 379 ff.

termination of a contract. Hence, the statement that '*Member States should not adopt or maintain additional national requirements in relation to matters falling within the scope of this Regulation, unless expressly provided otherwise* in *this Regulation*'[10] with a risk of prejudice to the direct and uniform application of the fully harmonised rules applicable to intermediary service providers in accordance with the objectives of this Regulation, without prejudice to the possibility of applying other national rules where the provisions of national law pursue legitimate public interest objectives different from those pursued by this Regulation.

Consistent with the foregoing, the possibility of facilitating this exploration through simple means of access and exit from the platform itself by users, whether commercial or not, must be affirmed, as well as the possibility for providers of intermediation services themselves to propose innovative formulas and services[11] possibly even permanently discontinuing the platform that is no longer adequate or performing to make it more efficient and improve the competitiveness of the services.[12] The concrete discipline applicable to the digital platform is shaped, according to the principle of subsidiarity,[13] by its ability to provide services that are appreciated by the market and the consequent dimension.[14] Different rules are stable for providers of digital platforms that qualify as micro or small enterprises under European law, for providers of medium-sized platforms and for providers of very large digital platforms,[15] i.e. those that have acquired systemic value for the Union's market involving at least 10% of the European population, the termination of which, it must be assumed, is subject to a special procedure modelled on the crisis response

[10] Recital 8 of Regulation 2019/1150 which goes on to state that Member States remain free to apply national rules prohibiting or sanctioning unilateral conduct or unfair commercial practices insofar as the relevant aspects are not, however, covered by the Regulation.

[11] On the subject, see Perlingieri (2014), pp. 30 ff.; Ammannati (2021), pp. 3 ff.; Petruso (2017), pp. 451 ff.

[12] On this point, Carleo (2022), p. 80, highlights how also the case Angela Bolger vs Amazon.Com LLC, (2020 WL 4692387) Cal. Court of Appeal, 8/13/20 in which the California Court of Appeal ordered Amazon to be jointly and severally liable for the damages suffered by a person who had purchased a product from a third-party seller and manufacturer, which was 'recommended' by the platform, becomes a guarantee for the buyer and induces him to prefer this digital platform over others by enhancing its competitiveness.

[13] Carleo (2022), p. 81, points out how the necessary concrete application of the principle of subsidiarity emerges as a space for the responsible formation of rules created by private individuals or social institutions closest to the interests to be protected, which are delegated by the legislator to dictate rules also of general interest. On this point, also Fusco (2015), pp. 153 ff., according to whom, in the context of modernity, trade and economic phenomena are normally the recipients of '*different regulatory mechanisms, often entrusted to the initiative of private parties and more capable of adapting promptly to the rapid evolution of the matter to be regulated*'.

[14] Amidei (2023), pp. 1542 ff.

[15] These are, pursuant to Art. 33 of Regulation 2022/2065, those which have an average monthly number of active recipients of the service in the Union of 45 million or more and which are designated as such under the Regulation.

mechanism and must therefore be managed in compliance with the decisions adopted by the Commission.

On an even higher level, the most recent regulation on market and digital products seems to suggest a reflection on the topicality of the exceptional nature of withdrawal. The increasing complexity, standardisation, speed and frequency of contracts concluded predominantly through digital systems and tools further reduce, and on several occasions, as noted, reset to zero, the time and space for the formation of the negotiating will that should precede the manifestation of the will.[16] It is therefore necessary to preserve this reflection, shifting it to a moment subsequent to the stipulation, through the provision of the ordinariness of withdrawal within a congruous term, in respect of the fair balance of the interests of the parties involved in the legal transaction, which, on the contrary, might not be adequately ensured by a possible rigidity of the system closed in a predetermined and exclusive exceptional function of withdrawal.

The limitation of this flexibility is marked by the Regulation itself in the need to guarantee the legal certainty of the relationships established between the platform operators, avoiding sudden changes or actions that risk prejudicing traders or consumers.

The actual operation of the institute under consideration, therefore, does not find its specific discipline in the regulatory acts establishing the platforms, but it is mainly to be reconstructed through reference to the regulatory provisions provided for by the domestic laws on the subject of negotiating relationships and weak subjects, both in the relationship of dependence between service provider and commercial user and consumer, in light of the objectives of the Regulation as defined above.

In this perspective, the verification of compatibility and coordination between the regulatory provisions already present in the legal system and the specific discipline introduced by the EU legislation on digital platforms is entrusted to the interpreter and the relevant criterion identified within the Regulation itself.

The line of this investigation is twofold: the first aimed at defining the withdrawal from the platform, as a place where market players meet and where information, evaluations and negotiation exchanges take place;[17] the second, dealing with the right of withdrawal from the individual contract signed between operators on the platform.

The difference is substantial. In the case of the digital platform, in fact, as an open place which, by its very nature, market players must be able to access and withdraw freely, withdrawal is presented, at least in the first instance, as a natural and functional element whose possible limitation represents an exception that must be adequately justified. In this case, moreover, one of the two subjects of the

16 Irti (1998), pp. 347 ff.; Finocchiaro (2018), pp. 192 ff. On the specific topic of digital platforms, Battelli (2022), p. 563.

17 Di Sabato (2020), p. 11.

relationship, the provider of the digital intermediation services, is constant, varying only in the qualities and characteristics of the other subject of the relationship.

The second, on the other hand, is an exclusive and private relationship between two parties in which any withdrawal constitutes, according to the general rules, either the subject of a specific agreement between the parties or a regulatory exception justified by the particularities of the transaction, as in the case of contracts signed off-premises, or by the imbalance of bargaining power between the parties involved as in the case of consumer contracts.

The two cases, therefore, require an in-depth analysis of the function and effects that the possible exercise of the withdrawal power may have in either context.

2 Structure and Function of Withdrawal in *Online* Platforms and Intermediary Services

The definition of a digital platform or *online* platform as a *hosting* service provider which, at the request of a recipient of the service, stores and disseminates information to the public, with the sole exception of cases in which this activity is a minor and purely ancillary function that cannot be separated, is extremely broad and encompasses very different configurations.

As noted, since they are not all equal, they should therefore not receive the same legal treatment. Some platforms present themselves as marketplaces where people exchange information, emotions and opinions. Other platforms constitute virtual marketplaces where all kinds of goods and services can be purchased directly from producers, retailers or the platform operator.

Still others defined as large are characterised by having a significant impact on the internal market, such that they can lead to systemic effects on the entire Union and involve a very large number of active recipients.

Platforms are relevant for the construction of the internal digital market and the growth of business user services for consumers, but platforms that are qualified as large are crucial and systemic.

The already congenital fragmentary nature of withdrawal is thus enriched by further non-homogeneous contractual cases, requiring an analysis of the function and overall practical effect of its exercise with respect to the various hypotheses of the concrete.[18]

---

[18] Padovini (2012), pp. 86 ff., clarifies how the view that the figure of withdrawal is only apparently unitary has long been shared and how the functions assigned to withdrawal are plural. Beyond an initial bipartition between ordinary and extraordinary withdrawal a tripartition has now been affirmed, which distinguishes between: (1) determinative withdrawal, intended to mark the end of contracts of duration without a term, thus identifying the extent of the performance; (2) penitential withdrawal, intended to allow a party to regret the conventional rule already shared, thus negating the commitment made, such as that of the consumer; (3) appeal withdrawal, intended to allow a

Withdrawal, therefore, cannot be dealt with in the same way or with a single discipline in the different hypotheses, as it is characterised not only by the two types of platforms, but also by the subject, intermediary service provider, consumer or business user, to whom this power is attributed.

From a subjective point of view, as mentioned, the 2022 European legislator expressly speaks of termination of the relationship, particularly termination of the service or closure of the *account*, only in favour of the provider of the digital services. The Regulation P2B, in this respect, appears more complete by adding to this hypothesis the termination of the contract in the case of a declaration of termination of the relationship by the business user because of changes in the terms and conditions of the service.

Particularly, pursuant to the 2019 Regulations, in the event of a decision by the *online* intermediary service provider to determine the complete termination of the provision of services to a particular business user, the notice provided for in the relevant procedure must be at least 30 days to allow the user subject to the decision to prepare an adequate defence in respect of a final fact as important as the termination of the service.

At the same time, however, the procedure now indicated for the definitive termination of the relationship with the business user may be derogated from, limited to the application of the aforementioned minimum notice period, in the event of the exercise of a right of termination based on compelling reasons under national law in conformity with Union law, thus introducing a distinction between the open formula of termination, which can be traced back to several institutions, and the exercise of the power of termination conferred by the individual laws of the Member States.

The power of withdrawal already provided for by the individual legal systems, therefore, arises upstream and as a possible cause for the definitive termination of the relationship, but obviously does not exhaust its hypotheses. This confirms the need to verify the possible existence of a power of withdrawal different and additional to those already present in national laws, with reference to the provider of *online* intermediation services.

This investigation must be carried out considering the nature of the relationship that is created between the *online* platform provider and the users who participate in it, whether commercial or not. The adhesion to the digital platform determines, in fact, the birth of a relationship of indefinite duration with continuous performance in which the withdrawal is the only element capable of determining the termination of the effects of the contract, thus qualifying as determinative. Its operability, as confirmed by established doctrine and jurisprudence with reference to so-called

---

party to react with respect to original defects in the contract or with respect to facts that have arisen during the implementation of the relationship to which is added the further figure of the right of reconsideration, again to protect the consumer.

perpetual contracts, therefore constitutes a general rule as a technical instrument aimed at preventing the creation of bonds without a term.[19]

In addition to the cases already regulated by the individual states, it would therefore seem necessary to affirm, in line with the nature of the legal relationship between the service provider and users, a general power of withdrawal of a legal nature, the prerequisites and boundaries of which must necessarily be defined in accordance with the aims and objectives of the sector regulation.[20]

This assertion does not appear diminished, and indeed may find useful indications, in the other powers that the law attributes to the *online* service provider, such as in the case of information storage service providers who, in addition to the power to suspend or terminate the account of the recipient of the service, also have the power to suspend or terminate the provision of the service to a particular business user, including by removing individual goods or services offered by that user from the platform or by effectively eliminating search results, or to restrict individual business user referrals, for instance by negatively affecting the appearance of a business user (‘*dimming*’) or by downgrading the ranking.

Although these actions pertain to the performance of the contract and not to its termination, and therefore lie in a different area of the legal relationship under consideration, it appears useful to point out that, already with reference to the supplier’s

---

[19] Padovini (2012), pp. 86 ff., in investigating the boundaries and points of contact between withdrawal and termination affirms the relevance of the right of withdrawal as a remedy against contractual defects, contrasting or, rather, adding in one case to cancellation and in the other case to termination instruments. Of particular relevance in this context is withdrawal as a remedy for resolutory defects, which is usually referred to as withdrawal for just cause, but sometimes has different terms, such as exclusion (from association relationships) or revocation (from relationships having as their object the performance of activities). The author questions whether it is possible to configure withdrawal for just cause as a general remedy in relationships of duration beyond the legal cases, arriving at affirming the possibility: ‘*it seems truly singular to admit an unlimited power of determinative withdrawal - and therefore, with notice - but to deny that it may be exercised for just cause, so as to compel a party to take legal action, but being able to oppose immediately a plea of non-performance. The very content of the relationship, destined to develop over time, must therefore lead to recognizing an indiscriminate applicability of termination for just cause in relationships of duration - in deference to the general principle derivable from the discipline on determinative termination - so as to avoid procedural superfetation, unsuitable to satisfy substantial requirements*’. A similar solution cannot, according to the Author, be recognised in relationships of instantaneous performance, which require a determination by the parties in their exercise of private autonomy.

[20] He investigates the issue, from the perspective of the abuse of withdrawal, Morotti (2020), p. 1370, highlighting the dimension of the problem of frequent returns in *online* trade in the total percentage of goods returned to the seller in the 2-year period 2018–2019 equal to about 30% of the total purchases on e-commerce portals, while it drops to 8% for purchases in traditional shops. The group of so-called ‘*serial returners*’, continues the author, is very broad, covering various categories of people: those who deliberately order more goods than they want to keep (‘*over-purchase*’) amount to 30% of *online* buyers, while the percentage of so-called ‘*bracketers*’, i.e. those who order several versions of the same good but with different sizes, colours, etc., with the intention of trying them on and returning those that do not fit, reaches 56%.

restrictive powers during the course of the relationship, both the 2019 and the 2022 Regulations, to minimise their negative impact on business users, establish the need to provide *legitimate reasons* in support of the decisions taken. Not only that, but these reasons must also be communicated to the addressee of the decision, as part of the internal complaint handling process, to allow the addressee to clarify the facts behind the decision and help the business user, where possible, to re-establish compliance. Particularly, the community legislator introduces a real binding procedure for the application of limitations aimed at creating an adversarial process with the business user, who, except in exceptional cases, must be given adequate notice providing him with the opportunity to clarify the facts and circumstances within the internal complaint handling process. To this end, the decision must contain a statement of reasons that enable the recipient to identify the reasons for the decision, based on the provider's prior statements in the terms and conditions of service, and make proportionate reference to the relevant circumstances, including third-party notifications, that led to the decision. And this was necessary to increase their chances of an effective appeal.

At the end of the procedure, the decision may be confirmed and enforced or revoked. Thus, for example, if the decision was made in error or if the breach of the terms and conditions that led to the decision was not committed in bad faith and has been satisfactorily remedied, reinstating the affected business user without delay, including in any access to personal data, other data, or both, that were available prior to the decision.

The ultimate aim of the regulation under consideration thus appears to be to reduce the cases of limitation, and even more so of definitive termination, of services in line with the aim of promoting the participation and exploitation of the new technology by all users.

The regulation of the commercial user's power to definitively terminate the relationship is different. Provided for the sole case in which the service provider modifies the terms and conditions of the same during the course of the relationship,[21] it may be exercised only within the notice period, fixed by the Regulation as a reasonable and proportionate period of time having regard to the significance of the modification and the consequences for the user on a technical or commercial level, and in any case not less than 15 days, provided that the user does not, during this period,

[21] The text of the Regulation expressly speaks of termination, but the power to terminate the relationship in this case, as before, seems more correctly to be termination. The modification of the terms and conditions of the service is in fact a lawful act of exercise of the power expressly attributed to the service provider by the Rules and has in fact no consequences either in terms of compensation for damages or any indemnity. The commercial user, therefore, is legitimised to interrupt the relationship on the basis of the different operating rules of the platform according to a logic of convenience and possibly confirm his personal interest in participation. The configuration of this power seems consistent with what was said earlier on the role and function of withdrawal in legal relationships in which the formation of the will has strongly compressed spaces and times.

declare to renounce it or engages in conduct, such as the sale of its products or services, which by virtue of the factual circumstances can be considered conclusive.

The power seems to configure a hypothesis of protective withdrawal (or liberation), as *ius poenitendi*, allowing the business user not to continue the relationship in derogation of the general principle of the binding nature of the contract. In this case, as noted, the function of withdrawal is to free oneself from onerous contractual obligations in open-ended contracts. This power of termination specifically granted to the business user in particular cases is therefore in addition to the general power of termination indicated above, differing in its casuistry and procedure.

An even different configuration must be recognised for the consumer whose protection, in the absence of specific regulatory provisions, does not provide for exceptions and must therefore be sought in the typical discipline expressly recognised for him.

Thus, distinct lines of investigation emerge.

The first aimed at declining the power of withdrawal from a legal source that exists generally for all participants in the platform by virtue of a legal relationship of a permanent nature with no limit in duration.

A second, again from a legal source, on the specific assumptions in favour of the individual subjective categories of *online* intermediary service provider, business user and consumer.[22]

A third, on possible hypotheses and related procedures, is unilaterally prepared by the supplier.

3 The Different Cases of Legal Withdrawal by the Supplier of Digital Platforms

The legal framework provides for different withdrawal hypotheses with different prerequisites, purposes and, consequently, operational disciplines.

One in accordance with the general principle of termination *ad nutum* in relationships of indefinite duration; one connected to the power, again provided for by the DSA Regulation, to definitively terminate the relationship with one or more users with adequate justification; and a third connected to the exercise of a right of termination provided for by national law.

[22] Battelli (2022), p. 572, points out that in *platform economy* contracts there are three different subjects: on the one hand, the *online* platform and, on the other, those who do business, i.e. the users/digital consumers and the suppliers/professionals, the latter two being qualified indiscriminately as users of the services provided by the platform with rights and duties in a tendentially symmetrical measure, making both categories responsible for the fulfilment of the obligations undertaken.

3.1 The Termination of the Online Platform

The discipline of determinative withdrawal, as mentioned above, corresponds to the need of the legal system to contain, by making them exceptional cases of perpetual obligations.

For this reason, it must be held that, while qualifying as a strong subject of the legal relationship, the provider of the brokerage service may, like the other subjects of the *online* brokerage relationship, withdraw from the relationship at any time in respect of the entire platform. The case of withdrawal in respect of one or more users, on the other hand, is different.

The possibility of definitively discontinuing the provision of the *online* intermediation service falls within the scope of the freedom of economic initiatives and therefore does not seem to require any justification provided that the discontinuance is definitive and total with respect to all users. In this sense, partial terminations of the service, i.e. limited to certain categories of products or categories of business users, should be placed in the context of amendments to the terms and conditions and thus subject to different procedures.

Even full permanent withdrawal, however, is subject to the principles of fairness and transparency, as well as fairness and good faith, which require the provider to adopt a procedure to protect the interests of users that considers their economic dependence on the platform.[23]

Since this hypothesis is not expressly provided for by the Community regulations, it must be declined by analogy, moving based on the seriousness of the case in relation to the interests involved with a reasonable and proportionate notice, the purpose of which, however, in this case, is not to allow users to clarify facts and circumstances, or in any case to contest the provider's decision, but to reorganise their activity by searching for possible different digital platforms to replace the service.

---

[23] On the balance of power between the operators of the digital platform, see Battelli (2022), p. 573, highlights how consumers, traditionally considered the weaker party in the relationship, in the bargaining through digital platforms take on the role of evaluators influencing the choices of subsequent consumers by directing them towards other goods or services that are more liked and appreciated. This 'judging community' mechanism alters the traditional balance of power, without however completely overturning it, introducing however an innovative factor that must be considered in order to concretely assess the conduct of the parties and the specific case. At the same time, the trader in turn experiences a position of economic dependence on the platform and a strong subject of the direct contractual relationship with the consumer. On this point, also Quarta (2019), pp. 85 ff., recalls how the same case law has affirmed how the presence on the large platform of certain operators '*appears indispensable for the survival*' of the plaintiff company, since it leads to the conclusion that '*the indefinite exclusion from the same platform does not simply result in a mere loss of customers, but has a much heavier impact that can go so far as to substantially exclude the company from the market itself*'.

In this perspective, even the minimum term of 30 days, subject to the exceptions of Art. 4(4) of the P2B Regulation, provided for the termination of the supply with respect to an individual business user between the date of the notice and the date of actual termination, does not appear to be adequate, as a longer term should be provided, also in consideration of the position of economic dependence, recognised by law, to protect business users.

The relevant communication must be offered on a durable medium, i.e. by any means that enables the business user to store the information addressed to him personally in such a way that he can access it in the future and for a period of time appropriate to the purposes for which it is intended, and in any event not less than 6 months, and that enables the information stored to be reproduced identically, and during that period it appears necessary for the service provider to offer adequate technical and informational support to users.

The notice, in turn, must be such as to allow all business users to regularly complete their orders, reorganise and move to another digital platform on which to conduct their business.

To do so, the supplier must reasonably foresee a progressive termination of the brokerage service and of the operation of the platform by promptly informing all users, commercial and non-commercial, starting with the discontinuance of new orders, progressively ceasing functionality until, finally, product guarantees, while still assuring purchasers, particularly consumers, the possibility of asserting their rights against commercial users.

Also for these reasons, the service provider shall transfer to the users the personal data and other data collected to which, in accordance with the terms and conditions of the service, they have given access (or ensure an adequate system for storing, consulting and extracting the same) that enables them to continue to access such data in the continuation of their activity on another digital platform without undue limitations or burdens.

Similarly, the *online* platform provider will have to guarantee the traceability of traders for at least 6 months as stipulated in Art. 30 of the DSA Regulation.

It is a different matter, as mentioned above, for the provider of very large *online* platforms whose systemic relevance strongly conditions their freedom of action due to the presence of obligations to assess and act to protect against possible risks and crises directly involving the European Commission itself to ensure a safe, predictable and reliable *online* environment and to enable citizens of the Union and other persons to exercise their fundamental rights, particularly freedom of expression and information, freedom to conduct business, the right to non-discrimination and the achievement of a high level of consumer protection.

It seems, therefore, correct to state that in the event that the provider of a large digital platform wishes to cease its activity, exercising withdrawal vis-à-vis all recipients of the services, it must inform the Commission in order to allow the latter to assess, as the case may be, the adoption of a decision under the risk mitigation or crisis procedure.

3.2 *The Legal Termination of the Service or of the Account of One or More Commercial Operators*

The termination of the supplier with respect to one or more traders must be characterised differently.

As said, this hypothesis, already expressly regulated by the 2019 Regulation through a specific procedure that begins with the communication by the supplier to the user, on a durable medium, of the reasons on which the decision is based, is supplemented in the 2022 Regulation in several respects, including that of the motivation, the traceability of the trader, and the terms of retention of the relevant information.

The motivation in this case differs from that provided for with reference to the terms and conditions established by the provider, and thus to the hypothesis of withdrawal from a negotiated source, involving all cases in which the user's conduct can be considered relevant according to the rules, principles and values of the order in itself in relation to unlawful or inappropriate content such as the security of a good or service, counterfeiting, fraud, malware, spam, data breaches, other risks to cybersecurity or the suitability of the good or service for minors.

The supplier is obliged to formulate clear communication in which the reasons are verifiable and contestable by the addressee, with the possibility of recourse to mediation, consistently with the predominantly sanctioning-remedial nature[24] of this form of termination aimed at reacting to conduct or a fact in any case attributable to the user.

---

[24] Franzoni (n.d.), pp. 3 45 ff. The case in point, however, is distinguished by the autonomy of the features that are not peculiar to either the former or the latter. Of the former because the sanction requires prior typification of the relevant conduct and the applicable penalty. Of the second because, although it can be linked to open cases, it requires in any event the violation of an obligation of the party of a 'serious' nature. On this point see Trib. Messina 7 July 2010 with note by Quarta (2019), pp. 79 ff, where, in investigating the legitimacy of an account suspension ordered by eBay following a certain number of negative feedbacks received by the plaintiff company, as a breach of some clauses of the contract unilaterally drawn up by eBay and signed by the plaintiff, the Court held that the feedbacks received by the plaintiff did not allow, by quantity and content, to appreciate a serious breach of eBay's rules, affirmed that '*the attribution to the hoster of a power to decide, even in the absence of any assessment as to the seriousness of the breach, the termination of the contract and the suspension of the account, would in reality attribute to the same a power to unilaterally withdraw from the relationship*', a clause to be considered certainly vexatious and therefore in need of specific approval. The A. then emphasises that the interpretation of the unilateral termination appears even clearer in the decision of 30 April 2012 of the Court of Catanzaro in which the Court held that the suspension could not be qualified as a termination for non-performance pursuant to Art. 1453 of the Italian Civil Code, since this has a judicial nature and requires a constitutive ascertainment by the judge, whereas, in the case examined, it had been directly executed by the creditor party. Similarly, the suspension could not be considered as a termination by virtue of an express termination clause which, in order to be validly affixed to the contractual regulation, requires a specific indication of the obligations that must be performed under penalty of termination. Since it was a unilateral termination, therefore, the suspension had to be specifically regulated by a clause to be submitted for signature by the debtor.

Communication that must therefore contain adequate evidence to support the facts and circumstances underlying the decision, allowing the user to verify and contest them by offering justifications or evidence to the contrary.

However, the reasoning does not seem to have to go so far as to configure a true allegation of tort with consequent allegation and proof of the unjust injury to the interests of the provider or other users, causal link and compensable damage, it being sufficient that the content contested by the provider to the operator appears illegal.

The Regulation P2B merely states that the definitive termination of the service with respect to a commercial user is the most serious decision that the provider may take when the limitation or suspension does not appear to be a sufficient decision to guarantee the regularity, fairness, transparency and correctness of the service or products.

It seems then to be sufficient for these purposes that there is a reasonable danger to the defence of *online* brokering services, its consumers or other business users attributable to a business user, or a category of business users or products, that cannot be adequately overcome or removed by the mere modification of the terms and conditions of the service pursuant to Art. 3 above.

The Regulation DSA complements this discipline regarding information storage service providers, including *online* platforms, by providing (reiterating) the obligation of a clear and specific motivation in the event of total or partial termination of the service or termination of the account of the recipient of the service in the event that the latter provides information that constitutes illegal content. In this case, the statement of reasons must contain at least a minimum set of information ranging from procedural aspects (prior indication of the extent of the decision, voluntary or third-party origin of the proceedings and possible use of automated tools in the assessment process, means of appeal available to the recipient) to substantive ones, i.e. the legal basis and explanation of the reasons why the information of the recipient of the service is considered illegal. Under this last profile, the Regulation DSA raises the rigour of the motivation by providing that these, in addition to being clear and easily understandable, must be '*as precise and specific as possible*', taking into account the circumstances to reasonably allow the recipient to make effective use of the possibilities of appeal.

The motivation, therefore, rather than supporting the decision based on the analysis that preceded it, is intended to provoke an adequate adversarial process with the addressee that enables the provider to adequately assess, at the outcome of this adversarial process, whether to confirm, modify or revoke it. This is an action that the platform provider must perform, without undue delay, under the supervision of suitably qualified personnel and not by using automated tools only, communicating the outcome to the addressee equally without delay to enable him to act for the out-of-court settlement of the dispute. In this respect, too, there seems to be confirmation of a tendency in Community law on the subject of the digital marketplace to support the need for speed in the establishment and termination of relationships by altering the traditional relationship between the time and depth of reflection preceding the decision and its subsequent confirmation.

When exercising the power to terminate the service or account vis-à-vis the commercial operator, the digital platform provider will have to verify that the operational modalities of the termination do not result in harm to consumers who, at the time of the termination, have contractual relations still pending by virtue of contracts concluded with them at a distance through the platform.

4 The Supplier's Negotiated Termination

Even wider is the room for withdrawal entrusted to the negotiating autonomy of the provider of the *online* platform service in configuring, through the terms and conditions of service, further hypotheses of termination of the service vis-à-vis one or more business users.

Broader because, in addition to the possibility of being able to define in detail in which cases the violation, or the danger of violation, of the assumptions of the law may determine the termination of the service, it also allows him to foresee all those types of conduct that, in his opinion, may contribute to determining the characteristics, quality and reliability of the intermediation service (such as, for example, information, quality and product guarantees, timing, payment methods and instruments, consequences in the event of violation of the minimum conditions of sale of the products or payments) updating these provisions whenever deemed necessary or appropriate. The digital platform, given the reference market, is, therefore, by its very nature, constantly evolving, having to accommodate both the technological and the behavioural evolution of its users, business and consumers.

This unilateral power to configure withdrawal also contributes, therefore, to determining the competitiveness of the digital platform in relation to the others, with the consequence that the provision of particularly easy or strict, *non-standard* or innovative conditions of conduct for business users, contributing to the improvement of *online* intermediation services, is also fully among the main objectives of the Community legislator are, consequently, entirely legitimate.

The limits set by the rule, in fact, pertain to the principles of fairness and transparency, which are followed by the operational rules of clarity and availability of terms and conditions, but not to the ease of performance or earnings, which may or may not constitute elements of a certain entrepreneurial strategy in the placement of the platform on the market by the service provider.

The same regulatory limits apply to the withdrawal procedures, which may be modified by the service provider to adapt them to its own interests, without, however, being able to aggravate or reduce the minimum protections provided by the legislator, including the obligations concerning justification, notice, durable medium, complaint procedures and traceability of the trader even after withdrawal to enable consumers to retain effectively.

In this sense, the special rule laid down in the Regulation P2B also seems to be understood, according to which, in the event of repeated breach of the terms and conditions by the commercial user, the obligation to give notice of the reasons ceases to apply, the latter's excessive difficulty in complying with the rules of the digital platform being sufficient in itself to justify the termination of the relationship.

4.1 The Termination of the Service or Account in Respect of One or More Consumers

The legal treatment of the consumer within digital platforms is, as is evident, structurally different. The entire regulation is aimed at reaching consumers with the twofold purpose of improving their welfare through greater choice and more competitive prices, on the one hand, and enabling the growth of the digital market by allowing the presence and growth of micro, small and medium-sized enterprises and the control of large platform providers, on the other. The hypothesis of withdrawal by the provider of the intermediation service vis-à-vis the individual consumer therefore appears to be at odds with the very purpose, function and structure of the digital platform and must therefore, contrary to the hypotheses seen thus far, be considered a wholly exceptional hypothesis.

This justifies a particularly attentive attitude towards any decisions that the service provider might take in this direction, both from the point of view of the certainty of the facts underlying the justification and the appropriateness of the measure in relation to the conduct.

This hypothesis, however, cannot be entirely excluded or denied when such a decision becomes necessary in order, for instance, to terminate the relationship with persons who repeatedly carry out actions maliciously aimed at abusing the platform, violating its rules, undermining its reliability, trust and prejudicing or risking prejudicing the interests of the other recipients of the service.[25] Even in these more serious cases, the service provider who decides to terminate the service will still have

[25] This point is the subject of express attention in recitals 53 and 54 of Regulation 2022/2065. In fact, the integrity of the system requires that, under certain conditions, *online* platform providers must temporarily suspend the service in relation to the person who has engaged in abusive conduct, recognising in any case, the power to activate all the complaint and out-of-court dispute resolution tools provided for by the Regulation. This is without prejudice to the freedom of *online* platform providers to determine their general conditions and to establish stricter measures in the case of manifestly illegal content related to serious crimes, such as child sexual abuse material, it being understood that a predetermined and specific list of all the individual violations that may constitute manifestly illegal content is inappropriate and unnecessary.

to explain in the justification why suspension of the service is not sufficient action to protect the digital platform and the interests of the other recipients of the service and why the more severe action of termination is necessary. This explanation must be even more solid and consistent, the greater the size of the platform itself, reaching its maximum degree in the case of large platforms.

4.2 The Withdrawal of the Commercial Operator from the Digital Platform

The continuous and indefinite nature of the relationship between the commercial operator and the provider of the digital platform, as mentioned above, also allows the former party to terminate at any time, subject to adequate notice to safeguard the interests of the other party. In this case, however, it should be noted that the party that risks seeing its interest adversely affected by the termination by the commercial operator is not so much the platform provider—which may at most complain of the absence of a certain brand, product or service and therefore of the reduced competitiveness of its platform in a purely commercial logic—as the possible counterparties to the individual contracts entered into by the commercial operator through the platform whose relationships have not been fully terminated. The latter, in fact, because of the withdrawal, run the risk of not seeing the services still being performed or of losing the agreed guarantees.

The systematic affirmation of withdrawal *ad nutum* as an expression of the commercial operator's freedom of economic initiative must therefore be tempered with the need, at the operational level, to preserve intact the interest of the other recipients of the services in the proper performance of the pending relationships by creating a secure, reliable and transparent *online* environment for consumers and other commercial operators. In concrete terms, it must be avoided that withdrawal from the platform becomes an instrument at the disposal of the commercial operator to evade its own contractual performance or the guarantees provided for by law or by the contract.

The applicable regulations do not provide for specific rules or procedures to protect these interests, which must therefore, again, be reconstructed through recourse to analogical reasoning and general principles.

It can then be stated first that withdrawal from the digital platform cannot take effect before the withdrawal, if any, from the contracts concluded through the platform itself and still in existence or, where this is not provided for, from their regular performance. Consistently, from the date of exercise of the withdrawal and during the entire pending period before its effectiveness, potential contractual counterparties should be adequately informed and warned of the trader's withdrawal status and of the particular dangerous conditions connected to the conclusion of contracts with a subject who, shortly, will no longer be present or reachable through the *online* platform.

An information obligation in addition to the traceability obligation, which, as is well known, requires providers of *online* platforms, with the sole exception of providers qualifying as micro or small enterprises, that allow consumers to conclude distance contracts with traders to trace the withdrawing traders and retain their data for 6 months. From this point of view, the shorter legal deadline than the established consumer protection guarantees is somewhat perplexing. Perplexity that, however, may be overcome by negotiation through specific provisions of the *online* platform provider itself in the terms and conditions of its service or systems that allow interested parties to acquire and retain data on the withdrawing party even beyond the aforementioned 6-month period.

5 The Events of the Individual Contracts Concluded on the Digital Platform

The regulation of individual contracts concluded on the digital platform does not find specific regulation in the Community legislation of reference and is therefore governed by the general rules. The withdrawal of the commercial operator, the strong subject of the contractual relationship, in the individual contract is therefore governed by the nature of the contract: it is therefore normally an exceptional hypothesis except in the case of contracts with continuous or periodic performance, where, by virtue of the principles already referred to in the preceding paragraphs, it constitutes an ordinary hypothesis. The Regulation DSA is limited, in these cases, to establishing the obligation of the supplier, who is not a micro or small enterprise, to retain the tracing data of the trader for a period of 6 months to ensure, to the persons who have ongoing dealings with him, adequate protection through the possibility of finding him to exercise the rights recognised in their favour by the legal system as a whole. In this case, too, the 6-month time limit gives rise to the same considerations already set out in the previous paragraph. In any event, the time limit must be understood as a minimum term that can be derogated from by negotiation or, in any case, by specific sectoral regulations provided for by Community or national law.

Similarly, the latter may provide for specific rules, burdens or procedures in relation to particular goods or services (e.g. pharmaceuticals or health services, electricity supply) from which the rules governing *online* platforms may derogate only by increasing the protections to protect the weaker party by reason of the specific context in which the contract is entered into. In turn, the commercial operator, on the other hand, has the right to access and collect all the data relating to its activity on the digital platform to be able to continue its activity through different solutions, including any competing digital platforms.

Withdrawal by the consumer is governed by special rules in favour of the consumer, as referred to and without prejudice to the rules governing digital platforms.[26] The consumer may therefore freely withdraw from the continued relationship having as its object participation in the *online* platform without any obligation to state reasons or give prior notice in view of the absence of a specific interest on the part of the other parties involved in his remaining within the *online* platform. In the event of withdrawal from individual contracts, the consumer therefore remains subject to the specific discipline for his protection already dictated by the Community system, supplemented and strengthened by the Regulation DSA, for example through the prohibition imposed on the suppliers of *online* platforms to adopt 'obscure paths' that have the effect of making a procedure for cancelling a service considerably more complex than that of joining it, or making it unreasonably difficult to interrupt purchases or to leave a given *online* platform.

References

Alpa G (2022) Sul potere contrattuale delle piattaforme digitali. Contr e impr 3:721 ff

Amidei A (2023) Tutela del consumatore-Il vaglio di validità delle clausole contrattuali di content moderation online. Giur it 7:1542 ff

Ammannati L (2021) Verso un diritto delle piattaforme digitali? In: Ammannati L, Canepa A, Greco GL, Minneci U (eds) Algoritmi, big data, piattaforme digitali. Torino, pp 3 ff

Battelli E (2022) Questioni aperte in materia di contrattazione nelle piattaforme online. Contratti 5:563

Bocchini R (2002) Il contratto di accesso ad Internet. Dir informazione e informatica 3:471 ff

Bocchini R (2021) La polivalenza delle posizioni contrattuali nella sharing economy. Nuovo dir civ 1:246 ff

Carleo R (2022) Piattaforme digitali e contratto. Eur J Privacy Law Technol 1:73 ff

Di Sabato D (2020) Il ruolo delle piattaforme digitali nello svolgimento delle attività economica in rete. Annali della Facoltà Giuridica dell'Università di Camerino-Studi 9:11

Donini A (2019) Il lavoro attraverso le piattaforme digitali, Bologna

Finocchiaro G (2018) Il perfezionamento del contratto on line: opportunità e criticità. Dir com scambi internaz 1/2:192 ff

Franzoni M (n.d.) Degli effetti del contratto. Efficacia del contratto e recesso unilaterale. Artt. 1372-1373, in Il Codice Civile – Commentario, directed by F Busnelli, pp 345 ff

Fusco GL (2015) Codici di autoregolamentazione, uso della rete e informazione dell'utente. In: Nuzzo M (ed) Il principio di sussidiarietà nel diritto privato, pp 153 ff

Gentili A, Battelli E (2011) I contratti di distribuzione del commercio elettronico. In: Bocchini R (ed) I contratti di somministrazione e di distribuzione, in Trattato dei contratti Rescigno-Gabrielli. Torino, pp. 379 ff

[26] Particularly, Regulations (EU) 2017/2394(13) and (EU) 2019/1020 of the European Parliament and of the Council (14), Directives 2001/95/EC (15), 2005/29/EC (16), 2011/83/EU (17) and 2013/11/EU (18) of the European Parliament and of the Council and Council Directive 93/13/EEC (19), and on the protection of personal data, particularly Regulation (EU) 2016/679 of the European Parliament and of the Council.

Giannone Codiglione G (2022) Il contratto dell'utente con il social network: i limiti dello schema negoziale nell'esercizio dei diritti fondamentali. In: Stanzione P (eds) I "poteri privati" delle piattaforme e le nuove frontiere della privacy. Torino, pp 283 ff

Irti N (1998) Scambi senza accordo. Riv trim dir proc civ, pp 347 ff

Morotti E (2020) I frequenti recessi del consumatore e il rifiuto di contrarre del professionista nel commercio elettronico. Nuova giur civ comm 6:1369 ff

Padovini F (2012) Risoluzione e recesso. Obbl contr 2:86 ff

Perlingieri (2014) Profili civilistici dei social networks. Napoli, pp 30 ff

Petruso R (2017) Responsabilità degli intermediari di internet e nuovi obblighi di conformazione: robo-takedown, policy of termination, notice and take steps. Eur dir priv, 2:451 ff

Quarta A (2019) L'espulsione del socio dal partito tra risoluzione e sanzione: nuovi profili civilistici della disattivazione dell'account. In: Sirena P, Zoppini A (eds) I poteri privati e il diritto della regolazione. Roma, pp 85 ff

Ruggeri F (2021) Regole di trasparenza e rapporti tra imprese nei mercati digitali: il regolamento (UE) 2019/1150 sull'intermediazione online e i motori di ricerca. Dir informazione e informatica:319

Smorto G, Donini A (2024) L'approvazione della Direttiva sul lavoro mediante piattaforme digitali: prima lettura. Labour Law Issues 10(1):C.23–C.44. https://doi.org/10.6092/issn.2421-2695/19855

Tosi E (2021) Diritto privato delle nuove tecnologie digitali. Milano, pp 283 ff

Extra-Judicial Protections in the Platform Economy

Pierfrancesco Bartolomucci

Contents

Abstract The chapter examines the aspects related to out-of-court dispute resolution systems that develop in digital platforms. Starting from an examination of existing empirical experiences and of the reference regulatory framework (European and national), it highlights the opportunity of guaranteeing, through such negotiation-type procedures, adequate instruments of protection for users operating within digital ecosystems that escape the dimensions of space and time that characterise legal systems.

P. Bartolomucci (✉)
University of Naples "Parthenope", Naples, Italy
e-mail: pfrancesco.bartolomucci@uniparthenope.it

R. Bocchini (ed.), *Digital Platforms - From Technical Foundations to Legal and Economic Implications*, https://doi.org/10.1007/978-3-032-07978-7_15

1 E-Agorà as a Privileged Framework for the Development of Alternative Dispute Resolution Mechanisms

The neologism e-Agorà appears particularly evocative, as it takes on very evocative meanings suitable for describing the phenomenal reality of the network.

Just as in ancient *poleis*, *cyberspace* platforms represent in contemporary society the political, economic, cultural and commercial context in which new dimensions of human relations unfold.[1]

Thus, just as in ancient Greece the *agorai* represented a meeting and entertainment place for holding events, games and theatrical performances, but also for the development of economic and commercial trades, reaching the pinnacle of the political and institutional life of the Hellenic communities, which gathered in assemblies to discuss their lives, as well as to exercise legislative and judicial power, in the hyper-connected world of digital platforms new dimensions of action are accommodated, both at the level of individuals, and at the collective level, up to the political-institutional level.

The increasingly massive recourse to the net transfers entire sectors of society onto digital platforms, to the point of constituting what economic science defines as veritable digital ecosystems;[2] like any ecosystem, in fact, the life of individuals unfolds in them, who can develop new dimensions of their personality, new profiles of their identity and new perspectives for the exercise of their fundamental rights; they also allow the expression of new styles and models of relational life.

At the same time, platforms are capable of constituting the infrastructures around which a dimension of citizenship takes place that is different from the traditional one, capable of imparting entirely original characteristics to the relationship with institutions: thus, on the one hand, the latter are modifying the ways and times of their action and, on the other hand, citizens are developing new ways of exercising their rights and innovative ways of using services.

The rapid technological progress and the proportional development of an ever-growing and diversified number of digital platforms[3] leads to the conclusion that each of them—due to the strong interaction and deep sharing of all participants, as well as the interdependence created both with regard to the subjects and the goods and services that are exchanged in it—represents a true *Agora*.

[1] Franceschelli (2001), pp. 4 ff., refers to this term to emphasise that the network phenomenon is not only relevant from a legal-economic point of view.

[2] Indeed, in the economic literature (especially in the area of *business management*) the term 'ecosystem', although it has experienced a strong momentum, is still at the centre of a debate in order to reach an agreed definition; with reference to its use with regard to digital platforms, inter alia, Barile et al. (2022), pp. 467 ff.; Ceccagnoli et al. (2012), pp. 263 ff.; Cusumano et al. (2019); Gawer and Cusumano (2014), pp. 417 ff.; McIntyre and Srinivasan (2017), pp. 141 ff.; Nachira et al. (2007); Selander et al. (2013), pp. 183 ff.; Senyo et al. (2018), pp. 206 ff.; Tiwana (2013); Weill and Woerner (2015), pp. 27 ff.

[3] Also, with regard to the economic literature, Rochet and Tirole (2003), pp. 990 ff.; Evans and Schmalensse (2016); Mazzucato et al. (2021), pp. 17 ff.

Despite this suggestive representation, which responds to the phenomenal perception of reality, it does not appear that the pervasive use of new technologies and the increasingly broad and complex use of Artificial Intelligence systems are leading to a mere formal transformation of the various dimensions of action, for the mere fact that they turn on telematic infrastructures.

The penetration of digital platforms into the heart of societies is, in fact, capable of reconfiguring individual behaviour and relational dynamics; of modifying the capacity to perceive and analyse reality; of introducing new habits and practices; of influencing lifestyles and cultural models; of reshaping organisations and institutions, both public and private.[4]

If we want to restrict the field of observation to the exchange market (and correspondingly to the negotiation dynamics underlying it), new forms of organising activities, new goods and services, new ways of creating value and new forms of circulating wealth emerge.

The market structure itself appears to be undermined by an economic model in which the rigid division between the production of goods and the supply of services is fading away; unprecedented modes of exchange are being created, characterised by ever-increasing interaction and interdependence and the consequent complementarity of supply and demand;[5] innovative rules of contract conclusion are being developed and negotiating models unknown to tradition are being created; new forms of liability are coming to the fore.[6]

From a legal point of view, the complexity of the phenomenon eludes a regulation that is actually capable of fully grasping the multiplicity of relationships and relations of a negotiating nature that take place in such ecosystems:[7] if, in fact, it appears useful to qualify that of the developers and managers of platforms as an intermediation activity between the users of the services offered in them, it must also be considered that such ecosystems appear capable of simultaneously generating bilateral markets (*two-sided markets*) or multilateral *markets* (*multilateral markets*),[8] thanks to this, the connection and interaction of different categories of users is made possible.[9]

[4] Floridi (2017), pp. 27 ff., states that it is man who has modified reality to adapt it to the characteristics of technology.

[5] Sickle (2023), pp. 61 ff.; Ead (2023), pp. 172 ff.

[6] Albanese (2024), pp. 9 ff.; Camardi (2021), pp. 870 ff.

[7] This scenario was foreshadowed by Barlow (1996).

[8] European Commission, *Public consultation on the regulatory environment for platforms, online intermediaries, data and cloud computing and the collaborative economy*, 2015, at *https://ec.europa.eu/digital-singlemarket/en/news/results-public-consultation-regulatory-evironment--platforms-online-intermediaries-data-and-cloud*; the foreign and Italian literature on competition profiles is vast on this point.

[9] On this point, see Trubiani (2025), p. 157 ff; Id. (2023), p 271 ff. For an analysis of legal profiles, Ammannati (2021), pp. 3 ff.; D'Agostino (n.d.), pp. 81 ff.; Canepa (2020); Quarta (2017b), pp. 556 ff.

In such markets, different and heterogeneous actors interact with each other and with the platforms to create value on them; within these interrelationships, economic and negotiation processes are initiated that require transforming electronic impulses into data and information that enable new achievements and knowledge; thanks to these, further relationships can be generated, in a network of relationships that is always in flux.

The fleeting and evanescent network of negotiating relations via the Internet makes the various protagonists of the transactions virtually present to each other, but at the same time prevents the behaviour they engage in and the statements they make from having a precise geographic location and a definite temporal determination.

After all, the dissolution of the space-time dimension is the *ubi consistam* of the network:[10] it can ensure efficiency, speed and economy to all relations, especially economic and contractual ones, regardless of the geographical location of the subjects that give rise to them and, consequently, of the legal systems to which they belong.

These characteristics constitute, therefore, the distinctive feature of *online* transactions, which stands in contrast to transactions that take place without the aid of technological tools and which opens up a different perspective (also) for private law,[11] as is also shown by the attention paid to it by the European legislator.

The intermediation activities of the platforms are also inspired by the same logic of time and cost reduction, in accordance with an efficiency that must be recovered in all phases of the relationship between the operators: from the first social contact, to the commercial communication, to the conclusion and execution of the contract, up to the pathology of the same that requires, precisely, a rapid, secure and reliable management of disputes.

In parallel, the development of these new markets also leads to the emergence of new conflicts.

If the absence of geographical boundaries and the speed of processes constitute the pillars of a system that claims its autonomy with respect to legal systems (national and supranational), to the point of determining its own rules of operation—which emerge 'from below' and are produced directly by the subjects that operate within it—the same logic inspires the objective of dictating rules for resolving conflicts that do not necessarily lead to jurisdiction.

It is not simply a question of verifying the resilience of principles and rules that have already been tried and tested (and are the subject of specific regulatory discipline, both at national and European level) in the changed technological scenario. On the contrary, it is a question of analysis. First, what is the distinctive and unifying element of the demand for justice underlying disputes relating to digital

[10] In relation to the transnationality of the network Franceschelli (2001), p. 23; Svantesson 2018, pp. 49 ff.

[11] The literature on the subject is boundless; let us simply refer Belli (2017); Quarta and Smorto (2024); Bargelli and Calderai (2022); Tosi (2021), pp. 210 ff. With regard to European private law principles, *ex multis*, AA.VV (2018); AA.VV(2016); Iamiceli (2021), pp. 392 ff.

markets, which appear to be extremely diversified; second, whether and to what extent out-of-court procedures can respond adequately to it.

Even in this case, therefore, the investigation cannot appear to be limited to the possibility of carrying out a check on the appropriateness—in the digital environment—of the techniques, methods and rules for conducting these procedures, but must go as far as analysing whether and how the digital revolution has imprinted a change (not only to the very nature of conflicts, but) also in the way in which the parties can reach their resolution.

The erosion of the spaces of intervention of state systems in the governance of online transactions entails an increasing difficulty in applying legal norms and the expansion of technical rules; within this relationship between law and technique,[12] it appears increasingly complex to resort to the former to qualify facts, acts and behaviour without a precise reference to space and time. This is also relevant in the event that disputes arise, in relation to which it does not appear easy to identify the provisions of the law (understood as national law) applicable to the case, nor those necessary to identify the competent judge.

This erosion would seem to occur precisely at the expense of the legal norm, which appears to be yielding to the technical one; the latter, on the other hand, appears to be more flexible and suited to resolving the disputes that arise in the environment that it itself helps to determine, inspired by the same canons of speed and efficiency that characterise the digital market.

In this perspective, there is then a need to establish the modalities and opportunities for access and determination of these technical rules and, at the same time, to ensure the establishment of a proper dialogue with the regulatory provisions, to guarantee that all parties involved can exercise the instruments of negotiating autonomy (to determine the rules applicable to contracts and to establish those for resolving conflicts relating thereto), without completely obliterating judicial protection.

2 Transnationality of Conflicts, Multiplicity of Normative Statuses and (Socio-Economic) Uniqueness of Cyberspace: Autonomy and Heteronomy in the Search for Dispute Resolution

What has been briefly observed with regard to the digital economy and the transactions that take place on *online* platforms makes it possible to state that this reality is extremely complex; within it, changes (both subjectively and objectively) appear rapid and unstoppable in their flow, since they are no longer subject to traditional generational processes that require long gestation and sedimentation times, but rather appear governed by the rhythm of technological progress, which is characterised by its nature of incessant rapidity.

[12] Irti and Severino (2001) and Mengoni (2011).

This level of complexity is all the more acute if one takes into consideration the context in which it is developed; even though the perception of users may make virtual space appear as a context endowed with a dimension of its own, it in fact reveals itself as a 'non-place', devoid of the spatial-temporal guidelines around which one usually observes reality,[13] lacking the spatio-temporal directrices around which reality is usually observed.

The breaking down of territorial barriers thus opens up a different dimension of globalisation, which is no longer so much constituted by the multiplication of exchanges that take place between subjects belonging to different countries and, therefore, to different legal systems between which the connecting rules applicable to the case must be identified, but rather by the interconnection that unites subjects and weaves relationships in an *Agora* that does not have the traditional 'urban' characteristics, but is characterised by its dimension devoid of the elements of space and time.

The freedom of access and the opportunities for use that are ensured to all economic operators on the network allow for the establishment of relations characterised by transversality that transcends geographical boundaries; consequently, the opportunity to conduct *online* transactions, regardless of the nationality of the contracting parties, makes them insusceptible to being traced back to a single legal system (even supranational).

From a legal point of view, this poses unprecedented challenges, on which scholars have already been reflecting for some time to identify a set of rules that would allow for a *governance*[14] appropriate to the regulation of the Internet market.

The difficulty of placing e-commerce in the right spatial and temporal dimension gives the impression that technology contributes, as mentioned, to the process of erosion of the state monopoly of the production of norms, which has already been put in crisis in recent decades, as if the network could endow itself with its own regulatory statute, with its own laws[15]—in the same way as a legal system[16]—which is structured entirely around rules of a technical nature that can cope with the narrowness of legal rules, even with regard to those of private international law (which presuppose the existence of a territoriality of trade), on the applicable law or the

[13] Irti (2001), pp. 65 ff.

[14] Rossello (2006); Antonucci (2019), pp. 20 ff.; Nuzzo (2019), pp. 42 ff.

[15] Camardi (2004), p. 554.

[16] *Contra.* Sbordone (2023), p. 41, who observes that such a reconstruction 'gives way both to the concrete needs of justice manifested by the parties before judges obliged to apply the law (state, in the broad sense) and to the applicative uncertainties to which it might give rise'. The author adds—after observing that the use of the telematic instrument does not take place within an area devoid of rules—that it 'multiplies, with respect to contracts concluded by traditional means of communication, the possibility of recognising in the contractual transaction various and numerous extraneous elements whose presence ends up making it difficult to coherently compose the regulatory framework of reference'.

procedural rules dictated to determine the rooting of the jurisdiction of the judicial authority.[17]

It does not appear, however, that the network is capable of self-determining the production of self-sufficient normative statutes and thus of governing itself.

It is true, however, that the absence of a unitary regulatory framework leaves wide margins of manoeuvre to private autonomy in establishing the rules for managing the relations that develop within it; relations that exponentially amplify the dynamics of mass economic and contractual relations, ontologically built around the unilateral predisposition of negotiation models.

The technological environment is not limited to determining a mere quantitative expansion of mass contracting, but profoundly affects its very nature, insofar as the techniques through which the parties enter into relations make it possible to conform upstream needs, demands, necessities and to adapt downstream the will that is manifested in the contracts stipulated on the network, through the use of platforms.

Commercial solicitation, *marketing*, advertising and their intrinsic capacity to influence economic and negotiation choices are certainly not new, nor are they connected to the development of the platform market alone. However, the different technological context, for the reasons mentioned above, is such as to create increasingly pervasive techniques capable of generating new forms of vulnerability with respect to which the traditional rules prove inadequate to respond to the new demands for protection of which a vast number of subjects are bearers, who find themselves in a state of true technological subordination.

It cannot be overlooked that these 'technological' forms of persuasion may appear to fundamentally alter (compress) the ability of users of Internet goods and services to self-determine with a sufficient degree of freedom.

Moreover, the increasingly widespread use of such techniques appears physiologically inherent to the digital market, which requires uniform conduct to develop according to a logic of speed and efficiency. Private autonomy unfolds, therefore, in a context that is constructed by a set of legal rules and technical rules:[18] the former assume as a premise that their recipients are still subjects capable of making rational, emotional, responsible choices that are based on will and relationship; the latter, on the other hand, exclude this mode of manifestation of the rationality of individuals. While law conceives of a space in which subjects are substantially free (to the point where they can also decide to violate it), technology does not recognise this space and only requires executive type behaviour, which conforms to the rule it has created, with the consequent impossibility of implementing a different type of behaviour (unless it is affected by *bias* or programming errors capable of generating harmful effects that must in any case be remedied).

---

[17] Generally, on the subject, Ballarino (1998); Bariatti (2001), pp. 6 ff.; De Cristofaro (2007), pp. 185 ff.; Draetta (2001); Finocchiaro (2001), pp. 571 ff.; Manucci (2002), pp. 81 ff.; Manucci (2002), pp. 49 ff.; Sbordone (2011), pp. 87 ff.; Vigoriti (2001), pp. 399 ff.

[18] On the relationship between law and technology in general, Irti and Severino (2001) and Mengoni (2011).

Digital markets, which are built around the standardised and uniform repetition of actions and models, seem to operate an overcoming of this dichotomy, where both technological and negotiation rules are welded together thanks to their unilateral predisposition: the former ensures the conformation of needs and interests (in the phase of social contact and commercial communication), establishes a computerised protocol that dictates the rules of conduct (in the phase of concluding the deed), ensures control over the compliance of the conduct with the model (in the phase of executing the relationship), also to prevent dissimilar conduct, disruptive contingencies, and non-performance. The second, for its part, makes the various aspects of this relationship, in all its phases, legally relevant.

The risk, then, is that negotiating autonomy—as the source of production of the rule governing exchanges in the platform market—unfolds according to dynamics that make the greater strength of the large *players* of the digital market prevail, who are the same subjects that hold the technological *know-how* and who, therefore, also govern the technical rule;[19] a risk that appears to be increasingly felt only if one considers that the conformation of the market is such as to concentrate in the hands of a very few subjects the ownership of platforms that, as previously mentioned, are capable of influencing individual and collective behaviour, and thus the economic and negotiating choices of millions of people.[20]

These operators are increasingly acquiring the role of sole providers, against whom the negotiating freedom of users is reduced.

To the already known forms of economic and contractual imbalance, typical of modern globalised market economies, new ones are being added.

First, the negotiation asymmetry may be caused by the lack of technical and IT expertise on the part of the users (consumers and/or professionals), which is necessary to correctly appreciate and evaluate the choices they are making.

Second, it may also result from manipulative practices[21] or from discriminatory initiatives[22] determined by the use of algorithms, which govern ever larger sectors of bargaining: the capacity of the same to analyse *big data* to an exponential extent, the increasingly sophisticated profiling techniques of millions of users, the predetermined setting criteria for their use can determine new forms of influence on the will to negotiate and discriminatory attitudes that condition the already reduced (and predetermined) spaces of bargaining, to the point of possibly leading to the exclusion of a significant number of subjects, especially the most fragile and, as such, in need of higher levels of protection.

---

[19] Criscuolo (2015), pp. 107 ff.; Fachechi (2015), p. 260.

[20] Pollicino (2023), pp. 410 ff.; Resta (2023), pp. 1008 ff.

[21] It is no coincidence that the European legislator paid the utmost attention to this aspect, which constitutes one of the most salient aspects of the so-called *Digital Service Act*; on this subject, Gorgoni (2024), pp. 915 ff.

[22] With particular regard to the legislation on the processing of personal data: Carapezza Figlia (2023), pp. 638 ff.; Messinetti (2019), pp. 890 ff.; Pellecchia (2018), pp. 1223 ff. Generally, on the topic, see Carapezza Figlia (2015), pp. 1405 ff.; Carapezza Figlia (2013); Neri (2021), pp. 983 ff.; Tommasi (2020), pp. 112 ff.; Tonazzi (2019), pp. 201 ff.

The organisation of platforms in entrepreneurial form makes it possible to analyse and manage these asymmetries (through the collection and analysis of data) and, also through reputational mechanisms, to increase the dominant position in the market of reference (already reserved for a small number of large *players*) with techniques that are not merely loyalty-building but true *lock-in*.[23]

In the global digital market, therefore, economic and contractual dynamics are unfolding that allow old and new economic and bargaining imbalances to emerge that disregard and go beyond the subjective qualification of the parties (such as that of consumer)[24] and that instead highlight an intrinsic weakness on the part of the contracting parties;[25] this is the case both in the event that they concern the relationship between users and providers of digital services offered by platforms, and in the event that the latter are simply the third-party infrastructure needed to connect two or more parties to regulate the sale of goods or the supply and provision of services (digital and otherwise).

The inadequacy of state and/or international regulatory frameworks to cope with the negotiation dynamics in the network and, at the same time, the impossibility of entrusting the governance of the system's operating rules to the subjects managing the telematic infrastructures, in a totally deregulated context, make emerge—alongside significant attempts at standardisation, such as those undertaken by the European Union with the *Digital Service Act* and the *Digital Market Act*, or most recently with the Artificial Intelligence Regulation—the appropriateness of self-regulatory initiatives, understood as forms of *soft law* capable of initiating a process of co-regulation that has the capacity, on the one hand, not to abandon negotiating relations to the dynamics of individual or collective private autonomy and, at the same time, to leverage informal processes capable of adapting with a high level of flexibility to the specificities of economic segments, the speed of technological evolution, and the technical characteristics of phenomena.[26]

This premise leads to a new approach to the theory of sources,[27] which—starting from the analysis of the rules put in place by national legislators, such as the European Union, as well as the inadequacy of those adopted by the model laws of international institutions, such as UNCITRAL—nevertheless leaves the production of rules by stakeholders, such as digital market operators, to emerge.

This layered production of norms escapes the traditional ordering criteria of sources and, rather, imposes a correlation between them that ends up drawing a heterogeneous framework that aspires to regulate such a complex phenomenon.

Since it is therefore not possible to imagine that the platform market—albeit empirically considered as a *unicum*—can be regulated by a unitary body of rules, in

[23] D'Agostino (n.d.), pp. 91 ff.; Martinelli (2022), pp. 15 ff.

[24] In relation to inter-company relations, Libertini (2023), p. 1.

[25] Camardi (2023), p. 217.

[26] Bellelli (2024), pp. 51 ff.; Busch (2019), pp. 115 ff.; Pollicino (2022), pp. 1049 ff.; Rossi (2016), pp. 47 ff.

[27] Ciacci (2023), pp. 11 ff.

the absence of a worldwide adherence of all countries, let alone by a new digital *lex mercatoria*, due to the fragmentation and diversification of the multiple sectors and segments of said market, the rules of Internet governance are forced to a difficult coexistence; with respect to it, it is up to the interpreter to identify each time the rule best suited to the solution of the concrete case, taking into account the specificities of an objective and subjective nature that characterise it.

The 'competition' of rules, abstractly applicable to concrete cases according to their own criteria, does not place them all on the same level; those of a regulatory nature (state and supranational, both European and international) are still characterised by the limitations of space and time that are ontologically connected to the heteronormative power of the subject that issues them; this physiological limitation consequently allows the digital market to let the rules that it itself, i.e. the subjects that operate in it, create autonomously prevail.

This competition does not necessarily appear destined to generate conflicts of rules; on the contrary, the very essence of the system, which needs its own order to ensure the efficiency and effectiveness of the transactions that take place within it, leads one to believe that a coexistence is realised that is capable of finding, from time to time, the best way to overcome inevitable contradictions, in the constant search for the most appropriate solution in the *mix* of rules of different formation.[28]

The difficulties connected to the reconstruction of a framework of rules applicable to individual cases and the aforementioned welding between technological rules and negotiating rules (which would also like to ensure an increasingly efficient level of conformation and repetition of conduct) mean that electronic commerce is still a context of the emergence of conflicts that cannot always be resolved through the automatic (*recte* automated) application of the technical rules on the basis of which the *online* economic transaction is constructed.

The digital marketplace, however, is not only the environment in which such conflicts can arise, but also the one in which resolution mechanisms can develop.[29]

On the other hand, to ensure the ever-increasing development of electronic commerce, it appears essential that all its participants can rely on the possibility that the resolution of any disputes will take place through recourse to mechanisms that ensure the same effectiveness that characterises that market, both with regard to the rules that can be used to pursue a satisfactory solution, and with regard to the timeframe for the settlement of the dispute, as well as with regard to the cost-effectiveness of recourse to such procedures.

[28] Rossello (2006) observes that 'the solution cannot be found either in pure normativism (the Irtian thesis) or in the creation of an autarchic regulatory enclave parallel to the real world. Probably, the approach destined to bear more fruit, and at the same time able to guarantee democratic control over decision-making processes, is that of an adjustment of the system of sources, and of a balanced mix between instruments of authoritative regulation and conventional discipline, and, within the latter, of self-regulation and "co-regulation" (or, if you prefer, of "controlled self-regulation")'.

[29] Mancini (2016), pp. 15 ff.

This trust seems all the more necessary if one takes into account the transnationality of relations and hence of the disputes that may arise in the digital market; if, as said, this assumes the nature of a non-place, the identification of the law applicable to the conflict, the recognition of the competent judicial authority and the determination of the modalities of execution of a decision (administrative or jurisdictional) may prove to be lengthy, complex and burdensome and, therefore, not in conformity with the need for speed and efficiency that the network informs negotiation and economic relations.

The aforementioned heterogeneity of e-commerce disputes thus opens up new spaces within which to develop the relationship between judicial and extrajudicial protection, in terms of mutual conditioning rather than opposition.[30]

3 Digital Platforms, Brokerage and ADR Systems

As noted above, platforms play a fundamental and increasingly expansive role in determining the shape of the digital marketplace and the negotiated transactions that take place within it.

The relevance of their role is determined by the fact that they—understood as intermediary infrastructures—are not limited to the organisation and management of the IT architecture made available to users, but take on the role of real regulators of the same.

Platforms, in fact, take on different and increasingly complex tasks:[31] they may perform the function of service providers made directly available to consumers or businesses, or through third-party producers with whom they conclude separate contracts for the purchase of rights of use (e.g. for content such as music, images, films). At the same time, they may act as true intermediaries, in the sense that they facilitate the matching of supply and demand and the subsequent conclusion of a contract between the parties (who may be consumers and professionals, professionals only, or individuals only, as in the case of *peer-to-peer* platforms).

In addition, platforms may act as containers to facilitate the retrieval of information (as in the case of search engines or comparison services) or interaction between users (as in the case of *social networks*); even in this case, the matter is not without relevance from a negotiating point of view, not so much in relation to the sponsorship agreements that some users may enter into with producers to advertise goods

---

[30] Although not with reference to *online* disputes, the doctrine has long captured the essence of this relationship: Carpi (2016), pp. 811 ff.; Comoglio (2000), pp. 318 ff.; Ghirga (2009), pp. 357 ff.; Silvestri (1999), pp. 321 ff. In foreign literature, with specific regard to consumer rights, Eidenmuller and Engel (2014), pp. 261 ff.; Loos (2016), pp. 61 ff.; Wagner (2014), pp. 165 ff.

[31] Quarta and Smorto (2024) classify platforms into distinct categories: advertising platforms (e.g. Facebook, X, Tik-Tok, i.e. search engines); service platforms (e.g. Spotify, Netflix, Dropbox); *e-commerce* platforms (Amazon, Alibaba, eBay) and *sharing economy* platforms (Uber, Airbnb).

and services, but also because the use of such a container is still on a contractual basis.

The various functions performed by the platforms unfold, therefore, in a network of relationships that are destined to condition each other, but whose distinctive feature is that of a unilateral type of negotiation regulation,[32] dictated by the developers themselves, through the use of general contractual conditions, regardless of whether the agreement is reached through the so-called *browse wrap* or *click wrap* model.

This is not the place to comment on the albeit relevant questions as to the spaces actually granted to the adherents, both with regard to their right of self-determination—necessary for the expression of private autonomy—and with regard to the content of such contracts.

For this discourse, however, it is worth noting that—within the framework of these contractual relationships—there is often provision for recourse to dispute resolution mechanisms between the parties;[33] the provision of such tools represents, in fact, an important instrument of user loyalty, indispensable—as already noted—to consolidate their trust in the platforms.

Several studies, also conducted at the international level,[34] have examined the various procedures put in place by the large global platforms, yielding a composite picture,[35] which is difficult to subsume under the dogmatic categories that have been elaborated on the subject of a.d.r. over the past decades, given the specificity of the phenomenon connected to the development of the digital market and the multiplicity of functions assumed by these platforms in the management of conflict resolution procedures.

From the empirical analysis conducted, however, some common guidelines emerge, both in relation to disputes arising from relationships in which the parties to a negotiation relationship are only intermediated by the platforms, and in relation to those in which they are instead involved in disputes concerning contracts directly concluded with users.

With reference to the first sphere, it should not be overlooked that—in the construction of a reputational system essential to their development—the platforms equip themselves with systems for evaluating those who sell goods or offer services, not only to increase buyers' trust in the system (which is thus able to select

[32] Alpa (2021b), p. 728. He doubts the configurability of a contract Quarta (2022), pp. 195 ff.; of the same opinion, Palka (2018), pp. 135 ff.

[33] Merone (2022), pp. 269 ff.

[34] These studies show that—without prejudice to the unilateral arrangement of the aforementioned out-of-court settlement procedures—there is a substantial difference in their regulation, depending on whether the transactions to which they refer take place with users residing within or outside the European Union.

[35] Casabona (2017), pp. 497 ff., classifies the various procedures into three models (weak, strong and very strong), depending on the existence or non-existence of contractual constraints committing the parties to resort to such compositional mechanisms, as well as the level of proceduralisation of the same.

professionals based on the reliability found), but also to prevent and limit the emergence of possible disputes *a priori.*[36]

These are, in any case, relationships established *online* and relating to goods and services that—due to their value and type—require a quick, efficient and cost-effective solution; for this reason, the procedures set up in connection with them are also managed electronically.

They involve, initially, a phase of direct negotiation between the parties, which is the most immediate form of solution, obviously based on an entirely self-compositional model.

The effectiveness of a direct negotiation between the disputants may, however, appear hardly feasible, given the disparity (informational, economic, negotiating, linguistic, cultural and psychological) between the parties, exacerbated by the 'distance' created by the digital network in which the relationship arose; for this reason, in some cases, it is the platforms themselves that make their infrastructures available to enable and facilitate dialogue.[37]

In the event of a negotiation failure, therefore, the platforms intervene to 'mediate' the management of the conflict; this activity, however, does not appear to be of a purely conciliatory nature, in the sense that the role assumed does not appear to be aimed exclusively at soliciting a solution that the parties can autonomously identify, according to the general principles of private autonomy.

On the contrary, they play a proactive role that can be more or less incisive,[38] being able to even go so far as to delimit the requests that can be put forward (in relation to the circumstance of whether or not the seller has used the platform's services to offer its goods and products), to dictate the timeframe within which these

---

[36] On the role of reputational systems and their litigation-preventing capacity, Casabona (2017); Giannone Codiglione (2015), pp. 169 ff.; Smorto (2016), pp. 199 ff.; Zeno Zencovich (2007), pp. 263 ff.: some of these authors also emphasise the direct reputational role that a dispute resolution system plays vis-à-vis users and in favour of platforms. For the foreign literature, *ex multis*, Rule and Singh (2021), pp. 176 ff.; Koulu (2019), pp. 74 ff. This selection is now entrusted to algorithms capable of analysing *big data,* which carry out a preventive selection that admits or prevents access to the platforms themselves; it appears evident that such a system—even if it is not only suitable for resolving but even for preventing possible disputes—appears opaque and risks creating discriminatory attitudes, with the consequence that extremely relevant problems arise with regard to the possible violation of fundamental rights and freedoms, including those of economic initiative.

[37] Si pensi, ad esempio, ai regolamenti previsti da Amazon, Booking.com, Airbnb, eBay; in caso di fallimento del negoziato le parti possono affidare alla piattaforma la gestione del confronto, in funzione valutativa e aggiudicativa; fanno eccezione alcune piattaforme, come ad es. Facebook, which—in its capacity as moderator of the contents and expressions conveyed by the users, intervenes directly and in the event of a conflict regarding the decision taken (as in the case of the removal of a certain content, and therefore, following a dispute that at this point directly concerns the platform)—provides for this to be managed by the *Facebook Oversight Board*, whose third party status, in the traditional sense, may be doubted, since it may in any case be considered to be an 'internal' procedure of the platform.

[38] In the case of Booking.com less incisive and more informal; in the case of Amazon, PayPal, eBay and Airbnb more proceduralised.

must be submitted, but also to prepare a possible range of feasible solutions. The role, therefore, appears to be of an evaluative-adjudicative nature, according to models that the national legislation on mediation of civil and commercial disputes also provides for.

What appears to be quite peculiar is the function assumed in the execution phase of the solution proposed and accepted by the parties; these measures, in fact, especially if they accept the customers' requests, can be executed directly and automatically on the platform. One thinks, for instance, of the case in which the dispute relates to the conformity of a good or a service for which the seller is acknowledged to be liable; in this context, the platform may oblige the latter to repay what has been paid by the customer, and—in the event of spontaneous non-compliance—to pay the amount due itself, and then withhold the relevant amounts from the price paid by the customer, perhaps through the use of the payment service made available by the platform itself (in fact, ensuring a sort of after-sales assistance to end users).

Similarly, if it is established that one of the parties is liable, the platform may order the suspension or restriction of the use of the *account*; the removal of advertisements, reviews or other content, etc.

In the latter case, it should be clarified that such a sanction constitutes not so much the consequence of the non-fulfilment of the solution proposed to settle the dispute *inter partes*, but a sort of reaction by the platform to the non-fulfilment of an obligation imposed by the contract concluded with it. It seems clear that in the event of dissatisfaction on the part of the addressee with the 'sanction' imposed, the latter may always activate the procedure provided for disputes arising directly with it.

This form of *private enforcement* highlights, once again, the decisive role of platforms even in the conflict management phase, which is functional to the efficiency of the intermediation system they employ, the parties' reliance on that system and the effectiveness of its operation.

With reference to the second sphere (i.e. that of conflicts relating to relations directly with the platform), the course of the procedural *process* is different; here the difference lies in the nature of this relationship, depending on whether it is established with persons who use the platform to sell goods or offer services, or whether it is established with persons who access it to make use of them.

In the former case, disputes may concern both the performance of services of access to and use of the platform itself, as well as ancillary services (e.g. logistics, which it may make available to sellers/suppliers).

In this hypothesis, the main negotiation protocols envisage—as the first stage of the procedure—a direct confrontation between the parties, managed by an in-house complaints department, which takes charge of the complaint, to which it responds within a short period of time; it is the applicable unilateral conditions themselves that identify the content and method of lodging complaints.

Where the evaluation carried out by the offices (often through the use of predictive algorithms) does not meet with the other party's satisfaction, recourse is envisaged to a third-party body, called upon to settle the conflict between platform and user in a manner that is, also in this case, evaluative and adjudicative, but conducted by a party other than the disputing parties, which—having carried out an admissibility check on the applications—may formulate a proposal for a solution that the parties are free to accept or reject.

The evaluative approach and, consequently, the role assumed by the third party in these procedures is also manifested by the particular form of cross-examination that is established between the disputants, which—unlike in conciliation procedures in the strict sense—does not contemplate any form of confrontation or cross-examination, but only an interlocution with the third party, which nevertheless ensures the confidentiality of the statements made and the documentation produced within the procedure.

In the second case, on the other hand, the management of the dispute with the customer—as a matter of course—is made to fall within the internal management by the platform's complaints department, which can also in this case take place through the use of predictive algorithms, capable of analysing very rapidly the data relating to disputes belonging to the same type; the contractual provision of recourse to these procedures responds to the aforementioned logic of customer loyalty, in respect of which the offer of a service for the resolution of possible conflicts is presented with a view to *customer satisfaction*. It is no coincidence, therefore, that—even in the absence of a transparent management of the complaint by the platform, which does not provide for any form of confrontation between the parties—these 'internal' procedures are the only ones, in fact, to be used for the resolution of disputes with end users (even though the general contractual conditions provide for the subsequent recourse to external conciliatory bodies in the event of failure to satisfy the outcome of the complaint).

4 Negotiating Relationships and Technological Subordination: Models of Business-to-Business and Business-to-Consumer Conflict Resolution in the Virtual Marketplace

It has been repeated several times that platforms have changed the market and its dynamics; it does not appear easy to transpose the traditional models usually used to qualify economic and negotiation relations in the transnational and global market, since the diversity of roles, the segmentation of the digital market, and the methods of entry into it do not fit into the categories that economic and legal science have hitherto used, or rather, they require an effort of reflection that allows the phenomenon to be framed, resorting both to traditional rules, suitably adapted to the new context, and to *ad hoc* rules, where the former do not appear sufficient.

In this context, a change in commercial and contractual relations has gradually taken place, both in business-to-business and business-to-consumer relations: a change that could be grasped under multiple profiles, now related to the competitive dimension, now to the dimension of technological innovation, now to the contractual dimension.

The new technological dimension allows the parties (businesses and professionals, as well as consumers and users) to exploit enormous opportunities, completely unknown in traditional markets: for businesses and professionals, for example, the use of digital ecosystems can lead to an expansion of supply on a global basis, a diversification of markets, products or services, the realisation of multichannel levels for the distribution of their services, and the realisation of enormous economies of scale. For consumers, on the other hand, access to platforms makes it possible not only to be able to deal with an increasing number of suppliers, thus being able to purchase goods or use services at a lower price (especially for standardised ones), but above all to be able to obtain them on terms that fully realise their individual expectations and needs, precisely because they are tailored to personal preferences and needs; without neglecting the further consideration that goods and services can be obtained and enjoyed quickly, conveniently and efficiently.

In the face of these undoubted benefits, however, the platform economy also entails certain disadvantages, especially if one reflects on the negotiation dynamics that develop with the various operators (businesses and consumers); these disadvantages are essentially connected to the way in which the activities of the platforms are carried out: profiling; collection, cataloguing and analysis of *big data*, *scoring* of business activities as well as of individual behaviour (through the use of increasingly sophisticated algorithms), attribution of the corresponding indices of reliability constitute an indispensable prerequisite for the full development of the digital market, which, however, attributes to them a technological and economic power that gives them a role of absolute pre-eminence, capable of conditioning not only tastes and preferences, but also economic choices and—consequently—negotiation choices.

With regard to companies, the global digital *marketplaces* have total control over the information that is fed into the network and that is 'processed' in the individual infrastructures, through which the 'digital reputation' of the operators is attributed and, therefore, market access is granted or denied; this creates an inevitable asymmetry that can also translate into a real dependence, both technologically and economically, which is further exacerbated by the lack of transparency regarding the procedures of processing these data and attributing the relative *score*.

With reference to consumers (i.e. customers), platforms contribute to the construction of a market that gives the perception that it is built entirely around the satisfaction and gratification of the individual; this, however, is the result of a strategy that—thanks to the analysis of the data of each subject—induces needs and necessities, or at least strongly conditions them, through the use of a model based on criteria of 'conformation' rather than 'normality'[39] (understood as an indispensable condition for the expression of individuality and the exercise of fundamental rights),[40] which amplifies the 'rational ignorance' with which consumption choices

[39] Rodotà (2012), p. 329.

[40] Alpini (2019), p. 1; Perlingieri (2020), pp. 379 ff.; Perlingieri (2021), pp. 70 ff.

are often made, exacerbated by the difficulty of knowing the digital environment or the very technical nature of the goods and services exchanged on the Net.

Moreover, the economic dynamics that develop within platforms entail the coexistence of multilevel bargaining, which may be isolated or interdependent: in fact, business-to-business bargaining, business-to-consumer bargaining, *business-to-private* (*peer-to-peer*) bargaining, and bargaining of these entities with the platform (where the latter directly offers services) coexist.[41]

In such a network of relationships that, as we said, can also coexist to construct a unitary economic operation, recourse to the known subjective categories of European derivation seems unsatisfactory, not only because these can be used between subjects to which the European legislation applies, but also between subjects residing outside the European Union,[42] but even more for the fact that they appear insufficient to legally frame the phenomenon of the digital market,[43] which instead gives rise to a figure of a weak contracting party,[44] which eludes a proper subjective qualification.

The noted weakness, in fact, resides in a subordination that is first technological, since the market structuring operated by the platforms prevents both companies and customers from escaping the analysis of their data and their subsequent cataloguing; technological subordination is then followed by that of an economic nature, since they cannot place themselves on an equal footing with the platforms. These forms of vulnerability are also associated with the cognitive one, given the ability of platforms to influence[45]—as mentioned—tastes and needs, and the informational one, given the substantial impossibility of accessing data evaluation processes, even if these are legitimately collected with the consent of the person entitled.

All this inevitably also affects the ensuing negotiation dynamics, which take on an asymmetrical characterisation,[46] from the phase of first social contact, to the pre-contractual phase and on to the phase of conclusion and execution of the contract.

This is true both with regard to the company that makes use of the services offered by the platforms, to which—despite some attempts made in doctrine[47]—it does not appear that a true subjective qualification can be attributed (i.e. weak

---

[41] Katsh et al. (2000), pp. 705 ff.

[42] Article *6a*(1)(b) of Directive 2011/83/EU, as amended by Directive 2019/2161/EU (so-called *omnibus*), imposes an obligation on the *online* marketplace provider to inform consumers whether or not the one offering digital goods, services or content is a professional; Smorto (2020), pp. 49 ff.; Iamiceli (2021), pp, 392 ff; Busch (2020) pp. 133 ff; Ruhl (2015), pp. 431 ff.

[43] Trubiani (2023), p. 271; Trubiani (2019), pp. 133 ff.

[44] Bocchini (2003), p. 25; Bocchini (2021), p. 212.

[45] Mazzucato et al. (2021), p. 17.

[46] On the concept of negotiation asymmetry, Benedetti (2012), pp. 370 ff.; Camardi (2005), pp. 581 ff.; Chiarella (2016), pp. 1 ff.; D'Amico (2019), pp. 1 ff.; De Poli (2002), pp. 1 ss.; Roppo (2001), pp. 769 ff.; Vettori (2012), pp. 1190 ff.; Zoppini (2008), pp. 515 ff.

[47] The reference is to the figure of the 'third contract', on which *ex multis* AA.VV (2008); Colangelo (2004); Parini (2015), pp. 308 ff.; Roppo (2011); *contra,* among others, Minervini (2009), pp. 493 ff.; Perlingieri (2006), pp. 341 ff.

professional),[48] comparable to that recognised by the European legislator to the consumer, but which is nevertheless in a condition of disadvantage; both with regard to the consumer in the strict sense of the term; and finally with regard to the subjects who, through the use of platforms, exchange goods and services among themselves, being able in fact to take on the characteristic traits of the professional due to the particular ways in which they operate in the digital environment.[49]

The asymmetrical nature of the relationship between users and platforms, like that of the relationship between parties only formally on an equal footing, is reflected, insofar as it is of interest here, in the way disputes relating thereto are handled, which is left to contractual determinations.

In the first case, the technological and economic pre-eminence entails the imposition by platforms of unilaterally prepared contractual models, albeit through the use of apparently confidential formulas and colloquial tones,[50] in relation to which operators are left with no choice but to *take it or leave it*.

The provision of recourse to out-of-court conflict resolution procedures—both relative to relations entertained directly with the platforms and those intermediated by them—responds, therefore, to a direct economic interest that is reflected in their 'internalisation'; impartiality, therefore, is not considered as a determining element for their proper conduct. It, in fact, yields before the maximisation of trust in the platform, both as a direct service provider and as manager of the negotiating relations between third parties.

In the latter case, in fact, the intervention (usually of an evaluative/decisive nature) is functional to build a trust that is necessary to strengthen the bond with the platform even after a dispute has been resolved; with regard to intermediate contractual relations, in fact, this also realises a concrete interest of the parties: that of the users, who can trust in a rapid and efficient solution to the dispute concerning conformity defects of the goods or total or partial non-fulfilment in relation to the provision of the services offered, and that of the suppliers, who can maintain—precisely through the recognition of the customers' right—high reputational levels, essential for the development of their *business* within the platform.

The development of such an *online* conflict resolution system leaves little room for the use of tools other than this one. Indeed, an alternative system to the one managed by the platform does not appear to be equally reliable, first because the latter has no interest in adhering to it (even though certain uniform contractual models, especially in the context of contracts concluded in the territory of the European Union, refer to them, in accordance with European Union law), second, because there is a lack of awareness on the part of the users that would enable them to reject the contractual model and, therefore, to have recourse to other procedures or other

[48] Minervini (2008), p. 10.

[49] In this respect, the definition of *prosumer* was coined, on which Toffler (1980). On this definition, Alpa (2021a), pp. 14 ff.; Maugeri (2015), pp. 406 ff.; Quarta (2017a), pp. 667 ff.; Ritzer and Jurgenson (2010), pp. 10 ff.

[50] Alpa (2021b), p. 728; Bygrave (2015), pp. 28 ff.; Momberg (2017), p. 189; Quarta (2017b), p. 566.

bodies, whose existence, procedural and decision-making rules, reference legislation, etc. should be known.

This information *gap* and—above all—the lack of real awareness on the part of the parties involved makes it preferable to have recourse to a direct, contractually 'imposed', and in any event rapid and effective means of settling disputes that primarily concern disservices or non-conformities: on the other hand, the compression of the spaces of private autonomy for settling the dispute appears justified by the concrete possibility of obtaining the replacement of the goods, the reduction of the price, compensation for the damage for the disservice suffered, etc., which substantially represent the object of the claims put forward by the parties.

This, however, does not detract from the fact that—again in the context of negotiation via platforms—there may be ample room for the development of alternative dispute resolution systems, whether *offline* or *online*, which concern contracts concluded directly between suppliers and customers that (by type or value) do not fall within the scope of contractual provisions, or which may be resorted to in a subsidiary manner, where the latter have not led to a mutually satisfactory solution.

Alongside this hypothesis, systems other than those operated directly by platforms can usefully be implemented in relation to a still wide range of negotiating relationships in which operators contract in the digital marketplace.

Suffice it to think of all the companies that—due to size or needs related to the type of goods sold or services offered—do not need (or do not have the opportunity) to place themselves within the ecosystem built by the platforms, being able to activate their own site or make use of a proprietary mobile application. From this perspective, there is no doubt that recourse to such tools can have a positive effect on the market, given that recourse to an out-of-court procedure available to customers can be considered an additional service, useful for building the loyalty of customers (professional and non-professional)[51] and for developing a sort of competition with other companies, including in the management of conflicts.

At the same time, and perhaps in a context that holds more interesting prospects, these systems offer the opportunity to alternatively resolve a number of disputes concerning the so-called collaborative (sharing) economy,[52] in which—as mentioned above—contractual relations take place between subjects to whom it is difficult to give a precise subjective legal qualification (as consumers or as professionals).

We particularly refer to all those so-called *peer-to-peer* transactions in which—through platforms—private individuals can offer goods and services (even without this being part of a professional activity) and at the same time make use of goods and services made available by other private individuals.

---

[51] Camardi (2006), p. 2.

[52] There are numerous contributions on the *sharing economy*; among them, Di Sabato (2018), pp. 2 ff.; Quarta (2017a), pp. 667 ff.; Ramella and Manzo (2019); Rossi (2019); Smorto (2015), pp. 245 ff.; Smorto (2017), pp. 119 ff. As to foreign contributions, *ex multis*, Busch (2016), pp. 225 ff.; Hatzopulos (2018), pp. 1067 ff.; Miller (2016), pp. 151 ff.; Vallejo (2019), pp. 995 ff.

In such cases, it appears evident that—beyond the formal qualification attributable to the seller/supplier who appears to be a private individual and, therefore, on an equal footing with his contractual counterpart—the latter still carries out his activity in a habitual, continuous manner, based on knowledge related to that specific market segment. This can lead to negotiating imbalances from which conflicts are generated that can be more usefully resolved out of court, where the platform does not intervene directly, especially if one takes into account the difficulty of establishing the boundaries within which the principles and instruments of consumer protection can be applied.

Also with regard to them, therefore, recourse to alternative dispute resolution mechanisms entrusted to a third party, in conditions of impartiality and independence, may represent an adequate response for the identification of a solution that (besides being rapid and effective) constitutes the fruit of a confrontation capable of remedying the original asymmetry that generated the conflict—thanks to the intervention of the third party—and thus of ensuring the achievement of an effectively satisfactory agreement.

With respect to these cases, business-to-consumer relations, as well as business-to-business or peer-to-peer relations, still require a system of out-of-court dispute resolution that ensures the rapid and efficient resolution of any disputes, which—for the reasons mentioned above—appears inherent to the very nature of e-commerce; at the same time, it requires that the principles and rules that inspire these procedures ensure the impartiality and independence of the body.[53]

In such hypotheses, it is not simply a matter of relying on a procedure directly managed by the platform—which reinforces the parties' trust in it and ensures their permanence in its ecosystem—but rather of having recourse to a procedure managed by a third party, which—whether it carries out an activity of a facilitative type or an evaluative/adjudicative type—requires the cooperation of the parties involved, which ensures a mutually satisfactory result, because it is based on the actual interest of the parties that allows them to safeguard, where appropriate, their future relations.

5 ADR and ODR: Ontological Characteristics, Structural Differences and Prospects for the Use of Artificial Intelligence

The use of the network's own computer technology has made it possible to qualify these procedures as o.d.r. (*online dispute resolution*), which compares with a.d.r. (*alternative dispute resolution*) that traditionally take place offline outside digital marketplaces.

---

[53] Mantovani (2013), p. 438; Lazzarelli (2015), pp. 134 ff.; Fachechi (2016), *passim*; Rossi (2015), pp. 72 ff.; Ead (2016).

This consideration appears sufficient in itself to exclude that the former can be considered as belonging to a dogmatic category that is distinct from that in which the latter are included;[54] in fact, they represent the transposition of procedures that—while maintaining distinct typological characterisations (adjudicative models, facilitative models, mixed models)—are the result of the transition to the 'computerised' environment.[55]

Moreover, both categories share the same purpose, which is to ensure the efficiency of the reference markets through the out-of-court settlement of conflicts whose distinctive features are consistent with the way they develop.

Whether we speak of a.d.r. or of o.d.r., we must recognise the coexistence of a multiplicity of procedures that can be counted in the two categories usually referred to in doctrine and that refer to how the parties reach a solution to the dispute: on the one hand, those of a self-compositional type, of a facilitative-conciliatory character; on the other hand, those of a hetero-compositional type, of an evaluative-adjudicative character.

From a functional point of view, they appear to be entirely equivalent in theory, since they can lead the parties towards an out-of-court settlement of the conflict. Moreover, there would be no apparent impediment to the use of these instruments, regardless of the nature of the contractual relationship that gave rise to the conflict, since disputes arising in connection with a contractual relationship concluded *online* can also be resolved by means of a traditional a.d.r.

Indeed, notwithstanding this formal functional equivalence, it must also be noted that markets (digital and otherwise) tend to resort to homologous mechanisms with respect to the economic dynamics that take place in them; nevertheless, the only hypothesis that appears reasonably practicable is that in which the parties, even if they have entered into a negotiation relationship outside the network, may nevertheless decide to have recourse to an o.d.r. for the resolution of a dispute arising from the execution of the same.[56]

With regard to disputes arising out of relationships entered into *online,* in fact, the only practicable route appears to be that of the o.d.r.; however, one cannot

---

[54] To this effect, Minervini (2016), p. 8.

[55] On the subject, AA.VV (2006); AA.VV (2015); Camardi (2004); Cassano (2005), pp. 883 ff.; Fachechi (2012), pp. 373 ff.; Forgillo (2011), pp. 475 ff.; Forgillo (2023), pp. 665 ff.; Marangon (2006), pp. 375 ff.; Peruginelli (2007), pp. 477 ff.; Pierani and Ruggieri (2002) pp. 1 ff.; Tripodi (2005), pp. 205 ff.; Vaccà (2009), pp. 1072 ff. The debate on the conceptual autonomy of ODR vis-à-vis ADRs is also much felt in the foreign literature: Menkel Meadow (2016), pp. 4 ff.; Rule (2016), pp. 8 ff.; generally, for a reconstruction of the debate, Katsh and Rabinovich Einy (2017), pp. 33 ff.; Koulu (2019), *passim*; see also Katsh (2021), pp. 10 ff. (who, in highlighting the autonomy of ODRs considers technology to be one of the parties to the negotiation); *contra* Lodder and Zeleznikow (2010), pp. 79 ff.; Lodder (2006), pp. 143 ff.

[56] Consider, for example, the conclusion of a hotel contract entered into by a foreign tourist *inter praesentes,* without any *online* booking, who wants to contest the non-performance of certain services during his stay; in the event that direct negotiation during the course of the holiday did not lead to an agreement, one could imagine that the tourist—once back in the foreign country of origin—decides to resort to an o.o.r. to try to settle the dispute anyway.

consider the marketplace on the *web* as a *unicum*. As noted above, a distinction must be made between negotiating relationships relating to e-commerce *tout* court and those relating to negotiating relationships intermediated by platforms.

While in the first case, in fact, the parties (provided they are both aware and informed) may freely resort to the model they deem most suitable to the nature of the dispute, the subject matter of the dispute, personal conditions, and so on, in the second case the choice appears instead conditioned by adherence to the general terms and conditions of the contract which—as said—impose predetermined models, essentially left to the managers of the platform itself.

This highlights a further characteristic; indeed, these are procedures in which the platform hardly assumes a true third-party role. It may be part of the negotiating relationship from which the dispute has arisen, and in that case, it is also part of the procedure, which, however, does not assume the connotations of a true direct negotiation, not even in the form best known to us of assisted negotiation.

The procedure, therefore, is similar to the handling of a complaint, which often restricts the initiative of the complainant, who—by virtue of the applicable general terms and conditions of the contract—may carry out his complaints provided that they fall within a predetermined scope, are presented within certain deadlines and in accordance with certain procedures, waive the right to an adversarial process, and bind himself in advance to what will be decided, not being able to choose whether to turn to an autonomously chosen third party body, if a law other than that provided for in the contract (perhaps that of his country of residence) applies.

Even in cases in which the platform assumes the function of intermediary, its role as a third party appears blurred, since a direct interest can always be recognised, both in the case in which it provides accessory services for the execution of the negotiated relationship between the parties to the dispute (e.g. logistics and transport services, or payment services), and in the case in which it—although completely extraneous to the negotiated relationship—implements a *policy* more favourable to the client, which induces it to exert some form of pressure intended to favour the latter.

In view of the differences noted, it seems more useful to identify a breakdown of the o.d.r., between those that develop *human-based* models (more likely to be adopted for disputes that do not concern platforms) and those that instead are informed by *machine-based* models.

Indeed, it seems intuitive that the development of o.d.r. procedures is intimately connected with the use of Artificial Intelligence systems that, through the use of increasingly sophisticated algorithms, can intervene at various stages and with different functions within them.

First, Artificial Intelligence can carry out the preliminary steps (presentation of the application and the counterparty's reply; selection of the third party to be entrusted with the management of the litigation, perhaps corresponding to the nature of the litigation); scrutinise any profiles of inadmissibility of applications (because they do not fall within the scope—objective and subjective—dictated by the body managing the procedure); facilitate communication between the parties (think of the information technologies that allow them to interact remotely, or to exchange allegations and documents using *chat* or *e-mail*) analysing and systematising the documents produced by the parties (especially in relation to particularly complex disputes, with a significant number of annexes, some of them of a strictly technical nature), or to translate them, where they are drawn up in different languages; transcribing the minutes of meetings or providing a simultaneous translation service of the statements made by parties who do not speak the same language.

It is, therefore, a use that is in any case subservient to the performance of procedures essentially based on human intervention (whether facilitative or evaluative procedures), made easier by technological tools; it is, in any case, the third party natural person who takes on the task of dialoguing with the parties, even when they are not simultaneously and physically present, having preferred to use remote communication platforms.[57]

Not even the use of *software* that uses Artificial Intelligence to detect any profiles of incompetence appears capable of performing a real conflict resolution function, nor of a conciliatory, nor of a decisional nature.

The discourse appears, on the other hand, quite different when Artificial Intelligence systems are employed precisely for the latter purpose; here, in fact, human activity is completely extraneous and is replaced by the predictive capacity of the machine to arrive at a solution to the conflict.

With this in mind, a distinction must be made between heteronomous and autonomous procedures; as is evident, in the former, the algorithms are used to formulate a proposal for the settlement of the dispute (which may, in some cases, also be binding on the parties), whereas in the latter, they are used in the facilitation of the negotiation, which is and remains at the full disposal of the parties.

Despite the noted differences, the use of Artificial Intelligence raises questions of no small moment.

As far as the evaluative-adjudicative activity is concerned, it is evident that the predictive capacity of the algorithms gives rise to a model that has rightly been defined as blind[58] since the solution is left to the Artificial Intelligence system itself, which draws up a solution proposal on the basis of the evaluation of the data and the conditions under which the parties involved have declared their willingness to settle the dispute.

Such mechanisms are precisely those used by the major global platforms in the described management of conflicts involving them with respect to the users of their services.

The purely empirical analysis, which takes into account quantitative data and the degree of perceived satisfaction, makes it possible to view the development of such use of Artificial Intelligence with some interest; beyond the aforementioned purposes to which the o.d.r. in this sector tend towards (maintenance of trust, preservation of reputational *standards*), the predictive capacities of algorithms for the

[57] Peruginelli (2007) highlights the limitation of communication that does not take place physically, especially with regard to self-compositional procedures in which the facilitation activity performed by the third party also requires the development and analysis of non-verbal communication.

[58] Mancini (2016), p. 18; Peruginelli (2007), p. 490.

construction of fully automated decision-making processes gives rise to strong perplexity, albeit with a lesser degree of concern in relation to disputes in which the distance between the parties is relative to a *range* predetermined by them, or to the existence of a defect in relation to which an asset must be replaced; on the contrary, it is precisely the ability to analyse an extraordinarily impressive amount of data from the standardised reports produced by the platforms that enables Artificial Intelligence to come up with a solution that comes close to the claims made.

Greater concerns, on the other hand, arise in relation to relationships in which the good of life at stake does not appear susceptible to being referred to the predictive assessment of the machine, without compromising the realisation of a justice of the concrete case that balances the requirements of flexibility and speed inherent in these markets and, at the same time, respect for the interests and protection of the rights of the subjects operating in them.

In this respect, also in view of the data management profiles of the parties and the assessment of the technological risk that such an activity might entail, the rules of the GDPR as well as those of the I.A. Act should come into play.

As far as facilitative activity is concerned, on the other hand, although its use is not yet noteworthy, the doubts that emerge are connected to the ability of Artificial Intelligence systems to actually interact with individuals, to perceive their needs, needs and feelings, and to grasp the meanings connected to non-verbal communication, which appear to be indispensable assessment tools for the third party to facilitate dialogue between the parties, to defuse sabotaging psychological mechanisms, to re-elaborate the terms of the issue, disengaging it from purely psychological elements that do not help the identification of a satisfactory solution.

Whether it is a matter of evaluative activity (outside the spheres in which it is already developed) or facilitative activity, the future use of predictive Artificial Intelligence in the context of o.d.r. can only be ensured by a system that can guarantee a bilateral intelligibility: that of the machine with respect to human language, especially if it is a technical language and referred to complex negotiation relationships (which escape, therefore, the deductive-linear approach proper to such algorithms), but also that of man with respect to algorithmic language, to ensure a certain understanding and, therefore, the full and conscious exercise of the freedom to accept or not the proposed solution to the dispute that has been elaborated.

In this context, the issue of possible errors made by the algorithm in analysing and interpreting human language is also relevant; the erroneousness of this process, or its manipulation (based on the pre-set data to which the machine responds) in fact determines problems that relate not only to the actual ability to put an end to the conflict, in a definitive and satisfactory manner, but also to the actual recognition of the fundamental rights of individuals.

As much as technology is making enormous strides in the development of relational capabilities (according to the model defined as *affecting computing*), in the imitation of behaviour, in the creation of empathy, in the analysis of behavioural elements,[59] it must be considered that the activity performed within the framework of such procedures is still aimed at identifying a solution that is not only economically satisfactory as well as legally valid and effective, but that is capable of offering them or at least of accompanying them towards a solution that is not based on conforming to predetermined standards, but that is actually receptive to the real interests of the parties (of whatever nature they may be) in a projection that also knows how to be creative and, as such, not only just, but also convenient.

6 EU Initiatives on Out-of-Court Settlement of Consumer Disputes: Prospects for Development

Ever since the early 1990s, the European legislator has shown great interest in alternative dispute resolution instruments, especially with regard to relations between professionals and consumers; this choice of legal policy appeared necessary not only to ensure forms of substantive justice (alternative and complementary to judicial justice) for the latter, but above all to contribute in this way to the establishment of an increasingly efficient single market.[60]

In this context, the attention given to their development in the context of e-commerce does not appear to be without significance, as evidenced by the provision in Art. 17 of Directive 2000/31/EC.[61]

Following this intervention, aimed exclusively at the settlement of *online* disputes, the European regulator then inaugurated a new phase in which the regulation of a.d.r. (although still linked to consumer relations, if one excludes the isolated regulation of certain aspects of civil and commercial mediation[62]) became part of a more comprehensive strategy, which concerned both the traditional and the digital market.

---

[59] On the subject in general, Incutti (2022), pp. 519 ff.

[60] Appiano (2009), pp. 59 ff.; Bartolomucci (2007), pp. 211 ff.; Capponi (1991), pp. 361 ff.; Capponi (1993), pp. 216 ff.; Carpaneto (2000), pp. 761 ff.; Danovi (1997), pp. 326 ff.; Martinello (1992), pp. 1619 ff.; Martinello (1994), pp. 340 ff.; Rossolillo (2008), pp. 349 ff.; Sticchi Damiani (2004); Vigoriti (2011), pp. 81 ff.

[61] Generally, on the European approach to a.d.r. in e-commerce, Cortes (2010); Lopez and Tarruella (2001), pp. 1337 ff. spec. 1374 ff. As is well known, the directive was transposed by the Italian legislator in Art. 19 of Legislative Decree No. 70/2003; in this regard, Camardi (2004), p. 594; Danovi (2003), p. 927; Fachechi (2016), p. 23; Menichino (2014), p. 798; Minervini (2016), p. 11.

[62] Ghirga (2009), pp. 1 ff.; Luiso (2015); Minervini (2005), pp. 427 ff.; Zucconi Galli Fonseca (2010), pp. 653 ff.; Bosnak (2011), pp. 625 ff.; Esplugues (2014).

The cornerstones of this new line of action[63] were Directive 2013/11/EU and the coeval Regulation 524/2013/EU;[64] the latter particularly regulates precisely the o.d.r. procedures, which are entrusted to an IT platform that, however, is limited to performing a mere coordination function between the various accredited bodies at the European level, following a screening of compliance with the principles contained in the directive on a.d.r. This coordination role allows the platform to receive any requests received from individual European consumers and (where this has not been identified personally, or by agreement between the parties) to refer them to the body competent to deal with the dispute.

To ensure accessibility to the platform, it provides not only the model documents for filling in the application, but also ancillary services such as translation, which is particularly useful in the case of cross-border disputes.

It therefore does not represent a body for the direct and telematic management of procedures, but simply a point of contact between the various bodies existing in the various Member States of the Union.

Such a mechanism, despite the emphasis with which its entry into force was accompanied and its placement within a framework of general principles inspiring the entire regulatory package on the subject, did not take long to show its intrinsic weakness, to such an extent that the Commission once again intervened and—following the report on the state of implementation of the legislation—supplemented the platform's functionalities, enabling it to facilitate direct negotiation between the parties, by means of an IT interface.

Nonetheless, the implementation of these new formulas has not allowed the European' o.d.r. system to develop effectively, sanctioning on the other hand its substantial failure; as appropriately emphasised, the reasons for this failure are not only linked to the procedural aspects regulated therein, but rather to 'the choice of the European Union legislator to push market operators towards a *human-based* model of out-of-court dispute resolution, instead of accepting the inevitable change of approach and beginning a work of regulation of the *technology-based* systems already in current use',[65] with specific reference to transactions involving platforms.

The legislation in question, therefore, has developed against the trend of the new digital markets, and this has forced the Brussels legislator to make a U-turn along two lines.

In October 2023, the Commission adopted a proposal for the revision of the so-called a.d.r. package, which provides for an amendment of the 2013 directive, the

---

[63] Gioia (2012), pp. 697 ff.; Appiano (2013), pp. 965 ff.; Bottino (2014), pp. 396 ff.; Bugiolacchi (2013), pp. 1403 ff.; Lombardi (2012), pp. 457 ff.; Rossi (2014), pp. 831 ff.; Vigoriti (2021), pp. 313 ff.

[64] Gabellini (2018), pp. 409 ff.; Luiso (2015); Mancaleoni (2017), pp. 1065 ff.; Galletto (2017). As known, the directive was transposed into domestic law by Legislative Decree No. 130/2015, which amended the Consumer Code: on this point, Bartolomucci (2016), pp. 494 ff.; Scannicchio (2019), pp. 971 ff.; Ferraris (2017), pp. 1631 ff. With regard to the o.o.r., Colombo (2021), pp. 256 ff.; Dalla Bontà (2021), pp. 191 ff.

[65] Felicetti (2023), pp. 197 ff.

repeal of the o.d.r. regulation and the adoption of a recommendation concerning quality requirements for dispute resolution procedures offered by *online* marketplaces.

For the discourse that is going to be carried out, it seems appropriate to point out that the discontinuation of the o.d.r. platform follows an empirical consideration on the irrelevance of the data of the appeals managed by it, which do not justify the use of economic resources for the continuation of this activity. It is surprising, however, that—when investigating the reasons for this lack of success—it is considered to be mainly due to the lack of information on the functioning mechanisms of the a.d.r. procedures, the lack of interest on the part of sellers of goods and providers of *online* services, and the difficulty for consumers in filing complaints.

One almost has the impression that the vision underlying this choice does not take into account the real structure of the so-called *platform economy* and the economic and negotiation dynamics that develop in it, with inevitable repercussions on dispute management.[66]

In September 2024, the proposal for a directive on a.d.r. was published, amending the 2013 legislation and partly taking into account the impact of new technologies on the use and management of out-of-court consumer dispute procedures, which—however—appear to be conceived on the model centred around the figure of a third party in charge of the procedure (regardless of the facilitative or evaluative role played by the latter), so that the use of new technologies is conceived as an auxiliary to the implementation of these procedures.

The new regulatory intervention takes into account three aims, explicitly mentioned by the Commission: *(i)* 'adapting the ADR framework to digital markets by explicitly including a wide range of EU consumer rights that may not be expressly described in contracts or that concern pre-contractual steps'; *(ii)* 'enhancing the use of ADR in cross-border disputes through more personalised assistance to consumers and traders'; *(iii)* 'simplify ADR procedures to the benefit of all actors involved, including by reducing the reporting obligations of ADR schemes and the information obligations of traders, while encouraging traders to increase their engagement in ADR complaints through the introduction of a duty to reply'.

To pursue these aims, the directive should provide for a significant broadening of the scope of application, both objectively and subjectively: in the first case, recourse to a.d.r. should also be recognised 'against any trader selling goods or services, including digital content and digital services, to consumers residing in the EU, and to disputes relating to the pre-contractual stages during which consumer rights exist irrespective of whether the consumer eventually concludes a contract. This concerns, for instance, misleading advertising, missing, unclear or misleading information, unfair terms or warranty claims. In addition, the extended scope is intended to

---

[66] Even though the document states 'the narrowly defined scope of the ADR directive is not suitable for resolving the emergence of a wide range of disputes, particularly in digital markets. The minimum harmonisation approach adopted in the ADR directive has allowed Member States to adapt their ADR framework to their own culture and investment, resources, infrastructure, level of awareness, etc.'.

cover disputes concerning other fundamental consumer rights under the law, such as the right not to be subject to geo-blocking practices, to change telecommunications provider or to access basic financial services' (Art. 2).

In the second case, the new provisions should also provide that 'traders established outside the EU may participate (on a voluntary basis) in ADR procedures. The Commission therefore proposes to introduce an obligation for Member States to establish ADR entities that will have the competence to deal with such disputes between consumers and traders from outside the EU' (Art. 5).

It must also be emphasised, for the reasons set out above, the prominence given to the 'vulnerable consumer', qualified as a person with 'limited digital literacy skills', who is granted the right to receive documents also in non-digital format, as well as to be able to access a.d.r. procedures by means of 'inclusive tools' and to be able to submit an automated decision to the scrutiny of a natural person.

The second guideline along which the European Union legislator has been moving, on the other hand, relates to the provision of certain provisions on the subject of conflict settlement mechanisms, both in the so-called *Digital Service Act* and in the *Digital Markets Act*, all inspired by the need to adapt the rules on e-commerce to the 'new' reality of platforms, for which specific obligations are envisaged; for this very reason, the two sets of rules do not appear to be limited solely to disputes involving consumers.

Particularly, whereas in the latter regulation the legislator merely provided for the obligation of the so-called *gatekeepers* to publish the general terms and conditions of access by business users 'to their shops of *software* applications, *online* search engines and *online social network* services', provided that these are fair, reasonable and non-discriminatory and include an 'alternative dispute resolution mechanism' (Art. 6(12)), in the former the regulation of this aspect appears more comprehensive.

Particularly, it is envisaged that recourse to an o.d.r. may be exercised following decisions taken by the platform in relation to the removal of information and content; the suspension or termination of the provision of the service or the suspension or removal of the account; and the limitation of the possibility of obtaining remuneration for the publication of content.

The regulation provides for a sort of *multi-step* pathway consisting, in the first instance, of the handling of the complaint (which must be lodged no later than 6 months after the decision has been communicated), in a manner that ensures, at the same time, ease of access and completeness of content.

The platform's decision on the claim must be reasoned and taken 'in a timely, non-discriminatory, diligent and non-arbitrary manner', by qualified personnel and 'not using automated tools exclusively'; this is with the obvious aim of reducing the impact of the platform's own interests in the management of this phase and in the processing of the *claim* by the customer.

The second *step* provides that, in the event of dissatisfaction with the outcome of the interlocution at the complaint stage, the customer may have recourse to an a.d.r. procedure, which may be either of the adjudicative or facilitative type; in this respect, the legislator intended to comply with the general framework on the subject of a.d.r, accepting a vision that is open to the coexistence of several models, provided that they are entrusted to third-party bodies that have obtained accreditation by the digital services coordinator, which represents the reference authority in each Member State, and provided that they are not procedures that end with a decision that is binding on the parties.

Lastly, a system of apportionment of the costs of the proceedings is also provided for, almost as if a sort of loss of earnings were recognised, which, however, is ill-suited to the case of procedures of a facilitative nature, given the conciliatory outcome that excludes the recognition of winners and losers.

Un'ultima chiosa, al riguardo, in merito alla legislazione di diritto interno; il legislatore domestico (che pure ha disciplinato sotto molteplici punti di vista le procedure di risoluzione alternativa delle controversie, anche ampliando il raggio d'azione delineato dalla trasposizione nell'ordinamento interno delle norme europee) non ha in alcun caso preso in considerazione, al momento, la possibilità di disciplinare la materia delle o.d.r. in general and, even less so, those relating to transactions that take place through the use of digital platforms, if we exclude the laconic reference contained in Art. 19 of Legislative Decree No. 70 on e-commerce.

Neither the provisions on civil and commercial mediation (as set forth in Legislative Decree No. 28/2010, as amended several times),[67] nor do those concerning consumer ADRs (governed by the Consumer Code) contain detailed rules on this point, limiting themselves to providing for the possibility that, in certain hypotheses, recourse to such procedures may also be made by telematic means.

It is clear from reading these provisions that—on the one hand—the intention is to refer only to procedural and managerial aspects and not also to those inherent in the adoption of the decision and that—on the other hand—there was (and there is currently) no clear intention on the part of the legislature to regulate the o.d.r. in the context of the digital platform economy.

References

AA.VV (2006) In: Camardi C (ed) Metodi on line di risoluzione delle controversie: arbitrato telematico e ODR. Atti Convegno, Venezia, 10 ottobre 2003. Padova

AA.VV (2008) In: Gitti G, Villa G (eds) Il terzo contratto. L'abuso di potere contrattuale nei rapporti tra imprese. Bologna

AA. VV. (2015)" In: Imbrenda M, Fachechi A (eds) Meccanismi alternativi di risoluzione delle controversie nel commercio elettronico, Napoli

AA.VV (2016) In: De Franceschi A (ed) European contract law and the digital single market: the implications of the digital revolution, Cambridge

AA.VV (2018) In: Grundmann S (ed) European contract law in the digital age, Cambridge

Albanese A (2024) Le categorie del diritto privato alla prova delle nuove tecnologie. Contratto e "torto" nell'economia digitale. Nuovo dir civ, pp 9 ff

[67] Riccio (2011), pp. 211 ff.

Alpa G (2021a) Consumatori e mercato. In: Capilli G (ed) I contratti del consumatore. Torino, pp 14 ff
Alpa G (2021b) Sul potere contrattuale delle piattaforme digitali. Contr e impr, p 728
Alpini A (2019) Sull'approccio umano-centrico all'intelligenza artificiale. Riflessioni a margine del "Progetto europeo di orientamenti etici per una IA affidabile". Comp dir civ, p 1
Ammannati L (2021) Verso un diritto delle piattaforme digitali? In: Ammannati L, Canepa A, Greco GL, Minneci U (eds) Algoritmi, Big Data, piattaforme digitali: la regolazione dei mercati in trasformazione. Torino, pp 3 ff
Antonucci A (2019) I non-luoghi di produzione delle regole. In: Antonucci A, De Poli M, Urbani A (eds) I luoghi dell'economia. Le dimensioni della sovranità. Torino, pp 20 ff
Appiano EM (2009) I sistemi di Adr nell'ottica del legislatore comunitario. Contr e impr/Eur, pp 59 ff
Appiano EM (2013) ADR e ODR per le liti consumeristiche nel diritto UE. Contr eimpr/Eur, pp 965 ff
Ballarino T (1998) Internet nel mondo della legge, Padova
Bargelli E, Calderai V (eds) (2022) A contract law for the age of digital platforms? , Pisa
Bariatti S (2001) Internet III) Diritto internazionale privato e processuale. Enc giur Treccani XVII:6 ff
Barile CS et al (2022) Platform-based innovation ecosystems: entering new markets through holographic strategies. Ind Mark Manag 105:467 ff
Barlow JP (1996) A declaration of the independence of cyberspace
Bartolomucci P (2007) Conciliazione extragiudiziale. In Dig. IV ed., Disc. priv., Sez. civ., Agg., 3, I, Torino, pp 211 ff
Bartolomucci P (2016) La nuova disciplina delle procedure di risoluzione alternativa delle controversie in materia di consumo: il d. lgs. n. 130/15 e le modifiche del codice del consumo. Nuove leggi civ comm, pp 494 ff
Bellelli A (2024) Soft law e co-regolazione. In: Bocchini R (ed) Manuale di diritto privato dell'informatica. Napoli, pp 51 ff
Belli L (2017) Law of the land or law of the platform? Beware of the privatisation of regulation and police. In: Belli L, Zingales N (eds) Platform regulations: how platforms are regulated and how they regulate us. Rio de Janeiro
Benedetti G (2012) Contratto asimmetrico, voce. In Enc dir, Annali, V, Milano, pp 370 ff
Bocchini F (2003) Nozione di consumatore e modelli economici. In: Bocchini F (ed) Diritto dei consumatori e nuove tecnologie, I, Gli scambi. Torino, p 25
Bocchini R (2021) La polivalenza delle posizioni contrattuali nella sharing economy (prima parte). Nuovo dir civ, p 212
Bosnak M (2011) The European Mediation Directive: more questions than answers. In: Ingen-Housz A (ed) ADR in business: practice and issues across countries and cultures, II. Alphen aan der Rijn, pp 625 ff
Bottino M (2014) La nuova normativa europea in materia di risoluzione alternativa delle controversie dei consumatori. Contr e impr/Eur, pp 396 ff
Bugiolacchi L (2013) Commercio elettronico e ODR (online dispute resolution) dopo il regolamento n. 524/2013 dell'Unione europea. Resp civ prev, pp 1403 ff
Busch C (2016) Crowdsourcing consumer confidence. How to regulate online rating and reviewed system in the collaborative economy. In: De Franceschi A (ed) European contract law and the digital single market. The implication of the digital revolution. Cambridge, pp 225 ff
Busch C (2019) Self-regulation and regulatory intermediation in the platform economy. In: Cantero Gamito M, Micklitz H (eds) The role of the EU. In transnational legal ordering: standards, contracts and codes, pp 115 ff
Busch C (2020) The P2B Regulation (EU) 2019/1150: Towards a "procedural turn" in EU platform regulation?. Journal of European Consumer and Market Law, pp 133 ff
Bygrave LA (2015) Internet governance by contract. Oxford, pp 28 ff

Camardi C (2004) Metodi "alternativi" di soluzione delle controversie: diritto, spazio e tempo nell'ambiente delle tecnologie informatiche. Eur dir priv, p 554

Camardi C (2005) Contratti di consumo e contratti tra imprese. Riflessioni sull'asimmetria contrattuale nei rapporti di scambio e nei rapporti "reticolari". Riv crit dir priv, pp 581 ff

Camardi C (2006) Metodi "alternativi" di soluzione delle controversie nelle reti telematiche. Una riflessione su diritto, spazio e tempo nell'ambiente delle tecnologie informatiche. In: Metodi on line di risoluzione delle controversie: arbitrato telematico e ODR. Padova, p 2

Camardi C (2021) Contratti digitali e mercati delle piattaforme. Un promemoria per il civilista. Jus Civile, pp 870 ff

Camardi C (2023) Dalla logica individualistica alla regolazione della complessità nella tutela del consumatore (e delle vulnerabilità) nell'ecosistema digitale. In: Grisi G, Tommasi S (eds) Mercato digitale e tutela dei consumatori. Prove di futuro. Torino, p 217

Canepa A (2020) I mercanti dell'era digitale. Un contributo allo studio delle piattaforme, Torino

Capponi B (1991) Libro verde e accesso dei consumatori alla giustizia. Doc giust

Capponi B (1993) Giustizia civile: nuovi modelli verso l'Europa. Foro it V:216 ff

Carapezza Figlia G (2013) Divieto di discriminazione e autonomia contrattuale, Napoli

Carapezza Figlia G (2015) Il divieto di discriminazione quale limite all'autonomia contrattuale. Riv dir civ, pp 1405 ff

Carapezza Figlia G (2023) Decisioni algoritmiche tra diritto alla spiegazione e divieto di discriminare. Pers Mercato 4:638 ff

Carpaneto L (2000) La tutela comunitaria del consumatore: il problema dell'accesso alla giustizia, con particolare riferimento all'Italia e all'Inghilterra. Contr e impr/Eur, pp 761 ff

Carpi F (2016) La metamorfosi del monopolio statale sulla giurisdizione. Riv trim dir proc civ, pp 811 ff

Casabona S (2017) Intermediazione digitale e composizione delle controversie: dall'alternative dispute resolution all'alien dispute resolution. Dir inform informatica, pp 497 ff

Cassano G (2005) Le nuove forme di Alternative Dispute Resolution (ADR) nell'era di Internet. Giur it 4:883 ff

Ceccagnoli M et al (2012) Co-creation of value in a platform ecosystem: the case of enterprise software. MIS Q 36(1):263 ff

Chiarella ML (2016) Contrattazione asimmetrica. Segmenti normativi e costruzione unitaria, Milano

Ciacci G (2023) Le fonti del diritto dell'informatica. In: Bocchini R (ed) Manuale di diritto privato dell'informatica. pp 11 ff

Colangelo G (2004) L'abuso di dipendenza economica, tra disciplina della concorrenza e diritto dei contratti. Un'analisi economica e comparata, Torino

Colombo GF (2021) What we talk about when we talk about consumer ODR: the EU ODR regulation and its preliminary lessons. Int J Procedural Law, pp 256 ff

Comoglio L P (2000) Mezzi alternativi di tutela e garanzie costituzionali. Riv dir proc, pp 318 ff

Cortes P (2010) Online dispute resolution for consumers in the European Union. Londra

Criscuolo F (2015) Il ruolo della prassi economica telematica: autosufficienza ordinamentale e lex mercatoria. In: Imbrenda M, Fachechi A (eds) Meccanismi alternativi di risoluzione delle controversie nel commercio elettronico. Napoli, pp 107 ff

Cusumano MA et al (2019) The business of platforms: strategy in the age of digital competition, innovation, and power. New York

D'agostino G (n.d.) Le piattaforme digitali come nuove forme di mercato. Alcune considerazioni in merito ai profili economico-giuridici alla luce del processo normativo. UE. In: Ammannati L, Canepa A, Greco GL, Minneci U (eds) Algoritmi, Big Data, piattaforme digitali: la regolazione dei mercati in trasformazione. Torino, pp 81 ff

Dalla Bontà S (2021) Una giustizia "co-esistenziale" online nello spazio giuridico europeo? Spunti critici sul pacchetto ADR-ODR per i consumatori. Giust consensuale, pp 191 ff

D'Amico G (2019) Giustizia contrattuale e contratti asimmetrici. Eur. dir. priv., pp 1 ff

Danovi R (1997) Le ADR e le iniziative dell'Unione europea. Giur it IV:326 ff

Danovi F (2003) La risoluzione stragiudiziale delle controversie tecnologiche. In: Tosi E (ed) Commercio elettronico e servizi della società dell'informazione. Le regole giuridiche del mercato interno e comunitario: commento al D. Lgs. 9 aprile 2003, n. 70. Milano, pp 927 ff
De Cristofaro M (2007) La tutela giurisdizionale statale nella virtualità del Cyberspazio. In: Rossello C, Finocchiaro G, Tosi E (eds) Commercio elettronico, documento informatico e firma digitale. Torino, pp 185 ff
De Poli M (2002) Asimmetrie informative e rapporti contrattuali, Padova
Di Sabato D (2018) Progredire tornando all'antico: gli scambi nella sharing economy. In: Di Sabato D, Lepore A (eds) Sharing economy. Profili giuridici. Napoli, pp 2 ff
Draetta U (2001) Internet e commercio elettronico nel diritto internazionale dei privati, Milano
Ead (2023) Piattaforme ed ecosistemi digitali. Scelte pro-concorrenziali. Riv dir ind, pp 172 ff
Eidenmuller H, Engel M (2014) Against false settlement: designing efficient consumer rights enforcement systems in Europe. Ohio State J Disput Resolut, pp 261 ff
Esplugues C (2014) Mediation in the EU after the transposition of the directive 2008/52/EC on mediation in civil and commercial matters, Cambridge
Evans D, Schmalensse R (2016) Matchmakers. The new economics of multisided platforms. Boston
Fachechi A (2012) Spunti di riflessione sulle tecniche di conciliazione telematica delle controversie. Corti salernitane, pp 373 ff
Fachechi A (2015) Net neutrality e discriminazioni arbitrarie. In: Perlingieri C, Ruggeri L (eds) Internet e diritto civile. Napoli, p 260
Fachechi A (2016) La giustizia alternativa nel commercio elettronico, Napoli
Felicetti AM (2023) La risoluzione extragiudiziale delle dispute nei mercati digitali: alcune novità dall'Europa. Riv trim dir proc civ, pp 197 ff
Ferraris F (2017) A.D.R. e consumatori: rapporti e interferenze. Nuova giur civ comm, pp 1631 ff
Finocchiaro G (2001) Lex mercatoria e commercio elettronico. Il diritto applicabile ai contratti conclusi su Internet. Contr e impr, pp 571 ff
Floridi L (2017) La quarta rivoluzione. Milano, pp 27 ff
Forgillo E (2011) La giustizia telematica. Le online dispute resolution. In: Valentino D (ed) Manuale di diritto dell'informatica. Napoli, pp 475 ff
Forgillo E (2023) La giustizia digitale Le online dispute resolution in Bocchini R (ed) Manuale di diritto privato dell'informatica, Napoli, pp 665 ff
Franceschelli V (2001) Premesse generali per uno studio del commercio elettronico. In: Franceschelli V (ed) Commercio elettronico. Milano, pp 4 ff
Gabellini E (2018) L'attuazione della direttiva alle ADR di consumo negli Stati europei: una breve panoramica. Riv arb, pp 409 ff
Galletto T (2017) Adr e controversie dei consumatori: un difficile equilibrio. Eur dir priv
Gawer A, Cusumano MA (2014) Industry platforms and ecosystem innovation. J Prod Innov Manag 31(3):417 ff
Giannone Codiglione G (2015) Reputazione online, sistemi di rating e anonimato in una recente decisione della corte di cassazione tedesca. Dir inf, pp 169 ff
Gioia G (2012) Il nuovo "pacchetto" della Commissione europea sull'ADR. Corr giur, pp 697 ff
Gorgoni A (2024) La vulnerabilità nell'ambiente digitale e la protezione della libertà del volere. Pers mercato 3:915 ff
Hatzopulos V (2018) The collaborative economy under EU law, Oxford
Iamiceli P (2021) Online platforms and the digital turn in EU contract law: unfair practices, transparency and the (pierced) veil of digital immunity. Eur Rev Contract Law, pp 392 ff
Incutti EM (2022) Sistemi di riconoscimento delle emozioni e ruolo dell'autonomia privata. Giust civ 2:519 ff
Irti N (2001) Norma e luoghi. Problemi di geo-diritto. Roma-Bari, pp 65 ff
Irti N, Severino E (2001) Dialogo tra diritto e tecnica. Roma-Bari
Katsh E, Rabinovich Einy O (2017) Digital justice: technology and the internet of disputes. Oxford, pp 33 ff

Katsh E et al (2000) E-commerce, E-disputes, and E-dispute resolution: in the shadow of "eBay Law". Ohio State J Disput Resolut, pp 705 ff

Katsh E (2021) Online Dispute Resolution (ODR): a Look at History, in Rainey D, Katsh E., Wahab M.A. (eds) Online Dispute Resolution: Theory and Practice, The Hague

Koulu R (2019) Law, technology and dispute resolution: privatisation of coercion, New York

Lazzarelli F (2015) ODR e rapporti asimmetrici tra non consumatori. In: Imbrenda M, Fachechi A (eds) Meccanismi alternativi di risoluzione delle controversie nel commercio elettronico. Napoli, pp 134 ff

Libertini M (2023) La presunzione di dipendenza economica nei mercati digitali. Un commento all'art. 33 della legge 5 agosto 2022, n. 118. Orizz dir comm, p 1

Lodder A (2006) The third party and beyond: an analysis of the different parties, in particular The Fifth, involved in online dispute resolution. Inf Commun Technol Law, pp 143 ff

Lodder A, Zeleznikow J (2010) Enhanced dispute resolution through the use of information technology. Cambridge, pp 79 ff

Lombardi EM (2012) La mediazione e lo spazio cibernetico: uno sguardo alle proposte della Commissione europea su ADR e ODR. Giust civ, pp 457 ff

Loos M (2016) Enforcing consumer rights through ADR at the detriment of consumer law. Eur Rev Priv Law, pp 61 ff

Lopez A, Tarruella (2001) A European Community Regulatory Framework for Electronic Commerce. Common Mark Law Rev, pp 1337 ff spec. 1374 ff

Luiso FP (2015) La direttiva 2013/11/Ue, sulla risoluzione alternativa delle controversie dei consumatori. judicium.it

Mancaleoni AM (2017) La risoluzione extragiudiziale delle controversie dei consumatori dopo la direttiva 2013/11/UE. Eur dir priv, pp 1065 ff

Mancini F (2016) Mercato, regula iuris e giurisdizione nazionale nel fenomeno delle ODR. In: Minervini E (ed) Le online dispute resolution (ODR). Napoli, pp 15 ff

Mantovani MP (2013) Sistemi di Alternative Dispute Resolution a livello europeo e internazionale fra modelli di regolazione del mercato e tutela dei contraenti in condizioni di asimmetria negoziale. In: Favale R, Gambini M (eds) Mediazione civile e strumenti alternativi di composizione delle liti. Itinerari. Napoli, p 438

Manucci A (2002) Il diritto applicabile ai contratti on line. In: Maschio F (ed) Il diritto della nuova economia. Padova, pp 81 ff

Marangon A (2006) I sistemi online di risoluzione delle controversie. Dir inf, pp 375 ff

Martinelli S (2022) Platform economy: the nature of the platform and the regulation of this new disruptive actor. In: Bargelli E, Calderai V (eds) A contract law for the age of digital platforms? Pisa, pp 15 ff

Martinello P (1992) Accesso dei consumatori alla giustizia. Un progetto pilota. Doc giust, pp 1619 ff

Martinello P (1994) Libro verde sull'accesso dei consumatori alla giustizia: appunti per un'analisi critica, ivi, pp 340 ff

Maugeri M (2015) Elementi di criticità nell'equiparazione, da parte dell'AEEGSI, dei "prosumers" ai "consumatori" e ai "clienti finali". Nuova giur civ comm II:406 ff

Mazzucato M et al (2021) Reshaping platform-driven digital market. In: Moore M, Tambini D (eds) Regulating big tech: policy responses to digital dominance. Oxford, pp 17 ff

McIntyre DP, Srinivasan A (2017) Networks, platforms, and strategy: emerging views and next steps. Strateg Manag J 38(1):141 ff

Menichino C (2014) Sub art. 19 (Composizione delle controversie). In: Finocchiaro G, Delfini F (eds) Diritto dell'informatica. Torino, pp 798 ff

Mengoni L (2011) Diritto e tecnica, ora. In: Castronovo C, Albanese A, Nicolussi A (eds) Scritti I. Metodo e teoria giuridica, Milano

Menkel Meadow C (2016) Is ODR ADR? Reflections of an ADR Founder from 15th ODR Conference. Int J Online Dispute Resolut, pp 4 ff

Merone A (2022) Online dispute resolution, intermediari digitali e il nuovo paradigma della composizione preventiva e self-executing. Riv arb, pp 269 ff
Messinetti R (2019) La tutela della persona umana versus l'intelligenza artificiale. Potere decisionale dell'apparato tecnologico e diritto alla spiegazione della decisione automatizzata. Contr e impr, pp 890 ff
Miller SR (2016) First principles for regulating the sharing economy. Harv J Leg, pp 151 ff
Minervini E (2005) La proposta di direttiva comunitaria sulla conciliazione in materia civile e commerciale. Contr e impr/Eur, pp 427 ff
Minervini E (2008) Status delle parti e disciplina del contratto. Obbl contr, p 10
Minervini E (2009) Il "terzo contratto". Contr, pp 493 ff
Minervini E. (2016) I sistemi di ODR in Minervini (ed), Le online dispute resolution, Napoli, pp. 7 ff
Momberg R (2017) Standard terms and transparency in online contracts. In: De Franceschi A (ed) European contract law and the digital single market. The implication of the digital revolution. Cambridge, p 189
Nachira F et al (2007) Digital business ecosystems. Publications Office of European Commission
Neri A (2021) Uso di un algoritmo discriminatorio nella contrattazione privata. Nuova giur civ comm II:983 ff
Nuzzo A (2019) Algoritmi e regole. An giur econ, pp 42 ff
Palka P (2018) Terms of service are not contracts. Beyond contract law in the regulation of online platforms. In Grundmann S (ed) European contract law in the digital age, pp 135 ff
Parini M (2015) "Terzo contratto" e tutela dell'imprenditore debole. Studium iuris, pp 308 ff
Pellecchia E (2018) Profilazione e decisioni automatizzate al tempo della black box society: qualità dei dati e leggibilità dell'algoritmo nella cornice della responsible research and innovation. Nuove leggi civ comm, pp 1223 ff
Perlingieri P (2006) Il diritto civile nella legalità costituzionale secondo il sistema italo-comunitario delle fonti. Napoli, pp 341 ff
Perlingieri P (2020) Relazione conclusiva. In: Perlingieri P, Giova S, Prisco I (eds) Il trattamento algoritmico dei dati tra etica, diritto ed economia. Napoli, pp 379 ff
Perlingieri C (2021) Diritto privato delle nuove tecnologie: contenuti e competenze. Tecn diritto, pp 70 ff
Peruginelli G (2007) Le Online Dispute Resolution: un'evoluzione delle Alternative Dispute Resolution. Inf dir, pp 477 ff
Pierani M, Ruggieri E (2002) I sistemi alternativi di risoluzione delle controversie online, Milano, 2022; R. Sali, ODR: la risoluzione online delle controversie. In Commercio elettronico, autodisciplina e risoluzione extragiudiziale delle controversie", edited by S. Azzali, Milano, pp. 71 ff
Pollicino O (2022) I codici di condotta tra self-regulation e hard law: esiste davvero una terza via per la regolazione digitale? Il caso della strategia europea contro la disinformazione online, in Simposio sulla regolazione digitale nell'Unione europea. Riv trim dir pub, pp 1049 ff
Pollicino O (2023) Potere digitale (voce). In Enc. dir. (I Tematici), directed by M. Cartabia-M. Ruotolo, Milano, V, pp 410 ff
Quarta A (2017a) Il diritto dei consumatori ai tempi della peer economy. Prestatori di servizi e prosumers: primi spunti. Eur dir priv, pp 667 ff
Quarta A (2017b) Il ruolo delle piattaforme digitali nell'economia collaborativa. Contr e impr/Europa, pp 556 ff
Quarta A (2022) Some light remarks on the legal qualification of websites' terms of use. In: Bargelli E, Calderai C (eds) A contract law for the age of digital platforms?, 195 ss.
Quarta A, Smorto G (2024) Diritto privato dei mercati digitali, Firenze
Ramella F, Manzo C (2019) L'economia della collaborazione. Le nuove piattaforme digitali della produzione e del consumo. Bologna
Resta G (2023) Poteri privati e regolazione. In Enc. dir. (I Tematici), directed by M. Cartabia-M. Ruotolo, Milano, V, pp 1008 ff

Riccio GM (2011) La mediazione on-line. In: Riccio GM, Pera A (eds) Mediazione e conciliazione. Diritto interno, comparato e internazionale. Padova, pp 211 ff
Ritzer G, Jurgenson N (2010) Production, consumption, prosumption. The nature of capitalism in the age of the digital “prosumer”. J Cons Cult, pp 10 ff
Rochet JC, Tirole J (2003) Platform competition in two-side markets. J Eur Econ Assoc, pp 990 ff
Rodotà (2012) Il diritto di avere diritti. Roma, p 329
Roppo V (2001) Contratto di diritto comune, contratto del consumatore, contratto con asimmetria di potere contrattuale: genesi e sviluppi di un nuovo paradigma. Riv dir priv, pp 769 ff
Roppo V (2011) Parte generale del contratto, contratti del consumatore e contratti asimmetrici (con postilla su “terzo contratto”) in Roppo V (ed) Il contratto del duemila. Torino, pp 102 ff
Rossello C (2006) Il commercio elettronico. La governance di Internet tra diritto statuale, autodisciplina, soft law e lex mercatoria, Milano
Rossi T (2014) Effettività della tutela nella recente regolamentazione europea di Adr e Odr. Rass dir civ, pp 831 ff
Rossi T (2015) La tutela dei diritti nel mercato digitale. Le corti salerintane, pp 72 ff
Rossi T (2016) Nuovi profili dei rapporti tra imprese nel commercio elettronico. Inf dir 1:47 ff
Rossi EA (2019) La sharing economy nel diritto internazionale, Torino
Rossolillo G (2008) I mezzi alternativi di risoluzione delle controversie (Adr) tra diritto comunitario e diritto internazionale. Dir un Eur, pp 349 ff
Ruhl G (2015) Alternative and online dispute resolution for cross-border consumer contracts: a critical evaluation of the European legislature’s recent efforts to boost competitiveness and growth in the internal market. J Consumer Policy, pp 431 ff
Rule C (2016) Is ODR ADR? A response to Carrie Menkel-Meadow. Int J Online Dispute Resolut, pp 8 ff
Rule C, Singh H (2021) ODR and online reputation systems: maintaining trust and accuracy through effective redress. In: Rainey D, Katsh E, Wahab MSA (eds) Online dispute resolution. A treatise on technology and dispute resolution. The Hague, pp 176 ff
Sbordone F (2011) La legge applicabile. In Valentino D (ed) Manuale di diritto dell’informatica. Napoli, pp 87 ff
Sbordone F (2023) Contratti telematici e transnazionalità della rete. In: Bocchini R (ed) Manuale di diritto privato dell’informatica, p 41
Scannicchio N (2019) La falsa attuazione della finta direttiva per l’adr di consumo in Italia. Contr e impr/Eur, pp 971 ff
Selander L et al (2013) Capability search and redeem across digital ecosystems. J Inf Technol 28(3):183 ff
Senyo PK et al (2018) Understanding behaviour patterns of multi agents in digital business ecosystems: an organisational semiotics inspired framework. In International conference on applied human factors and ergonomics, Cham, pp 206 ff
Silvestri E (1999) Osservazioni in tema di risoluzione alternativa delle controversie. Riv trim dir proc civ, pp 321 ff
Smorto G (2015) Verso la disciplina giuridica della sharing economy. Mer conc reg, pp 245 ff
Smorto G (2016) Reputazione, fiducia e mercati. Eur dir priv, pp 199 ff
Smorto G (2017) Economia della condivisione e antropologia dello scambio. Dir pubbl comp eur, pp 119 ff
Smorto G (2020) La tutela del contraente debole nella platform economy dopo il regolamento UE 2019/1150 e la direttiva UE 2019/1261 (c.d. Omnibus)
Sticchi Damiani S (2004) Sistemi alternativi alla giurisdizione (ADR) nel diritto dell’Unione europea, Milano
Svantesson DJB (2018) Digital contracts in global surroundings. In: Grundmann S (ed) European contract law in the digital age, pp 49 ff
Tiwana A (2013) Platform ecosystems: aligning architecture, governance, and strategy
Toffler A (1980) The third way, New York

Tommasi S (2020) Algoritmi e nuove forme di discriminazione: uno sguardo al diritto europeo. Revista de Direito Brasileira 27:112 ff

Tonazzi A (2019) Discriminazione e collusione tacita tra lessico, intelligenza artificiale e algoritmi. Analisi giur econ, pp 201 ff

Tosi E (2021) Diritto privato delle nuove tecnologie digitali: riservatezza, contratti, responsabilità tra persona e mercato. Milano, pp 210 ff

Tripodi EM (2005) I sistemi di conciliazione online: dalla soluzione delle controversie alla gestione dei rapporti tra imprese e tra imprese e consumatori. Dir internet, pp 205 ff

Trubiani F (2019) I soggetti del commercio elettronico: limiti delle attuali definizioni legislative e prospettive future. Nuovo dir. civ., pp 133 ff

Trubiani F (2023) I soggetti giuridici del contratto digitale. In Bocchini R (ed), Manuale di diritto privato dell'informatica, Napoli

Trubiani F (2024) I soggetti giuridici dell'economia digitale. In: Bocchini R (ed) Manuale di diritto privato dell'informatica

Trubiani F (2025), I soggetti giuridici dell'economia digitale. In Bocchini R (ed), Le piattaforme digitali e-Agorà, p 157 ff.

Vaccà C (2009) Il punto su ODR, online dispute resolution. Contr, pp 1072 ff

Vallejo AO (2019) Contractual relationship in collaborative economy. Eur Rev Priv Law 5:995 ff

Vettori G (2012) Il contratto senza numeri e aggettivi. Oltre il consumatore e l'impresa debole. Contr e impr, pp 1190 ff

Vigoriti V (2001) E-commerce e tutela giurisdizionale: giudice, legge, processo. In: Sica S, Stanzione P (eds) Commercio elettronico e categorie civilistiche. Milano, pp 399 ff

Vigoriti V (2011) Europa e mediazione. Problemi e soluzione. Contr e impr/Eur, pp 81 ff

Vigoriti V (2021) Superabili ambiguità. Le proposte europee in tema di ADR e ODR. Nuova giur civ comm, pp 313 ff

Wagner G (2014) Private law enforcement through ADR: wonder drug or snake oil? Priv Mark Law Rev, pp 165 ff

Weill P, Woerner SL (2015) Thriving in an increasingly digital ecosystem. MIT Sloan Manag Rev 56(4):27 ff

Zeno Zencovich V (2007) Comunicazione, reputazione, sanzione. Dir inf, pp 263 ff

Zoppini A (2008) Il contratto asimmetrico tra parte generale, contratti di impresa e disciplina della concorrenza. Riv dir civ I:515 ff

Zucconi Galli Fonseca E (2010) La nuova mediazione nella prospettiva europea: note a prima lettura. Riv trim dir proc civ, pp 653 ff

Liability

The Internet Service Provider's Liability

Laura Guffanti Pesenti

Contents

Abstract The chapter sets out to represent the problem and the discipline of the civil liability of Internet service providers for damage caused by network users. Particularly, Dir. 2000/31/EC and the subsequent Regulation 2022/2065/EU (Digital Services Act) are examined, highlighting both the lines of continuity and some profiles of distinction between the two regulatory episodes.

L. G. Pesenti (✉)
Catholic University of the Sacred Heart of Milan, Milan, Italy
e-mail: laura.guffanti@unicatt.it

R. Bocchini (ed.), *Digital Platforms - From Technical Foundations to Legal and Economic Implications*, https://doi.org/10.1007/978-3-032-07978-7_16

1 Foreword

The *Internet service provider*'s liability is part of the broader framework of torts linked to the Internet phenomenon.[1] In fact, the *Internet service provider* is anyone who facilitates the connection between several subjects by allowing them access to the network.[2]

Regardless of their specific characteristics,[3] *Internet service providers* can be described as the subjects that provide connection, storage and transmission services of the most varied 'contents', making available the means necessary for that purpose.[4] As it has been observed, in fact, whatever activity is carried out on the network, it always passes through the intermediation of a provider:[5] in whose *servers* data and contents transit and put users in contact.

In terms of classification, it is worth pointing out that there is no full overlap between *Internet service providers* and so-called 'digital platforms'. The latter is a wide-ranging expression that has led the doctrine to question its meaning also in the

---

[1] As Castronovo (2018), p. 285, points out, the information society and computer technology have given rise in recent years to a series of cases hitherto unknown precisely because they are the offspring of the information society, centred on the use of the telematic network, i.e. on the services known as the information society. A distinction is made in doctrine between Internet offences, offences against the Internet, and offences by means of the Internet: see on this point Magni and Spolidoro (1997), p. 61; Ponzanelli (2002), p. 363; Di Ciommo (2003), *passim*.

[2] Cf. Franzoni (2023), pp. 224 ff., describes the *provider* as the intermediary that allows the ordinary user to connect to the network' It in fact, having the availability of telephone lines, it is able to allow them to be temporarily allocated to the user who has requested them.

[3] Marsico (2024), p. 278—after observing that by provider is meant a subject who, operating in the information society, freely offers services of connection, transmission and data storage—highlights how the technological evolution has led to a division of the unitary figure of the *provider*, being able, generally, to identify three types of intermediary on the basis of the role played in the process of transmission and diffusion of data in telematic networks. Particularly, a distinction can be made between the *access* provider, who guarantees access to the Internet putting users in a position to access the web; the *content* provider who prepares and places the content of a website on the net on behalf of an end user by organising material produced by him or sent to him by the client, but of which he knows, or in any case must know, the type and content; and finally, the *host provider* who provides *content providers* with hospitality by making available a portion of his hard disk, of which, however, he remains the owner in order to convey the information that he intends to disseminate on the net. The articulation of the *provider* category is even broader, for those who identify, alongside the figures mentioned above, those of the *network provider*, the *service provider* and the *cache provider*. For these further typologies, see D'Arrigo (2012), p. 11.

[4] The *provider* was defined in Art. 2(b) of Directive 2000/31/EC as any natural or legal person who provides an information society service. Allegri (2018), *passim*, observes that the extreme breadth of this definition makes it possible to refer it not only to *Internet service providers* as they operated at the beginning of the 2000s, but also to subjects that today provide services of a more modern and evolved type, such as search engines and social network providers (Snp).

[5] D'Arrigo (2012), cit., p. 11.

light of the recent and prolific European legislation that, in various respects, concerns platforms.[6]

The digital platform seems to be characterised specifically by the fact that it allows several parties to enter into a relationship via the Internet[7] for different purposes and with different aims, where the *Internet service provider*[8] is any entity that allows others to operate via the network, carrying out data transmission and storage activities and allowing access to the network itself.[9]

The problem of the regulation of the Internet and the relations between its actors has been perceived since the 1990s[10] and initially concerned the choice of whether

---

[6] This is the subject of Irti (2025), pp. 151 ff., who, after having analysed the definitions of 'digital platform' in recent European legislation, concludes that for the European Union legislator digital platforms are nothing more than tools for accessing, transporting and storing data, i.e. infrastructures designed, prepared and intended for the processing of digitalised data, with respect to the use of which the question of the protections to be guaranteed to users remains central. On platforms, for a general survey, see Palmieri (2019), *passim*; Contaldo (2021), *passim*.

[7] Galasso (2023), cit., p. 162, in describing the phenomenon of platforms, observes that according to a definition provided by economic doctrine, platforms are digital infrastructures that allow two or more groups to interact. The latter definition, however, is in danger of being vague, for the author, who underlines that the European Commission has provided a more precise definition: 'Online platforms can be described as software based facilities offering two or even multi-sided markets where providers and users of content, goods and services can meet'. The same author considers how, in any case, one characteristic remains central, both in the doctrinal definition and in that of the Commission: *interaction*. In order for an IT infrastructure to be defined as a *digital platform*, it must be characterised by interaction between users or, it should be added, between users and the platform itself.

[8] In confirmation of the fact that these two entities, the platform and the *Internet services provider*, do not fully overlap, Regulation 2022/2065/EU (known as the Digital Services Act), to which we shall return below, after having outlined a series of general rules, valid for all *Internet services providers* without distinction, contemplates in Section II a series of additional rules applicable to providers of information storage services, including online platforms. And in the same definitions with which the aforementioned Regulation opens, the 'online platform' is considered as an item in need of a specific definition: it is 'an information storage service which, at the request of a recipient of the service, stores and disseminates information to the public, except where that activity is a minor and purely ancillary function of another service or a minor functionality of the main service and, for objective and technical reasons, cannot be used without that other service and provided that the integration of that function or functionality into the other service is not a means of circumventing the applicability of this Regulation' (Art. 3(1)(i)).

[9] Palmieri (2019), cit., p. 27, speaking of Regulation 2019/1150/EU—but with generally valid considerations—observes that between platform and *Internet service provider* there are profiles of distinction: it is not only a solid network of contractual relationships; the further aspect relates to it playing the role of 'facilitator'. In this capacity, the platform in a sense takes on the task of directing traffic by enabling interested parties to enter the virtual space under its control in order to be able to operate effectively within it.

[10] On this point, Finocchiaro (2023b), cit., p. 135, recalls that from the 1990s to the present day large digital companies have dictated legal rules, mainly by using the instrument of the contract or

to adopt a specific regulatory apparatus for the phenomenon. From the initial intolerance of any form of regulation, we moved on to the consideration of a sort of *lex mercatoria* valid for network operators, which contributes to consolidating relations between them and their users; however, from another point of view, this was considered, especially in the European Community sphere, harmful to the democratic process of law-making.[11] This was followed, in Europe, by a regulation of electronic commerce that, in addition to contractual profiles of the matter, also dealt with civil liability.[12]

This chapter deals with the issue of non-contractual liability of the *provider*. We will consider, however, not the liability of the *provider* for damage caused directly by him to the user, but the liability of the *provider* for the wrongful act of another user, through the network.

The problem arises since the network constitutes an instrument through which harmful conduct of various kinds can be carried out.[13] The question then arises as to whether the *Internet service provider*, which makes that network available to users, can in turn be held liable (and if so, to what extent) for the damage caused to its users through the network itself.

This question is particularly significant also because, in a context such as that of the Internet, it is not easy to identify the author of the offence, who is often 'hidden' behind the thick curtain of a technology that is difficult to understand and penetrate.[14] Hence the question is whether, instead of the damaging party, or even in conjunction with him, the person who made available the telematic tool by means

---

by channelling legal rules through technology itself, and the two phenomena are often referred to as lex mercatoria or lex informatica, respectively.

[11] D'Arrigo (2012), cit., p. 3, outlines the transition from the original idea of a self-regulation of a private matrix to the discipline of a supranational source, and represents a scenario in which the regulatory evolution of the entire matter is based on a polycentrism of sources, coordinated on several levels (starting from a legislative framework among all the states that intend to regulate the matter, with a subsequent specification of rules through national regulations, and a further adoption of self-regulatory codes).

[12] This is Directive 2000/31/EC, through which—as Leocani (2000), p. 623, observes in one of the first analyses—the Commission intended to regulate analytically only certain sectors of electronic commerce: the directive in fact brings together a series of heterogeneous provisions united only by the requirement of the medium, the telematic network, used for negotiations in the broad sense.

[13] To summarise, Ponzanelli (2002), p. 367, pointed out that apart from infringement of private rights, almost all offences committed on the Internet can be attributed to the *genus* 'defamation'; Franzoni (2023), cit., p. 225, nt. 51, gives the example of one of the first cases brought to the attention of Italian courts, in which an *Internet* user had placed an e-mail message on the *Internet* damaging the honour and reputation of another user of the service, and it was therefore a question of establishing whether the company in charge of managing the site could also be held liable.

[14] On this point, see Troiano (1998), pp. 400 ff., who delves into the problem of the imputation of unlawful activity carried out through the Internet, even before that of the imputation of the liability that follows from it. The author particularly dwells on the modalities and problems connected with the identification of the owner of an Internet address and the employer's liability for the offence committed by the employee through the use of telematic means made available to the organisation headed by him.

of which the user was able to cause the damage can also be called to restore the damage: the *Internet service provider* is in fact a more easily identifiable subject than those who make use of it to carry out the most varied activities.

The profiles deserving consideration, which were immediately placed at the centre of the debate, firstly concerned the criterion for attributing liability to the *Internet service provider*, i.e. whether it should be liable for fault or according to an objective criterion;[15] subsequently, as we shall see, the opportunity of placing liability on this subject: that is to say, in a nutshell, whether it should be called to restore the damage for the wrongful act committed by means of the network or whether it would be preferable to exclude its liability, and if so, under what conditions.[16]

In this alternative, as we shall see, the European legislator opted for a regime of exclusion of liability with Directive 2000/31/EC,[17] which was followed by the transposing domestic legislation (D.lgs No. 70 of 9 April 2003). This was an arrangement, however, that with the gradual evolution of Internet-related technology, and due to its extension, required some adjustments in its interpretation and application, favouring jurisprudential orientations of varying tendencies along the borderline between liability or not of the *Internet service provider.*

This has not, however, led to a radical change in the structure of the discipline in *question*: so that, as will be said, even in its most recent reformulation by means of Regulation 2022/2065/EU (DSA), the fundamental choices made by the European legislator in 2000 have been confirmed. It is to all these profiles that the following paragraphs will be devoted.

2 The Problem of Prejudice Suffered Online

The question of the *provider*'s civil liability has arisen due to the fact that the interactions that take place via the Internet are capable of generating various types of damage.[18] The damage for which the question arises, as to whether it should be compensated and by whom, is generated by the fact that the information put on the

[15] Riccio (2002), pp. 45 ff., reviews the various rules of strict liability, but considers the general model of fault-based liability preferable (ibid., pp. 57 ff.). See also De Cata (2010), pp. 83 ff.

[16] As Albanese (2010), p. 355, observes, the provision of *ad hoc* rules [such as those introduced by Directive 2000/31/EC] is not due to the impossibility of finding a legal solution on a logical level, but derives from an assessment of opportunity that leads to regulating the cases in question differently, derogating for certain aspects from the general discipline by reason of precise choices of legal policy.

[17] Again Albanese (2010), p. 355, recalls that the declared purpose of the special legislation is to favour the development of the network as a means of free manifestation of thought and an instrument of social communication through an appropriate delimitation of the provider's liability, functional to reduce the management costs of the service and consequently improve the economic conditions of access by users.

[18] Bocchini (2023), p. 534, speaks of 'telematic incidents'.

net through the *Internet service provider* can sometimes infringe the legal sphere of other people.[19]

The topic is not that of the loss suffered by a user as a result of the breach of an obligatory relationship by another user: when, for example, in the contractual relationship that takes shape on the network there is a breach, or there is a delay in the fulfilment of the obligation: in this case, the discipline will be contractual.[20]

It is not even a question of the damage that the *Internet service provider* may cause to the user in the provision of the service; for example, because the connection fails, generating economic losses to those who were using it to perform their activity. Here, too, the law of contract (between the *online* service provider and the user who has suffered the disservice and the damage) will apply.[21]

Speaking of the civil liability of the *Internet service provider,* one rather considers the problem of the damage that a person causes to another by making use of the Internet connection, but outside of a contractual relationship.[22] In fact—as it has been observed—the extreme ease of uploading written or visual content (which becomes usable in almost real time by anyone consulting a website, or participating in a newsgroup) on the one hand represents an exceptional realisation of the constitutional right to free expression of thought, on the other hand it disproportionately increases the possibility of commission of unlawful acts for the violation of protected situations of third parties, damaged by the data uploaded.[23]

Indeed, damage does not appear among the elements that the rules dedicated to the subject matter deal with:[24] it thus represents a requisite without any specific characterisation by the special legislation. It may therefore be assumed that the general rules of non-contractual liability[25] apply in this respect, and thus that any damage that is relevant to them gives rise to a question of compensation, in respect of which the question arises as to who should be liable, and particularly whether the provider of the electronic service (*Internet service provider*) may also be held liable.

Among the offences that can be perpetrated on the Internet, consider in particular the violation of the provisions of copyright or industrial property law (to which

[19] Cf. Nivarra (2003), *passim*, for whom 'given that the network is capable of hosting data and information of all kinds, it is only natural that on the network, or rather through the network, all offences based on the dissemination or use of data or information can be committed'.

[20] On this topic, see Camardi (2021), p. 870.

[21] He devotes particular attention to network access contracts and the provision of telematic services by the *Internet service provider*, Pasquino (2003), *passim*.

[22] Cf. Di Ciommo (2002), pp. 206 ff., who points out on the one hand how the network is a candidate to be both the most powerful and the most dangerous of the information and communication media; on the other hand, how both information and communication activities are likely to cause damage, particularly to personality rights.

[23] See Bugiolacchi (2000), p. 831.

[24] Nor is the injury. Again, Nivarra (2003), cit., observes that it is totally irrelevant that the lesion is aimed at this or that legal good: if anything, as we shall immediately see, the truly decisive point is represented by the type of service that the provider himself concretely provides.

[25] On the subject of which, see Castronovo (2018), particularly ch. III. For determinate compensation, Civil Code rules or the relevant special legislation can be applied.

Section III is devoted); or also, still on the economic side, acts of unfair competition; but also, moving on to the non-pecuniary side, the unlawful processing of personal data, or more broadly the violation of personal rights, such as the right to honour, reputation, image, and name. Through such violations, Internet users can cause economic and non-economic damage, characterised, moreover, by a particular intensity, due to the breadth and speed of dissemination in the network, which also increases the extent of the damage.[26]

3 The Civil Liability of the *Internet Service Provider* Before Directive 2000/31/EC

Before the introduction of Directive 2000/31/EC, authors and jurisprudence had tried to solve the problem of the *Internet service provider*'s civil liability under the Italian civil code. In fact, in the presence of the new phenomenon, the question arose of whether the *ius positum* was sufficient to deal with the problems following the spread of the Internet.

In this respect, the interpretation offered in the 1990s was not unequivocal,[27] as was also the case in other jurisdictions.[28] The essential problem was to establish whether the *provider* was liable for fault or according to strict liability rules, and in the latter direction, both Art. 2051[29] and Art. 2049[30] were taken into consideration as possible solutions. The viability of the path marked out by Art. 2050,[31] dedicated, as it is well known, to the exercise of dangerous activities, has also been

---

[26] The presence in the new Regulation 2022/2065/EU of the category 'illegal content', defined as 'any information that, in itself or in relation to an activity, including the sale of products or the provision of services, is not in compliance with Union law or the law of any Member State which is in compliance with Union law, irrespective of the precise subject matter or nature of that law', does not seem capable of altering these general premises. In fact, it does not appear that this definition and the very category of illegal content aim at, or in any case, have the effect of circumscribing the characteristics of the harm that may arise from the offence committed on the network. It is instead aimed at describing the object of the preventive duties of diligence, as well as the subsequent duties of communication to which *Internet service providers* are subject according to the new discipline.

[27] Among others, Pasquino (2003), cited above, pp. 213 ff.; Riccio (2002), cited above, *passim*; De Cata (2010), cited above, *passim*.

[28] For a review of the main solutions adopted by European and other legal systems, see Bugiolacchi (2000), cit., pp. 836 ff. For a look at US jurisprudence, see Troiano (1998), cit., pp. 407 ff.; Ponzanelli (2002), cit., p. 367.

[29] Franzoni (1997), p. 250, who considered the possibility of grounding the *provider*'s liability on a duty of care for the site, by means of a 'summary check' by the provider himself.

[30] He considers this provision, but denies its applicability to the civil liability of the *Internet service provider*, Pasquino (2003), cited above, pp. 272 ff.

[31] Facci (2002), pp. 268 ff., with, however, negative conclusions on the applicability of Art. 2050 to the matter at hand.

considered, although it does not textually introduce strict liability, it comes close to it in its interpretation.[32]

Strict liability, however, was not considered convincing in the final analysis,[33] both because from an economic point of view it would have entailed a significant burden[34] also in terms of insurance (given the particularly high risk that the *provider* would have faced[35]), and because from the point of view of the legal basis, it was held that it was not possible for the *provider* to comprehensively control the content present on the network,[36] and strict liability should necessarily be rooted, instead, in the power—if not the duty—to avoid the damage of the person to be held liable.[37]

Different from that perspective, based on the application of the rules of the civil code,[38] there was a further interpretation of the phenomenon, which held that it could be traced back to the liability of the print media publisher.[39] In this logic, liability has sometimes been recognised in the hands of the *provider* as a liability for

[32] On this point, see Castronovo's (2018) extensive reflection, cit., p. 454.

[33] Lastly, they consider that a strict liability rule of the *provider* should be reconsidered: see Benatti and Portonera (2024), p. 480.

[34] And it would have been able, therefore, to 'cause *overdeterrence* pathologies', writes Ponzanelli (2002), cit., p. 371, referring to considerations by Guido Calabresi (on medical liability).

[35] See D'Arrigo (2012), cit., p. 15.

[36] See again Bugiolacchi (2000), cit., p. 856.

[37] Cf. Castronovo (2018), cit., p. 489, where it is stated that whatever the criterion of imputation, the fact for which one is liable is considered to be a fact that should have been or could have been avoided by the person who is made responsible for it; subjective liability corresponds to the first hypothesis, objective liability to the second: in the latter, it is indeed true that among the conditions of the sanction, the rule does not include the conduct of the person made liable, as happens in cases of liability for damage caused by others, but if the connotation of power or duty that we have indicated is not introduced, no discretionary criterion is provided between objective liability and insurance.

[38] It has also recently been recalled that it was not unrelated to the activity carried out by ISPs' precise 'dangerousness' profiles, linked to the illicit use that certain users could make of the services available to them (although this perspective has not been followed up in the field of enforcement), see Benatti and Portonera (2024), p. 479. The same authors observe how in the recent copyright law, resulting from the transposition of Art. 17, Directive 2019/790/EU, there is a formulation not far from that of our Art. 2050 of the Civil Code. In the same way as the latter, in fact, the current Art. 102-septies l. dir. aut. is also constructed in terms of making the subject liable, with the possibility of exonerating himself by demonstrating that he has fulfilled those obligations that the law itself imposes on him.

[39] Astone (2022), p. 1054, reports on this again recently, summarising the debate at the time in the search for a compromise solution between the positions of those who equated the IT service provider with the editor of a newspaper, and those who instead placed him on the same level as a newsagent. The issue basically consisted either in excluding any involvement of the provider from the illicit acts committed on the network, or in admitting his liability and, in this case, it was a question of understanding its nature (see also, by the same author, *La responsabilità del prestatore di servizi della società di informazione nella direttiva 2000/31/CE*, in *Europa dir. priv.*, 2003, 431 ff.).

culpa in vigilando by virtue of his position as a subject who can control what is published by his users, and therefore obliged to answer for it.[40]

However, the gradual realisation of the *provider*'s lack of power to effectively control the content uploaded by users has, over time, suggested a different path, marked by the alternative not so much between fault and strict liability, but between affirmation and denial of liability on the *Internet service provider.*

And so, alongside some pronouncements in which the outcome was liability based on fault,[41] other pronouncements ended up denying liability itself, holding that the person who merely provided the means for the tort to be committed could not be required to pay compensation for the damage caused by others.

On closer inspection, however, the difference in the outcomes (of liability or irresponsibility) did not arise from opposing views as to whether the *provider* should also be liable, but rather from the different factual situations on which the court was called upon to intervene from time to time.[42] In fact, while at times the *Internet service provider* limited himself to making the line available for the mere transmission of the message judged to be harmful, at other times the provider of the telematic service cooperated with the third party that caused the damage in the formulation of the message, thus participating in the illicit act: so that, on the basis of this distinction [it was] possible to explain the different orientation that was recorded in the case law of merit,[43] in the sense of the irresponsibility of the *provider* in the first case, and his liability in the second case.

[40] See e.g. Trib. Napoli 8 August 1997 (but also Trib. Macerata 2 December 1998 and Trib. Roma 22 March 1999). It is stated in the conclusions of the judgment that 'in the present case, the lack of diligence of the two defendant companies integrates the subjective element of fault, which is an inescapable presupposition for the purposes of the configurability of a concurrence of the extraneous in the entrepreneur's unlawful act. The lack of vigilance is, in our case, all the more reprehensible in view of the exceptional diffusion of the communication tool used (modern telematic techniques on the "Internet" network), which imposed on the diligent professional a more intense control activity'.

[41] In some cases, it has been pointed out that 'there is the provider's liability for negligence if the content of the communications appears to be clearly unlawful'; in this case, the *provider*, by setting up the connection, contributes to the unlawful act insofar as he makes a causal contribution to its commission: this was a case in which this subject was held liable for not having detected, according to ordinary diligence, the use of a well-known acronym by an unauthorised person: cf. Trib. Roma 22 March 1999, in *Dir. informazione e informatica*, 2000, 66 with note by Sammarco.

[42] Castronovo (2018), pp. 286 ss. The two pronouncements referred to by the author are Trib. Cuneo 23 August 1997 (ord.), in *AIDA*, 1997, pp. 500 ss. and the already mentioned Trib. Napoli 8 August 1997 (ord.), in *Giust. civ.* 1998, pp. 259 ss.

[43] As observed again by Castronovo (2018), pp. 286 ff., it is necessary to specify the features of the fact because the modalities of access to the network are basically two. One, in which the service provider limits himself to making the telematic route available for a simple passage of the message; the other is constituted by the cooperation of the telematic service provider itself in the formulation of the message. It is on the basis of this distinction that it is possible to explain the different orientation of the two cited rulings.

4 The Directive 2000/31/EC and Its Transposition: The Exclusion of Liability

The jagged interpretative framework that thus emerged was later recomposed with Directive 2000/31/EC.[44]

The discipline introduced by the European legislator was animated by the perceived need, at that time, not to curb the technological development connected with the Net, favouring, on the contrary, the activity of *online* intermediation, to facilitate, through it, economic exchanges and communications between market players.[45]

This led to the European institutions' decision to formulate a directive regulating *online* intermediation, characterised first of all by the exclusion of the *Internet service provider*'s civil liability[46] for offences committed on the Internet by users, in the terms that will be described below;[47] furthermore, by the absence of any obligation on the part of the *provider* itself to monitor the content that throngs the Internet, also due to the abundance of the same, which is considered to preclude any possibility of effective verification.[48]

The aforementioned directive was transposed into Italian law by D.lgs No. 70 of 9 April 2003, which incorporated its framework and, albeit with some variations, also its rules. It contemplated, in addition to a series of rules that the 'information society service provider' was required to comply with in electronic commerce,[49] also a number of provisions concerning the civil liability of the *provider*,[50] which

---

[44] To the outcome of which, according to Nivarra (2003), cit., esp. text at nt. 13, also contributed the severity with which case law had treated the *Internet service provider* up to that point.

[45] Piraino (2017), 470 reports on the economic analysis of law underlying the choices of the European legislator. Also, the Supreme Court, in its judgment No. 7708 of 19 March 2019, states in this regard that in the regulation of European origin has been applied the maxim of experience, drawn from the economic analysis of law, according to which delimiting the liability regime has the effect of supporting business choices.

[46] Exclusion of liability is the category on which European legislation is based, in the wake—Piraino (2017), cit., p. 475—of the Safe Harbor concept of the US *Digital Millennium Copyright Act* of 1998.

[47] Articles 12, 13, 14, Directive 2000/31/EC.

[48] Article 15, Directive 2000/31/EC.

[49] Leocani (2000), cited above, pp. 615 ff.

[50] Again Piraino (2017), cit., p. 472, observes, moreover, how the regulation of Internet intermediaries should not be considered so much in the *focus of* liability (as a special liability regime or, rather, as a special liability exclusion regime). In fact, the discipline introduced by the directive aims primarily to draw the contours of the sphere of lawfulness of action of intermediaries, rather than to remove prejudice. This is all the more true in the new discipline introduced by Regulation 2022/2065/EU (DSA), the purpose of which is to create, first and foremost, a predictable and reliable safe online environment, through the provision of rules of conduct of varying content imposed on *Internet service providers*. Nonetheless, Regulation 2022/2065/EU (like Directive 2000/31/EC) also provides for rules expressly dedicated by the legislator to the 'liability of intermediary service providers' (Articles 4, 5, 6, 7, 8): and thus, aimed at addressing the problem of providers' civil liability.

modulated the latter (or more precisely, the exclusion of liability) according to the service provided by the operator (these were Articles 14–17, D.lgs No. 70/2003).

These rules have, however, been recently repealed by D.lgs No. 50 of 25 March 2024[51] but they were revived, with similar content, in Regulation 2022/2065/EU (DSA), Articles 4, 5, 6, 8. It is therefore worthwhile to consider them as well to outline the system of civil liability of the *provider* as structured by the first source of law that dealt with it in the (then) European Community, and then to verify how much new, if anything new, there is in the more recent legislation.

The liability of intermediary providers (this was the heading of Section 4 of Chapter II of Directive 2000/31/EC) is regulated differently depending on the type of service performed by the *provider*.[52] The directive, in this regard, as well as the transposing regulation, contemplated three types of activities performed by the *provider*, which remain such today in the new Regulation 2022/2065/EU. There is, first, that of the *mere conduit*, which must therefore be understood as a technical intermediary whose activity consists in the mere passage of data through the network.[53] Then there is that of the person who, on the other hand, stores the data: according to a modality that varies, however, and which may be automatic, intermediate and temporary (so-called *caching*); or permanent (so-called *hosting*).[54]

The first of these two hypotheses occurs when the storage of information is aimed solely at its transmission to other recipients who request it, without there being any processing of the information itself on the part of the *provider*: the latter merely copies it and forwards it to third parties by means of purely technical and automatic processes.[55]

---

[51] On the basis of the repeal of the corresponding Art. 12, 13, 14, 15 of Directive 2000/31/EC by Regulation 2022/2065/EU, Art. 89, which refers instead to its Articles 4, 5, 6, 8.

[52] Bocchini (2003), pp. 128 ff., speaks in this regard of a proportionality relationship between the extent of the intermediary service performed by the *provider* and the extent of liability.

[53] This is the activity that enjoyed and still enjoys the most favourable regime, also because—as recalled by D'Arrigo (2012), cit., p. 25—given the merely passive role of the service provider (as a possible instrument through which the offence of others is perpetrated), an obligation cannot be imposed on him to set up systems to prevent the offence, nor of a possible interruption and/or removal of the offending activity itself *motu proprio*. This is confirmed by the last paragraph of Art. 14 of D.lgs No. 70/2003, for which the duty to prevent or put an end to an infringement can only be imposed by a judicial or administrative authority having a supervisory function.

[54] Stella (2022), pp. 838 ff., exemplifies the three roles: *mere conduit* activity is carried out by telephone companies or concessionaires of bandwidth services to allow users to connect to the network; *caching* activity is carried out by search engines (e.g. Google), which scan the net and 'photocopy' the contents of web pages on their servers, to speed up the search service offered by their own engine, an activity also liable to generate the provider's liability, as emerges from the case history on the subject of the right to be forgotten. The *hosting* activity is carried out by the owners of online platforms (to mention other illustrious names: YouTube, Amazon, eBay), which allow users to upload information that sometimes interferes with or infringes the private rights of third parties.

[55] As such, they do not in any way entail the involvement of the *Internet service provider* in the processing of the information: if this were to happen, it would undermine the irresponsibility regime. On this point, see Leocani (2000), cit., p. 617.

In the second case the intermediary's relationship with the information is more intense than in the *caching*: in this case, in fact, the intermediary provides users with a space in which the information is retained on a lasting basis, with the intermediary's own consequent possibility of easily knowing its content.[56]

Despite the differences that have been highlighted, in all three cases the *provider* has a passive position with respect to the formulation of the information by the user, and is merely instrumental to its circulation and dissemination, which justified the common regime of irresponsibility envisaged for the different types of intermediary service providers.[57]

Even on this common basis, however, the cases in which the exclusion of liability ceases to apply vary (in the former as well as in the present rules), and liability reverts to the three categories mentioned.

With regard to *the mere conduit* intermediary, liability returns to[58] whenever the provider, from being a mere passive transmitter as it should be, interferes instead in the transmission, either by originating it, or by identifying its recipients, or by affecting its content.[59] For the other two categories of network operators (performing *caching* and *hosting* activities, respectively), the discipline is more articulated.

---

[56] For a detailed description of the characteristics of the two storage activities, temporary and durable, see Bocchini (2023), cit., p. 538.

[57] In our legal system, by virtue of Art. 14, 15, 16, D.lgs No. 70/2003 (now repealed), which transposed respectively Articles 12, 13, 14, Directive 2000/31/EC. They all opened with similar wording: 'In the provision of an information society service consisting of the transmission, over a communication network, of information provided by a recipient of the service, or of the provision of access to the communication network, *the service provider shall not be liable for the information transmitted* on condition that ...' (Art. 14); 'when providing an information society service consisting of the transmission in a communication network of information provided by a recipient of the service, *the service provider shall not be liable for the automatic, intermediate and temporary storage of that information*, performed for the sole purpose of making more efficient the subsequent transmission of the information to other recipients of the service upon their request, on condition that ...' (Art. 15); 'in the provision of an information society service consisting of the storage of information provided by a recipient of the service, *the service provider shall not be liable for the information stored at the request of a recipient of the service*, on condition that the service provider …' Directive 2000/31/EC, also because of this, seemed rather to fix with certainty that sphere of lawfulness of action, within the scope of which the services performed do not expose *Internet service providers* to any unlawfulness with respect to possible unlawful acts committed by users (Piraino (2017), cit., p. 478).

[58] Not automatically, but after ascertaining the prerequisites of general private law, as Albanese (2010), cit., p. 357, observes. According to the author, the argument 'to the contrary' by virtue of which the law, in the hypotheses in which it did not exclude the *provider*'s liability, intended instead to make him always and in any case liable, is misleading. Such a conclusion would, moreover, end up surreptitiously translating into a rule of strict liability, which has no basis either in the letter of the rule or in the legal policy aims pursued by the legislature.

[59] Article 14 of D.lgs No. 70/2003 provided that '1. When providing an information society service consisting of the transmission over a communication network of information provided by a recipient of the service, or the provision of access to the communication network, the service provider shall not be liable for the information transmitted provided that: (a) he does not originate the transmission; (b) he does not select the recipient of the transmission; (c) he does not select or modify the information transmitted. 2. The acts of transmission and of providing access referred to in

The *caching provider* enjoys the aforementioned exemption as long as, in a nutshell, it does not modify the stored information; complies with conditions and rules on access to the information valid in the relevant sector; and finally, it 'acts promptly to remove the information it has stored, or to disable access to it, as soon as it becomes effectively aware that the information has been removed from its initial location on the network or that access to the information has been disabled or that a court or administrative authority has ordered its removal or disabling'.[60]

For what concerns the provider who performs *hosting* activities, the provider is not liable for the information stored at the request of a recipient of the service, on condition that the provider (a) does not have actual knowledge that the activity or information is unlawful and, as far as actions for damages are concerned, is not aware of facts or circumstances that make it apparent that the activity or information is unlawful; (b) as soon as it becomes aware of such facts, upon notice from the competent authorities,[61] acts immediately to remove the information or to disable access to it.[62]

With regard to the rules referred to, not always clear in their wording, it appears that the *provider*'s liability in the latter case—but the same applies to the former—is based on the electronic service provider's 'actual knowledge' of the offence to which the stored information gives rise, and its failure to take action to remove it from the network or in any case to preclude access to it.[63]

---

paragraph 1 include the automatic, intermediate and transient storage of the information transmitted in so far as this takes place for the sole purpose of carrying out the transmission in the communication network and provided that its duration does not exceed the time reasonably necessary for that purpose'.

[60] Article 15, D.lgs 70/2003.

[61] It is worth noting that such an aside ('upon notification of the competent authorities') was not present in Art. 14, Directive 2000/31/EC. It is therefore an addition made by our legislator at the time of transposition, which, however, at least in the case law of the Supreme Court that has ruled on this matter (Cass. 19 March 2019, no. 7708) does not seem to have been taken into particular consideration. In any case, it disappeared with the repeal of Art. 16 of D.lgs 70/2003, and does not appear in the corresponding Art. 6 of Regulation 2022/2065/EU.

[62] Thus, Art. 16 of D.lgs No. 70/2003, which closes with a para 3, pursuant to which 'the judicial authority or the competent administrative authority may demand, also as a matter of urgency, that the service provider, in the exercise of the activities referred to in paragraph 1, prevent or put an end to the violations committed'. The same provision is inserted at the end of the previous Articles 14 and 15, D.lgs No. 70/2003.

[63] In this regard according to the Court of Cassation, the liability of the *hosting provider* arising from the aforementioned Art. 16, D.lgs No. 70/2003 'subsists in the liability of the service provider who has not immediately removed the unlawful content, or has continued to publish it, when the following conditions are jointly met (a) it has legal knowledge of the unlawful act perpetrated by the recipient of the service, having been informed by the owner of the infringed right or *aliunde*; (b) the unlawfulness of the conduct of others is reasonably ascertainable, so that the *hosting provider* is seriously at fault for not having positively ascertained it, in the light of the degree of diligence that can reasonably be expected of a professional network operator at a given historical moment; (c) it has the possibility of taking useful action, since it has been made sufficiently specifically aware of the unlawfully posted content to be removed…' (Cass. civ, 19 March 2019, no. 7708).

Also in this case, as is already the case for the intermediary who performs *caching* activities, the fact that the *provider*'s liability is based on the 'actual knowledge' of the offence committed on the network by one of its users (in the presence of which the *provider* is required to take action in the sense indicated by the former Articles 15 and 16 of D.lgs No. 70/2003) has prompted interpreters to question the meaning to be attributed to this syntagma.[64]

In addition, it has led to questions being raised as to how the *provider* can gain 'actual knowledge': whether it is sufficient for the *provider* to be informed by others of the presence of the offence, and thus passively await the communication of others, or whether he himself must gain this knowledge, through an activity of verification and control personally carried out on the content present on the network.[65]

4.1 The Absence of a General Obligation to Monitor

With regard to the latter problem, the rules themselves answer the question, where they also provide the rule that the *provider* is not obliged to monitor or control what happens on the network.[66]

Pursuant to Art. 17 of D.lgs No. 70/2003, in fact, 'When providing the services referred to in Articles 14, 15 and 16, the service provider shall not be subject to a general obligation to monitor the information which he transmits or stores, nor to a general obligation actively to seek facts or circumstances indicating illegal activity. Without prejudice to the provisions of Articles 14, 15 and 16, the service provider shall in any event be obliged: a) to inform without delay a judicial authority or an administrative authority having a supervisory role, when he becomes aware of alleged unlawful activities or information concerning one of his recipients of the Information Society service; b) to supply without delay, at the request of the competent authorities, information in his possession enabling the identification of the

[64] Given that the expression 'actual knowledge' is in itself sufficient to exclude the relevance of the *provider*'s abstract knowledge of the offence, as Servida (2024), p. 147, recalls Delfini and Finocchiaro (2014), p. 785.

[65] According to Riccio (2002), cit., p. 43, to admit that intermediary providers—and, particularly, those who carry out a *hosting* activity—have an effective power of control over the information appears to be disproportionate. To reach this conclusion, it is sufficient to bear in mind the fact that, daily, hundreds of messages are circulated in each of the forums offered by the same *provider*. According to the same author, considering that a preventive control is technically impossible for the *provider*, it would not be only strict liability, but it would be 'absolute liability'.

[66] Already before the directive, the point was reflected upon in doctrine—Troiano (1998), cit., p. 414—observing that in the majority of cases, the index finger is pointed at offences committed in the context of information services constituted by the great mass of users, with the impossibility of a blanket control of the information. The risk, then, is that when the *service provider* sets up a control system, it is systematically deduced that the offence is knowable and therefore that he is responsible for it. In fact, if it appears desirable that the *service provider* should not disregard what happens in his own structures … it is also true that only sample checks are possible, which do not exclude the presence of undiscovered offences because one cannot sift through everything.

recipient of his services with whom he has storage agreements, for the purpose of identifying and preventing unlawful activities'.[67]

It should also be pointed out that the Italian regulations transposing directive 2000/31/EC had added a third paragraph to Art. 17, absent in the source of European law (and not reproduced in the new DSA Regulation), which affirmed the civil liability of the *provider* in two further cases, particularly providing that 'the provider shall be civilly liable for the content of such services where, requested by a judicial or administrative authority with supervisory functions, he has not acted promptly to prevent access to that content, or if, having become aware of the unlawful or prejudicial nature for a third party of the content of a service to which he provides access, he has failed to inform the competent authority'.

The supplement left open a number of questions.[68] On the one hand, it was considered that it had intended to enhance the dialogue between the *provider* and the competent administrative authority 'through the provision of a very restrictive formal (specific notice) and cognitive (qualified knowledge) requirement'.[69] It would thus have introduced a further limit to liability, consisting in the fact that the *provider* would only have to act (and would incur liability if he failed to do so) in cases of formal notice from the competent authority.[70]

However, the interpretation of this rule has not been unanimous, in the sense that in the absence of intervention by the authority, the *Internet service provider* would not be required to take any action, nor would it be liable. In fact, an interpretation more in line with the solution of European origin,[71] considers the *hosting provider*'s inertia in removing illicit content to be a sufficient element for the assertion of its liability, even in hypotheses in which the request to remove the content comes from people other than the authority, for example, from the injured party himself.[72]

---

[67] Some critical remarks on this rule and its dubious usefulness can be found in Pino (2004), pp. 832 ff., who considers the first paragraph pleonastic, the second superfluous and the third a harbinger of multiple interpretation problems.

[68] Particularly, Pino (2004), cit., p. 836, observes that this provision, partially inherited from the directive, is however destined to give rise to considerable interpretative and applicative controversies: one may ask, in fact, when and under what conditions is it possible to affirm that the provider has had knowledge of the 'unlawful or prejudicial nature for a third party'; is a formal notice required? Is it necessary to notify a final judgment? Is even an anonymous e-mail sufficient? On this point, perhaps the delegated legislator could have said something more.

[69] This is reported by Signoretta (2023), p. 118.

[70] Ibid., where it is stated that the competent authority is the only party empowered to impose specific activation and/or removal obligations. The hosting provider is subject to an obligation to report only to the authority and to remove only by order of that authority. Since the knowledge requirement is the prerequisite for the attribution of the charge, the hosting provider is only burdened with those obligations which the authority was first able to define in content.

[71] This can already be deduced from a comparison between the text of Art. 14, Directive 2000/31/EC and that of Art. 16, D.lgs No. 70/2003, concerning the parenthesis (missing in the European source, present in the Italian one) relating to the need for a 'communication from the competent authority' for the provider to take action to remove the illicit content or to disable access to it.

[72] Imbruglia (2024), p. 160, with some jurisprudential references. This discipline, in any case, disappeared with the repeal resulting from Regulation 2022/2065/EU, in which it does not seem to find any specific reference.

4.2 On the Requirement of 'Actual Knowledge' and the Criterion of Imputation of Liability

Returning to the rules on the exclusion of liability, particularly to the case of Art. 16, D.lgs No. 70/2003, it provided—as mentioned above—that the *hosting provider* was not liable on condition that it was not actually aware that the activity or information was unlawful and, as regards actions for damages, it was not aware of facts or circumstances that made the unlawfulness of the activity or information manifest; furthermore, Art. 16 provided that, as soon as it became aware of such facts, upon notice from the competent authorities, the provider acted immediately to remove the information or to disable access to it.

The problem that arose with this provision, as mentioned above, was mainly that of establishing the meaning of 'actual knowledge' of the offence as the primary prerequisite for the *provider*'s liability: both in terms of the source of this 'actual knowledge' and in terms of the modalities.

As to the first aspect (although based on para 3 of Art. 17 of D.lgs No. 70/2003, it could be assumed that an information notice from the competent authority was necessary), it is a consolidated opinion that a communication from the injured party would suffice. The Court of Cassation stated that knowledge of another person's wrongdoing, as a constituent element of the liability of the service provider, coincides with the existence of a communication made by the third party whose right is alleged to have been infringed.[73] For the second profile, relating to the manner of the communication, it does not matter so much that it takes a certain form,[74] such as that of the notice to remove the unlawful content, but rather that it is sufficiently circumstantiated[75] and that it reaches the addressee in accordance with the general rules laid down by the civil code.[76]

---

[73] Cass. 19 March 2019, no. 7708 (5.4.).

[74] Cass. no. 7708 of 19 March 2019 (5.4.) further states that 'the incurring of the obligation (which will be discussed further below) on the part of the service provider does not require a "warning" in the technical sense - such as a request for the fulfilment of the obligation to remove the unlawful documents - the mere "communication" or notice of the infringement of the right being sufficient'.

[75] And which therefore allows the *provider* to understand and identify the illicit content in order to be able to remove it or block access to it. But these are mainly technical-informatics profiles, aimed at establishing—as recalled by Court of Cassation No. 7708 of 19 March 2019—whether the content in question 'is identifiable through the mere indication of the name of the transmission from which it is taken and similar descriptive elements, or whether it is also necessary to precisely indicate the so-called "url" (uniform resource locator) address, as a sequence of characters identifying the address sought'.

[76] Cass. 19 March 2019, no. 7708 (n. 5.4) specifies, in fact, in this respect that 'in the event of information provided by the holder of the injured right himself [it is sufficient] to use ordinary means capable of ensuring the communication of the event, in accordance with the system of simple presumption under Article 1335 of the Civil Code, under which a person is legally aware of an event where he has been made aware of it by means of written or verbal communication'.

Once *the provider* has been made aware of the unlawfulness of the information present on the network, it is obliged to take steps to remove it (or to prevent users from accessing it), in order to benefit from the exemption from liability placed in its favour by the *aforementioned* rules.

The problem that arises in this regard, however, is whether the *provider* is called upon to remove any content whose unlawfulness is reported to him, *sic et simpliciter*, or whether he must first sift through the information: in this case the further difficulty arises of his ability to recognise the unlawful nature of the data or information reported to him.[77]

To avoid attributing to the *provider* 'a role that does not belong to him, that of judge of doubtful cases',[78] however, it is of help the qualification of the unlawfulness whose removal is requested as 'manifest' (Art. 16 of D.lgs No. 70/2003): that is, verifiable 'without particular difficulty, in the light of the experience and knowledge typical of the operator in the sector and of the professional diligence required of him'.[79] Only if the *provider*—put in a position to know the information and also to recognise its unlawful nature—does not take action in the terms indicated by the law, the exclusion of liability will cease to apply: and it will be called upon to restore the damage according to the general rules of civil liability.[80]

In this regard, however, referring to the subjective element that connotes liability in the albeit limited spaces in which it returns to operate, in the face of the

[77] It was already observed prior to Directive 2000/31/EC (Troiano (1998), cit., p. 414) that the requirement of knowledge should operate on a twofold level: that of knowledge of the information and also that of knowledge—*recte*: recognisability—of its illicit character when it becomes objectively difficult for the *provider* to ascertain the injury, he cannot be required to censor the information by slavishly executing what the alleged injured party requests, without the endorsement of a judicial order.

[78] Ibid., resulting in the 'dry alternative' of censure or assumption of pecuniary responsibility.

[79] Cass. 19 March 2019, no. 7708 (n. 5.6).

[80] Trib. Milano 15 February 2023, no. 1208, recently expressed its opinion on this point, stating that Article 16 cited above, as regards the objective profile, contemplates a case of civil liability of an omissive nature that takes shape if the hosting provider omits to remove the contents of which it is aware that they are manifestly unlawful. On this point, see Bocchini (2023), cit., p. 553, for whom the telematic tort is to be considered a permanent tort, in which the *provider* contributes from the moment he has omitted to behave as required by the directive. This entails the joint and several liability of the tortfeasor and the *provider*, governed by Art. 2055(2) (again Bocchini, ibid., pp. 551 ff.). Also, according to Piraino (2017), cit., p. 498, the *provider*'s omission of the obligation to remove the illicit content entered by the user concurs with the latter's damaging conduct, prolonging the damaging effects over time. On this subject, see also recently Marsico, 2024, pp. 281 ff.

widespread consideration of it as liability for fault,[81] some have envisaged its necessarily intentional nature.[82]

According to this thesis, it emerges from the body of law that the *provider*'s tort is substantiated by the failure to remove the unlawful content (or in any case the failure to block access to it) only once the *provider* itself had actual knowledge of it. It is therefore a matter of the *provider*'s failure to adopt an active conduct, on the assumption of actual knowledge, on its part, of the unlawful activity. This omission, according to this thesis, could only be the result of malice on the part of the *provider* itself because he knew of the unlawfulness and he did nothing to deal with it.[83]

4.3 Some Observations on the Regime of Irresponsibility

From the framework outlined above, it emerges that *Internet service providers* are not liable for offences occurring via the network, nor is there a general duty to monitor content. This is the case as long as the *provider* is not made aware of the presence of an offence on the network, in which case it is obliged to take action to remove it.[84]

[81] D'Arrigo (2012), cit, p. 39, speaks of a liability for 'professional negligence'; according to the a. a balance can be found between the opposing interests of the victims of telematic offences and of the intermediary precisely in the reference to professional diligence, to which the latter must adapt the performance of his activity, functional (also) to the identification and prevention of illegality: the author refers to recital 48 of Directive 2000/31/EC for which 'this Directive does not affect the possibility for Member States of requiring service providers, who host information provided by recipients of their service, to apply duties of care, which can reasonably be expected from them and which are specified by national law, in order to detect and prevent certain types of illegal activity'.

[82] And some consider that the responsibility of the provider is configured in the same way as a subjective responsibility: culpable, when the service provider, aware of the presence of suspicious material on the site, refrains from ascertaining its unlawfulness and, at the same time, from removing it; fraudulent, when he is also aware of the unlawfulness of the user's conduct and, once again, fails to intervene (thus Nivarra (2003), cit.).

[83] Cf. Bocchini (2019), p. 2611, points out that inaction following knowledge of a wrongful act entails liability for intent and not for fault. The criterion for imputation of liability, then, is certainly subjective—for the author—and not objective, but, contrary to what the doctrine holds, it is based not on fault, but even on the intermediary's wilful misconduct. Malice (but together with it gross negligence) constitute a subjective element of the *provider*'s liability for Court of Cassation no. 7708 of 19 March 2019, which, however, considers that such subjective states do not so much concern the *provider*'s failure to act, subsequent to the actual knowledge of the unlawful act (as the a. referred to considers); but rather the failure to recognise a manifest unlawfulness. Such an adjective would be worth 'in essence, to circumscribe the liability of the provider to the case of gross negligence or wilful misconduct: if the unlawfulness must be 'manifest', it means that it would be possible to detect it without particular difficulty, in the light of the experience and knowledge typical of the operator in the sector and the professional diligence required of him, so that not to have done so at least integrates serious negligence on his part' (ibid., n. 5.6).

[84] The Supreme Court of Cassation describes it in terms of a 'balancing, by the legislator, of the interests involved in the internet phenomenon … achieved by sanctioning a regime of irresponsibility of the provider up to the limit of his direct involvement or of his knowledge of the offence: in this way, therefore, circumscribing, but not completely annulling, the control over the content

With regard to the irresponsibility regime on which the regulation is based (Arts. 14, 15, 16 D.lgs No. 70/2003, now repealed by Regulation 2022/2065/EC and replaced by its Arts. 4, 5, 6, 8), it has been noted in doctrine that the choice made by the legislator is anomalous with respect to the usual rules formulated in positive terms. And it has been observed how this reversal leads to considering irresponsibility the rule, and liability an exception: which, as such, is subject to the regime of exceptional rules, and particularly to the preclusion of any analogical application.[85]

On the dogmatic level, then, it has been highlighted how the regime of irresponsibility induces one to consider that the conduct of the *provider* is assisted by a cause of justification ascribable to the legitimate exercise of a right, in turn a manifestation of the freedom of private economic initiative.[86] It must therefore be understood as the provision of a fact preventing the case from proceeding, which attributes relevance to a different and opposing interest with respect to that of the injured party, considered prevalent on the basis of a balancing according to criteria of reasonableness and proportionality.[87]

Where, moreover, the Internet service provider has implemented one of the conducts that exclude exemption from liability—for example, with regard to the activity of mere conduit, when the service provider has originated the transmission, or selected its recipient (according to the now repealed Art. 14, para 2, D.lgs No. 70/2003)—in this case, it has been pointed out by interpreters that the *provider* should not automatically be held liable, but that it is necessary to ascertain, in any

---

entered that may integrate telematic offences' (Court of Cassation, 19 March 2019, no. 7708, no. 5.5.). Some reflections on the evidentiary burdens relating to liability thus configured can be found in Stella (2022), cit., who specifies that the injured party will have the burden of proving: (a) the existence and ownership of the right injured; (b) the content on the hosting provider's platform that violates the right; (c) the ISP's actual knowledge of such content, acquired through the injured party's complaint or *aliunde*; on the other hand, the *Internet service provider* will have the burden of proving one or more extinguishing, modifying or impeding facts of the credit right of the holder of the exclusive right, and thus: (i) the fulfilment of the *ex lege* obligation to remove the unlawful content (or the timeliness of the fulfilment, if the dispute concerns the delay accumulated by the ISP in effectively following up the complaint); (ii) the impossibility of fulfilment for reasons not attributable, due to technical impossibility or to the excessive onerousness of the effort required (iii) the fulfilment of the third party, and thus the extinction, with a satisfactory outcome here, of the removal obligation incumbent on the ISP, following the spontaneous removal of the content by the users (this would instead be a mere defence, if the spontaneous removal has already taken place ante causam and the defendant intends to contest the constitutive fact alleged by the damaged plaintiff) (iv) the existence of exculpatory acts or causes of justification for the use of the work by third parties under copyright law, here 'subrogatorily' expendable by the ISP.

[85] It has been written that rules constructed in this way serve to prevent the analogical application—to which provisions constructed in a positive key might call for. That is to say, if the legislator had placed a rule of the tenor: "the IT service provider is liable when", etc., it would have allowed the interpreter to broaden the scope of the case by analogy, whereas the affirmation of liability in terms of exception with respect to non-liability renders the instrument of analogy useless, in view of the prohibition of Art. 14 'disposizioni sulla legge in generale', to broaden the various cases: thus Castronovo (2018), cited above, p. 290.

[86] Cf. Albanese (2010), cit. pp. 355 ff.

[87] Ibid.

case, the existence of the requirements of Art. 2043 of the Civil Code.[88] Otherwise, a strict liability regime would be introduced, albeit limited to those hypotheses, whereas this is not the intent of the European legislator, nor was it the intent of the transposing domestic discipline.[89]

5 The Figure of the 'Active' *Hosting Provider* in European and Italian Case Law

In the years following the transposition of Directive 2000/31/EU – which brought about the regime of irresponsibility referred to above and the absence of any obligation for the *provider* to monitor the contents placed on the network by its users – case law had to decide on cases in which the role of the *Internet service provider*, because of the continuous technological evolution,[90] was characterised by a more intense participation than the position of mere intermediary or mere passive host of the data and information circulating on the network.

The figure of the so-called 'active' *hosting provider*[91] has thus entered the jurisprudential landscape: a name used to qualify the provider of electronic services who is not merely neutral and inert with respect to the content conveyed, but, on the contrary, is aware of it and is also interested in making some profit from it.[92]

---

[88] See also Leocani (2000), cit., p. 652, who notes that if a supplier does not meet the conditions to benefit from this limitation, the nature and extent of his liability will have to be determined on the basis of the rules laid down by the national law applicable in each case.

[89] Cf. Albanese (2010), cit. This is also affirmed by case law, in the aforementioned Cass. 19 March 2019, no. 7708 (n. 5.3).

[90] An example of this can be found in Imbruglia (2024), cit., p. 155, who refers to the first video posted on YouTube, which dates back to 2005 and thus to a time later than the entry into force of Directive 2000/31/EC and also the transposition rules.

[91] In this regard, Bocchini (2019) p. 2607, writes that the peculiar concept of active *hosting* is not to be found in any normative source since no such distinction of active or passive *hosting* is profiled in the enucleation of *hosting* liability in the e-commerce directive, but is ascribable to a, by now, consolidated jurisprudential practice, of European matrix, to such an extent that, as highlighted by the judgment, this notion can, by now, be considered an acquired landing place in the Community context.

[92] Although the presence of remuneration is not considered determinant for the purposes of qualifying the provider as 'active': cf. Imbruglia (2024), cit., p. 157, where he points out that the circumstance that the service offered by the *provider* is remunerated is compatible with the *safe harbour*. See also Allegri (2018), cit., p. 66, who refers to some important judgments on the topic. The first was the order with which the Court of Rome in 2009 prevented, as a precautionary measure, the insertion and dissemination through the YouTube platform of audiovisual content relating to the television programme 'Big Brother', of which RTI held exclusive rights of economic use. Although YouTube claimed its position as a neutral *hosting provider*, unaware of the unlawfulness of the content uploaded by users, the judge held that the massive presence of advertisements on the web pages where the unlawfully inserted videos appeared, as well as RTI's repeated requests for the unlawful material to be removed, were elements that demonstrated the non-neutral position of the provider and its awareness of the unlawfulness of the audiovisual content in question.

The category, indeed, was formulated by the European Court of Justice from recital 42 of Directive 2000/31/EC itself. In this recital, in fact, it is made clear that the exemption from liability on which Directive 2000/31/EU hinges only concerns those intermediaries who perform an automatic, passive and technical role, without knowledge or control of the information transmitted or stored.[93] Similarly, recital 43 confirms this attitude of the European legislator, where it specifies that *caching* and *mere conduit* services may only benefit from the exemption if the service provider is not involved in any way with the information transmitted.

These premises allowed the European Court[94] first to specify that where the service provider 'has not played an active role of such a kind as to give him knowledge or control of the data stored. ... that service provider cannot be held liable for data which he has stored at the request of an advertiser, unless, having become aware of the unlawful nature of that data or of the activities of that advertiser, he failed to promptly remove that data or disable access to it'.[95]

Subsequently, on those assumptions, the Court came to distinguish more sharply between 'cases where the activity of information society service providers is merely technical, automatic and passive, with the consequence that those providers do not know or control the information transmitted or stored by the persons to whom they provide their services (judgments of 23 March 2010, Google France and Google, C-236/08 to C-238/08, … paragraph 113, and of 15 September 2016, Mc Fadden, C-484/14, … paragraph 62)',[96] and cases 'in which an information society service provider plays an active role, enabling its customers to optimise their *online* sales activity (see, to that effect, judgment of 12 July 2011, L'Oréal and Others, C-324/09, … paragraphs 113, 116 et 123 and case law cited)'.[97] In the first case, the limitations of liability originating in Directive 2000/31/EC apply; in the second case, these limitations of liability do not apply, and the general rules on civil liability become operative.[98]

[93] Recital 42, Directive 2000/31/EC 'The exemptions from liability established in this Directive cover only cases where the activity of the information society service provider is limited to the technical process of operating and giving access to a communication network over which information made available by third parties is transmitted or temporarily stored, for the sole purpose of making the transmission more efficient; this activity is of a mere technical, automatic and passive nature, which implies that the information society service provider has neither knowledge nor control over the information which is transmitted or stored'.

[94] On the development of *hosting provider* liability by the jurisprudence of the European Court of Justice, see Smorto and Quarta (2020), pp. 287 ff. The same authors embark on a path of investigation to examine the most recent developments of hosting provider liability in various fields of application.

[95] Court of Justice. EU, 23 March 2010, C-236/08 (No. 120).

[96] Court of Justice EU, 7 August 2018, C-521/17 (Nos. 47–48).

[97] Ibid.

[98] For an analysis of the early rulings of the European Court of Justice on the subject, see Petruso (2012), p. 1175. For a further jurisprudential review on the topic, see also Grisanti (2020), 5, pp. 491 ff.

Also in Italy (albeit in the knowledge that the European legislator had chosen to exempt the *provider* from liability, unless the conditions dictated for the different types of intermediaries by Articles 14, 15, 16, D.lgs No. 70/2003) Tribunals decided to verify the actual involvement of the *Internet service provider* in the unlawful act, thus going along with the attitude of the European Court of Justice, in favour of recognising the figure of the active *hosting provider* as a subject excluded from the benefits of the irresponsibility discipline.[99]

The figure was finally approved by the Court of Cassation, although it was not unanimously endorsed by the jurisprudence of merit.[100] Particularly, Cass. 19 March 2019, no. 7708[101] recognised the category of *active hosting provider* as a provider of network services that is not merely inert,[102] and therefore subtracted from the favourable regime sought by Directive 2000/31/EC.

More precisely, we read in Cass. no. 7708/2019 that the elements suitable to delineate the figure of the *active provider*, also called 'interference indexes', are—by way of example—'the activities of filtering, selection, indexing, organisation, cataloguing, aggregation, evaluation, use, modification, extraction or promotion of the contents, operated through an entrepreneurial management of the service, as well as the adoption of a technique of behavioural evaluation of the users in order to increase their loyalty: conduct that has, in essence, the effect of supplementing and enriching in a non-passive manner the use of content by indeterminate users'.

In the presence of these factual elements, it is considered that 'the provider of information society services [performs] an activity that goes beyond a merely

---

[99] For the most significant domestic case law references, and more generally for the debate developed in the case law on the merits, see Imbruglia (2024), cit. p. 159.

[100] On this point, Bocchini (2019) cit. p. 2608, observes that 'it seems evident at least until the pronouncement [of the Supreme Court], a jurisprudential conflict regarding the creation of a real dogmatic figure of active hosting'. This is also highlighted by Allegri (2018), cit., p. 68. See, for instance, the well-known decision—contrary to this orientation, considered by the same court to be misleading—of the Court of Appeal of Milan, 7 January 2015, no. 29. In this decision, the court of second instance held that 'the current advanced technologies, in the absence of other elements capable of giving a glimpse of real manipulation of the data entered by the hosting provider, are not alone capable of determining the change in the nature of the passive type of *hosting provider* service (according to the classification used by the national case law referred to by the appealed judgment), into an active type of hosting provider service'. Referring to the case law of the Court of Justice, the Court of Appeal of Milan ruled that 'it is certainly not in accordance with the interpretation given by the Court of Justice to identify for the "evolved" hosting provider a regime of full liability for data entered by third parties and not of limitation of liability.'

[101] On the same date, the Supreme Court of Cassation issued another ruling, Cass. 19 March 2019, no. 7709, also dedicated to the liability of the provider, but with a focus on the *caching* service. Zanovello (2020), p. 557; Cassano (2019), p. 364; Gambini (2020), p. 186; Tormen (2019), p. 1039; Scrofani (2024), p. 553.

[102] It is stated in Signoretta (2023), cit., p. 119, that one glimpses in this a consideration of the activity of the *provider* as a dangerous activity, apt and prone in itself to create harm to third parties. In fact, what the courts seem to be condemning, by reducing the provider's chances of defence, is a form of recklessness, resulting from the decision to pursue a business model potentially damaging to the rights of others, without providing the necessary safeguards to ensure that such injuries do not occur.

technical, automatic and passive service of order, and instead engages in active conduct, participating with others in the commission of the offence'. For this reason, the active *hosting provider* remains 'exempt from the general exemption regime provided for in Article 16 of D.lgs No. 70 of 2003, since its civil liability must be governed by the common rules'.[103]

In doctrine, alongside favourable opinions,[104] some doubts have been expressed concerning this figure[105] and the uncertainty to which it would give rise,[106] with some considering it preferable to adopt a classification that takes into account the objective profile of the offence committed by the *provider* rather than the subjective qualification of the provider itself as an 'active' or 'passive' *provider.*[107]

However, the latter alternative seems to be consolidated in jurisprudence, also because the so-called *active hosting providers* derive considerable profits from their intermediation activities, which make the outcome of liability in the event of damage suffered by users[108] more plausible than it might have been at an early stage of their development.

---

[103] Cass. 19 March 2019, no. 7708 (n. 7).

[104] See, e.g. Tosi (2019a), pp. 234 ff., who retraces the jurisprudential course that led the Supreme Court to the aforementioned approach, approving it. By the same author, on the subject, see also the essay *L'evoluzione della responsabilità civile dell'*Internet service provider *attivo e passivo* (2019b), p. 590.

[105] See Tescaro (2020), p. 1475.

[106] First of all of a technical nature: notes Bugiolacchi (2015), p. 1269, that until it is not understood, from a technical point of view, in what way the setting up of software and algorithms intervenes on the hosted materials, it is also difficult to understand whether the functionalities offered by the hosting providers managing the large content aggregators or by the search engines produce such an intervention on the content, whether stored or linkable, as to really exceed the neutrality of the provider's conduct.

[107] Cf. Piraino (2017), cit., p. 514, for whom what jurisprudence, with considerable insight and sensitivity, has conceived in a subjective key, elaborating the figure of the active intermediary, should instead be more profitably and rigorously reworked in an objective key: distinguishing between concrete cases in which intermediaries are aware or could have been aware of factual elements that manifestly reveal the commission of an offence by their users, and concrete cases in which there is no such evidence. The point, therefore, that differentiates the liable intermediary from the one immune from liability is not its character as an active, or passive, subject, but the condition of knowledge (of the unlawfulness or manifest unlawfulness). The author confirms his doubts in the more recent Piraino (2023), p. 153.

[108] Notes Bocchini (2019), cit., p. 2609, that in reality, the real point of relevance is not the mere definition of active *hosting*, as ascertained by the Supreme Court but the real focus of the issue is to identify—outside of the entities referred to in Articles 14, 15 and 16 and outside of a real obligation to monitor—those network intermediaries who, by carrying out activities, illustratively identified by the Supreme Court, derive an economic advantage in the activity of filtering, selecting, indexing, organising, cataloguing, aggregating, evaluating, using, modifying, extracting or promoting content on the network. In such cases, in fact, the ISP, far from carrying out an activity of mere transmission, storage or 'hosting', of the content on the network, carries out a true and proper entrepreneurial management of the service which, therefore, generates wealth on a par with any lucrative activity. And this unlawful wealth takes the ISP out of the *sicheren Hafen*, identified in German doctrine, to make him 'end up' on the rocks of liability.

This is also reflected in a more recent ruling by the Court of Cassation,[109] in which it is observed that 'the sorting and reordering of content, far from being absorbed by the notion of mere storage, are nowadays the core of the economic activity of a hosting provider'. In fact, continues the Supreme Court, thanks to a series of techniques that allow them to extract information from large quantities of data, as well as their use and processing for various purposes (whether scientific, business, industrial), *providers* can make huge profits from their *hosting* activity. Particularly, through the activity of so-called user 'profiling', 'operators have the ability to intercept users' preferences, to vary the offer of content according to the recipients and to disproportionately increase views, in fact contributing, in a causally decisive way, to the dissemination or otherwise of illicit products'.[110]

In this framework, more generally, one can understand the need felt, also at the legislative level, for a recalibration of the original *favour for online* intermediaries, to protect users who may be affected in various ways by their activities.

6 The European Tension Towards a New Discipline and the *Digital Services* Act Regulation

With the passage of time, the market for *online* services has largely consolidated,[111] and the Internet has thus assumed the centrality that is well known.[112] This has led to the need to rethink the regulatory discipline of the *Internet service provider*,[113] according to a different balance from the original one, which would certainly still take into account the driving role of this subject in the digital market, and the need not to frustrate its development and growth; but at the same time would not neglect the protection of those who might suffer prejudice from this context.[114]

[109] Cass. 13 December 2021, no. 39763 (n. 1.6).

[110] Ibid.

[111] Finocchiaro (2023a), p. 730, describes the essential points of change.

[112] And which has made the creation of a European digital single market a primary objective of the Commission since 2008. Sgueo (2023), p. 746, dwells on this point, observing, however, that the European digital economy in 2010 was still composed of an archipelago of 27 markets, disconnected from each other, each with its own independent consumer protection rules, tax regimes and payment systems. It will take another ten years for the framework to evolve partially in line with European objectives.

[113] Finocchiaro (2023b), cit., pp. 135 ff., observes that over the last 30 years, regulation from private sources has been consolidated with regard to contracts, liability, the use of platforms, and many other issues. This has led to talk of private digital sovereignty, thus referring to a strong presence of private powers on the web. In reaction to this phenomenon, in recent years, public power has tried and is trying to regain digital sovereignty through new regulations.

[114] The aim was to create a digital environment in which all users [could] exercise and have guaranteed their fundamental rights, particularly freedom of expression and information, the right to respect for private and family life, the right to protection of personal data, the right to non-

Thus, a work of enrichment of the original discipline, and of its reworking, was initiated, which resulted in the adoption in recent years of a series of regulatory acts aimed at governing the digital market more precisely.[115] With particular regard to the liability profile of electronic service providers, Regulation No. 2022/2065[116] (DSA) was adopted on 19 October 2022, amending Directive 2000/31/EC.

As stated in Art. 1 of the Regulation, its primary objective is to 'contribute to the proper functioning of the internal market for intermediary services by establishing harmonised rules for a safe, predictable and reliable *online* environment that facilitates innovation and in which fundamental rights enshrined in the Charter, including the principle of consumer protection, are effectively protected'.

The intention is thus to strike a balance between technological innovation, which Europe intends to continue promoting, and the protection of individual rights recognised by the Charter of Fundamental Rights, which the former might undermine.[117]

The change in intentions, however, was followed by only a partial restatement of the rules, which – for the most part – repeat those of Directive 2000/31/EC. The choice of the European legislator of the DSA, as already anticipated, was in fact to confirm the general regime of the *Internet service provider*'s irresponsibility for unlawful acts committed on the network, also confirming the absence of any duty to monitor the contents that transit on the network.

Added to this general indication of irresponsibility, however, is the provision of numerous rules with which the *provider* must comply[118] to ensure that the *online*

discrimination and finally the right to protection of property, including intellectual property (Servida (2024), p. 136).

[115] Bocchini (2025), cit., p. 31, gives an extensive account of this.

[116] From a formal point of view, the choice of regulation instead of directive is aimed at avoiding the fragmentation that the previously chosen source allowed. Suffice it to recall our legislator's addition of para 3, Art. 17, D.lgs. No. 70/2003 and the interpretative difficulties to which it gave rise (see *supra*, par. 4). According to Piraino (2023), pp. 154 ff., it is clear that the European legislator intended to prepare a uniform 3.0 regulation, without granting anything to the discretion of the Member States.

[117] This is a changed perspective compared to that of Directive 2000/31/EC, in which, partly because of the greater sensitivity to a technology that was to be encouraged, the objective was essentially (Art. 1, Directive 2000/31/EC) 'to contribute to the proper functioning of the internal market by ensuring the free movement of information society services between the Member States'; to approximate, 'to the extent necessary for the achievement of the objective set out in paragraph 1, certain national provisions on information society services relating to the internal market, the establishment of service providers, commercial communications, electronic contracts, the liability of intermediaries, codes of conduct, out-of-court dispute settlements, court actions and cooperation between Member-States'; and finally to complement 'Community law applicable to information society services without prejudice to the level of protection for, in particular, public health and consumer interests, as established by Community acts and national legislation implementing them in so *far as this does not restrict the freedom to provide information society services*'. This last consideration appears particularly significant of the different intentions of that time compared to those of today: since the protection of consumers and public health took second place to the guarantee of the freedom to provide information society services.

[118] Astone (2022), cit., p. 1058, points out that a new strategy emerges from this regulatory statute. In fact, the technique used is no longer based on reparation, but rather on prevention and on the

environment in which users move is 'transparent and secure'.[119] These rules vary according to the activity performed and the size of the service provider, and are designed to prevent the occurrence of offences and to remedy them, including through the intervention of public authorities set up or appointed for this purpose.[120]

Before considering some of the contours of the new regulation, however, it is appropriate to dwell on its scope of application, particularly on the characteristics of those against whom the regulation is intended to operate.

6.1 *The Subjects to Which the Regulation Applies*

In this respect, one immediately notices a greater articulation compared to Directive 31/2000/EU.[121] The sections that follow one another, particularly in Chapter III of the Regulation—and which follow Section I on *Provisions applicable to all intermediary service providers*—are in fact each referred to a particular type of network operator, by reason of the services offered to users and the size.[122]

---

empowerment of the providers of online platforms; this is achieved through the provision of obligations to draw up codes of conduct and the signing of self-regulation and co-regulation agreements to carry out content moderation activities. With this, the DSA Regulation intends not so much to tighten the liability regime, but to promote the active role of the *provider*: overcoming, one might add, what had seemed to some a 'contradiction in the system devised by the European legislator': the fact that the subjects relieved of responsibility by Community legislation are at the same time the subjects that are in the best position to put an end to the illicit activities committed by third parties through the services provided (Petruso (2012), cit., p. 1193).

[119] These are the two poles around which the most substantial part of the Regulation revolves, respectively regulated in Chapter II, under the heading *Liability of intermediary service providers*, and in Chapter III, under the heading *Duty of care for a transparent and secure online environment*.

[120] On the institutional profiles of the DSA, whose set-up he defines as 'reticular and collaborative', see again Sgueo (2023), cit., pp. 748 and 751, who first considers the role of the Commission and of two administrative articulations that support it in monitoring, investigating and sanctioning functions: one national, the other European. These are the Digital Services Coordinators and the European Digital Services Committee, respectively. Extra-judicial dispute resolution bodies, as well as so-called 'trusted reporters' and 'independent auditors' are also regulated.

[121] It is also due to the development of intermediaries in terms of their size and the services they offer. Suffice it to consider on this point the necessity and, at the same time, the difficulty of framing the services provided by some well-known *online* intermediaries: see Court of Justice. EU, 20 December 2017, C-434/15; ECJ. EU, 10 April 2018, C-320/16; ECJ. EU, 3 December 2020, C-62/19; ECJ. EU, 19 December 2020, Case C-390/18.

[122] Following the first section (which as mentioned in the text covers all *Internet service providers*), there is Section II, which provides for *Additional provisions applicable to providers of information storage services, including online platforms*; this is followed by Section III, which introduces *Additional provisions applicable to providers of online platforms*; Section IV provides for *Additional provisions applicable to providers of online platforms that allow consumers to conclude distance contracts with traders;* Section V concerns additional obligations incumbent on 'very large' platforms and 'very large' search engines 'for the management of systemic risks'. Finally, there is a Section VI devoted to *Other provisions on due diligence obligations*. For some considerations on this graduation, see Pinelli (2024), pp. 452 and 455.

There is, however, even in these differences, a minimum common denominator that must characterise all the subjects to which the regulation is intended to apply: they must have the character of so-called 'intermediary services' (see Art. 2(1), heading *Scope*), since as Art. 2(2) redundantly specifies, 'this regulation shall not apply to any service that is not an intermediary services'.

What an 'intermediary service' is, as usual, one learns from the definitions, which are contained, in numerous instances, in Art. 3 of the Regulation: particularly, under sub-paragraph (g) it is stated that an 'intermediary service' means 'one of the following information society services': (i) a *mere conduit* service, consisting of the transmission in a communications network of information provided by a recipient of the service, or the provision of access to a communication network; (ii) a *caching* service, consisting of the transmission in a communication network of information provided by a recipient of the service, involving the automatic, intermediate and temporary storage of that information, performed for the sole purpose of making more efficient the information's onward transmission to other recipients upon their request; (iii) a *hosting* service, consisting of the storage of information provided by, and at the request of, a recipient of the service.

The definition of intermediary service does not differ in substance from the tripartition that also characterised Directive 2000/31/EC: what is new among the definitions contained in the recently approved Regulation is rather the distinction—within the broad area of 'intermediary services'—of the figures of the '*online* platform' and the '*online* search engine'.

Both belong to the *genus of* 'intermediary services', but the former 'stores and disseminates information to the public' (Art. 3(i)); the latter 'allows users to input queries in order to perform searches of, in principle, all websites, or all websites in a particular language, on the basis of a query on any subject in the form of a keyword, voice request, phrase or other input, and returns results in any format in which information related to the requested content can be found' (Art. 3(j)).

Even beyond its scope, the DSA is characterised by a richer structure than the previous Directive 2000/31/EC.

The regulation of liability is indeed confined to Chapter II of the Regulation (Articles 4–10). It is preceded, however, by a Chapter I of an introductory nature[123] , and followed by: a Chapter III, devoted to the obligations imposed on network intermediaries 'for a transparent and safe online environment', which vary according to the characteristics and functions performed on the network by *Internet service providers*; a Chapter IV devoted to the implementation of the Regulation (with an indication of the Authorities competent to verify compliance and provision for appropriate sanctions); a Chapter V with the usual closing rules.

[123] Containing, as usual in European legislation, the subject matter, scope, and numerous definitions.

6.2 The Exclusion of Liability of Intermediary Service

In terms of civil liability, as already mentioned, Regulation 2022/2065/EU takes up what was already provided for in Directive 31/2000/EC. And so Art. 4 concerns the activity of so-called 'mere conduit', for which it is provided that 'Where an information society service is provided that consists of the transmission in a communication network of information provided by a recipient of the service, or the provision of access to a communication network, the service provider shall not be liable for the information transmitted or accessed', except on the conditions indicated by the same rule.[124] Articles 5 and 6, on the other hand, concern the activity of temporary storage[125] and durable storage,[126] respectively, and they too repeat the rules already present in the previous framework.

[124] It particularly provides that the exclusion of liability is waived on the condition that the provider (a) does not initiate the transmission; (b) does not select the receiver of the transmission; and (c) does not select or modify the information contained in the transmission. In cases (a) and (c), the lack of responsibility is explained because the recipient affects the information it transmits, either by putting it into the network, where the transmission originates, or by selecting and modifying the content transmitted. In case sub b), the explanation for the assertion of liability instead of irresponsibility lies in the fact that, as Bocchini (2023), cit., p. 543, observes, 'the selection [of the recipient] entails, on the one hand, knowledge of the information and, on the other hand, an economic interest ... since it can offer its customers a more efficient service and therefore more attractive than competing companies'.

[125] According to Art. 5, in particular, '1. Where an information society service is provided that consists of the transmission in a communication network of information provided by a recipient of the service, the service provider shall not be liable for the automatic, intermediate and temporary storage of that information, performed for the sole purpose of making more efficient or more secure the information's onward transmission to other recipients of the service upon their request, on condition that the provider: (a) does not modify the information; (b) complies with conditions on access to the information; (c) complies with rules regarding the updating of the information, specified in a manner widely recognised and used by industry; (d) does not interfere with the lawful use of technology, widely recognised and used by industry, to obtain data on the use of the information; and (e) acts expeditiously to remove or to disable access to the information it has stored upon obtaining actual knowledge of the fact that the information at the initial source of the transmission has been removed from the network, or access to it has been disabled, or that a judicial or an administrative authority has ordered such removal or disablement. 2. This Article shall not affect the possibility for a judicial or administrative authority, in accordance with a Member State's legal system, to require the service provider to terminate or prevent an infringement'.

[126] Article 6 is set out later in the text. It should also be pointed out how the classification of the *provider* according to one or the other qualification (*caching* or *hosting*) is not an immediate operation, as highlighted by Amidei (2024), p. 471, who observes that it does not seem to be possible to endorse an automatic correspondence between *caching activity,* on the one hand, and neutrality on the other, for the mere fact that the first would be of a merely temporary nature and, above all, automatic: the automatic nature of any intervention on the contents conveyed does not exclude its potential incisiveness, nor its traceability to the provider who makes use of the automatic tool. It will be another matter—and this is the real issue on which to reflect, also in order to overcome the problematic distinction between 'active' and 'passive' *hosting*—to verify whether the type and level of intervention put in place are such as to determine the actual loss of neutrality on the part of the provider.

For what particularly concerns the *hosting provider*, Art. 6 provides, echoing the previous Art. 14 of the directive, that 'Where an information society service is provided that consists of the storage of information provided by a recipient of the service, the service provider shall not be liable for the information stored at the request of a recipient of the service on condition that the provider: (a) does not have actual knowledge of illegal activity or illegal content and, as regards claims for damages, is not aware of facts or circumstances from which the illegal activity or illegal content is apparent; or (b) upon obtaining such knowledge or awareness, acts expeditiously to remove or to disable access to the illegal content'.[127]

On the other hand, the figure of the 'active' *hosting provider*, which has been developed in case law, does not find explicit recognition in the rules of the DSA. However, its exclusion from the immunity regime of the Regulation is confirmed by recital 18, which states that 'the exemptions from liability established in this Regulation should not apply where, instead of limiting themselves to a neutral provision of services by means of a purely technical and automatic processing of the information provided by the recipient of the service, the intermediary service provider plays an *active* role which gives it knowledge or control over that information. Consequently, such exemptions should not be available as regards liability for information provided not by the recipient of the service but by the intermediary service provider itself'.

A provision that seems significant, and which is not found in the directive previously in force, is that set forth in the new para 3 of the same Art. 6, under which the provisions of the preceding paragraphs 'shall not apply with respect to the liability under consumer protection law of online platforms that allow consumers to conclude distance contracts with traders, where such an online platform presents the specific item of information or otherwise enables the specific transaction at issue in a way that would lead an average consumer to believe that the information, or the product or service that is the object of the transaction, is provided either by the online platform itself or by a recipient of the service who is acting under its authority or control'.

This provision seems to mean that where the average consumer may be led to believe that the product or service he intends to purchase—or the information provided about it—comes directly from the platform, or from its auxiliaries, this is sufficient to neutralise the platform's liability exclusion regime.

This provision, which tightens up the legal system's attitude towards platforms, while favouring consumer protection, thus strikes a new balance between expansion of the digital market (underlying the irresponsibility regime[128]) and protection of

[127] It is not present—as indeed it was not in Directive 2000/31/EC—the clause whereby the *provider*, once the illegal content is known 'upon notification by the competent authorities' is obliged to take action to remove it. This was an insertion on the initiative of our legislator when transposing the directive (D.lgs. No. 70/2003), which, however, generated uncertainty in interpretation and was not particularly followed up in application, and which today, due to the Regulation, is outdated.

[128] See Bocchini (2016), p. 518, for whom the European Union, as has always been the case in the history of economics, had eased the position of providers to help private economic initiative in the pioneering phase of the sector.

the weaker contracting party who ventures into the terrain of platforms,[129] nominating the latter as the prevailing reason.[130]

Another novelty with respect to Directive 2000/31/EC lies in the provision of Art. 7 DSA, according to which the *Internet Service Provider* may (but is not obliged to) carry out its own network control and surveillance activities.[131] This, however, in no way alters the operation of the preceding articles;[132] it is, in fact, a virtuous behaviour that the *provider* himself may decide to adopt, in order to protect users and in cooperation with the competent institutions: for the creation of a safe and reliable *online* environment, but without this entailing the loss of the special regime of exclusion of liability[133] placed in his favour by Articles 4, 5 and 6.

---

[129] Bocchini (2023), cit., p. 2615, also gives an account of the progressive change in the attitude of the legal system (first and foremost of the jurisprudence, even before the DSA) with regard to the *hosting provider*'s liability, p. 2615. He observes that we have gone from the beginnings of the phenomenon with the law of the sector in 2003—when the legislation had as its precise objective the protection and promotion of the growth and development of the market and of the economic operators who invested in the 'new world' of the Internet—to today's setback: where the true affirmation of the evolved electronic market could not disregard a greater protection of the user of the network. It corresponds, conversely, to a worsening of the forms of liability borne by the intermediary of electronic commerce.

[130] As Tommasi (2020a), p. 113, observes, the objective of promoting the development of the network and the digital market has favoured *providers* for a long time. Today, however, the *online* dissemination of content that may violate the foundations of democratic values and people's fundamental rights, the technological innovations, which allow for the detection and removal of content on the net, seem to incentivise the identification of a more stringent responsibility and an obligation to act proactively.

[131] The article is headed *Voluntary own-initiative investigations and legal compliance* and provides that 'Providers of intermediary services shall not be deemed ineligible for the exemptions from liability referred to in Articles 4, 5 and 6 solely because they, in good faith and in a diligent manner, carry out voluntary own-initiative investigations into, or take other measures aimed at detecting, identifying and removing, or disabling access to, illegal content, or take the necessary measures to comply with the requirements of Union law and national law in compliance with Union law, including the requirements set out in this Regulation'.

[132] The purpose, as recital 26 states, is to ensure 'legal certainty, and not to discourage activities that aim to detect, identify and act against illegal content that providers of all categories of intermediary services undertake on a voluntary basis'. Particularly, F. Piraino (2023), cit., p. 156, observes that this provision was intended to prevent the provider from being considered active merely because he had activated within the terms indicated in Art. 7. This is why it was decided to reiterate the application, also in this case, of the rules on the exclusion of liability set out in the previous articles.

[133] Moreover, it has been observed by S. Tommasi (2020b), pp. 936 ss. that this arrangement could also act as a disincentive to the provider himself. This is because although the exemptions from liability are not lost by the mere fact that providers carry out their own voluntary investigations, these actions may give rise to the liability of the hosting service if they result in the actual knowledge of the unlawfulness of such content or activities, and they have not acted immediately to remove them or disable access to the same. This could lead to hosting services either being discouraged from taking voluntary measures or being very strict in removing content to the detriment of the protection of freedom of expression.

6.3 *Absence of a General Obligation to Monitor: Presence of Obligations to Cooperate with the Public Authority*

The DSA also confirms the absence of an obligation to monitor he information which providers of intermediary services transmit or store; the *Internet service provider* is therefore not obliged to check the content that passes through it and spreads among users.[134]

Nevertheless, it is expected to be involved in what has been described as a collaboration between *private enforcement* and *public enforcement*, where the former sees the *provider* himself as the main actor. Among the relevant rules in this regard can be considered Articles 8 and 9 of the Regulation, which place obligations on the *provider* to counter illegal content, and obligations to inform the authority if the latter so requests.[135]

But also, moving on to more specific provisions, there is, for example, Art. 18 of the Regulation, for which, 'Where a provider of hosting services becomes aware of any information giving rise to a suspicion that a criminal offence involving a threat to the life or safety of a person or persons has taken place, is taking place or is likely to take place, it shall promptly inform the law enforcement or judicial authorities of the Member State or Member States concerned of its suspicion and provide all relevant information available'.

More generally, it has been observed how public supervision, in the architecture of the Regulation, also passes through the obligation of cooperation by *Internet Service Providers*: first of all because providers of very large online platforms and very large online search engines are required to provide the coordinator of digital services of the place of establishment or the Commission with access to the data or

[134] Article 8 of the Regulation.

[135] More precisely, the two aforementioned articles are expressed in terms of 'orders' that the public authority issues and which the *provider* is required to comply with. Art. 9, entitled *Orders to act against illegal content*, provides in para 1 that 'Upon the receipt of an order to act against one or more specific items of illegal content, issued by the relevant national judicial or administrative authorities, on the basis of the applicable Union law or national law in compliance with Union law, providers of intermediary services shall inform the authority issuing the order, or any other authority specified in the order, of any effect given to the order without undue delay, specifying if and when effect was given to the order'; it further provides in subsection 5 that 'At the latest when effect is given to the order or, where applicable, at the time provided by the issuing authority in its order, providers of intermediary services shall inform the recipient of the service concerned of the order received and to the effect given to it. Such information provided to the recipient of the service shall include a statement of reasons, the possibilities for redress that exist, and a description of the territorial scope of the order, in accordance with paragraph 2'. Of almost identical content is Art. 10 of the Regulation, entitled *Orders to provide information* and referring to the receipt by the *provider of* an order to provide specific information on one or more individual recipients of the service to the competent national judicial and administrative authorities. Bocchini (2023), cit., p. 548, states that these are the most important obligations for intermediaries who, once they have received such orders [to counter illegal content and to inform the authority], are obliged to execute them without 'undue delay'. They are part of a broad strategy of the European legislator, which called for the widest possible cooperation from intermediaries with the public authority (ibid., 551).

explanations necessary to monitor and assess compliance with the Regulation.[136] Moreover, the providers themselves are required to provide tools to monitor their compliance with the Regulation through the establishment of an independent compliance function.[137]

7 Some Observations on the Nature of the Liability of the *Internet Service Provider*

The regulation of the civil liability of the *Internet service provider*—or rather, of its irresponsibility—has therefore not radically changed with the DSA, which has retained the essential features imprinted at the time by Directive 2000/31/EC.

It is still based on the presence of a general rule of exclusion of liability, governed by the absence of an obligation to monitor the contents on the part of the *provider*: this is due to the impossibility on the part of the *provider* himself to know first, and therefore to examine and qualify, the multiplicity of said contents in terms of lawfulness or unlawfulness.

The meaning of these rules, read in conjunction, is that if the *Internet service provider* is not obliged to check in advance the lawfulness of content published by third parties, then it cannot even be held liable if that content is harmful to the legal sphere of other network users.

---

[136] Finocchiaro (2023b), op. cit., p. 143, also points out that the express provision of such *private enforcement* measures of the DSA distinguishes the latter from the DMA (*Digital Markets Act*), where, although implicit reliance is placed on the *private enforcement* of the Regulation itself, no express measures are identified.

[137] Ibid. In this framework of cooperation, the provision of Art. 45 of the Regulation also seems to fit in, whereby the drafting of codes of conduct at Union level is encouraged and facilitated to contribute to the correct application of the Regulation itself. So-called self-regulation is not a new experience for *online* platform operators (cf. Cinà (2023), pp. 313 ff.). However, it shows some critical profiles. It has recently been observed that self-regulation is still promoted by private actors that have almost as much influence and important economic interests as states, and thus, having defined their own interests, can choose how to pursue them and at what cost. See on this point Benatti (2023), pp. 82 ff. In the field of information, this implies, for the author, the possibility of censoring or restricting content that is not considered advantageous for one's own purposes. Particularly, given the importance of *online* information in our time, it means giving social media control over political debate and democratic life: it is they who define the limits of acceptable public discourse and legitimise it. Second—as the same a. considers—this profile is accentuated by the characteristics of the codes of conduct, which use generic, often rhetorical language. Above all, one notices paternalistic overtones with the intention of guiding the citizen/consumer towards the news one wishes to legitimise. The ambiguous effects of these self-regulatory codes seem evident if one takes into account that the absence of criteria that are not only objective but also rationally justifiable has allowed the censoring of various messages on *social networks* with questionable content, depending on the person from whom they came and according to the ideas or ideologies upheld. Finally—she concludes—self-regulation through codes of conduct can become a strategic tool for companies to avoid regulations that could penalise them or impose greater burdens on them.

Only if the *provider* itself has actual knowledge (from the competent authority, but also possibly from its users and from the injured party himself) of the unlawful nature of that content, and in that circumstance does not take action to remove it: only then can it be held liable for the damage suffered by the user.

It has also been observed,[138] in this regard, that the centrality and strength acquired by *Internet service providers*, particularly by digital platforms, could also justify strict liability, as happened in the twentieth century in the face of the economic consolidation of the industries, which led, inter alia, to the formulation of producer liability. Particularly, a reference to Art. 2049 of the Civil Code has been suggested,[139] although not in the sense of a bland assimilation between the position of the user-author of the damaging content and that of the servant (and, correlatively, of the platform with the master), but rather to bring out—after a structural reduction of the rule to its fundamental nucleus: the organisation—the possibility of qualifying the question of responsibility also by reason of the relationship between the platform and the user, within which the typical business risk is also realised.

From a different point of view, but still in the direction of a rethinking of the *provider*'s liability,[140] it has also been considered that it could be ascribed to the area of contractual liability,[141] emphasising the presence of a reliance of the service users on the professional *status of* the provider, such as to give rise to obligations on the part of the latter to protect the legal sphere of the former.[142]

This interpretation has been considered to be proposed, for example, in the context of a *provider*'s liability for a product, where the intermediary, although neither producer nor seller, is considered obliged to protect the legal sphere of the user who

---

[138] Cf. Benatti and Portonera (2024), cit., p. 480, who note, with respect to the latter, a significant difference in the fact that in the reality of the Internet, unlike in the case of product liability, the damage is not caused directly by the *Internet service provider*, as it is instead by the producer to the third party: the damage derives instead from the conduct of a different subject, also a user of the platform like the injured party, and who has uploaded on the platform, and who through the platform has disseminated, the illicit content. The platform is a mere intermediary, therefore, and not an active subject in the verification of the damage.

[139] Ibid.

[140] Which, in the limited spaces remaining for it, is held to be non-contractual liability under Art. 2043 of the Civil Code.

[141] See Trib. Torino, 3 June 2015, according to which 'the relationship linking the owner of the infringed right and the provider of information society services, not bound to each other by any contractual relationship... seems appropriately catalogued in terms of 'social contact' relationship, thus calling on the parties concerned to behave in accordance with fairness and good faith, in a solidarity perspective': for the Court, the qualification of the relationship in the key of 'social contact' determines its ascription to the extra-contractual liability area, while it is quite well known that the elaboration of the category has entailed the allocation in the contractual area of those hypotheses of damage placed on the borderline between contract and tort (cf. Castronovo (2018), cit, ch. X). See also Trib. Roma 20 January 2021, which refers to the previously cited judgment on the figure of qualified social contact.

[142] Cf. Albertini (2023).

is damaged by the defective product purchased through him.[143] A similar interpretation has also been proposed for cases in which the damage, although originating from the conduct of a third-party network user, is directly attributable to the functioning of the algorithm referable to the platform (because, for example, it reproposes the damaging content over and over again to its users).[144] In both cases we are talking about *providers* who, in the language derived from the case law of the European Court of Justice, would be defined as 'active', i.e. characterised by a position that makes them participants in the injurious conduct of others, and therefore places them outside the scope of the exemption from liability provided for, today, by Regulation 2022/2065/EU.

Even with reference to the merely 'passive' *provider*, however, the dimension of the relationship that binds him to his users seems to be enhanced today thanks to the aforementioned Regulation, which, as we have seen, places a series of new obligations on providers of intermediary services.[145]

According to Art. 54 DSA, in fact, 'Recipients of the service shall have the right to seek, in accordance with Union and national law, compensation from providers of intermediary services, in respect of any damage or loss suffered due to an infringement by those providers of their obligations under this Regulation'.

This rule, which does not affect the immunity of the electronic service provider originating in Directive 2000/31/EC, does, however, introduce a new provision of liability, which arises from the *provider*'s breach of the obligations under the Regulation to protect the user, for a 'safe, predictable and trusted' *online* environment.[146]

These obligations—to which the *Internet Service Provider* is not bound by virtue of the contract with the user of the service, but by virtue of the regulation under consideration, and which may be considered in the same way as 'duties of

[143] Cf. Rossi (2023), *passim*, which highlights how more than one circumstance could be relevant in order to identify a possible breach of the obligations to protect the other party, such as obligations of fairness and good faith, incumbent on the provider. Those circumstances are the absence of controls on the identity, solvency or presence of insurance coverage of third-party sellers who are authorised to sell their products on the platform; the lack of adequate controls on the safety of products (especially those with an inherent danger to people's health) sold on the platform; the methods of storage and preservation of certain products which, although sold by third parties, are held by the platform (e.g. Amazon) in its own warehouses before being shipped; as well as the enticing display of wording, banners, indications and evidence in correspondence with certain items in the list of search results (such as, for example, 'Amazon's recommended item', 'Amazon's Choice', 'sponsored', 'featured offer', 'suggested', 'top offer').

[144] It is stated again in Benatti and Portonera (2024), cit., 484, that the space of good faith as a mechanism of integration and conformation of the relationship is also identified in those hypotheses in which the provision of the services offered by the platform may constitute an occasion of damage for the user. The reference is to the category of obligations of protection, which is capable of adding, alongside the creditor's interest in the performance, also an interest in the protection of both parties, who, because of the relationship, are exposed to a specific danger of damage to person or property.

[145] On the liability of the service provider and its nature, see Castronovo (2006), p. 768.

[146] This is the formula to be found in Art. 1 DSA, devoted to the *subject matter of* the Regulation.

status'[147]—are, however, intended to prevent the user from suffering harm in the course of using the network, even possibly by third parties, or in any case to curb the extent of such harm.

With the consequence that, in the classic alternative between the two types of civil liability, as is the case for obligations that are therefore said to be 'protective',[148] their presence reveals a legally relevant relationship, the breach of which should give rise to liability of a contractual nature.[149]

8 Liability for Unfair Commercial Practices

The issue of Internet service providers' liability for an offence committed by one of its users also arises in the different field of unfair commercial practices: this happens when the illicit conduct falls within those prohibited by Directive 2005/29/EC, transposed into Italian law in Art. 18 et seq. of D.lgs No. 206 of 6 September 2005 (Consumer Code).

In cases in which the conduct qualifying as commercial practice unfair has been implemented directly by the *Internet service provider*, there is no doubt as to the existence of liability on the part of the latter (with the consequent activation of the remedies of public and private law connected thereto: Art. 27 of the Consumer Code): as when, for example, the platform is reticent with regard to the costs of the intermediation service provided by the same.

However, when the unfairness of the commercial practice is not committed by the provider of the *online* service, but once again by one of its 'users', is different and more difficult to define[150] who—making use of the network made available by

[147] Castronovo (2018), cit., p. 238, recalls the expression, regarding the civil liability of the public administration, which is bound to comply with the rules of the administrative procedure.

[148] On which see again Castronovo (1991), p. 1; Nicolussi (2015), p. 659; Albanese (2021), p. 31; Nicolussi and Portonera (2023), *passim*.

[149] Astone (2022), cit., pp. 1059 ff., observes that the provision of obligations commensurate with the breadth and size of the platforms confirms the legislative intention to protect the users to whom the services rendered by such Internet operators are addressed in the phase of the programming of the contents, before they are made available to the general public or to the addressees, to avoid the commission of the offence itself. Consequently, their infringement will give rise to contractual liability, with the consequent obligation to pay compensation for the damage suffered by the recipients of the service. It will then be for the law of the Member States to determine the methods of compensation.

[150] To give a significant example—also because it is inherent to the COVID-19 pandemic—one may consider a case decided by the Italian Competition and Market Authority in which, on a digital platform intermediary in the sale of goods and services, there had been the 'publication of advertisements for the sale of health and/or parasanitary products including filtering masks and *test kits* for self-diagnosis, connoted by *claims* relating to the alleged ability to prevent COVID-19 infection or to detect the *virus* in human blood', with also the indication of prices 'in an ambiguous way and significantly increased compared to the period before the pandemic'. The case is PS11734, which was closed by order 28445, at the meeting of the Competition Authority on 10 November 2020.

the intermediary—engages in conduct ascribable to the kind of misleading or aggressive conduct prohibited by Art. 20 ff. Consumer Code. In certain cases that have been brought to its attention, the Italian Competition and Market Authority (Autorità Garante della Concorrenza e del Mercato) has seemed inclined to affirm that the *hosting provider* can also be held liable. And the 'gigantism of the platforms'[151]—both for the reasons of 'digital' asymmetry that characterises them with respect to users, and for the profit that they derive from the exchanges (or more broadly from the interactions) that they can host—would seem to put platforms themselves in the best position to restore the damage.[152]

Nonetheless, the legal framework underpinning the assertion of the liability of platforms for unfair commercial practices engaged in by users exhibits some fragilities worth dwelling on.

The Authority's decisions sometimes state that the platform would be liable for unfair commercial practices, by reason of the fact that the platform would be obliged—'also on the basis of the *standard* of professional diligence referred to in Article 20 of the Consumer Code'—'to adopt measures aimed at avoiding speculative phenomena such as those detected, or to prevent the use of claims and statements intended to mislead consumers in the purchase of products presented'.[153]

But the adoption of measures aimed at 'avoiding speculation phenomena' as well as 'preventing the use of claims and statements intended to mislead consumers' would presuppose surveillance by the platform of the contents proposed to users through it: surveillance which, however, the platform is not obliged to carry out, by express provision of law (Art. 17, D.lgs No. 70/2003, now Art. 8 DSA), as mentioned above.

The question therefore arises as to whether affirming the liability of the platform for unfair commercial practices, when the unfairness is committed by third parties, does not conflict with the structure of the aforementioned discipline, which, on the contrary, seems to exclude such liability, on the assumption of the absence of any duty of supervision on the part of the *provider*.

The issue has been addressed in precisely these terms in a number of rulings by the Council of State, e.g. in Judgment No. 3851 of 18 May 2021. In it, on the one hand, it is observed that 'there is no objective incompatibility between the figure of professional, within the meaning of the unfair commercial practices legislation, and

[151] Already evoked in the opening (according to the expression found in Irti (2025), cit., p. 159).

[152] See C. State, 18 May 2021, no. 3851 (n. 3.7) which observes how 'in the current legal system, if on the one hand, the importance of these subjects is recognised both from an economic point of view - they intermediate most of the entrepreneurial activities that take place on the net - and from a socio-cultural point of view - they allow the circulation of and access to information - on the other hand, it is complained from several quarters that telematic offences occur precisely because of the activity carried out by Internet intermediaries, who must therefore be involved in the liability or at least in the prevention and removal of such offences'.

[153] PS11734, closed by order 28445, at the meeting of the Competition Authority, 10 November 2020.

that of *hosting provider*, within the meaning of the e-commerce legislation';[154] on the other hand, however, the Council of State states that these disciplines 'must be coordinated, in the sense that it is possible to penalise conduct that violates the rules of professional correctness, but it is not permitted that, through the application of the rules on unfair practices, services are imposed on the *hosting provider* that are not provided for by the rules on electronic commerce'.[155]

This does not imply, however, the radical immunity of digital platforms for unfair commercial practices carried out by their professional users. What should be verified according to the Council of State is whether there is any involvement of the digital platform in the commercial practice: since, in the hypothesis that the latter exists, the liability of the platform may also be affirmed, for the improper conduct engaged in cooperation with another entity operating on it.[156]

Administrative case law thus follows civil case law, also considered in the preceding paragraphs, and particularly the case law of the Court of Cassation,[157] which, as recalled, has distinguished between two possible ways of performing the *hosting* service, to which different outcomes in terms of liability would be linked. Alongside the passive *hosting provider*, who does not participate in the processing of the content published by its users, and who is therefore not liable, one must also consider the figure of the active *hosting provider*,[158] who instead carries out 'activities of filtering, selection, indexing, organisation, cataloguing, aggregation, evaluation, use, modification, extraction or promotion of the content published by users, carried out through an entrepreneurial management of the service, as well as the adoption of a

[154] Within the meaning of Directive 2005/29/EC, a trader is considered to be any natural or legal person who, in commercial practices covered by that Directive, is acting for purposes relating to his trade, business, craft or profession and anyone acting in the name of or on behalf of a trader (Art. 18(b) of the Consumer Code.), i.e. 'the natural persons who come into contact with consumers in their capacity as agents (with or without representation), agents or auxiliaries of that person, as well as entrepreneurs who, on behalf of the latter, disseminate such messages by addressing them and making them available to the consumer public': thus De Cristofaro (2012), p. 1083.

[155] C. State, 18 May 2021, no. 3851 (3.6).

[156] Elsewhere, with regard to the liability of the seller of goods who is not also the author of the unfair advertising message, it was held that 'it is still necessary, in order for liability for unfair commercial practices to arise against [it] ... that [it] participates [...] in the unfairness of the practice, and that it is therefore ascertained, on [it]'s part, that the violation of Articles 20 et seq. of the Consumer Code has been committed: therefore, the mere intermediary of the message who has not contributed with his own conduct to the commission of the offence cannot be considered liable, but it will be necessary to verify, in the case of whoever is to be sanctioned, participation in the infringement of the prohibition', see Guffanti Pesenti (2020), p. 245.

[157] Cass. 19 March 2019, no. 7708, to which Bocchini (2019), p. 2606, devotes an extensive commentary.

[158] This is a figure developed by the European Court of Justice, as can be inferred from the reconstruction made by Cass. 19 March 2019, no. 7708 (n. 4.2), where it is stated that 'the notion of "active hosting provider," [is] referred to all those cases which go beyond an "activity of information society service providers (which) is of a merely technical, automatic and passive nature, with the consequence that those providers do not know or control the information transmitted or stored by the persons to whom they provide their services," whereas "limitations of liability are not applicable where an information society service provider plays an active role."'

technique of behavioural evaluation of users to increase their loyalty'.[159] The decisive factor in establishing what type of *hosting* we are talking about is whether or not the *provider* engages in 'conduct that ... has the effect of completing and enriching in a non-passive manner the users' enjoyment of the contents'.[160]

This distinction (by means of which a figure of active *hosting* has been definitively theorised, overcoming the jurisprudential conflicts on this point, and outlining a form of liability better suited to the development of the network)[161] is thus considered valid by administrative jurisprudence also for the liability for unfair commercial practices,[162] which can and must be affirmed in the 'presence of elements, in the professional's activity, capable of demonstrating a 'prior knowledge and control' of the contested information, or the power of 'manipulation' of the content stored by third parties'.[163]

References

Albanese A (2010) Trasferimento di dati e responsabilità del prestatore di servizi telematici: dal «diritto secondo» al «diritto primo». AIDA, p 355

Albanese A (2021) Buona fede contratto legge. Europa Dir Priv p 31

Albertini L (2023) La responsabilità civile degli internet service provider per i materiali caricati dagli utenti (con qualche considerazione sul ruolo di Gatekeepers della comunicazione). In: medialws.eu, Law and Media working papers series

Allegri MR (2018) Ubi Social, Ibi ius. Milano

Amidei A (2024) Vecchi e nuovi problemi in tema di motori di ricerca, tra oblio e informazione. Giur It

Astone M.A (2003) La responsabilità del prestatore di servizi della società di informazione nella direttiva 2000/31/CE. Europa Dir Priv pp 431 ff

Astone MA (2022) Digital Services Act e nuovo quadro di esenzione dalla responsabilità dei prestatori di servizi intermediari: quali prospettive? Contr e impr p 1054

Benatti F (2023) Un diritto privato neofeudale? Banca, Borsa, Tit Cred pp 82 ff

Benatti F, Portonera G (2024) La responsabilità di diritto civile degli Internet Service Providers. Spunti dalla comparazione con la giurisprudenza statunitense. NGCC, p 480

Bocchini R (2003) La responsabilità civile degli intermediari del commercio elettronico. Napoli, pp 128 ff

Bocchini R (2016) La centralità della qualità del servizio nel dibattito in tema di network neutrality. Dir Inf 3:518

Bocchini R (2019) La responsabilità civile plurisoggettiva, successiva ed eventuale dell'ISP, Giur it., p 2606

[159] C. State, 18 May 2021, no. 3851 (3.8).

[160] C. State, 18 May 2021, no. 3851 (3.8).

[161] Thus, again, Bocchini (2019), cited above, p. 2609.

[162] The latter is first and foremost an administrative liability since, if ascertained, it leads to the imposition of a sanction by the Competition and Market Authority pursuant to Art. 27 of the Consumer Code, as has been illustrated in greater detail elsewhere (see Guffanti Pesenti (2020), pp. 112 et seq. and 132 et seq.)

[163] C. State, 18 May 2021, no. 3851 (3.9.4).

Bocchini R (2023) La responsabilità extracontrattuale del provider. In: Bocchini R (ed) Manuale di diritto privato dell'informatica. Napoli, p 534
Bugiolacchi L (2000) Principi e questioni aperte in materia di responsabilità extracontrattuale dell'internet provider. Una sintesi di diritto comparato. Dir Inf p 831
Bugiolacchi L (2015) Ascesa e declino della figura del provider 'attivo'? Riflessioni in tema di fondamento e limiti del regime privilegiato di responsabilità dell'hosting provider. Resp Civ Prev p 1269
Camardi C (2021) Contratti digitali e mercati delle piattaforme. Un promemoria per il civilista. Jus Civile, p 870
Cassano G (2019) La Cassazione civile si pronuncia sulla responsabilità dell'internet service provider. In: Il diritto industriale, p 364
Castronovo C (1991) voce Obblighi di protezione. In: Enc Giur Treccani, XXI, Roma, p 1
Castronovo C (2006) La nuova responsabilità civile. Milano, p 768
Castronovo C (2018) Responsabilità civile. Milano, p 285
Cinà G (2023) Il "disordine informativo" sulle piattaforme digitali: un confronto tra i modelli europeo e statunitense. Riv Dir Civ pp 313 ff
Contaldo A (2021) Le piattaforme digitali. Profili giuridici e tecnologici nel nuovo ecosistema. Pisa
D'Arrigo R (2012) Recenti sviluppi in tema di responsabilità degli Internet Services Providers. Milano, p 11
De Cata M (2010) La responsabilità civile dell'internet service provider. Milano, pp 83 ff
De Cristofaro G (2012) Pratiche commerciali scorrette. Enc Dir, Milano, p 1083
Delfini F, Finocchiaro G (2014) Diritto dell'informatica. Milano, p 785
Di Ciommo F (2002) La responsabilità civile nell'era di internet. In: Ponzanelli G (ed) La responsabilità civile. Tredici variazioni sul tema. Padova, pp 206 ss
Di Ciommo F (2003) Evoluzione tecnologica e regole di responsabilità civile. Napoli
Facci G (2002) La responsabilità extracontrattuale dell'Internet provider. Resp Civ Prev pp 268 ff
Finocchiaro G (2023a) Responsabilità delle piattaforme e tutela dei consumatori. Giorn Dir Amm p 730
Finocchiaro G (2023b) Il Digital Services Act e il Digital Markets Act tra private e public enforcement. In: Il diritto privato nell'economia digitale. Tutele giurisdizionali e autorità indipendenti, Torino
Franzoni M (1997) La responsabilità del provider. AIDA, p 250
Franzoni M (2023) Dalla colpa grave alla responsabilità professionale. Torino, pp 224 ff
Galasso G (2023) Piattaforme digitali, autonomia contrattuale e condotte delle imprese. In: Il diritto privato nell'economia digitale. Tutele giurisdizionali e autorità indipendenti, p 162
Gambini M (2020) La responsabilità dell'Internet service provider approda al vaglio della Cassazione. Corr Giur p 186
Grisanti S (2020) Internet Service Providers: una rassegna giurisprudenziale europea ed italiana ai tempi del Covid-19. Dir Ind 5:491 ff
Guffanti Pesenti L (2020) Scorrettezza delle pratiche commerciali e rapporto di consumo. Napoli, p 245
Imbruglia D (2024) La responsabilità degli intermediari. In: Battelli E (ed) Diritto privato digitale. Torino, p 160
Irti C (2025) La protezione dei dati personali degli utenti nelle piattaforme digitali. In: Il diritto privato nell'economia digitale. Tutele giurisdizionali e autorità indipendenti. Torino, pp 151 ff
Leocani P (2000) La direttiva UE sul commercio elettronico: cenni introduttivi. In: Europa Dir Priv p 623
Magni S, Spolidoro SM (1997) La responsabilità degli operatori in Internet: profili interni e internazionali. Dir Inf, p 61
Marsico GM (2024) La fattispecie a formazione progressiva della responsabilità dell'Internet Service Provider: tra politica del diritto e innovazione digitale. Danno e Resp 3:278, 281 ff
Nicolussi A (2015) Obblighi di protezione. In: Enc Dir Annali. Milano, p 659
Nicolussi A, Portonera G (2023) Buona fede e correttezza nel rapporto obbligatorio. Torino

Nivarra L (2003) La responsabilità del provider. In: Dig Disc Priv, Torino
Palmieri A (2019) Profili giuridici delle piattaforme digitali. La tutela degli utenti commerciali e dei titolari di siti web aziendali. Torino, p 27
Pasquino T (2003) Servizi telematici e criteri di responsabilità. Milano
Petruso R (2012) Fatto illecito degli intermediari tecnici della rete e diritto d'autore: un'indagine di diritto comparato. Europa Dir Priv, p 1175
Pinelli C (2024) Poteri e diritti nelle piattaforme. Problemi di una prospettiva costituzionale. Giur It, pp 452, 455
Pino G (2004) Assenza di un obbligo generale di sorveglianza a carico degli Internet service providers sui contenuti immessi da terzi in rete. Danno e resp, pp 832 ff
Piraino F (2017) Spunti per una rilettura della disciplina giuridica degli internet service provider. AIDA, p 470
Piraino F (2023) La responsabilità dei prestatori di servizi di condivisione e di contenuti online. Nuove leggi Civ Comm, pp 153, 154 ff
Ponzanelli G (2002) Verso un diritto uniforme per la responsabilità degli internet service provider. In: Sica S, Stanzione P (eds) Commercio elettronico e categorie civilistiche. Milano, pp 363, 367
Riccio G.M (2002) La responsabilità civile degli internet providers. Torino, pp 45 ff
Rossi EA (2023) Danni da prodotto e commercio elettronico. La problematica internazionalprivatistica sullo sfondo di una recente giurisprudenza nordamericana. Europa Dir Priv
Scrofani M (2024) Il ruolo e la responsabilità degli Internet Service Provider nella "Post Truth Era." Danno e resp, p 553
Servida BS (2024) La responsabilità degli internet service provider dal safe harbour al principio di accountability. Nuove leggi Civ Comm pp 136, 147
Sgueo G (2023) L'architettura istituzionale del Digital Services Act. Giorn Dir Amm p 746
Signoretta C (2023) La responsabilità civile degli intermediari internet. Danno e Resp 1:118
Smorto G, Quarta A (2020) Diritto privato dei mercati digitali. Firenze, pp 287 ff
Stella M (2022) Responsabilità degli internet providers: rifrazioni dell'onere della prova. Riv Dir Civ, pp 838 ff
Tescaro M (2020) La responsabilità civile dell'hosting provider e il dialogo fra le Corti. Studium Iuris, Spec, p 1475
Tommasi S (2020a) Algoritmi e nuove forme di discriminazione: uno sguardo al diritto europeo. In: Revista de Direito Brasileira, Florianópolis, p 113
Tommasi S (2020b) The liability of internet service providers in the proposed digital services act. Eur Rev Priv Law, pp 936 ff
Tormen L (2019) La linea dura della Cassazione in materia di responsabilità dell'hosting provider (attivo e passivo). NGCC, p 1039
Tosi E (2019a) La disciplina applicabile all'hosting provider per la pubblicazione di contenuti digitali protetti dal diritto d'autore, tra speciale irresponsabilità dell'ISP passivo e comune responsabilità dell'ISP attivo, alla luce di Cassazione 7708/2019 e 7709/2019. Riv Dir Ind II:234 ff
Tosi E (2019b) L'evoluzione della responsabilità civile dell'Internet service provider attivo e passivo. Dir Ind p 590
Troiano O (1998) Gli illeciti attraverso internet: problemi di imputazione e responsabilità. AIDA, pp 400 ff
Zanovello F (2020) La responsabilità dell'Internet Service Provider. Brevi note a Cass.19 marzo 2019, nn. 7708 e 7709. In: Studium Iuris p 557

Artificial Intelligence and Tort Law

Antonio Albanese

Contents

Abstract Technologies based on the use of Artificial Intelligence lead to a statistical reduction of damages resulting from human error, but at the same time, they give rise to new risks, which must be managed. From this perspective, the chapter examines the role played by civil liability in preventing damages, allocating their cost according to criteria of justice and efficiency.

A. Albanese (✉)
Catholic University of the Sacred Heart of Milan, Milan, Italy
e-mail: antonio.albanese@unicatt.it

R. Bocchini (ed.), *Digital Platforms - From Technical Foundations to Legal and Economic Implications*, https://doi.org/10.1007/978-3-032-07978-7_17

1 The Legal Issues

The progressive development of mechanical and/or computer systems capable of carrying out an increasing number of activities independently from human decisions has led to the question of whether 'Artificial' Intelligence could be, in this regard, comparable to that which is a distinctive feature of human 'nature'.

Although it has not yet been defined with sufficient conceptual precision, the phenomenon has also assumed importance from a legal point of view, raising several questions, among which the one concerning the identification of liable parties for any damage caused using intelligent machines has attracted particular attention.[1]

The reasons for this focus on the applicable liability regime are manifold.

First, the use of Artificial Intelligence systems not only serves to produce more utility in a more efficient manner, but also to reduce the risk of damage due to human error. However, this increased safety does not rule out the possibility of damage occurring, nor does it eliminate the problem of ascertaining responsibility.

On the contrary, the gradual introduction of previously unknown technologies generates new risks that were not there before or increases others that already existed.

One thinks first of the security of personal data: Artificial Intelligence systems exploit technologies characterised by their enormous capacity to process a huge amount of information. But this increases the risk of cyber-attacks and, in any case, of unlawful exploitation and disclosure of personal data. In addition, the use of data poses problems of data reliability and may give rise to discrimination between subjects.[2]

On the other hand, so-called generative Artificial Intelligence facilitates possible infringements of intellectual property by enabling the processing of texts, music, and images, which exploit works accessible on the web.

In the face of these risks, civil liability and the imputation criteria on which it is based contribute to implementing regulatory strategies to prevent or reduce damage, without halting technological development,[3] but ensuring that it is directed in a way that respects the fundamental rights of individual human beings and the interests of society.

Regarding this new taxonomy of harmful events, it will therefore be necessary to verify whether the compensatory remedies offered by the law constitute an adequate instrument for achieving the twofold objective of preventing damage and, where

[1] This was also expressed by the European Parliament in its resolution of 16 February 2017, with recommendations to the Commission concerning private law rules on robotics.

[2] On the latter, see Parenzo (2022), pp. 335 ff.

[3] From a more general point of view, Baldwin et al. (2012), pp. 20 ff., highlight the risk that overly rigid or detailed rules may hinder innovation.

damage has occurred anyway, of allocating its cost according to criteria of justice and efficiency.[4]

To fully understand the preventive function of civil liability, it is essential to realise that damage once it has occurred cannot be eliminated. Compensation does not make it go away, but shifts its cost from the person who suffered it to the person who must compensate for it.[5]

From this perspective, the rule of liability is efficient to the extent that it places the damage in the hands of the person who is in the best position to assess the expediency of the actions to be taken to avoid it, by comparing the respective costs of prevention and compensation. In this way, in fact, on the one hand, the overall loss of resources will be reduced to a minimum,[6] on the other hand, the probability that the prevention measures, precisely because of their lower cost, will be adopted will increase, with a correlative decrease in the risk of the harmful event occurring.

These rules, moreover, if properly interpreted, can provide an efficient and rational system of disincentives, capable of guiding and governing technological development. Even before the occurrence of any damage to be compensated, in fact, these rules constitute evaluation criteria, which are assumed by business processes, influencing the economic and organisational choices of enterprises that offer the market goods and services based on new technologies, through the evaluation and management of the relative risks in the interest of *shareholders* and *stakeholders*.[7]

In this sense, the possible compensatory consequences do not prevent the development and use of intelligent systems, but operate as an incentive to make them safer, combining and balancing the protection of individuals against possible injury with the collective interest in favouring technical innovations capable of improving the conditions of human life, also with regard to fundamental interests and values such as health and personal freedom.

[4] With regard to these aspects, see Koch (2020), p. 122, according to whom '*it should not depend upon the technology involved whether a loss is allocated in a fair and efficient manner, thereby considering inter alia who benefited from the activity that ultimately led to harm, who was in control thereof, who deviated from appropriate conduct or failed to employ technology according to acknowledged standards, or who was the cheapest cost avoider*'. The thought of Mataja (1888), pp. 19 ff., revitalised by Calabresi (1970), pp. 47 ff., is therefore still current with respect to these new liability figures.

[5] See, for all, Trimarchi (1990), pp. 8 and 302.

[6] Thus, Calabresi (1975), p. 666, reformulates the criterion of the 'cheapest cost avoider', clarifying the one previously elaborated in Calabresi (1970).

[7] Trimarchi (1990), cit., pp. 303 ff.

2 Liability in a Damage Prevention System

But the legal system also implements other prevention strategies, making use of instruments other than civil liability, which, however, as will be seen,[8] may indirectly affect the criteria for imputation of the latter.

A way of law intervention is by imposing risk management procedures and systems, which have a preventive effect on the organisational structure of the company, through positive duties, the violation of which is sanctioned irrespective of the actual occurrence of damage.[9]

This is, moreover, the approach followed by the EU regulation on Artificial Intelligence (Regulation (EU) 2024/1689), the so-called *AI Act*, which classifies activities involving the use of Artificial Intelligence according to their level of risk, establishing, depending on the case, different technical and organisational measures that companies must take to manage and mitigate risks.[10]

In this context, civil liability contributes to forming an integrated system of damage prevention instruments.

Liability rules are, in fact, disincentives to carrying out activities deemed excessively risky and incentives to adopt risk-containment measures, and, as such, they become evaluation criteria in corporate decision-making processes.

From this point of view, the criteria for attributing liability, because of their ability to adapt to different situations, without rigidly predetermining what conduct is required, have undoubted advantages over the more specific duties of *risk management*.

Such rules first and foremost reduce the risk of economically inefficient legal solutions, as they result in organisational choices, which are decided by the individual company on a case-by-case basis and not uniformly imposed by central authorities,[11] sometimes lacking sufficient knowledge of the problems.[12]

In the latter cases, on the other hand, the company is not free to self-determine its organisation, which is instead hetero-determined on the basis of an abstract risk assessment, so that the costs of protective measures may exceed those of possible damage, thus discouraging the introduction of technologies capable of procuring benefits and utilities greater than the resulting risks.[13]

---

[8] See below, para 3.

[9] On the differences between such preventive measures and civil liability, see Mulgan (2000), p. 558.

[10] Calvano and Calzolari (2021), p. 7.

[11] This dirigiste aspect is particularly pronounced in the AI Act, which does not even leave it to the regulated entities to assess the risks of their activities, directly identifying and classifying them in pre-established categories, according to an approach defined as 'top-down' by Tommasi (2023), p. 293.

[12] In this sense, the limits of the normativist approach are already highlighted by Mengoni (2011), pp. 65 ff.

[13] These aspects raise serious doubts as to the appropriateness of a strategy aimed at preventing possible injuries solely through the provision of risk management rules, instead entrusting civil

Liability, on the other hand, forces the entrepreneur to perform a cost-benefit analysis himself, choosing the most cost-effective solution between preventing the damage and compensating for it.

Compensation, on the other hand, could not perform this function of efficient cost allocation, where it follows a punitive logic, which determines its quantification to an extent exceeding the prejudice suffered by the injured party.[14] In such a case, in fact, certain costs of prevention could exceed those of possible damages.[15]

Conversely, compensation commensurate with the actual damage is consistent with the logic of the market, rewarding the most efficient companies in managing the relevant risk.[16] The costs of compensation, also in terms of liability insurance and of prevention, are in fact reflected in the price of products and services offered to the market.[17]

Obviously, this cost-benefit analysis encounters a limit in the protection of fundamental rights and values, which cannot be balanced by private actors, nor can they be sacrificed based on a purely economic calculation. In such cases, the provision of security requirements specifically established by the regulatory authorities with which AI systems must comply is appropriate.

However, compliance with the regulations is not subject to prior assessment by the control authority, but must be ensured, both at the time of placing on the market and subsequently, by the supplier, who is subject to significant sanctions in the event of non-compliance.

These are, however, rules that affect the organisational choices of the company from the outside, translating into economic costs, which are justified on the grounds of the anticipated protection of fundamental rights and values.

The analytical nature of these provisions also highlights, in differential terms, another strong point of civil liability, given the great elasticity of the legal concepts on which it is based and of the related imputation criteria.

A striking example of this can be found in the comparison with the AI Act, which defines Artificial Intelligence as 'a machine-based system that is designed to operate with varying levels of autonomy and that may exhibit adaptiveness after deployment, and that, for explicit or implicit objectives, infers, from the input it receives, how to generate outputs such as predictions, content, recommendations, or decisions that can influence physical or virtual environments'.[18]

---

liability solely with the task of compensating victims for the damages suffered. See in this sense, Bertolini (2022), pp. 416 ff.

[14] In this regard, see the well-known pronouncement in which Cass., sez. un., 5 July 2017, no. 16601, affirmed that the so-called punitive compensation is not ontologically incompatible with the Italian legal system.

[15] For other critical aspects inherent in the attribution of a sanctioning function to civil liability, see Castronovo (2018), pp. 897 ff.

[16] An approach aimed at fostering innovation, relying mainly on competitive market mechanisms, is the one adopted in the United States: Calvano and Calzolari (2021), cit., p. 6.

[17] See especially Coase (1960), p. 44 and Calabresi (1970), cit., pp. 47 ff.

[18] Thus, Art. 3(1), Regulation (EU) 2024/1689.

This extremely broad formula is then specified with regard to so-called high-risk systems by means of a case-by-case listing of them in Annex III to the European regulation.

However, this approach of the legislator increases the possibility of gaps, since the more detailed the list, the greater the probability that some assumptions have not been provided for.[19]

The need for continuous updating of legislation then clashes with the difficulty of the law keeping up with the pace of technological progress.[20]

The regulation of civil liability, on the other hand, disregards problematic definitions of Artificial Intelligence and relies on imputation criteria based on well-established legal concepts with considerable elasticity, capable of adapting to different situations and social and technological changes.

It is not a matter of 'pouring new wine into old wineskins',[21] but of updating legal institutions by welcoming innovations into a system[22] that, as Luigi Mengoni taught us, is not closed, but rather open to the critical contributions of new points of view and ready to introduce corrections, modifications or additions to the doctrinal edifice already constructed, which is never final.[23]

3 Fault as a Defect of Organisation

In this sense, fault, while constituting the most traditional of the criteria for attributing liability, run through history of law (not only civil law), reflecting new social needs in each era, so much so as to represent a paradigmatic example of the interaction between dogmatic categories and protection instances, which find recognition in the legal system through the intervention of the legislator and the activity of the interpreter.[24]

Modern codes inherit the nineteenth-century conception of guilt, which, according to the cultural approach of liberal individualism, is understood as the foreseeability and avoidability of damages.

[19] On the general problem, see Tarello (1980).

[20] Calvano and Calzolari (2021), cit., p. 7, also point out this criticality. On the general problem of the so-called pacing gap, i.e. the misalignment between the development of new technologies and their regulation, see Marchant et al. (2011).

[21] On this point, Ruffolo (2019), p. 1690, speaking of the plastic capacity of Western codification systems to adapt to new cases, states that they are conditioned by the systematic effects (even if not foreseen or foreseeable) of any non-essential legislative over-regulation.

[22] Albanese (2024b), p. 12.

[23] Thus, Mengoni (1985), pp. 90 ff.

[24] On this role of dogmatics in relation to the problems posed by technological innovation, see Castronovo (2024), pp. 145 ff.

This conception takes as its fundamental value the will and freedom of the individual, thought of as a natural person, responsible only for harmful events that are within his direct control.

Already in the early years of codification, this conception proved to be inadequate in relation to the demands of industrial society and the machine civilisation, where the harmful act is not always attributable to the conduct of a single individual.[25]

Therefore, strict liability cases are increasingly affirming themselves, concurrently with the recognition of fault in the normative sense, which also includes the objective violation of precautionary rules through conduct and acts directly resulting in damage.

The concept evolves and expands in today's mass consumer society, in which people are part of a complex system which connects them also through new technologies.

The actions and choices of some individuals often have unpredictable consequences, which cannot always be attributed to the conduct of a single person.[26]

The concept of risk becomes central: human activities, especially those of big business, bring benefits, but also generate risks that cannot be foreseen ex ante.[27]

Protection against damage requires a paradigm shift. Not only strict liability, but also a new understanding of fault, as a failure of adequate organisation.

Hence, hypotheses in which those who carry out activities that are likely to generate risks must adopt organisational arrangements suitable for monitoring, preventing and mitigating any harmful materialisation of these are gradually being recognised by law.[28]

From this perspective, the failure to adopt the organisational measures provided for by the EU regulation on Artificial Intelligence, in addition to triggering the application of the financial penalties provided for therein, may constitute a criterion for the fault imputation of damages which are causally attributable to the use by

---

[25] Castronovo (2021), p. 687, states in this sense that the machine undermines the traditional imputation of such events to the simple will of man, because the logic of the relationship between the man who works and the tools he uses is inverted: these are no longer functional tools as man's *longa manus*, therefore adapted to his action, but are increasingly complicated machines, to which man and his actions must adapt [...]. If it is man who must now respond to the logic of the machine, the imputation of what their symbiosis produces is now up to the latter, and therefore in this context the idea of responsibility as a corollary of an wrong-exercised freedom [...] disappears, but rather that which now dominates him with its objectivity, not only opposed to individual subjectivity, but which has become the dominant and therefore decisive element of the question of responsibility.

[26] Similarly, Franzoni (2025), p. 203, emphasises the inadequacy of a notion of guilt, based on the assessment of conduct in terms of mere negligence, with respect to activities that have a technical basis and a strong social impact, such as those that precisely involve the use of AI.

[27] On the legal treatment of negative externalities produced by new technologies, see Calabresi and Al Mureden (2021), p. 29.

[28] This principle, as Finocchiaro (2012), p. 731, observes, consists in making the party benefiting from the use of Artificial Intelligence accountable by requiring it to take the necessary measures to avoid or mitigate the associated risk.

third parties of high-risk intelligent systems and which could have been avoided if the supplier[29] and/or the deployer[30] had complied with the risk management rules.

In this sense, the 'supplier' of high-risk systems must take organisational measures to ensure that this risk is reduced to acceptable levels. These requirements include the adoption of precise governance and management practices for training datasets; the preparation of procedures for monitoring and correcting any distortions; the drafting of constantly updated technical documentation; and d) the chronological listing of significant events occurring in the life cycle of the system.[31]

In turn, the deployer must, among other things, take appropriate technical and organisational measures ex ante to ensure that the systems are used in accordance with the accompanying instructions; monitor the operation of the AI and inform the supplier or the competent authorities in the event of particular risks; entrust the supervision of the systems to persons who have the necessary competence and training.[32]

Failure to take such organisational measures gives rise to fines and, where it causes damage, gives rise to civil liability in tort.

Another hypothesis relates to the administrative liability of entities for certain offences committed in their interest and to their advantage by natural persons who have a governing role within them. In these cases, the entity can escape liability if it has adopted and effectively implemented an appropriate organisational model to prevent offences of the kind committed, entrusting a special body with the task of supervising the observance and adequacy of the model.[33]

Conversely, where adequate organisational measures have not been implemented, it is reasonable to configure not only administrative, but also civil liability of the entity towards those who have been harmed because of this defect in internal organisation.

These and similar regulatory provisions, which require the adoption of risk management procedures and systems, can alternatively take on a twofold systematic value.

On the one hand, they could be regarded as exhausting the range of duties to be performed by operators, so that no liability could be imputed to them for organisational failures outside the cases provided for.

---

[29] Article 3(3) of Regulation (EU) 2024/1689 defines a supplier as a natural or legal person, public authority, agency or other body which develops an IA system or an IA model for general purposes or which has an IA system or an IA model developed for general purposes and places that system or model on the market or puts it into service under its own name or trademark, whether in return for payment or free of charge.

[30] Article 3(4) of Regulation (EU) 2024/1689 defines it as a natural or legal person, public authority, agency or other body using an AI system under its own authority, except where the AI system is used during a personal, non-professional activity.

[31] Article 9, Regulation (EU) 2024/1689 (Risk Management System).

[32] Article 26, Regulation (EU) 2024/1689 (Obligations of deployers of high-risk IA systems).

[33] Article 6(1), Legislative Decree No. 2001/231.

On the other hand, the individual rules could be reconstructed as points of emergence of a more general concept of fault, also relevant as failure to adopt measures that are not typified by the law, but which are required, in relation to each activity, according to criteria of diligence and expertise inferable respectively from the social and professional context. In this case, non-compliance does not give rise to the application of sanctions, but only in the event of damage constitutes a criterion for attributing civil liability.

Both interpretative solutions confirm, moreover, albeit with different degrees, the character of guilt, as a criterion that follows the evolution of the legal system, adapting with it to the changing needs of the social and economic context.

4 The Negligent Use of Artificial Intelligence, the Evidential Difficulties of the Injured Party and the Proposal for a Uniform Regulation in the European Union

Regardless of whether an organisational fault on the part of the entity can be established, the traditional fault-based liability for damages attributable to the wrongful act of the natural person using the Artificial Intelligence system may still apply.

The adoption of preventive risk assessment and risk management measures presupposes that the concrete results of the activities autonomously performed by the IA must be subject to constant human supervision, to guarantee the safety of persons with respect to possible harm, also by resolving possible ethical dilemmas, which require choices based on criteria that cannot be internalised in an algorithm.[34]

In this sense, the European Commission, in the document *Ethics Guidelines for Trustworthy AI*, recommended that the use of AI should promote the fundamental rights of the individual, always allowing for full and effective determination of the human being interacting with them.[35]

Moreover, irrespective of the configuration of guilt, man's interaction with intelligent systems, characterised by a high degree of autonomy and at the same time by the complexity and opacity of their operating mechanisms, may make it more difficult to prove the causal link between the damage and the negligent conduct of the person who is hypothetically liable for it.

From the point of view of compensatory protection, there is therefore a need to ensure that those harmed by Artificial Intelligence are no less protected than those harmed by traditional technologies.

To remedy these drawbacks and to ensure the effectiveness of the protection against damages, the introduction of new rules to ease the burden of proof on the injured party has been proposed.

---

[34] For some concretisations of this principle, see Albanese (2023), pp. 442–443 and id. (2024a).

[35] https://digital-strategy.ec.europa.eu/en/library/ethics-guidelines-trustworthy-ai.

It has also been pointed out that a uniform supranational regulation, which would reduce uncertainties regarding the applicable liability regime, is desirable to encourage the dissemination of Artificial Intelligence systems, thus reducing a factor that could negatively affect the production and use of new technologies.[36]

The European Institutions intended to give an initial response to these demands with a 'Proposal for a Directive of the European Parliament and of the Council' of September 2022 on the adaptation of tort law to Artificial Intelligence.

The declared aim of this measure is to progressively harmonise the systems of the countries of the European Union without reducing the compensatory protection granted by each of them to injured parties, but, on the contrary, strengthening its effectiveness at a procedural level.

The proposal for a directive, moreover, on the basis of the principle of proportionality, is intended to harmonise only the regulation of tort liability in cases where the damage was caused by the output produced by an AI system or by the failure of that system to produce an *output* through the fault of a person.[37]

The application of these rules therefore presupposes that the damage, which is allegedly attributable to the culpable conduct of a certain natural person, was caused through the use of an 'Artificial Intelligence' system and, in this respect, reflects the same uncertainties already highlighted with respect to the definition adopted by the EU regulation on Artificial Intelligence, which is expressly referred to therein.

Having affirmatively resolved this issue, on the assumption therefore that the harmful result is attributable to an activity carried out through the use of Artificial Intelligence, the legislation under consideration presumes until proof to the contrary that the harmful event was caused by negligent human conduct, where it is proved or may reasonably be presumed, as the case may be (i) the breach of a duty of care by the defendant or another person for whom he is responsible, (ii) that such negligent conduct affected the operation of the machine and (iii) that the damage complained of by the plaintiff resulted therefrom.

Where, however, the defendant is a non-professional user who makes use of Artificial Intelligence for personal purposes, the reversal of the burden of proving causation operates only in cases where his conduct has materially interfered with the operating conditions of the system, e.g. by not complying with the instructions for use or by violating the obligations regarding the scope of use or the operating conditions of the system.

Moreover, if the damage is suspected to have been caused by a so-called 'high-risk' Artificial Intelligence system, as defined by the aforementioned European regulation, the proposal for a directive has laid down an obligation for the provider and the user to disclose the relevant evidence, also providing that the national courts may order the disclosure of such evidence, at the request of the plaintiff, if the latter has previously made every proportionate effort to obtain it and demonstrates the

[36] For a critical analysis of the policy objectives of EU law, see Salanitro (2020), pp. 1246 ff.

[37] In this sense, Art. 1(2) states that this Directive shall apply to non-contractual liability actions based on fault aimed at obtaining compensation for damage caused by an IA system.

plausibility of his claim. In such cases, to balance the interest of the injured party with that of the manufacturer or supplier in the preservation of industrial and commercial secrets, measures may be taken to ensure the confidentiality of the information disclosed during or after the proceedings. In the event of non-compliance with the court's injunction, the breach of the duty of care alleged by the plaintiff is also presumed, until proof to the contrary.

The draft directive is, however, without prejudice to the rules of the DSA, which regulate in a comprehensive and fully harmonised manner the due diligence obligations relating to the algorithmic decision-making process of online platforms, including the related exemption from liability of providers of 'intermediary services'.

From a different perspective, but still in a logic of proportionality and minimum harmonisation, the European legislator also admits that the injured party may benefit from the more favourable national rules, also by invoking the rules of strict liability that may be applicable.

It is precisely with reference to these cases, however, that a review of the directive is foreseen five years after the finalisation of its transposition to assess the appropriateness of introducing uniform rules, possibly in combination with compulsory insurance, without prejudice, of course, to the EU provisions with regard to damage caused by defective products.

5 The 'Supplier' of Artificial Intelligence Systems and Producer Liability

In this regard, it has been debated whether AI systems can be considered products even when they are not structurally embedded in a physical device.[38] An affirmative conclusion is rationally justified by the fact that 'Artificial' Intelligence, precisely because it is not 'natural', is a 'product' of human beings.[39]

This is also the direction taken by the European legislator, who, by resolving the interpretative doubts that had arisen with regard to the previous rules, extended the application of the new product liability directive to the developer of the software.[40]

---

[38] In affirmative terms, Montinaro (2020), p. 372, considers that it is not decisive that the immaterial component is incorporated in a physical support and/or can bring about some tangible effect, affecting the material reality (e.g. making a robot move to enable it to operate an assembly line).

[39] The opinion of Leanza (2021), p. 1021, according to which it would be impossible to have recourse to the discipline of product liability when the automaton is endowed with such 'freedom' as to enable it to make decisions and act completely independently of the original programming, cannot be shared. In that case, the automaton should not be regarded as a product.

[40] Article 4(1) of Directive (EU) 2653/2024 defines a product as any movable property, even if incorporated into or interconnected with another movable property or immovable property, including electricity, digital manufacturing files, raw materials and software.

This development by way of legislation also confirms the elasticity of liability criteria and the ability to respond to social demands for justice in an efficient manner.

This regulatory choice is also consistent with the fact that Artificial Intelligence, as an object of rights, although it tends to come close to the concept of service, is not identified with it, but is substantiated in the utility objectively obtainable from a complex of assets (tangible and otherwise) integrated and/or connected in various ways, capable of procuring certain results independently of human conduct, which can be considered in the same way as a performance deduced in an obligatory relationship between two specific parties.[41]

It follows that any defects in the Artificial Intelligence and the resulting damage assume relevance in a logic unrelated to that of non-performance, giving rise to a liability, potentially attributable to each of the parties participating in the realisation of the smart product, also towards third parties other than the user.

This, of course, does not exclude that the latter may be held liable for non-performance if the defective functioning of the system it used, without rendering performance impossible, adversely affected its proper performance.

If, on the other hand, only the user's creditors are entitled to claim compensation for such damage, the extra-contractual and objective nature of the producer's liability[42] makes it possible to extend the relevant compensation protection to all those who have been harmed by Artificial Intelligence.[43]

In this respect, it should also be noted that the introduction of technologies capable of reducing risks associated with human error generates a growing social expectation for safer products. One thinks, for example, of technological driver assistance devices or high-precision surgical and diagnostic instruments.

The interaction between the legal rule and the new technologies, due to the impact they have on social expectations, is therefore destined to result in a corresponding extension of manufacturers' liability for damage caused by intelligent machines and systems that, although they comply with the specific technical standards that may be provided for by the sectoral legislation regulating their marketing and use, do not offer the safety that may reasonably be expected (average consumer expectation) and must therefore be considered defective.[44]

The manufacturer will therefore be held liable for the malfunctioning of the machine on the basis of a rule of strict liability, which is independent of a fault attributable to a concrete natural person operating in its business organisation.

On the other hand, if the manufacturer cannot be held liable for defects arising from compliance with regulatory requirements, this does not mean that compliance

---

[41] Regarding software, Di Rosa (1999), pp. 725–726, sees the prevalence or otherwise of a *facere* performance as the distinguishing criterion between services and goods.

[42] See in this sense the reconstruction by Carnevali (1990), p. 6.

[43] For an expansive interpretation of these rules, from the point of view of the parties entitled to act against the manufacturer of highly automated vehicles, see Albanese (2019), pp. 1014–1018.

[44] This is the definition of a defective product provided for in the Italian legal system by Art. 117(1) of Legislative Decree 6 September 2005 (Consumer Code) implementing the harmonised European Union rules.

with these is sufficient to exclude the product from being defective if it does not ensure, in other respects, a level of safety commensurate with a reasonable expectation.[45]

Consequently, the presence of the defect logically ends up being ascertained ex post because only in relation to the concrete circumstances in which the damage occurred can it be assessed whether the product was sufficiently safe or not at the time it was placed on the market, according to a judgment of so-called posthumous prognosis.[46] Thus, for example, in the case where the system was unexpectedly exposed to easy attacks by hackers, who alter its functioning in a potentially damaging manner.

This liability is therefore based on an objective criterion of imputation that, leaving aside proof of negligent human conduct, offers adequate compensation protection to injured parties, who can discharge their burden of proof by simply demonstrating that the Artificial Intelligence system does not correspond to social expectations of safety, without having to reconstruct its specific technical modes of operation, which most often remain opaque and difficult to ascertain.[47]

From this perspective, there is no reason to fear that the judge may lack the necessary knowledge to ascertain whether the safety standards required for technologically advanced products are met or not.[48] He, in fact, through a hermeneutic procedure analogous to that which is followed regarding other general clauses (e.g. good faith and morality),[49] can act as an interpreter of social conscience to establish whether the product is safe to the extent considered proper by the community of reference.[50]

In the extra-contractual logic of this liability, the lack of the safety that can be legitimately expected and that renders the product defective cannot be related to the expectation that is generated on the occasion of contact between two specific persons, but must be assessed on the basis of a more general and abstract criterion of social expectation, which appropriately takes into account all those who could be harmed.

---

[45] For similar considerations, with reference to traditional vehicle production, Owen (2008), pp. 1134 ff. and, regarding self-driving vehicles, Schellekens (2015), p. 510.

[46] The defect, however, remains the subject of a judgement that tends to be autonomous from that of the ascertainment of the damage occurred, as Italian jurisprudence has had occasion to clarify, excluding that the former element can be deduced from the latter (Court of Cassation, 13 December 2010, no. 25116, in *Foro it.*, 2012, p. 1589).

[47] Albanese (2024a), cit., p. 1020.

[48] In this sense, see the concerns expressed, with specific regard to highly automated vehicles, by Evas (2018), p. 33.

[49] On the product defect as a general clause, Loi (1989), pp. 545 ff. For similar considerations, see in Belgian Law Van de Gehuchte (2000), p. 37.

[50] In this regard, De Mari Casareto dal Verme (2024), pp. 227 ff., relates the safety assessment to a criterion of reasonableness. From this point of view, the fear expressed by the European Parliament in its resolution of 16 February 2017, with recommendations to the Commission concerning civil law rules on robotics, proves unfounded.

On the other hand, an assessment of the safety of the product in relation to the expectations of its user would almost inevitably end in the condemnation of the manufacturer, since the very use of the product by the injured party normally presupposes that the latter trusted in the absence of danger.[51]

From this point of view, it is plausible to assume that an 'intelligent' product, precisely because of the safety objectives underlying its introduction, will be deemed defective when its use has resulted in damage that would not have occurred had traditional tools been used or had there been active human participation.

The use of such a criterion, moreover, would significantly reduce the risk that the protection of injured parties would be made less effective by the time and cost of technical consultations, which would otherwise be necessary to ascertain whether the standards designed to ensure the safe operation of Artificial Intelligence systems are met or not.[52] A further reduction in the administrative costs of ascertaining the existence of a defect could also be achieved by making it mandatory for certain activities to introduce 'data recorders', which would make it possible to establish the causes of damaging events in a certain and rapid manner.

On the other hand, the fear that strict producer liability could hinder technological progress would lack any real rational basis. On the contrary, the very rule that identifies the criterion of imputation of damage in the safety defect that can legitimately be expected from the product, referring to an objectively verifiable standard, far from impeding research and development of new technologies, constitutes an incentive to orient such activities towards the production of increasingly safer systems.

From the point of view of compensation, too, producer liability is both a fair and efficient solution to the problem of any damage caused by Artificial Intelligence.

On the one hand, it responds to a criterion of justice, according to which the social utility produced by Artificial Intelligence must be matched by the collectivisation of the costs of the resulting damage. In this sense, the compensation or insurance premium paid by the producer, like the other costs of his productive activity, will be reflected in the selling price of the products and thus shared among all buyers.

On the other hand, the producer is the entity that is best able to carry out the cost-benefit analysis, investing in safety as often as the relative costs are lower than those of preventable damage, while competitive mechanisms will reward in the market

---

[51] This model of adjudication has been criticised in common law systems for the practical inconveniences it leads: see Stapleton (1994), pp. 234–236.

[52] On the contrary, the reconstruction proposed by De Mari Casareto dal Verme (2024), cit., pp. 251 ff. seems to meet this drawback, who considers that the injured party must prove the 'deviation' of the concrete operation of the intelligent system from that hypothetically referable to an abstract exemplary agent, on the basis of a judgement corresponding to that which leads to the ascertainment of fault. However, this approach does not consider the difficulties, even probative ones, connected to the opacity of the mechanisms and procedures through which the AI arrives at certain outputs, making it almost impossible to compare with an alternative model, which in turn is problematic to identify.

those companies that can minimise the costs necessary, as the case may be, to prevent or compensate for possible damage.[53]

This economic assessment, however, remains at the discretion of the producing company, and does not translate into a legal rule that it only bears the costs of compensation in cases where the total amount exceeds that of the investments to be made to prevent or reduce the damage.

In fact, the so-called risky/utility test, which seems to be recognised in the States with the Restatement (Third) on Product Liability of 1997, has not found acceptance in European Union law risky/utility test, which seems instead to be recognised in the States with the Restatement (Third) on Product Liability of 1997, which, by making the ascertainment of the *design defect* dependent on the existence of a 'reasonable alternative', enables a comparative evaluation of all the costs and benefits deriving from the use of the product with respect to the available alternatives to be introduced into the liability judgement, which could lead to deeming it safe by reason of a general interest prevailing over that of the individual injured party.[54]

In fact, the assessment of the legitimately expected safety is not resolved in a mere economic calculation balancing the collective benefits of the use of a given product, albeit in terms of increased safety from a general point of view, against the damage that, despite this, individual persons might suffer because of a defect that becomes apparent in its actual use.

Similarly, the criterion based on legitimate social expectations provides a more extensive compensatory protection than that resulting from the application of the well-known 'cheapest cost avoider' criterion developed by Guido Calabresi, which instead places the cost of the damage on the person who, taking into account the information available to him at the time he acted, was in the best position to assess, through a cost-benefit analysis, the most convenient choice between preventing the damage and compensating him.[55]

In our legal system, on the other hand, the assessment of the conduct by which the user could have avoided the damage does not exclude *erga omnes* the existence of the defect, but has relevance limited to the relationship between the latter and the manufacturer, depending on the case, as an interrupting factor of the causal link or as a contributory negligence of the injured party, determining in the latter case a mere reduction of the compensation due by the manufacturer, on the assumption therefore that he is liable.

The rule in this sense, laid down in Art. 122(1) of the Consumer Code, is therefore incompatible with the criterion of the cheapest cost avoider, which could instead lead to the exclusion of the producer's liability even towards third parties damaged by the circulation of the vehicle, who are however completely uninvolved

---

[53] Albanese (2024a), cit., pp. 1022–1023.

[54] Cf. on this point the opinion of Rajneri (2016), p. 617, who correctly notes that equating the interests of the community with those of the parties involved … sometimes leads to results that clash with common feeling.

[55] For the complete elaboration of this rule Calabresi and Hirschoff (1972), pp. 1060 ff.

in the choices relating to the production and use of a good, which in hypothesis does not correspond to legitimate safety expectations.

Consistently, the European framework on general product safety defines 'safe' as that which, irrespective of a comparative assessment with those already existing on the market, 'presents no risk or only minimal risks [...] that are considered acceptable in accordance with a high level of protection for the health and safety of persons'.[56]

However, the defect concept outlined so far must also be related to the self-learning capability that specifically characterises intelligent products and enables them to evolve autonomously, drawing information directly from external reality, independently of updates installed under human control.[57]

With reference to these hypotheses, the manufacturer could abstractly invoke the exemption from liability provided for in Art. 120 of the Consumer Code when, having regard to the circumstances, it may be assumed that the defect that caused the damage did not exist when he put it into circulation or arose subsequently.[58]

However, such a conclusion would be incompatible with the aims of the aforementioned directive, which, while proposing the same grounds for exemption from liability,[59] also with a view to overcoming possible resistance in the social context to the introduction of these new technologies, aims to ensure the injured party a level of protection that is not less than that provided in the case of damage caused by traditional products.[60]

It is therefore possible (and necessary) to interpretatively adapt the meaning of the rule under consideration to the socially expected safety requirement. Indeed, given the characteristics of an Artificial Intelligence system, it is reasonable to expect it to develop its self-learning capacity to satisfy human needs, while avoiding harmful results for the user or third parties. In this sense, a product that, being intelligent, has been designed and manufactured without the appropriate provision of limits and operating 'blocks' to prevent uncontrolled and dangerous developments must be considered defective.[61]

According to this logic, precisely regarding such possible contingencies, the European Artificial Intelligence Regulation lays down specific duties for the supplier of high-risk systems, who must take organisational measures to monitor the functioning of the product after it has been placed on the market, to intervene promptly in the event of defects that have occurred.[62]

---

[56] Thus, Art. 103(1)(a) of the Consumer Code, which slavishly transposes into Italian law Art. 2(b) of Directive 95/2001, itself enacted to implement Art. 153 of the Treaty of the European Union.

[57] See Calvano and Calzolari (2021), cit., p. 6.

[58] Amidei (2020), p. 140.

[59] Thus, Art. 11(c), Directive (EU) 2653/2024.

[60] It emphasises that the exclusion of liability is contrary to the purpose of the directive Machnikowski (2020), p. 146.

[61] In this sense, see Amidei (2020), cit., p. 142 and Bertolini (2013), p. 235.

[62] In this regard, Art. 72, Regulation (EU) 2024/1689 requires that the post-market monitoring system be proportionate to the nature of the AI technologies and the risks of the high-risk AI sys-

On the other hand, the indemnity protection of persons harmed by the use of Artificial Intelligence is limited by the so-called development risk, which operates as a cause of exoneration of the producer's liability in cases where the state of scientific and technical knowledge available at the time when the product was put into circulation, pursuant to Art. 118(e) of the Civil Code, did not yet allow it to be considered defective.

This rule, in fact, excludes compensation for damage caused by products that, while not offering the safety that could legitimately be expected at the time they were marketed, turned out to be defective only in the light of knowledge acquired at a later date.

6 The Use of Artificial Intelligence as a Non-Hazardous Activity

In this regard, some scholars maintain that this gap in protection can be filled by Art. 2050 of the Civil Code about liability for the exercise of dangerous activities,[63] which is considered applicable to the cases at hand precisely because establishing a development risk would imply that the product is not safe.

The application of this rule, although abstractly allowed by the European directive, which leaves intact the rights that the injured party may exercise under the rules of contractual and non-contractual liability of each national legal system, cannot, however, be implemented automatically and indiscriminately. The lack of safety, in fact, especially if recognised only in the light of subsequent technical and scientific developments, cannot be equated per se with the dangerousness referred to in the rule of the Civil Code, which must instead be verified in the individual case and in relation to the characteristics of the activity concretely carried out using Artificial Intelligence in a non-occasional or sporadic manner.[64]

On the other hand, if this were considered dangerous in all cases where there is a risk from development, the rule of the Consumer Code, which provides for such a ground for exemption from liability, would inexplicably be abrogated by an earlier regulation which, moreover, having a broader scope of application, could not prevail even on the basis of a logical criterion of specialty.

---

tem. The regulation is expressly referred to in Art. 9, which lays down obligations to set up a risk management system.

[63] Ruffolo (2020). See also Procida Mirabelli di Lauro (2020), pp. 334–335.

[64] In this sense instead Ruffolo (2020), cit., p. 1697, according to which the very existence of a high development risk, i.e. the case in which the defect of the product derives from the non-observance of the technical knowledge absent at the time of its marketing, but which occurred (and which is capable of classifying it as defective) when that product is still on the market - could in itself constitute an indication, if not proof, of the dangerousness of the activity connoted by that risk, if particularly incidental in the case of smart products.

From the point of view of legal policy evaluations, moreover, this conclusion would lead to an excessive extension of producer liability, paradoxically ending up by hindering the introduction of technologically advanced tools, also designed and manufactured to enable these activities to be carried out in a safer (as well as more efficient) manner than the traditional ones.

An incentive to produce goods offering higher safety standards can, moreover, only operate where this result is concretely attainable on the basis of the technical and scientific knowledge available. However, it would be contradictory, on the one hand, to admit ex ante the development and trade of intelligent goods on the grounds of their greater reliability and lower risk of human error and, on the other hand, to assert ex post that they are intrinsically dangerous in the light of subsequent scientific discoveries.

By contrast, Art. 2050 of the Civil Code itself logically presupposes an activity that can be considered risky from the outset, where it excludes the liability of the person who, in exercising it, has taken all appropriate measures to prevent damage.

However, it does not seem possible to apply this rule to 'high risk' systems, considering that the adoption of the risk management measures imposed by the European regulation implies that the latter has been brought down to acceptable levels and that, vice versa, the failure to comply with such provisions, integrating in itself an organisational fault on the part of the supplier,[65] makes it possible to hold him responsible according to the general rule of Art. 2043 of the Civil Code, irrespective of Art. 2050 of the Civil Code, thus radically excluding the possibility of giving the exonerating proof provided for therein of having adopted all appropriate measures to avoid the damage.

Outside these cases, Artificial Intelligence, even if it introduces ex novo a risk factor, precisely because of the objectives it aims at, does not in itself make dangerous the activity in which it is used.

The more stringent rule of liability provided for in Art. 2050 of the Civil Code and the related evidentiary regime therefore only applies with respect to those activities that are dangerous due to their characteristics, where the use of intelligent systems is not sufficient to reduce their potential harmfulness within normal risk limits.

Conversely, the introduction of new and safer technologies may in some cases lead to an activity carried out with traditional tools that are now considered unsafe precisely because of the high risks involved in their use.

Where, moreover, the Artificial Intelligence system is set up to carry out acts that are intrinsically damaging,[66] its use, in addition to being prohibited and sanctioned ex ante, will entail the civil liability of all those who, by using it, have contributed to causing the damaging event.

---

[65] See above, para 3.

[66] Take, for example, AI practices that are considered unacceptable and, as such, prohibited in absolute terms by Art. 5, Regulation (EU) 2024/1689.

But, apart from such cases, what prompts one to consider (erroneously) risky the use of intelligent things is once again the autonomy that characterises their functioning, removing them from human control.[67] This characteristic, however, is not sufficient to rationally ground a judgement of the dangerousness of the technologies in question any more than it justifies it regarding the freedom that naturally characterises human actions.

7 The Functional Autonomy of Artificial Intelligence and the Liability of the 'Custodian'

Rather, the autonomy of the machine is to be considered from the point of view of the traceability of the damage to its operation, independent of human intervention.

From this point of view, Art. 2051 of the Civil Code may be applied, according to which 'everyone is liable for the damage caused by things he has in his custody, unless he proves a fortuitous event'. In fact, the machine or intelligent system, precisely because of its capacity for autonomous operation, may constitute the direct cause of the damage and not the instrument of harmful human conduct. In other words, the damage is caused not 'with' but 'by' the thing and therefore falls within the scope of Art. 2051 of the Civil Code insofar as it derives from the dynamism inherent in the thing or from the occurrence in it of a damaging agent, excluding the case that the thing constituted the mere means used to perform an autonomous action per se capable of causing the damage.

It is therefore an autonomous and distinct case of liability, involving negligent human conduct interacting with the intelligent system, and it can be characterised, depending on the circumstances, as contractual[68] or as non-contractual.[69]

However, the applicability of this discipline could not be questioned by pointing out that it was conceived with reference to 'traditional' things that, although endowed with autonomous dynamism, are nonetheless devoid of decision-making and self-learning capacities. This objection can in fact be easily overcome if we consider that, in the system outlined by the Civil Code, liability for damage caused by things in custody, both from the point of view of its historical origin and on a logical level, constitutes a generalisation of the more specific rule provided for by Art. 2052 of the Civil Code with regard to damage caused by animals, which are

[67] In this sense, Castronovo (2018), cit., p. 175, points out how recourse to liability for the exercise of dangerous activities represents a way of escaping the sharp and awkward antithesis between person and thing, which is posed to the interpreter in the qualification of Artificial Intelligence.

[68] This hypothesis occurs where the intelligent system has been used for the performance of an obligation, adversely affecting the performance offered to the creditor, who has thus been damaged not directly by the 'thing', but by the conduct of the debtor who made use of it.

[69] On this subject, see above, para 4.

also endowed with an intelligence different from human intelligence, although still natural and therefore characterised by a greater degree of unpredictability.[70]

Moreover, both rules establish the same objective criterion of imputation, which disregards the fault of the liable party and is limited by the fortuitous event, and their *rationale* is commonly found in the principle expressed by the proverb *cuius commoda eius et incommoda*, according to which the party who benefits from the use of the thing or animal must consistently bear any costs, including compensation.

From this perspective, therefore, it cannot be rationally excluded that the concept of 'thing', resulting from the systematic combination of Articles 2051 and 2052 of the Civil Code, *a fortiori* also includes robots and, more generally, Artificial Intelligence systems, which are indeed capable of autonomously performing their activities, but always according to pre-established programs. For the purposes of liability, therefore, what matters is not the noun 'intelligence' but the adjective 'artificial', which allows it to be assimilated to other 'things' produced by man.[71]

In these cases, too, the justifying reason for the rule exists, whereby the person who makes use of the thing, exercising a de facto power over it, must be objectively responsible for the harmful consequences arising therefrom.

In this regard, it does not seem acceptable the objection, according to which the capacity for autonomous functioning of things with Artificial Intelligence would not allow one to find a person who could be blamed for failing to preserve or maintain these things.[72]

In fact, the liability provided by Art. 2051 of the Civil Code is not based on the breach of a legal duty of surveillance,[73] which could enable us to assess, in terms of negligent omission, the conduct of the custodian, who is instead liable on the basis of the mere factual relationship linking him to the thing that caused the damage.[74] The omissive conduct of the custodian, in fact, even if it assumes relevance on a merely factual level as the cause of the damage, it is not, however, the criterion of imputation pursuant to Art. 2051 of the Civil Code, since it is not contemplated in this article among the constituent elements of the case of liability.

This must therefore be distinguished from the liability arising from the breach of duties that the EU Artificial Intelligence Regulation imposes on the user of high-risk

---

[70] On this point, see Ruffolo (2020), cit., p. 99.

[71] For further arguments to this effect, see Bertolini (2022), cit., pp. 370–371.

[72] Against the application of Art. 2051 of the Civil Code, Costanza (2020), p. 414, according to which the harmful action of Artificial Intelligence does not depend on improper maintenance or use, since, if it is the efficient cause, the search for the responsible party must reasonably be traced back to its intrinsic defectiveness, or to its own defective and insecure mind.

[73] In contrast, Santarpia (2018), p. 1237, considers that the rule is applicable when the harm occurs as a function of the man's lack of supervision.

[74] Cass., sez. un., 30 June 2022, no. 20943. Laghezza (2016), pp. 3162 ff., appropriately points out that the only prerequisites for applying Art. 2051 of the Civil Code are custody and the derivation of the damage from the thing.

systems and which, in the event of damage, constitutes a concurrent liability, based on an organisational fault criterion.[75]

In this second case, however, the culpable title of the user's liability may be relevant for the purpose of apportioning the cost of compensation in relation to other jointly and severally liable parties (e.g. the producer).[76]

But irrespective of the violation of specific regulatory requirements, the mere use of the smart thing abstractly contributes to creating a risk, and it is therefore fair that the cost of any damage should be borne by those who take advantage of it.

The rule under consideration, however, does not necessarily imply the absence of any human conduct in the damaging event, as it can also be configured when this assumes a non-exclusive role with respect to other causal factors directly linked to the autonomous functioning of the thing.[77]

If, in fact, the prerequisite of Art. 2051 of the Civil Code is mere de facto power over the thing, irrespective of its legal availability; this factual situation of 'custody' cannot, however, be resolved in the mere enjoyment or use of the good, in the absence of any possibility of interference in its destination.[78]

In this sense, a doctor,[79] for instance, who works as an auxiliary of a health facility and who, because of a business choice made by others, uses the intelligent machine for certain activities of diagnosis and treatment of patients, cannot be considered a custodian. He may therefore be liable for fault, but certainly not based on an objective criterion of imputation as custodian.[80]

On the other hand, the liability of the custodian is borne by the person who, irrespective of the ownership of a right, has full de facto availability of the thing, being able in concrete terms to permit or prevent its use, and has thereby contributed to generating the abstract risk that has materialised in the damage to be compensated, irrespective of any assessment of his subjective conduct.[81]

---

[75] See above, para 3.

[76] See below, para 10.

[77] Cass. 12 July 2022, no. 21977.

[78] Cassation 10 August 2004 no. 15429 and Cassation 30 November 2005 no. 26086 refer to the control of the way the thing is used and stored as characteristic elements of 'custody'.

[79] D'Adda (2022), p. 815, attributes this liability to the business risk, thus excluding that this case can be configured with respect to a doctor who makes use of a machine entrusted to him by a hospital in performance of a work contract concluded with the latter.

[80] This conclusion is confirmed by Art. 7, para 3, Law No. 24 of 8 March 2017 (Provisions on the safety of care and the assisted person, as well as on the professional liability of healthcare professionals), according to which the healthcare professional... is liable for his or her actions pursuant to Art. 2043 of the Civil Code, unless he or she has acted in the performance of a contractual obligation undertaken with the patient.

[81] In this regard, Salvi (1988), p. 1227, points out that the legislative datum does not require, for the purposes of imputation, either the inclusion of the thing in an organised economic activity, or its particular dangerousness, it being sufficient the existence of the relationship of custody between the person responsible and the thing that gave rise to the damaging event. A somewhat different opinion is expressed by Comporti (1965), who, while ascribing the provision of Art. 2051 of the Civil Code to the category of objective liability, sees its rationale in the creation of a situation of

In this sense, the guardians of the Artificial Intelligence system must be the owner and the people appointed by him, who can influence its operation and possibly prohibit its use. To them must also be equated the possible trainer who, having the task of controlling and directing the evolution of the machine during the cycle of its existence, can determine its choices. Therefore, without prejudice to his possible liability 'for fault' pursuant to Art. 2043 of the Civil Code, he may also be held liable for damages on the basis of the objective position of a custodian, with the limit of fortuitous events.

According to this rule, the injured party does not need to prove that the thing in custody was defective or dangerous,[82] while the defect of the product or its dangerousness constitutes instead the prerequisites for the different (and possibly concomitant) liability of the producer or of the person carrying out dangerous activities examined above.

The different rules applicable in this case, however, referring to the same harmful event, do not lead to an accumulation of damages, but give rise to a concurrence of actions that, as will be seen, the injured party may bring, depending on the case, against the same or different parties.

The custodian may, however, be released from liability by proving the existence of a specific, objectively unforeseeable and unavoidable interruptive factor in the causal link,[83] which takes the form of a 'fortuitous event' outside his sphere of risk.[84]

Scholars and judges moreover substantially agree in excluding a merely subjective notion of fortuitous event, as any cause not depending on the fault of the custodian.[85] Consistent, in fact, with the objective nature of the liability in question, which disregards an assessment of the conduct of the liable party,[86] the relevant lack of foreseeability does not concern the damaging event, which excludes fault,[87] but is

---

danger, from which the damage was derived. Franzoni (2010), p. 440, and Monateri (1998), p. 1038, have also expressed themselves in favour of the objective nature of liability for things in custody.

[82] The literal wording of the rule, corroborated by legal comparison, excludes that the liability of the custodian can in any way be linked to profiles of non-compliance of the thing with the normatively or socially required safety standards, as Belfiore (2018), p. 1580 footnote 82, seems to believe.

[83] On this notion, see recently Court of Cassation no. 3739 of 8 February 2023.

[84] As Belfiore (2018), cited above, p. 1580 at footnote 82, the fortuitous event does not result in a mere interruptive factor of the causal link, but implies a further value judgement of a different kind.

[85] In this sense, see, for all, Salvi (1988), cit., p. 1230 and Monateri (1998), p. 1059. In case law, among many others, see Cass. 13 January 2015, no. 295 and Cass. 21 November 2014, no. 24845.

[86] On the contrary, Santarpia (2018), cit., p. 1242, considers that the custodian can free himself from liability by proving that his conduct is free from fault. But the identification between fortuitous event and no fault is erroneous since the former implies the latter, but not vice versa. In this sense see also Di Rosa (2013), pp. 98–99.

[87] On the extraneousness of liberating evidence to the scope of fault, Scognamiglio (1968). In case law, see Cass. 1 February 2018, no. 2477.

linked to the extraordinary nature of the supervening event, which enters the causal series, interrupting it.[88]

The causal link, the interruption of which must be proved, is not that which links the damage to subjective conduct,[89] but has directly in the thing in custody its initial term of reference.[90]

Moreover, in the event of doubt as to the causal traceability of the damage to negligent human conduct or to an objective defect in the safety of the product, the application of this rule simplifies the injured party's procedural choices, allowing him to assert the liability of the custodian in the first instance, as an immediately identifiable subject, leaving this one with the burden of deciding whether and against whom to act in recourse among the various co-responsible subjects. The victim will thus be able to avoid the embarrassment of having to choose whether to sue only one of them, risking that the judge will hold another liable, or to act against all of them, aggravating the court costs, which, at least in the first instance, he will have to bear.[91]

Furthermore, this regulation also strengthens the protection of the injured party in terms of patrimonial guarantees, giving priority to his interest in compensation over that of those who, deriving benefit from Artificial Intelligence and exercising, albeit without fault, a de facto power over it, must consistently bear the risk that the damage caused by its malfunctioning will not be concretely compensated by the manufacturer or other (jointly) liable party.[92]

Far from being anachronistic, 'custodian' liability that has its origins in Roman law continues to play a central role in the system of allocating the (primary and secondary) costs of damage.

Such a rule, moreover, cannot constitute a real disincentive to using intelligent tools, since, on the contrary, failure to use them could constitute culpable conduct due to failure to comply with technical rules relating to the profession practised, which attest ex ante to the greater safety of new technologies on the basis of comparative risk assessments.

From this point of view, the use of Artificial Intelligence does not offer a convenient expedient to escape liability for damages, which would otherwise be imputed to the human agent.

---

[88] On the extraneousness of exculpatory evidence to the scope of fault, see Court of Cassation 1 December 2022, no. 35429.

[89] The assertion of Costanza (2020), cited above, p. 414, which bases the liability under consideration on the failure to control or to preserve the thing in custody, cannot therefore be accepted.

[90] See in this sense, with specific reference to self-driving cars, Albanese (2019), cit., p. 1013.

[91] For similar considerations regarding liability for damage caused by vehicles, see Albanese (2019), cit., p. 1006.

[92] From this point of view, the current rules on jointly and severally liability, being able to leverage the assets of a plurality of parties, constitute a remedy with a greater degree of effectiveness than the proposal, formulated by Bertolini (2022), cited above, pp. 401 ff., to identify a single party as the entry point, addressee of actions for damages, leaving to this party the task of acting in recourse against the other parties responsible, who have contributed to causing the damage. It is in fact clear that if such a person were insolvent, the indemnity protection could not be realised, as it could he could easily escape liability.

Custodian liability, however, unlike vicarious liability, does not presuppose a judgment on (actual or potential) human conduct, nor does it provide for a right of recourse against another party who has caused the damage. Neither of these aspects is present, moreover, in cases involving damages caused by Artificial Intelligence systems independently of human intervention, where liability is instead assessed based on the risk situation objectively created by the user (or custodian)., who is liable for the relevant damaging realisations, appears more appropriate, unless he proves that their causal derivation from the autonomous functioning of the intelligent thing was interrupted by a fortuitous event.

It is also clear that this provision grants the injured party a higher level of protection than that which they would enjoy if they had to prove that the harmful event was due to negligent human conduct attributable directly to the person responsible or to one of his assistants.

However, the liability of the custodian as such cannot determine the final allocation of the cost of the damage in cases where a malfunction objectively attributable to the producer has occurred.

If this were left to the user, the preventive function of liability would not be efficiently realised. For one thing, the custodian is not the party best placed to prevent damage resulting from a defect in the intelligent system. On the other hand, it is the manufacturer who is best placed to carry out an efficient cost-benefit analysis.

On the other hand, the sole and final liability of the custodian could be a disincentive to the use of AI and an obstacle to technological progress.

In this sense, the liability of the producer is more efficient, against whom the custodian may take recourse where the damage has resulted from a defect in the product.[93]

8 Why Tort Liability Cannot Be Directly Assigned to Artificial Intelligence as a Legal Person

The presence of this rule, moreover, renders useless any attempts to configure liability for the act of other persons on the basis of a questionable anthropomorphic view, which equates the automatic operation of the machine with the human conduct of an auxiliary.[94] Pursuant to Art. 2049 of the Civil Code, in fact, the fact of 'servants and employees' is imputed to their 'masters and principals' not because of the intelligence with which they are endowed, but because of the legal subjectivity inherent in them as human beings, which allows their conduct to be qualified, from a moral point of view before even before the legal point of view, as a voluntary or negligent

[93] On this point, see below, para 10.

[94] This is Karner's (2019) reconstruction, p. 120, according to which no one can escape the rule on vicarious liability by employing technical instruments in place of any helpers.

offence.[95] In this sense, vicarious liability is based on an assessment of human conduct (actual or hypothetical), which cannot be assimilated to the criterion of imputation of custodian liability, which instead implies the mere existence of a causal link between the autonomous functioning of the thing and the damage. It is precisely this finding of unlawfulness that justifies, moreover, the principal's right of recourse against the employee who caused the damage, further differentiating the treatment of the two hypotheses in our legal system.

The idea of recognising the legal personality of intelligent robots,[96] endowing them with autonomous assets[97] (or suitable insurance coverage) with which they could be liable for possible damage to third parties[98] has so far lacked the necessary legislative implementation.

Such a solution would, however, imply a choice of legal policy that cannot be fully justified in terms of rationality and consistency with our legal system which, according to a clear anthropocentric approach, characterises entities endowed with legal subjectivity (associations, foundations, companies, etc.) essentially by reason of the necessary dependence—for the exercise of their activity—on the intervention of natural persons, who act as their organs. The acts performed by them are therefore part of, and governed by, relations between human beings that serve to indirectly and mediately satisfy their interests. Thus, if it is true that the rights owned by an association cannot be considered to belong to its members even in the form of a community, it is also true that the ownership of the collective entity translates into a series of rights, obligations and powers of its members and third parties, who for various reasons enter into relations with it.

On the other hand, a similar human substratum would be lacking in the case of the personification of robots and intelligent machines, which are created to operate without the need for organic identification with the natural person,[99] who is not the means but the end to which Artificial Intelligence immediately and directly tends.

---

[95] Castronovo (2024), pp. 143–144, emphasises the defect of will and in any case of self-consciousness as characteristics that prevent the adoption of categories such as guilt and voluntary misconduct, but raises the question of whether, in the absence of culpable conduct, one can still think of a liability for the act of others, even if not configurable as a tort.

[96] On this issue, see Teubner (2019). Similarly, Leanza (2021), cit., p. 1021, considers that the responsibility for the damage caused should no longer be of the manufacturer, but of the robot itself, thus recognising the legal personality of the machine to make it responsible for its actions, to reconcile the safety needs of the system with technological evolution.

[97] In this sense, the European Parliament resolution of 16 February 2017 on recommendations to the Commission concerning civil law rules on robotics, while noting that, at least at the current stage, liability must be of a human being and not of a robot, recommended the establishment of a specific legal status for robots in the long term, so that at least the most sophisticated autonomous robots can be considered as electronic persons responsible for any damage caused by them.

[98] In favour of this possibility, Fazio (2023), pp. 166 ff.

[99] As, on the other hand, Kelsen (1934), p. 19, notes, the presence of a psychic will, however attributable to the human being, is an essential characteristic of legal persons.

The latter, therefore, also from the point of view of liability for damage caused to third parties, consistently assumes relevance as the product or instrument of a human activity and not as the author of a tort.

9 The Potential Concurrence of Different Forms of Liability

Liability for custody may be concurrent with producer liability where the damage caused by the autonomous functioning of Artificial Intelligence manifests a safety defect. This causal series may also include a dangerous activity carried out by means of the use of the intelligent machine and/or other voluntary or negligent conduct of the user of the machine, which contributed to causing the harmful event.

Therefore, if the constituent elements of the different cases exist, the injured party may alternatively bring an action, on the basis of the respective disciplines, against each of the jointly liable parties.

Joint and several liability, in fact, according to the dominant opinion in Italian jurisprudence and doctrine, does not necessarily imply a single damaging fact; the uniqueness of the damaging event resulting from a plurality of conduct being sufficient for this purpose. Although the rule of the Civil Code textually refers to a 'harmful event attributable to several people', it is commonly held that there is no need for a single joint action of the various competitors, but that autonomous cases of liability may concur in causing the same damage, depending on the case, by fault or strict liability.[100]

A similar conclusion may also be drawn, independently of an extensive interpretation of Art. 2055 of the Civil Code, on the basis of the general rules on causality. Indeed, where facts subjectively or objectively attributable to several persons must be considered—from a legal as well as a naturalistic point of view—to be the cause of the same harmful event, each of those responsible will be obliged to compensate the entire damage, with consequences substantially corresponding to those of joint and several liability.[101]

Moreover, this is a solution that satisfies a need for greater protection of the injured party, in that on the one hand it broadens the number of parties incentivised to prevent damage, and on the other hand it mitigates the difficulties of determining, in the exercise of their compensation claims, the origin of the harmful event and its traceability to a specific liable party, thus achieving in both respects an objective expressly pursued by the European institutions on.[102]

---

[100] In doctrine, see for all Scognamiglio (1968), p. 652 and in case law, Cass., sec. un., 15 July 2009, no. 16503 and Cass. 21 June 2013, no. 15687. To the contrary, however, Castronovo (2018), cit., pp. 375 ff. Also in US common law, the prerequisite for contributory liability is the uniqueness of the damage and not of the conduct: see Fleming (1983), pp. 175 ff. On the different solutions adopted in European legal systems, von Bar (1998), pp. 70 ff.

[101] Albanese (2019), cited above, p. 1037.

[102] On this subject, see D'Adda (2022), cit. p. 827.

If, however, the negligent conduct of the holder/user of an intelligent defective product has contributed to causing damage to other people's property, Art. 122, para 3 of the Civil Code, by derogating from the rule of joint and several liability for the entire damage provided for by Art. 2055 of the Civil Code, establishes that the compensation due by the producer is reduced on the basis of the same criteria that apply in the different hypothesis of fault of the injured party provided for by Art. 1227, para 1 of the Civil Code. On the contrary, this exception does not apply to personal injuries, for which the manufacturer, according to Art. 121, para 1 of the Civil Code, will be fully liable, jointly and severally with the person who has culpably contributed to causing them.

10 The Apportionment of Compensation in the Internal Relations Between the Parties Jointly and Severally Liable

In these cases, the problem arises of identifying a criterion according to which the cost of compensation may be allocated in internal relationships between subjects, who are indeed jointly and severally liable, but based on different types of liability, not always based on fault. Accordingly, the aim is to assess which criteria drawn from positive law permit a just and efficient distribution of damages.

In this respect it does not appear that a satisfactory solution can be drawn from the rule provided for, in the matter of producer liability, by Art. 122(2) of the Code of Civil Procedure, which, while assuming a plurality of parties liable in various capacities, to determine the extent of the right of recourse of the one who has compensated the entire damage against the other jointly liable parties, attributes relevance to the size of the risk objectively referable to each, as well as to the gravity of the faults and the entity of the consequences resulting therefrom, but does not establish the 'specific weight' of each criterion with respect to the others.[103] The question, therefore, remains unresolved as to how a comparative assessment can be made among elements that are heterogeneous and therefore not susceptible to providing unequivocal indications as to the share of compensation to be borne by the various co-responsible parties.[104]

Since it is impossible to proceed to a graduation of the respective responsibilities in internal relations, the damage would always be apportioned in equal measure, as provided for by the rule itself, with reference to doubtful cases.[105] But this would

[103] On this point, you can see Albanese (2019), cit., p. 1040.

[104] On the impossibility of a quantitative comparison between heterogeneous entities such as fault and strict liability, see Trimarchi (1961), p. 304.

[105] This solution had already been formulated regarding similar situations by Scognamiglio (1968), cited above, p. 653, who proposed to extend by analogy to joint and several strict liability Art. 2055, section 3, Civil Code, whereby in case of doubt the individual faults are presumed to be equal.

mean attributing to the provision, dictated for residual hypotheses, an exclusive and all-encompassing application that does not concern it, standardising the discipline of situations that, instead, according to the intentions of the law, should 'as a rule' be treated differently.[106]

Nor does the doctrine seem correct that, in the case of different titles of liability, in domestic relations, the cost of the damage must always fall entirely on the party liable for fault, through a simplified and reductive reading of Art. 2055, section 2, of the Civil Code, which recognises that the party who has compensated for the entire damage has the right of recourse against each of the other jointly and severally liable parties, to the extent determined by the gravity of their respective negligence.[107]

First, this decision criterion could not even be applied if the damage was caused exclusively by concurrent cases of objective liability, which are independent of an assessment of the conduct of the concurring parties in terms of fault.[108]

But even in other cases, to make only the guilty subjects responsible would mean distorting the letter and the rationale of the law, ignoring the significant differences that may exist between the various cases of strict liability.

The attribution of the cost of the damage to the guilty person is in fact admissible only when the strict liability of the other responsible party has essentially a function of financial guarantee or of facilitation of the procedural position of the injured party, as occurs in the case of 'custody' responsibility of the owner or user of the intelligent machine or of any other person who exercises a mere de facto power over it, regardless of any evaluation of his subjective conduct.[109] In fact, as noted, this rule, while attributing relevance to the risk introduced by the custodian, does not have a preventive purpose, but serves to strengthen and make more effective the protection of the injured party on a substantial level, extending the patrimonial guarantee offered by the liable parties, and, from a procedural point of view, shifting onto the custodian the expenses and risks relating to ascertaining the causes of the harmful event, the cost of which is however destined to be borne definitively by the producer and/or any other party who culpably contributed to causing it.[110]

Obviously, a different assessment will have to be made in cases where the user of the Artificial Intelligence system is concretely attributable to the breach of organisational duties provided for by the AI Act.[111] Such negligent conduct will, in fact, take on relevance in determining, on the basis of its seriousness pursuant to Art. 2055, para 2, of the Civil Code, the share of compensation to be borne by him in internal relationships with the other people who are jointly and severally liable.

---

[106] See to that effect Albanese (2019), cit., p. 1041.

[107] De Cupis (1979), p. 181.

[108] Thus Salvi (<1988), cit., p. 1255.

[109] Similar considerations in Albanese (2019), cit., p. 1042.

[110] See above, para 7.

[111] See above, para 3.

But even in these cases, it would be neither fair nor appropriate to hold the negligent person, where there are cases of strict liability, who performs a similar preventive function with respect to the occurrence of potentially harmful events.

For instance, it cannot be doubted that the manufacturer of an Artificial Intelligence system or whoever developed the software or the algorithm regulating its autonomous operation must bear pro rata the cost of the damage it has caused with the (concretely) negligent complicity of a third user.

In such a case, given the impossibility of comparing fault and strict liability in terms of lesser or greater seriousness, the compensation can only be apportioned based on the contribution that each case has objectively made to the production of the damage.

The same conclusion must also be reached where all concurrent cases concern strict liability (e.g. in the case of several producers of defective components).

It is clear, however, that from a logical point of view, the various causal factors must all be considered equivalent ex post since, in the absence of each of them, the harm would not have occurred. The extent to which each factor contributed ex ante to increasing the risk must therefore be considered for the purposes of internal damages allocation.

In this sense, the defective functioning of the intelligent product will constitute, together with the possible negligent conduct of the user, the object of a judgment aimed at establishing the extent to which each of these causal antecedents has contributed to increasing the risk of damaging events of the same type as the one that materialised.[112]

11 Conclusions

Consistent with the aim of making the use of Artificial Intelligence safer, the cost of compensation will thus be borne exclusively by those who, among those jointly and severally liable, could have played a role in preventing the harmful event, regardless of whether this is attributable to them on an objective or negligent basis.

Through the recourse action, on the other hand, those persons who could not have prevented it (for example the blameless user) will be exempted from the burden of compensation, but who are responsible for the sole purpose of strengthening the protection of the injured parties, also because the former are better able than the latter to identify the various 'producers' that have contributed to creating the 'intelligent system', to whom the damage caused by its defective operation must be definitively borne.

This discipline, on the one hand, guarantees the effectiveness of compensation without disincentivising the 'demand' for Artificial Intelligence and, on the other

[112] This is the solution proposed in Albanese (2019), cit., p. 1043. In a similar vein, Trimarchi (1990), cit., pp. 448 ff., but with exclusive reference to strict liability.

hand, encourages the 'supply' of safer technology, within the limits allowed by the scientific knowledge available at the time the product is put into circulation.

References

Albanese A (2019) La responsabilità civile per i danni da circolazione di veicoli ad elevata automazione. Eur Dir Priv, pp 1006, 1013, 1014–1018, 1020, 1022–1023, 1037, 1040–1043
Albanese A (2023) Mobilità del futuro e funzione preventiva della responsabilità civile. Eur Dir Priv, pp 442–443
Albanese A (2024a) Digitalizzazione delle cure e intelligenza artificiale: i nuovi obblighi verso i pazienti. In: Il Sole 24 Ore online, 14 giugno
Albanese A (2024b) Le categorie del diritto privato alla prova delle nuove tecnologie. Contratto e torto nell'economia digitale. In: Nuovo diritto civile, p 12
Amidei A (2020) Intelligenza artificiale e responsabilità da prodotto. In: Ruffolo U (ed) Intelligenza artificiale: il diritto, i diritti, l'etica. Milano, pp 140, 142
Baldwin R, Cave M, Lodge M (2012) Understanding regulation: theory, strategy, and practice. Oxford University Press Oxford, pp. 20 ff
Belfiore A (2018) Responsabilità (Struttura del giudizio e prestazione risarcitoria). In: Le parole del diritto. Scritti in onore di Carlo Castronovo, III, Napoli, p. 1580 nota 82
Bertolini A (2013) Robots as products: the case for a realistic analysis of Robotic applications and liability rules. Law Innov Technol 5(2):235
Bertolini A (2022) Artificial Intelligence does not exist! Defying the technology-neutrality narrative in the regulation of civil liability for advanced technologies. Eur Dir Priv pp 370–371, 416 ff
Calabresi G (1970) The cost of accidents: a legal and economic analysis. Cambridge University Press, New Haven, pp 47 ff
Calabresi G (1975) Optimal deterrence and accidents. Yale Law J 84:666
Calabresi G, Hirschoff JT (1972) Toward a test for strict liability in torts. Yale Law J 81:1055 ff
Calabresi G, Al Mureden E (2021) Driverless Cars. Intelligenza artificiale e futuro della mobilità. Bologna, p 29
Calvano E, Calzolari G (2021) AI and policy: what makes AI different? Economic Policy, pp 6–7 https://academic.oupcom/economicpolicy/advance-article/doi/10.1093/epolic/eiae067/7951937
Carnevali U (1990) Art. 1. Responsabilità del produttore. In: La responsabilità per danno da prodotti difettosi. Milano, p 6
Castronovo C (2018) Responsabilità civile. Milano, pp 897 ff
Castronovo C (2021) Diritto positivo dogmatica e teoria generale nella responsabilità oggettiva. In: Eur Dir Priv, p 687
Castronovo C (2024) Dogmatica del diritto. Milano, pp 145 ff
Coase RH (1960) The problem of social cost. J Law Econ 3:44 ff
Comporti M (1965) Esposizione al pericolo e responsabilità civile. Napoli, pp 1 ff
Costanza M (2020) L'AI: De iure condito e de iure condendo. In: Ruffolo U (ed) Intelligenza artificiale: il diritto, i diritti, l'etica. Milano, pp 414 ff
D'Adda A (2022) Danni da robot (specie in ambito sanitario) e pluralità di soggetti responsabili tra sistema della responsabilità civile ed iniziative di diritto europeo. Riv Dir Civ pp 815 ff
De Cupis A (1979) Il danno, III edn. II. Milano, p 181
De Mari Casareto Dal Verme T (2024) Intelligenza artificiale e responsabilità civile. Napoli, pp 227 ff
Di Rosa G (1999) Linee di tendenza e prospettive in tema di responsabilità del prestatore di servizi. Eur Dir Priv, pp 725–726
Di Rosa G (2013) Problemi di diritto privato, II ed. Torino, pp 98–99

Evas T (2018) A common EU approach to liability rules and insurance for connected and autonomous vehicles. European Added value Assessment, p 33
Fazio E (2023) Intelligenza artificiale e diritti della persona. Napoli, p 166 ff
Finocchiaro G (2012) Intelligenza artificiale e responsabilità. In: Contr. e impr., II, p 731
Fleming J G (1983) The Law of Torts. VI ed., Sydney, p 175 ff
Franzoni M (2010) L'illecito. In: Tratt. resp. civ., II ed., I, Milano, p 440
Franzoni M (2025) Danni da intelligenza artificiale. In: Albanese A, Guffanti Pesenti L, Tommasi S (edited by), Il diritto privato nell'economia digitale. Tutele giurisdizionali e autorità indipendenti, Torino, p 203
Gehuchte D van de (2000) Productaansprakelijkheid in Belgiëi. Gent, p 37
Karner E (2019) Liability for Robotics: Current Rules, Challenges and the Need for Innovative Concepts. In: Lohsse S, Schulze R, Staudenmayer D (eds.), Liability for Artificial Intelligence and the Internet of Things, Baden-Baden, p 120
Kelsen H (1934) Reine Rechtslehre. Wien, pp 23 ff
Koch B A (2020) Liability for Emerging Digital Technologies: An Overview. In: JETL, 11, n.2, p 122
Laghezza P (2016) Responsabilità da cose in custodia e fortuito soggettivo. In: Foro it., p 3162 ff
Leanza C (2021) Intelligenza artificiale e diritto: ipotesi di responsabilità civile del terzo millennio. In: Resp. civ. prev., p 1021
Loi M L (1989) Art.5 Prodotto difettoso. In: Le nuove leggi civ. comm., p 545 ff
Machnikowski P (2020) Producers' Liability in the EC Expert Group Report on Liability for AI. In: Journal of European Tort Law, 11, n.2, p 146
Marchant G E et al. (2011) The Growing Gap Between Emerging Technologies and Legal-Ethical Oversight: The Pacing Problem. Berlin
Mataja V (1888) Das Rechtdes Schadensersatzes vom Standpunkte der Nationalökonomie. Leipzig, p 19 ff
Mengoni L (1985) Ancora sul metodo giuridico. In: Diritto e valori, Bologna, p 90 ff
Mengoni L (2011) La questione del «diritto giusto» nella società post-liberale. In: Castronovo C, Albanese A, Nicolussi A (edited by), Scritti I. Metodo e teoria giuridica, Milano, p 65 ss
Monateri P G (1998) La responsabilità civile. Le fonti delle obbligazioni, III. In: Tratt. dir. civ., Torino, p 1059
Montinaro R (2020) Responsabilità da prodotto difettoso e tecnologie digitali tra soft law e hard law. In: Pers. merc., p 372
Mulgan R (2000) 'Accountability': An Ever-Expanding Concept? In: Public administration, p 558
Owen D G (2008) Products Liability. II ed., West Academic Publishing, p 1134 ff
Parenzo B (2022) Profilazione e discriminazione: dal GDPR alla proposta di regolamento sull'intelligenza artificiale. In: Camardi C (edited by), La via europea per l'intelligenza artificiale, Padova, p 335 ff
Procida Mirabelli di Lauro A (2020) Le intelligenze artificiali tra responsabilità civile e sicurezza sociale. In: Perlingieri P, Giova S, Prisco I (edited by), Rapporti civilistici e intelligenze artificiali: attività e responsabilità, Napoli, p 334–335
Rajneri E (2016) Prodotto difettoso. In: Dig. disc. priv. (sez. civ.) Agg., p 617
Ruffolo U (2019) Intelligenza artificiale machine learning e responsabilità da algoritmo. In: Giur. it., p 1690
Ruffolo U (2020) Intelligenza artificiale: il diritto, i diritti, l'etica. Milano, pp 1 ff
Salanitro U (2020) Intelligenza artificiale e responsabilità: la strategia della commissione europea. In: Riv. dir. civ., p 1246 ff
Salvi C (1988) entry Responsabilità extracontrattuale (dir. vig.). In Enc. del dir., XXXIX, Mi-lano, p 1203 ff
Santarpia D (2018) Un'indagine subiettiva sulla responsabilità da custodia. In: Resp. civ. e prev., p 1237
Schellekens M (2015) Self-driving cars. In: Comput. Law Secur. Rev., 31, p 510

Scognamiglio R (1968) Responsabilità per colpa e responsabilità oggettiva. In: Studi in memoria di A. Torrente, II, Milano, p 652
Scognamiglio R (2023) Intelligenza artificiale e responsabilità civile. Eur Dir Priv pp 433 ff
Stapleton J (1994) Product Liability. Butterworths, p 234-236
Tarello G (1980) L'interpretazione della legge. Milano
Teubner G (2019) Soggetti giuridici digitali? Sullo stato giuridico degli agenti software autonomi. Napoli
Tommasi S (2023) Digital Services Act e Artificial Intelligence Act: tentativi di futuro da armonizzare. In: Pers. merc., p 293
Trimarchi P (1961) Rischio e responsabilità oggettiva. Milano, p 304
Trimarchi R (1990) Categorie giuridiche e scienza del diritto civile. Milano, pp 55 ff
von Bar C (1998) The common European law of tort, I. Clarendon Press, Oxford, p 70 ff

Civil Liability for Infringement of Intellectual and Industrial Property Rights

Francesca Morri

Contents

Abstract In the event of infringement of intellectual property rights by users of online platforms, the platform operator may be the recipient of an injunction order even if 'non-responsible'. On the other hand, for the compensation of damages, in the application of the liability rules provided for in the e-commerce provisions, different solutions have been envisaged depending on the role of the platform and the knowledge of the illegal activities.

F. Morri (✉)
Catholic University of the Sacred Heart of Milan, Milan, Italy
e-mail: francesca.morri@unicatt.it

R. Bocchini (ed.), *Digital Platforms - From Technical Foundations to Legal and Economic Implications*, https://doi.org/10.1007/978-3-032-07978-7_18

1 Introductory Remarks

As is well known, Intellectual and Industrial Property rights[1] consist of the faculty to use the subject matter of the right under exclusive rights, which may consist of a distinctive sign[2] or a creation of an intellectual nature having as its object a technical innovation (such as patents for inventions[3] and utility models[4] and new plant

---

[1] In this work the term Intellectual Property will be used to refer to both Intellectual Property and Industrial Property, following the terminology of European Union law and the most recent international treaties (see, for example, the TRIPS Treaty signed in Marrakesh on 15 April 1994 and Directive 2004/48/EC of the European Parliament and of the Council of 29 April 2004 on the enforcement of intellectual property rights—henceforth, also the Enforcement Directive), which simply speak of Intellectual Property Rights.

[2] The most important distinctive signs are the trademarks, consisting of 'any signs, in particular words, including personal names, drawings, letters, numerals, sounds, the shape of goods or of the packaging of goods, colours or combinations of colours [...], provided that they are capable of distinguishing the goods or services of an undertaking from those of other undertakings' (Art. 7, Legislative Decree No. 30 of 10 February 2005—c.p.i.—and, in substantially the same terms, Art. 4 Regulation (EU) 2017/1001 on the European Union Trade mark). The proprietor of a trademark has the right to prohibit third parties from using in their economic activity signs identical for goods identical to those for which the trademark has been registered, or signs even only similar to the registered trademark in relation to identical or similar goods, where this leads to a likelihood of confusion or association for the public. Where the trademark enjoys a reputation, the proprietor may prohibit the use of identical or similar signs in relation to goods or services that are not similar, where such use would allow a third party to take unfair advantage of, or be detrimental to, the distinctive character or reputation of the trademark. For a more detailed discussion on the regulation of trademarks and other distinctive signs, see Vanzetti et al. (2021), pp. 147 ff.; Ricolfi (2015).

[3] The patent for invention grants the holder, for the 20 years following the filing date of the application and subject to the limitations set out in Art. 68 IPC, the 'exclusive right to implement the invention and to profit from it' (Art. 66 IPC). The subject of the patent is therefore the '*invention*', a concept for which there is no normative definition, but only, in Art. 45 IPC, a catalogue of what cannot be included in it. This lack of normative definition is compensated for by scholars, which unanimously define an invention as an 'original solution to a technical problem' (Vanzetti et al. 2021, p. 387) 'reproducible with constant results by an expert in the field, by means of an activity that is merely executive of the teachings provided by the applicant in his patent application' (Ghidini and Cavani 2022, p. 3).

[4] The patent for a utility model protects, for 10 years from the date of filing of the application and in the same way as a patent for an invention (to which Art. 86 of the IPC makes explicit reference), 'new models capable of conferring particular efficacy or convenience of application or use on machines, or parts thereof, instruments, tools or objects of use in general, such as new models consisting of particular conformations, arrangements, configurations or combinations of parts' (Art. 82 of the IPC). See Vanzetti et al. (2021), pp. 527 ff., for an in-depth examination of the IP right at issue.

varieties[5]), the appearance of a product (industrial designs[6]) or an artistic/cultural work (copyright on creative works and related rights, such as those of singers and actors on their performances, or broadcasters on their broadcasts[7]).

The rights in question are mainly governed at national level by Legislative Decree No. 30/2005 (Industrial Property Code or c.p.i.) and by Law No. 633 of 22 April 1941 on copyright (l.d.a.), to which is added, on the subject of audiovisual rights on sports events, Legislative Decree No. 9 of 9 January 2008 (the so-called Melandri Law).[8]

The discipline has a strongly international character, the subject matter being one of the first for which multilateral international conventions were concluded (Paris Union Convention for the Protection of Industrial Property of 1883 and Berne Union Convention for the Protection of Literary and Artistic Works of 1886). There have also been numerous interventions by the European Union, with directives and

---

[5] A new plant variety is, pursuant to Art. 100 of the IPC, 'a plant grouping of a botanical taxon of the lowest known rank' that can be 'defined on the basis of the characters resulting from a certain genotype or a certain combination of genotypes', that is distinguished 'from any other plant grouping on the basis of the expression of at least one of the aforesaid characters' and that is suitable for 'being reproduced' while maintaining unchanged the characters on the basis of which the plant grouping is defined. New plant varieties are the subject of a so-called *sui generis* right, which grants the holder the exclusive right of exploitation, which under certain conditions may also extend to the harvested products. See Morri (2012) for an in-depth analysis more detailed discussion on the subject.

[6] Pursuant to Art. 31 of the IPC, 'the appearance of the whole or a part of the product as it appears, in particular, from the features of the lines, contours, colours, shape, surface texture or materials of the product itself or its ornamentation may be registered as a design, provided that they are new and individual in character', i.e. they produce in the informed user a different overall impression from earlier designs. Registration as a design confers on the holder the right to prohibit third parties from commercial use of any form that produces the same overall impression on the informed user as the registered design. On this subject, see Vanzetti et al. (2021), pp. 531 ff.; Fabbio (2024), pp. 329 ff.

[7] Works protected by copyright are 'intellectual works of a creative nature belonging to literature, music, fine arts, architecture, theatre and cinematography, whatever may be the mode or form of their expression' as well as 'computer programs' and 'database that, due to the choice or arrangement of the material thereof, constitute an intellectual creation of the author' (Art. 1, Law No. 633 of 22 April 1941, hereinafter Italian Copyright Act; a non-exhaustive list of protected works is contained in Art. 2). The Law grants the author of the work a series of exclusive moral and economic rights. The latter consist in the exclusive rights to publish and exploit the work; to reproduce it; to transcribe it; to perform, represent or recite it in public; to communicate it to the public; to distribute it; to translate it; and to rent it (Art. 12 to *18-bis* of the Italian Copyright Act). While the author's moral rights cannot be transferred (Art. 22 of the Italian Copyright Act), the economic rights may be, even separately, 'acquired, alienated or transmitted in all the ways permitted by law' (Art. 107 of the Italian Copyright Act). The transmission of these rights must be proven in writing (Art. 110 of the Italian Copyright Act). The Italian Copyright Act also grants exclusive rights to those who make creative works available to the public, such as performers, producers of phonograms, cinematographic or audiovisual works, radio and television broadcasters, etc. These rights are called 'related rights'. For more on copyright and related rights and their protection, see Cogo (2024), pp. 497 ff.

[8] For an in-depth discussion on the reform of sports audiovisual rights following the Melandri law, see Morelli (2012).On this topic, see also Poddighe (2001).

regulations that have considerably standardised the matter, even if not completely (see, for example, Regulation (EU) 2017/1001 on the European trademark, Regulation (EU) 2012/1257 on the European patent with unitary effect and the very recent Regulation (EU) 2024/2822 and Directive (EU) 2024/2823 on designs).[9]

The subject-matter of the Intellectual Property rights are very different from the goods, to which classic property law refers. In fact, we speak in this regard of 'immaterial' goods, since they do not have a physical consistency, even though they require physical supports to 'materialise' each time an act of reproduction or communication is performed. It is therefore very easy to appropriate them and make use of them that would be reserved for the rightsholder.

For this reason, the legal system provides for very strong legal safeguards, also at the level of the search for evidence. To name but a few relating to civil protection: measures, including precautionary ones, of injunction,[10] seizure,[11] description of the products/procedures and accounting records of the alleged infringer,[12] right to information,[13] orders to exhibit.[14] Special rules are laid down on the subject of compensation for damages[15] and, in relation to industrial property rights, the sanction of the restitution of the infringer's profits is provided for, as an alternative to compensation for loss of profit or to the extent that they exceed the amount paid under this title.[16]

Civil enforcement tools for Intellectual Property rights are well-proven and have, over time, proven their effectiveness in 'physical' markets and territories and against localised and localisable counterfeiters.

The system of protection of Intellectual Property rights has, however, been put to the test with the development of digital technology and related markets, no longer physical, but online. This is first and foremost because, for some creations, digitisation and uploading onto the Internet network have allowed them to be reproduced and circulated free of material supports, to an indefinite number of recipients and without territorial constraints (think of the phenomenon of cinematographic and musical works placed on the Internet network without the consent of the rightsholder). Moreover, even for creations that still need to materialise on, or in, a physical product (as is the case for product trademarks or design objects)[17] online

[9] Which, respectively, replace the previous Regulation (EC) 2002/2246 and amend Directive 98/71/EC.

[10] Sections 131 IPC and 156 Italian Copyright Act.

[11] Articles 129 IPC and 161 Italian Copyright Act.

[12] Articles 129 IPC and 161 Italian Copyright Act.

[13] Articles *121-bis* IPC and *156-ter* Italian Copyright Act.

[14] Articles 121(2) IPC and *156-bis*(1) Italian Copyright Act. For more on the procedural protection of intellectual property rights, see Bertani (2024), pp. 619 ff.

[15] Articles 125 c.p.i. and 158 Italian Copyright Act

[16] Article 125(3) IPC For more on civil sanctions, see Cogo (2024), pp. 613 ff.; Vanzetti et al. (2021), pp. 539 ff.; Vanzetti (2013a), pp. 1176 ff.

[17] Even for these rights, however, the evolution of technology and marketing techniques have enabled 'dematerialised' exploitation. For trademarks, for example, there have been cases of use in

counterfeiting is particularly insidious, since in the digital world it is not always possible to identify the infringer, and when an infringer is identified and an injunction is obtained against him, there is no guarantee that it will be enforced or that the same infringement will not be immediately repeated elsewhere, i.e. at another web address, in a continuous rat-hunt that may frustrate the expectations of rightsholders.

For these reasons, an effective protection of Intellectual Property in digital markets cannot disregard the collaboration (*recte*: involvement) of Internet service providers (ISPs), i.e. the subjects who, each according to their activity, actually make online infringements possible.[18] Moreover, as is well known, the legal system recognises ISPs, under certain conditions, an exemption from liability for any illegal acts committed by the recipients of their services: this is the safe harbour already provided for by Art. 12 to 15 of Directive 2000/31/EC of the European Parliament and of the Council of 8 June 2000 on certain legal aspects of information society services, in particular electronic commerce, in the Internal Market (henceforth: E-Commerce Directive) and now contained, substantially unchanged, in Articles 4, 5, 6 and 8 of Regulation (EU) 2022/2065 of the European Parliament and of the Council of 19 October 2022 on a single market for Digital Services (DSA).

This exemption, which is 'horizontal', also covers offences consisting in the infringement of Intellectual Property rights,[19] for which intermediaries could under certain conditions be held liable, even if only by way of complicity with the users of the service, if the ordinary rules of the offline sectors were followed. Addressing the issue of the civil liability of ISPs (and thus also of digital platforms[20]) for

---

the Metaverse as NFT (Non-Fungible Token). See in this regard Trib. Roma, ord. 20 July 2022, with footnote by Iaia (2022) and with footnote by Raffaelli (2022), pp. 287 ff., which ordered an injunction against the defendant company that marketed, produced and offered for sale NFTs bearing the photograph of a well-known former footballer, also reproducing the Juventus Club uniform and brand, in the absence of a licence from the latter.

For more on this topic, see Spolidoro (2022), pp. 515 ff.

[18] On the role of Platforms in the fight against illegal content placed online, see Communication from the Commission to the European Parliament, the Council, the European Economic and Social Committee and the Committee of the Regions, *Tackling Illegal Content Online, Towards an enhanced responsibility of online platforms* of 28 September 2017, COM/2017/0555 final.

[19] As now expressly stated in the DSA, recital 12 of which is quoted: 'in order to achieve the objective of ensuring a safe, predictable and trustworthy online environment, for the purpose of this Regulation the concept of "illegal content" should broadly reflect the existing rules in the offline environment. In particular, the concept of "illegal content" should be defined broadly to cover information relating to illegal content, products, services and activities. In particular, that concept should be understood to refer to information, irrespective of its form, that under the applicable law is either itself illegal [...] or that the applicable rules render illegal in view of the fact that it relates to illegal activities. Illustrative examples include [...] the sale of non-compliant or counterfeit products [...] the non-authorised use of copyright protected material'.

[20] Defined by the DSA as 'a hosting service that, at the request of a recipient of the service, stores and disseminates information to the public, unless that activity is a minor and purely ancillary feature of another service or a minor functionality of the principal service and, for objective and technical reasons, cannot be used without that other service, and the integration of the feature or

infringements of Intellectual Property rights, therefore, requires coordinating the provisions protecting these rights (including those that have strengthened their protection in the digital sector[21]) with those on e-commerce, keeping the sanction of injunction separate from that of damages.

2 The General Rules on the Civil Liability of Internet Service Providers Under the E-Commerce Provisions (Overview)[22]

As is well known, in outlining the liability regime of ISPs for unlawful acts committed by the recipients of their services, European and Italian rules (the latter not enforce anymore)[23] consider three types of service providers: the so-called 'mere

---

functionality into the other service is not a means to circumvent the applicability of this Regulation' (Art. 3(i)).

[21] See Directive (EC) 2001/29 of the European Parliament and of the Council of 22 May 2001 on the harmonisation of certain aspects of copyright and related rights in the information society (InfoSoc Directive, implemented in Italy by Legislative Decree No. 68 of 9 April 2003, commented in Sena et al. (2003), as well as Directive (EU) 2019/790 of the European Parliament and of the Council of 17 April 2019 on copyright and related rights in the Digital Single Market (Copyright Directive, implemented in Italy by Legislative Decree No. 177 of 5 November 2021, on which see Lavagnini (2022b). See also, for administrative protection, AgCom's *Regulation on the protection of copyright on electronic communication networks and implementation procedures pursuant to Legislative Decree No. 70 of 9 April 2003*, adopted by Resolution No. 680/13/CONS (on which Ubertazzi (2014), which has been amended several times, most recently in 2023 by Resolution No. 189/23/CONS, which introduced specific precautionary measures for the protection of sports events broadcast live, pursuant to Art. 2(3) of Law No. 93 of 14 July 2023, *Provisions Relating to the Prevention and Suppression of the Unlawful Dissemination of Copyright-Protected Content through Electronic Communication Networks*. The aforementioned regulation, in its various versions, has been the subject of appeals before the Administrative Court: see Council of State, 15 July 2019, No. 4993 (in *Dir. inf*, II, 1215), which found well-founded and legitimate the Authority's power to issue administrative injunctions in the event of copyright infringement, but not also that of accompanying such measures with fines for non-compliance (sanctions now expressly provided for by Art. 5, Law No. 93/2023) and TAR Lazio-Roma, 22 January 2024, in portali.giustizia-amministrativa.it, which dismissed an appeal seeking, inter alia, to have the recent amendments to the Regulation declared illegitimate, as well as the automated technological platform called *piracy shield* (on this subject Lorusso (2024); see also Renna (2014) pp. 111 ff.). It should be noted that by Law Decree No. 123 of 15 September 2023 on *Urgent measures to combat youth discomfort, educational poverty and juvenile crime, as well as for the safety of minors in the digital sphere*, converted with amendments into Law No. 159 of 13 November 2023, AgCom was designated as the Coordinator of Digital Services for Italy (Art. 15) pursuant to Art. 49(2) DSA.

[22] See sect. I of this Title II, edited by L. Guffanti Pesenti, for a comprehensive discussion of the subject.

[23] The E-Commerce Directive was implemented in Italy by Legislative Decree No. 70/2003. The provisions relating to the liability of Internet service providers were contained, before their abrogation by Legislative Decree No. 50 of 25 March 2024, as a consequence of the entry into force of the DSA, in Articles 14 to 17, and had given rise to various interpretation problems, to which we

conduit' intermediaries, such as telecommunication companies, which simply transmit on a communication network information provided by a recipient of the service or provide access to the network (Art. 12 of the E-Commerce Directive, now Art. 4 DSA); intermediaries who, like search engines, perform services of temporary storage of information entered by the recipient of the service (so-called 'caching providers') carried out for the sole purpose of making more efficient or more secure the subsequent forwarding of the information to other recipients of the service at their request (Art. 13 E-Commerce Directive, now Art. 5 DSA); 'hosting providers', who provide services consisting of 'the storage of information provided by a recipient of the service' (Art. 14 E-Commerce Directive, now Art. 6 DSA).[24]

Focusing, for what is of interest here, on the position of the hosting provider, a category to which online platforms belong, the system of liability for content/information transmitted and/or uploaded and/or disseminated by recipients of the service outlined by the E-Commerce Directive, and reiterated by the DSA, establishes that such liability can only arise if the hosting provider is 'actually aware that the activity or information is unlawful and, as regards actions for damages, […] of facts or circumstances that make manifest the illegality of the activity or information' or if, 'as soon as it becomes aware of such facts', it does not act 'immediately to remove the information or to disable access to it'.

As already enshrined in Art. 15.1 of the E-Commerce Directive, and reiterated in Art. 8 DSA, 'no general obligation to monitor the information which providers of intermediary services transmit or store, nor actively to seek facts or circumstances indicating illegal activity shall be imposed on those providers'.

It is important to emphasise that the so-called Internet content providers are unquestionably outside the safe harbour, as they are subjects that directly put content on the net and therefore, in relation to third parties' protected material, make uses reserved to the owner that require his consent. In the absence of consent, they will be subject to the ordinary liability regime.

---

will return later, highlighted for example by Lavagnini (2022a). As a result of the DSA, the national and European provisions are now perfectly aligned.

[24] Since the adoption of the E-Commerce Directive, Internet services have been enriched with new types, and it was unclear whether the new services would fit into the taxonomy of the aforementioned directive. In recital 29 of the DSA, it was specified that mere conduit services include 'internet exchange points, wireless access points, virtual private networks, DNS services and resolvers, top-level domain name registries, registrars, certificate authorities that issue digital certificates, voice over IP and other interpersonal communication services'; that caching services also include 'the sole provision of content delivery networks, reverse proxies or content adaptation proxies'; that hosting services include 'services such as cloud computing, web hosting, paid referencing services or services enabling sharing information and content online, including file storage and sharing'. Recital 29 of the DSA states that 'whether a specific service constitutes a "mere conduit," "caching" or "hosting" service depends solely on its technical functionalities, which might evolve in time, and should be assessed on a case-by-case basis'.

On the development of the digital platform market and its impact on competition, see *ex multis* Falce (2022), pp. 172 ff.

3 Digital Platforms, Infringement of Intellectual Property Rights and Injunctions

The injunction is one of the most important civil sanctions for the case of infringement of Intellectual Property rights, provided for in both the IPC and the IPL. Particularly, the owner of the right 'may request that an injunction be ordered against any imminent infringement of his right and the continuation or repetition of the infringements under way, and in particular may ask for an injunction against manufactoring, trading and using the items constituting an infringement of the right, and an order to withdraw them from the market, against a party who is the owner of who has them in any way available, in accordance with the provision of the code of civil procedure concerning precautionary proceedings. The injunction and the order to withdraw from the market may be requested, on the same preconditions, against any person whose services are used to infringe an industrial property right' (Art. 131 IPC; see also, for copyright and related rights, Art. 156, para 1, l.d.a. on the definitive injunction, and Art. 163, para 1, l.d.a. on the precautionary injunction, of similar tenor).

The rule is in line with Art. 11 of Directive 2004/48/EC on the enforcement of intellectual property rights (Enforcement Directive), which provides that 'Member States shall ensure that, where a judicial decision is taken finding an infringement of an intellectual property right, the judicial authorities may issue against the infringer an injunction aimed at prohibiting the continuation of the infringement. Where provided for by national law, non-compliance with an injunction shall, where appropriate, be subject to a recurring penalty payment, with a view to ensuring compliance. Member States shall also ensure that rightholders are in a position to apply for an injunction against intermediaries whose services are used by a third party to infringe an intellectual property right, without prejudice to Article 8(3) of Directive 2001/29/EC' on the harmonisation of certain aspects of copyright and related rights in the information society (InfoSoc Directive). The latter provision, which concerns only copyright, states that 'Member States shall ensure that rightholders are able to apply for an injunction against intermediaries whose services are used by a third party to infringe a copyright or related right'.

It is important to emphasise that the injunction, as opposed to compensation for damages, can be based on the mere ascertainment of the infringement, regardless of the subjective status of its author. Its purpose is, in fact, to make the infringement of the intellectual property right cease and/or not be repeated.[25]

Digital platforms, as ISPs, are undoubtedly 'intermediaries whose services are used by third parties to infringe an intellectual property right'. After all, the particular liability regime of ISPs provided for by the e-commerce directive is 'without prejudice to the possibility, in accordance with the legal system of the Member

[25] For more on inhibition in intellectual property rights, see Ubertazzi (2019), pp. 832 ff.; Vanzetti (2013b), pp. 1400 ff.; Spolidoro (2008), pp. 86 ff.; Fabbio (2021b), pp. 57 ff.

State, for a judicial or administrative authority to require the service provider to terminate or prevent an infringement' (Articles 4.3, 5.2, 6.4 DSA).[26]

The sanction of injunction, therefore, deserves a separate discourse, since it applies not only to 'responsible' intermediaries, but also to 'non-responsible' ones[27] (so-called accountability without liability), who may, like the former, be the

[26] See also, in this respect, recital 45 of the E-Commerce Directive, according to which 'The limitations of the liability of intermediary service providers established in this Directive do not affect the possibility of injunctions of different kinds; such injunctions can in particular consist of orders by courts or administrative authorities requiring the termination or prevention of any infringement, including the removal of illegal information or the disabling of access to it'. The principle was reiterated and clarified in recital 25 of the DSA, which states that 'The exemptions from liability established in this Regulation should not affect the possibility of injunctions of different kinds against providers of intermediary services, even where they meet the conditions set out as part of those exemptions'. Also, the InfoSoc Directive, in recital 59, notes that 'in the digital environment, in particular, the services of intermediaries may increasingly be used by third parties for infringing activities' and that 'in many cases such intermediaries are best placed to bring such infringing activities to an end. Therefore, without prejudice to any other sanctions and remedies available, rightholders should have the possibility of applying for an injunction against an intermediary who carries a third party's infringement of a protected work or other subject-matter in a network. This possibility should be available even where the acts carried out by the intermediary are exempted under Article 5'.

[27] The principle that an injunction may also be pronounced against 'non-responsible' persons within the meaning of the E-Commerce Directive and the corresponding national provisions is now well established. See, among European decisions, ECJ. EU 7 August 2018, C-521/17, *Coöperatieve Vereniging SNB-REACT U.A.* v. *Deepak Mehta*, where it is stated that 'if the referring court were to come to the conclusion, at the end of its examination, that the activity of the service provider at issue in the main proceedings can benefit from the limitations of liability set out in paragraph 43 of this judgment, it would be open to it, in accordance with Articles 12(3), 13(2) and 14(3) of Directive 2000/31 to adopt, in cases where the existence of an infringement or a risk of infringement of an intellectual property right has been sufficiently established, an injunction aimed at bringing that infringement to an end or preventing that risk from occurring'. In the same vein, ECJ. EU 15 September 2016, C-484/14, *Mc Fadden*.

Among the national decisions, see, inter alia, in the matter of copyright, Trib. Milan 24 July 2024 in *Giurisprudenza delle imprese*, according to which 'Given the admissibility of the extension of the so-called pure injunction to persons exempt from the subjective element of guilt and fraud, which is a requirement only for the protection of damages, the mère conduit, in their capacity as intermediaries pursuant to Article 156 of the Italian Copyright Act, may be the addressees of the prohibitory measure, without there being any contradiction between their irresponsibility and their being the passive subjects of the prohibitory measure'; Trib. Milan 5 June 2023, ibid., according to which 'If Internet service providers, although not liable for the offence, are qualified as intermediaries, they can be recipients of injunction orders regardless of the existence of wilful misconduct or fault'; Trib. Milan 12 April 2018, in *Giur. ann. dir. ind*, 2019, no. 6749/3, with note by Bertani (2018) and with note by Galli (2018), pp. 3 ff; Trib. Milano 25 July 2017, in *AIDA*, 2019, no. 292; Trib. Milano, ord. 8 May 2017, *ivi*, 2018, no. 266; Trib. Torino, ord. 3 June 2015, commented, together with other measures, by Tosi (2017), pp. 6 ff.; Trib. Roma 15 April 2010, in *AIDA*, 2010, no. 1382. On trademarks, see Trib. Milano, ord. 13 June 2017, in *Giur. ann. dir. ind.*, 2017, no. 6544 and Trib. Milano, ord. 31 August 2021, *ivi*, 2022, no. 7108.

addressee of a judicial (or administrative[28]) order requiring them to cease the offence by removing or obscuring the content that infringes an Intellectual Property right.

Since it has been clarified that there is no mandatory joinder of parties,[29] in relation to online infringements of Intellectual Property rights the owner may take action not only against the infringer, but also, or only, against the Internet Service Provider (and therefore also the online platforms),[30] to obtain from the Judicial Authority a measure ordering the 'upstream' removal of the infringing content. And this, as the EU Court of Justice has recently clarified,[31] even in the absence of a prior out-of-court warning, unless in implementing the E-Commerce Directive the Member State has expressly provided for this.[32]

Since, as has been said, the provisions on ISP liability exclude a general and preventive surveillance obligation on the part of ISPs, the rightsholder requesting an injunction must indicate the content whose removal from the platform he is requesting, with an indication of the relevant URL[33] or the link for each. On the other hand, there have been cases in which, in view of the easy availability on the provider's site of unlawful content, for instance, through the search tools made available by the

[28] As mentioned in footnote 21, AgCom has the power to issue administrative orders to prevent or stop online infringements of copyright and related rights. On this topic, see Cogo and Ricolfi (2020), pp. 586 ff.

[29] See, e.g. Trib. Milan 12 April 2018, cit.

[30] It should also be noted that the DSA, in recital 27, recalls that 'despite the generally important role played by such [intermediary service] providers, the problem of illegal content and activities online should not be dealt with by solely focusing on their liability and responsibilities. Where possible, third parties affected by illegal content transmitted or stored online should attempt to resolve conflicts relating to such content without involving the providers of intermediary services in question. Recipients of the service should be held liable, where the applicable rules of Union and national law determining such liability so provide, for the illegal content that they provide and may disseminate to the public through intermediary services. Where appropriate, other actors, such as group moderators in closed online environments, in particular in the case of large groups, should also help to avoid the spread of illegal content online, in accordance with the applicable law. Furthermore, where it is necessary to involve information society services providers, including providers of intermediary services, any requests or orders for such involvement should, as a general rule, be directed to the specific provider that has the technical and operational ability to act against specific items of illegal content, so as to prevent and minimise any possible negative effects on the availability and accessibility of information that is not illegal content'. On the issue of so-called overfiltering or overblocking, see below.

[31] ECJ. EU 22 June 2021, Cases C-682/18 and C-683/18, *Peterson* v. *YouTube* and *Elsevier* v. *Cyando*, para 130, with notes by Anselmi (2021) and Tassone (2021), p. 838.

[32] Mansani and Simoni (2017), pp. 565 ff., consider that the conduct of the rightsholder that initiates an injunction action not preceded by an out-of-court request to remove the content, even according to the *notice and takedown* procedure possibly set up by the platform operator, should be taken into account for the purposes of the award of costs.

[33] The URL (Uniform Resource Locator) corresponds to a sequence of characters that uniquely identifies the address of an Internet resource on a host server within which certain content is located.

provider to users, the injunction has been granted on the mere indication of the content to be removed, without the need to specify the URL or provide the link.[34]

Obtaining an order against the provider to remove the infringing content may not be sufficient to ensure effective protection to the rightsholder, since it is possible, and in fact very frequent, that the prohibited content is re-uploaded online. For this reason, it is in the interest of rights owners to obtain orders with contents broader than the simple removal of the contents already uploaded on the platform, which also prevent the subsequent (re)uploading; that is, measures that impose on the intermediary an obligation to verify the specific prohibited content, which is activated after the removal order by the Authority and requires him to adopt the necessary technical measures to prevent, or hinder, the consultation of the prohibited contents. Measures have also been requested against certain intermediaries, especially those offering mere conduit services, to extend the judicial order to *alias* sites, i.e. to sites which, although not expressly indicated in the injunction, make available the same content (generally sporting events or live shows that can be enjoyed in streaming mode) considered unlawful in the injunction (so-called 'dynamic' injunctions).[35]

---

[34] In the sense that the plaintiff seeking an injunction has the burden of alleging and proving which are the specific Internet addresses (URLs) or links to which the challenged content is available, see Trib. Torino 24 January 2018, in *AIDA*, 2018, no. 1866; Trib. Milano, ord. 8 May 2017, *ivi*, 2018, 266; App. Milan, 7 January 2015, in *Riv. dir. ind.*, 2017, II, 4.

In the sense that the indication of the unlawfully reproduced content identified by name or commercial title of the work is sufficient, see Trib. Rome 22 January 2021 and Trib. Rome 20 January 2021, both with a note by Colaruotolo (2021), pp. 50–51; Trib. Rome 15 February 2019, *ivi*, 2019, II, 296 and Trib. Milan 9 September 2011, in *AIDA*, 2012, no. 1505.

[35] On dynamic inhibitions, see at length Bertani (2018) and the note to Trib. Milano 12 April 2018, in *Giur. ann. dir. ind.*, 2019, no. 6749. The main problem of the 'elastic' inhibitions concerned their compatibility with the prohibition to impose on online intermediaries a general and preventive surveillance obligation on the content uploaded by their users. Particularly, ECJ. EU, 24 November 2011, C-70/10, *Scarlet*, in *AIDA* 2012, no. 1461, had ruled out that the judge on the merits could impose on the intermediary extensive monitoring obligations for the prevention of future infringements of intellectual property rights. Moreover, the same Court, in its judgment of 27 March 2014, C-314/12, *Telekabel* (ibid., 2014, no. 1588 and with note by Cottino (2014), pp. 2754 ff.) then paved the way for dynamic injunctions, noting, on the one hand, that an injunction serves not only to stop ongoing infringements, but also to prevent future infringements (para 37); and on the other hand, admitting the legitimacy of injunction orders imposing on the provider the blocking of the current domain name 'as well as any other future address of which that company may become aware' (para 12), in a general way, that is, without the identification of concrete measures (paras 42 ff.). Also, the Italian Courts that have granted 'elastic' injunctions (with more or less broad content) have emphasised their full compatibility with the ISPs' liability regime, since they deal with specific and not general surveillance obligations, a posteriori and not preventive. See, e.g. Trib. Torino, ord. 3 June 2015, in the case *Delta TV v. Dailymotion*, in *Riv. dir. ind.* 2017, II, 6 ff., ibid. 36, point 3.5. of the reasoning, according to which 'the intervention required from the hosting provider does not take the form at all … of a preventive screening of all the content present or being uploaded on its platform, aimed at identifying videos infringing the rights of the applicant. Instead, it is a subsequent and targeted check. Subsequent because it was preceded by a complaint in which the specific URLs of the allegedly infringing content were identified. Targeted because it was aimed at preventing new uploads of that content that was present at the URLs already com-

Thus, for example, in a recent case pitting two well-known film companies against a 'pirate' site that allowed streaming of recently released films, the (mere transport) providers were ordered to prevent 'access to [...] second level domain names even where a top level domain other than those already indicated is associated that makes available to the public the same unlawful content that is the subject of this measure, ordering the blocking' and 'access to *alias* resulting from changes to the second level domain relating to all the portals indicated, provided that, in addition to referring to the same unlawful content considered, the subjective link with those responsible for the unlawful activity [...] in place is objectively detectable, with the burden borne by the parties'.[36] The same happened in relation to sports broadcasting, through an order that ordered providers to prevent access not only to the sites indicated by the appellant, but also to those *alias* 'which, also in the future, make available to the public the same unlawful content that is the subject of these proceedings and are subjectively and objectively referable to the same services' indicated in the appeal.[37]

municated'. Even the order issued in the complaint (Trib. Turin 19 October 2015, ibid.), while partially reforming the measure, admitted 'the inhibition of any new future unlawful uploading of the same content already subject to specific out-of-court warning - through the use of technical measures (so-called fingerprinting) available for the identification of the unlawful content uploaded - with the indication of the relevant URL, when research activities implementing the aforementioned warning'.

Currently, recital 30 of the DSA, in reiterating that 'providers of intermediary services should not be, neither *de jure*, nor *de facto*, subject to a monitoring obligation', specifies that 'this does not concern monitoring obligations in a specific case and, in particular, does not affect orders by national authorities in accordance with national legislation, in compliance with Union law, as interpreted by the Court of Justice of the European Union, and in accordance with the conditions established in this Regulation'. Moreover, previously, the European Commission's communication of 20 November 2017 (COM/2017/708), *on guidance on certain aspects of directive 2004/48/EC of the European parliament and of the Council on the enforcement of intellectual property rights*, had acknowledged that the adoption of dynamic injunctions could be an effective measure if the content of an Internet site infringing an intellectual property right and already inhibited is made available with new IP addresses or URLs.

With regard to elastic injunctions in administrative protection, it suffices to recall that Law No. 93/2024 gives AgCom the power to order 'service providers, including network access providers, to disable access to abusively disseminated content by blocking the DNS resolution of domain names and blocking the routing of network traffic to IP addresses uniquely intended for unlawful activities', including 'the blocking of any other future domain name, sub-domain, or IP address, to whomsoever traceable, including variations of the name or of the simple declination or extension (so-called top level domain), which allows access to the same abusively disseminated content and to content of the same nature' (Art. 2, paras 1 and 2).

[36] Trib. Milan, ord. 23 July 2024, in *Giurisprudenza delle Imprese* (*Disney Enterprises Inc.* and *Columbia Pictures Industries Inc.* v. *Tim and Others*).

[37] Trib. Milano, ord. 3 June 2023, in *Giurisprudenza delle Imprese* (*Lega Calcio* and *Dazn* v. *Tim and others*). Among the compliant measures, see Trib. Milano, 12 April 2018, in *Giur. ann. dir. ind.*, 2019, no. 6749/6, cit., which is notable for being one of the first decisions that issued an injunction extended to the *so-called alias* sites and Trib. Milano, ord. 13 June 2017, *ivi*, 2017, no. 6544/3. Conversely, in the sense that the injunction can only have as its object the contested IP address and not also any other future address, thus excluding that the command can be extended to

Extended injunction orders have also been granted to copyright holders against platforms hosting content uploaded by users, in the event of an ascertained violation of copyright or related rights. For example, the Court of Rome,[38] in a case relating to television broadcasts, ordered the online platform 'the immediate removal [...] of the damaging content specifically identified in the grounds', inhibiting 'the continuation or repetition of any further infringement of RTI's rights by publishing the same content on the platform or otherwise making it available to users'.

With regard to the perimeter of the precautionary injunction, case law has resorted in various cases to mechanisms for identifying future infringements based on cooperation between the addressee of the injunction and the rightsholder, who has the burden of identifying and notifying the provider of infringements subsequent to the injunction. According to this mechanism, which has been defined by a scholars as the 'Italic variant of the notice and takedown procedure' provided for in the USA,[39] the precautionary injunction consists in the order 'to prevent access to the same content that has previously been found to be unlawful regardless of the continuous change of the domain name, desired by the offender, provided, however, that the infringement is reported to the Internet Service Provider by the holder of the intellectual property right unlawfully infringe'.[40]

Precisely to ensure, also in consideration of the cross-border context in which the online platforms operate, that the intermediaries of the Internet services can comply with the orders of the (judicial and/or administrative) Authorities 'effectively and efficiently' without being 'subject to disproportionate burdens', the DSA, while making 'without prejudice to Union law in the field of judicial cooperation in civil or criminal matters [.... and national criminal or civil procedural law]' (see recitals 31 to 38) has established in Art. 9(2) the minimum conditions that the 'orders to counter illegal content' issued by the competent national judicial or administrative authority must meet. In particular, the order (also judicial) must contain, in addition to information on the issuing Authority and the mechanisms of appeal, reference to the legal basis of the order, the reason for which the content is illegal, and 'clear information enabling the provider of intermediary service to identify and locate the illegal content concerned, such as one or more exact URLs and, where necessary, additional information'.

---

the so-called *alias* sites, see Trib. Milano, ord. 11 March 2019, in *Giur. ann. dir. ind.*, 2019, no. 6781. Also to the contrary to *dynamic* orders Trib. Milano, ord. 31 August 2021, ibid., 2022, n. 7108 and Trib. Milano, ord. 27 July 2016, in *AIDA*, 2017, n. 1814.

[38] Trib. Rome 26 September 2019, *RTI* v. *Bit Kitchen Inc.*, in *Giurisprudenza delle imprese*. Trib. Turin 23 June 2014, cited above, ordered Yahoo to remove content unlawfully uploaded by its users and specifically indicated by URL, as well as to inhibit its further uploading.

[39] Bertani (2018), p. 882, where we also read, on pp. 877 and 878, an exhaustive description of the American system (§ 512 17 US Code).

[40] Thus, Trib. Milano 12 April 2018, in *Giur. ann. dir. ind.*, 2019, cit., in whose ample note it is highlighted, among other things, how the Court, in the case at hand, in a manner defined as 'rational' from the point of view of the economic basis, has charged the monitoring expenses to the rightsholder. In the same sense Trib. Milan, ord. 8 May 2017, in *Repertorio AIDA*, 2018.

It should be noted that the failure to comply with the judicial order entails, in addition to the application of penalties pursuant to Art. 156, para 1, of the Italian Copyright Act and Art. 124, para 2, of the Code of Criminal Procedure, also the non-applicability of the hosting provider's exemption from liability, since the condition set out in Art. 6(b) of the DSA (formerly Art. 14 of the E-Commerce Directive) is met.

4 Infringement of Intellectual Property Rights and 'Active' Hosting

As seen above, the e-commerce provisions state that the hosting provider is not liable for infringements of Intellectual Property rights committed by its users as long as it 'does not have actual knowledge of illegal activity or information and, as regards claims for damages, is not aware of facts or circumstances from which the illegal activity or information is apparent' or 'is not 'actually aware of facts or circumstances from which the illegal activity or information is apparent or 'upon obtaining such knowledge or awareness, acts expeditiously to remove or to disable access to the information'.

In applying this provision, the Courts had to face with various interpretative problems: not only on the concept of 'actual knowledge' of the offence (on which see below) but, even before that, on the subjective scope of application of the exemption. In fact, certain activities of the hosting providers, gradually made possible by the evolution of technology (such as cataloguing, indexing, sending targeted offers or advertisements based on profiling, inserting advertisements, monitoring views, contractual content moderation policies, etc.), did not seem entirely compatible with the principle of technological neutrality that constitutes the prerequisite for the exemption of liability (already) provided for by the E-Commerce Directive.[41] Hence, the well-known jurisprudential distinction between passive hosting provider, exempt from liability under the conditions indicated above, and active hosting provider, to which the exemption does not apply.

At the European level, the distinction is based on the EU Court of Justice, Grand Chamber, 23 March 2010, No. 236[42] which was asked to interpret Art. 14 of the

[41] See for all Musso (2010), pp. 795 ff.

[42] Cases C-236/08 to C-238/08, *Google France*, paras 113 and 120, in *Giur. ann. dir. ind.*, 2010, no. 5608, with note by Ricolfi (2010) pp. 1603 ff. and with note by Tavella and Bonavita (2010), pp. 429 ff. These were three references for preliminary rulings made by French courts in relation to disputes concerning Google's offering of the plaintiffs' trademarks as keywords within its service called 'Adwords', which allows advertisers to place their ads next to the natural results that appear when a user types a keyword into the search engine. The Court was first asked to determine whether, by offering its advertisers the plaintiffs' trademarks as keywords, Google was directly making use 'in the course of trade' of those trademarks. If the answer was in the negative, whether it could benefit from the exemption from liability under the E-Commerce Directive for possible acts of infringement by advertisers. The Court, after having ruled out the possibility of Google

E-Commerce Directive in a case concerning trademarks. According to the Court 'it follows from recital 42 in the preamble to Directive 2000/31 that the exemptions from liability established in that directive cover only cases in which the activity of the information society service provider is 'of a mere technical, automatic and passive nature', which implies that that service provider 'has neither knowledge of nor control over the information which is transmitted or stored'. The Court concluded that 'Article 14 of Directive 2000/31 must be interpreted as meaning that the rule laid down therein applies to an internet referencing service provider where that service provider has not played an active role of such a kind as to give it knowledge of or control over the data stored'.

From then on, the distinction between active and passive hosting provider, even if opposed by some Italian case law,[43] has been constantly referred to by the decisions on infringement of Intellectual Property rights,[44] also with the aim of clarifying the boundaries, particularly by indicating the elements from which to deduce the

---

directly using the plaintiffs' trademarks, stated the principle set out in the text in relation to the search engine's liability regime for possible trademark infringements committed by users of the 'AdWords' service.

On the use of others' trademarks as key-word, see in doctrine Spedicato (2010), pp.731 ff.; Tosi (2009), pp. 387 ff. Among the Italian decisions, again in the sense of denying that the service provider makes direct use of another person's trademark and can be held liable in the absence of actual knowledge of the offence and prompt activation following such knowledge, see Trib. Palermo 7 June 2013 and Trib. Milan 23 April 2013, with note by Guardì (2014), pp. 179 ff.

Generally, on the unlawfulness of an advertiser's use of another's trademark as a key-word, see ECJ. EU 25 March 2010, C-278/08, *BergSpechte*, according to which 'the proprietor of a trade mark is entitled to prohibit an advertiser - on the basis of a keyword identical with or similar to that trade mark, chosen by him, without the consent of that proprietor, in the context of an internet referencing service - from advertising goods or services identical with those for which that trade mark has been registered, where such advertising does not enable the average internet user, or enables him only with difficulty, to ascertain whether the goods or services referred to by the advertisement originate from the proprietor of the trade mark or from an undertaking economically connected to him or, on the contrary, originate from a third party'. Among the Italian decisions Trib. Bari 27 April 2021, in *Giur. ann. dir. ind.*, 2021, no. 7015; Trib. Milano 6 May 2013, *ivi*, 2014, no. 6092; Trib. Bologna 1 July 2011, in *Le sezioni specializzate italiane della proprietà industriale e intellettuale*, 2012, 51 and Trib. Milano 11 March 2009, in *Giur. ann. dir. ind.*, 2009, no. 5409.

[43] See, e.g. App. Milan, 7 January 2015, with footnote by Anselmi (2015) and with footnote by Iaselli (2016), pp. 166 ff. and therein, with footnote by Tosi (2017), pp. 4–6. Moreover, as highlighted by Lavagnini (2022a), p. 225, even measures that have emphasised the figure of active hosting have often configured its liability as having remained inactive after receiving a notification from the rightsholder. See in this sense Trib. Milano 9 September 2011, in *AIDA*, 2012, 740 and with a note by Saraceno (2011), II, pp. 364 ff., who pointed out that there is an 'impossibility also for the provider of active hosting services to be able to proceed with a prior check of the material entered daily by users' with the consequence that 'appropriate importance must be attributed to the receipt of a warning'.

[44] See first ECJ. EU, Grand Chamber, 12 July 2011, *L'Oréal*, C-324/09, para 113, in *Jur. ann. dir. ind.* 2011, no. 5775 with extensive notes. The case (on which see below, para 7) was also in the field of trademarks and was occasioned by a reference for a preliminary ruling by the *High Court of Justice (England and Wales)* in a case discussing the possible liability of the eBay platform for commercial transactions of goods bearing counterfeit trademarks that took place within it. See in this regard Rodean (2011), pp. 1594 ff.; Schrijvers (2011), pp. 723 ff.; Lievens (2012), pp. 68 ff.

loss of the provider's neutrality requirement, with consequent application of the ordinary liability regime.

It was thus clarified, also in a trademark case involving a well-known perfume and cosmetics manufacturer against the eBay platform, that 'the mere fact that the operator of an online marketplace stores offers for sale on its server, determines the terms of its service, is remunerated for it and provides general information to its customers cannot have the effect of depriving it of the exemptions from liability provided for in Directive 2000/31'[45] whereas, on the contrary, 'where that operator has provided assistance consisting, inter alia, in optimising the presentation of the offers for sale in question and in promoting those offers, he must be regarded as not having occupied a neutral position between the selling customer concerned and the potential purchasers, but as having played an active role capable of giving him knowledge of or control over the information related to those offers. In that case, he cannot rely on the liability exemption in Article 14 of Directive 2000/31 in respect of those information'.[46]

The principle has recently been reiterated in the field of copyright, stating that it is for the national court to determine whether hosting providers 'contribute, beyond the mere provision of their platform, to giving the public access to protected content in breach of copyright' and that, if this is the case, 'the operator in question could not rely on the exemption from liability provided for in Article 14(1) of the e-Commerce Directive'.[47]

The figure of active hosting has also been emphasised by the CJEU. EU 15 September 2016, *Mc Fadden*, C-484/14, in copyright; CJEU. EU 7 August 2018, *Coóperative Vereniging v. Deepak Mehta*, C-521/17, in trademark matters; ECJ. EU, Grand Chamber, 22 June 2021, *Peterson* v. *Youtube and Elsevier* v. *Cyando*, Joined Cases C-682/18 and C-683/18, cited above. As regards Italy, the figure of active *hosting* was consecrated by Cass. 19 March 2019, no. 7708, with note by Novelli (2019), pp. 500 ff., with note by Di Ciommo (2019), p. 2072 and with note by Tosi (2019), pp. 202–270 and with note by Bocchini (2019), pp. 2604 ff. The Supreme Court defined 'active' as 'the provider of information society services who performs an activity that goes beyond a merely technical, automatic and passive service and, instead, engages in active conduct, concurring with others in the commission of the offence, so that he is exempt from the general exemption regime provided for in Article 16, Legislative Decree No. 70 of 2003, since his civil liability must be governed by the common rules'. Among the decisions on the merits, see *ex multis*, in addition to Trib. Milano 9 September 2011, cit. and Trib. Milano 7 June 2011, cited by Saraceno (2011), p. 386, Trib. Roma 27 April 2016, in *Riv. dir. ind.*, 2017, II, 3 ss., Trib. Roma 20 January 2021 and Trib. Roma 22 January 2021, *ivi*, 2021, II, 50 ss.

[45] ECJ. EU 12 July 2011, *L'Oréal*, cited above, para 115. See also CJEU. EU 2 April 2020, *Coty Germany*, C-567/18, para 43, also on trademarks, whereby 'the fact of creating the technical conditions necessary for the use of a sign and of being remunerated for that service does not mean that the person rendering that service uses the sign himself, even if he is acting in his own economic interest'.

[46] ECJ. EU 12 July 2011, *L'Oréal*, cited above, paras 115–116.

[47] ECJ. EU 22 June 2021, cited above, para 107, according to which if the national court were to find that 'YouTube or Cyando contribute, beyond the mere provision of their platform, to giving the public access to content protected in breach of copyright, the operator in question could not rely on the exemption from liability provided for in Article 14(1) of the E-Commerce Directive'.

The Italian Supreme Court,[48] after stating that it is up to the Judge of the merits to establish whether a hosting provider plays an active or passive role, has outlined a series of so-called 'interference indexes' on the illicit content that 'by way of example and not necessarily all coexisting' may indicate an active role. Particularly, these are the following elements: 'activities of filtering, selection, indexing, organisation, cataloguing, aggregation, evaluation, use, modification, extraction or promotion of content, operated through an entrepreneurial management of the service, as well as the adoption of a technique of behavioural evaluation of users to increase their loyalty: conduct that has, in substance, the effect of completing and enriching in a non-passive manner the use of content by unspecified users'.[49]

The distinction between active and passive intermediary, already endorsed by the EU Commission in its Communication of 28 September 2019,[50] is now enshrined at the legislative level in the very recent DSA. This Regulation has indeed preserved the 'horizontal framework of conditional exemptions from liability for providers of intermediary services, laid down in Directive 2000/31/EC' but, in 'view of the divergences when transposing and applying the relevant rules at national level', has

---

[48] Cass. 19 March 2019, no. 7708, cited above.

[49] Similar criteria can be found in decisions on the merits, even prior to the decision of the Supreme Court indicated in the text: for example, for Trib. Roma 10 January 2019, in *Giurisprudenza delle imprese*, 'the platform operator will be subtracted from the benefits of irresponsibility in the event that its activity is configured in an assistance consisting in the optimisation of digital content and has contributed to the editing of material damaging to the interests protected within the internet network'; Trib. Rome 27 April 2016 held 'not applicable the regime of limitation of liability' provided by Art. 14 of the E-Commerce Directive 'to the provider of information society services that [...] allows an easy and varied choice with a simple consultation of thousands of videos not randomly entered by users but catalogued and organised in specific categories. Such an advanced system [...] is completely incompatible with the figure of simple hosting'. On the subject of videosharing platforms, Trib. Rome 20 January 2019 and 22 January 2019, cit., have recently considered as indices of interference forms of intervention of the ISP on the data 'aimed at exploiting the contents of the individual materials stored by the users, through the control, knowledge and profiling in an automated way'; or the fact that the provider 'has provided to analyse and select the contents stored on the site, cataloguing, indexing and organising them by sections and topics [...], contributing to the dissemination of illicit contents' due to the fact of making 'considerably easier for the user to identify the contents searched, among millions of documents'. Moreover, again on the subject of video-sharing platforms, Trib. Turin 24 January 2018, in *AIDA* 2018, no. 1866, denied that the owner of the platform loses its neutral character 'for the mere fact of implementing operations aimed at improving the usability of the platform and the content poured into it' for example through activities of 'indexing or individualised search suggestions for similar or sequential products or of advertising insertion and matching of targeted advertising messages [...]. Only if the Internet service provider manipulates or transforms the information or content transmitted or stored does it become so-called active hosting and full civil liability under the common rules subsists'. On the figure of active hosting, see *ex multis* Lavagnini (2022a), pp. 223 ff.; Zincone (2012), pp. 149 ff.; Saraceno (2011).

[50] COM/2017/0555 final. Paragraph 10 of that Communication states that the liability exemption in the E-Commerce Directive 'is only available to hosting service providers who comply with the conditions set out in Article 14 of the Directive; such service providers are those whose activities consist of the storage of information at the request of a third party and who do not play an active role enabling them to gain knowledge of, or control over, that information'.

clarified 'certain elements [...] having regards of the case law of the Court of Justice of the European Union'.[51]

On the issue at hand, the DSA clarifies that 'the exemptions from liability established in this Regulation should not apply where, instead of confining itself to providing the services neutrally by a merely technical and automatic processing of the information provided by the recipient of the service, the provider of intermediary services plays an active role of such a kind as to give it knowledge of, or control over, that information' (recital 18), nor should they apply 'where the recipient of the service is acting under the authority or the control of the provider of a hosting service' (art. 6(2)), for example where 'the provider of an online platform that allows consumers to conclude distance contracts with traders determines the price of the goods or services offered by the trader' (recital 23).

It is important to recall that the DSA 'is without prejudice to Union law on copyright and related rights, including Directives 2001/29/EC (21), 2004/48/EC (22) and (EU) 2019/790 (23) of the European Parliament and of the Council, which establish specific rules and procedures that should remain unaffected' (recital 11).

In fact, as we will see better below, for copyright, the Copyright Directive excludes from the application of the safe harbour a particular kind of hosting provider, the so called 'online content sharing service provider' ('OCSSP'), defined as 'an information society service of which the main or one of the main purposes is to store and give the public access to a large amount of copyright-protected works or other protected subject matter uploaded by its users, which it organises and promotes for profit-making purposes' (Art. 2(6)).

For such a service provider, which has features in common with the category of active hosting provider, Art. 17 of the Copyright Directive requires Member States to provide that it 'performs an act of communication to the public or an act of making available to the public [...] when it gives the public access to copyright-protected works or other protected subject-matter uploaded by its users' and must 'therefore obtain an authorisation from the rightholders'.

Consistent with the provision that the provider of online content-sharing services who gives public access to such content directly performs an act that would be reserved to the rightsholder, regardless of whether the content has been uploaded by its users, the Copyright Directive provides that for such acts 'the limitation of liability set out in Article 14(1) of Directive 2000/31/EC shall not apply' (Art. 17(3)).

A specific paragraph will be devoted to the particular regime of (direct) liability of the online content sharing service provider, as outlined by the Copyright Directive in Article 18(4) and unaffected by the DSA, with the caveat that until the implementation in Italy of the Copyright directive (which took place by Legislative Decree No. 177[52] of 8 November 2021), the liability of such service providers for

[51] See recital 16.

[52] Legislative Decree No. 177/2021 introduced a new Title *II-quater* (Articles *102-sexies* to *102-nonies*, which, except for a few aspects, reproduce Art. 17 of the Copyright Directive almost verbatim) into the Italian Copyright Act.

copyright infringement by their users is to be treated according to the rules then applicable to hosting providers.[53]

5 Infringement of Intellectual Property Rights, Knowledge of the Infringement and Obligation to Activate

Even passive hosting, however, incurs liability if, being aware of the unlawfulness of the content uploaded by its users, it does not take immediate action to remove the unlawful content or prevent access thereto.

In relation to possible infringements of Intellectual Property rights, the interpretation to be given to the condition (already) provided for in Art. 14(1)(a) of the E-Commerce Directive, according to which the exclusion of liability of passive hosting operates if the service provider in question 'does not have actual knowledge of illegal activity or information' and 'as regards claims for damages, is not aware of facts or circumstances from which the illegal activity or information is apparent'. The problem has arisen especially for platforms that provide systems for indexing, searching and recommending content and/or contain clauses in their general terms and conditions that allow the service provider to remove or suspend content that does not comply with the platform's policies, up to and including disabling the account in the event of repeated violations. The increasingly complex business model of certain operators, combined with the need to comply with 'dynamic' injunction orders, has led the main platforms to equip themselves with (more or less) automatic filtering systems of the content entered by users in order (also) to combat the uploading and/or dissemination of illegal content.

To avoid the paradox of excluding from the safe harbour precisely the most cooperative operators,[54] thus discouraging the voluntary adoption of systems that are instead considered very useful in view of an effective fight against online counterfeiting, it has been specified that the adoption of such measures does not automatically affect the liability regime of the provider,[55] which will therefore have to be

---

[53] ECJ. EU 22 June 2021, *Peterson* v. *YouTube and Elsevier* v. *Cyando*, cited above, para 59: 'the questions raised in the present cases relate to the Copyright Directive, the E-Commerce Directive and the Enforcement Directive, applicable at the time of the facts in the main proceedings. The interpretations given by the Court in response to those questions do not concern the regime, which entered into force after that time, established by Article 17 of Directive (EU) 2019/790 of the European Parliament and of the Council of 17 April 2019 on copyright and related rights in the digital single market and amending Directives 96/9/EC and 2001/29'.

[54] See, among others, Di Ciommo (2010), pp. 829 ff.

[55] See now expressly in this regard the DSA, which in Art. 7 provides that 'Providers of intermediary services shall not be deemed ineligible for the exemptions from liability referred to in Articles 4, 5 and 6 solely because they, in good faith and in a diligent manner, carry out voluntary own-initiative investigations into, or take other measures aimed at detecting, identifying and removing, or disabling access to, illegal content, or take the necessary measures to comply with the require-

verified on a case-by-case basis according to the actual knowledge of the infringement of Intellectual Property rights.

On this aspect, it is now well established that 'As regards the condition laid down in Article 14(1)(a) of the Directive on Electronic Commerce, that condition cannot be regarded as not being satisfied solely on the ground that that operator is aware, in a general sense, of the fact that its platform is also used to share content which may infringe intellectual property rights and that it therefore has an abstract knowledge that protected content is being made available illegally on its platform', since the hypotheses envisaged by that Article 'refer to specific illegal information and activities'. Indeed, 'it is only in relation to specific content that such a provider is able to fulfil' the obligation to take action (already) laid down in Art. 14(1)(b) of the E-Commerce Directive.[56]

It has thus been clarified that 'the fact that the operator of an online content-sharing platform automatically indexes content uploaded to that platform, that that platform has a search function and that it recommends videos on the basis of users' profiles or preferences is not a sufficient ground for the conclusion that that operator has 'specific' knowledge of illegal activities carried out on that platform or of illegal information stored on it'. On the contrary, 'it is sufficient that the service provider concerned has become aware, in one way or another, of facts or circumstances on the basis of which a diligent economic operator should have identified the illegality in question and acted in accordance with Article 14(1)(b). That includes, inter alia, the situation in which such a provider uncovers, as the result of an investigation undertaken on its own initiative, an illegal activity or illegal information, as well as a situation in which the operator is notified of the existence of such an activity or such information'.[57]

---

ments of Union law and national law in compliance with Union law, including the requirements set out in this Regulation'.

Moreover, the aforementioned Commission Communication COM/2017/0555 of 28 September 2017, points 10 and 11, had provided that 'proactive measures taken by an online platform in order to detect and remove illegal content could result in it becoming aware of illegal activities or information, which could lead to the loss of the exemption from liability under Article 14(1)(a) of the E-Commerce Directive. In such cases, however, the online platform remains free to act immediately to remove or disable access to the information concerned as soon as it becomes aware of such facts. If it does so, the online platform continues to benefit from the exemption from liability pursuant to Article 14(1)(b). Concerns about the loss of the benefit of the exemption from liability should therefore not discourage or preclude the application of the effective voluntary proactive measures that this Notice seeks to encourage'. Again: 'The Commission strongly encourages online platforms to take voluntary proactive measures aimed at detecting and removing illegal content and to increase cooperation and investment in automated detection technologies and their use', as it does not consider that such measures '- including the use of automated tools and tools to ensure that previously removed content is not re-uploaded - in themselves entail a loss of the benefit of the exemption from liability'.

[56] See most recently ECJ. EU 22 June 2021, *Peterson* v. *YouTube and Elsevier* v. *Cyando*, cited above, paras 111–113.

[57] Ibid., points 114–116.

In relation to the second situation indicated by the EU Court, i.e. that of the sending of a communication by the rightsholder denouncing the unlawfulness of a certain content for infringement of an Intellectual Property right, a peculiar interpretative problem has arisen in Italy, due to the choice of our legislator to implement the *E-Commerce* Directive by providing that the hosting provider was indeed liable for failure to take action to remove the content 'as soon as it becomes aware' of the unlawfulness of the activity or information uploaded by the user, but only in the case of 'notice by the competent authorities' (Art. 16(1)(b), Legislative Decree No. 70/2003).[58]

The provision was thus initially interpreted in the sense that the hosting provider who had simply received a warning/communication (notice) from the rightsholder would not incur liability, an order from the Authority, judicial or administrative[59] being necessary for this purpose. This interpretation, corroborated by Art. 17 of Legislative Decree No. 70/2003 concerning the exemption from the general surveillance obligation, also implementing in a peculiar way the corresponding provision of the E-Commerce Directive,[60] was however at a certain point overtaken, having been clearly expressed on this point by the Italian Supreme Court in the decision *Reti Televisive Italiane v. Yahoo!*[61] In this decision the Supreme Court emphasised the fact that the wording of the provisions in question suggests that the prompt activation following the 'communication of the competent authorities' is only one of the two alternative conditions for the exclusion of the provider's liability, the other being the lack of actual knowledge of the infringement (which for actions for

[58] As Musso (2010), pp. 795 ff., points out, having made the activation obligation subject to a communication from the Authority responded to the need to avoid placing on the provider the burden of assessing the unlawfulness of content/activities that it was instead appropriate to have carried out elsewhere, precisely in the judicial/administrative sphere. On this aspect, see, *infra*, para 7.6.

[59] Trib. Milan 20 March 2010, with note by Sammarco (2010), pp. 908 ff., in a case concerning an infringement of audiovisual rights on sporting events, which acquitted the provider of the claim for damages for not having taken action after the warning received from the rightsholder. In the same sense, see, for example, Trib. Rome 20 October 2011, cited by Zincone (2012), pp. 149 ff.; App. Rome 19 February 2018 in *AIDA* 2018, no. 1868/3; Trib. Florence, ord. 25 May 2012, with note Scannicchio (2012), p. 1210.

[60] That the corresponding European provision added that 'the service provider shall be civilly liable for the content of such services where, having been requested to do so by a judicial or administrative authority having a supervisory function, he has not acted promptly to prevent access to that content, or where, having become aware of the unlawful or prejudicial nature for a third party of the content of a service to which he provides access, he has failed to inform the competent authority'. The national provision seemed to confirm that the obligation to activate the ISP was conditional upon the sending of a request by the judicial or administrative authorities and that the mere warning or communication by the rightsholder was only capable of producing the obligation to inform the competent authorities.

[61] Cass. 19 March 2019, no. 7708, cited, point 5.2. of the grounds; in the same sense, among the decisions on the merits, App. Rome 29 April 2017, in *AIDA* 2018, no. 1843/2 and *Dir. aut.*, 2017, 240 ff.; App. Milan 7 January 2015, in *Riv. dir. ind.* 2016, II, 166 ff.; Trib. Roma 27 April 2016, *ivi*, 2017, II, 3 ff., cit.; Trib. Torino, ord. 23 June 2014, in *AIDA* 2015, no. 1685/4. Trib. Rome, ord. 22 March 2011, with note by Colangelo (2011), pp. 894 ff., later reformed on appeal by Trib. Rome, ord. 11 July 2011 (cited by Saraceno (2011), pp. 385–386).

damages must be 'manifest'). And it clarified that, 'with regard to the interpretation and application of Article 16(1)(a) of Legislative Decree No. 70 of 2003, knowledge of another person's wrongdoing, as a constitutive element of the liability of the provider itself, coincides with the existence of a communication to that effect made by the third party whose right is alleged to have been infringed'.[62]

The principles just mentioned were reaffirmed in the DSA,[63] which, moreover, adds a piece of information in the part where it specifies that 'the provider can obtain such actual knowledge or awareness of the illegal nature of the content, inter alia through its own-initiative investigations or through notices submitted to it by individuals or entities in accordance with this Regulation'.

In this respect, the DSA has imposed organisational rules on platforms, particularly to set up mechanisms allowing anyone to report allegedly illegal content (Art. 16 DSA) and to handle with particular speed the reports made by the so-called 'trusted flaggers' (Art. 22 DSA), i.e. by persons in possession of the necessary requisites[64] and accredited by the Supervisory Authorities acting within the designated area of competence for submitting reports on 'illegal contents' stored and disseminated to the public by online platforms.[65]

According to the DSA, online platforms must then take measures to counter both the frequent uploading of manifestly illegal content and abusive reporting,[66] also

---

[62] The Court clarified that the knowledge of the unlawfulness of the content gives rise, in the case of passive hosting, to 'liability for one's own culpable act, moreover in the face of a situation of 'manifest' unlawfulness of the conduct of others, the continuation of which is not prevented by removing the information or disabling access'; in the case of active hosting, liability is for 'complicity through active conduct in the unlawful act [...] which likewise presupposes, according to the general rules, knowledge of the unlawfulness of another's act': point 5.3 of the grounds.

[63] V. recital 22, which states that 'in order to benefit from the exemption from liability for hosting services, the provider should, upon obtaining actual knowledge or awareness of illegal activities or illegal content, act expeditiously to remove or to disable access to that content', clarifying that 'such actual knowledge or awareness cannot be considered to be obtained solely on the ground that that provider is aware, in a general sense, of the fact that its service is also used to store illegal content' and that 'the fact that the provider automatically indexes information uploaded to its service, that it has a search function or that it recommends information on the basis of the profiles or preferences of the recipients of the service is not a sufficient ground for considering that provider to have "specific" knowledge of illegal activities carried out on that platform or of illegal content stored on it'.

[64] Pursuant to Art. 22(2) DSA, the applicant for the status of credible reporter must demonstrate that he/she has special skills and expertise for the purpose of detecting and reporting illegal content, that he/she is independent from any online platform provider, and that he/she can guarantee that he/she can carry out his/her activity in a diligent, accurate and objective manner.

[65] Following the designation as Digital Services Coordinator, AgCom adopted Resolutions No. 282/24/CONS (on certification procedure of bodies for the out-of-court dispute resolution between online platform providers and recipients pursuant to Art. 21 of the DSA) and No. 283/24/CONS (procedural guidelines for recognising trusted flaggers pursuant to Art. 22 of the DSA).

[66] The problem of combating possible abuses in the reporting of infringing content to platforms arises especially in relation to copyright-protected content, due to the fact that the legal system provides for a number of exceptions and limitations to the right, which allow, for example, the use of protected material for the purpose of criticism, quotation and parody. The topic is well treated

making them known in their general terms and conditions (Art. 23 DSA). It is also provided that online e-commerce platforms, if they 'become aware, irrespective of the means used, that an illegal product or service has been offered by a trader to consumers located in the Union' through their services, shall notify purchasers and/or the public (Art. 32 DSA).

Very large platforms[67] are, moreover, subject to even stricter obligations. In fact, the DSA requires such operators to carry out a self-assessment (Art. 34 DSA) to identify systemic risks (such as the dissemination of illegal content[68]), to adopt 'reasonable, proportionate and effective' mitigation measures and 'content moderation processes, including [...] where appropriate, the expeditious removal of, or the disabling of access to, the content notified' (Art. 35 DSA[69]) and to submit at their own

---

by, among others, Bertani (2018). We will come back to this topic in the section on Art. 17 of the Copyright Directive, which sought to strike a balance between the legitimate protection aspirations of holders of related copyrights and the fundamental rights guaranteed not only by the Italian Constitution but also by the Charter of Fundamental Rights of the European Union, through a system of counterweights aimed at preventing possible abuses of the right.

[67] Very large operators are 'online platforms and online search engines which that a number of average monthly number of active service recipients of the service in the Union equal to or higher that 45 million' (Art. 33.1 DSA). Based on the information received or collected, as of 25 April 2023, the Commission has qualified the following services as 'very large' platforms and search engines: AliExpress (Decision of 25 April 2023, C/2023/2736 final), Amazon Store (Decision of 25 April 2023, C/2023/2746 final), App Store (Decision of 25 April 2023, C/2023/2726 final), Bing (Decision of 25 April 2023, C/2023/2728 final), Booking.com (Decision of 25 April 2023, C/2023/2748 final), Facebook (Decision of 25 April 2023, C/2023/2756 final), Google Maps (Decision of 25 April 2023, C/2023/2737 final), Google Play (Decision of 25 April 2023, C/2023/2738 final), Google Search (Decision of 25 April 2023, C/2023/2731 final, with correction of 13 July 2023, C/2023/4883 final), Google Shopping (Decision of 25 April 2023, C/2023/2733 final), Instagram (Decision of 25 April 2023, C/2023/2734 final), LinkedIn (Decision of 25 April 2023, C/2023/2735 final), Pinterest (Decision of 25 April 2023, C/2023/2729 final), Pornhub (Decision of 20 December 2023, not yet available), Snapchat (Decision of 25 April 2023, C/2023/2730 final), Stripchat (Decision of 20 December 2023, not yet available), Shein (Decision of 26 April 2024, C/2024/2842 final2), Temu (Decision of 31 May 2024, not yet available), TikTok (Decision of 25 April 2023, C/2023/2720 final), Twitter/X (Decision of 25 April 2023, C/2023/2721 final), X Videos (Decision of 10 July 2024, not yet available), XNXX (Decision of 20 December 2023, not yet available), YouTube (Decision of 25 April 2023, C/2023/2725 final), Wikipedia (Decision of 25 April 2023, C/2023/2742 final) and Zalando (Decision of 25 April 2023, C/2023/2727 final).

[68] Article 34 DSA does not provide a definition of 'systemic risk', but lists four categories of it, including precisely 'the dissemination of illegal content' through the services of the very large platform (para 1(a)). As seen in footnote 19, the concept of 'illegal content' is very broad and, according to recital 12 of the DSA, also includes 'the sale of [...] counterfeit products' and 'the unauthorised use of copyrighted material'.

In their risk assessment, platforms must consider, inter alia, the impact of 'the design of their recommendation systems on any other relevant algorithmic systems' (Art. 34(2)(a)) and their 'content moderation systems' (Art. 34(2)(b)).

[69] Concerns about these obligations have been expressed by several parties regarding the protection of freedom of expression and information, which is taken into account by the DSA in the part where it categorises as a systemic risk that very large platforms have to assess the 'actual or foreseeable negative effects for the exercise of fundamental rights, in particular [...] freedom of

expense and at least once a year to independent audits' to assess compliance with their obligations under the DSA and any commitments made thereunder (Art. 37 DSA). Very large operators must also establish an internal compliance function that is independent of their operational functions (Art. 41 DSA).[70]

6 On the Content of the Notice by the Rightsholder

Recalling principles already expressed by the EU Court,[71] recital 22 of DSA requires that the reports capable of triggering the provider's liability be 'sufficiently precise and adequately substantiated to allow a diligent economic operator to reasonably identify, assess and, where appropriate, act against the allegedly illegal content'.

In cases of infringement of Intellectual Property rights, particularly of copyrighted or related content, the issue of the content of the report has given rise in Italy to two jurisprudential orientations.

While it was common ground a generic report of possible infringements of rights were not sufficient to make the provider aware of the unlawfulness of specific content uploaded by users, part of the case law did not consider it sufficient to report a specific infringing work, identified by its title, requiring instead the identification of the specific location of the infringing content within the platform, by indicating the URL or providing the link.[72]

---

expression and information' (Art. 34(1)(b) DSA). See, inter alia, Palumbo and Piemonte (2023), no. 3; Ciliberti (2024), no. 2.

[70] As is well known, the obligations under the DSA are assisted by a system of public enforcement divided between the Commission and the Member States. For an overview in this respect, see Sabia (2023), no. 2.

[71] ECJ. EU 12 July 2011, *L'Oréal*, cit., para 122: 'although such a notification admittedly cannot automatically preclude the exemption from liability [...] given that notifications of allegedly illegal activities or information may turn out to be insufficiently precise or inadequately substantiated, the fact remains that such notification represents, as a general rule, a factor of which the national court must take account when determining, in the light of the information so transmitted to the operator, whether the latter was actually aware of facts or circumstances on the basis of which a diligent economic operator should have identified the illegality'; CJEU, 22 June 2021, Peterson, para 122. EU 22 June 2021, *Peterson* v. *YouTube and Elsevier* v. *Cyando*, cited above, para 116: 'a notification that protected content has been illegally communicated to the public via a video-sharing platform or a file-hosting and -sharing platform must contain sufficient information to enable the operator of that platform to satisfy itself, without a detailed legal examination, that that communication is illegal and that removing that content is compatible with freedom of expression'.

[72] See, e.g., App. Milan 7 January 2015, in *Riv. dir. ind.*, 2016, II, 166 ff, which overturned the first instance judgement for considering that a notice containing the titles of illicitly published television programmes (Amici, Big Brother, Le Iene, Striscia la notizia and Zelig) was suitable to give rise to the liability of the platform, considering that such a generic indication did not violate the requirement of neutrality, since the *provider* had to actively search for the exact location of the illicit content in contrast with the general surveillance prohibition established by the E-Commerce Directive. In the same sense, among others, Trib. Torino 24 January 2018, in *AIDA*, 2018, 796 and Trib. Torino, ord. 3 June 2015, in *Riv. dir. ind.*, 2017, II, 6 ss. On the contrary, Trib. Roma 27 April

In this regard, the aforementioned decision of the Italian Supreme Court in the case of *Reti Televisive Italiane v. Yahoo*[73] established that the issue must be addressed on a case by case basis by the lower Court, without preconceived solutions, having to 'assess whether the legal knowledge - a constituent element of the case of liability of the provider pursuant *to* Article 16 Legislative Decree No. 70 of 2003 - (is) integrated by the communication of the infringement of the right on the transmissions indicated in the notice' and therefore whether this is 'suitable to allow the recipient to understand and identify the unlawful content: to this end, regard must then be had to the technical-informatics profiles to assess whether, in the case of transmission of video products in violation of another person's copyright, these are identifiable by mere indication of the name of the transmission from which they are taken and similar descriptive elements, or is it also necessary to indicate the precise so-called "URL" address, such as the "URL" address, which is the name of the transmission from which the video is taken and the description of the content, so-called "URL" address, as a sequence of characters identifying the address sought [...] in the light of the technological development at the material time'.[74]

2016, in *Riv. dir. ind.*, 2017, II, 3 ss, in a case involving *Reti Televisive Italiane* against a platform, *Break Media*, which hosted the plaintiff's programmes uploaded by users, affirmed that the notice 'does not necessarily have to indicate the unlawful contents to be removed with the indication of the respective telematic addresses (Uniform Resource Locator or related links) in order to allow the hosting provider a prompt removal, since a notice containing the indication of unlawfully reproduced contents indicated by name or commercial title of the work is also suitable for this purpose'.

[73] Cass. 19 March 2019, no. 7708, cited above. Moreover, subsequent decisions have reiterated the need, always and in any case, for the URL to be indicated: see App. Turin 18 November 2021, in *Giur. business*, which, while considering it true 'that the illicit content can in abstract be identified through various modalities of decreasing precision, namely the URL, the URN and, finally, the indication of the title of the work' pointed out that 'without the URL the process of elimination inevitably remains entrusted to heuristic processes'. It also pointed out that 'without the URL, the process of deletion inevitably remains entrusted to heuristic processes, running the risk of being characterised by a margin of error such as not to guarantee the correctness and completeness of the process' and also how 'the request for generalised interventions of contrast by the hosting provider' translates into 'at a closer look, into the imposition on the provider of an active and indiscriminate control on the contents circulating on the platform managed by the ISP'. This rearguard position seems, moreover, to be surpassed, for online platforms, by the DSA.

[74] Interesting is the reference in the judgment to the already mentioned Commission Communication COM (2017) 555 of 28 September 2017, particularly in the part where it notes that online platforms 'usually have the technical means to identify and remove' illegal content and that, also in light of 'technological progress in information processing and machine intelligence, the use of automatic detection and filtering technologies is becoming an ever more important tool in the fight against illegal content online. Many large platforms are now making use of some form of matching algorithms, based on a range of technologies, from simple metadata filtering, to hashing and fingerprinting content'; adding that 'for instance, in the field of copyright, automatic content recognition has proven an effective tool for several years' (p. 13). Moreover, 'technological tools can be used with a higher degree of reliability to fingerprint and filter out (take down and stay down) content which has been already identified and assessed as illegal', through automatic content recognition and automatic permanent removal procedures (p. 20).

7 The Special Liability Regime of Online Content Sharing Service Providers

As mentioned above, the Copyright Directive, also to promote the market of copyright and related rights licences, introduced the category of 'online content sharing service providers' (OCSSP), establishing that they perform an act of communication to the public when they 'gives the public access to copyright-protected works or other protected subject matter uploaded by its users' (Art. 17(1), Copyright Directive. See also the corresponding national provision: Art. *102-sexies* Italian Copyright Act).

The communication to the public of protected material is an act reserved for the owner of the relevant rights[75] and therefore gives rise, in the absence of authorisation,

[75] Communication to the public is one of the faculties reserved exclusively to the rightholder under national and European copyright law. Communication to the public means, according to Art. 3(1) of the InfoSoc Directive, 'any communication to the public of their works, by wire or wireless means, including the making available to the public of their works in such a way that members of the public may access them from a place and at a time individually chosen by them' (in Italy, the right of communication to the public is provided for in Art. 16, l.d.a., of similar tenor). The EU Court of Justice has ruled on the interpretation of this provision on several occasions to clarify the concepts of 'act of communication' and 'public', also in relation to the indications contained in the recitals of the InfoSoc Directive, including the one according to which communication to the public is to be understood 'in a broad sense covering all communication to the public not present at the place where the communication originates. This right should cover any such transmission or retransmission of a work to the public by wire or wireless means, including broadcasting' (recital 23). Thus, the Court has given a very broad interpretation of the concept of 'act of communication to the public', encompassing not only cases of transmission or retransmission of a protected work but also any act capable of enabling its direct access to an audience not present (thus ECJ. EU 13 February 2014, C-466/12, *Nils Svensson and others*, ECJ. EU 8 September 2016, C-160/15, *GS Media* v. *Sanoma Media Netherlands*), requiring, however, that the person granting access be aware that he or she plays an essential role (CJEU. EU 14 June 2017, C-610/15, *The Pirate Bay*, para 26 and ECJ. EU 26 April 2017, C-527/15, *Filmspeler*), since 'the mere provision of physical facilities for enabling or making a communication does not in itself amount to communication' within the meaning of the InfoSoc Directive (recital 27). The notion of the public has also been interpreted broadly: it covers an indeterminate number of potential recipients, as long as they are not too small (see, among many others, ECJ. EU 14 June 2017, C-610/15, *The Pirate Bay*, cited above, para 27), and it generally occurs whenever the act increases the audience of potential recipients of the protected content, for instance—under certain conditions—through the use of hyperlinks (for a careful and up-to-date reconstruction of the right of communication to the public and the copious European case law formed in this regard, see Cogo (2024), pp. 562–269.

Article 17 of the Copyright Directive relates to specific acts of communication to the public for providers of online content-sharing services and 'does not affect the concept of communication to the public or making available to the public in other areas of Union law, nor the possible application of Article 3(1) and (2) of Directive 2001/29/EC to other service providers using content protected by Union law' (see recital 64 of the Copyright Directive). It is a provision that innovates the orientation expressed by the EU Court on the basis of the previous system (in this sense also Cogo (2024), p. 568), since in the decision of 22 June 2021, case C-682/18 and C-683/18, *Peterson* v. *YouTube and Elsevier* v. *Cyando*, cited above, the operator of a platform that has not encouraged infringements and has taken steps to limit them also by promptly removing the reported illegal content was excluded from carrying out an act of communication to the public.

to an infringement hypothesis. Indeed, Art. 17(1) of the Copyright Directive and Art. *102-sexies*(3) of the Italian Copyright Act require the provider of online content sharing services to obtain 'an authorisation from the rightholders [...] in order to communicate to the public or make available to the public works or other subject-matter'.

The authorisation also covers the acts of the user who uploaded the content, if he does not act for commercial purposes or if his activity does not generate significant revenue (Art. 17(2) Copyright Directive and Art. *102-sexies*(4) Italian Copyright Act).

Online content sharing service providers that make available unlicensed content are subject to a special liability regime, different from that of hosting providers (formerly) provided for in Art. 14 of the E-Commerce Directive and now contained in Art. 6 DSA.[76] This special liability regime is, in turn, based on an exemption, conditional on the fulfilment of three cumulative conditions. A 'lighter' liability regime is reserved for 'new' OCSSPs, i.e. those that have been offering services in the Union for less than 3 years.

Before examining the conditions for the exemption from liability of online content sharing service providers for possible infringements of copyright and related rights deriving from protected material uploaded by their users, it is appropriate to indicate their subjective scope of application, defined by Art. 2(6) of the Copyright Directive and, in Italy, by Art. *102-sexies*, paras 1 and 2, of the Italian Copyright Act. These are information society service providers whose main purpose, or one of the main purposes, is to store and give public access to large quantities of protected works uploaded by users, which the service organises and promotes for profit, with the express exclusion of non-profit online encyclopaedias, non-profit educational or scientific repositories, open source software development and sharing platforms, providers of electronic communication services within the meaning of Directive (EU) 2018/1972, providers of online marketplaces, business-to-business cloud services and cloud services that allow users to upload content for personal use.

The assessment as to whether the subjective requirements for the application of Art. 17 Copyright Directive are met should be made on a 'case-by-case basis', taking into account a combination of elements, such as the audience of the service provider and the total number of copyright-protected files uploaded by users (recital 63). It should, however, only apply to 'service providers that play an important role in the online content market by competing with other online content services, such as online audio and video streaming services' (recital 62).

An important element for the identification of the providers of content-sharing services to which the special liability regime of Art. 17 of the Copyright Directive applies is the 'profit aim' understood as profit obtained, directly or indirectly, from the organisation and promotion of the content uploaded by users to attract a wider public, for example, by placing advertisements. Therefore, service providers that do not have such a profit aim do not fall within the definition of OCSSPs, even if they

[76] That the liability system outlined by the Copyright Directive for OCSSPs constitutes a *lex specialis* also with respect to DSA, can be considered unquestionable: on this point, see e.g. Peukert et al. (2022), no. 53, pp. 358–376, pp. 360–361.

do not belong to the categories that are undoubtedly excluded, pursuant to Art. 2(6) of the Copyright Directive, from the application of Art. 17.[77]

Moreover, some scolars[78] pointed out that this provision, due to the 'open' nature of concepts such as 'main purpose' and 'large amount of works', will certainly give rise to litigation in 'grey' cases, i.e. relating not only to sharing platforms that do not fall within the expressly excluded categories, but also to platforms that, due to their importance and size (such as YouTube or Instagram), certainly fall within the definition of OCSSP.

Turning to the objective part of the (new and special) liability case, providers of online content sharing services are 'liable for unauthorised acts of communication to the public, including making available to the public, of copyright-protected works and other subject matter', unless they prove that they have cumulatively fulfilled the following conditions having:

(a) made 'best efforts' to obtain an authorisation;[79]
(b) made, in accordance with high industry standards of professional diligence, best efforts to ensure the unavailability of specific works and other subject matter for which the rightholders have provided the service providers with the relevant and necessary information;
(c) acted expeditiously, upon receiving a sufficiently substantiated notice from the rightholders, to disable access to, or to remove from their websites, the notified works or other subject matter, and made best efforts to prevent their future uploads in accordance with point (b)' (para 4, Art. 17 Copyright Directive and Art. *102-septies*, Italian Copyright Act).[80]

[77] Doubts as to the appropriateness of the legislative choice to apply what appears to be favourable treatment to providers of completely free sharing services have been expressed by Lavagnini (2023), pp. 759 ff., spec. p. 766. It should also be pointed out that, as also noted by the author, the exclusion from the scope of application of Art. 17 of the Copyright Directive does not amount to unaccountability of the platform: it simply makes it subject to the regime of Art. 6 DSA.

[78] Quintais et al. (2024), no. 55, pp. 157 ff. On the difficulty of giving unambiguous content to the concept of 'profit motive', see also Lavagnini (2023).

[79] It should be noted that Art. *102-septies* (1) of the Copyright Act, unlike the corresponding provision of the Copyright Directive, requires that the 'utmost efforts' to obtain an authorisation be made 'in accordance with high standards of professional diligence in the sector'.

[80] As mentioned above, for 'new' online sharing service providers the liability regime is mitigated, in the sense that if they have an annual turnover of less than ten million euro they simply have to make best efforts to obtain a licence from the rightsholder and act 'expeditiously, upon receiving a sufficiently substantiated notice, to disable access to the notified works or other subject matter or to remove those works or other subject matter from their websites'; if they have an average of more than five million unique visitors per month, 'they shall also demonstrate that they have made best efforts to prevent further uploads of the notified works and other subject matter for which the rightholders have provided relevant and necessary information' (Art. 17(6) Copyright Directive and Art. *102-octies* 102-octiesItalian Copyright Act).

It is also expressly excluded that a service provider 'the main purpose of which is to engage in or to facilitate copyright piracy'[81] (recital 62, Copyright Directive).

It is also reiterated that the application of the above provisions 'shall not lead to any general monitoring obligation' (Art. 17(8) Copyright Directive), since the liability system outlined in Art. 17(4) is based on 'cooperation between online content-sharing service providers and rightholders', with the aim, inter alia, of preventing access 'of works or other subject-matter uploaded by users which do not infringe copyright and related rights, including in cases where such works or other subject-matter are covered by an exception or limitation' (Art. 17(7) Copyright Directive).

In fact, the main concern regarding the liability regime under Art. 17 of the Copyright Directive relates to the risk of overblocking,[82] with the consequent compression of users' freedom of expression and information: this concern was at the origin of the troubled approval process of this directive[83] and of the appeal submitted by Poland to the EU Court of Justice to have Art. 17(4)(c) or, alternatively, the entire Art. 17 annulled. The appeal was rejected by the Court,[84] enhancing the obligations (of result) to ensure the lawful uses of protected subject-matter provided for in Art. 17(7) of the Copyright Directive. In order to 'support a correct and consistent transposition of Art. 17 of the Copyright Directive in all Member States, paying particular attention to the need to strike a balance between fundamental rights and the use of exceptions and limitations', in 2021, the Commission published its guidelines,[85] which should be reinterpretedin light of the aforementioned decision of the Court of Justice, which came later.

---

[81] The reference is to cases, such as that of the Pirate *Bay* (on which see EU Court of Justice 14 June 2017, C-610/15, *The Pirate Bay*, cit.), characterised by the intentional element of the infringement by the platform operator, which also determines its exclusion from the safe harbour (already) provided for by the E-Commerce Directive. Again in relation to copyright infringements committed by peer-to-peer platforms, see the recent Trib. Milan, 8 September 2022, with a note by Lavagnini (2023).

[82] As has been rightly pointed out by Faglia (2022), pp. 712 ff., 'the risk of preventing the availability of lawful content (the so-called risk of overblocking) is inherent in any liability regime that requires the web intermediary to comply with a notice and action mechanism', i.e. 'procedures aimed at removing unlawful content from the network through the involvement of the provider of an information society service' (p. 713). As we shall see, the legislator has placed in the OCSSP an obligation, defined by the Court of Justice as a result, to allow the uploading of lawful content, which reduces the risk of overblocking. On this subject, see also Kuczerawy (2020).

[83] A timely account can be read in Falce and Faraone (2021), no. I, pp. 12 ff, and in Thiem (2022), pp. 2 ff.

[84] Court of Justice. EU 26 April 2022, C-401/19, *Republic of Poland* v. *European Parliament and EU Council*, with note by Faglia (2022), n. 1 988. For some comments abroad, see Jütte and Priora (2022), pp. 631 ff.; Krokida (2023), p. 348; Jütte (2022), pp. 693 ff. See also Senftleben (2024), pp. 347 ff.; Quaedvlieg (2024), pp. 359 ff.

[85] Communication from the Commission to the European Parliament and the Council of 4 June 2021, comm/2021/288, *Guidance on Article 17 of Directive 2019/790/EU on Copyright in the Digital Single Market.*

The OCSSPs' liability regime thus revolves around the concept of 'best efforts': to obtain the necessary authorisations from rightholders; to prevent the uploading of content reported by rightholders themselves, if they do not wish to grant licences; and to promptly remove illegally uploaded content and prevent new uploads in the future.

These are therefore obligations of 'means', which require OCSSPs to take action and/or organise themselves to (try to) achieve the result desired by the standard.

In its guidelines, the Commission made it clear that the concept of 'best efforts' constitutes 'an autonomous notion of EU law' that should be 'interpreted in light of the aim and the objectives of Article 17' and its entire text, particularly with the obligation 'of result', to ensure the uploading of lawful content.

With regard to efforts to obtain a licence, the Commission recommends a case-by-case assessment, taking into consideration the specific market practices of the various sectors, but indicating as a minimum requirement that OCSSP 'engage proactively with rightholders that can be easily identified and located', as is the case with collective management organisations under Directive 2014/26/EU.[86]

It is worth noting that the Commission has expressed the view that, in verifying whether the online content sharing service provider has made best effort to obtain authorisation from the rightholders, it should be considered that licensing agreements 'should be fair and keep a reasonable balance between both parties', bearing in mind that 'Recital 61 also states that rightholders should receive appropriate remuneration for the use of their protected works or other subject matter' and that 'service providers should be transparent with rightholders' about 'the criteria they intend to use to identify and remunerate the content covered by the agreement, in particular when service providers use content recognition technology to report on the uses of content under licenses'.[87]

---

[86] Directive 2014/26/EU of the European Parliament and of the Council of 26 February 2014 on collective management of copyright and related rights and multi-territorial licensing of rights in musical works for online use in the internal market. On this topic, see most recently Barbone (2022), pp. 349 ff.

[87] With regard to the issue of licence negotiation, it is worth mentioning the case concerning the negotiations between the SIAE, a well-known Italian collective management organisation, and Meta, in relation to the use of musical works included in the repertoire managed by the aforementioned organisation within the Facebook and Instagram platforms. The case did not deal with a possibile liability of Meta under the Copyright Directive, but rather with a possible abuse of economic dependence in the digital environment, pursuant to Art. 9 of Law No. 192/1996 on subsupply agreements, as amended by Law No. 118/2022, which introduced a (relative) presumption of economic dependence of the company that uses the intermediation services provided by a digital platform (on this provision, see Libertini (2023), pp. 36 ff). Anyway, the Copyright Directive was an important issue of this case because [a] it requires the negotiation of a fair licence between the provider and the rightholders, being the OCSSP obliged to provide rightholders with information on the use of their works within the platform; and [b] the Copyright Directive emphasises that authors, artists and the collective organisations representing them are usually in a weak position vis-à-vis the platforms (recital 72). The case at issue arose because META interrupted the negotiation of a license agreement with SIAE and, in order to avoid any possibile liability for infringement of copyright and related rights, removed from its platforms all the musical works managed by the

There is currently only one court decision on the obligation of the operator of an online platform falling under the definition of OCSSP to make its 'best efforts' to obtain a licence for the content used on its platform. This is a decision of the Munich District Court[88] rendered in a case between the owner of rights to cinematographic works and the platform TikTok. In the case at issue the negotiation of a license agreement failed, the platform then blocked the unlicensed contents, but the issue of past uses remained. The German court condemned the platform for copyright infringement, as in its opinion the platform had not made every effort to obtain a licence under the provision implementing Art. 17(4) of the Copyright Directive in Germany.

With regard to the other conditions for the exclusion of liability for copyright infringement of online content sharing service providers, the concept of 'best efforts' requires, as we have seen, that when providing filtering systems for the uploading (*ex-ante* or *ex-post*) of content infringing copyright or related rights, the service provider acts 'in accordance with high standards of professional diligence'. In this regard, recital 66 of the Copyright Directive requires it to take 'all the steps that would be taken by a diligent operator to achieve the result of preventing the availability of unauthorised works or other subject matter on its website, taking into account best industry practices and the effectiveness of the steps taken in light of all relevant factors and developments, as well as the principle of proportionality'.

The industry practices in force in the market at a given time are therefore the key, guaranteeing the service provider the freedom to choose the most suitable technology or solution to fulfil the duty of care, also with the cooperation of the rightsholder.[89]

SIAE. SIAE requested the intervention of the italian antitrust authority (Autorità Garante della Concorrenza e del Mercato - AGCM), complaining of an abuse of economic dependence pursuant Art. 9 of Law No. 192/1996. By order No. 36060 issued on a urgent bases in proceeding A-559, the AGCM ordered Meta, as a precautionary measure, to resume the negotiations and to provide SIAE with the necessary information. In this regard the authority established the appointment of a 'trustee' to identify the quantity and quality of the information to be provided to SIAE. Furthermore the AGCM ordered Meta to restore the usability of the content managed by SIAE, subject to SIAE's authorisation. The precautionary measure, which was confirmed by TAR Lazio, section I, with decision no. 16069 of 30 October 2023, was however annulled by the Council of State, with decision no. 5824 of 2 July 2024.

For a commentary on the AGCM measure, see Lopopolo (2023), no. III, pp. 432 ff.; on the subject, see also Scalzini (2022), pp. 113 ff.

[88] The decision is dated 9 February 2024, Case No. 42O1079/22, and is available in German in the link at the bottom of Braun's short commentary note (2025).

[89] In the aforementioned Communication to the European Parliament and the Council of 4 June 2021, comm/2021/288, *Guidance on Article 17 of Directive 2019/790/EU on Copyright in the Digital Single Market* (para 2), the Commission states that the dialogue with stakeholders has made it possible to identify the content recognition technologies currently most widely used by the main service providers in relation to copyright-protected content. These are fingerprinting-based technologies, although other technologies such as hashing, watermarking, use of metadata, keyword searches, or a combination thereof, may also be used. The Commission points out, for the purpose of the case-by-case assessment of the fulfilment of the obligations, that while 'larger service providers with a significant audience may be expected to deploy more advanced solutions/

Such cooperation is, moreover, of paramount importance since the obligations to prevent the uploading of infringing content and to remove it provided for in Art. 17(4) Copyright Directive and Art. *102-septies*(1) Italian Copyright Act presuppose that, depending on the case, rightholders provide service providers with 'relevant and necessary information' for *ex ante* or *ex post* monitoring or 'sufficiently reasoned reports' to take blocking measures.

Particularly, information aimed at obtaining monitoring on specific content must be precise on the 'ownership rights of the work or material' and contain what is necessary to enable *providers* to fulfil their obligations, taking into account the 'solutions used by service providers'.[90] The Commission calls for cooperation between rightholders and online content sharing service providers, also to find shared solutions on the issue of the identification of works to be protected.

In this regard, it is worth mentioning the very topical issue of the protectability by copyright of works generated by so-called generative Artificial Intelligence systems in a legal system such as the european and italian ones (but also in other legal systems), in which copyright arises only in 'human' authors, whose personality the work is an expression of.[91] On this topic a debate is going on, but in a nutshell, it can be said that (at the moment) copyright cannot be claimed on such works when a sufficient creative contribution by a human being cannot be identified.[92]

As the number of works created with, or by, I.A. circulating on the Internet is increasing, a problem will arise for platforms in the management of possible

---

technologies' it may be 'more proportionate to expect smaller service providers to resort to simpler solutions (like metadata or keyword search) as long as these solutions do not result in over-blocking of content'. In addition, 'the availability of suitable and effective means and the related costs' should be considered.

[90] When using fingerprinting technology, rightholders should 'provide an electronic fingerprint of the work [...] or a file that the service provider itself will fingerprint, together with information about the ownership of the rights. When using metadata-based solutions, the information provided may include, for example, the title, author/producer, duration, date': see Communication *Guidance on Article 17 of Directive 2019/790/EU on Copyright in the Digital Single Market*, cit., para 2).

[91] Pursuant to Art. 6 of the Italian Copyright Act, 'the original title of the acquisition of copyright is the creation of the work, as a particular expression of intellectual work'; pursuant to Art. 8 of the Italian Copyright Act, 'the author of the work [...] shall be considered the person who is indicated as such', and 'the pseudonym, artistic name, acronym or conventional sign known to be equivalent to the real name' shall be considered 'as the name'; above all, Art. 25 of the Italian Copyright Act links the duration of the economic exploitation rights to the life of the author, establishing that they 'last for the author's entire life and until the end of the seventy calendar years after his death' and that they 'last until the end of the seventy calendar years after his death'. Above all, Art. 25 of the Italian Copyright Act links the duration of exploitation rights to the life of the author, establishing that they 'last throughout the author's life and until the end of the 70th calendar year after his death', and Art. 23 of the Italian Copyright Act entrusts the protection of very personal rights, such as the paternity of the work, to the deceased author's family members. In short, currently only a person can be the 'author' of a work, whereas a machine cannot be.

[92] See in this regard Cass., ord. 16 January 2023, no. 1107 with note by Iaia (2023) and with notes by Bettoni (2023), no. 2, p. 391 and Leanza (2023), no. 2, p. 391. For further insights into the protection of creations, not only aesthetic/cultural, obtained using AI systems, see, among others, Posteraro (2023), no. 2; Fabbio (2021a), no. I, pp. 129 ff.; Sena (2020), no. I, pp. 151 ff.

blocking or filtering requests related to such kind of works. The solution may not be easy, also in the light of what the Court of Justice ruled in the *Republic of Poland* case regarding the obligation to guarantee users the right to upload lawful content.

In this regard, a suggestion may arise from the obligation to 'mark' content generated by Artificial Intelligence systems under Art. 50, para 2, of Regulation (EU) 1689/2024 (the so-called AI Act).[93] When a work is 'marked' in such a way, a (*juris tantum*) presumption of non-protectability with copyright applies. Indeed, the solution currently adopted to assess whether a work created by a generative AI system may be protected under copyright, is based on a case-by-case approach, verifying the existence of a 'creative contribution that directly and immediately affects the representative form of the work', and excluding such a creative contribution when the work, in its individuality of representation, is 'generated by the machine according to its logic and algorithmic capacity'.[94]

In other words, the 'AI marking' of the work should allow the platform to treat the work as 'free of rights',[95] unless the work is already recognised as deserving protection or the owner accompanies the Platform's request for intervention with sufficient evidence to prove that there has been a human creative contribution that has affected the representative form of the work itself, making it worthy of copyright protection.

As anticipated, a fundamental issue concerns the balance between the need for effective protection of online copyright and the need to guarantee users' freedom of expression and information. This balance is imposed by para 7 of Art. 17 of the Copyright Directive (implemented by Art. *102-nonies*, para 1 of the Italian Copyright Act), whereby the cooperation between service providers and rightholders must not prevent the availability of lawful content, including content for which the user may benefit from 'an exception or limitation' to copyright or related rights.

In this regard, the aforementioned provision of the Copyright Directive has obliged Member states to ensure that users of an OCSSP may use protected works in the content they generate, upload and make aviailable on online content-sharing

[93] On the possibility of 'tagging' content generated by AI systems, see also *Commission Guidelines for providers of Very Large Online Platforms and Very Large Online Search Engines on the mitigation of systemic risks for electoral processes pursuant to Article 35(3) of Regulation (EU) 2022/2065* (C/2024/3014).

[94] Cogo (2024), p. 522. Using musical compositions as an example, the author emphasises how 'the protection of [them] can be excluded without too many qualms' when they are 'created by a so-called generative artificial intelligence application on the basis of the author's textual input'', not even the selection of the results presented by the application being sufficient to affect the creative representation of the work; on the other hand, 'there does not seem to be any reason to deny protection of a composition created by the machine when the author has stimulated it with his own specific inputs, has selected it from among several proposals and has substantially intervened on the final representative form of the work, without prejudice to the rights on the prior works that may be recognisable in the work thus obtained'.

[95] And unless, in the future, a *sui generis* right is provided for these creations, or they are granted copyright protection even in the absence of sufficient human creative input, or it becomes technically feasable to define a standard that 'certifies' which works are the result of sufficient human creative input to grant them copyright protection.

services, when the use is for the purposes of quotation, criticism and review or for the purpose of caricature, parody or *pastiche*,[96] since it is important to 'strike a balance between the fundamental rights laid down in the Charter of Fundamental Rights of the European Union, in particular the freedom of expression and the freedom of the arts, and the right to property, including intellectual property' (recital 70).

In fact, the Court of Justice, in its decision on Poland's appeal against Art. 17(4) of the Copyright Directive, clarified that users have the right to upload lawful content (para 88) and that Art. 17(7) of the Copyright Directive provides for an obligation of result (para 78). Therefore, when an OCSSP employ automated technologies to prevent the uploading of infringing content, they must take particular precautions since 'in order to prevent the risk which, in particular, the use of automatic recognition and filtering tools entails for the right to freedom of expression and information of users of online content-sharing services, the EU legislature laid down a clear and precise limit […] on the measures that may be taken or required in implementing the obligations laid down in point (b) and point (c), in fine, of Article 17(4) of Directive 2019/790, by excluding, in particular, measures which filter and block lawful content when uploading'.[97]

In this context, as already emerged from the Commission's guidelines, the organisational mechanism for fulfilling the obligations, provided for by Art. 17 of the Copyright Directive requires the adoption of different procedures depending on the type of suspected infringement of copyright.[98] Indeed, only for content that definitely constitutes an infringement (i.e. 'manifestly infringing copyright or related rights') will it be possible to proceed with automatic blocking, subject always to the notification of the user who uploaded the content and the possibility for the same to

[96] Article 70(1) of the Italian Copyright Act already provided for the possibility of freely 'summarising, quoting or reproducing passages or parts of works and communicating them to the public […] for the purpose of criticism or discussion', provided that 'within the limits justified by these purposes' and on condition that 'they do not constitute competition with the economic use of the work'. The literal tenor of the provision has, however, made its application to works other than literary works, particularly works of the visual arts, uncertain, and in any case the exception operates when the indicated conditions are met. As for parody, although it is not the subject of a specific exception in Italian law, jurisprudence has traditionally considered it lawful, as an autonomous work, endowed with its own creative character, although recently this approach seems to have been challenged by Cass., ord. 30 December 2022, no. 38165, with a note by Toni (2023), n. 2004. In implementing the Copyright Directive, the Italian legislator introduced Art. *102-nonies*, para 2, requiring online content sharing platforms to ensure their users the possibility to freely use protected works for the purposes of quotation, criticism and review or for the purpose of caricature, parody or *pastiche*, without further conditions, and this seems to overcome, even if only for the online environment (Toni (2023), p. 708, also speaks of the 'specific and sectorial character' of the new exceptions), the exception regime provided for the offline environment. On the impact of the exceptions in the Copyright Directive, see Musso (2020), pp. 411 ff.; generally, on exceptions to copyright, see for all Cogo (2024), pp. 573 ff.; on quotation and parody in the system outlined by the Infosoc Directive, see Court of Justice. EU 29 July 2019, C-476/17, *Pelham*, with note by Banterle (2020), n. 1914.

[97] ECJ. EU 26 April 2022, C-401/19, *Republic of Poland*, cited above, para 85.

[98] See also, on the subject of measures against illegal online content, Commission Recommendation of 1 March 2018, (EU) 2018/334.

file a complaint to obtain the restoration of the blocked content. In the case of content that is not manifestly infringing copyright and related rights, its removal may only be ordered after a human *ex post* verification and provided that the rightsholders, having been informed of the presence of such content on the platform, request the OCSSP to remove it by sending a notice explaining why the content is unlawful.[99]

Of course, it is always possible that the 'human verification' leads to errors. On the other hand, even in the case of an exact match to the protected work, which constitutes an indication of a 'manifest infringement' for which the automatic filtering mechanism is allowed, it could be a lawful use (for instance because the user has negotiated an authorisation with the rightsholder). For this reason, complaint mechanisms have been provided for against the platform operator, with the possibility of further submitting the matter to the competent authority (Art. 17(9), Copyright Directive and Art. *102-decies*, Italian Copyright Act). In Italy, the procedure takes place before the Autorità per le Garanzie nelle Comunicazioni (AgCom), according to the rules laid down in the AgCom Resolution No. 115/23/CONS of 18 May 2023. It will be a matter of understanding, when put to the test, whether the legal framework put in place will actually allow users' rights to be protected.[100]

8 Marketplace Platforms and Intellectual Property Rights

As seen, the liability regime outlined in Art. 17 of the Copyright Directive applies only to the online use of copyright-protected material, and marketplace platforms, 'the main activity of which is online retail, and not giving access to copyright-protected content' (recital 62, Copyright Directive) are expressly excluded from the definition of online content-sharing service provider by Art. 2(6) of the Copyright Directive.

However, the question of the possible direct liability of marketplace platform has arisen in relation to the sale on such platforms of counterfeit products by their users. Particularly, the EU Court of Justice has ruled several times in cases relating to trademark counterfeiting, setting out principles that can be applied *mutatis mutandis* to the offer for sale on the marketplace of any product infringing any Intellectual Property right (such as patented medicines or devices, design objects, plants, etc.).

In *L'Oreal v. eBay*,[101] concerning the unauthorized sale on said platform of goods bearing trademarks owned by L'Oreal,[102] the Court had addressed among others, the

[99] In this sense, see *ampus* Quintais et al. (2024).

[100] In this regard, see the interesting considerations, also stemming from empirical research, by Quintais et al. (2024), p. 171, on the self-censorship practised by creatives who disseminate their works through online platforms in order to avoid the preventive and automatic blocking of their creations. Also on the subject, from a different perspective, Moscon (2020), no. 51, pp. 977–982.

[101] ECJ. EU 12 July 2011, *L'Oreal v. eBay*, cited above.

[102] These were samples, not intended for trade, because the owner of the trade marks had provided them for demonstration purposes to its authorised distributors. The samples were, among other

following questions: [1] whether, by purchasing from Google (through AdWords corresponding to L'Oreal's trademarks) services for the placement of its users' product listings offered on its platform, eBay was making a 'use' of someone else's trademark 'in the course of trade', which under the trademark rules the owner can prevent; [2] whether, by hosting listings for goods bearing the plaintiff's trademarks, eBay was likewise making use of the trademark 'in the course of trade'.

On the first question, the Court, in line with its rulings in *Smirnoff*[103] and *Google France*,[104] held that eBay can be considered an 'advertiser' that makes 'use' of another person's trademark in the course of trade, having 'used keywords corresponding to L'Oréal trade marks to promote its own service of making an online marketplace available to sellers and buyers of products' (para 89). The Court therefore ruled that 'on a proper construction of Article 5(1)(a) of Directive 89/104 and Article 9(1)(a) of Regulation No. 40/94[105] the proprietor of a trade mark is entitled to prevent an online marketplace operator from advertising – on the basis of a keyword which is identical to his trade mark and which has been selected in an internet referencing service by that operator – goods bearing that trade mark which are offered for sale on the marketplace, where that advertising does not enable reasonably well-informed and reasonably observant internet users, or enables them

things, sold on eBay without packaging, thereby harming the image of the trademarks, which are very well known. Trademark law provides that, in the case of original goods, i.e. originating from the trademark owner, the latter may not oppose their circulation if the first act of placing on the market in the EU territory (or in the EEA area) was done by him or with his consent, unless there are legitimate reasons. Part of the questions submitted to the Court concerned precisely the application of this rule (so-called principle of exhaustion of trademark rights), which also applies to other Intellectual Property rights. For further precedents on exhaustion, also in relation to the repackaging of original goods, see ECJ. EU 27 October 2022, Case C-197/21, *Soda-Club*, in *Giur. ann. dir. ind.*, 2022, no. 7178; Trib. Milano 10 May 2021, *ivi*, 2021, no. 7020 and Trib. Milano 17 January 2019, *ivi*, 2019, no. 6767. In doctrine, see Di Cataldo (2022), no. I, pp. 20 ff.

[103] Court of Justice. EU, ord. 19 February 2009, C-62/08. The case concerned the possible liability for trademark infringement of the operator of an Internet site who published anonymous offers to buy or sell and concluded the relevant contracts in his own name but on behalf of sellers, charging a commission, and who had used in his business correspondence a sign identical to the plaintiff's trademark. The Court held that the latter was making 'use' of someone else's trademark, considering it irrelevant that the goods did not belong to the site operator. The Court gave weight, inter alia, to the fact that 'the use of that sign by the third party, in a situation such as that at issue in the main proceedings, is likely to be interpreted by the public targeted as designating or tending to designate the third party as the undertaking from which the goods originate and is therefore such as to create the impression that there is a material link in trade between those goods and the undertaking from which they originate' (para 49). Generally, on the notion of 'use' of the trademark relevant to infringement, ECJ. EU 12 November 2002, case C-206/01, *Arsenal Football Club*, in *Giur. ann. dir. ind.*, 2003, no. 4602; ECJ. EU 16 November 2004, Case C-245/02, *Anheuser-Busch, in Dir. ind.*, 2005, 355; ECJ. EU 25 January 2007, Case C-48/05, *Adam Opel, in Jur. ann. dir. ind.*, 2007, no. 5188; 11 September 2007, Case C-17/06, *Céline*, ibid. 2007, no. 5195; 12 June 2008, Case C-533/06, *O2 Holdings and O2 (UK)*, ibid. 2008, no. 5324.

[104] Court of Justice. EU 23 March 2010, C-236-238/08, cit.

[105] Now replaced by Directive (EU) 2015/2436 to approximate the laws of the Member States relating to trade marks and Regulation (EU) 2017/1001, respectively.

only with difficulty, to ascertain whether the goods concerned originate from the proprietor of the trade mark or from an undertaking economically linked to that proprietor or, on the contrary, originate from a third party'.

On the second question, the Court ruled out that the platform could be held liable for infringement only because, by making its services available, it in fact allows its advertisers to offer for sale products that counterfeit other trademarks. The principle expressed in this regard is that 'the operator of an online marketplace does not "use" [...] of signs identical with or similar to trade marks which appear in offers for sale displayed on its site' and can only be liable indirectly when it has played an 'active' role enabling it to have knowledge or control over the data stored (i.e. it 'provides assistance consisting in particular in optimising the presentation of the offers for sale in question or in promoting them') or when, while having a passive role, 'was aware of facts or circumstances on the basis of which a diligent economic operator should have realised that the offers for sale in question were unlawful and, in the event of it being so aware, failed to act expeditiously' (paras 123 and 124).

Later on, the Court ruled in a case concerning the sale of allegedly infringing goods on Amazon's marketplace.[106] The Court had been asked whether the operator of a marketplace that not only offers a space for the advertisements of its customers, but also stores the goods and organises their delivery through a third party, even in a situation where the sale is made directly by the advertiser, makes 'use' of the trademark.

Even taking into account the literal wording of the European provisions configuring the content of the rights conferred by the registration of a trademark,[107] which allow it to prohibit 'the offering of goods, their putting on the market, their storage "for those purposes" or the offering or provision of services under the cover of the sign in question', the Court replied in the negative, holding that 'in order for the storage of goods bearing signs identical, or similar to trade marks to be classified as 'using' those signs, it is also necessary [...] for the economic operator providing the storage itself to pursue the aim referred to by those provisions, which is offering the goods or putting them on the market (para 45).

The Court also stated that the notion of use 'involves active behaviour and direct or indirect control of the act constituting the use', since only a person who has such control 'is effectively able to stop that use and therefore comply with that

[106] ECJ. EU 2 April 2020, *C-567/18*, *Coty Germany v. Amazon*, in *Jur. ann. dir. ind.*, 2020, no. 6956 (max.) with note by Andreoletti and La Rocca (2018), no. II, pp. 303 ff. See also Howard and Hyland (2020), pp. 849 ff. The case had been instituted by Coty Germany, which complained that Davidoff-branded perfumes were being sold on Amazon in infringement of its trademark rights.

[107] Currently, Art. 9(3)(b) of Regulation (EU) 2017/1001, which in this respect reproduces Art. 9(2) (b) of Regulation (EU) 207/2009 previously in force. For Italian precedents holding the forwarding agent liable (also), in a case, moreover, of belonging to the same corporate group as the owner of the e-commerce website selling the infringing products, see Trib. Milano, ord. 13 June 2013, in *Giur. ann. dir. ind.*, 2017, no. 6544. Trib. Genova 29 November 2016, ibid., 2016, n. 6449 held liable for counterfeiting a company in whose warehouses counterfeit products of other people's trademarks had been found, with a view to subsequent marketing on its own together with original products.

prohibition'. And it enunciated the principle that 'a person who, on behalf of a third party, stores goods which infringe trade mark rights, without having knowledge of that infringement, stocks those goods in order to offer them or put them on the market for the purposes of those provisions, even if it is only the third party who intends to offer those goods or put them on the market'.

Another element was added by the EU Court of Justice in 2022 in the decision rendered in *Louboutin v. Amazon*.[108] The dispute arose because high-heeled shoes with the famous red sole were on sale on Amazon, infringing the trademark rights of the plaintiff company. The relevant advertisements, from third-party sellers, were similar to those of products directly sold by Amazon and could be perceived by the public as advertisements of Amazon itself. Moreover, the third-parties products were delivered to customers by Amazon, whose business model has changed over time and includes offering to sellers its own logistics services.

The question was whether, in the circumstances described by the referring courts,[109] Amazon made direct use of the plaintiff's trademark, and the Court answered in the affirmative.

It is worth retracing the reasoning of the decision. In fact the Court, while declaring itself to be in continuity with the previous judgments, reaches different conclusions in view of the changed context offered by the referring judges (and, probably, of the changed attitude of the EU legislature towards large platforms, as can be seen from the DSA). According to the Court, 'in order to determine whether the operator of an online sales website incorporating an online marketplace does itself make use of a sign which is identical with a trade mark of another person, which appears in advertisements relating to goods offered by third-party sellers on that marketplace, it is necessary to assess whether a well-informed and reasonably observant user of that website establishes a link between that operator's services and the sign in question' such as to consider "that the operator is marketing, in its own name and on its own account, the goods for which the sign in question is being used"' (paras 43 and 48).[110]

In the context of that assessment, 'the method of presenting the advertisements, both individually and as a whole [...] and the nature and scope of the services provided by the operator of the website are particularly important' (para 49). In that regard, the Court observes, first of all, that 'a uniform method of presenting the offerings published on its website', which displays 'both its own advertisements and those of third-party sellers and placing its own logo as a renowned distributor on its own website and on all those advertisements, including those relating to goods offered by third-party sellers', is liable to give 'the well-informed and reasonably observant user the impression that that operator is marketing, in its own name and on its own behalf, the goods offered for sale by those third-party sellers. Consequently,

108 ECJ. EU 22 December 2022, Cases C-148/21 and C-184/21, *Louboutin v. Amazon*, in *Jur. ann. dir. ind.*, 2022, no. 7179 (max.), with extensive notes. See also Riis (2023), pp. 337 ff.

109 Amazon was sued in Belgium and Luxembourg.

110 On the role of public perception in the judgement of trademark infringement, see Sironi (2013).

when those goods bear a sign which is identical with a trade mark of another person, that uniform presentation may establish a link, in the eyes of those users, between that sign and the services provided by that same operator' (para 51).

The Court also points out that 'presentation is likely to strengthen the impression of the well-informed and reasonably observant user that those goods thus promoted are being marketed by that operator, in its own name and on its own behalf' when 'the operator of an online sales website describes the various offerings, from itself or a third party, without distinguishing them as to their origin, as 'bestsellers' or 'most sought after' or 'most popular' for the purpose inter alia of promoting some of those offerings' (para 52).

Lastly, the 'nature and scope of the services provided by the operator' of the marketplace, 'such as the services consisting inter alia in dealing with the questions of the users relating to those goods or to the storage, shipping and management of returns of those goods, are also likely to give the impression, to a well-informed and reasonably observant user, that those same goods are being marketed by that operator, in its own name and on its own behalf, and may thus establish a link, in the eyes of those users, between its services and the signs placed on those goods and in the advertisements of those third-party sellers' (para 53).

Accordingly, the Court concluded that 'the operator of an online sales website incorporating, as well as that operator's own sales offerings, an online marketplace may be regarded as itself using a sign which is identical with an EU trade mark of another person for goods which are identical with those for which that trade mark is registered, where third-party sellers offer for sale, on that marketplace, without the consent of the proprietor of that trade mark, such goods bearing that sign, if a well-informed and reasonably observant user of that site establishes a link between the services of that operator and the sign at issue, which is in particular the case where, in view of all the circumstances of the situation in question, such a user may have the impression that that operator itself is marketing, in its own name and on its own account, the goods bearing that sign. In that regard, the following are relevant: the fact that that operator uses a uniform method of presenting the offers published on its website, displaying both the advertisements relating to the goods which it sells in its own name and on its own behalf and those relating to goods offered by third-party sellers on that marketplace; the fact that it places its own logo as a renowned distributor on all those advertisements; and the fact that it offers third-party sellers, in connection with the marketing of goods bearing the sign at issue, additional services consisting inter alia in the storing and shipping of those goods' (para 54).

In Italy, too, there have been cases, mostly relating to precautionary proceedings, which have seen owners of mostly luxury brands pitted against marketplace platforms, alleging a direct trademark infringement activity.

Among these, it is worth mentioning Trib. Milano, ord. 3 July 2019, case *Sisley v. Amazon*.[111] In this case the well-known luxury cosmetics manufacturer took pre-

[111] Trib. Milan 3 July 2019, with note by Sironi (2021) pp. 389 ff. Also on the subject of selective distribution, see Mansani (2021), vol 1, pp. 347 ff.

cautionary action against Amazon, which had placed Sisley products on sale on its online marketplace in a manner that the owner of the brand, which had set up a selective distribution system that reserved the sale of the products only to authorised retailers,[112] considered detrimental to the image of the brand. The appeal had been rejected by the Court of Milan on the ground that the selective distribution agreements between Sisley and its resellers were contrary to Art. 101 TFEU on the grounds that they did not allow online sales.[113]

In the complaint, after Sisley had changed the terms of its contracts to allow its retailers to sell products online on their e-commerce sites but not on third-party sites, the injunction was granted. Amazon was, in fact, held liable for trademark infringement because the sales methods on its marketplace were deemed to debase Sisley's trademarks.

Particularly, the Court considered as damaging the brand the offer for sale and advertising of Sisley products 'alongside advertising material of other brands, even of lower market segments, on the same internet page', putting them 'next to products not belonging to the sphere of luxury' and 'links to sites of totally different products'. Moreover, the Court emphasised the 'lack of appropriate customer service, similar to that ensured by the presence in the brick-and-mortar-shop of a person capable of adequately advising or informing custumers'.

Still on the subject of online sales of branded products sold through selective distribution systems, the Court of Milan, in a precautionary proceeding that pitted the fashion house Chanel against an online retailer not belonging to the official

[112] In a selective distribution system 'the supplier undertakes to sell the contract goods or services, either directly or indirectly, only to distributors selected on the basis of specified criteria and where these distributors undertake not to sell such goods or services to unauthorised distributors within the territory reserved by the supplier to operate that system' (Art. 1(1)(g), Regulation (EU) 2022/720). It is a system that is mainly used in sectors that require specialised personnel at the sales stage, such as high-tech products, and in the case of luxury brands, whose value is (also) preserved through the careful selection of retailers, so that the outlets provide the public with an image consistent with that of the brand. Containing clauses restricting intrabrand competition, the compatibility of such distribution systems with Art. 101 TFEU, which as is well known prohibits restrictive agreements of competition, depends mainly on the fulfilment of the conditions currently contained in Regulation (EU) 2022/720 on vertical agreements, on which see Commission Notice Guidelines on Vertical Restraints (2022/C 248/01) of 30 June 2022, para 4.6.2 and in doctrine, among others, D'ostuni and Beretta (2021), pp. 675 ff.

[113] Clauses prohibiting online sales to resellers from a selective distribution system *tout court* are contrary to Art. 101 TFEU: see in this respect ECJ. EU, 13 October 2011, C-439/09, *Pierre Fabre*, 13 October 2011, C-43909, in *Foro it.*, 2012, IV, 414, concerning the legitimacy of clauses that, by requiring the reseller to market products in a physical space and in the presence of a pharmacist, in fact prohibited online sales; see also the Commission's Communication Guidelines on Vertical Restraints (2022/C 248/01), cit., which considers obligations, of whatever nature, that prevent the use of the online channel as serious restrictions. On the other hand, in a case concerning the resale of luxury goods, clauses were found to be compatible with competition rules if they allowed the retailer to sell on its own e-commerce channel, but prohibited it from using third-party marketplaces over which it had no control and which could harm the image of the brand (ECJ. EU 6 December 2017, *C-230/16*, *Coty Germany*, in *Jur. ann. dir. ind.*, 2017, no. 6592). On this topic, see also Colangelo and Torti (2018); Giani (2019), no. I, pp. 432 ff.; Ricolfi (2015), p. 1323.

network, held that the trademark owner had a legitimate reason to oppose the resale of its products, having ascertained an 'alteration of the codes affixed to the packaging' and the presentation of the products 'with blurred images and crowded content, next to products of a different merchandising nature and with lower profile brands' with consequent prejudice 'to the luxury or prestige image of the brand due to the marketing carried out by third parties outside the selective distribution network'.[114]

References

Andreoletti MA, La Rocca F (2018) Considerazioni generali in tema di distribuzione selettiva. Riv Dir Ind II: 303 ff

Anselmi L (2015) Nota a App Milano, 7 gennaio 2015. AIDA 1701

Anselmi L (2021) La Corte di Giustizia sul caso Youtube: avanti (ma non troppo) con giudizio. AIDA, p 1954

Banterle F (2020) Libertà di sampling ed equilibrismi tra espressione artistica e diritti esclusivi nel caso Pelham. AIDA, p 1914

Barbone M (2022) Diritto d'autore e collecting societis in internet. In: Cassano G, Tassone B (eds) Diritto industriale e diritto d'autore nell'era digitale. Milano, pp 349 ff

Bertani M (2018) L'ultima frontiera contro la pirateria online: ingiunzioni dinamiche ai gatekeepers della rete definite con procedure di notice and take down. AIDA, p 1875

Bertani M (2024) Disciplina del processo sulla proprietà intellettuale, In: Bertani M, Cogo A, Fabbio P, Genovese A, Ottolia A (eds) Lineamenti di diritto industriale. Padova.

Bettoni A (2023) Tutela dell'opera d'arte algoritmica. Spunti comparatistici a margine di una recente pronuncia italiana. Arte e Diritto 2:391

Bocchini R (2019) La responsabilità civile plurisoggettiva, successiva ed eventuale dell'ISP. Giur it, pp 2604 ff

Braun S (2025) Munich District Court rules on TikTok's duty to negotiate licences seriously. In Iris 2024-4:1/14, European Audiovisual Observatory (Council of Europe)

Ciliberti L (2024) DSA e EMFA: speciale responsabilità delle piattaforme online e tutela della libertà dei media. Riv it informatica e dir 2

Cogo A (2024) Diritti d'autore e connessi. In: Bertani M, Cogo A, Fabbio P, Genovese A, Ottolia A (eds) Lineamenti di diritto industriale. Padova

Cogo A, Ricolfi M (2020) Administrative enforcement of copyright infringement in Europe. In: Frosio G (ed) Oxford handbook of online intermediary liability. Oxford University Press, Oxford, pp 586 ff

Colangelo G (2011) La responsabilità del service provider per violazione indiretta del diritto d'autore nel caso Yahoo! Italia. Giur comm II:894 ff

Colangelo G, Torti V (2018) Selective distribution and online marketplace restriction under EU competition rules after Coty prestige. Eur Compet Law Rev

Colaruotolo A (2021) Diffusione di opere protette senza autorizzazione: c'è responsabilità dell'ISP in caso di editing del materiale immesso dagli utenti. Riv dir ind II:50–51

Cottino G (2014) La corte di Giustizia si pronuncia sulla tutela del diritto d'autore online. Giur it, pp 2754 ff

D'Ostuni M, Beretta M (2021) Il diritto della concorrenza in Italia. Torino, pp 675 ff

[114] Trib. Milano, ord. 28 February 2022, in *Giur. ann. dir. ind.*, 2022, no. 7138 and, in the previous phase, Trib. Milano, ord. 10 May 2021, *ivi*, 2021, no. 7020.

Di Cataldo V (2022) Importazioni parallele di farmaci confezionati, farmaci sfusi, principi attivi. Vale anche in questi casi il principio dell'esaurimento del diritto di marchio? Giurisprudenza commerciale I:20 ff
Di Ciommo F (2010) Programmi-filtro e criteri di imputazione/esonero della responsabilità on-line. A proposito della sentenza Google/Vivi Down. Dir inf inf, pp 829 ff
Di Ciommo F (2019) Oltre la direttiva 2000/31/CE, o forse no. La responsabilità dei provider di Internet nell'incerta giurisprudenza europea. Foro it, p 2072
Fabbio PH (2021a) Intelligenza artificiale e disciplina dei disegni e modelli. Riv dir ind I:129 ff
Fabbio P (2021b) La questione della proporzionalità dell'inibitoria nel diritto della proprietà intellettuale e dei brevetti in particolare. Riv dir ind I:57 ff
Fabbio P (2024) In: Bertani M, Cogo A, Fabbio P, Genovese A, Ottolia A (eds) Lineamenti di diritto industriale, Padova
Faglia F (2022) La Corte di Giustizia e l'enforcement algoritmico del diritto d'autore. AIDA, pp 712 ff
Falce V (2022) Piattaforme ed ecosistemi digitali. Scelte pro-concorrenziali. In Riv. dir. ind., p 189
Falce V, Faraone N (2021) Spunti di diritto positivo sull'art. 17 della Direttiva Copyright. In: Riv. dir. ind., I, p 12 ff
Galli M (2018) Dynamic injunction, obblighi di sorveglianza e siti "alias": il caso Mondadori. Riv dir media, pp 3 ff
Ghidini G, Cavani G (eds) (2022) Proprietà intellettuale e concorrenza, Torino
Giani S (2019) Distribuzione selettiva tra regolamento di esenzione ed esaurimento del diritto. Riv dir ind I:432 ff
Guardì D (2014) La responsabilità dell'inserzionista e del service provider nell'ambito del keyword advertising. Giur comm II:179 ff
Howard M, Hyland M (2020) The boundaries of "use": when do e-commerce platforms become liable for trade mark infringement? Coty Germany GmbH v Amazon Services Europe Sarl (C-567/18). Eur Intellect Prop Rev, pp 49 ff
Iaia V (2022) La tutela del marchio Juventus si spinge nel Metaverso. Dir & giust 5
Iaia V (2023) Il "maggior rigore" nell'esame di originalità delle opere dell'ingegno realizzate con l'ausilio del software. Riv dir ind 2:247
Iaselli M (2016) Caso Yahoo! Video: la Corte di Appello di Milano non vede responsabilità nell'operato dell'internet provider. Riv dir ind II:166 ff
Jütte BJ (2022) Poland's challenge to Article 17 CDSM Directive fails before the CJEU, but Member States must implement fundamental rights safeguards. J Intellect Prop Law Pract, pp 693 ff
Jütte BJ, Priora G (2022) CJEU rejects Poland's challenge to preventive upload filtering to combat copyright infringement on online platforms. Eur Intellect Prop Rev, pp 631 ff
Krokida Z (2023) Deciphering article 17 of the digital copyright directive and its compatibility with freedom of expression and information following Republic of Poland v European Parliament. Eur Law Rev, pp 348 ff
Kuczerawy A (2020) From 'Notice and Takedown' to 'Notice and Stay Down': risks and safeguards for freedom of expression. In: Frosio G (ed) Oxford handbook of online intermediary liability. Oxford
Lavagnini S (2022a) La responsabilità degli Internet service provider e i prestatori di servizi online. In: Lavagnini S (ed) Il diritto d'autore nel mercato unico digitale. Torino
Lavagnini S (ed) (2022b) Il diritto d'autore nel mercato unico digitale, Torino
Lavagnini S (2023) La responsabilità civile delle piattaforme online: il ruolo del fine di profitto. AIDA, pp 759 ff., spec.766
LEANZA S (2023) Il diritto d'autore tra ingegno umano e intelligenza artificiale, nota a Cass., in Arte e Diritto, 2, 391.
Libertini M (2023) La presunzione di dipendenza economica nei mercati digitali. Un commento all'art. 33 L. 5 agosto 2022, n.118. Orizzonti dir comm, pp 36 ff

Lievens D (2012) L'Oréal v. eBay—welcomed in France, resented in England. Int Rev Intellect Prop Compet Law, pp 68 ff
Lopopolo S (2023) L'abuso di dipendenza economica a prova di mercati digitali tra presunzione e misure cautelari (nota a Autorità Garante della Concorrenza e del mercato, ord.caut.20 aprile 2023, n.30606). Foro it, pp 432 ff
Lorusso A (2024) Poteri pubblici e privati nella tutela del diritto d'autore online. La piattaforma "antipirateria" di AGCom al vaglio del giudice amministrativo. MediaLaws 2
Mansani L (2021) Distribuzione selettiva, esaurimento del marchio e difesa dell'immagine di lusso nella giurisprudenza europea. In: Studi di diritto commerciale per Vincenzo Di Cataldo. Torino, vol 1, pp 347 ff
Mansani L, Simoni M (2017) Il danno arrecato dall'Internet Service Provider al titolare del copyright su materiali caricati dagli utenti. Analisi giur economia 2:565 ff
Morelli E (2012) I diritti audiovisivi sportivi, Milano
Morri F (2012) Nuovi brevetti e varietà vegetali, Napoli
Moscon V (2020) Free circulation of information and online intermediaries—replacing one "value gap" with another. Int Rev Intellect Prop Compet Law (IIC) 51:977–982
Musso A (2010) La proprietà intellettuale nel futuro della responsabilità sulla rete: un regime speciale? Dir inf inf, pp 795 ff
Musso A (2020) Eccezioni e limitazioni ai diritti d'autore nella direttiva UE n. 790/2019. Dir inf inf, pp 411 ff
Novelli C (2019) La Cassazione su responsabilità del provider e contenuto della notifica. Dir inf Inf, pp 500 ff
Palumbo A, Piemonte I (2023) Delega di funzioni regolamentari e lotta ai rischi sistemici causati dalla disinformazione nel Digital Services Act: quali rischi per la libertà di espressione? MediaLaws 3
Peukert A, Husovec M, Kretschmer M, Mezei P, Quintais JP (2022) European Copyright Society – comment on copyright and the Digital Services Act proposal. Int Rev Intellect Prop Compet Law 53:358–376, 360–361
Poddighe E (2001) "Diritti televisivi" e teoria dei beni. Padova
Posteraro F (2023) Il copyright al tempo dell'IA generativa. MediaLaws 2
Quaedvlieg A (2024) Monitoring after Poland. In: Thouvenin F, Peukert A, Jaeger T, Geiger C (eds) Kreation Innovation Märkte – creation innovation markets, pp 359 ff
Quintais JP, Katzenbach C, Schwemer SF, Dergacheva D, Riis T, Mezei P, Harkai I, Magalhães JC (2024) Copyright content moderation in the European Union: state of the art, ways forward and policy recommendations. Int Rev Intellect Prop Compet Law 55:157 ff
Raffaelli O (2022) La tutela del marchio nel Metaverso. Riv dir ind II:287 ff
Renna M (2014) Le questioni di legittimità del regolamento dell'Agcom sulla tutela del diritto d'autore on-line. AIDA, pp 111 ff
Ricolfi M (2010) Motori di ricerca, link sponsorizzati e diritto dei marchi: il caso Google di fronte alla Corte di Giustizia. Il dir ind, pp 1603 ff
Ricolfi M (2015) Trattato dei marchi. Torino, p 1323
Riis T (2023) Primary liability of intermediaries for trade mark infringement in light of the decision in joined cases Louboutin (C-148/21) and (C-184/21). Eur Intellect Property Rev, pp 337 ff
Rodean N (2011) Responsabilità del gestore del mercato online per le violazioni ai diritti di marchio altrui. Dir pubbl comp eur, pp 1594 ff
Sabia R (2023) L'enforcement pubblico del Digital Services Act tra Stati membri e Commissione europea: implementazione, monitoraggio e sanzioni. MediaLaws 2
Sammarco P (2010) Le partite di calcio in TV e la loro ritrasmissione non autorizzata via WEB in un caso relativo ad una violazione di diritti audiovisivi su eventi sportivi. Dir inf inf, pp 908 ff
Saraceno A (2011) Note in tema di violazione del diritto d'autore tramite Internet: la responsabilità degli Internet Service Provider. Riv dir ind II:364 ff
Scalzini S (2022) Abuso di dipendenza economica, mercati digitali e libertà di impresa. Orizzonti dir comm, pp 113 ff

Scannicchio T (2012) La responsabilità del motore di ricerca per la funzione "autocomplete". Dir inf inf, p 1210
Schrijvers M (2011) European Court rules on the position of eBay regarding the sale of infringing products: L'Oréal v eBay. Eur Intellect Prop Rev 33:723
Sena G (2020) Invenzioni brevettabili e Intelligenza artificiale. Riv dir ind I:151 ff
Sena G, Frassi AE, D'Ammassa G, Giudici S, Minotti D, Morri F (2003) Diritto d'autore e diritti connessi nelle società dell'informazione, Milano
Senftleben M (2024) UGC creation and dissemination. The role of platforms, copyright holders and the Court of Justice in safeguarding freedom of expression and information. In: Thouvenin F, Peukert A, Jaeger T, Geiger C (eds) Kreation Innovation Märkte – creation innovation markets, pp 347 ff
Sironi GE (2013) La percezione del pubblico nel diritto dei segni distintivi, Milano
Sironi GE (2021) Marchi, distribuzione selettiva e marketplace on line. Riv dir ind II:389 ff
Spedicato G (2010) La sottile linea di confine tra esclusiva sul segno e usi leciti del marchio altrui: prime riflessioni sulla giurisprudenza comunitaria in materia di keyword advertising. Dir inf inf, pp 731 ff
Spolidoro MS (2008) Profili processuali del Codice della Proprietà Industriale. Il dir ind, pp 86 ff
Spolidoro MS (2022) Dal Metaverso ad Acchiappacitrulli? Riflessioni in tema di NFT. AIDA, pp 515 ff
Tassone B (2021) Quando un hosting provider è responsabile per le violazioni del copyright? La parola, di nuovo alla grande Sezione della Corte di Giustizia. Resp civile e prev 2021:838
Tavella M, Bonavita S (2010) La Corte di Giustizia sul caso "AdWords": tra normativa marchi e commercio elettronico. Il dir ind, pp 429 ff
Thiem T (2022) Iter della Direttiva 2019/790 e sua implementazione in Europa e in Italia. In: Lavagnini S (ed) Il diritto d'autore nel mercato unico digitale. Torino, pp 2 ff
Toni AM (2023) La parodia di Zorro fu vera parodia? Ai posteri l'ardua (ma giustamente equilibrata) sentenza. AIDA:2004
Tosi E (2009) Contraffazione di marchio e concorrenza sleale in Internet: dal classico "domain grabbing" all'innovativo "keyword" marketing confusorio. Riv dir ind II:387 ff
Tosi E (2017) Contrasti giurisprudenziali in materia di responsabilità civile degli hosting provider – passivi e attivi – tra tipizzazione normativa e interpretazione evolutiva applicata alle nuove figure dei motori di ricerca, social network e aggregatori di contenuti. Riv dir ind, II
Tosi E (2019) La disciplina applicabile all'hosting provider per la pubblicazione di contenuti digitali protetti dal diritto d'autore, tra speciale irresponsabilità dell'ISP passivo e comune responsabilità dell'ISP attivo, alla luce di Cassazione 7708/19 e 7709/2019. Riv dir ind II:202–270
Ubertazzi LC (ed) (2014) Il regolamento AGCOM sul diritto d'autore. Torino
Ubertazzi LC (ed) (2019) Commentario breve alle leggi su proprietà intellettuale e concorrenza, 7th edn. Padova, pp 832 ff e pp 2358 ff
Vanzetti A (ed) (2013a) Codice della proprietà industriale. Milano, pp 1176 ff
Vanzetti M (2013b) Commento all'art. 131 del Codice della proprietà industriale. In: Vanzetti A (ed) Codice della proprietà industriale. Milano, pp 1400 ff
Vanzetti A, Cataldo V, Spolidoro MS (2021) Manuale di diritto industriale, 9th edn, Milano
Zincone A (2012) Hosting attivo e violazione del copyright: cosa cambia nella responsabilità dell'Internet provider. Il dir aut, pp 149 ff

Platforms and Digital Ecosystems, IP Profiles

Overview

Valeria Falce

Contents

Abstract This contribution intends to examine digital platforms and ecosystems in the framework of the European Data Strategy, identifying data as a strategic business asset. The European Union, through the regulatory season that has seen the approval of some relevant measures, such as the Data Governance Act and the Data Act, aims at using data as an 'engine' of transformation and an 'antidote' to monopolies. The European Strategy promotes the opening, sharing and re-use of public and private data, 'crossing' new products and services (interconnected through the Internet) and new business models, centred on data and enabling technologies. At the same time, the protection of intellectual property is strengthened, seeking a balance between the openness of data and the protection of rights to enhance investments, the value of innovation and know-how.

V. Falce (✉)
European University of Rome, Rome, Italy
e-mail: valeria.falce@unier.it

R. Bocchini (ed.), *Digital Platforms - From Technical Foundations to Legal and Economic Implications*, https://doi.org/10.1007/978-3-032-07978-7_19

1 Platforms (and Ecosystems) in the Context of the European Data Strategy

As part of the dual path of economic transformation (ecological and digital)[1] undertaken in Europe, the digital one is characterised by the primacy of data as a strategic business *asset*, the prevailing disintermediation and decentralisation in relations,[2] also with respect to the use of content, the contamination and consequent integration between activities, products and services, and hence in the emergence of new players, the platforms.[3]

Platforms, data and Artificial Intelligence are (not by chance) elevated to the hallmark of the industrial revolution: new (the fourth) and unique (because, while the previous ones were 'ignited' by a single technology—steam engine, electricity, computer—the new revolution is characterised by a set of technologies that, thanks to the Internet, are aggregated in a systemic way). New intermediaries (the platforms), new products and services (interconnected via the Internet) and new business models, centred on data and enabling technologies (*big data*, *data analytics* and cognitive systems, but also *Internet of Things*, *cloud*, augmented reality, enabling technologies and advanced robotics) enabling the creation and sharing of content in a disintermediated manner, are emerging on the market.

Digital platforms, in this sense, affect every sphere of the economy and society; they present themselves as the new 'interface' of (and on) the market and, through services and products that comprehensively meet the needs of demand, offer enormous potential for growth and increased prosperity.

This ushers in the first phase, in which data is the new oil, platforms refine it and extract value from it. Thanks to *data analytics* and I.A. systems, platforms are increasingly and better trained to offer better services. Competition is 'between' and 'within' platforms, markets are dynamic, processes innovative, disruptive and 'fast'. Due to a process of unstoppable creative destruction, context and dynamics evolve rapidly.[4] Platforms spring up quickly and are quickly swept away.

---

[1] European Commission-Directorate-General for Communication-Leyen (2019–2024); Opening statement in the European Parliament plenary session 16 July 2019; Speech in the European Parliament plenary session 27 November 2019.

[2] On this topic, see Falce (2023); Falce et al. (2020); Falce et al. (2018); as well as Falce (2021a, b); Falce and Genovese (2021); Falce and Finocchiaro (2019); Falce (2021a, b).

[3] OECD (2024), *Competition Policy in Digital Markets. The Combined Effect of Ex Ante and Ex Post Instruments in G7 Jurisdictions*; OECD, *Big data: bringing competition policy to the digital era, Background note by the Secretariat*, 8; OECD, Hearing on Competition Economics of Digital Ecosystems held during the 134th Meeting of the Competition Committee on 1–3 December 2020.

[4] For an initial survey of the literature on the topic, see Robertson (2021), pp. 3–9; Jacobides and Lianos (2021), pp. 1199–1229; Crane (2019), p. 412 ff.; Jacobides (2022), p. 99 ff.; Jacobides et al.

This phase is succeeded by a second one characterised by the persistence of a few digital ecosystems offering technologically connected and functionally complementary products and services.[5] Examples of 'accomplished' ecosystems are Google, which, in addition to its search engine, expands into related products and services, such as browsers, i.e. software for surfing the Internet, operating systems and video streaming, or even Facebook, which from the social network 'expands' into contiguous but also distant products and services, from gaming to messaging, from retail to *devices*.

In the new context, the ecosystem excels and sizes up the market because it is unequally trained. The innovation that is introduced is the one that sustains the ecosystem and not the one that can interfere with, if not disrupt, its *business* models. The reasons for the primacy of ecosystems are different but all converging. The ecosystem, first, because it offers both integrated and complementary products, can generate substantial economies of scale, because different goods and services can be produced with the same production factors and savings increase as the quantities increase. Moreover, the more it extends into different markets, the stronger it becomes, because the value of the ecosystem and its services increase as the number of users increases. And it consolidates its position thanks to data, which, processed and refined with sophisticated AI techniques, can intercept, first, and create, then, new needs, classify emotions, and direct orientations. Moreover, since the forms of 'preventive occupation' of spaces and areas of possible commercial interest ensure a competitive advantage, it prefers intersectoral collaborations and strategic acquisitions, but also innovative forms of appropriation of intangible assets.[6]

It is these 'genetic' characteristics that facilitate integration between services and the convenience of remaining within the ecosystem, prompting a new reflection.[7] Reflection that focuses on a double market dimension: the one that takes place

---

(2018), p. 2255 ff.; Fletcher (2020), p. 2; Petropoulos (2020), p. 5; Bourreau (2020), p. 5; Bourreau and de Streel (2019), pp. 9–10; Crane (2020), p. 67.

[5] Please also refer to Faraone and Falce (2023a), p. 37.

[6] For a general survey, see Cusumano et al. (2019). See Faraone and Falce (2023a), cit., p. 37 ff.

[7] In the Union, reference is made, inter alia, to the decision in Case AT.40099 – Google Android, rendered on 18 July 2018 and the subsequent appeal ruling rendered by the General Court, judgment of 14 September 2022, Case T-604/18, Google and Alphabet v Commission (Google Android), § 268 ff.; or also European Commission, Case AT.40437, Apple – App Store Practices (music streaming), 16 June 2020; European Commission, Case AT.40652, Apple – App Store Practices (e-books/audiobooks), 16 June 2020; European Commission, Case AT.40452, Apple – Mobile payments, 16 June 2020. In the US, see Epic Games, Inc. v. Apple Inc., Case No. 4:20-cv-05640-YGR (N.D. Cal.), Judge Y. Gonzalez Rogers, 10 September 2021, 1 ("Epic v. Apple"), subsequently appealed: Epic Games, Inc. v. Apple Inc., case 21-16506-21-16695, 15 July 2022 (9th Cir). For further discussion, Competition and Markets Authority, Mobile Ecosystems Market Study, 10 June 2022. See also Bosteon and Mândrescu (2020), p. 7 ff.

between ecosystems and the one that unfolds within them. While the latter recurs when companies offering an ecosystem of products and/or services face a competitive constraint also exerted by 'specialised' companies, which are placed on another level of the value chain, the former refers to a competitive race between incompatible systems of products and services, which inevitably keeps the consumer,[8] who prefers to remain within it.[9]

2 Open Data and Industrial Property Rights: Balancing Perspectives and Convergence

As a response to the economic phases of first platform emergence and then imposition of ecosystems, Europe leverages data not only as an 'engine' of transformation[10] but also as an 'antidote' to monopolistic concentrations.[11,12]

The subject of investment programmes[13] and the pivot of a profound regulatory overhaul, it is precisely on data and enabling technologies that the Union decides to

---

[8] Matutes and Regibeau (1988), pp. 221–234.

[9] See Aghion et al. (2005), p. 701 ff. and Marty and Warin (2020), p. 4, according to which a dominant firm, even if protected by barriers to entry, may have incentives to innovate, especially outside the digital world, when, for instance, it markets durable goods and innovation is necessary to induce customers to renew their equipment. Second, they may have incentives to innovate especially when competing with other digital platforms. In this regard, such companies have an incentive to innovate in order to ensure the continuity of their data streams and, thus, increase the predictive capabilities of their algorithms. The predictive capabilities of algorithms are all the greater the more up-to-date and diversified the data. The more a platform diversifies its services, the better its 'predictive performance'. Finally, innovation can be a means to sustain and expand one's dominant position. Moreover, innovation is also an essential factor for the provider company operating within the ecosystem, as the success of its *business* strategy and inclination depends on being part of a dynamic ecosystem. At the same time, a low innovation rate may expose them to being replaced by other firms operating within the platform or even excluded from the platform. Finally, there are three further reasons why 'complementary' firms operating within the ecosystem have an incentive to innovate. The first reason is competition among the 'complementary' providers themselves. The second reason lies in the risk of the platform integrating the service provided into its own offering if it is not satisfied with the quality of the product or the performance of the service. The third reason is the need to diversify the risk if a strategic change driven by the platform/ecosystem is abstractly capable of challenging the sustainability of its technology or *business* model.

[10] On the role of data and big data: Cannataci et al. (2020), cit., *passim*; Delmastro and Nicita (2019); on the concentration of data by ecosystems: Polo and Sassano (2021), p. 529, who consider that '*in this architecture, the data collected remains in the availability of the platform, accelerates the dynamics of strengthening its dominance and constitutes a barrier to entry*'; Mannoni and Stazi (2021); Ghidini et al. (2020), p. 114.

[11] Let me refer in this regard to Falce (2024a, b), *passim*.

[12] Let me refer, in addition to the contributions in footnote 2, to Falce (2022a, b); Falce (2021a, b); Falce and Finocchiaro (2019).

[13] Please refer to the *link*: https://eic.ec.europa.eu/eic-2025-work-programme_en.

'bet' first and then 'accelerate' to recover, if not ensure, market openness, digital autonomy and technological sovereignty, to free itself from the state of technological subordination and dependence on non-European economies[14] and, hence, relaunch the European model.

The start would seem to be uphill: the data market generates, according to European Commission estimates, a decidedly unsatisfactory economic value (equal to 2.6% of EU-27 GDP) due to uncertainties over ownership of rights, imbalances in bargaining power, limited availability of reliable *cloud* services and lack of cross-sector interoperability of data in the EU. In addition to this, despite its value approaching EUR 82 billion in 2023, thus surpassing China (whose market is around EUR 50 billion), Europe lags significantly behind both the US (whose data market is worth EUR 350 billion) and China in terms of development and exploitation for reasons attributable to a slower rate of adoption of digital technologies, structural barriers to investment in digitisation, fragmented policy approaches, lack of recognition of the benefits of digital and a continuing digital skills gap.

The path and the goal to be achieved are defined: reversing the march and overcoming the criticalities encountered also through the introduction of facilitating and enabling rules, together with the injection of capital and huge investments, to enable the data market to reach a value of almost EUR 120 billion in 2030[15] and the AI and new technologies market a value of over USD 200 billion in 2030.[16]

The actions planned and implemented on the regulatory front are part of the *European Data Strategy*. The focus is on uniform rules (oriented towards the principle of maximum harmonisation), both to orient digital markets and services towards transparency, fairness and contestability,[17] and to foster access and re-use of public and private data. Particularly, with the *Data Governance Act* Regulations[18] and the *Data Act*,[19] Europe opts for a horizontal and cross-sectoral regulatory system for data access, re-use and sharing, promoting the creation of *Common Spaces* in strategic sectors and areas of public interest. With the *AI* Act, it regulates the placing of Artificial Intelligence systems on the EU market, following a risk-based

[14] Cusumano et al. (2019); Faraone and Falce (2023b), cit. p. 87 ff.

[15] IDC, European Data Market Study 2021–2023, 2024, accessible at https://digital-strategy.ec.europa.eu/en/library/results-european-data-market-study-2021-2023.

[16] For an initial indication, please refer to the information and materials available at https://www.assonime.it/Events/Groups/Pages/Group-Data-Strategy-Europe.aspx.

[17] Most recently: Digital Market Act Regulation 2022/1925/EU; Digital Service Act Regulation 2022/2065/EU. On which, see, for an introduction, Caggiano et al. (2022), p. 205 ff. as well as essentially on the former, Falce (2021a, b), cit.

[18] Assonime, Circular 17/2024 - Data Governance Act: areas of implementation and policy ideas for companies, available at https://www.assonime.it/attivita-editoriale/circolari/Pagine/Circulars.aspx.

[19] Assonime, Circular 9/2024 - The new European rules on data access and use ('Data Act'). Opportunities and challenges for companies, available at https://www.assonime.it/activities/editorial/circulars/pages/circulars.aspx.

ex-ante approach.[20] With Eidas 2, it aims to provide businesses and citizens with a European digital identity to facilitate relationships and enable new ones on a transnational basis.[21] With the *cybersecurity* package, it creates the conditions to safeguard the security and integrity of data within Europe's borders.[22]

However, at the same time and in an apparently diachronic sense, Europe insists on the introduction of efficient, transparent and balanced forms of protection in favour of those who, by investing in innovation and creativity, contribute to technological progress and the dissemination of culture. With the 2020 Council Conclusions[23] the Commission, in fact, promotes the creation of European rights (such as the European patent), the modernisation of existing institutes (such as those on copyright), the pro-competitive *by design* curvature of proprietary rights (such as the proposal for a regulation on essential patents[24]) and the promotion of an *enforcement* capable of combating piracy and abuse (also through the DSA) at EU level.[25]

In extreme synthesis and at the cost of some simplification, the Strategy is proposed as innovative and at times propulsive: it now forces the principle of free negotiation by obliging the opening up of certain categories of data and administering the relationships; it now brings back to unity the status of data, which, regardless of its nature, is qualified as a *commodity* and, in this way, codifies the principle of monetisation; it now elevates the data intermediary to a new status, who, provided specific requirements are met, enjoys special legitimacy to give impetus to markets and *data space*,[26] now directs the markets in the direction of greater order, more pronounced protection of rights and clearer accountability of relations, now finally regulates them in line with the principles of fairness and competition.

In the light of this double thrust, Europe, in containing the spaces of autonomy of states, seems to follow an undulating if not schizophrenic trend on the *policy*

---

[20] Assonime, Circular 14/2024 - The European Regulation on Artificial Intelligence: a reasoned analysis of the new rules and policy perspectives for companies, available at https://www.assonime.it/attivita-editoriale/circolari/Pagine/Circolari.aspx. For all, on this subject see A. Pajno-F. Donati-A. Perrucci (ed.), *Artificial intelligence and law: a revolution*, vol. 1. *Fundamental rights, personal data and regulation*; vol. 2. *Administration, liability, jurisdiction*; vol. 3. *Intellectual property, society, finance*, Bologna, 2022.

[21] Assonime, Circular 20/2024 - From EUDI to IT wallet: prospects for enterprises from digital identity to attribute wallet, available at https://www.assonime.it/attivita-editorial/circulars/pages/circulars.aspx.

[22] Regulation (EU) 2019/881 of the European Parliament and of the Council of 17 April 2019 on ENISA, the European Union Cybersecurity Agency, and on cybersecurity certification for information and communication technologies, and repealing Regulation (EU) No 526/2013 ('Cybersecurity Regulation').

[23] Accessible at https://single-market-economy.ec.europa.eu/industry/strategy/intellectual-property/intellectual-property-action-plan-implementation_en.

[24] Proposal for a Regulation of the European Parliament and of the Council on Essential Patents, amending Regulation (EU) 2017/1001 Brussels, 27.4.2023 COM(2023) 232 final 2023/0133 (COD).

[25] For an examination of the European trajectories and seasons of intellectual property discipline, let me refer to Falce and Ghidini (2018), p. 335.

[26] See Falce (2024a, b), p. 61.

front. On the one hand, it seems to want to subvert classical paradigms, imposing or, at any rate, directing Member States and stakeholders to open up, share and re-use data, to nurture European spaces and their markets, foster intra- and inter-sectoral collaborations and facilitate the recovery of the competitive gap with the USA and China. On the other hand, it seems to renew a certain (hyper)protectionist drift, reinforcing proprietary protection, its prerogatives and the forms of protection of intangible assets, on the assumption that, in the new economy, they are at the heart of companies' market positioning.

On closer inspection, and as will be said immediately, the aporia is only apparent and the two forces converge in a new legal order of the market[27] in which the new digital society,[28] having created the conditions to reduce the distance in terms of economic and commercial strength vis-à-vis the non-European superpowers, can in the meantime exploit the benefits of open and contestable data markets, if and insofar as they recognise their specific and overall value.[29]

2.1 *Towards Data-Aware Governance*

Turning to the first direction, the renewal moves from the framework, i.e. the definition of rules that would lead the Member States towards a single, shared model of data governance and circulation.[30]

Anticipated by the *Open Data* Directive, the *Data Governance Act* is a Regulation that adds a further building block to the creation of the single market for the exchange and re-use of (publicly held) data, establishing a lowest common denominator to facilitate their circulation at the intra-European level.

The objective of the DGA is to establish: (a) conditions for the re-use within the EU of certain categories of (entity-held) public data; (b) a legal basis for digital operators facilitating the sharing and exchange of these same data; (c) a framework for the voluntary registration of entities collecting and processing data for altruistic purposes; and (d) a framework for the establishment of a European Data Innovation Board (Art. 1).

Within the perimeter of the Regulation are the categories of data (held by public bodies) that are covered by the regulations on intellectual property rights, commercial or statistical secrecy, or the protection of personal data (Art. 3). The scope of the *Data Governance Act* therefore includes any public data that can be considered 'sensitive', whether in relation to the personal sphere or to the business dimension.

Without prejudice to national prerogatives in strategic sectors (public security, defence and national security), the regulation, on the one hand, broadens the basis

---

[27] Frosini (2000), p. 271 ff.; Frosini (2022), p. 5 ff.

[28] Cf. Codeluppi (2022).

[29] Already in this sense, Falce (2024a, b).

[30] For an analysis, for all, Assonime Circular, cit.

of the data market and, on the other hand, affects national freedoms to regulate relations, bringing them back to a common, indeed uniform basis.

The basic premise is that public bodies (state, regional or local authorities, bodies governed by public law or associations formed by one or more such authorities or one or more such bodies governed by public law) are free to allow or deny access to, use and re-use of public data.

Where they exercise this option, public bodies 'that hold protected data for reasons of (a) commercial confidentiality; (b) statistical confidentiality; (c) protection of intellectual property rights of third parties; (d) protection of personal data' are burdened with certain obligations. Particularly, at the cross-border level, they must direct their conduct in the direction of:

(a) waive, in line with *antitrust* law principles, exclusive agreements or other practices for the re-use of data, unless the exclusivity is necessary for the provision of a service or product of general interest that would not otherwise be possible. The period of exclusivity of the right to re-use data shall not exceed three years (Art. 4);
(b) make public and transparent the conditions for re-use, which are anchored in competitive principles (they must be 'non-discriminatory, proportionate and objectively justified in relation to the categories of data, the purposes of re-use and the nature of the data for which re-use is allowed') (Art. 5(1));
(c) address relations with third parties, to oblige them to: (1) only re-use pre-anonymised/pseudonymised data; (2) only access and re-use data within a secure, public-sector-provided and controlled processing environment, including a physical processing environment, thus bringing even data with limited openness and in respect of which technical solutions are required to be implemented under common rules;
(d) guarantee through uniform conditions the integrity of the technical systems and of the secure processing environment used, the confidentiality of the data and the respect of intellectual property rights. In addition, the public sector body must be able to verify the results of the data processing carried out by the re-user and reserve the right to prohibit the use of results that contain information that jeopardises the rights and interests of third parties (Art. 5(5)).

The standardisation of conditions extends to economic profiles, both by providing that the charges (Art. 6) for data transfer are public, non-discriminatory, objective and proportionate, also in methodology, and by opening the way to the so-called altruistic use, i.e. the voluntary sharing of data for general interest objectives, which the DGA advocates.

Strict obligations are then imposed on intermediaries who facilitate the sharing and exchange of data. In this regard, to avoid situations of unfair competitive advantage and improper use of data, the *Data Governance Act* requires digital operators to assume a purely neutral behaviour in the activity of intermediation, both by requiring them not to 'use the data for which they provide services for purposes other than making such data available to the users of the data' and to use '*the metadata collected in the course of the provision of the data sharing service only for the development of such service*' (Art. 11).

The scope of the new framework further extends to data sharing for altruistic purposes, i.e. the use of data to pursue general interests, such as scientific research or the improvement of public services. Provision is therefore made for the creation of a 'register of recognised data altruism organisations' (Art. 15) in which the organisations concerned may only register if a series of requirements (Art. 16) and specific obligations (Art. 18) of transparency and protection of the rights of the concerned are met.[31]

Through the Regulation, Europe underpins the fairness and transparency of relationships, respect for competition and fundamental freedoms in the data market. But above all, it confirms *fairness* as a general principle and litmus test of the *Data Strategy.*[32]

In the wake of the framework and procedural rules, Europe has gone further on the substantive front. The enabling framework has been enriched with a further piece, which undermines the proprietary paradigm, imposing access to and facilitating the use and reuse of data (for the moment only) from the Internet of Things (IoT), establishing who can use the data generated by *smart* products, under what conditions and in what contexts.[33]

The *Data Act* regulates access and use of data generated by the use of related products and services, differentiating between B2C and B2B relationships. In relation to the former, both free, simple, secure and structured-format accessibility to the data that the user has contributed to create is ensured, and the possible commercial use and re-use of those same data under market conditions is guaranteed. Data and information that assume commercial value for the producer and that, because of that value, are kept confidential escape the paradigm of openness and remain covered by the protection offered by trade secrets.

For the latter (B2B relations), an effective system of protection against contractual imbalances and *unfair contractual terms* is provided. The Regulation separates *the black* clauses, which, unilaterally imposed, are null and void as manifestly abusive or unfair, from the *grey* clauses, the unfairness of which is presumed and, as such, can be overcome with proof to the contrary. The reasonableness of any fees for the provision of data is enshrined, with the option of recourse to out-of-court dispute settlement bodies (for issues relating to the fee or unfairness of the clauses).

Escaping this bipartition is the public sector, which, in the case of exceptional circumstances and public emergencies, can claim access to the data of private individuals, also for statistical processing and the creation of interoperability standards (B2G context).

---

[31] With regard to *enforcement*, the establishment of a 'European Data Innovation Board' is envisaged, which is entrusted with the tasks of advising and assisting the Commission in enhancing the interoperability of data brokering services and drawing up guidelines on how to facilitate the development of data spaces (Art. 27).

[32] Pharaoh and Falce (2023), cit. p. 37.

[33] For an initial analysis, Circolare Assonime, cit.

New rules are intended to facilitate the transition between *cloud*, *edge* and other *data processing services* (DPS), and the development of interoperability *standards* for data to be transferred and reused between different industries. In the transition between providers, functional equivalence is preserved, without imposing technical interfaces and interoperability *standards*, but steering the market towards open *standards*, if any, that comply with European law. Guarantees are provided against the illegal transfer of non-personal data. For data spaces, the *Data Act* lays down minimum rules for interoperability and for *smart contracts* in line with the trend to reduce the spaces of free negotiation, which in the Copyright Directive has found a very important first landing.[34]

2.2 The Pivot of the Balancing of Interests

The drive towards openness, use and re-use of data seems to be held back by the second trajectory, the Intellectual Property Strategy, which, by marking the stages of a process of modernisation of proprietary institutions in favour of intangible assets, on both the genetic and functional fronts, seems to be steering the European Union towards a protectionist drift.

Approaches on the first front are, as is well known, the new rules on authorship (with which it was intended to adapt the matter to the new enabling technologies, to reconcile the system of exceptions in a dynamic and uniform manner and to favour the forms of circulation of intellectual works in the digital economy), anticipated by those on the subject of industrial secrecy (with which it was intended to standardise the notion and harmonise the rules for civil law protection in the event of infringement) and those relating to the creation of a new proprietary title, the unitary patent (which, overcoming the principle of territoriality, was created as a title with European curvature directly enforceable and protectable in the 27 Member States). Significant expressions of the second front are, inter alia, the European rules for the protection of intellectual property rights, which, on the one hand, make platforms and intermediary providers liable and, on the other hand, impose burdens of timely intervention for the removal of illegal or counterfeit content.

On closer inspection, however, each of the actions declining the Data Strategy and the IP Strategy moves from a fixed point: that the owner of intangible assets (data or content) disposes of them, deciding what to use them for and with what remuneration.

Limiting ourselves to commercial data, the *Data Governance Act* stipulates that public and private entities may grant—on market terms or even free of charge and

[34] With regard to governance, the regulation refers the provision of the necessary guarantees for compliance and the handling of complaints and claims to each Member State. The Commission, on the other hand, is reserved for the definition of standard contractual clauses for access and re-use of data, the adoption of delegated acts for the control of switching costs in DPSs, and requirements for interoperability.

for the purposes they authorise—access to data and content protected by intellectual property rights, which they may have at their disposal.

The *Data Act* moves in the same direction, which introduces at the EU level a new right in favour of users of data generated by products or within the scope of intelligent services. This is the right to obtain them free of charge, and then to exploit them either directly or via third parties, for uses to be granted free of charge or on market terms.

The *AI Act*[35] follows in the same wake and, indeed, continues it, especially in relation to a specific technology, that of general models, which are designed, set up and developed to be trained with data, images and sounds. Particularly, under the new Regulation, owners of data and content must retain control through intellectual property rights, also with respect to the providers of AI systems and models, which, as we know, cannot be designed, set up and developed without constant training with quality data (also text, images, sounds).

Without prejudice to compliance with Union law for all systems and models, the *AI Act* burdens these providers with a twofold obligation to perform: (i) to implement a policy to comply with Union law on copyright and, particularly, to identify and respect, including through state-of-the-art technology, the reservation of rights regulated by the Copyright Directive; (ii) to draw up and make available to the public a sufficiently detailed summary of the content used for training.

These are organisational and process obligations that do not interfere with the substance and protection of rights, nor do they exhaust the intersections and interferences with author protection, which remains intact, merely encouraging compliance with rules that already exist on data mining, requiring them to be enforced regardless of where the models are trained and in which jurisdiction, how they are disseminated (open and closed licences) and the size of the providers.

Why introduce them then? Because Europe is pushing for equal treatment between the different providers and demands that the rules that already exist on the extraction of data, text, content, sound and images be applied irrespective of where

[35] To understand its scope, it is useful to recall that the new regulation defines the regulatory framework for placing AI systems and models on the market in Europe. It defines the minimum characteristics of Artificial Intelligence (software with inferential capacity), recognises transparency and literacy as the minimum rules with which suppliers and users must comply, and graduates the obligations on the basis of their dangerousness to the point of prohibiting certain systems and models (if, for example, their object or effect is *social scoring* or manipulative practices). Precisely because it does not introduce the European code of AI nor does it propose itself as a single text on enabling technologies, it is not surprising that the regulation refers to the mark for the sole purpose of qualifying the person who affixes it as the party responsible for the obligations that fall on the supplier of the system or model and to make the subjects of the value chain responsible, including the *deployer*, i.e. the professional user, who, by modifying the system in terms of functions or purposes, takes over the status of supplier. In short, to the use of the trademark, the AI *Act* corresponds a specific subjective quality and from this it makes a specific statute descend, the statute of the AI supplier. Nor is it surprising that the Regulation reaffirms and confirms industrial secrecy, because the obligations of transparency incumbent on suppliers, scaled down in the event that systems are released in open and open source mode, must not interfere with and prejudice industrial property.

the models are trained and in which jurisdiction, irrespective of the mode of dissemination (open and closed licences) and irrespective of the size of the providers. No provider, recital 106 recalls, should be able to gain a competitive advantage in the Union market by applying less stringent copyright rules than in the Union.

To this end, the exception for the extraction of text, data, sounds and images, i.e. *Text and Data Mining*, already regulated at European level both for research purposes (which must be carried out on a non-profit basis and must not conflict with the interests of the right holders) and for commercial and lucrative purposes (such as for the making of 'complex commercial decisions and the development of new applications or technologies') is reaffirmed. It is also confirmed, in line with EU law but also with international principles, that this is not an absolute[36] exception, nor unconditional, but subject to compliance with specific and general prerequisites. Among the first: that the content is legally accessible (through contractual conditions or subscriptions), that the content is not confidential, and that access for the purpose of *text and data mining* is granted. Among the latter: that the use of those materials does not conflict with the normal exploitation of the works or other materials and does not unduly prejudice the legitimate interests of the right holders.[37]

The Regulation, therefore, does not innovate the substance, but helps to guard it. For the benefit of third parties and especially copyright holders, it requires providers to introduce, comply with and enforce design and development measures, including those for the automatic identification of possible reservations of rights,[38] as well as to publish a summary of private or public databases and data repositories used for training and a description of other main sources.[39]

In short, Europe, through the guidelines that will be discussed immediately, channels innovation to safeguard everyone's right to innovation and in this way sanctions an obligation to do, i.e. to introduce active measures (technical, design and system development), which ensure compliance with the authorship discipline

[36] 'All exceptions, in fact, are subject to limitations', first and foremost that of being conditional on compliance with the three-step *test* (in the sense that they must be precisely defined and narrowly construed, must not interfere with the 'normal exploitation of the work' and must not 'unreasonably prejudice the legitimate interest of the rights holder'. See Strowel and Ducato (2021). See also Quintais (2019).

[37] See Schonwette (2003); Guibault (2002); Ficsor (2002); Gervais (2005), pp. 1–37; Ginsburg (2001), pp. 1–16; Oliver (2002), pp. 119–170; Ricketson (1987); Ricketson (2003); Senftleben (2004); WTO Copyright Panel decision (2000), case WT/DS160, United States - Section 110 (5) of the US Copyright Act.

[38] Peukert (2024).

[39] To close the circle, the AI *Act* calls for AI systems to be designed in such a way as to inform users both when we are interacting directly with an AI system and in relation to the outputs of the AI system, which must be marked in a machine-readable format and detectable as artificially generated or manipulated. Moreover, professional users themselves must make it clear that they are using artificially generated or manipulated content to inform the public. Finally, to seal compliance with the European discipline, the Regulation stipulates that the latter obligation does not apply if the synthetic content has been subjected to a human review process or editorial control and a natural or legal person therefore assumes editorial responsibility for it.

both upstream (in the training phase) and downstream, when synthetic content is released.

Moreover, in favouring the sharing and exchange of data, it does not renounce its own model of balancing interests, clarifying in the actions of the European Strategy that the price of the race for innovation cannot consist in the expropriation of rights nor in the undue appropriation of the investments underlying the creation of the data that constitute the *quid proprium* of entrepreneurial activity. The AI Regulation is the most recent confirmation of this, reaffirming that strengthening European competitiveness in digital is not a matter of depriving companies of their *know-how*, of arbitrarily taking away data and content without compensation in favour of new enabling technologies, nor of allowing free training of new models.

Rather, it is a matter of first identifying and recognising and then maximising the value of data, extracting it every time and for every use under the best possible conditions in the strategic interest of the company and for the benefit of the community.

References

Aghion P, Bloom N, Blundell R, Griffith R, Howitt P (2005) Competition and innovation: an inverted-U relationship. Q J Econ 120(2):701 ff

Bosteon F, Mândrescu D (2020) Assessing abuse of dominance in the platform economy: a case study of app stores. Eur Compet J 431(16):7 ff

Bourreau M (2020) Some economics of digital ecosystems. DAF/COMP/WD(2020)89, p 5

Bourreau M, De Streel A (2019) Digital conglomerates and EU competition policy. CERRE Report, pp 9–10

Caggiano G, Contaldi G, Manzini P (eds) (2022) Verso una legislazione europea su mercati e servizi digitali. Bari, p 205 ff

Cannataci J, Pollicino O, Falce V (2020) Legal challenges of Big data. Cheltenham (UK), p *passim*

Codeluppi V (2022) Mondo digitale. Roma-Bari

Crane DA (2019) Ecosystem competition and the antitrust laws. Nebraska Law Rev 98(2):412 ff

Crane DA (2020) Ecosystem competition. DAF/COMP/WD(2020)67

Cusumano MA, Gawer A, Yoffie DB (2019) The business of platforms: strategy in the age of digital competition, innovation, and power. HarperBusiness

Delmastro M, Nicita A (2019) Big Data. Come stanno cambiando il nostro mondo. Bologna

European Commission – Directorate-General for Communication – Leyen U (2019) Political guidelines for the next European Commission 2019–2024

Falce V (2021a) Competition law enforcement in digital markets. Torino

Falce V (2021b) Financial Innovation tra disintermediazione e mercato. Torino

Falce V (2022a) Intelligenza artificiale e Fintech. Consulenza decentrata tra algogovernance ed elemento fiduciario. In: Pajno A, Donati F, Perrucci A (eds) Intelligenza artificiale e diritto: una rivoluzione? Bologna

Falce V (2022b) Le regole sulle banche dati nella strategia europea: (molti) diritti e (poche) responsabilità. In: Pajno A, Donati F, Perrucci A (eds) Intelligenza artificiale e diritto: una rivoluzione? Bologna

Falce V (2023) Strategia dei dati e Intelligenza artificiale. Verso un nuovo ordine giuridico del mercato. Torino

Falce V (ed) (2024a) Digital ecosystems. market challenges and pro-competitive solutions. Torino, *passim*

Falce V (ed) (2024b) Competition law enforcement in digital markets, cit.

Falce V, Finocchiaro G (2019) Fintech: Diritti, Concorrenza, Regole. Bologna
Falce V, Genovese A (2021) La portabilità dei dati in ambito finanziario. Quaderno FinTech, CONSOB
Falce V, Ghidini G (2018) Disciplina della proprietà intellettuale: un volto spiccatamente europeo. In: Amato G, Moavero Milanesi E, Pasquino G, Reichlin L (eds) Europa. Roma, p 335
Falce V, Ghidini G, Olivieri G (2018) Informazione e Big Data tra Innovazione e Mercato. In: Quad. romani dir. comm.
Falce V, Pollicino O, Cannataci J (2020) Legal challenges of big data. Cheltenham (UK)
Faraone N, Falce V (2023a) Digital ecosystems in the wake of a legislative/regulatory turmoil: a first (tentative) antitrust assessment of the Italian (and European) experience in the AGCM case law. World Compet 46(1):37
Faraone N, Falce V (2023b) Digital ecosystems in the wake of a legislative/regulatory turmoil, cit., p 87 ff
Ficsor M (2002) The Law of Copyright and the Internet – The 1996 WIPO Treaties, their Interpretation and Implementation. Oxford
Fletcher A (2020) Digital competition policy: are ecosystems different? DAF/COMP/WD(2020)96, p 2
Frosini TE (2000) L'orizzonte giuridico dell'Internet. Dir. inf., p 271 ff
Frosini TE (2022) L'orizzonte giuridico dell'intelligenza artificiale. Dir. inf., p 5 ff
Gervais D (2005) Towards a new core international copyright norm: the reverse three-step test. Marquette Intellect Prop Law Rev 9(1):1–37
Ghidini G, Manca D, Massolo A (2020) La nuova civiltà digitale. L'anima doppia della tecnologia. Milano, p 114
Ginsburg JC (2001) Toward supranational copyright law? The WTO Panel Decision and the "Three-Step Test" for Copyright Exceptions. Working Paper No. 181, Columbia Law School – Revue Internationale du Droit d'Auteur, pp 1–16
Guibault L (2002) Copyright limitations and contracts – an analysis of the contractual overridability of limitations on copyright. The Hague
Jacobides M (2022) How to compete when industries digitize and collide: an ecosystem development framework. Calif Manag Rev 64(3):99 ff
Jacobides MJ, Lianos I (2021) Ecosystems and competition law in theory and practice. Indus Corp Change 30(5):1199–1229
Jacobides M, Cennamo C, Gawer A (2018) Towards a theory of ecosystems. Strategic Manag J 39(8):2255 ff
Knights R (2020) Limitations and exceptions under the "three-step test" and in national legislation – differences between the analog and digital environments. WIPO document WIPO/DA/MVD/00/4. Geneva
Mannoni S, Stazi G (2021) Sovranità.com. Potere pubblico e privato ai tempi del cyberspazio. Napoli
Marty F, Warin T (2020) Innovation in digital ecosystems: challenges and questions for competition policy. CIRANO Cahier Scientifique, 2020S-10, p 4
Matutes C, Regibeau P (1988) "Mix and Match": product compatibility without network externalities. RAND J Econ 19(2):221–234
OECD (2020) Hearing on Competition Economics of Digital Ecosystems held during the 134th Meeting of the Competition Committee on 1–3 December 2020
OECD (2024) Competition Policy in Digital Markets. The Combined Effect of Ex Ante and Ex Post Instruments in G7 Jurisdictions
OECD (s.d.) Big data: bringing competition policy to the digital era. Background note by the Secretariat, p 8
Oliver J (2002) PANEL DISCUSSION: Copyright in the WTO: the panel decision on the three-step test. Columbia J Law Arts 25:119–170

Pajno A, Donati F, Perrucci A (eds) (2022) Intelligenza artificiale e diritto: una rivoluzione. Vol. 1. Diritti fondamentali, dati personali e regolazione; Vol. 2. Amministrazione, responsabilità, giurisdizione; Vol. 3. Proprietà intellettuale, società, finanza. Bologna
Petropoulos G (2020) Competition economics of digital ecosystems. DAF/COMP/WD(2020)91, p 5
Peukert A (2024) Copyright in the Artificial Intelligence Act – a primer. Disponibile su: https://papers.ssrn.com/sol3/papers.cfm?abstract_id=4771976
Polo M, Sassano A (2021) DMA: Digital Markets Act o Digital Markets Armistice? Merc. conc. reg., p 529
Quintais JP (2019) The new copyright in the digital single market directive: a critical look. Disponibile su: https://papers.ssrn.com/sol3/papers.cfm?abstract_id=3424770
Ricketson S (1987) The Berne Convention for the Protection of Literary and Artistic Works: 1886-1986. The Hague
Ricketson S (2003) WIPO study on limitations and exceptions of copyright and related rights in the digital environment. WIPO publication SCCR/9/7. Geneva
Robertson VHSE (2021) Antitrust market definition for digital ecosystems. Concurrences 2:3–9. In: On-Topic/Competition policy in the digital economy
Schonwette T (2003) The three-step test within the copyright system. Disponibile su: http://pcf4.dec.uwi.edu/viewpaper.php?id=58&print=1
Senftleben M (2004) Copyright, limitations and the three-step test – an analysis of the three-step test in international and EC copyright law. The Hague
Strowel A, Ducato R (2021) Ensuring text and data mining: remaining issues with the EU copyright exceptions and possible ways out. Disponibile su: https://papers.ssrn.com/sol3/papers.cfm?abstract_id=3829858. Ultimo accesso 15 dicembre 2024
Unione Europea, Commissione Europea, Direzione Generale per la Comunicazione – von der Leyen U (2019) Political guidelines for the next European Commission 2019-2024
WTO (2000) Copyright Panel decision, case WT/DS160, United States – Section 110 (5) of the US Copyright Act

Platforms and Artificial Intelligence: The blind side of the moon

Valeria Falce

Contents

Abstract This chapter intends to analyse the tensions between access to data for training AI systems and the control of content by intellectual property rights owners, framed in the European Data Strategy. This overlap focuses on the use of protected works as input for training, regulated by the Text and Data Mining (TDM) exception of the Copyright Directive. The application of this exception is only legitimate if it complies with the so-called Three-Step Test and the rightholders' right to expressly reserve the use of their works ('opt-out'). In addition, the AI Act requires providers of generative AI systems to implement appropriate policies to respect copyright by identifying and observing such reservations of rights, including through advanced technologies.

1 Tensions Between Data Access and Control for Artificial Intelligence Systems and Models

It is in the context of the European Data Strategy, therefore, that the intersections and interferences of the Union's legislation on intellectual property (IP) with the season of technological innovations, starting with enabling technologies and AI, which make use of platforms and ecosystems *in the first place,* are framed.

V. Falce (✉)
European University of Rome, Rome, Italy
e-mail: valeria.falce@unier.it

R. Bocchini (ed.), *Digital Platforms - From Technical Foundations to Legal and Economic Implications*, https://doi.org/10.1007/978-3-032-07978-7_20

These interferences are only apparently new, because they refer to the never-ending tension between the push for the opening up of data, as the driving force behind dynamic competition and social access to information, culture and innovation, and the resistance of intellectual property rights holders, who claim a *ius excludendi alios* on data and content, on pain of misappropriation and the exercise of an unjustified *free-rider* behaviour against investment and creative and inventive efforts.

On the other hand, a new chapter in this story, under the banner of modern balancing, is underway and can be appreciated by looking at Artificial Intelligence systems, now defined in the European AI Regulation, which constitute its most recent litmus test. If, in fact, such systems in the IP perspective attract a combination of IP subjects and rights (in terms of know-how, industrial secrets, patents, authorship and database protection), on the other hand, it is their very modes of operation that call for a new reflection with respect both to the works/results produced by the AI—the *output*—and to the data, contents, sounds and images on which these same systems must feed to train themselves and to achieve a certain result—the *input.*

In this specific perspective, the intersections and interferences between AI and data can be appreciated at least at two levels and in two distinct phases: 1. 'Upstream', when data, information and content are used to train AI systems and models. In this sense, systems are fed by *copyrighted* works, whose digital version—linked to the original, be it analogue or digital[1]—must be acquired by the system in compliance with the author's prerogatives; 2. On the basis of the data, content and information extracted from an original work, it elaborates a synthesis or provides a new data processing, which cannot be directly and specifically traced back to any of the content used except as a source of inspiration, thus generating a new work or one bearing (at least) a 'transformative' content.

Limiting ourselves for the time being to the first level of intersection (*copyright-protected* works as training material), the balancing act lies in the reconciliation of the provisions of Directive (EU) 2019/790 on Copyright and Related Rights in the Digital Single Market ('Copyright Directive'),[2] with particular reference to the exception of *Text and Data Mining* ('TDM')[3] with those of the AI Regulation.

The lowest common denominator between them is, in fact, that any exception to copyright, including that of TDM—an extraction technique that consists of three main steps: (i) access to texts and/or data; (ii) extraction and/or copying of content; (iii) extraction of texts and/or data and discovery of knowledge—must be applied in compliance with the conditions underlying the *Three-Step Test*, on pain of violation of national, European and international law.[4]

---

[1] See Hugenholtz and Quintais (2021), p. 1190; Gervais (2020), p. 2053; Ginsburg (2018), p. 131; Ginsburg and Budiardjo (2019), p. 343; Guadamuz (2021), p. 147.

[2] See Chapter V *below* for a detailed analysis of the Copyright Directive.

[3] See Drexl et al. (2019); Guadamuz (2024), p. 111; Lucchi (2023).

[4] See *supra*, footnote 34.

But let us proceed in order. The starting point for framing the exceptions system in general, and hence TDMs, is the provisions introduced by Chapter II of the InfoSoc Directive, adopted in 2001 to adapt EU copyright law to the challenges posed by digital and *online* environments. With the aim of harmonising copyright laws across EU Member States, reducing legal fragmentation and ensuring that copyright rules are applied uniformly across the EU, the InfoSoc Directive strengthens the protection of copyright and related rights within the internal market by balancing them with fundamental rights and the public interest.

Recital 31 specifically calls for a 'fair balance' to be struck between the rights and interests of the various categories of rightholders as well as between those of the various rightholders and those of the users of the protected subject matter. In pursuing this objective, the InfoSoc Directive intervenes not only with respect to ensuring a high level of protection for rightholders through the protection of technological measures (such as DRM systems that prevent unauthorised access to or copying of *copyright-protected* works) but also with respect to the definition of a harmonised framework of rules governing the exploitation of works and other protected subject matter while also taking into account other and equal interests.

Following this trajectory, Art. 5(5) of the InfoSoc Directive[5] introduces a set of E&Ls defined on the basis of the three conditions set out in Art. 9(2) of the Berne Convention (1886) and known cumulatively as the *Three-Step Test*, according to which limitations to copyright are allowed: a) in particular cases; b) when they do not conflict with the normal exploitation of the work; and c) when they do not unreasonably prejudice the author's legitimate interests.

Under Art. 5(2) of the InfoSoc Directive, EU Member States enjoy the discretion to decide whether to incorporate an E&L from the list into their own laws. This freedom is, however, limited and conditioned in two distinct and related respects: (i) E&Ls must be consistent with Art. 5(5) and, thus, comply with the conditions set out in the *Three-Step Test*;[6] (ii) in complying with the *three-step-test*, exceptions

[5] Article 5(5), InfoSoc Directive: The exceptions and limitations provided for in paras 1, 2, 3 and 4 shall apply only in certain special cases that do not conflict with a normal exploitation of the work or other subject-matter and do not unreasonably prejudice the legitimate interests of the rightholder.

[6] In so doing, the European legislature has, among other things, incorporated into European law the treaties of the World Intellectual Property Organisation (WIPO), which, in turn, require adhering countries to comply with Articles 1–21 of the Berne Convention and thus also with the *Three-Step Test*. In addition, by adhering to the 1995 TRIPs Agreement (Agreement on Trade-Related Aspects of Intellectual Property Rights), the EU reaffirmed its adherence to the *Three-Step Test*, incorporated in Art. 13, according to which: 'Members shall limit limitations or exceptions to exclusive rights to certain special cases that do not conflict with a normal exploitation of the work and do not unreasonably prejudice the legitimate interests of the right holder'.

must be interpreted restrictively.[7] Indeed, in the Infopaq judgment,[8] the Court of Justice ruled that any exception to copyright, in so far as it derogates from the general rule that authors' original creations deserve adequate protection, must comply with a strict necessity test, in the sense that unauthorised uses are permissible to the extent strictly necessary, appropriate and proportionate to achieve the objective of overriding interest (Painer judgment).[9]

The Copyright Directive, continuing along the same trajectory: i) makes the system of exceptions mandatory and subordinates the legitimacy of each one, including that of TDM, to the respect of the Berne conditions, reaffirming in Art. 7(2) and its Recital 6 that the E&L, aiming at achieving a fair balance between the rights and interests of authors and other rightholders, on the one hand, and users, on the other hand, are not subject to the Berne conditions. [10] and its Recital 6 that the E&L, aiming at achieving a fair balance between the rights and interests of authors and other rightholders, on the one hand, and users, on the other hand, '[s]upply only in certain specific cases that do not conflict with the normal exploitation of the works or other subject matter and do not unduly prejudice the legitimate interests of the rightholders'; ii) renews the 'fair balance' paradigm as a parameter for balancing rights and interests through Art. 17(4),[11] which establishes the liability of *online* content sharing service providers ('OCSSPs') for the use of copyright-protected content,

---

[7] Court of Justice, Kapper, C-476/01, para 72, and Court of Justice, Commission v. Spain, C-36/05, para 31. With reference to the strict interpretation *standard* of E&Ls, see: Court of Justice, Spiegel Online, C-516/17, EU:C:2019:625, para 53; Court of Justice, Funke Medien, C-469/17, EU:C:2019:623, para 69; VCAST, C-265/16, EU:C:2017:913, para 32; AKM, C-138/16, EU:C:2017:218, para 37; Court of Justice, Stichting Brein, C-527/15, EU:C:2017:300, para 62; Court of Justice, Vereniging Openbare Bibliotheken, C-174/15, EU:C: 2016:856, para 50; Court of Justice, Ranks and Vasiļevičs, C-166/15, EU:C:2016:762, para 42; Court of Justice, Public Relations Consultants Association, C-360/13, EU:C:2014:1195, para 23; Court of Justice, Deckmyn and Vrijheidsfonds, C-201/13, EU:C:2014:2132, para 22; Court of Justice, ACI Adam and others, C-435/12, EU:C:2014:254, para 22.

[8] Court of Justice, InfopaqInternational, C-5/08, EU:C:2009:465, 58; Court of Justice, ACI Adam and Others, C-435/12, EU:C:2014:254, 26.

[9] ECJ, Painer v. Standard Verlags GmbH and Others, C-145/10, paras 105 and 106.

[10] Article 7(2), Copyright Directive: 'Article 5(5) of Directive 2001/29/EC shall apply to the exceptions and limitations provided for in this Title. Article 6(4), first, third and fifth subparagraphs, of Directive 2001/29/EC shall apply to Articles 3 to 6 of this Directive'.

[11] Article 17(4) Copyright Directive: 'Where no authorisation is granted, providers of online content-sharing services shall be liable for unauthorised acts of communication to the public, including making available to the public, of copyrighted works and other subject-matter, unless they prove that they

(a) having made every effort to obtain an authorisation;
(b) have made, in accordance with high standards of professional diligence in the industry, their best efforts to ensure that specific works and other subject-matter for which they have received the relevant and necessary information from rightholders are not available; and in any event
(c) having acted promptly, after having received a sufficiently reasoned notice from the rightholders, to disable access to or remove from their websites the works or other subject-matter referred to in the notice and having made utmost efforts to prevent their upload in the future in accordance with point (b)'.

while also providing for exclusions. According to this provision, OCSSPs (e.g. *social media* platforms, video sharing platforms and other *online* content sharing services) may only exclude their liability for copyright infringement if they prove that they: (a) they have made utmost efforts to obtain an authorisation; (b) they have made utmost efforts, in accordance with high industry standards of professional diligence, to ensure that specific works and materials for which they have received the necessary and relevant information from rightholders are not available; and (c) they have acted promptly, after receiving a sufficiently reasoned notice from right-holders, to disable access or remove content from their *websites* and have made their best efforts to prevent the future uploading of works subject to the notice.[12]

Accordingly, access to and extractions from works or other materials,[13] even when carried out for commercial activities (bearing in mind that recital 18 makes clear that, in addition to their relevance to science, TDM techniques 'are widely used by both public and private entities to analyse large amounts of data in various areas of life and for various purposes, including public administration services, complex business decisions and the development of new applications or technologies') are legitimate insofar as they comply with specific conditions, laid down by the directive, and general conditions, laid down by the tripartite *test*.

---

[12] The Commission's 2021 guidelines clarify that Art. 17(4) of the Copyright Directive introduces a specific regime that allows CSPBs, under certain conditions, to avoid liability arising from the act of communication to the public within the meaning of Art. 16(1). As pointed out in recital 66, this specific regime takes into account the fact that CSPBs provide access to material uploaded not by themselves but by users and that these conditions must be explicitly transposed into national law, since the notion of 'best efforts' is not defined and there is no reference to national law. The notion of 'best endeavours' therefore constitutes 'an autonomous concept of EU law that should be transposed by the Member States' in accordance with the guidelines provided by the Commission and interpreted in the light of the purpose and objectives of Art. 17. The Commission's guidelines further specify that: 'The obligations arising from the "best endeavours" paradigm are subject to respect for the freedoms of users, as provided for in Article 17(7). In particular, they stipulate that measures taken by OCSSPs, such as the removal of reported content, must not result in a violation of freedom of expression and the right of access to information. This implies avoiding forms of undue censorship or excessive restrictions that may limit access to legitimate content (so-called "*overblocking*"), ensuring a balance between copyright protection and the fundamental rights of users. Proportionality (Art. 17(5)) is central to the assessment of compliance, especially to distinguish between large platforms and smaller operators'.

[13] Article 4 Copyright Directive: '1. Member States shall provide for an exception or limitation to the rights provided for in Articles 5(a) and 7(1) of Directive 96/9/EC, Article 2 of Directive 2001/29/EC, Article 4(1)(a) and (b) of Directive 2009/24/EC and Article 15(1) of this Directive in respect of reproductions and extractions made from works or other subject matter to which access is legally obtained for the purpose of text and data extraction.

2. Reproductions and extractions made pursuant to paragraph 1 may be retained for as long as necessary for the purpose of text and data extraction.

3. The exception or limitation referred to in paragraph 1 shall apply on condition that the use of the works and other subject matter referred to in that paragraph has not been expressly reserved by the rightholders in an appropriate manner, such as through tools allowing automated reading in the case of content made publicly available *online*.

4. This Article is without prejudice to the application of Article 3 of this Directive'.

Concerning the general conditions: A) To balance exclusive rights and digital innovation as a public interest protected by EU law,[14] Art. 4(3). 3, of the Copyright Directive requires Member States to provide E&L to copyright for reproductions and extractions made from works or other subject matter to which access is lawfully obtained for the purposes of the TDM activity, provided that the use of the works and other subject matter has not been expressly reserved by the rightholders in an appropriate manner (‘*opt-out*’), for example through tools enabling automated reading of content made publicly available *online*, in respect of which the rightholder has decided to waive the exclusionary rights; B) With respect to research, Recital 14 of the Copyright Directive specifies that the notion of ‘lawful access’ should be understood as access to content on the basis of an open access policy or contractual arrangements, such as subscriptions, between rightholders and research organisations or cultural heritage institutions, or by other lawful means; C) With respect to commercial activities, Recital 18 specifies that the exception should apply (i) ‘only in the case of legal access to the work or other subject matter by the beneficiary, including when the work or other subject matter has been made available to the public *online, and* (ii) to the extent that the rightholders have not appropriately reserved the rights to make reproductions and extractions for the purpose of text and data extraction. In the case of content made available to the public *online*, it should be considered appropriate to reserve such rights only through the use of tools that allow for automated reading, including metadata and the terms and conditions of a *website* or service’; (iii) allowing users to keep copies made for as long as necessary for the activity.

As widely recognised in doctrine, ‘the scheme is clear in its apparent simplicity. TDM can be carried out for any purpose, commercial or non-commercial (e.g. investigative journalism, software, etc.), as long as limits acts of reproduction (and adaptation in the case of software)’.[15] However, rightholders can ‘defuse’ the operation of the exception by expressly reserving the use of such works in an appropriate manner,[16] e.g. by machine-readable means in the case of content made publicly available *online* (Art. 4(3) Copyright Directive).

[14] Article 3 TEU states that the EU aims to promote sustainable development, economic growth and technological progress. These objectives are intrinsically based on the promotion of innovation. Furthermore, Art. 179 TFEU specifically addresses the role of the EU in strengthening its scientific and technological base and in establishing an internal market conducive to research, technological development and innovation.

[15] Margoni (2024).

[16] Ibid.

2 AI Act Choices with Respect to Data and Content Extraction

On the TDM exception is *the AI Act*, which, at Art. 53, regulating the obligations of the providers of generative AI systems, requires them to implement 'a policy aimed at complying with Union law in the area of copyright and related rights and, in particular, at identifying and respecting, including through state-of-the-art technology, an express reservation of rights pursuant to Art. 4(3) of the [*Copyright*] Directive' (para 1(c)).[17]

Assuming that both the 'storage' of data and the development and implementation of downstream AI systems[18] can affect author's prerogatives, Art. 53(1) is, in short, 'the way to operationalise, at least within the sub-category of generative A.I., the possibility for right holders to monetise the use of their works once they have opted out (or presumably denied access to them)'.[19]

Recital 105 specifies in this respect that 'any use of copyright-protected content requires the authorisation of the relevant right holder, unless exceptions and limitations relevant to copyright apply'. This implies that, if providers of generative AI systems intend to use TDM, they must verify whether the rightholders have reserved the use of their works for TDM using 'machine-readable means, including metadata and the terms and conditions of a website or service' or through 'contractual agreements or a unilateral declaration' (Art. 4(3) and Recital 18 of the *Copyright* Directive) and in any case that the conditions of the tripartite *test are met.*

It should be added that the transparency obligation under Section 53(1)(d) of the *AI Act*[20] allows rightholders to determine whether or not their works have been used in the training datasets and, if necessary, to exclude them, thanks to the obligation for providers to draw up and make available to the public a sufficiently detailed summary of the content used for general-purpose AI model training, according to a template provided by the *AI Office*.

Finally, the analysis of the regulatory framework must consider the second draft of the General Code of Conduct for AI, which, according to Section 53(4) of the IA Act, can be used by providers of generative AI systems 'to demonstrate compliance with copyright obligations, until a harmonised standard is published'. The draft contains specific provisions on generative AI systems, emphasising that the *AI Act* and the Code 'shall be without prejudice to standards established by Union and national law'. Particularly, the need to interpret the Code in compliance with the Union rules on copyright is emphasised, with reference to the E&L introduced by the *Copyright* Directive.

---

[17] Peukert (2024).

[18] Ibid.

[19] Margoni (2024), cit.

[20] Article 53(1)(d), IA *Act*: '1. Providers of general-purpose IA templates shall: (d) draw up and make available to the public a sufficiently detailed summary of the content used for the training of the general-purpose IA template, according to a template provided by the IA Bureau'.

The draft Code specifies, in fact, that the *Copyright* Directive 'introduced exceptions and limitations that allow reproductions and extractions of works or other subject matter, for the purpose of text and data extraction, under certain conditions. Under these rules, rightholders may choose to reserve their rights in their works or other subject matter to prevent the extraction of texts and data, unless it is for the purpose of scientific research. If the rights have been expressly reserved in an appropriate manner, providers of generic A.I. templates must obtain permission from the right holders if they wish to perform text and data extraction on those works'.

Finally, the Code refers to Section 53(1)(c) of the *AI Act*,[21] which imposes an obligation on suppliers of generic AI systems placed on the Union market to implement a policy of compliance with Union copyright and related rights. Particularly, providers must: (i) detect and, where appropriate, comply with an express reservation of rights under Art. 4(3) of the *Copyright* Directive; (ii) ensure such compliance with this provision regardless of the jurisdiction in which the copyright acts underlying the formation of such generic AI systems take place.

Among the measures put in place to enforce the limits of the TDM exception, the Code provides at sub-measure 2.6[22] the obligation for signatories to use only *crawlers* 'that read and follow the instructions expressed in accordance with the Robot Exclusion Protocol (robots.txt)'[23] and, at sub-measure 2.7,[24] the commitment of the signatories to make 'best efforts', in accordance with widely disseminated industry *standards*, to identify and comply with other appropriate expressions of reservation of rights at the aggregate level.

[21] Article 53(1)(d), AI Act: 'Providers of general purpose AI models shall: (c) implement a policy to comply with Union law on copyright and related rights and, in particular, to identify and respect, including through state-of-the-art technology, an express reservation of rights in accordance with Article 4(3) of Directive (EU) 2019/790'.

[22] Sub-measure 2.6.: 'If signatories engage in text and data mining within the meaning of Article 2(2) of Directive (EU) 2019/790 for the training of their general-purpose AI models, they undertake, as a minimum measure to identify and comply, including through state-of-the-art technology, with an express reservation of rights within the meaning of Article 4(3) of Directive (EU) 2019/790, to employ web-crawlers that read and follow express instructions in accordance with the robot exclusion protocol (robots.txt), as specified in Internet Engineering Task Force (IETF) request for comments No. 9309'.

[23] *Web crawling* (or '*spidering*') is a process whereby an automated programme (the *crawler*) explores *the web* by crawling links between pages. The goal is to build an index for the *web*. *Crawlers* are commonly used by search engines to speed up the association between available pages and what the user is looking for.

[24] Sub-measure 2.7.: 'Signatories undertake to use their best efforts, commensurate with their size and capacity, in accordance with widely used industry standards, to identify and comply with, including through state-of-the-art technology, other machine-readable means of appropriately expressing a reservation of rights at source or work level pursuant to Article 4(3) of Directive (EU) 2019/790 in the case of content made publicly available online. This commitment is without prejudice to the right of the relevant rightholders to expressly reserve the use of works and other legitimately accessible material for the purpose of text and data extraction in any appropriate manner pursuant to Article 4(3) of Directive 2019/790/EU. [...]'.

With regard to sub-measure 2.6, it seems appropriate to point out that *web-crawling* consists of a phase of *web-scraping*[25] that includes 1) analysing the *website*, 2) *web-crawling* and 3) organising the data.[26] As is well known in doctrine, since '*copyright* law does not prevent the collection of data per se, nor does a website necessarily own the data on its site, particularly when it is user-generated (e.g. content from *social media* sites),'[27] *web-scraping* can lead to copyright infringements. To contain these risks, tools have been developed to regulate the access of *crawlers/robots* to *web* pages, first the robots.txt, a programme that informs *the web-scraper* about access restrictions to the *website*, with a significant impact on copyright protection.[28] More precisely, the presence or absence of such *files* can be used to determine whether a *website* owner allows access to *web-crawlers* (e.g. Field v. Google).[29]

A significant limitation of the robots.txt tool is direct access to a URL. In the case where a restricted-access subsection of a site ('site A') is reached through a direct *link* from another site ('site B'), the *bot* will not be able to retrieve the robots.txt file of site A, and will therefore be able to access it.[30] Precisely because of this limitation, the General Code of Conduct for AI, while recognising that the robots.txt tool represents an initial defence against *web-scraping*, introduces the additional measure 2.7, thus highlighting that robots.txt still needs refinement to effectively protect copyright.

Precisely for this purpose, sub-measure 2.7 offers a further level of protection, explicitly recalling Art. 17(4) of the *Copyright* Directive, which, as seen above, incorporates the 'best endeavours' paradigm into EU law, establishing *standards of* conduct for platforms to prevent copyright infringements and ensure a balance between the interests of rightholders and users. Particularly, signatories are encouraged to implement tools in line with widely used industry *standards* that allow for the 'identification of and compliance with [...] other machine-readable means of appropriately expressing a reservation of rights at source or work level within the

---

[25] *Web scraping* is a process whereby an automated programme (the so-called '*scraper*') extracts unstructured data from *web* pages and renders them structured in such a way that their subsequent processing is possible. In this way, *scrapers* enable the collection of information that is not immediately available or difficult to extract manually.

[26] Krotov and Silva (2018).

[27] Krotov et al. (2020).

[28] Placed on the initial directory of a *website*, the robots.txt indicates which sections of the site can be visited and which cannot, restricting access to files, individual pages and entire *directories*. The robots.txt file is optional: if the bot does not find this file, it implicitly assumes that it can explore and retrieve data from all the pages that make up a site.

[29] Field v. Google Inc., Case 2:2004cv00413 (2006), United States District Court for the District of Nevada.

[30] The judgment in case C-466/12 (known as the Svensson case) of the Court of Justice ruled that it is permissible to share links to *websites* with free content without the prior authorisation of the rights holder, making it de facto difficult to restrict the dissemination of content through *linking*. However, this possibility is excluded if the content is only accessible through a *paywall* or after registering with the *website*.

meaning of Article 4(3) of Directive (EU) 2019/790 in the case of content made publicly available *online*'.

Pending a stance by the Court of Justice and the Supreme Court, the German case of Robert Kneschke v. LAION e.V (Hamburg District Court[31]), although debatable in its conclusions, deals with the issue correctly, scanning it from the perspective of the biphasic test and thus ultimately referring to the compatibility of the conduct under and for the purposes of the tripartite test.[32]

Therefore, the provisions of the *Copyright* Directive, read in conjunction with Section 53 of the *IA Act*, recognise the legitimacy of TDM conduct, even for the purpose of training AI systems, only where the conditions underlying the *Three-Step Test* are met. And in so doing, systematic consistency is emphatically reaffirmed and confirmed.

---

[31] Hamburg Regional Court, Judgment 310 O 227/23 (2024).

[32] The case addresses the issue of the use of copyright-protected data for the training of AI systems, examining the compatibility with the TDM exceptions provided by European law and establishing that the use of protected works for the training of AI systems can fall within the exceptions provided by Art. 3 of the Copyright Directive and Art. 60d of the German Copyright Act (TDM for scientific research purposes). In the present case, the plaintiff is a photographer who has made one of his photos freely available to the public via the Bigstockphoto website, subject to the following terms of service: 'The user may not use any automated programmes, applets, bots or the like to access the Bigstock.com website or any content therein for any purpose whatsoever, including but not limited to downloading content, indexing, *scraping* or caching of any content on the website'. The defendant, a non-profit organisation dedicated to promoting research activities in the field of AI, creates and provides open datasets consisting of ready-to-use text-image pairs to train generative AI. By matching a large number of text and images, AI is able to learn the appearance of people, animals or objects, on the basis of which AI can be authorised to distinguish and artificially create people, animals or objects on its own. For the purposes of AI's training activities, he downloaded and stored a copy of a series of images from publicly available resources. If there is a mismatch, the software removes the particular image from the dataset as the dataset must be reliable and consistent to ensure proper AI training. The defendant's dataset comprises nearly six billion text-image pairs, including a photo created by the plaintiff. Robert Kneschke therefore asked LAION to stop any reproduction of the photo in question. The court held that the type of TDM carried out by LAION could be considered TDM within the meaning of Section 60d of the German Copyright Act, which also applies when rights are expressly reserved. LAION's analysis of the image file to match it with a pre-existing description of the image would amount to an analysis aimed at obtaining 'correlation' information (i.e., the issue of non-concordance between images and image descriptions), which, insofar as it is made available free of charge, would not pursue any commercial purpose. Whilst it is true that the dataset thus created can subsequently be used to train artificial neural networks and that the content generated by the AI can compete with the works of (human) authors, this does not justify the creation of datasets being regarded as an infringement of the exploitation rights of works within the meaning of Art. 5(5) of the InfoSoc Directive. The application of the TDM limitation would also be compatible with the *Three-Step Test* because it is not evident, nor has it been argued by the applicants, that the possibilities of exploitation of the works in question by Robert Kneschke would be affected by the creation of datasets by LAION. This appears to be in line with settled case law of the Court of Justice, according to which in assessing whether a national TDM provision is applicable in a given case, a court should not only focus on the specific conditions for its application but should also consider whether the requirements of the *Three-Step Test* are met.

References

Drexl J, Hilty RM et al (2019) Technical aspects of artificial intelligence: an understanding from an intellectual property law perspective. Max Planck Institute for Innovation and Competition Research Paper, n. 19-13. In: https://ssrn.com/abstract=3465577

Gervais D (2020) The machine as author. Iowa Law Rev 105:2053

Ginsburg JC (2018) People not machines: authorship and what it means in the Berne Convention. IIC – Int Rev Intellect Prop Compet Law 49:131

Ginsburg JC, Budiardjo LA (2019) Authors and machines. Berkeley Technol Law J 34(2):343

Guadamuz A (2021) Do androids dream of electric copyright? Comparative analysis of originality in artificial intelligence generated works. In: Hilty RM, Lee JA, Liu KC (eds) Artificial intelligence and intellectual property. Oxford, p 147

Guadamuz A (2024) A scanner darkly: copyright liability and exceptions in artificial intelligence inputs and outputs. GRUR Int 73(2):111. Disponibile su: https://academic.oupcom/grurint/advance-article/doi/10.1093/grurint/ikad140/7529098?login=false

Hugenholtz PB, Quintais JP (2021) Copyright and artificial creation: does EU copyright law protect AI-assisted output? IIC – Int Rev Intellect Property Compet Law 52:1190

Krotov V, Silva L (2018) Legality and ethics of web scraping

Krotov V et al (2020) Tutorial: legality and ethics of web scraping. Commun Assoc Inf Syst, 47, art. 22

Lucchi N (2023) ChatGPT: a case study on copyright challenges for generative artificial intelligence systems. Eur J Risk Regul 1. Disponibile su: https://doi.org/10.1017/err.2023.59

Margoni T (2024) TDM and generative AI: lawful access and opt-outs. Disponibile su: https://papers.ssrn.com/sol3/papers.cfm?abstract_id=5036164

Peukert A (2024) Copyright in the Artificial Intelligence Act – a primer. GRUR Int 73. In: https://ssrn.com/abstract=4771976

References

[illegible]

The Protectability of AI Systems

Emanuela Arezzo

Contents

Abstract Artificial intelligence systems are complex products comprising several hardware and software components, and as such, they fall under the protection of several intellectual and industrial property instruments. In this chapter, we will focus, in particular, on patent law as it applies to AI inventions in accordance with the well-known case law on *mixed-type claim inventions.*

1 Artificial Intelligence Systems As Complex Products

Artificial intelligence systems are complex products brought to life through the contribution of several parties that provide technical components, *hardware* and *software*, processes, *know-how* and, above all, large quantities of data.[1] Intelligent

[1] See Regulation of the European Parliament and of the Council laying down harmonized rules on artificial intelligence and amending Regulations (EC) 300/2008, (EU) 167/2013, (EU) 168/2013,

E. Arezzo (✉)
University of Teramo, Teramo, Italy
e-mail: earezzo@unite.it

R. Bocchini (ed.), *Digital Platforms - From Technical Foundations to Legal and Economic Implications*, https://doi.org/10.1007/978-3-032-07978-7_21

systems are, in turn, capable not only of interacting with humans but also of producing a series of information, data, recommendations, and 'outputs' that can be likened to works of genius or inventions. It is therefore necessary to consider two distinct sets of problems: first, how to protect the intelligent system itself, given the co-presence of various inventive/creative contributions. Second, it is necessary to consider what kind of protection should be afforded to any *outputs* produced by the intelligent system. In other words, this is the issue commonly referred to as generative AI.[2]

Upon closer examination, the second question splits into at least two intrinsically connected questions in both patent law and copyright law.[3] A first profile concerns, in fact, the possibility of attributing the status of author/inventor to the intelligent machine, while a second profile concerns the protectability of 'outputs' produced through a significant contribution of the intelligent system—i.e., by the intelligent system in a more or less autonomous manner[4]—according to the rules on inventions and intellectual creations.

(EU) 2018/858, (EU) 2018/1139 and (EU) 2019/2144 and Directives 2014/90/EU, (EU) 2016/797 AND (EU) 2020/1828, *Regulation on Artificial Intelligence*, (hereinafter referred to as Ai *Act* for brevity), *G.U.* L 2024/1689, 12 July 2024, recitals 63, 83, 88.

[2] On the contrary, the issue does not seem to arise in cases where the AI falls within the so-called '*partly-generative machine*' category, i.e. in those cases where the intelligent machine serves merely as a *toolkit*, albeit a very sophisticated one, used by the human being, under their own input, to create a work of genius. See Frosio (2020), p. 54 who recalls the distinction originally made by Denicola (2016), pp. 251, 269 ff. Indeed, there are many examples in which the work of genius is produced by the machine (hardware or software: consider, for instance, a word-processor program or a camera), even though no one doubts that it merely functions as a tool enabling human creativity. On this point Ginsburg and Budiardjo (2019), pp. 343, 428.

[3] I addressed this in detail in *Gli investimenti in "attrezzature per produzioni di avanguardia tecnologica" come strumento di ripartenza economica. La tutela dell'ia e dei suoi prodotti tramite diritto d'autore e diritti connessi*, in *AIDA*, 2022, 333.

[4] Indeed, there is a widely held view in the literature that, although apparently endowed with a very high degree of autonomy, the work of the intelligent system still responds to human input and the result produced is to some extent adapted, chosen, tested, etc. by the flesh-and-blood person. Ginsburg and Budiardjo (2019), p. 401 and footnote 219, in which they state that even the most sophisticated intelligent machines simply execute orders given by the human programmer; Kim (2020), pp. 443, 446, who states that it would be more accurate to speak of automation and not autonomy when referring to intelligent systems, as the latter also implies the machine's ability to self-regulate and self-determine, characteristics that are absent in intelligent systems. See Dornis (2021), pp. 1, 12.

2 The Protection of Artificial Intelligence Systems Through the Classic Instruments of Intellectual and Industrial Property

According to the data,[5] the protection of the intelligent system as such does not appear to pose any particular problems. And indeed, a large part of the components of the intelligent system—particularly the application that interfaces with the user, as well as the software instructions that enable its operation—are undoubtedly covered by the authorship discipline applicable to computer programs.[6] Similarly, regarding the patent profile, the EBU was quick to clarify that the concepts of artificial intelligence and machine learning are, in fact, assimilable to mathematical methods and, consequently, patenting is conditional on the invention, as a whole, being able to produce a technical contribution.[7] Inventions concerning A.I. would therefore also fall within the well-established category of so-called *mixed-type claim inventions,*[8] where the inventor claims both technical and non-technical portions of an invention together (the non-technical ones being unpatentable as such: data compilations, algorithms, etc.), and where protection is granted as long as the invention, as a whole, makes a further technical contribution to the state of the art that can be considered worthy of protection.[9]

The Technical Boards of Appeal have taken a similar line. In case T 702/20, the EB clarified that a neural network defines a class of mathematical functions and,

[5] This has been extensively discussed, in relations to inventions, by Straus (2021), p. 615.

[6] While the algorithms detailed in the programme listing are in fact protected by trade secrecy. On this subject, allow me to refer to Arezzo (2012), p. 26 ff.

[7] Epo, *Guidelines for Examination in the European Patent Office*, March 2023, https://www.epo.org/en/legal/guidelines-epc, Part G, Chap. II - Inventions, § 3.3.1. It is useful to point out that the sub-section is inserted within the section on mathematical and computational methods. Indeed, artificial intelligence and machine learning are based on computational models and algorithms; hence the challenge of identifying technical character arises, since—like mathematical formulae—they are not patentable as such. See also *therein*, Part G, Chap. II, 3.6.4., where the EPO, when discussing databases, refers to the subsection dedicated to artificial intelligence, and also in this case the Office refers to the necessity of the technical contribution that must be made by the program in order for it to be considered an invention and, therefore, patented.

[8] For this type of invention, which now encompasses very heterogeneous fields, from chemistry to information technology, see Arezzo (2011), p. 106.

[9] The approach based on demonstrating the further technical contribution, produced through the interaction between the technical and non-technical means of the invention, was developed, as is known, with reference to *computer implemented inventions*. It was then established, beginning with the EPO decision, *26 September 2002, COMVIK/TWO IDENTITIES, T0641/00*, [2004] E.P.O.R. 10, as the methodology to be followed in all cases where elements not patentable as such, from scientific discoveries to business methods, are claimed in the patent application. With regard to the EPO approach as refined in *Comvik,* may I refer to my article *Nuove invenzioni e rapporti tra i diversi requisiti di brevettabilità nella giurisprudenza EPO*, in *Dir. ind.*, 2016, 158. For the development of this methodology with specific reference to software inventions, see at length E. Arezzo, *Tutela brevettuale e autoriale dei programmi per elaboratore: profili e critica di una dicotomia normative,* 162–165.

consequently, since such knowledge *is* not patentable, it should be *excluded* from patentable *subject matter*. Nonetheless, as with other "non-technical" elements, an invention based on a neural network can be considered non-trivial when the network is concretely used to solve a technical problem, e.g., when it is trained with a precise data set to address a specific (technical) task.[10] Similarly, in case T 598/07, the Technical Commission held patentable an invention concerning a method for monitoring heartbeats, based on a neural network, for the purpose of identifying irregular heartbeats.[11]

In the case of the patenting of the intelligent system, no problems are foreseen specifically regarding the analysis of the requirement of novelty, since the state of the art will be enriched by the inventions of intelligent systems already patented or in any case accessible, inasmuch as in use and available on the market, before the filing date of the invention for which protection is sought.[12] Nor does the assessment of the inventive step with respect to the state of the art seem to be particularly complex here, since the latter includes the knowledge accessible to the average technician in the branch operating in that particular field of technology and therefore, in all likelihood, familiar with the most common training or learning *methods* of intelligent systems.[13] Similarly, the requirement of industrial application does not seem to pose any obstacle, since intelligent systems take the form of finished products with a specific application or mode of use, clearly claimed in the patent application; otherwise, they would incur the aforementioned prohibition of patenting under Art. 52, para. 2, lett. (a), EPC (i.e., our Art. 45, para. 2, lett. (a), Italian Intellectual Property Code).

Unlike computer-implemented inventions, however, the patenting of intelligent systems could raise concerns regarding the lawfulness of the invention, which, as is well known, aims to prevent the protection of inventions whose *implementation* would conflict with principles of morality and common sense or jeopardize the protection of public order.[14]

In this respect, however, while it is true that the AI Regulation does not address industrial and intellectual property issues (except those related to the protection of

[10] See EPO, 7 November 2022, *Sparsely connected neural network/MITSUBISHI*, T 0702/20, ECLI:EP:BA:2022:T070220.20221107.

[11] Cf: EPO, 19 May 2010, *Cardionetics Limited/BIOTRONIK*, T598/07, ECLI:EP:BA:2010:T059807.20100519.

[12] In this regard, see, however, the timely observations of Hattenbach and Glucoft (2015), pp. 19, 38, where it is emphasized that not all accessible information is per se invalidating, as it often lacks the degree of detail necessary to illustrate how the invention was implemented. In the authors' words "[...] The issue here is that even if a page displaying a computer-generated claim does technically qualify as a printed publication, it would also need to be enabling in order to constitute invalidating prior art".

[13] In fact, when analysing and evaluating the patenting of the intelligent system as such, the average technician in the field will be identified as the operator (i.e. the *team of* people) with highly qualified IT skills. On this point, see Kim et al. (2022), p. 295.

[14] On the requirement of lawfulness, see Spada (2000), pp. 5–19; Muciaccia (2021), pp. 222, 238 ff.; Adcock and Beyleveld (2016), pp. 2–5; Ricolfi (2003), pp. 31–32. Ottolia (2019), p. 440.

authorial content accidentally used to train the intelligent system), on the other hand, the document is strongly attentive to the ethical aspects connected with the use of artificial intelligence, robotics, and all related technologies, aiming to promote the adoption of a legal framework that supports investment and the dissemination of safe, reliable, and ethical AI.[15]

The EU therefore proposes an approach focused on the comprehensive protection of the individual, both in terms of the health, safety, and security of citizens, and with regard to the most personal aspects of human life such as the protection of privacy, image, dignity, and protection from all forms of discrimination.

It is with these aims in mind that the EU legislator has carefully mapped out those technologies that considered particularly harmful to humans, those posing a risk defined as 'unacceptable' and therefore always prohibited, while introducing specific regulations for so-called 'high-risk' technologies, whose circulation in the European single market is subject to compliance with certain requirements.[16]

It is thus prohibited, for instance, to place on the market—or even to merely use—intelligent systems that employ subliminal techniques capable of acting without a person's knowledge, or 'deliberately manipulative or deceptive techniques with the purpose or effect of materially distorting the behaviour of a person or group of persons', thereby significantly impairing their autonomy of judgement and inducing them to make choices and decisions that they would not otherwise have made.[17] All the more so is the distribution of AI systems prohibited when they exploit the vulnerabilities of a single person or a specific group of individuals for the purpose of massively influencing their behaviour, causing them significant harm.[18]

[15] Cf. *Explanatory Memorandum to the Proposal for a Regulation*, § 1.1., where the Commission endorses the concerns previously expressed by the Council and the European Parliament regarding the ethical aspects of AI. See European Council, Extraordinary meeting of the European Council (1 and 2 October 2020), Conclusions, EUCO 13/20, 2020, 7; European Parliament resolution of 20 October 2020 with recommendations to the Commission regarding the framework for the ethical aspects of artificial intelligence, robotics and related technologies (2020/2012(INL)). A. Del Ninno, *La proposta di Regolamento UE sull'Intelligenza Artificiale: I profili operativi del nuovo quadro normativo europeo. Parte prima,* in *Dir. & giust.*, 2021, 1, 3, highlights that one of the objectives proposed Regulation is the protection of fundamental human rights put at risk by the use of AI systems. The author emphasizes the usefulness of the proposal's strict transparency requirements, particularly when individuals interact with it. See also Schepisi (2022), p. 330, who stresses that the EU has chosen to regulate these aspects of AI *ex ante* through *hard regulation*, while also highlighting the criticalities and difficulties of conducting an a priori assessment of the possible risks of an AI system, 332 and 341 ff. For a discussion of the *risk approach* see Casonato and Marchetti (2021), p. 415.

[16] High-risk includes, for example, AI systems that enable biometric identification of natural persons 'in real time' and 'a posteriori'; AI systems intended to determine access or assignment of natural persons to educational and vocational training institutions; and AI systems intended for recruitment or selection of individuals, in particular for advertising vacancies, screening or filtering applications, and assessing candidates in interviews or tests. See Annex III, Ai *Act*.

[17] This, of course, to the extent that the decision taken by the person or group of persons causes them significant harm. See Section 5(a), Ai *Act*.

[18] *Idem*, Art. 5(b).

References

Adcock M, Beyleveld D (2016) Morality in intellectual property law: a concept-theoretic framework. Intel Prop Rights 1:2–5

Arezzo E (2011) Nuovi scenari in materia di brevettabilità delle invenzioni attuate a mezzo di elaboratore elettronico: dal tramonto della Proposta di direttiva europea alla recente Opinione della Commissione allargata dei Ricorsi dell'UEB nel caso G 0003/08. Riv. dir. ind., p 106

Arezzo E (2012) Tutela brevettuale e autoriale dei programmi per elaboratore: profili e critica di una dicotomia normativa. Giuffrè, Milano, p 26 ff

Casonato C, Marchetti B (2021) Prime osservazioni sulla proposta di regolamento dell'Unione europea in materia di intelligenza artificiale. BioLaw J:415

Denicola R (2016) Ex Machina: copyright protection for computer-generated works. Rutgers Univ Law Rev 69:251, 269 ff

Dornis TW (2021) Authorless works and inventions without inventor—the muddy waters of AI autonomy. Eur Intellect Prop Rev 1:12

Frosio G (2020) L'(I)Autore inesistente: una tesi tecno-giuridica contro la tutela dell'opera generata dall'intelligenza artificiale. AIDA:54

Ginsburg JC, Budiardjo LA(2019), Authors and Machines, in 34 Berkeley Tech. L. J. 428.

Hattenbach B, Glucoft J (2015) Patents in an Era of Infinite Monkeys and Artificial Intelligence, in Stanford Technology Law Review, 32, 19.

Kim D (2020) AI - Generated Interventions: Time to Get the Record Straight? in Grur Int., 69, 443.

Kim D et al (2022) Clarifying assumptions about artificial intelligence before Revolutionising patent law. GRUR Int:295

Muciaccia N (2021) Ordine pubblico e clausola di moralità nella brevettazione delle armi autonome e ad uso civile-militare. AIDA:222, 238 ff

Ottolia A (2019) Commento all'art. 50 c.pi. In: Ubertazzi LC (ed) Commentario breve alle leggi su proprietà intellettuale e concorrenza. CEDAM, Padova, p 440

Ricolfi M (2003) La brevettazione delle invenzioni relative agli organismi geneticamente modificati. Riv dir ind 5:31–32

Schepisi C (2022) Le "dimensioni" della regolazione dell'intelligenza artificiale nella proposta di regolamento della Commissione. Quaderni AISDUE:330

Spada P (2000) Liceità dell'invenzione brevettabile ed esorcismo dell'innovazione. Riv dir priv 5:5–19

Straus J (2021) Artificial intelligence and patenting: from lessons from "DABUS" patent applications. In: Costa C et al (eds) Studi di Diritto Commerciale per Vincenzo di Cataldo. Giappichelli, Torino, p 615

The Protectability of AI-Generated Works

Emanuela Arezzo

Contents

Abstract This chapter examines the possibility of granting copyright protection to products created—allegedly—autonomously by intelligent systems. The question arises, inter alia, whether the current concept of creativity can extend to goods produced by machines.

1 The Protectability of AI-Generated Products As 'Intellectual Works'

In the Italian legal system, intangible assets that can be protected by copyright are those belonging to literature, music, figurative arts, architecture, theatre, and cinematography (and specifically those that take the form of one of the works listed in Article 2 of the Italian Copyright Law), regardless of the manner or form they are

E. Arezzo (✉)
University of Teramo, Teramo, Italy
e-mail: earezzo@unite.it

R. Bocchini (ed.), *Digital Platforms - From Technical Foundations to Legal and Economic Implications*, https://doi.org/10.1007/978-3-032-07978-7_22

expressed, provided they are endowed with a creative character.[1] From a merely phenomenological point of view, it would therefore seem that the products of the AI can indeed fall within the *genus* of intellectual works, since they usually take the form of goods that appear to belong to those fields of art and culture traditionally protected by copyright and, moreover, are undeniably endowed with a representative form[2]: for example, consider the paintings of the intelligent system Aaron[3] or the portraits of Ai-Da.[4] Indeed, many have pointed out the practical impossibility of distinguishing works created by the human author from those produced by the intelligent machine.[5]

The picture, however, is not complete. Indeed, the discipline of authorship expressly requires that a protectable intellectual work must be creative (or original, in Anglo-Saxon legal systems) and represent the result of the author's intellectual effort[6]: elements that, in both doctrinal and judicial analysis, often merge into the same notion of protectable work, almost becoming nuances of the same concept.[7]

The requirement of creativity in Italian copyright law has historically been understood as the expression of human intellectual effort.[8] The work must be the

---

[1] The Italian law—which describes artistic forms in great detail, including theatre, cinematography, architecture—adds the element of creativity. The works protected by copyright law, Article 1 of the Copyright Act (which incorporates Article 2575 of the Italian Civil Code) are those that possess a creative character.

[2] On this point, among others, De Sanctis (2012), p. 30, who argued that the creative character as a requisite of protectability necessarily refers to the *representative form* that all intellectual works possess and in any case must possess, since they are "communications of information" about their author's thoughts on the subject.

[3] Aaron is an intelligent system created by Harold Cohen, a painter and expert in *computer-generated art*, capable of creating figurative works on canvas as well as drawings. For a more in-depth look at https://www.wired.com/2001/05/aaron-art-from-the-machine/.

[4] V. Mazzoni (2022) and Ippolito (2022).

[5] Thus Denicola (2016), pp. 251, 272; Yu (2017), p. 1257; Ginsburg and Budiardjo (2019), p. 401 ff.

[6] See Arts. 2575 Italian Civil Code and 1(1) Copyright Act with reference to the requirement of creativity, and Arts. 2576 Civil Code and 6 Copyright Act where it is specified that the constituent event of the right is the creation of the work *as a particular expression of intellectual work"* ("quale particolare espressione del lavoro intellettuale").

[7] Cf. Fabiani, for whom the elements the intellectual work must posses in order to constitute the object of copyright, are, *in addition to its creative character*, its belonging to one of the fields of art and culture and the "concreteness of its expression". Fabiani (2004), p. 39. For De Sanctis, the creative character is the requirement that intellectual works must possess together with the expressive form "in which creativity must be expressed" (in order to be protected under Article 2575 of the Italian Civil Code). De Sanctis (2012), cit., p. 31. Similarly, Auteri holds that the definition of intellectual work protected by copyright also clarifies the meaning of the requirement of creative character that the work must possess in order to merit copyright protection. Auteri (2023), pp. 623, 639.

[8] See Art. 2576 of the Italian Civil Code and Art. 6 Italian Copyright Act. In this sense Oppo (1964), p. 191. More recently, Musso argues that art. 2576 of the Civil Code, with its reference to the creation of the work as a "particular expression of intellectual work", would constitute an indissoluble link between the element of the personal creation of the intellectual work by its author, as per art.

result of author's intellectual activity, who is entitled to exclusive rights by virtue of the creative act (Art. 2576 of the Civil Code)[9] and must further reflect their personal imprint[10]—creativity in this sense also meaning the originality or individuality of the work.[11] This second nuance of the concept of creativity appears to have been accepted at European level both by the European Union legislator and by the case law of the Court of Justice. Indeed, if at first the parameter of the "author's own intellectual creation" was only introduced by law with reference to certain specific types of intellectual works (i.e. the so-called useful creations[12] and photographic

---

2575 of the Italian Civil Code, and the (original) acquisition of the right by the author, *as* per art. 2580 of the Italian Civil Code (by reason of the creation) Musso (2008), p. 126.

[9] Since every conception comes, by definition, from a creative act of its author, whose imprint it bears, it will be subjectively new in the sense of being different from all other existing works of the intellect (a diversity which, obviously, relates to the different manner of expression and not to the object of such representation that which might well be known to the community). Thus Auteri (2023), *Il diritto d'autore*, cit., 497. In this sense, subjective novelty is an important aspect that characterizes the (broader) requirement of creativity. Thus Are (1963), p. 52. On the other hand, the idea that authorship protection also requires proof of the so-called objective novelty of the work, as authoritative doctrine once held, in particular Are (1963), p. 53; Ascarelli (1960), p. 705; Greco and Vercellone (1974), p. 47 ff. Today Bertani (2011), p. 126 ff. seems to lean towards this thesis, holding that such a conception of the creativity requirement would have the merit of resolving problematic situations, such as the case of chance encounters, thereby restoring a greater level of legal certainty.

[10] On this point, see De Sanctis (1971), p. 38, who considers the requirement satisfied when the creation represents the 'reflection' of the author's own personality insofar as it is the image of the latter's characteristic traits at a given time and in a given direction sedimented in an objective quid that crystallises in a certain sense the dynamic configuration of the individual. Similarly on the point, even earlier, Stolfi (1932), p. 518 ff.

[11] Thus Auteri (2023), p. 639. This is, therefore, a conceptual nuance that differs from the Anglo-Saxon notion of originality in which the term is understood as synonymous with origin, the origin of the work by its author: this notion leads to considering the requirement fulfilled whenever the creation can be traced back to a certain author, who conceived it in a completely independent manner (i.e. without copying). This, in turn, justifies the doctrine of so-called *independent creation*, according to which even identical creations will not be considered infringing where the authors (*recte:* the second author) can prove that they conceived them independently. For all see. Leaffer (2004), pp. 59 and 408.

[12] The reference is to computer programs and databases, so defined by P. Frassi to highlight their typically functional connotation. V. Frassi (1997). These are in fact intangible assets whose protectability has in some cases been ruled out by some national courts. On this subject, see Aplin (2009), p. 49.

works),[13] this initial "vertical" harmonisation[14] of the notion of creativity/originality by the legislator was subsequently followed by a harmonisation work, this time "horizontal", by the Court of Justice. Starting from the well-known *Infopaq* ruling, the Court proposed extending the requirement of originality—understood as "the *result of the author's own intellectual creation"*—to all types of intellectual creations.[15,16]

The result was a jurisprudential line of cases that, starting from the element of the author's own intellectual creation as a reflection of their creative spirit, gradually developed the notion of creativity around the parameter of the freedom of choice, arrangement and combination of the elements that make up the representative form of the work,[17] establishing it as the general canon of the entire discipline of authorship.[18] From this perspective, the Court has clarified that the element of creativity is

[13] See Art. 1(3) of Directive 2009/24/EC of the European Parliament and of the Council of 23 April 2009 on the legal protection of computer programs, in *O.J.* L 111, 5 May 2009; Art. 3(1) of Directive 96/9/EC of the European Parliament and of the Council of 11 March 1996 on the legal protection of databases, in *O*.J. L 077, 27 March 1996.*U.* L 077, 27 March 1996; Art. 6, Directive 2006/116/EC of the European Parliament and of the Council of 12 December 2006 on the term of protection of copyright and certain related rights, in *O.J.* L. 372, 27 December 2006, 12 (with reference to photographic works).

[14] The expression is from Fabbio (2016), pp. 281, 285.

[15] Cf. Court of Justice. EU, 16 July 2009, in Case C-5/08, *Infopaq International v. Danske Dagblades Forening, [2009] ECR* I-6569, § 37.

[16] On this point, Kur et al. (2019), p. 338 ff., note how the Court of Justice succumbed to the temptation to fill the regulatory gaps still largely present in the European copyright landscape. Indeed, as rightly noted by doctrine prior to *Infopaq*, the introduction of a specific notion of originality only for certain intellectual goods, although largely justified by a strong need for harmonisation regarding the treatment (and perhaps even before the recognition of protection) accorded to certain types of works, carried with it the risk of breaking the unity of the system (see Casas Valles 2009a, b, pp. 103 and 132). The Court's decision in *Infopaq* should, therefore, be framed as a first and important recognition by the Court of the need to adopt a single concept of originality (together, it will be seen, with a single notion of intellectual work) valid across all EU countries and transversal to all the different types of intellectual works (cf. Fabbio (2016), p. 293 ff.). However, it is important to remember that the notion of author's own intellectual creation actually had very heterogeneous nuances within the three directives in which it was initially introduced. On this point Ramalho (2018), p. 26ff.; Rosati (2013), p. 63; Van Eechoud et al. (2009), p. 41.

[17] It should also be recalled, moreover, that such a concept of creativity, referring to the specific choice and arrangement of material (even in itself made up of non-protectable elements) was introduced with reference to the regulation of creative databases (Art. 3 of Directive 96/9), finding its antecedent in the protection of collective works (see Art. 3 of the Copyright Law).

[18] Indeed, it is recalled that in *Infopaq*, the question concerned the protectability by copyright of extremely small fragments of works (i.e. extracts of as few as eleven words). The Court ruled in favour of the protectability of such excerpts where, through the choice, arrangement and combination of simple words, even if not individually protectable, the author was able to express his creative spirit in an original manner, obtaining a result that constituted an intellectual creation. *Infopaq*, C-5/08, cit., § 45. The principle that copyright applies whenever the work "[...] constitutes an intellectual creation of the author which reflects his personality and is manifested through his free and creative choices [...]." has been reaffirmed by the Court in many subsequent cases. See Court of Justice. EU, 12 September 2019, in Case C-683/17, *Cofemel - Sociedade de Vestuário SA*

to be excluded whenever the author is, for any reason, constrained within specific parameters or rules, compliance with which imposes a certain path on them, thereby depriving them of discretion.[19] And again, based on somewhat similar reasoning, the Court has likewise ruled to exclude protection for those works (or portions of works) in which the form cannot be freely determined by the author because it is dictated by technical or functional reasons, and where the necessity of use effectively results in a "fusion" between idea and expression.[20]

---

v. G-Star Raw CV; ECJ. EU, 13 November 2018, in Case C-310/17, *Levola Hengelo v. Smilde Foods BV*, (hereinafter for brevity, CJEU, C-310/17); CJEU. EU, 7 August 2018, in Case C-161/17, *Land Nordrhein-Westfalen v. Dirk Renckhoff*; CJEU,7 August 2018, in Case C-161/17, *Land Nordrhein-Westfalen v. Dirk Renckhoff*; CJEU. EU,1 March 2012, in Case C-604/10, *Football Dataco and others v. Yahoo! UK Ltd and others*; Court of Justice. EU, 1 December 2011, in case C-145/10, *Eva-Maria Painer v. Standard VerlagsGmbH and others*; ECJ. EU, 4 October 2011, in Joined *Cases* C-403/08 and C-429/08, *Joined Cases Football Association Premier League Ltd and Others v QC Leisure and Others,* and *Karen Murphy v Media Protection Services Ltd* (hereinafter for brevity: *Football Association Premier League*, C-403/08 and C-429/08) § 97.

[19] As in the case of sports matches, for which the Court ruled out protectability by copyright (note: while leaving the way open for related rights), holding that the latter "[...] cannot be regarded as intellectual creations classifiable as works within the meaning of the Copyright Directive [...]" because they are " subject to rules of the game, leaving no room for creative freedom for the purposes of copyright". See Court of Justice. EU, *Football Association Premier League*, in Cases C-403/08 and C-429/08, cited above, § 98. Thus, the impossibility of falling within the category of works protected by copyright is attributed to the absence of the creativity requirement. On the element of creativity—understood also as synonymous with discretion—see M. Bertani, *Diritto d'autore europeo*, cit., 122, who argues that copyright protection is reserved exclusively for intellectual works that meet the legal requirement of demonstrating a creative character and, at the same time, the element of discretion. The latter is described as the condition in which the forms are not "necessary" in relation to the ideational or informative content they are meant to express. On this point, see also Casas Valles, who maintains that the requirement of creativity encompasses both the fact that the work originates from its author and, above all, that it results from the freedom to choose among different possible forms of expression. Cf. Casas Valles (2009a, b), p. 113.

[20] Cf., with reference to the issue of the protectability of graphical user interfaces, the ruling of the ECJ in the *BSA case*. The ECJ in the *BSA* case specified that if the expression of graphical components is dictated solely by their technical function, the criterion of originality would not be satisfied and protection would consequently be denied ("...*since the different methods of implementing an idea are so limited that the idea and the expression become indissociable.* "). See. ECJ. EU, 22 December 2010, in Case C-393/09, *Bezpenostní softwarová asociace - Svaz softwarové ochrany/ Ministerstvo kultury*,§49. It should be noted that authoritative doctrine had already expressed a similar view. See Giovanni Guglielmetti (1997), p. 299 ff., who argues that graphic user interfaces are protectable where they show a certain degree of creativity in relation to the particular choice, arrangement, organisation, sequence, graphic elaboration etc. of the set of images, words and sounds that compose it.

In addition, see also the later ruling *SAS Institute Inc. v. World Programming Ltd*, where, on the basis of similar considerations, the ECJ denied copyright protection for the mere functionality of a computer program, its programming language and the format of the data files used to exploit some of its functions holding that these do not "constitute a form of expression of that program for the purposes of Article 1(2) of Directive 91/250.". The Court further warned that granting protection to such purely functional aspects of software would be tantamount to making it possible to monopolise ideas, to the detriment of technological progress and industrial development.". See Court of Justice, 2 May 2012, in Case C-406/2010, *SAS Institute Inc. v. World Programming Ltd.*

In light of the framework thus outlined, which has now also found recognition in national case law,[21] and embracing the notion of creativity understood as the fruit of the author's free and individual choices, through which they imprint their personal mark on the work, and reflexively understood as the absence of any constraint that could in any way dictate the author's path or confine them within pre-established tracks, several authors have considered it appropriate to exclude that a machine is capable of 'creating' in the same manner as a human author. First, the machine would not be able to choose from an infinite number of possibilities, albeit an enormously vast number for the human mind.[22]

Indeed, the intelligent machine, even one based on the most sophisticated techniques of *machine learning*, where the level of decision-making autonomy makes the creative outcome unpredictable, always moves along the track predefined by the author and will always create according to the criterion and following the parameters with which its informational enrichment was configured.[23] Second, unlike the human being, the programmed apparatus, however intelligent, would not be able to reflect its own personality[24] (which it does not possess) and imprint its own touch on

[21] See Court of Cassation, 29 May 2020, no. 10300, in *AIDA*, 2020, 369 (case law published in headnotes only); Court of Cassation, 30 April 2020, no. 8433, in *AIDA*, 2020, 1922, with note by Schneider.

[22] In this sense see Rossi (2018), pp. 275, 276, according to which 'the new and original result is by no means an outcome of the creativity of the system, but simply of the fact that it has given application to the algorithm'. See also Yanisky Ravid and Velez Hernandez (2017), p. 691, who argue that current copyright law is not able to embrace the kind of production and creativity expressed by A.I. Similar conclusions are also reached by other authors, according to whom some A.I., in particular those based on deep learning mechanisms, are indeed capable of making countless choices in total autonomy; nevertheless, the result they reach is not original in the sense required by copyright. See Hristov (2017), p. 436 ff.; Gervais (2019), p. 52 who states that assets would fall into the public domain. An intermediate position is held by Bridy, who, while considering it unthinkable to attribute the ownership of rights over the intangible goods produced to the machine, considers it impossible to deny creative nature to the works produced by the Bridy (2012), p. 26. He goes further Banterle (2016), p. 71, arguing that A.I. machines would be capable of expressing creative choices in a completely autonomous manner and their creations would therefore be intellectual works to be protected by *copyright*.

[23] See Ramalho (2017), p. 3 ff., who identifies the absence of the creative capacity in the intelligent machine as lying in its lack of imagination, stating that A.I. can only represent what has been imparted to it through a set of abstract rules identified by the programmer, since the software is not capable of modifying the style of the creations it will compose unless specially reprogrammed by man. Similar considerations have been expressed by Rossi (2018), p. 276, who argues that not even the most sophisticated machine capable of self-learning could be said to be able to create, since "its actions will always be bounded, in an insurmountable way, by the starting database and the algorithm". See also Ginsburg and Budiardjo (2019), cit., p. 402 ff. On this point, see also the reflections of Burk (2020), pp. 263 and 266, according to which the products of A.I., even if they represent unique and completely unpredictable creations, are always the direct result of the process implemented by the machine, which is obviously the fruit of human intellectual work.

[24] With reference to the subject of A.I. see Rossi (2018), p. 275, who even evokes a causal link between author and work. Similarly, Gervais (2019), p. 52, speaks of "causation of originality". See also Frosio (2020), p. 74 who notes that in order to allow the authorial protection of "algorith-

the works produced[25] (if anything, it would convey the characteristic features of the creations that constitute the data set on which it has been trained).[26]

2 On the Link Between Creativity and the Human Nature of the Author

The reflections recently formulated lead one to wonder whether the requirement of the creativity of a work, as most recently outlined by the Court of Justice, presupposes, as a corollary, that the protectable work is necessarily and solely created by a human being.[27]

Even if one were inclined to agree with those who hold that the AI is capable of creating in the same way as a human being,[28] to imagine attributing the status of

mic creativity" one would have to change the existing subjective and anthropocentric interpretation of the notion of originality and replace it with a formal and objective approach.

[25] Thus Musso (2008), cit., p. 126 ff., argues that the element of creativity as an expression of the author's intellectual work must necessarily manifest itself in the form of the author's personal imprint on the original work: an imprint that would be completely lacking in the case of artificial intelligence, where the creative act would be entirely delegated to programs, even if very sophisticated.

[26] Spedicato (2019), p. 270 ff. also agrees on this point. See also Antikainen (2018), p. 257, who doubts that an A.I. system can possess its own personality or, more banally, be able to make choices that can be said to be genuinely free and creative.

[27] This is certainly the direction taken by the practice of the North American Copyright Office, which has refused to register works whose author turns out to be a machine and has sealed this principle in specific "Best Practices", where it explains that "[...] the Office will not register works produced by a machine or mere mechanical process that operates randomly or automatically without any creative input or intervention from a human author [...]". See *Copyrightable Authorship: What Can Be Registered U.S. Copyright Office*, *Compendium of U.S. Copyright Office Practices*, 3 ed., 2021, para. 300, § 313.2., available at: https://copyright.gov/comp3/chap300/ch300-copyrightable-authorship.pdf. Again, in section 306 (entitled "The Human Authorship Requirement"), it specified that "[...] the Copyright Office will register an original work of authorship, provided that the work was created by a human being. The copyright law only protects "the fruits of intellectual labour" that "are founded in the creative powers of the mind" Trade-Mark Cases, 100 U.S. 82, 94 (1879), see https://supreme.justia.com/cases/federal/us/100/82/. Because copyright law is limited to "original intellectual conceptions of the author" the Office will refuse to register a claim if it determines that a human being did not create the work.

[28] See Guizzardi (2018), p. 58 (footnote 38), who considers that the process of creation of an intellectual work entirely entrusted to technology cannot in itself, merely by virtue of the fact that is carried out by A.I., be said to be constrained and therefore so predetermined in its final outcome as to deprive the final result of such processes of creativity. In some ways similar positions have also been formulated by Spedicato (2019), p. 273 ff., who argues that if it is true that the A.I. does not operate entirely free of rules, the degree of freedom that it is able to express - while complying with the system of rules that govern its functioning—would generally be analogous to the type of creativity that characterizes a human being.

author to a machine seems arduous and, in some respects, not even desirable (especially in the absence of a commonly accepted definition of what is meant by AI).[29]

Indeed, the intelligent machine not only lacks individuality capable of being reflected in the work but also lacks legal personality and capacity to act.[30] These two aspects, which will not be discussed in detail in this chapter, are in fact of predominant importance. An entity without legal capacity can hardly be regarded as a bearer of rights and economic prerogatives, let alone held responsible for any violations that might arise from the dissemination, in a broad sense, of works produced by AI.[31]

Similar considerations apply to a subject lacking the capacity to act, who may be abstractly regarded as the holder of rights, but is nevertheless precluded from exercising them personally.[32]

In the case of the intelligent machine, it seems obvious that it lacks both elements. Not only that. It is incapable, autonomously, of either wisely exploiting its products (for example, by selecting the best results, evaluating the most suitable modes of commercial exploitation, etc.) or of taking any responsibility for any damage caused (within the scope of this discussion) by the commercialisation of such goods.[33]

A recent North American position, which was then explicitly recognised in the guidelines of the U.S. Copyright Office,[34] firmly rejected the possibility of recognising the authorship of the intelligent machine. Consequently, it denied protection to

[29] The European Parliament has also expressed this view in its recent Resolution on intellectual property rights for the development of artificial intelligence technologies, text adopted on 20 October 2020, available at https://www.europarl.europa.eu/doceo/document/TA-9-2020-0277_EN.pdf, where, after expressing scepticism about the possibility of attributing authorial protection to A.I. products, in § 15 the body recommends that the ownership of any rights should eventually be assigned only to natural or legal persons who have lawfully created the work.

[30] The general possibility of assigning rights to an intelligent system was questioned by Solum (1992), pp. 1231, 1258.

[31] See Frosio (2020), p. 63, who argues that without legal personality, A.I. could neither acquire ownership of the copyrights on the creative products it generates, nor enforce those rights against third parties. Similar thoughts have been advanced by Senftleben and Buijtelaaar (2020), p. 14. On this point, see also the reflections of Sena, who maintains that the absence of legal capacity on the part of A.I. prevents it from becoming the owner of the rights, since it is not disputed that it is the author of its creations. Sena (2020), p. 327.

[32] On this point, see also Sena's reflections to the effect that it is precisely the absence of legal capacity on the part of the A.I. that prevents it from becoming the owner of the rights, since it is not disputed that the latter is the author of its creations. Sena (2020), p. 327.

[33] Consider the case where A.I.-generated products represent an infringement of another's copyright. How would the author of the infringing work sue the A.I.? See on this point Gervais (2019), p. 37 ff., who emphasizes the close link between *authorship/rights* attributed to the author of the work and *responsibility* for their own creations. Similarly: Senftleben and Buijtelaaar (2020), p. 15.

[34] See Guidance copyright registration, 16 March 2023, Federal Register, vol. 88, No. 51, Rules and Regulations, 16190, where it is stated that the term 'author', as understood by the U.S. Constitution and Copyright Act, cannot include non-human subjects.

those products for which only an artificial author was indicated,[35] as well as those portions of works for which it was not possible to identify a human contribution that could be separated from that of the machine.[36] On the other hand, this rejection led the office to conclude that it is indeed possible to recognise a form of authorship protection for a human being who claims to be the author of a product made to a certain extent with the help of an intelligent system, provided that they expressly declare having used it and are able to distinguish their own creative contributions from those—which cannot be regarded as such —generated solely by the intelligent system.

The protection, therefore, would not extend to the entire product, but only the human creative contributions, possibly covering only to those results that were initially produced by the AI, but on which the author has deeply intervened, submitting a significant number of additional customisation requests (the so-called *prompts*).[37]

This latter approach also appears to have been accepted in Chinese jurisprudence, where the Beijing Court recognised the existence of copyright in an image

[35] Cf. *Thaler v. Perlmutter*, Case 1:22-cv-01564-BAH (D.D.C., Aug. 18, 2023) in which the District Court of the Circuit of Columbia upheld the validity of the refusal by U.S. Copyright Office to register the work "A Recent Entrance to Paradise", the author of which was an intelligent system called "Creativity Machine", owned by the inventor Stephen Thaler.

[36] The case of the comic strip 'Zarya of the Dawn' written by Kris Kashtanova and illustrated entirely by A.I. is already famous. In 2022, the author applied for registration and was granted copyright protection for the entire work. The protection was, however, revoked when the Office realized that the author had used an intelligent system (MidJourney) for image generation. At the same time, the Office ordered that the product be registered, but that only the author's creative contributions, i.e. the texts and the selection, coordination, and arrangement of the images generated by the intelligent system, be granted copyright protection. The Office specified that the images produced by A.I., as such, did not benefit from any protection as they lacked the requirement of 'human authorship'. See *U.S. Copyright Office, Cancellation Decision re: Zarya of the Dawn* (VAu001480196) (21 February 2023), https://www.copyright.gov/docs/zarya-of-the-dawn.pdf. Less famous is the case, shortly afterwards, of the novel by Elisa Rae Shupe, later published under the pseudonym Ellen Rae, in which the U.S. Copyright Office (USCO) initially rejected the application for registration in which the author stated that she had made extensive use of the ChatGPT system for the writing of the work. On appeal by the author, the Office reconsidered the case and finally granted registration limited to the selection, coordination, and arrangement—by the author—of the texts generated by the intelligent system. See Copyright Office USA, 10 September 2023, Registration No. TX0009377452 / 2023-10-10, *AI Machinations Tangled Webs and Typed Words, Copyright Claimant: Elisa Rae Shupe*.

[37] On the other hand, protection could not exist when human intervention is limited to a single command given to the system which then produces, in response, a complex output with textual and/or audiovisual elements (literally, "When an AI technology receives solely a prompt from a human and produces complex written, visual, or musical works in response, the 'traditional elements of authorship' are determined and executed by the technology-not the human user"). Consequently, protection cannot be granted. See Copyright Review Board, 5 September 2023, No. 1-5T5320R, *Space opera theatre by Jason Allen*, concerning the two-dimensional digital image "Théâtre D'opéra Spatial", created by the artist Jason Allen through the application Midjourney, with which the artist won the Colorado State Fair's annual fine art competition in 2022, for the category "Digital Art". The principle was later codified in the USCO Guidelines. See Guidance copyright registration, 16 March 2023, cited above, 16192.

generated by artificial intelligence.[38] Alternatively, the author could obtain protection for the resulting whole, derived from the selection, coordination, and arrangement of "*human-authored* content", created by the author, and machine-generated content (AI *content*).[39]

The foreign approach outlined likely draws on a doctrinal view that emphasised the significance of the human creative contribution during the so-called refinement phase, intended both as the final stage of refinement of the work, involving modifications or additions by the author, and as the phase of selecting (among many possible options) the result that best reflects the author's creative flair and can therefore be intended for dissemination.[40] Indeed, even in the case of a product entirely conceived and produced by the intelligent system, the AI would still be unable, without human intervention, to select which works to place on the market (let alone disseminate them and derive profit from them). One might consider, in Aaron's case, the decisions made by Cohen regarding which paintings to release to the market or in the case of translation or text-generation programmes, the revisions carried out by the human author before approving the final text.[41]

According to this interpretation, then, the human author of a work produced—to varying extents—with the contribution of the AI would not coincide with the creator/inventor of the intelligent system itself, as has also been authoritatively argued,[42]

---

[38] The Court specified that for the purposes of the recognition of copyright, both the intellectual contribution of the human author (given by the prompts they designed through the selection of words and the decision on the order of the prompts to be adopted) and the originality of the result obtained, which must reflect the author's personal expression, were present in this case. Moreover, the Court generally stated that this requirement is present when the image generation process is very detailed, to the point that each element in the final work reflects a precise human choice. See Beijing Internet Court, 27 November 2023, Jing 0491 Min Chu No. 11279, *Li v. Liu*. On this point, see the considerations made by Fritz (2024), pp. 552, 552–553; Yu (2024), pp. 101, 113 ff.

[39] *See Guidance copyright registration*, 16 March 2023, Federal Register, vol. 88, No. 51, *Rules and Regulations*, cit., 16,193.

[40] See, however, to *the contrary*, Antikainen (2018), cit., p. 258 ff., who argues that the role of the machine user is often limited to the initial command ("pushing a button") and therefore even when the result produced by the machine has some aesthetic value, such a product could not be considered an intellectual creation of its author, as it lacks the latter's personal touch.

[41] This, mind you, applies even when "[...] the Ai system has played a significant or even predominant role in the entire creative process". Cf. Hartmann et al. (2020), pp. 76 and 83, where it is added that even in the case of products with characteristics completely unpredictable for the author of the A.I., due to the machine learning techniques employed, the role of the latter still becomes predominant in the final phase of the work's "redaction", which requires various creative inputs.

[42] See Grimmelmann (2016), p. 412. See also Samuelson (1986), pp. 1185 and 1205, who although arguing for a different solution, emphasizes that, at least in the first instance, it seems clear that the contribution made by the programmer towards the product generated by the A.I. (although she spoke of a "generator programme") is often the more substantial and significant one. See also Ginsburg and Budiardjo (2019), cit., p. 401 ff, who, while acknowledging that A.I. products seem to be in every way "creative" and very similar to human-generated works, warn against attributing the expressive value of the products to the machine that generated them, since any "creativity" in the output produced by A.I. is directly attributable to the code written by the programmer who designed and *trained* it or to the instructions given by the user operating the machine. See also the

given that the latter provided, through the various phases of the production process leading to the creation of the intelligent machine, the creative inputs that define it both as a product in itself and in terms of its creative capacities.[43] Rather, the author would be the user of the intelligent system, understood here as any application that can be accessed through a licence (from ChatGPT to MidJourney).

And indeed, in most cases, the intelligent system is not designed for the personal and exclusive use of its author (as in Aaron's case), but it is instead designed for the entire digital market. In this context, the legitimate user of the generative intelligent system interacts with the AI to create content, entering as many commands as needed to achieve the desired result.[44] And, as the North American controversies analysed above show, it is precisely the author/legitimate user of the AI who has an interest in protecting that product which results from a successful fusion of human and algorithmic creativity.[45]

Commission's White Paper on Artificial Intelligence which explains that: "In case of machine learning techniques, which constitute a subset of AI, algorithms are trained to enter certain patterns based on a set of data in order to determine the actions needed to achieve a given goal. Algorithms may continue to learn when in use. While AI-based products can act autonomously by perceiving their environment and without following a predetermined set of instructions, their behaviour is largely defined and constrained by their developers. Humans determine and programme the goals, which an Ai system should optimise for'. V. European Commission, *White paper on Artificial Intelligence - A European approach to excellence and trust*, 19 February 2020, at https://ec.europa.eu/info/sites/default/files/commission-white-paper-artificial-intelligence-feb2020_en.pdf, 16.

[43] In fact, it is believed that such creativity can indeed reverberate in the product generated by the A.I., since these instructions profoundly affect the *modus agendi* of the A.I. On this point, see Ginsburg and Budiardjo (2019), cit. p. 407 ff., who argue that even in the case of self-learning machines, equipped with the most sophisticated self-learning programs, the machine still operates on the basis of the information initially provided by its programmer. A similar point is expressed by Rossi (2018), p. 276, who observes that the key moment remains the preparation of the algorithm, i.e. the logical path that the system will follow to rework the basic material until arriving at an original result. According to the author, this scenario does not change even in the case of self-learning systems, since their actions will always be incontrovertibly limited by the initial database and the programming algorithm. A contrary position was, on the other hand, expressed by Yanisky Ravid and Velez Hernandez (2017), cit., p. 693 ff., who argue that none of the parties involved in the creative process of the A.I. could claim any legal prerogative over the works produced by the intelligent machine.

[44] On the subject of originality in *prompts* see Mazzi (2024), pp. 410, 413 ff.

[45] On the other hand, as noted in doctrine, a right granting exclusive prerogatives over the products of A.I. solely to the designer of the intelligent machine would frustrate the economic incentives of the user of creative A.I.. See Senftleben et al. (2020), cit., p. 18. As far back as 1985, Pamela Samuelson explained that output generation was the purpose for which *generative programs* (i.e. the ancestors of A.I.) were created. Consequently, if the inventors then transferred the generative program to third parties, receiving fair financial consideration for such a transfer or licence, it seemed appropriate that they also (con)ceded to the legitimate users of the program (at least some of them) the rights to the goods produced through the use of the generative software: and this in order to create incentives for users to exploit the technology. See Samuelson (1986), p. 1207. Similar considerations on this point have recently been elaborated by Yanisky Ravid and Velez Hernandez (2017), p. 682.

References

Antikainen M (2018) Copyright protection and AI-generated works—a fight we have already lost? AIDA:257

Aplin T (2009) Subject matter. In: Derclaye E (ed) Research handbook on the future of EU copyright. Edward Elgar, Cheltenham, p 49

Are M (1963) L'oggetto del diritto di autore. Milano, p 52

Ascarelli T (1960) Teoria della concorrenza e dei beni immateriali. Milano, p 705

Auteri P (2023) Il diritto d'autore. In: AA.VV (ed) Diritto Industriale, proprietà intellettuale e concorrenza, 7th edn. Giappichelli, Torino, pp 623–639

Banterle F (2016) Ownership of inventions created by Artificial Intelligence. In: AIDA, 1, p 71

Bertani M (2011) Diritto d'autore europeo. In: Quad. di AIDA, Torino, p 126 ff

Bridy VA (2012) Coding creativity: copyright and the artificially intelligent author. Standford Technol Law Rev 5:1, 26

Burk DL (2020) Thirty-six views of copyright authorship, by Jackson Pollock. Houston Law Rev 58:263, 266

Casas Valles R (2009a) The requirement of originality. In: Derclaye E (ed) Research handbook on the future of EU copyright. Edward Elgar, Cheltenham, p 103, 132

Casas Valles R (2009b) The requirement of originality, cit., p 113

De Sanctis V M (1971) Il carattere creativo delle opere dell'ingegno. Milano, p 38

De Sanctis VM (2012) Il diritto di autore. Del diritto di autore sulle opere dell'ingegno letterarie e artistiche, artt. 2575-2583. In: Schlesinger P, Busnelli FD (eds) Il Codice Civile Commentato. Giuffrè Editore, Milano, p 30

Denicola R (2016) Ex Machina: copyright protection for computer-generated works. Rutgers Univ Law Rev 69:251, 272

Fabbio P (2016) Opere protette e requisiti di tutela nel diritto d'autore UE. AIDA 281:285

Fabiani M (2004) Diritto d'autore e diritti degli artisti interpreti o esecutori. Milano, p 39

Frassi PAE (1997) Creazioni utili e diritto d'autore. Programmi per elaboratore e raccolte di dati. Giuffrè, Milano

Fritz J (2024) The notion of 'authorship' under EU law-who can be an author and what makes one an author? An analysis of the legislative framework and case law. J Intellect Property Law Practice 19(552):552–553

Frosio, L'(I)Autore inesistente: una tesi tecno-giuridica contro la tutela dell'opera generata dall'intelligenza artificiale, in AIDA, 2020, p. 54.

Gervais DJ (2019) The machine as author. Iowa Law Rev 105:1, 52

Ginsburg JC, Budiardjo LA (2019) Authors and Machines, cit., p 401 ff, 402 ff

Greco P, Vercellone P (1974) I diritti sulle opere dell'ingegno. Torino, p 47 ff

Grimmelmann J (2016) There's no such thing as a computer-authored work—and it's a good thing, too. Columb J Law Arts 39:412

Guglielmetti G(1997) L'invenzione di software, 2nd edn. Giuffrè, Milano, p 299 ff.

Guizzardi S (2018) La protezione d'autore dell'opera dell'ingegno creata dall'Intelligenza Artificiale. AIDA:58. (nota 38)

Hartmann C, Allan J, Hugenholtz P, Quintais J (2020) Trends and developments in artificial intelligence—challenges to the intellectual property rights framework—final report. Publications Office of the European Union, p 76, 83

Hristov K (2017) Artificial intelligence and the copyright dilemma. IDEA 57, 3:436 ff

Ippolito L (2022) Ai-Da, a Venezia la robot-artista con ritratti e opere ispirate a Dante, 4 aprile, https://www.corriere.it/video-articoli/2022/04/04/ai-da-venezia-robot-artista-ritratti-opere-ispirate-dante

Kur A, Dreier T, Luginbuehl S (2019) European intellectual property law—text, cases & materials, 2nd edn. Edward Elgar Publishing, Cheltenham, p 338 ff

Leaffer MA (2004) Understanding Copyright Law. USA, p 59, 408

Mazzi F (2024) Authorship in artificial intelligence-generated works: exploring originality in text prompts and artificial intelligence outputs through philosophical foundations of copyright and collage protection. J World Intellectual Property 27:410, 413 ff
Mazzoni G (2022) La Biennale di Venezia apre le porte ai Robot. Attesa la partecipazione dell'umanoide Ai-Da e le sue performance, 4 aprile, https://insideart.eu/2022/04/04/ai-da
Musso A (2008) Diritto d'autore sulle opere dell'ingegno letterarie e artistiche. Art. 2575–2583. Roma, p 126
Oppo G (1964) Creazione ed esclusiva nel diritto industriale. Rivista di diritto commerciale 5-6:191
Ramalho A (2017) Will robots rule the (artistic) world? A proposed model for the legal status of creations by artificial intelligence systems. J Internet Law 1:3 ff
Ramalho A (2018) Originality redux: an analysis of the originality requirement in AI-generated works. AIDA:26 ff
Rosati E (2013) Originality in EU Copyright. UK, p 63
Rossi G (2018) L'intelligenza artificiale e la definizione di opera dell'ingegno. AIDA:275, 276
Samuelson P (1986) Allocating ownership rights in computer-generated works. Univ Pittsburgh Law Rev 47:1185, 1205
Sena G (2020) Intelligenza artificiale, opere dell'ingegno e diritti di proprietà industriale e intellettuale. Riv Dirit Ind I:327
Senftleben M, Buijtelaaar L (2020) Robot creativity: an incentive-based Neighbouring rights approach. Eur Intellect Prop Rev 1:14
Solum LB (1992) Legal personhood for artificial intelligences. North Carolina Law Rev 70:1231, 1258
Spedicato G (2019) Creatività artificiale, mercato e proprietà intellettuale. Riv Dirit Ind 1:270 ff
Stolfi N (1932) Il diritto d'autore. Milano, p 518 ff
Van Eechoud M, Hugenholtz PB, Van Gompel S, Guibault L, Helberger N (2009) Harmonizing European copyright law. The challenges of better law making. Wolters Kluwer, p 41
Yanisky Ravid S, Velez Hernandez LA (2017) Generating Rembrandt: artificial intelligence, copyright, and accountability in the 3A era—the human-like authors are already here—a new model. Mich State Law Rev:691
Yu R (2017) The machine author: what level of copyright protection is appropriate for fully independent computer-generated works? Univ Pa Law Rev 165:1257
Yu PK (2024) Artificial intelligence, autonomous creation, and the future path of copyright law. Brigham Young Univ Law Rev 50:101, 113 ff

The Protectability of Inventions Generated with A.I. Systems

Emanuela Arezzo

Contents

Abstract This chapter analyses the possibility of patent protection for findings conceived in an—allegedly—autonomous manner by an intelligent system. The chapter begins by analyzing recent cases on the subject of inventorship, and then examines how traditional patenting requirements apply to the output of AI.

1 The Presence of a Human Inventor As a Condition for the Eligibility of the Patent Application

Similarly to what has happened in the field of copyright, the question has repeatedly arisen in the field of patents as to whether it is compatible with patent law to name an artificial, rather than a human, inventor in a patent application. The multitude of controversies that have affected the majority of industrialized countries stems, in fact, from the same story involving inventor Stephen Thaler (not by chance defined by the *Economist* as "the inventor who fell in love with his AI") and his intelligent

E. Arezzo (✉)
University of Teramo, Teramo, Italy
e-mail: earezzo@unite.it

R. Bocchini (ed.), *Digital Platforms - From Technical Foundations to Legal and Economic Implications*, https://doi.org/10.1007/978-3-032-07978-7_23

machine Dabus (acronym *for Device for Autonomous Bootstrapping of Unified Sentience*), which had already been patented as an intelligent system by Thaler himself.[1]

In 2018, Thaler had filed two patent applications with the EPO and UKIPO in which his "creativity machine" was named as the inventor of a fractal geometry container for food or liquids and a neural light signaling system, respectively.[2] Thaler claimed that both inventions were generated entirely independently by the intelligent system, which even assessed the novelty of the findings. Nevertheless, Thaler was listed as an applicant and therefore the future holder—where granted—of the economic exploitation rights to the inventions produced by Dabus. Thaler, in fact, described himself as the "assignee" of the intelligent system, justifying the derivative acquisition of the patent right in the first instance by briefly invoking to the so-called *work for hire doctrine,* equating the intelligent system to a sort of inanimate employee.[3] In a second step, however, he specified that his status of "assignee" derived from his being the owner (as owner of the patent rights) of the intelligent system, implicitly recalling the theory of accession[4]: just the owner of the

[1] The story has attracted media attention in several parts of the world, with protection being sought even in Australia. See, for all, the Economist, *The inventor who fell in love with his AI*, 4 April 2023.

[2] Thaler applied for a patent for two allegedly machine-invented products: a product for preserving food and a system (consisting of a machine and a method) of light signaling applicable in various products. Respectively EP 18275163, "food container" and EP 18275174, "Devices and Methods for Attracting Enhanced Attention". *See Designation of inventor/DABUS*, Case J 0008/ 20, Board of Appeal of the EPO, 21 December 2021, 1.

[3] *See Designation of inventor/DABUS*, Case J 0008/ 20, Board of Appeal of the EPO, 21 December 2021, 1, where it is stated that Thaler initially declared that he had acquired the right to the patent as the 'employer' of the intelligent system. In favor of recognizing inventorship for the intelligent system are, first and foremost, Abbot, defender of Thaler. See Abbott (2016), p. 1104; Davies (2011), pp. 601, 606; Banterle (2018), p. 24. A more moderate position has been expressed by Picht and Thouvenin (2023), pp. 916, 919, who sympathize with the idea of recognizing the machine as the inventor; however, they consider that the machine should appear in the patent application as the 'proxy inventor', whereas a natural or legal person should then be indicated in the section of the application relating to the person authorized to exercise patent rights, once protection has been granted. Interesting on this point is the position of G. Sena who argues that there would be no obstacle, in theory, to recognizing the paternity of the invention for the intelligent system, since there are examples in patent law that *originally* attribute the right to the patent to the employer (which may be a legal person) or allow such rights to accrue to the body financing the research (as happens when research financed by third parties is conducted by researchers employed by public institutions). According to Sena, however, where one is faced with a work or invention generated independently by the intelligent system, it would belong to the public domain, since the need to attribute an exclusive right for intangible goods is justified only where there is an intersubjective conflict of interest. Where there is no connection with the human person, the right would not exist. See Sena (2020), pp. 329–330. Similar considerations have been expressed by Heinz Meitinger (2023), p. 484, who considers that if an invention were obtained in total autonomy by the machine, it would not be patentable, because any fiction of identifying a human author would amount to an abuse of the patent system in the absence of the inventive contribution by the latter.

[4] *See Designation of inventor/DABUS*, Case J 0008/ 20, EB Board of Appeal, 21 December 2021, 2 and 5.

vineyard owns the grapes growing there, so too would the owner of the intelligent system would become the owner of the products created by the machine.[5]

The European Patent Office, in a decision upheld by the Legal Board of Appeal, firmly rejected the patent applications, clarifying that a patent application cannot validly name an entity other than a human being as the inventor. In this regard, the Commission made it clear that the provision in Article 81(1) EPC, which sets out the obligation to designate the inventor in the patent application, must be read in conjunction with Articles 60 and 62 EPC, which respectively establish the inventor's right to the patent and the right to be named as the author of the invention in the application.[6] The Commission makes it clear that both rules unequivocally presuppose the existence of a real inventor,[7] with legal personality[8] and capacity to act.[9] This also applies where, as in this case, there is no coincidence between the inventor and the applicant, and it is therefore necessary to specify under what title the latter acquired the right to the patent (by submitting the so-called *declaration of origin*, required by Article 81, paragraph 2, EPC).[10] Even in this second case, the Board of Appeal explains, one cannot disregard a combined reading of Article 81(2) EPC

[5] See Gibson (2022), pp. 401, 405.

[6] These rules find their counterpart in Art. 2588 of the Italian Civil Code and Art. 63(2) of the Italian Industrial Property Code where the principle that the right to a patent belongs to the author of the invention is enshrined. On rights arising from the conception of the invention, see Arezzo (2017), p. 47 ff.

[7] Cf. the remarks of the President of the EPO, reported in the decision, who recalls, as further confirmation of the requirement that the inventor be a natural person, as incontrovertibly shown by the preparatory works to the EPC, that Rule 19 of the EPC (on the designation of the inventor) requires that the designation contain mention of the inventor's first name, surname, country and place of residence. See *Designation of inventor/DABUS*, Case J 0008/ 20, cit., 11. On the normative relevance of the provision of Rule 19, given that the EPC Implementing Regulations form an integral part of the Convention and its provisions would, therefore, therefore have equal authority to those of the Convention itself. Stierle (2020), pp. 918, 920 and 923.

[8] The lack of legal personality on the part of the intelligent machine is decisive in determining whether A.I. can be regarded as a subject entitled to legal prerogatives and rights. On this point in general, see Ruffolo (2020), p. 213. Critical on this point is Stierle (2020), pp. 918, 921, who argues that it would instead be appropriate to distinguish the concept of "inventorship", understood as the recognition of a subject's capacity to invent and thus be qualified as an inventor, by virtue of having created a particular invention, from the notion of a subject's capacity to be the centre of imputation of the rights arising from the conception of the invention.

[9] *See Designation of inventor/DABUS*, case J 0008/20, cit., 21 ff., in particular §§ 4.3.1 and 4.3.2, and § 4.3.9. As pointedly observed in the literature, in the case of the intelligent machine we are not indeed speaking of an incapacitated subject, but rather of an 'incapacitated object', so that an analogy with the legal institutions of guardianship, parental authority, or similar forms of administration does not seem conceivable. On this point, see more extensively, Vessia (2022), pp. 36, 373.

[10] In such a case, the declaration indicating how the applicant acquired the right to the patent becomes an integral part of the designation of the inventor. That, the Commission explains, creates a strong link (the Commission refers to it as a 'normative link') between the provisions of Article 81 and Article 60(1) EPC. Consequently, a valid declaration must necessarily identify the origin of the patent right in a manner consistent with Article 60(1) EPC. *Designation of inventor/DABUS*, Case J 0008/ 20, cit., 19 ff., in particular § 4.2.2.

with the provisions of Article 60 EPC, which state that the right to the patent belongs to the inventor or their successor in title.[11] Even in this second circumstance, indeed, regardless of the legal nature of the successor in title—which could also be a legal person—the validity of the transfer of the patent right still requires that the inventor be a (natural) person with legal personality and capacity to act; otherwise, any act transferring the proprietary right would be invalid.[12]

A similar outcome was reached in England, where the two patent applications had been rejected by the Ukipo because they were contrary to the requirements of Section 13(2) of the *UK Patent Act* of 1977 on the designation of the inventor.[13] The Office's decision was upheld by the *High Court of England and Wales*[14] at first instance and subsequently by the Court of Appeal.[15] Most recently in 2023, the UK Supreme Court also upheld the decisions of the lower courts, concluding that—under the *UK Patents Act* 1977—only a "natural person" can be designated as an inventor.[16]

Finally, a sign of openness appears to have come from a recent ruling of the German Federal Court of Justice. In June 2024, the *Bundesgerichtshof* confirmed the position, now established in almost all of the jurisdictions involved—with the exception of South Africa[17]—that only a natural person, and not an AI system, can

[11] *Designation of inventor/DABUS*, Case J 0008/ 20, cit., 17 ff., in particular § 4.2.2.

[12] In this regard, the Commission clarified that if, on the one hand, the EPO is required to carry out only a check of regularity, it cannot, however, exempt itself from verifying whether the application identifies an inventor in the meaning adopted by the EPC, that is, in line with the provisions of Article 60, paragraph 1, EPC. Such an inventor can only be a human person endowed with legal capacity, since the machine — which, moreover, lacks legal personality — is not a subject capable of possessing rights or transferring them to third parties, as Thaler himself acknowledges. *Designation of inventor/DABUS*, case J 0008/ 20, cit., 20 ff., in particular § 4.2.3.

[13] Ukipo, Decision of 4 December 2019, BL O/741/19, on Stephen L. Thaler's patent applications No. s GB1816909.4 and GB1818161.0 dated 17 October and 7 November 2018 respectively. Decision available at Patent decision (O/741/19).

[14] England and Wales High Court (Patents Court) Decisions, *Thaler v The Comptroller-General of Patents, Designs And Trade Marks*, No. 2412(Pat), 21 September 2020, available at https://www.bailii.org/ew/cases/EWHC/Patents/2020/2412.html.

[15] Judgment of the England and Wales Court of Appeal (Civil Division), (L.J. Richard Arnold and Elisabeth Laing in favour, L.J. opposed by Colin Birss), *Thaler v. Comptroller General of Patents Trade Marks And Designs*, No. 1374, 21 September 2021, available at http://www.bailii.org/ew/cases/EWCA/Civ/2021/1374.html.

[16] Judgment of the Supreme Court of the United Kingdom, *Thaler (Appellant) v. Comptroller-General of Patents, Designs and Trade Marks (Respondent)*, No. UKSC 49, 20 December 2023, available at https://supremecourt.uk/uploads/uksc_2021_0201_judgment_3f445a5dc7.pdf, see §§ 54-73. It should be noted that the English courts also rejected the applicability of the Anglo-Saxon doctrine of accession in the present case, considering it applicable only to tangible goods. Ibid. §§ 74-90.

[17] In July 2021, the South African patent office, operating on the Companies and Intellectual Property Commission (CIPC), granted Thaler's patent application without substantive examination, specifying that "the invention was autonomously generated by an artificial intelligence" and thus naming Dabus as the inventor. See Patent Journal of South Africa, July 2021, vol. 54 No. 7, /3242, 255. In 2020, Thaler also filed the same patent application with the Australian Patent Office.

be designated as the inventor in a patent application.[18] On the other hand, however, the Court clarified that a human-made invention developed with the help of an intelligent system may receive protection, provided that the system is designated solely as a technical means and the former is designated as the inventor.[19]

The Court explains the fact that an artificial intelligence system has made a significant contribution to the search, for a technical solution does not preclude the identification of a human inventor,[20] who typically intervenes in the programming or data preparation phase, instructs the research process that led to the required teaching or is involved in the final phase of verification and selection among the inventive results proposed by the intelligent system.[21] Indeed, the Court maintains that, according to current scientific knowledge, there is no system capable of researching and producing technical results without any preparation or instruction by a human being.[22]

The Court therefore concluded that an invention developed through the use —and even significant contribution—of an intelligent system was protectable, provided that a contribution from a human inventor can be identified.[23] On this basis,

---

The Office refused the patent application on the ground that there was no indication of a human inventor, as required by Article 15 of the Australian Patent Act. Thaler appealed the decision to the Federal Court of Australia, which initially upheld his claims, interpreting "inventor" in an "evolutionary" sense, i.e., stating that the notion of inventor should be broadened in line with the evolution of the technological context. See Thaler v. Commissioner of Patents, 2021, FCA879. In 2022, however, the Australian Federal Court's ruling was overturned in a restrictive sense by the full Federal Court. The latter overturned the Federal Court's ruling, stating that the inventor is 'the person who is responsible for the inventive concept'. Consequently, it ruled that Australian patent law provides for the grant of the exclusive right only to an invention conceived by the intellectual effort of one or more human minds. See Commissioner of Patents v Thaler [2022] FCAFC 62, §§ 101–116. For further discussion see Zoboli (2023), p. 99; Kenneth Southworth and Yahong (2023), pp. 58, 62–63; Lim and Li (2022), pp. 376, 382–383.

[18] Judgment of the German Federal Court (Bundesgerichtshof), X ZB 5/22, 11 June 2024, ECLI:DE:BGH:2024:110624BXZB5.22.0, § 42.

[19] Ibid, §§ 63–64.

[20] Ibid, § 44. On this point, see Blok (2017), pp. 39, 72, who points out that A.I. is a tool, however sophisticated, at the disposal of the human inventor.

[21] Ibid, § 39. Cf. on this point the 2020 Aippi (International Association for the Protection of Intellectual Property) resolution which sets out a list of the activities carried out by the researcher during the inventive process that are considered sufficient to make "an intellectual contribution to the inventive concept", therefore supporting recognition of the right to the patent even if the researcher used an intelligent machine during the process. AIPPI Resolution Q 272-RES-2020, § 4.

[22] Ibid. § 40. In this context, therefore, the applicant must necessarily indicate (at least) a human inventor, even if they consider that the main contribution was made by an artificial intelligence system. Ibid. § 44.

[23] On the nature and extent of the human contribution, especially in relation to that of the machine, the Court does not seem to provide precise findings. In some passages, it limits itself to stating in general terms that this contribution must have been decisive in achieving the technical teaching, and must have influenced the success of the result. Ibid. § 38. In other passages, however, it seems to contradict itself by saying that the important thing is that the contribution exists, but its quantification is completely irrelevant. Ibid, § 39. Finally, the Court does not require that the author of

and confirming the ruling of the Federal Patent Court, it was finally recognized that it was possible to validly file a patent application for the invention produced with the aid of the Dabus intelligent system and naming Thaler himself as the author, albeit on the basis of auxiliary claims filed during the various stages of the proceedings.[24]

2 On the Patenting Requirements Applied to the Invention Conceived with the Aid of an Intelligent System

The position of the *Bundesgerichtshof*, which, moreover, finds many points of contact with the North American one,[25] appears to be widely shared, especially with reference to the assumption that fully autonomous intelligent machines do not yet exist. Although the usefulness of employing intelligent systems to achieve the

---

the product made with the support of A.I. is also the author of the intelligent system as such. By contrast, Ghidini and Austoni (2022), pp. 43, 49, express the contrary view, arguing that the inventor of the invention generated by the intelligent system necessarily coincides with the inventor of the system *tout court*, since the authorship of the robotic invention is the same as that of any other "software" invention.

[24] During the first instance proceedings before the Federal Patent Court, Thaler also filed ancillary claims to the main claim to designate DABUS as an inventor in the patent applications, proposing himself as the inventor, as the natural person who had created the prompt that enabled DABUS to generate the invention. In 2021, the Federal Patent Court decided to grant the patent on the basis of this auxiliary claim, designating Thaler as the inventor with the addition of the formula "who induced the artificial intelligence Dabus to generate the invention". Judgment of the Bundespatentgericht, No. 18 W (Pat) 28/20, of 21 June 2023, ECLI:DE:BPatG:2023:210623B18 Wpat28.20.0.

[25] The two Uspto decisions were respectively affirmed in *Thaler v. Hirshfeld*, 558 F. Supp.3d 238 (E.D. Va. 2021), and later in *Thaler v. Vidal*, 43 F.4th 1207, 1213 (Fed. Cir. 2022), cert. Denied, 143 S. Ct. 1783 (2023), where the Federal Court established the principle that "[...] *only a natural person can be an inventor, so AI cannot be*."

The recent North American guideline also holds, however, that an invention developed with the aid of the intelligent system may be patented where a significant contribution by a human inventor in the conception of the inventive idea can be discerned. See *Inventorship Guidance for AI-Assisted Inventions*, by the Department Of Commerce, Patent and Trademark Office [Docket No. PTO-P-2023-0043], published in the Federal Register, vol. 89, No. 30, 13 February 2024, 10043 ff. and entered into force on the same date. The guidelines reiterate and apply to the case of inventions made with the use of an intelligent system certain principles concerning inventions conceived by several inventors (*joint inventorship*) establishing that in order to qualify as a co-inventor it is necessary (a) to have made a significant contribution to the conception or implementation of the invention; (b) to have made a contribution that is not insignificant, in proportion to the invention as a whole; (c) not to have merely shared with other co-inventors known concepts already part of the state of the art. These are the so-called *Pannu factors,* developed in the wake of the Federal Court's ruling in *Pannu v. Iolab Corp.,* 26,155 F.3d 1344 (Fed. Cir. 1998). For a more detailed discussion see Holman (2024), p. 116.

desired technical solution more efficiently and quickly is undeniable,[26]much of the doctrine holds that—at least at the time of writing—AI systems remain strongly anthropocentric. The technical problem that the invention proposes to solve, going beyond the knowledge that constitutes the state of the art, will always be formulated by man and then proposed to the machine.[27] It will always be a human who, on the basis of the formulated problem, provides the intelligent system with the necessary tools (*recte*: the operating algorithms and training *datasets*), and it is then generally the human who tests the validity of the proposed solution and makes the final decision as to which of the results, if any, to submit for patenting.[28]

Consequently, even if a patentable result can be achieved through AI's computational capacity and its ability to process enormous amounts of data, that result certainly cannot be attributed solely to the machine.[29]

The approach taken by the *Bundesgerichtshof* also seems to suggest, as a corollary, a second assumption that is equally acceptable and desirable: namely, that if a natural person must be designated as the inventor, on account of their own inventive contribution, separable from that of the machine, it is also necessary, at least in the description of the invention,[30] to acknowledge the contribution made by the

[26] On this point, see Asay (2022), pp. 1187, 1193, who argues that despite considerable technological progress, mainly due to increased computational capacity and the availability of huge amounts of data, intelligent systems are still calibrated to solve specific tasks and remain far from having autonomous thinking capabilities. See also Blok (2017), cit., p. 70.

[27] In this sense see Ramalho (2021), p. 78 who stresses the necessary presence of the human being who establishes the technical problem to be solved. In a similar vein: Banterle (2018), cit. pp., 4 and 21. Drexl (2018) agrees, emphasizing even more strongly the need for such intervention with reference to additional passages. By contrast, see Abbott (2017), p. 324, who relies on the self-learning capacity of the most advanced A.I. systems, which, by modifying even their own operating algorithms, could achieve results unpredictable by humans. This circumstance, however, does not exclude the fact that such results still respond to an initial technical question formulated by the human being.

[28] Thus in doctrine, see Bogni and Galli (2020), pp. 127, 129; Shemtov and Gabison (2022), pp. 423, 426; Hartmann et al. (2020) *Contra* Abbott (2017), cit., p. 1094, who argues that providing the machine with data for training and giving it a technical problem to solve would not be sufficient to impute authorship of the invention to the human being. It should be noted, however, that even strong proponents of recognizing the authorship of the intelligent system, such as Abbott, agree on the need to identify a different subject as the owner of the proprietary rights to the invention, since the intelligent system does not have legal personality or capacity to act (ibid., 1114 ff.).

[29] As properly noted in the literature, Thaler did not explain in the patent application who formulated the technical problem to be solved and how he submitted it to the intelligent system. Likewise, the patent application did not mention the prior art and, in particular, the prior art used to train the algorithm. These are all essential elements to demonstrate human interaction with the machine and, in particular, the inventor's intervention in the *problem-solution-approach, which is* necessary to articulate the assessment of the invention's originality. Thus Straus (2021), cit., p. 624.

[30] On this point, the position expressed by the Legal Board of Appeals in the *Dabus* case does not seem persuasive, as it considers it unnecessary to include this information because it is not expressly required, interpreting the provisions of Article 83 EPC on the sufficiency of the description. According to the BoA, the applicant may, if they consider it necessary, explain how the invention was made in the description, but this is not required by the standard (the standard does not

intelligent system in developing the invention. This is not for reasons of "fairness," as argued by Thaler before the Legal Board of Appeals of the EPO,[31] but because the use of the intelligent system could have an impact on the reconstruction of the state of the art, in the form of "*general* knowledge"[32] available to the average technician in the field, with obvious repercussions for the assessment of the invention's originality.[33]

The implications are far from trivial. Scholars have rightly pointed out that an assessment of the state of the art that does not include intelligent systems already in use will ultimately make it easier to establish the originality of a technical solution: this could lead to an excessive proliferation of patents.[34] Conversely, if the state of the art were to include such prior art, there would be the opposite risk of considering all technical solutions arrived through the use of AI[35] as obvious.

The decisive point, therefore, remains how to define the pool of knowledge that constitutes the state of the art, available to the average technician in the field, with particular reference to knowledge relating to AI tools or systems, and whether it is relevant, in this regard, whether these systems have themselves been patented. Since the law clearly states that the state of the art must necessarily include everything that has been made accessible before the filing date of the application, whether by written or oral description, use or any other means (art. 46 and art. 54, Italian Industrial Property Code), common sense would seem to suggest that if the invention falls within a technical field where AI tools are widely used, for examples the biotech sector, then such tools will certainly be "accessible," known to the average

require it, nor does it prohibit it, so it remains at the applicant's discretion). *Designation of inventor/DABUS*, Case J 0008/ 20, cited above, 22 ff.

[31] In the European Dabus case, Thaler argued that the designation of the intelligent system as an inventor met the requirements of justice (*fairness*) based on an alleged right of the public to know who the real inventor was and how the invention was created.. The Legal Board of Appeal rejected this argument on the grounds that there was no statutory basis in the EPC to justify such a right of the public to obtain such information, nor was this relevant under Article 83 EPC on the requirement to describe the invention sufficiently clearly to enable the average technician in the field to implement it. *Designation of inventor/DABUS*, Case J 0008/ 20, cit., 22 ff., §§ 4.3.6. ff.

[32] In EPO case law, the so-called 'common general knowledge' coincides with manuals, monographs, encyclopaedias, and treatises; in short, it is the background knowledge that the skilled person working in the field should have or can easily access.. Case Law Board of Appeal, para. § 2.8.1. EB Guidelines, sec. G, Ch. VII, § 3.1.

[33] Several authors agree on the necessity of disclosing A.I. as a technical means employed to achieve the inventive result. Plotkin (2009), pp. 105–107; Abbott (2018), p. 6. Ebrahim (2020), pp. 147–158.

[34] Bonadio (2021), pp. 48–66. Most recently, Plotkin (2009), cit., pp. 102, 111, points out that the failure to include knowledge relating to A.I. tools in the state of the art, in a sector where they are widely used, would unfairly reward companies that employ intelligent means by allowing them to hoard patents.

[35] Thus Libertini (2022), p. 89, Abbot who argues that the more the contours of the prior art expand, the lower the likelihood of finding an invention inventive. Abbott (2016), cit., pp. 20 and 37; Abbott (2017), cit., p. 1124.

technician in the field, and should therefore be included within the perimeter of "*common general* knowledge."[36]

Similarly, one would reasonably be inclined to think that where the intelligent system used to arrive at the inventive result has itself been patented, it must automatically form part of the state of the art,[37] since prior patent applications, including—if only to examine the novelty of the invention—those that are still secret, represent precisely the classic example of "written descriptions" referred to in the provision and which, above all, are available to the Patent Office examiners.[38]

This conclusion, however, is not at all obvious if the inventor is under no obligation to mention the use of the intelligent system in the patent application. Consider, for example, a pharmaceutical company that, to identify a compound with certain therapeutic properties, employs a *roboscientist*: without any obligation to disclose the technical means used, the company could simply file a patent application for the compound, more or less new, depending on the novel therapeutic application.[39]

Complementary to this theme is the question of how to construct the figure of the average expert in the field.[40] Here too, various solutions have been hypothesized, including the rather fanciful one of the average technician who is also artificial, robotic.[41]

This hypothesis seems to be rejected for the reasons already expressed with reference to the designation of the inventor, who must be a natural person. Just as the inventor must be human, so too must the benchmark for testing the non-obviousness

---

[36] Thus Zoboli (2023), cit., p. 159 ff. See also the eloquent words of the president of the EPO who stated that '*if Ia is used in the relevant field of technology, it will be used by the skilled person and their skills will rise accordingly*'. In Shemtov and Gabison (2022), cit., p. 428.

[37] Shemtov and Gabison (2022), cit., p. 428, for whom '*the state of the art will depend on whether the information on Ai tools, techniques and application is publicly available at the priority date*'.

[38] On the difference between the assessments of novelty and inventive step, and the possibility of combining prior art only in the latter, *ex multis,* Holman et al. (2018), pp. 131, 145. Arezzo (2017), cit., p. 158. V. Acquafredda (2003), pp. 415, 419; Franzosi (2001), p. 75.

[39] On the patenting of new uses in the pharmaceutical sector Arezzo (2023), p. 81 ff.

[40] Remember that the EPO guidelines describe the average technician in the branch as a "[...] *skilled practitioner in the relevant field of technology who is possessed of average knowledge and ability (average skilled person). The person skilled in the art is aware of what was common general knowledge in the art at the relevant date*'. See Guidelines, sec. G, ch. VII, § 3.

[41] A somewhat futuristic proposal is put forward by Fabris (2020), pp. 685, 692 ff., according to which the notion of the 'PHOSITA' (i.e. the *person having ordinary skills in the arts*) should be replaced with that of the 'MOSITA' (i.e. the *machine of ordinary skills in the arts*), which thanks to its computational capacity would be able to map all existing prior art and make all possible correlations, even with knowledge from apparently distant technological fields. The possibility that the spread of computational innovations will lead to the figure of the average branch technician being replaced by that of the average robotics technician (so-called 'skilled computer') is anticipated by several authors: Abbott (2017), cit., pp. 1124–1125; Bonadio (2021), cit., p. 48; Schuster (2018), pp. 1945–2004. See also Romm (2021), pp. 1413, 1449, who, however, argues that if the average technician in the field were to be completely replaced by a machine, the assessment of inventive step should focus only on the data the machine can understand, thus ignoring the role of humans in designing and implementing the machine and ultimately interpreting such information.

of the invention be human. The well-known *problem solution approach,* in fact, requires answering the question of whether the average technician in the field, having certain technical knowledge at their disposal, would (*would* and *could not*!) have arrived at the technical solution as a matter of course. The average technician, not the machine.[42] Especially since, as pointed out, the machine never sets itself the inventive goal, the technical problem, nor does it sift and test the validity of the proposed result.

Consequently, the question comes back to what knowledge and know-how should be attributed to the average technician: that is, whether to assume that they must possess, in addition to the basic skills of a practitioner in that technical field, notions of programming, of "know how" regarding the training and the use of intelligent systems.

Clearly, even with reference to this question, the doctrine has shown that if it is assumed that an average technician capable of using AI for inventive purposes is taken as a benchmark, such a technician would certainly have more advanced skills than the average technician in the so-called "traditional" branch.[43] Even in this case, the risk could be that of raising the bar, leading the average technician, with advanced skills in the use of AI, to find the contribution made with the aid of the intelligent machine[44] scarcely inventive.

It seems fair to conclude that even in this case, the solution cannot disregard a case-by-case analysis of the technological *trend* in the relevant sector. Considering that the average technician is often constructed as an imaginary person with interdisciplinary and cross-sector knowledge, it would be illogical to deny them AI skills where it is customary in that particular sector to use artificial intelligence tools.[45]

---

[42] Blok (2017), cit., p. 70. Of the same opinion, see Romm (2021) who states that machines are tools used by the average technician. See also Heon (2023), p. 381, who states that it is still reasonable today for the average technician to be a human being, as intelligent machines are not yet autonomous during the inventive process.

[43] Ramalho (2021), cit., p. 94. The latter points out that the perspective chosen for the average technician in the field would also influence the weight to be given to the so-called indicia of non-evidence, which would clearly have to be analyzed differently if interpreted in the light of an average robotic technician or one using A.I. systems.

[44] Thus, Picht and Thouvenin (2023), pp. 916, 919 ff., argue that it is appropriate to supplement the competences of the average technician in the branch with 'AI system abilities' and view favorably the consequent raising of the bar for the originality requirement, which would avert the risk of excessive proliferation of patents on intelligent system technologies. See also Abbott (2016), pp. 1079, 1125; Bonadio (2021), cit., p. 54; Fabris (2020), cit., p. 691 ff. *Contra* Simon (2013), pp. 101, 118 ff.; Burk (2020), pp. 301, 309–310, who argue that A.I. can certainly simplify research and experimentation but that such simplification would not affect the assessment of inventive step.

[45] On this point, Zoboli (2023), cit., p. 159, who points out that to fall within the notion of common general knowledge available to the average technician, A.I. tools must be commonly used in the sector. They must not, on the other hand, be of a pioneering or experimental nature. See also Heon (2023), cited above, who states that knowledge about commonly used A.I. should be included in the capabilities of the average technician in the sector, thus imposing a standard in the field. Abbott (2018), pp. 4, 6 also adds that, when determining whether an intelligent machine is commonly used in an industry, there should be an obligation for patent applicants to indicate the technology used

Similarly, it certainly seems possible that different AI tools could be combined with each other, as well as with other prior art from different fields, to arrive at a finding of obviousness regarding the invention.[46]

References

Abbott RB (2016) I think, therefore I invent: creative computers and the future of patent law. Boston Coll Law Rev 57:1079–1125

Abbott RB (2017) Artificial intelligence, big data and intellectual property: protecting computer-generated works in the United Kingdom. In: Aplin T (ed) Research handbook on intellectual property and digital technologies. Edward Elgar, Cheltenham, p 324

Abbott RB (2018) Everything is obvious. UCLA Law Rev 66(4):6

Acquafredda V., (2003) Nuove invenzioni e rapporti tra i diversi requisiti di brevettabilità nella giurisprudenza. Dir ind 5:415–419

Arezzo E (2017) I diritti nascenti dalla brevettazione. In: Clemente A, Gambino A, Falce V (eds) Trattario di Diritto Civile edited by Cendon P, Proprietà intellettuale, mercato e concorrenza. Giuffrè, Milano, p 47 ff

Arezzo E (2023) Patent portfolios and pharmaceuticals: a European perspective. Quaderni di AIDA, 33, Torino, p 81 ff

Asay CD (2022) *Artifificial Stupidity, in William & Mary Law Rev*, 61, 1187.

Banterle F (2018) Ownership of inventions, p 4, 21, 24

Blok P (2017) The inventor's new tool: artificial intelligence – how does it fit in the European Patent System?, in European Intellectual Property Rev, 69, 39

Bogni M, Galli C (2020) Intelligenza artificiale. Nuove dinamiche della ricerca e "problem and solution approach". Dir. ind. 2:127–129

Bonadio E (2021) A.I. As inventor: exploring the consequences for patent law. IPQ 1:48–66

Burk DL (2020) AI patents and the self-assembling machine. Minn Law Re Headnotes:301, 309–310

Davies CR (2011) An evolutionary step in intellectual property rights. Artificial intelligence and intellectual property. Comp Law Secur Rev 27:601–606

Drexl J (2018) Data access and control in the era of connected devices. Study on behalf of the European Consumer Organisation BEUC. Disponibile su: https://www.beuc.eu/sites/default/files/publications/beuc-x-2018-21_data_access_and_control_in_the_area_of_connected_devices.pdf

Ebrahim TY (2020) Artificial intelligence inventions & patent disclosure. Penn State Law Rev:147–158

Fabris D (2020) From the PHOSITA to the MOSITA: will "secondary consideration" save pharmaceutical patents from artificial intelligence. In: I.I.C.—international review of intellectual property and competition law, vol 51. Springer, p 685, 692 ff

Franzosi M (2001) Novità e non ovvietà, lo stato della tecnica. Riv dir ind 62:75

in the inventive process, if any. Of the same opinion is Ramalho (2018), pp. 25, 25–26, who distinguishes between the use of artificial intelligence as standard practice and its pioneering use, which determines whether or not it is relevant for the notion of common general knowledge. Consequently, she affirms that use of the tool should be specified. In contrast, Romm (2021), cit., p. 1447, argues against the obligation to specify use of the intelligent machine in the inventive process in the patent application, stating that declaring the use of A.I. could lead to identifying the average technician in the field on a case-by-case basis, rather than by assessing the average use of that type of intelligent machine in the relevant field

[46] See Shemtov and Gabison (2022), cit. p. 430.

Ghidini G, Austoni I (2022) Intelligenza artificiale e proprietà intellettuale. In: Pajno A, Donati F, Perrucci A (eds) Intelligenza artificiale e diritto: una rivoluzione? Proprietà intellettuale, società e finanza, vol III. Il Mulino publishing company, Bologna, pp 43–49
Gibson J (2022) Artificial intelligence and patents: DABUS and methods for attracting enhanced attention to inventors. Queen Mary J Intellectual Prop 11:401–405
Hartmann C, Allan J, Hugenholtz P B, Quintais JP, Gervais D (2020) EC Report on Trends and Developments in AI, final report. Disponibile su: https://opeuropa.eu/en/publication-detail/-/publication/394345a1-2ecf-11eb-b27b-01aa75ed71a1/language-en
Heinz Meitinger T (2023) Artificial intelligence as an authority for testing the inventive step of an invention. A view from Germany. J Intellectual Property Law Practice 18:484
Heon L (2023) Artificially obvious but genuinely new: how artificial intelligence alters the patent obviousness analysis. Seton Hall Law Rev 53:381
Holman CM, Minsen T, Solovy EM (2018) Patentability standards for follow-on pharmaceutical innovation. In: Biotechnology Law Report, p 131, 145
Holman CM (2024) *The U.S. Patent and Trademark Office's Response to Recent Developments in Artificial Intelligence, in Biotechnology Law Report*, 43, 116.
Kenneth Southworth E, Yahong L (2023) AI inventors: deference for legal personality without respect for innovation? J Intellectual Property Law Practice 18:58, 62–63
Libertini M (2022) I prodotti inventivi dell'intelligenza artificiale. In: Pajno A, Donati F, Perrucci A (eds) Intelligenza artificiale e diritto: una rivoluzione? Proprietà intellettuale, società e finanza, vol III. Il Mulino publishing company, Bologna, p 89
Lim PH, Li P (2022) Artificial intelligence and inventorship: patently much ado in the computer program. J Intellectual Property Law Practice 17:376, 382–383
Picht PG, Thouvenin F (2023) AI and IP: theory to policy and back again—policy and research recommendations at the intersection of artificial intelligence and intellectual property. IIC - Int Rev Intellect Prop Compet Law 54:916, 919 ff
Plotkin R (2009) The genie in the machine: how computer-automated inventing is revolutionizing law & busineff Stanford, p 105–107
Ramalho A (2018) Patentability of AI-generated inventions: is a reform of the patent system needed? Inst Intell Prop, Found For Intell Prop Japan:25–26
Ramalho A (2021) Intellectual property protection for AI-generated creations. Europe, United States, Australia and Japan. London, p 78
Romm C (2021) Putting the person in PHOSITA: the human's obvious role in the artificial intelligence era. Boston Coll Law Rev:1413, 1449
Ruffolo U (2020) La "personalità elettronica". In: Ruffolo U (ed) Intelligenza artificiale, il diritto, i diritti, l'etica, Milano, p 213
Schuster WM (2018) Artificial intelligence and patent ownership. Washington Lee Law Rev 75:1945–2004
Sena G (2020) Intelligenza artificiale, p 329–330
Shemtov N, Gabison GA (2022) The inventive step requirement and the rise of the AI machines. In: Abbott R (ed) Research handbook on intellectual property and artificial intelligence. Edward Elgar, Cheltenham, p 423, 426
Simon BM (2013) The implications of technological advancement for obviousneff. Mich Telecommunications Technol Law Rev 19:101, 118 ff
Stierle M (2020) Artificial intelligence designated as inventor—an analysis of the recent EPO case law. GRUR Int 69:918, 920–923
Straus J (2021) *Artificial Intelligence and Patenting: from lessons from "DABUS" patent applications, in C. Costa, M. Aurelio, R. Pennisi, P. M. Sanfilippo, R. Vigo (a cura di), Studi di Diritto Commerciale per Vincenzo di Cataldo*, G. Giappichelli, Torino, 615
Vessia F (2022) *Riflessioni sulla brevettabilità delle «invenzioni computazionali» a margine del caso Dabus*, in AIDA, 363.
Zoboli L (2023) Diritto dei brevetti e intelligenza artificiale. EGEA S.p.A, Milano, p 99

Copyright Law As a Balancing Tool in Content Intermediation

Maria Letizia Bixio

Contents

Abstract The chapter analyses copyright law in the digital era as a means for balancing the rights of rightholders and the broader public interest, especially with regard to content -sharing platforms. Through a focus on the innovations introduced by the EU Directive 790/2019 while offering a critical analysis of its transposition into Italian domestic legislation. In conclusion, a reflection on the redistribution of revenue in the digital single market is proposed.

M. L. Bixio (✉)
European University of Rome, Rome, Italy
e-mail: Marialetizia.bixio@unier.it

R. Bocchini (ed.), *Digital Platforms - From Technical Foundations to Legal and Economic Implications*, https://doi.org/10.1007/978-3-032-07978-7_24

1 Digital Single Market and Copyright Between Compromises and Remedies

The aforementioned *Copyright* Directive[1] may be viewed as a closing a specific season in the history of copyright law, wich has been strongly characterised by the complex interactions between rightholders and the new leading players in the digital era, who are in the business of making coopyright-protected works available to the public through so-called content-sharing platforms.

Recital 83 of the directive, in fact, has established as its principal objective "the modernisation of certain aspects of the Union coyright framework to take account of technological developments and new channels of distribution of protected content in the internal market"; an objective that, due to the scope, effects and cross-border dimension of the content-sharing phenomenon, required a centralised Europe-wide harmonisation intervention that could not be achieved by the individual Member-States.

This kick-started the aptly defined process of modernisation[2] of copyright law, needed to align *copyright* rules with the challenges posed by the broader digital ecosystem and the new technologies. The main lines of intervention of the European legislator have followed a twofold trend: on the one hand, by addressing the need to once again strengthen the effectiveness of exclusive rights, confirming the rightholders' right to exclude all other parties from using their intellectual property (*ius exclendi alios*) in the face of the growing and uncontrolled potential forms of exploitation driven by digitalisation; on the other hand, by promoting, in the name of a broader public interest, an improved balance between the interest of rightholders and the general interest, while safeguarding fundamental freedoms, such as freedom of expression, the public's right to access culture and information, or other free market and competition rights. It is precisely from this latter instance that the topic of exceptions and limitations has become part of the Digital Single Market Strategy launched by the European Commission in May 2015, and has led to a radical rethinking of the whole copyright system. Suffice it to say that, in the previous directive on this subject (2001/29/EC),[3] only one of the 23 optional exceptions for Member-States was mandatory; conversely, under Directive 2019/790, all the exceptions provided with the intention of adapting the copyright rules in order to overcome possible obstacles to the cross-border circulation of intellectual works for

[1] Directive (EU) 2019/790 of the European Parliament and of the Council of 17 April 2019 on copyright and related rights in the digital single market and amending Directives 96/9/EC and 2001/29/EC, text available at: https://eur-lex.europa.eu/legal-content/IT/TXT/?uri=CELEX:32019L0790.

[2] Among the very first comprehensive analyses of the complex updating process that would await the First Copyright Directive (2001/29/EC) cf. Falce (2012). Cf. also Hilty and Moscon (2017) and Rosati (2021).

[3] Directive 2001/29/EC of the European Parliament and of the Council of 22 May 2001 on the harmonisation of certain aspects of copyright and related rights in the information society, text available at: https://eur-lex.europa.eu/legal-content/it/TXT/?uri=CELEX%3A32001L0029.

reasons of public interest[4]— i.e. new mandatory exceptions in the areas of research (Article 3–4),[5] new exceptions in the field of education (Article 5),[6] new mandatory exceptions in the fields of cultural heritage conservation (Article 6)[7] —have become binding on the Member-States.

An attempt to improve coordination between copyright protection and unrestricted access to knowledge, and therefore encourage the circulation of culture by way of a series of exceptions, had already been made at the international and European level through, the WIPO Marrakesh Treaty,[8]aimed at facilitating the making available of works to persons with disabilities, Directive 2012/28 wich introduced a mandatory exception to encourage greater cross-border access to the so-called orphan works, and Directive 2017/1564 implementing the Marrakesh Treaty, aimed at guaranteeing persons with visual impairments or other difficulties

[4] Musso (2020), pp. 411– 464.

[5] The Directive has been transposed into national law in Article 70-ter and quater of Law No. 633/1941 (the Italian copyright law, abbreviated as LDA). For a comment on the regulations, cf. Caso (2020). More specifically, Article *70-ter*, paragraphs 1 to 8, implements Article 3 of the directive by allowing cultural heritage institutions and research organisations (the definition of which is made explicit in paragraph 4), the activities of extraction of parts of text and data (so called *"text and data mining*" or TDM) of works and other protected material, contained in networks or databases to which these subjects have access, for scientific research purposes. Paragraphs 5 and 6 relate to measures to ensure the security and integrity of networks and databases defined on the basis of agreements between rightholders' associations, research organisations and cultural heritage institutions. On the other hand, Article *70-quater* transposes Article 4 of the Directive and, without prejudice to Article *70-ter*, allows the same extraction operation to anyone having legitimate access to works and other subject matter contained in databases or networks provided that the use has not been expressly reserved by the rightholders, without prejudice to the security levels provided for TDM allowed to research organisations.

[6] Article 5 provides that Member States shall provide for an exception or limitation to the rights provided for in Article 5(a), (b), (d) and (e) and Article 7(1) of Directive 96/9/EC, Articles 2 and 3 of Directive 2001/29/EC, Article 4(1) of Directive 2009/24/EC to permit digital use of works and other subject-matter solely for the purpose of illustration for teaching purposes, to the extent justified by the non-commercial purpose pursued, provided that such use: takes place under the supervision of a person who has been authorised to use the work for the purpose of teaching; and that the use is not in breach of the right to use the work for teaching purposes. 1 of Directive 2009/24/EC to permit the digital use of works and other subject-matter solely for illustrative purposes for educational use, to the extent justified by the non-commercial purpose pursued, provided that such use: takes place under the responsibility of an educational establishment, on its premises or elsewhere, or through a secure electronic environment accessible only to the pupils or students and teaching staff of that establishment; and is accompanied by an indication of the source, including the author's name, except where that is impossible. Cf., for a more detailed commentary on the Directive and the national transposition - embodied in Article *70-bis*, Law No. 633/1941 - cf., respectively: Falce (2019), p. 375; Massa (2024), p. 31 ff.

[7] The Italian transposition includes the new exceptions to Article 68(*2-bis*) of Law 633/1941. For an initial comment cf. Maiello et al. (2024), cit., p. 51 ff. Therefore, cultural heritage institutions—broadly defined in the new Article *70-ter*(3)—are entitled to reproduce and make copies of protected works, permanently present in their collections, for preservation purposes, in any format and medium to the extent required for their preservation.

[8] The Marrakech Treaty was adopted on 27 June 2013 and entered into force on 30 September 2016.

access to books and other printed material in suitable formats; upon closer scrutiny, a crescendo that fostered the above-described implantation of Directive 2019/790. A trend that seems to have narrowed the gap between the traditional continental "*droit d'auteur*" system and the Anglo-Saxon "*copyright*".

In the former system, based on the idea that a work belongs to the author, being a sort of extension of their personality, the law afforded broader protection to the exclusive rights of the author, compared to relevant limitations, considered more restrictively. In the Anglo-Saxon system, instead, greater importance is given to the economic profiles of the exploitation of the authors' rights, which are useful for stimulating scientific and cultural progress and guaranteeing social wellbeing. Therefore, there is a restrictive enucleation of exclusive rights and a more open definition of the limits to these rights.

The Anglo-Saxon approach, characterised by the centrality of market dynamics, sometimes to the detriment of the ability to fully exercise the copyright, while distant from the *droit d'auteur* model in *civil law*, has nevertheless influenced the European legislator tasked with implementing a strategy for tacklingthe "single digital market",[9] in wich the priority is the proper redistribution of revenues to the industry as a whole and only subordinately to the individual rightholders.

At the core is the need to create a truly single market, strengthening creative ecosystems, implementing policies to support investment, ensuring a virtuous cycle of reinvestment in European works, boosting economic and employment growth, media pluralism, and cultural diversity.[10]

Again this backdrop, updating the copyright regulation becomes first and foremost as the cornestone for boosting the entire culture industry by rebalancing the market dynamics tending toward the impoverishment of the creative supply chain.[11] And here the reference goes to the two most contentious provisions emerging during

---

[9] The European Commission made its first comments on the digital single market in 2009, a reflection that culminated in 2015 with the publication of the Communication of the Commission and the Parliament on the Strategy for Europe's Digital Single Market, available: https://eurlex.europa.eu/legalcontent/EN/TXT/PDF/?uri=CELEX:52015DC0192&from=FI in which the digital environment was seen as an opportunity for creative content markets as well as a lever for boosting the overall European economy.

[10] Broad objectives already outlined in the Commission report, *Creative Content in a European Digital Single Market: Challenges for the Future. A Reflection Document of DG INFSO and DG MARKT*', 2009, 14–20; similarly in the Commission Communication *A Single Market for Intellectual Property Rights. Boosting creativity and innovation to provide economic growth, high quality jobs and first class products and services in* Europe, 2011, 287 final, 9–10.

[11] These provisions are designed to close the so-called value gap, i.e. the gap in value between the revenues from the online circulation of protected content *online* and the revenues actually collected by rightholders. The gap between the value produced online by cultural content through *User Generated Content* (UGC) platforms, and the lack of economic return in terms of revenues for the content creators, as well as its overall impact on the cultural and creative industry, was highlighted in Roland Berger's research commissioned by Gesac in 2015, which highlighted how in Europe at least 23% of the revenues generated by cultural content for Internet intermediaries (equal to EUR 4,980 million), does not accrue to the authors of that content. Cf. R. BERGER, *Cultural content in the online environment: Analysing the value transfer in Europe*, 2015. The text can be found at the

the negotiations of the directive, namely Article 15, on the protection of press publications concerning online uses — which will be adressed in the following subsection—as well as Article 17 protecting all rightholders whose work is disseminated on content-sharing platforms without the conclusion of prior profit-sharing arrangements.

2 The Problem of the Fair Redistribution of Profits Generated by Platforms

The regulation process has focused more specifically on the players who act as industry drivers, suggesting specific tools for enabling authors and performers to monitor and recover their online and offline remuneration also in the long term.[12]

Thesetools develop along two lines, only partly converging, to respond to the same request for redistribution of the revenues from the economic exploitation of protected content.

Regarding the redistribution aimed at recovering remuneration for the specific benefit of creatives broadly speaking, attention should be paid to Chapter 3 of the directive, wich, not surprisingly, is titled without any reference to online content: *Fair remuneration in exploitation contracts of authors and performers.*[13]

Here, the regulations introduce four new areas of protection, governed by Article 18 et seq. of the Directive[14]; firstly, the right for authors and performers who have assigned or transferred their rights to receive adequate and proportionate remuneration (Article 18),[15] envisaging a sort of right to share in the revenue actually generated by the circulation of the work; secondly, the article provides a transparency obligation to ensure the contractual balance effective,[16] the right to transparency is

following *link:* http://authorsocieties.eu/uploads/Report%20for%20GESAC_Online%20Intermediaries_2015%20Nov_EUR(1).pdf.

[12] *Cf. amplius* Bertani (2020), p. 457.

[13] For a commentary on the whole structure of Chapter 3 of the directive, cf. Fabbio (2019), p. 90 ff.; Falce and Bixio (2020), p. 261 ff.

[14] For a commentary on the Italian transposition cf. Ghiretti (2024), cit. p. 227 ff.

[15] The rule has been transposed in Article 107(2) of Law No. 633/1941, which expressly provides that authors and the AIEs may claim their right to fair compensation directly or through the collective management organisations and independent management entities to which they have thus conferred the appropriate mandate. For the purposes of determining the appropriate and proportionate remuneration, the Italian legislation makes explicit reference to the value of the rights licensed or transferred, as well as to the revenues deriving from their exploitation, specifying, moreover, that existing collective bargaining, the particularities of the reference sector and the right to remuneration provided for by articles *46-bis* and 84 of the LDA must also be taken into account. For an initial comment on article 18 of the directive see V. Falce-M.L. Bixio, *Brief notes on the principle of* fair remuneration *and* fair contract *in the Copyright Directive*, cit., 269.

[16] More extensively, cf. Bura (2022), p. 281 ff.

enshrined, requiring the receipt of "updated, relevant and complete information" at least annually.

The aim of this provision is to determine the value of the economic exploitation of the transferred rights(Article 19)[17] and possibly, also to activate the third protection provided for, i.e. the right to claim a "contract adjustment" if the originally agreed remuneration upon turns out to be disproportionately low compared to the subseq*uent succes*s of the work ("best seller" clause) (Article 20), a frequent hypothesis in cases of *lump-sum* remuneration in the licensing process. 20),[18] a frequent hypothesis in cases of lump-sum remuneration in licensing[19]; finally, a right of revocation is introduced,[20] when a right that has been transferred has not been exploited within a reasonable time (Article 22).[21] To date, the transposition of these provisions hass not radically changed the existing models—which, moreover, in the Italian system already included very similar measures to protect authors and performes—and, contractual freedom has been preserved, in accordancet with the final rules of the directive in which prohibit the circumvention or evasion of the principles of *fair remuneration* and *fair contract.*

2.1 New Policies and Enforcement: From the Copyright Directive to National Transposition—Critical Notes

However, the transposition of the directive provisions into Italian copyright law raises several interpretative and applicative doubts, which are expected to give rise to judicial and doctrinal debates.

One of the most problematic issuesvitiating Article 18 or, better, by now the last paragraph of Article 107 of Law no. 633/1941, is the provision of nullity of any stipulations contrary to the wording of the article, which, it is surmised refers to the contractual provisions that provide for an inadequate and non-proportionate remuneration. The question arises as to whether the nullity of a clause contrary introducing to the principle of appropriate and proportionate representation affects the entire contract, constituting a "lack of consent". Evidently, such a prospect could significantly deter potential purchasers of the rights.[22]

---

[17] The rule has been transposed in Article *110-quater*, Law No. 633/1941, cf. Falce and Bixio (2020), cit., p. 273.

[18] Cf. Falce and Bixio (2020), cit., p. 279.

[19] On this point, cf. Mazzoni (2023), p. 614 ff.

[20] *Cf., amplius*, D'Ammassa (2024), cit. p. 261 ff.

[21] Cf. Falce and Bixio (2020), cit., p. 283.

[22] Among the resolutive hypotheses F. Ghiretti, *La disciplina dell'equa remunerazione e gli obblighi di trasparenza*, cit. Suggests that "the mandatory rule aimed at supplementing the content of the null clause could be found in Article 2225 of the Civil Code on the subject of self-employment contracts which, as is well known, empowers the courts to determine the consideration that has not been agreed upon by the parties and cannot be determined according to professional rates or cus-

Another interpretational shortcoming could arise from the misalignment between Article 18 and Article 20, regarding the the parties affected by the new provisions. In fact, while Article 20 expressly refers to the contractual counterparties and their assignees, Aricle 18 is limited to the former, suggesting a restrictive interpretation as to any claims lodged by an assignee in relation to non-appropriate and non-proportionate remuneration. If this interpretation were to be considered definitive, this would undoubtely significantly restrict the scope of the provision, in view of the fact that in many sectors of the creative industry (music, cinema, etc.) the first assignee of the rights is not necessarily the party that will go on to directly exploit the work over time.

This aspect is crucial in respect of the two macro remedial measures put in place by the directive to address the objective of profit redistribution objective, which, as mentioned above, do not always converge.

Before outlining the rationale of intervention of the cited Articles 15 and 17, where the focus is on the "*online*" exploitation of protected content through platforms and aggregators, we must ask whether the principle of appropriate and proportionate remuneration, apparently developed for the offline content, should also be applied to online content. Suffice it to mention the endless subsequent exploitations of a film or a song on the so-called "*sharing platforms*", which translates into indirect revenues for the online content sharing service providers in the form of advertising revenue shares associated with the content.[23] In order to do so, it is necessary to overcome the restrictive interpretation of the liable persons in Article 18 and to apply Article 20 more extensively.

As things stand, in fact, authors and performers appear to be precluded from significantly recovering the value collected by *web* intermediaries through the tools indicated in Articles 18 et seq. Therefore, the rightholders' objective of receiving truly proportionate remuneration compared to the revenues from the dissemination of their work seems to have been missed, especially with regard to the online uses of certain works.[24]

---

tomary practice, "in relation to the result obtained and the work normally required to obtain it'". See also Ghiretti and Milani (2022), p. 331.

[23] *Cf.*, *amplius*, Montagnani et al. (2011), according to which: "*Furthermore, distribution systems based on advertising incomes are the point of contact between traditional distribution and the recent phenomenon constituted by the UGCs. UGC platforms that support themselves by generating advertising incomes make content freely available to users, who are in turn exposed to advertising messages that generates income to support the operation of the platform*'.

[24] In the music and film industry, the digital exploitation of the work usually represents a second phase of exploitation; clearly if the apprpriateness and proportionality of the remuneration is assessed with respect to the revenues that the film producer or publisher receives from its digital distributors, the remuneration paid to authors and performers may be fair; on the other hand, if it were related to the overall revenues from the sharing platforms, there would once again be a significant *value gap*. Cf. Marzano (2024), op. cit., p. 240, who points out how industry practice seems to be difficult to reconcile with the regulatory requirement to recognise appropriate and proportionate remuneration to the value of the rights licensed or transferred *and* commensurate with the revenues recived from their exploitation therof. Specifically, the author clarifies that "the producer mesure the value of the rights in accordance with Article 107 according to their budget,

2.2 For a Redefinition of the Degree of Liability of Intermediaries in the Communication to the Public of Protected Works

In order to enhance the protection of copyright and related rights in relation to the dissemination of content on sharing platforms, the European legislator has, in fact, introduced another measure in Article 17,[25] aimed at radically modifying the intermediary's exemption from liabilityaccording to the directive on elettronic commerce (or e-Commerce Directive 2000/31).

Article *102-sexies* of Law No. 633/1941 transposed the key innovation introduced by Article 17 of the directive 790/2019, i.e. the requirement whereby content-sharing service providers that share content uploaded by their users shall obtain prior authorisation [26] before any copyright-protected content is made available to the public on their platforms in order not to be held liable for copyright infringements. Basically, albeit with an initial subjective barrier, under certain conditions and with a series of exceptions explicitly set out in the text, the intention was to clarify that the liability of these operators becomes direct in the event of copyright infringement, excluding the applicability of the liability limitation regime set forth in Article 14 of the E-commerce Directive, transposed into Article 16 of Legislative Decree No. 70 of 9 April 2003.

The limitation is evident from a subjective point of view in the combined provisions of Article 2 and recital 62[27] where the perimeter of the notion of online

---

covered by the purchase price of the rights that the first licensees of the work are willing to pay; and this "first cycle of exploitation" is taken into account precisely when preparing the budget. It could be objected that the pre-sales of a work's rights could generate unexpected revenues for the producer.But this is just a textbook case because the fame of the author(s), the director, the actors determines both the consideration that all of them have received from the producer during negotiations, and the revenues generated during the first cycle of exploitation. Most of the revenues will actually be generated, if it at all further downstream, during further exploitations of the work". On this point, the author also refers to Cogo (2022), p. 1300 ff. and concludes his reflections by supporting the exemplary interpretation according to which the assignees of the producer -an not the producer- should inevitably be the parties obliged to recognise the extra sums due to them as referred to in Article 107.

[25] For an examination of the standard and a reconstruction of the decision-making *process* that led to the final text, cf. Falce and Faraone (2021), p. 12 ff.

[26] "Online content-sharing service providers, when giving the public access to copyright-protected works or other protected subject matte uploaded by its users, perform an act of communication to the public or an act of making available to the public for which they shall obtain an authorisation from the rightholders, for instance by concluding a licensing agreement either directly or through a collec- tive management organisation and the independent management entities referred to in Legislative Decree No. 35 of 15 March 2017."

[27] In Article 2(1)(6) of the directive, an "online content-sharing service provider" for the purposes of Article 17 is defined as "a provider of an information society service of which the main or one of the main purposes is to store and give the public access to a large amount of copyright-protected works or other protected subject matter uploaded by its users, which it organises and promotes for profit-making purposes". Moreover recital 62 of the directive further restrictss the definition of

content-sharing service providers is defined. The effect of these definitional shortcomings is that the burden of the new obligation[28] essentially lies squarely on the providers alone whose main purpose is to store and make available to the public large amounts of copyright protected works, wich they organise and promote works for profit-making purposes.[29]

Among the many balances introduced by the new rules, is a release from liability in cases where an online content-sharing service provider, lacking prior authorisation (*pursuant to* Article *102-septies* of Law no. 633/1941), is able to prove that it had made its "best efforts"[30] to obtain the required authorisation to use the works from the rightholders in accordance with high industry standards of professional diligence and it had made its "best efforts" to prevent the availability of those works *online*, and, after receiving a sufficiently reasoned notice from the rightholder, had promptly disabled access to or removed the works or other content referred to in the notice, from its websites, and made its best efforts to prevent their uploading in the future. On closer inspection, the latter provision introduces both a *notice-and-takedown* mechanism and a *notice-and-stay-down* obligation.[31]

---

online services to those services "that play an important role on the online content market by competing with other online content services, such as online audio and video streaming services, for the same audiences". Such services have as their main purpose to ' store and enable users to upload and share a large amount of copyright-protected content with the purpose of obtaining profit therefrom, either directly or indirectly, by organising it and promoting it in order to attract a larger audience*store and* [...]'.

[28] The nature of the obligations imposed on intermediaries would appear to be one of result, both in the light of recital 66 which expressly clarifies that such activity must have as its aim "to avoid the availability on their services of unauthorised works or other subject-matter on its *website*", and of the reconstruction suggesteded by the European Court of Justice in Case C-314/12, *Telekabel*, where the Court specified that "as regards the protection of copyright, the Oberlandesgericht Wien held that UPC Telekabel could only be required, in the form of an obligation to achieve a particular result, to forbid its customers access to the website at issue, but that it had to remain free to decide the means to be used" (subsection 14), and that "an injunction such as that at issue in the main proceedings leaves its addressee to determine the specific measures to be taken in order to achieve the result sought, with the result that he can choose to put in place measures which are best adapted to the resources and abilities available to him and which are compatible with the other obligations and challenges which he will encounter in the exercise of his activity" (subsection 54). a

[29] The profit-making aspect as a qualifying element of the act of communication to the public had been explored by the Court of Justice (Cases C-527/15, *Stichting Brein*, subsections 34 and 49 and C-610/15, *The Pirate Bay*, subsection 29).

[30] The reference to their 'besti efforts' was long disputed during the negotiations as leading to the weakening on the degree of harmonisation of the measure. The different translations in the Member States and the vagueness of the concept as such, lacking objective parameters, raised concerns about the risk of impairing the evaluation of efforts, and it was therefore advocated to direct the examination of best efforts through a proportionality *test* and through case-by-case assessments of the types of service offered, the amount of content uploaded by users, the availability of information on rights holders and the complexity of authorisation procedures. On this point, see Ercolani (2024), cit., p. 179.

[31] For a very first commentary on the *stay-down* obligation, see Romero Moreno (2019), p. 20.

However, there are significant mitigating circumstances alongside the new, apparently rather strict set-up.. First of all, a preferential scheme is adopted in the case of online content-sharing service providers that have been operating for less than 3 years and have an annual turnover of less than ten million euros, who, in order to obtain release from liability, must be able to prove that they had made their best efforts to obtain a licence and, in the event of a report from the relevant rightholder, that they had disabled access or removed the reported works from their websites. Moreover, such providers will be subject to a *stay-down* obligations only if the average number of their monthly unique visitors exceeds 5 million.

Among the most relevant exclusions from the newly introduced regime is the express exemption from application of the rules of providers of electronic communication services and *business-to-business cloud* services or providers who allow their users to upload content for personal use, such as *cyberlockers*, providers of *online* marketplaces, whose main business is *online* retailing, and who therefore do not make availale copyright-protected content finally, for service providers such as *open source software* development and sharing platforms, non-profit scientific or educational repositories and non-profit *online* encyclopaedias.

Last but not least, it should be noted how the legislator, in reconstructing roles and responsibilities, strived to cause as little damage as possible to users; in fact, Article 17 also specifies that where a licensing agreements has been concluded between the rightholders and the online content-sharing service provider, the relevant authorisation shall also cover acts carried out by individual users of the services, provided that they are not acting on a commercial basis.. Furthermore, the aforementioned acts of uploading shall also be covered by the exceptions and limitations already provided in Directive 2001/29/EC on the subject of quotation, criticism, review, and use for the purpose of caricature, parody, and pastiche. This latter inclusion still entails a misalignment in the domestic legal system between the protections afforded for the *online* and *offline* exploitation of works. Taking a step back, it can be recalled that Article 5(3)(k) of Directive 2001/29 on the harmonisation of certain aspects of copyright and related rights in the information society had introduced the parody exception, however leaving its transposition to the discretion of the Member-States. Since Italy has never transposed this exception, the lawfulness of parodying a copyright protected work has remained the subject of oscillating case law interpretations over time.

As mentioned above, the Italian legislator, in application of Article 17 of the Directive, have introduced in Article 102-nonies of Law No. 633/1941, the provision, regarding online platforms, whereby "users, when uploading and making available content generated by them through an *online* content sharing service provider, may avail themselves of the following exceptions or limitations to copyright and related rights: (a) quotation, criticism, review; (b) use for the purpose of caricature, parody or pastiche". Although this exception is mandatory, the European legislator seems to have limited its application to *online* use only.

The provision, in fact, is unequivocally applies to exploitation through online platforms, and the exceptions provided for therein can only apply within this perimeter. Today, in the aftermath of the national implementation, since the discrepancy between the two planes of application remains, it must be questioned whether the new provision could be extended to also include conventional contexts and uses, if only to avoid unequal treatment in clearly identical cases.

In conclusion, it should be remembered that in order to guarantee users' freedom of thought, as much as possible, it was decided, in connection with the transposition of the last subsection of Article 17 into Article *102-decies* of Law No. 633/1941, to introduce a threefold mechanism for protecting the rights of the parties involved, which provides for a *claim* and *counterclaim* mechanism directly set up by the platform, a dispute resolution mechanism set up by third-party authorities (wich in Italy is the Authority for Communications), and finally a judicial pathway.

Regarding the first mechanism, the Italian legislator departed from the text of the directive by introducing an extension aimed at ensuring, in the event of any claims by the rightholder, that the platform operator must stop making the content available to the public until a decision is taken on the merits of the counterclaims received from the user.

This approach can be criticised, insofar as it impairs the full application of the exceptions and limitations granted to users; althought it can hardly be blamed if interpreted in the light of the complex framework[32] for redefining the liability of intermediaries exposed to direct claims for compensation, which will be discussed in the following sections.

References

Bertani M (2020) Tra paternalismo ed autonomia negoziale: il nuovo assetto dei rapporti fra autore, artista ed impresa culturale nel digital single market. In: Orizzonti dir. comm., p 457

Bura A (2022) L'equa remunerazione di autori ed artisti ed impatto sul diritto dei contratti. In: Lavagnini S (ed) Il diritto d'autore nel mercato unico digitale. Giappichelli, Torino, p 281 ff

Caso R (2020) Il conflitto tra diritto d'autore e ricerca scientifica nella disciplina del text and data mining della direttiva sul mercato unico digitale. In: Trento LawTech Research Paper, 38, disponibile su SSRN: https://ssrn.com/abstract=3533401

Cogo A (2022) Il diritto d'autore nel mercato unico digitale. Giur it 5:1300 ff

Fabbio P (2019) Il diritto del creativo ad una remunerazione adeguata e proporzionata nella Direttiva Digital Copyright. Ann it dir aut:90 ff

Falce V (2012) La modernizzazione del diritto di autore. Giappichelli, Torino

Falce V (2019) La spinta adeguatrice della Direttiva Copyright. Il caso dell'eccezione di insegnamento. Riv. dir. ind.:375

Falce V, Bixio ML (2020) Brevi note sul principio di fair remuneration e fair contract nella Direttiva Copyright. Riv. dir. ind. I:261 ff

Falce V, Faraone N (2021) Spunti di diritto positivo sull'art. 17 della Direttiva Copyright. In Riv dir ind. I:12 ff

[32] In particular, the recent Law No. 93 of 14 July 2023, discussed *below*, which contains provisions for the prevention and repression of the unlawful dissemination of copyright-protected content through electronic communication networks, as well as the two European regulations, the *Digital Services Act*, Regulation (EU) 2022/2065 and the *Digital Markets Act*, Regulation (EU) 2022/1925.

Ghiretti F, Milani M (2022) Il nuovo "Statuto" di autori ed artisti nel mercato unico digitale. In: Dir. ind., p 331

Hilty R, Moscon V (2017) Modernisation of the EU Copyright Rules. Position Statement of the Max Planck Institute for Innovation and Competition. Max Planck Institute for Innovation and Competition Research Paper No. 17–12, disponibile su: https://www.ipmpg.de/en/publications/details/modernisation-of-the-eu-copyright-rules-position-statement-of-the-max-planck-institute-for-innovation-and-competition.html

Maiello R, Mazziotti G, Sappa C (2024) Qualche spunto sull'eccezione per la conservazione del patrimonio culturale. In: Bixio ML (ed) Crisi e resilienza del diritto d'autore. Giappichelli, Torino, p 51 ff

Massa F (2024) L'insegnamento a distanza: l'accademia italiana può essere competitiva? In: Bixio ML (ed) Crisi e resilienza del diritto d'autore. Giappichelli, Torino, p 31 ff

Mazzoni EC (2023) Gli effetti dell'attuazione in Italia della Direttiva (UE) 2019/790 sulla trasmissione dei diritti di utilizzazione spettanti agli autori e artisti (interpreti o esecutori). Nuove leggi civ comm 3:614 ff

Montagnani ML, Nuccio M, Borghi M (2011) Online distribution of digital goods: empirical evidence from bottom-up cluster analysis. Disponibile su SSRN

Musso A (2020) Eccezioni e limitazioni ai diritti d'autore nella Direttiva UE n. 790/2019. Il Dir informazione e informatica XXXV(4):411–464

Romero Moreno F (2019) 'Notice and stay down' and social media: amending article 13 of the proposed directive on copyright. Int Rev Law Comp Technol 33(2):20

Rosati E (2021) Copyright in the digital single market. Article-by-article commentary to the provisions of directive 2019/790. Oxford Academic Press, Oxford

Copyright Law and Access to Journalistic Information Through Digital Platforms

Maria Letizia Bixio

Contents

Abstract This chapter examines the corrective measures introduced by the EU Directive 2019/790 with regard to the online publishing sector, focusing in particular on its impact on the national legal systems. The introduction of a new related right to protect publishers of press publications was, in fact, intended to counter the phenomenon of digital free-riding by online platforms and news aggregators. The regulation aims to rebalance economic relations in the information market, ensuring fair remuneration for the digital use of editorial content.

1 Publishing Industry and Platforms: The New Tools to Prevent Content Free Riding

The European legislator has decided to introduce, within the copyright law modernisation process, an ad hoc reform of online press publications, be-cause the contribution of publishers of press publications needs to be recognised and further

M. L. Bixio (✉)
European University of Rome, Rome, Italy
e-mail: Marialetizia.bixio@unier.it

R. Bocchini (ed.), *Digital Platforms - From Technical Foundations to Legal and Economic Implications*, https://doi.org/10.1007/978-3-032-07978-7_25

encouraged "to ensure the sustainability of the publishing industry and thereby foster the availability of reliable information"[1].

Since 2010, the print media sector[2] has been facing a severe crisis, partially due to the involuntary damage caused by the new *online* sharing practices by the publishers of press publications themselves. Making available, free of charge, a large part of their content on the online versions of newspapers has led to a fall in the consumption of printed newspapers and the failed recovery of revenue through *online* advertising and subscriptions. In the face of the increase in press content on portals and of consumer demand for news via digital devices, business models have been developed based on the offer of information services by so-called *news aggregators*, which are services that collect and organise content from news websites into single, easy-to-view platforms that meet the information needs of users.[3] This has substantially diverted the flow of user access from the newspaper portals to third party platforms.

This new practices has therefore, led to questionable forms of content *free riding on*, and, at the same time, to copyright infringements, throught communicating and making available an author's work to the public. The inevitable domino effect has caused a decline in user access to the primary sources of information, with ensuing direct and indirect loss of revenue across the entire press publishing industry.

Against this backdrop, it became necessary, at Union level, to adopt harmonised rules at Eu level, regarding *online* uses of press publications by information society service providers; this led to the formulation of Article 15 of Directive 2019/790, which, while sharing certain basic objectives, according to the *rationale of* Articles 17 et seq.— as commented in the preceding paragraph—takes on an autonomous configuration due to the specificity of the sector to which it applies.

The main distinguishing feature is the introduction of a new rights for the protection of press publications concerning online uses, for a two-year term,[4] provided to the relevant publishers established in a Member-State in relation to cases of online

---

[1] Cf. recitals 55 and 58 of Directive No. 790/2019.

[2] "With the decline of print, publishers have become increasingly dependent on the monetisation of their digital content, but they manage to do so today only to a limited extent. Paywalls and B2C digital-subscription offers are being increasingly proposed, in particular by the main newspaper and magazine brands, but today they only account for around 10% of news publishers' online revenues. Freely-available content remains crucial as it attracts advertising revenues, which are today still the main contributor to press publishers' digital revenues". Cf., 'The impact of web traffic on revenues of traditional newspaper publishers. A study for France, Germany, Spain and the UK', Deloitte, March 2016. http://www2.deloitte.com/content/dam/Deloitte/uk/Documents/technology-mediatelecommunications/deloitte-uk-impact-of-web-traffic-on-newspaper-revenues-2016.pdf.

[3] Cf. *Impact Assessment on the modernisation of EU copyright rules*, 156 ff. Available at: https://digital-strategy.ec.europa.eu/en/library/impact-assessment-modernisation-eu-copyright-rules. Cf. Sganga (2021), p. 159.

[4] Pursuant to Article 15(4) of Directive 2019/790, the two-year period "shall be calculated from 1 January of the year following the date on wich that press publication is published".

use of the press publications by information society service providers[5] or media *monitoring* and review platforms. Broadly speaking, the definition of "press publication" covers only press publications, such as, for instance, daily newspapers, magazines (including subscription-based magazines), and news websites, while periodical publications published for scientific or academic purposes, *blogs*, private or non-commercial uses, *hyperlinks*, and, lastly, single words or very short extracts sourced from such publications are not included in the scope of the directive.

Especially appreciable are the conceptualisation efforts firstly of the European legislator, followed by the Italian legislator[6], with regard to the definition of press publication, as well as in relation to the boundaries of the "short extract", and to identifying the reference criteria for fair compensation, since their aim is to provide the parties with a valid toolkit for conducting their negotiations, based on the principles of fairness and good faith.

In this regard, the choice of a quality-based, rather than quantitaty-based, criterion for determining the concept of a "very short extract"[7] seems worthy of support; in fact, if one had based the assessment of the damaging scope of the extract on a mere word count, the results would not have been reliable. On the other hand, the extent to which the sourcing can be considered as alternative to reading the original source should inevitably be assessed on a case-by-case basis. If the extract enables the user to dispense with consulting the "source material", i.e. the press article in its entirety, then the alternative offered by the aggregator becomes a parasitic link to the publisher's product and should require compensation to the latterfor loss of users.

The directive has introduced new rights in publication precisely for the purpose of concretely and effectively preventing such a parasitic operation.[8] Of course, the balancing of the interests involved is the result of the complex debate on the various aspects of the regulatory framework of which Art. 15 is a part, which, in any case, highlights the desire of the European legislator to ensure that publishers of press publications (just like authors and performers), obtain an adequate remuneration for the use of their content, through negotiations conducted with the news aggregators, in accordance with the broader purpose, as outlined in the previous paragraph, of bridging the value gap and restoring a level playing field between the digital market players.[9]

---

[5] For the definition of information society service, cf. reference should be made in the national transpositionto Article 1(1)(b) of Legislative Decree No 223 of 15 December 2017.

[6] Article 15 has been transposed into Article *43-bis* of Law No. 633/1941.

[7] Cf, Banterle and Ghidini (2021), p. 253.

[8] It should be noted that the new right does not preclude the excercise of the rights of authors and other rightholder under the copyright law concerning works included in press publications and in the case of a non-exclusive licensing, the possibility of a different uses of such publications by other authorised parties remains unaffected. For a very first commentary on the intent of the reform brought about by Article 15 in the publishing field, cf. Falce and Bixio (2016).

[9] Also on the topic of the recovery of the '*value gap*' in redefining the roles and responsibilities of new players, cf. Priora (2019), p. 330 ff.

It is interesting to note how the final choices made by the European legislator, to provide a reorganisation toolkit for the publishing industry, are based on the lectio learned, a few years ago, in Germany and Spain following the adoption of national regulations that have proved counterproductive compared to the expected outcomes.[10]

Also important in this sense were the characterisations of the Italian transposition[11] where, in an attempt to respond as a matter of priority to the need to make the protection of the weaker party effective during negotiations with the aggregator, the cause of the failure of the Spanish law, an important and concrete role was given to the Authority for Communications (abbreviated as AGCOM), which not only identified in a special regulation objective criteria for the conduct of such negotiations and the determination of fair compensation[12], but is also invested with deterrent supervisory and sanctioning powers. Last but not least, in addition to protecting of a "perfect" subjective right (such as the "new" related right envisaged by the directive), there is a special focus on balancing protection of a patrimonial right with the aim of preserving freedom of expression, in accordance with the Italian Constitution (Articles 3(2) and 21) and the European Convention on Human Rights (Article 10)..

---

[10] Both attempts to ensure the disbursement of fair compensation for rightsholders by the news aggregators have failed, causing even greater distorsions such as the closure of services such as 'Google News' and the consequent de-indexing of multiple sites with which the platforms refused to enter into licences upstream. Cf. critically Rosati (2016), p. 569 ff.

[11] The Italian transposition model was strongly supported by ENPA-European Newspaper Publishers' Association and EMMA-European Periodicals Publishers' Association, as *it introduced the 'assisted negotiation' mechanism, inspired by the Australian News Media Bargaining Code,* to give effectively implement to the new *related right of newspaper publications.*

[12] With resolution No. 3/23/CONS, AGCOM approved its Regulation on determining fair compensation for the online use of press publications, in application of Article 43-bis of the copyright law. At the heart of the Regulation, resulting from a lengthy public consultation process, for implementing copyright protection as defined by the law, is the principle of respect for the negotiating freedom of the parties, whereby it encourages the conclusion of mutually beneficial agreements between publish- ers and information society service providers, including media monitoring and press review platforms (IMMRS). The procedure established by the Regulation provides that, if the parties fail to agree on the amount of the fair compensation, within 30 days of the request to commence negotiations, either party may refer the matter to the Authority, without prejudice to its right to bring an action before the courts. Within 60 days of the request, the Authority shall indicate, in accordance with the Regulation, which of the economic proposals complies with the said criteria or, if it does not consider any of the proposals to be compliant, it shall officially establish the amount of fair compensation. In the case of IMMRS, fair compensation is established on the basis of their turnover from any media monitoring and press review activities. Regarding the other types of providers, the Regulation adopts a more detailed revenue-sharing calculation model, as the result of a balancing act performed by AGCOM between a multiplicity of private and public interest, also in light of the diverse structural character- istics of providers and publishers. Lastly, the Regulation governs the communication and information obligations incumbent on the Platforms and the IMMRS, to obtain the necessary data for applying the reference criteria and therefore determine the measure of the fair compensation. AGCOM, which oversees this obligation, has the authority to apply a fine of up to 2 per cent of the turnover recorded in the latest financial year prior to the notification of the dispute.

2 Innovations in the Internal System in the Implementation of the European *Lectio*

Wanting to highlight two further characterisations of Article *43-bis* with respect to the text of the directive, it will be noted how the national provision has provided that the related right includes the entire right of communication to the public, and not only the right to make it available to the public as indicated in the European context[13]; furthermore, whereas in the directive and in Article 43-bis, a discipline tended to be consistent for all providers (news aggregators), AGCOM, through its Regulation distinguishes between press review agencies and media monitoring and other providers of news aggregators. *43-bis* had been outlined in the directive and in Article 43-bis, AGCOM decided to distinguish in the regulation between press review and media *monitoring* agencies and the other providers.[14] This was due to a proper differentiation between the *business* models adopted: that of press review and media *monitoring* companies, which in fact "providetheir services generally for a fee to customers who enter into contracts for supplying customised services to a multiplicity of end users belonging to the contractor's organisation"[15], and the typical modelof platforms, revenue sharing.

The focus of the Italian legislator on press reviews, expressly referred to Article *43-bis*, could be justified by the many lawsuits between newspaper publishers and-press review service providers[16] as a result of the anti-competitive behavior of the latter over the former. Going forward the wording of the new article may clear the field of the uncertainties generated by the lengthy litigation[17] concerning the

[13] For a more complete commentary on transposition, cf. Giordanelli et al. (2024) cit., 127 ff.

[14] Cf. footnote 43 in more detail.

[15] AGCOM, Resolution 3/23/CONS, 12, of 19 January 2023 available at: https://www.agcom.it/sites/default/files/migration/delibera/Delibera%203-23-CONS.pdf.

[16] The national disputes were between FIEG-registered publishers, represented by the company Promopress 2000, and the two main national reviewers, Eco della Stampa and Data Stampa.

[17] For a more exhaustive reconstruction, cf. Marzano (2024). With judgment no. 816 of 18.1.2017, the Court of Rome, held that the prohibition on reproduction and communication to the public in Article 65 of the LDA was not applicable, recognising the full lawfulness of the conduct of reviewers, given the alleged non-competitiveness with the activity of publishers. Subsequently with sent. of the App. Rome 12 June 2019, no. 3931, the Court, while denying the possibility of an analogical interpretation of the rules on exceptions and limitations, admitted an extensive interpretation, admitting press reviews among the media on which it is possible to republish articles. Subsequently, Fieg, Promopress and the other publishers appealed to AGCOM, so that, in application of the 'anti-piracy regulation', it would inhibit the use of 'reserved' articles in press reviews. This solution turned out to be successful and the publishers' arguments were accepted by AGCOM with decisions 16/2020/Pres, 96/20/Csp., then again confirmed by the Lazio Regional Administrative Court, with its own judgement 4263/21, and finally by the Council of State, with judgement no. 2586/2022. Finally, to round off the matter, the Supreme Court of Cassation intervened with Order No. 1651 of 19 January 2023, which, if on the one hand brought the terms of the matter *ratione temporis* back to the parameters of Article 65 of Law No. 633/1941 should apply, while also acknowledging that Article *43-bis introduced*: "a new right in favour of publishers of journalistic publications, in order to obtain a fee for the digital use of the pieces they edit. [...]. As things stand at present,

lawfulness of press review activities in the light of the combined provisions of Articles 65 and 101 of Law No. 633/1941.

Summing up the new internal set-up that has redefined the rules for making available information to the public via platforms, some elements can be emphasised. Firstly, a concrete simplification of the granting of licences for the exploitation of publishing products with the consequent contribution to the remuneration of the financial investment made by publishers.

Article 65 (a) and (b)and 101 of Law No. 633/1941, the rationale of the AGCOM Regulation and the Court of Cassation's conclusions ruling in the litigation between publishers and review platforms all feature an important common denominator: the desire to protect the investments made by publishers to secure their position as the first to break and disseminate news. Since the economic value of these activities is understandably limited to a very short time span, any reuse of such information, in conjunction with its first dissemination, is inevitably harmful to the interests of publishers [18]. The reform, its transposition, and especially the rules of the AGCOM Regulation seem to provide the press publication industry with the means for recover from the 2010 crisis, and to offer them the possibility of rebalancing their economic and negotiating relations with the large web operators, while continuing to make reliable information available online to the public.[19]

therefore, publishers of journalistic publications are granted exclusive reproduction and communication rights for the online use of their publications by information society service providers, including media monitoring and press review platforms, and are entitled to fair compensation as established by a fair and controlled negotiation".

[18] Eduardo Piola Caselli already expressed the matter in these terms back in 1941: '*Moreover, it should be remembered that their commercial value vanishes in an extremely variable space of time, depending on the importance and nature of the news and information, so that it appears very difficult to cover this information or news with a fixed term intellectual property right*'. Piola Caselli (1943). The reference to the time-based commercial value of certain news items have brings to mind the US '*Hot News Doctine*', developed by the US Courts as early as 1918 with the case *International News Service v. Associated Press, 248 U.S. 215* (1918).

[19] According to the text of the regulation, cf. footnote 43, in the case of *web* giants it will be advertising revenues that will be the basis for calculating the amount of the publisher's share. The aim of the regulation is therefore to effectively bridge the *gap* between the revenues received by the platforms for publishing press content and those received by the publishers and rightholders,—which until now have been very low indeed.

References

Banterle F, Ghidini G (2021) Copyright, news, and "information products" under the new DSM copyright directive. In: Mirone A, Costa C, Sanfilippo PM, Pennisi R, Vigo R (eds) Studi di diritto commerciale per Vincenzo Di Cataldo. Giappichelli, Torino, p 253

BIXIO M.L., FALCE V., Verso un nuovo diritto connesso a favore degli editori on line. Brevi note su recenti derive (iper)-protezionistiche, in Diritto Mercato e Tecnologia, 2016

Giordanelli F, Marzano P, Splendore I (2024) La via italiana per i diritti connessi degli editori di pubblicazioni giornalistiche. In: Bixio ML (ed) Crisi e resilienza del diritto d'autore. Giappichelli, Torino, p 127 ff

Marzano P (2024) Applicazione della norma interna e primo vaglio giurisprudenziale. In: Bixio ML (ed) Crisi e resilienza del diritto d'autore. Giappichelli, Torino, p 135 ff

Piola Caselli E (1943) Codice del Diritto d'Autore. Unione Tipografico-Editrice, Torino

Priora G (2019) Catching sight of a glimmer of light: fair remuneration and the emerging distributive rationale in the reform of EU copyright law. JIPITEC 10(3):330 ff

Rosati E (2016) Neighbouring rights for publishers: are national and (possible) EU initiatives lawful? IIC 47:569 ff

Sganga A (2021) Evoluzioni e trasformazioni dei diritti connessi nei percorsi di armonizzazione del diritto d'autore europeo. Riv dir ind 3:159

The Scope of Platforms' Liability and Accountability for Content Intermediation Services

Nicola M. F. Faraone

Contents

Abstract This chapter analyses the evolution of the liability of online intermediaries (ISPs, platforms) concerning the circulation of copyright protected content in the digital era. It aims at reviewing the transition from a regime of conditional irresponsibility (E-commerce Directive) to new and more stringent obligations introduced by the Copyright Directive (Art. 17) and the Digital Services Act (DSA). The Copyright Directive introduces direct liability for platforms, imposing the need for authorisations or to make so-called "best efforts" to prevent the availability of illegal content, with the adoption of technical filtering measures. The DSA adds new duties of care and accountability for platforms in the fight against illegal content and disinformation, while reaffirming the absence of a general obligation to monitor.

N. M. F. Faraone (✉)
European University of Rome, Rome, Italy
e-mail: NicolaMariaFrancesco.Faraone@unier.it

R. Bocchini (ed.), *Digital Platforms - From Technical Foundations to Legal and Economic Implications*, https://doi.org/10.1007/978-3-032-07978-7_26

1 Introduction

It is now well established fact that the innovative leap generated by the digital transformation has led to a new perspective on the distribution and enjoyment of creative content.

We have witnessed the emergence of new markets and *online* services, as well as the development of new *players* and new innovative *business* models. The widerange *of* services offered by *online* platforms has enabled them to play an intermediary role, managing, de facto, the circulation, processing, storage, and archiving of protected works and data.

Large platforms have thus assumed a position of unprecedented power in the copyright market by indiscriminately exploiting the works of other market actors and making the management of advertising (on third-party content) and the unregulated processing of users' data their core business. On the other hand, the progressive spread of highly innovative technologies have produced contrasting effects for industrial sectors characterised by a high exploitation of intellectual property rights (so-called "IPR-intensive").

While consumers have wider access to digital content and, therefore, new and potentially greater opportunities for its exploitation by right holders arise, dematerialisation has also facilitated the emergence of new forms of unauthorised exploitation that have proven difficult to combat.

The points from which this unavoidable process of modernisation of copyright law has taken its cue are undisputed: (i) adapting *copyright* to the digital ecosystem and the challenges of new technologies and (ii) strengthening the effectiveness of rights and promoting a more mature balance between the interests of authors/publishers and the general interest.[1]

The complexity of the situation is further exacerbated by the adoption, following Directive (EU) 790/2019 of 17 April 2019, on copyright and related rights in the digital single market (*Copyright* Directive), of several "horizontal" legislations, including, but not limited to, the new Audiovisual Media Services Directive (AVMS),[2] the recent European Media Freedom *Act* (*European Media* Freedom *Act*),[3] the *Digital Services Act* (DSA),[4] which although not specifically related to

[1] On this topic, see Falce (2012), p. 204 ff.; Ghidini and Falce (2022).

[2] On 10 December 2021, Legislative Decree No. 208/2021 concerning the new Consolidated Text on Audiovisual Media Services was published in the *Official Gazette* No. 293/2021 SO 44. The decree implements the Directive (EU) 2018/1808 of the European Parliament and of the Council of 14 November 2018 amending Directive 2010/13/EU on the coordination of certain provisions laid down by law, regulation or administrative action in Member States concerning the single text for the provision of audiovisual media services in the light of changing market realities.

[3] Regulation (EU) 2024/1083 of the European Parliament and of the Council of 11 April 2024 establishing a common framework for media services in the internal market and amending Directive 2010/13/EU (European regulation on media freedom).

[4] Regulation (EU) 2022/2065 of the European Parliament and of the Council of 19 October 2022 on a single market for digital services and amending Directive 2000/31/EC (Digital Services Act).

copyright, are helpful in retrospectively interpreting the new directive on copyright protection in the digital market, and, are in a dialectical relationship between *lex generalis* and *lex specialis* with, for example, a "key" provision of the Copyright Directive such as Art. 17.

It therefore becomes clear how all these issues revolve around responsibility and the "central" function of the *provider*, which can be defined as an intermediary that provides a link between those who intend to communicate information and the recipients of that information.[5] This contribution reflects critically on this figure within a network of newly introduced regulations that stand in a dialectical relationship with each other, ultimately pointing to a need for harmonisation that is (obviously) not yet fully achieved, both at the Union and domestic level.

2 The Role of the Intermediary in the E-commerce Directive and the Doctrinal Elaboration on the ISP's Liability

The regulatory references to start from are the well-known Directives 2001/29/EC (*InfoSoc Directive*) and 2000/31/EC (*E-commerce* Directive), which have outlined the prerequisites that must be met in order for the liability of Internet Service Providers (ISP) to be affirmed, depending on the activity carried out by the same, which is categorised as "*mere conduit*", "temporary storage", (or "*caching*") and "information storage" (or "*hosting*") services as per Articles 12, 13, and 14, implemented without substantial amendments by Legislative Decree no. 70/2003.

It is also well known that it was jurisprudence that drew up the aforementioned distinction between passive and active hosting, which allows the liability of the ISP to be affirmed based on different rules where the ISP has not merely "hosted" the unlawful content made available to the public by other parties, mainly on account of the relationship that can be established between its activity and the content itself.

In light of this taxonomy, it is immediately clear that the most relevant figure is that of the *content provider*, without prejudice to what case law has recently established regarding the "dynamic injunction", which shifts the emphasis to the role played by the *access provider*.[6]

[5] For an introduction about the taxonomy of *online* intermediaries and so-called *service providers*, see Dinwoodie (2020), pp. 37–56; Geiger et al., *Intermediary Liability and Fundamental Rights*, in Frosio (2020) p. 138; Angelopoulos and Smeth (2017), p. 266 ff.; Frosio and Husovec (2020), cit., pp. 613–630; Van Eecke (2011), p. 1479 ff.

[6] See Galli (2021); Frosio and Bulayenko (2021), p. 1128 ff.; Husovec (2017); Stella (2023), p. 891 ff.; as well as, more generally, what is reported in Cassano et al. (2023), *passim*. According to the Court of Milan, 18 June 2018: 'the European Commission affirmed the admissibility of orders, called "Dynamic Injunction", which extend also to sites not expressly indicated in the precautionary command; effective and efficient measures, which avoid the need for the establishment of subsequent judgments to strike and chase identical violations'. Thus Cassano and Tassone (2021), p. 115. Other jurisdictions have been ahead of their time, going so far as to devise said *dynamic*

Since the aforementioned rules on e-commerce and the case law emerging from the latter have been accompanied by endless scholarly work and judicial case law, rather than elaborating on the *technicalities* connected with the identification of the individual types of ISPs, it appears helpful to retrace some moments of the doctrinal elaboration on the subject.

In this regard, when the *E-Commerce* Directive was originally conceived, the entrepreneurial activities connected to Information Society services were at an early stage and the economic analysis of the law recalls that the reasons for resorting to limitations of liability to favour entrepreneurial sectors at a "nascent" stage is anything but new.[7]

It is precisely in the light of this consideration that we can explain the general principle of the absence of a general obligation to monitor and the rules on individual types of ISPs.At the same time, academia, legal scholars, and commentators have pointed out that *the E-Commerce* Directive sought to establish "an area without national borders for the services of the European information society" characterised by a system of "conditional irresponsibility".[8]

On this basis, both the European and the domestic legislator through the transposing legislation have ensured a form of "*safe harbour provisions*" to pursue a series of social purposes of special relevance.

In particular, these provisions are characterised by a preferential treatment and aimed at promoting the development of *e-commerce*, which would have been reasonably limited in the presence of an exceptionally rigid liability regime for market operators.[9]

In the United States, before the promulgation of the *Digital Millennium Copyright Act* of 1998 (hereinafter referred to as "DMCA") and the *Communications Decency Act* of 1996, a *report* prepared by the *Commerce Committee* was published, which pointed out that *e-commerce* constituted the form of emerging economy capable of ensuring a considerable increase in national wealth by 2002.[10] This prediction, which has come true today, called for the identification of forms of exemption from liability for ISPs that would ensure the operation of this business sector and facilitate substantial investments that would soon yield a significant social advantage.[11]

---

blocking injunctions in earlier times: see English judgment Cartier International AG & Others v. British Sky Broadcasting Limited and Others, 17 October 2014, EWHC 3354.

[7] Cooter et al. (2006), *passim*; Pardolesi and Tassone (2003), *passim*.

[8] For example, Parisi (2012), p. 388. See also Bocchini (2003), *passim*; Ponzanelli (2002), p. 87 ff.; Gambini (2006), p. 290.

[9] In this regard, the *E-commerce* Directive, Recital 2, highlights how 'the development of electronic commerce within the information society offers significant employment opportunities in the Community, particularly in small and medium-sized enterprises, and will stimulate economic growth and investment in innovation by European companies and can also enhance the competitiveness of European industry'.

[10] Dinwoodie (2017), p. 93 ff. On this topic, see also Farano (2012); Montagnani (2018), p. 75 ff., who recalls, on the subject of duty of care, a contribution by Ullrich (2017), p. 111 ff.

[11] The reference to the so-called *safe harbour* refers to the 'safety net' that has historically marked the development of digital platforms concerning the liability of network intermediaries for the

On the other hand, in the face of these social demands and in the absence of liability waiver provisions, ISPs would have had no incentive to improve their network systems. Still, they would have been concerned only with safeguarding their advantage and rent-seeking positions, adopting a defensive and anti-innovation approach.[12]

Moreover, in this direction, it is emphasised that, among the *rationale* of the discipline, there is also the one aimed at guaranteeing in the digital environment the widest freedom of information and free expression of thought, often emphasised in the rulings of the CJEU itself, as well as by the European Court of Human Rights.[13]

Therefore, the European rules on electronic commerce led to recognising service providers with a broad exemption from liability and the inexistence of any form of prior control over the information uploaded by their users, who remain solely responsible for any damage caused to third parties by the dissemination of this information.[14]

On the other hand, this legislative framework merely serves to adapt the general rules on civil liability to the new telematic context, without providing for a general principle of freedom and irresponsibility, so that for all the aspects not "covered" by it, the general rules on civil liability *pursuant to* under Art. 2043 et seq. of the Italian Civil Code became applicable and effective.[15]

At the procedural level, it is easy to conclude that, in the first case, it is the plaintiff (the injured party) who must prove that there are good reasons for derogating from the general rule of "freedom and irresponsibility" (i.e. that the conditions of exemption provided by the special rules do not apply). In contrast, in the second

---

content hosted on their services (which may be illegal and damaging to personal rights and freedoms). The DSA appears to overcome the attitude of protection towards platforms to the detriment of users and consumers and to prioritise a primacy of protection for the latter. It should be emphasised, however, that in the DSA's regulatory framework, the *safe harbour* instruments do not disappear. Under Art. 6 of the DSA, intermediaries cannot be held liable 'for information stored at the request of a recipient of the service' (and thus for 'hosted' content) provided, however, that they are not aware of illegal content, or that they promptly remove it or block access to it once they become aware of it. According to part of the doctrine, the need for the protection and safety of users and *online* consumers goes hand in hand with a minimum level of protection for platforms to stimulate innovation and competitiveness. On this topic see, *ex multis*, Englisch and Priora (2019), p. 128 ff.; Stucchi (2024), p. 271 ff.; Saavedra Servida (2024), p. 135 ff.

[12] Lemley and Reese (2004), pp. 1386–1390. See, also, Holland (2007), p. 101 ff.

[13] CJEU, Grand Sect., 9 March 2021, Case C-392/19, VG Bild-Kunst, in *Foro it*, 2021, IV, 447, with a footnote by Caso (2021), p. 2385, with a footnote by Boggio (2021); while on the relationship between violation of exclusive rights and free manifestation of expression under Arts. 10 ECHR and 21 Const., Corte Edu, 19 February 2013, Ref. no. 40397/12, FredrikNeij, Peter SundeKolmisoppi, in AIDA 2014.

[14] See Pagallo (2009), p. 733; Angelopolous and Senftleben (2021); . van Hoboken, Quintais, Poort, van Eijk (2018).

[15] according to The requirement of knowledge of the unlawfulness of the activity or of the information transmitted pursuant to Articles 16 and 17, Legislative Decree no. 70/2003, by the *provider* must be assessed according to the general criterion of fault and proven on a case by case basis. The system outlined by the EU legislator would be "incomplete", so that Article 2043 of the Italian Civil Code remains the reference standard on the matter.

case, it is the defendant (obviously the ISP) who must prove the existence of real "objective causes".

However, this interpretative option has remained confined mainly to theoretical reflections,[16] although there have been few judgments that have sought to aggravate the ISP's procedural position by placing on it the evidentiary burdens illustrated by the second thesis;[17] and there has been at least one ruling inclined to extend, in the opposite sense, the scope of Legislative Decree No. 70/2003.[18]

It is precisely in the light of this scenario that an epochal change occurred when some of those companies that were previously "nascent" and to be protected, became global and multinational companies, if not centres of power even more "powerful", in various respects, than the national States or countries (with a simultaneous proliferation of acronyms, such as Big Tech and GAFAM, used to identify essentially Google, Amazon, Facebook, Apple, Microsoft, the pioneers of the *tech economy*). This has led to a general and progressive tendency to consider exemption from liability as an exception to the rule, emphasising the shift from the "notice and take down" rule to the "notice and stay down" rule.[19] In this regard, the final decisive factor materialised in the "replacement" of the *E-commerce* Directive with the DSA and with the addition to the *puzzle* (already articulated in itself) of the piece of the *Copyright* Directive,[20] especially, with reference to Art. 17.

The following paragraphs will focus on these two regulations.

[16] See again Sartor (2020), p. 3; Bertolini et al. (2021), p. 26; Pasquale (2016), p. 494; Gillespie (2018), p. 32.

[17] See Tribunal Catania 29 June 2004, in *Foro it.*, 2005, I, 1259, which affirmed the liability of the *provider* who failed to prove its status of *service provider* and, therefore, its extraneousness to the creation of a site where an original work was present without consent, i.e. that he did not act as a *content provider.*

[18] Although this is a minority orientation, it should, however, be recalled that also App. Rome, 19 February 2018, no. 1065 rendered in the Previti/Wikipedia case, supported the extensive scope of Legislative Decree No. 70/2003 in place of the traditional criteria aimed at ascertaining liability for defamation by means other than the press.

[19] Kuczerawy (2024), cited above, pp. 525–543; Husovec (2019), pp. 53–84. See also, as to the change of perspective, European Commission Communication, *Tackling Illegal Content Online. Towards an enhanced responsibility of online platforms*, COM(2017) 555 final, s. 6; Kritkos (2021), p. 26.

[20] On the origin of the Copyright Directive and for a detailed commentary on it, see Rosati (2021), pp. 9–15; Id. (2023), pp. 118–122.

3 The *Copyright* Directive and the New Liability Structure Resulting from European Case Law (YouTube/Cyando and Poland v. Parliament and Council)

In the regulatory, doctrinal, and jurisprudential framework stratified over time, the *Copyright* Directive intervenes in a disruptive manner, whit Art. 17 essentially establishing that operators of platforms used for sharing content uploaded by users must obtain authorisation from the right holders (e.g. in the form of license agreements), at the time when protected content is made available to the public, unless they run the risk of being held directly liable for infringements of copyright and related rights of third parties.[21]

Although it is beyond the scope of the present discussion to analyse in detail the *Copyright* Directive[22] and the Legislative Decree No. 177 of 8 November 2021,[23] it should be noted that, after providing for the need for an authorisation, the *Copyright* Directive establishes the right to adequate and proportionate remuneration, so that many tensions are transferred towards the negotiation phase and the "supplementary" mechanisms in the event of failure to reach an agreement (the role that collecting societies will play shortly remaining in the background).[24]

Given the above, it seems premature to assess the real impact of Legislative Decree No. 177/2021. Notwithstanding, it has to be noted that rules already adopted are in line with those that contribute to addressing the issue of the filtering activities: according to Art. 102-septies of the Italian Copyright Law (Law No. 633 of 22 April 1941), providers of online content sharing services (hereinafter "OCSSPs"), in the

[21] On the liability regime of the directive mentioned in the text, let us refer to Falce and Faraone (2021), p. 12 ff.; Ercolani and La Rosa (2024), p. 169 ff.; Cogo (2019), p. 68 ff.; Spoerri (2019); Frosio (2020), p. 709; Lambrecht (2020); Spindler (2019), p. 334; Dussolier (2020), p. 979; Husovec and Quintais (2021); Schwemer and Schovsbo (2020); Grisse (2019), p. 887; Rendas (2022), p. 54. As a preliminary remark, it is important to note that Art. 17(10) tasks the EU Commission with organising stakeholder dialogues to ensure the uniform application of the obligation of cooperation between OCSSPs and right holders, as well as to establish best practices regarding the appropriate industry standards of professional diligence. These stakeholder dialogues resulted in the publication of the EU Commission Guidance on the interpretation of Art. 17. The Guidance was adopted as a Communication, and is therefore not binding. (at least in principle). Still, it is a useful document to assist in the interpretation of Art. 17. See Reda and Keller (2021). For an overview of different national implementations of Art. 17 and their implications, see Angelopoulos (2022).

[22] While only touching on some of the policy areas outlined in the 2015 Digital Single Market Strategy, the text of the directive is longer and significantly more detailed and complex than the European Commission's original 2016 proposal. Communication from the Commission to the European Parliament, the Council, the European Economic and Social Committee and the Committee of the Regions, Strategy for a Digital Single Market in Europe, Brussels, 6 May 2015 COM(2015) 192 final. See Proposal for a Directive of the European Parliament and of the Council on Copyright in the Digital Single Market, Brussels, 14 June 2016 COM(2016) 593 final 2016/0280(COD).

[23] Rosati (2023), pp. 31, 46–48; Cogo and Lavagnini (2024), p. 1 ff.

[24] Ginsburg (2022), p. 125 ff.

absence of the authorisation referred to in Art. 102-sexies and after having received a sufficiently reasoned report, are liable, among other things, if they have not "*promptly disabled access to or removed from their websites the works or other subject-matter of the report and have made* [...] *their utmost efforts to prevent their uploading in the future*", although paragraph 4 makes it clear that this is not intended to impose a general obligation to monitor.[25]

In any case, when, in the absence of an agreement, the liability of this particular type of ISP arises (at least potentially), we assist to an epochal paradigm shift.[26] In this context, we are referring to a form of "liability" of platforms and ISPs whenever they play an "active role" also through the "optimisation of the presentation of materials or their promotion".[27]

Indeed, the CJEU, in Case C-401/19 (Republic of Poland v. Parliament and Council), ruled on the compatibility of the new liability regime of OCSSPs for the unlawful uploading by their users of content protected by copyright or other similar rights, introduced by Article 17 of the *Copyright* Directive, with the protection of the fundamental right to freedom of expression.[28] The ruling stemmed from an action for annulment brought under Article 263 of the Treaty on the Functioning of the European Union (TFEU) by the Republic of Poland, which argued that the aforementioned provision, by requiring platforms, as a condition for obtaining exemption from liability, to adopt automatic content filtering and blocking systems, would result in an infringement of the freedom of expression and information protected by Article 11 of the Charter of Fundamental Rights of the European Union. The Court of Justice dismissed the action stating that the burden imposed on OCSSPs to verify and filter content that users wish to disseminate to the public is accompanied by sufficient safeguards to ensure its compatibility with respect to freedom of expression and information.

Before examining the Court's arguments, it is necessary to briefly summarise the essential elements of the new—and stricter—liability regime of OCSSPs for users uploading material that infringes copyright or other similar rights.[29]

The new regime applies to providers of *online* content-sharing services, defined in Art. 2(6) of the same directive as providers "of *information society services whose principal purpose or one of the principal purposes is to store and give public*

---

[25] Furthermore, for paragraph 2 '[t]o determine, in accordance with the principle of proportionality, whether the provider of online content-sharing services is exempt from liability, the type, audience and size of the service and the type of works or other material uploaded by the users of the service, as well as the availability of adequate and effective tools and the cost thereof for the service providers shall also be taken into account on a case-by-case basis. In any event, the provider of online content sharing services that practices or facilitates copyright piracy is not exempt from liability'.

[26] See Di Ciommo (2019), p. 557; Panetta and Rovati (2019), p. 261. For European case law on *hosting provider* liability, see Court of Justice 7 August 2018, C-521/17, Cooperatieve Vereniging SNB-REACT U.A.; Court of Justice 11 September 2014, C-291/13, Sotiris Papasavvas; Court of Justice 12 July 2011, C-324/09, L'Oréal.

[27] See Bently and Sickle (2017); Sickle (2017).

[28] Jütte and Priora (2022), pp. 44, 631, 635; Husovec (2023), pp. 60, 173, 104–195.

[29] Cf. Guzel (2021), p. 205 ff.

access to large amounts of copyright-protected works or other protected subject-matter uploaded by its users, which it organises and promotes for profit". Some particular subjects, such as non-profit online encyclopedias, platforms for developing and sharing *open source* software and other cases expressly provided for remain excluded.

In its final version, Art. 17 of the *Copyright* Directive clarifies that OCSSPs, when they allow the public to access works uploaded by users that are protected by copyright or other similar rights, are performing an act of communication to the public or an act of making available to the public. This is a substantial novelty; previously, it was held that OCSSPs did not carry out any communication to the public of the material uploaded onto their platforms as long as their role was only technical, automatic, and passive. In fact, the CJEU had clearly come to this conclusion in its judgement in Youtube and Cyando (judgment of 22 June 2021, Joined Cases C-682/18 and C-683/18),[30] in which it had brought the liability of OCSSPs for the uploading of content infringing intellectual property rights under the regime provided for in Article 3 of Directive 2001/29/EC and Article 14 of the E-Commerce Directive, which, as the CJEU had held that OCSSPs were not liable for the uploading of content infringing intellectual property rights. Art. 14 of the *E-Commerce* Directive, which, as well known, provides that the provider of an information society service consisting in the storage of information provided by a user (hosting provider) is not liable for the uploading of unlawful content by users provided that provider: "(a) does not have actual knowledge that the activity or information is unlawful and, as regards actions for damages, is not aware of facts or circumstances which make manifest the unlawfulness of the activity and information, or (b) as soon as it becomes aware of those facts, acts immediately to remove the information or disable access to it".

In the above-mentioned Youtube and Cyando judgement, in particular, the CJEU stated that the operator of a content-sharing platform does not carry out a communication to the public and, therefore, its activity falls within the scope of the exemption from liability provided for in Article 14, provided that the operator does not play a role defined as "active" in the commission of the infringement. It is considered that a "hosting provider" plays an active role when it does not limit itself to carrying out merely technical and automatic activities, but actively contributes to making unlawful content available to the public, for instance by carrying out indexing or cataloguing operations or by failing to promptly disable access to content of whose unlawfulness it is fully aware.[31]

The current qualification of the conduct of OCSSPs as an act of communication to the public implies, as confirmed by the third paragraph of Art. 17, that the entities referred to in the directive can no longer benefit from the exemption regime provided for in Art. 14(1) of the *E-Commerce* Directive. Consequently, in order to be

[30] See Geiger and Jütte (2021), pp. 625–635; Id. (2021), p. 517; Reda (2021); Angelopoulos (2021).

[31] On the notion of active *hosting provider* in Italian jurisprudence see, most recently, Cass., sec. I, ord. 13 December 2021, no. 39763.

exempt from liability for the publication of infringing content on their platform, OCSSPs would have to obtain authorisation from the right holders involved, e.g. by concluding a special license agreement.

However, since OCSSPs allow a great deal of content to be shared directly by users, the Directive provides for certain conditions under which *providers* are exempted from liability even in the absence of such authorisation.

In particular, in the event of the uploading of illegal content by the users, OCSSPs are not held liable if they can prove the cumulative fulfilment of three conditions set out in paragraph 4 of Art. 17: "(a) having made best efforts to obtain an authorisation; and (b) having made, in accordance with high standards of professional industry diligence, best efforts to ensure the unavailability of specific works and other materials for which they have received relevant and necessary information from the right holders are not available; and in any event (c) having acted expeditiously, after having received a sufficiently reasoned and substantiated notice from the right holders, to disable access to or remove from their websites the works or other subject-matter in respect of which they have received a notice and having made utmost efforts to prevent their future uploading in accordance with subparagraph (b)".

It seems clear that the liability exemption regime provided for in Art. 17 is stricter than the one provided for in Art. 14 of the *E-Commerce* Directive; in fact, the OCSSPs must not only undertake immediate action to disable access to content after receiving a report but must also do everything in their power to ensure the unavailability of specific works and subject matter for which right holders have provided them necessary and relevant information , as well as to prevent the future uploading of content already reported as illicit: the obligation to take action, therefore, does not arise only after a copyright infringement has occurred, but must also be acted upon in advance to prevent the occurrence and recurrence of such infringements.[32]

Returning to the merits of the issue,[33] the CJEU, therefore, while rejecting the appeal, agrees with Poland on a fundamental point: compliance with the conditions

[32] Quintais (2020), pp. 39–43; Falce and Faraone (2021), cit., p. 12 ff; Husovec and Quintais (2021), p. 325.

[33] The Republic of Poland had requested, principally, the annulment of only para. 4(b) and (c) limited to the obligation to make 'utmost efforts to prevent future loading in accordance with (b)' and, in the alternative, the annulment of the whole of Article 17. Considering subparagraphs (b) and (c) of Article 17(4) to be inseparable from the remaining paragraphs of the same provision, the Court of Justice held that the application for annulment brought as a principal claim was inadmissible and, therefore, focused on the application for annulment of the whole of Article 17. The Polish action was essentially based on the alleged incompatibility between the preventive measures imposed on OCSSPs in order to obtain exemption from liability for the uploading of illegal content by their users and the right to free expression and information protected by Article 11 of the EU Charter of Fundamental Rights. That right, as emphasised by the Court in paragraphs 44 and 46 of the judgment under review, includes both the freedom to hold opinions and to 'receive and impart information or ideas without interference by public authorities and without frontiers' and protects not only the content of the information but also the means by which it is disseminated. In the applicant's view, compliance with the conditions imposed in order to benefit from the exemption from liability would impose a burden of prior monitoring of the content that users would wish to upload onto the platform and would necessarily entail, in the state of the art, the obligation to use auto-

laid down in Article 17 requires, in fact, the adoption of automatic tools for recognising and filtering content that may result in a restriction on the dissemination of *online* content and, in general, on the full exercise of freedom of expression. Therefore, the CJEU, in line with the Advocate General's reasoning, recognises, at para. 58, that the liability regime introduced by Art. 17(4) of the *Copyright* Directive "entails a limitation on the exercise of the right to freedom of expression and information of users of those content-sharing services, guaranteed in Art. 11 of the Charter".

However, the CJEU does not stop there, but recalls that a restriction on fundamental rights can be legitimate if it meets all the requirements of Article 52(1) of the European Charter on Human Rights. In fact, according to that provision, in compliance with their essential content, fundamental rights may be subject to restrictions laid down by law, in accordance with the principle of proportionality, if these are "necessary and genuinely meet objectives of general interest recognised by the European Union or the need to protect the rights and freedoms of others".

In order to assess the legitimacy of the balancing act carried out between freedom of expression and the protection of the interests of right holders and other related rights, it is necessary to examine paragraph 4 not in isolation, but in the light of Art. 17 as a whole, and taking into account that the legislation has the legitimate aim of protecting intellectual property rights, protected by Article 17(2) of the Charter of Fundamental Rights of the European Union.

The most delicate point is the respect of the principle of proportionality: limitations on the rights and freedoms guaranteed by the Charter may not exceed what is "appropriate and necessary" to achieve the legitimate aims pursued or to protect the rights and freedoms of others, and, among the many appropriate measures, the least restrictive one that does not cause disproportionate inconveniences in relation to the aims pursued must be adopted; moreover, the law providing for a limitation to a fundamental right—in particular when such a restriction derives from automated processing—should set minimum requirements as well as clearly establish the circumstances and conditions under which the restriction may be applied.[34]

---

matic filtering and blocking *software*. Such systems, however, are often unable to take into account the context in which the alleged infringement takes place and to clearly distinguish lawful from unlawful content. Thus, the use of automatic systems based on 'comparison' algorithms would risk preventing the uploading and dissemination to the public of content that is, in fact, perfectly lawful, resulting in an infringement of the essential content of freedom of expression. Advocate General Henrik Saugmandsgaard Øe, in a non-binding opinion issued last year, had agreed, at least in part, with Poland's arguments, admitting that, in fact, the new regime requires the adoption of automatic filters that may not be able to perfectly distinguish lawful from unlawful content. However, the Advocate General, in the same opinion, also emphasised that, provided that all the guarantees provided for in the remaining paragraphs of Article 17 are respected, the new regime is compatible with the rights protected by the European Charter of Human Rights; a reasoning that, as will be seen shortly, was reiterated by the CJEU in the judgment under review. See Husovec (2023), p. 173.

[34] CJEU (Grand Chamber), judgment of 16 July 2020, C-311/18, *Data Protection Commissioner* v Facebook Ireland Limited and Maximillian Schrems, paragraph 176.

In this ruling, the CJEU notes that while, on the one hand, it is true that Art. 17 does not clearly identify the measures that content-sharing service providers must adopt, resorting to the imposition of an obligation to carry out so-called "*best efforts*" to be assessed in accordance with professional diligence in the sector, on the other hand, it cannot be ignored that, in a constantly changing field such as the one under consideration, the wording adopted may be better suited to ensure constant adaptation to technological evolution.[35]

The CJEU, however, draws certain limits regarding the technical measures to be taken. Indeed, even if the directive leaves discretion, according to paragraphs 7 and 9 of Art. 17 as well as Recitals 66 and 70 of the directive, all measures that risk blocking even lawful content during the *upload* phase must be excluded. An automatic selection system unable to distinguish between lawful and unlawful content does not respect the right balance between freedom of expression and the protection of intellectual property of the right holders.

Indeed, the first paragraph of Section 7 clarifies that "cooperation between *online* content-sharing service providers and right holders shall not result in the prevention of the availability of works or other subject-matter uploaded by users, which do not infringe copyright or related rights, including where such works or other subject-matter are covered by an exception or limitation". This provision—to be read in conjunction with the third paragraph of Section 9 (which states that the Directive in no way affects legitimate uses such as under exceptions or limitations)—provides for a specific obligation of result: the system concretely adopted by the platforms must be able to clearly distinguish between unlawful and lawful content, including statutory exceptions to copyright (quotation, criticism, review, caricature, parody or *pastiche*).

The CJEU emphasises that Art. 17, as reiterated in Section 8 and in accordance with what has already been established by Article 15(1) of the *E-Commerce* Directive, does not impose a general obligation of prior surveillance and monitoring, but liability arises only where right holders "provide relevant and necessary information about such content"; in the absence of such information, service providers are not led to block material uploaded.[36] Furthermore, the CJEU, referring by analogy to the Glawischnig-Piesczek judgement, emphasises that OCSSPs are not obliged to filter and block content whose unlawfulness should be established by means of "an independent assessment [...] in the light of the information provided by the right holders as well as any exceptions and limitations to copyright".[37]

With this ruling, the CJEUourt, although not explicitly, seems to affirm that the monitoring obligation imposed on OCSSPs would, in fact, only concern manifestly infringing content, in line with the Advocate General's argument. Following this interpretation, the CJEU emphasises, in paragraph 91, that the notification made by

[35] This is also in light of the case law of the CJEU, Judgment 16 June 2015, Delfi AS v. Estonia (No. 64569/09).

[36] See also the contribution of Senftleben and Angelopoulos (2020).

[37] CJEU (Third Chamber), judgment of 3 October 2019, Case C-18/18, Eva Glawischnig-Piesczek v Facebook Ireland Limited. See Monti (2019) and Rauchegger and Kuczerawy (2020).

right holders must contain sufficient elements to enable the provider to ascertain the unlawful nature of the content "without the need to carry out an in-depth legal examination". Interpreting the provision in the terms just set out, the CJEU considers that the liability regime provided for in Art. 17 does not implyl an infringement of the essential content of freedom of expression and is appropriate and necessary to ensure effective protection of intellectual property rights in the *online environment*.

Art. 17 contains additional procedural safeguards to ensure that the instruments adopted by OCSSPs do not result in an infringement of freedom of expression. In particular, in order to reduce the risk that providers disable lawful content by mistake or, in any case, without justification, OCSSPs must render available a complaint mechanism that operates without undue delay and that provides, in any case, for a human review; this mechanism must be accompanied by the availability of out-of-court dispute resolution means as well as the possibility to appeal to the courts.

Lastly, Section 10 of Art. 17 entrusts the Commission with the task of organising meetings between interested parties aimed at establishing best practices for cooperation between OCSSPs and right holders taking into account, in particular, 'the need to balance between fundamental rights and the use of exceptions and limitations'.

The CJEU, therefore, while agreeing with Poland that the automatic upload filters made necessary in order to comply with the conditions imposed by Article 17(4) pose a risk to the protection of freedom of expression, considers that Article 17, as a whole, contains sufficient safeguards to make the filtering obligation justified and proportionate in the light of EU law.

A key point in the argument proposed by the CJEU to defend Art. 17 is the prospect of a hierarchy between the obligations laid down by Art. 17: the conditions imposed by Section 4 are mere obligations of '*best efforts*'; on the other hand, the obligation, laid down in Sections 7 and 9, to prevent the unavailability of lawful content constitutes a specific obligation of result. It seems, therefore, also in the light of the Advocate General's conclusions and the EU Commission's guidelines, that the use of upload filters should be limited to manifestly illegal content (or content whose unlawfulness has already been ascertained in court) and, instead, should be excluded with reference to cases in which ascertaining the unlawful nature would require an *ad hoc* investigation of the context in which the alleged infringement takes place. Loading filters should therefore be used in such a way as to minimise the risk of censoring even content that is in fact lawful.

4 The DSA and the New Obligations for Platforms

The DSA, through the publication of which a fundamental part of the European Digital Strategy was implemented, is a very complex text.[38] This is demonstrated by the Commission's Accompanying Report to its own Proposal, which devoted almost four pages only to the illustration of its contents[39]: not to mention that—as emerges from the Legislative Resolution of the European Parliament of 5 July 2022—this text was then incisively enriched, reaching a length of 312 pages.[40]

The DSA, which was published in the Official Journal of the European Union in October 2022, represents the biggest change of rules for the liability of *online* intermediaries in twenty years, bringing in a new and composite regulatory framework that—through the introduction of significant obligations and duties of diligence for *providers*—aims to reconcile different needs: providing a response to the risks caused by user-generated content, protecting fundamental rights, with particular regard to freedom of expression, while finding solutions to the practical limits of content moderation.[41]

This intervention is part of the European Union's strategy aimed at laying the foundations, anticipating other countries and non-EU countries, for the affirmation of a complete digital public policy, pursuing both the consolidation of global leadership in the field of platform regulation, and the containment of the proliferation of national disciplines on the subject that could lead to a problematic lack of homogeneity of approaches in the internal market.[42]

Without needing to dwell on its articulated regulatory framework, only the first of the two main areas of which it is composed—Chapters II and III (Arts. 4-48), while Chapter I is devoted to the scope of application and general definitions—revolves around the issue of ISPs' liability and the obligations incumbent upon them.

In this regard, it is immediately apparent that—in line with other normative provisions, including the *Copyright* Directive—an asymmetrical and vertical approach (linked to the size of the economic operator and, in part, to its *business* models) is

[38] For a recent overview of the DSA (Regulation (EU) 2022/2065), see M. Husovec (2024), p. 17; Id. (2024); Frosio and Geiger (2023), pp. 29(1–2), 31–77; Husovece and Roche Laguna (2022); the collected volume edited by Von Ungern-Sternberg (2023), as well as that edited by Van Hoboken et al. (2023); Manganelli and Nicita (2022). In the Italian context, see Morgese (2021), p. 32 and the various contributions published in Issue No. 1/2023 of the *Internet Law Review*.

[39] COM(2020) 825 final.

[40] P9_TA(2022)0269.

[41] This is the effective summary of Church and Pehlivan (2022), p. 53, who call the DSA "the biggest shake-up to the rules for online intermediary liability in twenty years". For an analysis of the Regulation with a *focus on* its ethical-social impact, see Turillazzi et al. (2023), p. 83 ff.

[42] Buttarelli (2023), p. 120, recalls, in particular, the German Netzwerkdurchsetzungsgesetz, NetzDG of 2017 on the subject of obligations to remove or block illegal N

accompanied and sustained by an approach that is symmetrical and horizontal (concerning illegal content per se considered).[43]

However, in Chapter II (Arts. 4-10) containing the rules applicable to all intermediary service providers (i.e. ISPs according to the above-mentioned typologies outlined by the *E-Commerce* Directive), the issue of ISP liability is addressed by reiterating the absence of a general obligation of monitoring (Art. 8).[44]

Moreover, among the provisions dictated only for the passive *hosting provider* by Section II of Chapter III (Arts. 16-18)—and on this point lies the main difference from the previous discipline, with the 'step backwards' mentioned above—there is one requiring that the report must include 'a clear indication of the exact electronic location of such information, such as the exact URL address(es) and, if necessary, additional information enabling the identification of illegal content appropriate to the type of content and the specific type of information storage service' (Art. 16). In essence, all platforms must also set up an 'effective reporting mechanism' for allegedly illegal content, adequately justify the service recipient's information restriction decisions with respect to their illegality or inconsistency with their general terms and conditions (Art. 17), and provide for an internal complaints handling system (Art. 20) relating to their own decisions to restrict illegal content or information (inconsistent with their general terms and conditions).

The European Union's intention to achieve even greater 'standardisation' on the matter clearly emerges and is testified by Recital 9 of the DSA.

[43] The DSA differentiates its prescriptions on the basis of the 'size' of the interested party. Thus, a distinction is made between generally applicable rules, rules that apply to 'online platforms' (excluding micro and small enterprises) and, finally, rules that apply only to 'very large online platforms' (the so-called Very Large Online Platforms or "VLOPs") or to "very large search engines" (so-called Very Large Online Search Engines or "VLOSEs"), i.e. those platforms or search engines providing their services to an average monthly number of active recipients of the service in the Union of forty-five million or more. Nineteen digital service providers were designated as Vlops and Vloses by designation decisions of 25 April 2023: seventeen are large platforms (Alibaba AliExpress, Amazon Store, Apple AppStore, Booking.com, Facebook, Google Play, Google Maps, Google Shopping, Instagram, Linkedin, Pinterest, Snapchat, TikTok, Twitter, Wikipedia, You Tube, Zalando) and two are large search engines (Bing and Google search). The adoption of the designation decisions led to the lodging of two appeals by Zalando—according to which the Commission did not use "standardised criteria or a clear methodology" to identify Vlops, making a selection in a "causal and uneven manner"—and by Amazon, which does not consider that its online platform has the characteristics indicated in the DSA to be considered Vlop. See, on this subject, https://digital-strategy.ec.europa.eu/en/policies/list-designated-vlops-and-vloses. See, in general, on this approach, Eifert et al. (2021), p. 987; De Gregorio and Dunn (2022), p. 473.

[44] According to which 'no general obligation is imposed on intermediary service providers to monitor the information that such providers transmit or store, or to actively seek out facts or circumstances indicating the presence of illegal activities'. However, they are obliged, if they receive an order to counteract one or more illegal contents from a judicial or administrative authority, to inform the same authority without delay of the action taken on the order. Senftleben and Angelopoulos (2020), p. 23; Frosio (2022), pp. 1145–1148; Quintais and. Schwemmer (2022), pp. 191, 197.

Moreover, although such a dynamic is not unusual when one wants to achieve a greater uniformity of rules, the intention of the EU legislator is, however, implemented with a peculiar legislative technique, because Arts. 4, 5 and 6 of the DSA duplicated Arts. 12, 13, and 14 of the *E-commerce* Directive, which is not even repealed (and, on the contrary, its survival is at least partly predicted by Recital 9).[45]

In this complex regulatory architecture, the DSA inserts an important model of co-regulation.[46]

First of all, the regulation not only takes into consideration "codes of conduct" (Art. 45 and 46), but significantly accompanied them with other soft regulation measures (to use the nomenclature illustrated in the Better Regulation Toolbox); some of them are already known, such as the "voluntary standards" established by the "competent European and international standardisation bodies" (Art. 44); others are innovative, such as the 'crisis protocols' (Art. 48), a new source, which is not easy to qualify, provided to deal with extraordinary circumstances affecting public health or safety.[47] The drafting of such protocols constituting 'atypical' acts of co-regulation[48] is initiated by the Commission and envisages the involvement, in the

[45] Indeed, according to the Recital referred to in the text, 'Member States should not adopt or maintain additional national requirements in relation to matters falling within the scope of this Regulation, unless expressly provided otherwise herein, as this would affect the direct and uniform application of the fully harmonised rules applicable to intermediary service providers in accordance with the objectives of this Regulation', but it is considered immediately thereafter 'appropriate that this should not preclude the possibility of applying other national rules applicable to intermediary service providers in accordance with Union law, including Directive 2000/31/EC, in particular Article 3 thereof, where the provisions of national law pursue legitimate public interest objectives other than those pursued by this Regulation'. For an up-to-date overview, see Frosio (2025).

[46] See, among others, Simoncini (2022), p. 1031; Pollicino (2022), p. 1051.

[47] Recital 91 DSA reads as follows: 'In times of crisis, certain specific measures may need to be taken urgently by providers of very large online platforms, in addition to the measures they would take in view of their other obligations under this Regulation. In this regard, a crisis should be considered to occur when exceptional circumstances arise that may lead to a serious threat to public safety or public health in the Union or significant parts thereof. Such crises could result from armed conflicts or acts of terrorism, including emerging conflicts or acts of terrorism, natural disasters such as earthquakes and hurricanes, as well as pandemics and other serious threats to public health of a cross-border nature. The Commission should be able to request very large online platform providers and very large online search engine providers, on the recommendation of the European Digital Services Committee, to initiate a crisis response as a matter of urgency. Measures that these providers may identify and consider applying may include, for instance, adjusting content moderation processes and increasing resources allocated to content moderation, adjusting the general conditions, algorithmic systems and relevant advertising systems, further intensifying cooperation with trusted beacons, adopting awareness-raising measures, promoting trustworthy information and adjusting the design of their online interfaces'.

[48] See Recitals 99 and 108, as well as Article 48 of the DSA.

drafting, testing and application phase, of the VLOPs as well as, where necessary, of civil society organisations.

Two examples of (already existing) codes of conductmay be expressly mentioned: the 'code of conduct against illegal forms of online hate speech'[49] and the 'reinforced' code of practice on disinformation'. [50]a new version of the first 2018 Code ofPractice on Disinformation of 2018.[51]

This new model of co-regulation, which takes the form of an encouragement towards the elaboration of codes of conduct,[52] in conjunction with the traditional *notice and action* provisions introduced in Art. 14 of the DSA and the *notice and take down and notice and stay down* procedures of "illegal" content in Art. 17 of the *Copyright* Directive, can certainly represent a significant novelty in view of a subsequent "readjustment" to the protection towards *online* investors.[53]

Furthermore, reading through the text of the DSA, the provisions on *trusted flaggers*, i.e. those third parties who make use of the tools made available by *online* service providers to report content which, in their opinion, must be subject to moderation or removal,[54] may be useful and encouraged.

---

[49] In May 2016, to prevent and counter the spread of illegal online hate speech, the Commission agreed with Facebook, Microsoft, Twitter and YouTube on a 'Code of Conduct to counter illegal online hate speech'. During 2018, Instagram, Snapchat and Dailymotion joined the Code of Conduct; Jeuxvideo.com in January 2019; TikTok in 2020 and LinkedIn in 2021. In May and June 2022, Rakuten Viber and Twitch finally joined, respectively. See also Recital 62 of the DSA.

[50] The Code of Practice on Disinformation 2022, available at the following link: digital-strategy.ec.europa.eu/en/library/2022-strengthened-code-practice-disinformation. The Code currently has over 40 signatories, including the following VLOP and VLOSE designees: Google Search & YouTube (Google), Instagram and Facebook (Meta), Bing and LinkedIn (Microsoft) and TikTok.

[51] Code of Practice on Disinformation 2018, in digital-strategy.ec.europa.eu/en/library/2018-code-practice-disinformation.

[52] The co-regulatory model of the DSA is different. Unlike the GDPR model, there is no mandatory control over codes of conduct. Nevertheless, Art. 45 expressly attributes to the Commission and the Committee, in addition to the promotion role, the function of ensuring compliance with the principles concerning the purpose and content of the codes themselves, as well as their concrete application. It is thus preferred to a formal control centred on 'subjective' requirements, a substantial control on the 'objective' requirements of the proposed legislation. Finally, there is no mention of 'publicity' or 'transposition' functions in the DSA draft. On the other hand, the Committee (and not the Commission) is entrusted with a specific function of *ex-post* monitoring of the achievement of the objectives of the codes and publication of the results.

[53] The Code of Conduct to counter illegal *online* hate speech, first, on 20 January 2025, and the Code of Conduct on Disinformation, later, on 20 February 2025, were integrated by the Commission and the European Digital Services Committee within the framework of the DSA, constituting the so-called 'Code of Conduct on Disinformation', in force since 1 July 2025. For further details, please refer to the following *link:* https://digital-strategy.ec.europa.eu/en/policies/dsa-codes-conduct.

[54] See Article 22 of the DSA. See, on this, Davola and Monti (2023), p. 59 ff.

The status of trusted reporter is granted by the digital services coordinator of each Member-State at the request of entities "that [have] demonstrated, inter alia, that they have special skills and expertise in the fight against illegal content and that they carry out their activities in a diligent, accurate and objective manner".[55]

Finally, it is obvious that the CJEU may be more "directly" involved in the various theoretical questions whicht revolve around the rules defining the ISP's liability[56] and the structure of the powers regarding content moderation.

Nevertheless, although these provisions are formulated in general terms, they seem to introduce at least an incentive, if not an obligation,[57] to be proactive in content moderation in order to mitigate certain types of systemic risks. This interpretation seems to be confirmed by the opening of the Commission of a proceeding for violation of the DSA, and in particular of Arts. 34 (1), 34 (2) and 35 (1), against X (Twitter) for not having put in place effective measures against illegal content and disinformation[58] and by the requests for information sent concerning the cutback of staff dedicated to moderation.[59] More specifically, with regard to the first investigation opened in December 2023, the Commission focused on the following profiles: (i) compliance with the DSA's obligations relating to the fight against and the dissemination of illegal content within the Union, in particular in relation to the risk assessment and the mitigation measures adopted by X, as well as the functioning of the mechanism for notifying illegal content, also in the light of X's content moderation resources; (ii) the effectiveness of the measures adopted to counter the

[55] Recital 61 of the DSA. The same Recital mentions as examples of trustworthy reporters Europol—a public entity—and INHOPE—a global network of hotlines—which have proven over the years to reliably and accurately carry out their *web* monitoring activities for the removal of terrorist and child pornography content respectively. As for the Italian case, recently, on 22 January 2025, the AGCOM, designated as Digital Services Coordinator, pursuant to Article 49, paragraph 2, of the DSA, The Council of the Authority, in its session of 22 January last, approved the first resolution recognising the qualification of reliable reporter pursuant to Article 22 of the DSA (resolution No. 26/25/CONS) to the company Argo Business Solutions S.r.l., in relation to the issues of infringement of intellectual property rights and other commercial rights, as well as the fight against online fraud and scams.

[56] Frosio and Geiger (2023), cit., pp. 31–77.

[57] For a critique of this approach see, for example: Helberger (2020), pp. 842–854; Frosio and Geiger (2023), cit., p. 45.

[58] V. European Commission, DSA.100100 - X (formerly Twitter) - Investigation into compliance with articles 34 (1) and (2), 35 (1), 16 (5) and (6) of Regulation (EU) 2022/2065, 18.12.2023, C (2023) 9137final. The same remarks can be made with regard to the letter that Commissioner Thierry Breton sent to TikTok (but also X and Meta) concerning terrorist content after the Hamas attack on 7 October 2023 (www.x.com/ThierryBreton/status/.1712472108222329056?lang=en).

[59] See Commission press release dated 8 May 2024, 'Commission requests information from X on decreasing content moderation resources under the Digital Services Act', available at: www.digital-strategy.ec.europa.eu/en/news/commission-requests-information-x-decreasing-. content-moderation-resources-under-digitalservices.

manipulation of information on the platform, in particular the effectiveness of the so-called "Community Notes", of X within the Union[60] and the effectiveness of the related risk mitigation policies for civil discourse and electoral processes; (iii) the measures taken by X to increase the transparency of its platform; and (iv) the suspicion of a misleading design of the user interface, in relation to the legal tick marks to certain subscription products (the so-called "Blue checks").[61] Shortly thereafter, the Commission followed up with the opening of further investigations against

[60] In January 2025, Meta announced that it would start experimenting, at least in the United States, as of 18 March 2025, with the Community Notes system, already used by X (Twitter), on Facebook, Instagram and Threads. See the New York Times article, *Meta Says It Will End Its Fact-Checking Program on Social Media Posts*, 7 January 2025, available at: https://www.nytimes.com/live/2025/01/07/business/meta-fact-checking. With the acquisition by Elon Musk, X has in fact introduced radical changes in content moderation, moving towards a model based on user participation. At the heart of this transformation are Community Notes, a system that allows users to add annotations to posts deemed misleading, validating them through a diverse group of reviewers (X Help Center). This decentralised approach presents both opportunities and risks: on the one hand, it favours transparency and direct involvement of users, reducing the risk of censorship; on the other, to be truly effective, it requires broad and competent participation. In the absence of adequate control, inaccurate results may emerge, while disinformation may continue to spread before corrective annotations are added, temporarily compromising the reliability of the information. It also casts doubts on the ability of platforms to contain disinformation at critical times, such as during election campaigns or health crises. Moreover, Meta's decision risks influencing other platforms, pushing them towards less stringent and more self-regulating models that could reduce public trust in *online* information. The new system will replace the *fact-checking* system, i.e. the one introduced in 2016 and based on collaboration with external organisations certified by the *International Fact-Checking Network* (IFCN) to identify and verify potentially false or misleading content. Demonstrating that digital platforms themselves are at the heart of the European strategy to combat disinformation, the Commission has included the issue of content tracking and transparency in the DSA, imposing precise obligations on VLOPs, including the obligation to collaborate with certified *fact-checkers* and to actively mitigate systemic risks related to disinformation.

[61] The preliminary findings of the investigation, published on 12 July 2024, confirmed the violation of the DSA in relation to the last two aspects. Furthermore, on 17 January 2025, the Commission extended the investigation to the suggestion algorithm and requested that documentation be kept on certain changes made up to that date. Finally, the Commission submitted a request for access to some of X's commercial APIs, technical interfaces for its content that allow a direct investigation into the moderation of content and the 'virality' of *accounts*. For further details, see Daily News, 17 January 2025 'Commission addresses additional investigatory measures to X in the ongoing proceedings under the Digital Services Act', available at: https://ec.europa.eu/commission/presscorner/detail/en/mex_25_287 and press release dated 12 July 2024 'Commission sends preliminary findings to X for breach of the Digital Services Act', available at: https://ec.europa.eu/commission/presscorner/detail/en/ip_24_3761.

TikTok in February,[62] in April[63] and December 2024,[64] AliExpress in March 2024,[65] Temu in October 2024,[66] Meta and Instagram in April[67] and May 2024.[68]

It should be noted, however, that in these cases, no real liability is established for harmful content disseminated on the platform, as immunity remains applicable; rather, it has been witnessing an increased level of accountability for this content, accompanied by a crucial role of the Commission in setting the required *standard of* care.[69]

5 Public Powers as a Counterbalance in the Relationship with Private Parties in the Protection of Copyright Online: The Case of the AGCOM's "Anti-Piracy" Platform

A rapid overview of the most recent evolution of copyright shows that, although it is very challenging to balance it with other constitutionally protected rights, which must also be weighed in light of the European Union's principle of proportionality, the "pendulum" has recently swung in favour of the former.

This aspect becomes clear if we bear in mind the aforementioned institution of the "dynamic injunction" (as well as the provisions of Law No. 93/2013 that strengthen Italian Communications' (AGCOM) powers in the field of copyright protection, which will be discussed below), to which we can add, for example, the

[62] See Commission press release dated 19 February 2024 "Commission opens formal proceedings against TikTok under the Digital Services Act", available at: https://ec.europa.eu/commission/presscorner/detail/en/ip_24_6487.

[63] See Commission Press Release dated 5 August 2024, following the acceptance of commitments to remedy concerns raised at the opening of the investigation on 22 April 2024 'TikTok commits to permanently withdraw TikTok Lite Rewards programme from the EU to comply with the Digital Services Act', available at: https://ec.europa.eu/commission/presscorner/detail/en/ip_24_4161.

[64] See Commission press release dated 17 December 2024 'Commission opens formal proceedings against TikTok on election risks under the Digital Services Act', available at: https://ec.europa.eu/commission/presscorner/detail/en/ip_24_6487.

[65] See Commission press release dated 14 March 2024 "Commission opens formal proceedings against AliExpress under the Digital Services Act", available at: https://ec.europa.eu/commission/presscorner/detail/en/ip_24_1485.

[66] See Commission press release of 31 October 2024 'Commission opens formal proceedings against Temu under the Digital Services Act', available at: https://digital-strategy.ec.europa.eu/en/news/commission-opens-formal-proceedings-against-temu-under-digital-services-act.

[67] See Commission press release of 30 April 2024 'Commission opens formal proceedings against Facebook and Instagram under the Digital Services Act', available at: https://ec.europa.eu/commission/presscorner/detail/en/ip_24_2373.

[68] See, Commission press release dated 16 May 2024 'Commission opens formal proceedings against Meta under the Digital Services Act related to the protection of minors on Facebook and Instagram', Available at: https://ec.europa.eu/commission/presscorner/detail/en/ip_24_2664.

[69] Failure to comply with which may result in the imposition of heavy fines under Article 74 DSA.

recent change of course concerning the relationship between the disclosure under Art. 154-bis of the Copyright Law and the right to privacy with respect to what is provided for in Art. 154-bis of the Copyright Law. and the right to *privacy* concerning what was established in the Peppermint case, or the new orientation of the Italian Supreme Court on the subject of the extension of the right of paternity under Art. 20 of the aforementioned law:[70] it broadens the sphere of protection of the moral right and resolves the conflict between anonymity and paternity in favour of the latter, which confirms that the time is now ripe to attribute full legitimacy to copyright itself as a fundamental right.[71]

Regarding the current regulatory framework on copyright protection on electronic communication networks and AGCOM's most recent determinations, it is worth noting that the legislator has recently revised the relevant regulations.

Law No. 93 of 14 July 2023,[72] in compliance with the provisions of Law No. 19 of 19 February 2007,[73] redefined the structure of public functions to make control activities more effective and combat the unlawful dissemination of copyright-protected content.

The aforementioned Law No. 93/2023, in fact, provided that AGCOM, by its own measure, orders[74] service providers—uploaders, page managers and of the Internet site, network access intermediaries—to disable access to content illegally disseminated *online*. According to Art. 2, this can be achieved by blocking domain names and "the routing of network traffic to IP addresses uniquely intended for the performance of illegal activities".[75] These powers are intended to inhibit the

[70] Trib. Turin, 3 June 2015, in *AIDA*, 2016, 951.

[71] On the second aspect referred to in the text Cass. civ., 5 July 2019, no. 18220, in *Foro it.*, 2019, I, 3957, with a contribution by Casaburi (2019), according to which 'art. 20 l.d.a., which recognises the moral right of authorship, must be interpreted in the sense that "the right to claim authorship of the work" consists not only in the right to prevent the abusive self- or hetero-attribution of authorship by others, but also in the right to be recognised as the author of the work, regardless of the parallel, albeit only possible, attribution to others, and that the violation of the right entails the obligation of the person responsible to compensate for the non-pecuniary damage caused".

[72] Enacting "Provisions for the prevention and repression of the unlawful dissemination of copyright protected content through electronic communication networks".

[73] Law ratifying the Convention on the Protection and Promotion of the Diversity of Cultural Expressions signed in Paris on 20 October 2005.

[74] It should be noted, indeed, that it was only with Law Decree No. 123 of 15 September 2023 that a real obligation to intervene was introduced for AGCOM. In fact, pursuant to aArt. 2, Law No. 93/2023 as amended by Art. 15-ter, Legislative Decree No. 123/2023, the Authority "shall order service providers, including network access providers, to disable access to content disseminated abusively". In its original wording, on the other hand, Article 2, Law No. 93/2023 provided for the mere possibility (and not the obligation) for the Authority to intervene upon notification. Moreover, as a result of Decree-Law No. 123/2023, the taxability of the blocking phase is also reinforced by the elimination of the sentence "where technically possible". The Law Decree provided that communications and updates to the addressees of the measure—with regard to the list of domain names and IP addresses—would no longer be carried out by the Authority but by the platform itself.

[75] See Article 2, Law No. 93/2023.

well-known phenomena of illegal *online* dissemination of content, such as sports events, entertainment programmes, movies, etc.[76]

It is well known, in fact, that those who organise such "broadcasts" on so-called pirate sites often derive direct remuneration from the sale of advertising space on the relevant pages and an "indirect" advantage deriving from the routing of traffic and from access to certain user navigation data. This, occurs in violation of copyright, to the considerable detriment of the economic operators who disseminate the same paid content and who see their customer base reduced, fatally attracted by the free nature of "pirate" sites.

Indeed, the illicit conducts are often carried out while the "paid" event is in progress, so that, in order to combat the relative phenomenon, it was necessary to provide for instruments that would allow an effective repressive intervention in real time. Moreover, considering that the offences are often carried out through sites that escape Italian jurisdiction and the exercise of the administrative powers of the national authorities, providing only *ex post* sanctioning mechanisms—such as the imposition of a fine—would have rendered the system of safeguards ineffective.

In the light of these brief considerations, then, it can be understood why Art. 2(3) of Law No. 93/2023 provided that "in cases of seriousness and urgency, which concern the making available of content broadcast live, first viewings of cinematographic and audiovisual works or entertainment programmes, audiovisual content, including sports content, or other similar intellectual works, sporting events as well as events of social interest or of great public interest (…) by means of a precautionary measure adopted in an abbreviated procedure without an adversarial procedure, the Authority shall order service providers, including network access service providers, to disable access to the abusively disseminated content by means of blocking of domain names and IP addresses".

In this context, AGCOM—also on the basis of a recommendation of the European Commission aimed at strengthening the fight against *online* piracy of sporting events[77]—has started work for a timely update[78] of the Regulation on the protection of copyright *online* (resolution 680/13/CONS of 12 December 2013, already

[76] These are hypotheses concerning the making available of contents broadcast live—first releases of cinematographic and audiovisual works or entertainment programmes, audiovisual contents, including sports contents, as well as events of social interest or of great public interest, as defined by Article 33, paragraph 3, Legislative Decree No. 208 of 8 November 2021. In such cases, i.e. where live broadcasting of the event is envisaged, the administrative authority's measure is adopted and enforced before the beginning or, at the latest, during the broadcast itself; where no live broadcast event is involved, the measure is adopted and enforced before the beginning or, at the latest, during the broadcast itself.

[77] See European Commission Recommendation No. 2023/1018 of 4 May 2023 on combating piracy.

[78] In compliance with the provision of Art. 6, paragraph 1, Law No. 93/2023 where it is provided that "within sixty days of the entry into force of this law, the Authority shall, in compliance with the provisions of Law no. 241 of 7 August 1990, amend the regulation on the protection of copyright on electronic communication networks, referred to in Resolution No. 680/13/CONS of 12 December 2013, in order to adapt it to the provisions of this law."

previously amended with the introduction of new supervised subjects, of an abbreviated procedure, as well as of precautionary powers), in order to adapt it to the new requirements for risk containment and mitigation arising from the spread of pirate sites.

With Resolution No. 189/23/CONS of 26 July 2023—just a few days, therefore, after the publication of Law No. 93/2023—the Authority regulated the precautionary procedure aimed at ending violations of copyright and related rights concerning the unlawful broadcasting of audiovisual content transmitted live.[79]

In particular, Art. 9-bis, paragraph 4-ter, of the regulation provides that "the precautionary order referred to in paragraph *4-bis* is adopted within three days of receipt of the application or of the supplementary documents requested by the management for the purposes of the admissibility of the same application and executed by the addressees of the measure within the term established by the Authority and, in any case, within 24 hours of its notification".[80] or within 30 min from the notification in the case of subsequent notifications, as already provided for, in general, by Art. 2(4) of Law No. 93/2023.

Even this super-accelerated procedure risked, however, being ineffective if (only) AGCOM was invested with the (almost impossible) task of looking into the *web* in search of pirate sites.

Appropriately, the law provides that the owner or licensee of the right allegedly infringed can submit a blocking request to the Authority, attaching the necessary documentation "including the list of domain names and IP addresses through which the abusively disseminated contents are made available" (Art. 2, paragraph 4).

Furthermore, Law Decree No. 123/2023 amended Law No. 93/2023 by providing that this list must be "directly and simultaneously communicated through the platform to the Authority and to the addressees of the measure, who must promptly remove or disable it, in any case within a maximum period of 30 minutes from the communication" (Art. 2, paragraph 4).

---

[79] Cf. Art. 9-bis, paragraph 4-bis, of the regulation on the protection of copyright on electronic communication networks (AGCOM Resolution 680/13/CONS), as amended by Resolution 189/23/CONS, provides that "with the application referred to in art. 6, paragraph 1, a reasoned request may be made to the Authority to order as a precautionary measure the providers of mere conduit services operating in the Italian territory to put an end to the infringement of copyright or related rights concerning audiovisual works concerning live broadcasting and similar sports events, pursuant to Article 8, paragraph 4". Paragraph *4-ter* of the same Article also provides that, unless the infringement is manifest and the Directorate may proceed directly with the issuance of the precautionary order, the latter "shall be adopted within three days from the receipt of the application or of the supplementary documents requested by the Directorate for the purpose of the admissibility of the application and shall be executed by the addressees of the measure within the term established by the Authority and, in any case, within 24 hours from the notification thereof".

[80] Cf. Art. 9-bis, paragraph 4-ter, Resolution 680/13/CONS, which currently provides that "the precautionary order referred to in paragraph 4-bis is adopted within three days from the receipt of the petition or of the supplementary documents requested by the Directorate for the purposes of the admissibility of the same petition and executed by the addressees of the measure within the term established by the Authority and in any case within 24 hours from the notification thereof".

The "blocking" measure, by which the Authority orders service providers, including network access service providers, to disable access to abusively disseminated content by blocking domain names and blocking the routing of network traffic to IP addresses uniquely intended for unlawful activities, is notified immediately by the Authority to network access service providers, search engine operators, and information society service providers involved in any capacity in the accessibility of the illegal website or services (Art. 2(5), Law No. 93/2023).

In the event that they are involved in any capacity in the accessibility of the illegal website or services, these subjects shall execute the Authority's measure without any delay and, in any case, within a maximum period of 30 min from the notification, by disabling the DNS (Domain Names System) resolution of domain names and the routing of network traffic to the IP addresses indicated in the list or, in any case, by adopting the necessary technological and organisational measures to make the content disseminated unlawfully inaccessible to end users.[81]

In order to allow the report to be followed by an injunction measure promptly adopted, notified, and enforced by "disabling" the pirate site, the law provided for the introduction of an automated system. Pursuant to Art. 6(2) of Law No. 93/2023 (in its version resulting after the amendments of November 2023), "the Authority, in cooperation with the National Cybersecurity Agency, shall convene a technical roundtable with the participation of service providers, Internet access providers, rights holders, content providers, audiovisual media service providers and the most representative associations in charge of protecting copyright and related rights, in order to define the technical and operational requirements of the tools necessary to enable a timely and effective disabling of domain names or IP addresses, as provided for by Article 2 of this law, through the definition of a single technological platform with automated operation for all recipients of disabling measures".[82]

As a result of the discussion that took place at the technical roundtable, the Authority adopted a platform (called *Piracy Shield*) designed to enable the automated management of notifications by rights holders and to ensure timely and effective protection. The platform—realised by the Lega Calcio Serie A and donated to AGCOM—allows, in fact, service providers to proceed, following AGCOM's precautionary order,[83] to directly and automatically disable access to the reported

---

[81] Against AGCOM's decision, a complaint may be lodged with the same Authority within five days. Although the lodging of a complaint does not have the effect of suspending the precautionary order, it does imply the initiation of a procedure that must be defined within seven days by the Authority with the participation of the persons entitled to lodge a complaint and of the person who submitted the petition referred to in Art. 6, paragraph 1, of the regulation. See Art. 9-bis, paragraphs 5 and 7, regulation annexed to Resolution 680/13/CONS, as amended by Resolution 180/23/CONS.

[82] See Art. 6, Law No. 93/2023.

[83] Art. 9-bis, paragraph 4-quater, Resolution No. 680/13/CONS, provides that with the application referred to in paragraph 4-bis, a qualified person may also request that, once the precautionary order has been adopted, the addressees of the measure proceed, by means of subsequent notifications, to block any other future domain name and sub-domain, or IP address, including variations of the name or of the simple declination or extension, referable to the same contents and through

telematic addresses within 30 min from the communication, pursuant to aArt. 4, paragraph 2, Law No. 93/2023 and Art. 9-bis, paragraph 4-sexies, of the regulation on the protection of copyright *online* in its consolidated version.

The system should, therefore, allow for the timely adoption of measures aimed at repressing unlawful conduct, although the very celerity of the procedure and the automation of the same risk giving rise to decisions in which the dissemination of content could be prevented on the false assumption of its unlawfulness.

References

Caso R (2021) Intelligenza artificiale e diritto d'autore. In: Ghidini G, Simoni A (ed) Proprietà intellettuale e innovazione digitale. Milano, p 205

Sartor G (2020) I diritti sulle informazioni. In: Ghidini G, Simoni A (eds) Proprietà intellettuale e innovazione digitale. Milano, p 157

---

which the violations take place. The report may be filed on condition that the right holders, also providing certain documentary evidence as to the actuality of the unlawful conduct, indicate, under their own responsibility, that the IP addresses identifying the "Main servers" and the "Delivery Servers" of the sites in question and the domain names associated with them, have the character of univocity. The Authority, also by means of the technological platform, verifies the conformity and completeness of the reports received, which must be promptly received by the service providers in order to guarantee blocking within the 30 min provided for by law.

Personal Data Protection

Digital Identity and User Profiling

Mauro Tescaro

Contents

Abstract The problem of adequate protection of personal identity has become more and more serious with the increasing spread of mass media and has inevitably taken on new relevance in the digital age, with the related online sharing of huge amounts of information and personal data. Thus, personal identity becomes increasingly digital and the need to protect it arises especially with regard to profiling.

M. Tescaro (✉)
University of Verona, Verona, Italy
e-mail: mauro.tescaro@univr.it

R. Bocchini (ed.), *Digital Platforms - From Technical Foundations to Legal and Economic Implications*, https://doi.org/10.1007/978-3-032-07978-7_27

1 Personal Identity

The right to personal identity has two fundamental meanings: the first, older and tending to be static, concerning identification; the second, more recent (but already established before the digital era) and dynamic, concerning identity.[1]

Traditionally, the notion in question served, in fact, essentially to summarise the findings of public registers necessary to identify a subject in relations with the public administration, distinguishing it from others.

In more recent times, in line with a broader sensitivity—which developed particularly after the Second World War—aimed at extending the protection of the personality towards ever new horizons, the idea that each individual has the right to the truth of his or her own life and ideas[2] has gradually asserted itself, i.e. to be represented as he or she really is even beyond the above-mentioned identification aspects and therefore with regard to the entire complex of his or her activities and positions, of the most diverse nature (intellectual, political, social, religious, ideological, professional, etc.).

This right, lacking any specific regulation in the Italian Civil Code, was justified initially on the basis of that of the right to one's name (and the right to one's image), with related injunctive and compensatory remedies (Article 7 and, as regards the right to image, Article 10 of the Italian Civil Code), applied by analogy and then even directly on the basis of Article 2 of the Italian Constitution, which, according to a widespread opinion, would allow the judge to defend aspects of one's personality endangered by the evolution of society even without any specific provisions of ordinary law.[3]

There are, however, several such Italian provisions, such as Article 8 (as amended by Article 42 of Law no. 416 of 5 August 1981) of the Press Law (Law no. 47 of 8 February 1948) on the subject of replies and corrections, as well as those that we will discuss below with regard to digital identity, which should therefore be seen as the main regulatory basis of our right.[4]

From a case law point of view, the new right of personality—which had already been the subject of doctrinal studies and a number of avant-garde judgments of lower level[5]—was definitively confirmed by a famous Supreme Court ruling in 1985.[6] In that controversy, the well-known oncologist Umberto Veronesi complained

[1] See, also for further references, Zeno-Zencovich (1993), p. 294 ff.; Fusaro (2002), p. 51 ff.; Resta (2007), p. 511 ff.; Finocchiaro (2010), p. 721 ff.; Livi (2012), p. 20 ff.; as well as the extensive monograph by La Spina (2022), p. 2 ff.

[2] Bianca (2002), p. 200.

[3] Cf. among others Lino (2023), p. 399 ff; Leanza (2023), p. 1809; Cocuccio (2016), p. 949 ff and spec. p. 968.

[4] For a similar perspective, see Zeno-Zencovich (1993), p. 294 ff.

[5] We refer, also for further quotations, to the works already cited *supra*, note 1, to which should be added Tescaro (2014), p. 825 ff., and Tescaro (2014), p. 316 ff.

[6] Cass. 22 June 1985, no. 3796, in *Nuova giur. civ. comm.*, 1985, I, 647 ff.

about the inclusion in an advertisement for cigarettes of a statement of his, concerning the lesser evil represented by cigarettes with a low nicotine content, which he had in fact expressed, however, in the context of a broader interview aimed at highlighting the danger of smoking. The extrapolation of that statement and its insertion in a considerably different advertising context would therefore have harmed the oncologist's personal identity. The Court of Cassation adopts this perspective by giving the following clear definition of the violated right: "Every person has an interest, generally considered worthy of legal protection, in being represented, in the life of relationships, with his true identity, as it is known or could be known in the social reality, general or particular, with the application of the criteria of normal diligence and subjective good faith; that is, he has an interest in not seeing altered, misrepresented, obfuscated, contested outside his intellectual, political, social, religious, ideological, professional, etc. heritage, which had been expressed or appeared, on the basis of concrete and unequivocal circumstances, destined to be expressed in the social environment".

2 Digital Identity

The problem of adequate protection of personal identity has become more and more serious with the increasing spread of the mass media and has inevitably taken on new relevance in the digital age, with the relative sharing of huge amounts of information and personal data on the net. Hence, personal identity is becoming increasingly digital in both of the above-mentioned profiles, that of identification and that of identity.[7]

As regards the first profile, in Article 1, paragraph *u-quater* of the Italian CAD (Digital Administration Code, pursuant to Legislative Decree no. 82 of 7 March 2005, as amended), digital identity is defined as "the computerised representation of the correspondence between a user and his or her identifying attributes, verified through the set of data collected and recorded in digital form according to the methods laid down in the decree implementing Article 64".[8] Although a person may have several digital identities to access different online services,[9] legislation (both Italian domestic and of the European Union) has long pursued the objective of a univocal

[7] Among many, see Finocchiaro (2012), p. 383 ff; Alpa (2017), p. 723 ff; Tardia (2017), p. 53 ff; Pasquino (2019), p.93 ff; Perchinunno (2020), p. 1430 ff; Perlingieri (2021), p. 86 ff; Alpa (2022), p. 620 ff; La Spina (2022), p. 265 ff; Messina (2023), p. 89 ff; Ruggiero (2023), p. 79 ff; as well as, most recently, Pasquino (2024), p. 19 ff.

[8] This definition is then taken up and deepened in the d.p.c.m. of 24 October 2014 (the so-called SPID decree), of which see especially Art. 1(1)(o).

[9] V. La Spina (2022), p. 294 ff., who, after recalling that 'real doubles or [...] avatars' are 'to be considered absolutely inherent to the digital dimension', examines in depth the particularities of the right to online anonymity. On this subject see also Nazzaro (2024), p. 135 ff.

digital identity at least in dealings with the public authorities, with greater security requirements than those of common private credentials.[10]

In this perspective, we should first of all point out Articles *3-bis* and 64 of the CAD, which enshrine the right to access the services of public administrations (and of some subjects treated as equal to them) through the SPID (Public System for the Management of the Digital Identity of Citizens and Businesses), the CIE (Electronic Identity Card), and the CNS (National Services Card).

Not only from an Italian point of view, of great relevance was also Regulation (EU) 910/2014 (eIDAS), aimed at introducing a uniform common framework for electronic transactions within the European Union, fostering the development of interoperable and secure electronic identification systems.[11] Most recently, moreover, Regulation (EU) 2024/1183 intervened to amend eIDAS reg. and especially to establish a European digital identity framework centred on the *European Digital Identity Wallet* paradigm.[12]

The identity profile also presents itself with new features in the digital age, as demonstrated, for instance, by the fact that the "Declaration of Rights on the Internet", drawn upon 2015 (XVII Legislature) on behalf of the Italian Chamber of Deputies by a special study commission chaired by Stefano Rodotà, qualifies the "right to identity" as the "right to the full and up-to-date representation of one's identity on the Net" (Art. 9, para. 1).

In this regard, privacy comes into the limelight, which extends far beyond the traditional right to secrecy, mainly concerning the power to control one's personal data also online and thus assuming fundamental importance also for the construction and protection of digital identity.[13]

The reference framework is therefore to be found primarily in Regulation (EU) 2016/679 (GDPR) and the Italian Personal Data Protection Code (Legislative Decree No. 196 of 30 June 2003, as amended for the purpose of adaptation to the GDPR in 2018 by Legislative Decree No. 101), although their actual effectiveness in protecting the right to digital identity is the subject of numerous doctrinal doubts, easily understandable, from a more general point of view, just in view of the very rapid and incessant technological evolution, which would require ever new measures in order to supplement if not modify a regulatory framework inevitably destined to remain unsatisfactory, at least to some extent.

---

[10] See, for example, Lucarelli Tonini (2024), p. 69.

[11] See, for all, Zaccaria et al. (2020).

[12] See e.g. Leanza (2023), p. 1814 ff., where it is emphasised that it is a wallet with numerous functions in addition to the storage of user identification data and that the underlying objective is to improve the eIDAS Regulation to take into account the latest technological developments by broadening the trust services covered and harmonising security systems in the EU.

[13] See, among others, Piraino (2017), p. 401; Cuffaro (2018), p. 1105; Franzoni (2021), p. 1105, where the 'right to control the flow of information concerning the individual' is discussed; Franzoni (2021), p. 4 ff; La Spina (2022), p. 352, 362 and 365 ff; Giova (2023), p. 335; Morace Pinelli (2024), p. 488. It is to this power of control that the various rights or remedies contemplated by the GDPR (on which we will elaborate *below*, paras. 7 ff.) may be said to be functional.

The main problem is that the aforementioned rules seem to have been conceived especially with a view to making a single data controller responsible for planning the processing, assessing in advance the risks concerning only his own activity and minimising them right from the design phase, thus proving inadequate to the increasingly widespread and relevant phenomenon of big data managed through artificial intelligence, i.e. mass processing that spreads far beyond the sphere of a single data controller.[14] Precisely in order to extend regulatory protection beyond the logic of making a single operator responsible and controlling individual processing, new rules have become necessary, in addition to the previous ones, enriching them in this respect.

This concerns above all (but not only)[15] Regulation (EU) 2024/1689 on Artificial Intelligence (the so-called A.I. Act),[16] which complements the first legal framework with an aspiration of completeness on this topic worldwide.[17] The regulation in question is centred on different levels of risk (minimal or nil, limited, high and unacceptable), to which corresponds a gradually more incisive regulatory intervention, which may go as far as prohibiting the artificial intelligence system.[18] On the whole, this seems to result in enhanced preventive protection of personal identity,[19] albeit within the framework of an approach that focuses almost exclusively on the

---

[14] See e.g. La Spina (2022), p. 449 ff; Fazio (2023), p. 310 ff; Barela (2023), p. 159 ff.

[15] Another relevant text from the point of view of digital identity protection is Regulation (EU) 2022/2065 (the so-called *Digital Services Act* or DSA), on which see Di Cerbo (2023), p. 260 ff., who especially dwells on Articles 26 (on the subject of advertising on online platforms) and 27 (on the subject of recommender system transparency) highlighting the connection with Article 22 GDPR (on which see *below* in the text, para. 8). See also, with particular attention to the interaction between Regulation (EU) 2022/2065 and Regulation (EU) 2024/1689, Tommasi (2023), p. 279 ff. Regulation (EU) 2022/868 (the so-called *Data Governance Act* or DGA) is also of some interest, at least if its function of promoting not only the data market but also the dignity of the individual is emphasised, as done by Morace Pinelli (2024), p. 489 ff.; Poletti (2024), p. 533 ff. But see also the critical perspective of Owusu (2023), p. 217 ff. To this legislation was then added Regulation (EU) 2023/2854 (the so-called *Data Act*), on which see Ricci (2024), p. 799 ff.

[16] Applicable in principle only from 2 August 2026: see, more extensively, Art. 113.

[17] Substantially in line with the aforementioned EU Regulation was therefore the Council of Europe Framework Convention on Artificial Intelligence (CETS 5 September 2024, no. 225), recently signed by many countries (including the Vatican) and by the EU itself, which incorporates the first legally binding international agreement on the subject.

[18] For more on this, see Battelli (2022), p. 1115 ff; Messina (2023), p. 288 ff; Bravo (2024), p. 1070 ff; Gentili (2024), p. 1043 ff; Smorto (2024), p. 208 ff; Petruso and Smorto (2024), p. 989 ff; Orlando (2024b), p. 815 ff; Natale (2024a), p. 201 ff; Natale (2024b), p. 289; Proietti (2024), p. 882 ff; Finocchiaro (2024), p. 25 ff; Andò (2024), p. 119 ff; Imbruglia (2024), p. 301 ff; Taddei Elmi and Contaldo (2024); Martini and Wendehorst (2024); Necati Pehlivanet al. (2024); Gabrielli and Ruffolo (2025), p. 438 ff; Pollicino et al. (2025).

[19] Particularly noteworthy are the rules on the requirements for high-risk artificial intelligence systems, in the context of which, on the one hand, Art. 10, aimed at setting quality criteria for the data used for profiling, and, on the other hand, Art. 12-14 of Regulation (EU) 2024/1689, which express a general principle of explainability from the outset of decision-making processes centred on the concepts of traceability, intelligibility and monitorability of artificial intelligence by humans, stand out. See also for further references Parenzo (2023), p. 126 ff.

accountability of those who produce or make use of artificial intelligence systems and that instead leaves both public authorities and, above all, individual users on the margins of action.[20] Moreover, the most relevant part of the new rules for our purposes concerns the various requirements, regulated in detail, of high-risk artificial intelligence systems, a category that Article 6 of Regulation (EU) 2024/1689 configures, however, in narrow and rigid terms.[21]

With the aim of integrating European legislation into the areas of competence of domestic law, placing Italy—also in view of its presidency of the G7 in the year 2024—in the vanguard on this issue, on 20 May 2024 the d.d.l. no. 1146 on "Provisions and delegation to the Government on artificial intelligence"[22] was also presented in the Senate and was then definitively approved, giving rise to Law no. 132 of 23 September 2025.

If the legislator, despite all efforts, will inevitably remain inadequate to meet the digital challenge, one can be more optimistic at least with regard to the scholars. Already in earlier times, when the protection of the moral personality still concerned only the analogue world, valuable investigations were in fact also carried out for the present context, as is, for instance, the case with the elaboration of the category of extra-patrimonial rights.[23]

3 The Different Types of Profiling

The need to protect personal identity, in today's digital society, arises above all with regard to profiling and automated decision-making relating to natural persons (whether or not including profiling), activities which have spread enormously through the increasingly widespread use by network operators of sophisticated mega-data analysis and artificial intelligence technologies.[24]

As pointed out, inter alia, in the "Guidelines on Automated individual decision-making and Profiling"[25] of the Article 29 Data Protection Working Party,[26] such activities, on the one hand, are useful for both users and organisations, deriving undeniable advantages in terms of improving efficiency and saving resources, but, on the other hand, entail numerous risks, which we shall return to below.

Beginning by illustrating the different types of profiling, Article 4(4), GDPR defines it generally as "any form of automated processing of personal data

[20] On a similar line of thought, see Fazio (2023), p. 335; Messina (2023), p. 299.

[21] See, more extensively, Parenzo (2023), p. 130 ff. See also *infra*, footnote 64.

[22] For a concise commentary, see Cassano (2024), p. 601 ff.

[23] See especially Zaccaria (1988).

[24] See extensively Adinolfi and Simoncini (2022).

[25] These Guidelines were adopted on 3 October 2017 and then, in an amended version, on 6 February 2018.

[26] Working Party established under Article 29 of Directive 95/46/EC as an independent advisory body of the European Union for the protection of personal data and privacy.

consisting of the use of such personal data to evaluate certain personal aspects relating to a natural person, in particular to analyse or predict aspects concerning that natural person's performance at work, economic situation, health, personal preferences, interests, reliability, behaviour, location or movements".[27]

There are therefore three elements that characterise profiling in general, i.e. not only an automated processing and use of personal data but also the purpose of assessing personal aspects. Therefore, the mere classification of subjects that does not involve some form of assessment of a natural person does not constitute profiling.

That being said, three different types can be distinguished: (i) profiling in general, defined as above; (ii) decision-making based on profiling; (iii) decision-making based *solely* on automated processing, including profiling, which produces legal effects concerning the data subject or similarly significantly affects him or her, within the meaning of Article 22(1) GDPR.

Already profiling in general, as explained in recital 72, must comply with the data protection principles and legal bases for processing set out in the GDPR.

These principles, which are set out in more detail in Article 5(1) GDPR, concern lawfulness, fairness, and transparency (subpara. a; on transparency see also the rights under Articles 12-14), further processing and purpose limitation (subpara. b), data minimisation (subpara. c),[28] accuracy (subpara. d), storage limitation (subpara. e), and integrity and confidentiality (subpara. f).[29]

The legal bases for processing are instead listed in Article 6(1) GDPR, which requires at least one of them between the consent of the data subject (sub-para. a; we will come back to this in section 6 *below*) and the necessity of the processing: for the performance of a contract (sub-para. b), for compliance with a legal obligation (sub-para. c), in order to protect vital interests (sub. d), for the performance of a task carried out in the public interest or in the exercise of official authority (sub. e) or for the pursuit of the legitimate interests of the data controller or a third party (sub. f).[30]

Moreover, it frequently happens that an automated decision-making process, per se different from profiling, derives from it or partially overlaps with it, in which case it is necessary to establish whether the decision is based solely on automated processing (i.e. whether any significant human intervention is excluded) and whether the further conditions indicated under iii are met, in which case the limitations and

---

[27] On the notion of profiling present in the Italian system before the GDPR, see Cass. ord. 8 November 2021, no. 32411, with note by Accoto (2023), p. 191 ff.

[28] On the principle of data minimisation, see, in case law, Cass. 21 October 2019, no. 26778, in *Dir. informazione e informatica*, 2020, 207; as well as Cass. 25 July 2023, no. 22338, in *Ilcaso.it*.

[29] On these and other principles concerning the matter at hand, see extensively Bravo (2023).

[30] On the legal basis of processing, see Court of Justice EU, 4 July 2023, Case C-252/21, at www.curia.europa.eu, as well as the note by D'Ippolito (2023), p. 323 ff., where further references. With more specific regard to the notion of legitimate interest, see also Court of Justice EU 4 October 2024, Case C-621/22, in *www.curia.europa.eu*, as well as the 'Guidelines 1/2024 on processing of personal data based on Article 6(1)(f) GDPR' of the European Data Protection Board—EDPB.

further protections set out in Article 22 GDPR (to which we shall return *below*, para. 8) apply, in addition to the rules on profiling in general.

4 Risks and Possible Abuses to the Detriment of the User

On the whole, the regulation under consideration aims to address the numerous risks for users, to which correspond as many possible abuses to their detriment, connected with profiling and automated decision-making processes relating to natural persons (including or not profiling).

As explained inter alia in the aforementioned Guidelines, non-transparent procedures may in fact lead, first of all, to data subjects not knowing that they are being profiled or not understanding the consequences.[31]

Moreover, profiling may even lead to social segregation, confining a natural person to a specific category, with detriment to his or her freedom to choose goods and services.[32]

The evaluations inherent in profiling may also prove to be inaccurate due to the erroneous nature of the data on which they are based or due to the shortcomings of the algorithm used to identify correlations between them,[33] with the risk of unjustified discrimination.[34]

Even in the absence of the aforementioned criticalities, in the light of its inevitable partiality and tendency to be static, the profile always ends up being different, and therefore false, compared to the real personal identity of a subject.[35]

Given the absence of any meaningful human involvement, the most serious dangers of damaging digital identity characterise, moreover, decision-making processes based solely on automated processing, which justifies the already mentioned special protection of Article 22 GDPR (see paragraph 8 *below*).

[31] Thus, 'personal identity undergoes a progressive depersonalisation', ending up becoming 'in some ways inevitably false and yet perceived as true and trustworthy' (La Spina (2022), p. 419 and p. 421).

[32] This is reasoned, for instance, in relation to the mechanism of the so-called filter bubble, i.e. the digital cage of information that increasingly sophisticated algorithms create by collecting the personal information of internet users, with the consequence that search engines end up selectively proposing the answers that are most likely to be liked, isolating the subject from the others: see, among others, Bianca (2019), p. 1 ff.

[33] See, among many, Pellecchia (2018), p. 1209 ff; Battelli (2022), p. 1103 ff; Troisi (2022), p. 953 ff; Fazio (2023), p. 320s; Parenzo (2023), p. 105 ff.

[34] See also for further references Fazio (2023), p. 303 ff.; Carapezza Figlia (2023), p. 638 ff., who points out that it is necessary to face the challenge in question not only with data protection legislation but also with anti-discrimination legislation; as well as, most recently, Parenzo (2024), p. 197 ff.; Grasso (2024), p. 489 ff.

[35] See very clearly La Spina (2022), p. 432 ff; Guzzardi (2023), p. 524 ff; Di Landro (2020), p. 97 ff.

5 Cookies and Other Identifiers

As explained in recital 30 of the GDPR, profiling is often (though not necessarily) carried out by means of cookies,[36] which are defined by the "Cookies and other tracking tools guidelines" of 10 June 2021 of the Italian *Garante per la protezione dei dati personali* (GPDP) as "text strings that websites (cd. publishers, or 'first parties') visited by the user, or different websites or web servers (so-called 'third parties') place and store—directly, in the case of publishers, and indirectly, i.e. through them, in the case of 'third parties'—within a terminal device available to the user".

For purposes such as those of cookies, which are "active identifiers", in that they presuppose the storage of information in the user's device (who therefore, in addition to benefiting from the legal protections of the GDPR, can also directly remove cookies), "passive identifiers" such as fingerprinting are also sometimes used, which are not based on such storage but on the simple observation of the configurations of the user's device (with the consequence that the profile created remains in the sole availability of the data controller).

In any case, it is essential to distinguish cookies—and other tracking tools, including "passive" ones—that are technical, i.e. "any technical storage of or access to information already stored if their sole purpose is to carry out the transmission of a communication over an electronic communication network, or to the extent strictly necessary for the provider of an information society service explicitly requested by the contracting party or user to provide such service" (Article 122, paragraph 1, Legislative Decree no. 196/2003), from cookies—and other tracking tools, including "passive" ones—of profiling, i.e. "used to link specific actions or behavioural patterns recurring in the use of the offered functionalities (pattern) to specific identified or identifiable subjects, in order to group the different profiles within homogeneous clusters of different size, so that it is possible for the data controller, inter alia, to modulate the provision of the service in an increasingly personalised manner beyond what is strictly necessary for the provision of the service, as well as to send targeted advertising messages, i.e. in line with the preferences expressed by the user while surfing the net" (thus the aforementioned "Cookie Guidelines").

---

[36] In a not too distant future, however, it is likely that cookies will be mostly abandoned in favour of other instruments: see more extensively Aiello (2024), p. 793 ff.

As we shall see, Italian law tends to approach the issue of cookies from the point of view of the protection of personality. Different is the approach of German law, which prefers instead the rights in rem perspective, highlighting the insertion of external computer material made by cookies in the device owned by the user, which then becomes opposable, where it is not justified, with instruments of the type of *actio negatoria*: see, for example, Fritzsche (2025). The latter approach, although formally unexceptionable, grants a protection that, at least from a functional point of view, however, seems excessive, considering how cookies, compared to other tracking tools even if not invasive of the user's property, have the advantage that they can be removed by the user himself, without the need to activate legal protections.

6 Profiling Cookies and Consent of the Person Concerned

Pursuant to paragraph 1 of Article 122 of Legislative Decree No. 196/2003, if it uses simple technical cookies (or similar tools), the data controller is not obliged to obtain the consent of the data subject, as it is merely required to provide specific information on the same, even if only within the general one. Other cookies, on the other hand, "are allowed only on condition that the contract party or user has given consent after being informed in a simplified manner".

It is therefore the Italian Personal Data Protection Code that provides (as well as the aforementioned exemption in the case of simple technical cookies) the obligation to obtain consent for the use of profiling cookies (or similar tools), but the characteristics of such consent are now to be found in the GDPR.

Without dealing in more detail with consent to the processing of personal data in general,[37] which should strictly be speaking being distinguished from the declaration with which one communicates the same data,[38] one should first recall recital 32, according to which "Consent should be given by a clear affirmative act establishing a freely given, specific, informed and unambiguous indication of the data subject's agreement to the processing of personal data relating to him or her, such as by a written statement, including by electronic means, or an oral statement. This could include ticking a box when visiting an internet website, choosing technical settings for information society services or another statement or conduct which clearly indicates in this context the data subject's acceptance of the proposed processing of his or her personal data Silence, pre-ticked boxes[39] or inactivity should not therefore constitute consent.

Consent should cover all processing activities carried out for the same purpose or purposes. When the processing has multiple purposes, consent should be given for all of them. If the data subject's consent is to be given following a request by electronic means, the request must be clear, concise and not unnecessarily disruptive to the use of the service for which it is provided".

---

[37] See chapter "The Conditions for the Lawfulness of Personal Data Processing" by Scola (2025) in this handbook.

[38] La Spina (2022), p. 336 ff. considers the latter declaration, when it consists only in the sharing of content concerning one's private life, to be a mere declaration of knowledge or sentiment, unless the object of the declaration is personal data necessary for the provision of a service to which the subject requests access, in which case it would be a declaration of will not consisting in a legal act (*negozio giuridico*) and especially an authorisation, and unless it is the communication of personal data that are not necessary for the performance of an agreement and are in substance the consideration for the service or good presented as free, in which case it would be a legal act (*negozio giuridico*). Consent to the processing of personal data, on the other hand, would always be a declaration of will, sometimes consisting in a legal act, sometimes not (in which case, once again, it would be an authorisation). For more details, see, among others, Irti (2021), p. 37 ff; Alpa (2022), p. 626 ff; Orlando (2022), p. 527 ff; Pinelli (2022), p. 1322 ff; Versaci (2022), p. 1130 ff; Bachelet (2023), p. 27 ff; Tosi (2023), p. 198 ff; Orlando (2024a), p. 333 ff.

[39] Cf. in this regard Court of Justice EU, Grand Chamber, 1 October 2019, Case C-673/17, in *Dir. fam. e pers.*, 2020, 133.

Therefore, as explained, inter alia, by the aforementioned "Cookie Guidelines", mere scrolling, in itself (unless it is one of the elements of a more articulated process), is not suitable for the collection of a consent justifying the installation and use of profiling cookies.

A similar reasoning must also be applied with regard to the so-called cookie wall (a mechanism that requires the user to consent to cookies or else it is impossible to access the site), which is in principle incompatible above all with the requirement of freedom of consent (Article 4(11) GDPR), unless the person concerned is offered the possibility of accessing equivalent content without consenting to profiling cookies.

In the aforementioned Guidelines, the GPDP, while respecting the entrepreneurial autonomy and accountability of each data controller (who may well, therefore, prefer different modalities), suggests the adoption of an online consent acquisition mechanism that is certainly in line with the GDPR. This is a banner that, besides presenting additional features (aimed, inter alia, at facilitating the modification or updating of the choices previously made by the user) on the details of which it is not appropriate to dwell here, on the one hand, does not prevent the retention of the default settings and therefore the denial of consent to profiling cookies simply by closing the banner itself (without the need to access other content) and, on the other hand, also allows a positive action in which any consent is substantiated, which—pursuant to para. 3 of Art. 7 GDPR—must be withdrawable at any time and *ad nutum.*[40]

As regards analytical cookies, i.e. those that serve to monitor the use of a website by users for the purpose of optimising it, according to the 2021 "Cookie Guidelines" it is not excluded that they are equated with technical cookies and that, consequently, they may be employed without acquiring the consent of the data subject. However, in light of the GDPR, this only applies in the event that such cookies do not lead to the direct identification of the user.

If special categories of personal data are involved (which replaces and extends the scope of sensitive data),[41] even in the case of profiling (which could result in data that were not originally included becoming such by combining them with other data), the processing of such data is only permitted if one of the conditions set out in Article 9(2) of the GDPR is also met.[42]

That being clarified, going back more generally to the obligation to obtain consent for profiling cookies, it should also be recalled that such an obligation is normal, but not always present, given, on the one hand, the possible existence in the case in point of a different legal basis for processing under Article 6(1) GDPR (see paragraph 3 *above*) and, on the other hand, the vagueness and breadth of the

---

[40] In general, on the importance of the right to withdraw consent, its aforementioned characteristics and its autonomy from the right to object to processing, see Bravo (2017), p. 161 ff, as well as La Spina (2022), p. 408 ff.

[41] See among many La Spina (2022), p. 396 ff.

[42] See for example Fazio (2023), p. 317; Siniscalchi (2023), p. 52; as well as, with specific regard to emotion recognition systems, Montinaro (2024), p. 847 ff.

formulas used by the regulations in question.[43] Especially the case of the performance of a task in the public interest or in connection with the exercise of official authority (Article 6(1)(e)) should not be interpreted restrictively: in this matter, perhaps more than in others, a balanced equilibrium must always be sought, but the public interest, if it is really such, deserves in principle to prevail already because of its collective dimension alone.[44]

7 User Protection and Especially the Right to Object

The traditional protections of the right to personal identity are, as already recalled (*supra*, par. 1), the injunction[45] and the compensation for damages,[46] the latter being the subject in the GDPR of the complex and controversial rules of Article 82.[47]

Moreover, with regard to digital identity, the GDPR significantly innovates the framework, contemplating further rights[48] for data subjects to which particular

[43] On this last circumstance, see La Spina (2022), p. 346. It is well known, however, that the GDPR marked a reduction of the role of consent and at the same time an enhancement of data circulation: see also for further references Caggiano (2018), p. 75 ff; Di Landro (2020), p. 180 ff; as well as Siniscalchi (2023), p. 48 ff.

[44] Similar reflections were formulated by R. Carleo in the open lecture *Questioni attuali in tema di trattamento dei dati personali* organised by F. Trubiani at the University of Naples 'Parthenope' as part of the Course in *Diritto del commercio elettronico* on 29 November 2023. As an emblematic example in this sense, the case dealt with by Court of Cassation no. 6177 of 1 March 2023, in *De Jure*, was cited, which annulled a measure pronounced by the *Garante per la protezione dei dati personali* against the INPS (*Istituto nazionale della previdenza sociale*) in order to sanction the latter's use of anti-fraud software aimed at guiding inspection visits. The fundamental reason why the data subject's consent (which could also be deemed implicit in the employee's presentation of the illness certificate) was not deemed necessary for such processing is that it concerns a control based on the law (in implementation of the indication of paragraph 2 of Article 97 of the Italian Constitution in the sense of the good performance of administrative activity).

[45] See most recently Fazio (2023), p. 363. Although the GDPR does not expressly regulate any action for an injunction, the right to lodge a complaint with a supervisory authority under Art. 77 could be similar to it, albeit with a particular conformation.

[46] See Tescaro (2014), p. 343 ff. See also *infra*, footnote 48.

[47] See for all chapter "Liability for Unlawful Personal Data Processing" by Faccioli (2025) in this handbook.

[48] Part of the scholars, however, prefers to avoid talking in this regard about proper rights (considering a different qualification more appropriate, mostly in terms of remedies) in order to emphasise that their infringement does not give rise to an autonomous compensation for damages with respect to the one possibly deriving only from the contextual infringement of the right of personality to which the final protection is addressed: on this subject see, also for further references, La Spina (2022), p. 475, who, moreover, advocates a consideration of the matter that is not analytical but systematic.

As for the complicated question, which always arises in matters such as ours, of the interaction between the new protections deriving from EU law and the purely national ones, although it is not possible to deal with it fully here, it seems that the remedies on which we will focus in the following generally add to and do not replace the domestic ones (which, in light of the probable *lex spe-*

obligations correspond for data controllers, who, as explained in the already mentioned (*supra*, par. 3) "Guidelines on Automated individual decision-making and Profiling", could be either the data controller creating the profile or the data controller making an automated decision on a data subject (with or without human intervention), where they are different entities.

Relevant first of all are the right to be informed—for what is of most interest here—under Articles 13(1)(f) and 14(1)(g) (rules distinguishing personal data collected from the data subject from those obtained indirectly)[49] and the right of access under Article 15 (including, pursuant to paragraph 3, the right to receive a copy of the personal data undergoing processing), not to be confused with the innovative right to data portability under Article 20, the latter right having, unlike the former, as its object the profile itself and not only the personal data composing it.

Leaving aside to delve into these subjective legal situations,[50] it is necessary to examine here a right—at least according to the intention of the European legislator—of central importance for the protection of digital identity, that to object under Article 21 GDPR.

This is a right that the data controller must "explicitly" bring to the attention of the data subject, presenting it "clearly and separately from any other information", 'at the latest at the time of the first communication" (Art. 21(4) GDPR).

---

cialis nature of Art. 82 GDPR, should instead not apply to the aforementioned action for damages, while more doubtful—see *above*, footnote 45—is the discourse concerning the action for injunction).

[49] Although it is materially impossible for the ordinary user to know the operating mechanism underlying an algorithmic decision in full (see, *ampus* Messinetti (2019), p. 861 ff.), he should be informed about it, otherwise his consent might not be freely given (nor specifically with reference to a clearly identified processing of personal data) and therefore invalid (see Court of Cassation 25 May 2021, no. 14381, with critical note by Bravo (2021), p. 1001 ff., which held that, 'in the case of a web platform [...] designed to draw up reputational profiles of individual natural or legal persons, centred on a calculation system with an algorithm at its base aimed at establishing reliability scores, the requirement of awareness cannot be regarded as satisfied where the algorithm's implementation scheme and the elements of which it is composed remain unknown or cannot be known by the persons concerned'). However, the statement should not be taken to extremes, since it is necessary to consider, and balance with this interest of the user, also that of the programmer to protect personal data as well as commercial or technical secrets (see Fazio (2023), p. 305; as well as Cons. Stato 2 January 2020, no. 30, in *Guida al dir.*, 2020, 13, 106). In any case, as clarified by the scholars (see above all Bravo (2021), p. 1017 ff., where copious administrative case law to the contrary is also cited), the transparency of the algorithm should not require the source code to be disclosed, but the illustration of the algorithm's operation in a form comprehensible to the average person, not necessarily endowed with computer skills. Italian case law of last resort has also recently conformed to this indication: see Court of Cassation, 10 October 2023, no. 28358, in *Dir. informazione e informatica*, 2024, 103 ff., with a note of adhesion and comparative in-depth analysis by Falletti (2024), p. 408 ff., and with a partially critical comment by Brutti (2024), p. 402 ff., judgment which precisely specified that it is not necessary "that the mathematical and computer language be shown to users, nor that it be effectively understood by them". A similar line of thinking has now been adopted by Court of Justice EU, 27 February 2025, Case C-203/22, at *www.curia.europa.eu*. We will also return to this subject *infra*, para. 8.

[50] See chapter "Rights of the Data Subject" by Troiano (2025) in this handbook.

The data subject therefore has "the right to object, on grounds relating to his or her particular situation,[51] at any time" to processing (and thus also to profiling, which the provision expressly refers to), however only where the latter is based on points (e) or (f) of Article 6(1) GDPR, i.e. where it is necessary for the performance of a task carried out in the public interest or in the exercise of official authority or in the pursuit of the legitimate interests of the data controller or of a third party. This is a relevant applicative limitation, which entails the exclusion of the right under consideration in the different hypotheses referred to in sub-paragraphs (a)-(d) of the same Art. 6 (those of processing based on the data subject's consent or necessary for the performance of a contract or in order to comply with a legal obligation or even to safeguard vital interests), in which the data subject may therefore object not to the processing, including profiling, but only to its functionalisation for direct marketing purposes within the meaning of Article 21(2) (which we will discuss shortly).[52]

If, on the other hand, there is an objection to processing, "the controller shall no longer process the personal data" and therefore avoids starting or stops profiling (as well as may have to delete personal data pursuant to Article 17(1)(c) GDPR), unless he "demonstrates compelling legitimate grounds[53] for the processing which override the interests, rights and freedoms of the data subject or for the establishment, exercise or defence of legal claims" (Art. 21(1) GDPR).

Hence, the need for a balance between the interests of the user and those of the data controller, with the latter bearing the burden of proving the aforementioned "compelling legitimate grounds".

As pointed out in the aforementioned Guidelines on Profiling, this is a more onerous balancing act for the data controller than the one required by Article 6(1)(f) of the GDPR on the subject of legitimate interests in general, requiring in the case in point, in order for the right to object to prevail, the further demonstration of the compelling nature of the legitimate interest. This notion is, moreover, only generically outlined, which, in addition to the aforementioned limitation in its application, contributes to making the right to object "*de facto* very circumscribed".[54]

---

[51] The latter reference serves to base the objection on any personal reason of the interested party, even irrespective of possible violations of the law, as pointed out by La Spina (2022), p. 482.

[52] See very clearly La Spina (2022), p. 484.

[53] As an example of 'compelling legitimate grounds', the Profiling Guidelines mention the purpose of detecting the spread of contagious diseases in advance. It does not seem, however, that super-individual interests must necessarily come into play, which recital 69 does not mention in this regard (see La Spina (2022), p. 484).

[54] La Spina (2022), p. 444 and p. 485, who concludes that "the right to object results, *de facto*, in a reconsideration, probably motivated by unexpected events in favour of the data subject, of the balance between his interest and that of the data controller, already carried out at the time of the initiation of the processing itself to verify the lawfulness pursuant to art. 6 paragraph 1 letter f, with the sole favour of the imposition of the burden of proof on the data controller. But [...] the data subject also bears the burden of adequately justifying his objection, since it cannot be considered, in the light of the entire regulatory framework and its axiological foundation, that it can consist in a merely arbitrary claim". Doubtful about the real incisiveness of Article 21 GDPR is also Piraino (2017), p. 339 ff., where he reasons of a "right to object [...] partly resized" and "rather unfortunate".

The user has, on the other hand, an unconditional right to object to the processing of his personal data, including profiling insofar as it is related to it, "for direct marketing purposes" (Article 21(2) GDPR).[55] In this eventuality, in other words, no balancing of interests is required, since the data controller must certainly respect the wishes of the data subject.

The right in question may be exercised "at any time" and, as stated in recital 70, "free of charge". The Guidelines on Profiling add, moreover, that in order to fully comply with Article 12(2) GDPR (according to which "the controller shall facilitate the exercise of data subject rights"), the data controller should offer users an easy way to indicate that they object to the use of their data for direct marketing purposes already at the time of collection,[56] rather than inducing them to exercise their right to object at a later stage.

It does not appear that the rules in question can be applied by analogy[57] to purposes that are certainly different from the one indicated, especially if they have no direct economic connotation. One thinks of political activity, which in the past case law has sometimes[58] questionably equated with commercial activity.

8 The General Prohibition of Decisions Based Solely on Automated Processing

In the same Section (Section IV, on the subject of "Right to object and automated individual decision-making", again under Chapter III, on the "Rights of the data subject") of Article 21 just examined, we also find the already mentioned (*supra*, para. 3) Article 22 GDPR.

As pointed out inter alia in the Guidelines on Profiling, despite the different terminology of para. 1 of Art. 22, there should be inferred from these rules not merely a right of the data subject, but even a general (subject to exceptions) prohibition (i.e. to be complied with even irrespective of the exercise of any subjective legal situation) on the adoption of decisions based solely (i.e. without any meaningful human involvement)[59] on automated processing, including profiling, albeit only where

---

[55] The aforementioned purposes, however, are not always easy to grasp. Just think of the multiform and not yet fully regulated role of influencers, on which see for all Trubiani (2024), p. 385 ff.

[56] Cf. in case law Cass. 2 July 2018, no. 17278, in *Guida al dir.*, 2018, 31, 20.

[57] This is also without taking into account that it is highly doubtful that EU provisions can be applied by analogy as is usual for national ones: in this regard Stürner (2021), p. 163 ff.; Baldus and Raff (2022), p. 173 ff.

[58] This is the case of Trib. Bari 31 December 2012, with note by Pastore (2013), p. 59 ff.

[59] As underlined by the Guidelines on Profiling, the data controller cannot circumvent Article 22 GDPR through a purely symbolic human involvement. Moreover, protection seems to be excluded in all the hypotheses in which profiling integrates only one of the parameters, even if perhaps the main one, at the basis of the decision-making outcome, which (in addition to what we will specify immediately following in the text) contributes to limit its relevance to a considerable extent, as

there is the further specific assumption that such decisions (or even only preparatory activities that are fundamental to the same)[60] produce legal effects concerning the data subject or affect him or her in a similar significant way.

The latter assumption, in the light of the Guidelines on Profiling, would seem to cover only cases where the person has been deprived of one of his rights or of the concrete possibility of acquiring another,[61] thus excluding the infringement of a personality right, such as the right to personal identity. Such a restriction, which would make the protection offered by the rule in question almost irrelevant for our purposes, sounds moreover paradoxical and is therefore contested by the scholars who advocate an interpretation that is not literal but systematic and axiological.[62]

In any case, the above-mentioned conception of Article 22 in terms of a general prohibition aims at strengthening the protection of users, making it automatic in the context at hand, in line with the more general purpose of the GDPR to guarantee data subjects control over their personal data (see *above*, para. 2).

The relevance of the general prohibition in question is further limited by the fact that it suffers from exceptions when it is a decision: necessary for entering into or performance of a contract; based on the "explicit consent" of the data subject;[63] or authorised by the law of the Union or of the competent Member- State, with specification of suitable measures to protect the data subject (Art. 22(2) GDPR).

Even if the first two exceptions among those listed above apply, suitable measures must still be taken to protect the data subject, i.e. "at least the right to obtain human intervention on the part of the controller, to express his or her point of view and to contest the decision" (Art. 22, para. 3, GDPR). This right, on the one hand, is more modest than the right to the ineffectiveness of the automated decision contemplated by Art. 22(1) and, on the other hand, in order to be really exercised, requires

---

highlighted by La Spina (2022), p. 486, among others, although an orientation of part of the scholars supports a broad interpretation of Article 22 GDPR such as to include all automated decisions in substance, i.e. with human intervention that is not essential to the content of the decision (so Fazio (2023), p. 326).

[60] The notion of 'decision' in Article 22 GDPR is in fact understood in a broad sense by the Court of Justice EU, 7 December 2023, Case C-634/21, in *Nuova giur. civ. comm.*, 2024, I, 416 ff. (with adhesive commentary by D'Orazio (2024), p. 416 ff, who points out, inter alia, how this reading is in line with the aim of protection of persons that characterises the rules in question), according to which 'the automated establishment, by a credit information agency, of a probability value based on personal data relating to a person and concerning his or her ability to meet payment commitments in the future constitutes "automated individual decision-making" [...] where a third party, to which that probability value is transmitted, draws strongly on that probability value to establish, implement or terminate a contractual relationship with that person'. See also, among the scholars, in favour of such an extensive reading, Bravo (2021), p. 1022 ff. Albeit in hypothetical terms, Ruggieri (2023), p. 823 ff. also seemed to lean towards a similar position. With specific regard to emotion recognition systems, see also Montinaro (2024), p. 871 ff.

[61] This seems also to be the orientation of recital 71, which mentions, as examples, 'automatic refusal of an online credit application or e-recruiting practices without any human intervention'. On the first hypothesis, see also the previous footnote.

[62] La Spina (2022), p. 487 and p. 493; and Fazio (2023), p. 328.

[63] See *supra*, footnote 49.

that the data subject knows the reasons for the decision and the relevant procedure in its entirety, something that the letter of the law does not assure him but that part of the scholars affirms through a systematic interpretation of the GDPR (in the light also of its principles and recitals) according to which the right to human intervention would include precisely that to the explanation of the aforementioned circumstances.[64] In this perspective, if the system adopted is not fully intelligible, i.e. precludes the aforementioned explanation, the conclusion would again be the ineffectiveness of the automated decision.[65]

If the automated decision-making process involves the use of special categories of personal data within the meaning of Article 9(1) GDPR, the processing is permitted only if the special requirements of Article 22(4) GDPR are met.

Recital 71 further specifies that automated decision-making "should not concern a child", although the use of the conditional tense suggests that this is not an absolute prohibition of which, moreover, there is no trace in Article 22 GDPR.[66]

---

[64] See again La Spina (2022), p. 488 ff, to whom it therefore seems "that through the right of access under Art. 15 the data subject can claim to know not only the circumstances relating to the initial phase of the automated processing (inputs, the data used, the system's operating mechanism), but also the situations relating to the intermediate phase in which the information is processed and, therefore, the outputs generated by the system itself, i.e. the data derived from it generated and then processed together with those collected from the data subject or from third parties, as well as the conditions relating to the final phase and, in particular, the deductive logical mechanisms (the reasons) that led to the final decision". On a similar line of thought, see also Troisi (2022), p. 965 ff; D'Orazio (2024), p. 414. The point is moreover controversial, especially since artificial intelligence algorithms seem to be characterised by an intrinsic and ineradicable opacity: see also for further references Bravo (2021), p. 1012; as well as Parenzo (2023), p. 124 ff and 132 ff, where a mismatch between regulations is also noted insofar as the principle of human surveillance laid down by Art. 14 of Regulation (EU) 2024/1689 for high-risk artificial intelligence systems seems to place them outside the scope of Art. 22 of the GDPR (which, as we have seen, concerns decisions based solely on automated processing) and the related right to an explanation, thus arriving at 'a vicious blind circle: where explainability can be had, the data subject would no longer seem to have a right to an explanation; where, on the other hand, a right to an explanation still seems to be able to be claimed, a guarantee of explainability is lacking'.

[65] La Spina (2022), p. 494; Fazio (2023), p. 333.

[66] Nor does an absolute prohibition result from Art. 28 (see especially para. 2) of the DSA. Children are also addressed in recital 38 of the GDPR, according to which they 'merit specific protection with regard to their personal data, as they may be less aware of the risks, consequences and safeguards concerned and their rights in relation to the processing of personal data. Such specific protection should, in particular, apply to the use of personal data of children for the purposes of marketing or creating personality or user profiles and the collection of personal data with regard to children when using services offered directly to a child. The consent of the holder of parental responsibility should not be necessary in the context of preventive or counselling services offered directly to a child'.

More generally on the processing of the personal data of a minor (processing for which Article 8 GDPR attributes legitimising value to the consent of a person at least 16 years old, without prejudice to the possibility for Member States to choose a lower age as long as it is not less than 13 years old, which for Italy in Article *2-quinquies*—introduced by Legislative Decree no. 101/2018—of Legislative Decree no. 196/2003 has been indicated as 14 years old), see Giandoriggio (2024), p. 296 ff; Agostinelli (2023), p. 397 ff; La Spina (2022), p. 386 ff; Senigaglia (2020), p. 75 ff; as well as Cinque (2007), p. 19 ff.

On the subject of the personalised price, the regulation in question is explicitly exempted by Article 49(1)(e)-*bis*) of the Italian Consumer Code, pursuant to which, before the consumer is bound by a distance or off-premises contract or a corresponding offer, the trader shall provide him, in a clear and comprehensible manner, among other information, if applicable, that the price has been personalised on the basis of an automated decision-making process.[67]

9 The General Right of Review

Various provisions also give rise to what may be summarised as the user's general right of review.

In addition to the already mentioned (*supra*, para. 6) withdrawability of consent under Art. 7(3), Art. 5(1)(d) GDPR, with regard to the accuracy of personal data, states in fact that, at the data controller's expense, they must be "where necessary, kept up to date", adding that "every reasonable step must be taken to ensure that personal data that are inaccurate, having regard to the purposes for which they are processed, are erased or rectified without delay". As clarified in the Guidelines on Profiling, in the light of this provision, it is particularly important that the data subject receives clear information on the data processed, so that he/she is in a position to correct any inaccuracies. Furthermore, Article 5(1)(e) GDPR, on the subject of storage limitation, requires, inter alia, the "implementation of the appropriate technical and organisational measures [...] in order to safeguard the rights and freedoms of the data subject", which, as clarified in the aforementioned Guidelines, means that the data controller should also keep the data updated during the storage period so as to reduce the risk of errors.

Implementing the indications just recalled, Section III (on the subject of "Rectification and erasure") of Chapter III of the GDPR contemplates, in addition to the right to erasure of personal data under Article 17 (which, although the legislative heading might suggest otherwise, is only a particular aspect of the broader right

[67] See extensively Caloiaro (2024), *passim* and spec. p.75 ff; as well as Parenzo (2023), p. 133 ff.

to be forgotten recognised by the current case law)[68] and the right to restriction of processing under Article 18,[69] the right to rectification regulated by Article 16.

The latter provision allows the data subject to obtain not only the review or correction, i.e. "without undue delay the rectification of inaccurate personal data concerning him or her" but also, "taking into account the purposes of the processing", the integration of incomplete personal data, "including by means of providing a supplementary statement".

This second aspect is particularly emphasised by scholars, both for its valuable innovativeness with respect to the pre-GDPR rules and because the aforementioned integration is functional to remedy not the lack of truthfulness of the event narrated, but its lack of historicisation, thus configuring itself as a relevant articulation of the right to be forgotten (understood in the broad sense)[70] as a way of exercising the right to personal identity.[71]

As pointed out in the Guidelines on Profiling, this applies both to input personal data, i.e. those used to create the profile, and to output personal data, i.e. the profile itself.

References

Accoto F (2023) Il confine tra profilazione online e condizioni generali di contratto. Tecn Dir 1:191 ff

Adinolfi A, Simoncini A (eds) (2022) protezione dei dati personali e nuove tecnologie. Ricerca interdisciplinare sulle tecniche di profilazione e sulle loro conseguenze giuridiche. Napoli, passim

Agostinelli B (2023) Minori in rete: l'illusione del consenso e l'equivoco della privacy. Familia:397 ff

[68] See, for instance, Trabucchi (2025), p. 482, where he briefly points out that, 'in reality, there are at least three declinations of the right to be forgotten found among scholars and in case law [...]: (a) the most classic conception is the one according to which the right to be forgotten is to be understood as the right not to see past events re-emerge once a certain lapse of time has passed; (b) the second meaning of oblivion concerns information disseminated on the internet, for which the most problematic point is given by the fact that the news placed on the web cannot be erased; (c) the last of the meanings of the right to be forgotten (and the one closest to the provision of art. 17 GDPR) concerns the actual deletion of information, carried out at the request of the person concerned, within the scope of which it is also possible to include the so-called right to de-indexing'. Recently, see also Belmonte (2023), p. 1 ff; as well as, in case law, Cass. ord. 1 February 2024, with comment by Conte (2024), p. 271 ff.

With regard to the comparison between the right to de-indexing under Art. 17 and the right to object under Art. 21 GDPR, see La Spina (2022), p. 511 ff., where it is clarified that the former should be considered more elastic than the latter, as we have seen (*supra*, para. 7) instead very weak.

[69] See again Troiano (2025), cit.

[70] See *supra*, note 68.

[71] See in this sense La Spina (2022), p. 514 and p. 527, who points out how this reading is corroborated by recital 65, where the right of rectification is precisely coupled with the right to be forgotten.

Aiello M (2024) L'ultima stagione dei cookies di terze parti nel settore della profilazione online: dall'esperienza sui cookie banners al nuovo progetto privacy sandbox. Dir Int, 793 ff
Alpa G (2017) L'identità digitale e la tutela della persona. Spunti di riflessione. Contr. e impr., 723 ff
Alpa G (2022) proprietà privata, funzione sociale, poteri pubblici di "conformazione". Riv Trim Dir Pubbl, p 620 ff
Andò B (2024) (Cor)relazioni pericolose: identità personale e inferenza algoritmica. In: Salanitro G (ed) Scenari dell'intelligenza artificiale. Uomo e Algoritmo nelle scienze sociali, Pisa, p 119 ff
Bachelet V (2023) Il consenso oltre il consenso, Pisa, p 27 ff
Baldus C, Raff T (2022) Richterliche Interpretation des Unionsrechts. In: Gebauer M, Teichmann C (eds) Europäisches privat- und Unternehmensrecht, 2a ed., Baden-Baden, p 173 ff
Barela V (2023) Accezione aggregata del dato: shuffle degli interessi in gioco e necessità di un approccio interdisciplinare a presidio del diritto di autodeterminazione della persona. Dir Informazione e Informatica, p 159 ff
Battelli E (2022) Necessità di un umanesimo tecnologico: sistemi di intelligenza artificiale e diritti della persona. Dir Fam. e Pers., p 1103 ff
Belmonte E (2023) La tutela dinamica dell'identità personale in rete: sarà vero oblio?. Rass Dir Civ, p 1 ff
Bianca CM (2002) *Diritto civile*. La norma giuridica. I soggetti, Milano, 2nd ed., Vol. 1, p 200
Bianca M (2019) La filter bubble e il problema dell'identità digitale. MediaLaws 2:1 ff
Bravo F (2017) Il consenso e le altre condizioni di liceità del trattamento di dati personali. In: Finocchiaro G (ed) Il nuovo Regolamento europeo sulla privacy e sulla protezione dei dati personali, Bologna, p 161ff
Bravo F (2021) Rating reputazionale e trasparenza dell'algoritmo. Il caso "mevalutate". Dir. informazione e informatica, p 1001 ff
Bravo F (ed) (2023) Dati personali. protezione, libera circolazione e governance, Principi. Pisa, vol.1, passim
Bravo F (2024) Intelligenza artificiale, autonomia contrattuale e meccanismi di controllo. Contr e impr, p 1070 ff
Caggiano IA (2018) Il consenso al trattamento dei dati personali nel nuovo Regolamento europeo. Analisi giuridica e studi comportamentali. Oss Dir Civ e comm, p 75 ff
Caloiaro LA (2024) Il prezzo personalizzato. Il consumatore e le insidie del mercato digitale, Torino, passim e spec.75 ff
Carapezza Figlia G (2023) Decisioni algoritmiche tra diritto alla spiegazione e divieto di discriminare. Pers. e Merc 4:638 ff
Cassano G (2024) Note minime sul d.d.l. in materia di intelligenza artificiale. Vita Not, p 601 ff
Cinque M (2007) Il minore e la contrattazione telematica tra esigenze del mercato e necessità di apposite tutele. Nuova giur. Civ Comm II:19 ff
Cocuccio MF (2016) Il diritto all'identità personale e l'identità "digitale". Dir Fam Pers., p 949 ff, spec. p 968
Conte F (2024) La natura del diritto all'oblio: analisi della tutela inibitoria e risarcitoria. Dir Int, p 271 ff
Cuffaro V (2018) Il diritto europeo sul trattamento dei dati personali. In Contr. e impr., p 1105 ff
D'Ippolito G (2023) Data economy: la Corte di giustizia precisa il rapporto tra concorrenza e protezione dei dati personali e le norme sulla pubblicità personalizzata. MediaLaws 2:323 ff
D'Orazio F (2024) Il credit scoring. Nuova Giur Civ Comm, p 410 ff
Di Cerbo A (2023) La tutela dell'identità nell'ambiente digitale alla luce delle norme europee. Eur J Priv Law Technol 2:260 ff
Di Landro AC (2020) Big Data. Rischi e tutele nel trattamento dei dati personali, Napoli
Faccioli M (2025), Liability for Unlawful Personal Data Processing. In this handbook
Fazio E (2023) Intelligenza artificiale e diritti della persona, Napoli.
Finocchiaro G (2010) Voce Identità personale (diritto alla). In Dig Disc Priv, Sez. Civ, V Agg., Torino, p 721 ff

Finocchiaro G (2012) Identità personale su internet: il diritto alla contestualizzazione dell'informazione. Dir informazione e informatica, p 383 ff

Finocchiaro G (2024) Diritto dell'intelligenza artificiale, Bologna, p 25 ff

Franzoni M (2021) Lesione dei diritti della persona, tutela della privacy e intelligenza artificiale. Jus Civ p 4 ff

Fritzsche J (2025) Sub § 858 BGB. In Hau W, Poseck R (eds) BeckOK BGB, 73a edN. Monaco di Baviera, Rn. 15

Fusaro A (2002) Nome e identità personale degli enti collettivi. Dal "diritto" all'identità uti singuli al "diritto" all'identità uti universi. Nuova Giur Civ Comm II:51 ff

Gabrielli E, Ruffolo U (eds) (2025) AI Act: gli effetti settoriali. Giur It, p 438 ff

Gentili A (2024) Regole per l'intelligenza artificiale. Contr. e Impr 1043 ff

Giandoriggio M (2024) I minori d'età e i social network: l'insostenibile leggerezza del post. Danno e Resp, p 296 ff

Giova S (2023) La persona nel contesto digitale: considerazioni conclusive. Tecn Dir 2:335

Grasso AG (2024) Processi decisionali automatizzati discriminatori: tra pericoli inediti e misure di contrasto. Studium Iuris, p 489 ff

Guzzardi G (2023) Il paradigma identitario nella società digitale. Pers. e merc., 3:524 ff

Imbruglia D (2024) La regolazione della intelligenza artificiale. In: Battelli E (ed) Diritto privato digitale, p 301 ff

Irti C (2021) Consenso "negoziato" e circolazione dei dati personali, Torino, p 37 ff

La Spina A (2022) Complessità e identità personale. Napoli

Leanza C (2023) L'identità personale nell'era telematica: l'identità digitale. Dir Fam Pers, p 1809 ff

Lino V (2023) Dal prenome e cognome all'identità digitale. Not., p 399 ff

Livi MA (2012) Il diritto al nome nel prisma dell'identità personale, Torino, p 20 ff

Lucarelli Tonini LM (2024) Persona, identità e strumenti nella società dei dati. In: Battelli E (ed) Diritto privato digitale, 2nd edn, Torino, p 69

Martini M, Wendehorst C (eds) (2024) KI-VO.Künstliche Intelligenz-Verordnung. Kommentar. Monaco di Baviera, passim

Messina D (2023) La tutela della dignità nell'era digitale. Napoli

Messinetti R (2019) La tutela della persona umana versus l'intelligenza artificiale. potere decisionale dell'apparato tecnologico e diritto alla spiegazione della decisione automatizzata. Contr. e Impr., 861 ff

Montinaro R (2024) Riconoscimento delle emozioni e marketing personalizzato. Pers. e merc. 3:847 ff

Morace Pinelli A (2024) Dalla Data protection alla Data Governance: il Regolamento UE 2022/868. Nuova Giur Civ Comm II:488 ff

Natale G (2024a) Il nuovo Regolamento Europeo AI ACT. Dir Int, p 201 ff

Natale G (2024b) Intelligenza artificiale, neuroscienze, algoritmi. Pisa, p 289 ff

Nazzaro AC (2024) Soggettività dell'avatar tra profilazione e identità personale. Tecn Dir, 135 f

Necati Pehlivan C, Forgó N, Valcke (2024) The EU Artificial Intelligence (AI) Act. Alphen aan den Rijn, passim

Orlando S (2022) Per un sindacato di liceità del consenso privacy. In Pers e merc., 4:527 ff

Orlando S (2024a) Consenso al trattamento e liceità. Pers. e Merc 2:333 ff

Orlando S (2024b) Sulla necessità di un controllo di liceità sostanziale per tutte le basi del trattamento dei dati personali. Pers. e merc. 3:815 ff

Owusu A (2023) Data sharing in the personal data economy. Does sharing mean caring? Eur J Priv Law Technol 2:217 ff

Parenzo B (2023) Profilazione e discriminazione. Dal GDPR alla proposta di Regolamento sull'IA. Tecn Dir 1:105 ff

Parenzo B (2024) La profilazione algoritmica nel prisma dell'autonomia privata, Napoli.

Pasquino T (2019) Identità digitale della persona, diritto all'immagine e reputazione. In: Tosi E (ed) privacy. Digitale. Riservatezza e protezione dei dati tra GDPR e nuovo Codice privacy, Milano, p 93 ff

Pasquino T (2024) Dall'identità personale all'identità algoritmica: la tutela del sé e dell'altro da sé nella dimensione reale e virtuale della persona. Nuovo Dir Civ, p 19 ff
Pastore M (2013) L'immagine di Totò e la lesione dell'identità personale… a quanto ammonta il danno? In Dir. informazione e informatica, p 59 ff
Pellecchia E (2018) Profilazione e decisioni automatizzate al tempo della black box society: qualità dei dati e leggibilità dell'algoritmo nella cornice della responsible research and innovation. Nuove Leggi Civ Comm., p 1209 ff
Perchinunno MC (2020) Identità personale, identità digitale e diritto di cronaca. Contr. e impr., p 1430 ff
Perlingieri C (2021) Diritto privato delle nuove tecnologie: contenuti e competenze. Tecn Dir 2:86 ff
Petruso R, Smorto G (2024) Il Regolamento europeo sull'intelligenza artificiale: una prima lettura. Nuova Giur Civ Comm II:989 ff
Pinelli AM (2022) La circolazione dei dati personali tra tutela della persona, contratto e mercato. Nuova Giur Civ Comm II:1322 ff
Piraino F (2017) Il regolamento generale sulla protezione dei dati personali e i diritti dell'interessato. Nuove leggi civ. comm., p 339 ff
Poletti D (2024) Il quadro normativo del Data Governance Act: l'esercizio dei diritti dell'interessato nell'attività di intermediazione dei dati. Nuove Leggi Civ Comm, p 533 ff
Pollicino O, Donati F, Finocchiaro G, Paolucci F (eds) (2025) La disciplina dell'intelligenza artificiale, Milano, passim
Proietti G (2024) Definire l'indefinibile? I sistemi di intelligenza artificiale alla ricerca di un inquadramento sistematico. Contr. e Impr., p 882 ff
Resta G (2007) Identità personale e identità digitale. Dir informazione e informatica, p 511 ff
Ricci A (2024) Introduzione al regolamento europeo sull'accesso equo ai dati e sul loro utilizzo. Nuove leggi civ. comm., p 799 ff
Ruggieri L (2023) La dicotomia dati personali e dati non personali: il problema della tutela della persona nei c.dd. dati misti. Dir fam. e pers., 823 ff
Ruggiero DG (2023) Persona e identità digitale, Napoli, p 79 ff
Scola S (2025), The Conditions for the Lawfulness of Personal Data Processing. In this handbook
Senigaglia R (2020) Minore età e contratto. Contributo alla teoria della capacità, Torino, p 75 ff
Siniscalchi AM (2023) Big Data e digitalizzazione del sistema sanitario. Nuovo Dir Civ, p 48 ff
Smorto G (2024) Distribuzione del rischio e tutela dei diritti nel regolamento europeo sull'intelligenza artificiale. Una riflessione critica. Foro it., 208 ff
Stürner M (2021) Europäisches Vertragsrecht, Berlino-Boston, p 163 ff
Taddei Elmi G, Contaldo A (eds) (2024) Intelligenza artificiale. AI Act - Regolamento (UE) 1689/2024. Il nuovo scenario giuridico europeo, Pisa, passim
Tardia I (2017) L'identità digitale tra memoria e oblio, Napoli, p 53 ff
Tescaro M (2014) La tutela postmortale della personalità morale e specialmente dell'identità personale. In Studi in onore di Maurizio Pedrazza Gorlero, I, I diritti fondamentali fra concetti e tutele, Napoli, p 825 ff; also in Jus civ. 2014, p 316 ff
Tommasi S (2023) Digital Services Act e Artificial Intelligence Act: tentativi di futuro da armonizzare. Pers. e merc 2:279 ff
Tosi E (2023) Circolazione contrattuale dei dati personali tra GDPR e nuovo Codice del consumo. Dir. informazione e informatica, p 198 ff
Trabucchi G (2025) Istituzioni di diritto civile, 51ª ed., (eds) Delle Monache-G. Trabucchi-S. Tro iano-M. Tescaro, Milano, p 482
Troiano S (2025), Rights of the Data Subject. In this handbook
Troisi E (2022) Decisione algoritmica, Black-box e AI etica: il diritto di accesso come diritto a ottenere una spiegazione. Jus Civ p 953 ff
Trubiani F (2024) Influencer marketing: libertà della scelta di consumo nel mondo digitale. Dir. informazione e informatica, 385 ff

Versaci G (2022) Consenso al trattamento dei dati personali e dark patterns tra opzionalità e condizionalità. Nuove leggi Civ Comm, p 1130 ff

Zaccaria A (1988) Diritti extrapatrimoniali e successione. Padova, passim.

Zaccaria A, Schmidt-Kessel M, Schulze R, Gambino AM (eds) (2020) EU eIDAS-Regulation. Article-by-Article Commentary, München-Oxford-Baden-Baden-Chicago, passim

Zeno-Zencovich V (1993) Voce Identità personale. Dig Disc Priv Sez Civ, IX, Torino, p 294 ff

Rights of the Data Subject

Stefano Troiano

Contents

Abstract The chapter critically illustrates the multiple tools, both substantive and remedial in nature, that the European General Data Protection Regulation, in the form of 'rights of the data subject', recognises to the user of a digital platform in order to prevent violations of the right to personal data protection or react to them, in increasingly proactive terms.

S. Troiano (✉)
University of Verona, Verona, Italy
e-mail: stefano.troiano@univr.it

R. Bocchini (ed.), *Digital Platforms - From Technical Foundations to Legal and Economic Implications*, https://doi.org/10.1007/978-3-032-07978-7_28

1 Foreword. The Rights of the Data Subject as Internal Articulations of the Unitary Right to Personal Data Protection

The General Data Protection Regulation (EU) 2016/679 (GDPR),[1] the cornerstone of personal data protection legislation within the European Union, outlines in its Chapter III, Articles 12–23, the rules governing the 'rights of the data subject'.

Rather than listing autonomous subjective rights (of the personality), this is a summary formula intended to indicate the powers, faculties, and claims, both substantive and remedial in nature, into which the unitary right to the protection of personal data[2] is divided. This right, enshrined in general terms in Article 1 of the Regulation and reinforced by Article 8 of the Charter of Fundamental Rights of the European Union,[3] is a fundamental legal position with a broad and heterogeneous content.

Not all the prerogatives into which this right is broken down are substantive in nature; some of them function primarily as protective mechanisms— remedies[4] or procedural tools—granting individuals the ability to act, whether within or outside judicial proceedings. The articulation of the content of the right reflects, indeed, the complexity of the very evolution of the right to the protection of personal data. Once centered on a 'static' or 'passive' safeguard against intrusions into private life via personal data, the right has gradually expanded to include 'dynamic' and 'active' prerogatives,[5] which,

---

[1] Regulation (EU) 2016/679 of the European Parliament and of the Council of 27 April 2016 on the protection of individuals with regard to the processing of personal data and on the free movement of such data and repealing Directive 95/46/EC (General Data Protection Regulation).

[2] See, in particular, Piraino (2017), p. 2790.

[3] Article 8 of the EU Charter (Protection of Personal Data) not only enshrines this right but also outlines its essential principles, features and contents, moreover expressly stating its specific declination as the right to access. According to this provision: '1. Everyone has the right to the protection of personal data concerning him or her. 2. Such data must be processed fairly, for specified purposes and on the basis of the consent of the person concerned or some other legitimate basis laid down by law. Everyone shall have the right of access to the data collected concerning him or her and the right to have them rectified. 3. Compliance with these rules shall be subject to control by an independent authority'.

[4] See also Piraino (2017), p. 2790.

[5] The, so to speak, 'negative' dimension of confidentiality, understood as the right to exclude others from knowledge of events in one's personal and family life (commonly referred to in Anglo-American legal contexts as the *right to privacy* or the right *to be left alone*), has been complemented, over time, by a broader conception. This expanded view encompasses a set of prerogatives aimed at reserving to the person concerned also, in a proactive key, *control* over the information that concerns them and over the relative flow of data, in close contiguity with the need to guarantee them the power to affect the external projection of their personal identity. This positive declination, in addition to being implicitly derived from Article 2 of the Constitution, found explicit recognition

throughout all stages of data processing, affect from different perspectives and different levels of intensity the processing itself,[6] regardless of concrete violations taking place, and also attributing to the data subject useful tools to prevent them.

The data subject's rights are also to be read as a reflection of the processing principles set out in Article 5, since they are intended, depending on the case, to ensure compliance with them, to prevent their infringement or to react to the infringement of those principles that has occurred in any event.[7]

2 The Right to Transparency and Information

Following the structure of Chapter III, one first encounters the data subject's rights to transparency (see Article 5(1)(a)) and to information—rights that the Regulation, in line also with the principle of accountability,[8] has significantly expanded compared to the former Directive 95/46/EC.

This extension is evident, first and foremost, from a quantitative perspective: the list of information that the data controller must provide to the data subject— either from the time of collection of the data from the data subject (Art. 13) or even when the data are not obtained from the data subject (Art. 14)—is now extensive and detailed, and must be supplied irrespective of a specific request by the latter.

In the former case, the required information—provided that the data subject does not already possess it—include, above all, the identity and contact details of the data controller and, where applicable, of its representative and the data protection officer,

---

in Directive 95/46/EC (Directive 95/46/EC of the European Parliament and of the Council of 24 October 1995 on the protection of individuals with regard to the processing of personal data and on the free movement of such data), implemented in Italy by Law no. 675/1996 (Law no. 675 of 31 December 1996, Protection of persons and other subjects with regard to the processing of personal data), later absorbed by Legislative Decree no. 196/2003 (Legislative Decree no. 196 of 30 June 2003, Personal Data Protection Code, so called *Privacy* Code), as well as in the aforementioned Art. 8 EU Charter.

[6] For an overview of the evolution of the right to personal data protection over time, prior to the EU Regulation, see Finocchiaro (2012).

[7] The reference is to the principles, set out precisely in Art. 5(1), of 'lawfulness, fairness and transparency', 'purpose limitation', 'data minimisation', 'accuracy', 'limitation of storage', 'integrity and confidentiality' (on which see Dell'Utri (2019), p. 179 ff; Colapietro and Iannuzzi (2017), p. 85 ff). To these must added the so-called principle of 'accountability' or, in the Italian version, of 'responsabilizzazione', enshrined in para. 2, according to which 'the data controller is responsible for compliance with para. 1 and able to prove it', on which we refer, *infra*, to S. Gatti, Sec. VI.

[8] The intimate connection between transparency and accountability is highlighted by the *Guidelines on Transparency under Regulation 2016/679*, prepared by the Article 29 Working Party on 29 November 2017 and amended on 11 April 2018, 4. See also Ricci (2019), p. 395.

the purposes[9] and legal basis of the processing; the recipients or categories of recipients of the personal data, if any; and any intention of the data controller to transfer personal data to a third country or international organisation, including a reference to appropriate or adequate safeguards. In addition to this information, and specifically for the purpose of 'ensuring fair and transparent processing',[10] information must also be provided concerning, inter alia, the retention period of the personal data or, where this is not possible, the criteria used to determine that period, as well as the rights of the data subject[11] and the existence of an automated decision-making process, including profiling.

In the second case, the data controller is required to provide the data subject with information (largely coinciding with that required by Art. 13) as to where the data originated, within a reasonable period of time after obtaining the personal data, but at the latest within one month, having regard to the specific circumstances in which the personal data are processed, or, where the personal data are intended for communication with the data subject, at the latest at the time of the first communication to the data subject, or, finally, where communication to another recipient is envisaged, no later than the first communication of the personal data.[12]

Even at a qualitative level, however, emphasis is placed on the detailed definition and proceduralisation of the ways in which the information must be provided.[13] The data controller is required to take 'appropriate measures' to provide the data subject with all the information referred to in Articles 13 and 14 and the communications referred to in Articles 15 to 22 and Article 34 relating to the processing 'in a concise, transparent, intelligible and easily accessible form, in plain and intelligible language, in particular in the case of information specifically addressed to children'.[14]

---

[9] Pursuant to para. 3, where the data controller intends to further process personal data for a purpose other than that for which it was collected, it shall, prior to such further processing, provide the data subject with information as to that other purpose and any further relevant information referred to in para. 2.

[10] See recitals 39 and 60.

[11] Access, rectification, erasure, restriction of processing, objection, portability, withdrawal of consent and complaint to the supervisory authority.

[12] In this case, however, the obligation to provide information does not exist when: communicating such information would be impossible or would involve a disproportionate effort; for processing for archiving purposes in the public interest, for scientific or historical research or for statistical purposes, or insofar as the obligation might render impossible or seriously jeopardise the attainment of the purposes of such processing; the obtaining or disclosure is expressly provided for by Union or Member State law to which the controller is subject and which provides for appropriate measures to protect the data subject's legitimate interests; or where the personal data must remain confidential pursuant to an obligation of professional secrecy laid down by Union or Member State law, including an obligation of secrecy laid down by law. See, in this respect, also recitals 61 and 62.

[13] V. Ricci (2019), p. 395.

[14] See on this point the aforementioned *Guidance on Transparency under Regulation 2016/679*, WP29, where it is specified (3 f.) that the transparency obligation 'is not legalistic, but rather user-centred' and that, 'in any case, the quality, accessibility and comprehensibility of the information

Transparency, which was previously an implicit requirement derived from the duty of fairness, now emerges as an explicit and essential dimension within which the duty to inform must be fulfilled throughout the entire duration of processing, in a manner that, as required by the principle of *accountability*, must be modulated in a flexible form according to both the concrete circumstances and the subjective qualities of the data subject.

As a rule, information is provided in writing or, where appropriate, by electronic means, unless the data subject requests that it be provided orally. The information may, however, also be provided in combination with standardised icons in order to give, in an easily visible, intelligible and clearly legible manner, an overview of the intended processing. If presented electronically, the icons must be machine-readable (Art. 12(7)).[15]

Finally, the information must be provided free of charge.[16]

3 The Right to Access

While transparency and information are primarily addressed in the Regulation in their passive dimension, i.e. as obligations incumbent upon the data controller, the first right that the Regulation expressly recognises as such for the data subject is the right of access (Article 15). The right is also mentioned, as noted above, in Article 8 of the EU Charter, and can arguably be seen as an evolution of the right to information, representing a more robust and incisive expression of it.

It consists in the right to obtain confirmation from the data controller confirmation[17] as to whether or not one's personal data are being processed and, if so, to access those data along with a reasonably detailed set of information concerning them—information that, broadly speaking, corresponds to what the data controller

is just as important as the actual content of the information aimed at transparency that is to be provided to data subjects'.

[15] The Commission is empowered to adopt delegated acts in accordance with Article 92 to determine the information to be presented in the form of icons and the procedures for providing standardised icons (Art. 12(8)).

[16] Only if the data controller demonstrates that the data subject's requests are manifestly unfounded or excessive, in particular because of their repetitive nature, may it charge a reasonable fee taking into account the administrative costs incurred in providing the information or refuse to comply with the request (Art. 12(5)).

[17] The term 'confirmation' is, however, not to be understood in a literal sense. It is not required that the data subject has already received prior information (even from third parties) and is merely seeking its verification from the data controller: see, for example, Lo Surdo (2003), p. 121. And see also Cass. 9 January 2013, no. 349.

is already obliged to provide under Articles 13 or 14, depending on whether the data were collected from the data subject or from another source.[18]

The right of access also includes the right to obtain, free of charge[19] (and in the case of a request submitted by electronic means) in a commonly used electronic form, a copy of the personal data undergoing processing. The explicit recognition of this aspect represents a novelty introduced by the Regulation, intended to strengthen the right of access.[20] However, the exercise of this right must not infringe upon the rights and freedoms of others,[21] and in such cases, a careful balancing of interests must be carried out on a case-by-case basis.[22]

The data subject exercises the right of access by submitting a request to the data controller, who, pursuant to Article 12, must reply without undue delay and, in any event, within one month of receipt of the request. If the request is made by electronic means, the prescribed information must also normally be provided in the same form, in a commonly used electronic format.

In the broad terms in which it is framed, the right of access may be seen as a (substantive) position with a primarily informational content,[23] offering the data subject a minimum yet essential protection. Full and accurate knowledge of which data are processed and how they are being processed constitutes an indispensable prerequisite for the data subject to be able to exercise the other (substantive and, above all, remedial) positions recognised by the Regulation.[24]

---

[18] In this respect too, there is a (albeit slight) extension, compared to the previous regime, of the information that the data subject is entitled to receive, which also includes the data retention period and the existence of the data subject's other rights (see Ricci (2019), p. 395).

[19] Again, this is without prejudice to the case of repeated exercise of the right, in which case the data subject may be charged a reasonable fee based on administrative costs.

[20] See Ricci (2019), p. 399, who recalls how the Italian Data Protection Authority had therefore, on several occasions, denied that the right of access also included the right to obtain a copy of the data, except in cases where obtaining a copy of the data was the only way for the data subject to acquire knowledge of them.

[21] Including any industrial or intellectual property rights.

[22] The issue has been dealt with on several occasions by the Italian Privacy Guarantor, not infrequently with regard to the hypothesis in which the right of access is exercised by heirs with respect to bank accounts in the name of the deceased. As a rule, in these cases, the information must be provided 'taking care, however, to obscure any personal information referring to third parties' (thus, e.g. Garante per la protezione dei dati personali 20 May 2004 [web doc. no. 1098787]). However, it was specified that 'in certain cases... the need may arise to produce and hand over copies not only of individual personal data, but also of entire acts or documents that might also concern third parties. This only if the personal data relating to the applicant and any other news or information relating to third parties are intertwined to such an extent as to render the former incomprehensible, or distorted in their content, if deprived of certain essential elements for their comprehension, which may include, as in the case in point, information relating to joint holders who carry out relevant transactions in the common relationship" (Garante per la protezione dei dati personali 3 aprile 2002, in *Bollettino*, n. 27, 20 [doc. web n. 1065256]).

[23] A "right to know", therefore: see Alpa (1998), p. 719.

[24] See Ricci (2019), p. 398; Di Genio (2016), p.170.

It should be emphasised that, precisely because of its instrumental nature, the exercise of the right is in no way conditional on the data subject's allegation of a breach, either actual or potential, is not subject to time limits[25] and does not have to be justified.[26]

4 The Right to Rectification and Supplementation

In contrast to the merely 'static' protection afforded by the right of access, the other rights enshrined in the Regulation confer upon the data subject a set of powers enabling direct intervention on the processing. These rights thus fully embody the 'dynamic' and proactive content of the right to personal data protection. This dynamic nature also highlights the underlying connection with the right to personal identity, also understood as the individual's capacity to shape the accurate representation of their identity in the external world, including its projection into the digital world sphere.[27]

In this perspective, the right to rectification (Article 16) is of primary relevance. It entitles the data subject to obtain from the data controller, without undue delay and in any case within one month from receipt of the request, the rectification of inaccurate personal data concerning him as well as the integration of those that are incomplete in the light of the purpose of the processing, also by providing a supplementary statement. This right represents a concrete application of the principle of accuracy, as set out in Article 5(1)(d) of the Regulation.

The former directive did not expressly provide for the right to obtain the supplementation of data, now explicitly provided for by the Regulation. Nonetheless, such right could arguably have been implied within a broad meaning of rectification, encompassing any modification intended to restore the truthfulness of the data, and

---

[25] On this point see Court of Justice. EU 7 May 2009, C-553/07 - *College van burgemeester en wethouders van Rotterdam v M. E. Rijkeboer*, for which Article 12(a) of Directive 95/46/EC 'requires Member States to provide for a right of access to information on the recipients or categories of recipients of the data as well as on the content of the information disclosed not only for the present, but also for the past'. It is therefore for the Member States to lay down a time-limit for the storage of that information and the corresponding access to it which strikes a fair balance between, on the one hand, the interest of the person concerned in protecting his privacy, in particular by means of intervention and the possibilities of bringing legal proceedings provided for by the directive, and, on the other hand, the burden which the obligation to store that information places on the controller. In the present case, it was held that legislation which limits the retention of and access to information to a period of one year, even though the basic data are retained for much longer, does not strike that balance, unless it can be shown that retaining that information for longer would impose an excessive burden on the controller.

[26] See Ricci (2019), p. 402.

[27] See, of course, M. Tescaro, *supra*, Sec. I. On the intimate connection between rectification/integration and the protection of personal identity see also Ricci (2019), p. 403.

therefore also including supplementation, in cases where inaccuracy consisted in the lacunae, incompleteness or even the lack of contextualisation of the information.[28]

Since rectification is a remedy granted to address the inaccuracy of information, it presupposes that the information in question contributes to the objective construction of the individual's identity profile in its social dimension. Conversely, rectification cannot be invoked to request the modification of subjective and discretionary assessments or judgements (e.g. a negative evaluation in an examination report), except insofar as it concerns the supplementation or correction of objective information on which those judgements are, or may be, based.[29]

5 The Right to Erasure

As we move up the scale of possible interventions to ensure compliance with data processing requirements, Article 17 introduces the right to erasure, also referred to, by the Regulation itself, as the 'right to be forgotten', a concept which, as will be said, deserves however a separate discussion (*infra*, *sub* 5).

The right to erasure entitles the date subject to obtain from the data controller, without undue delay (i.e. as quickly as possible),[30] the erasure of their personal data when one of the grounds listed in Article 17 is met, which render the processing no longer justified, either for objective reasons or based on the data subject's own will. Such conditions include situations where the personal data are no longer necessary in relation to the purpose of the processing; the processing is unlawful; a legal obligation laid down by Union or Member-State law to which the data controller is subject requires the erasure; or, again, the processing concerns children's data collected (pursuant to Article 8(1)) in connection with the provision of information society services.

Reasons dependent on the data subject include the case of withdrawal of consent by the data subject, provided no other legal basis for processing exists, and the case of exercise by the data subject of the right to object to the processing under Article 21.[31]

In all such cases, the data subject shall have the right to obtain from the controller the erasure of personal data concerning them without undue delay, and the controller shall be obliged to erase the personal data without undue delay. Moreover, taking

---

[28] Ricci (2019), p. 403.This is confirmed by the fact that the possibility of integration was provided for, in Italy, both by Article 13 of Law No. 675/1996 and by Article 7(3)(a) of the Privacy Code.

[29] See, e.g., Garante per la protezione dei dati personali 17 June 1999, doc. web 48067, with specific regard to objective information underlying assessments of an employee's performance. In this regard, the Garante clarified that rectification may only be requested with respect to such data and, in any case, only after the assessment has been completed.

[30] Di Ciommo (2019), p. 356.

[31] Provided that, since the opposition is requested on the basis of Article 2(1), there is no overriding legitimate reason to proceed with the processing.

into account available technology and the cost of implementation, the controller must take reasonable steps, including technical measures, to inform other controllers processing the data of the data subject's request to erase any links to, copy or reproduction of their personal data.[32]

The peculiar content of the right, centered on the removal of data whose processing is not (or is no longer) justified, highlights its primarily remedial function.[33] However, in cases where the lack of justification derives solely from the will of the data subject, as in the case of revocation of consent, the right to erasure also assumes a substantive dimension. In this sense, it can be understood as the extension of the (substantive, precisely) right to personal identity, serving as a means for individuals to reclaim and assert control over the intimate aspects of their identity.

As for the concept of 'erasure', it includes, according to the prevailing opinion, both the removal/deletion of data in the strict sense (which results in the cessation of any further processing by the data controller) and anonymisation,[34] due to the capacity of the latter to achieve the same practical outcome as deletion: namely, the exclusion of data from the scope of application of the Regulation.[35]

Deletion, however, must be kept distinct from the restriction of processing (which will be discussed shortly), which is not an equivalent measure. Consequently, in situations where Article 17 imposes an obligation on the data controller to delete personal data, that obligation cannot be satisfied merely by restricting the processing of the data. Finally, de-indexing, i.e. the technical operation by means of which an Internet search engine removes certain content from its indexations, does not amount to full data erasure. In this way, the data associated with them are not completely removed from the network, where they remain usable, but are prevented from being found by querying that particular search engine. While it prevents the data from being retrieved via that particular search engine, the information itself remains on the web and can still be accessed by other means. On whether de-indexing can be regarded as an appropriate response, under certain conditions, to a request for erasure (particularly in the context the right to be forgotten), however, the EU Court of Justice expressed a favourable opinion in the landmark *Google Spain* judgement of 2014, which will be discussed shortly.

Like all fundamental rights, the right to erasure—conceived as a specific expression of the broader right to personal data protection—is subject to the principle of balancing. This means that it must be weighed against other potentially conflicting

[32] This additional obligation constitutes a novelty of the Regulation compared to the previous legislation, aimed, as recital 66 specifies, at strengthening the right to be forgotten in the online environment. It is considered that the data controllers to whom the information must be addressed are those who process the same data by reason of the publication of those data by the obligatory data controller (and not also those who process those data for having obtained them independently): Di Ciommo (2019), p. 359.

[33] Piraino (2017), p. 2794.

[34] On these concepts see D'Acquisto and Naldi (2017).

[35] This cannot be said, however, of pseudonymisation, which always leaves open the possibility of recovering the link between the data and the identity of the data subject.

interests and may, in certain circumstances,[36] wholly or partially be limited or overridden where compelling justifications exist for doing so.

This elementary balancing requirement is met by the provisions of Article 17(3), which provide for five situations in which the right to erasure does not operate,[37] most of which have already emerged extensively in the course of the decades-long application, in domestic and EU law, of data protection legislation.

This is the case, in particular, when processing is necessary: (a) for the exercise of the right to freedom of expression and information; (b) for compliance with a legal obligation or for the performance of a task carried out in the public interest or in the exercise of official authority vested in the data controller; (c) for reasons of public interest in the field of public health; (d) for archiving purposes in the public interest, scientific or historical research or statistical purposes; or (e) for the establishment, exercise, or defence of legal claims.

With regard to the relationship with freedom of information, recital 153 and Article 85(1) of the Regulation are also relevant, as they require Member-States to reconcile the rules governing freedom of expression and information, including journalistic, academic, artistic, or literary expression, with the right to protection of personal data under the Regulation. With specific regard to processing carried out for journalistic purposes or for the purposes of academic, artistic or literary expression, Member-States may therefore provide for exemptions or derogations from the rules of the Regulation, including those relating to the rights of the data subject, where they are necessary to reconcile the right to the protection of personal data with freedom of expression and information,[38] by notifying the Commission of the adopted derogations without delay.[39]

It is worth recalling that Italian jurisprudence, like that of other European countries, has long developed criteria for establishing when the right to privacy and, specifically, the right to the protection of personal data must yield to the exercise of freedom of information (in the form, in particular, of the right to report news). These criteria include the truthfulness of the fact, the existence of a public interest in their knowledge,[40] the essential nature of the dissemination of the data, which must be contained within the necessary limits with respect to the news, and the objectivity

---

[36] It goes without saying that the balancing must be carried out in relation to the peculiarities and concrete circumstances of each case, according to the prudent appreciation, ultimately, of the judge.

[37] The fact that such a provision is not repeated with regard to the other proactive rights of defence of the data subject (rectification, restriction of processing, objection to processing) is probably justified by the particularly drastic and invasive nature of erasure, which requires greater precautions to safeguard the interests of others that conflict with it. See Di Ciommo (2019), p. 361.

[38] For a critique of this 'blank' delegation, whose dangers are denounced particularly in relation to the risk of fragmenting national regulations, Di Ciommo (2019), p. 363.

[39] It should be noted that, unlike the general limits enshrined in Article 17(3) of the Regulation, derogations from national sources may concern not only the right to erasure but also the other rights of the data subject (rectification, restriction of processing, objection to processing, etc.). This is noted by Di Ciommo (2019), p. 368.

[40] The public interest in question, as will be clarified shortly with specific regard to the right to be forgotten, must also be assessed in terms of its present-day relevance.

of the information with respect to the informative purpose pursued, thus avoiding suggestive or hyperbolic methods.[41]

6 In Particular, the 'Right to be Forgotten'

One of the main innovations introduced by Regulation (EU) 2016/679 with regard to the rights of data subjects is represented by the express reference, in the heading of Art. 17, to the 'right *to be forgotten*'. This legal concept, initially developed through the case law of many European national courts (including the Italian Court of Cassation)[42] and later affirmed by the EU Court of Justice itself, has evolved into the right of an individual to have information relating to a past event no longer available to the public, provided that, also due to the time that has elapsed since the event took place, the information is no longer of public interest. The right to be forgotten thus protects a fundamental dimension of personal identity: the interest in avoiding indefinite exposure to outdated representation of oneself, due to republication (or continued publication) over a long period of time of information relating to past events that no longer hold current relevance.[43]

This marks the first formal recognition of this right in European legislation. However, its mention alongside the 'right to erasure' in Article 17, as if to imply that it is a synonym or, at most, a specific declination of it, is misleading in many respects. It should be noted, in fact, that, on the one hand, the wording of this provision does not contain a definition of the meaning of the phrase[44] and that, on the other hand, the concept of oblivion that has been emerging in national legal experiences does not seem to coincide entirely with that of (mere) erasure.

In particular, in the absence of an express definition, it has to be established whether the interest underlying the request for oblivion can also be satisfied through tools such as de-indexing from search engines, anonymisation of data or their better contextualisation. These alternatives may have a far less disruptive impact on the competing interests of information and press reporting and could therefore offer a more proportionate means of balancing the conflicting interests, without sacrificing the protection of the identity of the data subject. The exercise of the right to erasure has, in fact, an undoubted impact on *online* platforms and search engines,

[41] In this sense, see, in Italy, the "Code of ethics relating to the processing of personal data in the exercise of journalistic activity", issued by order of the Garante per la protezione dei dati personali of 29 July 1998. In case law, see, for all, Cass., un. sec., 22 July 2019, no. 19681.

[42] See, among many others, the already cited Cass., un. sec., no. 2019/19681.

[43] See, above all, Bianca (2019), p. 22, who sees in the right to be forgotten a manifestation of the *diachronic* dimension of personal identity, consisting in an individual's right to prevent information concerning them, which, due to the time that has elapsed since it was made public, has now lost its informational relevance, from continuing to be associated with them.

[44] Di Ciommo (2019), p. 371.

which must manage users' requests by balancing the right to erasure with other fundamental rights, such as precisely, access to information.

The EU Court of Justice's response on this point, formulated in 2014 in the Google Spain case,[45] even though it concerned a case governed by the rules prior to the Regulation, was clear in the sense of opening up space for de-indexation as a tool to respond to requests for oblivion.[46] In that case, the applicant had sought an order against Google Spain and Google Inc. for the removal or concealment from the search engine of information relating to forced sale of real estate at public auction, following foreclosure proceedings initiated for the recovery of social security debts. Although the events had taken place many years earlier and although the related newspaper article had been lawfully published at the time, reporting on the forthcoming auction in compliance with an order from the competent authority, the information remained readily accessible via the search engine. This persistent availability, despite the clear loss of public relevance over time, was found to unjustifiably infringe the applicant's right to privacy.

Among the many profiles of interest, the ruling is therefore noteworthy because it clarifies the contours of the right to be forgotten, well grasping its only partial overlap with the right to erasure and better defining its relationship with the right to information (and therefore to memory).

Similar considerations are also found in the Guidelines of the *European Data Protection Board,*[47] which clearly specify the legal bases of the right to de-indexing, as a way of implementing the right to be forgotten.

7 The Rights to Restriction of Processing and to Object to Processing, Including Profiling (Referral)

Article 18 of the Regulation grants the data subject the right to obtain from the controller the restriction of processing, which, according to Article 4, no. 3, consists in the marking of the stored personal data, with the aim of limiting the processing of the marked data to the mere storage of those data in the future or only to the processing expressly permitted by the data subject or necessary for the establishment, exercise, or defence of legal claims or the protection of the rights of another natural or

[45] CJEU, Grand Chamber, 13 May 2014, C-131/12. The issue also came back to the Court's attention in CJEU, Grand Chamber, 24 September 2019, C-507/17, to which we owe the clarification that the operator of a search engine does not have to comply with the request for de-indexing in all versions of its platform, but only in those corresponding to the Member States of the European Union.

[46] On the reflection of this ruling on the civil liability of the Internet provider see Tescaro (2020), p. 172 ff.

[47] EDPB, *Guidelines 5/2019 on criteria for the exercise of the right to be forgotten in the case of search engines, under the GDPR (Part 1)*, Version 2.0, Adopted 7 July 2020 (at *https://www.edpb.europa.eu/sites/default/files/file1/edpb_guidelines_201905_rtbfsearchengines_afterpublicconsultation_en.pdf*).

legal person or for reasons of substantial public interest of the Union or a Member-State. The effect aimed at by the exercise of the right is not, therefore, the erasure of the data, but rather the imposition of a lien on them[48] limiting their availability and use.[49]

This right arises in four cases, considered exhaustive:[50] when (a) the data subject contests the accuracy of the personal data, for the period necessary for the data controller to verify the accuracy of those personal data; (b) the processing is unlawful and the data subject objects to the erasure of the personal data, requesting instead that their use be restricted; (c) although the data controller no longer needs the personal data for the purposes of the processing, the personal data are necessary for the establishment, exercise, or defence of a legal claim; (d) the data subject has objected to the processing pursuant to Art. 21(1) of the Regulation, pending verification as to whether the legitimate grounds of the data controller override those of the data subject.[51]

This list highlights the essentially remedial function of the right to restriction of processing, like the right to erasure.[52]

Recital 67 identifies, by way of example,[53] the modalities that data controllers may resort to in order to restrict the processing of personal data, which could consist, inter alia, in temporarily transferring selected data to another processing system, making selected personal data inaccessible to users or temporarily removing data published by a website.[54]

Logically related to the right of restriction is, again, the right to object to processing, provided for by Article 21 and extended by Article 22 also, with more specific

---

[48] Directive 95/46/EC, in the Italian version, provided for the possibility of obtaining data '*congelamento*' ('freezing'), a suggestive expression intended to translate the English '*blocking*'. The Italian transposing legislation had, however, preferred to adopt the formula '*blocco*' ('blocking'), more in keeping with the English version (see Article 7(3) of the Privacy Code). Compared to data blocking, data restriction is however a more precise concept and better defined in its (peremptory) application prerequisites, expressly requiring, moreover, the 'marking' of the data as a guarantee of effectiveness and publicity of the restriction (see Di Ciommo (2019), p. 367).

[49] Ricci (2019), p. 429.

[50] See also Ricci (2019), p. 429.

[51] These assumptions are largely taken from those already indicated in Regulation (EC) No 45/2001 of 18 December 2000 on the protection of individuals with regard to the processing of personal data by the Union institutions, bodies, offices and agencies and on the free movement of such data, now repealed and replaced by Regulation (EU) 2018/1725 of the European Parliament and of the Council of 23 October 2018.

[52] See in this sense Piraino (2017), p. 2795, who frames it properly among the means of reaction to unlawful or improper processing.

[53] The choice is therefore ultimately left to the data controller, who, in line with the principle of *accountability*, assumes responsibility for identifying the most appropriate means to the end. See Di Ciommo (2019), pp. 366 and 368.

[54] With specific regard to automated files, it is also stipulated that the restriction of the processing of personal data should in principle be ensured by technical devices in such a way that personal data are not subject to further processing and can no longer be modified. The system should also clearly indicate that the processing of personal data has been restricted.

provisions, to the sensitive case of automated processing of personal data, which includes profiling. This right, in view of its unquestionable importance in today's digital information society, and its strategic importance in curbing what can be considered, today, among the most insidious conducts in terms of the risk of an attack on individuals' digital identity, has already been discussed at length in Chapter I of this Part II, to which we therefore refer.[55]

8 The Right to Portability

Finally, *a sui generis* position, among the data subject's rights, is occupied by the right to data portability, introduced for the first time, marking a significant innovation,[56] by the Regulation in the European framework for personal data protection (Article 20). This is a legal situation with a complex content, which includes at least two distinct claims.

First, the data subject is entitled to receive the data in a structured, commonly used and machine-readable format, the personal data concerning him provided to a data controller. According to the principle of technological neutrality by which the Regulation is inspired, there are, however, no technical indications from a legislative source on specific technological choices: the common use of a format must therefore be determined on the basis of the technical state of the art.

Second, the data subject has the right to transmit those data to another data controller without any impediment (or expense) and can be opposed by the data controller to whom he provided them.

A third, optional facet of the right to portability may also come into play: the right to obtain the *direct* transmission of personal data from one controller to another, if technically feasible.[57] It is important to note that such a request does not necessarily imply or entail the deletion of the data from the first controller.[58]

If we consider the first component, the right under scrutiny may be viewed as an evolution of the right to access,[59] from which, however, it already differs in that it aims at obtaining a copy of personal data not in any format but in a format that, by its characteristics, facilitates its further re-use by the data subject. When we turn then to the second element, namely the claim to the transmission, possibly even direct, of personal data to another data controller, the innovative character of this

---

[55] *See supra*, M. Tescaro, Sec. I.

[56] Underlined by most commentators: Kühling and Martini (2016), p. 450; Scudiero (2017), p. 119; Wong and Henderson (2019), p. 173.

[57] Somaini (2018), p. 165, speaks of a right with threefold content. Instead, Pezza (2018), p. 203, speaks of a twofold content, evidently not considering the last claim as autonomous from the first two.

[58] See recital 68.

[59] Ricci (2019), p. 229.

right becomes more apparent. Unlike the 'static' nature of the right to access,[60] data portability aims at achieving the maximum enhancement of the right to dynamic and active control over one's own data,[61] at the same time facilitating the transition from one service provider to another (e.g. in social networks, by allowing people to move their *online* profiles from one platform to another in a single operation) and rebalancing the relationship between data subjects and data controllers (see recital 68).

Because of these peculiarities, the right to portability lies along the ridge between the protection of the individual (whose power to control data is maximised) and the need to regulate the data market,[62] insofar as, by removing the constraints (so-called 'lock-in') that bind the data subject to a given digital service provider,[63] it allows the data subject to exercise his or her right to privacy, while strengthening competition between companies[64] (as in the precursor institution, i.e. that of telephone number portability: see directive 2002/22/EC on universal service). Positive competition is thus fostered, which is hoped will also facilitate the creation of new digital services and the development of technologies that are attentive to the protection of *privacy* and based on interoperable formats.

The second 'soul' of the Regulation, namely its ambition to foster the development of a (certain and secure) data market,[65] that the legislator seeks to reconcile with its properly personalistic dimension, becomes particularly evidente in the provision of this right. It cannot be overlooked, however, that the broad scope of the data subject's powers of use and (re)transfer, even in bulk, of their own data risks, by means of an unintended heterogenesis of ends, multiplying the opportunities for harm to individual rights associated with data circulation. This is in clear contradiction with what is suggested by the general principle of data minimisation set out in Articles 5 and 6 of the Regulation.

In order at least partially to meet these concerns, but also, conversely (and therefore in a perspective unrelated to the concern for the protection of the data subject), to contain the heavy burdens that the obligation to comply with requests for portability may impose on data controllers, the Regulation therefore subjects the exercise of this right to several limitations.

---

[60] See, *amplius*, Troiano (2025), p. 159, and Troiano (2019), p. 198.

[61] As explicitly stated in Recital 68. On the right to portability as a fundamental right see Pelino (2016), p. 250 and Somaini (2018), p. 171. On the dynamic nature of the right to portability see Battelli and D'Ippolito (2019), p. 193.

[62] See Monteleone (2017), p. 205 And see also Fenwick et al. (2023).

[63] The point is highlighted in Working Party Article 29, *Guidelines on the right to data portability*, adopted 13 December 2016, amended version and adopted 5 April 2017, 16/IT, WP 242 rev.01, 4. On the similarity with the right to telephone number portability see Graef et al. (2018), p. 1359.

[64] However, the effectiveness of the instrument in terms of promoting competition is controversial. See the perplexities of Weber (2016), p. 67. and Krämer et al. (2020), p. 55 ff and p. 272 ff.

[65] For Piraino (2017), p. 2796, portability implies the 'recognition of a typical power of disposition, such as the prerogative of ceding to third parties the right to exploit an entity over which control can be exercised that overrides another's interest in exclusive use'.

First of all, it operates only where the processing is based on the data subject's consent (pursuant to Article 6(1)(a) or Article 9(2)(a)) or on its necessity for the performance of a contract or for the performance of the pre-contractual phase of a contract (pursuant to Article 6(1)(b)), and, moreover, on the further condition, which is also necessary, that the processing is carried out by automated means. These are therefore cases in which from the outset the processing is based, to some extent, on intentional conduct on the part of the data subject: data processed on other legal grounds (e.g. legitimate interest) are, by contrast, excluded from the right to portability.

Furthermore, in order to fall within the right to portability, the data must be clearly referable to the person invoking the right and have been provided by the data subject. Hence, the inapplicability of this measure to anonymous or anonymised data, whereas its applicability to pseudonymised data does not seem to be ruled out, as these are data that remain linkable, albeit with certain expedients, to a specific data subject.[66]

More controversial is the requirement that the data must come from the data subject. The fact that the data must be 'provided by the data subject' leads to the conclusion that the data controller is not obliged to comply with requests for portability relating to data that the data controller has autonomously obtained on the basis of further processing of raw data provided by the data subject[67] (so-called 'inferred' or 'derived' data, i.e. data obtained by inference from data processed on the data subject's instructions). It is not clear, however, whether the concept of data provided by the data subject is to be understood in a narrow sense, i.e. with reference to the data that the data subject has knowingly handed over to the data controller, or in a broad sense, as referring to all the data that the data controller obtains also through the observation of the activities carried out by the data subject in using the service.[68]

Again, the right to portability must not infringe the rights and freedoms of others (Article 20(4)), including both the rights of other data subjects (think of the extremely frequent case where a user's data in a social profile also contains the personal data of several people) and the rights of other third parties or of the data controller or processor itself (intellectual property, trade secrets, etc.). In these situations, a careful case-by-case balancing exercise is required.[69] This assessment should consider the nature of the conflicting rights and the type of harm that the exercise of

[66] As already mentioned, pseudonymised data are personal data within the meaning of the GDPR.

[67] One thinks of a heartbeat, from which, with appropriate algorithmic processing, it is possible to derive information on the state of health or habits of the data subject.

[68] On this point, the *WP29* has argued for the most extensive interpretation (WP29, *Guidelines on the right to* data *portability*, cit., 9 f.; the view that includes 'observed data' within the scope of portability is shared by Krämer (2021), p. 290), but the conclusion may raise some doubts, especially considering the greater risks it entails for the protection of the data subject's personal data (nor should it be overlooked that the distinction between observed personal data and inferential data is, in practice, very blurred) (see Pezza (2018), p. 204). A reading in accordance with the general principles of the Regulation, in particular that of minimisation, should perhaps lead to a different conclusion.

[69] The unpredictability of this procedure is emphasised by Somaini (2018), p. 184.

portability might cause to them Preference should be given to solutions — to which data controllers must make themselves available where technically feasible — that allow the data subject to select the relevant data and exclude (or anonymise) those relating to other individuals whose exposure could result in harm.[70]

Finally, another limitation to portability is that the right is excluded where processing is necessary for the performance of a task carried out in the public interest or in the exercise of official authority vested in the data controller.[71]

The limitations identified not only reduce the effectiveness of the right to portability[72] but also contribute to the still relatively limited adoption of this instrument, which, moreover, is not always adequately known by the potential data subjects themselves.[73]

It should, however, be pointed out that, in recent years, thanks to other European Union regulatory measures already in force or still in preparation, portability is undergoing a major evolution.

From being the content of a specific right of the data subject with respect to his or her own personal data, in the terms contemplated by the aforementioned Article 20 of the Regulation, portability is increasingly becoming a commonly used concept also outside the specific sphere of personal data, where it does not necessarily present itself as the subject of a specific subjective right. Moreover, data portability is receiving specific consideration in some areas from which it was initially excluded or for which more detailed regulation is needed, such as health data[74] or consumer

[70] According to the *WP29* guidelines, the decisive factor is whether the processing serves an exclusively personal purpose of the data subject: WP29, *Guidelines on the right to* data *portability*, cit., 13: "in order to avoid infringing the rights and freedoms of the third parties concerned, the processing of the personal data in question by a different controller is only allowed to the extent that the data remain in the exclusive availability of the user who had requested their portability and are used exclusively for personal or domestic purposes. The 'new' controller who has received such data (even directly, if the user so requests) may not use the data referring to third parties for its own purposes—for example, to propose marketing offers and services to the said third parties, or to enrich the profile of the third parties concerned and reconstruct their social context without their knowledge and consent. Nor can it use them to derive information about the third parties in question and create specific profiles, even if it already holds their personal data'.

[71] On this point, however, the WP29 guidelines have established that even in these cases where the public interest prevails, it is still desirable that good practices be established whereby the data controller puts in place processes capable of automatically following up on requests for portability. Think of systems allowing the data subject to receive from the government data on the income taxes he or she will have to pay over the years: Article 29 Working Party, *Guidelines on the Right to* Data *Portability*, cit., 8.

[72] Defined as a blunt weapon by Kuebler et al. (2021), p. 268.

[73] A recent survey on German users' knowledge of their GDPR rights showed that data portability is the data subject right, among those under the GDPR, that is known to the lowest percentage of respondents (Kuebler et al. (2021), p. 266.). There are also few rulings concerning the right to portability in the EU (and none from the Court of Justice).

[74] See Regulation (EU) 2025/327 of 11 February 2025 on the European Health Data Space and amending Directive 2011/24/EU and Regulation (EU) 2024/2847.

protection.[75] Therefore, it increasingly appears as a multifaceted and versatile concept that can take on variable functions and content. For this reason, some authors today prefer to decline the concept in the plural, speaking of 'portabilities', thus outlining the existence in European legislation of different forms of portability.[76]

References

Alpa G (1998) La normativa sui dati personali. Note esegetiche sulla Legge 31 dicembre 1996, n. 675 e successive modifiche, Roma, p 719

Battelli, D'Ippolito G (2019) Il diritto alla portabilità dei dati personali. In: Tosi E (ed) Privacy digitale. Riservatezza e protezione dei dati personali tra GDPR e nuovo Codice della Privacy, Milano, p 193

Bianca M (2019) Memoria ed oblio: due reali antagonisti?. Medialaws, p 22

Colapietro C, Iannuzzi A (2017) I principi generali del trattamento dei dati personali e i diritti dell'interessato. In: Califano L, Colapietro C (eds), Innovazione tecnologica e valore della persona. Il diritto alla protezione dei dati personali nel Regolamento UE 2016/679, Napoli, p 85 ff

D'Acquisto G, Naldi M (2017) Big data e privacy by design. Anonimizzazione, Pseudonimizzazione, Sicurezza, Torino

Dell'Utri M (2019) Principi generali e condizioni di liceità del trattamento dei dati personali. In: Cuffaro V, D'Orazio R, Ricciuto V (eds), I dati personali nel diritto europeo, Torino, p 179 ff

Di Ciommo F (2019) Diritto alla cancellazione, diritto di limitazione del trattamento e diritto all'oblio. In: Cuffaro V, D'Orazio R, Ricciuto V (eds) I dati personali nel diritto europeo, Torino, pp 356–371

Di Genio G (2016) Trasparenza e accesso ai dati personali. In: Sica S, D'Antonio V, Riccio GM (eds) La nuova disciplina europea della privacy, Padova, p 170

Fenwick M, Jurcys P, Minssen T, (2023) Data portability revisited: toward the Human-Centric, AI-Driven data ecosystems of tomorrow (June 10, 2023). Vanderbilt J Entertain Technol Law, Forthcoming, Available at SSRN https://ssrn.com/abstract=4475106

Finocchiaro G (2012) Privacy e protezione dei dati personali. Disciplina e strumenti operativi, Bologna

Gatti S (2024) Dalla portabilità alle "portabilità": l'evoluzione al plurale di un diritto (e concetto) chiave nella disciplina europea dei dati. Eur J Priv Law Technol 1:157 ff

Graef I, Husovec M, Purtova N (2018) Data portability and data control: lessons for an emerging concept in EU law. German Law J 19(6):1359

Krämer A, Senellart J, De Streel P (2020) Making Data Portability more effective for the Digital Economy. Centre on Regulation in Europe (Cerre), available at SSRN: https://ssrn.com/abstract=3866495, p 55 ff e 272 ff

Krämer J (2021) Personal data portability. The platform economy: economic implications and policy recommendations. J Compet Law Technol 17, 2, 290

Kuebler S, Wachendorff LR, Kranz J, Mager S, Syrmoudis E, Mayr S, Grossklags J (2021) The Right to Data Portability: conception, status quo, and future directions. Informatik Spektrum 44:266–268

[75] The right to portability also appeared in the European directives that modernised consumer protection in the digital market, in particular in Directive (EU) 2019/770 on certain aspects of contracts for the supply of digital content and services, and in Directive (EU) 2019/2161 so-called *omnibus*, in particular in the rules on distance and off-premises contracts, when the contract concerns digital content or services and the consumer exercises the right of withdrawal.

[76] Gatti (2024), p. 157 ff.

Kühling J, Martini M (2016) Die Datenschutz-Grundverordnung: Revolution oder Evolution im europäischen und deutschen Datenschutzrecht? EuZW 27(12):450
Lo Surdo C (2003) Dati personali e strumenti di tutela del soggetto "interessato". Danno e resp, p 121
Monteleone AG (2017) Il diritto alla portabilità dei dati. Tra diritti della personalità e diritti del mercato. LUISS Law Rev 2:205
Pelino E (2016) I diritti dell'interessato. In: Bolognini L, Pelino E, Astolfi C (eds), Il regolamento privacy europeo. Commentario alla nuova disciplina sulla protezione dei dati personali, p 250
Pezza F (2018) Art. 13 GDPR. In: Riccio GM, Scorza G, Belisario E (eds) GDPR e normativa privacy. Commentario, Milano, pp 203–204
Piraino F (2017) Il regolamento generale sulla protezione dei dati personali e i diritti dell'interessato. Nuove leggi civ. Comm pp 2790–2796
Ricci A (2019) I diritti dell'interessato. In: Finocchiaro G (ed) La protezione dei dati personali in Italia. Regolamento UE n. 2016/679 e d.lgs. 10 agosto 2018, n. 101, Bologna, pp 229–429
Scudiero L (2017) Bringing your data everywhere: a legal reading of the right to portability. Eur Data Protect Law Rev 3(1):119
Somaini L (2018) The right to data portability and user control: ambitions and limitations. Riv Dir Media pp 165–184
Tescaro M (2020) Una proposta ricostruttiva contrastante con il diritto vivente in tema di responsabilità civile dell'internet provider nel diritto italiano tra direttiva 2000/31/CE, regolamento UE 2016/679 e direttiva UE 2019/790. In: Pasquino T, Rizzo A, Tescaro M (eds) Questioni attuali in tema di commercio elettronico, Napoli, p 172 ff
Troiano S (2019) Il diritto alla portabilità dei dati. In: Zorzi N (ed) Persona e mercato dei dati. Riflessioni sul GDPR, p 198 s
Troiano S (2025) Potential and limitations of the right to data portability eight years after the adoption of the GDPR. In: Anzenberger P, Schwaighofer K (eds) Recht der Digitalisierung II, Internationalisierung der Justiz im digitalen Zeitalter, Tübingen, p 159
Weber RH (2016) Data portability and big data analytics. New competition policy challenges. Concorrenza e Mercato 59:67
Wong J, Henderson T (2019) The right to data portability in practice: exploring the implications of the technologically neutral GDPR. Int Data Priv Law 9(3):173

The Conditions for the Lawfulness of Personal Data Processing

Sara Scola

Contents

Abstract This chapter is dedicated to the conditions for the lawfulness of personal data processing envisaged by the GDPR and focuses on their application in the digital world, particularly within platforms. A special investigation is devoted to the consent of minors online.

1 Introduction

For the protection of *privacy*—by which is meant, according to its most modern meaning, not so much the right to exclude others from interfering in one's private life,[1] but, rather, the right to dispose of one's personal data and to protect one's personal

[1] Cf. in this regard ("diritto alla riservatezza"), *ex multis*, De Cupis (1959), p. 256 f., according to whom " la riservatezza può definirsi come quel modo di essere della persona il quale consiste nella esclusione dalla altrui conoscenza di quanto ha riferimento alla persona medesima".

S. Scola (✉)
University of Verona, Verona, Italy
e-mail: sara.scola@univr.it

R. Bocchini (ed.), *Digital Platforms - From Technical Foundations to Legal and Economic Implications*, https://doi.org/10.1007/978-3-032-07978-7_29

identity[2]—stands out, in Article 5 of the GDPR,[3] the principle of lawfulness of personal data processing, which is followed, in Article 6, by the *conditions* of lawfulness of the processing.[4]

The double provision of lawfulness—in both Article 5 and Article 6 of the GDPR—may appear pleonastic[5] but, in fact, it seems to be motivated by a precise intention. The principle of lawfulness in Art. 5 makes it possible to select the presuppositions thus legitimising the processing; moreover, in an overall view of the principles inspiring the legislation, it constitutes the general parameter on the basis of which to assess the lawfulness of the processing in compliance with the further requirements—set out in Art. 6—identified by the law.[6] Rather, as reasonably observed in the literature, the relationship between the two provisions should be read in inverted numerical progression, given that, before defining the *manner in which* processing should be carried out, the *conditions* that make it *ex ante* lawful should be identified.[7]

Art. 6 GDPR, therefore, while not exhausting the normative apparatus of reference,[8] intends to give substance to the principle of lawfulness by detailing a list

---

[2] Battelli (2024), p. 130. Therefore, the processing of personal data, although it may indirectly touch upon the other profile, mainly concerns the proper circulation of personal data: on this topic see also Caggiano (2018), p. 4; see also Bianca (2019), p. 151 f., who also points out that the right to privacy has a two-faced nature, both private and publicistic, since it protects not only the person, but also the market.

[3] "Regulation (EU) 2016/679 of the European Parliament and of the Council of 27 April 2016 on the protection of natural persons with regard to the processing of personal data and on the free movement of such data, and repealing Directive 95/46/EC (General Data Protection Regulation)".

[4] These provisions are in turn aligned with the supranational precepts of Article 8 of the Charter of Nice ('Charter of Fundamental Rights of the European Union', proclaimed in Nice on 7 December 2000, in *OJEC* 18 December 2000, No. C 364; for a commentary on Article 8 already before the advent of the GDPR see, among others, Piroddi (2014), p. 1682 ff.) and Article 16 of the TFEU (Treaty on the Functioning of the European Union)—according to which everyone has the right to the protection of personal data concerning him or her, taking into account that data protection also includes the provision—expressly provided for in paragraph 2 of the aforementioned Art. 8—for which 'data must be processed fairly for specified purposes and on the basis of the consent of the person concerned or some other legitimate basis laid down by law' (the reference to Art. 8 of the Charter of Nice and Art. 16 TFEU is made, right at the outset, by the GDPR, in recital 1): see also Dell'Utri (2019), p. 184, as well as Bianchedi (2023a), p. 58.

[5] See, already with reference to the former legislation, Piraino (2006), p. 750.

[6] Achille (2019), p. 105 f. In a substantially similar sense, Resta (2022a), p. 63 f., 0pointing out that the principle of lawfulness can also represent a more general parameter for assessing the compliance of processing with the law. See also Bravo (2019a), p. 116, who points out that the existence of a condition of lawfulness of the Art. 6 GDPR is a necessary but not sufficient prerequisite, "occorrendo poi completare il processo valutativo in ordine alla liceità del trattamento, in rispondenza del principio di cui all'art. 5, par. 1, lett. a), Reg. cit.".

[7] Thus Poletti (2019), p. 2783. On the function of the two rules and the relationship between them see also Dell'Utri (2019), p. 188 ff.

[8] In addition to the other references found in the GDPR itself (see, e.g., for Art. 9 GDPR, Tosi (2023), p. 31), for italian law, reference must first be made to the new rules of the *Privacy* Code (Legislative Decree No 196 of 30 June 2003) introduced by Legislative Decree No 101 of 10 August 2018. Particularly relevant are Articles *2-ter*, *2-quinquies*, *2-sexies*, *2-octies*, as well as Part II of the Decree for processing in specific areas. For a summary of the relevant legal framework, both before and after the GDPR, see Bianchedi (2023a), p. 56 ff.

of hypotheses, considered exhaustive,[9] in the presence of which processing may be defined as lawful, and thus offering a solid and uniform bulwark for the protection of personal data at European level.

2 The Conditions of Lawfulness Envisaged by Article 6 GDPR

The conditions of lawfulness set out in Article 6 GDPR have a similar value and are equivalent and alternative to each other,[10] with the exception of what is set out in recital 46, which evokes a tendential residual nature, compared to the other hypotheses, of the case of data processing necessary to protect a vital interest of the data subject or of third parties.[11]

As in the past, the data subject's consent is only one of several conditions for the lawfulness of processing, although, as its very placement (at the beginning of the list) reveals, it is the hypothesis most frequently used in practice.[12] At the same time, unlike previously—where the data subject's consent was the rule and the other hypotheses appeared as exceptions— today the cases of Article 6 are, as mentioned, all on the same level, without any hierarchical order.[13]

The different conditions of lawfulness of Article 6 GDPR can be structurally grouped into two categories, one based on the will of the data subject, the other centred on the necessity of the processing.[14]

On the one hand, there is, in fact, the consent of the data subject (Art. 6.1(a)), which in turn presupposes an assessment of convenience and expediency already carried out by the data subject; on the other hand, we have all the other hypotheses, which, albeit with different nuances and connotations, are based on an objective necessity of processing (and this irrespective of the data subject's will).[15]

Starting with the latter hypotheses, which in turn can be divided into three categories depending on whether the justification for processing is based on (1) contractual legitimacy (lett. b), (2) legal legitimacy (lett. c), d), e) or (3) comparative legitimacy (lett. f),[16] it should first of all be pointed out that the parameter of necessity of processing is to be understood in a particularly strict sense, excluding that processing is lawful

---

[9] V. Bosa (2019), p. 122.

[10] On the topic, also Troiano (2023), p. 123 f.; Bravo (2019a), p. 115 f.; Bianchedi (2023b), p. 67 f.

[11] Poletti (2019), p. 2783.

[12] Troiano (2023), p. 124.

[13] D'Agata (2019), p. 81 ff. who highlights the different wording (compared to that of Art. 6 GDPR) of Articles 23–24, Italian Legislative Decree no. 196/2003 prev. On the subject, see also Basunti (2020), p. 868 f.; Bravo (2019a), p.130 ff; Barbujani and Carollo (2019), p. 64. See, finally, Bachelet (2023a), p. 39 f.

[14] Lucchini Guastalla (2019), p. 67. Also on the subject Poletti (2019), p. 2784.

[15] Troiano (2023), p. 123.

[16] Dell'Utri (2019), p. 221.

in all cases where it transpires that the purposes of the processing can also be pursued by alternative means that do not invade the sphere of confidentiality of the data subject.[17]

The first condition covers cases where processing is necessary for the performance of a contract to which the data subject is party for the performance of pre-contractual measures taken at the data subject's request (Article 6(1)(b)).

It is true that this hypothesis is still linked, albeit indirectly, to the will of the data subject, the necessity being linked to the instrumentality of the processing in relation to a contract, and therefore associated with a voluntary choice by the data subject.

However, the prerequisite for this condition of lawfulness, unlike all the other hypotheses, lies in purely contractual logic.[18] In the cases taken into consideration here, it may in fact be considered that, with a view to simplifying legal transactions, the contractual agreement between the parties also implies a willingness to supply the data instrumental to its implementation, making a further and separate unilateral manifestation of will by the person concerned unnecessary.[19] The *ratio* of the provision, therefore, consists essentially in allowing the contractor offering services to carry out activities functional to the conclusion of economic transactions encouraged by the same party to whom the data refer.[20]

At the same time, however, the instrumentality of the processing in relation to the contract must be rigorously ascertained, requiring an assessment of the adequacy, relevance, and strict necessity of the processing in relation to the envisaged objectives. Moreover, processing will not be extended to all the data of the data subject, but only to those that are instrumental to the execution of operations necessary for the performance of the contract or pre-contractual measures whose adoption is referable to an express request of the data subject.[21]

---

[17] In this sense, *Opinion* No 6/2014 of the Article 29 Working Party, WP29, had already expressed itself, in the force of the previous Directive 95/46/EC: Troiano (2023), p. 127, also highlights this profile, pointing out how this is also appropriate in order to avoid circumventing the need to protect the person of the data subject, on which the Regulation is based (Art. 1 GDPR).

[18] Here the contractual matter prevails over the regulation of data processing (which is merely functional to the former) and the consent to the conclusion of the contract or to the completion of negotiations absorbs the consent to data processing (think of the hypothesis of online purchase of airline tickets or other goods or services where the acquisition and use of personal data is indispensable for the performance of the service due; see also below, in the text and in the following footnotes). Moreover, it has been observed that, precisely because it hinges on the will, this rule is deemed applicable only in cases where the data subject has the capacity to act, thus excluding persons under age: Bosa (2019), p. 126 f., highlights both aspects.

[19] Troiano (2023), p. 128.

[20] Poletti (2019), p. 2786.

[21] Dell'Utri (2019), p. 222.

On the concept of necessity in this context, to be understood here in a restrictive sense, see also European Data Protection Board (EDPB) Guidelines 2/2019 'on the processing of personal data under Article 6(1)(b) GDPR in the context of the provision of online services to data subjects', Version 2.0, esp. paras. 2.4 f.

See, also, in relation to Article 6(1)(b) GDPR, ECJ. EU 9 January 2025, C-394/23, *Mousse* v. *Commission nationale de l'informatique et des libertés* (CNIL), *SNCF Connect*, according to

For these reasons too, it is often appropriate in such cases to base processing on the data subject's consent (Art. 6(1)(a)) or on one of the other conditions listed in Art. 6.[22]

Also linked to this hypothesis is the case where personal data become the object of a real 'exchange' in the context of a contractual transaction presented, at least formally, as free of charge (so-called *non-monetary transactions*); this aspect will be examined elsewhere.[23]

The conditions of lawfulness mentioned in Article 6(1)(c) and (e) GDPR may then be examined jointly, relating respectively to processing necessary for compliance with a legal obligation to which the data controller is subject (point (c)) and to processing necessary for the performance of a task carried out in the public interest or in the exercise of official authority vested in the data controller (point (e)).

In both cases, in fact, there emerges that social function of data processing (referred to in recital 4 GDPR) that justifies going beyond the data subject's consent.[24]

The provisions should be read in the light of recitals 41 and 45. Recital 41, while specifying that as a general rule no *ad hoc* legislation is required from Member-States, makes it clear that the legal basis or legislative measure to which the GDPR refers must be clear, precise, and its application must be foreseeable for the persons subject to it; Recital 45 specifies that even a single legislative act may be sufficient as a basis for several processing operations, while declining the characteristics of such an act and what, in this context, is a matter for Union or Member-State law.[25]

The provisions are then completed by Paragraph 2, which leaves a margin of discretion to Member-States as to whether to maintain or introduce more specific rules on the matter and Paragraph 3, which requires that the basis for processing, which must also contain the purposes of processing, be established by the law of the

---

which 'the processing of personal data relating to the title of the customers of a transport undertaking, the purpose of which is to personalise the commercial communication based on their gender identity, does not appear to be either objectively indispensable or essential to enable the proper performance of a contract and, therefore, cannot be regarded as necessary for the performance of that contract'. See also ECJ. EU 12 September 2024, Joined Cases C-17/22 and C-18/22.

[22] This aspect is also highlighted by Guidelines 2/2019, cited above, esp. para. 2.2.

A further critical point is also highlighted by Troiano (2023), p. 128, who observes that in the different situation in which the processing of personal data is functional to the achievement of purposes *other* than or in *addition to* those covered by the contract (e.g. indirect *marketing* or advertising), ' non solo il contratto non può da solo fondare la liceità del trattamento ma un distinto consenso al trattamento rischierebbe finanche di essere considerato invalido, perché non libero, ove alla sua prestazione fosse indebitamente condizionata la stipulazione o l'esecuzione del contratto' (see Art. 7(3) GDPR, on which see below).

[23] See *infra*, Sect. 4.

[24] See Bosa (2019), p. 129.

Zorzi Galgano (2019), p. 53, also elaborates on the concept of social function in this context. On Article 6(1)(c) GDPR cf. ECJ. EU 12 September 2024, Joined Cases C-17/22 and C-18/22, cited above. On Article 6(1)(e) GDPR cf., instead, ECJ. EU 7 March 2024, C-740/22, *Endemol Shine Finland Oy*.

[25] For further discussion, Resta (2022b), p. 86.

Union or of the individual Member-State. The latter rule is further clarified in Italian law by Article *2-ter* of Legislative Decree no. 196/2003,[26] which states that the legal basis referred to in Article 6(3)(b) GDPR is a provision of law or regulation, or general administrative acts.[27]

With regard to the condition of lawfulness that refers to processing necessary for the protection of the vital interests of the data subject or of another natural person (point (d)), it may be considered that the assessment of the interests at stake and their balancing are in this case carried out upstream by the legislator itself, thus making consent unnecessary.[28]

It emerges from recital 46, in addition to the already mentioned residual nature of this condition in relation to the others, that the interest taken into consideration here is the interest essential to the life of the data subject or of a third party, with the clarification that certain processing operations may respond both to important public interest reasons and to the vital interests of the data subject.

Lastly, there is the condition of lawfulness inherent in processing necessary for the pursuit of a legitimate interest of the data controller or of a third party (point (f)).[29]

Here, a balancing act is required between the interests of the data controller or of third parties and those of the data subject, the assessment of which, unlike under Directive 95/46/EC, is now, under the GDPR, left entirely to the data controller himself;[30] by making the data controller responsible also for identifying the legal basis of the processing, the provision therefore represents a clear manifestation of the principle of *accountability*.[31]

The—rather vague—wording of the provision, which does not clarify the concept of 'legitimate interest' to be adopted in this context and which, as mentioned above, leaves the choice as to the use of such a condition to the exclusive assessment of the data controller, in fact makes the scope of the provision extremely broad. At the same time, it is precisely the vagueness of the concept of 'legitimate interest' that

[26] Article introduced by Legislative Decree No 101 of 10 August 2018 and subsequently amended by Decree-Law No 139 of 8 October 2021, converted with amendments by Law No 205 of 3 December 2021.

[27] Resta (2022b), p. 89 f. Mulazzani (2019), p. 200 ff. offers an initial analysis of the rule (prior to the 2021 novellation).

[28] Bravo (2019a), p. 184.

[29] On the systemic significance of this provision see Dell'Utri (2019), p. 227.

[30] Indeed, the 2018 italian Budget Law (see Art. 1, comma 1022-1023, Law no. 205 of 27 December 2017) had provided, for the data controller who intended to use the 'legitimate interest' as a condition of lawfulness, the obligation to promptly notify the *Garante per la protezione dei dati personali* (Italian Data Protection Authority) and to wait, within the following fifteen days, the *Garante*'s reply, if the processing was carried out with new technology or automated tools. The scope of the provision was subsequently circumscribed by Legislative Decree No. 101 of 10 August 2018, which clarified that it applies exclusively to the processing of personal data functional to the authorisation of the change of the name or surname of minors (see Article 22(5)). On the subject, among others, Poletti (2019), p. 2787 f., as well as Bianchedi (2023b), p. 82.

[31] For a discussion of the topic see, *infra*, Sect. 6.

puts a brake on the frequent use of this hypothesis, particularly in view of the risks that the data controller may face.[32]

Recitals 47 to 49 of the GDPR, while not providing any exhaustive definition of the concept of legitimate interest, offer some further indications: with regard to the balancing act in question, it is appropriately specified that the existence of a legitimate interest also requires a careful assessment as to whether the data subject, at the time and in the context of the collection of personal data, could reasonably expect processing to take place for that purpose;[33] furthermore, a number of examples are outlined in which the operation of this condition of lawfulness may be envisaged, which are in addition to those indicated by the explanatory relation to Italian Legislative Decree No. 101/2018, as well as those previously identified by the *Garante* (Italian Data Protection Authority) and in the list contained in *Opinion* 6/2014 of the WP29.[34]

Finally, two further elements enrich the picture.

On the one hand, the provision of point (f) is accompanied by the clarification that the case does not come into play when the processing of data is carried out by public authorities in the performance of their duties; in such cases, in fact, the processing will have to be based on a provision of law that circumscribes the scope of action of the public administration in a more rigorous and less vague manner.[35]

At the same time, where the interest opposed to that of the data controller is that of a person under the age of majority, the same provision of point (f), while not denying its operability also in this hypothesis, requires special attention, which is

---

[32] On this point see, e.g., Troiano (2023), p. 129.

With regard to this provision, a recent ruling clarified that 'the processing of personal data which consists in the disclosure, for consideration, of personal data of the members of a sports federation, in order to satisfy a commercial interest of the controller, may be regarded as necessary for the purposes of the legitimate interests pursued by that controller, within the meaning of that provision, only on condition that that processing is strictly necessary for the purposes of the legitimate interest in question and that, in the light of all the relevant circumstances, the interests or fundamental rights and freedoms of those members do not override that legitimate interest. While that provision does not require that such an interest be determined by law, it requires that the alleged legitimate interest be lawful' (thus ECJ. EU 4 October 2024, C-621/22).

See also ECJ. EU 9 January 2025, C-394/23, cited above, according to which the data processing referred to there (see. *supra, sub* footnote 21) 'cannot be regarded as necessary for the purposes of the legitimate interests pursued by the controller or by a third party, where: – those customers were not informed of the legitimate interest pursued when those data were collected; or – that processing is not carried out only in so far as is strictly necessary for the attainment of that legitimate interest; or – in the light of all the relevant circumstances, the fundamental freedoms and rights of those customers can prevail over that legitimate interest, in particular because of a risk of discrimination on grounds of gender identity'.

[33] On this topic also D'Agata (2019), p. 85, as well as Barbujani and Carollo (2019), p. 67 f.

[34] Moreover, *Opinion* 6/2014 of the WP29 also identifies the steps of the balancing test to be performed (on this point see again Poletti (2019), p. 2788 f.).

[35] Troiano (2023), p. 129.

justified by the—at least potential—vulnerable condition of the minor in relation to any other subject.[36]

3 The Consent of the Data Subject

The data subject's consent finds its citizenship in the GDPR, as it is transversally intertwined among several provisions; among them, first and foremost, Article 4(11), which offers its definition, Article 6(1)(a), which envisages it as the first—though not necessarily the most important— condition for the lawfulness of the processing, and Article 7, which also lays down rules for the phase immediately preceding it, as well as the phase following its possible revocation.[37]

Although there are no marked differences with respect to the previous system, a number of elements—including, for example, the broader configuration of the condition defined in point (f) —resize the scope of consent, causing it to lose the centrality it had in the past.[38]

Underlying the provision of Article 6(1)(a) is evidently the will of the data subject, who, as a result of an assessment of convenience and expediency made by himself, expresses his will, in terms that must not, however, be generic but related to one or more specific purposes of the processing.[39] It is, moreover, a manifestation of will that can be revoked at any time, with the same ease with which consent was previously given and without the revocation affecting the lawfulness of the processing carried out before it (Article 7(3)).[40]

---

[36] Poletti (2019), p. 2788 ff.; see also Troiano (2023), p. 130.

[37] Lucchini Guastalla (2019), p. 71.

[38] Troiano (2023), p. 124; see also Basunti (2020), p. 872 ff. See also *sub* para. above.

[39] In the background, then, remains the question of whether consent to data processing is only of an authorising nature (Astone (2019), p. 33 ff., seems to move in this direction, although showing perplexity, especially with regard to data processing linked to the circulation of data, e.g. through profiling activities; see also, Bravo (2019b), p. 52 ff., who excludes that the consent to data processing is a negotial consent, specifying at the same time that 'il consenso contrattuale alla fornitura del servizio ed allo scambio dei dati non si sostituisce al consenso autorizzatorio al trattamento: anzi, quest'ultimo coesiste con il primo, senza precludere la commerciabilità dei dati personali'), or even of a negotial nature, also taking into account the growing economic dimension of personal data, which has in fact created a veritable market (see, on these aspects, Garaci (2021), p. 800 f.). The information concerning a natural person, in fact, especially as regards the particular categories of personal data outlined in Article 9 GDPR (relating to racial or ethnic origin, political opinions, religious and philosophical beliefs, etc.) incorporate an economically appreciable utility that is of interest to market operators; such utilities are therefore attracted to the category of "bene giuridico" and lend themselves to being the subject of contractual relations (see the precise observations of Senigaglia (2020b), p. 95 ff. and Senigaglia (2020a), p.765; on personal data as goods subject to economic and legal relations see also Vulpiani (2021), p. 103, as well as Matta (2024), p. 477 ff. On these aspects see also Irti (2021), p. 74 ff.; Bianchedi (2023b), p. 70 f.; Bosa (2019), p. 124 ff.

[40] See on this point Omodei Salé (2023), p. 452 f.

As mentioned above, the requirements that consent must meet in order to be able to outline the condition of lawfulness in question are set out, at a definitional level, in Article 4(11) GDPR, which identifies the 'consent of the data subject' as that freely given, specific, informed, and unambiguous manifestation of will by which the data subject indicates his or her assent, by a statement, or by a clear affirmative action that personal data relating to him or her are to be processed.[41]

Freedom of consent is the first and main requirement, to which the others are functional. Taking into account its purposes, which go beyond the purely negotiating level and embrace even the personal interests of the individual, freedom is to be understood in a broad sense and implies that the manifestation of will is not the result of constraints or conditioning, irrespective of whether or not there is a flaw in consent in the strict sense.[42]

The GDPR also lays down a rule of an interpretative nature (Art. 7(4)): 'When assessing whether consent is freely given, utmost account shall be taken of whether, *inter alia*, the performance of a contract, including the provision of a service, is conditional on consent to the processing of personal data that is not necessary for the performance of that contract'.[43]

The legislator has provided that where consent has been given under the conditions outlined in the aforementioned provision, it is reasonably plausible that it has not been freely given. As has been persuasively observed, this is not a presumption, but rather an invitation from a legislative source to pay attention, among the other circumstances of consent, to this peculiar form of conditioning, which is a potential indicator of an impaired freedom of decision of the user.[44]

This hypothesis must obviously be kept distinct from that in which the processing is instead instrumental to the performance of the contract, in which case the legal basis of the processing will be represented not by consent, but by the case under Article 6(1)(b).[45] Moreover, the fact that a performance is made conditional on consent to the processing does not in itself preclude the lawfulness of the latter (and the freedom of the manifestation of consent) in all cases where the performance being conditioned is not infungible and unwaivable on the part of the data subject.[46]

---

[41] For an illustration of the requirements of consent to the processing of personal data see, e.g., under different perspectives, Zorzi Galgano (2019), p. 59 ff.; Omodei Salè (2023), p. 449 ff.; Bravo (2019a), p. 151 ff.; Bosa (2019), p.122 ff.; Seminara (2021), p. 861 ff.; Vivarelli (2019), p. 57 ff.: Pisapia (2018), p. 60 f. Instead, Orlando (2024), p. 342 ff. dwells on the 'lawfulness of privacy consent' as a requirement so to speak implicitly, i.e. not expressly contemplated by the GDPR, but at the same time autonomous with respect to the parameters of Article 4(11) GDPR.

See also the guidance provided by the European Data Protection Board (EDPB): Guidelines 05/2020 'on consent under Regulation 2016/679', Version 1.1, esp. para. 3.

[42] Troiano (2023), p. 124. In this direction also Bosa (2019), p. 122 f.

[43] Lucchini Guastalla (2019), p. 72 ff.

[44] Thus Lucchini Guastalla, *ibid.* Of the same opinion Bachelet (2023b), p. 492.

[45] See *sub* para. 2.

[46] Cass. it., 2 July 2018, no. 17278, with note by Thobani (2019), p. 530 ff.

A further indication as to the freedom of consent is to be found in recital 43, according to which consent should not be a precondition for valid processing where there is a 'clear imbalance between the data subject and the controller', especially in cases where the latter is a public authority or where it may be presumed that consent has not been freely given.[47] Moreover, the last part of recital 42 makes it clear that consent should not be considered freely given if the data subject is not in a position to make a genuinely free choice or is unable to refuse or withdraw consent without detriment.

Article 4(11) requires that the manifestation of will also be specific. This requirement is further developed in Art. 7(2) GDPR, where it is specified that, if the data subject's consent is given in the context of a written declaration that also relates to other matters, the request for consent must be made 'in a manner which is clearly distinguishable from the other matters, in an intelligible and easily accessible form, using clear and plain language;, failing which the (part of the) declaration that is made in breach of the Regulation will not be binding.[48]

The specification that the manifestation of the will must also be informed indicates not only that, in general terms, consent must be preceded by appropriate information[49] but also that, again prior to the expression of consent, the data subject must be informed about the right to withdraw that the Regulation grants him (Art. 7(3) GDPR).

Lastly, the requirement of unambiguity implies that consent can never be inferred from mere silence or merely inactive behaviour (see recital 32); on the other hand, a tacit manifestation of will is not excluded, i.e. the possibility of inferring consent from conclusive behaviour,[50] except in cases where the GDPR prescribes unambiguous and even 'explicit' consent.[51]

Moreover, unlike in the past,[52] consent does not necessarily have to be given or documented in writing, although drafting it in writing may obviously facilitate the data controller's fulfilment of the burden of proof that consent has been obtained, also in accordance with the principle of *accountability*.[53]

---

[47] On the subject also Barbujani and Carollo (2019), p. 65.

[48] Troiano (2023), p. 124. For online consent see *sub* para. s.

[49] On this point, even before the advent of the GDPR and also with particular reference to consent given within the digital platforms of *social networks*, see Perlingieri (2014), p. 69.

[50] Troiano (2023), p. 125 f.

[51] These are cases of: a) processing of special categories of personal data of Art. 9, b) automated processing of personal data, including profiling (Art. 22), c) transfer of personal data abroad (in accordance with the provisions of Art. 49(1)(a)). On the subject also Resta (2022c), p. 102.

[52] See Art. 23(3) and (4), Italian *Privacy* Code prev.

[53] This aspect is also clarified by Troiano (2023), p. 126. On *accountability*, see also Sect. 6.

4 *Next*. The Consent of the Data Subject Online

In the context of the condition of lawfulness laid down in Article 6(1)(a), particular attention must be paid to the consent of the data subject online.

The GDPR offers some, albeit meagre, indications in recital 32, clarifying that consent may also be expressed by electronic means and also specifying (a) that the manifestation of consent may take place by 'ticking a box when visiting an internet website, choosing technical settings for information society services or another statement or conduct which clearly indicates in this context the data subject's acceptance of the proposed processing of his or her personal data'; (b) that, conversely, silence, inactivity or pre-ticked of boxes should not constitute consent; (c) that, 'if the data subject's consent is to be given following a request by electronic means, the request must be clear, concise and not unnecessarily disruptive to the use of the service for which it is provided'.

Therefore, the passive adherence to an option pre-set by the data controller on the *web* page activating an *online* service cannot constitute valid consent, whereas, on the contrary, it is possible for the manifestation of consent to processing to be inferred from unequivocal positive conduct, such as a click in the space of the page set up for this purpose.[54]

In addition to this, there are further normative references placed outside the GDPR and relating to particular hypotheses.

It is worth mentioning, first, the *e-privacy* directive (Directive 2002/58/EC),[55] which is still in force, although its replacement by a regulation has been under discussion for some time.[56] But mention may also be made, for instance, of the provision of Article 5(2) of the *DMA*,[57] which prohibits *gatekeepers* from a number of activities, including processing and combining personal data from the relevant core platform service with personal data from any further core platform services or from any other services provided by the gatekeeper or with personal data from third-party services, unless the end user has been presented with the specific choice and has given consent pursuant to GDPR;[58] or, again, Article 26(3) of the *DSA*,[59] concerning

[54] Troiano (2023), *ibid.* On recital 32 in relation to Article 4(11) GDPR, see Puddu (2019), p. 70 f. On this point, see also *infra*, in the text.

[55] For some regulations see below, in the text.

[56] This is the 'Proposal for a Regulation of the European Parliament and of the Council concerning the respect for private life and the protection of personal data in electronic communications and repealing Directive 2002/58/EC (Regulation on Privacy and Electronic Communications) COM/2017/010 final': on the subject see also Marino (2020), p. 406.

[57] 'Regulation (EU) 2022/1925 of the European Parliament and of the Council of 14 September 2022 on contestable and fair markets in the digital sector and amending Directives (EU) 2019/1937 and (EU) 2020/1828 (Digital Markets Act)'.

[58] On the topic, Irti (2024), p. 7.

[59] "Regulation (EU) 2022/2065 of the European Parliament and of the Council of 19 October 2022 on a Single Market for Digital Services and amending Directive 2000/31/EC (Digital Services

targeted advertising, a provision that limits the legal basis of consent for data under Article 9 GDPR.[60]

Supplementing the reference scenario are then some significant rulings of the Court of Justice.

Among these, mention may be made, for example, of the judgement in the so-called Planet 49 case,[61] which, dealing with the problem of the acceptance of *cookies* by the user browsing the web, clarified the meaning of Article 5(3) of Directive 2002/58/EC—a provision amended by Directive 2009/136/EC and from which derived the insertion of the new Article 122 in Italian Privacy Code—specifying that consent 'is not validly constituted if, in the form of cookies, the storage of information or access to information already stored in a website user's terminal equipment is permitted by way of a pre-checked checkbox which the user must deselect to refuse his or her consent'. Therefore, a so-called *opt-in* procedure is necessary, instead of the more generic—but precisely impermissible—possibility of *opt-out.*[62]

Moreover, the same ruling recalls that, also in this context, the data subject's consent must be specific and refer precisely to the data taken into consideration, since it cannot be inferred from a manifestation of will having a distinct object.[63]

The most recent ruling in the so-called Meta case[64] had a particular resonance. The CJEU addressed, in particular, the issue of whether the consent of users can be considered truly free, when it is given as a condition for accessing the service provided by a dominant platform, such as *Facebook*, in a monopolistic context where there are few alternative providers of similar services.

The Court stated that the operator of an online social network occupies a dominant position on the market in that sector does not, in itself, preclude the users of

---

Act)": for an initial illustration of the framework outlined therein, let us refer to Scola (2022), p. 127 ff.

[60] For the links between the *Digital Services Act* and the GDPR, see Pelino (2023), p. 9 ff.

[61] This is ECJ. EU (Grand Chamber), 1 October 2019, C-673/17. Marino (2020), p. 410 ff. offers an extensive discussion. See also Reinalter and Vale (2020), p. 79 ff., as well as Modica (2023), p. 97 ff. On these issues see also ECJ. EU 11 November 2020, C-61/19, *Orange* Romania SA v. ANSPDCP.

[62] See also Reinalter and Vale (2020), p. 81. Again with regard to *cookies*, see also *Resolución* de la Agencia Española de Protección de Datos, Proc. n° PS/00300/2019 (available at: https://www.aepd.es/documento/ps-00300-2019.pdf): see in this regard Modica (2023), p. 96 f. On the issue of consent to data processing in relation to *cookies*, extensively Seminara (2021), p. 866 ff., who also traces the significant case studies of the *Garante per la protezione dei dati personali*, prior to the GDPR, on the subject of consent to data processing in the digital context.

[63] See again ECJ. EU (Grand Chamber), 1 October 2019, C-673/17, esp. para. 58. He elaborates on the point Marino (2020), p. 414 f., persuasively observing that from the Court's indication we obtain 'il principio del consenso *separato*. La volontà contrattuale e il consenso all'installazione di *cookie*, e in generale alle attività di trattamento di dati personali, non possono coincidere, ossia non possono confondersi in un'unica manifestazione di volontà'.

[64] ECJ. EU (Grand Chamber), 4 July 2023, C-252/21, for commentary on which see the thorough contribution of Bachelet (2023b), p. 483 ff. See also Bellomo (2024), p. 573 ff. Finocchiaro (2024), p. 9 f., as well as Iamiceli (2024), p. 33 ff., also deal with the ruling in the context of a more comprehensive analysis of European case law in this area.

such a network from being able validly to consent to the processing of their personal data by that operator. However, that circumstance constitutes 'an important factor in determining whether the consent was in fact validly and, in particular, freely given, which it is for that operator to prove'.[65]

In this regard, it has been observed that the Court, by evoking the conditionality of Article 7(4) GDPR,[66] has appreciably oriented the interpreter towards a more liberal reading of this rule;[67] at the same time, given that the data subject's freedom should be considered as restricted when consent is given to access a service that can be qualified as 'essential', the delicate question arises as to whether a digital platform such as *Facebook* now constitutes a truly 'essential' service.[68]

5 *Next.* The Consent of Minors Online

A special provision, which supplements the more general provision of Article 6(1)(a) GDPR, is set out in Article 8 GDPR for minors.

The provision, based on the observation that 'children merit specific protection with regard to their personal data, as they may be less aware of the risks, consequences and safeguards concerned and their rights in relation to the processing of personal data'[69] thus fills a gap in Italian legal system, since the Italian *Privacy* Code did not provide for anything on this point, opening the way for different reconstructions of the problem.[70]

The minor is, in fact, so-called digital native who often moves with agility and ease through the internet and, moreover, under the legislation in question, he/she has a—albeit limited—capacity to consent to the processing of his or her data;[71] but, at the same time, he/she's a vulnerable subject[72] and can also be considered a

---

[65] See point 8) of the judgment.

[66] For a more detailed discussion of this rule see *infra*, sub Sect. 4.

[67] Bachelet (2023b), p. 493 f., who observes that an overly strict reading of Article 7(4) GDPR would end up 'per escludere sempre e comunque – o quasi – la libertà, e liceità, del consenso al trattamento "non disinteressato"'.

[68] See again Bachelet (2023b), p. 494, who highlights that, according to the interpretation of the Courts (see in particular Cass. it., 2 July 2018, no. 17278, cited above) one should consider 'la libertà dell'interessato effettivamente coartata soltanto quando il consenso è prestato per accedere a un servizio non solo infungibile (nel senso di non conseguibile altrove senza acconsentire al trattamento), ma altresì irrinunciabile senza gravoso sacrificio, il che accade se esso è "essenziale": si pensi ai servizi sanitari o bancari'.

[69] See Recital 38 GDPR, which provides further clarifications on the protection to be provided to the child in this context: on this point see, among others, Vulpiani (2021), p. 106. See also Capilli (2019), p. 253.

[70] See in this regard Caggiano (2018), p. 11.

[71] On this point see *below* in the text.

[72] Cf. Andreola (2021), p. 849, who considers the minor a weak subject of the online network, as he needs protection because of a fragility linked to his condition of psychological inferiority

consumer, and precisely the weakest of consumers, specifically because of the possible lack of mental requirements that would allow him or her to adequately understand and give valid consent.[73]

These are probably the main reasons that prompted the European legislator, not only to outline the rules in Article 8 GDPR but also to further specify certain aspects, including the fact that the language must be plain and clear and the information addressed to the child easily comprehensible,[74] and that the protection of the child must also be the subject of specific attention by the supervisory authorities,[75] as well as by the data controller when adopting risk management measures.[76]

However, the laudable legislative intent of regulating a phenomenon— that of consent to the processing of children's data in the digital context— which would otherwise lack protection, clashes with the inevitable consideration that the current regulatory apparatus still appears insufficient to guarantee effective protection of the so-called *best interest of the child* while preserving the efficiency of the digital system.[77]

Article 8, GDPR, in fact, in circumscribing its scope of application 'to child's consent in relation to information society services',[78] establishes only a criterion based on the age of the data subject, specifying that 'the processing of the personal data of a child shall be lawful where the child is at least 16 years old'. This is, however, a parameter that can be modified by the Member-States, which may set a lower age, provided that it is not below 13 years of age.[79]

---

related to age; on this subject see also Caggiano (2018), p. 7 ff, who illustrates some tools, also of the so-called *soft law*, to protect minors online; on these profiles, see also Senigaglia (2020b), p. 81, as well as Garaci (2021), p. 801.

[73] See again Andreola (2021), p. 851; see also Garaci (2021), p. 802, who points out that the child is a particularly vulnerable consumer.

[74] Cf. recital 58 and Art. 12(1) GDPR; Vulpiani (2021), p. 108 also elaborates on the point. See also Capilli (2019), p. 254.

[75] Art. 57 GDPR.

[76] Cf. Recital 75 GDPR; see on this point Caggiano (2018), p. 9.

[77] The inadequacy of the regulation prepared by the GDPR is also highlighted by Bianca (2019), p. 166 ff.

[78] That is, according to the definition offered by Directive (EU) 2015/1535, Article 1, services normally provided for remuneration, at a distance, by electronic means and at the individual request of a recipient of services, which certainly includes social networks and sharing platforms: see on this point also Caggiano (2018), p. 12, who points out that the "contratto *online* relativo a beni o servizi da consegnarsi o prestarsi fisicamente, coerentemente con quanto previsto dalla giurisprudenza della Corte di Giustizia" can also be considered an information society service. On the fact that Article 8 GDPR does not refer to any hypothesis of *online* processing of data concerning children, but circumscribes the cases, see Struzzi (2019), p. 80 f.

[79] Limit, that of 13 years of age, already accepted since 1998 also in the US system by the so-called C.O.P.P.A.—*Children's Online Privacy Protection Act*, available on the website of the *Federal Trade Commission*—www.ftc.gov.

Obout the *ratio* of the provision of Article 8 GDPR, which allows lowering the threshold age of 16, see Struzzi (2019), p. 81. See also Capilli (2019), p. 251 ff., who expresses perplexity both with regard to the choice of the GDPR to set a limit based solely on age, and with regard to the

This is what has also happened in Italian system by Article *2-quinquies* of the *Privacy* Code (introduced by Article 2, Legislative Decree No 101 of 10 August 2018). The Italian legislator, in fact, after an initial proposal that tended to maintain the age limit of 16 years,[80] has established that a minor who has reached the age of 14 years[81] may independently give consent to the processing of his or her personal data.

However, a number of non-negligible questions arise.

First, the mechanism set up by Article 8 GDPR is easily circumvented by minors, who, especially in the digital world, can easily conceal their age.[82]

This is also acknowledged by the AGCOM (Italian Communications Regulatory Authority) —which is also called upon to supervise the rules protecting minors in communication—which, in order to extend its range of action beyond the traditional systems, drew up a White Paper in 2013 on the relationship between the media and minors, which was followed by the more recent White Paper of 2018.[83] Even in the White Paper, in fact, the critical issues arising from the lack of transparency on digital identity emerge, taking into account the fact that 'soltanto l'identità digitale consente la trasparenza, la riconoscibilità di chi accede in Rete, per un proprio diritto e, conseguentemente, la possibilità di fruire di strumenti di tutela efficaci'.[84]

A further problematic issue concerns the boundaries of the capacity of the under-18-year-old subject, taking into account that Article 8 GDPR is potentially able to open a not insignificant breach in the minor's codified incapacity to act, shaped by Article 2 of the Italian Civil Code.

One could, in fact, say that the minor authorised to give consent to data processing enjoys a real, albeit special, capacity.[85] This capacity would not only concern the

---

possibility (allowed by the Regulation) for Member States to adopt different solutions, bearing in mind that it would have been preferable to standardise the legislation also in this area.

[80] See Opinion of Italian *Garante privacy* on the draft legislative decree containing provisions for the adaptation of national legislation to the provisions of Regulation (EU) 2016/679—22 May 2018 and Parliamentary Opinion of 27 June 2018.

[81] Article *2-quinquies* Italian Privacy Code also states that "il titolare del trattamento redige con linguaggio particolarmente chiaro e semplice, conciso ed esaustivo, facilmente accessibile e comprensibile dal minore, al fine di rendere significativo il consenso prestato da quest'ultimo, le informazioni e le comunicazioni relative al trattamento che lo riguardi". It has been observed in this regard that the rule seems to take a cognitive psychology approach in the part where it requires the minor's consent to be meaningful. The *ratio* is to make consent an effective tool with respect to the interest it is intended to protect (Lucchini Guastalla (2019), p. 77).

[82] On this subject see Astone (2019), p. 41 ff., and Battelli (2024), p. 136.

The problem is also taken note of by the "Tavolo tecnico sulla tutela dei diritti dei minori nel contesto dei *social networks*, dei servizi e dei prodotti digitali in rete", including among its proposals for action the one concerning the importance of an effective age verification system: see the Final Report of the aforementioned Technical Table, published in *Dir. di internet*, 2024, 219 ff. (esp. 224 and 234 ff.).

[83] *Libro Bianco Media e Minori 2.0*—Review, available on the AGCOM website—www.agcom.it; for a concise illustration of AGCOM's work in this context see Votano (2021), p. 245 ff.

[84] V. *Libro Bianco* 2018, p. 152.

[85] Cf. Garaci (2021), p. 802.

personal sphere but also, in some cases, the patrimonial one; in particular, according to some authors, it would be a capacity that goes beyond the performance of the so-called minute acts of daily life, embracing those acts of a patrimonial nature that are an expression of the minor's personal identity (such as contracts for the provision of services or digital content in exchange for the provision of personal data).[86]

On the aforementioned issue is then grafted the further profile of the validity of the acts performed by the child, which, especially in a contractual perspective, would find a barrier in Article 1426 of the Italian Civil Code.

Article 8(3) GDPR expressly states that the rules on the minimum age of consent are without prejudice to the general provisions of the contract law of the Member-States, such as the rules on the validity, formation, or effect of a contract in relation to a child. In the case of a child over the age of 14, it is therefore abstractly possible that the consent given by that child for the processing of his or her personal data is valid for the purposes of the GDPR, but entails instead, pursuant to Article 1425 of the Italian Civil Code, the annullability of the contract by reason of which that consent was given.[87]

At the same time, with reference to Article 1426 of the Italian Civil Code, it has been observed that this rule was coined in a social, economic, and cultural context that was profoundly different from today's and still unaware of the telematic contractual modalities that would develop over time, thanks to the progress of technology. Therefore, an interpretative and evolutionary reading of the rule should be imposed today, especially in the context of *e-commerce*, in order to circumscribe the hypotheses of annullability. In particular, Article 1426 of the Italian Civil Code expressly states that the mere declaration of the minor being of age is not an obstacle to challenging the contract, presupposes that the other party has the possibility of looking at the face of his interlocutor and realising his young age, an aspect that, for obvious reasons, cannot take place in the digital context.[88]

Article 8 GDPR also deals with consent to the processing of a child's data given by parents (*i.e.* those exercising parental responsibility).

However, an initial, delicate problem arises as to the qualification— contractual rather than personal—to be attributed to the provision of consent. If the thesis of the contractual nature is accepted, it could be affirmed that, pursuant to Art. 320 of the Italian Civil Code, the consent given by the parents is an act of representation relating to acts of extraordinary administration; if, on the other hand, the personal nature

[86] Senigaglia (2020b), p. 136 ff.

[87] Aspect also highlighted by Troiano (2023), p. 127.

[88] See in this regard Senigaglia (2020b), p. 181 f.; in a partially different sense Vulpiani (2021), p. 119, according to whom the mere declaration of the minor as to his or her age would render the contract annullable, unless the minor's efficient machination in perpetrating the deception is recognised; at the same time, however, the author seems to envisage the possibility of preserving the validity of the contract whenever it can be considered that the minor has acted as the parent's representative by tacit power of attorney.

of the consent is affirmed, a contradiction could emerge, since it would be a very personal act and as such insusceptible of representation.[89]

Equally in the shade is the question whether, in the aforementioned hypothesis, the consent must be given by both parents or is the intervention of only one of them sufficient.

The jurisprudence seems to favour the first solution, considering that 'la nuova disciplina comunitaria impone che il consenso necessario ai fini del trattamento dei dati personali del minore, e dunque anche per le immagini che possano identificarlo, nel caso di minori di anni sedici, sia prestato dai soggetti esercenti la responsabilità genitoriale, in vece dei propri figli, concordemente fra loro e senza arrecare pregiudizio all'onore, al decoro e alla reputazione dell'immagine del minore'.[90]

More generally, however, the question arises as to whether the increasing number of rights and duties incumbent on parents as a result of their children's digital activities does not contribute to determining different educational tasks and responsibilities than those that were incumbent on them before the digital age, also bearing in mind that Article 30 of the Italian Constitution appropriately does not lay down educational rules. Probably, technology has changed the content of the educational duty of parents, highlighting new aspects of the limit indicated in Article 147 of the Italian Civil Code regarding the capabilities, natural inclinations, and aspirations of children, so that the concept of parental education must now also include education in the proper use of *social networks*, to compose a proper balance between opportunities and risks.[91]

Against the backdrop of these issues, there remains the question of how to verify that, in these hypotheses, the consent is actually given by the person exercising parental responsibility, and not by others.

Article 8 GDPR does not address this issue, leaving it to the data controller to take steps to verify that consent has been given by those entitled to it.[92] Conversely, in other jurisdictions, attempts have been made to address the problem by outlining a number of verification methods.[93]

Indeed, the European Data Protection Board has also intervened on the issue, in particular recommending the adoption of a proportionate approach, aiming at obtaining a limited amount of information, such as the contact details of a parent or guardian, and pointing out that "what is reasonable, both in terms of verifying that a user is old enough to provide their own consent, and in terms of verifying that a person providing consent on behalf of a child is a holder of parental responsibility, may depend upon the risks inherent in the processing as well as the available

[89] V. Bianca (2019), p. 159, who points out how the problem is relativised by those who affirm the two-faced nature, both personal and patrimonial, of the right to the processing of personal data.

[90] Trib. Rieti 7 March 2019, in *Dejure*; of the same opinion also Trib. Rieti 17 October 2022, no. 443, in *Dejure*. See also Trib. Mantova 19 September 2017, with note by Nitti (2018), p. 380 ff.

[91] Bianca (2019), p. 159 ff.; in this direction also Thiene (2018), p. 1621.

[92] See Art. 8(2); on the subject also Struzzi (2019), p. 82.

[93] This is the case of the aforementioned US *Children's Online Privacy Protection Act*; elaborates on the point, providing some examples outlined by C.O.P.P.A., Caggiano (2019), p. 19.

technology'; depending on the risk, which may be more or less high, different verification mechanisms may therefore be put in place (from e-mail contact with the parent, to the request for a symbolic transfer of €0.01 to be sent by the parent to the data controller, etc.).[94]

In any case, it now seems clear that the law must take responsibility for effectively combating elusive practices aimed at circumventing the rules on consent and identification of the person giving consent; at the same time, technology must also put in place increasingly efficient mechanisms to protect the child in the digital world.[95]

References

Achille D (2019) Sub art. 5 GDPR. In: Barba A, Pagliantini S (eds) Delle persone, II. In: Gabrielli E (ed) Commentario del Codice civile, Milano, p 105 f

Andreola E (2021) Misure cautelari a tutela dei minori nei social network. Fam. e dir., p 849 ff

Astone A (2019) I dati personali dei minori in rete. Dall'internet delle persone all'internet delle cose. Milano, p 33 ff

Bachelet V (2023a) Il consenso oltre il consenso. Dati personali, contratto, mercato, Pisa, p 39 f

Bachelet V (2023b) La Corte di giustizia sul caso Meta: trattamento dei dati e "prezzo" del consenso, in Pactum, p.483 ff

Barbujani E, Carollo V (2019) Sub art. 6 GDPR. In: D'Agostino A, Barlassina L R, Colarocco V (eds) Commentario al Regolamento UE 2016/679 e al Codice della privacy aggiornato, Milano, pp 64 ff

Basunti C (2020) La (perduta) centralità del consenso nello specchio delle condizioni di liceità del trattamento dei dati personali. Contr. e impr., p 868 ff

Battelli E (2024) Minori, privacy e consenso digitale. In Id. (ed) Diritto privato digitale, Torino, p 130 ff

Bellomo (2024) La Grande Sezione interviene sul principio di leale cooperazione tra autorità garanti e sul principio di liceità dei trattamenti di dati personali attuato da Facebook. DPCE online, p 573 ff

Bianca MI (2019) *Il minore e i nuovi* media. In: Senigaglia R (ed) Autodeterminazione e minore età. Itinerari di diritto minorile, Pisa, p 151 ff

Bianchedi G (2023a) Inquadramento normativo. In: Bianchedi G, Modica C (eds) Il principio di liceità. In: Bravo F (ed) Dati personali. Protezione, libera circolazione e governance, Pisa, vol. 1, p 56 ff

Bianchedi G (2023b) Portata applicativa del principio. In: Bianchedi G, Modica C (eds) Il principio di liceità. In: Bravo F (ed) Dati personali. Protezione, libera circol*azione e* governance, Pisa, vol. 1, p 67 ff

Bosa S (2019) Sub art. 6 GDPR. In: Barba A, Pagliantini S (eds) Delle persone, II. In Gabrielli E (ed) Commentario del Codice civile, Milano, p 122 ff

Bravo F (2019a) Le condizioni di liceità del trattamento di dati personali. In: Finocchiaro G (ed) La protezione dei dati personali in Italia. Regolamento UE n. 2016/679 e d.lgs. 10 agosto 2018, n. 101, Bologna, p 115 ff

Bravo F (2019b) Lo "scambio di dati personali" nei contratti di fornitura di servizi digitali e il consenso dell'interessato tra autorizzazione e contratto. Contr. e impr., p 52 ff

[94] V. Guidelines 5/2020, cited above, esp. para. 7.1.4.

[95] In this direction see also the reflections of Caggiano (2018), p. 22.

Caggiano I (2018) Privacy *e minori nell'era* digitale. Il consenso al trattamento dei dati dei minori all'indomani del Regolamento UE 2016/679, tra diritto e tecno-regolazione. Familia, p 4 ff
Capilli G (2019) La tutela dei dati personali dei minori. In: Panetta R (ed) Circolazione e protezione dei dati personali, tra libertà e regole del mercato. Commentario al Regolamento UE n. 2016/679 (GDPR) e al novellato d.lgs. n. 196/2003 (Codice Privacy), Milano, p.251 ff
D'Agata C (2019) Il legittimo interesse del titolare o di un terzo nel quadro dei diversi presupposti di legittimità del trattamento. In: Panetta R (ed) Circolazione e protezione dei dati personali, tra libertà e regole del mercato. Commentario al Regolamento UE n. 2016/679 (GDPR) e al novellato d.lgs. n. 196/2003 (Codice Privacy), Milano, p 81 ff
De Cupis A (1959) I diritti della personalità, I, Milano, p 256 f
Dell'Utri M (2019) Principi generali e condizioni di liceità del trattamento dei dati personali. In: Cuffaro V, D'Orazio R, Ricciuto V (eds) I dati personali nel diritto europeo, Torino, p.184 ff
Finocchiaro G (2024) Consenso al trattamento e libertà. In Persona e Mercato, p 9 f
Garaci I (2021) Il "superiore interesse del minore" nel quadro di uno sviluppo sostenibile dell'ambiente digitale. In Nuove leggi civ. comm., p 800 ff
Iamiceli P (2024) Il consenso al trattamento dei dati personali e la giurisprudenza europea tra tutela dei diritti fondamentali e giustizia contrattuale. In Persona e Mercato, p 33 ff
Irti C (2021) Consenso "negoziato" e circolazione dei dati personali, Torino, p 74 ff
Irti C (2024) Piattaforme digitali, contratti e protezione dei dati personali. In Contratti, p 7
Lucchini Guastalla E (2019) Privacy *e* Data protection*: principi generali.* In: Tosi E (ed) Privacy Digitale. Riservatezza e protezione dei dati personali tra GDPR e nuovo Codice Privacy, Milano, p.67 ff
Marino G (2020) Internet e tutela dei dati personali: il consenso ai cookie. In Jus civile, p 406 ff
Matta N (2024) Circolazione dei dati personali e regolazione dei mercati digitali. In Rass. dir. civ., p 477 ff
Modica C (2023) Applicazione del principio nella casistica. In Bianchedi G, Modica C, Il principio di liceità. In: Bravo F (ed), Dati personali. Protezione, libera circolazione e governance, Pisa, vol 1, p 96 ff
Mulazzani G (2019) Il trattamento di dati personali effettuato per l'esecuzione di un compito di interesse pubblico o connesso all'esercizio di pubblici poteri. In: Finocchiaro G (ed) La protezione dei dati personali in Italia. Regolamento UE n. 2016/679 e d.lgs. 10 agosto 2018, n. 101, Bologna, p 200 ff
Nitti M (2018) La pubblicazione di foto di minori sui social network tra tutela della riservatezza e individuazione dei confini della responsabilità genitoriale. In Fam. e dir., p 380 ff
Omodei Salé R (2023) Lo scambio dei dati personali dell'utente. In: Bocchini R (ed) Manuale di Diritto privato dell'informatica, Napoli, p 449 ff
Orlando S (2024) Consenso al trattamento e liceità. In Persona e Mercato, p 342 ff
Pelino E (2023) L'interazione tra DSA e GDPR. In: Bolognini L, Pelino E, Scialdone M (eds) Digital Services Act e Digital Markets Act. Definizioni e prime applicazioni dei nuovi regolamenti europei, Milano, p 9 ff
Perlingieri C (2014) *Profili civilistici dei* social networks, Napoli, p 69 f
Piraino F (2006) *La liceità e la correttezza.* In: Panetta R (ed) Libera circolazione e protezione dei dati personali, vol. 1, Milano, p 750
Piroddi P (2014) Sub art. 8 Carta dei diritti fondamentali dell'Unione europea. In: Pocar F, Baruffi MC (eds) Commentario breve ai Trattati dell'Unione europea, Padova, p 1682 ff
Pisapia A (2018) La tutela per il trattamento e la protezione dei dati personali, Torino, p 60 f
Poletti D (2019) Le condizioni di liceità del trattamento dei dati personali. In Giur. it., p 2783 ff
Puddu S (2019) Sub art. 6 GDPR. In: D'Agostino A, Barlassina LR, Colarocco V (eds) Commentario al Regolamento UE 2016/679 e al Codice della privacy aggiornato, Milano, p 70 f
Reinalter A, Vale S (2020) Cookie e consenso dell'utente. In Giur. it., p 79 ff
Resta F (2022a) Sub *art. 5 GDPR*. In: Riccio G M, Scorza G, Belisario E (eds) *GDPR* e Normativa Privacy. Commentario, Milano, vol 1, p 63 ff

Resta F (2022b) Sub *art. 6 GDPR*. In: Riccio G M, Scorza G, Belisario E (eds) GDPR e Normativa Privacy. Commentario, Milano, vol 1, p 86 ff

Resta F (2022c) Sub *art. 7 GDPR*. In: Riccio G M, Scorza G, Belisario E (eds) GDPR e Normativa Privacy. Commentario, Milano, vol 1, p 102

Scola S (2022) Digital Services Act: occasioni mancate e prospettive future nella recente proposta di regolamento europeo per il mercato unico dei servizi digitali. In Contr. e impr./Eur., p 127 ff

Seminara AP (2021) Cookie e libertà del consenso al trattamento dei dati personali. In: Persona e Mercato, p 861 ff

Senigaglia R (2020a) La dimensione patrimoniale del diritto alla protezione dei dati personali. In Contr. e impr., p 765

Senigaglia R (2020b) Minore età e contratto. Contributo alla teoria della capacità, Torino, p 81 ff

Struzzi (2019) Sub *art. 8 GDPR*. In: D'Agostino A, Barlassina LR, Colarocco V (eds) Commentario al Regolamento UE 2016/679 e al Codice della privacy aggiornato, Milano, p 80 ff

Thiene A (2018) Ragazzi perduti online: illeciti dei minori e responsabilità dei genitori. In: Nuova giur. civ. comm., I, p 1621

Thobani (2019) Operazioni di tying e libertà del consenso. In Giur. it., p 530 ff

Tosi (2023) Circolazione dei dati personali tra contratto e responsabilità. Riflessioni sulla fragilità del consenso e sulla patrimonializzazione dei dati personali nella società della sorveglianza digitale, Milano, p 31

Troiano S (2023) La tutela della riservatezza. In: Bocchini R (ed) Manuale di Diritto privato dell'informatica, Napoli, p 123 ff

Vivarelli A (2019) Il consenso al trattamento dei dati personali nell'era digitale. Sfide tecnologiche e soluzioni giuridiche, Napoli, p 57 ff

Votano (2021) Il libro bianco Media e minori: l'età del consenso digitale tra consapevolezza e responsabilità. In: Bianca MI (ed) The best interest of the child, Roma, p 245 ff

Vulpiani G (2021) L'utente minore online: tutela della privacy e attività negoziale. Tecn. dir., 2:103 ff

Zorzi Galgano N (2019) Le due anime del GDPR e la tutela del diritto alla privacy. In: Ead. (ed), Persona e mercato dei dati. Riflessioni sul GDPR, Milano-Padova, p 53 ff

The Exchange of Personal Data with Digital Content or Digital Services

Riccardo Omodei Salè

Contents

Abstract The chapter aims to provide an overview of the operation "exchange of personal data with digital content or digital services", focusing in particular on the requirements for valid consent to the processing of personal data and the remedies for the failure to supply and for lack of conformity of digital content or services.

R. Omodei Salè (✉)
University of Verona, Verona, Italy
e-mail: riccardo.omodeisale@univr.it

R. Bocchini (ed.), *Digital Platforms - From Technical Foundations to Legal and Economic Implications*, https://doi.org/10.1007/978-3-032-07978-7_30

1 The Economic-Contractual Dimension of Personal Data and the So-Called "Non-Monetary Transactions"

Over the last few years, personal data have acquired an ever-increasing economic value, having become a medium of exchange to obtain digital content or digital services of the most varied kind (e.g. e-mail services, use of social networks, newsletter services, etc.).[1] Indeed, this is an increasingly widespread business model, by virtue of which, to be more precise, the user, in order to make use of digital content or services, gives his consent to the processing of his data by the provider, for purposes other than those strictly necessary for the performance of the service, for instance, advertising, marketing or other purposes.[2] Thus, although the content or service appears to be "free", the consideration is, in reality, the personal data provided by the user (so-called "non-monetary transaction").[3]

The economic exploitation of personal data, however, poses several critical issues. On the one hand, the data companies that manage the main digital platforms dominate the market by hindering the entry of new players and have ended up acquiring enormous power not only economically but also politically.[4] On the other hand, there is the increasing intrusion into the private sphere of individuals and the risk of commodification of the human person, with the consequent debasement of his dignity.[5]

---

[1] In this regard, D'Ippolito (2020), p. 647, highlighted the tendency of users to exchange their personal data also to access 'services that are apparently of no use or that confer an ephemeral benefit', recalling, in particular, the success obtained in 2019 by *FaceApp*, an application that, based on a user's photo, through special filters returned an image of the user as if he had aged, rejuvenated or looked as he would have if he had been of a different sex. See, in the same vein, also De Franceschi (2019), p. 1384, who pointed out that 'individuals often underestimate the value of their personal data and therefore tend to consent, without adequate prior reflection, to the transmission of large masses of data, obtaining in exchange only a counter-performance of marginal value'.

[2] On this phenomenon, see, among many others, Thobani (2016b), p. 532; Basunti (2020), p. 890 ff; D'Antonio (2022), p. 155. See also what has been observed, in this regard, by D'Ippolito (2020), p. 660: 'whereas originally the processing of personal data was an ancillary phenomenon even though intrinsic to the main activity, such as the sale and delivery of a physical good, access to a service, etc., today it is increasingly the central element of the contractual relationship. In other words, there has been a shift from the processing of data as a means of performing a certain activity, to processing aimed at obtaining the data themselves. The processing is thus aimed at exploiting the data and would not be a necessary consequence of the performance of other activities'.

[3] See, in particular, Resta (2020), p. 59; Gallo (2022), p. 1056; Battelli (2022), p. 335 ff.

[4] Cf., in this regard, Morace Pinelli (2023), p. 3 ff., who recalled how, 'precisely for the purpose of circumscribing and functionalising such power, combining the right of individuals to control their own data with the need for their circulation, preparatory to the development of the market', the DSA and the DMA have recently been approved (for a comment on which, see Bolognini et al. 2023).

[5] Stanzione (2022), p. 6 highlighted, in particular, the dangers inherent in the so-called 'commodification' of privacy: 'if, in fact, the services versus data bargaining scheme is by now standard practice, admitting the possibility of remuneration for consent, however, runs the risk of leading to

It should also be recalled that, especially in Italy, the traditional linking of personal data to the (sole) protection of the person has long hindered the idea that a market for personal data could exist,[6] an idea that has, however, more recently gradually asserted itself, in conjunction with the progressive recognition of the above-mentioned economic-contractual dimension underlying the phenomenon concerning the processing of personal data.[7] Indeed, just as, in the field of copyright, image rights, and other personality rights, a distinction has gradually been drawn between a non-patrimonial right of a non-transferable nature and a patrimonial right to the economic exploitation of personality attributes, a similar reasoning has also been put forward with regard to personal data, now considered susceptible to commercialisation and exchange.[8]

Attention to the market and to the negotiability of data is, moreover, a feature of Regulation (EU) 2016/679 (henceforth, GDPR), which significantly specifies that "the free movement of personal data within the Union shall be neither restricted nor prohibited for reasons connected with the protection of natural persons with regard to the processing of personal data" (Article 1(3)). According to the European legislator, in fact, "the right to the protection of personal data is not an absolute right; it must be considered in relation to its function in society and be balanced against other fundamental rights", which also include the "freedom to conduct a business" (see recital 4).[9]

An important role in the recognition of the economic-patrimonial dimension of personal data has therefore been played not only by part of the legal science but also by the Competition and Market Authority (*Autorità Garante della Concorrenza e del Mercato*), as well as by case law. In particular, the AGCM, in sanctioning the web giants for unfair commercial practices, affirmed the existence of a data market and the lawfulness of the economic transaction "exchange of personal data against digital services", recognising a consumer relationship, with the consequent applicability of consumer law (in this case, of the protection against unfair commercial practices).[10]

---

the formation of a digital under-proletariat, i.e. of social strata willing to surrender, with their own data, the essential core of their own freedom'.

[6] See, in this regard, Ainis (2023), p. 53: 'according to the traditional approach of private law scholarship, in fact, personality rights have antithetical features compared to those typical of patrimonial rights (inalienability, irretrievability, imprescriptibility, etc.). One can therefore understand the theoretical difficulties in admitting that personal data can represent not only the object of a personal right, but also real economic resources and utilities, and that the same can be exchanged for non-pecuniary counter-performances: in short, that there is an economic/contractual dimension underlying the phenomenon of personal data processing, even more so in the new model of the digital economy'.

[7] They have placed the capitalisation of personal data at the centre of their reflection, taking a position in favour of their economic relevance, in particular Ricciuto (2018), p. 689 ff; Ricciuto (2020), p. 642 ff; Resta and Zeno Zencovich (2018) p. 411 ff; De Franceschi (2017); De Franceschi (2019), p. 1381 ff; Senigaglia (2020a), p. 760 ff.

[8] See, in this regard, D'Ippolito (2020), p. 637; Gallo (2022), p. 1062.

[9] Cf., in this regard, D'Ippolito (2020), p. 656, according to whom "in this choice one could find the will to place the moral approach and the contractual approach on the same level, aiming at a constant balancing of them".

[10] See AGCM, Order of 29 November 2018, No. 27432, as well as already AGCM, Order of 11 May 2017, No. 26597.

Such an approach was subsequently confirmed by the administrative judge, who, on the one hand, recognised the commercial value of personal data and, on the other hand, pointed out that the rules protecting consumers and those protecting personal data are "complementary, imposing, in relation to their respective purposes of protection, specific information obligations, in one case functional to the protection of personal data, understood as a fundamental right of the personality, and in the other case to the correct information to be provided to the consumer in order to enable him to make an informed economic choice"[11] And even the Supreme Court of Cassation (*Corte di Cassazione*), in a significant ruling, held that "the law does not prohibit the exchange of personal data, but nevertheless requires that such an exchange be the result of full and in no way coerced consent".[12]

The "exchange of personal data against digital content or digital services" was then regulated by the European legislator, through Directive (EU) 2019/770, in particular from the point of view of the conformity of the aforementioned content or services with the contract, as well as the remedies for the failure to supply and for lack of conformity. This directive in fact considers, alongside contracts in which the consumer, in exchange for the digital content or service, pays or undertakes to pay a price, also "cases" in which the consumer provides or undertakes to provide personal data to the trader (see Article 3(1)).[13] Unlike the proposal for a directive, which in both cases referred to "contracts", expressly qualifying, in recital 13, personal data as a "counter-performance other than money", the final version no longer mentions "contract" with regard to the transaction "exchange of personal data against digital content or services". As is well known, the modification of Article 3 of the directive was carried out following the critical remarks made by the European Data Protection Supervisor, who was concerned to reaffirm the concept that personal data do not constitute a monetisable commodity.[14] However, the notion of "contract", with regard to the operation "exchange of personal data against digital content or services", is expressly referred to in recital 24 of the directive,[15] and, on the other hand, the fact that the contract having as its object the aforesaid exchange

---

[11] V. TAR Lazio, 10 January 2020, nos. 260 and 261, with note by Solinas (2020), p. 320 ff cf. Cons. Stato 29 March 2021, nos. 2630 and 2631., with note by D'Alberti (2021), p. 1079 ff.

[12] Cf. Cass., 2 July 2018, No. 17278, with note by Zanovello (2018), p. 1175 ff; with note by Thobani (2019a), p. 530 ff. Cf. also the reflections made, starting from that judgment, by Bravo (2019), p. 34 ff.

[13] As stated in recital 24 of the Directive, 'The personal data could be provided to the trader either at the time when the contract is concluded or at a later time, such as when the consumer gives consent for the trader to use any personal data that the consumer might upload or create with the use of the digital content or digital service'.

[14] See EDPS, *Opinion 4/2017 on the Proposal for a Directive on certain aspects concerning contracts for the supply of digital content*, 14 March 2017, § 11 ff.

[15] Where it is precisely stated that 'this Directive should, therefore, apply to *contracts* where the trader supplies, or undertakes to supply, digital content or digital services to the consumer and where the consumer provides, or undertakes to provide, personal data' (italics ours).

has a synallagmatic structure does not seem to be really open to doubt, given the mutual performances of the parties.[16]

Finally, with Directive (EU) 2019/2161 (the so-called *omnibus* directive), the European legislator, moving from the observation that "digital content and digital services are often supplied online under contracts under which the consumer does not pay a price but provides personal data to the trader" (cf. recital 31), extended also to the transactions at issue the protections provided for by Directive (EU) 2011/83 on consumer rights (such as in particular, the right to obtain pre-contractual information and to withdraw from the contract within a period of 14 days).[17]

It is therefore clear from the foregoing that the economic dimension of the processing of personal data, which underlies non-monetary transactions, is not to the detriment of the individual, since it entails, on the contrary, that the latter is also protected as part of an economic transaction, with the consequent possibility of availing oneself—as already mentioned and as will be seen further below[18]—even of contractual remedies, which otherwise cannot be exercised by the data subject as such.[19]

2 The Transaction "Exchange of Personal Data Against Digital Content or Digital Services". Personal Data as Goods in the Legal Sense

At this point, we can consider in more detail the performances that characterise the transaction in question, and, starting with the provision of personal data by the user, it is necessary, on a preliminary basis, to point out how personal data, considered in isolation, do not generally have a particular economic value, which is, moreover, acquired by the same following their aggregation and processing, capable of

[16] See Morace Pinelli (2023), p. 22; Senigaglia (2020a), p. 766 ff.; Speziale (2021), p. 616; Bachelet (2024), p. 1140. The presence of a bargain also appears to be confirmed by the so-called 'pay-or-consent' option, recently outlined by the CJEU (Grand Chamber), 4 July 2023, C-252/21 (on which see below, par. 4), and is also admitted by some decisions of the national courts (see, in this regard, Barbi (2023), p. 1227). Otherwise, in the opinion of Viterbo (2023), p. 318 ff., the granting of consent to the processing of personal data should be assessed, rather than as a counter-performance, as a procedure, necessarily compliant with the GDPR, that may arise in relation to the contract for the supply of digital content or services according to variable negotiating schemes.

[17] See Irti (2021), p. 158 ff; Ainis (2023), p. 56.

[18] See below, par. 7.

[19] See, in this sense, Giannone Codiglione (2017), p. 419; D'Ippolito (2020), p. 638 and p. 671. See also Langhanke and Schmidt-Kessel (2015), p. 218: 'While commercialisation has brought about new risks for consumers as to their personal data, we will argue that the law should tackle these risks by establishing two layers of consumer protection, i.e. data protection rules and particular contract law rules in parallel'. For the application, in particular, of the prohibition of unfair terms in the forms pre-formulated by the data controller for the declaration of consent to processing, see Alvisi (2019), p. 690 ff.

transforming them into Big Data, thus enabling their subsequent use for the most varied commercial purposes.[20]

The fact that a market for personal data has been found to exist has therefore led to the question of whether such data can be qualified as goods. Although this is a rather controversial issue, one part of the legal science has come to believe that personal data do indeed constitute goods in the legal sense (albeit of an intangible nature), within the meaning of Article 810 of the Civil Code, insofar as they are capable of being object of a right to economic exploitation.[21]

In this perspective, the peculiar nature of the assets in question has also been emphasised, given that, on the one hand, their enjoyment does not imply their consumption and that, on the other hand, they are consequently susceptible of being used simultaneously by a plurality of subjects.[22]

3 The Granting of Consent to the Processing of Personal Data

As regards, then, the granting of consent to the processing of personal data in exchange contracts for the supply of digital content or services, it should first of all be clarified that the consent in question does not relate to the very personal and inalienable right to personal data, but only to the exercise thereof, on the basis of the purposes identified from time to time.[23]

It is debated, however, whether the consent, in the economic transaction under consideration, is a single one, i.e. concluding the contract for the exchange of personal data, at the same time authorising the processing thereof, or whether a distinction must be made between the consent to the processing of personal data and the consent that finalises the contract.

The latter approach, motivated by the desire to reconcile the full freedom of consent to processing with its necessity for the purposes of the contract, is essentially divided into two variants, namely the linked acts thesis and the conditional

[20] Cf. Mula (2021), p. 38; Pignataro (2024), p. 19. On the technical characteristics of Big Data, as well as the legal issues arising from them, see also Faini (2019), p. 160 ff.

[21] Cf. Ricciuto (2020), p. 656; Gallo (2022), p. 1064; Morace Pinelli (2023), p. 9; see, perspicuously, also Senigaglia (2020a), p.765: "data circulate in the market, which attributes to them a use value and an exchange value, and turns them into economic goods and therefore into legal goods, thus disposing them to contractualisation".

[22] The peculiar nature of the goods in question, which ultimately constitute information pertaining to the person, have therefore led some to consider that they are 'goods that have many features in common with public goods' (thus Gallo [2022], p. 1064). While others have considered, also in light of the characteristics briefly mentioned in the text, that the recurring assimilation of data to oil (new oil) is actually misleading (cf. Morace Pinelli [2023], p. 2; in critical terms of such a metaphor, see also Gambino and Stazi [2020], p. XVII f.).

[23] Cf. Morace Pinelli (2023), p. 13; Senigaglia (2020a), p. 782. See also, at length in this regard, Bravo (2018), passim.

exchange thesis. According to the first thesis, the user's consent to the use of data would constitute the prerequisite of the contract for the supply of digital content or services, so that there would be two functionally linked acts: the first, unilateral and of a personal nature, with which the subject exercises his informational self-determination, and the second, bilateral and with a patrimonial content, which perfects downstream the exchange between personal data and digital content or services.[24] On the other hand, according to the conditionality thesis, the user's consent to the processing of his or her own data would be a conditional performance, i.e. a performance that cannot be compelled, but which the subject would nevertheless need to perform in order to obtain the digital contents or services.[25]

Both of the aforementioned constructions therefore end up placing consent to the processing of personal data outside of the contract,[26] and consistently assert that the user's capacity should be subject to a differentiated discipline, given that while consent to processing could be given from the age of 14 (cf. art. 2-*quinquies*, par. 1, Personal Data Protection Code), consent to the exchange contract would, on the other hand, require, according to the general rule, the completion of the 18th year of age (art. 2, para. 2, Civil Code).[27]

The aforesaid separation between two consents (to the processing and to the contract) is, however, rejected by those who, highlighting its artificiality and various critical aspects, consider that consent is, in reality, only one, constitutive of a synallagmatic contract,[28] and then hold that the attainment of the capacity to express valid consent to the processing of personal data, in Italy fixed—as mentioned—at the age of 14, may also apply to the profile concerning the exchange between data and digital content or services, in line with the most recent tendency to differentiate the capacity on the basis of the different types of contract (think, precisely, of the different maturity required to register with a social network or to conclude a real estate sale).[29]

[24] See, in this sense, Resta (2020), p. 74 ff; Bravo (2019), p. 44; Quarta (2020), p. 308. He downgraded the separation between the two types of consent, Senigaglia (2020b), p. 139, in whose view consent to processing and contractual consent would constitute elements of a single case, giving rise to an objectively complex act.

[25] See, for this view, Irti (2021), p. 102 ff.

[26] As pointed out, in particular, by Ricciuto (2022), p. 140.

[27] Cf. Resta (2020), p. 110.

[28] See, in particular, Ricciuto (2024), p. 24; Gallo (2022), p. 1067 and p. 1071; Morace Pinelli (2023), p. 13; Bachelet (2023b), p. 101 ff, who considered it possible to reconcile the contract's synallagmatic structure with the persistent freedom of consent to data processing by placing the latter in the genetic phase of the relationship (rather than in the executive phase, as hypothesised by the thesis of conditional exchange mentioned earlier in the text), so that the contract would be perfected with the provision of consent, without any obligation for the subject to give it, just as real contracts (*contratti reali*) are perfected with the delivery of the thing.

[29] See, in this sense, Gallo (2022), p. 1070; Ricciuto (2022), p. 138 ff.

4 The Requirements of Consent to the Processing of Personal Data

Apart from what has been observed in the previous paragraph, consent to the processing of personal data must, in any case, meet the requirements set out in Article 4(11) GDPR, where the "consent of the data subject" is defined as a manifestation of will that is "freely given, specific, informed and unambiguous".[30]

Beginning, therefore, with the requirement of freedom, it is generally considered that, in the area of contracts concerning personal data, a greater degree of freedom of consent is required than is generally deemed sufficient for the conclusion of a contract, so that it is not sufficient that the consent itself is not vitiated by lack of capacity, mistake, duress, or fraud.[31]

In particular, according to Article 7(4) GDPR, "when assessing whether consent is freely given, utmost account shall be taken of whether, *inter alia*, the performance of a contract, including the provision of a service, is conditional on consent to the processing of personal data that is not necessary for the performance of that contract" (so-called "tying operations").[32]

This provision, if strictly understood, could, moreover, lead to excluding the very possibility of entering into exchange contracts in which the required consideration is, precisely, consent to the processing of personal data for purposes other than those necessary for the performance of the contract, since consent given in this way could not be considered truly free.[33] Thus, the model of the circulation of personal data would end up, in this perspective, being substantially similar to that of the circulation of parts of the human body, since in both cases, the act must be characterised by gratuitousness (see Article 3 of the Charter of Fundamental Rights of the European Union).[34]

However, to the contrary of such an approach, which would end up making the aforementioned type of contracts indiscriminately unlawful (indeed—as

[30] See, in this regard, the monographic contributions by Thobani (2016a) and Vivarelli (2019).

[31] See Resta and Zeno Zencovich (2018), p. 426; Thobani (2016b), p. 517; De Cristofaro (2020), p. 151.; Addante (2020), p. 903 ff.

[32] For an analysis of consent with specific regard to the so-called 'tying' phenomenon, see Thobani (2019b), p. 137 ff. D'Antonio (2022), p. 164.

[33] See, to this effect, Voigt and Von dem Bussche (2017), p. 95. See also the restrictive positions in this regard taken, respectively, by the Italian *Garante per la protezione dei dati personali*, according to which 'consent to further processing of personal data that the data subject "must" give as a condition for obtaining a requested service cannot be defined as "free"' (GPDP, *Linee guida in materia di attività promozionale e contrasto allo spam*, 4 July 2013, doc. *Web* No. 2542348, at www.garanteprivacy.it, § 2.6), as well as by the European Data Protection Board (EDPB, *Guidelines 05/2020 on consent under Regulation 2016/679*, 4 May 2020, § 3.1.2), according to which, with very few exceptions, the provider 'cannot prevent data subjects from accessing a service on the basis that they do not consent'.

[34] See, on this model, Resta (2011), p. 510 and p. 516 ff.

noted—widespread in today's economic and social reality),[35] it has been pointed out, on the one hand, that in the system of the Charter of Fundamental Rights of the European Union, while in relation to the human body and its parts, it is expressly provided that they cannot constitute, as such, a "source of financial gain", nothing similar is provided for with reference to personal data.[36] On the other hand, it has been specified that not even the above-mentioned provision of Article 7(4) GDPR introduces a prohibition, but establishes a mere evaluation parameter, to be considered together with other criteria.[37] So that, from this perspective, consent could not be deemed unfree merely because the supply of the digital content or service is conditional upon the granting of consent to the processing of personal data, but rather to be assessed on a case-by-case basis, taking into account all the relevant circumstances, for instance, the absence of alternatives, the essential nature of the good or service, the unfairness of the contractual conditions, and so on.[38]

The Court of Cassation, moreover, has also taken this view, and has held that it is possible to make the provision of digital services conditional upon the granting of consent to the processing of the user's personal data, provided, however, that the services in question are fungible and can be waived without serious sacrifice for the person concerned.[39] And even the Court of Justice, in its recent ruling on the so-called "*Meta* case",[40] seemed to guide the interpreter in the direction of a more liberal reading of Article 7(4) GDPR, as opposed to the overly rigid reading referred to above, given that only by considering consent to be potentially free would it make sense to ask the question, addressed by the Court, as to whether consent is compelled in the specific case in which it is given in order to access a service offered by a dominant platform.[41] To this question, the Court of Justice answered by stating that the latter circumstance is not, in itself, an obstacle to free consent, but constitutes

[35] See above, par. 1.

[36] See Resta (2020), p. 69, who added that 'Article 8 [of the Charter of Fundamental Rights of the European Union], after having reaffirmed the fundamental nature of the right to the protection of personal data, mentions consent as one of the possible bases to justify processing, but does not set any limit in terms of content comparable with that of Article 3'.

[37] Cf. Lucchini Guastalla (2018), p. 113; in the sense that the rule in question avoids offering an 'aprioristically negative' solution, see Zorzi Galgano (2019), p. 71; cf. also Solinas (2022), p. 92.

[38] See, again, Resta (2020), p. 70, who has, therefore, concluded that "the 'monetisation' of data [has] in itself nothing particularly disreputable or legally 'suspect', provided, however, that the consent in question represents an effective expression of informational self-determination and not a fictitious legitimisation clause of another person's negotiating or technological power". See, similarly, also Gallo (2022), p. 1077.

[39] See Cass., 2 July 2018, no. 17278, cited above. But see also, in this regard, the remarks of D'Antonio (2022), p. 167, according to whom "it is not easy to establish the level of importance that a service may have for a given individual, a situation that is susceptible to change depending on the moment and the environmental context. Irrenounceability therefore risks being a "difficult" parameter to which to anchor the verification of a judgment, to be conducted, obviously, through a casuistic and *a posteriori* approach".

[40] CJEU (Grand Chamber), 4 July 2023, C-252/21, for a comment on which see Bachelet (2023a), p. 483 ff; D'Ippolito (2023), p. 323 ff.

[41] See, in this sense, Bachelet (2023a), p. 493.

an "important factor" in determining whether consent has been validly and, in particular, freely given. On the other hand, with reference to the processing of data concerning users' behaviour outside the platform (so-called "external data"), since consent must be presumed not to have been freely given where users cannot refuse it without giving up the service,[42] the Court has clarified that, in order to make such a choice free, the economic operator is required to offer, if necessary for an appropriate fee, an "equivalent alternative" not accompanied by such data processing operations.[43]

Consent to the processing of personal data must, moreover, be specific,[44] with the consequence that the user, in addition to having to be aware that the consent to the processing of personal data relates to purposes other than those necessary for the performance of the contract,[45] must be able to express his or her consent separately for each processing purpose targeted by the provider of the digital content or service.[46]

It is also necessary to bear in mind the provisions of Article 7(2) GDPR, according to which, "where the data subject's consent is given in the context of a written declaration which also concerns other matters, the request for consent shall be presented in a manner which is clearly distinguishable from other matters, in an intelligible and easily accessible form, using clear and plain language". This provision, which applies, in particular, when consent to data processing is included in general terms and conditions, is intended to ensure the clarity and transparency of the declarations, and thus to prevent the data subject from giving consent by mistake.[47]

A further requirement for consent to data processing is, therefore, its informed nature, as the GDPR provides for a series of information that the data controller is obliged to provide to the data subject (see, in particular, Articles 13 and 14), within the scope of which a minimum nucleus of information to be provided prior to the

---

[42] According to the Court of Justice, the presumption in question would be justified, in relation to so-called 'external data', since such data are those most remote from the perception of users, and whose processing determines a 'significant impact'.

[43] According to Bachelet (2024), p. 1132, 'the circumstance that payment of a price constitutes the alternative to consent to processing, so-called "pay-or-consent", suggests that consent is now a mode of payment'. In contrast, the European Data Protection Board (EDPB) has more recently urged large online platforms to offer their services without behavioural advertising even free of charge, e.g. with a form of advertising involving the processing of less or no personal data (see EDPB, *Opinion 8/2024 on Valid Consent in the Context of Consent or Pay Models Implemented by Large Online Platforms*, 17 April 2024, § 180 f.).

[44] Cf., in this regard, Senigaglia (2020a), p. 771, who held that, "in contracts in which the object consists of data [...], the rule of determinability cannot be applied since, due to the interference of the discipline of consent, the rule of *necessary determinateness* must operate (so as to restrict the scope of application of Article 1346 of the Civil Code)"; in the latter sense, see also Sciancalepore (2022), p. 125.

[45] See Gallo (2022), p. 1072.

[46] In this sense, see also Art. 6(1)(a) GDPR, according to which processing is lawful only if 'the data subject has given consent to the processing of his or her personal data for one or more specific purposes'. See, in this regard, A. Gentili (2022), p. 711.

[47] V. De Franceschi (2017), p. 53.

request for consent is identified, for the purposes of its validity, such as those relating to the identity of the data controller, the purposes of the processing, the possibility of withdrawing consent, etc.[48]

Finally, consent must be unambiguous, since Article 4(11) GDPR requires that it be given "by a statement or by a clear affirmative action", so that mere inactivity on the part of the data subject, for example, failure to tick a box pre-selected by the data controller in favour of certain types of processing, should be deemed unsuitable for this purpose;[49] nor could valid consent be detected in the fact that the data subject continues to surf online in the face of information that such conduct would be interpreted by the data controller as a tacit manifestation of consent.[50]

In any case, in view of the possible difficulty of establishing, especially in the context of a technological dimension that is not always easy to decipher, whether the data subject has actually consented to his or her personal data being processed, it should be recalled that, pursuant to Article 7(1) GDPR, the burden of proof that consent has been given lies with the data controller. So that, where there is a dispute in this regard, and the data controller is unable to provide any evidence in this sense, it should be presumed that no consent to the processing of the data has been given.[51]

5 The Consequences of the Lack of One of the Requirements of Consent to Process Personal Data, as Well as of the Communication by the User of Untrue Data

If the data subject's consent lacks one of the requirements mentioned in the previous paragraph, it cannot be deemed to have been validly given, with the consequence that the processing of personal data based on it must be considered unlawful.

In the legal science, it has been pointed out that this circumstance also appears capable of affecting the contract for the supply of digital content or services, in particular in the sense of rendering it voidable, given that the invalidity of the consent would affect, depending on the various theses put forward,[52] respectively, the object or consideration of the contract, or the event made conditional, or even a prerequisite thereof.[53]

Since, moreover, in most cases, the absence of freedom, specificity, information, and unambiguity in relation to the data subject's consent is due to conduct consciously put in place by the professional, it has been hypothesised by some, with a view to making the latter liable, and as a solution preferable to the termination of the

---

[48] See Gentili (2022), p. 712; Addante (2020), p. 908.

[49] See Gallo, (2022), p. 1074; Stanzione (2022), p. 89.

[50] Cf. Alvisi (2019), p. 687.

[51] See De Franceschi (2017), p. 50.

[52] See above, par. 3.

[53] See, for a more detailed overview of the various theses, Bachelet (2023b), p. 138 ff.

contract, that it be preserved, where this corresponds to the user's interest.[54] So that the user, faced with the inhibition of the processing of his personal data by the provider of digital content or services, could continue to benefit from the latter free of charge.[55]

It should, however, be borne in mind that the user of digital content or services could also behave improperly, in particular if he or she provides untruthful personal data (e.g. age, first and last name, sex, etc.), as such useless for the trader.[56] With regard to such a case, some have argued that this is a circumstance capable of entailing the invalidity of the contract for the supply of digital content or services, with the consequent possibility of challenging it on the grounds of vices of will[57] while others have held that the trader would be entitled to payment of a fee in lieu of the "transfer" of the data.[58]

6 The Withdrawal of Consent to Personal Data Processing

In addition to the requirements mentioned in the previous paragraphs, consent to the processing of personal data is also characterised by its revocability: according to Article 7(3) GDPR, the data subject "shall have the right to withdraw his or her consent at any time" and "it shall be as easy to withdraw as to give consent". Therefore, if consent has been granted, for example, via the Internet, its revocation must be able to take place in the same way, excluding that it may be required to send registered letters or comply with other formalities. From the point of view of greater user protection, however, the existence of a principle of symmetry of forms seems to be denied, with the consequence that, where consent has been given, again by way of example, in writing, it should also be possible to revoke it orally, except in that case the burden of proof would be on the data subject.[59]

The revocability of consent to the processing of personal data evidently entails an intrinsic precariousness of the contract concerning the supply of digital content

[54] See, in this regard, Addante (2020), p. 910 ff.

[55] Such an orientation, as also observed by Bachelet (2023b), p. 140, is also transversal, in that it is shared both by some of those who qualify the exchange of "services against data" as a synallagmatic contract, and by some of the supporters of the thesis of the negotiated link or conditional promise (see, again, above, par. 3). The outcome mentioned in the text has, however, been criticised by Pagliantini (2022), p. 1530, as the same would end up surreptitiously imposing an obligation to contract on the platform operator.

[56] See Addante (2020), p. 911.

[57] See Gallo (2022), p. 1082.

[58] Cf., in this sense, De Franceschi (2019), p. 1405, who added that, "in such a case, the professional should already make it clear in the pre-contractual phase (Art. 49(1)(e) of the Consumer Code) that the party, in the event of "payment" by means of untrue data, will be required to make a "substitute" payment in money. The criteria for calculating that "substitute payment" must also be indicated in advance by the trader, in the context of the pre-contractual information".

[59] See Gallo (2022) p. 1088.

or services,[60] which, moreover, is justified in the light of the unenforceability of consent not only in the initial phase of the conclusion of the contract but also throughout the duration of the contractual relationship.

From the aforementioned unenforceability, then, it follows that, just as the original refusal to give consent to data processing cannot entail adverse consequences for the data subject, so too the subsequent withdrawal of consent cannot give rise to any obligation to pay compensation or indemnity on the revoking party,[61] except, in the opinion of some, the case of contradictory conduct or abuse of the right of revocation (e.g. a user who enters into a contract in order to immediately and definitively acquire the digital content, thereby creating an expectation in the other party that he will "continue" to consent to the processing of the data, and who subsequently, within a very short period of time, revokes the consent previously given).[62]

Turning, then, to consider the effects of withdrawal of consent, it must, first of all, be borne in mind that withdrawal operates *ex nunc*, in that it does not affect the lawfulness of the processing carried out in the meantime (see Article 7(3) GDPR). Since, however, any subsequent processing must be considered unlawful, the economic operator is obliged to comply with its obligations under the GDPR, and thus, in particular, to erase the user's personal data (see Art. 17(1)(b)). If, then, the data in question have been transferred by the data controller to third parties (e.g. as is often the case, for marketing purposes), the economic operator is obliged to notify each of the recipients to whom the personal data have been disclosed of their erasure, unless this proves impossible or involves a disproportionate effort (see Art. 19 GDPR).[63]

Withdrawal of consent to the processing of the user's personal data also entails consequences with regard to the contract for the supply of digital content or digital services, which, moreover, appear to differ to some extent depending on the type of performance to be fulfilled by the supplier.

Where, in fact, it is a service (e.g. subscription to a newsletter or access to a social network), the supplier, against the failure of the original counter-performance, may legitimately interrupt the performance of its service,[64] or, if it intends to

---

[60] V. De Franceschi (2017), p. 116; Addante (2020), p. 917.

[61] See Resta (2020), p. 79; Magli (2023), p, 2264 f.

[62] Cf. Gallo (2022), p. 1089; Langhanke and Schmidt-Kessel (2015), p. 222.

[63] See, in this regard, also Pignataro (2024), p. 22, who, after having pointed out that 'the right to erasure is not, however, capable of guaranteeing *the ius excludendi alios*, inherent in the absoluteness of the fundamental right of the individual, once the personal data have been placed on the network', recalled how 'the difficulty or impossibility of removing the data from the network [has] made necessary the codification of the right to be forgotten or de-indexed by search engines as a preventive precautionary measure, analogous to the function of the injunction and of compensation in specific form in the protection of personal rights, adapted to the sharing of the data as a means of exercising the right'.

[64] However, it does not seem to be possible to invoke the *exceptio inadimpleti contractus* envisaged in Art. 1460 of the Civil Code in order to suspend the performance of the relationship, given that the withdrawal of consent does not constitute a breach of contract by the user (see Bachelet [2024], p. 1154; on the contrary, Irti [2021], p. 112 ff.; Gallo [2022], p. 1090).

continue the service, request, for the future, the payment of a fee by the user.[65] Where, on the other hand, a digital good has already been definitively forfeited by the user (e.g. an e-book), it seems difficult to imagine that the latter would be under an obligation to return the good received or to pay a fee for it, since—as mentioned above—withdrawal of consent, on the one hand, has no retroactive effect and, on the other hand, cannot entail any disadvantage for the revoking party.[66] With particular regard to such cases, it should, therefore, be evident how the withdrawal of consent to data processing ends up constituting a risk for the provider of digital content: a risk which, however, should in any case be calculable, as it is known to the data controller, given that, among the information that the latter is required to communicate to the data subject (see Article 12 GDPR), there is, precisely, also the right to withdraw consent to processing.[67]

7 The Supply of Digital Content or Digital Services and the Remedies for the Failure to Supply and for Lack of Conformity

After having examined the granting of consent to the processing of personal data by the user, it is also necessary to briefly consider the promise by which the economic operator is bound, consisting in the supply of digital content or digital services.

In this regard, the aforementioned Directive (EU) 2019/770, "on certain aspects concerning contracts for the supply of digital content and digital services" (implemented in Italy by Legislative Decree no. 173 of 4 November 2021, which amended the Consumer Code) comes into consideration, which has, in particular, extended also to consumers not paying with money, but with personal data, the same remedies due to consumers who have entered into a traditional contract for reward. As previously mentioned,[68] the directive in question applies, in fact, not only to contracts in which the consumer, in exchange for the digital content or service, pays or undertakes to pay a price but also to "cases" in which the consumer provides or undertakes to provide personal data to the trader, except where the personal data provided by the consumer are exclusively processed by the trader for the purpose of supplying the digital content or digital service in accordance with the Directive or for allowing the trader to comply with legal requirements to which the trader is subject

[65] Cf. Gallo (2022), p. 1090. See also Bachelet (2024), p. 1153, in whose opinion the introduction of the pay-or-consent option by the aforementioned Court of Justice ruling on the so-called '*Meta* case' (see above par. 4), if considered in a systematic way, "would seem [...] to preclude the typical extinction effect of withdrawal, generating instead a pecuniary obligation on the revoking user".

[66] See, again, Gallo (2022), p. 1090.

[67] See, in the latter sense, Senigaglia (2020a), p. 773.

[68] See above par. 1.

(see Article 3(1) of Directive 2019/770, transfused in Article *135-octies*(3) and (4) of the Consumer Code).

The remedies provided by the rules under review concern, in short, both failure to supply and lack of conformity: while in the first case, the consumer is entitled to terminate the contract (see Art. 13, Directive 2019/770, merged into Art. *135-septiesdecies* of the Consumer Code), in the second case, the means of protection are, on the contrary, more articulated, starting from the restoration of conformity, moving on to the reduction of the price, up to the termination of the contract (see Art. 14, Directive 2019/770, transfused into Art. *135-octiesdecies* of the Consumer Code).

In this last respect, it is worth pointing out that, while in the case of the supply of digital content or services against payment of a price, the consumer is entitled to terminate the contract only if the lack of conformity is not minor (see Art. 14(6), Directive 2019/770, merged into Art. 135-octiesdecies, para. 6, of the Consumer Code), where, on the other hand, the consideration for the supply consisted in the consent to the processing of personal data, it should be understood that the consumer is entitled to terminate the contract even if the lack of conformity is minor, since, in the latter case, he cannot benefit from the price reduction (see recital 67 of the Directive).[69]

It is even more important, from the point of view of the complementary nature of contractual protection with respect to the protection of personal data, to emphasise that any breaches of security, transparency, etc. in the processing of data by the trader are also liable to be qualified as lack of conformity (e.g. in the case of inadequate encryption software, leading to the disclosure of data to unauthorised recipients, or in the case where the consumer's personal information is exposed to malware or spyware, with the consequent risk of misuse by third parties).

Such an assertion, although lacking an explicit reflection in the articles of Directive (EU) 2019/770, can nevertheless be found in the recitals (cf, in particular, recital 48),[70] and is deemed to be supported by further normative indications which state, on the one hand, the applicability of EU data protection law to any personal data processed in connection with supply contracts under consideration (see Article 3(8) of Directive 2019/770, and, in the same sense, Article *135-novies*(6) of the Consumer Code), and, on the other hand, require the trader to comply with the obligations laid down in the GDPR (see Article 16(2) of Directive 2019/770, and Article *135-noviesdecies*(3) of the Consumer Code).[71]

[69] See, in this regard, Senigaglia (2020a), p. 775; Addante (2020), p. 924; Gallo (2022), p. 1084 f.

[70] In that recital we read that: Facts leading to a lack of compliance with requirements provided for by Regulation (EU) 2016/679, including core principles such as the requirements for data minimisation, data protection by design and data protection by default, may, depending on the circumstances of the case, also be considered to constitute a lack of conformity of the digital content or digital service with subjective or objective requirements for conformity provided for in this Directive".

[71] See, in this sense, Camardi (2019), p. 514; Irti (2021), p. 136 ff; Versaci (2020), p. 192 ff; Pagliantini (2022), p. 1527; D'Onofrio (2023), p. 2255.

It follows that, if the way in which the digital content or service is provided does not comply with the requirements of the GDPR, the consumer will be able to invoke, in addition to the data protection legislation, the contractual remedies for lack of conformity provided by Directive (EU) 2019/770 (see, again, recital 48 of the Directive).[72]

References

Addante A (2020) La circolazione negoziale dei dati personali nei contratti di fornitura di contenuti e servizi digitali. Giust Civ, p 889 ff

Ainis M (2023) Circolazione dei dati personali e disciplina del mercato. In: Morace Pinelli A (ed) La circolazione dei dati personali: persona, contratto e mercato. Pisa, p 53 ff

Alvisi C (2019) Dati personali e diritti dei consumatori. In: Cuffaro V, D'Orazio R, Ricciuto V (eds) I dati personali nel diritto europeo. Torino, p 669 ff

Bachelet (2023a) La Corte di giustizia sul caso Meta: trattamento dei dati e "prezzo" del consenso. Pactum, p 483 ff

Bachelet V (2023b) Il consenso oltre il consenso. Dati personali, contratto, mercato. Pisa

Bachelet V (2024) Il contratto di scambio di "servizi contro dati" (o contro prezzo). Riv Dir Civ, p 1130

Barbi L (2023) Sui contratti di scambio servizi contro dati: prime riflessioni della giurisprudenza di merito. Contr. e Impr., p 1216 ff

Basunti C (2020) La (perduta) centralità del consenso nello specchio delle condizioni di liceità del trattamento dei dati personali. Contr. e Impr., p 860 ff

Battelli E (2022) I modelli negoziali di business degli operatori digitali a "prezzo zero" non sono "gratuiti". Contr. e Impr., p 355 ff

Bolognini L, Pelino E, Scialdone M (eds) (2023) Digital Services Act e Digital Markets Act. Definizioni e prime applicazioni dei nuovi regolamenti europei. Milano

Bravo F (2018) Il "diritto" a trattare dati personali nello svolgimento dell'attività economica. Padova

Bravo F (2019) Lo "scambio di dati personali" nei contratti di fornitura di servizi digitali e il consenso dell'interessato tra autorizzazione e contratto. Contr. e Impr., p 34 ff

Camardi C (2019) Prime osservazioni sulla Direttiva (UE) sui contratti per la fornitura di contenuti e servizi digitali. Operazioni di consumo e circolazione di dati personali. Giust Civ, p 499 ff

D'Alberti D (2021) Tutele "multilivello" e l'effettività dei rimedi per gli utenti online. Nuova Giur. Civ. Comm I, p 1079 ff

D'Antonio V (2022) Il consenso al trattamento dei dati personali tra autodeterminazione informativa e dinamiche remuneratorie. In: Stanzione P (ed) I poteri privati delle piattaforme e le nuove frontiere della privacy. Torino, p 151 ff

D'Ippolito (2023) Data economy: la Corte di giustizia precisa il rapporto tra concorrenza e protezione dei dati personali e le norme sulla pubblicità personalizzata. MediaLaws 2, p 323 ff

D'Ippolito G (2020) Commercializzazione dei dati personali: il dato personale tra approccio morale e negoziale. Dir Inf, p 635 ff

[72] The aforementioned recital closes, in fact, by stating that: "Where the facts leading to non-compliance with requirements under Regulation (EU) 2016/679 also constitute a lack of conformity of the digital content or digital service with subjective or objective requirements for conformity as provided for in this Directive, the consumer should be entitled to the remedies for the lack of conformity provided for by this Directive, unless the contract is already void or voidable under national law".

D'Onofrio M (2023) L'illecito trattamento dei dati come difetto di conformità del contenuto digitale. Giur It, p 2253 ff

De Cristofaro G (2020) Die datenschutzrechtliche Einwilligung als Gegenstand des Leistungsversprechens. In: Pertot T (ed) Rechte an Daten. Tübingen, p 151 ff

De Franceschi A (2017) La circolazione dei dati personali tra privacy e contratto. Napoli

De Franceschi A (2019) Il "pagamento" mediante dati personali. In: Cuffaro V, D'Orazio R, Ricciuto V (eds) I dati personali nel diritto europeo. Torino, p 1381 ff

Faini F (2019) Data society. Governo dei dati e tutela dei diritti nell'era digitale. Milano

Gallo P (2022) Il consenso al trattamento dei dati personali come prestazione. Riv Dir Civ, p 1054 ff

Gambino AM, Stazi A (2020) Introduzione. Datificazione dei rapporti socio-economici, circolazione dei dati e diritto. In: Gambino AM, Stazi A (eds) La circolazione dei dati. Titolarità, strumenti negoziali, diritti e tutele. Pisa, p XI ff

Gentili A (2022), La volontà nel contesto digitale. Riv Trim Dir Proc Civ., p 701 ff

Giannone Codiglione G (2017) I dati personali come corrispettivo della fruizione di un servizio di comunicazione elettronica e la "consumerizzazione" della privacy. Dir Inf, p 390 ff

Irti C (2021) Consenso "negoziato" e circolazione dei dati personali. Torino

Langhanke C, Schmidt-Kessel M (2015) Consumer Data as Consideration. EuCM, p 218 ff

Lucchini Guastalla E (2018) Il nuovo regolamento europeo sul trattamento dei dati personali: i principi ispiratori. Contr e Impr, p 106 ff

Magli C (2023) La revoca del consenso e le ripercussioni sul contratto di fornitura di contenuti e servizi digitali. Giur It, p 2264 ff

Morace Pinelli A (2023) Introduzione. In: Morace Pinelli A (ed) La circolazione dei dati personali: persona, contratto e mercato. Pisa, p 1 ff

Mula D (2021) La tutela dei dati personali sulle piattaforme digitali. In: Contaldo A (ed) Le piattaforme digitali. Profili giuridici e tecnologici nel nuovo sistema. Pisa, p 37 ff

Pagliantini S (2022), L'attuazione minimalista della dir. 2019/770/UE: riflessioni sugli artt. 135 octies – 135 vicies ter c. cons. La nuova disciplina dei contratti b-to-c per la fornitura di contenuti e servizi digitali. Nuove leggi civ. comm, p 1527 ff

Pignataro G (2024) Circolazione dei dati tra modelli proprietari e contrattuali. MediaLaws 2, p 18 ff

Quarta A (2020) Mercati senza scambi. Le metamorfosi del capitalismo di sorveglianza. Napoli

Resta G (2011) Danni non patrimoniali. Enc Dir Annali IV. Milano, p 510 ff

Resta G (2020) I dati personali oggetto del contratto. Riflessioni sul coordinamento tra la Direttiva (UE) 2019/770 e il Regolamento (UE) 2016/679. In: Gambino AM, Stazi A (eds) La circolazione dei dati. Titolarità, strumenti negoziali, diritti e tutele. Pisa, p 55 ff

Resta G, Zeno Zencovich V (2018) Volontà e consenso nella fruizione dei servizi in rete. Riv Dir Proc Civ, p 411 ff

Ricciuto V (2018) La patrimonializzazione dei dati personali. Contratto e mercato nella ricostruzione del fenomeno. Dir Inf, p 689 ff

Ricciuto V (2020) Il contratto ed i nuovi fenomeni patrimoniali: il caso della circolazione dei dati personali. Riv Dir Civ, p 642

Ricciuto V (2022) L'equivoco della privacy. Persona vs dato personale. Napoli

Ricciuto V (2024) Consenso al trattamento e contratto. Pers Merc, p 13 ff

Sciancalepore G, (2022) I dati come oggetto del contratto tra la direttiva sui contenuti digitali e il GDPR. In: Stanzione P (ed) I poteri privati delle piattaforme e le nuove frontiere della privacy. Torino, p 115 ff

Senigaglia R (2020a) La dimensione patrimoniale del diritto alla protezione dei dati personali. Contr. e Impr., p 760 ff

Senigaglia R (2020b) Minore età e contratto. Contributo alla teoria della capacità. Torino

Solinas C (2020) Circolazione dei dati personali, onerosità del contratto e pratiche commerciali scorrette. Giur It, p 320 ff

Solinas C (2022) Autonomia privata e regolazione pubblica nel trattamento dei dati personali. Bari

Speziale I (2021) L'ingresso dei dati personali nella prospettiva causale dello scambio: i modelli contrattuali di circolazione. Contr e Impr, p 602 ff

Stanzione P (2022) Introduzione. In: Stanzione P (ed) I poteri privati delle piattaforme e le nuove frontiere della privacy. Torino, p 1 ff

Thobani S (2016a) I requisiti del consenso al trattamento dei dati personali, Santarcangelo di Romagna

Thobani S (2016b) La libertà del consenso al trattamento dei dati personali e lo sfruttamento economico dei diritti della personalità. Europa Dir Priv, p 513 ff

Thobani S (2019a) Operazioni di tying e libertà del consenso. Giur It, p 530 ff

Thobani S (2019b) Il mercato dei dati personali: tra tutela dell'interessato e tutela dell'utente. MediaLaws 3, p 131 ff

Versaci G (2020) La contrattualizzazione dei dati personali. Napoli

Viterbo FG (2023) Oltre il valore economico dei dati personali, tra autonomia negoziale e gestione aziendale. Annali SISDiC, p 301 ff

Vivarelli A (2019) Il consenso al trattamento dei dati personali nell'era digitale. Sfide tecnologiche e soluzioni giuridiche, Napoli

Voigt P, von dem Bussche A (2017) The EU general data protection regulation (GDPR). A practical guide. Cham

Zanovello F (2018) Consenso libero e specifico alle e-mail promozionali. Nuova giur. civ. Comm, I, p 1175 ff

Zorzi Galgano N (2019) Le due anime del GDPR e la tutela del diritto alla privacy. In: Zorzi Galgano N (ed) Persona e mercato dei dati. Riflessioni sul GDPR. Milano, p 35 ff

Digital Succession

Silvia Bonetti

Contents

Abstract The chapter analyses the post-mortal dynamics involving digital objects, with particular regard—among these—to personal data, with a view to identify the instruments, starting from Article 2-*terdecies* of the *Codice della privacy*, that the legal system offers to ensure their protection, management and, eventually, circulation after the death of the person to which they refer to.

S. Bonetti (✉)
University of Verona, Verona, Italy
e-mail: silvia.bonetti@univr.it

R. Bocchini (ed.), *Digital Platforms - From Technical Foundations to Legal and Economic Implications*, https://doi.org/10.1007/978-3-032-07978-7_31

1 The So-Called Digital Succession: A Simplified Expression Identifying a Complex Phenomenon

The relentless advancement of technological development and the related advent of digitalisation are recognised as the driving forces behind the phenomenon that, more than any other, characterises the evolution of contemporary society, namely the gradual but rapid and, in all likelihood, irreversible transformation of both the nature and the structure of social and economic relations, with inevitable and tangible effects also in terms of the related legal regulation.

This radical transformation is accompanied by the continuous creation of new digital goods by individuals to whom those goods relate, who, consciously or unconsciously, place them into circulation in the legal traffic in carrying out common daily activities, both personal and professional, which to an increasing extent are nowadays carried out online.[1]

This process has also led to a transformation of the very concept of wealth, which has progressively changed in both composition and characteristics, taking on, in a large part of it, a fully digital form and nature. In the context of inheritance law, the consequence is that the estate is already today, and will presumably be even more frequently in the future, made up of intangible digital objects.[2]

The new meaning that wealth is acquiring in the digital world must also be linked to the dynamics of online exploitation of personal data (and, with them, of personality attributes), which increasingly become an inexhaustible source of information also of economic relevance, which can be extracted, in fact, from almost every aspect of everyone's life.[3]

The technological evolution outlined above justifies the growing interest, in recent years, in reconstructing the legal framework applicable to digital objects

[1] Among these: files containing documents, images, videos, books, music tracks, but also digital goods over which one can exercise a sole right (websites, domains, licences, etc.), digital goods generated by online contractual relationships entered into with an internet service provider, such as those for the purchase of goods and services on the net, those concluded with social networks and those concerning an instant messaging service or e-mail. Relevant are also all activities, both professional and non-professional, that are carried out more and more frequently on the net and that are likely to create a very significant flow of digital information and personal data. See Alpa (2017), p. 724 and Gambino and Stazi (2020), p. XI.

[2] For this idea see Resta (2019), p. 976. Relevant in their digital form—with obvious effects also in the context of succession law—are, for instance, all banking activities carried out through apps and home banking services, online payment instruments and virtual currencies.

[3] This refers, for instance, to all personal information that can be obtained through profiling activities (as defined in Article 4(1)(4) of Regulation (EU) 2016/679) carried out by monitoring search engines, e-mail, instant messaging services, social networks, e-commerce platforms, apps, clouds, film, television and music streaming services, digital assistants, smart TVs, all electronic devices such as smartphones, tablets and computers and, more generally, all Iinternet of Things (IoT) devices. See Tescaro, Ch. I.

following the death of the individual who hold them.[4] So much so that the legal literature, in order to summarise this lively debate under a title that is both simplified and evocative, increasingly uses the expression "digital succession", deliberately referring directly to the legal institution of "succession upon death" associating with it the attribute of "digitality", which properly pertains only to the assets.[5]

Precisely with the expression "digital succession" or "digital inheritance"[6] which corresponds to analogous terms such as *eredità digitale*, *digitaler Nachlass*, *mort numérique* and *herencia digital*, used in other legal systems, commonly refers to the broader phenomenon of the protection, management and post-mortem circulation of digital data, objects and relationships.

Although, as previously noted, the "digitality" formally characterises the objects rather than the succession itself, the prevailing perception in the debate is that this peculiar connotation of assets confers upon them specific capabilities that may also alter the relationship between regulatory norms and factual realities. In other words, the digital nature of the objects implies, or at least could imply, a distortion of succession rules, thereby amplifying its significance and making it a matter deserving deeper examination.[7]

2 The Object of So-Called Digital Succession: A Classification

Digitality, as noted, is the common feature of all legal situations that may fall within the scope of so-called digital succession.

It is, in fact, modern information and communication technologies, along with the resulting process of digitalisation, that give digital resources certain peculiar characteristics: immateriality, mediality and immortality.

[4] The first paper in Italy on the topic dates back to 2017: Bechini (2017). From the same year is the book by Ziccardi (2017), p. 97 ff, which addresses the topic from a social and political point of view.

[5] On the subject of "digital succession", the contributions of Arcella (2021), p. 608 ff; Barbierato (2022), p. 2103 ff; Camardi (2018) p. 65 ff; Cinque (2012), p. 645 ff; Cinque (2020), p. 72 ff; Confortini (2023); Confortini (2021), p. 1187 ff; De Rosa (2021), p. 495 ff; Di Lorenzo (2021), p. 138 ff; Magnani (2014), p. 519 ff; Maiorano (2023), p. 248 ff; Maniaci and D'Arminio Monforte (2020), p. 1367 ff; Marino (2022); Marino (2018), p. 167 ff; Maspes (2020), p. 583 ff;. Mollo (2020), p. 430 ff; Mollo (2021); Pinto (2021), p. 701 ff; Putortì (2021), p. 163 ff; Resta (2019), p. 975 ff; Resta (2014), p. 891 ff; Spangaro (2021), p. 574 ff; Spatuzzi (2020), p. 402 ff; Tampieri (2021), p. 543 ff; Trolli (2019), p. 313 ff; Zaccaria (2020), p. 1368 ff.

[6] Defined by Bianca (2022), p. 164, as "insieme di documenti, dati e contenuti digitali dei quali il defunto aveva il diritto di godere e di disporre in via esclusiva".

[7] See Camardi (2018), p. 66 and Confortini (2023), p. 17 ff.

As for the immateriality, it is evident, and has been widely pointed out, that digital utilities are intangible and not perceptible in physical form, except through a computational process carried out by specifically programmed machines.[8]

Furthermore, it is noted that the effectiveness of the rules governing the protection, management and circulation of digital objects is often mediated by the activity of a third party, an internet service provider, who has the control over them and can materially enable the exercise of rights over such assets, even after the death of the *de cuius*.[9]

Digitisation makes digital objects continuously replicable and immanent, allowing the information they carry to become, for all intents and purposes, immortal, and enabling the rights and claims associated with them to be exercisable by numerous parties even after the death of the person concerned. Digital resources, in other words, may survive and circulate even after the death of the *de cuius*, within an undefined space and for a potentially unlimited time period.[10]

Beyond these shared characteristics, the numerous objects that take digital form are ontologically different from each other and, in some respects, not easily comparable.

This, however, does not preclude the attempt to outline an internal classification; the qualification of the nature of digital objects, which are heterogeneous among themselves, is a necessary logical prerequisite in the process of identifying the applicable regulatory framework governing their fate after the death of the holder, whether this framework is based on rules of inheritance law or on other provisions, different from inheritance law, which complete (or replace) that discipline.[11]

In order to identify the categories within which digital objects can be placed, the literature has effectively distinguished the category of *offline* digital objects and that of *online* digital objects.[12]

[8] See, in particular, Orlandi (2009), p. 493, who observes that: "la *res* informatica [...] non è costituita da materia sensibile, ma è l'esito di un calcolo combinatorio svolto attraverso l'applicazione di criteri algoritmici e di istruzioni interne e dinamiche [...] la foto e il testo che vedo sul video non sono ciò che vedo, ma informazioni binarie (codici acceso/spento) prive di senso comune, che la macchina, calcolando, traduce in immagini o dati percepibili e dotati di senso".

[9] On this matter see Confortini (2023), p. 31. Even digital data stored on a physical support (CDs, USB keys, memory cards, etc.) are not exempt from the requirement of mediateness, since their creation also involves the use of software and applications supplied and managed by a *provider* under a service agreement concluded with the user. However, the mediation seems to surface mainly during the creative phase and is instead less prominent in the subsequent post-mortem exercise of rights over such data.

[10] On the topic of immortality of digital objects see, among others, Resta (2019), p. 86; Camardi (2018), p. 69; Delle Monache (2020), p. 460; Confortini (2023), p. 34 and Maiorano (2023), p. 256.

[11] Many scholars, even before identifying the rules governing the protection, management and post-mortem devolution of digital objects and relationships, feel the need to classify them and identify their characteristic traits. See, Resta (2014), p. 904 ff; Camardi (2018), p. 75 ff; Marino (2022), p. 42 ff and p. 67 ff; Confortini (2023), p. 25 ff; D'Arminio Monforte (2020), p. 67 ff.

[12] On the distinction between *offline* and *online* goods see, in particular, Barba (2018), p. 282 ff, as well as Confortini (2023), p. 30.

The first class includes not only digital objects stored in physical media (such as PCs, USB sticks, CDs, hard disks, and memory cards) that were exclusively available to the deceased and may be transferred, either inter vivos and mortis causa, possibly also through the circulation of the physical medium on which they are contained,[13] but also other digital objects over which the deceased may claim an exclusive right (such as personal websites domain names, as well as photos, videos, files, documents constituting works of authorship). Despite not always being embodied in a physical medium, these objects are nonetheless eligible for transfer under specific rules, by virtue of the exclusive relationship established with the deceased.[14]

The second class, on the other hand, encompasses all digital objects stored and managed by a third party, an internet service provider, which acts as an intermediary in the exercise of the rights associated with these objects and who not only stores them, but also provides the user with a related service.[15]

Moreover, considering that digital objects are not only characterised as instruments for the fulfilment of ideal, affective and commemorative needs, but also, and with increasing frequency, for their economic and profit-making nature, it is possible to draw a further distinction between digital objects with personal relevance and those of economic or patrimonial relevance.[16] Investigating the non-patrimonial or patrimonial nature of the interests involved is above all useful in assessing whether such a distinction may have any relevance in determining the most suitable legal instrument for the protection, management and post-mortem circulation of digital objects.[17]

---

[13] See, in particular, Camardi (2018), p. 75; Resta (2014), p. 905 and Bechini (2017), p. 3.

[14] Relevant, in particular, is the regulation on copyright (l. 22 April 1941, no. 633), which identifies specific rules for the post-mortal circulation of rights connected to such peculiar objects, also in their digital form. In the literature see Camardi (2018), p. 76; Resta (2014), p. 906 and Marino (2022), p. 173 ff.

[15] These include, among others, contractual relationships aimed at the purchase of goods or services through platforms, contractual relationships in the context of social networks and contractual relationships aimed at the use of e-mail services. See Camardi (2018), p. 76 ff.

[16] All scholars who have addressed the issue of so-called digital succession acknowledged the dual nature—both personal and patrimonial—of many digital objects. To clarify the classification described, some examples may be helpful: on the non-economic side, we can place digital family films, personal memoirs written in a digital document and photographic portraits; on the other hand, items with a purely economic connotation include projects or writings in digital form drawn up by a professional, software, domain names, digital goods purchased online, patentable digital inventions, the management data of an online bank account and so on.

[17] Indeed, if it is true that the rules of succession upon death are closely linked to the concept of patrimony, it would not be possible to apply any succession rule with respect to digital objects where the interests underlying their circulation are in no way economic and are rather personal in nature. On the patrimoniality *of mortis causa* transmissions see, *ex multis*, Bianca (2022), p. 2., where it is stated that "la morte estingue la capacità giuridica della persona ed. estingue i diritti ad essa inerenti, cioè i diritti personali. La morte della persona non estingue, invece, di massima i suoi diritti patrimoniali, e ne impone piuttosto la trasmissione ad altri"; Schlesinger (1971), p. 748 ff, according to whom the word inheritance identifies "il complesso dei rapporti patrimoniali trasmis-

It seems, however, difficult to definitively assign to only one of the alternative classes those particular digital objects that are also relevant as personal data. This is primarily because such objects—even after the death of the individual—may take an offline form, and thus be entirely and exclusively under the control of the deceased; they may, at the same time, be classifiable as intellectual works protected by Law No. 633/1941 on the protection of copyright and other related rights; and they may also be linked to an *online* contractual relationship. Secondly, the difficulty arises because the data may simultaneously involve both personal elements related to the data subject and economically relevant profiles. In other words, the personal nature of the data may also have a patrimonial relevance and, conversely, its economic exploitation is inseparable from its personal component.

For this reason, personal data have been the subject of the most intense scholarly debate. Specifically, an attempt has been made to answer the question whether, in the context of the digital economy, information connected to personal data can possess not only an innate personal relevance, but also an economic value in itself, regardless of the interest hidden behind the exercise of the rights referable to it.

In addressing this question, it should first of all be noted that personal data, individually considered (i.e. not in relation to other goods or rights), are an essential element of many products and services in the online market and can be the source of a significant competitive advantage, from the perspective of providers, especially in their aggregate form.[18]

Indeed, some digital services, such as e-mail, access to a social network, cloud services, apparently offered free of charge, are actually remunerated through the transfer of personal data that is communicated, directly or indirectly, through the activation and use of the service itself.[19]

Observations on the patrimonialisation of personal data pertain primarily to other areas of law and involve the so-called digital succession only to a limited extent.

---

sibili, attivi e passive, facenti capo al *de cuius* al momento della morte"; Bonilini (2009), p. 8 adds that "il fenomeno successorio *mortis causa* si connette al concetto di patrimonio, quale insieme dei rapporti giuridici di una persona suscettibili di valutazione economica. Il patrimonio, che cade in successione, comprende sia diritti, vale a dire rapporti attivi, sia rapporti passivi, vale a dire debiti. Detti rapporti debbono potersi ridurre a valore pecuniario, sicché non cadono in successione i diritti insuscettibili di valutazione economica, e ne sono pure esclusi taluni diritti che, pur valutabili in denaro, si estinguono con la morte del titolare, in quanto a stretto carattere personale". See also Grosso and Burdese (1977), p. 14; Mengoni (1984), p. 11 ff. On the other hand, the principle of patrimoniality of succession is questioned especially by Zaccaria (1998), who affirms the idea of an extra-patrimonial succession.

[18] In general, on the so-called patrimonialisation of personal data see Moretti (2022), p. 93 ff; D'Ippolito (2022), p. 51 ff; Ricciuto (2019), p. 95 ff, Ricciuto (2018,), p. 689 ff.

[19] See, among others, Resta (2020), p. 58 ff. It is for this reason that Directive (EU) 2019/770 applies not only to contracts according to which the consumer, in exchange for the supply of digital content or service, pays a price, but also to contracts through which, pursuant to Article 3, Directive (EU) 2019/77 "the trader supplies or undertakes to supply digital content or a digital service to the consumer, and the consumer provides or undertakes to provide personal data to the trader".

What is relevant for our purposes, however, is the observation that, in the context of the exchange of products and services against personal data, the economic value of the data is hardly quantifiable in monetary terms. As a result, for the data subject who provides them (often unconsciously) they are not taken into account as an asset of his or her own (even hereditary) heritage, but rather as elements and expressions of their personal identity, to be subject to the control, in the processing activity, of the data controller according to the rules of Regulation (EU) 2016/679 (GDPR).[20]

Therefore, although the new European Union rules on contracts for the supply of digital content and services recognise the negotiability and exchange of personal data, it does not seem that one can conclude from this premise that the deceased is allowed to dispose of such data and of the economic benefits deriving therefrom as elements of their estate, after his or her death, either in terms of attribution or transfer.

At the present stage of the regulation, it therefore does not seem possible to assert the potential patrimonial nature of personal data—and consequently the full applicability of succession law—based solely on their inclusion in the category of data, since this is a completely neutral qualification in this respect. Rather, the inquiry must focus on the interest underlying the data, as it is this interest alone that can give the information also economically significant features. Indeed, while the full recognition of so-called primary patrimoniality of personal information seems to be an outcome that is still a long way off, nothing prevents the attribution of some also economic relevance to information, at least in those cases in which it serves as means for exercising rights of a patrimonial nature or is also otherwise relevant to the legal system. In such cases, it is certainly appropriate to speak in terms of a secondary patrimoniality of personal data.[21]

---

[20] Confortini (2023), p. 48 agrees on this point. Moreover, according to Camardi (2018), p. 69, “dal punto di vista della persona che genera questi dati, essi sono il prolungamento della sua dimensione; ma dal punto di vista di chi invece li ‘vede’ e li intercetta essi sono semplicemente ‘dati’, informazioni codificate suscettibili di essere usate o cedute (o anche ‘vendute’)”.

[21] Zaccaria (1988), p. 37 ff doesn’t speak in terms of secondary patrimoniality, but, in any case, recognises some economic relevance to rights of a personal nature. The author, going beyond the distinction between patrimonial rights and non-patrimonial rights, identifies a third class, consisting of so-called personal-patrimonial rights, i.e. rights that, not qualifying as either only patrimonial or only personal, include and mix elements of both personal and patrimonial content. The author, while maintaining the category of patrimonial rights, states that “alla categoria di quelli non patrimoniali viene sostituita la categoria dei diritti personali; e, infine, fra questi due poli, quale ‘Zwischenform’, va inserita la categoria dei diritti ‘nuancés’: diritti né propriamente patrimoniali né puramente personali, in cui elementi attenenti alla persona del titolare e contenuti patrimoniali coesistono e si mescolano”.

3 The Approach to the Problem: Current Conceptual Models

Based on the regulatory framework currently in force,[22] and taking into account the thoughts of the literature elaborated so far, it is possible to summarise the conceptual models within which it is possible to frame the so-called digital succession: (1) the personalistic (or personal data protection) model; (2) the inheritance (or real-proprietary) model; (3) the model of private (or contractual) autonomy.[23]

The first conceptual model approaches the so-called digital succession from the perspective of the individual interests of the person arising in the context of the digital environment.

It has already been pointed out how modern technologies are today capable of transforming attributes and characteristics of the personality into data, i.e. into information that also has personal relevance, with the consequence of multiplying "i casi in cui l'effetto successorio è posto di fronte a (diritti su) oggetti – porzioni del mondo fenomenico – che sono anche (ma non solo) rappresentazioni della personalità dell'individuo (del soggetto)".[24]

Indeed, particularly in the realm of personal data protection, there is a clear and growing interest in controlling and protecting—even post-mortem—certain aspects of the deceased's digital personality, who may have an interest in expressing determinations as to the management and circulation of his or her digital traces on the internet.

In this context, a key reference within the Italian legal system is the recently introduced Article 2-*terdecies* of *Codice della privacy*,[25] which, in paragraph 1, provides that the rights governed by Articles 15 to 22 of Regulation (EU) 2016/679 on the protection of personal data—when they refer to the personal data of deceased persons—may be exercised "da chi ha un interesse proprio, o agisce a tutela dell'interessato, in qualità di suo mandatario, o per ragioni familiari meritevoli di protezione".

---

[22] From a regulatory point of view, there are legal systems, such as the English, Swedish and Irish ones, which expressly exclude the applicability of the European General Data Protection Regulation to personal data of deceased persons. Other legal systems, for instance Germany, don't introduce a legislative solution one way or the other. On the contrary, Italy, France and, above all, the United States of America, have expressly regulated the particular case of personal data of deceased persons. See Cinque (2012), p. 78 ff on regulatory developments in the USA and 90 ff for an analysis of the regulations of European countries, as well as Resta (2019), p. 94 ff.

[23] For a summary of the models developed so far, see Resta (2019), p. 89 ff and Schmidt-Kessel and Pertot (2019), p. 901 ff.

[24] The quotation is from Confortini (2023), p. 39. Camardi (2018), p. 65 ff also reflects on this matter. More generally, on personal identity in the context of digitalization, see Alpa (2017), p. 723 ff and, in this volume, Tescaro, Sec. I.

[25] Article 2-*terdecies* was introduced into *Codice della privacy* (Legislative Decree No. 196 of 30 June 2003) by Legislative Decree No. 101 of 10 August 2018, a regulation adapting the Italian data protection law to Regulation (EU) 2016/679 on the protection of individuals with regard to the processing of personal data and on the free movement of such data.

However, looking at the so-called digital succession having regard only to the personal aspects would be extremely reductive, as the element of personality is increasingly intertwined by patrimonial components of various kinds, which are more closely connected to other areas of law. As a result, failing to take these aspects into account in the analysis of the models for the protection, management and circulation of digital objects would mean not addressing the issue in its entirety.

This leads to the second model, which equates intangible assets (and, among them, digital objects) with any other movable good and, as a consequence, states that they are capable of being object of rights, as are tangible assets, and of being transferred, both inter vivos and mortis causa, according to the rules governing the circulation of such goods.[26]

The succession-based model also includes the idea that the *post-mortem* protection of data and, more generally, of digital objects, may be recognised and ensured through the heirs' succession into the contractual positions held by the *de cuius* relating to those objects.[27] In other words, in the context of a contract entered into by the deceased, while he was alive, with an internet services provider, the protection, management and circulation of the digital elements shared with that provider could be adequately ensured through the heirs' taking over the contractual position held by the deceased and to which those objects are connected, in accordance with

[26] With regard to personal data the reflection has been further deepened. Although there is authoritative literature that affirms that even personal information may be object of real rights and, in particular, that a property right can be established over it, which—upon the death of the data subject—would be transferred to heirs like any other property right over movable assets (see Zaccaria (2020), p. 1370), this proposal raises some objections. In addition to the remark that personal data have peculiarities and protection needs that distinguish them from ordinary movable goods, it should also be considered that such an approach would hardly seem compatible with Article 8 of the Charter of Fundamental Rights of the European Union, which recognises the nature of a fundamental right to the right to personal data protection. Such a classification of the right to personal data protection would conflict with the idea that it can be qualified as a property right, and can therefore also be exercised even against the data subject (see, for this critical remark, Schmidt-Kessel and Pertot (2019), p. 904 If one then takes as true the assertion that "la dimensione digitale è un prolungamento della dimensione umana, e come alla persona non si consente di alienare parti del corpo che potrebbero compromettere la funzionalità, allo stesso modo si dovrebbe proibire la cessione volontaria di dati personali che sono particolarmente 'sensibili'" (cf. Alpa (2017), p. 727), the proprietary thesis turns out not to be entirely satisfactory, at least not in relation to those categories of digital objects (among them, above all, personal data) that also reveal the personality of the deceased.

[27] In general, on the succession in the account of the deceased, see Marino (2022), p. 83 ff; Confortini (2023), p. 63 ff; Carleo (2022), p. 127 ff; De Rosa (2021), p. 498 ff; Delle Monache (2020), p. 460 ff; Marino (2022), p. 179 ff; Maspes (2020), p. 583 ff and De Francesco (2022), p. 649 ff. Also agrees with the succession-based model the well-known 2018 *leading case* decided by the *Bundesgerichtshof* (BGH 12 July 2018, III ZR 183/17, in *NJW*, 2018, 3178 ff), which, applying the principle of universality of succession—expressly codified in § 1922, *Abs.* 1, *BGB*—according to which "mit dem Tod einer Person geht deren Vermögen als Ganzes auf eine oder mehrere andere Personen über", applies the succession law in order to solve the disputed questions that the so-called digital succession involves.

the general principle of transmissibility to the heirs of the contracts concluded during the deceased's lifetime.[28]

Lastly, the third model, highlighting the choices made by the deceased during his lifetime, encompasses all the hypotheses in which it is the *de cuius*' indications as to the fate of his or her digital objects for the time after death that regulate, through the use of models made available by private autonomy, the so-called digital succession.[29]

3.1 Legitimation *Iure Proprio* and Succession *Mortis Causa*: An Alternative Still Debated

As a result of the analysis of the various approaches summarised above none of them seems to definitively prevail over the others in regulating the so-called digital succession, given the complexity of the objects involved and the legal questions each of them raises.

In particular, doctrinal discussions have focused on the opposition between the personalistic model and the succession model, an issue which reflects the long-standing debate concerning personality rights,[30] namely the choice between the

[28] Even this model, however, although suitable to encompass both aspects of protection and management as well as those of circulation and transmission, has been criticised, above all when the subject of succession concerns personal data. Precisely, it has been pointed out how the heirs' succession in the contractual relationship would concern only the obligatory aspect, thus excluding from the succession of all rights of fundamental rank, among which is also the right of personal data protection, which is more closely connected to the personalistic dimension of digital objects (see Schmidt-Kessel and Pertot (2019, p. 908).

[29] Address the topic from this perspective, among others, Confortini (2023), p. 206 ff; Marino (2022), p. 263 ff; Camardi (2018), p. 82 ff; Maiorano (2023), p. 265 ff; Putortì (2021), p. 163 ff; Resta (2019), p. 104; Spangaro (2021), p. 594 ff; Spatuzzi (2020), p. 402 ff; Tampieri (2021), p. 568 ff; Trolli (2019), p. 313 ff.

[30] The theory of *iure proprio* acquisition excludes the *mortis causa* transmissibility of personality rights, asserting instead their extinction upon the death of the individual to whom they refer. As a consequence, in the time period following the death of the first rights-holder, only forms of *iure proprio* acquisition may be admitted, by means of the recognition, in favour of certain specifically identified subjects, of a *post-mortem* legitimation to exercise rights that arise anew in their legal sphere, but still are linked with the personality of the deceased original holder. On this matter, the literature is extensive. See, among many others, Grosso and Burdese (1977), p. 17; De Cupis (1982), p. 85 ff and Zeno-Zencovich (1995), p. 437 ff. Alternative to legitimation *iure proprio* is the thesis that affirms succession *mortis causa* in personality rights. The resulting framework would therefore be that of succession *mortis causa* in the rights of the *de cuius*, limited to those of a patrimonial nature and aimed at the economic exploitation of the elements of personal identity. This is the theory of those who admit the configurability of an inheritance event concerning only those aspects of the subjective legal situation that are economically evaluable (the separate devolution of personal and patrimonial prerogatives is traditionally attributable to an interpretation developed by German case law and is expressed in two important rulings of the *Bundesgerichtshof*, both concerning the unauthorised economic exploitation of the name and image of the famous German

acquisition *iure proprio* of a new right and the succession in the same right held by the deceased.

In order to understand the post-mortal regulation of personal data, these theories have recently been developed and re-elaborated with regard to the new rule available today, i.e. Article 2-*terdecies Codice della privacy*. This provision, while expressly introducing the idea of protection of rights over the deceased's personal data for the period after death, does not expressly clarify the nature of the legal matter regulated therein, nor the modalities through which these rights may be exercised.

In the light of the lack of a clear stance by the legislator, which, moreover, is consistent with the wording of the previous provisions on the protection of the deceased's personal data,[31] interpreters have identified three possible solutions concerning the legal situation described in the provision.

The first solution affirms the non-transferability upon death of the rights over the deceased's personal data and recognises the *iure proprio* acquisition of new rights, with legitimation to their exercise by the persons identified in the first paragraph of Article 2-*terdecies*.[32]

According to this approach, the rights that the data subject was able to exercise during his or her lifetime would be extinguished, and new rights would arise with respect to the same data. These new rights would allow certain individuals to act either on the basis of their own interest, for the protection of the data subject, as legislative representatives, or for family or emotional reasons.[33]

---

actress Marlene Dietrich. See BGH, 1 December 1999, Marlene Dietrich and BGH, 1 December 1999, *Der blaue Engel*, in *Neue Juristische Wochenschrift*, 30, 2000, 2201). Another theory affirms the *mortis causa* succession also in personal or personal-patrimonial rights. This legal doctrine considers the dogma of the purely patrimonial nature of succession to be outdated and admits that such rights may persist even after the death of their holder and may therefore be transmitted to their heirs (see, for this second approach, Zaccaria (1988), p. 10 and p. 23 ff).

[31] Reference is made to Article 13, par. 3, of law no. 675/1996, according to which "i diritti di cui al comma 1 riferiti ai dati personali concernenti persone decedute possono essere esercitati da chiunque vi abbia interesse", later replaced by Article 9, par. 3, legislative decree no. 196/2003 (*Codice della privacy*), which stated that "i diritti di cui all'articolo 7 riferiti a dati personali concernenti persone decedute possono essere esercitati da chi ha un interesse proprio, o agisce a tutela dell'interessato o per ragioni familiari meritevoli di protezione".

[32] Delle Monache (2020), p. 469 supports the theory of the *iure proprio* acquisition of rights over the personal data of the deceased, asserting that "quando ci si collochi al di fuori del perimetro dei diritti patrimoniali del defunto" are only possible "forme di tutela *iure proprio*, con legittimazione attribuita dalla legge o comunque da riconoscere, secondo i princìpi, a determinati terzi, in base, per lo più, al loro legame con il *de cuius*"; see also Sasso (2019), p. 163; Maniaci and D'Arminio Monforte (2021), p. 666; Ziccardi (2017), p. 143; Pinto (2021), p. 717.

[33] The most recent case law also seems to confirm this solution. See, in particular, Trib. Bologna, ord. 25 November 2021, with a comment by Vignotto (2022), p. 701 ff; with a comment by Feleppa (2022), p. 19 ff as well as Trib. Roma, ord. 10 February 2022, with a comment by Maniaci and D'Arminio Monforte (2022), p. 561 ff, where it is stated that "la ricorrente agisce *iure proprio* sulla base di un interesse meritevole di protezione di natura familiare che la legittima all'esercizio della prerogative prevista e giustifica il diritto di acquisire i dati riferibili al defunto". A more neutral position is instead taken by the ruling of Trib. Milano, ord. 10 February 2021, which, although applying Article 2-*terdecies*, does not express itself clearly on the legal nature of the situation

This solution has been criticised as inconsistent, based on the argument that the extinction of rights and the *iure proprio* acquisition of newly derived rights reflect a defensive qualification of the right to the protection of personal data, as a reaction to possible violations, whereas the powers and safeguards guaranteed by the GDPR seem to frame the protection of personal information in a more attributive meaning (this is especially evident with regard to the right to data portability, Article 20 GDPR), which seems to be overlooked within the perspective that considers the data subject's rights extinguished upon their death.[34]

It remains, however, a firm and indisputable normative point that the EU rules provide for the death of the data subject as the time limit for the protection of personal data, given that, on the basis of what is stated in recital No. 27, the GDPR does not apply to the data of deceased persons. The post-mortem exercise of the rights regulated by Articles 15 to 22 of the GDPR should therefore be incompatible with a continued existence of such rights, unchanged in their content, in the legal sphere of the successor. Rather, it should be interpreted as an extraordinary legitimation to exercise such rights after the death of the original right-holder as a form of *iure proprio* legitimation granted to certain categories of individuals expressly identified in Article 2-*terdecies*.[35]

Consistent with this solution is also the *ratio* underlying the recognition of these rights to the data subject—and, more generally, of the right to personal data protection in its meaning of *control of information about yourself.* These rights grant the data subject control over the third-party processing activities concerning their personal information, which seems far removed from the attributive logic typical of succession law.

It is, however, undeniable that, despite the Regulation's effectiveness being limited to the life of the data subject, the data remain in the material availability of the data controller with whom they have been shared and they survive the event of death.

Based on this observation, two paths have been explored by literature to assert that a *mortis causa* succession can be realised with regard to the rights under Articles 15 to 22 of Regulation (EU) 2016/679: (i) the inclusion of the rights related to the deceased's *privacy* in the ordinary succession, with concurrent legitimation to exercise them of the subjects identified by Article 2-*terdecies Codice della privacy*; (ii) the qualification of the provision itself as a rule of *successione anomala.* In both these perspectives the death of the person concerned would initiate a real

described therein. For commentary on this ruling see, in particular, Maniaci and D'Arminio Monforte (2021), p. 658 ff; Maspes (2021), p. 1600 ff; Spangaro (2022), p. 1363 ff; Mastroberardino (2021), p. 622 ff; Vigorito (2021), p. 27 ff. Lastly, *si vis*, Bonetti (2021), p. 560 ff.

[34] See Confortini (2023), p. 192.

[35] It could, on the other hand, be argued that the fact that, by express provision of recital No. 27, the *GDPR* does not apply to the data of deceased persons does not preclude Member States from adopting provisions that extend the protections of the Regulation beyond its scope of application, including beyond the death of the data subject. This idea is the basis of theories that support the solution of the succession under Article 2-*terdecies*.

succession, through which the real rights held by the deceased, which have not been extinguished upon their death, would pass to their successors.[36]

The first thesis is the one that admits the transmissibility *mortis causa* of the rights over the deceased's data in accordance with the ordinary succession rules. In addition—acknowledging the need to reconcile the power to exercise the rights on the basis of Article 2-*terdecies Codice della privacy* for a very broad category of persons, not necessarily also heirs of the deceased—it is recognised the concurrent legitimation to exercise those rights of the individuals indicated in paragraph 1 of Article 2-*terdecies*.[37]

The ownership of the rights would therefore belong to the heirs or legatees; the legitimation to exercise them, however, would lie with a broader group of individuals, which includes other—sometimes different—persons who do not always also hold the status of universal or particular successors in the estate of the deceased, but who nonetheless have a qualified interest.

Another solution, which also lies in the field of succession law, is the one that affirms that Article 2-*terdecies Codice della privacy* introduces a new rule of *successione anomala*, with the consequence that those who are legitimised to exercise the rights under the first paragraph would also become successors of the deceased.[38]

3.2 The Instruments of Self-determination of the Individual

Lastly, also important is the reflection on the instruments of private autonomy available to the data subject for regulating the post-mortal fate of their digital objects and personal data, whether such instruments serve merely to provide instructions of a managerial nature, or entail the attribution of patrimonial rights in the context of succession.

The tension between data protection and inheritance law is also reflected in the identification of the respective sphere of application of the legal instrument under

---

[36] This is also the solution recently adopted by Trib. Como, ord. 26 July 2023, with a comment by Bertolini (2023), where it is stated that with regard to the rights on digital contents it is more consistent "una ricostruzione unitaria del fenomeno ereditario, che riconosca la trasmissibilità *iure successionis* dei diritti aventi ad oggetto *digital contents* nella loro integrità, ossia nelle indissociabili implicazioni personali e patrimoniali", thus excluding the application of Article 2-*terdecies* and affirming the exclusively succession nature of post-mortem legal events concerning digital contents, including those referring to personal data. The ruling is also commented by Pertot (2024), p. 453 ff.

[37] This is the solution of Marino (2022), p. 222 ff, which, considering the distinction between ownership of the right and legitimation to exercise it, affirms the occurrence of a succession phenomenon concerning the personal data rights of the *de cuius*, though to some extent "mitigated" by the concurrent legitimation of other, sometimes different, individuals.

[38] This is the theory developed by Zaccaria (2020), p. 1370 ff and followed also by Martone (2020), p. 113.

consideration. Accordingly, while some may be more coherently attributed to the first sphere, others belong more properly to the second.

From the perspective of data protection, mention must first be made of the significant innovations introduced in the new version of *Codice della privacy*, aimed at regulating the post-mortem management of the rights set out in Articles 15 to 22 of the Regulation or, conversely, at prohibiting their exercise.

Reference is made, in the first instance, to the provisions set out in paragraphs 2, 3 and 4 of Article 2-*terdecies*, through which the deceased is granted the right to prohibit the exercise—by means of a specific written declaration submitted to the data controller, which must be unambiguous, specific, free and informed, as well as revocable and modifiable at any time—of the rights relating to their personal information after death.[39] Such declarations, addressed to the data controller (and not to all the deceased's survivors), are however limited in their content to non-patrimonial indications, which do not amount to institutions of heirs or legatees, given the mandatory nature of the testamentary form for *mortis causa* dispositions concerning the share or specific assets of the hereditary estate. These declarations may, at most, constitute the so-called atypical content of a will, if included therein.

Secondly, express reference is made to the figure of the agent as the person entitled to exercise the rights related to the deceased's data after their death. There is no doubt in the literature that the legal construct referred to corresponds to the *mandato post mortem exequendum*, i.e. a "contractual" post-mortem mandate, entered into while the deceased was still alive but intended to be performed after, and by reason of, their death. However, the scope of application of this legal instrument appears to be limited to cases in which the mandate concerns the management of personal data rights solely in their personality-related dimension, since only in such cases would the mandate differentiate from a succession agreement (*patto successorio*) and would not fall within the prohibition of concluding such agreements.[40]

For both perspectives, the personality-based and the succession-based, the testamentary disposition assumes particular relevance. As a suitable instrument for including both typical and atypical provisions (i.e. patrimonial and extrapatrimonial),[41] the will seems to be valid encompassing not only personal

---

[39] On this matter, Trib. Roma, 10 February 2022, clarifies that, although Article 2-*terdecies*, in paragraph 3, involves the possibility for the data subject to prohibit, by means of a specific, freely given and informed declaration, the exercise of the rights relating to their personal data for the period following their death, it cannot be held that the mere acceptance of general terms and conditions, without any specific approval of the clauses unilaterally drafted by the producing company, meets the requirement that such a declaration of prohibition must have. Such acceptance does not demonstrate a clear, free and autonomous choice of the individual, as required by the provision.

[40] On the limits of *mandato post mortem exequendum* see, Ieva (2010), p. 93 ff. More generally, on *mandatum post mortem* as a legal transaction connected to death, the literature is extensive. See, in particular, Moncalvo (2009), p. 232 ff; Bianca (2022), p. 42; Palazzo (2008), p. 241 ff; Luminoso (1984), p. 123 ff; Minervini (1952), p. 24; Gradassi (1990), p. 827 ff.

[41] In the literature, on the atypical content of the will, see Giampiccolo (1954), p. 15 ff; Cicu (1942), p. 7 ff and Bianca (2022), p. 262 ff.

provisions, such as those relating to data rights, but also true attributive provisions, such as the institution of heirs and legatees.

Among the testamentary dispositions relevant for our purposes is also that which entrusts a specific managerial task to third parties to be carried out after the death of the *de cuius*, namely the appointment of an executor, entrusted with fulfilling the testator's last wishes, whether these relate to personal interests or involve attributive dispositions concerning the entire estate or a portion thereof.

However, beyond the will, there are other instruments of private autonomy in the matter of succession that may validly encompass provisions expressing the testator's digital last wishes. Consider, for instance, the legal construct known as the "legacy of passwords" (*legato di password*)[42] or the non-testamentary writings regulated by Law No. 633/1941 on the protection of copyright, which likewise seem to be relevant where the individual intends to provide instructions regarding the post-mortem fate of their digital objects.[43]

4 A Brief Final Reflection

In conclusion, if the various instruments of private autonomy merely highlight the essential important role of individual's self-determination in regulating the post-mortal protection, management and circulation of one's digital resources, this does not allow for the affirmation of a substitutive, rather than merely complementary, function of acts of self-determination.

Indeed, it must always be possible to identify a rule applicable in cases in which the deceased has not expressed any indications during his or her lifetime, whether

[42] The subject of the so-called legacy of passwords concerns the issue of which interpretative solution should prevail: whether such a provision entails the automatic transfer of the resource to which the password grants access, or whether, instead, credentials—serving merely to identify the account holder and to authorise access—should be understood as designating the person entitled to manage the password-protected resources, without producing any legal effects in terms of the *mortis causa* transfer of rights over them. The majority view in legal doctrine seems to favour the first interpretation. See, among others, Di Lorenzo (2014), p. 144 ff. However, the choice between these two theories does not seem to admit a uniform solution and must instead be based on the interpretation of the testator's intention, as expressed through the specific wording of the testamentary provision (see also Nardi (2020), p. 161 ff). In other words, it will be necessary to determine whether, by means of the so-called legacy of passwords the *de cuius* intended, for instance, (i) to bequeath the physical resource protected by access credentials; (ii) to dispose of the rights relating to its content; (iii) to assign, by way of a particular legacy, the contractual position linked to the resource accessible through the alphanumeric key; (iv) to appoint an executor or a post-mortem agent tasked with managing the credentials, with the duty of safeguarding and transmitting them to the heirs, without thereby attributing any proprietary effect; (v) to include in the will a legacy of a thing to be taken from a specific place, pursuant to Article 655 of the Civil Code.

[43] Reference is made to Articles 24, 93 and 96, which set out the rules governing instruments of private autonomy that, within the framework of this regulation, may be used to regulate the post-mortal fate of (also) creative digital content.

such indication derives from the right to the protection of personal data or from the law of succession. In any case, particular attention must be paid to the relationship between the general rule and the one established by individuals in their last will.

And since the objects described are very often comparable solely by their digital form, while differentiating entirely in other characteristics, the formal element alone can hardly justify the application of a single regulatory framework capable to identify one uniform model for their protection, management and circulation among the many possible. Rather, the post-mortal exercise of the rights seems to follow different rules whose application depends on the nature of the specific digital object, the legal position of the subjects legitimised to such exercise and the protected interests they represent, particularly when the object of the so-called digital succession consists of personal data.

References

Alpa G (2017) L'identità digitale e la tutela della persona: spunti di riflessione. In Contr. e impr., No.3, p 723 ff

Arcella G (2021) La tutela della personalità del defunto e la protezione post mortem dei dati personali. In Notariato, No.6, p 608 ff

Barba V (2018) Contenuto del testamento e atti di ultima volontà, Napoli

Barbierato D (2022) Osservazioni in tema di "eredità digitale". In Resp civ. prev., No. 6, p 2103 ff

Bechini U (2017) Password, credenziali e successione mortis causa. In Studio n. 6–2007/IG, http://home.datacomm.ch/ugobechini/password_morto.pdf

Bertolini P (2023) La tutela dell'eredità digitale fra successione nel contratto di cloud computing e trasmissibilità dei digital contents. In Pactum online. Riv. dir. contratti

Bianca CM (2022) Diritto civile, 2.2., Le successioni, Milano

Bonetti S (2021) Dati personali e tutela post mortem nel novellato Codice privacy: prime applicazioni. In Nuova giur. civ. comm., No.3, p 560 ff

Bonilini G (2009) Concetto, e fondamento, della successione mortis causa. In: Bonilini G (ed) Trattato di diritto delle successioni e donazioni, La successione ereditaria, vol I, Milano

Camardi C (2018) L'eredità digitale. Tra reale e virtuale. In Dir. informazione e informatica, No.1, p 65 ff

Carleo R (2022) "Eredità digitale" o diritto di accesso dei congiunti ai dati personali del de cuius? Prime decisioni e primi dubbi. In Nuovo dir. civ., No.3, p 127 ff

Cicu A (1942) Il testamento, Milano

Cinque M (2012) La successione nel "patrimonio digitale": prime considerazioni. In Nuova giur. civ. comm., No.10, p 78 ff

Cinque M (2020) L'"eredità digitale" alla prova delle riforme. In Riv. dir. civ., No.1, p 72 ff

Confortini V (2021) L'eredità digitale (appunti per uno studio). In Riv. dir. civ., No.6, p 1187 ff

Confortini V (2023) Persona e patrimonio nella successione digitale, Torino

D'Arminio Monforte A (2020) La successione nel patrimonio digitale, Pisa

D'Ippolito G (2022) Monetizzazione *patrimonializzazione e trattamento dei dati personali*. In: Cremona E, Laviola F, Pannelli V (eds) Il valore economico dei dati personali tra diritto pubblico e diritto privato, Torino

De Cupis A (1982) I diritti della personalità. In: Cicu A, Messineo F, Mengoni L (eds) Trattato di diritto civile e commerciale, 2nd edn. Milano

De Francesco F (2022) La successione mortis causa nei rapporti contrattuali: spunti interpretativi sull'art. 2-terdecies Codice privacy e sull'eredità "digitale". In Contr. impr., No.2, p. 640 ff

De Rosa R (2021) Trasmissione mortis causa del "patrimonio digitale". In *Notariato*, No.5, p 495 ff
Delle Monache S (2020) Successione mortis causa e patrimonio digitale. In Nuova giur. civ. comm., No. 2, p 460 ff
Di Lorenzo L (2014) Il legato di password. In Notariato, No. 2, p 144 ff
Di Lorenzo L (2021) L'eredità digitale. In Notariato, No. 2, p 138 ff
Feleppa M (2022) L'accesso ai dati del defunto conservati su smartphone: soluzioni emergenti e problemi aperti. In Dir. informazione e informatica, No. 1, p 19 ff
Gambino AM, Stazi A (2020) Introduzione, Datificazione dei rapporti socio-economici, circolazione dei dati e diritto. In: Gambino AM, Stazi (eds) La circolazione dei dati. Titolarità, strumenti negoziali, diritti e tutele, Pisa
Giampiccolo G (1954) Il contenuto atipico del testamento. Contributo ad una teoria dell'atto di ultima volontà, Milano
Gradassi F (1990) Il mandato post mortem. In Contr. impr., No.2, p 827 ff
Grosso G, Burdese A (1977) Le successioni. Parte generale. In: Vassalli F (ed) Trattato di Diritto Civile Italiano, vol XII, Torino
Ieva M (2010) I fenomeni successori. In: Rescigno P (ed) Trattato breve delle successioni e donazioni, vol 1, Padova
Luminoso A (1984) Mandato, spedizione, commissione. In: Cicu A, Messineo F, Mengoni L (eds) Trattato di diritto civile e commerciale, Milano
Magnani A (2014) L'eredità digitale, in Notariato, No.5, p 519 ff
Maiorano C (2023) Digitalizzazione nelle relazioni umane e successione mortis causa. In Dir. fam. pers., No. 1, p 248 ff
Maniaci A, D'Arminio Monforte A (2020) L'eredità digitale tra silenzio della legge ed esigenze di pianificazione negoziale. In Corr. giur., No.11, p. 1367 ff
Maniaci A, D'Arminio Monforte A (2021) La prima decisione italiana in tema di "eredità digitale": quale tutela post mortem dei dati personali?. In Corr. giur., No.5, p 658 ff
Maniaci A, D'Arminio Monforte A (2022) "Eredità digitale" e accesso ai dati personali del defunto. In Dir. di internet, No.2, p. 561 ff
Marino G (2018) La "successione digitale". In Osservatorio dir. civ. e comm., No.1, p 167 ff
Marino G (2022) *Mercato digitale e sistema delle successioni* mortis causa, Napoli
Martone I (2020) Sulla trasmissibilità a causa di morte dei "dati personali": l'intricato rapporto tra digitalizzazione e riservatezza. In: Ballerini L, Buset G, Pertot T, Rega L (eds) Nuovi modelli di Diritto Successorio: prospettive interne, europee e comparate. Atti del convegno, Trieste
Maspes I (2020) Successione digitale, trasmissione dell'account e condizioni generali di contratto predisposte dagli internet services providers. In Contratti, No. 5, p. 583 ff
Maspes I (2021) Morte "digitale" e persistenza dei diritti oltre la vita della persona fisica. In Giur. it., No, 7, p. 1600 ff
Mastroberardino F (2021) L'accesso agli account informatici degli utenti defunti: una prima, parziale, tutela. In Fam e dir., No.6, p 622 ff
Mengoni L (1984) Successioni per causa di morte. Parte speciale. Successione legittima, I. In: Cicu A, Messineo F (eds) Trattato di diritto civile e commerciale, vol XLIII, Milano
Minervini G (1952) Il mandato. La commissione. La spedizione. In: Vassalli F (ed) Trattato di diritto civile italiano, Torino
Mollo AA (2020) Il diritto alla protezione dei dati personali quale limite alla successione mortis causa nel patrimonio digitale. In Jus civile, No. 2, p. 430 ff
Mollo AA (2021) Eredità digitale e piattaforme online. Tutela e profili di pianificazione, Napoli
Moncalvo FA (2009) I negozi connessi alla morte. Il mandato post mortem. In: Bonilini G (ed) Trattato di diritto delle successioni e donazioni, La successione ereditaria, vol 1
Moretti A (2022) Il valore dei dati nell'European Data Strategy: sviluppo della persona, dinamiche di mercato e benessere sociale. In: Cremona E, Laviola D, Pannelli V (eds) Il valore economico dei dati personali tra diritto pubblico e diritto privato, Torino
Nardi S (2020) La successione nel patrimonio digitale. In: Cassano G, Previti S (eds) Il diritto di internet nell'era digitale, Milano

Orlandi M (2009) Diritto nel mondo virtuale. In Enc. Treccani XXI Secolo, Roma
Palazzo A (2008) Testamento e istituti alternativi, Milano
Pertot T (2024) Sorte postmortale degli oggetti digitali e questioni di diritto successorio. In Pactum, No.4, p 453 ff
Pinto F (2021) Sulla trasmissibilità mortis causa delle situazioni giuridiche soggettive "digitali". In Riv. not., No.4, p 701 ff
Putortì V (2021) Patrimonio digitale e successione mortis causa. In Giust. civ., No.1, p 163 ff
Resta G (2014) La 'morte' digitale. In Dir. informazione e informatica, No.6, p 891 ff
Resta G (2019) La successione nei rapporti digitali e la tutela post-mortale dei dati personali. In: Arroyo Amayuelas E, Baldus C, de Carvalho GE, Leroyer A, Lu Q, Rainer JM (eds) Casi controversi in materia di diritto delle successioni, vol II, Napoli
Resta G (2020) I dati personali oggetto del contratto. Riflessioni sul coordinamento tra la Direttiva (UE) 2019/770 e il Regolamento (UE) 2016/679. In: Gambino AM, Stazi A (eds) La circolazione dei dati. Titolarità, strumenti negoziali, diritti e tutele, Pisa
Ricciuto V (2019) I dati personali come oggetto di operazione economica. La lettura del fenomeno nella prospettiva del contratto e del mercato. In: Zorzi Galgano N (ed) Persona e mercato dei dati, Milano-Padova
Ricciuto V (2018) La patrimonializzazione dei dati personali. Contratto e mercato nella ricostruzione del fenomeno. In Dir. informazione e informatica, p 689 ff
Sasso I (2019) Privacy post-mortem *e "successione digitale"*. In: Tosi E (ed) Privacy *digitale.* Riservatezza e protezione dei dati personali tra GDPR e nuovo Codice Privacy, Milano
Schlesinger P (1971) Successioni (diritto civile): parte generale. In Noviss. dig. it., Torino, vol. XVIII
Schmidt-Kessel M, Pertot T (2019) "Donazione" di dati personali e risvolti successori. In: Arroyo Amayuelas E, Baldus C, De Carvalho GE, Leroyer A, Lu Q, Rainer JM (eds) Casi controversi in materia di diritto delle successioni. Esperienze straniere, vol II, Napoli
Spangaro A (2021) La tutela postmortale dei dati personali del defunto. In Contr. e impr., No.2, p 574 ff
Spangaro A (2022) La successione digitale: la permanenza post mortem di aspetti della personalità. In Giur. it., No.6, p 1363 ff
Spatuzzi A (2020) Patrimoni digitali e vicenda successoria. In Notariato, No.4, p 402 ff
Tampieri M (2021) Il patrimonio digitale oltre la vita: quale destino?. In Contr. e impr., No.2, p 543 ff
Trolli F (2019) La successione mortis causa nei dati personali del defunto e i limiti al loro trattamento. In Jus civile, No.4, p 313 ff
Vignotto A (2022) La successione digitale alla luce delle prime pronunce giurisprudenziali italiane. In Fam.dir., No.7, p 710 ff
Vigorito A (2021) La 'persistenza' postmortale dei diritti sui dati personali: il caso Apple. In Dir. informazione e informatica, No.1, p 27 ff
Zaccaria A (1988) Diritti extrapatrimoniali e successione. Dall'unità al pluralismo nelle trasmissioni per causa di morte, Padova
Zaccaria A (2020) La successione mortis causa nei diritti di disporre di dati personali digitalizzati. In Studium iuris, No.11, p 1368 ff
Zeno-Zencovich V (1995) Personalità (diritti della). In Dig. disc. priv., sez. civ., Torino, vol. XIII
Ziccardi G (2017) Il libro digitale dei morti. Memoria, lutto, eternità e oblio nell'era dei social network, Torino

Accountability Principle and Its Implementation in the General Data Protection Regulation

Stefano Gatti

Contents

Abstract The chapter examines the salient aspects of the accountability principle-approach in the General Data Protection Regulation (Art. 5(2) GDPR), delving into the instruments that, in the logic of the legislation, contribute to its implementation. What emerges is the centrality of the assessments required of the data controller, also in relation to risks, with consequent repercussions on the *liability* rule.

S. Gatti (✉)
University of Verona, Verona, Italy
e-mail: stefano.gatti@univr.it

R. Bocchini (ed.), *Digital Platforms - From Technical Foundations to Legal and Economic Implications*, https://doi.org/10.1007/978-3-032-07978-7_32

1 The Principle of Accountability As a Cultural Approach (Not Only in the General Data Protection Regulation (GDPR))

Among the most celebrated innovations of Regulation (EU) 2016 /679 (GDPR), the principle of accountability is undoubtedly the distinguishing feature of the current data protection regulation.[1] As attested by the elastic wording of the rules that enunciate it (Art. 5(2) GDPR) and of those that concretise it (Art. 24 and 32 GDPR), as well as by the numerous mechanisms that can be said to be related or instrumental to it, this principle aims to establish a culture of personal data protection in all activities subject to the scope of the Regulation. We are therefore not dealing with the simple illustration of an aim that guides the interpretation of a set of detailed rules, but with a real "approach", with a model that, although it underpins the regulatory framework of the General Data Protection Regulation (GDPR), it is primarily up to the data controller to implement, by adopting "appropriate technical and organisational measures" to suit the specific circumstances of the case. Nor is this a merely programmatic view: the accountability system is, in itself, mandatory and entails, for the data controller, an inextricable web of discretion and responsibility. In this regard, it is worth noting already here that the breach of the principle, even if not accompanied by the infringement of a right of the data subjects or by non-compliance with a further provision of the Regulation, is independently sanctioned through public enforcement.[2]

Neither the term nor the concept of accountability was new at the time the GDPR was drafted. However, the Regulation was responsible for the legal formalisation of this principle-approach in the field of data protection[3] in one of the most evolved forms in the debate.[4]

---

[1] On the principle, see at least Lucchini Guastalla (2018), p. 120 ff; Finocchiaro (2019a), p. 2778 ff; (2019b), p. 513 ff; Maio (2019), p. 503 ff; Amore (2020), p. 414 ff; Docksey (2020), p. 555 ff; Carleo (2021), p. 359 ff; Resta (2022), p. 77 ff; Siano (2022), p. 300 ff; Albanese and Cardinali (2023), p. 501 ff;. Roßnagel and Richter (2023), p. 288 ff; Dumortier and Gryffroy (2023), p. 564 ff.

[2] Art. 83(5) GDPR; see Dumortier and Gryffroy (2023), p. 566.

[3] An expression of the accountability principle symmetrical to that of the GDPR can be found in Art. 4(4), Directive (EU) 2016/680, with regard to personal data processed by competent authorities for the prevention, investigation, detection and prosecution of criminal offences or the execution of criminal penalties. In Italy, the transposition of Article 3(4) of *decreto legislativo* No. 51 of 18 May 2018 runs the risk of being seen as an oversimplification (which appears, however, to be correctable by way of interpretation), insofar as it translates the content of the principle into the simple "responsibility" of the data controller for compliance with the principles set out in the same article.

[4] The word "accountability" already appears in the original 1980 version of the OECD (Organisation for Economic Co-operation and Development) *Recommendation of the Council concerning Guidelines Governing the Protection of Privacy and Transborder Flows of Personal Data*: "A data controller should be accountable for complying with measures which give effect to the principles stated above". This first embryonic version of the principle, moreover, does not stray very far from

In the Anglo-Saxon language and culture, the term "accountability" represents an effective synthesis of the main aspects underlying this idea. In Italy, too, this word is substantially preferred to the official translation (*responsabilizzazione*): this term evokes, at once and above all,[5] responsibility, the assumption of responsibility, and the demonstration of responsibility—all aspects that are highlighted in the GDPR framework.

A feature of the accountability principle, which is also central to the Regulation, is that the regulated activity, while in itself lawful, is inevitably characterised by a certain level of risk. Therefore, an approach to activity based on the analysis and management of that risk is an integral part of this principle (risk-based approach).

Accountability, in its minimal meaning—linking one or more parties responsible for an activity to a set of processes aimed at ensuring compliance with a given legal framework, in a "proactive" and preventive logic—is, moreover, a recurring idea in many regulatory areas: a recent example concerns the obligations that Regulation (EU) 2022/2065, Digital Services Act, has imposed on intermediary service providers, according to a scalar model (with increasing protections), based on the type of service, the size of the provider and, therefore, the risks related to the activity.[6]

Indeed, when it is the legislator who guides the definition of risks and consequent obligations, there is a certain "hardening" of the accountability model. Such an evolution is reflected in Regulation (EU) 2024/1689, Artificial Intelligence Act. This legislation, while based on a model focused on the systematic management of risks associated with AI systems,[7] partially reduces the technical and organisational

---

the static idea of *responsibility* already known from Directive 95/46/EC (Art. 6(2): "It shall be for the controller to ensure that paragraph 1 is complied with", i.e. compliance with the basic principles of personal data processing). What distinguishes the modern understanding of accountability is the "proactive" approach, which encompasses both the responsible choice of measures to ensure compliance with the general principles of processing, and the ability of the data controller to demonstrate such compliance through these measures: see Docksey (2020), p. 561. The evolved meaning of accountability, openly encouraged by the Article 29 Working Party (WP29) in its *Opinion 3/2010 on the principle of* accountability (13 July 2010), can be found in the international debate both before and after the GDPR—e.g., in the International Standards on Data Protection and Privacy adopted at the International Conference of Data Protection and Privacy Authorities held in Madrid in November 2009, in the version of the aforementioned OECD Guidelines as amended in 2013, and in Convention 108+ adopted by the Council of Europe on 18 May 2018.

[5] Further aspects branch off from this multifaceted concept, in addition to those indicated in the text: transparency, liability (in the sense of being held liable for the harmful consequences of one's actions: see *infra*, Sect. 7), controllability (within the organisation of the subject obliged to comply with the principle), responsiveness (understood as attention to respond to the requests of stakeholders): see Docksey (2020), p. 561, in the wake of Koppell (2005), p. 96 ff.

[6] Camardi (2021), p. 907 ff; Servida (2023), p. 149 ff. Particular attention is paid to the issue of accountability with regard to hosting providers and, among these, to online platforms, of which a de facto, paranormative power is recognised (in order to decline it according to the model of a responsible exercise).

[7] Smorto (2024), p. 208 ff; Finocchiaro (2022b), p. 303 ff. On the importance of the accountability approach in IA regulation, with particular regard to liability rules, see Comandè (2019), p. 181 ff.

discretion of operators, to the extent that it predefines the risk levels[8] to which such systems are classified (unacceptable, high, specific, limited) and links each level to a corresponding regulatory regime.[9]

Nonetheless, the essential features of the principle (in particular, autonomy in determining technical and organisational measures, albeit informed by the objectives and minimum requirements established by the Regulation, attention to monitoring the effectiveness of such measures and accountability) emerge clearly in several places in the legislation. Examples can be found, with regard to the regulation of high-risk AI systems, in the risk management system (Art. 9), in the quality management system (Art. 17), and in the obligations of the deployers of such AI systems (Art. 26 and 27).[10]

2 The Accountability Principle in the GDPR: Responsibility, Accountability and Proof of Responsibility

Focusing on the processing of personal data, the accountability principle is crystallised in Article 5(2) GDPR.[11] According to this provision, "The controller shall be responsible for, and be able to demonstrate compliance with, paragraph 1" of the same Article, i.e. the general principles of processing set out therein.

The starting point is that, already known, of "responsibility", which the Regulation attributes in a general way (and peremptorily)[12] to the data controller, even when it is a matter of activities on the data performed on its behalf by other subjects (data processors).[13] At this stage, we do not intend to refer to the rules governing compensation for damages (liability: Art. 82 GDPR),[14] but rather to the close link that the GDPR establishes between the person who initiates a personal data

---

[8] Finocchiaro (2022a), p. 1094 ff; Finocchiaro (2024), p. 49 ff.

[9] To each risk band the legislator associates a proportionate regulation, from prohibition to obligations and the incentive of self-regulation. Moreover, there are rules on "general-purpose AI models", where the "systemic" risk is particularly taken into account. For an overview, see Petruso and Smorto (2024), p. 989 ff.

[10] See De Hert and Lazcoz (2022), p. 37 ff.

[11] In contrast to Commission Proposal COM(2012) 11 *final*, the principle now emblematically occupies an ad hoc paragraph of Art. 5 GDPR, which follows the listing of general processing principles in the previous paragraph, thus becoming a real pivot point: P. De Hert and Lazcoz (2022), p. 39.

[12] Roßnagel and Richter (2023), p. 288.

[13] Recital 74, in its *incipit*, is clear in this regard: "The responsibility and liability of the controller for any processing of personal data carried out by the controller or on the controller's behalf should be established".

[14] Art. 82 GDPR nevertheless establishes a rule consistent with the underlying idea of accountability, creating a general liability rule for the data controller. The processor is liable only in cases of breach of the obligations specifically addressed to it and of the lawful instructions of the controller (see *infra*, Sect. 7).

processing operation, determining its means and purposes (Art. 4(7) GDPR: the data controller), and compliance with the rules and principles governing these activities. Since the Regulation explicitly ties this responsibility to compliance with principles (and not only, therefore, with specific provisions), the modalities for ensuring genuine (and not just formal) compliance must, to a large extent, be determined and filled in by the data controller itself.[15] The discretion thereby conferred upon the controller in the decision-making process has the effect of rendering it "responsible" both for the organisation of its own activity and for the decisions to be taken in relation to issues arising in the course thereof; where necessary, it shall be required to account both for those decisions and the measures implemented.

The perspective adopted by the legislation explains why accountability lies primarily with those who are in charge of the processing.[16] The processor, for its part, is subject to specific obligations. It is true that some of these obligations coincide with those that are the expression of the principle under consideration here; however, this circumstance does not diminish the responsibility of the controller, who, as inferred from Article 28 GDPR, is instead required, in addition, to conduct a prior technical and organisational assessment of the entity to which material processing activities are to be delegated (para. 1), and to supervise and direct its activities based on a contract (or another binding legal act) (para. 3). Finally, the controller is responsible for authorising the engagement of other processors (para. 2).

The normative logic underlying accountability is widely defined as "proactive" in the personal data protection[17]: it is the result of the need, already felt under Directive 95/46/EC, to move "from theory to practice", from formal-bureaucratic compliance to proportionate, result-oriented measures that are subject to constant monitoring.[18]

---

[15] See the reflections of Carleo (2021), p. 373 ff., who interprets this framework as a sign of the "crisi della fattispecie" and of the "delega legislativa ai privati" for detailed regulation, which leads to the emergence of the trend towards the "*procedimentalizzazione* delle condotte" and the search for *best practices* (which, indeed, are encouraged in the Regulation: see infra).

[16] Joint controllership is common, and its regulation (Art. 26 GDPR) requires data controllers, among other things, to specify, "their respective responsibilities", "by means of an arrangement between them, which must be made available to data subjects for its essential content". Although the provision links these responsibilities to the exercise of data subjects' rights, the aforementioned arrangement may also specify aspects of accountability, for instance by indicating which entity is responsible for implementing which technical and organisational measures, pursuant to Art. 25 and 32 GDPR (discussed infra), and at which stage: see Hartung (2020a), p. 653; see also EDPB, *Guideline 07/2020 on the concepts of data controller and data processor under the GDPR*, Vers. 2.0, adopted on 7 July 2021, 48 f. That said, the principle of accountability, in the dual sense of ensuring compliance with the GDPR and being able to prove it, applies to every joint controller: see Dumortier and Gryffroy (2023), p. 570.

[17] The term, used by the Regulation in the Spanish language version (*responsabilidad proactiva*), is indeed recurrent in the doctrine that has dealt with the principle: see, by way of example, Siano (2022), p. 303; Maio (2019), p. 510; Amore (2020), p. 421; Docksey (2020), p. 557 (*proactive action*).

[18] See, in particular, WP29, *Opinion 3/2010*, 1 and *passim*.

The concrete and substantive turn imposed by accountability is further reflected in the need for the assessments made concerning the processing events and the consequently adopted measures to be demonstrable. The data controller must be able to demonstrate the compliance of its actions with the Regulation, in all circumstances and at all times, both when requested by a supervisory authority and when a data subject raises a complaint alleging a breach of the rules to their detriment (see below, Sect. 7). Finally, by linking up with the principle of transparency, accountability contributes to building confidence among data subjects in the effective protection of their personal data by the data controller.[19]

3 The Concretisation of Accountability in "Appropriate Technical and Organisational Measures" Implemented by the Data Controller

The key provision for understanding the functioning of the accountability principle-approach is contained in Article 24 GDPR, which mandates the data controller to implement—as well as review and, where necessary, update—"appropriate technical and organisational measures" to ensure the compliance of processing activities with the Regulation, and to demonstrate it.

The appropriateness of the measures with respect to the twofold purpose indicated by the rule is to be tailored to the individual case, on the basis of normative criteria dictated by Article 24 GDPR itself: the characteristics of the data processing in question ("taking into account the nature, scope, context and purposes of processing") and the related risks for individuals (the likelihood of occurrence and severity of which must be evaluated).[20] The provision does not refer to the resources

[19] The principle of accountability does not, however, imply "completa accessibilità, da parte dell'interessato, alle informazioni circa l'attività di un dato operatore": Lucchini Guastalla (2018), p. 121.

[20] The assessment of risks, in particular, in order to understand whether they are present and whether they are "high", must be objective and should be referred to the characteristics of the processing (Recital 76). Beyond this indication, the Regulation is silent on the methodologies to be used for risk assessment (Dumortier and Gryffroy (2023), p. 572); Recital 77 suggests the importance of referring, also for the "identification of best practices to mitigate risk", to "approved codes of conduct, approved certifications, guidelines provided by the Board or guidance provided by a data protection officer". Finally, the same Recital provides that "the Board may also issue guidelines on processing operations that are considered to be unlikely to result in a high risk to the rights and freedoms of natural persons and indicate what measures may be sufficient in such cases to address such risk". Apart from the notable cases to which the GDPR associates a high risk (Art. 35(3)), such silence is also to be found in the rules on data protection impact assessment (DPIA). Central to this aspect are the guidelines of the supervisory authorities, which, according to the aforementioned Article 35 GDPR, have, inter alia, the power to draw up black and white lists of processing operations in relation to the degree of risk (paras. 4 and 5).

available to the data controller, nor to the size of this entity,[21] nor to the costs of implementation and state of the art[22]: the focus here is solely on the nature of the processing and the associated risks.

The appropriateness of the measures is not to be assessed according to a purely formal yardstick, but takes into account their effectiveness, which must be predicted, documented and monitored by the data controller[23]; it is quite possible that measures and instruments put in place at an early stage prove to be no longer appropriate over time. The Regulation does not specify any temporal reference, thereby highlighting the decision-making autonomy of data controllers also in this respect.[24] On this point, it is undoubtedly preferable to consider that a review is "necessary" even when there is no change in the characteristics of the processing (which would otherwise make the need for a new assessment a foregone conclusion), since, under the same conditions, the related risks and the instruments for containing them may vary.[25]

The focus on the appropriateness of measures according to a substantive, iterative and dynamic logic highlights the idea of accountability as a model to be adopted and shaped according to the needs of the individual case, in a gradual and proportional approach. However, the problem remains open as to which measures, in concrete terms, can (and should) be adopted.

Although the illustrative list in the Commission's proposal has not been maintained,[26] some guidance can be derived from the legal text, which still contains and regulates, albeit in several articles, some of these so-called typical measures.[27] These measures, in some cases made mandatory by the Regulation, on the one hand do not exhaust the range of possibilities open to the data controller,[28] who is thus

[21] Docksey (2020), p. 565.

[22] Dumortier and Gryffroy (2023), p. 573. The state of the art and the costs of implementation are, however, taken into account in some of the provisions that further concretise the accountability approach: see, in particular, Art. 25 and 32 GDPR (see infra, Sect. 5).

[23] See Recital 74 GDPR, which, with respect to Art. 24 of the same Regulation, adds the adjective "effective" to the measures under consideration and specifies that effectiveness must also be subject to the controller's accountability. In the Commission's Proposal, COM(2012) 11 *final*, Article 22(3) required the data controller to implement mechanisms to ensure the effectiveness of the measures adopted, including, where appropriate, independent audits.

[24] According to Article 24(1) GDPR, "those measures shall be reviewed and updated when necessary". In its first-reading amendments, the European Parliament had proposed, with specific regard to compliance policies and procedures ("that persistently respect the autonomous choices of data subjects"), which are in addition to (or specify) the technical and organisational measures referred to in paragraph 1, a review every 2 years.

[25] See Dumortier and Gryffroy (2023), p. 576 ff.

[26] Art. 22(2).

[27] Amore (2020), p. 424.

[28] The data controller could also decide to apply, as a precaution, a measure that the Regulation envisages as mandatory in other circumstances (e.g., the appointment of a data protection officer even if not required under Art. 37 GDPR, or the keeping of records even if not mandatory under Art. 30 GDPR, or the carrying out of a data protection impact assessment even if the processing is not related to a high risk, under Art. 35 GDPR). This is what the Article 29 Working Party (WP29,

encouraged to devise or follow new, "atypical" solutions, and on the other hand they do not shield the controller from possible challenges regarding compliance with the principle under consideration.[29]

That said, the first indication comes from Article 24(1) of GDPR itself. From the wording of the provision, it emerges that the measures in question are both "technical" and "organisational" in nature. It is a matter, then, on the one hand, of the instruments deployed by the data controller (e.g. the records of processing activities under Article 30 GDPR, but also the software used to manage the data) and, on the other, of the models and procedures adopted within its organisation (e.g. the appointment of a data protection officer, but also the specific training of employees).

Article 24(2) GDPR, moreover, mentions, as a more complex organisational measure—the necessity of which in the specific context, consistent with the principle of accountability, is for the data controller to assess—the "implementation of appropriate data protection policies".

The Regulation does not specify, even in its minimum requirements, the content of these policies, which must also be articulated in the light of the specific features of the processing activities.[30] In short, and broadly speaking, it is a description of a set of procedures to be followed (e.g. for handling access or portability requests, or complaints), which the data controller may adapt according to the complexity of its organisation and share within it (or parts thereof).[31]

Finally, Article 24(3) GDPR refers to the adherence to approved codes of conduct and certification mechanisms. These instruments, which are entirely voluntary, are widely encouraged by the Regulation as valuable tools for demonstrating compliance with the GDPR.[32]

In particular, codes of conduct, governed by Articles 40 and 41 GDPR, are prepared and submitted for the approval of the competent supervisory authority by

---

Opinion 3/2010, 6) has defined as the "second tier" of accountability, consisting in the adoption of "voluntary accountability systems that go above and beyond the minimum legal requirements", or in methods for implementing or ensuring the effectiveness of measures that go beyond the minimum level. This tier includes the adoption of measures that the Regulation itself envisages as voluntary, such as codes of conduct and certification (see infra, in the text).

[29] It has been suggested that the adoption of typical measures would have the effect of triggering a rebuttable presumption of compliance in favour of the data controller (Amore (2020), p. 424). However, the Regulation lacks clear indications supporting this conclusion, reflecting maximum accountability of the data controller, including from the perspective of demonstrability. The same applies to codes of conduct or certification mechanisms (see infra): the literal wording does not seem sufficient to support the idea of a rebuttable presumption (see Resta (2022), p. 77; see also Dumortier and Gryffroy (2023), p. 579).

[30] Dumortier and Gryffroy (2023), p. 578.

[31] WP29, *Opinion 3/2010*, 13. Recital 78 makes clear that the internal policies adopted by the data controller should, like the various measures it implements, contribute to fulfilling the principles of *privacy by design* and *privacy by default* set out in Art. 25 GDPR (see infra, Sect. 5).

[32] See Art. 24(3), 25(3), 28(5) and 32(3) GDPR. Moreover, pursuant to Art. 83(2)(j) GDPR, such measures are positively taken into account as part of the factors to be weighed by the supervisory authority when deciding whether to impose an administrative fine and, if so, to determine its amount.

associations and other bodies representing categories of data controllers and data processors in certain sectors. If it does not concern processing by a public body, the proposed code, as part of the mechanisms for verifying compliance and intervening in the event of violations, must also identify a monitoring body, which is accredited by the supervisory authority based on the requirements set out in Article 41 of the Regulation.

The codes help to translate the rules on personal data protection into concrete, practical applications,[33] specifying and calibrating them in the light of the specific needs (and risks)[34] of the sector to which they refer.[35] Their main value lies in standardising and consolidating good practices in the various areas, offering an initial test bed for verifying and documenting compliance with personal data protection rules.[36] However, on the one hand, the supervision and intervention of the monitoring body does not prejudice the corrective—and consequently, sanctioning—powers of the supervisory authority; on the other hand, adherence to an approved code of conduct does not guarantee data controllers (and data subjects) full compliance with the Regulation .[37]

Certifications, on the other hand, are declarations made by third parties with specific requirements of competence and independence (the certification bodies accredited,[38] or, according to the letter of the GDPR, also the supervisory authorities),[39] attesting, based on mechanisms and criteria approved[40] by the supervisory authority,[41] to the compliance of a processing operation or set of processing

[33] Such codes may be useful, in particular, for micro, small and medium-sized enterprises, reducing the costs of compliance: see EDPB, *Guidelines 1/2019 on Codes of Conduct and Monitoring Bodies under Regulation (EU) 2016/679*, Vers. 2.0, 4 June 2019, 9; see also Art. 40(1) GDPR.

[34] See *supra*, footnote 20.

[35] "Specifying" the application of the Regulation (Art. 40(2) GDPR) and "calibrating the obligations" (Recital 98) are activities fundamentally aimed at filling with content regulatory provisions that are indeterminate and leave room for discretion: see Bergt and Pesch (2020), p. 884.

[36] The relevance of codes of conduct in the analysis and management of processing-related risks is made clear by Art. 32(3) (in relation to the identification of appropriate security measures) and 35(8) (in the context of the DPIA) GDPR.

[37] EDPB, *Guidelines 1/2019*, 8, fn. 17.

[38] According to Art. 43(1) GDPR, such bodies may be accredited either by the supervisory authorities or by the national accreditation body designated under Regulation No. 765/2008 (in Italy, *Accredia*). In the latter case, the criteria to be met for accreditation are supplemented by additional requirements established by the competent supervisory authority under Articles 55 and 56 GDPR.

[39] Art. 42(5) GDPR. This is an optional power, since, as is the case in Italy, it is possible for certificates to be issued by certification bodies only: EDPB, *Guidelines 1/2018 on certification and identifying certification criteria in accordance with Articles 42 and 43 of Regulation*, Vers. 3.0, 4 June 2019, 10.

[40] Certification criteria and procedures are either prepared by the certification body or by a different entity that develops them, "scheme owner", and "are an integral part of any certification mechanism" (EDPB, *Guidelines 1/2018*, 12 f.).

[41] On the draft decision, the European Data Protection Board (EDPB) issues an opinion (Art. 64(1)(c)). On the basis of the intention of the "owner" of the scheme or the certification body, through the supervisory authority to which the criteria are submitted, an application may be made for their

operations with the Regulation, thus helping to create and strengthen trust in the public of data subjects and in the market.[42] The positive attestation may be summarised by a logo or symbol (so-called seal or mark).

Even in this case, however, while constituting an important piece of evidence in this sense, the measure is not, in itself, able to guarantee to the controller (and processor) that its activity actually complies with the Regulation, nor can it shelter them from possible sanctions by the supervisory authority or actions for damages by data subjects.[43]

4 Accountability As Demonstrability of Compliance with the Regulation. In Particular, the Records of Processing Activities

As is already clear from the analysis of voluntary measures, accountability, according to a model that permeates every mechanism that the data controller adopts to comply with the principle, is an approach that takes the form of demonstrable processes. A crucial point is indeed to be able to prove compliance of one's actions with data protection legislation.

As part of this purpose, the Regulation provides, at least in certain contexts, for mandatory measures, among which records of processing activities are of particular importance. This is a novelty introduced by the GDPR, which has thus replaced the previous mechanism of *ex ante* notification to the supervisory authorities, provided for in Directive 95/46/EC,[44] in line with the new approach based on the autonomy and accountability of the data controller.

Article 30 GDPR requires data controllers (and, where applicable, their representatives) to keep a record in written form (also in electronic form) of processing

---

approval by the Board, resulting in a "common certification", valid in all Member States, which is called the "European Data Protection Seal" (Art. 42(5) GDPR).

[42] The certificate has a more or less general scope (e.g. all processing operations carried out by a data controller, with the exception of certain special categories of personal data) and a precise object of assessment ("data, processes and technical infrastructure"), which must be "meaningful with respect to the message or claim made on/by the certification and should not mislead the user, customer or consumer": EDPB, *Guidelines 1/2018*, 17. The purpose is to allow a quick assessment (according to a principle of transparency) of the level of data protection offered within a given processing: see Recital 100 GDPR.

[43] The certification obtained should not have the effect of weakening the vigilance of data controllers (or processors) or relieving them of responsibility: on the contrary, it is emphatically stated that a certification under Art. 42 "does not reduce the responsibility of the controller or the processor for compliance with this Regulation" (Art. 42(4) GDPR).

[44] Recital 89. The reference is to the provisions contained in Section 9 of Chapter II of Directive 95/46/EC.

activities,[45] which contains the main information, in a perspective that is not only static, but also dynamic, as it must be constantly updated.[46] Moreover, the controller's obligation extends to documenting "any personal data breaches, comprising the facts relating to the personal data breach, its effects and the remedial action taken" (Art. 33(5) GDPR).

While the latter fulfilment has a general scope of application, the record-keeping under Article 30 GDPR does not, in principle, concern entities with fewer than 250 employees. Indeed, the counter-exceptions that reintroduce the rule are very broad in scope, especially since they operate in an alternative relationship (para. 5). For the obligation in question to arise, it is sufficient that the processing "includes" data under Articles 9 or 10 GDPR, or "is likely to result in a risk to the rights and freedoms of data subjects" or even "is not occasional".[47]

Indeed, the dual function of the records of processing activities proves to be fundamental in the accountability system[48]. On the one hand, the structured nature of the record-keeping (imposed by the form-content requirements of Art. 30 GDPR), almost like a checklist, is a tool that enables data controllers (and data processors) to gain awareness of the processing taking place within their activity, of the risks associated with it, and to pay due attention to the compliance of their work with the Regulation in the most delicate aspects; on the other hand, what is documented may be useful to the supervisory authorities (but also to the data controller or the

[45] Pursuant to Art. 30(2) GDPR, moreover, even the data processor is obliged to keep its own records, the contents of which are declined according to the specificity of its role (e.g. it is not necessary to indicate the purposes of the processing, since these are established and therefore documented by the controller).

[46] The fact that the records must be kept up-to-date (although the European Parliament's proposal to include this obligation verbatim was not followed up) is a consequence of the principle of accountability: see Hartung (2020b), p. 739 f.

[47] WP29, *Working Party 29 position paper on the derogations from the obligation to maintain records of processing activities pursuant to Article 30(5) GDPR*, 19 April 2018. The *paper* emphasises, however, that where a counter-exception applies (e.g. a micro-enterprise processes certain categories of data on a non-occasional basis), the records may only cover the processing activities that justify this counter-exception.

[48] Even when maintaining records is not mandatory, the obligation of the data controller to be able to report on the measures taken to ensure compliance and their effectiveness remains unaffected: see Kotschy (2020), p. 618. For this reason, maintaining records is recommended even when it is not mandatory. This recommendation is endorsed in the FAQ published by the Italian *Garante per la Protezione dei Dati Personali* (GPDP), where it is argued that such a measure "fornendo piena contezza del tipo di trattamenti svolti, contribuisce a meglio attuare, con modalità semplici e accessibili a tutti, il principio di accountability e, al contempo, ad agevolare in maniera dialogante e collaborativa l'attività di controllo del Garante stesso".

processor) when carrying out ex post verifications of such work.[49] The data controller (as well as the data processor) is in fact obliged, in line with a more general obligation to cooperate with the supervisory authorities laid down by the Regulation (Art. 31 GDPR), to make the records available to them, upon request (Art. 30(4) GDPR).

5 The Risk Orientation of the Data Controller's Assessments. Security Measures. *Privacy by Design* and *by Default*

As has already been noted, accountability is oriented towards a risk-based approach. The need to consider risks to individuals is, therefore, a constant factor when determining the measures to be taken to comply with the Regulation.[50]

According to Article 32 GDPR, these risks are specifically addressed by some of these measures (security measures).[51] It is up to the data controller to identify the measures that are "appropriate" to the objective, which, according to the Regulation, corresponds to "a level of security" that is not absolute but "appropriate to the risk".[52] This assessment, in addition to reflecting the parameters set out in Article 24 GDPR, also takes into account the "state of the art" and the "costs of implementation".

The accountability model is therefore reiterated and further emphasised by this provision, insofar as it lists some useful measures for illustrative purposes, without specifying when they must be adopted. Moreover, it describes such measures,

[49] Recital 82 GDPR directly links processing records to the function of demonstrating compliance with the Regulation.

[50] Art. 24, 25, 32, 35 GDPR (see also supra, footnote 20). The risks directly taken into account, whose likelihood of occurrence and impact or severity must be assessed, are those affecting "the rights and freedoms of natural persons". A broad but not exhaustive illustration of these risks can be found in Recital 75. Finally, in Art. 32(2) GDPR, events are presented that may generate such risks in the context of processing activities (destruction, loss, alteration, unauthorised disclosure of data, or access to them: these are "data breaches" as defined in Art. 4(12) GDPR). For a multi-functional perspective of the security of processing in the Regulation's approach, which requires also taking into account the prerogatives of the data controller and the interests of the market, see Bravo (2019), p. 782 ff.

[51] The rule is an expression of the general principle of integrity or security of processing (Art. 5(1)(f) GDPR).

[52] The GDPR does not require zero risk, nor does it oblige the data controller to achieve such a result: CJEU 14 December 2023, C-340/21, *Natsionalna agentsia za prihodite*, (on that occasion, the Court clarified that national courts may carry out an examination of the substance of measures taken by the controller); CJEU 25 January 2024, C-687/21, *MediaMarktSaturn*.

except for pseudonymisation, in rather generic terms,[53] serving mainly to illustrate the objectives to be achieved.[54]

Notwithstanding the general responsibility of the data controller, the obligation under Article 32 GDPR is also incumbent on the data processor: this is also specified at a contractual level, pursuant to Article 28(3)(c) GDPR.[55]

Within this framework, the European legislator identifies a valuable tool for ensuring an appropriate level of security, making it compulsory for cases where, also because of the "use of new technologies", the risk associated with the processing is likely to be high[56]: the *Data Protection Impact Assessment* (DPIA). This is, in short, an in-depth and formalised analysis, according to an articulated and iterative procedure, aimed at identifying and effectively managing the risks related to one or more processing operations with similar characteristics (Art. 35(1) GDPR). This procedure is the responsibility of the data controller and involves, if present, the data protection officer (DPO) (para. 2).[57] The framework also provides for prior consultation of the supervisory authority in the event that, despite the measures envisaged, the expected risk remains high (Art. 36 GDPR).

In line with the not merely formalistic approach of accountability, assessing the risk associated with processing and the appropriateness of the technical and

[53] A broad and generic formulation also characterises the indications contained in Art. 25 GDPR (and in particular its para. 1, on which see infra). This remark is often emphasised by doctrine (e.g. Bravo (2019), p. 827 ff) and is in line with the accountability perspective and the technologically neutral language of the Regulation. Of particular relevance is the state of the art, which is useful to determine the standards of feasibility and proportionality given the specificities of the processing activities under consideration (on the so called PET—*Privacy Enhancing Technologies* and their limitations see again Bravo (2019), p. 793 ff and p. 814 ff). Moreover, this explains the usefulness of certifications (referred to in Art. 25(3) GDPR), which, while not affecting the responsibility of the data controller, can function as test-beds, based on external assessments, of the conformity of the technical and organisational measures adopted. On the practical side, an evaluation of the Board's guidelines (see EDPB, *Guidelines 4/2019 on Article 25. Data protection by Design and by Default*, Vers. 2.0, 20 October 2020, 4) and with the practice of supervisory authorities is undoubtedly useful. For these reflections, see Almada et al. (2023), p. 581 ff; Ratti (2021), p. 418 ff.

[54] For instance, "the ability to restore the availability and access to personal data in a timely manner in the event of a physical or technical incident" (Art. 32(1)(c) GDPR); see Renna (2019), p. 632.

[55] In fact, within the scope of the activity delegated by the controller, the measures adopted by the processor are relevant. See Jandt (2020), p. 753.

[56] Still from the perspective of accountability, the assessment of the level of risk and, consequently, of whether DPIA is mandatory or not falls under responsibility of the data controller, who is obliged, if necessary, to review its decision periodically in light of the evolution of the risks. Art. 35(3) GDPR sets out cases in which the DPIA is required. Even outside these cases, the DPIA, the complexity of which can be adapted depending on the processing activities, is nevertheless recommended as a voluntary measure, especially in conjunction with possible grey areas, where the need for such a measure might be controversial: WP29, *Guidelines on data protection impact assessment and determining whether processing is "likely to result in a high risk" for the purposes of Regulation 2016/679*, adopted 4 October 2017, 8.

[57] The processor is obliged to assist the controller in carrying out the assessment by providing the relevant information available to it (Art. 28(3)(f): WP 29, *Impact Assessment Guidelines*, 15).

organisational measures adopted does not take place in a single moment, but characterises the whole range of activities.[58]

With regard specifically to the security of processing, this entails not only the obligation—implicit here—to review and, where appropriate, update the measures, but also the requirement for the data controller and processor to have the capacity to react promptly and effectively to personal data breaches, following a formalised procedure (Art. 33 and 34 GDPR).[59]

The permanent perspective of accountability also requires, according to Article 25 GDPR, that data controllers assess the risks and, along with them, the characteristics of the processing, in order to determine appropriate measures to implement the data-protection principles in an effective manner and the "necessary safeguards" useful to "meet the [regulatory] requirements" and "protect the rights of data subjects", right from the design phase of their activities with regard to personal data (*privacy* or *data protection by design*). The Regulation, in essence, anticipates the moment from which the data controller is made responsible, from the beginning of the processing, to the preliminary stage of determining the "means" of processing. *Privacy by design* describes an essential feature of the accountability model and of the design and preventive logic inherent in it,[60] to the point of connoting, in substance, the very qualifying activity of the "data controller". Starting from the definition according to which a "controller" is a person who determines the means of processing based on the purposes (Art. 4(7) GDPR), what Article 25(1) GDPR adds is that this operation cannot be conceived as unrelated to the assessment of the technical and organisational measures[61] suitable to ensure full compliance with the Regulation, including the management of the associated risks.[62] Moreover, these two aspects tend to overlap when the means chosen are technological in nature.[63]

---

[58] See Mollo (2019), p. 263. Bravo (2019), p. 790.

[59] See Nuzzolo (2025).

[60] See, on this point, Mollo (2019), p 271 ff; Bravo (2019), p. 793 ff; Failace (2022), p. 1123 ff; Ratti (2021), p. 414; in Italian case law, see Cass., 10 October 2023, no. 28385, in *Onelegale*.

[61] A broad meaning is generally given to the notion "means of the processing": see Pizzetti and Greco (2021), p. 403. Art. 25 GDPR, while identifying the "state of the art" and the "cost of implementation" as relevant parameters for its materialisation (together with the parameters laid down in Art. 24 GDPR) has no exceptions and applies to any processing: see EDPB, *Guidelines* 4/2019, 4.

[62] The link between Art. 25 GDPR and the security principle is underlined by Recital 78 GDPR and the literature: see Bravo (2019), p. 848; Finocchiaro (2019b), p. 521. Although the data processor is not a direct addressee of the obligations under Article 25 GDPR, it remains nevertheless required to identify appropriate security measures and to comply with the instructions of the data controller. The controller, in turn, bears the responsibility of entrusting processing activities only to processors that provide sufficient guarantees to implement appropriate technical and organisational measures to safeguard the rights of data subjects (Art. 28(1) GDPR).

[63] In the sense of further widening the fronts of the data controller's responsibility, it should be considered the possibility, recognised *in claris verbis* by Recital 48 of EU Directive 2019/770, concerning contracts with consumers for the provision of digital content or services, that the data controller's failure to take appropriate measures may result in a lack of conformity that allows the consumer-data subject to exercise the remedies provided for in that legislation (at least in those cases, more frequently encountered in platform services, where the processing of personal data is

The data controller must only resort to means that enable the effective protection of personal data and the rights of data subjects, possibly compensating for any weaknesses that cannot be overcome on this level (due to technical limitations, the inability of influencing aspects prepared by external parties) with further appropriate (technical and organisational) measures.[64]

Article 25 GDPR links the principle of *privacy by design* to the idea of *privacy by default*. The two concepts, as highlighted by the European Data Protection Board (EDPB) Guidelines, are closely related.[65] *Privacy by default* is a basic approach which, through an application of the principle of minimisation to the organisation and technical equipment deployed by the data controller, aims to maintain the highest possible security profile. In particular, this approach orients the starting settings, in relation to the amount of data collected, the scope of the processing, the time of data storage and its accessibility, towards a criterion of strict necessity in relation to the purposes set. In this way, *privacy by default*, at the same time, illuminates a key aspect of the data controller's accountability, and reinforces its responsibility: it is up to the data controller to identify the minimum levels of necessity with respect to the purposes and to apply them as a standard at every stage of the processing and in all related technical and organisational aspects.

6 The Evaluative Moment As the Hallmark of *Accountability* in the Fabric of the GDPR. The *Data Protection Officer* (DPO)

As emerged in the previous sections, the principle of accountability requires the data controller to make delicate evaluations that are rarely confined to a single moment in time, instead demanding continuous and careful monitoring.

The scope of this approach does not concern only the technical and organisational measures discussed so far: accountability also entails the controller's ability to make correct decisions in the face of concrete issues arising in the course of

an integral part of the contractual performance, rather than a mere accessory: see Schmidt-Kessel (2023), p. 152 ff.).

[64] This, of course, within the limits of what is possible: Almada et al. (2023), p. 588. This consideration makes it clear that for the effective implementation of a data protection *by design* approach, it is crucial to raise awareness among the producers of the technologies and providers of the digital services used by the data controller to carry out data processing operations. This need is expressly recognised in Recital 78 GDPR (as well as by the EDPB, *Guidelines 4/2019*, cit, 5 ff.). However, unlike what happened—in another context—in the *Data Act* (Regulation (EU) 2023/2854), this does not result in a subjective extension of the *by design* obligation to these actors.

[65] EDPB, *Guidelines 4/2019*, 5 ff. On the relationship between Art. 25 GDPR and the rules of the *Digital Services Act*, see Pelino (2023), p. 9 ff. Finally, for an application of the principles to the reality of *social networks*, see EDPB, *Guidelines 03/2022 on deceptive design patterns in social media platform interfaces: how to recognise and avoid them*, Vers. 2.0, adopted on 14 February 2023.

processing, right from its conception.[66] The examples in the text of the Regulation are numerous, and there is no space here to review them all; however, at least some paradigmatic cases deserve to be mentioned, in which the required assessment takes the form of a balancing of opposing interests.

As is well known, by virtue of Articles 5(1) and 6 GDPR, it is the task of the data controller to identify the legal basis that makes the processing of personal data lawful in the light of the stated purposes. Except consent, whose prerequisites for validity (Art. 4(11) and 7 GDPR) must, in any case, be verified by the data controller itself,[67] the legal bases all underlie an assessment of "necessity" in relation to an objective (the performance of a contract, the compliance of a legal obligation, etc.) that defines the scope of their legitimising effect. This assessment, which depends on the individual case, is still the responsibility of the data controller. Among the legal bases, furthermore, there is one whose suitability to render processing lawful depends precisely on a balance: the "legitimate interests pursued by the controller or by a third party".[68]

Equally exemplary are the cases where a data subject exercises a right under the Regulation (Chapter III).[69] For all of them, consider the example of the right to erasure of data (Art. 17 GDPR): the request for erasure opens up a wide range of issues for the data controller, given that such a request must only be complied with if one of the conditions referred to in paragraph 1 is met (which underlie further assessments such as the absence of necessity in relation to the purposes [sub-para a], or of an "overriding legitimate ground for the processing" [sub-para. c], unlawfulness [sub-para. d]) and one of the exceptions in paragraph 3 does not apply (including the case, indicative of the sensitivity of the underlying assessments, of the "exercise of the right to freedom of expression and information" [sub-para. a]).

The complexity of the architecture of the processing, as well as the many legal and technical issues that may arise at each stage, makes it particularly useful for the data controller (but also for the data processor) to designate a person (internal or external to its organisation) as *data protection officer* ("DPO"). Due to the

[66] See, also for further examples than those given infra, Finocchiaro (2019a, b), p. 2780 (according to whom: "è certamente il principio di accountability da intendersi richiamato anche in ogni altro caso in cui al titolare sono rimesse decisioni"); Amore (2020), p. 427 ff.; Albanese and Cardinali (2023), p. 510 ff.

[67] This also applies with regard to the proof of consent and its characteristics. Although the Regulation does not place any formal requirement on this point, Art. 7(1) GDPR provides that the data controller must be able to prove that consent has been given by the data subject.

[68] Indeed, Art. 6(1)(f) GDPR requires that "legitimate interests pursued by the controller or by a third party" are not "overridden by the interests or fundamental rights and freedoms of the data subject": see Finocchiaro (2019a, b), p. 2780 f. On the subject, of particular relevance, CJEU 4 July 2023, C-252/21, *Meta Platforms*. On the principle of lawfulness, see Scola (2025).

[69] Art. 12 GDPR, which opens Chapter III, is already relevant: see Carleo (2021), p. 368. On such rights, see Troiano (2025).

competence and independence requirements, this figure is rightly regarded as a tool for implementing accountability.[70]

Given that in some cases the appointment of this person is compulsory (Art 37(1) GDPR), the data controller (as well as the data processor) may also identify a DPO on a voluntary basis, and may also grant him or her additional powers beyond those assigned to this figure by the Regulation[71]; in any case, if present, the DPO becomes an indispensable aid for taking decisions on data protection issues, also serving as a safeguard for third parties, especially data subjects.[72]

7 Accountability and Liability: How Does Accountability Influence the Liability Regime (Art. 82 GDPR)?

The influence of the accountability principle on the framework of the Regulation has some relevant implications on the civil liability regime dictated by Article 82 GDPR.[73] The most immediate implication concerns the burden of proof: since the relevant damage derives from an infringement of the Regulation (Art. 82(1) GDPR), the data subject may simply allege that infringement, while it will be up to the data controller to prove that the processing complies with the Regulation.[74]

The influence of accountability seems, in truth, much deeper. In fact, on the one hand, the principle in question affects the element of unlawfulness beyond the question of proof, shaping, in particular, the very concept of "violation" of the Regulation. On the other hand, it directs the interpretation of the exemption dictated by Article 82(3) GDPR, according to which the controller or processor shall not be held liable if it proves that it is in no way responsible for the event causing the damage.[75]

As regards the first aspect, the discretion inherent in accountability, which is expressed, as we have seen, in the parameters of appropriateness and proportionality, has the consequence that the principle, for a wide range of decisions, becomes a

[70] In these terms, e.g., Amore (2020), p. 426; see also Dumortier and Gryffroy (2023), p. 573, according to whom the adaptability in the organisational structure of the DPO's office and the resources available to it exemplifies the proportional approach to the specific needs of the case, as required by the accountability principle. In Art. 22(2) of the Commission's Proposal COM(2012) 11 *final*, the designation of a DPO was cited as an example of an appropriate organisational measure to ensure compliance with the Regulation.

[71] See Art. 38(6) as well as WP29, *Guidelines on Data Protection Officers (DPOs)*, adopted on 13 December 2016 (last revised on 5 April 2017).

[72] Art. 38 and 39 GDPR. In relation to the DPIA see *supra*, Sect. 5.

[73] On the liability rules dictated by Art. 82 GDPR, see Faccioli (2025).

[74] See already Caterina and Thobani (2019), p. 104; Van Alsenoy (2019), p. 104; more recently, see Salanitro (2023), p. 431 and, in European case law, CJEU 14 December 2023, C-340/21, cited above (fn. 52) and CJEU 25 January 2024, C-687/21, cited above (fn. 52).

[75] See Cuffaro (2024), p. 1366.

measure of compliance with the law and, therefore, of the conformity of the activity with the Regulation.[76]

An exemplary case is the liability of the data controller for personal data breaches by third parties. Having made it clear that the security obligation does not imply, for the data subjects, an absolute guarantee against unauthorised disclosure or access of data, an "infringement" of the Regulation only occurs if the technical and organisational measures put in place were, based on a concrete (but ex ante) assessment, actually inappropriate. This circumstance is not proven by the data breach: rather, this event has the effect of triggering a presumption of non-appropriateness, which can be rebutted, in line with the principle of accountability, by evidence to the contrary provided by the data controller (or data processor).[77]

Developing the reasoning in relation to this group of cases, the description of the "liberating proof" ends up overlapping, in the discourse of European jurisprudence, with the exemption of Article 82(3) GDPR. In practice, objective and subjective interpretations of this evidence tend to align. By demonstrating that it has made appropriate (and therefore diligent) choices, the data controller also proves its extraneousness, also in terms of legally relevant causation, from the unlawful act, which, at this point, will be entirely attributable to the third parties who have breached the data processed.[78]

More generally with regard to the exemption under Article 82(3) GDPR - which also covers breaches of specific obligations or breaches of general obligations that, while generic in nature, give rise to concrete duties in specific contexts - [79] the approach summarised by the principle of accountability seems to have made inroads into the reasoning of the European Court of Justice. The European judges have concluded, in general terms (thoughnot yet with full precision),[80] that the liability framework designed by the GDPR constitutes a liability for fault, characterised by a reversal of the burden of proof.[81]

A limit to this approach should concern those cases in which the damage is caused by the conduct of a person within the organisation of the data controller

[76] Cf. Salanitro (2023), p. 439 ff., for a reconstruction of the Regulation's framework in terms of a clear preponderance of the obligations of conduct, which are generic, over those of result. As CJEU 21 December 2023, C-667/21, *Krankenversicherung Nordrhein* explains, the very basis of the obligations under Art. 24 and 32 GDPR would be called into question "if the controller were then required to compensate for any damage caused by processing carried out in breach of the GDPR". See already Caterina and Thobani (2019), p. 2808.

[77] CJEU 14 December 2023, C-340/21, cited above (fn. 52).

[78] See also CJEU 14 December 2023, C-340/21, cited above (fn. 52).

[79] For example, a security measure, although correctly identified among those concretely appropriate to prevent a risk, was not then concretely adopted due to intervening circumstances.

[80] Alonzo (2024), p. 615.

[81] CJEU 21 December 2023, C-667/21, cited above (fn. 76) (disregarding, on this point, the Advocate General's conclusions). Of course, it remains possible to prove that the origin of the damage is external to the alleged infringement and that the latter did not contribute to such damage in any way (break in the causal link). On the debate on the imputation criterion, see Faccioli (2025), p. 887 ff.

(including the DPO). In such cases, the reference made by the Regulation to the entity as a whole to identify the data controller (as well as the data processor) is consistent with a strict liability criterion (similar to that of Art. 2049 of the Italian Civil Code), so that the human error of an employee should always result "in some way" attributable to the data controller (or the data processor).[82]

Moreover, in doctrine, a similar conclusion has been held to apply to the cases where the breach is attributable to the data processor. In fact, it has been stressed that a different solution would clash with the idea of the general liability of the controller "involved" in the processing (Art. 82(2) GDPR) and would undermine the effectiveness of the data subject's right to compensation for damage, which is the purpose of the rule of joint and several liability (Art. 82(4) and (5) GDPR).[83]

References

Albanese F, Cardinali I (2023) Il principio di responsabilizzazione (accountability). In: Bravo F (ed) Dati personali. Protezione, libera circolazione e governance, vol 1. Principi, Pisa, p 501 ff

Almada M, Maranhao J, Sartor G (2023) Sub art. 25. In Spiecker gen. In: Döhmann I, Papakonstantinou V, Hornung G, De Hert P (eds) General data protection regulation. Article-by-article commentary. Hart, Baden-Baden, p 580 ff

Alonzo E (2024) Il risarcimento del danno per violazioni del GDPR (art. 82 Reg. UE 2016/679). La tutela della persona nelle logiche del diritto privato regolatorio?. In Nuove leggi civ. comm., p 601 ff

Amore G (2020) Fairness, Transparency e Accountability nella protezione dei dati personali. In St. iuris, p 414 ff

Bergt M, Pesch PJ (2020) Sub art. 40 GDPR. In: Kühling J, Buchner B (eds) Datenschutz-Grundverordnung. Bundesdatenschutzgesetz. Kommentar, 3rd edn. CH Beck, München, p 876 ff

Bravo F (2019) L'"architettura" del trattamento e la sicurezza dei dati e dei sistemi. In: Cuffaro V, D'Orazio R, Ricciuto V (eds) I dati personali nel diritto europeo. Giappichelli, Torino, p 775 ff

Camardi C (2021) Contratti digitali e mercati delle piattaforme. Un promemoria per il civilista. In Jus civile, p 870 ff

Carleo R (2021) Il principio di accountability nel GDPR. Dalla regola alla auto-regolazione. In Nuovo dir. civ., p 359 ff

Caterina R, Thobani S (2019) Il diritto al risarcimento dei danni. In Giur. it., p 2805 ff

Comandè G (2019) Intelligenza artificiale e responsabilità tra liability e accountability. Il carattere trasformativo dell'IA e il problema della responsabilità. In Analisi giur. economia, p 169 ff

---

[82] See Salanitro (2023), p. 449; Hellgardt (2022), p. 26; Van Alsenoy (2019), p. 105. CJEU 11 April 2024, C-741/21, *juris*, ruled out that the failure of a person acting under the authority of the data controller can be considered as an exemption under Article 82(3) GDPR and held that the violation of the instructions of the controller is equally irrelevant. According to this ruling, the data controller could only free itself by demonstrating that "there is no causal link between any breach of the data protection obligation incumbent on him or her (...) and the damage suffered by the data subject".

[83] See the authors cited above in fn. 82; see also Caterina and Thobani (2019), p. 2808 and Albanese and Cardinali (2023), p. 523.

Cuffaro (2024) Risarcimento del danno e trattamento dei dati personali. In Enc. dir., I tematici, Responsabilità civile, Milano, vol VII, p 1360 ff
De Hert P, Lazcoz G (2022) When GDPR-principles blind each other: accountability, not transparency, at the heart of algorithmic governance. Eur Data Protection Law Rev:31 ff
Docksey C (2020) Sub art. 24. In: Kuner C, Bygrave LA, Docksey C, Drechsler L (eds) The EU general data protection regulation (GDPR). A commentary. Oxford University Press, Oxford, p 555 ff
Dumortier J, Gryffroy P (2023) sub art. 24, In Spiecker gen. In: Döhmann I, Papakonstantinou V, Hornung G, De Hert P (eds) General data protection regulation. Article-by-article commentary. Nomos, Baden-Baden, p 564 ff
Faccioli M (2025) Liability for Unlawful Personal Data Processing. In this Book
Failace (2022) La natura e la disciplina delle obbligazioni di cui all'art. 25 del GDPR, espressione dei principi di privacy by design e di privacy by default. In Contr. impr., p 1123 ff
Finocchiaro G (2019a) Il principio di accountability. In Giur. it., p 2778 ff
Finocchiaro G (2019b) Approfondimento sub art. 24. In: Barba A, Pagliantini S (eds) Delle persone. Leggi collegate, vol II. In: Gabrielli E (ed), Commentario del codice civile. Legal Utet, Milano, p 513 ff
Finocchiaro G (2022a) La regolazione dell'intelligenza artificiale. In Riv. trim. dir pubbl., p 1085 ff
Finocchiaro G (2022b) La proposta di regolamento sull'intelligenza artificiale: il modello europeo basato sulla gestione del rischio. In Dir. informazione e informatica, p 303 ff
Finocchiaro G (2024) Diritto dell'intelligenza artificiale. Zanichelli, Bologna
Hartung (2020a) Sub art. 26 GDPR. In: Kühling J, Buchner B (eds) Datenschutz-Grundverordnung. Bundesdatenschutzgesetz. Kommentar, 3rd edn. C. H. Beck Verlag, München, p 635 ff
Hartung (2020b) Sub art. 30 GDPR. In: Kühling J, Buchner B (eds) Datenschutz-Grundverordnung. Bundesdatenschutzgesetz. Kommentar, 3rd edn. C. H. Beck Verlag, München, p 725 ff
Hellgardt (2022) Die Schadensersatzhaftung für Datenschutzverstöße im System des unionalen Haftungsrechts. In ZEuP, p 7 ff
Jandt S (2020) Sub art. 32. In: Kühling J, Buchner B (eds) Datenschutz-Grundverordnung. Bundesdatenschutzgesetz. Kommentar, 3rd edn. C. H. Beck Verlag, München, p 750 ff
Koppell JCS (2005) Pathologies of accountability: ICANN and the challenge of "multiple accountabilities disorder". Public Adm Rev:94 ff
Kotschy W (2020) Sub art. 30. In: Kuner C, Bygrave LA, Docksey C, Drechsler L (eds) The EU general data protection regulation (GDPR). A commentary. Oxford Academic, Oxford, p 616 ff
Lucchini Guastalla E (2018) Il nuovo regolamento europeo sul trattamento dei dati personali: i principi ispiratori. In Contr. impresa, p 106 ff
Maio (2019) Sub art. 24. In: Barba A, Pagliantini S (eds) Delle persone. Leggi collegate, vol II. In Gabrielli E (ed), Commentario del codice civile. UTET Giuridica, Milano, p 503 ff
Mollo (2019) Gli obblighi previsti in funzione di protezione dei dati personali. In: Zorzi Galgano N (ed) Persona e mercato dei dati. Riflessioni sul GDPR. Wolters Kluwer, Milano-Padova, p 255 ff
Nuzzolo A (2025) Data Processing Security and Personal Data Breach Notification System. In this Book
Pelino E (2023) L'interazione tra DSA e GDPR. In: Bolognini L, Pelino E, Scialdone M (eds) Digital Services Act e Digital Markets Act. Definizioni e prime applicazioni dei nuovi regolamenti europei. Giuffre, Milano, p 9 ff
Petruso R, Smorto G (2024) Il Regolamento europeo sull'intelligenza artificiale: una prima lettura. In Nuova giur. civ. comm., II, 989 ff
Pizzetti F, Greco L (2021) sub art. 24. In: D'Orazio R, Finocchiaro G, Pollicino O, Resta G (eds) Codice della privacy e data protection. Giuffrè, Milano, p 398 ff
Ratti M (2021) Sub art. 25. In: D'Orazio R, Finocchiaro G, Pollicino O, Resta G (eds) Codice della privacy e data protection. Academia, Milano, p 412 ff
Renna M (2019) Sub art. 32 GDPR. In: Barba A, Pagliantini S (eds) Delle persone. Leggi collegate, vol II. In Gabrielli E (ed), Commentario del codice civile. Wolters Kluwer, Milano, p 618 ff

Resta F (2022) Sub art. 5. In: Riccio GM, Scorza G, Belisario E (eds) GDPR e Normativa privacy. Commentario, 2nd edn. Wolters Kluwer, Milano, p 60 ff

Roßnagel A, Richter P (2023) sub art. 5, in Spiecker gen. In: Döhmann I, Papakonstantinou V, Hornung G, De Hert P (eds) General data protection regulation. Article-by-article commentary. Nomos Verlagsgesellschaft, Baden-Baden, p 261 ff

Salanitro U (2023) Illecito trattamento dei dati personali e risarcimento del danno nel prisma della corte di giustizia. In Riv. dir. civ., p 426 ff

Schmidt-Kessel M (2023) La responsabilità contrattuale del gestore di una piattaforma per la protezione dei dati personali del cliente nella prospettiva dei requisiti di qualità dell'adempimento. In Pactum, p 153 ff

Scola S (2025) Conditions of Lawfulness in Data Processing and User Consent within Digital Platforms and Social Networks. In this Book

Servida BS (2023) La responsabilità degli internet service provider: dal safe harbour al principio di accountability. In Nuove leggi civ. comm., p 135 ff

Siano M (2022) sub art. 24. In: Riccio GM, Scorza G, Belisario E (eds) GDPR e Normativa privacy. Commentario, 2nd edn. Wolters Kluwer, Milano, p 300 ff

Smorto G (2024) Distribuzione del rischio e tutela dei diritti nel regolamento europeo sull'intelligenza artificiale. Una riflessione critica. In Foro it., V, p 208 ff

Troiano S (2025) Rights of the Data Subject. In this Book

Van Alsenoy B (2019) Data protection law in the EU: roles, responsibilities and liability. Cambridge University Press, Cambridge

Data Sharing Services in the European Data Economy

Abigail Owusu

Contents

Abstract This chapter, after some due introduction, aims to provide a general overview of the merits and limits of the regulatory approach, adopted by the *Data Governance Act* (DGA), to the issue of data sharing, from a private law perspective. The chapter identifies the issues that need to be addressed in order to ascertain whether the regulation is really suitable to pursue the promised benefits.

1 The Legal Framework of the DGA: Subject Matter, Scope and Definitions

The proliferation of products related to the *Internet of Things* (IOT) has increased the amount and potential value of data, to the benefit of consumers, businesses and society at large.

A. Owusu (✉)
Verona, Italy
e-mail: abigail@studiolegaleowusu.it

R. Bocchini (ed.), *Digital Platforms - From Technical Foundations to Legal and Economic Implications*, https://doi.org/10.1007/978-3-032-07978-7_33

The ability to store, organise and analyse data in order to derive information from it is what gives data their enormous economic value.[1]

Recognising the economic and societal value of data, in 2023 the European Commission published a communication entitled 'A European Strategy for Data', announcing the goal of creating 'a single European data space - a true single market for data, open to data from all over the world - in which both personal and non-personal data, including commercially sensitive data, are secure and businesses have easy access to an almost infinite amount of high quality industrial data, stimulating growth and creating value, while minimising our carbon and environmental footprint'.[2]

Regulation (EU) 2022/868 of the European Parliament and of the Council of 30 May 2022 on European data governance and amending Regulation (EU) 2018/1724 (*Data Governance Act*, henceforth, DGA), applicable from 24 September 2023, is the first legislative instrument announced in the European Data Strategy to enter into force.

The DGA aims at 'improving the conditions for data sharing in the internal market by creating a harmonised framework for data exchanges and establishing some basic requirements for data *governance*, paying particular attention to facilitating cooperation between the Member States',[3] with the ultimate goal of 'further developing the borderless digital internal market and a human-centric, trustworthy and secure data society and economy'.[4]

According to the European legislator, 'providers of data brokering services, which may also include public bodies, offering services linking different actors have the potential to contribute to the efficient pooling of data as well as to the facilitation of bilateral data sharing. Specialised data brokering services, which are independent of data subjects, data owners and data users, could facilitate the emergence of new data-driven ecosystems independent of any player with a significant degree of market power, while providing non-discriminatory access to the data economy for companies of all sizes, in particular SMEs and start-ups with limited financial, legal or administrative means. This will be particularly important in the context of the creation of common European data spaces, i.e. interoperable sector-specific or cross-sectoral frameworks of common standards and practices to share or jointly process data, including for the development of new products and services, scientific research or civil society initiatives'.[5]

In addition to regulating data intermediaries (Art. 10–15), the DGA also deals with data reuse in the public sector (Art. 3–9), including special rules for organisations requesting and using personal data for altruistic purposes (Art. 16–25).

---

[1] OECD, *Data-Driven innovation: Big data for growth and well-being*, 2015, 150.

[2] 'Communication from the Commission to the European Parliament, the Council, the European Economic and Social Committee and the Committee of the Regions. A European strategy for data [COM(2020)86 final]'.

[3] See recital 3 DGA.

[4] Ibid.

[5] See recital 27 DGA.

This chapter focuses exclusively on the regulation of data brokering services, investigating in particular the objectives pursued by the European legislator, the application criteria and, above all, the conditions for the provision of data brokering services.

The main activity regulated by the DGA, i.e. data sharing, is defined as 'the provision of data by a data subject or data owner to a data user for the joint or individual use of such data, on the basis of voluntary agreements or Union or national law, either directly or via an intermediary, e.g. within the framework of open or commercial licences, in return for remuneration or free of charge'.[6]

In addition to the data subject referred to in Article 4 (1) GDPR, there are two new subjects to whom the Regulation is addressed: the 'data owner' and the 'data user'.

A data controller is 'a legal person, including public bodies and international organisations, or a natural person who is not the data subject with respect to the specific data concerned and who, in accordance with applicable Union or national law, has the right to grant access to or share certain personal data or non-personal data'.[7]

A data user, on the other hand, is defined as 'a natural or legal person who has legitimate access to certain personal or non-personal data and who has the right, including under Regulation (EU) 2016/679 in the case of personal data, to use such data for commercial or non-commercial purposes'.[8]

In their joint opinion on the *Data Governance Act* proposal, the European Data Protection Board (EDPB) and the European Data Protection Supervisor (EDPS) expressed their concerns about the tension between data protection principles and the phenomenon of data sharing.[9] In particular, the two authorities highlighted a number of inconsistencies between the GDPR and the proposed regulation.

As regards terminology, the joint opinion noted confusion, if not outright incompatibility, between the notion of 'data owner' contained in the *Data Governance Act* proposal and that of 'data subject' contained in the GDPR, as well as between the notion of 'data user' contained in the Regulation proposal and that of 'data controller' contained in the GDPR. In particular, it was noted that in both cases, conflicts could arise between the rights and prerogatives arising from the aforementioned concepts, as they partially overlap.[10]

The EDPB and the EDPS pointed out that the proposed regulation did not take due account of the need to ensure and guarantee the same level of protection of

[6] Art. 2 (10) DGA.

[7] Art. 2 (8) DGA.

[8] Art. 2 (9) DGA.

[9] 'Joint EDPB-GEPD Opinion 03/2021 on the Proposal for a Regulation of the European Parliament and of the Council on European Data Governance (Data Governance Act)', 8 ff.

[10] Ibid, 9 ff.

personal data as under EU law, raising, on the contrary, serious concerns from the perspective of the protection of fundamental rights.[11]

These concerns were shared by part of the doctrine.[12]

Although the transition between the November 2020 version of the *Data Governance Act* proposal and the one that was subsequently dismissed shows a rethinking of the new language adopted, keeping the notion of 'data subject' in Art. 4(1) GDPR alongside 'data owner' and 'data user', the EU's regulatory evolution towards the so-called commodification of personal data is undeniable. As will be illustrated in the course of the discussion, the new trend is confirmed, among other things, by the reference to the possibility of data recovery in the event of insolvency of the provider of data intermediation services (Art. 12 (h) GDPR).

By stating that the 'data owner' has the right to grant access to or share certain personal or non-personal data for the benefit of data users, the GDPR also emphasises another relevant legal *status*, namely that of 'data users', who have their own individual legal position that can be qualified in various ways, depending on how the data processing takes place, and therefore difficult to define a priori.[13]

The reference to the GDPR indicates cases in which the 'data user' is the holder, as 'data controller', of autonomous legal situations over such data, by virtue of the legal bases in Articles 6 (1) and 9 (2) GDPR.[14]

The rights of users to access and use data generated by IoT devices and to share it with third parties are expressly governed by Regulation (EU) 2023/2854 of the European Parliament and of the Council of 13 December 2023 on harmonised rules on fair access to and use of data and amending Regulation (EU) 2017/2394 and Directive (EU) 2020/1828 (*Data Act, breviter* DA).[15]

Article 2 (11) DA, defines data brokering service as 'a service that aims to establish, through technical, legal or other means, business relationships for the purpose

[11] Ibid.

[12] V. Bravo (2021), p. 239 ff.

[13] Ibid, p. 241.

[14] Bravo (2022), p. 54.

[15] Art. 4 (1) DA 'Where the user cannot directly access the data from the related product or related service, data controllers shall promptly make available to the user the data and relevant metadata necessary to interpret and use those data without undue delay, in the same quality as the data controller, easily, securely, free of charge, in a comprehensive, structured, commonly used, machine-readable format and, where relevant and technically feasible, on a continuous basis and in real time. This shall be done on the basis of a simple request by electronic means, where technically feasible'.

Art. 5 (1) DA 'At the request of a user, or of a party acting on behalf of a user, the data controller shall make the readily available data, as well as the relevant metadata necessary to interpret and use these data, available to third parties without undue delay, in the same quality as the data controller, easily, securely, and free of charge to the user, in a comprehensive, structured, commonly used and machine-readable format and, where relevant and technically feasible, on a continuous basis and in real time. The data shall be made available to the third party by the data controller in accordance with Articles 8 and 9'.

of data sharing between an indeterminate number of data subjects and data owners, on the one hand, and data users, on the other hand'.

In order to be classified as a provider of data brokering services, it is therefore not sufficient to merely provide the technical means for data sharing, without the additional aim of establishing or collecting information on the commercial relationship between data controllers and data users.[16]

The DGA then identifies three types of data brokering services.

The first category relates to 'intermediation services between data controllers and potential data users, including the provision of technical or other means to enable such services; such services may include bilateral or multilateral data exchanges or the establishment of platforms or databases that enable the exchange or joint use of data, as well as the establishment of other specific infrastructure for the interconnection of data controllers with data users'.[17]

The definition in Article 2 (11) DGA includes first and foremost the *data marketplaces*.[18]

Open data marketplaces[19] may fall within the scope of Art. 2 (11) DGA if they help parties to establish business relationships, and do not merely offer assistance with the technical aspects of data sharing.[20]

Data brokers who do not establish direct relationships between data holders and data users—in particular, *data brokers*[21]—are excluded from the scope of the DGA.

Surprisingly, the DGA does not apply to the most established and commercially successful type of data intermediary.

As mentioned, it is necessary that a data broker aims to establish relationships between an indeterminate number of data owners and data users. It follows that the DGA does not cover so-called closed brokering services, i.e. only available to a single data owner or a pre-selected group of companies.[22]

Pursuant to Article 10(a) DGA, providers of technical or other tools necessary to enable the provision of data brokering services are themselves regarded as data brokers. Nonetheless, pursuant to recital 28 DGA, such providers only fall within the scope of the Regulation if the provision of such tools is for the purpose of establishing a business relationship between the parties or enables the acquisition of information on the establishment of such business relationship.

---

[16] See recital 28 DGA.

[17] Art. 10(a) DGA.

[18] On the subject see Koutroumpis et al. (2020), p. 647.

[19] *See Commission Staff Working Document on the free flow of data and emerging issues of the European data economy, Accompanying the document Building a European data economy. Commission, Free flow of data. SWD/2017/2 final*', 17.

[20] Von Ditfurth and Lienemann (2022), pp. 274, 280.

[21] OECD, *Enhancing Access to and sharing of data: Reconciling risks and benefits for data Re-use across societies*, 2019, 37.

[22] See Art. 2 (11) (c) and recital 28 DGA.

Common *cloud* services, data sharing *software*, *web browsers* and e-mail services do not fall within the scope of the Regulation.[23]

Article 10 (b) expressly addresses C2B data intermediaries who provide 'intermediary services between data subjects who intend to make their personal data available or natural persons who intend to make non-personal data available and potential users of the data, including the provision of technical or other means to enable such services, enabling in particular the exercise of data subjects' rights under Regulation (EU) 2016/679′.

This category includes *Personal Information Management Systems*[24] and related services.

These data intermediary service providers assist data subjects in exercising their rights under the GDPR, in particular with regard to the provision or withdrawal of consent to data processing, the right of access to one's own data, the right to rectification of inaccurate personal data, the right to erasure or the right 'to be forgotten', the right to restriction of processing and the right to data portability. In this regard, the DGA considers it essential that the business model of such providers ensures that there are no misaligned incentives for data subjects to use such services to make more data concerning them available for processing than would be in their interest.[25]

The language of the provision evokes the tenor of Article 80 GDPR, which allows data subjects to mandate a non-profit body, organisation or association to exercise their rights under the Regulation itself.[26]

Data subjects may now grant power of attorney to data intermediary service providers to exercise their rights under a mandate contract.

This provision has been introduced with a view to legal systems that do not regulate mandates and, in legal systems where such a contract is already expressly regulated,[27] in order to legally oblige providers of data intermediation services to comply promptly with such a mandate.

Thanks to this new provision, the possibility of using the mandate contract and the obligation on the part of the data intermediary to comply with it are clearly provided for by law.

Finally, Art. 10 (c) DGA includes in the scope of application of the Regulation data brokering services provided by data cooperatives, as defined in Art. 2 (15) DGA.

According to recital 31 DGA, data cooperatives aim to empower individuals to make informed choices before consenting to the use of data by influencing the terms and conditions of services established by data user organisations.

---

[23] See recital 28 DGA.

[24] Zingales (2017), p. 21.

[25] See recital 30 DGA.

[26] Kulms (2022), p. 140.

[27] See, e.g. Art. 1703 of the Civil Code, according to which: 'A mandate is a contract by which one party undertakes to perform one or more legal acts on behalf of the other'.

The work carried out by data cooperatives could also benefit sole proprietorships and SMEs, which, in terms of their knowledge of the data-sharing phenomenon, are often comparable to individuals.

Art. 2 (11) (b) and (d) of the DGA establish further exceptions to the applicability of the Regulation itself: sub-paragraph (b) exempts intermediaries whose main purpose is the intermediation of copyright-protected content from the obligations laid down therein, while sub-paragraph (d) excludes from the scope of application of the DGA data sharing services offered by public entities that do not aim at establishing commercial relationships.[28]

Finally, Art. 15 DGA excludes from the scope of the Regulation organisations recognised for their altruism of data that do not establish commercial relationships.

Despite the definition of the concept of data brokering, the role of data brokering service providers remains ambiguous: conceived as entities capable of guaranteeing the rights of data subjects in the technological context, they may instead end up increasing the profitability of personal data by encouraging their use for commercial purposes.[29] As will be further illustrated in the course of the discussion, this could lead to a reduction of the level of protection of personal data under EU law, resulting in the debasement of fundamental personal rights.

2 The Conditions for the Provision of Data Brokering Services

Article 12 DGA imposes 15 conditions for the provision of data brokering services.

Most of the obligations are aimed at protecting fair competition and ensuring a high level of security for users' data.

First of all, Section 12(a) DGA requires data brokers to refrain from using the data for which they provide brokering services for purposes other than making them available to users.

Data brokering service providers are thus prohibited from analysing and using data shared by data owners for their own purposes (or for any other purpose).[30]

This rule is complemented by the provision in point (c) of the same article prohibiting the use of certain types of metadata for purposes other than enhancing brokering services.

The prohibition of data brokering service providers from using both data obtained from their users and data otherwise collected is intended to avoid situations of conflict of interest.[31] More precisely, the requirement of neutrality addresses concerns

[28] See recital 29 DGA.

[29] Poletti (2022), p. 53.

[30] See recital 33 DGA.

[31] Von Ditfurth and Lienemann (2022), p. 283.

that vertically integrated platforms may in practice play a dual role, being both an intermediary between companies and users and a competitor of those companies in offering their services. An example is a company that, in addition to providing a *marketplace* where independent companies can sell products to consumers, itself sells its own products in competition with independent companies. Such situations leave room for self-preference practices, whereby a platform treats its own services more favourably than those of its competitors.[32]

As mentioned above, providers of data intermediation services may not use data for any purpose other than to make it available to users. It follows that data intermediaries are generally not allowed to offer additional services to their users.

Nevertheless, under Section 12(e) DGA, data intermediaries may offer data-related services whose purpose is to facilitate the exchange of data. For instance, data intermediary service providers may assist their users in anonymising their data.[33]

In order to ensure that the data for which brokering services are provided are not used for other purposes, Article 12(a) of the DGA requires structural separation of brokering services from other business units ('the provider of data brokering services [...] provides data brokering services through a separate legal entity').

Structural separation must ensure that the data or other knowledge gained through the provision of data brokering services cannot be used for other activities carried out by the parent company or other subsidiaries.[34]

Art. 12(b) DGA also prohibits intermediaries from making the commercial terms for the provision of data brokering services, including pricing, dependent on whether the data owner or data user uses other services provided by the same data brokering service provider or a related entity.

Section 12(d) DGA then requires data brokers to exchange data in the format in which they receive them from the data subject or a data owner. This should prevent intermediary service providers from imposing their own *standards* on their users with regard to data format, which could lead to so-called *user* lock-in.[35] Nevertheless, conversion of the data format is allowed if it improves interoperability, is requested by the data user or is necessary to comply with international or European *standards*. In such cases, data owners and data subjects must be offered an *opt-out* option. Alternatively, conversion of the data format may be imposed by Union law: in these cases, data owners and data subjects may not refuse conversion.

According to Article 12(i) DGA, data intermediaries must take appropriate measures to ensure interoperability with other data intermediary services through the use of common and open *standards* in the relevant field.

In this respect, the DGA framework is most recently supplemented by sections 33, 34 and 35 DA, which lay down the essential requirements and conditions for facilitating data interoperability, data sharing mechanisms, common European data

[32] Graef and Gellert (2021), p. 12.

[33] See recital 32 DGA.

[34] Von Ditfurth and Lienemann (2022), p. 284.

[35] Ibid, 285.

spaces and the interoperability of data processing services. Furthermore, Art. 36 DA specifies some essential requirements for data sharing in the context of *smart contracts*.

Data intermediary service providers are also required to adhere to procedures for access to their services that are fair, transparent and non-discriminatory for users, also with regard to the determination of prices and conditions of service (Art. 12 (f) DA).

Data intermediaries are therefore prohibited from treating their users differently without justification. The prohibition of discrimination is intended to prevent possible distortions of competition.

In view of the ability of industry players to exclude other providers from their platforms or otherwise penalise them,[36] Section 12(f) DGA recognises *the gatekeeper* position of data intermediary service providers, obliging them to ensure that the procedure for access to their services is fair, transparent and non-discriminatory for data subjects, data owners and data users, including with regard to prices and conditions of service.

This provision is intended to protect the right of users to simultaneously use several data brokering services offered by different providers (*multi-homing*), since exclusivity clauses imposed by providers on their users are considered unfair.[37]

A fortiori, in order to facilitate access and sharing of relevant data for companies that do not qualify as *gatekeepers*, the DA introduces an unfairness *test for* B2B contractual clauses, imposed on SMEs, on data sharing. More precisely, paragraphs 4 and 5 of Art. 13 DA list a number of unfair or allegedly unfair clauses contrary to good faith and fair dealing.

Section 12(l) DA requires providers of data intermediation services to take the necessary measures to ensure an adequate level of security for the storage, processing and transmission of non-personal data. The highest level of security must also be ensured for the storage and transmission of competitively sensitive information.

According to Article 12(j) DGA, the data intermediary shall implement appropriate technical, legal and organisational measures to prevent the transfer of or access to non-personal data where this is unlawful under Union law or the national law of the Member State concerned. In essence, providers of data brokering services are obliged to monitor their users' data transactions in order to detect possible violations of the law and prevent illegal data transactions.[38]

Focusing on the adequacy of the measures, the provision could be interpreted as meaning that it would be sufficient to implement, on the one hand, mechanisms for reporting violations by third parties and, on the other hand, procedures for the exclusion of unauthorised users.[39]

---

[36] '*Stigler Committee on digital platforms: Final Report*', 2019, 74.

[37] Von Ditfurth and Lienemann (2022), p. 286.

[38] Graef and Gellert (2021), p. 12.

[39] Von Ditfurth and Lienemann (2022), p. 287.

In the event of unauthorised transfer, access or use of shared non-personal data, the data intermediary service provider is obliged to inform the data owners without delay (Art. 12 (k) DGA).

In addition, under Art. 12 (g) of the DGA, data brokering service providers are required to have procedures in place to prevent fraudulent or abusive practices. Data intermediaries are therefore required to verify the reliability of the services available to potential users.

Where data brokers offer data sharing services to natural persons, there is an additional fiduciary duty towards the latter. The data intermediary service provider is indeed obliged to act in the best interests of data subjects when facilitating the exercise of their rights. This includes advising data subjects on the potential uses of their data and the applicable *standard* terms and conditions (Art. 12 (m) DGA).

An important data subject right, the use of which can be facilitated in the context of data sharing services, is the right to data portability.[40]

Scholars have emphasised the 'multifunctional value' of this right, which is capable, on the one hand, of maximising the data subject's control over his or her own data, thus representing the utmost expression of the right to personal data protection in its positive projection, and, on the other hand, being a right that finds its initial justification in the stimulation of the market and competition, the right to data portability represents a driving force for the free movement of data.[41]

Within the framework of the DGA, the right to data portability seems to place more value on the latter aspect, so much so that it appears to be more functional to data controllers than to data subjects.[42]

The intermediary is also required to specify the jurisdiction of the third country in which the data are to be used and to provide data subjects with tools to give and revoke consent and data controllers with tools to give and revoke authorisations to process the data (Art. 12(n) DGA).

In the event of insolvency of the provider of data brokering services, Art. 12 (h) provides for the imposition of reasonable continuity of the provision of such services. Whenever such services ensure the preservation of data, data controllers and data users also have the right to obtain access, transfer or retrieval of their data. Where the provision of data brokering services concerns data subjects on the one hand and data users on the other hand, the provider of data brokering services ensures that the former can exercise their rights.

It is not clear how data intermediaries can ensure the continuity of their services in the event of insolvency, given that, according to the insolvency laws of most Member States, once insolvency proceedings have been initiated, the authority to

---

[40] Art. 20 (4) GDPR. On this topic, see Troiano (2019), p. 197 ff; Pelino (2016), p. 246 ff; Graef et al. (2018), p. 1359 ff; Somani (2018), p. 164 ff.

[41] Troiano (2019), p. 199 ff.

[42] Poletti (2022), p. 55.

decide on the continuation of business activities is transferred to a liquidator or a receiver.[43]

Finally, under Art. 12 (o) DGA, providers of data brokering services are obliged to keep a register of data brokering activities.

3 The Risks of the Data Sharing Phenomenon and the Limits of the DGA

A part of the doctrine has expressed concerns about the adequacy of the DGA framework in relation to its multiple objectives, both questioning its actual potential in terms of achieving a competitive data market and pointing out its inconsistency and even harmfulness in terms of protecting the fundamental rights of data subjects.

Firstly, one cannot help but notice a certain tension between the approach adopted by the DGA to protecting horizontal and vertical competition and its aim of promoting the rise of data brokers.

The strict obligations imposed on data intermediaries to protect competition could result in a severe limitation of the potential value of the data sharing phenomenon. More precisely, by vertically unbundling data brokering services from other data-related services, on the one hand, and by restricting the use of data generated by intermediaries (Art. 12 (a) and (c) DGA), on the other hand, the DGA limits the ability of data brokering service providers to exploit economies of scope.[44] Put differently, data brokers are prohibited from combining data generated by different services in order to obtain valuable information that can increase the quality of data brokering services.

Because of its rigidity, the regulatory framework outlined by the DGA prohibits practices that are without exception competitive and efficient for the development of the EU data economy, thus reducing the value that data brokering services can provide to their users.[45]

Moreover, strict obligations to protect competition will increase the already heavy regulatory burdens placed on data intermediaries.

The aforementioned regulatory provisions could, in some cases, even hinder competitive business practices that favour non-dominant data intermediaries. The process of market experimentation would thus be interrupted at a time when there are still very few successful data intermediaries.[46] In this regard, it should be noted that the addressees of the DGA are young companies that have not yet developed relevant market power.

---

[43] Von Ditfurth and Lienemann (2022), p. 290. See, e.g. Arts. 128-129, Legislative Decree No. 14 ('Business Crisis and Insolvency Code') of 12 January 2019.

[44] Von Ditfurth and Lienemann (2022), p. 289.

[45] Ibid.

[46] Ibid, p. 292. See also Resta (2022), p. 990; Baloup et al.(2021), p. 32.

The scope of the regulatory framework addressed by the DGA can be compared to that of the Regulation (EU) 2022/1925 on fair and contestable markets in the digital area Digital Markets Act (DMA)[47]; however, it is worth noting its different context: whereas the markets addressed by the DMA are rather concentrated, with the presence of a few large US-based players, the data sharing market that the DGA intends to promote is still at a very infant stage.[48]

On the other hand, with regard to the compatibility between the DGA and the need to protect the personal data of data subjects from external aggression, on closer inspection, the new Regulation reproduces the issues relating to the conflict between the mass transfer of personal data through interoperable formats, for easy and rapid reuse of such data, and the principle of data minimisation set out in Article 5(1)(c) of the GDPR.[49]

The promotion of data sharing seems to be hopelessly at odds with the spirit behind the other data subject rights, i.e. the need to minimise data and the risks related to the processing of personal data.

In the new regulation, data subjects' rights seem to be inextricably linked to the stimulation of the market and competition: they appear to be more functional to the commercial activity carried out by intermediaries and data controllers than to the protection of the fundamental rights of data subjects.

The DGA is yet another confirmation of a new way of interpreting the Data Protection Act, whose personalistic principle gradually gives way to the need to promote the free movement of personal data.[50]

The regulatory approach chosen by the DGA, on the one hand, might prevent data brokering service providers from fully exploiting the potential of the data sharing phenomenon, on the other hand, brings with it a tension between data protection principles and *data sharing*, as noted by the EDPB and the EDPS in their joint opinion.

With regard to the latter, there is no doubt that coordination between the DGA and the GDPR requires going beyond general and abstract formulations such as the one contained in Article 1(3) DGA, according to which 'this Regulation is without prejudice to Regulation (EU) 2016/679'.

More generally, the counterbalances provided by the DGA do not seem sufficient to contain the risks of commodification of personal data inherent in data brokering services, especially in light of their vague wording.

At present, the compatibility of the DGA with the rest of the EU *acquis* seems to be a problem whose solution is left to market players. On the contrary, in order to

[47] Baloup et al.(2021), p. 32.

[48] Graef and Gellert (2021), p. 11.

[49] See, with regard to the right to portability, Troiano (2019), pp. 210-211

[50] According to Zorzi Galgano (2019), p. 36 ff., two fundamental rights would emerge from the GDPR, two souls that constitute the expression of the protection envisaged therein: on the one hand, the right of the natural person, the data subject, to the protection of data concerning him or her; on the other hand, the right of the data controller to the processing and circulation of data, both expressions of the freedom of economic initiative.

ensure that the DGA achieves its objectives, its compatibility with EU data protection law should have been considered earlier in the legislative process.

References

Babaloup J, Bayamlıoğlu E, Benmayor A, Ducuing C, Dutkiewicz L, Lalova-Spinks T, Miadzvetskaya Y, Peeters B (2021) White Paper on the Data Governance Act, in CiTiP Working Paper, p 32

Bravo F (2021) Intermediazione di dati personali e servizi di data sharing dal GDPR al Data Governance Act. Contratto e impresa/Europa (1):239 ff

Bravo F (2022) "Destinatario" dell'informazione e trattamento dei dati personali nell'evoluzione dell'ordinamento europeo. In: D'Auria M (ed) I problemi dell'informazione nel diritto civile, oggi. Studi in onore di Vincenzo Cuffaro. RomaTrE-Press, Roma, p 454

Graef I, Gellert R (2021) The European Commission's proposed Data Governance Act: Some initial reflections on the increasingly complex EU regulatory puzzle of stimulating data sharing. In TILEC Discussion Paper, No.006, pp. 11–12

Graef I, Husovec M, Purtova N (2018) Data portability and data control: lessons for an emerging concept in EU law. German Law J 19(6):1359

Koutroumpis P, Leiponen A, Thomas LDW (2020) Markets for data. Ind Corp Chang 29(3):647

Kulms R (2022) Data sharing and data protection. Romanian Rev Private Law (1):140

Pelino E (2016) Diritti dell'interessato. In: Bolognini L, Pelino E, Bistolfi C (eds) Il regolamento privacy europeo. Commentario alla nuova disciplina sulla protezione dei dati personali. Zanichelli, Milano, p 246 ff

Poletti D (2022) Gli intermediari dei dati. Eur J Privacy Law Technol (1):53

Resta G (2022) Pubblico, privato, collettivo nel sistema europeo di governo dei dati. Rivista trimestrale di diritto pubblico, 4, 990

Somani L (2018) The right to data portability and user control: ambitions and limitations. Rivista di diritto dei media (3):164 ff

Troiano S (2019) Diritto alla portabilità dei dati. In: Zorzi Galgano N (ed) Persona e mercato dei dati. Riflessioni sul GDPR. CEDAM, Milano, p 197 ff

Von Ditfurth L, Lienemann G (2022) The data governance act: promoting or restricting data intermediaries? Compet Regul Netw Ind 23(4):274 ff

Zingales N (2017) The rise of "infomediaries" and its implications for antitrust. ASCOLA:21

Zorzi GN (2019) Le due anime del GDPR e la tutela del diritto alla privacy. In: Zorzi Galgano N (ed) Persona e mercato dei dati. Riflessioni sul GDPR. CEDAM, Milano, p 36 ff

Liability for Unlawful Personal Data Processing

Mirko Faccioli

Contents

Abstract This chapter analyses the rules on civil liability for unlawful processing of personal data contained in Article 82 of Regulation 2016/679/EU (the General Data Protection Regulation; GDPR), focusing in particular on the subjective scope of application of the rule, on the delimitation of the concept of unlawful processing, on the reconstruction of the criterion of imputation of liability and on the identification of compensable damages. The discussion highlights the importance of the case law of the EU Court of Justice on the subject, especially in the light of the comparison with the principles and categories of Italian law.

M. Faccioli (✉)
University of Verona, Verona, Italy
e-mail: Mirko.faccioli@univr.it

R. Bocchini (ed.), *Digital Platforms - From Technical Foundations to Legal and Economic Implications*, https://doi.org/10.1007/978-3-032-07978-7_34

1 Introduction: From Article 23, Directive 1995/46/EC to Article 82 GDPR

The rules on civil liability for unlawful processing of personal data have undergone important changes in the succession of the various regulatory measures that have been adopted over the years to regulate the matter.[1]

Article 23, Directive 1995/46/EC originally obliged Member States to give 'any person who suffers damage caused by an unlawful processing operation [...] the right to obtain compensation for the damage suffered by the controller', who could remain wholly or partly exempt from liability by proving that 'the event giving rise to the damage' was 'not attributable to him'. This provision was initially implemented by our legislator with Articles 18 and 29(9) of Law no. 675 of 31 December 1996 on the 'protection of persons and other subjects with regard to the processing of personal data': the former made 'whoever' caused damage to others as a result of the processing of personal data subject to the obligation to pay compensation pursuant to Article 2050 of the Civil Code; the latter sanctioned the possibility of compensation for non-pecuniary damage in cases of violation of Article 9 of the aforementioned law, concerning the methods of data collection and requirements. These provisions were then brought together, without any significant variations in content, in Article 15 of the 'Personal Data Protection Code' set out in Legislative Decree No 196 of 30 June 2003, also known as the '*Privacy* Code'.

Constituting the implementation, moreover meagre and fragmentary, of a European directive, these provisions were naturally destined to be integrated with the Italian regulation of contractual and non-contractual liability, to which they made express reference through the reference to Article 2050 of the Civil Code on the subject of liability for the exercise of dangerous activities.[2]

Article 82, Regulation 2016/679/EU, 'on the protection of individuals with regard to the processing of personal data and on the free movement of such data', the General Data Protection Regulation, better known by the acronym GDPR, has recently distanced itself from the aforementioned provisions, introducing into the system the much more articulated discipline that will be analysed below.

Before proceeding, however, it is necessary to address a methodological issue, concerning the practicability of interpreting Article 82 GDPR in the light of domestic principles and categories and, therefore, in continuity with the previous discipline[3] as well as with the doctrinal and jurisprudential elaboration developed around

---

[1] The need to take this 'diachronic path' into account is well highlighted by Cuffaro (2024), p. 1360.

[2] See, also for further references of conforming doctrine and case law, Navone (2022), pp. 139, 150; Palmerini (2021), p. 2470; Bilotta (2019), p. 446.

[3] In fact, Article 15, Legislative Decree No. 196/2003 was repealed by Legislative Decree No. 101 of 10 August 2018, containing provisions for the adaptation of national legislation to Regulation

the latter. Such an approach, although suggested by some,[4] does not indeed appear to be acceptable, as it contrasts with the clear legislative policy objective pursued by the European Union with the transition from the harmonisation instrument of the directive to the standardisation instrument of the regulation, which is to introduce a unitary regulation of the subject matter in the Member States, which the interpreter is not entitled to reread in the light of the specificities of the national orders.[5]

In the light of these remarks, which have also been recently corroborated by the EU Court of Justice,[6] the gaps and ambiguities of the regulation dictated by Article 82 GDPR must therefore be tackled by looking at the indications coming from the overall framework of Regulation 2016/679/EU and the EU case law that has developed on this subject under the impetus of the preliminary reference tool.[7] Recourse to domestic principles and categories should not, however, be deemed to be excluded,[8] provided that 'the preservation of the correct direction of travel is guaranteed: which is that which starts from the regulation and not from the Italian legislation, from the principles and the ratio of the former, and not vice versa'.[9]

Intertwined with these reflections is the debate on the nature of liability for unlawful processing of personal data, which sees the—indeed more convincing—thesis clearly prevailing that brings Article 82 GDPR within the scope of non-contractual liability,[10] even though there is no shortage of scholars who attribute to the liability in question a contractual nature[11] or a variable nature depending on different criteria.[12] On a practical level, however, the relevance of the question is

2016/679/EU, in which our legislator decided not to include any further provision aimed at specifying or supplementing the provisions of Article 82 GDPR: see Ratti (2019), p. 773.

[4] See Sica (2021), p. 892; Riccio (2022), p. 723; Solinas (2021), p. 142.

[5] Navone (2022), p. 151 ff; Bilotta (2019), p. 448; Cuffaro (2024), p. 1365 ff; Camardi (2020), p. 801; Camardi (2020), p. 1137; Salanitro (2023), p. 429; Scognamiglio (2023), p. 1151; Alonzo (2024a, b), p. 601 ff.

[6] See, in particular, *below*, the EU Court of Justice pronouncements cited in Sect. 5.1.

[7] Salanitro (2023), p. 430.

[8] Salanitro (2023), p. 429; Alonzo (2024a, b), p. 606. Navone (2022), p. 157 ff., is of a different opinion, according to which the hermeneutic questions raised by Art. 82 GDPR could only be addressed by stimulating the clarifying intervention of the EU Court of Justice through the instrument of the preliminary reference.

[9] Camardi (2023), p. 1138.

[10] Among others see, also for the criticism of the opposite thesis that brings the liability *under* Art. 82 GDPR back to the area of non-performance of the obligatory relationship, Palmerini (2021), p. 2477 ff; Tosi (2019), p. 49 ff; Serravalle (2020), p. 44 ff; Gambini (2018), p. 121 ff; Gambini (2019), p. 1081 ff; Barbierato (2019), p. 2154 ff.

[11] Bilotta (2019), p. 450 ff. and Piraino (2017), p. 388 ff., express themselves in this sense, arguing that the articulated plot of normative obligations of conduct provided for in the GDPR in charge of the data controller and the data processor would end up placing the relationship between them and the data subject in the dynamics of an *ex lege* obligatory relationship, arising as a consequence of the data processing activity.

[12] See, in particular, Bravo (2019), p. 383 ff; Zecchin (2022), p. 569.

greatly reduced by the possibility of finding in the provision under examination the regulation of the main aspects of liability discussed,[13] to the examination of which we must now turn our attention.

2 The Subjective Scope of Application

The active legitimacy of the claim for compensation is, under Article 82 GDPR, attributed to 'any person' who suffers damage as a consequence of the unlawful processing of personal data, an expression already used by Article 23, Directive 1995/46/EC and in substance coinciding with the reference to the damage caused 'to others' contained in the previous domestic legislation.[14]

The main active legitimated person is of course the data subject, who in the light of the definition of personal data offered by Article 4(1) GDPR can only be a natural person.[15] In the event of death, the active legitimacy belongs *iure hereditatis* to the successors for damaging events occurring before the passing of the *de cuius*, while for injuries occurring afterwards the position of the person who, pursuant to Article 2-*terdecies*, paragraph 1 of Legislative Decree no. 196/2003, is entitled to exercise the rights of the deceased pursuant to Articles 15–22 GDPR because he 'has an interest of his own, or is acting to protect the data subject, in his capacity as his representative, or for family reasons worthy of protection'.[16]

According to a widespread approach, the reference to 'any person' would then also confer standing on all further persons, other than those mentioned so far, who indirectly suffer harm as a result of the unlawful processing of others' personal data.[17] A part of the doctrine, however, takes a contrary view, according to which the subjects in question could only act on the basis of Article 2043 of the Civil Code.[18]

In terms of passive legitimacy, Article 82 GDPR differs both from Article 23, Directive 1995/46/EC, which only mentioned the 'controller' of the processing, and from the previous domestic regulation, which contained a generic reference to

[13] Which ultimately leaves to the qualification of the nature of the liability under consideration only the aspects of prescription and compensability of unforeseeable damages.

[14] Thobani (2019), p. 1223.

[15] On the legitimacy of the child of age, legitimated to give consent to the processing at the age of 14 pursuant to Article 2-*quinquies*, Legislative Decree no. 196/2003, see Bilotta (2019), p. 456.

[16] Thobani (2019), p. 1223 ff; Tosi (2019), p. 49 ff; Gambini (2018), p. 45; Gambini (2019), p. 1030.

[17] Think, for example, of the damage that the processing of inaccurate or incomplete personal data, possibly contained in a database, may cause to those who have placed a legitimate expectation on the correctness of such data: see Tosi (2019), p. 102; Gambini (2018), p. 46; Gambini (2019), p. 1031; Riccio (2022), p. 725; Barbierato (2019), p. 2156.

[18] Bilotta (2019), p. 455; Thobani (2019), p. 1225.

'anyone' causing damage by processing personal data. Pursuant to the new rules, in fact, the controller and processor are liable for the damage in question, according to the coordinates set out in detail in paragraphs 2, 4 and 5 of Article 82 GDPR.[19]

Pursuant to paragraph 2, the controller, as the person who determines the purposes and means of the processing (Article4(7) GDPR),[20] is subject to a 'general' liability[21] that may arise both from his own conduct and from the conduct of the controller, that is, the person who carries out the processing on behalf of the controller (Article 4(8) GDPR), as well as from the conduct of any joint controller (Article 26 GDPR).[22] The data controller, on the other hand, is obliged to pay compensation when he has failed to fulfil the obligations specifically imposed on data controllers by the GDPR or when he has acted in a manner that is inconsistent with or contrary to the lawful instructions given by the data controller, from which he is therefore obliged to depart if he finds that they are contrary to the law.[23]

For the hypothesis that there is more than one party liable, paragraphs 4 and 5 of the rule provide, irrespective of their capacity, for a regime of joint and several liability aimed at better protecting the injured party and accompanied by the possibility, for those who have compensated the entire damage, of exercising a right of recourse against the others.

For the purposes of the internal division of the indemnification obligation between the owner and the person responsible, it will be necessary to consider what is provided for by the act regulating the relations between the two figures and defining the modalities of processing pursuant to Article 28(3) GDPR.[24] Where the damage was caused solely by the conduct of the data controller, the data controller who compensated the injured party should be able to recover the full amount, unless he in turn can be reproached for having entrusted the task to a data controller who lacked the 'sufficient guarantees' to perform it properly within the meaning of Article 28(1) GDPR.[25] Similarly, for the purposes of apportioning liability among several data controllers, the content of the agreement by which, pursuant to Article 26 GDPR, they are called upon to determine their respective responsibilities with

[19] In the case of different parties, one can therefore only act on the basis of Article 2043 of the Civil Code (Thobani 2019, p. 1226), even jointly with the data controller and data processor (Riccio 2022, p. 725).

[20] On the possibility of recognising this qualification and the consequent liability *under* Article 82 GDPR to *Internet service providers*, search engines and *social networks*, see Tosi (2019), p. 147 ff; Gambini (2018), p. 37 ff; Palmerini (2021), p. 2503.

[21] Sica (2021), p. 892.

[22] Thobani (2019), p. 1227.

[23] Sica (2021), p. 892; Thobani (2019), p. 1229.

[24] Tosi (2019), p. 88; Ratti (2019), p. 783; Palmerini (2021), p. 2503, who points out that the controller is also liable for breaches committed by other controllers to whom it has had recourse under Article 28(4) GDPR.

[25] Thobani (2019), p. 1230.

regard to compliance with their obligations under[26] must be taken into account. Although only the latter provision expressly states this, it must therefore be considered that both the agreement in question and the document referred to in Article 28 GDPR must be made available to the data subject.[27]

In terms of domestic law, the rules set out above appear to be in line with the provisions of Article 1294 of the Civil Code on joint and several obligations and may therefore be considered to be supplemented by Articles 1298 and 1299 of the Civil Code: the former, insofar as it provides that the parties of joint debtors are presumed to be equal, unless proof to the contrary is provided; the latter, insofar as it provides for the consequences of the insolvency of one of the joint debtors.[28]

3 The Unlawful Processing

From an objective point of view, the constituent elements of the liability envisaged by Article 82 GDPR are unlawful processing, consequential damage and the causal link between one and the other: on the basis of Article 2697 of the Civil Code (and net of the clarifications set out below) it is therefore incumbent on the injured party to prove their existence, failing which the claim for damages will be rejected.[29]

Article 23 of Directive 1995/46/EC expressly referred to 'unlawful treatment', whereas the previous national legislation referred only to harmful 'treatment', which was in any case considered to be unlawful by way of hermeneutics.[30] This approach is now confirmed by Article 82 GDPR, which in this regard speaks of 'an infringement of the [...] Regulation', an expression to be understood extensively, in the light of recital 146, so as to also include 'processing that is not in accordance with the delegated and implementing acts adopted pursuant to the [...] Regulation and with the provisions of the law of the Member States that specify provisions of the [...] Regulation'.[31]

On the evidential level, it is considered that it is moreover sufficient for the injured party to allege the infringement in question on the part of the defendant, the

[26] Tosi (2019), p. 88; Ratti (2019), p. 783; Thobani (2019), p. 1230.

[27] Gambini (2018), p. 34; Gambini (2019), p. 1025.

[28] Ratti (2019), p. 782.

[29] See, also in the light of the jurisprudence formed on the previous discipline, Thobani (2019), p. 1233; Gambini (2018), p. 88; Gambini (2019), p. 1060. Regarding the burden of proof of the damage suffered, see, moreover, the rulings of the Court of Luxembourg referred to *below*, in Sect. 5.1.

[30] Cf. Palmerini (2021), p. 2473; Serravalle (2020), p. 18, who also relies on the referral of the former discipline to Article 2050 of the Civil Code.

[31] Bilotta (2019), p. 448; Ratti (2019), p. 776; Gambini (2018), (2019), p. 1032.

latter being required to prove, on the basis of the principle of accountability,[32] that the processing is lawful since it complies with the rules on the subject matter.[33] The plaintiff's burden of allegation will, however, be all the more punctual the less well-defined the obligation whose breach is contested: whoever complains that, for example, the processing is not fair or transparent within the meaning of Article 5(1)(a) GDPR, cannot limit himself to generically alleging its unfairness or lack of transparency, but must indicate precisely for what reasons and in what respects the defendant's conduct does not comply with those parameters.[34]

It seems appropriate to specify, moreover, that the data subject is also required to prove that the harmful processing is attributable to the proprietor or manager allegedly causing the damage. Where the data subject ascribes to a particular data controller the detrimental processing carried out by third parties, he will therefore have to prove not only the latter circumstance, but also the fact that the event giving rise to the damage is referable to the processing carried out by the person against whom the claim for damages has been brought.[35]

4 The Criterion of Imputation of Liability

The liability regime in question has undergone significant changes over the course of time, although it has always been based on the provision of a mechanism for reversing the burden of proof aimed at protecting the injured party against the considerable probative difficulties he would encounter if he had to provide in court a complete and analytical reconstruction of the personal data processing operations carried out by the other party.[36]

As already mentioned, in this perspective, Article 23(2) of Directive 1995/46/EC allowed the defendant to be exempt from liability by providing proof of the non-attributability of the harmful event; and in the light of recital 55, according to which such proof could be provided 'in particular [...] by proving the existence of an error on the part of the person concerned or a case of force majeure', the measure under review seemed to configure a hypothesis of strict liability.[37] With a solution that was

---

[32] On which see Chapter 6.

[33] Thobani (2019), p. 1234, who notes that, otherwise opined, the plaintiff might also have to provide the (almost impossible to give) proof of a negative fact, such as, for example, proof of not having given consent to the treatment.

[34] See Thobani (2019), p. 1234.

[35] Caterina, and Thobani (2019), p. 2807.

[36] Palmerini (2021), p. 2498; Gambini (2018), p. 88; (2019), p. 1060.

[37] Thobani (2019), p. 1230; Navone (2022), p. 133.

appreciated by some,[38] but panned by others as a 'baroque [...] invention',[39] our legislature had transposed the above rule by referring to Article 2050 of the Civil Code, which obliges those who cause damage in the exercise of a dangerous activity to pay compensation unless they prove that they have taken all appropriate measures to avoid it. In this way, the reconstruction of the regime of liability for unlawful processing of personal data had inevitably ended up suffering from the uncertainty that has always characterised the identification of the criterion for imputation of the liability contemplated by the aforementioned codicistic rule.[40]

Article 82(3) GDPR, which provides that the defendant shall be exempt from liability 'if he proves that the event giving rise to the damage is in no way attributable to him', marks a return to the past, taking over in a stricter manner the imputation criterion originally employed by the European legislator and without adding anything else through the recitals. Such exonerating evidence only comes into play if the defendant fails to prove that the processing, contrary to the plaintiff's allegations, is lawful and is precisely aimed at demonstrating that the breach of the law on the processing of personal data cannot be imputed.[41] What this means in terms of the imputation criterion is, however, the subject of much debate.

According to some, the entrepreneurial and professional nature of the processing operations governed by Regulation 2016/679/EU and the markedly preventive approach of the principle of accountability, which underlies the entire regulatory framework of the European measure, would draw Article 82 GDPR into the orbit of strict liability for business risk,[42] from which the defendant could escape only by adducing evidence of unforeseeable circumstances, force majeure, the act of a third party[43] or of the injured party himself.[44]

Observing that 'it would be inconsistent to set up a system aimed at obliging those who process data to adopt an apparatus of measures and instruments aimed

[38] Sica (2021), pp. 890, 892; Riccio (2022), p. 723; Navone (2022), p. 136.

[39] Palmerini (2021), p. 2497.

[40] On this point see, *ampus*, Gambini (2018), p. 68 ff; Gambini (2019), p. 1048 ff.

[41] Cf. Thobani (2019), p. 1233, 1235; Bravo (2019), p. 415.

[42] Cass. 17 September 2020, no. 19328, cited above, also expresses the same view, recognising a line of continuity between the reference to Article 2050 of the Civil Code made by the previous regulations (applied pro tempore to the case at hand) and the wording of Article 82(3) GDPR.

[43] For such a case, see Court of Justice. EU 14 December 2023, Case C-340/21, *VB* v. *Natsionalna agentsia za prihodite*, in *Foro it.*, 2024, IV, 58, with notes by Renna (2024), p. 58 and Riccio (2024); Alonzo (2024a, b), p. 1132. In the present case, the Court of Luxembourg ruled that the data controller cannot be exempt from liability merely because the damage resulted from unauthorised disclosure of personal data or unauthorised access to such data by third parties, since that controller must then prove that the act causing the damage in question is in no way attributable to him.

[44] See, albeit with a variety of accents, Sica (2021), p. 893; Alonzo (2024a, b), p. 615; Tosi (2019), p. 115 ff; Bilotta (2019), p. 460 ff; Camardi (2020), p. 794 ff.

not only at guaranteeing the lawfulness of the processing, but also at demonstrating compliance with regulatory prescriptions, and then not to admit that such a demonstration would be suitable to exclude liability', another orientation, also shared by the most recent case law of the EU Court of Justice,[45] considers the one under consideration to be a liability for presumed fault, from which the defendant could therefore escape by demonstrating—not only the circumstances mentioned above, but also—that he had adopted adequate technical and organisational measures in compliance with the obligations laid down by the GDPR[46] for those who carry out activities involving the processing of personal data,[47] albeit with the exclusion of the relevance of the lack of *culpa in eligendo* or *in vigilando* on the controller or other persons employed by him.[48]

Lastly, according to a further hermeneutical direction, the literal wording of Article 82(3) GDPR would testify to the European legislator's desire to adopt an imputation criterion that varies from case to case, in consideration of factors such as the content—in terms of conduct rather than of result—of the obligation breached by the defendant, the type of data processed, the state of scientific knowledge at the relevant historical moment and, especially, the seriousness of the risk associated with the processing, the increase in which would above all justify the gradual transition from the presumed fault mechanism to the strict liability model.[49]

5 Indemnifiable Damage

Compensable damage is, together with the imputation criterion, the most controversial profile of liability for unlawful processing of personal data. Mentioned only in Directive 1995/46/EC, the subject was dealt with in greater detail by the previous domestic rules, which linked the liability in question to the compensability of non-pecuniary damage. The GDPR has then to some extent followed in the footsteps of our legislator, which in Article 82(1) grants the right to compensation to anyone

[45] ECJ. EU 21 December 2023, Case C-667/21, *ZQ* v. *Medizinischer Dienst der Krankenversicherung Nordrhein, Körperschaft des öffentlichen Rechts*; ECJ. EU 11 April 2024, Case C-741/21, *GP* v. *juris GmbH*; Court of Justice. EU 4 October 2024, Case C-200/23, *Agentsia po vpisvaniyata* v. *OL*, according to which an opinion of the supervisory authority of a Member State issued on the basis of Article 58(3)(b) GDPR is not sufficient to exempt from the liability under scrutiny. For a more in-depth analysis of these rulings, Locatello (2024), p. 1215 ff.

[46] See, in particular, paras 24, 25 and 32 of the Regulation.

[47] See, for this perspective, Thobani (2019), p. 1235 ff. (to which the words in the text belong); Gambini (2018), p. 75 ff; Gambini (2019), p. 1053 ff; Barbierato (2019), p. 2157.

[48] This is also in accordance with Art. 2049 of the Civil Code: see Salanitro (2023), p. 449; Cass., ord. 4 April 2023, no. 9313, with note Riccio (2023a, b), p. 1131. by G.M. Riccio.

[49] See Salanitro (2023), p. 444; Palmerini (2021), p. 2500.

who suffers 'material or immaterial damage' and in recital 146 specifies that 'the concept of damage should be interpreted broadly in the light of the case law of the Court of Justice in such a way as to fully reflect the objectives of the [...] regulation' as well as that 'the persons concerned should obtain full and effective compensation for the damage suffered'.[50]

Faced with such provisions, one must first ask oneself whether the unlawfulness of the processing is sufficient for the establishment of a claim for compensation under Article 82 GDPR, or is it also necessary that some subjective legal situation protected by the system belonging to the plaintiff must be damaged.

The first thesis has, in fact, been argued by some by relying on the autonomy and special nature of the discipline in question, which unlike Article 2043 of the Civil Code does not mention the requirement of the injustice of the damage[51] and would thus lend itself to performing, by operating following the mere violation of the regulations on the processing of personal data, a deterrent-sanctioning function in addition to repairing the damage suffered by the victim of the unlawful act.[52]

The majority doctrine and the practically unanimous case law, both national and European,[53] are, however, oriented in the opposite direction on the basis of a number of solid arguments.[54]

The first observes how it follows from the literal wording of Article 82(1) GDPR 'that the existence of "damage" that has been "suffered" constitutes one of the conditions of the right to compensation provided for in that provision' and that, on the other hand, the 'separate mention of a "damage" and an "infringement" [...] would be superfluous if the Union legislature had considered that an infringement of the provisions of the regulation in question could be sufficient, alone and in any event, to give rise to a right to compensation'. It also follows from a reading of recitals 75 and 85, moreover, that 'a breach of the GDPR does not necessarily entail damage and [...] there must be a causal link between the breach in question and the damage suffered by the data subject in order to found a right to compensation'.[55]

---

[50] For an in-depth reflection on the importance of this *recital* and the role it explicitly assigned to the Court of Justice of the European Union (CJEU). EU v. Cuffaro (2024), p. 1367 ff.

[51] For an extensive reflection on the point, see Buset (2024), p. 1008 ff.

[52] See, also for further references of compliant doctrine, Tosi (2019), p. 103 ff, 268 ff; Bilotta (2019), p. 462 ff (according to which this thesis would also find support in the literal wording of recital 85 of the regulation); Ramaccioni (2017), p. 190 ff; Thiene (2017), p. 443.

[53] See, in particular, ECJ. EU, 4 May 2023, Case C-300/21, *UI* v. *österreichische Post AG*, in *Foro it.*, 2023, IV, 268, with notes by Palmieri and Pardolesi (2023) by Pagliantini (2023); Federico (2023), p.809; with note by Rossi (2024), p.9809; with notes by Alonzo (2023), p.1971, and Baldini (2023).

[54] For the most part, they refer both to the former discipline and to the rule of Art. 82 GDPR, on which attention will however be focused in the remainder of this discourse.

[55] These are the words of ECJ. EU 4 May 2023, Case C-300/21, cit. For similar considerations, see also Cass., ord. 4 April 2023, no. 9313, cit. as well as, in doctrine, Gambini (2018), p. 111; Gambini

These observations, in substance consistent with the well-established domestic principle that recognises the compensability only of the damage-consequences and not of the mere damage-event,[56] are accompanied by the consideration that, otherwise opining, the sum paid under Article 82 GDPR would abandon its proper reparatory function to take on sanctioning connotations that conflict with the very notion of compensation for damage.[57] The fact that this would be an unacceptable distortion of the legal framework is confirmed, on a systemic level, by the provisions of Articles 77, 78, 83 and 84 GDPR, which provide for means of reaction and forms of protection in the event of a breach of the regulation which, irrespective of the occurrence of individual damage, pursue sanctioning and deterrent purposes that cannot therefore be attributed to the civil liability under Article 82 GDPR, otherwise there would be an undue overlapping of the different personal data protection techniques laid down by the law.[58]

Having ascertained that the liability under Article 82 GDPR presupposes the occurrence of damage, there emerges the need to find a selective criterion of the damages—or, if you like, of the subjective situations—that can be compensated, which, by performing a function similar to that assigned in our system to the unfairness of damage clause, avoids the unfair results to which the use of the sole requirement of a causal link could lead.[59] The fact that the protection of subjective positions affected by unlawful processing is not absolute and unconditional is confirmed, moreover, by reading the three paragraphs of Article 1 GDPR, from which it can be inferred that in the regulation the protection of the fundamental rights and freedoms of individuals is always balanced with the objective of guaranteeing and strengthening the free movement of personal data within the Union.[60]

However, the thesis that considers that the existence of a generic 'right to the protection of personal data' can be deduced from the system in the event of a breach of which the liability under Article 82 GDPR can be linked[61] does not appear to respond satisfactorily to the above requirement, because 'the terms of the question are thus reversed, creating a right concerning compliance with the rules of conduct, instead of analysing those rules in order to identify which interests are protected. The so-called right to the protection of personal data does not in itself represent an

(2019), p. 1068; Barbierato (2019), p. 2158.

[56] Camardi (2023), p. 1139; Scognamiglio (2023), p. 1154; Cuffaro (2024), p. 1369; Navone (2024), p. 182; Remotti (2023), p. 726 ff.

[57] Thobani (2019), p. 1242; Serravalle (2020), p. 62.

[58] ECJ. EU 4 May 2023, Case C-300/21, cited above; ECJ. EU 25 January 2024, Case C-687/21, *BL* v. *MediaMarktSaturn Hagen-Iserlohn GmbH*.

[59] Remotti (2023), p. 730.

[60] Camardi (2023), p. 802; Camardi (2020), p. 1140; Cuffaro (2024), p. 1365.

[61] For such an approach see, in particular, Palmerini (2021), p. 2486 ff.

asset to be protected, but is instrumental to the protection of other interests of both an individual and a super-individual nature'.[62]

It seems more reasonable, rather, to distinguish according to the interests protected by the processing rule in question and to focus attention on provisions that protect individual interests rather than those of the general public. In this context, a compensable prejudice may in particular be recognised not only in cases of violation of a rule directly and primarily intended to protect an individual's interest, but also in cases of non-compliance with obligations to adopt security measures followed by the materialisation of the risk that the obligation aims to avert, and in cases of violation of provisions intended to protect the interests of the individual, instrumental to the exercise of his or her individual rights, resulting in the difficulty or impossibility of exercising the rights in question.[63]

5.1 *In Particular, Non-asset Damage*

The issue of non-pecuniary damage deserves further investigation; indeed, the vast majority of claims for damages based on the unlawful processing of personal data are centred on[64] and, moreover, it is expressly mentioned and qualified as compensable, albeit using the syntagma 'immaterial damage', by Article 82 GDPR. In this way, the regulation integrates the reference to the 'cases determined by law' provided for the indemnifiability of this type of prejudice by Article 2059 of the Civil Code, even if in light of the consolidated jurisprudential orientation that considers non-asset damage indemnifiable even in the presence of the injury of rights and interests inherent to the person of constitutional rank—but we will return to this point later—this aspect may no longer be as relevant as in the past, if it is true that the protection of personal data falls within the scope considered above.[65]

Precisely by reasoning on the type of subjective prerogatives that may be injured by the unlawful processing of data, one must indeed ask oneself whether it is always correct to apply the principle of the irrelevance of the damage-event and of the compensability of only the damage-consequences.

[62] Thobani (2019), p. 1243.

[63] Thobani (2019), p. 1244.

[64] Which obviously does not exclude that the unlawful processing of personal data may cause pecuniary damage, such as, for example, the refusal to grant a loan following an unlawful report in the risk centre, unlawful discrimination in access to a job following profiling, or the loss of personal data useful for the economic activity of the person concerned: Caterina and Thobani (2019), p. 2809.

[65] See, on this point, Serravalle (2020), p. 67 ff; Bilotta (2019), p. 465; Zecchin (2022), p. 573 ff; Gambini (2018), p. 100 ff; Gambini (2019), p. 1072 ff.

This solution does indeed appear to be appropriate when a rule of a technical-organisational nature has been violated so as to allow the person concerned control over the circulation of his personal data by means of rights of information, access, rectification, complaint, objection, and the like: in these cases, that is, it seems entirely reasonable to condition the claim for compensation on the actual materialisation of negative repercussions in the personal sphere of the plaintiff, which are by no means certain to occur in the variety of individual cases.[66] However, when the unlawful treatment undoubtedly prejudices fundamental personal rights of constitutional importance, in particular linked to the expression of the freedom, identity and dignity of the individual,[67] it would be necessary, according to some, to recognise that the non-asset damage that can be compensated is *in re ipsa* since it consists precisely in the event constituted by the offence to the person, in relation to which it would not even be conceivable to have further prejudicial consequences to which only the right to compensation could be linked.[68]

All this, according to others, would find important confirmation in our jurisprudence, which even through the use of the presumptive mechanism would not actually require the plaintiff to prove that he had suffered harmful consequences of a non-pecuniary nature in relation to the injury to assets such as honour, reputation, personal identity and the private intimacy of the person, while outside of these cases it would subordinate the acceptance of the claim for damages to the demonstration of having actually suffered discomfort, disturbance, suffering or disturbance of some kind as a result of the unlawful treatment.[69]

Moreover, our judges are firm in subordinating the compensation of immaterial damage caused by the unlawful processing of personal data to the requirements, consistently applied by the courts to all hypotheses of non-asset damage, of the seriousness of the injury to the protected subjective situation and the seriousness of the prejudice suffered by the victim of the unlawful processing, the lack of which is considered to entail the non-recoverability of so-called trivial damages in order to balance the principle of solidarity under Article 2 of the Constitution.[70]

---

[66] A paradigmatic example of these hypotheses is the unlawful dissemination of the name and contact data of the interested party, who, in order to obtain compensation, will have to prove that he has suffered subsequent and further damaging activities (e.g. persecutory conduct by third parties or the massive reception of unwanted advertising material) or that, due to the peculiarities of the case, the mere dissemination of his data was the source of a state of anxiety and apprehension deserving to be compensated with a sum of money.

[67] Such as in cases of unlawful disclosure of data concerning the health, personal history or judicial history of the person concerned.

[68] Camardi (2023), p. 1141 ff; Camardi (2020), p. 804. For similar considerations, see also Alpa (2023), p. 13.

[69] Caterina and Thobani (2019), p. 2809; (2019), p. 1247 ff; (2017), p. 427 ff.

[70] For extensive references on the point, see Navone (2022), p. 140 ff.

Although shared by several scholars,[71] this approach has been criticised from two different points of view: on the one hand, for wishing to derive from an improper reference to the constitutional principle of solidarity the unacceptable result of deeming tolerable, within a certain threshold, violations of rights that are in reality constitutionally inviolable or in any case expressly qualified by law as indemnifiable pursuant to Art. 2059 of the Civil Code; on the other hand, to reshape by way of interpretation in the light of the principles of national law the meaning of a rule contained in a European regulation, as such incapable of being subjected to such hermeneutic operations.[72]

Relying precisely on the latter argument, as well as on the absence of any mention of a threshold for the extent of the damage to be compensated in Article 82 GDPR and on the invitation to interpret broadly the concept of damage contained in recital 146 of the regulation, the Court of Justice has also recently clarified that a national rule or practice that makes compensation for damage caused by unlawful processing of personal data subject to the condition that the damage suffered by the data subject has reached a certain level of seriousness is incompatible with the provision in question. To hold otherwise, the Court of Luxembourg added, would also run the risk of subordinating the compensability of non-pecuniary damage to the assessments of individual national courts, thus undermining the objective of the regulation of ensuring a consistent and high level of protection of natural persons with regard to the processing of personal data throughout the Union.[73]

Referring to essentially the same arguments, together with the observation that this reading is compatible with the literal wording of Art. 82 GDRP as well as with the mention of the 'loss of control of personal data' in recital 85 of the Regulation, the Luxembourg Court also ruled that even the fear of a mere potential misuse of one's own personal data by third parties, nurtured by the plaintiff as a result of the infringement of the regulation, may in itself constitute compensable immaterial damage, provided that the national court ascertains whether it is justified in relation

[71] Caterina and Thobani (2019), p. 1810; Thobani (2019), p. 1251; Barbierato (2019), p. 2158; Gambini (2018), p. 107 ff; Gambini (2019), p. 1071.

[72] Tosi (2019), p. 229 ff; Serravalle (2020), p. 84; Bravo (2023), p. 426 ff; Viglianisi Ferraro (2020), p. 85 ff.

[73] See, among others, ECJ. EU 4 May 2023, Case C-300/21, cit.; ECJ. EU 25 January 2024, Case C-687/21, cit.; ECJ. EU 14 December 2023, Case C-456/22, *VX, AT* v. *Gemeinde Ummendorf*. It seems to be in line with the orientation of the Court of Justice Cass. 12 May 2023, no. 13073 with note by Riccio (2023a, b), p. 1125, according to which the victim of an unlawful processing of personal data 'may obtain compensation for any damage occurred to him, even if the injury is marginal', while confirming that 'the right to compensation does not escape the verification of the seriousness of the injury and the seriousness of the damage'.

to the specific circumstances and in respect of the interested party[74] and with the exclusion of cases where the possibility of such misuse actually constitutes only 'a purely hypothetical risk'.[75] As has been observed in doctrine, compensation should not, therefore, be granted on the basis of the mere subjective appreciation of the person concerned, as such changeable depending also on character factors, but only on the basis of the verification of demonstrable objective elements that render the risk feared by the plaintiff effective and concrete, possibly also on the basis of a social-typical assessment of the harmful consequences of the violation committed.[76]

In order to avert the danger of a 'judicial flood' of pretextual claims for compensation triggered by these guidelines,[77] naturally destined to prevail over the various lines of Italian jurisprudence referred to above,[78] particular attention must indeed be paid to satisfying the burden of proof concerning the non-asset damage suffered by the plaintiff[79] as well as the connected profile of the quantification of the compensation to be awarded.

With regard to the first aspect, it has always been held that, by virtue of its very elusive and intangible nature, non-asset damage can be proved by means of presumptions, provided that all the elements necessary to reconstruct the concatenated series of known facts that allow the judge to go back to the unknown fact are adequately indicated by the injured party.[80] Even by resorting to this inferential mechanism, however, it appears rather difficult to establish, once the requirement of the seriousness of the damage complained of has been set aside, the threshold from which one passes from the allegation of a mere feeling of irritation and annoyance, as such irrelevant, to the demonstration of a genuine intangible prejudice compensable under Article 82 GDPR, the appreciation of which will in any case be largely

[74] ECJ. EU 14 December 2023, Case C-340/21, cited above. See also ECJ. EU 20 June 2024, case C-590/22, *AT*, *BT* v. *PS GbR*, *VG*, *MB*, *DH*, *WB*, *GS* as well as ECJ. EU 4 October 2024, Case C-200/23, cited above, according to which a loss of control of limited duration, by the data subject, over his personal data may be sufficient to cause compensable immaterial damage, provided that person proves that he has actually suffered such damage, however slight, but without that notion of immaterial damage requiring a demonstration of further tangible negative consequences.

[75] ECJ. EU 25 January 2024, Case C-687/21, cited above.

[76] Riccio (2024), p. 82; Scognamiglio (2023), p. 1157.

[77] The expression is from Riccio (2024), p. 76.

[78] Scognamiglio (2023), p. 1155 ff; Camardi (2023), p. 1145.

[79] On this subject see, in general, Maietta (2023).

[80] See Scognamiglio (2023), p. 1155; Gambini (2018), p. 113; Gambini (2019), p. 1075; Palmerini (2021), p. 2496; Riccio (2022), p. 728; Solinas (2021), p. 146. On the other hand, the isolated pronouncement of Cass. 4 June 2018, no. 14242, in *Giur. it.*, 2019, 41, according to which non-asset damage caused by unlawful processing of personal data should be considered *in re ipsa*, unless the damaged party proves that there was no such damage, or that it is an irrelevant or trivial damage, or that the damaged party has benefited from the unlawful processing.

left to the discretion of the judge, just as it would have been with the parameter of seriousness.[81]

As far as the liquidation of (non-pecuniary) damage is concerned, it should be noted that the Court of Luxembourg considers the issue to be left to national law since it is not governed by the GDPR and relates to the procedural modalities of judicial remedies,[82] with the limitation of compliance with the principles of equivalence and effectiveness of EU law[83] and with the clarification of the compensatory and not punitive function of the compensation under discussion.[84] It follows that, for the purposes of its quantification, no account must be taken of the degree of seriousness or of the possible intentional nature of the breach committed by the defendant[85] or of the fact that he has committed multiple breaches of the regulation in the unlawful processing of the plaintiff's data,[86] nor can the criteria for setting the amount of the administrative pecuniary sanctions provided for in Article 83 GDPR[87] be used. Instead, it is necessary to calculate the amount by looking at the need to fully compensate, that is, in a full and effective manner, the prejudice concretely caused by the infringement in question, bearing in mind that intangible damage is not to be considered, by its nature, less serious than a personal injury and that, in the event of minor damage, the national court may also award a minimum compensation, provided that it is such as to fully compensate the prejudice suffered by the plaintiff.[88]

In the light of these indications, evidently incapable of avoiding differences in the application of Article 82 GDPR in the Member States,[89] the guidelines of our case-law are therefore of decisive value, which settles the compensation in question, in conformity with the orientation generally adopted for all cases of non-asset damage, resorting to the equitable assessment *pursuant to* Article 1226 of the Civil Code[90] and considering elements such as, above all, the more or less 'sensitive'

---

[81] Cf. Alonzo (2024a, b), p. 619 ff; Pagliantini (2023), p. 292; Baldini (2023), p. 1994, who indeed consider that, in order to obviate the problem, it would be necessary to exclude the possibility of resorting to the presumptive mechanism in the matter under examination.

[82] See, for all, ECJ. EU 4 May 2023, Case C-300/21, cit. He criticises this stance Navone (2024), p. 190., who observes that liquidated damages are substantive and not procedural issues.

[83] Emphasises the vagueness of this formula, Patti (2023), p. 1148.

[84] See, among others, ECJ. EU 25 January 2024, Case C-687/21, cited above; ECJ. EU 20 June 2024, Cases C-182/22 and C-189/22, *JU* v. *SO*.

[85] ECJ. EU 20 June 2024, Cases C-182/22 and C-189/22, cit. In the same line of thought, see also ECJ. EU 14 December 2023, case C-456/22, cit. and ECJ. EU 4 October 2024, Case C-507/23, *A* v. *Patērētāju tiesību aizsardzības centrs*, which ruled out that the defendant's attitude and motivation could be taken into account in order to possibly grant the person concerned compensation less than the damage suffered.

[86] ECJ. EU 11 April 2024, Case C-741/21, cited above.

[87] ECJ. EU 11 April 2024, case C-741/21, cit.; ECJ. EU 20 June 2024, case C-590/22, cit.

[88] ECJ. EU 20 June 2024, Cases C-182/22 and C-189/22, cit.

[89] Baldini (2023), p. 1996; Rossi (2024), p. 814.

[90] Which is sometimes also necessary in the quantification of pecuniary loss, for example in cases of unlawful reporting to the Centrale Risks, where problems often arise in the liquidation of loss of profit: Palmerini (2021), p. 2504.

nature of the data subjected to unlawful processing; the duration of the processing itself; the degree of intrusiveness of the damaging conduct and the pervasiveness of the means used for processing; the intensity and persistence of the inner suffering suffered by the victim (also in the light of his social, economic and professional conditions); the radius of dissemination of the undue data processed; the public office, the institutional or professional role, or more generally the notoriety of the injured person; the nature, public or private, of the author of the unlawful processing.[91]

Observing the rulings issued so far on the subject, two aspects worthy of note can be highlighted in conclusion.

The first is the considerable lack of homogeneity in the compensation awarded, which is also favoured by the lack of tables useful for guiding judges, from which it seems to emerge that 'what is lacking is not so much the objective parameters for settling damages, albeit in the variability of concrete cases, but rather the orders of magnitude of the amounts to be associated with them'.[92]

The second is the punitive nature that, albeit only implicitly (if not unconsciously), the quantification of compensation takes on in some rulings, according to a hermeneutic trend that, if on the one hand has always characterised the compensation of non-pecuniary damage and has even recently been revived by the rekindling of the debate on the sanctioning and deterrent function of civil liability,[93] on the other hand clearly collides with the guidelines of the Court of Luxembourg, which we have seen decisively deny the possibility of attributing such a role to liability under Article 82 GDPR.

References

Alonzo E (2023) La risarcibilità del danno "bagatellare" in materia di violazioni della normativa GDPR. In Resp civ. prev., p 1971 ff

Alonzo E (2024a) Il risarcimento del danno per violazioni del GDPR (art. 82 reg. Ue 2016/679). La tutela della persona nelle logiche del diritto privato regolatorio?. In Nuove leggi civ. comm., p 601 ff

Alonzo E (2024b) Le interferenze tra liability e accountability nel regolamento sulla protezione dei dati personali. In Resp civ. prev., p 1132 ff

Alpa G (2023) Danno in re ipsa e tutela dei diritti fondamentali (diritti della personalità e diritto di proprietà). In Resp civ. prev., p 13 ff

Baldini R (2023) Danno da trattamento illecito di danni personali: non basta l'ingiustizia ma sono sufficienti danni conseguenza "bagatellari" (basta provarli). In Resp civ. prev., p 1985 ff

Barbierato D (2019) Trattamento dei dati personali e "nuova" responsabilità civile. In Resp civ. prev., p 2151 ff

[91] See Navone (2022), p. 146 ff; Tosi (2019), p. 241 ff: Gambini (2018), p. 114 ff; Gambini (2019), p. 1075 ff.

[92] Thus Palmerini (2021), p. 2506.

[93] Cf. Scognamiglio (2023), p. 1159; Palmerini (2021), p. 2508; Navone (2022), p. 150; Ramaccioni (2017), p. 1214 ff.

Bilotta F (2019) La responsabilità civile nel trattamento dei dati personali. In: Panetta R (ed) Circolazione e protezione dei dati personali, tra libertà e regole del mercato, Giuffrè, Milano, p 445 ff

Bravo F (2019) Riflessioni critiche sulla natura della responsabilità da trattamento illecito di dati personali. In: Zorzi Galgano N (ed) Persona e mercato dei dati. Riflessioni sul GDPR. CEDAM, Milano, p 383 ff

Bravo F (2023) Il principio di solidarietà in materia di protezione dei dati personali nelle decisioni del Garante e della Corte di cassazione. In Contr. impr., p 405 ff

Buset G (2024) Ingiustizia del danno e antigiuridicità del fatto nella responsabilità da trattamento di dati personali. In Riv. dir. civ., p 1008 ff

Camardi C (2020) Note critiche in tema di danno da illecito trattamento dei dati personali. In Jus Civile, p 801 ff

Camardi C (2023) Illecito trattamento dei dati e danno non patrimoniale. Verso una dogmatica europea. In Nuova giur. civ. comm., p 802 ff

Caterina R, Thobani S (2019) Il diritto al risarcimento dei danni. In Giur. it., p 280 ff

Cuffaro S (2024) Risarcimento del danno e trattamento dei dati personali. in Enciclopedia del diritto, I tematici, VII, Responsabilità civile, Giuffrè, Milano, p 1360 ff

Federico M (2023) "La tempesta perfetta": ultime dalla Corte di Lussemburgo su danno (non patrimoniale) da illecito trattamento dei dati personali e possibili risvolti in tema di tutela collettiva. In Foro it., IV, p 809 ff

Gambini ML (2018) Principio di responsabilità e tutela aquiliana dei dati personali. Edizioni Scientifiche Italiane, Napoli

Gambini ML (2019) Responsabilità e risarcimento nel trattamento dei dati personali. In: Cuffaro V, D'Orazio R, Ricciuto V (eds) I dati personali nel diritto europeo. Giappichelli, Torino, p 1017 ff

Locatello DM (2024) Adeguata gestione del rischio e presunzione di colpa nell'imputazione del danno da illecito trattamento di dati personali. In Contr. impr., p 1215 ff

Maietta A (2023) La prova del danno da illecito trattamento di dati personali. Cacucci editore, Bari

Navone G (2022) Ieri, oggi e domani della responsabilità civile da illecito trattamento dei dati personali. In Nuove leggi civ. comm., p 132 ff

Navone G (2024) La costruzione dello statuto eurounitario del "danno immateriale": la prima pietra della Corte di giustizia. In Ordines, p 182 ff

Pagliantini S (2023) Un altro palcoscenico della "guerra" tra le corti: il danno (immateriale) bagatellare dell'art. 82 Gdpr. In Foro it., IV, p 292 ff

Palmerini R (2021) Responsabilità da trattamento illecito dei dati personali. In: Navarretta E (ed) Codice della responsabilità civile, Milano

Palmieri A, Pardolesi R (2023) Mai futile il danno non patrimoniale da violazione della privacy (purché lo si provi!). In Foro it., IV, p 268 ff

Patti D (2023) Il risarcimento del danno immateriale secondo la Corte di giustizia. In Nuova giur. civ. comm., p 1148 ff

Piraino F (2017) Il regolamento generale sulla protezione dei dati personali. In Nuove leggi civ. comm., p 388 ff

Ramaccioni G (2017) La protezione dei dati personali e il danno non patrimoniale. Jovene, Napoli

Ratti M (2019) La responsabilità da illecito trattamento dei dati personali. In: Finocchiaro G (ed) La protezione dei dati personali in Italia. Regolamento UE n. 2016/679 e d.lgs. 10 agosto 2018, n. 101. Zanichelli, Bologna, p 773 ff

Remotti G (2023) Evento e danno nella responsabilità per trattamento di dati personali. In Pers. merc., p 726 ff

Renna M (2024) I dati personali al sicuro: diritti, responsabilità, tutele. In Foro.it, IV, p 58 ff

Riccio GM (2022) Art. 82. Diritto al risarcimento e responsabilità. In: Riccio GM, Scorza G, Belisario E (eds) GDPR e normativa privacy. Commentario, 2nd edn. Wolters Kluwer, Milano

Riccio GM (2023) Dati personali e rimedi: diritti degli interessati e profili risarcitori. In Nuova giur.comm., p 1125 ff

Riccio GM (2024) Danni non patrimoniali per violazione dei dati personali: verso un'alluvione giudiziaria?. In Foro.it, IV, p 58 ff

Rossi V (2024) Violazione dell'art. 82 GDPR: risarcimento del danno da illecito trattamento di dati. In Giur. it., p 809 ff
Salanitro U (2023) Illecito trattamento dei dati personali e risarcimento del danno nel prisma della Corte di Giustizia. In Riv. dir. civ., p 426 ff
Scognamiglio C (2023) Danno e risarcimento nel sistema del Rgpd: un primo nucleo di disciplina eurounitaria della responsabilità civile?.In Nuova giur. civ. comm., p 1151 ff
Serravalle S (2020) Il danno da trattamento dei dati personali nel GDPR. Edizioni Scientifiche Italiane, Napoli
Sica S (2021) Art. 82. Diritto al risarcimento e responsabilità. In: D'Orazio R, Finocchiaro G, Pollicino O, Resta G (eds) Codice della privacy e data protection. Giuffrè, Milano
Solinas C (2021) Danno non patrimoniale e violazione del diritto alla protezione dei dati personali. In Nuova giur. civ. comm., p 142 ff
Thiene A (2017) Segretezza e riappropriazione di informazioni di carattere personale: riserbo e oblio nel nuovo Regolamento europeo. In Nuove leggi civ. civ. comm., p 410 ff
Thobani S (2017) Il danno non patrimoniale da trattamento illecito dei dati personali. In Dir. inf., p 427 ff
Thobani S (2019) Art. 82. Diritto al risarcimento e responsabilità. In: Barba A, Pagliantini S (eds) Delle persone. Leggi collegate, II. In Commentario del codice civile, directed by E. Gabrielli. Wolters Kluwer, Torino
Tosi E (2019) Responsabilità civile per illecito trattamento dei dati personali e danno non patrimoniale, Giuffrè, Milano
Viglianisi Ferraro A (2020) Danno da illegittimo trattamento dei dati personali, tra "inasprimento sanzionatorio" europeo ed "interpretazioni restrittive" della giurisprudenza italiana. In Riv. dir. priv., p 85 ff
Zecchin F (2022) Molteplicità delle fonti e tutela dei diritti. Il danno non patrimoniale nella lesione della proprietà e dei dati personali. In Eur. dir. priv., p 517 ff

Data Transfer to Non-EU Countries

Matteo Ortino

Contents

Abstract This chapter carries out an analysis of the main aspects of the EU rules contained in Regulation 2016/679 on the circulation of data from the Union to third countries, highlighting some critical issues, including those related to the effectiveness of the Commission's supervisory role and the proportionality of the burdens imposed on the companies involved in the circulation of data.

M. Ortino (✉)
University of Verona, Verona, Italy
e-mail: matteo.ortino@univr.it

R. Bocchini (ed.), *Digital Platforms - From Technical Foundations to Legal and Economic Implications*, https://doi.org/10.1007/978-3-032-07978-7_35

1 Objectives, Tools and Scope of Regulation 2016/679 ('GDPR') on International Data Flows: Introduction

The legal regulation of international data flows is spoken of in terms of a 'dilemma', thinking of the inverse relationship between data protection and the promotion of international trade.[1] On the one hand, once data have been transferred to a third country, the protection of the relevant individual rights provided by European Union (EU) law and the supervisory authorities practically disappears, both in substantive terms and in administrative and jurisdictional terms. On the other hand, personal data flows to and from countries outside the EU are necessary for the expansion of international trade and international cooperation.

Faced with this dilemma, the choice of the EU legislator and the EU Court of Justice ('Court') has been to let individual rights prevail over commercial needs. The Court declared that individuals may not be deprived of their fundamental rights through the transfer of their data to third countries.[2]

The General Data Protection Regulation (hereinafter 'Regulation' or 'GDPR')[3] pursues both objectives: that of protecting the fundamental rights and freedoms of natural persons, in particular the right to the protection of personal data, and that of ensuring the free flow of such data (Article 1), both within the EU (Recital 166) and outside the EU (Recital 101). However, the protection of rights has priority: it constitutes the rule, which may be derogated from only within certain limits and under certain conditions, resulting, e.g. from the application of the principle of proportionality to state interference in fundamental rights.

According to the Regulation, and in particular Articles 44 to 50 (Chapter V) thereof, the transfer of personal data to a third country may in principle only take place if the third country in question ensures an 'adequate level of protection' for those data (Article 45).[4] As will be specified below, such a level of protection is achieved if the conditions laid down in the aforementioned articles are met, i.e. more concretely, if a level of protection of fundamental rights and freedoms, related

---

[1] Schantz (2023), p. 776.The Advocate General in his conclusions, 19 December 2019, *Schrems II*, Case C-311/18, pt. 7 expressed himself in terms of 'striking a balance between, on the one hand, the need to demonstrate "a reasonable degree of pragmatism to enable interaction with the rest of the world", and, on the other hand, the need to affirm the fundamental values recognised in the legal systems of the Union and its Member States, in particular by the Charter', quoting the speech of the former European Data Protection Supervisor, Hustinix (2015), p. 49.

[2] Court of Justice EU 6 October 2015, *Schrems I*, Case C-362/14, pt. 58.

[3] Regulation (EU) 2016/679 of the European Parliament and of the Council of 27 April 2016 on the protection of individuals with regard to the processing of personal data and on the free movement of such data and repealing Directive 95/46/EC (OJ 2016, L 119, p. 1). In the remainder of this writing, the articles indicated without reference to the legislative source are those of the Regulation.

[4] A third country is defined as a country that is not a Member State of the Union or of the European Economic Area (EEA). International organisations (Art. 4(26)) are treated as third countries, even if they are situated in the territory of the EU, due to the immunities and privileges granted by the host Member State.

to data processing, can be guaranteed in the third country that is 'substantially equivalent' to that guaranteed within the Union by virtue of the Regulation, read in the light of the Charter of Fundamental Rights of the European Union ('Charter').[5] The aim is therefore to prevent the transfer of data outside the Union from circumventing and thus nullifying the relevant rules provided for at data protection.[6]

Pursuant to Article 44, '[a]ny transfer of personal data that is undergoing processing or is intended for processing after transfer to a third country or an international organisation, including onward transfers of personal data from a third country or an international organisation to another third country or another international organisation, shall take place only if *the conditions laid down in this Chapter are complied with by the* controller and processor, without prejudice to the *other provisions of* this Regulation. All the provisions of this Chapter shall be applied in order to ensure that the level of protection of natural persons guaranteed by this Regulation is not adversely affected'.[7]

In addition to the conditions laid down in Chapter V, the Regulation contains further rules governing international transfers of data,[8] which Article 44 itself preserves. Moreover, as already mentioned, the provisions of Chapter V must be read in the light of the Charter, since, as confirmed by the Court, the applicability of EU law entails the application of the Charter.[9]

That said, with regard to the above dilemma, some further reflections, some of which are opposite to those just set out, are in order. First of all, the inverse relationship between data protection and international trade is, at least in some respects, only apparent. The protection of personal data in an extraterritorial dimension does not necessarily conflict with commercial interests. Such protection can also contribute to the smooth functioning of the market insofar as it avoids the distortions of international competition that companies subject to a stricter data protection regime have to suffer compared to competitors from more *business-friendly* jurisdictions.[10] Second, data protection in the international sphere is related not only to commercial interests, but also to other public needs, such as those related to national security. In this regard, after an examination of the relevant legislation, the focus at the end of this chapter will be on the issue of balancing personal data protection with other national public interests of third countries.

As regards the scope of application of the regulation, personal data means any information relating to an identified or identifiable natural person (Article 4(1)). The transfer of personal data carried out for commercial purposes by an economic operator established in a Member State to another economic operator established in a

---

[5] ECJ 16 July 2020, *Schrems II*, C-311/18, pt. 94.

[6] ECJ 6 October 2015, *Schrems I*, Case C-362/14, pt. 73, where the Court explicitly refers to the risk of circumvention of EU law. See also Opinion of the Court of Justice. EU 1/15, 26 July 2017, pt. 93.

[7] Italics added.

[8] Arts. 5 and 6, Arts. 13(1)(f), 14(1)(f), 15(2), 28(3)(a), 30(1)(2), 30(2)(c), 58(2)(j).

[9] ECJ 26 February 2013, *Åkerberg* Fransson, Case C-617/10, pt. 21.

[10] As Schantz (2023), p. 777.

third country falls within the scope of the Regulation. Thus, the link with the Union—which justifies the extraterritorial application of the regulation under review—seems to be the collection of data on the territory of the EU for further processing in a third country (or in an international organisation).

In the light of the protection objective of the Regulation, 'transfer' must be understood as meaning not only the movement of data in the strict sense of the term, including their storage in a computer cloud located in a third country or their transit through the EU, provided that they are unencrypted readable data; but also transfer understood as an act that, while not moving the data, makes them accessible from a third country.[11]

In addition, the Regulation also covers cases where, during or after the transfer, such data may be processed by the authorities of the third country in question for purposes of public security, defence and State security.[12] Indeed, the Court has made it clear that this type of data processing by the authorities of a third country cannot exclude such a transfer from the scope of the Regulation.

These rules also cover 'onward transfers', i.e. those where data, after having been transferred from the EU to a third country (or international organisation), are transferred back to another third country (or international organisation). The Court has made it clear that the same level of protection (equivalent to that guaranteed by EU law) must also be guaranteed for such retransfers in order to avoid, again, circumventing the protection regime provided by the EU.[13] How this guarantee is to be provided is not certain.[14] If the onward transfer is already foreseen, because it is planned in advance, or is in any case foreseeable, the first transfer and the onward transfer could be allowed if they fulfil the conditions set out in the Regulation (e.g. the 'onward' third country is the subject of an equivalence decision by the Commission *under* Article 45). In other cases, the controller/processor would have to provide the appropriate safeguards under Article 46 or one of the derogations under Article 49 must be applicable (see *below*).

According to the Regulation, the guarantee of adequate protection of personal data to be transferred to a third country can be provided in three ways.

First, the Commission may find that, thanks to its national legislation or international commitments, the third country ensures an adequate level of protection (Article 45). To this end, the Commission adopts an adequacy decision. Second, in the absence of such a decision, such a transfer may only take place if the data exporter, established in the Union, provides adequate safeguards and the data subjects have enforceable rights and effective remedies (Article 46). Third, the Regulation provides for derogations in specific situations by setting out the conditions under which a transfer of personal data to a third country may take place in the absence of an adequacy decision or adequate safeguards (Article 49).

[11] Kuner (2020), p. 755 ff.

[12] ECJ 16 July 2020, *Schrems II*, Case C-311/18, pt. 89.

[13] Opinion of the Court of Justice. EU 1/15, 26 July 2017, pt. 214.

[14] See to that effect Schantz (2023).

The Regulation (Articles 51(1) and 57(1)(a)) and the Charter (Article 8(3)) entrust the competent national supervisory authorities with the task of monitoring compliance with Union rules on the protection of natural persons with regard to the processing of personal data. Therefore, each of them is vested with the competence to verify whether a transfer of personal data from its Member State to a third country complies with the requirements of the Regulation. The exercise of this function is of particular importance in the context of a transfer of personal data to a third country, since, with cross-border transfers of personal data outside the Union, the risk may increase that the individual may not be able to exercise his or her right to data protection, in particular to protect himself or herself against unlawful use or disclosure of such information. Since these events take place outside the Union, supervisory authorities may be in the position of not being able to pursue complaints or carry out investigations relating to activities carried out across borders.[15] Developing international cooperation mechanisms in this respect is crucial.

The supervisory authorities are obliged to handle complaints about an alleged breach of the Regulation with the required diligence. In order to deal with the complaints lodged, the supervisory authorities have significant powers of investigation, and where they find that an adequate level of protection is lacking, they have a number of corrective powers that they can adopt on the basis of an assessment of appropriateness to be carried out with all due diligence (Article 58(2)).

In the event that the supervisory authority fails to deal with your complaint, it is provided that each data subject has the right to an effective judicial remedy (Article 78(1) and (2)). Reference is also made to that right to a judicial remedy under Article 47 of the Charter in the event that the supervisory authority fails to act when it is necessary to take action to protect the rights of the data subject (Recital 141).

2 Adequacy/Equivalence Decision

As said, the transfer of data to a third country may take place on the basis of an adequacy decision by the Commission. Pursuant to the second and third sentences of Article 45(1), the latter may decide that the transfer of personal data to a specific third country is permissible because it, a territory or one or more specific sectors within that country, ensures an adequate level of protection. In that case, the transfer of data to that country is authorised in a general way and does not require any further specific authorisation or involvement of the competent national authorities, thus ensuring legal certainty and uniformity throughout the Union vis-à-vis the third country (recital 103). Institutionally, the Commission's act is an implementing decision (Article 288 TFEU) adopted pursuant to Article 291(3) Treaty on the Functioning of the European Union (TFEU), under the comitology procedure *pursuant* to Article 93(2) ('comitology'), whereby the Commission is assisted by

[15] Recital 116.

representatives of the Member States. The Commission publishes its decisions in the Official Journal of the EU and on its *website*, with regular updates, from which the list of third countries that it considers to be in a position to ensure an adequate level of data protection in view of their national law or international commitments can then be found.[16]

Without requiring the third country in question to guarantee a level of protection identical to that guaranteed in the Union's legal order, the expression 'adequate level of protection' must be understood as requiring that, that country actually ensures a level of protection of fundamental rights and freedoms that is 'substantially equivalent'[17] to that guaranteed within the Union by virtue of that Regulation, read in the light of the Charter. In assessing the adequacy and therefore the equivalence of the level of protection, the Commission takes into consideration various elements indicated by way of non-exhaustive list in Article 45(2) such as: respect for human rights, data protection legislation, the existence and functioning of independent supervisory authorities and international agreements for the protection of personal data.

It is certainly not an easy assessment, and this for several reasons. First of all, it involves an examination of the foreign legal system from a comparative and functional perspective, which cannot be limited to the formal legislative datum, but must include the *law in action* and thus not only the legislative norms, but also those that give concrete effect to them, case law and administrative practices. This is evidenced by the explicit reference in Article 45(2)(a) to the 'implementation of such legislation' as an object of assessment.[18] The legislature makes repeated use of the adjective 'effective' (referring to rights, remedies, etc.) in order to link the object of the Commission's assessment to the concrete functioning of the foreign legal system (Recital 104). As explained by the Article 29 Working Party (WP29 for short), 'any meaningful analysis of the adequacy of protection must include two fundamental elements: the content of the applicable rules and the means to ensure their effective application. It is up to the European Commission to systematically verify that the rules in force are effective in practice'.[19]

Second, the Commission's decision must be 'legal' and not 'political' in nature. The EU institution has little margin of discretion, as it must in any case be based on

---

[16] Art. 45(3) and the Commission's website: https://commission.europa.eu/law/law-topic/data-protection/international-dimension-data-protection/adequacy-decisions_en#related-links.

[17] Recital 103.

[18] The same applies to the implementation of international obligations (Recital 105).

[19] Article 29 Data Protection Working Party, *Adequacy Benchmarks*. Adopted 28 November 2017. Version amended and adopted on 6 February 2018. WP 254 rev. 01, p. 2. In order to be able to capture the essential features of a foreign jurisdiction when making such an assessment, the Commission must hear the non-binding opinion of the European Data Protection Board (Board). In order to fulfil its task of advising the European Commission under Article 70(1)(s), the Committee must receive the necessary documentation, including correspondence with the government of the third country or international organisation (see also recital 105). Furthermore, the Commission makes use not only of official sources, but also of independent sources and expert advice.

legal criteria (such as those indicated by the legislature itself) and not political ones, resulting from a negotiation with the authorities of the foreign country. Consequently, when reviewing the Commission's compliance with the legal requirements, the Court is called upon to carry out a 'close review', aimed inter alia at sanctioning any political motives behind the adequacy decision, which would then be in breach of the 'narrow margin of appreciation' available to the Commission.[20] To this end, under Article 296(2) TFEU, the Commission must state the reasons for the decision *pursuant to* Article 45.[21]

The adequacy assessment in terms of equivalence of the level of protection must focus on the legal elements directly relevant for the protection of personal data. However, as already mentioned, the scope of the legal elements of the third country (or organisation) to be examined is much broader, including inter alia the rule of law, the protection of human rights and fundamental freedoms.

With regard to the specific regulatory protection of personal data, what is assessed of foreign law, and which must be equivalent to that deriving from EU law, is the final and concrete result—i.e. the degree, extent and effectiveness of protection—and not so much the specific regulatory and enforcement instruments to achieve it, which may be different.[22] For the purposes of comparison, the essential components—'the basic [...] requirements'[23]—of the data protection rules are taken into account. These are derived *primarily* from the rights and freedoms set out in the GDPR and the Charter. International data protection commitments must also be taken into account.[24]

The WP29 has identified in EU law a minimum core of substantive requirements that must be functionally reflected in the law of the third country. These requirements cover both the content dimension of the legislation (content principles) and the procedural and *enforcement* dimension.

The basic content principles cover: (1) the basic notions and/or principles of data protection consistent with those adopted in the Union (e.g. personal data, processing of personal data); (2) the criteria of lawfulness and fairness of data processing that establish the necessary basis of legitimacy (e.g. consent of the data subject, legitimate interest); (3) the principle of purpose limitation; (4) the principle of data quality and proportionality; (5) the principle of data retention; (6) the principle of security and confidentiality; (7) the principle of transparency; (8) the rights of access, rectification, erasure and objection; (9) restrictions on onward transfers.

---

[20] ECJ 6 October 2015, *Schrems I*, Case C-362/14, pt. 78 where it refers by analogy to Court of Justice EU 8 April 2014, *Digital Rights Ireland*, Joined Cases C-293/12 and C-594/12, pt. 47–48.

[21] Opinion of the Advocate General, 19 December 2019, *Schrems II*, Case C-311/18, pt. 302; ECJ 6 October 2015, *Schrems I*, Case C-362/14, pt. 96.

[22] ECJ 6 October 2015, *Schrems I*, Case C-362/14, pt. 73–74.

[23] Article 29 Data Protection Working Party (WP29), *Adequacy Benchmarks*, cit. In that document, the Working Party listed what it considers to be the essential requirements of EU law to be taken into account in the adequacy assessment *under* Article 45.

[24] Recital 105, which explicitly refers to Council of Europe Convention No 108 of 28 January 1981 for the protection of individuals with regard to automatic processing of personal data.

In the same document, the Working Party also considers it indispensable for foreign legislation to provide for additional (e.g. stricter) principles to be applied in specific cases of processing (e.g. in relation to special categories of data, corresponding to those provided for in Articles 9 and 10 of the Regulation, or in the case of automated decision-making processes).

On the other hand, as far as the enforcement aspect is concerned, the Working Party considers indispensable the presence of the following instruments: (1) the presence of independent supervisory authorities; (2) a monitoring and sanctioning system effective in terms of deterrence and repression of unlawful processing; (3) internal control systems within data controllers; (4) rapid, effective and accessible means of control and redress (administrative and judicial) available to data subjects in order to assert their rights, including the right to compensation for damages.

What emerges from an examination of EU data protection law—and which must somehow find its correspondent in the third country—is the 'classic' pattern of legal regimes protecting the weaker party, consisting of three elements. First, the regime is based on the information paradigm, and thus to a large extent on the ability of the weaker party (the data subject, in this case) to protect himself. The data subject's ability to retain control over personal data concerning him or her, which is one of the underlying objectives of the Regulation,[25] is made to depend first and foremost on his or her possession of, and ability to use, certain information, even of a purely legal nature, considered necessary for the protection of his or her interests. This information relates to the identity of the data controller, the purposes of the processing, any legitimate interests pursued by the former, any recipients of the personal data, the various rights of the data subject under the law, the existence of an automated decision-making process, etc.

In this respect, the principle of transparency and the right of access, functionally equivalent to those deriving from Article 13 et seq. are relevant and must be provided for and enforced in the third country.

Second, the system of protection, on the one hand, imposes on the data controller further material conduct, whether positive or negative, in order to avoid prejudice to the interests of the data subject and, on the other hand, grants the data subject other rights (apart from those of an informative nature) for the legal self-defence of his interests. This means that in order to be considered adequate and thus equivalent, in terms of personal data protection, the third country must, for instance, provide for legislation, equivalent to Art. 32 et seq. That guarantees the security of personal data,[26] protecting them from unauthorised access by third parties or unlawful access by the data controller himself or his employees, from accidental loss, destruction or damage. In addition, compliance with the limits of 'purpose limitation' and 'data minimisation' (equivalent to Art. 5(1)(a) and (b)) must be ensured, otherwise the transfer of personal data to that country would mean that the data subject would lose

[25] Recital 7. On the objective of the control, see Schantz (2023), p. 790 ff. Vrabec (2021).

[26] The necessary data security measures in the third country are explicitly referred to in Art. 45(2)(a) in connection with the adequacy decision.

control over them. Data protection in the sense of maintaining control over personal data must be provided in relation to (possible) onward transfers to other third countries or other organisations. In third countries, the protection of personal data must also include the recognition of other rights, such as the right of rectification and the right to be forgotten.

Third, in line with the typical 'enhanced' protection regime, the protection of personal data depends on safeguards that increase the effectiveness of the apparatus, both public and private, of monitoring, *enforcement* and remedies made available to the weaker party. First of all, Article 45(2)(b) itself provides for the need for the existence and effective functioning of independent supervisory authorities in the third country, competent to ensure and monitor compliance with data protection rules, including adequate enforcement powers. Furthermore, the data subject must have the right to effective judicial and administrative remedies, in order to have access to personal data concerning him/her, and, where appropriate, to obtain their rectification or erasure,[27] as well as the right to compensation for any damage caused by unlawful processing. The third country must therefore provide rights equivalent to those under Article 47(1) Charter, which presuppose enforceable rights such as those under Articles 7 and 8 Charter.

With regard to the adequacy/equivalence of data protection that does not derive from elements of the legal system relating specifically to the subject of data, the Regulation refers to legal elements such as the rule of law, respect for human rights and general legislation on public security, defence, national security, criminal law and public authorities' access to personal data (Article 45(2)(a)). In this respect, the guarantees actually provided in the third country for access to personal data by public authorities in pursuit of legitimate objectives, such as national security, are of particular relevance. The adequacy of the safeguards, in view of the possibility of data processing by public authorities, depends in particular on the respect of fundamental rights, such as those laid down in the Charter (e.g. Articles 7 and 8). The main guarantees to be checked, also in the light of the case law of the Court,[28] are easily identifiable in this respect: processing by public authorities must be provided for by law and be based on clear, precise and accessible rules; the proportionality of the pursuit of legitimate objectives must be demonstrated; there must be independent controls (Article 52) to which the processing must be subject; retained data must be protected against the risk of abuse, unauthorised access and unlawful use; data subjects must have effective remedies, in particular judicial remedies (Article 47(1) Charter), capable not only of ascertaining but also of effectively remedying the infringement of rights (e.g. by ordering the deletion of data).

In so far as they concern the processing of personal data by public authorities, these are particularly politically sensitive guarantees, in which respect for the *rule of law* is of central importance, applied both to vertical relations (State versus

[27] ECJ 6 October 2015, *Schrems I*, Case C-362/14, pt. 89–90, 95.

[28] ECJ 8 April 2014, *Digital Rights Ireland*, Joined Cases C-293/12 and C-594/12, pt. 54–55; 6 October 2015, *Schrems I*, Case C-362/14, pt. 91–92. Article 29 Data Protection Working Party (WP29), *Adequacy Benchmarks*, cit., 9.

private) and to horizontal relations (political authority versus independent jurisdictional or para-judicial bodies). One thinks of the guarantee deriving from the necessary limitation of public interference in fundamental rights, based on the constraints deriving from the principle of proportionality. The Court has made it clear, e.g. that those constraints are not respected by the third country system which provides for legislation authorising in a general manner the retention of all personal data of all persons whose data have been transferred from the Union to that third country without any distinction, limitation or exception according to the objective pursued, and without any objective criterion being laid down that allows public authorities' access to the data and their further use to be delimited to purposes that are precise, strictly limited, and capable of justifying the interference that both access to and use of those data entail.[29] We shall return to the principle of proportionality later, in particular in the last paragraph.

2.1 The Review of the Validity of the Adequacy Decision. The Schrems II Judgment

Pursuant to Article 288(4) TFEU, the Commission's adequacy decision is binding in its entirety on all Member States to which it is addressed and is therefore binding on all their organs. Accordingly, so long as the decision has not been declared invalid by the Court, the Member States and their bodies, which include their independent supervisory authorities, may not adopt measures contrary to such decisions, such as acts intended to make a binding finding that the third country concerned by that decision does not ensure an adequate level of protection and, consequently, to suspend or prohibit transfers of personal data to that third country.

However, a Commission decision on adequacy adopted on the basis of Article 45(3) cannot prevent persons whose personal data have been or could be transferred to a third country from referring, pursuant to Article 77(1), a complaint to the competent national supervisory authority concerning the protection of their rights and freedoms with regard to the processing of those data. Similarly, such a decision cannot override or diminish the powers expressly granted to national supervisory authorities by Article 8(3) Charter and Articles 51(1) and 57(1)(a). This means that even in the presence of an adequacy decision by the Commission, the competent national supervisory authority, when approached by a person with a complaint concerning the protection of their rights and freedoms with regard to the processing of personal data concerning him, must be able to examine, in full independence, whether the transfer of such data complies with the requirements laid down by the Regulation and, if appropriate, to bring an action before the national courts so that the latter may, if they share the doubts of those authorities as to the validity of the

[29] Court of Justice EU 6 October 2015, *Schrems I*, Case C-362/14, pt. 93. See also, 8 April 2014, *Digital Rights Ireland*, Joined Cases C-293/12 and C-594/12, pt. 57–63.

adequacy decision, make a reference for a preliminary ruling directed at examining that validity.[30]

This was most recently the case in the *Schrems II* judgment in relation to Adequacy Decision 2016/1250 adopted under Article 45(3) by the Commission, in which the Commission found the level of protection of personal data transferred from the Union to the United States to be adequate (the so-called privacy shield decision).[31] The Court was called upon to verify the actual adequacy of the protection required by Article 45 of the data transferred to the United States and consequently the validity of that decision with regard to the requirements of the GDPR, read in the light of the provisions of the Charter (Articles 7, 8 and 47) guaranteeing respect for private and family life, the protection of personal data and the right to effective judicial protection.

The Luxembourg judges first recalled the rights enshrined in Articles 7 and 8 of the Charter that are at issue in this case. The former guarantees everyone the right to respect for his private and family life, his home and his communications, while the latter explicitly recognises everyone's right to the protection of personal data concerning him. Access to a natural person's personal data for the purposes of their storage and use affects the fundamental right to respect for private life *under* Article 7, which relates to any information concerning an identified or identifiable natural person, and constituting processing of personal data within the meaning of Article 8 must necessarily comply with the protection obligations under that Article. Moreover, the disclosure of personal data to a third party, such as a public authority, constitutes an interference with the aforementioned fundamental rights, irrespective of the further use of the information disclosed. This also applies to the storage of and access to personal data for the purpose of their use by public authorities, irrespective of whether or not the privacy information in question is of a sensitive nature, or whether or not the persons concerned have suffered any inconvenience as a result of that interference.

Second, the Court reiterated both the relative nature of the fundamental rights at issue, which must be considered in the light of their social function, and the conditions laid down by the Charter to be observed in order to lawfully process personal data and to restrict the exercise of the rights and freedoms recognised by the Charter itself. Pursuant to Article 8(2) Charter personal data must be processed for specified purposes and on the basis of the consent of the data subject or some other legitimate basis laid down by law. Furthermore, according to the first sentence of Article 52(1) Charter, any limitations must be provided for by law and must respect the 'essential content' of rights and freedoms. Subject to the principle of proportionality, limitations may be placed on those rights and freedoms only where they are necessary and genuinely meet objectives of general interest recognised by the Union and the need to protect the rights and freedoms of others.

---

[30] ECJ 6 October 2015, *Schrems I*, Case C-362/14, pt. 62–65.

[31] Commission Implementing Decision (EU) 2016/1250 of 12 July 2016 pursuant to Directive 95/46 on the adequacy of the protection provided by the EU-US Privacy Shield regime (OJ 2016, L 207, p. 1).

Applying those rules to the Commission decision at issue, the Court found that the appropriate level of protection of personal data was not ensured, thus declaring Decision 2016/1250 invalid.

First of all, the Court notes that that decision enshrines the primacy of the requirements of national security, public interest and compliance with US law, thus making interference with the fundamental rights of persons whose data are transferred to that third country possible. In the Court's view, the limitations on the protection of personal data which result from the internal legislation of the United States concerning access to and use by the US authorities of such data transferred from the European Union, and which were assessed by the Commission in Decision 2016/1250, are not framed in such a way as to satisfy requirements which are substantially equivalent to those required, in EU law, by the principle of proportionality. In fact, the surveillance programmes based on that legislation are not limited to what is strictly necessary. In the case of certain surveillance programmes, it is not apparent from that legislation that there are any limits to the authorisation, contained therein, of the implementation of those programmes, nor are there any guarantees for foreign nationals who may potentially be subject to them. The Court adds that the same legislation, although it lays down requirements to be complied with by the US authorities when implementing the surveillance programmes in question, does not confer on the persons concerned any rights vis-à-vis that authority which are enforceable before the courts.

In addition to the requirement of judicial protection, the Court, contradicting the Commission's findings in the decision under review, finds that the mediation mechanism provided for by the latter does not provide a means of redress before a body offering guarantees substantially equivalent to those required under EU law. The mediator provided for by that mechanism does not provide guarantees of independence and does not have at his disposal rules enabling him to adopt binding decisions against the US intelligence services.

Where a third country, a territory or a specific sector within a third country does not (any longer) guarantee[32] an adequate level of data protection, the transfer of personal data to that third country must be prohibited, unless the requirements of that Regulation with regard to transfers subject to appropriate safeguards *under* Article 46 (on which see *below*) are fulfilled.

3 Adequacy Safeguards, Including Additional Ones

In the absence of an adequacy decision by the Commission *under* Article 45(3), it is for the controller or processor established in the Union to provide adequate safeguards. Pursuant to Article 46(1), the data controller may only transfer personal data

[32] On revocation, modification or suspension of the adequacy decision by the Commission, see Art. 45(4) and (5).

to a third country if it has provided 'appropriate safeguards' to protect the data subject and provided that the data subject has 'enforceable rights and effective legal remedies'. The safeguards may consist of: a binding legal instrument between public authorities or public bodies; binding corporate rules; standard contractual data protection clauses adopted by the Commission; standard data protection clauses adopted by a supervisory authority and approved by the Commission; a code of conduct; a certification mechanism.

What is the yardstick for determining the adequacy of the guarantee? Article 46 must also be read in the light of Article 44, entitled 'General Principle for Transfer', which provides that '[t]he provisions [of Chapter V] shall be applied with a view to ensuring that the level of protection of natural persons guaranteed by [that] Regulation is not adversely affected'. As already mentioned, the aim of the provisions of that chapter is to ensure the continuation of the high level of such protection in the event of transfer of personal data to a third country.[33] Thus, persons whose personal data are transferred to a third country must enjoy, as in the context of a transfer based *on* an Article 45 adequacy decision, a level of protection that is 'substantially equivalent' to that guaranteed within the Union. This level must be determined on the basis of the provisions of the Regulation itself, read in the light of the fundamental rights guaranteed by the Charter.[34] More specifically, the safeguards must ensure compliance with 'requirements' equivalent to those laid down in Union law on data protection and data subjects' rights and effective 'remedies', including administrative or judicial redress, and claims for compensation, in the Union or in a third country. They must address, in particular, compliance with the general 'principles' of personal data processing and the principles of data protection *by design* and *by default*.[35]

What is the subject of the assessment, i.e. where should the protection of personal data transferred to a third country be derived from? In the case of the adequacy decision under Article 45, as seen, protection must derive from the legal system of the third country in question. If there is no such decision, the answer to the above question is more articulated, since Article 46 provides for the possibility that protection is alternatively guaranteed by various instruments, different (and, in some cases, additional, as will be explained *below*) from the law of the third country. This is the aforementioned list of instruments of protection in Article 46, which is only indicative in nature, as it does not exhaust the possible guarantee measures. Moreover, as just mentioned, in the context of the cases covered by Article 46, the law of the third country is still relevant, since it must be included in the assessment of the level of protection guaranteed, together with the individual instruments *under* Article 46 used for the transfer of the data.

These instruments, in fact, do not operate independently of, and within, the legal system of the third country. Consequently, data controllers or processors, as

[33] Opinion of the Advocate General, 19 December 2019, *Schrems II*, Case C-311/18, pt. 117.

[34] Court of Justice EU 16 July 2020, *Schrems II*, Case C-311/18, pt. 101.

[35] Recital 108.

exporters, have to verify, on a case-by-case basis, whether the law or practice of the third country affects the effectiveness of the adequate safeguards contained in the instruments referred to in Article 46.[36]

Unlike the Commission's examination of the law of the third country under Article 45, in these cases the exporter, possibly in cooperation with the importer, conducts a more circumscribed and contextual analysis of the law of the third country. The examination must 'only' cover the law and practice that is relevant to the specific circumstances of the transfer in question. Such circumstances may relate, e.g. to the purposes of the transfer and processing, the nature of the entities involved in the processing, the sector in which the transfer takes place and the categories of personal data transferred. The relevant laws and practices to be assessed may be sectoral and/or general, and cover elements such as those listed in Article 45(2).

The assessment of the relevant regulations and practices of the third country, in turn, is instrumental in assessing the effectiveness of the protection instrument that the exporter intends to adopt under Article 46. Such an instrument is effective if it succeeds in compensating for any data protection shortcomings in the third country by providing appropriate safeguards to protect the data subject.[37] Conversely, the instrument is ineffective if the relevant rules and practices of the third country are found to be inconsistent and incompatible with the commitments made by that instrument. This may be the case when the obligations or powers deriving from those rules and practices prevent the achievement of personal data protection essentially equivalent to that guaranteed in the Union.

It is perhaps worth emphasising that the outcome of the assessment of the effectiveness of the protection instrument may vary from country to country, as the level of protection guaranteed by the rules and practices may vary depending on the individual jurisdiction in question. This variety clashes with the standard content of some Article 46 instruments, such as the standard data protection clauses adopted by the Commission, which per se apply uniformly in all countries, irrespective of the level of protection guaranteed by each of them.[38]

The most common hypothesis in which the third country does not guarantee the due protection of data is when, thanks to the rules or practices in force in that country, the public authorities *de jure* or *de facto* are able to access data from outside (even if only in transit) in a way that is incompatible with the essence of the fundamental rights and freedoms of the Charter or to an extent that does not comply with

[36] ECJ 16 July 2020, *Schrems II*, Case C-311/18, pt. 134; EDPB, *Recommendations 01/2020 on measures supplementing transfer instruments to ensure compliance with the EU level of personal data protection*. Version 2.0. adopted on 18 June 2021, 14 ff.

[37] Recital 108.

[38] Court of Justice. EU 16 July 2020, *Schrems II*, Case C-311/18, pt. 130 and 133. Unlike the adequacy decision adopted by the Commission under Article 45(3), the adoption of the standard data protection clauses by the Commission under Article 46(2)(c) does not imply a tailor-made assessment of individual third countries to which personal data could be transferred on the basis of these clauses.

the limits deriving from the principle of proportionality, pursuant to Article 23 of the Regulation and Article 52(1) Charter.

In the light of the above, if the data exporter considers that the Article 46 instrument is effective, and thus that the third country's law and practices do not prevent the data importer from complying with the obligations under the chosen instrument to adequately protect the data, the data exporter may adopt that instrument as the basis for transferring the data to that third country, subject to reassessment at appropriate intervals or when significant changes emerge.

In case of a negative assessment, however, the exporter must put in place additional measures to overcome incompatibilities of the third country's law/practice with the Article 46 protection instrument and more generally with relevant EU law (e.g. the Charter). It is therefore necessary for the exporter to find a way to compensate (also) for the shortcomings of the chosen instrument, due for instance to its contractual nature which makes it non-binding for foreign public authorities. The aim is to achieve the appropriate level of data protection *by* combining the Article 46(2) instrument with additional measures. With regard to the Article 46(2)(c) instrument, the Regulation expressly provides that '[t]he possibility for data controllers [...] to use standard data protection clauses adopted by the Commission [...] should not preclude data controllers [...] from adding other clauses or additional safeguards', specifying in particular that data controllers 'should be encouraged to provide additional safeguards [...] supplementing the standard protection clauses'.[39]

The additional measures may be contractual, technical and/or organisational in nature. Their effectiveness depends on the type of data protection shortcomings related to the rules and practices of the third country and on a number of other factors related inter alia to the characteristics of the data (e.g. format and nature), the chain of data transfer, the possibility of onward transfers, etc.[40] If the incompatibility stems, for instance, from the power of public authorities to disproportionately access personal data transferred or in transit, (only) contractual and organisational measures will generally be insufficient. In such situations, only the use of even technical measures may prevent or render ineffective access to personal data by third country authorities, in particular for surveillance purposes. If this is the case, it can be done by contractually obliging the exporter, and consequently the importer, to implement specific technical measures, such as reliable encryption of the data or their pseudonymisation, so as to enable their transfer.

Where the controller/processor cannot take sufficient additional measures to ensure essentially equivalent protection, it or, failing that, the competent supervisory authority, must suspend or terminate the transfer of personal data to the third country concerned.[41]

---

[39] Recital 109.

[40] EDPB, *Recommendations 01/2020 on measures supplementing transfer instruments to ensure compliance with the EU level of protection of personal data*, cit., 24–25.

[41] ECJ 16 July 2020, *Schrems II*, Case C-311/18, pt. 135.

With regard to the mechanisms for verifying compliance with the above-mentioned requirements, a distinction must be made between the powers/duties of national supervisory authorities and the judicial remedies available to the data subject and the controller/processor.

As mentioned above, the competent supervisory authority may/must suspend or prohibit a transfer pursuant to Article 58(2)(j) or not grant authorisation if it considers that data protection equivalent to that provided for by Union law, in particular Articles 45 and 46 and the Charter, is not guaranteed.[42] This assessment must be based on an examination of the law and practice specifically in force in that third country and/or in the light of the (inadequate) safeguards put in place by the exporter, as it cannot be an assessment of the Commission's decision, such as that *under* Article 46(2)(c).[43] In case of divergent decisions by supervisory authorities of different Member States, Article 64(2) provides for the possibility for a supervisory authority which considers that transfers to a third country should in general be prohibited to refer the matter to the European Data Protection Board (EDPB), which may, pursuant to Article 65(1)(c), adopt a binding decision, in particular when a supervisory authority does not comply with the opinion given.

According to Article 77(1), if the data subject considers that his rights have been infringed, he may lodge a complaint with a supervisory authority in the Member State where he normally resides, works or where the alleged infringement took place. The data subject himself, as well as any natural or legal person, has the right to a judicial remedy against the supervisory authority that has adopted a legally binding decision affecting him and which he considers unlawful. That action must be brought before the courts of the Member State in which the supervisory authority is established (Article 78(1)).

In addition, any data subject has the right to bring an action against the data exporter, pursuant to Art. 79(1), if he considers that his rights under the Regulation have been violated as a result of processing. The competent court shall be that of the Member State in which the data subject is habitually resident, unless the data controller is a public authority of a Member State in the exercise of its public powers.

---

[42] ECJ 16 July 2020, *Schrems II*, Case C-311/18, pt. 113 and 121.

[43] If, on the other hand, the doubts of lawfulness concern the Commission's decision, e.g. on the standard contractual clauses for the transfer of data, the national authority must resort to court action, as is the case for the Commission's adequacy decisions *under* Article 45. In that regard, 'it is for the national legislature to provide remedies enabling the national supervisory authority (...) to raise the complaints which it considers well-founded before the national courts so that, where they share that authority's doubts as to the validity of the Commission's decision, the latter may make a reference for a preliminary ruling with a view to examining the validity of that decision'. ECJ. EU 6 October 2015, *Schrems I*, Case C-362/14, pt. 65. An example of such a preliminary reference was discussed in *Schrems II*, where the Court upheld the validity of Decision 2010/87/EU ('CPT Decision') on standard contractual clauses in light of Articles 7, 8 and 47 Charter.

4 Derogations in Specific Situations

Article 49 provides for two situations of an exceptional nature in which the transfer of personal data to a third country or an international organisation is allowed in the absence of an adequacy decision *under* Article 45(3) and adequate safeguards *under* Article 46.[44]

Possible grounds under the first derogation include the data subject's explicit consent to the transfer, the necessity of the transfer for the performance of a contract between the data subject and the data controller or the implementation of pre-contractual measures taken at the data subject's request, and the necessity of the transfer for important grounds of public interest recognised by Union law or by the law of the Member State to which the data controller is subject.[45]

If none of the grounds referred to in the first paragraph of Article 49(1) apply, the data transfer is nevertheless possible, provided that it is not repetitive, involves a limited number of data subjects, is necessary for the purposes of pursuing compelling legitimate interests of the data controller which are not overridden by the interests or the rights and freedoms of the data subject and where the data controller has assessed all the circumstances surrounding the transfer and on the basis of this assessment has provided adequate data protection safeguards.[46]

5 The Balance Between EU Data Protection and Other Non-EU Requirements. The Legal Assessments Required from Undertakings

As repeatedly stated, the primary aim of the above-mentioned legislation is to ensure an adequate level of protection for individuals in relation to the transfer of personal data abroad. This level does not imply absolute protection, but allows limitations to the fundamental rights involved. Since certain limitations are accepted when data are processed within the Union, a 'substantially equivalent' regime of possible restrictions must also apply in the case of data transfers and processing in third countries.

Let us consider the hypotheses—analysed above—in which it is the exporter, possibly in cooperation with the importer, who has to put in place an adequate data protection regime, capable of compensating for the deficiencies of the law and practice of the third country and/or those resulting from the Commission's standard clauses, by taking additional measures if necessary. In such cases it is the responsibility of the importer, both to enforce EU law, and in particular fundamental rights,

---

[44] On this topic see, EDPB, *Guidelines 2/2018 on exemptions under Article 49 of Regulation 2016/679. Adopted on 25 May 2018.*

[45] See the list of possible exemptions in Art. 49(1)(1)(a)–(g).

[46] Art. 49(1), para. 2.

and to carry out the legal assessment of the third country's law and practice and the standard data protection clauses. This responsibility implies the exporter's ability both to have a clear understanding of the content of EU law on the protection of personal data and to identify possible shortcomings in the law and practice of the third country's legal system and thus to determine whether any foreign restrictions on fundamental rights meet the legal conditions required by EU law for their legitimacy. These legal assessment capabilities require, in turn, that the normative content of the rule (protection regime) and exception (permissible restrictions) be well defined, so that they can be applied without undue difficulty and cost by companies exporting personal data.

Some elaboration on the permissible restrictions regime is appropriate. Article 23 of the Regulation (as well as Article 52(1) of the Charter) allows limitations to the legal protection of personal data provided in general by the Regulation itself (and by the Charter). This means that the level of protection to be guaranteed in the third country of destination of the data may legitimately be lower than it would be in the absence of limitations. However, there is a minimum level of protection, below which one cannot go, constituted by the 'essence of fundamental rights and freedoms'. Limitations must respect that essence. Moreover, while remaining above this minimum limit, the limitations in question must be provided for by law, must serve to safeguard the public interests set out in Article 23 and must meet the requirements of necessity and proportionality (in a democratic society).

This is in a nutshell the regime of exceptions to the general obligations to protect personal data laid down in the regulation. The regime revolves around the principle of proportionality, from which derive the suitability test (understood as the ability to safeguard the public interests referred to in Article 23), the necessity test (understood as the prohibition to impose limitations to fundamental rights that are not strictly indispensable and replaceable with non-, or less-restrictive, measures), and the proportionality test in the strict sense (which includes, in the case of fundamental rights, the condition of non-injury to the essence of the right).[47,48]

The regime of legitimate limitations on fundamental rights, in the cases of Article 46, requires data exporting companies to make legal assessments that may not be easy, especially for companies (e.g. SMEs, start-ups) other than the large digital platforms.[49] These companies may thus be disadvantaged in terms of competition, to the detriment of global digital competition and technological and commercial innovation (as well as to the detriment of the legitimate need to protect a certain measure of digital sovereignty, with its political and economic implications, which depends on the existence of national companies capable of competing in these areas).

In this respect, the Court has been able to offer interpretative clarifications on certain aspects of the legal regime of limitations.[50] The requirement that any limitation on the exercise of fundamental rights must be provided for by law implies that

[47] The assessment of proportionality in the strict sense is sometimes made by recourse to the doctrine of the 'substance of the right' (Schutze (2015), pp. 418–419), in the sense that the judgment of the non-proportionality of an EU measure can be made on the basis of the impairment of the very substance of a right by that measure. These are the judgments in which the proportionality of a public measure is assessed in relation to the protection of a subjective right recognised by EU law, i.e. fundamental rights such as the right to property, the right to carry out an economic activity or the right to citizenship (ECJ, 8 March 2011, *Zambrano v. ONEm*, Case C-34/09), which EU action, in the pursuit—usually discretionary—of a public interest, may affect negatively, in the sense of restricting its free exercise. The question concerns actions specifically based on such rights and the assessment criterion adopted to draw the threshold of acceptability of the limits to the fundamental right resulting from the EU measure, beyond which the said measure is to be considered disproportionate. In such cases, the European Court often makes an explicit or implicit reference to the case law of the European Court of Human Rights. After specifying the non-absolute nature of the protection enjoyed by those rights, which may therefore legitimately be subject to limitations, the Luxembourg judges proceed to ascertain whether the restrictions applied 'actually correspond to objectives of general interest pursued by the [Union] and do not constitute, in the light of the objective pursued, a disproportionate and unacceptable intervention, such as to affect the very substance of the rights guaranteed' (see among many judgments containing this formula, CJEU, 3 September 2008, *Kadì*, joined cases C-402/05 P and C-415/05 P, pt. 355). In other words, in these cases, the Court qualifies certain faculties deriving from fundamental rights as 'untouchable', not susceptible to exclusion, since such exclusions would be tantamount to nullifying the right itself, to emptying it of all content—and not just limiting its exercise. EU measures depriving the holder of such faculties would be precisely disproportionate in that they would undermine the correct 'balance [fair balance] between the requirements of the general interest and the interest of the individual(s) concerned' (ECJ. EU 3 September 2008, *Kadì*, cit., pt. 360. The Court refers on this point to the case law of the European Court of Human Rights).

[48] This is not the place to address the question of the conceptual distinction between the principle of proportionality and the test of the essence of fundamental rights (Art. 51(2) Charter and Art. 23). Even those who—like Lenaerts (2019), pp. 779 ff., 781—argue that they are distinct concepts, however point to measures in violation of the latter test as 'disproportionate' measures and acknowledge the partial overlap between the two concepts.

[49] On the requirement that the rules governing the international transfer of data must be reasonably clear and predictable, both on the question of their applicability and in their content, see Milanovic (2015), p. 81 ff.

[50] ECJ 16 July 2020, *Schrems II*, Case C-311/18, pt. 175–177.

the legal basis allowing interference in those rights must itself define the scope of the limitation.[51] Moreover, in order to satisfy the requirement of proportionality, the contested legislation entailing the interference must provide 'clear and precise rules governing the scope and application of the measure in question'. These rules must indicate in particular in what 'circumstances and under what conditions a measure providing for the processing of such data may be adopted', thus ensuring that the interference is limited to what is 'strictly necessary'. Furthermore, the same rules must impose 'minimum requirements so that the persons whose data are transferred have sufficient safeguards to protect their personal data effectively against the risk of abuse'. These safeguards consist, in particular, of 'effective and enforceable rights of data subjects'.

The aforementioned requirements decry the principle of proportionality, explicitly referred to by the Court, in some of its interlinked components,[52] namely the imperatives relating to the rule of law (Article 45) and the essence of fundamental rights and freedoms (Article 23). On the one hand, it prohibits public authorities from having a space and constraints to interfere with fundamental rights that are not sufficiently clear, precise and predetermined. Lack of clarity and vagueness are in fact fertile ground for abuse. On the other hand, the same space for possible interference must be reduced to what is strictly necessary to safeguard the legitimate public interest and in any case such as not to undermine the minimum level of data protection, and in particular not to deprive the data subject of the 'essence' (or 'essential content'[53]) of fundamental rights.

The essence of those rights is undermined if the restriction on fundamental rights empties them of their content or calls their very existence into question. In the words of the Court, respect for the essence of a fundamental right means that that right is not 'called into question as such'.[54] A measure that limits the exercise of some aspects of a fundamental right while leaving others intact, or that applies only in specific circumstances, is not such as to undermine the essence of that fundamental right.[55] The essence of a right is not sacrificed by a restrictive measure if, because of its intensity, extent and duration, the right remains exercisable and capable of

[51] Confirming that the principle of proportionality is the lynchpin of the regime at issue, the Court expressed itself in the following terms: 'If the requirement that any limitation on the exercise of fundamental rights must be laid down by law implies that the legal basis permitting interference with fundamental rights must itself define the scope of the limitation on the exercise of the right in question, that requirement is to a large extent confused with the requirements of clarity and precision arising from the principle of proportionality', citing the judgment of the ECJ in Case C-311/18, Schrems II, Case C-311/18, Schrems II, paragraph 1.1.1. EU 16 July 2020, *Schrems II*, Case C-311/18, pt. 180 (Court, 5 May 2022, C-570/20, *BV*, pt. 31).

[52] The imperatives of the rule of law can contribute to the essential content of fundamental rights, see, e.g. Court of Justice EU 16 July 2020, *Schrems II*, Case C-311/18, pt. 187.

[53] ECJ 5 May 2022, Case C-570/20, *BV*, pt. 30.

[54] Among many rulings see ECJ 20 March 2018, *Menci*, Case C-524/15, pt. 43.

[55] Lenaerts (2019), p. 779 ff, p.785.

offering the holder a minimum level of protection that, even if reduced, is sufficiently congruous, effective, in relation to its *ratio*.[56]

For instance, with regard to the necessity requirement, the US legislation in the *Schrems II* case was found to be in breach of the 'strict necessity' limits, inter alia, because it allowed public authorities to access data in transit in the US without circumscribing in a sufficiently clear and precise manner the scope of the collection of personal data. It was a bulk, non-targeted collection of personal data, not associated with a specific purpose. Furthermore, the same Court held that a system that does not provide 'any possibility for the individual to avail himself of legal remedies in order to have access to personal data concerning him [used by public authorities], or to obtain the rectification or deletion of such data, does not respect the essential [i.e. minimum] content of the fundamental right to effective judicial protection', as set out in Article 47 of the Charter.[57] Other essential rights, i.e. essential levels of rights, again relating to the fundamental right to effective judicial protection *under* Article 47 Charter, found not to be guaranteed by the US system in the same case stem from the Ombudsman's lack of binding powers and independence from the executive power.[58]

The jurisprudence of the Court, such as that exemplified by the *Schrems II* judgment, if linear, should over time increase the certainty and precision with which the Union law in question is understood and applied. This would benefit, first and foremost, data exporters in the fulfilment of their responsibilities *under* Article 46, and data subjects. The possibility of increasing legal certainty applies especially with reference to the identification of the minimum or essential guarantees, which we have said constitute the minimum level of protection ('the essence of fundamental rights and freedoms' *under* Article 23 and Article 52(1) Charter) from which there can be no derogation. In fact, the identification of such minimum guarantees, substantially equivalent to those provided by the Union, should become clear and certain with the consolidation of the relevant jurisprudential interpretation.

More doubts remain, however, with regard to the application of the necessity test by companies. One thinks of the proportionality assessments of third-country law *under* Article 46 to ascertain whether national legislation does not go beyond what is necessary in a democratic society to safeguard in particular state security, defence and public safety.[59] The Regulation and the relevant case law of the Court essentially ask private undertakings to assess, on a case-by-case basis, what measures, e.g. in the field of national security or defence, of a third country are sufficient and thus to judge whether the legislation, institutions and practices of that country go beyond what is strictly necessary. The difficulty of such an assessment, especially for a private company (which does not—to continue with the above-mentioned

[56] The concept of the 'essence of fundamental rights' is controversial in doctrine. Among the various interpretative positions, see, by way of example, in addition to Lenaerts (2019), Tzanou (2021) and Gonzàlez (2022).

[57] ECJ 16 July 2020, *Schrems II*, Case C-311/18, pt. 187.

[58] Ibid, pt. 195–196.

[59] ECJ. EU 16 July 2020, *Schrems II*, Case C-311/18, pt. 141.

examples—deal with national security or intelligence), is exacerbated by the fact that it can only be targeted and contextualised, given that what is necessary, e.g. in terms of national security, can change, even radically, from country to country. If this is the case, while on the one hand we could have in the future a—more or less—precise and *uniform* picture of the legal and institutional data protection instruments that each third country must guarantee as a minimum level of protection, on the other hand, the application of the criterion of 'substantial equivalence' with regard to the assessment of the necessity of the restrictions in the third country would still be difficult, burdensome and uncertain.

References

González Fuster G (2022) Study on the essence of the fundamental rights to privacy and to protection of personal data. Prepared for the European Data Protection Supervisor (EDPS), EDPS 2021/0932, 2022

Hustinix P (2015) Le droit de l'Union européenne sur la protection des données: la révision de la directive 95/46/CE et la proposition de règlment général sul la protection des données, 49, available at https://edps.europa.eu/sites/edp/files/publication/14-09-15_article_eui_fr.pdf-

Kuner C (2020) Art. 44 general principles for transfers. In: Kuner C, Bygrave LA, Docksey C (eds) The EU general data protection regulation (GDPR). Oxford Academic, Oxford, p 755 ff

Lenaerts K (2019) Limits on legislation: the essence of fundamental rights in the EU. German Law J:779 ff

Milanovic M (2015) Human rights treaties and foreign surveillance: privacy in the digital age. In. Harv Int Law J 56:81 ff

Schantz P (2023) Art. 44. In: General data protection regulation. Article-by-article commentary. Bloomsbury, Baden-Baden, p 776

Schütze VR (2015) European constitutional law. Cambridge University Press, Cambridge, pp 418–419

Tzanou M (2021) Schrems I and Schrems II: assessing the case for the extraterritoriality of EU fundamental rights. In: Fabbrini-E F, Quinn C-J (eds) Data protection beyond Borders. Transatlantic perspectives on extraterritoriality and sovereignty. Bloomsbury Publishing, London

Vrabec HU (2021) Data subject rights under the GDPR. Oxford Academic Press, Oxford

Data Processing Security and Personal Data Breach Notification System

Agostino Nuzzolo

Contents

Abstract The data breach discipline is of growing importance in the regulation of the digital ecosystem, given the constant proliferation of criminal phenomena. The aim of the discipline is, on the one hand, to impose adequate measures for preventing and minimising the risks of intrusion, and on the other, to establish the methods and timing for communicating relevant events to the authorities. Both privacy legislation and cybersecurity legislation have intervened on the matter. Lastly, the matter is relevant from the point of view of liability towards the owners of the information subject to breach, where case law has sanctioned full liability of the owner/processor, subject to proof of the adoption of adequate measures.

A. Nuzzolo (✉)
General Counsel TIM, Milan, Italy
e-mail: agostino.nuzzolo@telecomitalia.it

R. Bocchini (ed.), *Digital Platforms - From Technical Foundations to Legal and Economic Implications*, https://doi.org/10.1007/978-3-032-07978-7_36

1 Some Preliminary Considerations on the Security Principle

Before delving into the examination of the *data breach* discipline, it may be useful to mention the relevance of the security measures to be adopted by the data controller, also in relation to the liability profiles he may have in the event of events damaging the integrity of the data.

In fact, before the European Regulation on the Protection of Individuals General Data Protection Regulation (GDPR),[1] security was not considered an essential element and a specific duty of the data controller. And so, while in the 'Convention for the Protection of Individuals with regard to Automatic Processing of Personal Data'[2] security is assumed to be a central factor and fundamental principle in the activity of data processing,[3] as such it is mandatory,[4] in the subsequent directive on the protection of natural persons[5] with regard to the processing of personal data and on the free movement of such data, the legislator departed from that Convention, by downgrading security to a mere rule of conduct, compliance with which was the sole responsibility of the controller (Article 17).[6] Thus, while it prescribed the adoption of appropriate technical and organisational measures capable of ensuring the protection of personal data in the event of accidental or unlawful destruction, loss or alteration, or unauthorised disclosure or access, it did not include any reference to the data subject's right to obtain *ex ante* protection, and merely established a generic right to compensation.

This *trend*, so to speak 'minimalist', was later confirmed by the Personal Data Protection Code,[7] which relegated security to Title V, with the provision of a security obligation (Article 31 Code) taken from the former Article 15(1) of Law no. 75/1996, while the minimum security measures, governed by Article 33 and Annex B of the Code, were kept separate.[8]

All this led to a flattening in favour of the minimum measures, although they were then periodically updated on the basis of technological developments.

A decisive turning point is due to the GDPR, which, in contrast to the past, assigns security the role of principle in the processing of personal data, in order to increase the breadth of protection of the rights and freedoms of natural persons.[9]

---

[1] Regulation (EU) 2016/679.

[2] Strasbourg Convention No 108/81.

[3] Rodotà (1984), p. 89 ff.

[4] According to the original text of Article 7, 'appropriate security measures shall be taken to protect personal data recorded in automated data files against accidental or unauthorised destruction or accidental loss as well as against unauthorised access to, alteration of or disclosure of the data'.

[5] Directive 95/46/EC.

[6] Zeno and Zenchovich (1998), p. 159 ff.

[7] Legislative Decree No 196/2003.

[8] See Riccio (2005), p.126 ff.; Troiano (2007), p. 682 ff.; Motroni (2007), p. 221 ff.

[9] Lucchini Guastalla (2019), p. 70; Mantelero (2019), p. 473 ff.

Hence the need for the constant use of suitable and up-to-date technical and organisational equipment capable of minimising risks and providing an immediate response in the event of a personal data breach, or, according to the text of Article 4(12) GDPR, of any '*breach of security leading accidentally or unlawfully to the destruction, loss, alteration, unauthorised disclosure of or access to personal data transmitted, stored or otherwise processed*'.

According to Article 32(1) GDPR, in order to ensure a level of security appropriate to the risk, technical and organisational measures must be in place, including: the pseudonymisation and encryption of personal data; the ability to permanently ensure the confidentiality, integrity, availability and resilience of processing systems and services; the ability to promptly restore the availability and access of personal data in the event of a physical or technical incident; and a procedure by which the effectiveness of technical and organisational arrangements is regularly tested, verified and assessed.

Finally, the assessment of the adequacy of the level of security will also be conditioned by the weight assigned to the risk of destruction, loss, modification, unauthorised disclosure of or access, whether accidental or unlawful, to personal data transmitted, stored or otherwise processed (Article 32(2) GDPR).[10]

From the aforementioned regulatory framework, there emerges, in addition to the decisive process of *accountability* with respect to the activity of the data controller and processor, a responsibility that goes beyond mere compensation, but requires preventive, operational and reactive activities.

2 Definition of Data Breach and Case Studies

Before analysing the rules on *data breach* reporting, allow me to introduce the definition applicable to it and the case studies of the phenomenon.

As for the definition, reference should be made to the GDPR, where *data* breach is defined as a breach of security leading accidentally or as a result of unlawful acts to the destruction, loss, modification, unauthorised disclosure of or access to personal data transmitted, stored or otherwise processed within a given system (Article 4 GDPR).

Still in an attempt to frame the phenomenon, it is useful to recall an intervention in 2018 by the Working Party 29[11]within which a distinction was made into three macro-categories:

[10] Fonderico (2018), p. 420.

[11] This is the Joint Working *Party* of National Supervisory and Data Protection Authorities (Article *29 Working Party*), an independent advisory body, composed of one representative from each authority, which according to Article 29 of Directive 95/46 had several tasks including providing expert advice to the states, promoting the consistent application of the Directive and providing recommendations to the public.

- *Confidentiality Breach*, when there is an accidental or abusive access to personal data.
- *Availability Breach*, when there is an accidental or unauthorised loss or destruction of personal data.
- *Integrity Breach*, when there is an accidental or unauthorised alteration of personal data.

As can be seen, the emphasis is placed on the consequences of the act, whether accidental or unlawful, distinguishing between cases where there is only access, and those where the data is also destroyed or altered. Needless to say, with regard to the first hypothesis, the problem that the operator must face is what use can be made of the data accessed by the third party and, therefore, how to protect the owner of the data itself; whereas, in the other two hypotheses, there is also the problem of restoring the original data. We will return to this point later.

Data breaches are a problem in and of themselves, but they are also symptoms of a vulnerable, possibly outdated data security regime; therefore, they indicate weaknesses in the system that need to be addressed. In general, it is always better to prevent data breaches by preparing in advance, as several consequences of a *breach* are by nature irreversible.[12] Before a data controller can fully assess the risk arising from a breach caused by some form of attack, it is necessary to identify the root cause of the problem, in order to check whether any vulnerabilities that gave rise to the incident are still present and, worse still, exploitable.

Below is a brief description of the main causes of *data breaches*:

- *Hacker* or *malware* attacks: these are the most common methods of data breach; attackers use techniques such as *phishing*, social engineering, brute force attacks or exploitation of vulnerabilities in software or systems to gain unauthorised access to sensitive data.
- Credentials stored in source code: developers make the common mistake of leaving credentials or access keys in code *repositories*.
- Malfunctioning authentication or authorisation systems: applications with vulnerabilities or any *cybersecurity* infrastructure with *bugs* could allow an attacker to gain unauthorised access.
- Eavesdropping: unencrypted traffic through a network is vulnerable to interception.
- Internal information leaks: a trusted user or an individual with privileged access can abuse their rights to steal or compromise data.
- Loss or theft: laptops, office computers, portable hard drives, files and other physical assets may be lost or stolen.
- Inadvertent disclosure: sensitive data may be exposed due to user error or negligence.

[12] In the aforementioned European guidelines, an elastic vision of security emerges, intolerant of being caged within predefined schemes and not susceptible to contextual constraints. Thus, Esposito (2021), pp. 503–505.

- Inadequate security: technological deficiencies, user behaviour and weak credentials are some of the most common reasons leading to *data breaches.*
- Unknown reasons: in a limited number of cases, the actual cause of a data breach may remain unknown.

Data breaches can occur both *offline* and *online*. *Hackers* may use channels such as the Internet, *Bluetooth*, text messages or *online* services to access sensitive data.

Below is a list of the main types of data breaches:

- *Malware*: these programmes are designed to infect the victim's computer and steal sensitive information.
- Ransomware payment of a ransom: this is a sophisticated type of *malware* that encrypts the victim's files and demands for the decryption key.
- *Keylogger*: this type of *malware* can be designed to record keystrokes made by the user, enabling the attacker to capture sensitive information such as passwords.
- *Phishing*: this form of *social engineering* consists of tricking users into revealing sensitive information, such as login credentials or credit card numbers, resulting in a data breach.
- *Hacking*: if an attacker gains access to users' devices or compromises internal infrastructure, they can install *malware* to steal data.
- Payment card fraud: payment card data is stolen using physical *skimming* devices or other methods.

Cybersecurity incidents have been on the rise for years, but have increased more than proportionally with the advent of *smart working*, also as a result of the policies adopted in the Covid pandemic. This change has led to an increase in *data breaches* as users have stored data on their personal devices and organisations have opened up *cloud* resources and internal infrastructures accessible via VPN.

3 The Obligation to Report

According to the GDPR, notification of data breaches must be made without undue delay and, where possible, within 72 hours of becoming aware of the breach (Article 33 GDPR), to the competent national supervisory authority (hereinafter 'SA—*Security Authority*'—in Italy the *Data* Protection Authority—Autorità Garante sulla Privacy).[13]

[13] In Italy, prior to the approval of the regulation, there were already notification requirements in four processing cases. In the electronic communications sector, the Garante's Measure No. 161 of 4 April 2013 prescribed the obligation of notification to the Garante (by means of a special notification form) by providers of telephone and Internet access services (and not, for instance, websites disseminating content, search engines, Internet points, corporate networks). According to the measure, in the event of a personal data breach, the Telecommunication (Tlc) and internet service provider (Isp) companies had to: within 24 h of discovering the event, provide the Garante with the information necessary to allow an initial assessment of the extent of the breach; within 3 days of

The duty to notify a personal data breach to the supervisory authority is placed on the data controller: the former's position is not isolated, as the data controller, in this context, is required to inform the controller without undue delay after learning of the breach (Article 33(2) GDPR).[14]

This principle is subject to an exception in cases where the aforementioned personal data breach does not present, according to a probabilistic criterion, a risk for the rights and freedoms of natural persons.[15] It is understood that any delay must be justified.

The new rules have replaced the previous rules that provided for a prior notification obligation, which has now been replaced not only by the aforementioned duty to notify the *data breach* event, but also by the new obligations to keep a register of processing operations and *data breaches*.

In addition, notification may also take place in a progressive manner, communicating known information immediately and postponing the transmission of further data until the risk and impact surrounding the breach have been fully assessed (Article 34 GDPR).

In some cases, then, there is the additional task of also informing the holders of the breach, by communicating the information referred to in Article 33 GDPR, (b), (c) and (d). These are the cases where, due to the nature of the information acquired, there is a risk of causing significant harm to data subjects, more particularly when the personal data breach is likely to entail a high risk for the rights and freedoms of natural people.

---

the discovery, also inform each user involved, communicating the elements provided for in Regulation No. 611/2013 and the Garante's Order No. 161 of 4 April 2013. Notification to the users was not due if it was proven that security measures, as well as encryption and anonymisation systems that rendered the data unintelligible had been used. In the most serious cases, the Garante could still require disclosure to the data subjects. In order to enable the Garante's investigations, telephone companies and Internet service providers had to keep a constantly updated inventory of breaches. In the field of biometrics, Order No. 513 of 12 November 2014 required data controllers (companies, public administrations, etc.) to notify the Garante (using the template attached to the Order) within 24 h of becoming aware of the fact, of all data breaches or IT incidents that could have a significant impact on the biometric systems installed or personal data stored. In the field of healthcare data, Order No. 331 of 4 June 2015 stipulated that within 48 hours of knowledge of the fact, public and private healthcare facilities were required to notify the Garante (using the template attached to the order) of all data breaches or IT incidents that could have a significant impact on the personal data processed through the healthcare file. In the area of data communicated between public administrations, the Order of 2 July 2015—'*Security* measures *and modalities for the exchange of personal data between public administrations*'—prescribed, pursuant to Article 154(1)(c) of the Personal Data Protection Code, that public administrations, as referred to in Article 1(2) of Legislative Decree no. 165 of 30 March 2001. 165, were to notify the authority, within 48 h of becoming aware of the fact, of all data breaches or computer incidents that could have a significant impact on the personal data contained in their databases, and that such notifications were to be drawn up in accordance with a specific template annexed to the provision and sent by e-mail or certified e-mail.

[14] Renna (2020), p. 197 ff.

[15] Finocchiaro (2020), p. 246 ff.

Think of the case of abusive access to a commercial database in which the names of customers are acquired, with their VAT number and address. But if, in addition to the aforementioned data, other information and documents are taken—e.g. financial/banking information and/or copies of personal documents—the company will not be able to avoid reporting the incident to the people concerned.

Pursuant to Article 34(3) GDPR, such notification will not be made if one of the following remedies is in place[16]:

(a) Implementation of appropriate technical and organisational protection measures and their application to the personal data affected by the breach, including in particular those designed to make the personal data unintelligible to anyone not authorised to access them, such as encryption.
(b) Adoption by the controller of measures aimed at preventing the occurrence of a high risk to the rights and freedoms of data subjects.
(c) Public communication or equivalent measure effectively informing the data subjects where direct communication would require disproportionate effort.

This second hypothesis of communication to interested parties is clearly even more burdensome for the company, *firstly*, in cases of a large number of individuals affected by the phenomenon; *secondly*, because of the publicity given to the event, which is still an indication of the inadequacy of the company and its systems.

On the subject of notifications, it is worth mentioning Guidelines *WP250*—adopted on 3 October 2017, and subsequently amended through the version of 6 February 2018, by the 'Article 29 Working Group'. This document addresses the notification and communication of personal data breaches under the GDPR, specifying that: (i) the controller must notify the controller of a personal data breach without undue delay, making available to the controller any information that may be useful for the decision whether or not to notify the controller of the personal data breach; (ii) the data protection officer (DPO), if any, has a duty to inform the controller, and the controller, and to advise them, as well as to cooperate with the supervisory authority and act as a point of contact with respect to any matter related to the data processing activity.

Notification may be omitted in cases where the data controller, having verified the consistency and impact of the breach, considers that the rights and freedoms of natural persons are unlikely to be adversely affected: central, once again, is the *risk assessment* activity.[17] Following the guidelines, a risk assessment should be carried out linked to the following factors: (a) type of breach; (b) nature, sensitivity and volume of personal data; (c) ease of identification of individuals; (d) seriousness of consequences for individuals; (e) particular characteristics of the data subject; (f) particular characteristics of the data controller; (g) number of individuals concerned.

[16] Thus, Parisi (2022), pp. 225–226.

[17] The text of recital 76 GDPR is quoted: 'the likelihood and severity of the risk to the rights and freedoms of the data subject should be determined with regard to the nature, scope, context and purposes of the processing. The risk should be considered on the basis of an objective assessment as to whether the data processing operations involve a risk or a high risk'.

Turning to the contents of the notification, pursuant to Article 33(3) GDPR, the notification must:

- Describe the nature of the personal data breach including, where possible, the categories and approximate number of data subjects concerned, as well as the categories and approximate number of personal data records involved.
- Provide the name and contact details of the data protection officer or other contact point where more information can be obtained.
- Describe the likely consequences of the personal data breaches.
- Describe the measures taken or proposed to be taken by the data controller to remedy the personal data breach and mitigate its possible adverse effects.

A valuable source of guidance for those involved in the processing is Guideline No. 1/2021 on examples concerning the notification of a personal data breach, adopted by the EDPB on 14 December 2021. For cases of *ransomware*, data exfiltration attacks, human error, loss or theft of devices or paper documents, as well as for misdirected correspondence and other cases (*social engineering*), the European *board* offers precise guidance and valuable help for the data controller in assessing the data breach that has actually occurred. Finally, the document confirms the need for continued accountability of those involved in data processing activities, emphasising the centrality of prevention and minimisation of the impact of *data breaches*. More concretely, according to the guidelines, each data controller and processor should have plans and procedures for managing data breaches, establishing a clear allocation of internal tasks and identifying the figures responsible for the stages of the recovery process. In the name of the principle of *accountability* and in deference to data protection by design, the preparation of a data breach management manual, prepared by the controller and processor, is advocated.

In this framework, one of the most important obligations for the data controller is precisely to assess these risks, not only *ex ante*, by implementing appropriate technical and organisational measures to address them, but also in the event of a *data breach*, in order to decide whether and what notification to make and what action to take to minimise the negative impacts.

It goes without saying that the SA remains competent to decide on the adequacy of the notification made by the data controller, intervening with corrective powers and possibly the adoption of sanctions.

Added to this is the right of the data subject to be compensated for the damages suffered as a result of the *data breach*, as we will see in one of the next paragraphs. Indeed, a breach can potentially have a number of significant negative effects on individuals, which may result in physical, material or immaterial damage. The GDPR gives examples of this in a number of hypotheses, including loss of control over one's personal data, limitation of the exercise of rights over such data, effects of discrimination, identity theft or fraud and financial loss, unauthorised cancellation of pseudonymisation, damage to reputation or loss of confidentiality of personal data protected by professional secrecy (think of medical data). More generally, any other significant economic or social disadvantages for data subjects must be taken into account in the risk analysis.

Another issue addressed by the *European Data Protection Board* is that of non-EU international companies and the way in which data holders communicate *data breaches* through representatives established in the EU.

On this point, after a public consultation phase that started in September 2022 (09/2022), the *European Data Protection Board* adopted, on 28 March 2023, a new version of the guidelines regarding personal data breach notification obligations focused on data controllers established abroad, who have a representative within one of the European Union countries, and therefore as such fall within the scope of the GDPR. They are therefore recipients of the obligations, by virtue of the *targeting* of the processing. In particular, data controllers established in a third country who nonetheless carry out activities that intentionally involve the personal data of data subjects within the territory of the European Union for the purpose of offering goods and services or otherwise monitoring behaviour, insofar as such behaviour takes place within the territory of the Union, are obliged to appoint a representative.

For these entities, the previously established application of the *one-stop-shop* principle is expressly superseded, i.e. the identification of the competent lead supervisory authority, coinciding with the one where the company's main establishment is located or where the company itself resides. Otherwise, the *European Data Protection Board* adopts the principle of proceeding with the notification for each supervisory authority of the countries where the data subjects involved in the *data breach* reside. Evidently, in order to be able to proceed in this way, non-EU foreign companies will be called upon to adopt specific technical measures to immediately associate the data subjects involved in a *data breach* with their respective jurisdiction. This association will have to be made precisely within 72 h of becoming aware of the incident.

It goes without saying that such a requirement is a harbinger of several critical issues, both with regard to the design of the *databases* and to the adoption of correct methods for acquiring the aforementioned geographic information; and also with regard to the associated costs and their sustainability when compared with the need for protection and the previous possibility of notifying only one EU country.

On this specific point, Article 33 GDPR envisages a generalised obligation for the data controller to notify any competent supervisory authority of a *data breach*, pursuant to Article 55 GDPR ff., i.e. the supervisory authority coinciding with the sole or main place of establishment of the data controller affected by the breach, or the place where the data subjects affected by the breach are established.

The minimum information to be included in the notification is included, as mentioned, in Article 33 and it is the responsibility of the competent authority to provide the forms with the mandatory information on its website. This documentation enables the control authority to verify compliance with the requirements.

4 The Compensation of the Damage to the Data Subject in Community and National Case Law

One of the most controversial points in case law has concerned the compensation of damage in favour of the interested party.

In this regard, it is worth recalling a recent decision adopted by the EU Court of Justice,[18] on some preliminary questions raised by the Bulgarian judicial authority.

The reference for a preliminary ruling concerned the interpretation of Articles 5(2), 24 and 32, as well as Article 82(1) to (3) of Regulation (EU) 2016/679 of the European Parliament and of the Council of 27 April 2016 on the protection of individuals with regard to the processing of personal data and on the free movement of such data, and was submitted in the context of a dispute between a citizen of Bulgarian nationality and the local tax authority.

The issue concerned the interpretation of the GDPR, which provides that a data controller is liable for the damage caused by a breach of the regulation, unless it proves that *the harmful event is in no way attributable to him.*

The case stemmed from a hacker attack on the authority's website that resulted in the theft and publication of personal data of more than six million individuals of Bulgarian or foreign nationality. The applicant sought compensation for the immaterial damage that would have resulted from the disclosure of his personal data, where the immaterial damage consisted of the fear that his personal data, which had been published without his consent, would be misused in the future or that he might suffer blackmail, assault or even kidnapping.

The authority in its defence argued, first, that the applicant in the main proceedings had not asked it for information concerning the precise data that had been disclosed. It then produced documents to show that it had taken all necessary measures, upstream, to prevent the breach of personal data contained in its computer system and, downstream, to limit the effects of that breach and to reassure the public. Moreover, according to the authority, there was no causal link between the intangible damage complained of and that breach. Finally, it argued that, since it had itself suffered malicious damage by people who were not its employees, it could not be held liable for the harmful consequences thereof.

By decision of 27 November 2020, the **Administrativen** *sad Sofia-grad* (Sofia City Administrative Court) dismissed the applicant's action in the main proceedings. That court held, on the one hand, that the unauthorised access to the database resulted from hacking committed by third parties and, on the other hand, that the appellant in the main proceedings had not proved that NAP had failed to take security measures. Furthermore, it held that the appellant had not suffered intangible damage such as to give rise to a right to compensation.

The appellant in the main proceedings appealed against that decision to the *Varhoven* administrativen *sad* (Supreme Administrative Court, Bulgaria), which then referred the following questions for a preliminary ruling. In support of its

[18] Court of Justice, 14 December 2023, No 340/21.

appeal, the respondent argued that the court at first instance had erred in law in its allocation of the burden of proof concerning the security measures taken by the authority and that the authority had failed to prove its lack of inaction in that regard. Moreover, the appellant in the main proceedings argued that the fear of possible misuse of its personal data in the future constituted real, and not hypothetical, intangible damage.

The European Court of Justice in answering the questions for a preliminary ruling gave some important indications.

First of all, it clearly stated that Articles 24 and 32 of the GDPR must be interpreted as meaning that an unauthorised disclosure of personal data or unauthorised access to such data by 'third parties', within the meaning of Article 4(10), of that regulation, are not sufficient, in themselves, to consider that the technical and organisational measures implemented by the data controller in question are not 'adequate', within the meaning of those Articles 24 and 32.

The reference in Article 32(1) and (2) of the GDPR to '*a level of security appropriate to the risk*' and to an '*adequate level of security*' demonstrates that, that regulation establishes a risk management regime and that it in no way purports to eliminate the risks of a personal data breach. Therefore, it follows from the literal wording of Articles 24 and 32 of the GDPR that those provisions merely require the data controller to take technical and organisational measures to prevent, as far as possible, any personal data breach. The adequacy of such measures must be assessed in concreto, by examining whether those measures have been implemented by that controller taking into account the various criteria laid down by those articles and the data protection requirements specifically inherent in the processing in question, as well as the risks posed by that processing.

The court has also ruled on the manner in which the adequacy of the security measures must be assessed and, in particular, whether it must be assessed by the national courts in concreto, taking account of the risks associated with the processing in question. As a result, on the one hand there is the discretion of the data controller as to the appropriate technical and organisational measures, and on the other hand the duty of the national court which must be able to assess the complex weighting carried out by the data controller and thus ensure that the measures adopted by the latter are appropriate to guarantee such a level of security.

In making this analysis, the national court must not consider itself bound by the conduct of a judicial expert opinion (and its results), which is not a necessary means of proof.

As regards the burden of proof as to adequacy, it follows unambiguously from Articles 5(2), 24(1) and 32(1) of the GDPR that the burden of proving that personal data are processed in such a way as to ensure their adequate security within the meaning of Articles 5(1)(f) and 32 of that regulation lies with the data controller.[19]

[19] See, by analogy, Court of Justice, 4 May 2023, C-60/22, paragraphs 52 and 53, as well as Court of Justice, 4 July 2023, C-252/21, paragraph 95.

According to the referring courts, that liability cannot be excluded by the mere fact that the damage was caused by an act of *hacking* by a third party, that is to say, by persons removed from the direct authority of the data controller, since, on the contrary, the data controller must demonstrate that it did not make that breach possible by infringing an obligation laid down by the GDPR, and in particular the duty of data protection to which it is subject under Articles 5(1)(f), 24 and 32 of that regulation. Therefore, in the event of a personal data breach committed by a third party, the data controller may exonerate itself from its liability, on the basis of Article 82(3) of the GDPR, by demonstrating that there is no causal link between its possible breach of the data protection obligation and the damage suffered by the natural person.

Finally, with regard to the nature of the reimbursable harm and whether the fear of potential misuse of his personal data by third parties could fall within that definition, the court concluded in the affirmative.

In this regard, the court stated that it is clear from the wording of Article 82(1) of the GDPR that the existence of 'damage' 'suffered' constitutes one of the conditions of the right to compensation under that provision, on a par with the existence of a breach of that regulation and a causal link between that damage and that breach, these three conditions being cumulative.[20]

Moreover, relying on considerations of literal, systematic and teleological order, the court has interpreted Article 82(1) of the GDPR as precluding a national rule or practice which makes compensation for 'immaterial damage' within the meaning of that provision subject to the condition that the damage suffered by the data subject has reached a certain degree of seriousness.[21]

That being said, it must be emphasised, in the present case, that Article 82(1) of the GDPR does not distinguish between cases in which, following an established breach of the provisions of that regulation, the 'intangible damage' complained of by the data subject is, on the one hand, linked to a third party's misuse of his personal data which has already taken place, on the date of his claim, or, on the other hand, is linked to that person's perceived fear that such use may take place in the future.

Accordingly, the wording of Article 82(1) of the GDPR does not preclude the concept of 'immaterial damage' contained in that provision from covering a situation, such as that considered by the referring court, in which the data subject invokes, in order to obtain compensation on the basis of that provision, his fear that his personal data will be subject to future misuse by a third party, on account of the infringement of that regulation which has already occurred.

Furthermore, recital 85, first sentence, of the GDPR indicates that '[a] personal data breach may, if not addressed in an adequate and timely manner, result in physical, material or immaterial harm to natural persons, such as loss of control over personal data concerning them or limitation of their rights, discrimination, identity

[20] See Court of Justice, 4 May 2023, C-300/21, para. 32.

[21] See also Court of Justice, 4 May 2023, C-300/21, para. 51.

theft or usurpation, financial loss, (...) or any other significant economic or social harm'. It follows from that illustrative list of 'damage' which may be suffered by data subjects that the European Union legislature intended to include in those concepts, in particular, the mere 'loss of control' over their data, following an infringement of that regulation, even if the misuse of the data in question has not actually occurred to their detriment.

On the issue of damages, it is also worth recalling the case law of the Italian Supreme Court.

The court dealt with the subject when it framed the liability of the credit institution in cases where unauthorised orders are made by the customer on a current account by means of abusive access to the *Internet banking* system, within the scope of liability for the processing of personal data.[22] In these cases, the burden of proof was founded according to the criteria prescribed by Article 15 of Legislative Decree no. 196/2003, which provides that 'whoever causes damage to others as a result of the processing of personal data shall be liable to pay compensation pursuant to Article 2050 of the Civil Code', with the possibility for the bank to offer proof releasing it from its liability by demonstrating that it had taken all appropriate measures to avoid the damage in accordance with the knowledge acquired on the basis of technical progress, the nature of the data and the specific characteristics of the processing, by adopting suitable and preventive measures to prevent unauthorised access or processing pursuant to Articles 31 and 36 of Legislative Decree No. 196/2003. According to the Supreme Court, in fact, 'on the basis of the reference to Article 2050 of the Civil Code, operated by art. 15 of the privacy code, the institution that carries out an activity of a financial or, in general, credit type [...] is liable, as the owner of the personal data processing, for the damages resulting from the fact of not having prevented third parties from illegally entering the customer's telematic system by capturing his access codes and the consequent illegitimate transfer instructions, unless it proves that the damaging event is not attributable to him because it descends from negligence, error (or fraud) of the person concerned or from force majeure'.

In particular, Article 8(1) of Legislative Decree No. 11/2010 provides that 'The payment service provider issuing a payment instrument is obliged to (a) ensure that the personalised security credentials are not accessible to persons other than the user entitled to use the payment instrument, without prejudice to the latter's obligations under Article 7 [which are: to use the payment instrument in accordance with the terms governing its issuance and use, and to notify the payment service provider without delay of the loss, theft, misappropriation or unauthorised use of the instrument as soon as he becomes aware of it]'.

Article 10 further provides that, 'where the payment service user denies having authorised a payment transaction that has already been executed, the onus is on the payment service provider to prove that the payment transaction was authenticated, correctly recorded and accounted for, and that it has not been affected by the

[22] See Cass. 23 May 2016, No. 10638, in *Resp. civ. Prev.*, 2017, 850.

malfunctioning of the procedures necessary for its execution or by any other inconvenience'. Paragraph 2 adds that 'when the payment service user denies having authorised an executed payment transaction, the use of a payment instrument registered by the payment service provider is not necessarily sufficient in itself to prove that the transaction was authorised by the payment service user, nor that the payment service user acted fraudulently or failed with malice or gross negligence to fulfil one or more of the obligations under Article 7. The onus is on the payment service provider, including, where applicable, the payment order service provider, to provide proof of the fraud, wilful default or gross negligence of the user'.

The legislation in question, therefore, establishes, as a general rule, a liability of the bank in the event of a transaction not authorised by the customer, unless it stems from the customer's wilful misconduct or gross negligence, with the clarification that the onus is on the bank operator to prove that the unlawful operation by a third party, with reference to the disputed provisions, was made possible by the customer's wilful misconduct or gross negligence.

The Court of Cassation also specified that 'on the subject of the bank's liability in the case of transactions carried out by means of electronic instruments, also with a view to guaranteeing the confidence of users in the security of the system (which is in the interest of the operators themselves), it is entirely reasonable to bring the professional risk of the payment service provider into the area of foreseeable and avoidable by means of appropriate measures designed to verify the traceability of the transactions to the customer's will, the possibility of third parties using the access codes to the system, which cannot be attributed to the holder's fraudulent intent or to conduct so reckless that it cannot be dealt with in advance'.[23]

Accordingly, it is up to the service provider to prove that it has taken all the best technical precautions to avert the risk of fraudulent use of the payment instruments and the fraudulent or grossly negligent conduct of the user, such as to exclude its liability.

Moreover, the Supreme Court has ruled that 'although the bank has no general duty to monitor the regularity of the transactions ordered by the customer, nevertheless, in the presence of anomalous circumstances capable of harming the interests of the account holder, the bank, in application of its duty to execute the mandate in good faith, must refuse to execute it or at least inform the customer'.[24]

It has in fact been stated that 'on the subject of the bank's liability in the case of transactions effected by means of electronic instruments, also in order to ensure the confidence of users in the security of the system (which is in the interest of the operators themselves), it is entirely reasonable to bring the professional risk of the payment service provider into the area of the foreseeable and avoidable by means of appropriate measures designed to verify the traceability of transactions to the

---

[23] See Cass. 3 February 2017, No. 2950, in *Civil Justice Maximum*, 2017. See also Cass. 23 May 2016, No. 10638, cited above; Cass. 12 April 2018, No. 9158, in *Civil Liability & Prev.*, 2019, 620; Cass. 12 April 2020, No. 26916, in *Dejure* and, most recently, Cass. 20 May 2022, No. 16417, in *Law & Justice*, 2022.

[24] See, among many, Cass. 31 March 2010, No 7956, in *Jur. comm.*, 2011, 601.

customer's will, the possibility of third-party use of the system access codes, which cannot be attributed to the holder's intent or to conduct so reckless that it cannot be dealt with in advance. It follows that, even before the entry into force of Legislative Decree No. 11 of 2010, implementing Directive No. 2007/64/EC relating to payment services in the internal market, the bank, which is required to exercise due diligence of a technical nature, to be assessed according to the yardstick of the shrewd banker, is required to provide proof that the transaction can be traced back to the customer';[25] it was previously stated that 'on the subject of the distribution of the burden of proof, the account holder authorised to carry out transactions "on line" who, in accordance with Article 15 of Legislative Decree No. 196 of 2003 and 2050 of the Civil Code, acts for the abusive use of the services provided by the banker, is obliged to prove that the transaction is attributable to the customer', acts for the abusive use (in the case in point, by means of unlawful transfer instructions) of his computer credentials, it is only for the proof of the damage as it relates to the processing of his personal data, while the credit institution is liable, as holder of the data processing of the damage resulting from the fact that it did not prevent third parties from unlawfully entering the computer system by capturing the account holder's access codes, if it does not prove that the damaging event is not attributable to it because it was caused by the account holder's negligence, error or fraud or by 'force majeure'.[26]

And again with regard to the profile of the proof of the customer's wilful misconduct or gross negligence, the same case law has also clarified that the same must be positively provided by the service provider, since it cannot be presumed on the basis of the suitability of the protections adopted by the bank in order to prevent the execution of fraudulent transactions. The Civil Cassation has ruled in this sense[27]: 'The bank's liability for transactions carried out by means of electronic instruments, with particular regard to the verification of their traceability to the customer's will by checking the unlawful use of the relevant codes by third parties, is contractual in nature and, therefore, is to be excluded only if there is a situation of gross negligence on the part of the user'.

---

[25] See Cass. 3 February 2017, No. 2950, cited above; See also Cass. 12 April 2018, No. 9158, cited above; Cass. 20 May 2022, No. 16417, cited above.

[26] Cass. 23 May 2016, No. 10638, cit.

[27] See Cass. 26 November 2020, no. 26916, in *Civil Justice Maxima*, 2020.

5 Data Breach Management and Prevention

Every data controller should have plans and procedures in place for the prevention and subsequent management of data breaches, establishing clear reporting lines and responsibilities for action, including for aspects relating to the recovery process, in the most serious cases.[28]

In the prevention phase, training and awareness on data protection issues is crucial, since most breaches depend on human error.

This training should be repeated regularly, depending on the type of business and size of the data controller, addressing the latest trends and warnings from cyberattacks or other security incidents.

The principle of *accountability (responsibility*) and the concept of data protection *by design* (*privacy by design*) require preventive analyses to be carried out, which feed into the *Handbook on Data Breach Handling*, where the actions to be taken for each aspect of the processing at each main stage are set out.

Alongside the hypothesis of human error, the other most common type of *data breach* depends on the backwardness of hardware and/or software systems, in respect of which the only possible solution is to continually update them: a solution that obviously presents the problem of being particularly costly. To this end, periodic penetration tests are essential.

Further prevention measures are:

- Transform the user from a weak link to the first line of defence.
- Applying the principle of least privilege with regard to data access.
- Adopt timely system *patching* policies.
- Encrypt sensitive data.
- Use two-factor authentication.
- Also pay attention to physical security.
- Carry out auditing activities by the DPO.

If, despite preventive measures, a *data breach* situation arises, the data controller must have determined the most appropriate response measures for each case, depending on the type of attack.

In this sense, the data controller must adopt a response protocol, based on procedures to be followed to manage and resolve any incidents of data destruction and/or loss. The adoption of the protocol must involve all the joints affected by the event and indicate in a consistent, systematic and proactive manner how to handle the various types of incidents. In addition, a precise and rapid flow of information must be foreseen in order to feed the reporting of the *data breach.*[29]

In this regard, it is necessary to set up a *cyber data incident response pack*, capable of.

---

[28] Thus Pizzetti (2016), p. 291.

[29] Burton (2017), p. 65 ff.

- Managing the incident and support the entity in its activities.
- Analysing the nature of the breach.
- Identifying the evidence, proof and technical information.
- Determining the type of compromised data.
- Determining which data has been compromised.
- Formalising the status of the security measures in place.
- Preparing the *remediation* plan.

In addition, the controller has a duty to keep all internal documentation relating to data breaches.

Then, in the case of *ramsower* attacks, there is the additional issue of data recovery and restoration.

Finally, it may be appropriate to take out an adequate insurance policy to insure the company against the risk of *data breaches*. The insurance compensates the costs that the company has to bear to repair the consequences of the breach and may also cover any legal costs that the company will have to face.

6 The Other Hypotheses of *Data Breach* Notification

That of the privacy legislation described above is not the only hypothesis of *data breach* notification. In fact, there are further specific ones in the *cybersecurity* rules.

In the Italian legislation, the *Cybersecurity* Decree Law[30] is relevant, which provides for the obligation for public administrations to report incidents impacting networks, information systems and IT services envisaged in the taxonomy referred to in Article 1, paragraph *3-bis*, of Decree Law No. 105/2019. The report must be made within 24 hours of becoming aware of the event, to be followed by a subsequent notification with all the elements collected within the next 72 h.

This legislation is flanked by one of European derivation with the directives called *Network and Information Security (NIS*), 1[31] and 2,[32] also implemented in Italy.

The aim is to strengthen cooperation between Member States and the exchange of information through the creation of a cooperation group and a network of Computer Security Incident *Response* Teams (CSIRT).

These bodies, set up at national level, have the task of monitoring incidents, providing early warning in the event of impacts beyond national borders, alerting and informing stakeholders on risks and incidents, and providing dynamic analysis to raise awareness among all market players. In Italy, this role is performed by the National Cybersecurity Authority (NCA).

---

[30] Law No 90/2024.

[31] Directive (EU) 2016/1148.

[32] Directive (EU) 2022/2555.

According to the first NIS directive, operators of essential services (OSE),[33] are required to notify, without undue delay, incidents that have a significant impact on continuity and service provision, respectively, to the CSIRT. For the purposes of the significance of the incident, they shall take into account.

- The number of users affected by the interruption of an essential service.
- The interval of time during which the essential service was not operational.
- The geographical extent of the area affected by the incident.

The provisions of the directive were then made applicable by Prime Ministerial Decree No. 81 of 14 April 2021, which provides for a differentiation of the obligation according to the impact of the incidents on the ICT assets of the entities included in the National Cyber Security Perimeter (PSNC).[34] The decree's taxonomy distinguishes two types of incidents according to their severity:

- The less serious ones listed in Table 1 of Annex A, including infections, failures, installations.
- The serious ones, listed instead in Table 2 of the same annex, characterised precisely by the fact that the incident has created a real disruption.

For the former, the reporting time frame is within 6 h of knowledge of the event, while for the latter, it must be done within 1 h. This is followed by an obligation to report any further relevant information on the incident without undue delay and without prejudice to any need for secrecy arising from ongoing investigations.

Outside the PSNC perimeter, incidents impacting computer networks, systems and services not included in the PSNC perimeter,[35] but nevertheless pertaining to included entities, must be notified within 72 h of knowledge of the incident.

Compared to the framework described so far, the NIS 2 amendment first of all changes the subjective classification: no longer OSE and digital service providers, but essential entities *(EE)*[36] and *important entities (IE)*.[37] Moreover, the classification no longer serves to distinguish reporting obligations, but rather the surveillance mechanisms applied.

---

[33] Essential services are defined as those services provided by public or private operators carrying out indispensable economic and social activities, such as: energy, drinking water, waste water, transport, banking, financial markets, digital infrastructure, healthcare, space. With respect to these, the directive distinguishes other digital service providers (FSDs), to which less stringent obligations apply.

[34] Decree-Law No. 105 of 21 September 2019.

[35] See Article 1, paragraph *3-bis*, introduced by Article *37-quater* of Decree-Law No 115 of 9 August 2022, converted, with amendments, into Law No 142 of 21 September 2022.

[36] These are those that operate in one of the highly critical sectors listed in Annex 1, have more than 250 employees or an annual turnover of more than EUR 50 m (energy, transport, banking, health, water, digital infrastructure, ICT services, public administration, space).

[37] These are those that fall within the sectors of Annex 1, but are below the size thresholds therein, i.e. all those operating in the sectors listed in Annex 2 (mail and courier, waste management, chemicals, food, manufacturing—medical and electrical/electronic products, digital services—search engines, online marketplaces and social networks, research).

With regard to the reporting of events, NIS 2 stipulates that it should only be done for significant events[38] and distinguishes between two steps:

- A preliminary notification within 24 h of knowledge of the event.
- A complete one within 72 h.

A third communication is then foreseen one month after the initial report, where it must be acknowledged that recovery has taken place and the measures taken to prevent future occurrences.

A final hypothesis on the subject of *data breaches* can be found in a sector regulation in the financial sector, namely the *Digital Operational Resilience Act (DORA)*,[39] which aims to harmonise for the sector[40] the reporting regime of incidents on ICT infrastructures and services. In this sense, the legislation provides for specific obligations to manage, notify and report *cyber* incidents across the entire *supply chain of* ICT services. In addition, financial operators are obliged to protect the availability, authenticity, integrity and confidentiality of all data, both personal and non-personal.

In the DORA system, notification must be made according to severity both to the regulatory authorities and to the customers and partners concerned.

For critical incidents, three different types of reports must be submitted: an initial notification report; an interim report on the progress made to resolve the incident; and a final report analysing the main causes of the incident.

References

Burton C (2017) Art. 33. In: AA.VV (ed) The EU general data protection regulation (GDPR). A practical guide. Springer, Berlin, p 65 ff

Esposito MS (2021) Art. 32 GDPR. In: Codice della privacy e data protection. Academia, Milano-Bologna-Roma, pp 503–505

Finocchiaro G (2020) Riflessioni su intelligenza artificiale e protezione dei dati personali. In: Ruffolo U (ed) Intelligenza artificiale. Il diritto, i diritti, l'etica. Giuffrè, Milano, p 246 ff

Fonderico G (2018) La regolazione amministrativa del trattamento dei dati personali. In Giorn. dir. amm., p 420

[38] Significant incidents are those that: have caused or are capable of causing direct financial damage to the affected entity; have caused or are capable of causing serious operational disruption to services. On the other hand, notification is not required for non-significant incidents, in respect of which the directive does not provide specific definitions, operating by difference from significant incidents. However, voluntary notification is also required for these events (Art. 29, NIS 2 directive).

[39] Regulation (EU) 2022/2554.

[40] It applies to all financial institutions, such as banks, investment companies and credit institutions, as well as non-traditional entities such as providers of cryptocurrency-related assets and *crowdfunding* platforms. It also applies to providers of ITC services to the aforementioned players.

Lucchini Guastalla E (2019) Privacy e data protection: principi generali. In: Tosi E (ed) Privacy digitale. Riservatezza protezione dei dati personali tra GDPR e nuovo Codice Privacy. Giuffrè, Milano, p 70

Mantelero A (2019) La gestione del rischio. In: La protezione dei dati personali in Italia, opera diretta da G. Finocchiaro. Zanichelli, Bologna, p 473 ff

Motroni R (2007) La sicurezza dei dati e dei sistemi. In: Cuffaro V, D'Orazio R, Ricciuto V (eds) Il Codice del trattamento dei dati personali. Giappichelli, Torino, p 221 ff

Parisi AG (2022) Illiceità del trattamento dei dati personali e rimedi (inibitori, risarcitori, satisfattivi e ablativi). In: Stanzione P (ed) I poteri privati e le nuove frontiere della privacy. Giappichelli, Torino, pp 225–226

Pizzetti F (2016) Privacy e il diritto europeo alla protezione dei dati personali. Dalla direttiva 95/46 al nuovo Regolamento europeo. Giappichelli, Torino, p 291

Renna M (2020) Violazione dei dati personali, sicurezza del trattamento e protezione dei rischi. In Dir. merc aff e fin., p 197 ff

Riccio GM (2005) Artt. 32-36. In: Sica S, Stanzione P (eds) La nuova disciplina della privacy. Commento al d.lgs. 30 giugno 2003, n. 196. Pacini Giuridiche, Bologna, p 126 ff

Rodotà S (1984) Tecnologie dell'informazione e frontiere del sistema socio-politico. In: Alpa G, Bessone M (eds) Banche dati, telematica e diritti della persona. Società editrice il Mulino, Padova, p 89 ff

Troiano P (2007) Artt. 31-36. In: Bianca CM, Busnelli FD (eds) La protezione dei dati personali. Commento al d.lgs. 30 giugno 2003, n. 196. CEDAM, Padova, p 682 ff

Zeno V, Zenchovich (1998) Una lettura comparatistica della l. 675/96 sul trattamento dei dati personali. In: Cuffaro V, Ricciuto V, Zeno-Zenchovich V (eds) Trattamenti dei dati e tutela della persona. Giuffrè, Milano, p 159 ff

The Privacy Risk in the New Frontier of Medical Apps and Telemedicine

Luigi Cameriero

Contents

Abstract This chapter investigates the recent frontier of telemedicine and medical apps in the wake of the most recent programmer of digital transition of the public administration with a view to highlighting, on the one hand, the historical-regulatory aspects of the processes of dematerialization of consent in health matters, and on the other hand, the delicate issues related to the privacy risk on data concerning the sensitive data relating to the person's state of health.

L. Cameriero (✉)
University of Rome "G. Marconi", Rome, Italy
e-mail: l.cameriero@unimarconi.it

R. Bocchini (ed.), *Digital Platforms - From Technical Foundations to Legal and Economic Implications*, https://doi.org/10.1007/978-3-032-07978-7_37

1 Foreword

Within the vast theme devoted to the digital transition of the public administration, which has aroused, and continues to arouse, so much attention within the public apparatus, among private economic operators, and among citizens, the sector that has clearly aroused the greatest interest is undoubtedly that of digital health..[1]

In fact, if one considers the public and private interests that intersect therein, together with the problems that the new digital platforms and technologies of recent conception bring with them[2] one immediately understands that this is a particularly delicate sector for the mere fact that its object is the organization of a service aimed at satisfying not so much a generic subjective legal situation as specific constitutionally protected situations such as the right to health or the principle of budgetary balance[3] from which, as a result of a combined reading, the rights-duties under Articles 81, 97, 117 and 119 of the Constitution arise.

If then, in addition to this preeminent aspect, one also associates the distinct, albeit connected, profiles relating to the needs of each individual to have the confidentiality of his or her health data protected, one also becomes irrevocably aware that one is faced with a bundle of complex legal cases that are difficult to resolve in concrete terms.

Therefore, the present contribution would like to have, at least in its intentions, the purpose of putting into sideways the different legal problems[4] both of a publicist rank[5] and of a private nature[6] that today coagulate around the theme of the *privacy* risk in that more specific niche of digital administration constituted by telemedicine

[1] The infrastructures and services gravitating in the orbit of digital health are quite varied if it is true that they include both the simple ones for everyday use by citizens, such as the electronic health card, the single booking center (CUP), and the electronic medical prescription; and the more complex ones, such as telemedicine and the electronic health record (FSE).

[2] Think of *big data*, artificial intelligence, and *machine learning*, just to name the most influential ones. On the risks arising from these technological innovations, see also for a more general overview Casini (2020a, b); Lalli (2019), p. 18.

[3] Constitutional Law No. 1/12—entitled 'Introduction of the principle of "Balanced Budget in the Constitutional Charter"'—reformulated Art. 81, 97, 117 and 119 of the Constitution, implementing the 'Euro Plus's Pact; With it, the Member States are committed to adopting measures aimed at pursuing the objectives of sustainability of public finances, competitiveness, employment and financial stability, and in particular to transposing into national legislation the EU budgetary rules set out in the Stability and Growth Pact, without prejudice to "the faculty to choose the specific national legal instrument" to be used, provided that it has "a sufficiently strong binding and sustainable nature (e.g., Constitution or framework legislation)" and such as to "ensure budgetary discipline at both national and sub-national levels".

[4] See Raposo (2016), p. 12.

[5] For a general reflection on these aspects with reference to the topic of health and big data, see Palladino and Farina (2023). On the technological development of public administration see, also for further references and bibliographical insights, Protto (2022).

[6] Marchese (2021).

and by the main mobile infrastructures through which healthcare[7] itself very often expresses its technological potential and its suggestive medical alternatives.

2 Defining Framework

It is well to clarify at once, both from a systematic epistemological point of view, and from a more simply deductive semantic point of view, that the digital health frontier finds its starting point in the framework of a growing and increasingly sophisticated development of the so-called ICT.

In the health sector, in fact, ICT has *been performing* well, constituting the infrastructural bed within which algorithms based on increasingly natural languages have gradually taken root, laying the foundations for a new technological era governed by the so-called AI.

The latter, from the English acronym *artificial intelligence*, undoubtedly represents the real stakes of our time.[8]

Whichever way things turn out from this point of view, it is already quite evident how powerful such a prospect is if one thinks that artificial intelligence, as the spearhead of a certain digital technology, and the anthropomorphized robotics that will be its natural consequence, enable, in the healthcare field operations *en abîme*, worthy of the best Magrittian symbolism,[9] such as those promising to monitor any pathology in time by suggesting the latest drug in universal *follow-ups*, or to perform *overplace* surgery, or even to favor precision rehabilitation after post-traumatic operations.

Dreamlike prospects that are not dreams, however, so much so that from the 1990s[10] onwards certain voices in the medical literature aimed at promoting, in the

[7] Even more so within a technological horizon of this topic, it remains in our opinion fundamental to assimilate a distinctly humanistic conception of care. For an interesting philosophical trajectory on this matter see Menga (2023).

[8] For a competent analysis of the present and possible future scenarios, marked by the artificial intelligence revolution, the struggles between companies engaged in AI development and the geopolitical repercussions in the global equilibrium, see the valuable work by Aresu (2024).

[9] In the sign of the great Belgian artist's pictorial poetics, where it is enchanting to note the dialogue in its pure state between internal and external reality where no logical parameter is respected, the vision surpasses reality, in a surreality that detaches itself from its signifying crust and lives free of constraints and limits. For those wishing to explore the painter's work and his instinct to couple two realities, see Magritte (2024).

[10] For the sake of accuracy of documentation, it should be noted that Nebraska Psychiatric Institute in Omaha and Norfolk State Hospital and Bird, in 1967, created the first prototype of an interactive telemedicine system, which connected the medical station at Logan International Airport in Boston and Massachusetts General Hospital. Telemedicine projects were mostly developed and carried out by NASA with the aim of monitoring astronauts' vital parameters and the effects of zero gravity on their bodies. But as space flights became longer, telemedicine progressed from what we would today call telemonitoring, to the diagnosis and treatment of diseases or intervention in various medical conditions that occurred during space flights. Cf. Bird (1971).

sign of its own time and in the farsightedness of the times to come, so-called telemedicine have generated more and more consensus.

A solution, the latter, which can be framed in the semantics of a typical digital infrastructure capable of allowing most healthcare services to be delivered at a distance, giving more specialists and healthcare professionals the opportunity to assist their patients in their homes.[11]

It is also within the orbit of such a programmatic framework of digital health within which, as is well known, a plurality of complex tools and services of the entire and fertile *mobile health market*[12] are stirring, so much so as to have determined the need to establish the so-called European health data space,[13] mention should also be made of the *medical apps*,[14] the operation of which, unlike telemedicine, designed in any case to be always efficient through the doctor-patient relationship, is based, by contrast on a more advanced technological relationship due to the fact that it operates through a *software-person* relationship which, far from necessarily having to *ex latere* present a patient, rather takes on the guise of an infosphere[15] that a user-consumer interrogates in order to benefit from an algorithmized healthcare service without any need to establish a prior therapeutic relationship with a doctor as a physical person.[16]

3 Health and *Smart Cities*

In a historical context such as today's where all the world's cities are taking on the appearance of so-called *smart cities*, the theme of health digitization is both a priority and a crucial one.

Health digitization therefore aims to be both an economic vector for increasing the *performance of* the system and a useful tool for ensuring greater social equity.

---

[11] We will dwell on the regulatory specificities and technical peculiarities of telemedicine in the remainder of this discussion by analyzing its four main declinations known as telehealth, teleconsultation, telemonitoring, and teleassistance.

[12] The size of the global mHealth market is calculated to be $81.71 billion in 2025 and is expected to exceed approximately $268.46 billion by 2034, expanding at a CAGR of 14.13% from 2025 to 2034. The North American healthcare market size reached $27.10 billion in 2024 and is expanding at a Compound average growt rate (CAGR) of 14.15% during the forecast period. The market sizing and forecasts are based on revenue (USD million/billion), with 2024 as the base year.

[13] The 2024 European Health Data Space (EHDS) is an EU initiative to improve health data management by promoting privacy, security, and interoperability. It aims to facilitate the exchange of data between Member States, improving research, prevention, and treatment.

[14] The plural is all the more compulsory considering that according to the latest Research2Guidance 2024 report, there are estimated to be over 100,000 health apps on the market.

[15] On the nature and potential of this concept see, Floridi (2017).

[16] For a reflection on the technical but also ethical consequences of such an approach and, above all, on the issues related to the (lack of) scientific validation of health apps see Spissu et al. (2017).

Before, however, talking about the existing *liaison* between digital health and the *senseable city*, it is most opportune, for the purposes of a more complete analysis of the theme we are discussing here, to dwell on the meaning of the word 'health' and, more specifically, on the ontological dislocation of the same determined precisely by the introduction and consequent use of the new technologies.

If on the surface the issue may seem tedious, the same cannot be said in substance as soon as one notices, medical and legal literature in hand, that the concept, in its human centrality, has undergone radical changes in interpretation and meaning over the years.

While in the 1950s the most common definition of health would have been *the condition to be restored when an illness arises*, in the mid-twentieth century, the WHO without delay defined the concept of health as *a state of complete physical, mental and social well-being and not simply the absence of disease or infirmity.*[17]

In that turn of the century, and up to 2011, the concept of health referred to a more complex set of things: life expectancy 80 years and healthy life expectancy lower than life expectancy, about 60 years well-being during life, and more. In essence, the effigy of a constitutionally guaranteed freedom expressed in freedom from curable diseases and avoidable mortality.[18]

Having reviewed the evolution of the concept of health, let us now return to the subject of health digitization to reiterate how it is closely connected with a certain idea of the technological development of our cities.

In a city developing in an interoperable way, digital health enables not so much and not only the improvement of the care provided by hospitals and family doctors, but also less visible tasks such as the prevention and control of communicable diseases, health promotion, personnel planning and the improvement of the economic or environmental conditions in which people live.

4 Public and Private Legal Implications of *Digital Health*

In the preceding paragraphs, we have seen the technical, medical, and legal categories that revolve within the orbit of *digital health*.

After having grasped the preliminary meanings of these new technological solutions in the medical environment, we have seen how digital health a valid programmatic-political promise for the renewal of our society in terms of smartness is, which in turn fully adheres to a broader new idea of our future cities.

What we wish to bring out at this point of the analysis concerns another important theme, the treatment of which is fundamental for the correct reconstruction of

---

[17] Preamble to the Constitution of the World Health Organization as adopted by the International Health Conference, New York, 19–22 June 1946, signed on 22 July 1946 by the representatives of 61 states and entered into force on 7 April 1948.

[18] Sic., Sen (1999). For some critical insights into the *pars destruens* of the concept, see Nobile (2013).

the overall tenor of the subject we are dealing with. The reference is, as can be guessed, to the topic of *big* data[19] and, more specifically, to the problem of data processing itself, i.e., *privacy* risk prevention..[20]

As a matter of fact, if the solutions we have just discussed offer on the one hand a good *chance of* success both from a public perspective of strengthening the protection of health and from a private perspective in the name of a virtuous *empowerment of* the patient, the same cannot be said on the other hand, i.e., from the one that casts shadow cones on the fact that the diffusion of medical apps and telemedicine, to an extent, theoretically, almost totalizing, postulates *ex se* the management and circulation of a huge amount of personal and health data, such that it would not be at all illegitimate to continue to wonder, on account of the possible extraction[21] of people's *modus vivendi*, whether we have not really entered a post-society[22] irritate rather than liquid[23] daughter of that community of risk[24] destined to be governed only by a dystopian capitalism of surveillance.[25]

In a general situation characterized by such profiles of uncertainty, the new technologies are becoming more and more urgent a stance in favor of a precise economic analysis of the law and of a courageous regulatory policy on the part of the same[26] that is as osmotic as possible, i.e., capable of making public and private dialogue[27] with a view to a correct synthesis of interests that is able, on the one hand, to enhance the potential of the technologies while also protecting, to the effect, the

---

[19] The varied cataloguing of the phenomenon, such as *e-health, m-health, digital health, health information technology, telemedicine*, highlights the connection with the collection, analysis, and application of big data in the health sector, showing that the relationship between technology and health protection is constantly evolving. Palladino (2023) reports it in these terms and agrees with it.

[20] In deference to the meaning that it has gradually taken on in the most attentive legal literature since Warren and Brandeis' (1980) idea of privacy as the *right to be left alone.* See also Solove (2017). For a reconstruction of the concept in the Italian literature, among others, see at least, Rescigno (1995). For an in-depth study of the topic more generally and for further bibliographical references on the subject, see for all De Franceschi (2017).

[21] From a perspective of legal-regulatory prophylaxis, *big data* can in our opinion be defined as the excarnated unconscious and, for this reason, from a more strictly psycho-sociological point of view they are called upon to definitively mark its end.

[22] On this perspective of de-socialization or the end of the social, see Bordoni (2021).

[23] I take up the icastic images of the two most authoritative and influential sociologists in the world: see, in this regard, Ferrarotti (2020).

[24] For all, Beck (2018).

[25] Zuboff (2019).

[26] On the contribution that jurists can make in the reflection on the development of tools for the management and analysis of *big data*, see the interesting work by Faro et al. (2020), Shapiro and Varian (1999). On how to understand private law today on the general theory side, see the ever timely work of Rescigno et al. (2017). For a more general overview of the problem, see the valuable work by Falce et al. (2017).

[27] A topical reading on administrative law and emerging technologies that does not neglect to consider certain private law implications can be found in the work of Protto (2022). But see also on the topic the useful work of Avanzini (2019).

information heritage generated by them; and, on the other hand, neutralize those equally potential negativities that could result from a non-compliant analysis of the data collected and managed.[28]

This assumption gives us the figure of the importance that data have within the new global policies and how decisive they have now become in the development of competitiveness in the various market sectors and at the same time in the improvement of the administrative organization of public services.[29]

Even the legal remedies often adopted to best develop the various technological solutions of the vast world of *digital health*, such as PPPs or PFs, and P4Ps, if on the one hand thanks to virtuous public-private collaboration they drain public resources with a view to accelerating results, on the other hand, in the face of private *payback* drives, they pose, conversely, further problems linked to the installation of truly *waterproof privacy* systems, i.e., to the execution of rigorous *assessment* processes of the *privacy* ecosystem, the quality of which, especially at the level of the accountability of civil offences generated for various reasons,[30] is often open to doubt.

5 Prolegomena and Prophylaxis of Dematerialized Consent

Ours is the time of technology[31] and because of this cultural horizon, which is by no means resolved in the understanding of specific technologies, information infrastructures of all kinds starting with those we have identified in this contribution are evolving so fast that they leave man in fear of even losing control over them.

Even if law is always in crisis, being by its very nature a *post-factum* phenomenon, it is nonetheless a fact that in the face of the challenges that life offers us in the course of history, it is always up to law to regulate the novelties that the various cultural experiences introduce into the world.

Well, among these novelties, which the law has had to take on the burden of understanding and regulating, there is to be considered, for the purposes that interest us with a view to offering as exhaustive a picture as possible of the issues that concern us here, the innovation of dematerialization, i.e., the possibility of circulating

---

[28] This sort of *check and balance* 5.0. is questioned by those who believe that from the data, *recte*: from their analysis, an unexpected effect of changing sovereignty itself may arise. See Casini (2020a, b) for an in-depth discussion of this issue.

[29] See on this point the extensive reflections of Carullo (2018).

[30] We can also dwell on these profiles for further bibliographic needs in Perlingieri (2018), Sica (2018), Di Ciommo (2023), Bocchini (2003) and Sica (2023).

[31] The long and fruitful dialogue held by Natalino Irti and Emanuele Severino on this philosophical-political and juridical-economic concept is well known among the attentive scholars of these topics. And since it is always useful to return to it, see among many others Irti and Severino (2001). For a scholarly update on where we have arrived with respect to that imperishable dialogue, see Benenti et al. (2025).

the forms of manifestation of one's will and thought, in a technological and digital environment, without the necessary aid of paper.

The dematerialization of informed consent represents, in fact, a fundamental and, moreover, not simple junction to be tackled in view of the overall grounding of health digitization. That being said, it is in any event worth recalling that, in the medical environment, consent, as is well known, is already at the basis of any human sharing, and constitutes a *condicio* sine qua non for the very lawfulness of the healthcare activity[32] and assumes, by reason of its constitutional relevance as a fundamental right of the person,[33] the nature of a true and proper contractual obligation[34] for the breach of which one may be called to answer, even regardless of the outcome of the intervention itself, both in terms of civil liability[35] and criminal liability.[36]

6 A 5.0 Endiad: The Digital Patient-Citizen

It has been rigorously asserted that AI constitutes only a new form of man's capacity to act in the third millennium precisely to signify that far from imposing itself *ab externo*, and from above, in the social nature, it will rather be integrated from below, giving rise to a new *documanity*.[37]

Person and data, in other words, will increasingly become one and the same thing, so that the citizen itself, far from remaining detached from the social fabric, will be, on the contrary, the primary digital element of a broader administrative interoperability of the entire city of the future, technologically advanced to the point of becoming, by analogue and digital means, a true *Cyborg Onlife*.[38]

[32] For an exception to consent, read in any case Art. 8 of the Oviedo Convention and Art. 35 of the code of medical ethics.

[33] In the Italian legal system, the principle of informed consent has a constitutional basis in the combined reading of *Art. 32*, *Art. 13*, and Art. 2.

[34] It was enshrined as early as 1947 in the Nuremberg Code and subsequently made explicit in the World Medical Association's Declaration of Helsinki. In Italy, on the other hand, it is Article 33 of Law no. 833 of 23 December 1978, establishing the National Health Service, that sanctions the doctor's obligation to acquire the patient's prior consent to undergo surgery.

[35] In compliance with and within the limits of what is stated in case law: *ex multis*, see recently, also for further pretrial supplementing, at least Cass. civ., sec. III, no. 12205/2015, Cass. civ., sec., III, no. 17649/2024. In doctrine, for all, see Franzoni (2012).

[36] Art. 50 states: anyone who injures or endangers a right with the consent of the person who can validly dispose of it shall not be punishable.

[37] The icastic power of the concept and its complex meanings are due to the ingenuity of Ferraris (2021).

[38] The term *Onlife* was coined by Luciano Floridi to represent the experience that human beings have in hyper historic societies where one no longer distinguishes between *online* and *offline* and where it is no longer reasonable to ask whether one is *online* or *offline*. The word explains the merging of the digital into the analogue caused by information and communication technologies

Man will be a great producer of data to the extent that he will increasingly be required to release it, even *obtorto collo*, before being able to access any public or private service that interests him, and the set of this digital data, in turn, will be continuously configured and reconfigured to create *social palimpsests* within which man will manifest himself to satisfy his own human needs.

Obviously, the data produced by digital devices, even embodied by humans, will be able, *ça va sans dire*, to be visualized, algorithmically interpreted, and thus shared with others if desired.

This means that *cyber-space* will no longer be, as it was until yesterday, a place of the imagination, an idea to be admired in some postcard or to be seen through some telescope, but, on the contrary, it will be the virtual mirror of man, a sort of archive of the body's data, and thus a possible *hyperreality* within which man will confront and resolve through those newly coined subjective situations whose identification and discipline, especially in the health ecosystem, will represent the real legal challenge of our time.

7 From the Invention *Ex Vetere* to the *Post Festum* Inventory of Telemedicine

Telemedicine is an application that makes the most of ICT technologies with a well-defined and declared objective: to remotely provide a series of medical activities useful for assessing a patient's state of health and for possibly administering a treatment proposal to the same.

It is, therefore, a medical activity, of a subsidiary nature, which allows the doctor and the patient to communicate interactively, remotely, benefiting, in essence, from the same value that the doctor provides in his usual and traditional interactions with his patient.

Telemedicine began to appear in Italy in the mid-1970s, although it was only after the Covid-19 epidemiological emergency that its undoubted usefulness became more evident.[39]

Future work should identify an optimal formula that exploits a hybrid care model that combines virtual and in-person visits to create a consistent care experience.[40]

As shown in telemedicine, not only doctor-patient, but also doctor-consultant, or doctor-nurse relationships are involved.

Specialist telemedicine applications can be classified, according to the actors involved, into the following categories:

(ICTs), demarcating the historical period from the hyper historical one. For an analysis of the visionary issue, see Floridi (2015).

[39] For a reconstruction of the issue see Sica et al. (2010). Cf., more recently, the interesting collection by Alovisio and Iannone (2024).

[40] As shared by Jercich (2021).

1. Telehealth: This is the healthcare act in which the doctor interacts remotely, and by video call, with the patient to assess, through the real-time exchange of all the necessary medical documentation, his clinical situation and to prescribe drugs, or further examinations.
2. *Teleconsultation*: This is the modality whereby a professional interacts remotely, also asynchronously, with one or more colleagues to share clinical data and images of a patient to discuss together the patient's clinical situation, which may be either present or absent during the activity.
3. *teleconsulting*: This is the healthcare activity, not always medical, but in any case, of a healthcare nature, which takes place at a distance, with or without the patient, and is performed by two or more persons who have different responsibilities with respect to the specific case. In such a case, the addressed health professional provides the other, or the others, with indications for the decision or for the correct execution of care actions addressed to the patient.
4. *Telecare*: This is the professional act whereby a health professional interacts, in real time, at a distance with the patient or with his or her *caregiver* through a video call, to which may be added, if necessary, the sharing of referral data or images.
5. *Telemonitoring*: This is the procedure through which it is possible to remotely transmit the vital and clinical parameters continuously measured on the patient by means of special sensors.
6. *Telecontrol*: This is the activity through which the doctor, after a constant series of contacts with the patient, remotely monitors, via video call, the patient's state of health.
7. *Telerehabilitation*: This consists in the remote and *pooled* provision by a health professional of services useful for monitoring or improving the psychophysical well-being of persons of all ages who have disabilities or disorders, whether congenital or acquired, transitory or permanent, or who are at risk of developing them.

Based on this rather diversified range of opportunities, telemedicine undoubtedly represents an opportunity for great political-programmatic renewal, in technological and digital terms, of the international and Italian health system in particular.[41]

Telemedicine, in a public health system that is increasingly in difficulty, especially in the south and in the inland areas of the country, can undoubtedly represent the keystone for infuturing a healthcare that is more timely and closer to people of all age groups and territorial origins.

The strategies that contribute to effective care that could be provided through telemedicine can in fact be summarized in three fundamental challenges:

(a) Promoting self-management.
(b) Optimizing treatment.
(c) Coordinating care.

[41] Bortugno (2018) questions these aspects and the reason for telemedicine.

If these are the objectives behind these specific opportunities within a more general design of digital transition of the public administration, it is no coincidence to discover that many countries within the OECD are investing in telemedicine initiatives of their own, considering it the most important promise of *digital health.*

In addition, however, to the certainties mainly acquired at a political and economic level regarding the usefulness and goodness of such a prospect of digitally renewing the health system, many legal risks remain unresolved, which the digital ecosystem within which telemedicine will have to move contributes in some respects to confusion and complication.[42]

One thinks again of profiles linked to the difficulties not so much concerning the entrenchment of various territorial and jurisdictional competences that could always find a synthesis in the patient's place of residence, but rather of the complications of putting a judgement *in executivis* if, as could happen, the patient finds himself before professionals who could reside on either side of the world.

Moreover, it is already apparent *from tabulas* that direct-to-consumer telemedicine is often misused, which can increase healthcare utilization and costs.[43]

A further factor of concern is security management starting with *privacy.*

In particular, the transmission of data from wired to wireless networks requires specific security guidelines for data processing and management and the development of medical devices.

The goal of telemedicine must be to increase the shared trust, comfort, and compassion involved in care, proving that telemedicine issues go far beyond the traditional *privacy* risks commonly referred to.

The ethical conundrum of telemedicine realizes the unique positive impact telemedicine can have on patients, *providers* and clinical outcomes, as well as the potential for harm and abuse that can result. *Providers* and systems using telemedicine should also consider how it affects patient relationships, access to healthcare, ability to treat patients fairly, costs, and quality of life.

The ability to address these concerns will be important for the future development and implementation of this important technology as one of the means to improve access and quality of healthcare for all members of our society.[44]

---

[42] For a detailed analysis of data protection and medical liability issues in the telemedicine environment, see Pisani (2024).

[43] Eze et al. (2020).

[44] In this regard, see the timely reflections of Fleming et al. (2009).

8 The Native Security of *Mobile e-Health*: About *Privacy by Design and by Default*

Among the various issues that *digital health* raises, patient safety is the key issue.[45]

This awareness underlies the complex regulatory legislation that has been increasingly refined in recent years with a view to creating a system of controls, transparency, and traceability of medical devices that is increasingly rigorous and at the same time increasingly osmotic with the *privacy* legislation itself, with the principles enshrined therein of *accountability*[46] and *safety by design.*[47]

It is precisely the principle of *safety by design* that deserves further highlighting for our purposes, insofar as it aims to achieve important processes of security of health infrastructures through its specific realization by means of two other important and peculiar principles that in some way become constituent elements of the *health mobile*, namely *privacy by design* and *privacy by default.*

With privacy *by design*, the protection of the rights and freedoms of natural persons regarding the processing of personal data requires the adoption of appropriate technical and organizational measures to ensure compliance with the provisions of this regulation. To be able to demonstrate compliance with this Regulation, the data controller should adopt internal policies and implement measures that meet in particular the principles of data protection by design and data protection by default.

Privacy by default means processing as little data as possible in relation to the purpose for which they are processed and processing for as long as is strictly necessary for the fulfilment of that purpose and of the related data protection obligations.

9 The Positive Domestic Experience of the Italian PNT

The idea behind the telemedicine platform is to create new remote care pathways on the Italian territory, to make it easier for local structures to take charge, thus favoring territorial care and de-hospitalization.

The public body of national interest, Agenas (National Agency for Regional Health Services), has announced the call for expressions of interest for the submission of public-private partnership proposals for the concession for the '*Design, implementation and management of the enabling services of the National PNT Telemedicine Platform*'.

---

[45] With reference to the problems of consensus see Irti (2021), Rodotà (1984), as well as Finocchiaro (2019).

[46] It is responsibility-proof at the same time. Finocchiaro (2019) agreeably emphasizes this. For an in-depth study of the principle and also for further useful bibliographical references, see the valuable work by Carleo (2021).

[47] I refer to the combined reading of the two relevant normative documents on the subject, i.e., the MDR regulation 2017/45 and the GDPR.

From a strictly administrative point of view, Agenas, by means of a public-private partnership procedure, and with the competent assistance of ANAC, entrusted the design, realization and management of the National Telemedicine Platform in concession to PNT Italia S.r.l., a company set up 60% by Engineering and 40% by Almaviva S.p.A., for a total duration of 10 years.

The contract was signed on March 2023 with the expressly stated goal of assisting approximately 330,000 patients on the Platform by 2025, and over 790,000 in 2026.

In view of achieving this goal, about 90,000 workstations have been implemented for healthcare professionals working in rural pharmacies, doctors' offices, community hospitals, territorial operations centers, and healthcare institutions so that everyone through a sophisticated interoperability can access the Electronic Health Record 2.0 and the more general Health Data ecosystem in one go.

From a technical and operational point of view, the National Telemedicine Platform consists of a national infrastructure and 21 regional infrastructures, which are interoperable with each other, and which oversee providing the minimum telemedicine, teleconsultation, teleassistance, and telemonitoring services, the features of which we have discussed in the previous paragraph.

The national infrastructure is designed in such a way as to ensure compliance with the international standards required to promote interoperability with European initiatives in view of the final consecration of the EU Health Data Space,[48] which should make it possible for all citizens to access their ESF by 2030.

Agenas emphasized that this project has at least four challenges to be met in the short term, which will certainly have to include the cultural change of healthcare personnel and the population; training the personnel so as to avoid as far as possible forms of *digital divide* or *digital shock*; interoperability, without which nothing could work; and last but not least, of course, security, both in terms of *waterproofing* and *privacy*.

[48] Primary objectives of the European Health Data Space are interoperability of health data among all European citizens and the use of data for research and public interest objectives. In this regard, it is worth remembering that Europe was the first to create rules with the IA Act precisely to guarantee the quality of data, which, moreover, is a prerequisite for the functioning of artificial intelligence. The IA Act has been operational since 2 February 2025, but 60 measures are still needed to implement the regulatory patchwork provided for in Regulation 2024/1689. Another important building block is the entry into force on 12 January 2025 of the European Health Technology Assessment Regulation 2021/2282, which will impact both drugs and devices, including AI devices that will be assessed with this methodology from 2026.

10 Conclusion: From Man to Robot One Way Only

Ours is a time that is technologically exciting and philosophically challenging, but also legally very complex if we consider the fact that we have before us the concrete possibility of living with the *robot*.[49]

In the society of our time, this observation is no longer just a reflection to be developed within a certain legal-epistemological or ethical-phenomenological horizon, but evidence of our times to which we need to give increasingly clear and precise answers in our everyday life.[50]

Artificial intelligence[51] and humanoid robotics[52] will, in other words, be the new terrestrial guests[53] with whom we need to develop a more up-to-date social pact in place of the physiological limitation of human control in relation to the power of technology and, above all, the speed with which technological evolution flows before our eyes day after day.

We are, i.e., informed by knowledge of the *law of accelerated returns* that the time taken by technology to improve is never linear, but always exponential.[54]

Famous in this regard is the response of Steve Jobs, who in a 2008 interview with the *Wall Street Journal*, referring to the digital world in general, said: '*I wouldn't trust any of our predictions, because so far reality has exceeded them to the point that we are now, like you, mere spectators*'.

In other words, we know, thanks to these studies on the law of accelerated returns, that the better the machine, the less time it will take to improve, and therefore the greater the possibility that in the meantime anomic spaces will open in this diaphragm time.[55]

Artificial intelligence, algorithms of the deep and robotics propose, from this cultural point of view, a great transformation without return of society, science, and medicine.

Precision diagnostics based on AI is just one of the most used examples to impress but also to testify to the citizen that a machine, perhaps a humanoid *robot*, if well programmed, could deliver a diagnosis as fast as the blink of an eye, processing all the world's *follow-ups* that have been recorded on that problem it is investigating and with no margin for error.

---

[49] The *Oxford English Dictionary* defines the *robot* not only in its purely technical aspect but also in its humanistic view as '*a machine that is made to look like a human and that can do some things that a human can do*'.

[50] To this end, read the dense and interesting pages of Longo (1998).

[51] D'Acquisto (2021).

[52] The term *Ròbot* was coined by the Czech writer Karel Čapek, in his work *Rossum's Universal Robots*. On the subject, see Catalano (2020). On the subject, read, however, the fundamental work of the first to elaborate the so-called laws of robotics, namely Asimov (1950). See in this regard the compelling contribution by Cingolani and Metta (2015).

[53] Reading the fine work by Anerdi and Dario (2022) is useful and educational on this idea.

[54] This is the trajectory traced in the late 1990s by Kurzweil (2024).

[55] On this interesting turn, the consultation of Immordino and Yang (2017).

The field of IA-controlled robotic surgery is the other *challenge of* the entire *digital health* ecosystem, and the idea in this field of an IA centaur is by no means an imagination, but a concrete and timely representation of numerous projects already in use in the world's best hospitals.

Consider that the new frontier we are talking about has already put in place the prospect of creating the virtual physiological man, i.e., a digital twin of ours on whom we can carry out all sorts of experiments to get to know everyone's physiome in depth with a view to creating a precision prophylaxis capable of eradicating diseases before they take on exacerbating forms.

In the face of these discoveries, we can be more than certain that the road taken towards this new hyperreal world will be one of no return. Precisely for this reason, the time has also come, in our opinion, to avoid lingering over the realization of what we have been able to recount in this chapter in the conviction that, after all, it is not technological progress in itself that is cause for concern, but if anything the legal framework within which it will develop if it is as true as it is true that a technological and epoch-making revolution of this magnitude can be as good as bad depending on the moral character of the men who will try to regulate it.

References

Alovisio M, Iannone MT (2024) Telemedicina, scenari digitali e protezione dei dati. Esperienze a confronto, Themis

Anerdi G, Dario P (2022) Compagni di viaggio, Robot, androidi e altre intelligenze, Torino

Aresu A (2024) Geopolitica dell'intelligenza artificiale, Milano

Asimov I (1950) Io, robot, Milano

Avanzini G (2019) Decisioni amministrative e algoritmi informatici. Predeterminazione, analisi predittiva e nuove forme di intelligibilità, Napoli

Beck U (2018) La società globale del rischio, Asterios

Benenti G et al (2025) Il Computer impossibile. Come il calcolatore quantistico cambierà il mondo, Milano

Bird KT (1971) Teleconsultation: a new health information exchange system, Massachusetts General Hospital, NTIS, the 03 a. rep, Boston

Bocchini R (2003) La responsabilità civile degli intermediari del commercio elettronico, Napoli

Bordoni C (2021) Post-società. Il mondo dopo la fine della modernità, Roma

Bortugno C (2018) Telemedicina e trasformazione dei sistemi sanitari. Un'indagine di bioetica, Roma

Carleo R (2021) Il principio di accountability nel GDPR: dalla regola alla auto-regolazione. In Nuovo dir. civ

Carullo G (2018) Gestione, fruizione e diffusione dei dati dell'amministrazione digitale e funzione amministrativa, Torino

Casini L (2020a) Lo Stato nell'era di Google, Milano

Casini L (2020b) Lo Stato nell'era di Google. Frontiere e sfide globali, Milano

Catalano A (2020) I robot di Karel Čapek: 100 anni di metamorfosi. I testi dell'autore su "R.U.R." e i documenti della ricezione italiana negli anni Venti e Trenta. eSamizdat. Journal of Slavic Cultures 13

Cingolani R, Metta G (2015) Umani e umanoidi. Vivere con i Ròbot. Bologna

D'Acquisto G (2021) Intelligenza artificiale: elementi, Torino

De Franceschi A (2017) La circolazione dei dati personali tra privacy e contratto, Napoli
Di Ciommo F (2023) Evoluzione tecnologica e regole di responsabilità civile, Napoli
Eze ND et al (2020) Telemedicine in the OECD: An umbrella review of clinical and cost-effectiveness, patient experience and implementation. In: Plos One
Falce V et al (2017) Informazione e big data tra innovazione e concorrenza. In: Quaderni Riv. dir. comm., Milano
Faro S et al (2020) Dati e algoritmi. Diritto e diritti nella società digitale, Bologna
Ferraris M (2021) Documanità. Filosofia del mondo nuovo, Milano
Ferrarotti F (2020) Dalla società irretita al nuovo umanesimo, Roma
Finocchiaro G (2019) Intelligenza artificiale e protezione dei dati personali. In Giur. it
Fleming DA et al (2009) Telehealth Ethics, New Rochelle, NY, vol. 15
Floridi L (2015) The Onlife Manifesto Being Human in a Hyperconnected Era, Berlin, 2015
Floridi L (2017) La quarta rivoluzione. Come l'infosfera sta trasformando il mondo, Roma
Franzoni M (2012) Dal consenso all'esercizio dell'attività medica all'autodeterminazione del paziente. In Resp civ
Immordino MH, Yang (2017) Neuroscienze affettive ed educazione, Milano
Irti C (2021) Consenso negoziato e circolazione dei dati personali, Torino
Irti N, Severino E (2001) Dialogo su diritto e tecnica, Milano
Jercich K (2021) Stanford researchers: Telemedicine optimization requires training, interoperability. In Healthcare IT News
Kurzweil R (2024) La singolarità è più vicina. Quando l'umanità si unisce con l'AI, Milano
Lalli A (2019) Il sapere e la professionalità dell'amministrazione pubblica nell'era dei big data e dell'intelligenza artificiale, relazione al Convegno AIPDA, p 18
Longo GO (1998) Il nuovo Golem. Come il computer cambia la nostra società, Milano
Magritte R (2024) Scritti, Vol. 1 e 2. Edited by André Blavier, tradotto da Libero Sosio, Abscondita
Marchese A (2021) Profili civilistici dell'IT in ambito sanitario, Napoli
Menga FG (2023) Cura, Parole della Filosofia, in Corriere della Sera
Nobile M (2013) *Riflessioni sulla definizione di salute dell'OMS*. Intervento presentato a: XIX edizione del Seminario Nazionale di Sociologia del diritto, Capraia
Palladino A (2023) Le politiche pubbliche nella società costituzionale data driven. Big data e tutela mobile della salute tra poteri pubblici e privati. DPCE, Fascicolo 1
Palladino A, Farina M (2023) Le politiche pubbliche nella società costituzionale data driven. Big Data e tutela "mobile" della salute tra poteri pubblici e poteri privati. In DPCE, fascicolo 1
Perlingieri P (2018) Privacy digitale e protezione dei dati personali tra persona e mercato. In Foro napoletano, 2
Pisani AA (2024) Telemedicina: quadro normativo, tutele e diritti, sistema delle responsabilità, Bologna
Protto M (2022) (edited by) Pubblica amministrazione e nuove tecnologie. In Giur. it
Raposo VL (2016) Telemedicine: The legal framework (or the lack of it) in Europe. In GMS Health Technology Assessment, Vol. 12
Rescigno P (1995) Il diritto all'intimità della vita privata. In Studi in onore di F. Santoro-Passarelli, IV, Napoli, 1972
Rescigno P et al (2017) Diritto Privato. Una conversazione, Bologna
Rodotà S (1984) Protezione dei dati e circolazione delle informazioni. In Riv. crit. dir. priv
SEN (1999) Health in Development, Bollettino dell'Organizzazione Mondiale della Sanità
Shapiro C, Varian H (1999) Information Rules. A Strategic Guide to the Network Economy, Harvard
Sica S (2018) La responsabilità civile per il trattamento illecito dei dati personali. In: A. Mantelero, D. Poletti, *Regolare la tecnologia: il Reg. UE 2016/679 e la protezione dei dati personali. Un dialogo fra Italia e Spagna*, Pisa
Sica G (2023) "Responsabilità" e "danno" da illecito trattamento dei dati personali. Il modello europeo all'indomani del caso VB c. NAP In DMT
Sica V et al (2010) Telemedicina. Approccio multidisciplinare alla gestione dei dati sanitari, Berlin

Solove DJ (2017) A brief history of information privacy law. In: Mathews KJ (ed) Proskauer on privacy: a guide to privacy and data security law in the information age, 2nd edn. Practising Law Institute, New York

Spissu M et al (2017) Le applicazioni mobili in Sanità: aspetti regolatori e review sul loro utilizzo nelle patologie croniche più frequenti. In Rassegna GTDN

Warren S, Brandeis LD (1980) The Right to Privacy. Harvard Law Review, 5

Zuboff S (2019) Il capitalismo della sorveglianza. Il futuro dell'umanità nell'era dei nuovi poteri, Roma

Correction to: Digital Platforms - From Technical Foundations to Legal and Economic Implications

Roberto Bocchini

Correction to:
R. Bocchini (ed.), ***Digital Platforms - From Technical Foundations to Legal and Economic Implications*****,**
https://doi.org/10.1007/978-3-032-07978-7

The book was inadvertently published with an incorrect copyright year of "2025," whereas it should be "2026". The copyright year has been updated in the book.

The updated version of this book can be found at
https://doi.org/10.1007/978-3-032-07978-7

R. Bocchini (ed.), *Digital Platforms - From Technical Foundations to Legal and Economic Implications*, https://doi.org/10.1007/978-3-032-07978-7_38

MIX
Papier aus verantwortungsvollen Quellen
Paper from responsible sources
FSC® C105338

If you have any concerns about our products,
you can contact us on
ProductSafety@springernature.com

In case Publisher is established outside the EU,
the EU authorized representative is:
Springer Nature Customer Service Center GmbH
Europaplatz 3, 69115 Heidelberg, Germany

Printed by Libri Plureos GmbH
in Hamburg, Germany